FIELDING
TRAVEL GUIDES

D1007256

FIELDING'S
FRANCE

Other Fielding Titles

Fielding's Alaska Cruises and the Inside Passage
Fielding's America West
Fielding's Asia's Top Dive Sites
Fielding's Australia
Fielding's Bahamas
Fielding's Baja California
Fielding's Bermuda
Fielding's Best and Worst — The surprising results of the Plog Survey
Fielding's Birding Indonesia
Fielding's Borneo
Fielding's Budget Europe
Fielding's Caribbean
Fielding's Caribbean Cruises
Fielding's Caribbean on a Budget
Fielding's Diving Australia
Fielding's Diving Indonesia
Fielding's Eastern Caribbean
Fielding's England including Ireland, Scotland & Wales
Fielding's Europe
Fielding's Europe 50th Anniversary
Fielding's European Cruises
Fielding's Far East
Fielding's France
Fielding's France: Loire Valley, Burgundy & the Best of French Culture
Fielding's France: Normandy & Brittany
Fielding's France: Provence and the Mediterranean
Fielding's Freewheelin' USA
Fielding's Hawaii
Fielding's Hot Spots: Travel in Harm's Way
Fielding's Indiana Jones Adventure and Survival Guide™
Fielding's Italy
Fielding's Kenya
Fielding's Las Vegas Agenda
Fielding's London Agenda
Fielding's Los Angeles Agenda
Fielding's Mexico
Fielding's New Orleans Agenda
Fielding's New York Agenda
Fielding's New Zealand
Fielding's Paradors, Pousadas and Charming Villages of Spain and Portugal
Fielding's Paris Agenda
Fielding's Portugal
Fielding's Rome Agenda
Fielding's San Diego Agenda
Fielding's Southeast Asia
Fielding's Southern California Theme Parks
Fielding's Southern Vietnam on Two Wheels
Fielding's Spain
Fielding's Surfing Australia
Fielding's Surfing Indonesia
Fielding's Sydney Agenda
Fielding's Thailand, Cambodia, Laos and Myanmar
Fielding's Travel Tool™
Fielding's Vietnam, including Cambodia and Laos
Fielding's Walt Disney World and Orlando Area Theme Parks
Fielding's Western Caribbean
Fielding's The World's Most Dangerous Places™
Fielding's Worldwide Cruises

FIELDING'S FRANCE

By

Nick Tonkin

and

Sean Doran

Fielding Worldwide, Inc.
308 South Catalina Avenue
Redondo Beach, California 90277 U.S.A.

Fielding's France

Published by Fielding Worldwide, Inc.

Text Copyright ©1998 Fielding Worldwide, Inc.

Maps, Icons & Illustrations Copyright ©1998 FWI

Photo Copyrights ©1998 to Individual Photographers

FIELDING WORLDWIDE INC.

PUBLISHER AND CEO	**Robert Young Pelton**
GENERAL MANAGER	**John Guillebeaux**
OPERATIONS DIRECTOR	**George Posanke**
ELECTRONIC PUBLISHING DIRECTOR	**Larry E. Hart**
PUBLIC RELATIONS DIRECTOR	**Beverly Riess**
ACCOUNT SERVICES MANAGER	**Christy Harp**
PROJECT MANAGER	**Chris Snyder**
MANAGING EDITOR	**Amanda K. Knoles**

PRODUCTION

Paul Carbo   **Craig South**

COVER DESIGNED BY	**Digital Artists, Inc.**
COVER PHOTOGRAPHERS — Front Cover	**Robert Young Pelton/Westlight**
Back Cover	**Robert Young Pelton/Westlight**
INSIDE PHOTOS	**Robert Young Pelton/Westlight, French Tourism Board**

Inquiries should be addressed to: Fielding Worldwide, Inc., 308 South Catalina Ave., Redondo Beach, California 90277 U.S.A., ☎ *(310) 372-4474*, Facsimile *(310) 376-8064*, 8:30 a.m.–5:30 p.m. Pacific Standard Time.
Website: http://www.fieldingtravel.com
e-mail: fielding@fieldingtravel.com

ISBN 1-56952-145-X

Printed in the United States of America

Letter from the Publisher

In 1946, Temple Fielding began the first of what would be a remarkable new series of well-written, highly personalized guidebooks for independent travelers. Temple's opinionated, witty and oft-imitated books have now guided travelers for almost a half-century. More important to some was Fielding's humorous and direct method of steering travelers away from the dull and the insipid. Today, Fielding Travel Guides are still written by experienced travelers for experienced travelers. Our authors carry on Fielding's reputation for creating travel experiences that deliver insight with a sense of discovery and style.

France can be a daunting place when it comes to choosing the perfect itinerary. Our focus is making sure you get the best experience for your time and money. To assist you we have created handy comparison tables for accommodations and restaurants complete with highest rated and budget listings so you can plan according to your taste and budget. You'll also find the introductions highlight the romantic and adventurous. Loyal readers will be pleasantly surprised to find the entire book rewritten and with every listing checked for accuracy just before presstime.

Today, the concept of independent travel has never been bigger. Our policy of *brutal honesty* and a highly personal point of view has never changed; it just seems the travel world has caught up with us.

Enjoy your French adventure with Fielding.

RYP

Robert Young Pelton
Publisher and CEO
Fielding Worldwide, Inc.

DEDICATION/
ACKNOWLEDGEMENTS

A Raquel, car elle pacienta.

Many thanks to Bruce Haxthausen and Air France for their generous help and support.

ABOUT THE AUTHORS

Nick Tonkin

Nick Tonkin is a writer and editor based in Santa Barbara, California. Born and raised in England, he has lived in many countries of Europe as well as the United States. When not traveling in or writing about France, he spends most of his time on the Internet, where he can be reached at http://www.silcom.com/~tonkin.

Sean Doran

Sean Doran is a Southern California native. His first taste of travel was after graduation from the University of California at Santa Barbara when he took off for the typical European vacation and his adventures through Turkey landed him on the pages of the Turkish national newspaper. His love for France began to emerge as he spent his first night in Paris enjoying a bottle of Beaujolais in the same courtyard where the Three Musketeers once caroused. Sean quickly developed an affinity for exotic travel, which, combined with his love of foreign languages, led him on jungle expeditions through Southeast Asia, a short-lived romance in South America and a new identity as "El Huero" in Central America. Sean's future trips will continue to include his only two criteria: having no planned itinerary and "getting the hell out of Los Angeles."

Fielding Rating Icons

The Fielding Rating Icons are highly personal and awarded to help the besieged traveler choose from among the dizzying array of activities, attractions, hotels, restaurants and sights. The awarding of an icon denotes unusual or exceptional qualities in the relevant category.

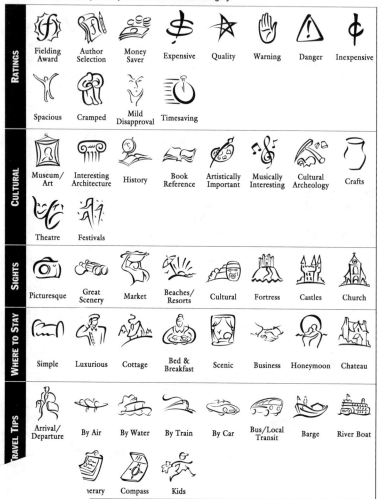

RATINGS
Fielding Award | Author Selection | Money Saver | Expensive | Quality | Warning | Danger | Inexpensive
Spacious | Cramped | Mild Disapproval | Timesaving

CULTURAL
Museum/ Art | Interesting Architecture | History | Book Reference | Artistically Important | Musically Interesting | Cultural Archeology | Crafts
Theatre | Festivals

SIGHTS
Picturesque | Great Scenery | Market | Beaches/ Resorts | Cultural | Fortress | Castles | Church

WHERE TO STAY
Simple | Luxurious | Cottage | Bed & Breakfast | Scenic | Business | Honeymoon | Chateau

TRAVEL TIPS
Arrival/ Departure | By Air | By Water | By Train | By Car | Bus/Local Transit | Barge | River Boat
Itinerary | Compass | Kids

Map Legend

Essentials

- 🏨 Hotel
- 🛏 Youth Hostel
- ✕ Restaurant
- 💲 Bank
- ☎ Telephone
- ℹ Tourist Info.
- ✚ Hospital
- 🍺 Pub/Bar
- 🎵 Music Club
- ✉ Post Office
- 🅿 Parking
- 🚕 Taxi
- Ⓢ Subway
- Ⓜ Metro
- 🏪 Market
- 🛍 Shopping
- 🎬 Cinema
- 🎭 Theater
- ✈ Int'l Airport
- ✚ Regional Airport
- ✴ Police Station
- ⚖ Courthouse
- 🏛 Gov't. Building
- ■ Attraction

- ✈ Military Airbase
- 🪖 Army Base
- ⚓ Naval base
- 🏰 Fort
- 🏫 University
- 🏫 School

Activities

- 🏖 Beach
- ⛺ Campground
- ⛱ Picnic Area
- ⛳ Golf Course
- 🚤 Boat Launch
- 🤿 Diving
- 🐟 Fishing
- 🎿 Water Skiing
- ⛷ Snow Skiing
- 🦅 Bird Sanctuary
- 🦌 Wildlife Sanctuary
- 🌲 Park
- 🏛 Park Headquarters
- ⛏ Mine
- 🗼 Lighthouse
- 🌾 Windmill

- ⚓ Cruise Port
- 🔭 View
- 🏟 Stadium
- 🏢 Building
- 🐘 Zoo
- 🌷 Garden

Historical

- ∴ Archeological Site
- ⚔ Battleground
- 🏰 Castle
- 🗿 Monument
- 🏛 Museum
- 🏛 Ruin
- 🚢 Shipwreck

Religious

- ⛪ Church
- 🛕 Buddhist Temple
- 🛕 Hindu Temple
- ☪ Mosque
- 🏯 Pagoda
- ✡ Synagogue
- ✝ Cemetery
- ✡ Hebrew Cemetery
- ☪ Muslim Cemetery

Physical

- — — — — — · International Boundary
- — · — · — · — County/Regional Boundary
- **PARIS** ⊙ National Capital
- **Montego Bay** ● State/Parish Capital
- **Los Angeles** ● Major City
- **Quy Nhon** ○ Town/Village
- ⟨5⟩ Motorway/Freeway
- ⟨163⟩ Highway
- 1AB⟍ Freeway Exit
- Primary Road
- Secondary Road
- — — — — Subway
- 🚋 Trolley/Street Car

- — — 🚲 — — Biking Routed
- 🚶 Hiking Trail
- ▪▪▪▪ Dirt Road
- ┽┽┽┽┽┽ Railroad
- **RR** Railroad Station
- — 🚤 — Ferry Route
- ▲ Mountain Peak
- Lake
- River
- Cave
- 🪸 Coral Reef
- Waterfall
- ♨ Hot Spring

©FWI

TABLE OF CONTENTS

LIST OF MAPS

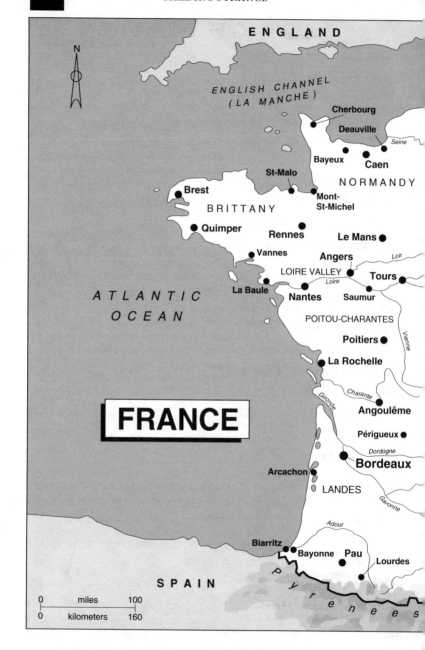

INTRODUCTION

The Eiffel Tower offers spectacular Paris views from 984 feet.

How to Use This Guide

In this edition of *Fielding's France* we have tried to provide a balanced diet for the traveler to the land of gastronomy. That is, a balance between specific detailed information you will need to plan your trip and make it a success, and the historical and cultural information to help you understand what you see as you explore. Our goal is to create a guide that you can read before your trip, while you are in France, and after you return…or even if you never set foot in the place. We have adhered to two assumptions about you, dear reader. The first is that you are an adventurous and curious person, and hungry for a memorable experience that you direct in large measure yourself. The second assumption is that France, as one of the world's top tourist destinations, has a superbly sophisticated and well-developed tourism industry. You can obtain more information than you could ever use from the network of French government tourist offices abroad and from the regional offices listed in this book, and, more importantly, you will find a tourist office staffed by friendly personnel armed with free maps, brochures and excursion-planning services in even the smallest of French towns. Based on these facts, we have declined to list every bank and laundromat in each town we describe: figuring that you will be able to find that out for yourself, we have concentrated on providing you with a detailed and rich historical, geographical and, yes, culinary overview of each region and city we recommend you visit.

We urge you to spend ample time reading through this book well in advance of your trip to France to get an idea of where you want to visit and what you want to see. Take your time and develop a theme or a list of destinations that appear particularly appealing. We have made suggestions on everything from hotels to restaurants and attractions, each listed with a critical description and a phone number (and in many cases a fax number). So that you can make your own reservations and plan your itinerary independently, we have also supplied the addresses and phone numbers for regional tourist offices and operators of boating and other specialty trips.

Once you arrive, we suggest you carry the book with you at all times, as it will provide vital information on the cities and regions you are visiting, as well as get you out of a linguistic jam with the dictionary of commonly used words and phrases. Even more valuable to the independent traveler are the insights and anecdotal information on all the major sights you will be touring. Whether you stick to the tried and true Paris-Loire Valley circuit or strike out across less-beaten paths, *Fielding's France* will be your most useful tool to get you there, ensure you have a wonderful experience, and bring you home safely. Bon voyage!

What's New

I have always been impressed that France has a Culture Ministry. The dangers of such governmental management of the arts are readily apparent, of course; one need only look at the Third Reich to see what such influence in the wrong hands can do. In France, however, the tradition of the state preserving and enhancing the national patrimony goes back two centuries or more, and it has always been a high priority in society and government. Each year France spends almost twice what it did the previous year on acquisition of artwork for public display. All of which means that you will see considerably improved collections of everything from Ancient Masters to Cubists and avant garde multimedia artists in France's myriad museums. This is truest of course in Paris, where the Richelieu and Denon wings of the Louvre recently reopened after a long refurbishment (other galleries continue to be restored at press time), but it is also true in smaller regional towns—the museum of fine art in Rouen, for example, just acquired two more Monets to add to its already impressive collection.

In Paris, work is nearing completion on the Bibliothéque Nationale du Ciné near the Trocadéro, which promises to be the most complete museum and archive of cinema in the world (don't forget it was the French who invented movies, not Hollywood!). The enormous national library, last of François Mitterand's great projects, was recently completed, and the advent of new government should bring forth additional monuments to France's prowess. All around the country museums and monuments are being refurbished to enter the 21st century—accessibility is a priority, finally. The renovation at the stunning Abbaye Royale de Fontevraud continues, and an entire third wing recently opened to the public. Concerts are now being giving in the refurbished dormitories there. In Strasbourg, a major new museum of modern art opened its doors in 1997, while Tours and Reims planned major celebrations of the 1500th anniversary of St. Martin's death and Clovis' baptism. Away from the arts, the country is gearing up for the 1998 soccer World Cup, with new stadiums being built in half a dozen cities.

It's always a good time to go to France, and there is much that is new for both first time travelers and seasoned visitors. For more up-to-date information that escaped our publishing deadlines, contact the French government tourist offices, whose addresses and phone numbers are on page 36.

Highlights

It's hard to pick a favorite thing to do or see in France; there's so much, and of such diversity, that it's like comparing apples to oranges. Personally, I find a thematic tour to be the most meaningful and lasting. Recognizing that many Americans stick to the traditional regions—Paris, the châteaux of the Loire, the Normandy beaches and maybe Brittany, I have focused on those regions, and heartily recommend a tour through them. Begin with Normandy and Brittany, work your way down the Atlantic to Nantes, then follow the Loire back to Paris. Along the way you'll trace both the history and the architectural development of France from prehistory to the modern age, in a fairly logical order. Despite the art in the museums, I find nothing more moving than standing in the nave of the cathedral at Chartres or Bourges, imagining the work of so many thousands of people, all driven by faith alone, as they erected these monuments to man's quest for meaning over centuries. I think if you take time in these temples to breathe in man's eternal spiritual quest, you'll better appreciate the long-haired, slightly odoriferous radical reading Sartre on the Left Bank when you get to the capital. And although I tend to shy away from that which is most popular, I have to say that the Louvre is the most exhilarating cultural experience of my life, no matter how often I visit. The grandeur of the palace only enhances the mastery of man's creation housed within, and I find myself moved in the same way I am in the cathedrals. Sure, I eat like a king in France, and could happily exist on cheeses and wines (without ever sampling the same combination twice) for the rest of my life. But when I return home, the things that I find have changed my life are the great accomplishments man has wrought, and there is surely no better place to find them than the places I have highlighted.

Prices

As discussed elsewhere in this book, France is not cheap. In fact, it's downright expensive. In spite of how much I love the place I have a hard time stomaching $4.50 for a gallon of gas (although I am saved from stomaching a Big Mac menu by its $8 price tag!). You need to be prepared for everything to cost considerably more than at home. Budget before you go, figure out how long you can afford to be there, then go and enjoy. Don't let mere money spoil your trip.

That having been said, here are a few pointers. There is a point of diminishing returns in budgeting. In searching for accommodations, don't be seduced by the signs advertising Formule 1 motels and others for FR140 a night. These are plastic sleeping chambers, many without even a bathroom or shower, cramped, stuffy and utterly, utterly devoid of character. Far better to spend the extra FR50 for a one-star or no-star hotel that may be ramshackle but cozy. The same holds true for eating out. It's hard to find any menu of the day for much under FR70, and when you do get down to FR55 or FR60, the portions will be small, or cold, or both, and you'll find yourself wishing you had ponied up the extra 10 or 15 francs to get a great meal that'll fill you up for the whole day.

Because our readers are from various nations, and because the exchange rates fluctuate considerably, the prices given here are in French francs. Consult your bank for current rates, as well as the sections in this book dealing with money, for how to obtain the most francs for your buck.

TRAVELER'S GUIDE

Aigues Mortes was created to give France a port on the Mediterranean.

Bird's-Eye View

Geography

The largest Western European nation, *la République Française* (as France is officially known) covers 220,668 square miles (551,670 square kilometers), a territory about four-fifths the size of Texas. France is bordered by the English Channel to the northwest, Belgium and Luxembourg to the northeast, Germany and Switzerland to the east, Italy to the southeast, the Mediterranean Sea and Spain to the south, and the Atlantic Ocean to the west. France has a diverse landscape, with more than 2000 miles of coastline, large tracts of forests and woodlands and several prominent mountain ranges. In the French Alps, Mont Blanc, Europe's highest peak, rises 15,771 feet (4807 meters) into the sky, while in the southwest, the Pyrénées form a rugged border between France and Spain. Off the southeast Mediterranean shore, lies the French island of Corsica. France's major rivers include the Seine, which flows through Paris; the Garonne in the province of Bordeaux; the long, curving Loire that arcs like a lifeline through the heart of the country; and the famous Rhône, which winds through Burgundy and Provence to empty into the Mediterranean. French vineyards are legendary—of course—but the French also supply much of Europe with beef, veal, poultry and dairy products. Crops include wheat and barley, as well as plants grown for the perfume industry, such as the fields of purple lavender that blanket the rolling hills in the south of France.

People

In 1997, France's population reached 58.3 million people, making it the 21st most populous country in the world. Almost three-quarters of the citizens live in urban areas. The capital, Paris, has about 2.2 million inhabitants; Marseille is the second most populous city, with just over 800,000 people.

Since prehistoric times, France has been shaped by trade, travel and invasion. Three basic European stocks—Celtic, Latin and Teutonic (Frankish)--have blended over the centuries to make up its present population. France's birth rate was among the highest in Europe from 1945 until the late 1960s, when it began to decline. Because of this growth and immigration, the population increased by fully one-third in the past 50 years, from 41 million in 1946. Traditionally, France also has had a high level of immigration. Fifty-two percent of France's noncitizens are southern Europeans. Another 26 percent of the country's people are North Africans, primarily Algerians. About 90 percent of the people are Roman Catholic, less than 2 percent are Protestant, and about one percent are Jewish. The more than 1 million Muslims are primarily immigrants.

Government

What is known as metropolitan France—the mainland and Corsica—is divided administratively into 22 regions, which are further divided into 95 *départments*, or departments. There are an additional five overseas departments located in Martinique, French Guiana and Réunion Island, as well as five overseas territories: New Caledonia, French Polynesia, Wallis and Futuna Islands, and the French Southern and Antarctic Territories. France maintains two special status territories, Mayotte and St. Pierre and Miquelon. France is currently a constitutional democratic republic, following the rise and fall of four previous republican regimes since the Revolution of 1789. The present Fifth Republic was established by General Charles de

Gaulle in 1958. The Constitution of the Fifth Republic was approved by a national referendum the same year. The constitution established a strong presidency within the joint presidential-parliamentary form of government. The constitution's preamble proclaims the rights of man, national sovereignty, and democratic evolution for the community.

Executive power is held by the president, who is popularly elected for a seven-year renewable term. The president appoints the prime minister, the second-most powerful governmental position. The prime minister, along with a nine-person Council of Ministers, directs the government. The bicameral *Parlement* consists of the *Senat* and the *Assemblée Nationale.* The Senate has 321 members, with 296 seats allocated for metropolitan France, 13 seats for the overseas departments and territories, and 12 seats for French nationals abroad. In the 577-seat National Assembly, 555 deputies serve metropolitan France and 22 deputies represent overseas departments and territories. The judicial system is headed by a Court of Cassation, which rules on the interpretation of law and the procedural actions of other courts. The *cours d'assises* are called upon to hear major criminal cases but have no regular sittings. Subordinate cases are tried by *tribunaux d'instance*, and by *tribunaux de grande instance* for more serious offenses.

Infrastructure

France has 964,040 miles of roads, of which 498,984 are paved. There are nearly 24 million passenger cars, almost 5 million trucks and buses, and 3 million motorcycles and mopeds. The French railway system is world-famous. With more than 21,000 miles (34,600 km) of track, the rail system provides efficient connections within France and to other European destinations. Fifty-four ports offer waterway links, while 461 airfields handle both passenger and freight airline service.

The French have a mania for keeping up with the news. More than 800 radio stations broadcast to a total audience of 51 million. Nearly half of all French people read a newspaper, choosing from 79 daily papers. Public television is carried on three channels, while *Canal Plus*, a private channel, shows films.

When to Go

Remember that France is one of the most popular tourist destinations in the world. This means that it gets crowded—extremely crowded—during the peak summer months. If you can, avoid planning your visit to France during the second half of July or August. On top of all the European and other tourists, the French themselves are all on vacation. All these tourists head for the same spots you're likely to want to visit. Besides, the climate is just as pleasant (more so in the south) during June or September.

Seasons

June has the advantage of long daylight hours. The sun doesn't set until well after nine o'clock, so you can enjoy a long day's sight-seeing and still have time to take a leisurely shower and even a short siesta at your hotel and make it to an evening dinner on a patio, where you can watch the sunset. During July and August prices rise, often astronomically, at the major tourist destinations, for everything from accommodations to food and souvenirs. France still employs the block vacation scheme, preferring to shut down businesses and factories for a month rather than stagger employees' time off, so in August especially you'll find the beaches completely overcrowded, the highways congested, and Paris empty. This makes August a good time to visit the capital, if you are planning to visit many of the museums and monuments, but during a hot year the city may be unbearably, sticky and damp. In September things change overnight—the Riviéra, Loire Valley and Provence become suddenly tolerable again, and hot days and warm evenings can last late into the month. Spring in France is beautiful, as it is everywhere, but be warned that March and April are the wettest months. May is really the best time to see "Paris in Springtime." In the Alps and the Pyrénées the ski season begins around Christmas time and lasts until early March. The best skiing is late in the season, when the snowpacks are deepest, but be aware that during the last two weeks in February and the first week in March, the slopes are the most crowded, as French schools break for vacation.

Festivals and Holidays

You should be aware of the major public holidays and festivals in France; the former because everything will be closed and the roads and trains will be packed, and the latter because you'll want to be there celebrating along with the locals.

The major national public holidays in France are:

New Year's Day

Easter Sunday

Easter Monday

Ascension Thursday

May 1st (Labor Day)

May 8th (Victory in Europe Day—1945)

Whit Monday

July 14th (Bastille Day)

August 15th (Assumption Day)

November 1st (All Saints' Day)

November 11th (Armistice Day—1918)

Christmas Day

There are festivals all over France at every time of the year—on any given weekend you'll find some small town somewhere celebrating its wine, its cheese, its dominant *légume*, or just for the hell of it. The following is a table of the major festivals and events by month. Inquire locally for events in the region you are visiting.

Nice has the largest Carnivale in France.

Month	Festival	Location	Notable
January	*Comic Book Festival*	*Angoulême*	The world's biggest comic book fair features many writers and artists, plus plenty of Asterix the Gaul material!
January	*Rally de Monte Carlo*	*Monte Carlo*	One of the premier stops on the World Championship circuit—it's thrilling to watch the drivers pilot their cars through the winding streets at breakneck speeds.

TRAVELER'S GUIDE

Month	Festival	Location	Notable
January	*Tournée de St. Vincent*	*Burgundy*	Serious debauchery is the point of this wine festival that rotates to a different village each year. You buy a cup for about $10 and get unlimited refills.
February	*Carnival*	*Nationwide*	In a colorful and musical prelude to Lent, many towns and villages organize a version of Carnival, with parades and dancing in the street. Nice has the largest celebration.
March	*Salon de Mars*	*Salon du Livre*	Paris Culture gets top billing in the capital during March with these twin festivals of modern art and books. Events are held at multiple locations throughout the city.
March-October	*Sound and Light Shows*	*Nationwide*	The fabulous palace at Versailles has nightly shows featuring illuminated fountains, lasers and fireworks. Many other *châteaux* throughout the country offer less-extravagant presentations.
May	*French Open Tennis Tournament*	*Paris*	Roland Garros Stadium plays host to one of four Grand Slam events of the year.
May	*International Film Festival*	*Cannes*	The granddaddy of them all, Cannes was drawing stars and starlets like moths to a candle before it became *de rigeur for every wanna-be hip town in the world to host a film festival.*
June	*Tour de France*	*Nationwide*	Over three weeks the world's most aerobically conditioned men pedal some 2300 miles around the country in pursuit of a yellow jersey. Culminates in the final chase down the Champs-Elysées in Paris.

Month	Festival	Location	Notable
July 14	*Bastille Day*	*Nationwide*	Celebration of the storming of the Bastille, start of the Revolution, takes all of France by storm. The major national holiday is marked by fireworks, parades and general partying.
July	*Sundry Arts Festivals*	*Nationwide*	They include the theater festival in Avignon, the jazz festival in Nice, the opera festival in Aix-en-Provence and countless smaller cultural events all over the country.
September	*Fête d'Automne*	*Paris*	The capital's major arts and music festival, with dozens of events held throughout the city for the next two months.
September	*Les Vendanges*	*Nationwide*	Festivals are held in towns in each of the country's wine-producing regions to celebrate the coming of the grape harvest.
October	*Prix de l'Arc de Triomphe*	*Paris*	The French love thoroughbred horse racing, and this is the race of races, the Gallic equivalent of the Kentucky Derby or the Grand National.
November	*Beaujolais Nouveaux day*	*Nationwide*	Slightly tongue-in-cheek festivals are held throughout the country on the third Thursday of the month to celebrate the unveiling of the usually very mediocre Beaujolais Nouveau wine. Bottles are airlifted to London by dawn, where the English enjoy their own affair.
November	*Les Trois Glorieuses*	*Burgundy*	The biggest wine festival of the year in France, this event is held to celebrate the end of the autumn harvest. Events are held throughout Burgundy, the highlight being the world's largest wine auction. Fun to watch, but don't raise your hand unless you're interested in a couple of hundred dozen cases!

Weather

When you consider that England is accurately thought of as gray and damp almost all of the time, and the Mediterranean region is pictured—again, accurately—as sunny beaches and sparkling blue waters, and that France fills the space between the two, you can appreciate France's range of climatic conditions. In general, the north of the country is wet and chilly, with temperatures from October to March rarely breaking above the 60°F mark. It rains often, mostly drizzles rather than heavy showers. This is not to say that the north is not beautiful—the rugged Brittany coastline and the greenness of Normandy and Picardie are, for many people, infinitely preferable to the sunny, semi-arid south. France's central heart is warmer than the north, and wetter than the south. French summers are long, defined properly as running from the second half of May through late September. Summer temperatures are warm, but rarely unbearably hot. South of Lyon, however, the topography and the weather change to a true Mediterranean clime. The winters can be pretty nippy, even though the sun will probably still be shining. The Mediterranean summers are baking, with an *average* daily temperature on the Riviéra of 80°F during July and August.

The following chart shows the average maximum and minimum daily temperatures (listed in Fahrenheit) in five key cities for each month of the year:

AVERAGE WEATHER IN FRANCE													
CITY		Jan.	Feb.	Mar.	Apr.	May	Jun.	Jul.	Aug.	Sep.	Oct.	Nov.	Dec.
BORDEAUX, southwest (46m/151 ft.)													
Avg High	°C	9	11	15	17	20	24	25	26	23	18	13	9
	°F	49	51	59	63	69	75	78	78	74	65	55	49
Avg Low	°C	2	2	4	6	9	12	14	14	12	8	5	3
	°F	35	36	40	43	48	54	57	56	54	47	40	37
Rainfall	mm	90	75	63	48	61	65	56	70	84	83	96	109
	in.	3.5	3.0	2.5	1.9	2.4	2.6	2.2	2.8	3.3	3.3	3.8	4.3
CHERBOURG, north/northwest (8m/26 ft.)													
Avg High	°C	8	8	10	12	15	18	19	20	19	15	12	10
	°F	47	47	51	54	59	64	67	67	65	60	53	49
Avg Low	°C	4	4	5	7	9	12	14	14	13	10	8	5
	°F	40	39	41	45	49	54	57	57	56	51	46	42
Rainfall	mm	109	75	62	49	41	39	55	71	79	99	133	119
	in.	4.3	3.0	2.4	1.9	1.6	1.5	2.2	2.8	3.1	3.9	5.2	4.7

TRAVELER'S GUIDE

AVERAGE WEATHER IN FRANCE

CITY		Jan.	Feb.	Mar.	Apr.	May	Jun.	Jul.	Aug.	Sep.	Oct.	Nov.	Dec.
EMBRUN, mountains (871 m/2858 ft.)													
Avg High	°C	5	7	12	15	19	23	26	25	22	16	10	6
	°F	41	45	53	60	67	73	79	77	71	61	50	42
Avg Low	°C	-5	-3	0	3	7	10	12	12	10	5	1	-3
	°F	24	26	33	38	45	50	54	53	49	42	33	26
Rainfall	mm	49	43	48	51	61	62	48	65	70	70	68	65
	in.	1.9	1.7	1.9	2.0	2.4	2.4	1.9	2.6	2.8	2.8	2.7	2.6
LYON, central/eastern (200 m/656 ft.)													
Avg High	°C	5	7	13	16	20	24	27	26	23	16	10	6
	°F	42	45	55	61	69	75	80	79	73	61	50	43
Avg Low	°C	-1	0	3	6	9	13	15	14	12	7	4	0
	°F	30	31	37	42	49	55	59	58	53	45	38	33
Rainfall	mm	52	46	53	56	69	85	56	89	93	77	80	57
	in.	2.1	1.8	2.1	2.2	2.7	3.4	2.2	3.5	3.7	3.0	3.2	2.2
MARSEILLE, Mediterranean coast (4 m/13 ft.)													
Avg High	°C	10	12	15	18	22	26	29	28	25	20	15	11
	°F	50	53	59	64	71	79	84	83	77	68	58	52
Avg Low	°C	2	2	5	8	11	15	17	17	15	10	6	3
	°F	35	36	41	46	52	58	63	63	58	51	43	37
Rainfall	mm	43	32	43	42	46	24	11	34	60	76	69	66
	in.	1.7	1.3	1.7	1.7	1.8	0.9	0.4	1.3	2.4	3.0	2.7	2.6
PARIS, central (75 m/246 ft.)													
Avg High	°C	6	7	12	16	20	23	25	25	21	16	10	7
	°F	43	45	54	60	68	73	76	75	70	60	50	44
Avg Low	°C	1	1	4	6	10	13	15	14	12	8	5	2
	°F	34	34	39	43	49	55	58	58	53	46	40	36
Rainfall	mm	56	46	35	42	57	54	59	64	55	50	51	50
	in.	2.2	1.8	1.4	1.7	2.2	2.1	2.3	2.5	2.2	2.0	2.0	2.0
AJACCIO, Corsica (4 m/12 ft.)													
Avg High	°C	13	14	16	18	21	25	27	28	26	22	18	15
	°F	55	56	60	64	70	77	81	82	78	71	63	58
Avg Low	°C	3	4	5	7	10	14	16	16	15	11	7	4
	°F	38	39	41	45	50	56	60	60	58	52	45	40
Rainfall	mm	76	65	53	48	50	21	10	16	50	88	97	98
	in.	3.0	2.6	2.1	1.9	2.0	0.8	0.4	0.6	2.0	3.5	3.8	3.9

TRAVELER'S GUIDE

How to Get There

By Air

Air travel to France from the United States and Canada can occur in several ways. Your flight can be nonstop, meaning you'll take off and not land again until you're in France. A direct flight means there'll be at least one stop (for refueling, most probably), during which you'll have to disembark and possibly change planes, although all legs of the trip will be under one flight number. A connecting flight means you'll be booked on at least two separate flights (with separate flight numbers as well as separate planes) and should ensure that you have enough time to collect your luggage (if it's not checked through to your final destination) before boarding your next flight. Connecting flights can be the most tiring, especially if you are connecting in one of today's mega-airports in which there may be as much as a mile of concourses separating the arrival gates from the departure gates. Flying time to France from the East Coast of North America is about seven-and-a-half hours; from the West Coast about 11 hours.

Airlines

Getting from point A to point B is the object of this exercise, after all, so the difficulty faced by airlines is distinguishing themselves from one another. There are very few ways in which one airline can claim to offer a different experience from the others that will be of interest to the vast majority of travelers. Will you really notice the difference between 34 and 35 inches of legroom, or the difference between 16° and 18° of reclination in your seatback? Probably not—unless you're planning to fly first class, where a round trip flight from Los Angeles to Paris can cost more than $8000.

That being said, there are some considerations *vis-a-vis* amenities that you may want to take into account when planning your flight. Virgin Atlantic Airways, for example, provides individual television monitors for every seat on the plane, offering a choice of six or seven movies and several popular Nintendo video games—this can make all the difference on an 11-hour crossing from Los Angeles, especially when compared with most airlines' offering of one barely visible movie during the entire flight. All United States-based carriers now forbid smoking on any section of the flight over American airspace, and an increasing number have outlawed it at all times, even on nonstop flights halfway around the world. If you are a smoker, this may make choosing Air France or another non-U.S. carrier worth considering. If money is no object, you may want to go with Air France's luxury package—New York to Paris via first class or Paris to New York on the Concorde. If you have to ask how much it is, you can't afford it.

Nevertheless, the major consideration in choosing an airline is always price. The major airlines serving France from North America are the following:

Air France
☎ *(800) 237-2747*

TransWorld Airlines
☎ *(800) 892-4141*

American Airlines
☎ *(800) 433-7300*

United Airlines
☎ *(800) 241-6522*

Continental Airlines
☎ *(800) 231-0856*

USAir
☎ *(800) 428-4322*

Delta Airlines
☎ *(800) 241-4141*

Virgin Atlantic Airways
☎ *(800) 862-8621*

(Note: Virgin Atlantic flies to London, connecting to Paris on British Midland Airlines; often the combined fare is as good as or better than flying directly to France. You'll also get to stop over in London for a day or two if you want.)

These airlines are in competition with each other, but it often seems as though they are actually competing with each other to see which airline's ad campaign can confuse you more fully. The plethora of restrictions, advance-purchase and length of stay requirements placed on ticket prices, which are advertised ambiguously anyway with lots of tiny type at the bottom of the ad, make it difficult to figure out what it's actually going to cost you to fly when you want to. Personally, I am convinced that this is intentional on the part of the airlines—the truth is that they all offer the same fares most of the time. And when one lowers or raises prices, the others quickly follow suit. All the while, each airline is really striving to make it seem that it is offering the best deal to snag your business.

Choosing a Carrier

If you have a favorite airline, or are a member of a frequent flyer bonus program offered by a particular carrier, your airline choice is clear. If you will be taking a connecting flight from your hometown to the hub where your international flight departs, you may find your best deal is to purchase a combined ticket on the regional carrier and its affiliated international carrier. I've always been partial to American Airlines, mostly because it has always been very helpful with my often convoluted travel plans, in addition to being competitive on pricing.

If you book your flight through a travel agent, you'll get a ticket at the same fare you'll be able to get from the airlines. You just need to make sure the agent checks every available option. Don't be afraid to insist that your agent looks through available fares "one more time." What you want is a fare known as APEX, or Advanced Purchase Excursion, a classification used by the airlines that means the ticket is their best current offer, usually requiring a two- or three-week advance purchase.

Charters

Until recently, charter flights were the best way to get cheap flights across the Atlantic, but of late they have largely been displaced by consolidators (see below). Nevertheless, there are still some opportunities to get a good deal from a charter company. Charters are convenient if you want to fly from a city other than New York or Los Angeles, such as Boston or Houston, and into a city other than Paris, such as Lyon, Nice or Marseille. The following are some reputable charter companies:

Corsair

> *5757 West Century Boulevard, Ste. 660, Los Angeles, CA 90045*
> ☎ *(800) 677-0720*

Council Charter

> *205 East 42nd Street, New York, NY 10017*
> ☎ *(212) 661-0311; FAX: (212) 972-0194*

Unitravel

> *1177 North Warson Road, P.O. Box 12485, St. Louis, MO 63132*
> ☎ *(314) 569-2501 or (800) 325-2222; FAX: (314) 569-2503*

Consolidators

A good source for really bottom-cost flights are the consolidators, fondly known in England as "bucket shops." These companies buy up unsold tickets from the airlines, as well as charter companies, and then sell them at reduced rates, usually on very short notice. Look in the Sunday paper travel section for their small ads. They usually only have a limited selection of seats, however, so don't leave it until the last minute to contact a consolidator if you have a firm departure date. Other things to bear in mind are that you will not be able to use your ticket on a different flight if you miss your scheduled departure. Since you bought your ticket from the consolidator and not the airline, the airline has no responsibility to you. Be aware that there have been numerous incidents of consolidators ripping people off. Pay with a credit card if you can—it's easier to get your money back— and see that the payment is held in escrow until your trip is over (a practice of all reputable consolidators that should be stipulated on your contract). Also call the airline as soon as you purchase your ticket to ensure that you are actually booked on the flight you're supposed to be on. Of course, don't forget to check the reputation of the consolidator you're considering using with the local Better Business Bureau. Some larger consolidators that historically have had a good reputation are the following:

Council Charter

> *205 East 42nd Street, New York, NY 10017*
> ☎ *(212) 661-0311; FAX: (212) 972-0194*

Travac

> *989 6th Avenue, New York, NY 10018*
> ☎ *(800) 872-8800*

Unitravel

> *1177 North Warson Road, P.O. Box 12485, St. Louis, MO 63132*
> ☎ *(314) 569-2501 or (800) 325-2222; FAX: (314) 569-2503*

By Sea

Yes, it's true, you can travel to France from North America by boat. You have to travel via England—the only regularly scheduled passenger steamer service across the Atlantic is now aboard the *Queen Elizabeth II*, which sails every two weeks or so between New York and Southampton between April and December. An Atlantic crossing is a once-in-a-lifetime experience, but it is a trip that requires trunkloads of money. If you're interested in getting brochures to get a peek at the lifestyles of the rich and famous, contact:

Cunard Line

555 Fifth Avenue, New York, NY 10017
☎ *(800) 528-6273*

Of course, if you are in England to begin with, you'll want to consider taking the ferry to France. This venerable method of crossing the English Channel (or *La Manche*, as the French call it) is in rapid decline thanks to the advent of the Channel Tunnel, but the ferry still has certain advantages. There's something about the view from the windswept deck of a ferry as the famous white cliffs of Dover recede or appear in the distance that 31 miles of tunnel blackness out the window can't quite match.

The major drawback to crossing on a ferry is its relative slowness. Dover-Calais, the shortest route, takes an hour and 15 minutes; Dover-Boulogne an hour and 40 minutes; other routes range from about two-and-a-half hours between Ramsgate and Dunkirk to six hours between Portsmouth and Le Havre. To these actual crossing times must be added the time necessary to board and disembark (half an hour on each end for pedestrians; four times that for cars), plus the time needed to get to and from the respective ports. This does not, indisputably, compare well with the three-hour London-to-Paris traveling time on Eurostar, the high-speed train that speeds through the Channel Tunnel. Nevertheless, speed and rushing around should not be your main preoccupation when traveling, and personally I've always enjoyed the ferry crossing for its bracing sea air, the excitement that mounts as you near land, and the opportunity it affords to just sit and relax for a couple of hours.

The other major advantage to crossing by ferry is the price: it's almost always cheaper than Eurostar, and during peak summer months the cost can be as much as £50 less per person. Most travel agencies in North America can give you up-to-date pricing and scheduling information on ferry crossings, as well as book tickets for you. Otherwise you can contact one of the operators in the U.K. at the telephone numbers below:

Britanny Ferries

☎ *(44) 1705-827701*

Hoverspeed (hovercraft crossings; unreliable in winter)

☎ *(44) 1843-595566*

P&O Lines

☎ *(44) 081-575-5555*

Sealink

☎ *(44) 1233-647047*

Sally Line

☎ *(44) 1843-595566*

By Rail
Eurostar

First debuted in 1994, Eurostar is the high-speed train service linking Paris with London (as well as Brussels) through the engineering marvel known as the Channel Tunnel. You can now travel from downtown London to the center of Paris in a "TVG" train. The "TVG" designation stands for *train à grande vitesse*, which translates from French as "high-speed train." In terms of speed and service, the train experience is more like what you'd expect from an airline. London to Paris takes just three hours, and travel time in the Channel Tunnel is only 20 minutes.

A service provided jointly by the railways of Belgium, Britain and France, Eurostar is the latest generation of the famous TGV trains. Eurostar trains are the most advanced in the world: each can smoothly transport 800 passengers (that's the equivalent of two jumbo jets!), at speeds of up to 200 miles per hour. From the time you check in at designated terminals at Gàre du Nord in Paris or Waterloo Station in London, to when you see the rakish, aerodynamic nose of the Eurostar locomotive, to the rush you experience as the train blasts out of the tunnel onto French soil at 100 miles per hour, you'll experience a train journey like none other in the world.

The Tunnel

Eurostar owes its existence to the Channel Tunnel project, a cooperative effort between France and Britain to establish Paris–London rail service. During construction, the "Chunnel" itself was plagued by cost overruns, financing shortfalls and delays, but in 1994 it opened, fulfilling the dream—or rather the fantasy—of generations of English and French. The tunnel is in fact three separate tunnels: two used by trains—one for each direction—and a third, smaller tunnel between the two used by service vehicles. The tunnels are 30 miles long and took seven years to build. Twin custom-designed boring machines amazingly managed to meet at the same spot under the seabed in 1992. An interesting note is that when the tunnels were completed, the machines became unusable, and were simply driven off to one side, where they now reside permanently in an underground tomb of their own making.

Technical problems were encountered while the new Eurostar trains were being tested on British rails. The archaic 750V third-rail power supply that Eurostar uses in Britain created electrical interference problems with the sensitive signalling system, causing the train unexpectedly to shut itself down. The delay in the tunnel opening was used to fix these problems, and in the summer of 1993, the first Eurostar train was run through the tunnel at reduced speed, pulled by a diesel locomotive. This was a major milestone, since until then Eurostar had used the boat and the road to get to Britain for testing. Eurostar service was officially inaugurated on November 14, 1994, and service has since been expanded.

The Trains

The Eurostar TGV is arguably the most complicated and sophisticated train ever to ride the rails. From the outside, the trains look distinctly different even from other TGVs, with a silhouette that can only be described, even today, as futuristic. They come in two kinds: long and short. Thirty-one of the 38 trains are long, with 18 cars between two locomotives. The remaining seven are short, with only 14 cars designed for service north of London, where platform lengths are insufficient to accommodate longer trains. The longer trains have a total capacity of 794 seats; 210 in first-class, 584 in second-class, and 52 folding seats. For safety reasons, the ninth and 10th cars do not ride on a common truck. Instead, they are coupled (not articulated) using an automatic coupler. This allows the train to be split in the middle in under two minutes should there be a serious emergency in the tunnel. Eurostar's nose is computer-optimized for running in the tunnel, where pressure waves can affect passenger comfort. The tunnel itself is passed at a "reduced" speed of 100 miles an hour. The tracks in Britain are also currently limited to 100 miles an hour because of the third-rail supply and tight curves. This leads to a rather embarrassing disparity in average speeds on either side of the Channel: in a run from Paris to London, the average speed on the French side is twice as fast as the speed on the British side—the TVG whisks along at 200 m.p.h.! The high-speed rail link from the tunnel to London, the Union Railway, is scheduled to open in 2002, and will make the British run significantly faster.

The Service

Eurostar is operated as a seamless service, which is something of a challenge because three countries, each with their own language, are served. In many ways, a trip on Eurostar feels more like an airplane trip than a conventional train trip. There are airportlike check-in procedures—the staff wears specially designed uniforms and speaks several languages, and on-board announcements are made in French, English, German and Dutch. The train engineer is also required to speak several languages, however, engineers can use their native tongue to communicate on the train's radio link with the dispatcher.

Fares and Schedules

At press time, the round-trip adult fare for a London–Paris trip ranged from a minimum of US$98 for a second-class APEX weekend ticket (with significant advance purchase requirements and other restrictions) all the way up to US$344 for first-class. Trains depart daily on the hour every hour, interspersed with **Le Shuttle**, the vehicle-transporting train, and twinned at night with service every three hours. You can get on the train far north of London and travel directly to the south of France, Lille in the north, or even Brussels without changing in Paris, in addition to the capital-to-capital service. For more information and to book seats, see your travel agent or contact Eurostar through the following agents:

BritRail Travel

> *1500 Broadway, New York, NY 10036*
> ☎ *(800) 677-8585*

Rail Europe

> *New York, NY*
> ☎ *(800) EUROSTAR*

Intercity Europe

> *Victoria Station, London, England*
> ☎ *(44) 071-828-8092*

Tour Operators

I encourage all visitors to France—all travelers anywhere, in fact—to strike out on your own. Get your own flights, make your own hotel reservations, set your own itinerary, rent your own wheels. In my opinion, you'll have a much more rewarding experience than being herded around on a tour bus. True, the days of "If it's Tuesday this must be Belgium" are pretty much gone, but even on the more culturally sensitive tours of today you'll miss out on a large part of what makes being in France so special: simply being in France.

Nonetheless, some travelers may want to go with an all-inclusive, no-worries trip to France, and there are hundreds of tour operators that offer everything from logistical assistance in getting across the water to fully comprehensive packages, including special interest tours for World War II veterans, cooking enthusiasts and wine lovers (of course!). Of the countless operators, I have selected a sampling of companies that offer very high quality services:

Abercrombie & Kent International

> *1520 Kensington Road, Ste. 212, Oak Brook, IL 60521*
> ☎ *(708) 954-2944 or (800) 323-7308; FAX: (708) 954-3324*

This company offers seven- to 13-day itineraries with stays in luxury hotels and country châteaux, minibus-escorted, private chauffeur-driven, guided or independent self-drive tours. "The Great France Express" features a 12-day itinerary with a two-day optional extension to Normandy, using first class and TGV high-speed trains. Walking and biking tours in the Dordogne, Provence and the Loire Valley are also offered. Private ski chalets in Val d'Isere, Meribel and Chamonix are available. Tours can be arranged to include travel on the Venice Simplon Orient Express and luxury barges.

Air France

> *142 West 57th Street, New York, NY 10019*
> ☎ *(212) 247-0100 or (800) 237-2747*

Working with major tour operators, Air France offers travel programs to all of France. Packages include Paris city programs, Riviéra programs, ballooning tours, barge cruising, fly-drive and more. For flight reservations and information call your travel agent or Air France direct.

Air Inter

142 West 57th Street, New York, NY 10019
☎ *(800) 237-2747*
This company offers special airfare discounts up to 65 percent for senior citizens, families, groups, youths and students. "France Visite" fares are offered in conjunction with APEX transatlantic fares. Travelers can take advantage of unlimited air travel in a one-month period with "Le France Pass," good for seven days, or the "Le France Air-Car Pass," good for two days' flight on Air Inter and one week Hertz rental car, or the "Le France Youth/Student Pass," good for five days between 31 French cities.

Alastair Sawday's Tours

44 Ambra Vale East, BS8 4RE Bristol, England
☎ *(44) 272-299921 or (800) 367-0303; FAX: (44) 272-254712*
Specializing in tailor-made tours throughout France for groups of six to 60, this company provides accommodations in châteaux, luxury bed-and-breakfast inns, and hotels. Luxury barge cruises are available in a wide range of prices, as well as moderately priced cycling tours.

American Airlines Fly AAway Vacations

☎ *(800) 832-8383, or contact your travel agent.*
The airlines offer "Fly AAway" vacations featuring city tours and fly-drive packages to Paris, Nice and many other French cities. Other packages include escorted motorcoach tours and winter tours from New York to Paris, air and land inclusive.

American Dream Vacations

46 Wyrertown Road, Sussex, NJ 07461
☎ *(800) 255-2376; FAX: (201) 7291706*
This company provides guided group tours, including "Paris for the First Time," designed for the first-time visitor. Other options include French wine country fly-drive tours, Paris hotels, Paris apartment rentals (five nights minimum), Riviéra programs, art-appreciation tours, ski programs, fly-rail packages and D-Day regional tours. All programs emphasize French culture and history.

American Express Vacations

P.O. Box 1525, Ft. Lauderdale, FL 33302
☎ *(800) 241-1700; FAX: (305) 357-4687*
Tour packages include escorted and independent vacations throughout France and tours combining Paris with other European cities. Specialty tours include 12- and 15-day packages and Euro Disney packages.

American Media Tours

16 West 32nd Street, New York, NY 10001
☎ *(212) 465-1630 or (800) 969-6344; FAX: (212) 465-1636*

This company can book stays in apartments, condos, villas, country houses and chalets throughout France. Packages including hotels, excursions and rent-a-car programs for semi-independent travelers. Special programs include cooking schools, skiing, and bike tours.

Annemarie Victory Organization

136 East 64th Street, New York, NY 10021
☎ *(212) 486-03 53; FAX: (212) 751-3149*
Catering to the luxury traveler, this firm offers deluxe gourmet tours to "The Very Best of France," all fully escorted. Packages include restaurant and hotel reservations, wine tastings in private cellars, lessons on art, culture, history and cooking demonstrations by three-star chefs. Specialty packages include the Paris *haute couture* showing, which features a trip on the Concorde, all transfers by limousines, dining in three-star restaurants, and private showings by Ungaro, Givenchy, Chanel, Vicky Tiel and Nina Ricci.

Autoventure

425 Pike Street, Seattle, WA 98101
☎ *(206) 624-6033 or (800) 426-7502; FAX: (206) 340-8891*
Specializing in self-drive and chauffeur-driven tours, this company houses clients in privately owned family châteaux and country inns.

Avalon Tours

P.O. Box 573, Jamestown, RI 02835
☎ *(714) 640-6963 or (401) 423-3730 or (800) 662-2628; FAX: (714) 640-6963 or (401) 423-3740*
Featuring deluxe custom food and wine tours in Bordeaux, Burgundy and other regions, this company specializes in small groups of four to 10 people. All tours are led by bilingual owners. Transportation in France is provided by private air-conditioned minibus, and accommodations include luxury châteaux and hotels. In-depth wine tours are offered for the connoisseur, aspiring connoisseur or those who just enjoy wine.

Club Med

40 West 57th Street, New York, NY 10019
or
P.O. Box 4460, Scottsdale, AZ 85261
☎ *(800) CLUB MED.*
Club Med features all-inclusive vacation packages that include a variety of sports and activities. Accommodations, meals, sports and entertainment are all part of prepaid price.

Le Cordon Bleu

8, rue Leon Delhomme, 75015 Paris, France
☎ *(33) 1-48-56-06-06; FAX: (33) 1-48-56-03-96*
In the United States:

404 Irvington Street, Pleasantville, NY 19570
☎ *(914) 741-0606 or (800) 457-CHEF; FAX: (914) 741-0869*
This famous school of French cuisine and pastry was founded in 1895 and today it welcomes tourists and groups of visitors. Groups may follow private demonstrations

and/or classes. Gourmet courses are offered on specific gastronomic themes including Parisian market tours, bistro cuisine, festive menus, lean cuisine and bread baking. Programs range from one to five days.

Cross-Culture

52 High Point Drive, Amherst, MA 01002
☎ *(413) 256-6303; FAX: (413) 253-2303*
Cross-Culture offers travel programs on French history, culture and contemporary life, including "Walks in the South of France" in Midi-Pyrénées and Languedoc-Roussillon. Other packages include the "Paris Plus" tour, as well as tours through Normandy and the Loire Valley. The "Autumn in the South of France" in Aquitaine, Midi-Pyrénées and Languedoc-Roussillon packages are other options. All tours include wine tasting and authentic French cuisine.

Dailey-Thorp Travel

330 West 58th Street, New York, NY 10019
☎ *(212) 307-1555; FAX: (212) 974-1420*
This company features the "Rambler Tours" program which offers quality fly-drive packages with Air France jet-transfer, car and seven nights' hotel accommodations. Flights are offered to any of 11 key cities in France. Extensions up to 21 days can be arranged in advance. Also available are special luxury escorted music festival tours to Paris, Aix-en-Provence, Orange, Nice and Strasbourg.

Distinctive Destinations Ltd.

P.O. Box 573, Jamestown, RI 02835
☎ *(401) 423-3730 or (800) 662-2628; FAX: (401) 423-3740*
Specialties include custom-planned tours for small groups to France, including transportation and accommodations. Packages offer luxury hotel barges, private country homes, wine tours in Bordeaux and Burgundy, as well as culinary adventures in Gascony.

Distrav

370 Lexington Avenue, New York, NY 10017
☎ *(212) 697-1133 or (800) 334-7872; FAX: (212) 983-8298*
This company offers two-week leisurely paced motorcoach tours with deluxe and first class accommodations, buffet-style American breakfast and other meals. Air travel is provided from New York and other U.S. gateways on Air France and other major airlines.

ETT Tours

198 East Boston Post Road, Mamaroneck, NY 10543
☎ *(914) 698-9426 or (800) 551-2085; FAX: (914) 698-9516*
ETT Tours offers independent tours by train and self-drive car, with accommodations in châteaux, hotels and country inns. The company specializes in eight-day tours to Brittany, Atlantic Coast-Loire Valley, and châteaux country. Optional packages offer travel on Venice Simplon Orient Express, or the Boulogne-Paris-Basle extensions.

European Car Vacations

9 Boston Street, Lynn, MA 01904

☎ *(617) 581-0844 or (800) 223-6764; FAX: (617) 581-3714*
This firm features self-drive, "go-as-you-please" programs with accommodations at France Accueil hotels and bed-and-breakfast properties throughout France.

European Holidays

137 South Pugh Street, State College, PA 16801
☎ *(814) 238-3557 or (800) 752-9578; FAX: (814) 238-3580*
Specializing in air-inclusive or land-only tours, this company offers "Paris Stay Put" packages that include hotels, transfers, sight-seeing with city tours and countryside excursions. "Go-as-you-please" hotel vouchers can be purchased separately or with car rental or rail passes. Combination Paris-London packages also are available.

EventNet

30 Exchange Street, Portland, ME 04101
☎ *(207) 879-9080 or (800) 729-8499; FAX: (207) 871-7675, (800) 795-7469*
This company provides special services for individuals and small groups, including ticket booking for opera, concerts, theater, sporting events in major cities; car-and-driver services in the Paris and Nice areas. Small inn and hostellerie/château accommodations are offered at selected properties. Yacht and self-drive houseboat charters also are available.

Expo Garden Tours

145 4th Avenue, New York, NY 10003
☎ *(212) 677-6704 or (800) 448-2685; FAX: (212) 260-6913*
Expo Garden Tours offers scheduled, escorted tour programs and custom-designed group itineraries to France for amateur and professional garden enthusiasts. A horticulturist or landscape architect accompanies each tour group.

Families Welcome

21 West Colony Place, Durham, NC 27705
☎ *(919) 489-2555 or (800) 326-0724; FAX: (919) 490-5587*
This firm specializes in tours of Paris and France designed especially for families. Arrangements are customized for each family. Two special escorted departures are offered each summer just for families. Apartments and hotels are provided in Paris. Private homes, cottages and villas are available in the countryside. The firm is a representative for the *Logis de France*, a self-drive program with accommodations in small, family-owned inns and guest houses throughout France.

Fenwick & Lang

100 West Harrison, South Tower, Seattle, WA 98119
☎ *(206) 216-2903 or (800) 243-6244; FAX: (206) 216-2904*
Specializing in luxury hotel and charter barge programs for individuals and small groups, this company also offers self-drive barges and ballooning. Other special interest charters include gastronomy, wine, golf, history and museum tours. Accommodations are provided in apartments, houses, villas, châteaux and exclusive estate rentals. Other services include private plane/helicopter transfers and custom self-drive or chauffeured auto transport.

France in Your Glass

814 35th Avenue, Seattle, WA 98122
☎ *(206) 325-4324 or (800) 578-0903; FAX: (206) 325-1727, (800) 578-7069*

This company offers wine and food vacations. Escorted tours for small groups include 10-day visits to Bordeaux, outstanding estates in Burgundy, the Rhône, Champagne, Alsace and the Loire. Cellar tastings are hosted by owners, and châteaux dining. Weeklong culinary programs in Paris and Provence are available.

France Vacations

9841 Airport Boulevard, Los Angeles, CA 90045
☎ *(310) 645-3070 or (800) 332-5332; FAX: (310) 645-1947*
This firm can book accommodations at more than 300 hotels, inns and resorts. All accommodations have two- to four-star ratings. Other packages include car rental and fly-drive programs.

The French Experience

370 Lexington Avenue, New York, NY 10017
☎ *(212) 986-1115; FAX: (212) 986-3803*
All travel needs for the independent traveler to France are arranged by this company. Specializing in five- to eight-day self-drive tours in the French provinces the company also offers a wine tour in Burgundy/Champagne and "The Châteaux Experience," a self-drive tour with stays in private châteaux in Brittany and the Loire Valley. À la carte accommodations in country inns and hotels and cottages throughout France, apartment rentals in Paris, and self-drive houseboats on French canals are available.

Galaxy Tours

P.O. Box 234, 997 Old Eagle School Road, Wayne, PA 19087-0234
☎ *(610) 964-8010 or (800) 523-7287; FAX: (610) 964-8220*
The company offers veterans' tours that follow actual routes and visit sites of World War I and II military importance. Custom-designed itineraries and seminars are available for military and other special-interest groups.

Gascony Tours

5 Ledgewood Way, Peabody, MA 01960
☎ *(508) 535-5738 or (800) 852-2625; FAX: (508) 535-5738*
The company offers an eight-day or longer "Country Kitchens of Gascony Tour," a culinary adventure into the heart of southwestern France that includes cooking demos and meetings with premier chefs at four-star properties. Large and small groups are welcome. First-class accommodations are provided. Other packages include visits to *foie gras* farms, goat cheese producers and wine/armagnac cellars. Historical and cultural tours of Gascony with customized itineraries from Bordeaux to Toulouse also are offered.

Grand Travel

6900 Wisconsin Avenue, Chevy Chase, MD 20815
☎ *(301) 986-0790 or (800) 247-7651; FAX: (301) 913-0166*
This firm offers two itineraries to France exclusively for grandparents and their grandchildren ages 7 to 17. Escorted tours provide activities for both generations with travel study guides for grandchildren. "The Glories of France" tour includes Normandy, Brittany, Loire and Paris. "The French Countryside" includes a three-night barge trip in Burgundy.

International Curtain Call

3313 Patricia Avenue, Los Angeles, CA 90064
☎ *(310) 204-4934 or (800) 669-9070; FAX: (310) 2049935*

Deluxe, fully escorted opera and music festival tours, include hotels, opera and concert tickets, customized sight-seeing with professional English-speaking guides and interesting excursions. Packages include air transportation, land transportation to airports, hotels, theaters and sight-seeing. Specialty packages include the July Tour: Paris Opera and Ballet, the Aix-en-Provence Air Music Festival tour, and the Avignon Orange Music Festival tour.

First Cultural Tours

225 West 34th Street, New York, NY 10122
☎ *(212) 563-1327 or (800) 833-2111; FAX: (212) 594-6953*

Cultural tours for escorted groups and individual travelers, using specialists from universities, institutes and museums with themed travel programs throughout France. Tour options include "From Impressionism to Modern Art," "From William the Conqueror to D-Day" and "The Good Life in Burgundy Barge Cruise." All packages feature specialized activities such as a painting session with an artist, a cooking demonstration with a master chef, or a wine tasting in the wine cellar of a château.

Loire Valley Travel

5, rue de la Pair, 41000 Blois
☎ *(33) 54-78-62-52; FAX: (33) 54-78-42-19*

This French firm specializes in classic and unusual travel for individuals and groups. Packages include bicycle touring in the Loire, Anjou, Brittany and Poitou-Charentes. With weekly departures, the bicycle tours include 15 routes, with accommodations, bike rental and luggage transport provided. Hotel-based walking tours and horseback tours in the Loire, along with mountain biking and hiking are available. Special interest group tours include gourmet, art, wine and music packages.

Maupintour

P.O. Box 807, 1515 St. Andrews Drive, Lawrence, KS 66047
☎ *(913) 843-1211 or (800) 255-4266; FAX: (913) 843-8351*

All-inclusive escorted tours including the 12-day "France Highlights" with stops in Paris, the Loire Valley and Normandy (Mt. St. Michel, Omaha Beach, Giverny). The 13-day "Southern France, Provence & the Riviéra" includes Paris, and TGV train transportation to Bordeaux, Carcassonne, Arles, Nice and Monte Carlo.

New Frontiers

12 East 33rd Street, New York, NY 10016
☎ *(212) 779-0600 or (800) 366-6387; FAX: (212) 779-1006*

This company specializes in custom-designed European vacations that include flights, hotels, city tours, rental cars, train passes and tickets, fly-and-drive packages, scheduled-air and charter inter-European flights. The firm is the American division of Nouvelles Frontieres.

Past Times Archeological Tours

800 Larch Lane, Sacramento, CA 95864

☎ *(916) 485-8140*
Small group tours: "Lascaux and the Dordogne," "Megaliths of Brittany," "European Art History in the Great Museums of Paris and France." One- and two-week tours are offered in June or by arrangement to Lascaux. Packages include tours to a dozen prehistoric painted caves and archeological sites in France and Spain. Visits are offered to the rural Pyrénées and Dordogne regions with small study-groups led by professional archeologists and art historians. All tours include travel by minibus with lectures on the history, language and customs of the region. Custom tours are offered for the fans of Jean M. Auel's *Clan of the Cave Bear*. Intensive museum and art history study in Paris.

Pilgrimage Tours and Travel
39 Beechwood Avenue, Manhasset, NY 11030
☎ *(516) 627-2636 or (800) 669-0757; FAX: (516) 365-1667*
Catholic pilgrimage tours include air and land travel. Packages include the "Pilgrimage to Lourdes," the "St. Bernadette Pilgrimage" and "Lourdes and Fatima." Customized pilgrimages are available for groups.

Privileges de France
36, rue Bernard Palissy, 37000 Tours
☎ *(33) 47-05-19-19; FAX: (33) 47-61-18-18*
This firm provides exclusive, tailor-made small-group programs in the Loire Valley and special-interest tours such as wine, golf and ballooning. First-class accommodations are provided in châteaux-hotels and private châteaux. Packages include gourmet French cuisine, wine tasting in private cellars, as well as visits to royal châteaux, medieval villages and offbeat private châteaux.

SAGA Holidays
222 Berkeley Street, Boston, MA 02116
☎ *(617) 262-2262 or (800) 343-0273; FAX: (617) 3755953*
Travel programs exclusively for adults over 50. All tours include air and land transportation. Cruise packages, hosted holidays, fully escorted motorcoach tours, week- and monthlong stays, and educational tours are available.

Swan Hellenic/Esplanade Tours
581 Boylston Street, Boston, WA 02116
☎ *(617) 266-7465 or (800) 426-5492; FAX: (617) 262-9829*
Small-group tours focus on the art and natural history of Provence, Côte d'Azur, Languedoc, the Pyrénées and Dordogne. All tours are accompanied by expert guest lecturers and local guides.

Touraine Welcome Organization
7, rue des Guetteries, 37000 Tours
☎ *(33) 47-64-54-37; FAX: (33) 47-05-25-50*
This regional agency in Western France offers tours of the Loire Valley, Anjou, Brittany, Normandy and Poitou-Charentes for individuals and groups. Tailor-made programs are available on subjects such as history, gastronomy, wine, music, golf, treasure hunts, cooking, bicycle tours and medieval receptions. Some tours feature gala evenings in royal châteaux and wine cellars. Off-the-beaten-track programs

include overnight stays in châteaux-hotels and private châteaux in the heart of France.

Tours of Historic & Important Places

134 Golf Club Drive, Longwood, FL 32779
☎ *(407) 862-4556; FAX: (407) 682-9039*
World War II tours, V-E Day tours, "Cold War" tours and seminars. Customized military tours are available.

Trafalgar Tours

11 East 26th Street, New York, NY 10010
☎ *(212) 689-8977 or (800) 854-0103; FAX: (212) 725-7776 or (800) 457-6644*
This company provides escorted motorcoach tours. Packages include the nine-day "Châteaux, Champagne and Normandy tour," the 14-day "Best of France tour," the 18-day "France and Spain tour," and the nine-day "Paris Week" city package.

Travel Bound

599 Broadway, New York, NY 10012
☎ *(212) 334-1350 or (800) 456-8656; FAX: (800) 208-7080*
Flexible, independent air/land or land-only packages with more than 60 hotels offered in Paris. Fly-drive programs throughout the country are available. Sight-seeing, rail passes, car rental, cabaret shows, airport transfers and more are included in package prices. Accommodations range from tourist class to deluxe. Multicity itineraries are available to link Paris with visits to other European cities.

La Varenne

P.O. Box 25574, Washington D.C. 20007
☎ *(202) 337-0073 or (800) 537-6486; FAX: (703) 823-5438*
This renowned culinary school features one- to three-week hands-on cooking programs. Located in Burgundy in the Château du Fey, the school offers packages with all-inclusive fees that cover classes, excursions, meals, accommodations, swimming pool and tennis courts. Travel to and from France is not included, however, the package includes pickup and drop-off in Paris.

XO Travel Consultants

38 West 32nd Street, New York, NY 10001
☎ *(212) 947-5530 or (800) 262-9682; FAX: (212) 971-0924*
This firm specializes in gastronomic and horticultural tours. All packages are customized, escorted programs for individuals and special interest groups. Deluxe arrangements include gourmet dining, authentic regional cuisine and special wine tastings. Also exclusive Aix-en-Provence/ Provençal countryside programs, and luxury sail-borne cruises on the Côte d'Azur to explore Provence and Languedoc. Special interest cruise and incentive packages are available for groups up to 60.

Before You Go

The Chinese say that the journey of a thousand miles begins with a single step. In reality, of course, the successful journey begins long before you ever leave your home. In this section you'll find lots of helpful hints and specific information that will assist you in making preparations for your visit to France. Taking care of your passport, visas, traveler's checks and insurance needs are all tasks that should be done well before you leave. Even seasoned travelers generally find it helpful to make a checklist of things to do before they leave—nothing can spoil a trip faster than not being prepared with the right documents. Plan ahead, and you'll avoid unpleasant surprises.

Documentation

All visitors to France must have a valid passport to enter the country, as well as to leave and return to their country of origin. If you've never traveled outside your country before or if your passport is expired, you will need to apply for a new passport. If your passport is current, check the expiration date to make sure the document won't expire during your trip—otherwise you might end up unable to return home, yet not legally permitted to remain on French soil. Most countries' governments claim to issue passports in three or four weeks, but most countries' governments take significantly longer than they promise to do *anything*, so allow six to eight weeks to receive your passport after you apply for it. Remember that April through July are the busiest times in most countries.

Passports
United States

You can apply for a new or renewed passport at most federal and state courthouses, post offices, many county courthouses, and at any of the State Department's Passport Agency offices in Boston, Chicago, Honolulu, Houston, Los Angeles, Miami, New Orleans, New York, Philadelphia, San Francisco, Seattle, Stamford (CT) or Washington, D.C. If you've never had a passport before, or if your current passport is 12 years old, or was issued to you before you turned 18 years old, you'll have to apply in person. You'll need to take proof of citizenship (original or certified copy of your birth certificate or naturalization documents), a separate picture identification, two passport photographs (they must be identical, full-face, against a plain background, in black-and-white or color), and a check or money order for $65 made out to Passport Services. If you have a passport that is less than 12 years old, you can renew it by mail by sending the old passport and a check or money order for $55 made out to Passport Services to the nearest authorized passport-issuing office. You'll receive your new passport by mail. Supposedly, you can get an emergency temporary passport on the spot if you can show proof that you'll be traveling within five working days (an airline ticket is about the only acceptable proof), but don't leave it that late! For more information, contact:

National Passport Center
> P.O. Box 371971, Pittsburgh, PA 15250-7971
> ☎ (603) 334-0500

Canada

You can get an application form for a five-year passport (nonrenewable; you must apply for a new passport every five years) at all passport offices, post offices and most travel agencies. Once you have completed the form, take it, along with two identical passport photographs, which you must sign on the back, and a check or money order for CDN$35 made out to Passport Office, to any one of the 28 regional passport offices throughout the country. The government claims to be able to process applications in person like this in five working days, but don't bet on it. In any case, you can also apply by mail by sending the completed form, photos and check or money order to:

Passport Office

> *Department of Foreign Affairs, Ottawa, ON K1A 0G3*
>
> *Information Line:* ☎ *(800) 567-6868*

Great Britain

You can apply for a 10-year full passport or a more restricted, one-year British Visitor's Passport (which is accepted for entry into France but only for a stay of no more than three months) from main post offices, offices of the Department of Social Security, or from the Passport Offices in London, Newport, Liverpool, Peterborough, Glasgow and Belfast. You can apply by mail to all the offices except the one in London, or in person at any of them. The fee for a full passport is £18. The Visitor's Passport fee is £12. The Visitor's Passport is usually issued on the same day you apply for it, and both partners of a married couple can be included on the same Visitor's Passport. For trips of up to 72 hours, an Excursion Document (which can also be obtained on the spot) is valid for entering France. Children up to 16 years of age can travel on their parent's passport, but they must be listed on the document. Follow the same procedures as when applying for a new passport to have your child's name added.

It's a good idea to make a photocopy of the 'business' page or pages of your passport that contain your name, the passport's number, and your photograph. Keep this copy in a safe place separate from the document itself. That way, if your passport is lost or stolen, you'll have an easier time proving to your country's consulate that you are entitled to a temporary replacement. If you do lose your passport, report it immediately to the nearest consulate or embassy, as well as the local police. It's also wise to store your passport in a safe or safety deposit box if your hotel provides such facilities.

Visas

Citizens of European Community nations, the United States, Canada and New Zealand do not need a visa to enter France so long as the trip is for no more than 90 days (this is true for both business and tourism visits). If you will be staying longer than 90 days, or if you are a citizen of Australia or any other country, you will need to obtain a visa from the French embassy or consulate in your home country before you will be allowed to enter France. There are three types of visas: a transit visa, which is valid for only three days; a *carte de séjour*, valid for up to 90 days, including unlimited entries and exits, and a *visa de circulation*, valid for any number of trips of up to 90 days' duration each over a three-year period. For information on student visas, see the Special Interests section.

Customs Regulations

Entering France

There should be no problem at French customs for most visitors entering the country, however, there are restrictions on the amount and value of goods you can bring with you. In keeping with European Community (EC) regulations established in 1993, there are two basic categories of import restrictions—one for goods purchased tax-paid in another EC country, and another for goods purchased in a non-EC country or purchased duty-free in another EC country.

In the first category, the duty-free limits are as follows: 300 cigarettes or 150 cigarillos or 75 cigars or 400 grams of tobacco; and five liters of table wine; and 1.5 liters of alcohol over 44 proof (i.e., most spirits or hard liquor) or three liters of alcohol under 44 proof (i.e., sparkling or fortified wine) or an additional three liters of table wine; and 90 milliliters of perfume; and 375 milliliters of toilet water; and additional goods up to a value of FR2400.

In the second category, the duty-free limits are similar but a little smaller all around: 200 cigarettes or 100 cigarillos or 50 cigars or 250 grams of tobacco (or, if you live outside the European Community, 400 cigarettes or 200 cigarillos or 100 cigars or 500 grams of tobacco); and two liters of table wine; and one liter of alcohol over 44 proof (i.e., most spirits or hard liquor) or two liters of alcohol under 44 proof (i.e., sparkling or fortified wine) or an additional two liters of table wine; and 60 milliliters of perfume; and 250 milliliters of toilet water; and additional goods up to a value of FR300.

It is the last section of the regulations that is of most import to visitors from other countries: if you are traveling with expensive photographic or computer equipment or other goods, be able to prove that they are personal belongings that will be re-exported when you leave France (the same holds true when you return home). A receipt indicating the date of purchase is helpful in this regard.

Under no circumstances may you import into France narcotics, material that constitutes a copyright infringement, counterfeit or fake artwork or other goods, and weapons or ammunition (unless you have previously secured a special import license from the French government). To avoid any confusion when you are traveling with prescription drugs, it is wise to carry them in clearly marked containers and also to carry a copy of the doctor's prescription for the medicine.

There is no restriction on the amount of money that may be imported into or exported from France, with the *caveat* that any amount over FR50,000 must be reported to the customs officials upon your arrival. This is true for French and foreign currency, as well as for bank notes, checks, traveler's checks, letters of credit, bills of exchange, bearer bonds, stocks and shares certificates, bullion, and gold and silver coins quoted on the official exchange.

You can bring your pets with you on your visit to France, with the following restrictions: Animals under three months old are not allowed into the country; a maximum of three dogs or cats over three months old are admitted, providing they have a certificate issued by a licensed veterinarian of having received an anti-rabies vaccination at least one month but no more than one year previous to entry. For more information, or for exceptions to the three-beast maximum rule, contact:

Ministère de l'Agriculture et de la Fôret

Direction Generale de l'Alimentation
Bureaux des Exchanges Internationaux
175, rue du Chevaleret, 75 Paris, cedex 13, France
☎ *01-45-84-13-13*

If you are a citizen of an EC country and you are entering France across the border from Belgium, Germany, Luxembourg or the Netherlands by car, you may proceed without stopping, provided you are only carrying law-abiding EC nationals, and money, animals and goods that you are legally entitled to bring into France as described above. All you need to do is display visibly on your windshield a green disk of at least 8 centimeters (approximately 3 inches) diameter. You should be able to get the windshield disk from your travel agent at home.

For more information on customs regulations, contact one of the French government's customs information centers:

Bordeaux
  ☎ *05-56-44-47-10. ext. 153*

Nantes
  ☎ *02-40-73-52-15*

Lyon
  ☎ *04-78-42-01-76*

Paris
  ☎ *01-40-01-02-06*

Marseille
  ☎ *04-91-08-60-50*

Strasbourg
  ☎ *03-88-32-48-90. ext. 211*

Returning Home

Every country has different customs regulations; you should be sure to familiarize yourself with your own before going on that shopping spree on the Champs-Elysées. The most important thing to remember is that any articles you purchase tax-free in France (see Shopping) or duty-free in the airports are subject to customs regulations and import duty in your homeland. "Duty-free" applies to where you buy the goods, not necessarily where they end up!

United States

The general rule for U.S. customs is the $400 per person limit. This is the value of goods purchased abroad that may be brought into the country free of duty by each person, provided that the importer has been out of the country for at least 48 hours (to discourage quickie shopping trips to Canada and Mexico) and has not taken advantage of this allowance in the past 30 days (to discourage repeated shopping trips to Canada or Mexico). The allowance applies to anyone, regardless of age, and family members traveling together are permitted to pool their allowances, so that a family of four can bring in $1600 worth of goods bought abroad. For the next $1000 worth of goods, there is a flat 10 percent tax rate; for goods over the combined $1400 threshold, the rate varies according to the nature of the goods. As noted above, carry copies of the receipts for expensive equipment or possessions so you don't get hassled by a zealous customs inspector upon your return. Or you can make up a list of serial numbers and descriptions of the articles before you leave and have the list stamped and dated by a customs officer at the airport you depart from. You can't carry a receipt for everything. When I was returning to the U.S. from Europe, I was once confronted by a customs agent who refused to believe that I had owned the leather jacket I was wearing since long before my trip. I was forced to resort to screaming and pleading to avoid paying duty on it. Remember, the customs agents will determine the value of your leather jacket/camera/laptop computer at their own discretion!

Additionally, anyone over 21 may import one liter of alcohol, 100 cigars (*not* from Cuba!) and 200 cigarettes. You may mail gifts from France so long as the value of the contents of each package does not exceed $50; only one package per addressee per day is allowed, and the parcel must be clearly marked as an "Unsolicited Gift" on the exterior. In keeping with its insular philosophy, the U.S. government is particularly paranoid about new bugs and parasites entering the country, so restrictions against importing food and plants are especially strict. Unfortunately for the visitor returning from France, fruits and cheeses are usually banned outright. You can get specific up-to-date information about which foods and plants you can and cannot import into the United States by ordering the brochure *Travelers' Tips on Bringing Food, Plant, and Animal Products into the United State* from the following address:

Animal and Plant Health Inspection Service

> *U.S. Department of Agriculture*
> *Public Information Office*
> *6505 Belcrest Avenue, Washington, D.C. 20250*
> For further general information, the Customs Service can send you a brochure called *Know Before You Go*; contact the service at the following address:

U.S. Customs Service

> *P.O. Box 7407, Washington, D.C. 20044*
> ☎ *(202) 927-6724*

Canada

Canadian residents or visitors entering Canada can import goods worth up to just CDN$300 duty-free, however, residents may only use this allowance once a year, and must have been out of Canada for at least seven days in order to claim it. (If you've only been outside Canada for a period between 48 hours and seven days, your allowance is only CDN$100, but at least you can use that allowance any number of times.) Any goods you import above the CDN$300 threshold will be taxed at a flat rate of 12 percent. You cannot pool your exemptions with other travelers, including members of your family.

You can mail part or all of the goods you want to import under your allowance, but you must still declare them when you enter the country. You can mail an unlimited number of gifts to people in Canada from France; the value of the goods in each package may not exceed CDN$60, and alcohol and tobacco may not be sent. Label the package clearly as "Unsolicited Gift—Value under CDN$60."

Alcohol and tobacco are included in the CDN$300 and CDN$100 allowances. People of age (under the individual provincial laws in effect at the point of entry) may bring into Canada 1.14 liters of wine or 24 12-ounce bottles or cans of beer; and 200 cigarettes and 50 cigars or cigarillos and 400 grams of tobacco.

More information is available in a brochure called *I Declare/Je Déclare*, available from the following address:

Revenue Canada Customs and Excise Department

Connaught Building, MacKenzie Avenue, Ottawa, ON K1A OL5
☎ *(800) 461-9999 or (613) 957-0275*

Great Britain

British citizens and others entering Britain who have traveled only in European Community countries since they left the country do not need to pass through customs. EC countries are France, Belgium, Britain, Denmark, Germany, Greece, Ireland, Italy, Luxembourg, the Netherlands, Portugal and Spain.

If you traveled in other countries, you may import goods purchased in those countries valued up to £136. Additionally, anyone over age 17 may bring into Great Britain up to 800 cigarettes and 400 cigarillos and 200 cigars and one kilogram of tobacco; and 90 liters of wine and 20 liters of fortified wine and 10 liters of spirits and 110 liters of beer.

More information is available in a brochure called *A Guide for Travelers*, which you can obtain from the following address:

HM Customs and Excise

Dorset House, Stamford Street, London SE1 9PY, England
☎ *(071) 928-3344*

Insurance

Insurance to cover the theft or loss of luggage or possessions may or may not be covered under your homeowner's or renter's insurance policy. Check with your agent to review your policy's restrictions. The risks of loss are no greater when you're abroad, so long as you employ the best prevention tool anywhere—common sense. Most medical insurance policies provide coverage for overseas emergency treatment—but be sure to review your policy for details. Be aware that overseas medical treatment is not provided by **Medicare**, the federal health insurance for senior citizens in the United States. Canadian citizens are covered by their national health insurance for up to three months after leaving the country.

You'll also want to look into the insurance provided through your credit card—**American Express**, for example, provides free flight insurance for tickets purchased with the card, and free collision damage waiver insurance for automobiles rented with it. This can represent quite a savings if you rent a car for a couple of weeks. If you purchase your auto insurance through the **American Automobile Association**, they will sell you an extension to provide comprehensive coverage while you are driving abroad.

Airlines provide life insurance for deaths under certain circumstances—check the fine print on your ticket for details. They are also responsible for $20 per kilogram for baggage lost or stolen in transit—this should be ample for most people, but you can buy additional coverage if you're carrying nothing but fancy electronics goods (see Customs Regulations above). If you are particularly paranoid, you can usually buy a last-minute flight insurance policy at the airport before you depart, but that has always seemed to me like gambling on your own demise. Most tour operators and travel agencies sell comprehensive travel insurance with their products that will cover you for medical expenses, baggage loss, property theft and personal liability. Inquire when you book your trip.

Some tips: Always carry a copy of your policies and a proof-of-insurance slip when you travel—you never know when it will simplify things. Report any loss or theft to police immediately, and insist upon a written incident report (even in French)—your insurance company will probably want to see one before settling any claim.

The following is a list of insurance companies that sell comprehensive travel insurance to independent travelers:

Travel Assistance International
1133 15th Street NW, Washington, D.C. 20005
☎ *(800) 821-2828; FAX: (202) 331-1530*

Travel Guard International
1145 Clark Street, Stevens Point, WI 54481
☎ *(715) 345-0505 or (800) 826-1300; FAX: (715)345-0525*

Travel Insured International
52-S Oakland Avenue, P.O. Box 280568, Hartford, CT 06128
☎ *(800) 243-3174; FAX: (203) 528-8005*

What to Take

You already know all the standard rules—pack your bag, then take two-thirds of the stuff out, take mostly dark clothing so it'll show the wear and tear less, take more layers of thin clothing rather than thick sweaters, as it will be more versatile, and so on. But there are some practical things to bear in mind that are specific to France. If you're going to be spending any time north of Lyon, and even if you're only going to be in the south in any month other than in July and August, it will be cold at least some of the time and it will almost certainly rain at least once. Take along enough layers of clothing to keep yourself warm, and don't forget a plastic raincoat and/or folding umbrella. Even on the Côte d'Azur in summer, the temperature gets a little chilly in the evening when the breeze comes in, so make sure you have at least a light pullover and a jacket. Most of the time, you'll want comfortable walking shoes. The tourist walks—a lot. This is especially true in France, where there are dozens of museums and hundreds of quaint villages you'll want to explore on foot.

Bear in mind that most things are more expensive in France than at home, so consider bringing with you supplies of things you might buy on the road elsewhere. This would include camera film, ladies' hosiery, and disposable razors. On the other hand, toiletries should be kept at a minimum: hotels have all the soap you need, and many provide shampoo as well. Unless you're going to the beach or are planning on spending a lot of time in really inexpensive rural hotels, there'll be plenty of towels available, too.

Some articles that I have found to be indispensable include: a Swiss Army knife (for the corkscrew, if for nothing else), a small backpack for day trips, a fannypack and/or money belt, a small calculator for currency conversion, ziplock-type plastic bags (for stinky tennis shoes, wet swimsuits, or leftover brie) and *Fielding's France*.

One last time: minimize, minimize. Remember that you'll be hefting that bag around with you for the duration! Although you can get laundry done at most hotels, remember it's expensive. There are coin-operated laundromats everywhere in France. Savvy travelers carry light-weight, handwashable clothes. Unless you are planning to dine at the most exclusive restaurants in Paris you won't need formal wear. Jeans are 'in' even at the Opera these days, and while shorts in the city are frowned upon, jacket and tie are not necessary outside of business meetings.

French Tourism Offices

France makes it easy for travelers to get information about the country as a whole, as well as about specific interests and geographic regions. Contact one of the offices listed below and they'll be happy to send you brochures, lists of hotels and attractions, and even coupons for discounts for museums and shows. In my experience, the national tourism offices are very helpful and will send out material free of charge, but be aware that the French Government Tourist Hotline in New York is a 900-number that costs 50 cents a minute to access. You can get around that by simply perservering until you get to speak in person with someone at one of the regional offices.

The regional offices in France are extremely cooperative—they are competing with each other for your visit—but as often as not you'll find that the staff there speaks very little English, so be prepared to ask for information in French (*"Je veux de l'information sur votre région"* should do it) and slowly spell out your address. Alternatively, you can send a letter in English requesting the information (they can always find someone to translate), but in that case you'll want to send a self-addressed envelope with international relay coupons that you can buy at any post office. Don't send stamps from your country; they can't use them in France!

United States

French Government Tourist Office
610 5th Avenue, New York, NY 10020
☎ *(212) 315-0888; FAX: (212) 247-6468*

French Government Tourist Office
676 North Michigan Avenue, Chicago, IL 60611

☎ *(312) 751-7800; FAX: (312) 337-6339*

French Government Tourist Office

9454 Wilshire Boulevard, Beverly Hills, CA 90212
☎ *(310) 271-2358; FAX: (310) 276-2835*

French Government Tourist Office Information Hotline

☎ *(900) 990-0040 (cost is 95 cents per minute)*

Canada

French Government Tourist Office

1981 Avenue McGill College, Bureau 490, Montreal, QC H3A 2W9
☎ *(514) 288-4264; FAX: (514) 845-4868*

French Government Tourist Office

30 St. Patrick Street, Suite 700, Toronto, ON M5t 3A3
☎ *(800) 361-9099 or (416) 593-4723; FAX: (416) 979-7587*

England

French Government Tourist Office

178 Picadilly, London W1V 0AL
☎ *(071) 491-7622; FAX: (071) 493-6594*

Ireland

French Government Tourist Office

35 Lower Abbey Street, Dublin 1
☎ *(01) 771871; FAX: (01) 747324*

Australia

French Government Tourist Office

12 Castlereagh Street, 12th Floor BNP Building, Sydney, NSW 2000
☎ *231-5244; FAX: 233-4576*

French Regional Tourism Offices

National Federation of Regional Tourism Committees

Fédération Nationale des Comités Régionaux de Tourisme

280 boulevard Saint-Germain, 75007 Paris
☎ *01-45-55-94-21; FAX: 01-45-51-20-42*

Alsace

Comité Régional du Tourisme d'Alsace

6 avenue de la Marseillaise - B.P. 219, 67005 Strasbourg cedex
☎ *05-88-25-0l-66; FAX: 05-88-52-17-06*

Aquitaine

Comité Régional du Tourisme d'Aquitaine

Cité Mondiale des vins et des Spiritueux - 23 parvis des Chartrons, 33074 Bordeaux cedex
☎ *05-56-0l-70-00; FAX: 05-56-0l-70-07*

Auvergne

Comité Régional du Tourisme Auvergne

43 avenue Julien - B.P. 395, 63011 Ciermont-Ferrand cedex 1
☎ *02-73-93-04-03; FAX: 02-73-34-11-11*

Bourgogne

Comité Régional du Tourisme de Bourgogne

12 boulevard de Brosse - B.P. 1602, 21035 Dijon cedex
☎ 03-80-50-10-20; FAX: 03-80-30-59-45

Brittany

Comité Régional du Tourisme de Bretagne

74b rue de Paris, 35069 Rennes cedex
☎ 02-99-28-44-30; FAX: 02-99-28-44-40

Champagne-Ardenne

Comité Régional du Tourisme de Champagne-Ardenne

5 rue de Jéricho, 51037 Châlon-sur-Marne cedex
☎ 03-26-64-35-92; FAX: 03-26-70-31-61

Corsica

Agence de Tourisme de la Corse

17 boulevard du Roi Jérôme-B.P. 19, 20181 Ajaccio cedex 1
☎ 04-95-21-56-56; FAX: 04-95-51-14-40

Franche-Comté

Comité Régional du Tourisme de Franche-Comté

9 rue de Pontarlier, 25044 Besançon Cdex
☎ 03-81-83-50-47; FAX: 03-81-83-35-82

Ile-de-France

Comité Régional du Tourisme d'Ile-de-France

26 avenue de l'Opéra, 75001 Paris
☎ 01-42-60-28-62; FAX: 01-42-60-20-23

Languedoc-Roussillon

Comité Régional du Tourisme Languedoc-Roussillon

20 rue de la République, 34000 Montpellier
☎ 04-67-22-81-60; FAX: 04-67-58-06-10

Limousin

Comité Régional du Tourisme du Limousin

Ensemble Administratif Régional
27 boulevard de la Corderie, 87031 Limoges cedex
☎ 05-55-45-18-80; FAX: 05-55-45-18-18

Loire Valley

Comité Régional du Tourisme Pays de la Loire

2 rue de la Loire - Ile Beaulieu - B.P. 2171, 44204 Nantes cedex 02
☎ 02-40-48-24-20; FAX: 02-40-08-07-10

Central Loire Valley

Comité Régional du Tourisme et des Loisirs de Centre Val-de-Loire

9 rue Saint Picue-Lentin, 45041 Orléans cedex 1
☎ 02-38-54-95-42/43; FAX: 02-38-54-95-46

Lorraine

Comité Régional du Tourisme de Lorraine

1 place Gabriel Hocquard - B.P. 1004, 57036 Metz cedex 1

☎ *03-87-37-02-16; FAX: 03-87-37-02-19*

Midi-Pyrénées

Comité Régional du Tourisme de Midi-Pyrénées

54 boulevard de l'Embouchure B.P. 2166, 31022 Toulouse cedex
☎ *05-61-13-55-55; FAX: 05-61-47-17-16*

Normandy

Comité Régional du Tourisme de Normandie

14 rue Charles Corbeaux Le Doyenné, 27000 Evreux
☎ *02-32-33-79-00; FAX: 02-32-31-19-04*

North Pas-de-Calais

Comité Régional du Tourisme du Nord Pas-de-Calais

6 place Mendes France, 59800 Lille
☎ *03-20-14-57-57; FAX: 03-20-14-57-58*

Picardie

Comité Régional du Tourisme de Picardie

11 mail Albert 1er - B.P. 2616, 80026 Amiens cedex
☎ *03-22-91-10-15; FAX: 03-22-97-92-96*

Poitou-Charentes

Comité Régional du Tourisme de Poiton-Charentes

62 rue Jean Jaurès - B.P. 56, 86002 Poitiers cedex
☎ *05-49-50-10-50; FAX: 05-49-41-37-28*

Provence-The Alps-Côte d'Azur

Comité Régional du Tourisme Provence-Alpes-Côte d'Azur

Espace Colbert
14 rue Sainte Barbe, 13001 Marseille
☎ *04-91-39-38-00; FAX: 04-91-56-66-61*

Riviéra-Côte d'Azur

Comité Régional du Tourisme de Riviéra-Côte d'Azur

55 promenade des Anglais - B.P. 602, 06011 Nice cedex 1
☎ *04-93-37-78-78; FAX: 04-93-86-0l-06*

Rhône Valley-The Alps

Comité Régional du Tourisme Rhône-Alpes

La Combe de Charbonnières
78 bis Route de Paris, 69260 Charbonnières-les-Bains
☎ *04-72-38-11-11; FAX: 04-72-38-44-94*

What to Expect

Getting Around

By Air

Air travel within France is expensive and not much faster than rail transportation unless you are traveling the whole length of the country in one shot, or aiming for one of the extremities not yet served by the TGV network. It's always a balance of time and money when making these decisions, and when you're traveling, time is money. But in general, I would recommend taking a few hours longer to arrive at your destination, thus seeing some of the countryside, and saving tens or even hundreds of dollars by taking the train. An exception would be for travel to Corsica, where the several-hour long ferry ride, coupled with your journey to the south coast, can cause you to lose an entire day each way in transit.

The main domestic carrier in France is **Air Inter Europe**, a subsidiary of **Air France**. Air Inter Europe covers 63 routes within France, serving 31 major cities. There are more than 400 scheduled daily departures, so you'll have no trouble getting a flight when you want so long as they fly to where you want. Purchasing a ticket when you arrive in France is extremely expensive. At press time, for example, a one-way weekend discounted ticket from Paris to Marseille was about US$170. On the other hand, planning ahead can get you some great deals. Because of Air Inter Europe's corporate relationship with Air France, the best deals on domestic flights are often to be had by booking ahead in your home country. This way, you can purchase a combined ticket to France and then to your other French destinations. Air Inter Europe also offers a number of passes and fly-drive programs. The "Le France Pass," US$339 at press time, is good for seven days of unlimited flights during any one month. The "Le France-Europe Pass," US$459, adds two European segments to the "Le France Pass" that must be flown within the seven days on the original pass. Air Inter Europe currently serves Alicante, Ibiza, Malaga, Madrid, Palma de Mallorca, Sevilla and Valencia in Spain; Casablanca and Oujda in Morocco; Alger, Algeria; Tunis, Tunisia; Dublin and Shannon in Ireland; Lisbon and Porto in Portugal; and London, England. The "Le France Air-Car Pass," US$359, is good for two day's unlimited flying plus a week's car rental from Hertz; and the "Le France Youth and Student Pass," US$219, is good for five days' unlimited flying over two months for students under age 27 or any youth under age 25. For more information contact Air Inter Europe at the following addresses:

Air Inter Europe

142 West 57th Street, New York, NY 10019
☎ *(212) 245-7578 or (33) 1-45-39-25-25; FAX: (212) 245-7585*

Minitel

☎ *36-15-AIRINTER*

Air Inter Europe

c/o Air France
☎ *(212) 830-4000 or (800) 237-2747; FAX: (212) 839-4431*

By Rail

Rail service in France is terrific. It's such a welcome change from North America (where trains are few and far between) and England (where trains are utterly unreliable) that it's worth making at least one segment of your intra-France journeys by train just for the experience. The SNCF *(Société Nationale de Chemins de Fer)* trains are frequent, on time, comfortable and fast. Very fast.

TGV and Other Services

France inaugurated its *Train à Grande Vitesse* (high-speed train) network in the early 1980s, and today the whole country, save the central region, is linked by TGV trains. The network is also connected to Belgium, Luxembourg, Germany, Switzerland, Italy and Spain, as well as Great Britain. Traveling at almost 200 miles an hour, the TGVs whisk passengers from Paris to Lyon or Nantes in the Loire Valley in just two hours, to Bordeaux in three hours, the Swiss border in three hours, and all the way to Nice in just six-and-a-half hours. In total, almost 120 cities and towns are served by the TGV system. The busiest route is the Paris-Lyon corridor, which has 25 scheduled daily departures. The traffic on this route has become so heavy that in 1996 SNCF introduced two-level TGV trains that are capable of carrying 545 passengers.

Most trains in France are comfortable and they are a great place to meet people. The compartments usually seat six people on the smaller, slower rural trains, and you will likely find yourself sharing with anyone from businesspeople to students or farmers. There are no cafeteria facilities on most trains (with the exception of TGVs, where the buffet food is underpriced and of low quality), so bring a sandwich and something to drink if you are traveling for more than an hour. On longer trips, you may want to save a day by traveling at night; if so, be sure to pay the extra FR100 or so and get a couchette. You'll probably have a bunk in a unisex compartment with five other people (an interesting experience itself when all are trying discreetly to dress in the morning!), but you'll sleep far better than if you try to doze in your seat all night.

Tickets and Reservations

Given the popularity of train travel, it is highly advisable to reserve seats on your train for main-line routes as far in advance as possible, especially during summer, and at all times for TGV service. This is true even when you are using one of the many rail passes—just because you have a pass does not mean you have a seat. Additionally, when you purchase an individual ticket from a travel agent or distributor abroad, it is likely to be an open ticket, meaning you can travel whenever you want (within designated seasonal limits and within two months of the initial date of validity), but also meaning you will need to reserve your seat before you travel. For travel on TGV and the Intercity trains you will be charged a reservation fee on top of your ticket price that will range from FR15 to more than FR100, depending on class and season.

For smaller, local routes, buy your tickets directly at the train station. Be careful to line up at the correct window, however—most stations offer different lines for domestic tickets, international tickets, seat reservations and general information. In the larger cities, the clerks may speak some English, but in the smaller towns it is likely that French will be the only language spoken. However, if you can pronounce your destination reasonably close to reality (or display it in writing), you shouldn't have too much trouble. A one way ticket is *aller*; roundtrip is *aller et retour*. Route information and timetables are usually posted in poster format at stations; the information window has timetables and brochures, some of which may be printed in English. You can also get information in English by calling ☎ *(33) 05-02-50-50 or* ☎ *(33) 1-43-80-50-50*, as well as from Rail Europe.

Once you have your ticket and are ready to board the train, you'll need to validate your ticket. This is done most often with an automated machine at the entrance to the platform, but in some rural stations there will still be an official doing it by hand. When your ticket is validated *(composté)*, hang on to it anyway, as you'll have to validate it again if you change trains and you will be required to produce it at any time on demand, as well as show it when you leave the station at your final destination.

Train Passes

If you are planning to travel far, but not necessarily often, a train pass is definitely the way to go. The passes offered by SNCF are not exactly cheap, but they are economical if you plan to travel from Paris to the south coast, to Bordeaux, or to château country and back. If you plan to travel only short distances by train, you will be better off buying individual point-to-point tickets.

The most comprehensive pass is the Eurailpass. For some strange reason, this pass is only offered in first class for adults. Travelers under age 26 may purchase the discounted Eurail Youthpass, which covers second-class travel. The basic Eurailpass is good for five-, six-, or seven-days unlimited train travel in France as well as in 16 other European countries—Austria, Belgium, Denmark, Finland, Germany, Greece, Holland, Hungary, Italy, Ireland, Luxembourg, Norway, Portugal, Spain, Sweden and Switzerland (note that England is **not** included) for 15, 21, 30, 60 or 90 days. Variations include the Eurail Flexipass and Eurail Youth Flexipass, which allow five, 10 or 15 days of train travel in two months, and the Eurail Saverpass (for adults only) which gives discounts to two or more people traveling together for 15, 30 or 60 days. At press time prices began at US$348 for a five-day Eurail Flexipass, or US$430 per person for a 15-day Eurail Saverpass, up to US$1398 for a three-month full Eurail pass; or US$255 for a five-day Eurail Youth Flexipass, up to US$768 for a full two-month Eurail Youthpass. You can also get a EurailDrive Pass, which is good for four days of train travel plus three days of Avis or Hertz car rental, starting at US$309 per person.

A scaled-down version of the Eurail pass is the Europass. (Confused yet?) This pass only covers five countries—France, Germany, Italy, Spain and Switzerland. The basic pass is good for five, six or seven days of unlimited train travel in three of the countries within a 60-day period. At press time, the rate for five days on this pass was US$210 per person for at least two people traveling together, rising to US$356 for a single traveler for seven days. If you buy 10 days, you can add a fourth European country free; for 15 days you can travel in all five Europass countries; this will cost you (at press time) US$495 per person for a couple or US$660 for an individual. Young people under age 26 get four countries with the basic Europass Youth pass for US$198 for five days, rising to US$478 for all five countries for 15 days out of a two-month period. The Europass Drive plan gives you five days of rail travel plus three days of car rental (to which you can add up to 10 rail days at US$38 each) for US$289 to US$519 per person, depending on how many people are traveling and what class car you rent.

Passes good for France only operate along the same basic system of a certain number of days of unlimited travel during a certain time period. The basic product, the France Railpass, costs at press time US$120 per person for two adults traveling together in second class for any three days of rail travel in a two-month period. The cost rises according to whether you are traveling alone or in first class up to a maximum US$378 for an individual for nine days of unlimited travel in first class. The France Rail 'n Drive pass gets you three rail days and two car rental days for anything from US$159 to US$359 per person, depending on how many people are in your group, which class train you want to ride, and what kind of car you rent. The France Rail 'n Fly pass is good for three rail days and one day of unlimited flying on Air Inter Europe for US$215 to $295 per person, again depending on how many travelers there are and what class you want to travel; and the grandpère of them all, (yes, you've guessed it) the France Fly Rail 'n drive pass that provides you with three days of unlimited rail travel, one day of unlimited Air Inter Europe flights, and two days of car rental, from US$259 to US$469 per person. In addition, you can add up to six rail days for US$30 each, additional flight days for US$99 each, and additional car days for anything from US$44 to US$84 each, depending on the vehicle you want.

Phew! As you can see, there is a wide variety of products available. Your best bet is to plan early and purchase your passes and make your flight reservations and car rental bookings before arriving in France. It is possible to buy the passes when you arrive but it'll be much, much simpler to do it at home. For information and sales, contact your travel agent or SNCF's overseas agent:

Rail Europe

> *226 Westchester Avenue, White Plains, NY 10604*
> ☎ *(800) 4EURAIL; FAX: (800) 432-1329*

By Bus

French buses are not much use to the foreign visitor. Buses are seldom used for long-distance travel. The only region where bus transportation is the primary mode of getting around is the French Alps. Most buses you see on the highways are privately chartered coaches hauling herds of unprotesting package-tourists around, or else they are trans-European shuttles. For routes and fare information in each city, inquire at the bus station, usually called the *gàre routière*, often found by the train station.

By Car

For the independent traveler, traveling around France is easiest by car. If you want true freedom to go where you like, when you like, a personal automobile is the only way to go.

Expense is likely to be the determining factor in deciding whether you should rent or lease a car for your trip. For one or even two people staying for just a week or two, a railpass will be cheaper. For larger groups, or for longer periods, renting, and especially leasing, a car may make more economic sense. You do need to bear in mind, however, that driving overall costs far more per mile in France than in North America or Britain. Most of the *Autoroutes* (expressways) are toll roads, and pretty expensive, too. You can easily run up a couple of hundred dollars in tolls in just a couple of weeks. Gasoline, meanwhile, is upwards of four dollars a gallon. Diesel is about a dollar a gallon cheaper than gasoline, plus diesel passenger cars are quite commonplace in Europe. If you don't mind a slight reduction in performance, you might want to rent a diesel model to save some money.

Driving Tips

In order to drive in France, you need a valid driver's license from your country of origin, as well as an International Driving Permit (available from the French Automobile Association and the American Automobile Association), although the latter document is never required to be shown and most people skip it. You drive on the right in France (if you have a car from England, readjust the headlights so they don't shine in oncoming drivers' faces. You also must give way to oncoming traffic from the right—the exact opposite of the custom in most other countries. This is the major difference to driving in France for most people. Be especially watchful at crossroads, where the driver coming from the right has the right of way even if your road is the major of the two. Watch out at traffic roundabouts, where you lose the right of way, rather than gaining it, once you have entered the circle. A sign portraying a yellow diamond with a black line through it indicates that you do not have the right of way, but the sign is not always present. The best policy is to give way whenever a car is approaching from the right. Ambulances, fire-engines, police cars and motorcycles, and public utility vehicles (Electricite, Gaz, Compagnie Generale des Eaux, Service de Nettoiement) all have the right of way. The single most flouted traffic law I have ever come across stipulates that it is forbidden to make any use of the horn in Paris and in the larger towns.

The speed limits are 130 kph (81 m.p.h.) on expressways, and 110 kph (68 mph) when it's raining; 110 kph (68 mph) on N- *Route Nationale* (major highways), and *Route Départemental*, or D-roads; 90 kph (56 mph) on minor rural roads, and 50 kph (31 mph) in urban areas. The French drive fast and aggressively—you will often be passed by cars traveling at up to 100 mph, especially on the *autoroutes*. My advice is do not copy this technique, as a speeding ticket for a visitor is infinitely more hassle than for a native. Often, the police officer will demand payment in cash on the spot. Conversely, there is a minimum speed limit of 80 kph (50 mph) for the outside lane on *autoroutes*, during daylight, on level ground and with good visibility.

Etiquette

A more flexible, popularly enforced minimum speed limit applies whenever someone behind you wants to pass. Flashing of headlamps is a complex language of the road. It can mean "Get the hell out of my way!" or "I'm about to pass you," or in the case of large trucks and buses, "You're past me, you can reenter the lane safely now." French drivers, especially bus drivers and truckers, also make use of the European convention of using the turn signals to indicate to someone behind them that it is safe to overtake. If the truck in front of you signals to turn right, the driver may not be exiting the road but instead may be signaling to you that you can pass safely. If the driver signals to the left, this can signal that you shouldn't pass because someone is coming the other way. It is customary to flash your lights or toot your horn after passing someone who has helped you this way. Try to get into the flow of this inter-driver communication, it makes driving in France a much more communal experience.

Accidents and Breakdowns

If you get in a minor accident, and no police officer is around, take down the number of the other car involved, lock your car and go with the driver of the other car to look for an officer. The *gendarme* will make out a report in triplicate, stating where the accident occurred, the names of both owners and insurance companies and the damage done. Try to obtain names and addresses of witnesses. Send the report to the correspondent of your insurance company. If the accident is serious, it is a good idea to take photographs. If someone is hurt, you can be held for up to three or four hours at a police station. If you have an accident on the road and only your car is damaged, the report is normally made by the *huissier* (bailiff) in the nearest community. If there are victims, or if the accident interferes with traffic, or if the *huissier* is not available, the *gendarme* can and should make the report. If neither is available, go to the nearest town hall (*mairie* or *hotel de ville*). If you breakdown on an *autoroute*, there are emergency phones every couple of kilometers; anywhere else, call or go to the nearest garage. Many rental companies and all leasing companies offer 24-hour roadside service; refer to your documentation for more information.

Parking

The parking situation in France is similar to that of many other countries—in the cities parking is almost impossible. Paris and the centers of other large cities are congested year-round, and most of the towns on the south coast lack parking during the tourist season. It is probably wise to not rent your car until you leave Paris. It's hell to find your way around the city, there's no parking, and besides, the Métro offers efficient transportation. If you do have a car in the capital (and the same holds true in other cities), be careful to obey the parking regulations, since violating a rule will result in the car being clamped (expensive and a big hassle) or towed (more expensive and a bigger hassle). Most areas operate with meters and pay-and-display machines, so keep a handful of one franc coins in the car. Parking is free in Paris during August since most Parisians leave town. In many small towns parking is free between noon and 2 p.m.

Gas

Unless you have a diesel vehicle, you should fill up with "super" gasoline or "sans plomb" (unleaded) fuel. Gasoline graded as "essence" is still sold but this will not adequately power your car. Gas is more expensive on *autoroutes*, and filling stations on minor roads can be few and far between, so make sure you don't let the tank get too low.

Maps

A good map is indispensable—the best are the Michelin maps, green-covered paperback books sold in every gas station that provide detailed regional maps indicating sights and Michelin-approved hotels as well as all roads.

For more information on driving in France you can contact the following organizations:

Automobile Club National

5 rue Auber, 75009 Paris, France
☎ (33) 01-44-51-53-99; FAX: (33) 01-49-24-93-99
This association joins together more than 40 French automobile clubs and will provide assistance and help to any tourist whose own club is affiliated.

Automobile Club de France

6 place de la Concorde, 75008 Paris, France

☎ *(33) 01-42-65-34-70; FAX: (33) 01-42-65-21-07*

Automobile Club de l'Ile-de-France

14 avenue de la Grande-Armee, 75017 Paris, France
☎ *(33) 01-43-80-68-58; FAX: (33) 01-43-80-90-51*

Rental Cars

Generally, it is better to rent your car before you leave home; once you arrive in France the rates will be much higher. All the principal air carriers, as well as SNCF and Rail Europe, offer fly-drive and rail-drive packages that considerably cut the cost of your car expenses. Also consider renting from one of the smaller U.S.-based companies, which will not have its own cars in France, unlike the big outfits, but can often offer better rates by subcontracting with smaller, local companies. Usually only the national or international companies will allow you to pick up your car in one city and leave it in another, and for that there is an additional charge. Avoid renting your car in Paris—wait until you strike out into the provinces.

Look into your insurance carefully—a basic rental agreement does not provide collision and damage insurance, but you may be covered if you pay for the rental with your credit card or through your own auto insurance policy. Under French law, you may not rent a car unless you are at least 21 years old and have had your driver's license at least one year, but many rental companies have their own restrictions that are even stricter.

The following is a list of companies renting passenger cars in France:

Aristo's Limousine

12, rue Martissot, 92110 Clichy, France
☎ *01-47-37-53-70; FAX: 01-47-37-91-99*
This firm offers private transfers and sight-seeing tours of Paris and the provinces by English-speaking chauffeur-guides in luxury sedans, limousines and minibuses. All cars are air-conditioned. Custom-made itineraries can be arranged.

Auto Europe

27 Pearl Street, P.O. Box 7006, Portland, ME 04112, U.S.A.
☎ *(207) 828-2525 or (800) 223-5555; FAX: (207) 828-1177 or (800) 235-6321*
This car rental firm has more than 300 locations in France. A wide variety of vehicles and services are available, including chauffeur service, transfer service, camper-vans and luxury autos. Leasing rates also are available with a 14-day minimum. No cancellation penalties.

Autorent

98 rue de la Convention, 75015 Paris, France
☎ *(33) 01-45-54-22-45; FAX: (33) 01-45-54-39-69*

Avis Chauffeur Driven Services

105 rue de Lourmel, 75015 Paris, France
☎ *(33) 01-45-54-33-65; FAX: (33) 01-45-54-16-98; Minitel: 36-15 AVIS*
This firm provides vehicles for business trips or excursions. Limousines, luxury minibuses and motorcoaches with chauffeur, air-conditioned vehicles and English-speaking chauffeurs are available. Assistance is provided at airports and train stations. Professional guides and hostesses are available on request. The firm maintains offices in Paris and the Riviéra.

Avis Motorhome Rentals

15 rue Fournier, 92110 Clichy, France

☎ *(33) 01-47-30-14-04; FAX: (33) 01-47-30-14-64; Minitel: 36-15 AVIS*

Avis provides motorhome rentals in France and Europe. The company's fleet of vehicles is renewed yearly. Pickup from Paris, Nice or Marseille.

Avis Rent-a-car

900 Old Country Road, Garden City, NY 11530, U.S.A.

☎ *(516) 222-3000 or (800) 331-1084; FAX: (516) 222-4671*

Avis Rent-a-Car

Tour Franklin, 92042 Paris-La-Defense cedex 11, France

☎ *(33) 01-49-06-68-68; FAX: (33) 01-47-78-98-98; Minitel: 36-15 AVIS*

Avis offers car rental, leasing, motorhome rentals and chauffeur-driven service. Packages include the "Supervalue," the "Discover Europe," the "French Drive" and the "Go-As-You-Please" fly-drive program. The "Rail & Drive Pass" and "Euraildrive" are offered in conjunction with Rail Europe. Avis has 520 rental locations in France (200 offices are located inside train stations). Economy, automatic, station wagons, minivans and luxury cars are available.

Budget Rent-a-Car

1 rue des Hauts-Flouviers, 94517 Paris, France

☎ *(33) 01-46-86-65-65; FAX: (33) 01-46-86-22-17*

Budget Rent-a-car

4225 Naperville Road, Lisle, IL 60532, U.S.A.

☎ *(708) 955-1900 or (800) 472-3325; FAX: (708) 955-7799*

Budget offers car rental programs for every need. Economy to luxury cars and minivansare available, with manual or automatic transmissions. The company has 200 rental locations throughout France and Corsica. Packages include the "Budget World Travel Plan" and the "Business Traveler."

Carey Limousine International

4530 Wisconsin Avenue NW, Washington, D.C. 20016, U.S.A.

☎ *(202) 362-7400 or (800) 336-4646; FAX: (202) 362-0942*

Citer

165 bis, rue de Vaugirard, 75015 Paris, France

☎ *(33) 01-44-38-60-00; FAX: (33) 01-40-56-08-80*

Economy to luxury sedans, pickup and return in Paris only.

Eurodollar Rent-a-car

100 North Sepulveda Boulevard, El Segundo, CA 90245, U.S.A.

☎ *(310) 410-2627 or (800) 800-6000; FAX: (310) 410-2634*

Eurodollar/Mattei

Parc des Reflets
Z.I. Paris Nord II, 165, avenue du Bois-de-la-Pie, B.P. 40002, 95911 Roissy-Charles-de-Gaulle cedex, France

☎ *(33) 01-49-38-77.00; FAX: (33) 01-49-38-77-02*

"Europe on Wheels" rates with three-day advance reservation from North America. Offices are located at all main airports in France. Reservations can be made through all airlines.

Europcar France/National/InterRent/Tilden

65 rue Edouard-Vaillant, 92100 Paris, France

☎ *(33) 01-49-10-55-55; FAX: (33) 01-49-10-99-46; Minitel: 36-15 EUROPCAR*

Executive Car

2 passage Douhasle, 75015 Paris, France

☎ *01-42-65-54-20; FAX: 01-42-65-25-93*

This worldwide, chauffeur-driven car network offers immediate confirmation, multilingual driver-guides and a fleet of fully air-conditioned cars, limousines, sedans and minibuses.

Foremost Euro-Car/Bon Voyage by Car

5658 Sepulveda Boulevard, Van Nuys, CA 91411, U.S.A.

☎ *(818) 786-1960 or (800) 272-3299; FAX: (818) 786-1249 or (800) 253-3876*

Rental or leased cars are available from this firm in all major cities in France. The fleet features economy to luxury vehicles, minibuses and station wagons. Camper and motorhome rentals also are available. Unlimited mileage.

Hertz

225 Brae Boulevard, Park Ridge, NJ 07656, U.S.A.

☎ *(800) 654-3001*

Hertz offers packages that include the "World on Wheels," the "Affordable France" and "Eurail/Drive and Chauffeur Service." Unlimited mileage. Maps and computerized directions are provided in English. Hertz maintains offices in 200 cities and provides an English-speaking staff. Also standard is 24-hour emergency service. Automatic cars, minivans, station wagons and luxury cars are available.

Holiday Autos U.S.

1425 West Foothill Boulevard, Upland, CA 91786, U.S.A.

☎ *(909) 949-1737 or (800) 422-7737; FAX: (909) 949-1450*

With many locations throughout France, this firm rents economy cars to minibuses, with either manual or automatic transmissions. Long-term rentals and agent discounts are available.

JKL

23 ave. de Neuilly, 75116 Paris, France

☎ *01-40-67-18-00; FAX: 01-40-67-13-52*

Complete transportation services are offered for individuals, corporate and incentive-groups of any size. Sedans, formal and stretch limousines, vans and coaches are available. Luxury chauffeured vehicles can be arranged. Services include out-of-town and airport transfers, multilingual guides and escorts, protocol service, and sight-seeing tours in Paris, the Loire Valley and the Riviéra.

The Kemwel Group

106 Calvert Street, Harrison, NY 10528, U.S.A.

☎ *(914) 835-5555 or (800) 678-0678; FAX: (914) 835-5449*

This firm offers car rentals, including unlimited mileage, full insurance coverage and all local value-added taxes. Packages include "Go-as-you-please" hotel accommodations, with preferred rates available to Air France passengers.

Leasing

If you're going to be in France for two weeks or more, look into leasing a car. The most obvious advantage of leasing is that you won't have to pay the exorbitant 20.5 percent sales tax charged for rental cars—a cost that over three or four weeks can easily amount to a couple of hundred dollars. Technically, most leases are not true leases at all but tax-free purchase-repurchase agreements. You buy a car from the company, then sell it back to them at the conclusion of the agreement for a predetermined price. In the case of the better companies, especially Renault Eurodrive, this is especially attractive because you'll be driving a new car. Renault Eurodrive delivers the car to your pickup point right from the factory. You can usually lease a car in this manner for about US$600 for three weeks, or for US$1000 for eight weeks. The longer the lease, the more the per-week price drops.

In most cases, the lease includes insurance and 24-hour roadside assistance. Most of the time, a customer under age 20 can lease a car where they would be unable to rent one and payment can be made with a personal check and a signed promissory note, meaning that the credit card-impaired are not excluded as they are from rental cars. You will, however, need to make leasing arrangements well in advance of your trip so the company can arrange for your car to be waiting for you at the airport.

Following are some companies that offer leasing services in France:

Auto France

139 Sherwood Drive, PO. Box 760, Ramsey, NJ 07446, U.S.A.
☎ *(201) 934-6994 or (800) 572-9655; FAX: (201) 934-7501*
Leases on tax-free new Peugeots for periods from two weeks to six months are available. Rates include full insurance, roadside assistance and unlimited mileage. Free pickup and return at Paris and most French airports.

Europe by Car

One Rockefeller Plaza, New York, NY 10020, U.S.A.
☎ *(212) 581-3040, (310) 272-0424, (800) 223-1516, or (800) 252-9401 (CA); FAX: (212) 246-1458*
This company specializes in tax-free leasing of cars, sedans and minibuses for two weeks to six months. Special programs are available for students, teachers and faculty members.

Renault Eurodrive USA

650 First Avenue, New York, NY 10016, U.S.A.
☎ *(212) 532-1221, (800) 221-1052 or (800) 477-7116 (western states); FAX: (212) 725-5379*
Renault Eurodrive offers a tax-free alternative to car rental, with packages that include a new Renault with complete insurance, unlimited mileage, 24-hour roadside assistance, free pickup and return locations within France and elsewhere in Europe. All services are backed by Europe's largest carmaker.

TT Car Transit

2 ave. de la Porte de Saint Cloud, 75016 Paris, France
☎ *(33) 01-46-51-51-70 or (33) 01-46-51-70-50; FAX: (33) 01-46-51-25-20*

This firm provides purchase-repurchase leases of temporary transit tax-free cars of all makes in France.

By Boat

France has the longest coastline of any European country. As such, many possibilities exist for tourists to travel by boat, to either go to Corsica or England (see the sections on Corsica and Getting There, respectively) or to simply enjoy the pleasures of the sea on a yacht or a sailboat. France also has many rivers and waterways, on which it is possible to rent boats and enjoy the life and beauty of the countryside. Along its 2130 miles of coastline, France has 254 yachting ports and 58,000 berths to shelter yachts. The North Sea, English Channel and Atlantic Ocean offer 126 yachting ports and more than 20,000 berths. On the Mediterranean Sea there are 128 yachting ports and 37,000 berths.

The following are companies that offer short cruises, yachting training, expeditions and boat rental, from luxury barge-hotels to charter yachts and self-drive riverboats. Many of these operators offer custom programs and optional extras:

Abercrombie & Kent International

1520 Kensington Road, Suite 212, Oak Brook, IL 60521, U.S.A.
☎ *(708) 954-2944 or (800) 323-7308; FAX: (708) 954-3324*
Packages include six-night cruises on the Seine and Yonne rivers; three- or six-night cruises on the Saone in Lower Burgundy; three- or six-night cruises in Alsace-Lorraine; six-night cruises in Central Burgundy; a newly refurbished hotel barge in the Loire Valley.

Alden Yacht Charters

1909 Alden Landing, Portsmouth, RI 02871, U.S.A.
☎ *(401) 683-1782 or (800) 662-2628; FAX: (401) 683-3668*
This company arranges charters on luxury private yachts on the Côte d'Azur, Corsica and other coastal cruising areas. Custom-planned charters are available on motor and sailing yachts. Also available are six-night luxury cruises aboard all major barge-hotels: *Le Papillon, The Alouette and The Hirondelle, La Belle Aventure, Genevieve, The Princess, Etoile de Champagne, Meanderer, Athos, Penelope, Julia Hoyt, La Reine Pedauque* and *Luciole*. Gourmet cuisine, wine connoisseurs, special excursions to fit visitors' special interests are available.

Athos Cruises, Ltd.

Penns Place, 3 Calverley Walk, Eastbourne, BN21 4SS, East Sussex, England
☎ *(44) 1323-412282; FAX: (44) 1323-722826*
Weekly barge cruises can be booked aboard *The Athos* on the Canal du Midi. Themed cruises for groups include painting, bridge, and wine tastings. The barge maintains a full crew and sleeps 12 in six cabins with en-suite facilities. All cuisine, drinks and excursions are included.

Bargain Boating/Morgantown Travel Service

P.O. Box 757, 127 High Street, Morgantown, WV 26507-0757, U.S.A.
☎ *(304) 292-8471 or (800) 637-0782; FAX: (304) 292-0819*
Self-drive canal cruising packages include Champagne, Alsace, Brittany, Burgundy, Franche-Comte, Charentes, Lot and Aquitaine-Midi-Camargue.

The Barge Lady

Suite 324, KLM Airlines, 225 N. Michigan Avenue, Chicago, IL 60601, U.S.A.
☎ *(312) 540-5500 or (800) 880-0071; FAX: (312) 540-5503*
This company books cruises on 20 canal barges in France. All barges have been personally inspected and the firm's emphasis is on recommending the right vessel in terms of price, amenities, accommodations, area sight-seeing, crew and special interests.

Centre Nautique des Glenans at Concarneau (Finisterre)

Facing 15, quai Louis-Bleriot, 75781 Paris cedex 16, France
☎ *(33) 01-45-20-01-40; FAX: (33) 01-45-27-61-54*

Crosieres Paquet

5, boulevard Malesherbes, 75008 Paris, France
☎ *(33) 01-49-24-42-00; FAX: (33) 01-49-24-42-01*

Crown Blue Line

Le Grand Bassin, 11401 Castelnaudary cedex, France
☎ *01-68-23-17-51; FAX: 01-68-23-33-92*
Crown Blue Line provides self-drive houseboats for the independent traveler. Packages emphasize relaxed touring on the waterways in Aquitaine, Midi, Lot, Charentes, Champagne, Camargue, Loire/Nivernais, Burgundy, Brittany and Alsace/Lorraine.

Dullien River & Canal Cruises

585 Paseo de Ante, Palm Springs, CA 92262, U.S.A.
☎ *(619) 864-9508 or (800) 925-0444; FAX: (619) 864-9798*
This firm offers "Botels" with full board, excursions and crew for four to 24 passengers. Self-skippered boats are available for two to 12 passengers. Packages include golf, châteaux, wine, gourmet, bike or cultural tours.

Etoile de Champagne

88 Broad Street, Boston, MA 02110, U.S.A.
☎ *(617) 426-1776 or (800) 280-1492; FAX: (617) 426-4689*
The company provides luxury canal barge packages that feature six- and 12-night cruises including Amsterdam-Paris, Moret-Auxerre, Paris-Epernay and Paris-Rouen. Cruises offer gourmet cuisine and regional wines. Options include hot-air ballooning, golfing and bicycling.

Euro Charters

1417 Brevard Avenue, Cocoa, FL 32922, U.S.A.
☎ *(407) 632-5610 or (800) 950-5610; FAX: (407) 632-5878*
Euro Charters feature six-night, all-inclusive barge cruises aboard the *Anjodi* in the Midi; the *Stella* and *La Vancelle* in Alsace-Lorraine; the *Crested Grebe, Hirondelle, Alouette, Reine Pedauque, Nymphea, Le Papillon,* and *Penelope* in Burgundy, *La Joie de Vivre* on the upper Loire, *Meanderer* in Champagne and the upper Loire; the *Julia Hoyt* and *Berendina* in Bordeaux; and *Le Belle Epoque* in Burgundy and Provence.

European Waterways

140 East 56th Street, New York, NY 10022, U.S.A.
☎ *(212) 688-9489 or (800) 217-4447; FAX: (212) 688-3778 or (800) 296-4354*

Specializing in luxury crewed barge-hotels, this firm offers cruises that include French chefs and cuisine, wine tastings and châteaux visits, minivan excursions, bicycles, regional shopping advice and hot-air ballooning. Independent and whole boat charters are available.

France Unlimited

133 Isabella Street, Toronto, ON M4Y 1P4, Canada
☎ *and FAX: (416) 920-6329*
Weekly luxury barge cruises aboard the *Crested Grebe* and the *Nymphea* in Burgundy and Canal du Midi, and the *Neeltje* and *La Belle Aventure* in Burgundy. Packages feature a breakfast-and-lunch meal plan, and bicycles and a van are provided for excursions. Hot-air ballooning is optional.

French Country Waterways Ltd.

P.O. Box 2195, Duxbury, MA 02331, U.S.A.
☎ *(617) 934-2454 or (800) 222-1236; FAX: (617) 934-9048*
This company offers exclusive representation of a premier fleet of owner-operated luxury barge-hotels. Packages include six-night cruises in Champagne and Burgundy with air-conditioned staterooms with private baths, provincial French cuisine, Premier and Grand Cru wines and champagnes, open bar, daily sight-seeing, bicycles and escorted transfers to-and-from Paris. Optional hot-air ballooning is available. Value season rates are available in April, July, August and October.

Inland Voyages Ltd.

23 Adlington Road, Cheshire Bollington, Cheshire SK1 O5JT, England
☎ *and FAX: (44) 1625-576880*
Specializing in individual and group tours, this firm offers weekly all-inclusive cruises aboard 14-berth *Luciole* on Burgundy and Nivernais waterways. Single-, twin and double cabins are available, all with low-level beds and en-suite facilities. Gourmet cuisine, wine tours are available. Paris transfers, special group and charter rates are offered.

Locaboat Plaisance

Port au Bois, B.P 150, 89300 Joigny, France
☎ *86-91-72-72; FAX: 86-62-42-41*
More than 300 self-drive mini-barges for two to 12 passengers with packages for two days or more. Charters offered in Lot, Garonne, Lauragais, Midi, Camargue, Burgundy, Nivernais, Franche-Comte, Alsace-Lorraine, Champagne-Ardenne, Nord-Picardie, Ile-de-France, Anjou, Brittany and Charentes.

Papillon-Croisieres Fluviales de Bourgogne

Conygre House, Farmborough, Bath, BA3 1AZ Avon, England
☎ *(44) 1761-470363; FAX: (44) 1761-472995*
This owner-operated firm offers six-night luxury barge cruises in Midi and Burgundy/Nivernais. One-week charters for private parties of up to six are also available. Barges carry a four-person crew and have three comfortable cabins with en-suite bathrooms. Fine wines and cuisine, excursions, wine tours, bicycles and tennis. Options include hot-air ballooning. Amenities include cellular phone, free bar.

Premier Selections

106 Calvert Street, Harrison, NY 10528, U.S.A.

☎ *(914) 835-5555 or (800) 234-4000; FAX: (914) 835-5449*

This firm offers luxury barge cruises on 19 barge-hotels that accommodate six to 24 passengers and one 50-passenger riverboat. Cruises in Burgundy, Alsace-Lorraine, Bordeaux, Midi, Provence and on the Seine River. Special interest itineraries on art, architecture, religion, opera and music, archeology, wine and cuisine, French language and bicycling.

Sonafho

Chateau la Chassagne, 21410 Pont de Pany, France

☎ *80-40-47-50; FAX: 80-23-66-28*

Sonafho provides luxury barge cruises in Burgundy aboard *La Reine Pedauque* and *MS Niagara* with packages that combine three nights in the Hotel Château la Chassagne. Amenities include half board, tennis, swimming pool, fitness, sauna, hot-air ballooning and a car fleet.

Spirit Cruises

501 Front Street, Norfolk, VA 23510, U.S.A.

☎ *(804) 627-2900; FAX: (804) 640-9315*

All cruises start from the Eiffel Tower, Pont d'Iena. Lunch and dinner cruises feature a three-course traditional gourmet menu on clear-glass windowed vessels, while sky-tracer and flood lights illuminate monuments, bridges and statues. The cruises feature a live band and dancing every night. Also available are one-hour guided sight-seeing cruises.

Syndicat National des Loueurs de Bateaux de Plaisance

Port de la Bourdonnais, 75007 Paris, France

☎ *(33) 01-45-55-10-49; FAX: (33) 01-47-53-94-75*

Voies Navigables de France

2, boulevard de Latour-Maubourg, 75007 Paris, France

☎ *(33) 01-49-55-60-00; FAX: (33) 01-47-05-81-38*

Yacht Club de France

4, rue Chalgrin, 75116 Paris, France

☎ *(33) 01-45-01-28-46; FAX: (33) 01-45-00-12-86*

By Taxi

Much as it is anywhere in the world outside London, taxi service in France is something of an adventure. Your driver will almost certainly speak little English and quite likely (especially in larger cities) only the most rudimentary French. The taxis themselves can be of any shape, size, color, make and model, so it's sometimes quite hard to spot one if you're trying to hail one on the street. It's generally better to try to get one at a taxi stand which are generally located at major street corners, as well as outside train stations and official buildings. At your hotel or at a restaurant, have someone call one for you.

Fares vary, but there should always be a meter visible to passengers. If there isn't, don't get in! Daytime rates are generally about FR3 per kilometer; about 50 percent more at night and a little higher outside the cities. There is a minimum fare of 12F and luggage is extra—generally about FR5 per piece. Due to the reduced size of most European cars (as compared with North American models and London cabs), you'll generally find a cab will only take three passengers, four in a pinch.

Taxi drivers expect a minimum 10 percent tip, even when they are a bit rude, as they are in France like everywhere. If you feel you have been ripped off or treated abusively, make a note of the license plate, date and time, and file a report with the local police. In Paris, the address is as follows:

Préfecture de Police
Service Taxis, 36 rue des Morillons, 75732 Paris cedex 15

By Bicycle

Bicycling through Côte d'Or

The Tour de France is not the only indication of the popularity of bicycling in France. Much of the country's terrain is ideal for pedal-powered transportation. Flat or gently rolling countryside abounds and in rural areas there are countless wide, relatively empty roads. No network of bicycle paths exists in France, but there are towpaths along most rivers that are free of cars and perfect for cycling. France is also accommodating toward bicyclists in other ways. You can always take a bike on the train, usually for a fee of about FR45, but often for free—look for the sign that says "*Votre vélo peut voyager avec vos gratuitement en cet train.*"

You can usually rent a cruiser, 10-speed or mountain bike *(vélo tout-terrain)* at the train station in most towns. If not, the station personnel will be able to tell you where in town you can. You can rent for half a day, a full day, or for several days. Rates start at around FR50 per day, and you'll get a discount for rentals of a week or more. You'll have to show your passport and leave a hefty deposit unless you're paying with plastic.

For more information, consult the following sources:

Cycling Europe: Budget Bike Touring in the Old World
Norman Slavinski. Available at most bookstores

Europe by Bike
Karen and Terry Whitehill. Available at most bookstores

Fédération Française de Cyclotourisme
8, rue de Jean-Marie Jégo, 75013 Paris, France
☎ *(33) 01-44-16-88-88*

Rail Europe
226 Westchester Avenue, White Plains, NY 10604
☎ *(800) 438-7245; FAX: (800) 432-1329*
Ask for the SNCF brochure *Guide to Traveling by Train with Your Bike.*

Money

Yes, unfortunately money *does* make the world go round, in France as much as anywhere else. The French may have plenty of *joie de vivre* and a well-deserved reputation as incurable romantics, but they also know the value of a franc, and traveling in France is definitely not cheap. Here are some guidelines to help you make sure you have enough of the green stuff, and to make sure you hold on to it until you want to hand it over.

The basic unit of currency in France is the *franc.* One franc is equal to 100 *centimes.* There are 20-, 50- (two types), 100-, 200- and 500-franc notes, and five-, 10-, 20- and 50-centime coins and one-, two-, five-, 10- and 20-franc coins. As with all numeration, in France the comma and the decimal point (or period) are transposed compared to their usage in most English-speaking countries, so while "one thousand francs and no centimes" would be rendered as FR1000.00 in the North America and Britain, for example, in France the figure would appear as 1.000,00F. Actually, in many shops and markets the 'F' for 'francs' appears between the francs and the centimes; for example 16F30, or 16,30 but not 16.30. At presstime US$1=5F44.

Traveler's Checks

Still one of the most convenient and most secure ways of taking money abroad, traveler's checks are well known and are widely accepted in France. The most widely recognized brands are also the most widely available for purchase in your home country—

American Express, Citicorp, Thomas Cook and Visa. These are available at most commercial banks—shop around before you buy, since the commission you pay to buy the checks can vary from zero (for example, for members of the American Automobile Association) to as high as five percent. You might also get hit up again when you go to cash your checks in France—some banks have been known to add a surcharge of as much as 20 percent of the face value. You're more likely to be charged a premium if the checks are denominated in a foreign currency other than U.S. dollars (for example, Australian or Canadian dollars), but even better than "dead presidents" is to get checks in French francs. Most larger banks and agencies sell them in francs, and franc-denominated checks can be cashed at Thomas Cook and American Express offices, as well as at many major banks, free of commission.

The main advantage of using traveler's checks, of course, is that the issuing agency or bank will replace them free of charge if you lose them or they are stolen. Keep the receipts separate from the checks themselves, but also make a separate list of the checks by number, crossing them out as you cash them. That way, if you file for a refund, you'll be able to tell the agency immediately which ones you've lost. Most of the big issuing agencies have numerous authorized refund-centers in France, so you shouldn't have a hard time finding a nearby center. Make things easier by requesting a list of refund centers and helpline telephone numbers from the issuing agency before you travel. If your checks are stolen, it will also expedite things to obtain a police report prior to filing for a refund.

Another advantage of using traveler's checks is that in most cases the issuing agency allows you to have a second person authorized to cash your checks. The second party must countersign when the checks are issued—countersigned checks are useful when one half of a traveling couple wants to linger just a bit longer in the Chanel store while the other is determined to find that certain special book in a funky store in the Latin Quarter. Be aware, however, that the only areas in which I guarantee you'll be able to cash traveler's checks are the big cities and high-traffic tourist destinations such as the Riviéra or the Alpine ski resorts. In rural areas, you'd be better off with a credit card (see below), or with previously exchanged currency.

Currency Exchange

In general, banks offer the most competitive exchange rates—and competitive is the key word. Be sure to shop around before changing your cash or traveler's checks. I'm not suggesting you dedicate a morning in each city you visit to changing your money, just that as you walk around you should pay attention to the signs outside the various money exchange places and compare them. You can exchange currency at banks, some post offices, airports, train stations, travel agencies and in the larger cities at specialty currency exchange storefronts. Remember the currency exchange shops will exact no commissions but they will offer deplorably exploitative rates.

There will usually be two rates posted, one (usually marked as *achète*) that represents what the bank/exchange house will pay you in francs for your foreign currency, and one (usually *vente*) that is the number of francs the bank/exchange house will charge to sell you one unit of foreign currency. The bank or exchange house makes money both ways, and you can assume that the official rate of the day is about halfway between the two rates quoted. So the closer together the buy and sell rates are, the smaller the piece of the action the bank or exchange house is taking.

The other way the bank/exchange house takes a cut is by charging you a commission. Ask before you hand over the cash—large banks, including Crédit Lyonnais and Crédit Agricole, charge just one or two percent, so anything over three percent or so is pretty much of a rip-off. Airports and train stations generally offer the poorest rates, and so take advantage of their convenience to the newly arrived and addled traveler. Hotels are even worse, and you can figure that any shopkeeper sharp enough to take foreign money in order to make a sale is definitely not doing you any favors. Do yourself a favor and change US$50 or so at home before your trip, and then you'll be able to bypass the gantlet at the airport in Paris. After that change large amounts at big banks in the big cities.

Automatic Teller Machines

Ah, the conveniences of modern technology! Unless you bank with an extremely iconoclastic establishment at home, you should find that your ATM card will work just fine in France. As you might expect in the age of the European Community, a card called *Euro-Card*, as well as its sister *EuroCheque* card, is very widely used in France. The EuroCard is the same as MasterCard, so a tourist with a MasterCard should see it readily accepted. The *Cirrus* card is associated with MasterCard, and most ATMs that accept EuroCard or MasterCard have now been adapted to accept Cirrus as well. Cards using the Plus network, however, are not able to be used in France.

You will find that the ATMs will usually give you a choice of several languages in which to conduct the transaction, but occasionally you may find some that automatically switch to your language by reading your card, which is all very well until there's a computer glitch. While most ATMs in France (and throughout Europe) are multilingual, there is a handful that do all transactions in French. This really should present no major problem, however, since it should be clear in any language that you are being asked for your PIN, or the amount you wish to receive.

I'm the last person who would presume to lecture anybody about profligate spending, but just bear in mind that the same self-control you exercise at home *vis-à-vis* the ATM should be employed in France. The convenience of being able to withdraw money at any corner can be a pitfall—it'll be no fun to get home and find your bank account empty—and remember that most banks charge for transactions not made at one of their own branches. One advantage to using an ATM card to get your money that compensates for any fees is that you'll receive an excellent exchange rate—the bank-to-bank wholesale rate—that will probably beat anything else you can find by at least five percent.

Credit Cards

Credit cards are accepted everywhere in France, and are invaluable—as at home—for their convenience and for the security they provide in the case of an unexpected emergency. Look for the *CB/Visa ou EC* or American Express signs in the windows of stores and restaurants that accept payment by plastic. *Carte Bleu (CB)* may be used alone in place of Visa; Eurocard *(EC)* is used exclusively for MasterCard. You can also use credit cards at ATM machines, although you will be charged interest on the money as soon as you withdraw it, just as if it were for a purchase. Visa and MasterCard cards (and the British Access and Barclaycard equivalents) can be used at ATMs in most banks—look for the same *CB/ Visa or EC sign. American Express* cards can be used to withdraw money from ATMs at Crédit Lyonnais banks as well as at American Express offices. Note that Discover cards are not able to be used anywhere outside the United States.

American Express offers an additional service to its members that is one of the most efficient and cheapest ways of accessing money in France. Using your American Express card and a picture identification, you can cash up to $1000 in personal checks per week at any of the hundreds of American Express offices around the country. Gold American Express cardholders can cash up to $5000 in a seven-day period.

If you lose your credit card, report it immediately to stop any unauthorized purchases. The telephone numbers in Paris for the three major companies are as follows:

American Express
> ☎ 01-47-77-72-00

MasterCard
> ☎ 01-45-67-84-84

Visa
> ☎ 01-42-77-11-90

Staying in Touch

Telephones

How to Dial

To call France from abroad, dial your country's international access code, then 33 for France, (then 1 for Paris only), then the eight-digit number. To call abroad from France, dial 00 for international access, then the country code, then the area code and number. Calling within France is a little more complicated. The country is divided up into five regions—Paris (area code 01), the northwest (area code 02), the northeast (area code 03), the southeast (area code 04) and the southwest (area code 05). To call from one region into another, use the area code followed by the eight-digit number. To call within a region just use the eight-digit number.

How to Pay

These days almost every public pay phone in France accepts only prepaid phone cards and, in some cases, credit cards. You can purchase *télécartes*, as they are called, at post offices, Métro stations, train stations, *tabacs* and at many retail stores. Look for the sign in the window with an icon of a telephone. The cards come in two denominations: FR40 and FR96. These are worth 50 and 120 *unités* respectively. Once you insert the card into the slot provided on the phone the amount of units remaining on the card will be displayed. After that, all you need to do is close the cover over the slot and dial your party. A FR96 card will last almost 20 minutes on a call to North America.

You'll get the best rates calling from pay phones in the street or at train stations. Bars and restaurants are allowed to put a surcharge of up to 30 percent on calls, and they do. I can think of no good reason to make a call from a hotel—the rates will often be twice what you'll pay at a pay phone. Pay phones in France accept incoming calls—the number is posted with *ici le* before it. A good plan is to call home and have your party return the call; phone rates overall are higher in France than in most English-speaking countries.

A collect call is known as *un appel en PCV*. However you'll be better off calling one of the U.S. long distance carriers or the Canadian or British telecommunications companies to place the call for you (see numbers listed below).

Some sample rates:

United States: 28F08 (3 minutes)

Canada: 28F08 (3 minutes)

Australia: 57F27 (3 minutes)

Britain: 4F50 (per minute)

Reduced rates are available from Monday to Saturday between 9:30 p.m. and 8 a.m., on Saturdays after 2 p.m., and all day on Sundays and during French public holidays.

Useful Numbers

Operator *(opératrice): 10*
International operator: *19-33-11*
Directory assistance: *12*
International directory assistance: *00-33-12 + country code*
Police emergency: *17 (free)*
Fire emergency: *18 (free)*
Ambulance emergency: *15 (free)*
AT&T: *0-800-99-00-11*
MCI: *0-800-99-00-16*
Sprint: *0-800-99-00-16*
British Telecom: *0-800-99-00-16*
Canada Dire t: *0-800-99-00-16*

Mail

The post office in France is called *le PTT* (which stands for *Postes, Télégraphes, Téléphones*). Its logo is a blue-and-yellow flying envelope and the letters PTT. Some maps mark post offices, some towns indicate where they are with signposts on nearby street corners. They are usually very busy, because in addition to mail, telegram and telephone services, post offices also offer banking and other services. If all you need are some stamps *(timbres)*, save yourself time standing in line and buying them up at a *tabac* or use one of the yellow automatic-vending machines on the outside wall of the post office.

Sending Mail

Thanks to the European Union, it costs the same to mail a letter or postcard to England or another European country as it does within France. At press time the basic rate of FR2.80 covers a letter up to 20 grams, i.e., a couple of sheets of paper and an envelope. Air mail to North America is reliable and fairly quick; letters and postcards cost FR4.30 and arrive in five to seven days. You need to write *Par Avion* clearly on the letter, though, otherwise it will likely wind up going by surface mail, which can take up to three months! Avoid that risk by using an *aerogramme*, a pre-paid, one-sheet, three-fold letter that is designed for air mail and costs FR5. Express mail *(exprés)* costs an additional FR28 and is guaranteed to arrive within five days. Or you can send a letter guaranteed to arrive within three days if you use *chronopost* and are willing to shell out a full FR280 for the extra two days. Most larger hotels sell stamps and also have a mailbox.

Receiving Mail

You can receive mail at any post office in France by having it sent to you *poste restante*. The sender should address it clearly with your last name in capitals first, then your first name, then on the second line the words *Poste Restante*, then on the third line the city name and the correct postal code. You will need your passport to pick up your mail, which will be held at the main post office in towns that have more than one, as well as a FR3 fee for each piece. You can also get mail delivered to American Express offices for a small fee (free to card holders), but they will only hold it for 30 days unless the sender specifies a longer period on the envelope. Be aware that during peak tourist periods, some American Express offices refuse to hold mail.

L'Internet

As more and more people get online every day, the Internet is an increasingly valuable tool for anyone planning a trip. Using your computer, a modem and an online service, you can find a wealth of useful information, tips and recommendations. You can even book hotel rooms and find out what's playing at the Paris Opera, all without leaving your home or office, and at considerable savings to you of time, effort and—in many cases—money. When you are in France, you'll be able to stay connected to friends and contacts at home with a temporary account at one of France's many commercial Internet service providers (ISPs), or through the nationwide Minitel network. The following section offers a (very) short list of hot links you can surf to on the World Wide Web before your trip, as well as information on the most responsive ISPs I have found, and an overview of the Minitel system.

New Internet services and servers come online daily, and those that currently exist but did not make this list may have added new and valuable information resources after this book was printed. Be sure to keep up-to-date on the latest offerings; as always, *Yahoo* is the best place to start. Check out *www.citynet or www.yahoo.com/Regional/Countries/France/*, the main Yahoo page of links to information on France. These pages, include official, semiofficial, unofficial and downright irreverent pages for cities including Auvergne, Gard, Grenoble Isere, Kemper, La Bourgogne, La Trinite sur Mer, Lingolsheim, Metz, Marseille, Nimes, Paris, Pays de Grasse, Toulouse and Monaco.

Useful (and Fun) Web Sites

French Travel Gallery and Reservation Center

http://www.webcom.com/~wta/hall_en_gif.shtml

Cut out the middleman! Using this service you can make, confirm, and even pay for hotel reservations in hundreds of hotels around France and Monaco without having to deal with a travel agent. You can do it without even getting out of your chair! The Travel Gallery contains comprehensive listings for more than 200 hotels. No pictures were included at press time, but this was supposed to be in the works—it would be nice to see what a room looks like before booking it. If you know the region where you want to stay, you can perform a search based on how many people are in your party, the amenities you want in the room, and how much you want to pay. For larger cities, including Paris, there are district or arrondissement categories. The system then finds out if your desired dates are available, takes your credit-card information using a secure encrypted commerce server, and books your room. Many hotels featured here are smaller, independent establishments, so this is a great way to discover lodgings that you might not hear about through regular travel agents or tour operators.

You don't need to stop at reserving a room, however. A second area of the Travel Gallery and Reservation Center is a virtual shopping mall. You can get information about, and with your credit card purchase, the Paris Visite travel pass for Paris that gives you unlimited trips on the Métro, the RER suburban trains, SCNF Ile de France trains, and several bus companies. Simply specify how many days and the various regions you want to pay for. You can buy a one-, three- or five-day pass that is good for entry at more than 60 Paris-area museums and monuments—breeze past interminable lines at the Louvre, say, or the Eiffel Tower. You can even prepurchase a local round-trip transfer on OrlyVal, the regional transportation authority's express shuttle-bus between Orly airport and your Paris hotel, or you can purchase an electric adapter to convert French 230-volt current for use with your 110-volt appliances. The OrlyVal tickets will be waiting for you at your arrival gate at Orly airport; the other purchases will be delivered to you at your hotel.

The Travel Gallery and Reservation Center also has decent links to general information pages for the visitor to France, as well as a link to The WebMuseum.

The Paris Pages

http://www.paris.org
Nonprofit sites are designated by the ".org" suffix. The Paris Pages contain a true treasure trove of information and resources about Paris. Contained within its well-ordered hierarchy are countless color photographs, thoughtfully saved at low resolution so they don't take forever to download, as well as a wealth of phone numbers, addresses and practical information.

There are home pages for a dozen famous open-air cafés and a dozen internationally renowned stores, including Cartier and Chanel, as well as general overview sections. Floor plans, upcoming exhibition schedules and other information are provided for the Musée du Louvre, Musée d'Orsay, Centre Georges Pompidou and several other major museums, as well as calendars of performances for l'Opéra de la Bastille, l'Opéra Comique, the Paris Opéra Ballet, le Théâtre de Champs-Elysées and other theaters. You will find page after page of tips on getting around and having fun in Paris, as well as a fairly decent list of restaurants and hotels, and a comprehensive and interesting section on the French Resistance. There's also a comprehensive practical guide for visitors to the capital, including useful details like a photograph of the phone card and which way to insert it into the pay phones! All in all, the Paris Pages are a wonderful resource for anyone planning a trip to Paris.

Subway Navigator

http://metro.jussieu.fr:10001/bin/select/english/france/paris
(Also.../lille,.../lyons,.../marseille,.../strasbourg and.../toulouse)

Although this is something you're likely to want to use more when you're actually in France than before you leave, I include it because (a) if you do have 'Net access in France you'll find it indispensable, and (b) it's so incredibly cool.

This Worldwide Web site allows you to use a search form to find out how to travel between any two Métro stations in any of France's major cities, as well as any city around the world that has a Metro or underground railway. You can even type in an approximation of the name of the station you are traveling to or from and the search engine will either handle it or tell you your request is ambiguous. I tested the Navigator on a point-to-point journey I knew to be complicated (involving two line changes) and possibly ambiguous. After typing in the names "Orsay" and "Roosevelt," I hit the return key, and quick as a flash, I got a message informing me that: "The station name you supplied (orsay) for the departure station is ambiguous. More than one station has been found. Choose the correct one: *Orsay-Ville, Musée d'Orsay*". After I clicked on Musée d'Orsay, and pressed the search button again, the Navigator came back in about three seconds with the following results:

"Route from 'Musée d'Orsay' to 'Franklin-D Roosevelt' in the Paris subway. Estimated time = 25 minutes

Line C, Direction 'Argenteuil' or 'Montigny/Beauchamp' or 'Versailles-RG' or 'Saint Quentin en Yvelines'

• Musée d'Orsay

• Invalides

Line 13, Direction 'Gabriel Péri' or 'Saint Denis-Basilique'

• Invalides

• Champs-Elysées/Clémenceau

Line 1, Direction 'La Grande Arche de la Défense'

• Champs-Elysées/Clémenceau

• Franklin D. Roosevelt

I was even offered a graphical depiction of my route superimposed on the official Métro map. Pretty impressive!

The Webfoot's Guide to France

http://www.webfoot.com/travel/guides/france/france.html

The Webfoot Travel Guides are something of a misnomer but nevertheless they are a tremendous resource for Internet surfers preparing a trip to another country. The France page is no exception. This site offers little in terms of endemic content, but is rich in links to other sites. Some 60 hyperlinks, many that transport you to other hotlists that each have dozens of pages, are presented in individual sections such as General Information, General Tips for Tourists, Food, Lodging, Culture, etc. Many of these sections are rather lame (the History section only had two entries, and the only one working was a link to a presentation on the siege of Paris during World War II), but others are dynamite. The Language and Literature section, for example, offers links to three distinct online French-English dictionaries, three interactive sites for picking up or brushing up on a little French before you go, including a very good one from Radio France International, and (extremely important to connoisseurs of fine comic art) a link to the unofficial *Asterix the Gaul* site.

The Web Museum

http://www.emf.net/wm/

This is the address for the mirror site in Berkeley, CA. Once you connect, you will be offered a choice of dozens of other mirrors around the world—pick the one that is closest to you and you will see a marked improvement in connection times.

Nicolas Pioch, the art-loving computer geek behind what was originally called Le Web Louvre (until the French Culture Ministry bureaucrats reminded him that the name "Louvre" is trademarked), has this to say—in his charmingly tortured English—about the Web Museum: "The WebMuseum was not made as part of any official or supported project. There's not grant behind that, it is total pleasurable. I decided to start working on this exhibit because I felt more artistic stuff was needed on the Internet... Some companies may be trying to get a monopolistic grab on arts and culture, developing a pay-per-view logic, shipping out CD-ROMs while trying to patent stuff which belongs to each of us: a part of our human civilization and history." Of course many thousands of Web authors have a similar philosophy, but the WebMuseum is no funky little home page. Rather, it is an incredibly deep resource for lovers of art and music, with thousands of high-quality reproductions of paintings and photographs of sculpture, categorized both by artist and genre. The site has become so huge that it is mirrored on dozens of servers around the world, and offers digitized collections of artwork from locations around the world. The core of this virtual museum is still its online presentation of the Louvre, as well as a number of virtual walking tours of Paris and other information about the city. If you plan to visit the great museum in Paris, it would be well worth it to spend some time at the WebMuseum to plan your tip to the real thing (see "Managing the Louvre").

Internet Service Providers

If you're hooked on reading your e-mail every day, or you can't leave your work completely at home and need to download or upload files while you're in France, you have two choices: Log in to your home server and pay the international toll calls, or set up a temporary account while you're in France. The following are the ISPs in France who said they would be happy to set up temporary accounts for visitors:

France-Teaser

☎ *01-47-50-62-48; FAX: 01-47-50-62-93*

E-mail: *sales@Cteaser.fr, info@teaser.fr*

Modem: *01-41-15-07-36*

Web: *http://www.teaser.fr*

Rates: *FR60 per month for 60 hours full Internet access; FR50 setup fee*

Comments: This large-scale, commercial service provider may lack the personal touch likely to be necessary for a temporary account, but it does offer the service. Connect speeds up to 33.6 kbps; local dial-up access only in Ville d'Avray outside Paris.

MNet

☎ *04-67-15-01-24*

E-mail: *info@mnet.fr*

Web: *http://www.mnet.fr/*

Rates: *FR250 per month for unlimited full Internet access*

Comments: There is no setup fee and no minimum contract on this service; in fact, when I inquired about a five-week temporary account, the company explained that they bill by the month but I could have the fifth week for free! Local dial-up access in the Montpellier area only.

NCTech

☎ *04-78-61-46-09; FAX: 04-78-61-46-99*

E-mail: *jlbernard@nctech.fr*

Web: *http://www.nctech.fr*

Rates: *FR2200 per month for unlimited full Internet access*

Comments: This service in Lyon has state-of-the-art equipment and offers ISDN connections, but unfortunately its rates are completely out of the ballpark.

Union-Fin

☎ *01-30-73-22-57*

E-mail: *alex@alex.union-fin.fr*

Modem: *01-30-38-11-00*

BBS: *01-30-38-44-72*

Web: *http://www.union-fin.fr/*

Rates: *US$30 per month for unlimited, full Internet access*

Comments: Denis Alexandre, operator of this small service, speaks excellent English. There is no setup charge for a temporary account, and the rates are reasonable, but local dial-up access is available only in Cergy-Pontoise (about 15 miles northwest of Paris).

Minitel

Although there is some debate now about whether or not the service is becoming rendered obsolete by the Internet itself, the Teletel videotext network was considered years ahead of its time when set up in 1980 by the French state telecommunications company, France Telecom. This nationwide network of some 600,000 microcomputers is accessible through more than 6 million videoterminals connected to the phone network. Teletel contains information provided by more than 25,000 service providers, covering everything imaginable—news, travel information, entertainment calendars, recipes, jokes of the day, and on and on. Naturally, most of the information is in French, but many services are available in English.

"Minitel" is the name of the terminal distributed by France Telecom for accessing the Teletel network. You'll find terminals connected to pay phones, in hotels, banks, train and bus stations, libraries and in special kiosks in city centers. You can also use a personal computer to connect to Teletel over the phone in France or on the Internet from anywhere in the world. You can access the services on a Minitel by first typing in a four-digit category code: 3616 and 3617 for business services, for example, or 3615 for consumer services such as tourist information, practical information, current affairs, news and games. The consumer service category offers the most English-language services. Once you've entered the category code, type in the service code identifying the service you want to access. This is usually a word or acronym. Lists of service codes are available anywhere there is a Minitel, and most hotels in the bigger cities can provide you with a list of the English-language services.

As I said, there are more than 25,000 individual services available through the Mintel network. Each service provider sets its own rates, which are collected by France Telecom as part of the fee you pay for using your system. Here are some examples of the services available that are of interest to visitors, and their respective fees:

Tourism (category number 3615): accommodation, restaurants, regional information, leisure parks

Service code	Tariff (F/min excludes VAT)
ANJOU	**1.24**

Tourism in Anjou, places of interest, leisure activities, events, accommodation, catering.

AUBERGEDEJ	**1.51**

Guide to all the youth hostels in France.

BOTTINGOUR	**1.51**

Selection of restaurants and hotels in France, Switzerland, Belgium, Monaco and Andorra.

BRETAGNE	**1.51**

Tourist information on Brittany. Sports and leisure activities, cultural events, accommodations.

CAMPANILE	**1.11**

Hotels in the Campanile chain and ideas for cultural and sporting activities arranged by region.

CAMPTEL	**2.30**

Guide to camping and caravan sites.

CORUS	**1.51**

Description of French mountain ski resorts.

COTEDAZUR	**1.51**

Tourist and cultural information on the Côte d'Azur.

DINAN	**1.24**

Accommodations, gastronomy, tourism, leisure activities and practical information such as outings, tours, geographical details.

ENFRANCE	**1.51**

Tourism in France, including places to stay, information on départements.

EURODISNEYLAND	**1.51**

General and practical information on Euro Disney.

FUTUROSCOP	**1.51**

Description of the Futuroscope Park at Poitiers, opening times, entry prices, hotels, restaurants.

GITEDEFRAN   1.51

List of farm accommodations, bed-and-breakfast inns, various rented accommodations.

ITOUR   1.24

Guide to Tourist Offices in France.

METEO   1.51

Daily weather forecasts and five-day forecasts for France and worldwide.

ORC   1.51

Search and reservations services for hotels in France and Italy.

PERIGORD   1.51

Tourist information, accommodations list, holidays, sites of interest, monuments, Perigord cookery courses.

RESINTER   1.24

Booking service for hotels in France and abroad.

SNCF   1.51

Information on the French railway system, including timetables, prices and availability.

Transport (category code 3615, except where noted):

Service code	Tariff (FF/min excludes VAT)

AIRFRANCE   1.51

Flight times in real time, prices and reservations.

ENGREVE   1.51

Services on strike in France including Air France, motorways, trains, etc.

EUROLINES   1.51

Coach travel across Europe.

EUROTUNNEL   1.51

News about the Eurotunnel, including progress of work, stock market information, information on shuttles and trains.

(3616) HORAV   1.51

Paris airports, timetable, practical information.

ITI   1.51

Choosing routes for driving, estimating traveling time (in English, German, Dutch, Italian).

LEPLAN   2.30

Calculation and faxing prepared routes for car journey within Paris, with maps showing nearby parking. Message service.

MICHELIN   1.51

Detailed road itineraries with mileage and distances. Hotel and restaurant information.

SEALINK 1.51

Sealink Company information, including timetables, prices, Channel and Irish Sea crossing reservations, prices for holidays.

SITU 2.30

SITU service of the *Régie Autonome des Transports Parisiens (RATP)*: route planning by bus, Metro or RER for Paris and its suburbs. (The service can locate the shortest routes and estimate time).

Once you connect to Teletel using a Mintel terminal, you'll have to navigate through the service using the commands on the keyboard. Here's a translation of the basic commands:

French	English
Envoi	Send
Annulation	Cancel
Suite	Next
Repetition	Repeat
Retour	Previous
Sommaire	Index
Correction	Correction
Guide	Help
Conexion/Fin	Connect/End

The only free Minitel service is the electronic-telephone nationwide directory, accessed by dialing 11 from any Minitel at a payphone. Other services are charged at the rate set by the service provider. You need either an account with *Intelmathique* (the France Telecom subsidiary that operates the service) or you must use a phone card in order to access Teletel services.

You can access the Mintel services over the Internet by opening an account with Intelmathique or one of its subsidiaries around the world—contact *Intelmathique at 16-18 rue du Dome, 92514 Boulogne-Billancourt cedex;* ☎ *(1) 47-61-47-61, FAX: (1) 46-21-22-40.* You can then Telnet to *mintel.fr* and log on with your user name and password. You can download free Minitel emulation software for the Mac, PC and Unix platforms at *http://www.minitel.fr/* or use a VT100 or VT220 terminal emulator. Use the following function keys to execute their corresponding commands:

Key	Command
F1	*Index*
F2	*Cancel*
F3	*Previous*
F4	*Repeat*

Key	Command
F5	*Correction*
F6	*Guide*
F7	*Next*
F8	*Send*
F9	*Connect/Clear*
F10	*Help/Quit*

For more information or to resolve a connection problem, you can contact Intelmatique via e-mail at *helpdesk@minitel.fr*.

The News

If you want to keep up with the news while you're vacationing in a wonderland like France, fear not—you'll be able to get your daily fix. The ubiquitous *Cable News Network* is available via satellite in many five-, four- and even three-star hotels, as are several other global networks including *British Sky Broadcasting* and, in many locations, the *BBC*.

Published in Paris jointly by the *Washington Post* and *The New York Times* since early this century, the *International Herald Tribune* is still the premier English-language newspaper for many Europeans and ex-patriots. A compact 12 pages or so, the *Herald Tribune* carries all the major international news, sports scores and even a regular arts page. The paper is available free in many hotels, and costs FR9 at newsstands. Many English dailies are available in Paris and in tourist resorts, and you'll find various English-language magazines on sale in larger cities.

Shopping

Shopping in France—for the French, at least—is more of an art form than a chore, whether it be for Louis Vuitton luggage on the Champs-Elysées or just the right slab of Brie for a *pique-nique* in Provence. After all, whether you're talking about fine luggage, clothes or, well, Brie, France's marketplaces are a study in chic, elegance and quality. Shopping for the French also has a ritualistic feel; the care and consideration given to choosing a purchase might seem like dallying to the American who is used to fast food, fast oil changes, and self-serve stores with express checkout lanes. But to the French *maman* it's an integral and vital part of the day to be savored and enjoyed as much as the purchase itself.

Service with a Shrug

The same air of careful consideration and leisurely selection prevails whether you visit one of the flagship boutiques in Paris—and it's definitely worth browsing in Cartier, Chanel, Hermès or Gucci, even if you don't have piles of money to spend—or whether you are in a *patisserie* in a small rural town. Your shopping experiences can be delightful so long as you go with the flow. For Americans in particular, service in French stores is generally, well, let's say minimalist. You certainly won't find an employee at the front of the store whose sole duty it is to smile at you and bid you welcome or farewell, as is the trend in many North American stores. The trick is to be polite yet firm. Don't give in to the air of rudeness that many store clerks, especially in larger department stores, exhibit. If you feel you're not getting what you need, ask for *le patron*—the salesperson's attitude will usually change at once, and if not, the boss is likely to be more worried about the store's image than the hired help.

When—and When Not—to Haggle

Many visitors to France, especially Americans, seem to believe that haggling is the accepted *modus operandi* for all situations, but nothing could be further from the truth. The only places where bargaining is considered normal practice is at the tourist souvenir stands. There you'll mostly find rather cheesy plastic Eiffel Tower statuettes and the same kind of tacky T-shirt merchandise that proliferates everywhere in the world. Bargaining is acceptable at antique swap meets and the open-air antique- and book-stalls found throughout France. If you're in a small store and are purchasing several items it won't hurt to ask *"Vous me faîtes un prix?"* ("Will you make me a deal?"), but it probably won't get you anywhere either. However, if you try this anywhere else you will be thought of as boorish and cheap.

Tax and Tax-free Shopping

The sales tax in France will definitely seem exorbitant to most visitors, especially those from the United States. Sales tax in France, like that in most European countries, is more properly known as Value Added Tax, or *VAT*. The rate varies, but on almost everything you will pay 18.6 percent. The tax rate is 20.5 percent on rental cars; 33 percent on luxury goods, including jewelry, watches, and cameras. In an indication of the French love of letters, books are exempt. The tax situation is especially distressing given that the price of most articles is already quite high compared to the country from which you are likely to be traveling. Fortunately, the sales tax is included in the price displayed for most goods. Look for a price tag with the letters TTC, for *toutes taxes comprises.*)

The good news is that, as a foreign visitor, you are entitled to purchase tax-free. However, in order to claim your exemption, you not only have to pay the tax upfront and later get it back as a refund; you also have to jump through several of France's notorious bureaucratic hoops. The process is so involved, in fact, that it would scarcely be worth going through for anything under a couple of hundred dollars. Perhaps, foreseeing this fact, the French government has set the minimum purchase at FR2000 (FR4200 for citizens of European Community countries). This is the amount that must have been spent in one store, so you can combine numerous purchases in one department store to meet the limit and still receive the credit. Many of the larger stores advertise this service, but you are entitled to it in any store. You need to fill out a form called the *formulaire de détaxe pour l'exportation.* The store should also give you a stamped envelope addressed to itself, along with one copy of the form. When you leave the country, you'll need to see a customs official at the *douane de détaxe* window, and allow at least an hour for the pleasure. Show the clerk your receipts, the form and quite possibly the merchandise itself (so don't pack it at the bottom of your bag). The clerk will stamp the form and the receipts, which you will then put in the envelope and mail back to the store where you bought the goods.

TRAVELER'S GUIDE

The store will then transfer the funds corresponding to the tax you paid to your bank account, according to the information you gave on the form. Generally you will receive the refund in about six months. If you've been through this process at the customs in England and received your refund in cash at the airport, you'll gnash your teeth at the convoluted French version, but it is nevertheless nice to get back what will be a minimum of US$70.

Staying Healthy

Getting sick in France is no more fun than falling ill anywhere, but the ill traveler in France has the reassurance of knowing that he or she is in a country with one of the most advanced health-care systems in the world.

Pharmacies are a good place to turn for help with minor ailments. French pharmacists are trained and authorized to provide basic medical advice and can tell you which medicine will alleviate your suffering.

In an emergency, dial 15 for the *SAMU* paramedic services. If you need help but not an ambulance, you can dial 17 for the police, who will tell you the name and location of the nearest doctor-on-call *(médecin)* or 24-hour pharmacy *(pharmacie de la garde)*. You will also find the name and location of the *pharmacie de la garde* posted in the window of other, closed, pharmacies and in newspapers. If you need to be taken to a hospital, the doctor will call an ambulance for you or you can look in the phonebook for "*Ambulances Municipales*".

There are two English-language hospitals in France:

American Hospital

> *63 boulevard Victor-Hugo, 92202 Neuilly*
> ☎ *(33) 01-46-41-25-25; FAX: (33) 01-46-24-49-38*

British Hospital Hortford

> *3 rue Barbes, 92300 Levallois*
> ☎ *(33) 01-46-39-22-22*

Remember to exercise caution and basic common sense during your trip and you will probably have no problems. Watch out for heat exhaustion in the south, which can become extremely hot in the summer, and allow yourself to acclimate to the high altitudes of the Alps before strenuous exertion. Eat sensibly, and drink bottled water wherever possible.

Food and Drink

General

That the French attach a good deal of importance to the subject of food and drink is a great understatement. They are understandably convinced of their country's position at the top of the world's list of great places to eat, and within France the arguments between the inhabitants of one region and another as to whose cheese or wine, or cuisine in general, is superior, are passionate and endless.

The national obsession with the gastronomic has resulted in a semiofficial pantheon of culinary styles and traditions. The bible of French cooking is the *Larousse Gastronomique* encyclopedia, the standard and definitive guide for chefs that was first published more than a century ago. There are three main branches of French cooking: *haute cuisine*, the style that originated with the prerevolution aristocracy and their gluttonous daylong eat-a-thons; *cuisine bourgeoise*, high-quality home cooking using expensive ingredients; and *cuisine des provinces*, country cooking that relies on basic ingredients and produces generous portions of hearty fare.

Seafood takes centerstage on most menus in France.

Today, *haute cuisine* is to be found only in expensive restaurants and banquets—unless your last name is Trump or Branson you won't be dining often in this style, but you should splurge at least once on a disgustingly expensive Paris restaurant just to see how the other half lives. Both *Cuisine bourgeoise* and *cuisine des provinces* will be used to prepare the food that you'll be served in most more reasonable restaurants, and a blend of the two traditional styles is what most French families create in their own kitchens. A newcomer to the palette is *cuisine nouvelle*, the minuscule artsy display of food that has also invaded North American restaurants. Although this style of "cooking" became trendy in Paris in the late '70s and '80s, a backlash has caused its purveyors to return to somewhat more moderate servings and styles.

The French usually eat a light breakfast *(le petit déjeuner)* consisting of coffee and milk, croissants, pastries *(brioches)* and maybe some bread and jam *(pain et confiture)*, and unless you're staying in an international chain hotel that's what you'll be doing too. Lunch *(le déjeuner)* is a bigger meal, taken at a leisurely pace—hence the two-hour lunch breaks. Note that the French word for both breakfast and lunch means "break-fast," with the former merely prepended by "small." Dinner *(le dîner)*, which does not begin until at least 7:30 or 8 p.m., is the main repast of the day.

Restaurants

The first thing you need to know is that the word *menu* does not mean the menu, but refers instead to the fixed three-course menu offered for an single price. If you want to see the menu, ask for *la carte*. There will also be specials posted on a chalkboard in most places—these are not special prices, but rather the fresh catch of the day or something the chef has been inspired to concoct.

The *menu* is the cheapest and least complicated way to go when dining out. Trying to get the waiter to explain which dishes are *à la carte* is rather tricky if you don't speak excellent French. Keep in mind that in France, waiters are just that—professional waiters. They are not wannabe actors or students holding down a second job, and they will not drip with smiles and ingratiating manner, coming by your table every five minutes to ask if everything is just fine. Personally, I find this most refreshing, but be prepared to order swiftly and bear in mind that in France, a waiter's primary goal is efficiency, not sycophancy. The *menu* will usually include an *entrée*, which means an appetizer, not the main dish as in North America, most often *pâté*, smoked ham *(jambon)* with bread, or fresh raw vegetables *(crudités)*. Salad is not common. The main dish *(plat)* will usually be fish *(poisson)* or seafood *(fruits de mer)* or meat, most often chicken *(poulet)*, duck *(canard)*, vea *(veau)*, lamb *(agneau)* or pork *(porc)*. The French are not big beef eaters, but you may be offered a steak *(bistec)*, which will be skinnier and rarer than you are used to. When the waiter asks how you want it done *(cuison?)*, go one level higher than you ordinarily would: the choices are well done *(très cuit)*, medium *(bien cuit)*, medium rare *(a point)* rare *(saignant)* and raw *(bleu)*. Also included in the *menu* will be dessert *(dessert)* and cheese *(fromage)*, as well as coffee and possibly your drink *(boisson compris)*, which means wine.

The French drink wine with everything and often all by itself. As a tourist you are expected to behave peculiarly, but to order a Pepsi with a fine meal is considered insulting. If you don't want wine *(du vin)* or beer *(une bière)*, ask for mineral water, either sparkling *(eau gazeuse)* or not *(eau plate)*. If you want ice *(de la glace)* you'll have to ask for it.

If you are in the mood for something lighter, you might want to steer for a *brassèrie*—also a restaurant, but serving less heavy food, and popular for lunch or a late dinner after a show.

When you want the bill ask for *l'addition*. Your meal is likely to be more expensive than you are used to paying, because the price includes 18.6 percent sales tax and, most likely, 15 percent service. If you do not see *service comprise* you should leave a 15 percent tip (see "Tipping"). You probably won't get a table for lunch after about 2 p.m. nor for dinner before about 7 p.m.

Cafés

There are a million cafés in France, and a million reasons to visit one. Whether you are tired, thirsty, lonely, hungry, bored, happy or sad, you'll find a café to suit your needs. Remember that location is what you pay for—the fare and the service is likely to be the same whether you are at an open-air spot on the Left Bank or on a side street in a market town; the prices, however, could be double in the former. *Café au lait*, as we were all taught in high school French, is no longer used; if you want a coffee with milk order a

afé *crème*. Ordering *café* or *café serré* only will get you a short shot of espresso; *café al-*
ongé gets it diluted with hot water; *café noisette* gets a splash of hot milk.

Cafés are easy places to forge new friendships.

Mineral water, a glass of wine or a cold beer are all rudimentary café drinks. *Du vin rouge* gets you a glass of red, often the cheapest item on the menu; *du vin blanc* is a glass of white. *Un demi* or *une pression* is a small glass of draft beer; imports are bottled. Mostly you'll find only lagers. If you want a lemonade order a *citron pressé*; *limonade* is Seven Up or similar. Coke, Pepsi and Tab are all common sodas.

The prices for everything should be posted. There are two prices, one for *salle*, or table service, and one for *comptoir*, where you stand at the counter. You will likely make conversation easily in a café, although you shouldn't try to chat with the bartender or waiter if it's busy. It's acceptable to ask to share a table if there are none free. Food in cafés is mostly unsatisfying; it's not their main bag, after all. You can get a *sandwich* (usually half a *baguette* sliced open with a slice of ham and nothing else), an *omelette*, or a grilled cheese and ham sandwich *(croque)*.

Grocery Shopping

It is fun, not to mention most economical, to put together a picnic meal for yourself especially for lunch. You can shop in the relatively new supermarkets *(supermarchés)*, which are much smaller than what you find in the United States or Canada. The very few true supermarkets are called *Hypers* or *Diplos* and are only found in big cities. Or you can do as the French have done for centuries—get your bread at the *boulangerie* (the basic loaf is a *baguette*), your cheese from a *fromagerie*, where you can choose from as many as 100 kinds, your cold cuts and *pâtés* at the *charcuterie*, your wine and other basics at the *epicerie*, your dessert at the *patisserie*, and your fresh fruit and vegetables at the street markets, or *marchés*.

Wine

Smaller wineries often allow visitors to view grape harvesting.

General

Wine is such a huge subject in France that it deserves its own book—and of course, hundreds of books have indeed been written on the subject. I will try here to give just a basic overview. I'm something of a wine snob even though I have absolutely no right to be—I'm as far from an expert on wines as one can be. But I grew up in England, where French was the only kind of wine, then spent eight years in Spain, where the soil and climate conditions are not as far removed from those in France as winemakers in the two countries would have us believe. So when I arrived in the United States, I scorned American wineries as interlopers, incapable of producing anything even close to a halfway decent *vin de table*. The great irony in this all too prevalent prejudice, of course, is that when the dreaded *phylloxera* bug destroyed virtually every vineyard in France during the 1870s, the vines were all replanted or regrafted with rootstock from hardier American strains.

Which just goes to prove what the French are always telling you—the climate and the soil have as much or more to do with the production of wine as does the grape. This is evidenced by the fact that identical grapes planted in different vineyards only a few miles apart will produce radically different wines. These soil variations and the "microclimates" the French winemakers find so important—but which are undiscernible to the average visitor—lead to the strictly controlled system of *Denomination d'Origine*, which ensures that the wine drinker knows exactly what he or she is getting. The French introduced the system in 1935, and have been battling fraud both domestically and abroad ever since. Cognac, for example, is a name that can only legally be applied to the double-distilled wine from the small region of the same name in Poitou-Charentes. Champagne, likewise, is a trademark-protected name that should not be used to describe anything but the bubbly from the Champagne region.

The top quality category for French wine is *Appellation d'Origine Controllée* (Controlled Place of Origin, often abbreviated AOC or AC). The wines that earn this title must meet extremely strict minimum and maximum requirements of production, alcohol content and geographic limits, as well as adhere to production standards defined by law. Only about 16 percent of French wines make the cut. The next category is *Vins Délimités de Qualité Superieur* (Restricted Wines of Superior Quality), accounting for a further 10 percent of national production. Next come *Vins de Pays* (Country Wines), and finally, *Vins de Table* (Table Wines). For most of us, a decent *Vin de Table*, despite its lowly standing in the hierarchy, is perfectly acceptable.

The main categories of grapes—and the terms that give names to the kinds of wine in North America—are *Pinot Noir*, from which Burgundies are made; *Cabernet-Sauvignon*, the main grape in Bordeaux; and *Chardonnay* and *Chenin Blanc*, from which white wines originate. White wines are made from the flesh of the grape, without allowing the skin to color the liquid. Rosés get their color from the skins being allowed to be present in the fermentation for just a while, while the red wines are the product of the entire grape, including even the stems.

Fielding

WINE
REGIONS

BORDEAUX The climate of this region varies more by year and by area than any other region of France, resulting in a wide variety of what are recognized as the finest wines in the world. Varieties include Cabernet Sauvignon, Cabernet Franc, Merlot, Petit Verdot, Malbec, Sauvignon and Semillon.

LOIRE VALLEY Cool Atlantic winds wash over the fertile Loire Valley, giving the Loire wines their characteristic acidity. The wines of this region are flavorful and aromatic but not as highly esteemed as those of Bordeaux or Burgundy. Varieties include Muscadet, Sauvignon, Chenin Blanc, Gamay and Cabernet Franc.

CHAMPAGNE Without a doubt, the most famous sparkling wines in the world come from the Champagne region. The cool yet mild climate helps to produce grapes that other vintners can only dream about. Varieties include Pinot Noir, Pinot Meunier and Chardonnay.

ALSACE Sharing a common border with Germany and a mild climate with Champagne, this region is fairly dry throughout the year. Wines from Alsace are predominately still, full-bodied, fruity and dry. Varieties include Gewurtztraminer, Riesling, Muscat, Pinot Gris, Pinot Blanc and Pinot Noir

BURGUNDY Sitting just above the Beaujolais region, Burgundy extends north along the Côte-d'Or. The wide variation in climate throughout the year here make for more of a variety of wines each year than in other regions. Varieties here include Pinot Noir, Gamay, Chardonnay, Aligote, Pinot Blanc and Sauvignon.

BEAUJOLAIS This region just south of Burgundy is famous for it's Pinot Noir, Chardonnay and Gamay grapes. Vineyards here are tucked away on the sunny hillsides of the Côte-d'Or. The south of Beaujolais is well known for its nouveau wines, while the north is better known for fine-quality Cru wines.

THE SOUTH Stretching along the Mediterranean coast, this region has a hot, dry climate, producing light, fruity wines. Known primarily for vast vineyards which mass-produce table and fortified wines, the area is starting to branch into smaller production of higher-quality wines. Varieties include Carignan, Aramon, Syrah, Mourvedre, Grenache, Cabernet Sauvignon, Merlot, Chardonnay, Blanc, Viognier and Muscat.

ENGLA

ENGLI

N12

Renne

Nant

La Rochell

ATLANTIC
OCEAN

Bordeaux

L

Bayonne

SPAIN

0   25   50
       miles

CHANNEL

Boulogne

BELGIUM

GERMANY

A26

CHAMPAGNE

Somme

LUXEMBOURG

A1

A26

Reims

Caen

A13

Seine

A4

Paris

Marne

A4

A31

LOIRE VALLEY

Strasbourg

A11

Troyes

ALSACE

Orleans

Colmar

Le Mans

Seine

Mullhouse

Angers

Loire

Auxerre

A6

Saone

Tours

Bourges

Dijon

A36

Poiters

BURGUNDY

Beaune

A10

A71

SWITZERLAND

Vienne

Macon

A6

Bourg-en

BEAUJOLAIS

A40

Limoges

A72

Lyon

A41

BORDEAUX

A47

A43

ALPS

aronne

Dordogne

Le Puy

Rhone

Grenoble

ITALY

Lot

A7

A62

Tarn

Nimes

Tarbes

Toulouse

A68

Montpellier

A51

Nice

A61

A9

A8

Monaco

Carcassonne

Narbonne

Marseille

Cannes

Perpignan

THE SOUTH

Toulon

MEDITERRANEAN SEA

Ordering

Even in France, not everyone is a wine expert (although everyone thinks he or she is). This is well known to wine waiters, or *sommeliers*, who are especially aware of the ignorance of the average tourist. Don't hesitate to ask for advice when choosing a wine—not only will this spare you the embarrassment of ordering something completely wrong, but the waiter's favorites are likely the best. If the waiter recommends something out of your price range, you can suggest, *"Peut-être quelque chose un petit peux moins cher?"* You can usually get the house wines by the carafe or half-carafe. Better quality wines are served by the bottle or by the glass.

The basic rules to follow are the same everywhere. Don't spring for the most exotic-sounding or expensive wine on the list; it's unlikely to be the best. Very dry whites go with seafood, fish and delicacies including snails, frog legs and cheese when served as an appetizer. Richer whites accompany chicken, richer fish dishes (including pasta seafood with heavy sauces). Light reds are served with roast lamb, pork and beef, as well as with the cheese plate. Heavy reds, including expensive vintage wines, are best with heavy red meat dishes such as stroganoff, and with the more odiferous cheeses. Sweet white and champagnes are drunk with dessert and alone. Follow these principles, and rely on your waiter, and you won't go far wrong.

Wine Cellars

It's a good deal of fun to visit wine cellars *(caves)*, both at the big châteaux and at smaller producers and distributors in the city. Many will offer a tour of the production rooms in action, as well as the rest of the facility. You can inquire at local tourist boards as to which wineries offer tours and where English is spoken. Personally, I prefer to visit the smaller wineries, where you are likely to be hosted by the owner. You'll be able to buy wines, or get information about distributors in your homeland that you can give to your local merchant. Bottle sizes are rather amusing in most *caves;* there will usually be wines on display in quarter-bottle, half-bottle, and bottle sizes, along with magnum (1.5 liters) and double magnum (3 liters) and the biblical jeroboam (5 liters), methuselah (6 liters), salmanazar (9 liters), balthazar (12 liters) and nebuchadnezzar (15 liters).

Tasting

Every *cave* that is open to visitors, as well as many city distributors, offers free wine tastings. This is not, however, a free booze-up. You are expected to be there because you are interested in wine and willing to make a purchase if you find a wine you like. You will annoy a merchant rather quickly if you just chug down a couple of glasses, ask no questions and make no comments, then leave. Don't feel obliged to go through the complex ritual you'll see the owner and perhaps other visitors indulging in, it's fine to simply drink the wine. If you want to sample like the natives, however, know that actually swallowing the wine is the last in a series of actions. First you look at the label, noting the classification (see above). Then, after you've been handed a glass, look at it in the light (*caves* have street level windows for this purpose), observing the clarity, consistency and hue. Next, take a while to savor the scent of the wine with your olfactory bulb—smell it. True connoisseurs can tell you the year, region and even vineyard by this point. Finally, take a mouthful, and let it sit against your palate for a moment—don't swill it around like mouthwash. If you're tasting several wines in succession, you'll spit it out so it doesn't color the tastebuds against the next one. Finally, when it's the last wine you are going to taste, you may swallow it.

Accommodations

Basics

There is a huge variety of types of lodgings in France, ranging in style, amenities and price across the whole spectrum. You'll find familiar hotel chains including Holiday Inn and Four Seasons, along with luxurious and unique accommodations in ancient châteaux, youth hostels and thousands of individual bed-and-breakfast spots. Give some thought first to the type of lodgings you want. Is price the most important consideration? Definitely a low price might be best if you are the type who just wants a bed and a shower and will be up and at 'em and on to the next town bright and early in the morning. On the other hand, if you plan to spend several days in one place, or you are on a romantic vacation and will be spending a great deal of time in your room or by the fireplace, you may opt to spend a little more for a place with more character or charm.

The price is always posted in the lobby of hotels and other lodgings, and the cost includes tax and service. Be aware that the general size of rooms in France is not what you may be used to—especially in the city hotels, where an emphasis is given to functionality over spaciousness. Always ask to see the room before agreeing to it. Most likely you'll be shown the best available rather than having the worst foisted upon you sight unseen. Breakfast is not included in the price you are quoted (although it should be posted separately) but much of the time it is taken as a given that you will be having it and you will be billed for it automatically. Breakfast is likely to be a minimal affair of coffee and croissants, unless it is advertised as buffet-style, which may include eggs and bacon, juice and other items. In that case, there may well be two prices, one for the typical continental breakfast and one for the buffet.

Types of Lodging

Hotels

Hotels are rated by the French government with from one to four stars. One star is really basic accommodation: you are unlikely to get a bathroom and, in some cases even a toilet, in your room. There'll be a ceiling light but no bedside lamp, and the lack of charm to the place will be almost complete. Two stars is a better bet if you are on a budget; being still fairly cheap (US$30–50), but with a good deal more comfort. Three-star hotels are very nice, but this category tends to be dominated by the big chains—there are very few independently owned three-star hotels left any more. The big chains include Altéa, Frantel, Holiday Inn, Mercure, Novotel, Pullman and Sofitel. Four-star hotels are the equivalent of five-star properties in the United States; the cost runs more than US$100 a night and the hotels are crammed with luxury conveniences, the majority of which the average holiday-maker may not need.

Three-star chain hotels often offer good rates on the weekends, when their business clientele has dispersed. In all cases do not be shy about asking for a reduction based on the fact that you are a regular guest of the chain, or if you are booking your room without

TRAVELER'S GUIDE

using an agent (to whom the hotel would have to pay a commission. It never hurts to ask for a discount. You also can sometimes get good rates by booking rooms through the airline you are flying to France, and the tourist boards mentioned in this book can let you know of any two-for-one or extra-day specials in their area. It's advisable to have reservations for your first night in France, as you'll be tired and grumpy after the flight, and you won't want the hassle of looking for a room then. You should also book rooms well in advance if you are traveling to the major tourist areas during summer, or you'll be left with a poor selection.

Châteaux

One of the most unique experiences you can have in France is that of staying in a centuries-old château or stately home. The best bet is to find a privately owned place whose owners are in financial straits and thus are renting out some rooms—these are the places where you'll get the most genuine feel for life in the French countryside, as well as personal attention and conversation. The level of service won't be as professional as that in the châteaux owned by corporations, but the price will probably be a good 20 percent less and the lived-in feel will more than compensate. A number of tour operators offering châteaux accommodations are listed in the preceding section ("Getting There"). You can also contact one of the following companies:

Châteaux Accueil

c/o Châteaux du Gerfaut, 37190 Azay-le-Rideau
☎ *(33) 01-47-45-40-16; FAX: (33) 01-47-45-20-15*
This is the best association of privately owned châteaux that accept guests. Most of its properties are quite delightful and you'll come away from the experience with a friend as well as good memories.

Châteaux-Hôtels Indépendents

15 rue Malebranche, 75005 Paris cedex 1
☎ *(33) 01-43-54-74-99; FAX: (33) 01-43-54-76-96*
This is an association of independently owned hotels set in châteaux and other homes. Confirm that you are actually going to a châteaux if that's what you want, and not somebody's rather ordinary house.

Relais & Châteaux

☎ *(800) 735-2478*
Offers booking services in extremely upscale châteaux accommodations, featuring delightful homes with amenities that include swimming pools, tennis courts, hot-air ballooning and more. Prices tend to be quite expensive.

Self-Catering Accommodations

You can rent a small cottage in the countryside in France for a week at a rate that will likely be cheaper than two rooms in a three- or even a two-star hotel. This is the perfect solution for families, groups of friends traveling together, and even couples who don't mind shelling out a little more for the privacy of an entire house. You get your bedrooms, a full kitchen, lounge and often even a garden for relaxing. This type of lodging is known in France as *Gîtes Ruraux*. You can rent by the week or the month, but it is advisable to book your cottage well in advance. Contact the French Government Tourist Offices for listings or contact:

Féderation Nationale Gîtes de France

35 rue Godot-de-Mauroy, 75009 Paris
☎ *(33) 01-49-70-75-75; FAX: (33) 01-49-70-75-76*

Bed and Breakfast

Known as *Chambres d'Hôte*, bed-and-breakfast spots in the French countryside are becoming more and more numerous. They represent an excellent option for the more adventurous traveler in search of inexpensive and comfortable accommodations with character and a real sense of French country living. Bed-and-breakfast inns are rated by the French government on the same scale as hotels except that the symbol for their rating is from one to four ears of corn, rather than stars. The ones that advertise *table d'hôte* offer dinner as well as a room. By definition, a host who opens up his or her home is likely to be friendly to guests, and you often will find the owner of a bed-and-breakfast to be the best guide to a region.

Youth Hostels

With the variety of inexpensive accommodations available in France, there is really no need to stay in a youth hostel unless you like the anarchic atmosphere or are particularly looking to meet fellow sojourners of the opposite or same sex for continued friendship. You can get a bed in a dormitory for perhaps US$20 a night, but for the same price you'll often find lodgings in a one- or even two-star hotel; and you won't have to bring a sleeping bag or share your room with 20 people. For more information on youth hostelling, refer to the following section ("Students and Youth") or contact:

Fédération Unie des Auberges de Jeunesse

4 boulevard Jules Ferry, 75011 Paris
☎ *(33) 01-43-57-02-60; FAX: (33) 01-40-21-79-92*

Camping

Camping and caravanning is a very popular method of tourism in France. There are more than 11,000 campsites located in all regions. In popular tourist areas, more visitors camp than stay in hotels. Campsites *(le camping)* vary in size from a few hundred square feet to several acres; locations range from flat fields to steep, terraced river- and lake-sides. The number of sites can vary from about 25 to more than 500. All but a few campsites accept tents, caravans and motor homes, although there may be separate areas for each type of unit.

Campsites are graded by a nationwide star classification that lays down minimum standards for each rating from one to four stars. In practice most sites exceed the minimum standards. "Pitch" *(emplacement)* or individual site sizes range from 90 to more than 100 square meters; they are usually marked out by posts, hedges or trees.

One-star campsites have basic facilities that are adequate for a short stay, suited in particular to visitors with a well-equipped caravan or motor home. Two-star campsites have facilities that provide for a comfortable stay of a longer duration and are more suited to tents as well as caravans and motor homes. Hot water is available at least in the showers and more often than not in hand basins *(lavabo)* and washing-up sinks *(bac à vaiselle)*. Most campsites run by the local town or village *(Camping Municipal)* are two-star properties. These include some of the cheapest and best-value campsites, providing excellent overnight stops when touring. Prebooking is not usually possible or necessary.

Campsites intended for visitors who wish to spend most or all of their time there are graded three- or four-star, and have at least 100 individual sites. They usually have someone at the reception point *(accueil)* who speaks English, and these campsites have electrical connection points for each pitch. These campsites also have well-appointed toilets blocks *(sanitaire)* with tiled showers and washrooms. Toilet facilities are often not segregated—men and women both use the same block. This typically French arrangement is particularly convenient for families with small children. Hot water is provided for washing up and for washing clothes *(lacà lique)*, in addition there may be a laundromat.

Swimming pools *(piscine)* are provided on most of the larger campsites and are well-maintained. Pools are fenced off for safety and hygiene reasons. Strict rules of conduct are displayed at the entrance to the pool area. Footwear is prohibited and often men are required to wear swimming trunks instead of shorts. It is not unusual for women to go topless in the pool area; a practice more common in the South of France. Other sports are often available, including tennis, volleyball, crazy golf and *petanque* (French bowls). Children's playgrounds are usually well-equipped and maintained.

Facilities provided at larger campsites often include shops for day-to-day needs and food. Fresh bread is often available, at least during high season, generally from 8 a.m.—and purchasing a loaf is a "must" for the native campers! *Camping Gaz International* is the standard fuel for cooking and canisters are stocked by most campsite shops. Often barbecues are provided near sites for visitor use. Private barbecue grills often are not allowed. Some campsites provide take-away food *(plats à emporter)* service. Bars and restaurants are often available, as is an entertainment service *(animations)*, which may range from guided walks to cinema shows. Competitions and events often are provided to keep the youngsters amused.

In addition to providing pitches for visitors bringing their own camping gear, many large campsites rent out accommodations such as static caravans and chalets. Booking in advance is strongly recommended.

For those who prefer a quieter camping trip, farm sites *(camping à la ferme)* are available, where the number of individual sites is restricted to 25. These also must meet minimum standards but are not star-rated. Set in rural surroundings, farm campsites provide basic facilities with a local flavor.

There are about 100 nudist campsites in France, popular with all European nudists. These campsites are usually full during the French holiday season. Nudist campsites are mostly graded two- or three-star and are well-screened and separate from conventional campsites.

A number of the travel companies listed under "Tour Operators" in the "How to Get There" section offer camping holidays in France in well-equipped ready-erected tents or static caravans.

Camping guidebooks are available in France and in most English-speaking countries. One of the best is the *Michelin Camping and Caravanning* guide. The *Michelin Motoring Atlas of France* is ideal for touring, and it shows the location of campsites listed in the guide, as well as other suitable campsites.

Large supermarkets and hyper-markets in France stock camping equipment. If you are thinking of using a caravan (or trailer) be aware that in Paris caravans are not allowed in the areas inside the orbital ring road, the Périphérique. In addition, motorhomes and vehicles pulling trailers (caravans) are restricted to designated parking places in Paris and most other large French cities.

During July and August, the French high season, many campsites are full. In June and September, individual sites will always be available but some facilities may not be available.

Special Interests

Travelers with Disabilities

France's infrastructure has evolved over centuries with little or no thought to the needs of those with developmental or physical disabilities. Like many other countries, France has recently begun taking steps to ensure easier, if not equal, access to most public places for the disabled. Access is generally much better in more modern buildings and institutions—ramps, elevators, special toilet facilities and other conveniences are much more likely to be found at those museums, hotels and monuments that have been built or renovated in the last decade.

Most airlines will provide assistance to disabled travelers in transit if you let them know in advance. Most airlines and all public transportation companies in France provide free transportation for seeing-eye dogs, but be sure to have your dog's certificate of anti-rabies vaccination with you when you travel. The SNCF provides special wagons on some trains (including all TGVs) for people using wheelchairs—but check in advance. The SNCF also provides free transit-assistance to the disabled who are transferring from one train to another, but you'll need to call in advance and request the help. Within Paris, accessibility to the Métro is limited to designated seats on the trains. Be aware that many stations do not have escalators, let alone elevators, for the descent below street-level. The RER network of surface trains that covers the Paris suburbs is a little more progressive—some of its stations are equipped with ramps and elevators—call in advance to find out which stations have been improved.

Resources

Lists of hotels and other accommodation published by the regional tourism authorities indicate facilities that provide handicapped access with the international symbol of a wheelchair. You can also get information in advance of your trip from a number of organizations including the following:

American Foundation for the Blind

11 Penn Plaza, Suite 720, New York, NY 10001, U.S.A.
☎ *(800) 232-5463 or (212) 502-7600*

Information Center for Individuals with Disabilities

Fort Point Place, 27-43 Wormwood Street, Boston, MA 02210, U.S.A.
☎ *(800) 462-5015 or (617) 450-9888; TDD (617) 424-6855*

Mobility International (World Headquarters)

228 Borough High Street, London SE1 1JX, England
(071) 403-5688

Mobility International USA

P.O. Box 3551, Eugene, OR 97403, U.S.A.
☎ *and TDD (503) 343-1284; FAX (503) 343-6812*

Royal Association for Disability and Rehabilitation

12 City Forum, 250 City Road, London EC1V 8AF, England
☎ *(0171) 250-3222*

Travel Industry and Disabled Exchange

5435 Donna Avenue, Tarzana, CA 91356, U.S.A.
☎ *(818) 368-5648; FAX (818) 344-0078*

Travelin' Talk

P.O. Box 3534, Clarksville, TN 37043, U.S.A.
☎ *(615) 552-6670; FAX (615) 552-1182*

There are a number of specialized tour operators that cater to travelers with disabilities. These operators offer individual, family and group trips and rates. These include:

Directions Unlimited

720 North Bedford Road, Bedford Hills, NY 10507, U.S.A.
☎ *(800) 533-5343 or (914) 241-1700*

Society for the Advancement of Travel for the Handicapped

347 Fifth Avenue, Suite 610, New York, NY 10016, U.S.A.
☎ *(212) 447-7284; FAX (212) 725-8253*

Wheelchair Journeys

16979 Redmond Way, Redmond, WA 98052, U.S.A.
☎ *(800) 313-4751 or (206) 885-2210*

Several organizations publish brochures and guides for the disabled traveler in France that will help you plan your trip with accessibility in mind. Among the most useful are the following:

Access Travel: Airports   **Free**

Consumer Information Center
Dept. 5804, Pueblo, CO 81009, U.S.A.
Airport Operators' Council
Description of the accessibility at more than 500 airports around the world.

Directory of Travel Agencies for the Disabled $19.95

Twin Peaks Press
P.O. Box 129, Vancouver, WA 98666, U.S.A.
☎ *(800) 637-2256 or (206) 694-2462*
Listings and contact information for almost 400 travel agencies and tour operators that offer specialized services for the disabled.

Travelin' Talk Directory $35

Travelin' Talk
P.O. Box 3534, Clarksville, TN 37043, U.S.A.
☎ *(615) 552-6670; FAX (615) 552-1182*
Resource guide for the disabled traveler, with the most comprehensive information I have seen; almost 500 pages.

Wheelchair Vagabond $19.95

Twin Peaks Press
P.O. Box 129, Vancouver, WA 98666, U.S.A.
☎ *(800) 637-2256 or (206) 694-2462*

When you arrive in France, you may want to contact one of the French organizations for the disabled. Most offer some literature and assistance in English. They include:

Association des Paralysées de France

Délégation de Paris, 9 boulevard Auguste-Blanqui, 75013 Paris, France
☎ *01-45-81-30-63*
This organization publishes the most comprehensive guide to hotels and motels in France that offer accessibility to persons with disabilities.

Comité National Français de Liaison pour la Réadaptation des Handicapés

236b rue de Tolbiac, 75013 Paris, France
☎ *01-53-80-66-66*

Union Nationale des Associations de Parents d'Enfants Inadaptés

15 rue Coysevox, 75018 Paris, France
☎ *01-42-63-84-33; FAX 01-42-63-08-45*

You can also consult the guide *Rousseau H. Comme Handicapés*, available at:

SCOP

4 rue Gustave-Rouanet, 75018 Paris, France
☎ *01-42-52-97-00; FAX. 01-42-52-52-50*

Gay and Lesbian France

In keeping with the generally wholesome French attitude toward sex; gays and lesbians in France endure less irrational contempt than in the more uptight societies of England or the United States. Although homophobic attacks and homophobic politicians have been somewhat in the ascendancy since the onset of the AIDS pandemic, the law—and usually, the culture—is on the side of personal freedom.

In fact, ancient anti-sodomy laws were abolished in France with the Revolution in 1791. This legal protection endured until the collaborationist Vichy government of World War II. Under the motto "Work, Family, Fatherland"—eerily reminiscent of the new right of the 1990s—gays, along with Gypsies, Jews and Communists, were targeted for harassment and extermination. The laws outlawing homosexuality adopted by the

Vichy government remained in force until 1981. The age of consent for gay sex was age 21 until 1978; and age 18 until 1981. For heterosexual liaisons, by way of discriminatory contrast, way back in 1945 the age of consent was set at 15. Beginning with the rise to power of the Socialist government of François Mitterrand in 1982, the oppressive laws have been rolled back, and the age of consent is now 15 for every sexual orientation, although minors are still under their parents' authority until age 18. Anti-discrimination protections were also made part of the law of the land during the first years of Mitterrand's government, and while full domestic partnership has not yet been adopted, since 1993, same-sex couples have been recognized for the purposes of employer-provided health insurance.

Despite the protections of the law and the general tolerance, gays and lesbians in France generally avoid open displays of affection in public. The gay activist community was decimated by the AIDS scourge in the 1980s; since then the community has been in a period of retrenchment, focusing on health education and lobbying for public funding of AIDS research.

Lingua Franca

In the French mainstream newspapers, "*homosexuel*" is still the most common word used, but *gai* (*gaie*, female) or *gay* is widely recognized, as in the influential magazine *Gai Pied* and the gay Paris radio station *Fréquence Gaie*. The abbreviation *homo* is more common, even more than *gay* in informal speech, and is thought of among French gays and lesbians as more unenlightened rather than purposefully derogatory. That intention is accomplished by the vicious epithet *pédé* (from the now obsolete *pédéraste* for child-lover), although, like "queer" in the United States, the term is used sardonically between members of the gay community themselves as well as by activists including members of ACT-UP France and others. The English word "queer" is not understood in France, even among gays and lesbians. On the other side, there is only one word for the non-gays used by gays and lesbians: *hétérosexuel*, rendered more often informally as *hétéro*, and sometimes, very facetiously, as *hétérote*. There is no real equivalent in French for "straight."

Resources

Tour operators specializing in services to the gay and lesbian community include the following:

Above and Beyond

3568 Sacramento Street, San Francisco, CA 94118, U.S.A.
☎ *(800) 397-2681 or (415) 922-2683*

Islanders/Kennedy Travel

183 West 10th Street, New York, NY 10014, U.S.A.
☎ *(800) 988-1181 or (212) 242-3222*

Skylink Women's Travel

746 Ashland Avenue, Santa Monica, CA 90405, U.S.A.
☎ *(800) 225-5759 or (310) 452-0506*

Publications of interest to gays and lesbians planning a trip to France may include the following:

Are You Two... Together? $18

Random House
Available in bookstores everywhere, this is the comprehensive guide to bars, restaurants, nightclubs, and hotels throughout Europe, with a good section on France, especially Paris.

Gai Pied Hebdo

Available everywhere at newsstands in Paris, this weekly newspaper of gay and lesbian advocacy also publishes a guide to the city. Copies sell for about FR50.

Paris Exit

Available everywhere at newsstands in Paris, this weekly newspaper provides feature articles (in French!) as well as entertainment reviews, listings of services, and a calendar of current events for the gay and lesbian community in the capital.

Spartacus International Gay Guide

Bruno Gmnunder
100 East Biddle Street, Baltimore, MD 21202, U.S.A.
☎ *(410) 727-5677*
A gay men's guide to lodgings and nightlife around the world.

Women Going Places $14

Inland Book Company
P.O. Box 120261, East Haven, CT 06512, U.S.A.
☎ *(203) 467-4257*
A guide to women-owned establishments around the world, geared toward lesbians.

When you get to France you'll want to check out some of the following organizations and resources:

ARIS

BP 1125, 16, rue Saint Polycarpe
69203 Lyon cedex 01, France
The umbrella gay and lesbian organization in Lyon, France's second city, can provide visitors with lots of information on gay resources and activities in the south of France.

ASMF (Association Sportive et Motocycliste de France)

BP 2, 75965 Paris cedex 20, France
Motorcycle club.

CGPIF (Comité Gai Paris-Ile de France)

BP 120, 75623 Paris cedex 13, France
☎ *01-45-83-58-78*
Athletic club that also provides gay games.

GAC (Gay Automobile Club)

BP 9, 91941 Les Ulis cedex, France

Centre Gai et Lesbien

3 rue Keller, 75011 Paris, France
☎ *01-43-57-21-47*

The biggest gay-and-lesbian community center in France, with many outreach services, as well as entertainment options and information for visitors.

Long Yang Club

c/o CGL, 3 rue Keller 75011 Paris, France
☎ *and FAX: 01-45-42-80-25*
☎ *in English: 01-40-20-06-72*
One of the largest social clubs for the international gay and lesbian community in Paris.

Les Mots à la Bouche

6 rue Ste Croix de la Bretonnerie, 75004 Paris, France
☎ *01-42-78-88-30; FAX: 01-42-78-36-41*
Paris' largest gay and lesbian bookstore, with English and German books, and lots of information.

Rando's IdF

BP 419, 75870 Paris cedex 18, France
☎ *01-42-26-08-04*
Hiking and cycling club.

Voile et Croisière en Liberté

BP 97, 92205 Neuilly cedex, France
Sailing club.

The Jewish Traveler

Like many Catholic countries of Europe, France went through its own anti-Semitic paroxysm during the Middle Ages, leaving its Jewish community scattered and decimated. During World War II, the collaborationist Vichy government put the faithful through further persecution, but in the intervening years the number of Jews in France has exploded, fueled by a mass influx of several hundred thousand from North Africa that began about 25 years ago. The Jewish community in France is now the fourth largest in the world; third largest outside Israel and largest in Europe. There are hundreds of synagogues in more than 120 cities throughout the country. Kosher markets and restaurants are also plentiful.

France has produced several notable writers and artists from its Jewish community, including Pisarro, Bonheur, Chagall, Jaques Offenbach, Claude Kahan, Henri Bergson, and René Cassin. Many areas in the south of France, especially the ancient city of Avignon, where the Jews were given refuge during the 15th-century persecution, are especially rich in Jewish heritage.

Resources

Most large cities, particularly Paris, Lyon and Marseille, have extensive Jewish cultural networks, including newspapers, radio stations and social clubs that welcome overseas visitors. A number of publications provide extensive information on services catering to the Jewish traveler in France, as well as listings of historical attractions and other places of interest.

The Jewish Travel Guide   US$11.95

Jewish Chronicle Publications

25, Furnival Street, London EC4A, England
☎ (071) 405-9252; FAX: (071) 831-5188

Sepher-Hermon Press

1265 46th Street, Brooklyn, NY 11219, U.S.A.
☎ (718) 972-9010
Publishes guides to travel opportunities and interests around the world.

France for the Jewish Traveler

Published by the French Government Tourist Office
A comprehensive 32-page guide for Jewish visitors to France.

Women

If you are a single woman or two single women traveling alone, you will indubitably receive the unsolicited attention of men throughout France. For some this can be fun and enjoyable, for others mildly bothersome, and for still others truly harassing. The same principles women employ at home should hold true in France—show no weakness nor fear, and use common sense and caution. The best way to discourage unwanted attention is make brief eye contact, say "*bonjour*," and then return at once to what you are doing—walking calmly down the street, reading your book, eating or whatever.

I certainly do not advocate having to modify your behavior because of others' rudeness, but it is simply a fact that if you dress modestly and do not act flirtatiously you will probably run into fewer problems.

If the situation does turn nasty, don't be afraid to raise holy hell. "*Au secours!*" means "Help!" and "*Laissez-moi tranquille!*" means "Leave me alone!" One thing about the male French sense of machismo is that if a Frenchman sees you being bothered by another man he'll willingly step in to help. If the worst happens, and you are assaulted or raped (*violée*), call the police immediately by dialing 15. You can also call a 24-hour hotline called *SOS Viol* toll-free at ☎ 01 (33) 05-05-95-95. You may also want to consult the following publications, which are available at most general and all specialty bookstores:

The Handbook for Women Travelers	**£8.99**
Piatkus Books	
The Virago Women's Travel Guides: Paris	**US$13.95**
Virago Press/Ullyses Press	
Women Going Places	**US$14**
Inland Book Company	

Students and Young People

Students and young people enjoy the advantage of discounts on many activities and places in France. Other discounts include reduced rates for airline tickets and discounts on train passes and other transportation within the country. The key to most of these discounts is an International Student Card (see below). You can also get an International Youth Card if you're not a student but are under 26 years of age. In either case, you'll need to present the card to receive the discount. For more information, check out the following resources:

Hosteling International — American Youth Hostels

733 15th Street NW, Washington, D.C. 20005, U.S.A.

☎ *(202) 783-6161*

This organization offers membership in the Hostelling International Association for US$15. Membership allows access to hundreds of youth hostels throughout France. Also publishes the *Guide to Budget Accommodation*, a comprehensive booklet that sells for US$13.95.

Council on International Educational Exchange

205 East 42nd Street, New York, NY 10017, U.S.A.

☎ *(212) 661-1450 or (310) 208-3551*

This organization issues the International Student Card and International Youth Card (US$14 each) and publishes *Student Travels* (US$2), a biannual publication that includes an application for the cards as well as a wealth of current information for student travelers.

Bits and Pieces

Tipping

Unless you're a true Scrooge, you'll want to tip when it's appropriate, right? There's nothing worse than the hostile glare and muttered epithets (especially in a language you don't understand) of someone who was expecting a small gratuity from you and received nothing but what appeared to them as a blasé smile. On the other hand, it's almost as embarrassing to leave a tip when local custom doesn't demand one. You may never know about it, but you'll be laughed at as a gullible or ostentatious foreigner. The French expect tips at certain times and places, are grateful for them on other occasions, and in certain settings where you might be used to leaving something, you don't really have to. Here are some tips on tipping.

Restaurants and Cafés

Service is always included in food and drink at restaurants and cafés; usually in the form of a 15 percent surcharge. You should see *service compris* on the menu confirming this. Nevertheless, it is customary to leave some small change, especially if the service has been particularly pleasant. This should be just a few centimes for a beer or coffee, and a few francs after a full meal. Five francs per person would be generous; FR10 per person extraordinary. If you are served by a wine waiter he or she will, however, expect about FR10.

Taxi Drivers

As noted below, taxicab rates do not include tips. You should tip the driver at least 10 percent of the metered fare.

Porters

Baggage porters in airports and train stations operate according to a tariff scheme that should be posted in plain view. Nevertheless, they expect a tip of five francs or so.

Hotels

Baggage porters in hotels (bell boys), on the other hand, expect about FR10 per piece of luggage carried. In fact, everyone who attends you in a hotel wants a tip; chambermaids should get about FR10 per day, plus an extra five francs when delivering dry cleaning or another service, room service waiters about five francs, even the switchboard operator will expect a few francs if she or he has placed some calls for you.

Theaters and Museums

Tip cloakroom attendants in theaters and restaurants at least five francs per item, unless there is a sign reading *Pourboire Interdite*, which means tipping is not allowed. You'll often see this in museums. Ushers and usherettes in theaters and cinemas expect a couple of francs whether they show you to your seat or simply collect your ticket stub. A guide who has proven particularly illuminating at a museum or monument should receive five francs or so.

General

Public toilet attendants (who in my mind are the most deserving) should get two or three francs unless there is a posted charge for using the facilities. Hairdressers expect about 10 percent of the bill. As always, the twin principles of "wait and see" and "do as the locals do" will serve you well: hang back and see what everyone else is doing, copy them, and you won't go far wrong.

Voltage

Most of France has switched to 220–230 volts AC, although a few parts may still run on 110–115 volts. Current alternates at 50 cycles, not the 60 cycles in use in the United States. Because of this, unless your appliances are dual voltage you will need a voltage transformer. Don't take chances—running 110 volts through a 200 volt appliance will merely cause it to not work, but running 220 volts through a 110 volt appliance will fry it. You should be able to buy one fairly cheaply at a drug store before you leave home, otherwise you can pick one up at your hotel in France. The only exception is for electric shavers, for which special outlets providing 110 volts are installed in most hotel bathrooms.

However, you'll also need a plug adapter. The wall sockets in France are the two round-pronged European kind, so neither the U.S. plugs (two square prongs) nor the British kind (three square prongs) will work. This is an awful lot of hardware to lug around, so if you can, bring appliances that run on batteries, and leave the electrical gadgets at home. Most larger hotels now provide hair dryers anyway (the most common appliance taken abroad by travelers, according to surveys).

Toilets

The first thing you need to know about this important subject is that the correct inquiry is *"Où sont les toilettes, s'il vous plaît?"* If you ask for *la salle de bain* (bathroom), you'll find yourself in a room with a bathtub. The nightmarish stereotype of toilets in France being basically just a hole in the ground is no longer reality except in older cafés and at public toilets in rural areas. Far more common these days are the famed self-cleaning pay toilets. Looking like a windowless payphone or perhaps Dr. Who's TARDIS, these are electronically controlled ablution units—insert two francs and the door swings open to a sterilized cubicle featuring equally sterile Muzak and offering 15 minutes of privacy for you to do your business. After you leave the unit cleans itself from top to bottom—hence the permanent smell of disinfectant.

Other public toilets are less attractive, especially in busy cafés and restaurants, although these are the places where you'll get away with using the facilities without ordering something to drink or eat. Toilets are also free at fast food restaurants, where the toilets are usually kept quite clean. Toilets in train stations and some larger restaurants have an attendant who will need to be paid or tipped a couple of francs.

Carry some change for toilets, and you might be wise to have on hand a supply of tissue paper as well. In some smaller towns, the public toilets are unisex. Otherwise, look for the signs reading *hommes* (men), *femmes* (women), *garçons* (boys) or *filles* (girls).

Lost Property

If you lose your property on the Métro, on a train or on a bus, go immediately to the terminal point, and you may find it there. Otherwise, 48 hours later, call the local police department's lost-and-found office. In Paris, the address is as follows:

Préfecture de Police

> *Bureau des Objets Trouvés, 36 rue des Morillons, 75015 Paris, France*
> ☎ *01-45-31-14-80*
> *Open weekdays from 8:30 a.m. to 5 p.m. (Tuesdays and Thursdays till 8 p.m.).*
> If your item is found, you will be required to pay 4 percent of the item's value for the service. Lost property is held for a year and a day.

Smoking

Even though a far higher proportion of adults smoke in France than in the United States, France has begun to adopt some of the American-style repressive measures against smokers. By law, as of November 1, 1992, all areas open to the public have been declared nonsmoking zones. You can still smoke in most restaurants, but only in designated areas. This is true even for outdoor patios. For those who do not smoke, this will be a welcome concession, since the Gauloise brand favored by most French smokers is, inarguably, among the most pungent of cigarettes.

Business Hours

You can generally depend on larger department stores to maintain regular opening hours from 9 or 9:30 a.m. to 7 or 8 p.m. without closing for lunch, but smaller stores, still owned independently to a far higher degree in France than in North America, may keep any or no regular hours at all. Normally, small stores will open early, by 8 a.m. in most cases, and not close until 7:30 or 8 p.m. However, they will close for at least two and possibly three hours for lunch, usually beginning at 12:30 or 1 p.m. Many stores don't open on Saturday, and if they do, will likely be closed on Monday. Until fairly recently, it was not permissible to do business on Sundays, but more and more stores in Paris and in tourist areas are open on Sunday.

Banks, post offices and government offices open only from Monday to Friday, usually from 8 a.m. to 4 or 4:30 p.m. with a "mere" hour or hour-and-a-half lunch break. Museums usually open both days on the weekend (although often only for half-a-day on Sunday) and are closed one weekday instead, usually Tuesday. Some of the smaller museums close for lunch, but larger ones are open right through from 9 or 9:30 a.m. to 5:30 or 6 p.m.

French Embassies

Foreign countries' embassies in France

U.S. Embassy

2 Avenue Gabriel, 75382 Paris, France; ☎ *(33) 01-42-96-12-02.*

U.S. Consulates

22, cours du Marechal Foch, 33080 Bordeaux, France; ☎ *(33) 05-56-52-65-95.*
12, boulevard Paul-Peytral, 13286 Marseille, France; ☎ *(33) 04-91-54-92-00.*
15, avenue d'Alsace, 67082 Strasbourg, France; ☎ *(33) 03-88-35-31-04.*

Canadian Embassy

35 ave Montaigne, 75008 Paris, France; ☎ *(33) 01-44-43-29-00.*

Australian Embassy

4 rue Jean-Rey, 75015 Paris, France; ☎ *(33) 01-40-59-33-00.*

Embassy of Great Britain and Northern Ireland

35 rue du Faubourg-St.-Honoré, 75008 Paris, France; ☎ *(33) 01-42-66-91-42.*

French Embassies Overseas

United States

Chancery 4101, Reservoir Road NW, Washington, DC 20007; ☎ *(202) 944-6000.*
10990 Wilshire Blvd., Los Angeles, CA 90024; ☎ *(310) 479-4426.*

Canada

42 Sussex Drive, Ottawa, Ontario K1M 2C9; ☎ *(613) 789-1795.*
1 Place Ville Marie, 26th Floor, Suite 2601, Montreal, Quebec H3B 4S3; ☎ *(514) 878-4381.*

Australia

6, Perth Avenue, Yarralumla, Canberra A.C.T. 2600; ☎ *(6) 270-5111.*

Great Britain and Northern Ireland

58, Knightsbridge, London SW1X 7JT; ☎ *(171) 201-1000.*

WHAT MAKES FRANCE SO FRENCH?

by Marael Johnson

The Champs-Elysées remains Paris' most famous promenade.

What other country on this planet conjures up the myriad sensory pleasures and cultural persuasions that France does? The land is a virtual border-to-border bastion of ooh-la-la's, viva-this-and-viva-that's, and joie de *everything*.

What's your pleasure? A taste (or a thousand tastes) of ambrosial wine? Pastries so fabulous they'll leave you crawling on your belly and speaking in tongues? Sinfully wicked underwear (make that *lingerie*) that will have you

95

doing the same? Soak up the sun on a flashy Riviera beach, then go through a pack of cigarettes and bowls of strong coffee while hiding in the corner of some people-watching cafe. How about the heavenly scent of made-just-for-your-earthly-flesh perfume? Or a skip through fields of lost-in-Monet-dreams flowers? Chase it down with Parisian-seasoned red lips and stiletto heels.

What's your pursuit? A long gawk through some of creations' most wondrous museums? Barflying around Paris, pretending it's the '30s and that *you're* Hemingway (or Anais or Henry)? Mingling with a zillion other tourists at the medieval isle of Mont St. Michel? Signing up for a French course, ballet lessons, or gourmet cooking classes—wishing your friends back home could see you *now* (but hoping they'll never *ever* show up)? All that wine gone to your head? Perhaps you'd like to sober up in Normandy—the ultimate reality check—follow an epic trail that spans the Scandinavian Vikings, William The Conqueror, World War II, the first major defeat of the H-word, and the bones and ghosts of D-Day dead.

It's all here—in *the* republic Francaise—art, sex, music, passion, literature, history, architecture, food and wine, language, sport, fashion, film, chateaux, and *many many* good hair days.

France—of course—does not always garner raves with everyone. Some cry that the people are arrogant, the prices are high. Others criticize the government. Probably *no one* is overjoyed about the country's policy of (usually secret) nuclear testing in the South Pacific. Nonetheless it is *très* doubtful that any visitor to France will leave without his or her blood pumping harder and faster, the juices flowing juicier.

Mon visiteur—think of your journey to France as good sex—*really* good sex. And—if you don't especially love everything French—then think of it as really good sex with someone you hate and will only see again when you want another fix. What could be better than that?

Bon voyage, baby!

Sex

Of *course*, sex! France practically *invented* sex and passion (as well as much of the vocabulary that goes with!). The rest of the uptight world might consider premarital, extramarital, extracurricular—whatever—encounters as being illicit or immoral. Not so on *this* fertile soil. Everything is done with style, aplomb and that oh-so-French *savoir-faire*. No "dirty deeds" or "no-tell motels" here, my sweet. Have an appointment for a secret rendezvous (French word) with your much younger or much older lover? A *ménage a trois* (three French words), perhaps, with one or more sexes? A nearby pensione will no doubt welcome you with fresh flowers, hot-and-cold running bidet, and a discreet smile. A weekend in the country with your husband's mistress or your wife's love slave might require no more preparation than making certain there's enough wine, pâté, croissants and chocolate to go around. Of course, when the whole thing goes bad, you can expect *plenty* of passionate outbursts as well as some glorious displays of slashed wrists, drug overdoses, and alpine mental hospitals (haven't you ever seen a French film?). And let's certainly not forget that France is also the acknowledged home of *soixante-neuf.* (If you need a translation, you don't deserve to have it!)

Art

Of *course*, art! With few exceptions, since the late Middle Ages when illuminated manuscripts and panel paintings became *très vogue*, France—up until World War II—has firmly held the lead on the fast, fickle, furious European art beast. Cutting edge styles have included Mannerism (actually brought in by a couple of prominent Italian artists), Neoclassicism, Romanticism, Impressionism, Post-Impressionism, Cubism and Surrealism. The School of Fontainebleau was the rage of the 16th century, the esteemed Academy of Painting and Sculpture became a major player during the 17th century, salon exhibitions were the darling of the 18th century, the Barbizon School a *plein-air* feature of the 19th century, and Dada was born a 20th-century war baby. The cast of artists who made their mark or brushed their stroke in France reads like the A-list at a post-Oscar Awards do: Lorrain, Poussin, Boucher, Delacroix, Corot, Rousseau, Courbet, Manet, Monet, Renoir, Degas, Cezanne, Gauguin, Van Gogh, Matisse, Picasso, Braque, Leger, Dali, etc. etc. etc. Even Da Vinci spent the last three years of his life working in France. Montmartre, Montparnasse—*viva!* Even though the "scene" more or less shifted to New York after World War II, France's six-century-long legacy of artistic creation continues to inspire even those who believe art is a paint-by-numbers donkey on a piece of cheap black velvet.

Music

Music in France is pretty much ditto with art. Debussy, Satie, Ravel—all major players who bequeathed strains of heaven upon the motley earth. More contemporary contributors include flautist extraordinaire Jean-Pierre Rampal, composer Pierre Boulez, pianists Claude Bolling and Michel Legrand. And what '20s lover doesn't throb when dreaming about (or reliving) the American-born black cabaret star, Josephine Baker? Josephine won the hearts (and lower-placed body parts) of many an adoring admirer. The likes of Hemingway, Piaf and Stravinsky fawned over her performances while certain significant others (such as the crown Prince of Sweden) became part of her entourage (French word) of husbands and lovers. Speaking of Edith Piaf, chanson-she, and other grass-rooters like Jacques Brel, were also bigwigs on the 1950s music circuit. Jazz (in all its forms) is a perennial Parisian favorite, while flavor-of-the-year (or decade) alternative group is French-born Spanish rockers Mano Negra. And, come to think of it, isn't the Phantom of the Opera *francais*???

Literature

Oh, *mon dieu*, the pen is mightier than the sword—and, in France, it's also wittier, nastier and one hell of a lot sharper. For sheer bulk, there's Marcel Proust's tome, *Remembrance of Days Past*. And—for you philosophers—how about Rene Descartes? Who else? Gustave Flaubert, Victor Hugo, Anais Nin, Emile Zola, Colette, Honore de Balzac, Jean-Paul Sarte, Jean Genet, Alexandre Dumas, Marcel Pagnol, among others and others and on and on. Simone de Beauvoir bequeathed the western world with an ahead-of-her-time (or long overdue—depending on your point of view) treatise on feminism. Francoise Sagan gave us tittery little fictions of love affairs gone lasciviously right, then horribly wrong. Poetry's your thing? Jarry and Apollinaire are your window to the French Avant-Garde, while Andre Breton was one of the deities of Dada. The expats (with their ex-pat lifestyles) are perhaps the most remembered and revered literary figures of France (even though none of them were French)—Hemingway (of course), Henry Miller (of course), Gertrude Stein (and Alice B.), F. Scott Fitzgerald, George Sand, amongst them. The literary glory days may be over—though you can still visit most of the settings (and, at least, soak up the atmosphere) penned by your favorite authors. Or just hang out in Paris, at the famous Shakespeare & Co. bookshop—thumb the secondhand books, take in a poetry reading, and tap into the literally and figuratively spirits.

Language

La langue d'amour. Really, doesn't *everyone* love the French language?? Such magnificent words and phrases, rolling sensuously off the tongue—or nasally through the *nez* (nose). Boring old underwear turns into *sous-vetement*, the simple umbrella transcends into a *parapluie*, a pair of ordinary slippers spin into *partoufles.* Do you have a sunburn? *Non!* You have *brule par le soleil!* Even a dreary highway warning sign such as *Ce chemin est glissant lorsqui'il est mouille* (this road is slippery when wet) comes off sounding like a luscious encounter. The French even have an official association, the *Academie Francais*—composed of 40 members (the immortals), and dating from 1634—to ensure that the sacred language is protected from linguistic (particularly English) rubbish and faux pas. Parisians, many of whom speak English, probably won't let on while you struggle to order dinner or understand a train schedule. And many won't even acknowledge your bad French either! Practically no one in the countryside speaks anything other than French but they are at least more tolerant toward your bad pronunciation. As for the French, the rule is: don't utter a sound in English if there is any French word that can be used instead. *Qu'est-ce que c'est* 'handcuffs' *mistresse?*

Food and Drink

Bourgogne Vineyards

Who can do food and drink like the French can? Anything your senses (and non-senses) might desire—hundreds of cheeses (extra high fat, of course—and more than 400 varieties!), the perfect *omelette* or *soufflé*, buttery and flaky *croissants*, sweet or savory *crepes*, heaven-sent breads and pastries, and indescribably delectable gourmet meals. Even the lowliest cheese sandwich or fried egg is somehow elevated to a special treat. Cuisine is an art form, chefs are designated artists (you can become somewhat of an *artiste* yourself, after a course at the famed **Le Cordon Bleu** or newer **Ritz-Escoffier Ecole**). Choose from cafes, pizzerias, brasseries and full-scale restaurants. *Prix-fixe* or *à la carte* menus. Each region proudly presents its own special eats—Bayonne ham and wild pigeon in Pays Basque, Mediterranean-type flavors in Provence, snails and Roquefort cheese in Languedoc, goose and duck in Dordogne, etc. etc. etc. Breakfast is usually a *croissant* and bowl of *cafe*, lunch a serious and lengthy (two-or-three hour) endeavor, and dinner is an event. Cheese comes before dessert and coffee is offered after the last bite. As for *other* drinks—do you even have to *ask?* Wines to die for are produced mainly in the areas of Bordeaux, Burgundy, Champagne, the Loire Valley and Rhone Valley—though just about any bottle is bound to beat out the comparative rot-gut you've become used to back home. And of course—for harder spirits—there are such wonders as Cognac, Pernod, Kir, Poire William. Even the water is cause for celebration—brands such as Evian, Vittel, Vichy, Volvic (mineral or spring, sparkling or still) are as famous as the spas from which they gurgle. The French drink the waters, take the waters, turn the waters into wine. What a country! And, a special word about smoking— nonsmoking sections in all restaurants have been mandated since late 1992. *However*—if you're asthmatic, indignant or freaked by secondhand smoke, you will soon learn that the French don't always take laws (*any* laws) very seriously. *Vive la France!*

Film

Bardot, Moreau, Deneuve, Signoret, Montand, Boyer and Depardieu all became international stars, not just in France. With films such as *Children of Paradise, Day for Night, Betty Blue, Jules and Jim, Diva, A Man and A Woman* and *La Cage aux Folles,* directed by the likes of Godard, Truffaut, Malle, Besson, Varda, Tavernier. And, *voila!* French films have almost always ended up more as cutting edge lore than on the cutting room floor. The Sixties, in particular, with its advent of "New Wave" cinema, saw a surge of oh-boy-it's-a-*French*-film popularity throughout the world. Sometimes shocking and *risqué* (who didn't pant over *Last Tango in Paris*—even though it was directed by Italian Bertolucci and starred American Brando?), and— sometimes—boringly abstract or repetitive, French films are at least *talked about*—each one of them worthy of an *apres-cinema* espresso or glass of wine (or a heated debate in the sack). The French love films, both domestic and international creations—there are local cinema clubs, an archives with the world's largest assemblage of silent films, practically zilch censorship, and— of course—the razzle-dazzle, paparazzi heaven, Cannes Film Festival.

Architecture

The old is fabulous, the new either controversial or appallingly ugly. The Romans left their mark in temple ruins at Nimes, amphitheaters at Arles and Nimes, gateways at Autun, Saintes and Reims. Many building styles made their way in from Italy and were later "Franco-philed." The basic rule was that whichever king or religious leader was in power dictated architectural styles of the time—Carolingian, Romanesque, Gothic, Renaissance, Baroque, Rococo—notably appearing on chateaux, churches and various religious and public edifices. Later came "engineering" type trends, the use of reinforced concrete, and a wave of Modernists—including famous 20th-century architect Le Corbusier. The Metro, in operation around 1900, was bestowed with some interesting entrances—Art Nouveau styling by Hector Guimard, classical-type porticos by Charles Garnier. Art Nouveau and Art Deco became prevalent styles, with the French rather brilliantly bypassing the mostly hideous '50s and '60s trends that were the rage in America and other parts of the world. Despite some really interesting contemporary architecture (Centre Georges Pompidou and the I.M. Pei pyramid addition to the Louvre, both in Paris), newer suburbs and (horrors!) housing developments are notoriously boring and ugly (and let's not even discuss those cargo-container motels!). Nonetheless, just about everywhere you look in France—be it Mont St. Michel, the Eiffel Tower, the town of Senlis, or the Paris Metro stop at Place des Abbesses, even the most tunnel-visioned visitor will get locked in a peripheral gape.

Sport

There are rugby and football, of course—both eliciting the usual religious zeal, combined with that special passion that the French do *so* well. The three-week **Tour de France** bicycle race and the 24-hour **Le Mans** auto race both draw huge crowds of spectators, and bullfighting is a hot ticket down around the Camargue. Skiing—in all its forms—is a favorite (albeit expensive) sport that garners a share of saved-up-for-this-all-year locals along with the Beautiful People from both France and elsewhere. The Alps, natch, rank highest with the ski and apres-ski buffs, but areas around Provence and the Pyrénées also have their followers. The Jura and Massif Central are the ranges favored by the cross-country circuit. Unique sports are the Basque-created pelota—still the heartstopper of the Basque country (hard leather balls, wicker baskets strapped to wrists, world's fastest ball game—you can't miss it), along with *boules* (*petanque*, in the south)—a kind-of British bowls game except on a much smaller (and rougher) bit of land. And, you surfers—some of the best waves in Europe (maybe even *the* best) are just north of Biarritz, on the Atlantic Coast. Name of the beach is *Sables d'Or*, but *don't* let on to the locals who told you!

Fashion and Hair

French women have always been synonymous with fashion chic.

Fashion is linked inevitably with France along with food and wine—but then surely you *knew* that unless you've been living under a rock! Haute couture, the chi-chi-est fashion shows, exotic (and very *thin*) catwalk models, and star-status designers have been the ooh-and-aah rage of the world (no matter if—upon close scrutiny—the season's debut fashions look suspiciously like belted burlap bags, or the foil you wrapped last night's chicken in!). And—*so* typical—the French have actually regulated the definition of *couturier*—a status that is only bestowed upon a relative few, depending upon the studio, number of staff, and design output. Just a few of the *couturiers* who have pioneered the French (and international) fashion world have included Coco Chanel (revolutionizing women's fashion with the "little black dress" and her signature collarless and braid-trimmed suit—not to mention the fabled Chanel No. 5 *parfum* to splash on those collarless necks), Christian Dior, Yves Saint Laurent and Christian Lacroix. Hermes scarves, Vuitton bags, Jourdan shoes and perfumes by *everyone* are all on hand to complete the perfectly status-symboled package. Not that local style is confined to big francs and designer labels—the French know how to wear a pair of ripped, secondhand jeans as though they were custom-fitted, one-of-a-kinds—accessorizing with belts, stiletto heels, cashmere pullovers, see-through blouses—and *no* white underwear! Speaking of which—the French *know* how to make *brassieres*—darting, molding, shaping to glorify a woman's born-with breasts—*real* wonder bras (usually black). As for hairstyles (make those *coiffures*)—where do you think the word *mousse* came from?

Dead or Alive People

In France, the dead people are as exciting as the live ones. Just take a trip over to the *cimetiere Pere-Lachaise*, on the outskirts of Paris. The guide to this "resting place," dating from 1804, reads like a Hollywood map to the stars' homes—Piaf, Colette, Balzac, Corot, Chopin, Modigliani, Proust and Oscar Wilde are just a handful-and-a-half of those whose bones are entombed. Since the 1970s, however, American rocker Jim Morrison, has been the star attraction of those grateful for the dead. His worshippers (most of whom weren't even born during his lifetime, and *never* saw him undulate in his skintight leather pants), come to write graffiti, smoke dope, have sex, and pass out on his grave—which is known, simply, *as* 'The Grave.' Morrison aside—or asunder—the French jaunt over to Pere-Lachaise and other cemeteries with picnic baskets, sketching pads, poetry journals, and trussed-out miniature poodles, freely soaking up some of the world's most creative, volatile and stylish spirits. In France, when people are dead, they're really still alive—and when they're alive, they're *really living*.

THE HISTORY OF FRANCE

War Museum, Paris, is well worth a visit for history buffs.

With its several faces turned towards the North Sea, the Atlantic and the Mediterranean, the very different lands and peoples of Britain, North Africa and Central Europe, France has been influenced by many and very diverse cultures and trends during its history. It has been a melting pot throughout the centuries, as it continues to be today, and nevertheless there are cogent and comprehensible historical threads running through the country. Major civilizations like the Romans and the Celts before them, and major players such as Eleanor of Aquitaine and Joan of Arc, are found all over the country even before France as we know it today ever existed. It should be remembered that the present incarnation of the country only came about just over

100 years ago, when the last piece of the jigsaw puzzle that is France—Savoie—became part of the nation in 1860. The history of France begins a long, long time ago; half a million years, more or less, as the earliest Stone Age hunters in Europe migrated to the area from Africa and Central Europe.

Ancient History

Much more recently, between 30,000 and 10,000 years ago, Cro-Magnon man was present in France, hunting bison, deer, rhino, and other beasts of the field to survive. The very term "Cro-Magnon man" derives from the French town of Cro-Magnon, where a 25,000-year-old human skull was found in 1968. Relics depicting a fertility goddess (often carved in mammoth ivory) from as long as 28,000 years ago have been found in France. The cave paintings in Lascaux and other areas, especially in the southwest, date from 18,000–15,000 years ago and are the best preserved and most extensive in the world.

By about 6000 years ago the Ice Age was over and wooly mammoths had become extinct, forcing the Stone Age peoples to become hunter-gatherers, relying more on the forest, which covered much of the country, for survival. Over the next two or three thousand years the "neolithic revolution" took place, as early man settled into villages and began farming. The stone megaliths at Carnac in Brittany, Corsica, and throughout the country, are evidence of the development of this culture, with its religion, science and social order.

Over the turn of the last millennium before Christ, from about 1200 to about 800 B.C., the Celtic peoples that would dominate France for centuries began to migrate from the east. This period contains the epochs referred to as the Bronze and Iron Ages, and society developed as man learned how to make and use tools and weapons. The Celtic culture flourished throughout modern France as well as the rest of western Europe for the next several hundred years, the only outside influence being the establishment of trading posts along the Mediterranean coast, notably at Marseille, and on Corsica by the ancient Greeks, who were happy to trade fine goods such as jewelry and textiles with the less developed Celts in exchange for slaves, tin, iron and copper. By the second century B.C. the Greek culture in the eastern Mediterranean had given way to the Romans, and Gaul—as it became known—was about to change dramatically.

Gallo-Roman Times

The Celtic civilization in Gaul had become quite advanced, albeit very splintered, by the second century BC. Ornamental jewelry and costumes, sculpture and religious statuary were all well developed throughout the region and can be seen throughout France, especially in Brittany, where the isolation of the region, as well as a second wave of migration from Britain a few centuries later, worked to preserve the culture more than in the rest of the country. The Romans, who had taken over the role of the ancient Greeks along the Mediterranean by the midpoint of the second century B.C., found the country to their liking and expanded their settlements inland, initially into what is today Provence. In 121 B.C. they annexed the region. Their territorial ambitions continued to grow, and in 58 B.C. Julius Caesar led his armies into Gaul to conquer the whole country. The division of the Celts into tribes and factions facilitated his task, and he advanced relentlessly through the country, encountering weak to insignificant resistance for the most part. Vercingétorix, a chieftain in the region that is now lower Burgundy, proved Caesar's most formidable opponent, defeating him once before finally being routed in 51 B.C., the date at which Roman Gaul is considered to have been established. In 31 B.C. Caesar Augustus divided Gaul into three provinces, counting present-day Belgium among the territories Gaul encompassed.

Roman rule was a steadying factor for the next 200 years or so, as the occupiers established the *pax romana* and dwelt in peace with the native peoples, intermarrying and combining the best of both cultures. Law and order, roads, vineyards, amphitheaters, aqueducts and temples are all evidence today of this period of intense development, as the combined culture known as "Gallo-Roman" developed. The first Christians were executed in the arena at Lyon in A.D. 177, but by A.D. 250 or so missionaries were spreading the gospel and the new religion was gaining a foothold, using its time-honored tactic of incorporating, rather than eradicating, existing local cults. Emperor Constantine declared Christianity the official religion of the Roman Empire in A.D. 313, and the first major churches were built in Gaul.

Forty years earlier the first barbarian raids from the east had taken place, and by the end of the fourth century A.D. Gaul was coming under increasing attack from Germanic tribes to the east. In A.D. 406 a major invasion took place, and big chunks of northeastern Gaul were lost to the marauding Visigoths, Vandals and Franks. Some of these tribes settled in relative peace with the Gallo-Romans, and when Attila the Hun came sweeping into Gaul in A.D. 451 after plundering his way across the entire continent, it was a coalition of Romans, Visigoths and Franks under Merovius that combined to defeat him in Champagne. The Roman empire was declining back home, however, and the dwindling influence of Rome, in tandem with the growing power of the Germanic tribes, made inevitable what finally took place in A.D. 476—the end of the western Roman empire and a free-for-all in Gaul.

The Merovingian and Carolingian Era

The Franks were the last ones left standing in the anarchy that followed the fall of the Roman empire, and Merovius' grandson, Clovis, was king of a relatively unified territory by A.D. 481, making his capital in Paris. In A.D. 496 he converted to Christianity and was baptized at Reims, thereby bringing the power and influence of the church behind his throne. Clovis and his armies expanded their territory westward and southward over the next several years, taking control over the Loire Valley, Burgundy and, in 507, when he defeated the Visigoths and drove them over the Pyrénées, Aquitaine and southwestern Gaul. After Clovis' death the kingdom split into several squabbling factions, and a long period of instability and confusion followed. The resettlement of Brittany by Christian Britons fleeing the Saxon invasions of their homeland began in the sixth century. In the political vacuum left by the fractious and fractured Merovingian dynasty, the power of the church grew exponentially, as did the local control of barons and lords. Monasteries sprung up throughout France, especially in Burgundy, and powerful fiefdoms allied with equally powerful bishops to create the rigidly defined feudal society that was to underlie all succeeding political dynasties for the next 1500 years.

Periods of stability were established briefly during the sixth and seventh centuries, notably from 628 to 637, when Dagobert ruled as the last effective Merovingian king, but generally instability was the order of the day. Beginning in the seventh century the Saracens swept northwards from North Africa, until they were stopped at the Battle of Poitiers by Charles "the Hammer" Martel in A.D. 732. Martel's son, Pepin le Bref ("the short"), overthrew his uncle in 751, convened a meeting of barons and bishops at Soissons, and got himself elected king of the Franks, beginning the Carolingian dynasty. Pepin's son, Charlemagne, was to become the greatest king the country had yet seen. He unified and subjected the Frankish kingdom, catching the eye of the Catholic church in Rome, where he was crowned emperor of the west on Christmas Day in A.D. 800. Charlemagne's territory included all of modern day France as well as parts of Germany, the low countries, Denmark and the Alps. From his capital at Aix-la-Chappelle (today Aachen, Germany), Charlemagne ruled with a steady and powerful hand. After his death in A.D. 814, however, things began to fall apart once more. His son, Louis the Pious, held things together for a few years, but in A.D. 842 Charlemagne's three grandsons swore the oaths of Strasbourg that marked the breakup of the Holy Roman Empire, the beginnings of modern Europe, and the first time a written language recognized as the ancestor of French was used. The following year the Treaty of Verdun split the kingdom between Charles the Bald, who took most of Gaul, and Louis the German, who took the eastern portion that now covers the low countries and Germany. The two sides began fighting among themselves immediately; renewed raids from the south by the Saracens and invasions of the north by Vikings (Norman) further threatened the unity of the kingdom. By the beginning of the 10th century, the Vikings had established a permanent presence in Nor-

The Kings of France

Prior to Hugh Capet, the Frankish Merovingian (481–751) and Carolingian (751–987) dynasties ruled the land. The dates below note birth-accession to the throne-death. The name of the queen follows if historically significant.

Hugh Capet
(Father of the Capetian Dynasty)
940–987–996

Robert II (the Pious)
970–996–1031

Henri I
1008–1031–1060

Philip I
1052–1060–1108

Louis VI (the Fat)
1081–1108–1137

Louis VII
1120–1137–1180
m. Eleanor of Aquitaine, 1137
m. Constance of Castille, 1154
m. Adèle of Champagne, 1160

Philip II (Augustus)
1165–1180-1223

Louis VIII
1187–1223–1226

Louis IX (St. Louis)
1214–1226–1270

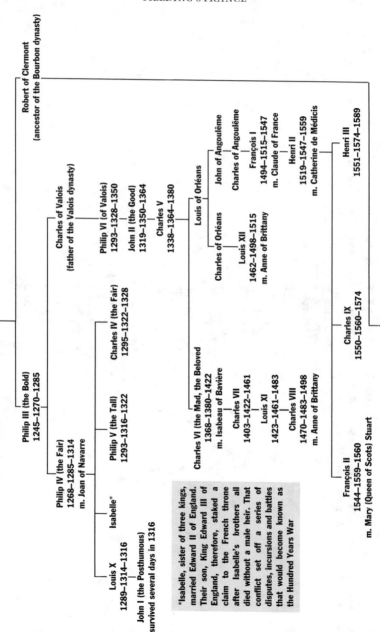

Robert of Clermont
(ancestor of the Bourbon dynasty)

Philip III (the Bold)
1245–1270–1285

Charles of Valois
(father of the Valois dynasty)

Philip IV (the Fair)
1268–1285–1314
m. Joan of Navarre

Isabelle*

Philip V (the Tall)
1293–1316–1322

Charles IV (the Fair)
1295–1322–1328

Philip VI (of Valois)
1293–1328–1350

John II (the Good)
1319–1350–1364

Charles V
1338–1364–1380

Louis of Orléans

Louis X
1289–1314–1316

John I (the Posthumous)
survived several days in 1316

Charles VI (the Mad, the Beloved
1368–1380–1422
m. Isabeau of Bavière

Charles VII
1403–1422–1461

Louis XI
1423–1461–1483

Charles VIII
1470–1483–1498
m. Anne of Brittany

Charles of Orléans

Louis XII
1462–1498–1515
m. Anne of Brittany

John of Angoulême

Charles of Angoulême

François I
1494–1515–1547
m. Claude of France

Henri II
1519–1547–1559
m. Catherine de Médicis

François II
1544–1559–1560
m. Mary (Queen of Scots) Stuart

Charles IX
1550–1560–1574

Henri III
1551–1574–1589

*Isabelle, sister of three kings, married Edward II of England. Their son, King Edward III of England, therefore, staked a claim to the French throne after Isabelle's brothers all died without a male heir. That conflict set off a series of disputes, incursions and battles that would become known as the Hundred Years War

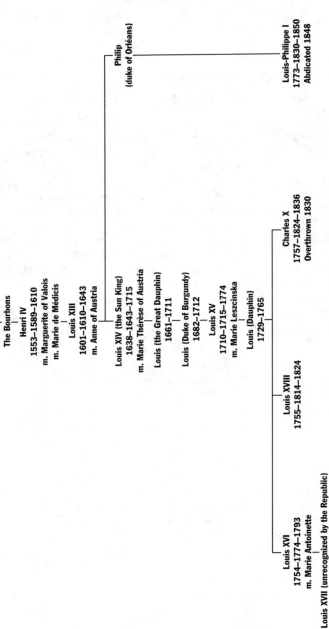

The Bourbons

Henri IV
1553–1589–1610
m. Marguerite of Valois
m. Marie de Médicis

Louis XIII
1601–1610–1643
m. Anne of Austria

Louis XIV (the Sun King)
1638–1643–1715
m. Marie Thérèse of Austria

Louis (the Great Dauphin)
1661–1711

Louis (Duke of Burgundy)
1682–1712

Louis XV
1710–1715–1774
m. Marie Leszcinska

Louis (Dauphin)
1729–1765

Philip
(duke of Orléans)

Louis XVI
1754–1774–1793
m. Marie Antoinette

Louis XVII (unrecognized by the Republic)
1785–1795

Louis XVIII
1755–1814–1824

Charles X
1757–1824–1836
Overthrown 1830

Louis-Philippe I
1773–1830–1850
Abdicated 1848

In addition, France has had two self-proclaimed emperors, Napoleon I (Bonaparte), 1769–1804–1821, abdicated in 1814, then returned for 100 days in 1815, and Napoleon III, his nephew, 1808–1852–1873, deposed 1870.

THE HISTORY OF FRANCE

mandy; in A.D. 911 a treaty between Carolingian king Charles the Simple and the Norse chieftain Rollo established the Duchy of Normandy. By the end of the 10th century the Carolingian "kingdom had been reduced to a small enclave around Paris, the rest of the country effectively in the hands of powerful independent dukes and counts.

The Middle Ages

After the century-long shakedown begun by the dividing of the empire among Charlemagne's grandsons, the long, slow process of assembling France into the single political entity it is today began with the ascendence of Hugues Capet. Capet, king of the Franks, took control in 987 and immediately set about expanding the kingdom. It was a slow process, especially at the beginning, when the Franks had little might or power, and at first Capet and his heirs had to content themselves with subjugating small counties and duchies. The duchies of Lorraine, Burgundy, Anjou, Normandy and Aquitaine, meanwhile, continued to be more powerful than the so-called crown even though they were in theory subjects of it. In 1066 William the Bastard of Normandy set off to invade England to capture the crown denied him by treachery, defeating the forces of King Harold at the Battle of Hastings and adding King of England to his title as Duke of Normandy. The relationship between England and France suffered due to William's schizophrenic role, however, and the seeds were sown for the Hundred Years' War.

Through all this the power of the church continued to grow, as local bishops and the hierarchy in Rome exploited and fostered the feudal system to keep control of the people. In 1095 at Clermont-Ferrand Pope Urban II ordered the first crusade to free the Holy Land from the Arabs who lived there, and for the next two centuries a succession of French kings as well as knights from the various duchies would take time out from their political endeavors to go east in the name of the Lord. At least one king, Louis XI, died in the effort (in Tunisia in 1270).

In 1137, the 15-year-old Eleanor of Aquitaine was married to Louis VII of France in an arrangement designed to vastly expand the French crown's holdings in and control of the west of the country. Disaster for the Capetian dynasty came 15 years later when Louis divorced Eleanor. Just two months afterward she married Henri Plantagenet, duke of Normandy and heir to the throne of England. Two years later he became king of England, controlling a kingdom reaching from north of London through Angers and the western Loire Valley down the west coast of France all the way to the border with Spain—a huge territory that vastly exceeded that of the king of France, to whom he was supposedly still a vassal. The inevitable war between France and England grew ever closer.

As always, the church continued to grow in power and wealth during this time. The rebuilding of the Abbaye St. Denis outside Paris signaled the beginning of the Gothic style of religious architecture; Notre Dame, Chartres and Bourges were not far behind as stunning opulent cathedrals reinforced the church's control over the peasant population. In the first half of the 13th century the desire of the church for absolute power and of the French crown for territorial expansion combined in the Albigensian Crusade against the Cathars, resulting in the expansion of the French kingdom into the south at Toulouse and Languedoc. Périgord and Limousin were added about the same time, and with the conquest of Anjou, Touraine and Poitou as well as Picardy and Artois by Phillipe Auguste, France now covered over half the territory it does today. This was not, however, to last.

The start of the Hundred Years' War, in 1337, was due to centuries-old political and territorial conflicts and tensions that surely could have had no other result. What finally set it off was the end of the Capetian line in 1328, marked by the death of Charles IV. His cousin, Phillipe of Valois, became king Phillipe VI, but Edward III of England, nephew of Charles IV, argued that he was the rightful heir. The war itself was a series of battles, alliances and other, nonmilitary influences that lasted three or four generations and reduced France to almost nothing. The English were formidable opponents, of course, defeating two successive French kings, Phillip VI and Jean le Bon, at Crécy and Poitiers, and taking the latter prisoner. Internal dissension added to the difficulties faced by the House of Valois, as the French crown was now known, as both Burgundy and Armagnac allied themselves with the English against France, even though the two duchies were also occupied with fighting each other. The Catholic church had undergone the most serious schism in its history in 1309, and rival popes were claiming divine authority in Rome and Avignon; the Black Death bubonic plague, lasting from 1347 to 1351, killed off a third of the population. The French were defeated yet again by the English under king Henry V at Agincourt in 1415. Starvation and peasant revolts further destabilized the situation, and to top it all off, the king from 1380 to 1422, Charles VI, went completely mad. By 1419 the English, with their Burgundian allies, controlled the entire northern third of France as well as the vast western swath of Aquitaine. Charles VI gave his daughter to Henry V of England in marriage, meaning the English would inherit the throne upon his death, and his son, the future Charles VII, went into hiding in the Loire Valley. Both Henry V and Charles VI died in 1422, however, and the war revved up again. By 1428 the English were advancing from the south and west as well as the north, where they had laid siege to Orléans, and the tiny remaining French territory was on the brink of succumbing.

The intervention of Joan of Arc in 1429 turned the tide, as she first convinced the dithering Charles VII that he was in fact destined to lead France back to its former glory, then rode at the head of the army that defeated the English at Orléans. At Joan's urging Charles traveled to Reims to be crowned, receiving safe passage from the Burgundians, who perhaps sensed that change was in the air. They reserved no such respect for Joan, however, whom they captured as she led a battle at Compiégne, north of Paris, later that year. Sold to the English, she was burned at the stake in 1431. Nevertheless Joan had set in motion the eventual rout of the English, and in 1436 Paris was retaken, and in 1453 the Battle of Castillone-la Bataille, won by the French, put an end to the Hundred Years' War, leaving only Calais in the hands of the English.

End of the Middle Ages, the French Renaissance

Once the Hundred Years' War with England was behind it, France entered a new era of peace and prosperity—and expansion. In 1477 Louis XI took over the duchy of Burgundy; in 1481 Anjou was reannexed into the French fold. In 1491 Charles VIII wed Anne of Brittany, bringing unification between France and the western peninsula closer to reality. Although many there would have it that Brittany remains a separate region to this day, it was finally annexed in 1532. Charles VIII and Louis XII embarked on military adventures in Italy, and in the early 16th century François I followed suit, concentrating his avarice on the independent kingdom of Naples. None of these brought any particular military success nor territorial expansion to France, but they did bring back—especially in the case of the last mentioned—the fresh winds that were beginning to blow through Europe at the time. Although the accepted word for the cultural and artistic revolution of the 15th and 16th centuries is "*Renaissance*," a French word, the movement had begun in Italy almost a century earlier. François I, especially, patronized the Italian artists and musicians he had encountered in Italy, bringing many of them to France. The most famous of these was of course Leonardo da Vinci, who spent the last three years of his life under François' tutelage at Amboise. Architecture was the most outwardly visible recipient of the Renaissance, as straight staircases replaced spirals, delicate carving in stone facades replaced the cumbersome statuary of yore, and the emerging bourgeoisie built themselves *hôtels particuliers* in cities throughout the country.

Under François I the building of the greatest château of all began at Chambord, and soon other royal palaces, as well as mansions and castles of the aristocracy, were being transformed from defensive strongholds into the pleasure palaces that are most well known in and around the Loire Valley. Accompanying the revolution in architecture and art, which saw a return to the use of perspective and the symbols of Greek mythology, was the Reformation, a revolution in thinking epitomized by Calvin, Rabelais and other writers and philosophers. The new ideas espoused by these men laid the foundation for the Révolution to come, as well as promoting the spread of Protestantism. The introduction of the printing press at the end of the 15th century facilitated the quick spread of these revolutionary ideas. Meanwhile, French explorer/genocidal conquerors joined the Spanish and Portuguese in settling in the "New World." In 1534 the explorer Jacques Cartier took possession of what is now Canada in the name of the French crown.

Another major Italian player in the development of Renaissance France, however, had very different ideas as to what was and was not permissible social change. Cathérine de Medici, widow of Henri II and mother of three other kings, was the virtual ruler of France for half a century, skillfully welding together religion and politics to stamp out the nascent popular liberation. The Wars of Religion, as the period between 1562 and 1598 is called, was really a return to internal division and bloody strife that pitted Catholic royalists against Protestant populists, with wealthy and powerful nobles on both sides. The Valois dynasty came to an end when Henri III was assassinated by a monk in 1589, himself having ordered the assassination of the Duc de Guise, a leading Catholic, in Blois some years earlier. The next to take the throne was Henri of Navarra, who, like his cousin Henri III, was a Protestant, but who escaped the bloody St. Bartholomew's Day Massacre a few days after marrying Marguerite of Valois in 1572 by temporarily renouncing the Reformation. He continued to waver throughout his reign while trying to bring about peace and tolerance, caught between the conflicting desires to stay alive and yet protect his Protestant countrymen in Navarra. He eventually converted again to Catholicism in 1593, but in 1598 issued the Edict of Nantes, stipulating religious tolerance as the law of the land. He was assassinated a few years later.

Le Grand Siècle

Under Louis XIII (whose reign was managed first by his mother, Marie de Medici, then by the enormously powerful cardinal Richelieu) the gains made by the Protestants were largely wiped out. Although the Edict of Nantes was not officially rescinded until the reign of Louis XIV, Richelieu, in the name of unifying the country under one monarch and one church, set about persecuting and rendering powerless both the Huguenot enclaves at La Rochelle and elsewhere, as well as the rebellious aristocracy that had risen up early in Louis XIII's reign. There were expansions of Paris and some of the major provincial cities, continued exploration and exploitation of North America, infrastructure development (canals, roads, etc.), and the always necessary military adventures as a side player in the Thirty Years' War. Descartes uttered his immortal "Cogito, ergo sum," the Academie Française was founded, and by the time Louis XIII and Richelieu died a year apart in 1642–1643 the stage was set for the most powerful monarch Europe had seen since the Caesars.

Louis XIV ascended to the throne at age five and reigned for 72 years, including 51 as an adult with absolute power. In his early years his prime minister, Mazarin, concluded several diplomatic coups to further strengthen France's position in Europe, ousting the Spanish from their position of influence in the Netherlands and purchasing the port of Dunkirk. Following a brief war across the Pyrénées, Louis made peace with the Spanish by marrying Marie-Thérèse. At this time France was the most powerful nation in Europe, if not the world, with a population of 20 million compared with 8 million in England and 6 million in Spain. Louis' finance minister, Colbert, expanded trade with the colonies in Canada and Africa and stabilized France's economy. The foreign empire expanded into the United States, with La Salle taking possession of Louisiana and naming it after the king. Partly to keep all his nobles in one place where he could keep an eye on them, and partly to satisfy his enormous egoism (he believed he was king by divine right and encouraged a cult of near deity, referring to himself as the Sun King), Louis built Versailles, the greatest palace in the world and the culmination of the opulent period France was enjoying. The construction of the palace, and costly wars against the Austro-Prussians, and again with the Spanish, famine and continued religious conflict sparked by Louis' revocation of the Edict of Nantes, however, left the kingdom broke and ripe for revolution by the time he died in 1715. Having outlived both his son and grandson, Louis passed the crown to his great-grandson, who became Louis XIV. His reign was marked by ineffectiveness; after an unnecessary seven-year war with the English, France lost the colonies in North America. As the economy continued to decline, the social inequities that characterized the supposedly extinct feudalism—the aristocracy and the powerful clergy were exempt from taxes, for example—continued to bring the country to its knees and the peasants to their feet.

The Revolution

When Louis XVI became king in 1774 there was probably nothing anyone could have done to avert the revolution that broke out a few years later. The economy was in tatters, famines were becoming annual events due to an inefficient agricultural sector, and news of the American Revolution (which France had supported) was filtering back from the New World. Enlightenment thinkers and writers such as Voltaire and Rousseau were calling for a new social contract. Another great finance minister, Necker, made the first steps towards the necessary drastic reform, but was fired as soon as he began advocating for reform of the aristocracy's privileges. A conference called the meeting of the Estates General was called for 1792 then pushed up to May

1789. Another famine in the winter of 1788 and the bread riots that followed drove tensions to the breaking point.

The Estates General meeting declared itself the National Constituent Assembly and called for an end to absolute monarchy. On July 14 a mob in Paris stormed the Bastille prison and the revolution was off and running. Privileges were abolished and the Universal Rights of Man proclaimed. Trying to keep some semblance of order, the Assembly tried to set up a constitutional monarchy, but Louis resisted the idea, then attempted to flee the country. He was arrested, and he and Marie Antoinette became the most famous of the guillotine's victims in 1793. The Prussians tried to take advantage of the disorder by invading from the east, but a number of generals, including one Napoléon Bonaparte, drove them back. In 1792 the Convention was signed, providing the revolutionary leadership for the next two years; the following year, which saw the beheading of the king, the Vendée rebellion, organized by royalists but supported by a populace tired of the excesses, was brutally crushed by Paris. The revolution began to take on a life of its own, as Robespierre and the Terror ruled the country, beheading anyone who was not revolutionary enough, as well as counterrevolutionaries. Robespierre himself was guillotined in 1794. The property of the church was confiscated and nationalized, the metric system and a new calendar with months named after the seasons was introduced, and the new Republic was ruled by a government called the Directory. Notoriously corrupt, the Directory itself was overthrown by Napoléon in 1799.

The Empire to the Third Republic

Napoléon declared himself First Consul in 1799, but by 1804 he had crowned himself Emperor in Notre Dame cathedral in Paris. Napoléon led the French to a series of glorious military victories in continental Europe, but was never able to assert French superiority over the British at sea. He also sold the Louisiana territory (recently reacquired from Spain) to the United States. In 1812 he marched on Russia, but was forced to retreat, and the following year he was routed by the Germans in alliance with all the armies of Europe. In 1814 he abdicated and went into exile on the island of Elba. Louis XVIII returned from exile in England to take the throne, but the people were unready to return to a monarchy, and a year later Napoléon returned to power and Louis fled once again. The emperor ruled for "a hundred days" but his ignominious defeat at Waterloo at the hands of the English and the Prussians forced him into exile again, this time permanently, on St. Helena. For all Napoléon's military prowess and bloody campaigns, France's territory at the end of his reign was the same as when he rose to power. Nevertheless he had several lasting influences on the country, besides the Louvre museum and the Arc de Triomphe in Paris: the Napoleonic Code is still the basis for law in France, and he reformed the banking and civil systems to a point they had never reached before.

Louis XVIII came back to the throne in a period known as the Restoration, during which some of the privileges of the aristocracy were reinvigorated, and the upper classes (who had largely escaped the Revolution precisely thanks to their wealth) grew fatter at the expense of the working classes, whom the Industrial Revolution did not benefit at all. Louis' successor, Charles X, tried to balance the interests of the restive masses with the powerful aristocracy, but the tightrope just wasn't there and in July 1830 a second revolution called "Three Glorious Days" drove him out of office and the country. Louis-Phillipe became king and held on until 1846. At that time the Napoleonic clan resurfaced, with the election of Louis-Napoléon to the presidency of the Second Republic. But in 1851 he dissolved the National Assembly and declared himself president for 10 years; the following year a thoroughly bogus referendum approved the Second Empire and Louis-Napoléon became Emperor Napoléon III. During this time France was modernizing fast: railways were criss-crossing the country, steel production was among the most important in the world, Indo-Chinese and Algerian colonies were being established and expanded, Paris was being rebuilt, and in 1855 the capital hosted its first World's Fair. In 1860 the final pieces of France's geographical puzzle fell into place as Savoie and Nice voted to join the nation. Napoléon dreamed of establishing a Catholic French empire in México to counterbalance the Protestant United States, but his dream was turned to ashes by fierce Mexican resistance and the intervention of the Americans. Meanwhile, the Prussians and Austrians were rising in power and war broke out in 1870. Napoléon was defeated and taken prisoner along with 100,000 men, and the Second Empire came to an end. The Prussians, however, were at the door of Paris.

The Third Republic to the Present

After the defeat of Napoléon another small revolt in Paris led to the creation of the Third Republic, with an elected president. The first order of business was to deal with the Prussians, poised outside the capital to completely take over the country. In 1871 the Treaty of Frankfurt brought a kind of peace as France gave up Alsace and Lorraine to the Prussians. Peace and modernization gripped the country for the next few decades, as social improvements at home (establishment of free compulsory secular education, legalization of trade unions, separation of church and state) contrasted with continued expansion of France's overseas colonies in Indochina, Africa and the Middle East. The Dreyfus Affair, a case of a Jewish captain falsely accused of espionage, brought antimilitarists and anticlerics into conflict with right-wingers, a foreshadow of the 30 percent of the vote the National Front now wins regularly in French elections.

In 1914 the First World War began, with the bloodiest fighting taking place on French soil, at Marne in the early days of the war, and at Verdun in its cataclysmic final months. The Treaty of Versailles of 1918 brought the conflict to an end, after 5 million French lives had been sacrificed, and Alsace and Lorraine were returned to France. History took unusual turns as Maréchal Phillipe Pétain led the French forces at Verdun, only to collaborate with Hitler 20 years later. The seeds were sown for a repeat of the conflict almost immediately, as the postwar government occupied the industrial heartland of Germany and exacted crushing reparations, only increasing the Germans' determination to rise up again in revenge. At the same time, France built the fortified border on its eastern flank known as the Maginot Line.

Cultural revolution was in the air between the wars, as the desperate economic times caused by the first war and the worldwide depression led to great unrest and the rise of socialism and communism. Avant garde writers, artists and musicians from home and abroad found a spiritual and physical home in Paris and the rest of France. The jazz age, Art Deco, Coco Chanel and another International Exhibition (in 1925) marked the era. In 1936 the Popular Front government of Léon Blum introduced radical social reforms, including paid vacations and early retirement.

In 1939 Hitler began invading countries to the east of Germany; in 1940 he marched swiftly around the Maginot Line through Belgium and invaded France. Resistance was weak and in six weeks the battle was over. Pétain agreed to the terms of an armistice dictated by Hitler whereby the north of the country was occupied by Germany and the south remained independent, with a collaborationist government based in Vichy. The Vichy government, perhaps believing it had no other option, grew more and more like the Nazis, eventually handing over Jews and resisters for deportation and extermination. General Charles de Gaulle led the Free French from England in coordinating the resistance and fighting alongside the allies in North Africa. In June 1944 the allied forces landed in Normandy and by August, De Gaulle was at the head of a new government—the Fourth Republic—in Paris and the Germans were defeated.

De Gaulle, having learned from the previous generation's mistakes, sought at once to bind France's and Germany's futures together so that conflict could never again erupt between them. In 1949 France joined NATO and formed the Council of Europe with Germany as the major partner. Over the next several years France gave up its colonies, usually not without a fight (80,000 French soldiers died in the war for independence in Madagascar), withdrawing from Vietnam in 1954 and Tunisia and Morocco a few years later. It refused to give up Algeria, and the bloody civil war that brought down the Fourth Republic began in 1954. In 1957 the Treaty of Rome es-

tablishing the European Community was signed. In 1958 the crisis in Algeria had grown so bad that De Gaulle resigned, but he was returned to power
soon after, setting up the Fifth Republic and calling for a strong, independent France. His proposed new constitution was adopted in a popular referendum in 1958. In 1962 Algeria won independence, and the following year
France exploded its first nuclear bomb. In 1967 it left NATO, only rejoining
in the Bosnia campaign of 1995. In 1968 major labor and student demonstrations spelled the beginning of the end for the autocratic De Gaulle, and
the following year he was forced to step down. In 1981 François Mitterand
was elected the first socialist president in France since the Second World
War, and in 1994, just before the end of his second seven-year term, the
Channel Tunnel connecting France and England, surely a symbol of the end
of a long era of French history, was opened by Mitterand and Queen Elizabeth II. In 1995 a conservative president, Jacques Chirac, was elected to join
the conservative legislative majority that took power a year earlier. The new
government attempted to implement a social reform plan akin to the Republican Revolution in the United States and the reconcentration of wealth
being attempted by right-wing governments throughout the world, but
found that the powerful French unions and students would not easily be
stripped of their rights. At press time a series of strikes and protests was calling into question the future of not only Chirac's reforms, but of his very government.

PARIS

This has been the site of Paris' city hall since the 14th century.

What Makes Paris So French?

1. *The millions of skeletons living beneath the city streets in the Catacombs—see some 30 generations worth of skulls and other bones neatly stacked for your viewing pleasure (sure to make your treasured shrunken head back home pale in comparison).*

2. *Two partial women on view at the Louvre—Mona Lisa minus body, Venus de Milo minus arms (but at least they're not French).*

3. *From some hotel rooms in the city, the Eiffel Tower is but a mass-produced image superimposed upon the windows. Want a room with Eiffel Tower view? Hey, no problem!*

121

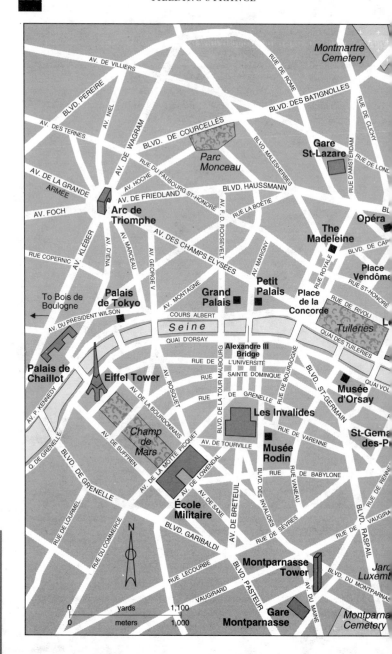

AV. DE VILLIERS

BLVD. PEREIRE

BLVD. DES BATIGNOLLES

RUE DE ROME

Montmartre
Cemetery

AV. DES TERNES

AV. NIEL

BLVD. DE COURCELLES

RUE DE CLICHY

RUE DE LOND

RUE D'AMSTERDAM

Gare
St-Lazare

Parc
Monceau

BLVD. MALESHERBES

AV. DE WAGRAM

RUE DU FAUBOURG ST-HONORE

AV. DE LA GRANDE
ARMEE

AV. HOCHE

AV. DE FRIEDLAND

BLVD. HAUSSMANN

RUE LA BOETIE

Opéra

BL

AV. FOCH

Arc de
Triomphe

AV. DE CHAMPS ELYSÉES

RUE COPERNIC

AV. KLÉBER

AV. D'IENA

AV. MARCEAU

AV. GEORGE V

RUE F. D. ROOSEVELT

AV. MARIGNY

RUE ROYALE

The
Madeleine

BLVD. DE CAP

Place
Vendôme

RUE DE ST-HONORE

To Bois de
Boulogne

Palais
de Tokyo

AV. MONTAGNE

Grand
Palais

Petit
Palais

Place
de la
Concorde

RUE DE RIVOLI

Tuileries

Le

AV. DU PRESIDENT WILSON

COURS ALBERT

Seine

QUAI DES TUILERIES

QUAI D'ORSAY

AV. P. KENNEDY

Palais de
Chaillot

Eiffel Tower

AV. DE LA BOURDONNAIS

AV. DE SUFFREN

Alexandre III
Bridge

RUE DE L'UNIVERSITÉ

SAINTE DOMINIQUE

DE GRENELLE

BLVD. DE LA TOUR MAUBOURG

RUE DE BOURGOGNE

BLVD. ST-GERMAIN

Musée
d'Orsay

QUAI VOL

Champ
de
Mars

AV. DE TOURVILLE

Les Invalides

RUE DE VARENNE

St-Gema
des-P

Q. DE GRENELLE

BLVD. DE GRENELLE

AV. DE LOWENDAL

AV. DE LA MOTTE PICQUET

École
Militaire

AV. DE SAXE

Musée
Rodin

RUE DE BABYLONE

BLVD. DES INVALIDES

RUE VANEAU

RUE DE RENN

BLVD. VAUGIRA

RUE DE LOURMEL

RUE DU COMMERCE

N

BLVD. GARIBALDI

AV. DE BRETEUIL

RUE DE SEVRES

BLVD. DE

RASPAIL

RUE LECOURBE

Montparnasse
Tower

Jard
Luxemb

VAUGIRARD

BLVD. PASTEUR

AV. DU MAINE

BLVD. DU MONTPARNAS

0 ____ yards ____ 1,100
0 ____ meters ____ 1,000

Gare
Montparnasse

Montparna
Cemetery

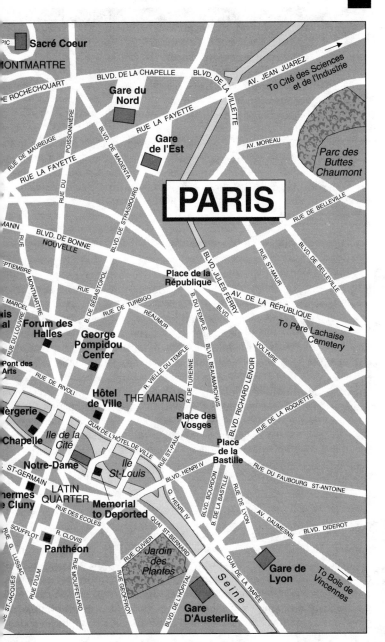

What Makes Paris So French?

4. *The Japanese ambassador now lives in the same circa-1718 home formerly occupied by Napoleon's family, as well as the king of Bavaria. Strangeness in the concept of hand-me-downs.*

5. *Cezanne's coat still hangs on the door peg of his old studio.*

6. *That* Champs-Elysées *notion that eventually you'll see someone you know if you hang out on the street long enough.*

7. *Marie Antoinette's head rolling over at* place de la Concorde.

8. *Scads of beret-clad "artists" painting pretty pictures over by the Seine—still able to wow tourists out of their hard-exchanged* francs.

9. *The Eiffel Tower erector set, the Louvre pyramid addition, and the inside-out Tinker-toy-ish Centre Georges Pompidou.*

10. Le Tango, *the authentic oldies-but-goodies club that will make you swoon over the memory of Maria Schneider (now dead) and Marlon Brando (now fat) in Bertolucci's erotic* Last Tango in Paris.

Paris, the capital of France, is one of *the* world's greatest cities. But its dominance of the country can only be understood by putting it into context. A good clue is the fact that France is officially known as *"Paris et les provinces"*—Paris and the provinces. Paris and the rest of the country. While this is in part a reflection of the elevated status the city and its residents consider themselves to have, it is also true that fully one-fifth of the entire population of France lives in the city and its suburbs. At one time the most important city in the art world by any measure, Paris still has the greatest museums; it is one of the most beautiful cities in the world architecturally; the top fashion designers in the world still make Paris their home—the reputation for chic and elegance the city enjoys is fully deserved. Everyone who comes to Paris has a dream, an image of what they think it will be like, derived from movies, books, friends who have traveled here, even stylized perfume ads. Everyone finds their dream to be true. The City of Lights, the City of Love is everything you imagined, and more. Overcrowded, overpriced, overvisited, yes. But also the most magical city in France, and, for many people, in the world.

History

Distances in France are measured from Point Zero, a plaque in the ground in front of Notre Dame cathedral. This is a singularly appropriate marker, since the Ile de la Cité is not only the geographical but the historical heart of the city. The island was settled about 200 years before Christ by a Gallic tribe of fishermen called the Parisii (from the Celtic for boat, *par*). The Roman general Labienus conquered the settlement in 52 B.C., burning it to the ground and founding a new encampment called Lutetia in its place. Soon extended to the south, where the remains of an amphitheater and baths still stand, Lutetia was a major strategic fort for the Romans in the early days of the campaign to establish *pax romana*. The first bishop, St. Denis, was martyred in the third century, and, perhaps in divine wrath, the Barbarians from the east destroyed the settlement. This incited the population to retire back to the safety of Ile de la Cité, where the Romans had set up their most important buildings, the forum and the temple. Today, Notre Dame and the police headquarters fulfill the same functions. About this time, as the Romans declined, the city was renamed Paris.

In 473 a basilica was erected over the tomb of St. Denis; this would become the first Gothic cathedral in France several centuries later. Clovis, king of the Franks, settled for a while in Paris beginning in 508. He built ramparts and his status as king caused other major buildings, including monasteries, to be built out from the city on the south and north banks of the Seine. By the time the Vikings sailed up the river and laid siege to Paris in 845, the city was strong enough to defend itself. Five successive Norse invasions were fended off, and the leader of the defenders in the final onslaught of 885, Eudes, was elected king of the Frankish realm, a small territory with Paris at its heart. Beginning with Hugues Capet, the Capetian dynasty ruled the growing kingdom of France as well as the city of Paris. Outlying swamps were drained and developed and the city grew rapidly, boosted by its position as a major trading port on the Seine. The abbey at St. Germain-des-Près was rebuilt in Romanesque style at the turn of the millennium; other construction quickly followed suit, including the Gothic renovation of St. Denis in 1136, and the initial work on Notre Dame beginning in 1163. Phillipe Auguste fortified the ever-expanding city from 1160 to 1210, with a ring of ramparts and the central defenses at the Louvre fortress (the foundations from this period can be seen inside the Louvre museum). The magnificent Sainte Chapelle was built at the far end of Ile de la Cité from Notre Dame by King Louis IX in 1246, originally to house the relics of the crucifixion he had purchased. Paris' position as an educational center was also beginning to become clear; the University of Paris, France's first, was founded in 1215, followed by the Sorbonne college a few years later. The schools as well as most of the important religious buildings not found on the island were located on the Rive Gauche, or Left Bank. The river merchants emerged as a powerful and wealthy class, binding together as the Watermen's Guild in 1210. This body exercised levying power on the port—which really meant the entire city—and evolved into a kind of city council. In 1355 the provost of the guild built a new headquarters just beside the main port on the right bank— the site is still the location of the Hôtel de Ville, Paris' magnificent City Hall.

In the early days of the Hundred Years' War, Paris remained the seat of the French monarch, albeit after Charles V put down a rebellion by the same

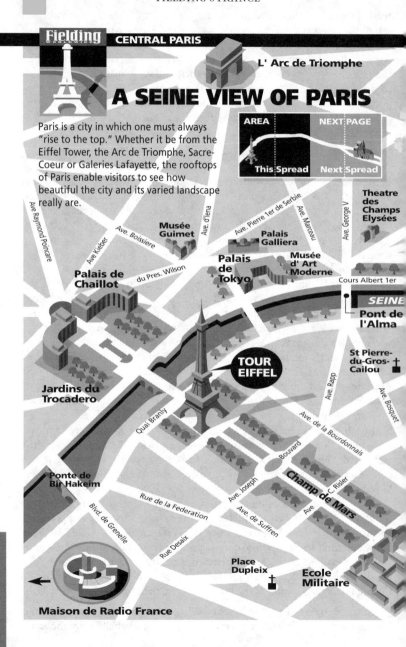

Fielding WORLDWIDE **CENTRAL PARIS**

L' Arc de Triomphe

A SEINE VIEW OF PARIS

Paris is a city in which one must always "rise to the top." Whether it be from the Eiffel Tower, the Arc de Triomphe, Sacre-Coeur or Galeries Lafayette, the rooftops of Paris enable visitors to see how beautiful the city and its varied landscape really are.

AREA   NEXT PAGE

This Spread   Next Spread

Theatre des Champs Elysées

Ave. Raymond Poincare

Ave. Boissiere

Ave. Kleber

Musée Guimet

Ave. d'Iena

Ave. Pierre 1er de Serbie

Ave. Marceau

Ave. George V

Palais Galliera

Palais de Chaillot

du Pres. Wilson

Palais de Tokyo

Musée d' Art Moderne

Cours Albert 1er

SEINE

Pont de l'Alma

TOUR EIFFEL

St Pierre-du-Gros-Cailou †

Jardins du Trocadero

Quai Branly

Ave. Rapp

Ave. Bosquet

Ave. de la Bourdonnais

Bouvard

C. Rider

Ponte de Bir Hakeim

Rue de la Federation

Ave. Joseph

Champ de Mars

Blvd de Grenelle

Ave. de Suffren

Ave.

Rue Desaix

Place Dupleix †

Ecole Militaire

Maison de Radio France

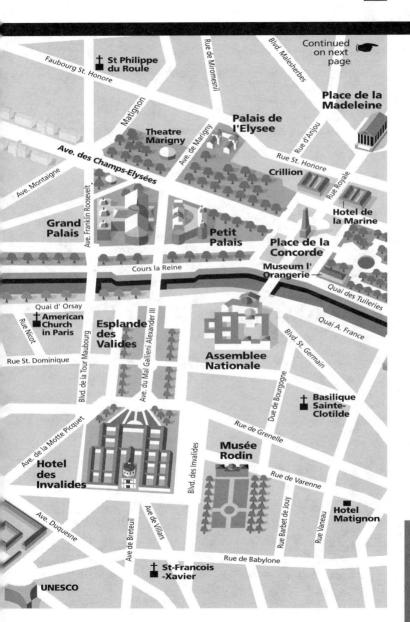

Continued on next page

Faubourg St. Honore

† **St Philippe du Roule**

Rue de Miromesnil

Blvd. Malesherbes

Place de la Madeleine

Matignon

Theatre Marigny

Ave. de Marigny

Palais de l'Elysee

Rue d'Anjou

Rue St. Honore

Ave. des Champs-Elysées

Crillion

Rue Royale

Ave. Montaigne

Ave. Franklin Roosevelt

Grand Palais

Petit Palais

Hotel de la Marine

Place de la Concorde

Museum l' Orangerie

Cours la Reine

Quai des Tuileries

Quai d' Orsay

Rue Nicot

† **American Church in Paris**

Esplande des Valides

Ave. du Mal Gallieni Alexander III

Quai A. France

Rue St. Dominique

Blvd. de la Tour Maubourg

Assemblee Nationale

Blvd. St. Germain

Due de Bourgogne

† **Basilique Sainte-Clotilde**

Ave. de la Motte Picquet

Rue de Grenelle

Musée Rodin

Blvd. des Invalides

Hotel des Invalides

Rue de Varenne

Ave. Duquesne

Ave. de Villars

Ave. de Breteuil

Rue Barbet de Jouy

Rue Vaneau

Hotel Matignon

Rue de Babylone

† **St-Francois -Xavier**

UNESCO

CENTRAL PARIS (continued)

Place de la Madeleine
Rue Tronchet
L'Opera Garnier
Blvd. des Italiens
Blvd. des Capucines
Rue de Quatre Septembre
Ave. de l'Opera
Rue Royale
Rue St. Honore
Hotel de la Marine
Place Vendome
Rue Castiglione
Bibliotheque Nationale
Rue des pts Champs
Rue de Rivoli
Jardin des Tuileries
Rue de Richelieu
MUSEE DU LOUVRE
Palais Royal
Quai des Tuileries
Ave du Gal Lemonnier
Quai A. France
SEINE
Quai du Louvre
Rue du Louvre
Rue de Bellechasse
Musée d' Orsay
Quai Malaquais
Ecole des Beaux-Arts
Bld St. Germain
Rue du Bac
Rue des Saints Peres
Rue Bonaparte
Institute de France
Rue de Seine
Rue Mazarine
Rue Dauphine
Rue de Grenelle
Saint Germain des Pres
Rue de Varenne
Blvd. Raspail
le Bon Marche
Rue de Rennes
Rue de Four
Saint Sulpice
Rue de Babylone
Rue de Serves
Rue Bonaparte
Palais du Luxembourg
Rue de Vaugirard
To Montparnasse

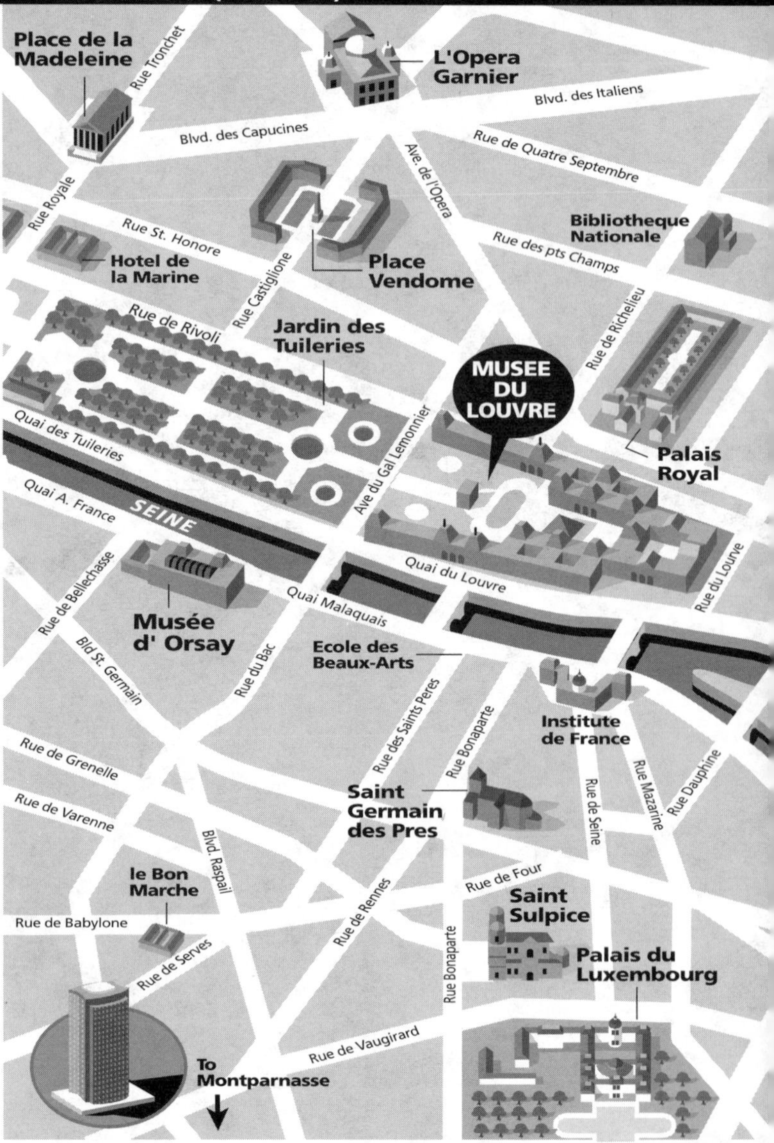

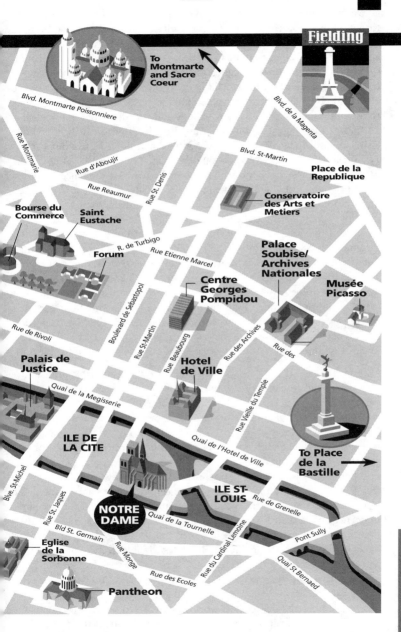

Fielding

To Montmarte and Sacre Coeur

Blvd. Montmarte Poissonniere

Blvd. de la Magenta

Rue Montmarie

Rue d'Aboujir

Rue St. Denis

Blvd. St-Martin

Place de la Republique

Rue Reaumur

Conservatoire des Arts et Metiers

Bourse du Commerce

Saint Eustache

R. de Turbigo

Rue Etienne Marcel

Forum

Palace Soubise/ Archives Nationales

Centre Georges Pompidou

Musée Picasso

Rue de Rivoli

Boulevard de Sebastopol

Rue St-Martin

Rue Beaubourg

Rue des Archives

Rue des

Palais de Justice

Hotel de Ville

Quai de la Megisserie

Rue Vieille du Temple

ILE DE LA CITE

Quai de l'Hotel de Ville

To Place de la Bastille

Blve St-Michel

Rue St. Jaques

NOTRE DAME

ILE ST-LOUIS

Rue de Grenelle

Quai de la Tournelle

Rue du Cardinal Lemone

Pont Sully

Bld St. Germain

Eglise de la Sorbonne

Rue Monge

Rue des Ecoles

Quai St Bernaed

Pantheon

above-mentioned provost. He moved off the Ile de la Cité into the Louvre,
turning it into a palace/fortress from the bleak military keep it had been. In
1370 he built himself another castle, the Bastille within new ramparts he
added to fortify the northern part of the growing city. By 1418 the confusion of the war had forced Charles VI to flee and go insane and the English
took over the city. Charles VII dithered in the Loire Valley until prodded
into action by Joan of Arc, who was injured while leading a force attempting
to recapture the capital in 1429. Charles eventually drove out the English in
1437, but the kings of France continued to dwell primarily in their Loire
châteaux until François I tired of Chambord and moved the court back to
Paris in 1546, ordering construction of the new Louvre palace. Architecture
dating from this period shows the incipient Renaissance influences, brought
to France by François and his two immediate predecessors. The Wars of Religion played out in Paris as much as anywhere at the end of the 16th century, with thousands of Huguenots massacred in the St. Bartholomew's Day
bloodbath in 1572. Henri III was forced out of the city by the Catholic
League in 1588, and although he engineered the murder of the League's
Duc de Guise at Amboise, he was soon killed also by a zealous Catholic
monk. His successor, Henri of Navarre, became Henri IV, who somehow
managed to tiptoe between Catholicism and Protestantism and not only stay
alive but return to Paris and the throne, in 1594. During his reign, the Arsenal and place des Vosges were constructed, along with the Pont Neuf (still
called "new bridge," it is now the oldest in the city), and by the time he, in
turn, was assassinated, the classical style was sweeping into the city.

   Under Louis XIII the Ile de St. Louis became the fashionable place to live
it is today, while the outskirts of the city continued to expand and new ramparts were added again. In 1642 the final piece in the great Cour Carré of
the Louvre, the Pavillon de l'Horloge, was completed; the following year the
Hospital for Incurable Diseases was built. After Louis' death the people re-
belled in an incident known as the Frondé; Anne of Austria took her son, the
young Louis XIV, out of the city until things calmed down. The long reign
of the Sun King was to have lasting effects on Paris, however, in spite of the
fact that he dedicated much of his time and most of the nation's money to
Versailles—some would say to avoid the dangers of another popular uprising. He had Le Vau finish the facade of the Louvre and the Institut de
France across the river, Le Notre designed and constructed the Tuileries gardens, Bruant built the magnificent Hôtel des Invalides for wounded soldiers,
and the place Vendôme and place des Victoires were also designed. Louis
XIV also gave huge patronage and support to the arts, and during his reign
the Royal Academy of Music was founded and theater flourished, with venues great and small built to show works by Racine, Molière and others. Louis' genius finance minister, Colbert, set up the manufacturing center at

Gobelins, and at the end of the Grand Siècle, Paris had blossomed. Louis XV, like his great-grandfather, was five years old when he took the throne, and it was largely the work of his ministers that saw the Esplanade des Invalides and the place de la Concorde built.

Louis XVI's reign was characterized by the opulence and excess that led to the revolution—and cost him his head. In Paris, great artisans flourished making furniture, tapestries, and artwork for the royal court and the rest of the aristocracy. It took less than an hour for the people of Paris to storm the Bastille on July 14, 1789; they did not find a large arms cache, as they had hoped, but they did set off the Révolution, which was to see its most dramatic scenes played out in the city. (See "History of France" for more information on the events of the revolution). Louis was beheaded in the place de la Concorde in January 1793, his profligate wife Marie Antoinette in October of that year. Thousands of heads rolled during the Terror, until finally Robespierre himself was guillotined and things began to calm down. Napoléon took over the country and substituted his imperial rule for the chaos of the Revolution in 1798. In between foreign military adventures he put his imprimatur on many of the monuments and great buildings of the city (look for the "N" and the strange insignia of the empty Roman armor). He also ordered a whole new swath of monumental construction in Paris, very much in the imperial style, with great showpieces including the Arc de Triomphe, Arc de Triomphe du Carousel, the round Bourse (stock exchange) at one end of the Halles, the National Assembly and the column in the place de Vendôme.

In the 19th century a new spirit of planned development gripped the city. New fortifications were added yet again, although the city proper had expanded to the Bois de Boulogne on the west and the Bois de Vicennes on the east and would grow no more (though the suburbs certainly would!). Baron Haussman, working on Napoléon III's orders, tore down large tracts of the city to make way for the elegant, wide boulevards and circles that so characterize Paris today. The Opéra Garnier was built, several ornate railway stations ringed the city, and a huge new wing was added to the Louvre; during the Second Empire two World's Fairs (in 1855 and 1867) showed off the city's progress. Napoléon was defeated by the Prussians in 1870 and the city was besieged; in the ensuing confusion and civil unrest several major buildings, including the city hall and the Tuileries, were destroyed. Once order was restored, Paris set about another building boom, this time in the age of iron, marked most awesomely by the Eiffel Tower (built for another World's Fair in 1889), and also by several Art Nouveau apartment houses around the city. The oddly out-of-place basilica Sacré Coeur atop Montmartre hill, which was beginning to be the Mecca for artists—including Van Gogh, Picasso and other greats—was begun in the late 1880s. The World's

PARIS METRO/RER

RER - A

RER - C

13 Gabriel Péri

St-Denis Basili **13**

St-Ouen
St-Denis Porte de Paris
Carrefour Pleyel
Mairie de St-Ouen
Garibaldi
Porte de St-Ouen

Mairie de Clichy
Porte de Clichy

Guy Môquet Abbes
Brochant
La Fourche Pigal

Pont de Levallois-Bécon
3 A. France
Louise Michel
Porte de Champerret
Péreire
Wagram
Malesherbes
Rome
Blanche
Pl. de Clichy St-Georges

1 Grande Arche de La Défense
Pont de Neuilly
Esplanade de La Défense
Les Sablons
Porte Maillot
Argentine
C. de Gaulle-Etoile

Villiers
Monceau
Courcelles
Ternes
Europe
St-Lazare
Havre-Caumartin
St-Augustin

Liège
Trinité
Notre de Lo
C. d'Antin
La Fayette

Miromesnil
St-Philippe du Roule
Auber
Ope

Porte Dauphine **2**
6
George V
F.D. Roosevelt
Madeleine
Concorde
Tuileries
Pyr

Av. Foch
Victor Hugo
Kléber
Boissière
Alma Marceau
Champs Elysées Clémenceau

Av. Henri Martin
Rue de La Pompe
Trocadéro
Invalides
Palais Royal Mus. du Louvre
Pont N
Mus. d'Orsay Ch

La Muette
Boulainvilliers
Ranelagh
Jasmin
Passy
Champ de Mars Tour Eiffel
Bir Hakeim
Pont de l'Alma
Latour Maubourg
Assemblée Nationale
Solférino
St-Germain des Prés
St-

Varenne
St-François Xavier
Rue du Bac
Vaneau
Mabillon
Odé
St-Sulpice

Boulogne Pont de St-Cloud
10
Boulogne Jean Jaurès
Michel-Ange Auteuil
Porte d'Auteuil
Kennedy Radio France
Eglise d'Auteuil
Javel
Dupleix
Ecole Militaire
Segur
Duroc
Sèvres Babylone
St-Placide
La S
Rennes

Michel-Ange Molitor
Chardon Lagache
Mirabeau
Charles Michels
Av. E. Zola
La Motte Picquet
Cambronne
Falguière
Sèvres Lecourbe
Montpar
Bienven
Nôtre-Da des Char
Vavi

Exelmans
Porte St-Cloud
Marcel Sembat
Billancourt
Commerce
Félix Faure
Pasteur
Edgar Quinet
Raspail

9 Pont de Sèvres

Bd. Victor
Boucicaut
Lourmel
Volontaires
Vaugirard
Convention
Gaîté
Pernéty
Denfert Rochereau

8 Balard
Porte de Versailles
Plaisance
Mouton-Duvernet
Issy-Plaine
Corentin Celton
Porte de Vanves
Alésia

12 Mairie d'Issy
Issy
Malakoff Plateau de Vanves
Malakoff Rue Etienne Dolet
4 Porte d'Orléans
Laplace

RER - C (Versailles R.G.)

13 Châtillon-Montrouge

RER - (Orlyva

Seine

Fair of 1900 gave the city the Grand Palais and Petit Palais exhibition halls and the Alexander III bridge, as well as the Métropolitain underground railway. Since the occupation of Paris by the Nazis in the Second World War (thanks to the stunning ease with which Hitler swept through France, and the relative ease with which the Germans were ousted from the capital, most of the great buildings and monuments escaped damage), Paris has turned to modern development, while keeping its old, beautiful face and its position as a cultural capital of the world. The Montparnasse tower, the tallest building in the city, was erected in the 1960s, while the innovative Georges Pompidou Center turned the concept of an art museum inside out, literally. The Form des Halles, nearby, is a faux Belle Epoque park atop a modern shopping mall on the site of the former wholesale market, while the Défense, west of downtown, has developed as one of Europe's most important business centers, crowned by the Grand Arch, a futuristic echo of the Arc de Triomphe (check out the view from the entranceway of the Louvre, where you can look through the Arc du Carousel, down the Champs-Elysées through the Arc de Triomphe, and through the Grande Arche of Défense several miles away).

Paris is breathtaking in the scope and beauty of its historical legacy—anywhere you look you see care and consideration given to conserving the patrimony of this 2000-year-old city. Consider for a moment that simply walking slowly around Paris with your eyes open can provide you with more history and culture than most.

How to See Paris

There are some very basic things to remember when planning your visit to Paris. First, the city is very, very big. Do not expect to be able to see everything unless you are going to be here several months. Trying to rush around and "do" Paris in three days or even a week will leave you with a very superficial and unsatisfying experience. Far better to sit down with this book and one of the excellent seasonal guides put out by the tourist authorities, available at all hotels, and decide which areas and which monuments you want to visit. Go for quality, not quantity.

Second, the city is very, very busy. Don't bring a car unless you actually enjoy driving in a European capital (there is nothing similar in North America; the cities just aren't old enough). There is a certain exhilaration at successfully negotiating the Arc de Triomphe or the place de la Concorde (eight or ten lanes of traffic, all unstriped, right of way from the right...), but generally you will be able to travel around the city much more quickly on public transportation or your own two feet. Parking is impossible, and most hotels charge an extra $20 to $40 per night to use their garage.

Many of Paris' premier attractions are found along the Seine.

Third, the city is very, very expensive. There's not much you can do about this fact; I just warn you so you won't have sticker shock. It's very hard to find anywhere to eat for less than $15 per person, and the quality of the meals for that price varies enormously, from excellent to a total rip-off. The idea of a picnic in the park or beside the river is romantic and it is in fact a charming way to have lunch, but recognize that by the time you've stocked up at the *boulangerie*, the *épicerie*, the *charcuterie* and the *patisserie* (especially the patisserie!), you'll still have spent what you might spend in a restaurant back home. Accept the fact that you're going to be spending at least $100 per day per couple on top of hotels and exclusive of major shopping, and you'll have a much better time than cursing through your teeth every time a (non-refillable) coffee costs you more than two dollars. One way you can cut costs is to get a three- or five-day museum pass, which gets you into almost every museum and monument in the city (with the notable exception of the Eiffel Tower) for FR140 or FR200 and plan your museum-going around those days. Outside your pass period you can see high-quality art at private galleries, where the work is for sale but visits by the public are encouraged. Look for the posters announcing the exhibits in cafés and *brasseries* around town. As far as shopping goes, unless you're quite wealthy you'll find the prices in the major department stores and name boutiques to be quite a bit more than at home. I'd recommend window-shopping and browsing in these places for fun, then doing your real souvenir hunting at the used book stands lining the Seine or the flea markets (translated literally as *marché des puces*) at Porte de Cligancourt and Porte de Montreuil (the latter is the more popular; the former more touristy and expensive).

Since you can´t get around by car in Paris (if you're going to rent a car, get one when you leave town or drop it off before you arrive, depending on whether your visit to the capital is at the beginning or the end of your trip), you'll have to rely on public transportation (which is excellent) or your two feet (which will get tired). Fortunately, in Paris, the river is the real main drag of the city and most of the major sights are along its banks. As long as your hotel is reasonably central and/or close to the Seine you'll be able to get to most of the main attractions on foot. Beginning at the Pont de Brenelle and the copy of the Statue of Liberty in the west you can pass the Eiffel Tower, the Trocadéro, the Palais de Tokyo (city modern art museum), the Grand and petit Palais, Place de la Concorde, the National Assembly, the Musée d'Orsay, the Jardin des Tuileries and the Louvre, the Hôtel de Ville, and the Ile de la Cité (with the Sainte Chapelle and Notre Dame), all within about five miles. If you want to go farther afield or save your shoes use the excellent Métro, which covers the entire city and runs from 5:30 a.m. to 12:30 a.m. The best bet is a book of 10 tickets called a *carnet*, which sells for FR40, compared with the individual ticket price of FR7; buy at the counter and ask for a *plan* or map of the routes. Buses are slower than the Métro but naturally you see more of the city as you travel. Ask at your hotel for a list of lines with routes nearby. You can buy various daily and weekly passes that give you unlimited access to the Métro, buses, and RER suburban trains.

The extensive listings found below give you all the information you'll need on the major attractions and museums of Paris. But, like any great city, the attractions only tell half the story. In order to experience the flavor of Paris, as lived day to day by its 20 million inhabitants, you'll need to venture farther afield. The surprises and more popular experiences to be had by wandering aimlessly through one of the less touristy neighborhoods will provide you with memories equally as lasting as a visit to the Louvre or a night out at the Moulin Rouge. Close in to the center of town, the city is divided roughly into the Left and Right Banks—the Rive Gauche and Rive Droite. The Rive Gauche has acquired a hip cachet over the years, and it is true that the major academic institutions—and the young, creative community they engender—can be found in the eastern half of the district, in an area roughly contained within the Seine to the north, boulevard Montparnasse-Port Royal-Saint Marcel to the south, rue de Rennes to the west, and boulevard de l'Hôpital to the east. The western half of the Rive Gauche, bordered by the Seine to the north and west, rue de Rennes to the east, and boulevard de Grenelle-Garibaldi-Pasteur to the south, can be roughly said to contain the government and administration centers. This is where all the embassies and government ministries are, as well as the Eiffel Tower and the Invalides. The Rive

Droite area has always been the city's center of commerce. The luxury shopping district spreads out from either side of the Champs-Elysées and into Opéra, from St. Lazare station south to the river. Historic place Vendôme is perhaps the heart of the district, with Cartier, Chanel, Dior, Gucci and other boutiques clustered together. Occupying the same district and expanding east, west and north a mile or two is the business and finance district, with lots of high-rent offices in elegant 19th-century buildings housing a modern world's money changers. East of the Louvre and Opéra, in a district stretching north almost to Montmartre and encompassing République and Le Marais, is the commerce district, i.e. regulation big-city businesses and stores, without the *je ne sais quoi* of the place Vendôme. The district also includes the Halles and the Pompidou Center, a fine place to spend an entire day watching the world go by and viewing the impressions of others who have done the same.

Outside this central portion of the city you begin to get into the more livable parts of Paris. Between the Seine and the Bois de Boulogne in the west, in a district bordered by boulevard Exelmans to the south and rue de Ranelagh to the north, Paris' hip new creative minds have set up shop. Yuppies to some, movers and shakers to others, these are the people who keep the city on the leading edge of graphic design, media and advertising. High-tech offices compete with converted apartments and trendy restaurants and nightclubs in this newly invigorated area of the city. One of the joys of visiting a great city is watching it reinvent itself, and this is true in Paris more than elsewhere. The demographic and sociological evolution of the city is as fascinating as any exhibit in its museums. Besides the southern Right Bank just mentioned, the Bastille area is also developing as a young, popular neighborhood. The twin icons of Paris' history—the monument to the Révolution on the site of the storming of the Bastille prison and the gleaming new opera house inaugurated on the revolution's 200th anniversary—stand guard over a thriving scene that is home to the largest concentration of a new phenomenon in Paris: bars. In the past bars that are just bars—with good music, hip decor and lots of people drinking and making merry—didn't exist in France; you had to go to a *brasserie* or coffee shop to just hang out. In the last few years Bastille has seen an explosion of the trendy places, most of which are open until dawn, and the breath of new life has turned the previously somewhat run-down neighborhood into a happening place. South of Montparnasse on the other side of the river, in a neighborhood bordered by the station, rue Vercingétorix, rue d'Alesia and boulevard du Maine, is the city's major Chinese neighborhood. Groceries, restaurants, crafts stores and cultural centers give this part of town a distinctly oriental flavor. Other cultural hot spots are the Jewish quarter between the place des Vosges and the Pompidou center and the Arab quarters in the east of the city near Montreuil and in the district north of the St. Lazare station and west of Montmartre. Montmartre itself is still the Bohemian hangout it was in the days of the Bateau-Lavoir when Picasso, Chagall, Lenin, Trotsky, Miller and Hemingway made it their home, although the Bohemians have changed a lot since the pre-beat days. Artists of varying talent congregate in the square atop the hill, on the steps of Sacré Coeur, and on the many steps that connect the hill to the rest of town. The lower reaches of the district are very popular, with a young and very nonconformist crowd renting apartments and studios and displaying their wares in storefronts. The boulevard Clichy area at the base of the hill is Paris' red light district, with myriad sex shops driving out the old style *Grandes Brasseries* that once filled the quarter (though a few still survive and should be visited). If you're still up for another neighborhood, you might head out to La Défense, the ultra-modern business district outside the Périphérique ring road to the northwest of town. There's nothing to do here but ogle the gleaming towers and wonder whether the architecture we now deem so important will last a tenth as long as the monuments you've seen on the banks of the river. Still, it is one of the most impressive collections of avant-garde architecture in the world.

What to Do

Historical/Architectural Sites

Arc de Triomphe   ★★★★

place Charles de Gaulle, ☎ *01-43-80-31-31.*
Public transportation: 1,2,6, A. Metro stop: Charles de Gaulle Etoile.
Hours open: 9:30 a.m.–6:30 p.m. Special hours: Off-season and holidays 10 a.m.–5 p.m.
Situated in the middle of place Charles de Gaulle (formerly L'Etoile), Napoleon's monument to his long-suffering troops is the largest triumphal arch in existence, standing 164 feet above the tomb of the Unknown Soldier (a re-lighting ceremony takes place each evening at 6:30 p.m.). Time is taking its toll, however, so don't be surprised to see scaffolding at its skirts. The top of the arch (admission FR31; students, children over 7 FR7; under 7 free), with an informative museum, offers another interesting view of Paris: some of its worst traffic jams. Enter through the underpass beneath the north side of avenue des Champs-Elysées and avenue de la Grande Armée.

Atelier de Cezanne   ★★★

9 avenue Paul Cezanne, ☎ *01-42-21-06-53.*
Hours open: 10 a.m.–5 p.m. Special hours: Closed from noon–2 p.m. Closed: Tue.
The interior of the studio where the father of cubism, Paul Cezanne, spent his last days, appears as if he were about to return at any moment. An unfinished canvas is propped up on an easel, and his coat hangs on a door peg. You can almost smell the coffee brewing. The Tourist Office, at *2 place du General de Gaulle (*☎ *01-42-26-02-93),* has devised an interesting walking tour of the city; follow its brochure, which will take you past all of the artist's favorite haunts, ending up at the Atelier, just outside of town. Just north from Aix is the Montagne St.-Victoire, a peak rec-

PARIS

ognizable in much of Cezanne's work. The Tourist Office is open from 8 a.m.–10 p.m., Mon.–Sat.; Sun. from 9 a.m.–10 p.m. Admission: FR12.

Avenue des Champs-Elysées ★★★★

Eighth arrondissement. Take Metro line #1 or 13 to Champs-Elysées.
Public transportation: 1, 13. Metro stop: Champs-Elysées.

Quite easily the most famous avenue in the world, the Champs-Elysées spans from the Louvre to the Arc de Triomphe to La Defense. Its origins were not inspired by a desire to create what many call the most beautiful avenue in the world. Instead, its much nobler beginnings stemmed from Le Notre planting trees here in 1667 to extend the royal promenade from the Tuileries. By the time of the Revolution, the avenue had been completed in full. Still, it was just a nice street to wander. Following the two world wars, it gained much notoriety with the staging of the victory parades. It has since become a symbol of luxury for tourists from around the world. In fact, most of the people watching from expensive cafes such as Foquet's are foreigners rather than Parisians. Regardless, the Champs-Elysées is as much a part of a visit to Paris as the Sunset Strip is to Hollywood, except with more of a grand historical background. One look down the magnificent 10-lane avenue is worth a thousand words.

Sacré Coeur was built on the highest part of the city.

Basilica Sacré-Coeur ★★

35 rue de Chavalier.
Metro stop: Abbesses.
Hours open: 6:45 a.m.–11 p.m.

This oft-painted, tall, white Romanesque-Byzantine church is visible from most of Paris. The view from the dome (admission, FR15, open 9 a.m.–7 p.m., winter until 6 p.m.) is practically endless. You can also visit the crypt, where Alexandre Legentil, one of the basilica's builders, literally left his heart. (Admission; FR10, same hours as dome) There are plenty of street entertainers and corny souvenirs can be bought on the steps of the church.

Cathedrale St.-Denis ★★

place de l'Hotel-de-Ville.
Public transportation: 13. Metro stop: St.-Denis-Basilique.
Hours open: 10 a.m.–7 p.m. Special hours: Winter until 5 p.m.

This Cathedral, the burial place of French royalty (from Clovis to Marie Antoinette), was begun in 1137. During the French Revolution, the regal quietude was disturbed by angry mobs, who went on a rampage, exhuming and reburying bodies indiscriminately outside. Fortunately, most of the sculpted tomb art was left undamaged, and these alone are worth a visit. Admission for children, seniors and students is FR13. Admission: FR24.

La Conciergerie ★

1 quai de l'Horloge, ☎ 01-43-54-30-06. Take Metro line #4 to Cite.
Public transportation: 4. Metro stop: Cité.
Hours open: 9:30 a.m.–6:30 p.m. Special hours: Oct.–Mar., 10 a.m.–4:30 p.m.

These empty halls and cells served as the administrative center and prison during the French Revolution. Death-by-beheading sentences were handed to 2780 condemned souls during its heyday. Among those who passed through here before the final walk to the place de la Concorde (place de la Revolution during the time) to greet the guillotine were Marie Antoinette, Robespierre and the poet Andre Chenier. A vivid historical imagination is needed to leave here with much of an appreciation of what the walls here saw. Admission: FR27.

Le Marais ★★★

Marais district.

A quarter brimming with proud 16th-, 17th- and 18th-century private mansions. Untouched by commercialism, it is one of the most interesting parts of the Right Bank for strolling.

Lido Cabaret ★★★

116 bis, avenue des Champs-Elysées, ☎ 01-40-76-56-10.
Metro stop: George V.
Special hours: Shows 10 p.m.–12:15 a.m.

The Lido stages what is probably the most elaborate spectacle in Europe today. Imaginative, grand, dynamic, the theater restaurant stuns its patrons with an ensemble of at least 50 dancers, showgirls, seminude performers and international headliners. In the spacious 1200-seat venue, located in the Normandie Cinema building, all have an adequate view of the stage, as the sloped design terminates at a ringside tier that sinks to navel level. Surprising fantasy effects have been introduced by extending mechanical equipment out over the audience. Dinner is served at 8:30 p.m. Admission FR640–FR810 with dinner, FR465 without.

Artists sell their works at Place du Tertre.

Montmartre
★★★

Montmartre district.
Metro stop: Abbesses.

Many tourists believe that Montmartre is the real Paris. Built on a steep hill, the neighborhood is known for its quaint cobblestone streets and painters' garrets. Old houses stand along narrow streets and lovely squares, of which the place du Tertre (behind the Sacré-Coeur) is one of the most picturesque. The area now seems a bit honky-tonk; but the savvy can usually spot a rip-off, especially from so-called "artists" hawking their bogus wares. Nighttime views of the city, though, are still magical from the top. There are several interesting ways to get here; take note of the Abbesses metro station—the Hector Guimard-designed entrance is one of only two left in Paris, and it's been re-created on many a fine-art poster of the city. From the end of rue Foyatier, to the west, you can ride the funicular (FR6, metro tickets valid) to the foot of the Sacré-Coeur, although there may be a wait. The terraced Square Willette, below the forecourt of the Sacré-Coeur, is a student hangout, and a lively scene in the evening.

Moulin Rouge
★★

place Blanche, ☎ *01-46-06-00-19.*
Metro stop: Place Blanche.

A sister to the Lido in spirit is the Moulin Rouge—sketched by Toulouse-Lautrec and later made infamous by its cancan. It is up at Montmartre, in a huge, tiered, theaterlike hall. The shows are stunning—a splash of glitter, feathers and chiffon—and still somewhat shocking. Dinner is served between 8 and 10 p.m. The shows are at 10 p.m. and midnight. Admission is FR670 with dinner; FR465 without.

Notre Dame Cathedral   ★★★★★

6 place du Parvis-Notre Dame.
Metro stop: Cité.
Hours: 8 a.m.–7 p.m.

Dating back to 1163, the Notre-Dame cathedral has the history of Paris virtually engraved in its stone. During the Crusade, many came here to pray; Napoleon was crowned here, as well. Today you can mount the towers (387 steps, Admission: FR31, seniors, students FR17, under 17 FR6) to see the bells and step outside on the roof platform for a peep at the cathedral roof, with its gargoyles, and the Seine and its bridges below. You can also visit the Treasury and its relics, manuscripts and ornaments for FR15. Daily organ concerts at 5:45 p.m., free tours on Wednesdays (in English), and history or theology lectures at 4:45 p.m. on Sundays, Oct.–May. Admission: free.

Palais de Justice   ★★

4 boulevard du Palais, Ile de la Cite.
Metro stop: Cité.
Hours open: 10 a.m.–5 p.m.

Hundreds of heads rolled during the Reign of Terror (beginning in 1793), and many fateful decisions were handed down from this imposing building, now home to the law courts of Paris. At present, a more benevolent form of justice is meted out, and the public is invited to attend courtroom sessions. Admission: free.

Pantheon   ★★★

place du Pantheon, ☎ 01-43-54-34-51.
Public transportation: B. Metro stop: Luxembourg.
Hours open: 10 a.m.–5:45 p.m.

At the summit of Mount St. Genevieve, the crypt of this national shrine contains the tombs of Victor Hugo, Voltaire, Rousseau, Emile Zola and heroes of liberty. Originally a church built by Louis XV in honor of the patron saint of Paris, it is modeled after the Pantheon in Rome. Admission: FR26.

Place de la Bastille   ★★★

Public transportation: 1,5,8. Metro stop: Bastille.

Now a major traffic intersection, this is where the infamous Bastille Prison stood. If you feel like risking your own life to taxis, cars and buses whizzing by, you can pace off the outline of the edifice by following the white periphery painted on the street surface. The July Column (Colonne de Juillet) at its center honors those Parisians killed during the July 14, 1830, uprising, as well as the destruction of the prison. The square is also the site of the annual Bastille Day revelry. At the south corner of the place de Bastille is the Opera de la Bastille (designed by a Canadian architect, Carlos Ott), a political football in its inaugural months (it cost more than a billion francs). Things have settled down a little, and the opera is adding to the city's musical life. Tours daily, 1 p.m. and 5 p.m.; admission FR20; students FR10 (☎ 01-40-01-19-17).

Voltaire, Rousseau, Marie Curie and Victor Hugo are among those entombed beneath the Panthéon.

Place des Vosges   ★★★

rue des Birangue, off rue St.-Antoine.
Metro stop: Bastille, St. Paul.
Completed during the reign of Henri IV, this was once a meeting place of aristocrats. Mme de Sevigne was born at No. 1; Victor Hugo lived at No. 6; and Cardinal

PARIS

Richelieu resided at No. 21. Today, as then, it is the most beautiful public square in Paris—perhaps the world. The three-sided square is surrounded by 36 old town houses built over arcades; the current occupants are quality cafes and shops.

The Sorbonne   ★★★

47 rue des Ecoles.
Public transportation: 10. Metro stop: Cluny-La Sorbonne.
Hours open: 9 a.m.–6 p.m. Closed: Sat., Sun.
Founded in 1253 to teach theology to a small number of impoverished students, the Sorbonne today is France's leading university, also known as the University of Paris. Cardinal Richelieu ordered the construction of the Church of the Sorbonne in the 17th century; it's the only original building left standing. The tomb of the crafty clergyman (who essentially ran the country for Louis XII) is in the church's south transept. Classes are not open to the public. The church is open for special events only.

Tour Eiffel   ★★★★

quai du Branly and avenue Gustave Eiffel.
Public transportation: 6. Metro stop: Bir-Hakeim.
Hours open: 9 a.m.–midnight Special hours: Winter 9:30 a.m.–11 p.m.

Reviled during its construction (completed in 1889 for the Universal Exposition) like the Beaubourg and the Louvre Pyramid after it, the Eiffel Tower remains Paris' leading tourist destination. There are three platforms from which to see the city. From the third level, which you can reach only by double-decker elevator (there's often a wait) you can sometimes see up to 40 miles in every direction. You can also take a stairway still higher, where there's an excellent (and expensive) restaurant, the Jules Verne (listed separately). After-dark-illumination makes it even more beautiful. If the admission fee to the top is too stiff, you can use the stairs to the first and second platforms for FR12. Admission: FR55.

Kid's Stuff

Jardin d'Acclimation   ★★★

boulevard des Sablons.
Public transportation: 1. Metro stop: Les Sablons.
Hours open: 10 a.m.–6 p.m. Special hours: Saturday, 2–6 p.m.
Tucked away in a far corner of the Bois de Boulogne is this modest-size park within a park, with kiddie rides, marionette shows (Thur., Sat.–Sun., holidays), a riding school and a minicar racing track. A fun way to enter the park is via a mini-train from the Porte Maillot (FR6). Admission: FR10.

Parc Zoologique de Paris   ★★

Bois de Vincennes, ☎ 01-43-43-84-95.
Metro stop: Porte Doree.
Hours open: 9 a.m.–5:30 p.m. Special hours: Sunday to 6 p.m.
France's largest zoo, located in the 2500-acre Bois de Vincennes, is also a kind and gentle place, with mostly uncaged animals roaming as freely as possible, in natural settings. Students, seniors, FR24; children under 18; FR10. Nearby, on the western edge of the Bois, *(293 avenue Daumesnil, ☎ 01-43-43-14-54)* is the Musée des Arts d'Afrique et d'Oceanie, with a crocodile room and an interesting, well-stocked

aquarium; open 10 a.m.–5:30 p.m., Saturday-Sunday 12:30 p.m.–6 p.m., closed Tuesday-Thursday. Admission FR27; students, seniors FR18; under 18, free. Sunday FR12. Includes admission to the museum; included in the Carte Musées et Monuments. Admission: FR40.

Museums and Exhibits

Espace Montmartre Salvador Dali   ★★

> *11 rue Poulbot.*
> *Metro stop: Anvers, Blanche or Pigalle.*
> *Hours open: 10 a.m.–6 p.m.*

Welcome to the bizarre though intriguing world of Salvador "The Mustache" Dali. This Montmartre gallery (off the place du Tertre) features more than 300 works by the flamboyant surrealist artist. Admission: FR35.

Georges Pompidou Center   ★★★★

> *rue du Renard,* ☎ *01-44-78-12-33.*
> *Public transportation: 11. Metro stop: Rambuteau.*
> *Hours open: Noon–10 p.m. Special hours: Sat.–Sun., 10 a.m.–10 p.m. Closed: Tue.*

Completed in 1977, the building bears the brunt of much criticism and controversy, but its collections and presentations offer a fresh, bright and unusual slant on art appreciation. The open space out in front of the Pompidou Center is the site of impromptu performances—music, mime, magic—and there are some pleasant cafes in its multiform shadows. Inside are galleries for temporary art exhibitions, a large performance space and the Musée National d'Art Moderne (on the third and fifth floors), featuring works by such 20th-century masters as Max Ernst, Kandinsky, Chagall, Leger, Pollock, Calder and Henry Moore. You may wish to visit Brancusi's Atelier, an atmospheric reproduction of the sculptor's studio. Museum hours are the same as the center. Admission is FR35-45. Free admission on Sundays, from 10 a.m.–2 p.m. Also housed in the Center are the Center for Industrial Design and the Institute for Research and Coordination of Acoustics/Music, offering concerts and seminars often open to the public.

Hotel Les Invalides   ★★★★★

> *place des Invalides,* ☎ *01-44-42-37-67.*
> *Metro stop: Invalides.*
> *Hours open: 10 a.m.–5 p.m.*

This vast complex, encompassing four museums and two churches, has functioned as lodgings and a hospital for wounded military veterans since 1670; hence, its name. Near the south entrance is the verdant Jardin de l'Intendant, from which you can see the Eiffel Tower. Under the gold-leafed Dome Church, designed by Mansart, lie the entombed remains of Napoleon, in not one, but six coffins (Apr.–Sept., 10 a.m.–6 p.m.; Oct.–Mar. until 5 p.m.) Nearby the Musée de l'Armée, begun in the 1700s, is perhaps the most impressive and comprehensive of its kind in the world. Naturally, a large portion of one of its two galleries is devoted to the exploits of the little general from Corsica. You'll see his death mask and stuffed horse here, as well as uniforms, medals and weapons. The rest of the museum contains weapons from the Stone Age through World War II (same hours as Napoleon's Tomb). For

FR35, you gain admittance to both museums, plus St. Louis Church and the Musée des Plans et Reliefs; tickets are good for two days.

La Villette/Cite des Sciences et de L'Industrie ★★★★★

30 avenue Corentin-Cariou, ☎ *01-36-68-29-30.*
Public transportation: 7. Metro stop: Porte de la Villette.
Hours open: 10 a.m.–6 p.m. Special hours: Wed., noon–9 p.m.; weekends, noon–8 p.m. Closed: Mon.

A shining mirrored orb rises out of the landscape as you approach this high-tech complex (built on the grounds of a failed slaughterhouse) dedicated to the dissemination of scientific knowledge. What you see is the Geode, an Omnimax movie theater with an 11,000-square-foot hemispheric screen that moves everyone, especially children, to open-mouthed wonder. But that's the kind of place this is; built on a massive scale, this 10-year-old park project employed some of the western world's more forward-thinking architects and planners. Exhibits run the gamut from astrophysics to biotechnology; attractions include a Planetarium with a multilensed, state-of-the-art projection system, hanging greenhouses, a Space Station, and a user-friendly, interactive "Science City" area for children. The admission price shown covers all exhibits, except the Geode, which costs FR55 for adults, FR40 for children under 17 (Hourly shows daily, except Mon., 10 a.m.–9 p.m.). The Cite is situated within the 136-acre La Villette park, the largest park in the city, and where you'll find a cafe and restaurant. Admission: FR45.

Musée Picasso ★★★

Hotel de Sale, 5 rue de Thorigny, ☎ *01-42-71-25-21.*
Public transportation: 8. Metro stop: St. Sebastien-Froissart.
Hours open: 9:30 a.m.–6 p.m. Closed: Tue., Wed.

Located in the Hotel Sale (former home of Aubert de Fontenay, a salt tax collector), this handsome palace dating to the late 17th century contains the greatest Picasso collection you'll see anywhere, in addition to many splendid pieces collected by or given to Picasso by other well-known artists of his time. Along with several thousand works by the Spanish master (paintings, ceramics, sculptures, engravings, sketches), on display are paintings by Cezanne, Rousseau, Miro and Braque, among others, and many African masks, also from his collection. Sunday admission: FR16. Admission: FR30.

Musée Rodin ★★★★

77 rue de Varenne, ☎ *01-44-18-61-10.*
Public transportation: 13. Metro stop: Varenne.
Hours open: 10 a.m.–5:45 p.m. Special hours: Winter until 5 p.m. Closed: Mon.

This is one of the loveliest small museums in Paris. The great sculptor (living through the talent of Camille Claudet, many think) lived here from 1910 until he died in 1917. His major works are on display within the 18th-century mansion or arranged outdoors in a parklike setting. One of the first things you'll see upon entering the courtyard is his immortal bronze statue of "The Thinker." Inside are smaller (but not lesser) pieces, letters and mementoes tracing the artist's life and times. Students, seniors, children under 18 FR17. Admission to garden only: FR4. Admission: FR26.

Musée Victor Hugo ★★★

6 place des Vosges.
Metro stop: Bastille.
Hours open: 10 a.m.–5:45 p.m. Closed: Mon.

These second-floor rooms in the house where Hugo courted his various muses are furnished as they were during the poet-author-playwright's time. Much of the furniture was created by this Renaissance Man, who wrote *Les Miserables* and *The Hunchback of Notre-Dame*. Among the displays are Hugo's memorable drawings, depicting scenes from his own works. Sunday admission: free. Admission: FR15.

Musée d'Orsay ★★★★

1 rue de Bellechasse, ☎ *01-45-49-11-11.*
Metro stop: Solferino.
Hours open: 10 a.m.–6 p.m. Special hours: Thurs. to 9:45 p.m. Closed: Mon.

Formerly the Gare d'Orsay, a splendid rail station designed by Victor Laloux, it was converted to this impressive museum in 1986. The museum houses a grand collection of art from 1850 to 1910; it's a teeming cauldron of some 1500 pieces of sculpture, 2300 paintings, 13,000 photographs, art objects and furnishings in the thousands. Orsay not only received the Jeu de Paume's Impressionist treasures (one of its main draws), but it also became heir to heretofore unseen assemblages from the Louvre's vaults, and other state sources. In short, it's a landmark restored for the preservation of landmark aesthetics. Under 18, free; Sunday admission, FR24. Admission: FR35.

Musée de Cluny ★★★

6 place Paul-Painleve.
Public transportation: 10. Metro stop: Cluny/La Sorbonne.
Hours open: 9:15 a.m.–5:45 p.m. Closed: Tue.

In this historic museum, you'll discover the 15th-century Thermes de Cluny, built upon third-century Gallo-Roman baths, coupled with a comprehensive collection of medieval art and artifacts. Most notable among its displays are some exquisite tapestries, including the 15th- and 16th-century series known as "The Lady with the Unicorn." Students and senior admission FR27; under 18 free; FR18 Sundays. Admission: FR27.

Musée de l'Orangerie des Tuileries ★★★★

Jardin des Tuileries, placede la Concorde, ☎ *01-42-97-48-16.*
Metro stop: Concorde.
Hours open: 9:45 a.m.–5:15 p.m. Closed: Tue.

Located in the southwest corner of the Jardin des Tuileries, this museum houses a section of one of the most famous series of paintings in the world, Monet's "Nympheas," or Waterlilies, which the artist completed toward the end of his life, while in his garden at Giverny. The canvases fill two lower-level rooms in the museum. There's more to see, however: Early works by Picasso, some 24 paintings by Renoir ("Young Girls at the Piano"), 14 by Cezanne, nine by Rousseau, and others round out the fabulous Walter-Guillaume Collection. Sunday admission: FR17. Admission: FR27.

A vast area beneath the Louvre's pyramid entrance houses the lobby and shops.

Musée du Louvre   ★★★★★

Rue de Rivoli. main entrance cour Napoleon
Metro stop: Palais Royale-Musée de Louvre.
Hours open: 9 a.m.–6 p.m. Special hours: Wed., to 10 p.m. Closed: Tue.

This world-famous museum, housing an abundance of art treasures, stretches nearly
one kilometer between the Seine River and the rue de Rivoli. The Louvre's main
entrance is via the controversial seven-story metal-and-glass pyramid designed by
I.M. Pei and completed in 1990. To avoid the inevitable queues, however, don't
enter the museum through the Pyramid—there's a more accessible entrance via the
Porte Jaujard (at the far end, near the Tuileries and the Seine). The structure began
as the residence of Francois I, and, as buildings were added and remodeled, it
remained a royal residence until the Court relocated at Versailles in 1682. There are
six galleries, with more than 300,000 priceless paintings, sculptures and objets d'art.
After you've seen Leonardo Da Vinci's "Mona Lisa," and other famous works like
the "Winged Victory at Samothrace," and the "Venus de Milo," head over to the
Cour Carree site, a dungeon conceived by Phillipe Auguste in the 12th century,
which is a change of pace from gallery hopping. Also awe-inspiring are the 25-ton
Assyrian alabaster bulls (five of them) in the reconstruction of Sargon II's palace in
the Cour de Zhorsabad (formerly the Cour du Louvre). Sunday and after 3 p.m.,
admission FR20, free entrance from the Pyramid to the Carrousel du Louvre, a series
of subterranean shops and galleries. Admission: FR40. (See 3-D map on page 150.)

Music

Free Concerts   ★★★

Various locations.

In addition to the plethora of street musicians in Paris, many prominent theaters,
parks, churches, museums and galleries hold regular musical events scheduled

throughout the year. Classical concerts and recitals are held weekly at the St.-Roch Church, the burial place of Corneille, in the first arrond *(rue St.-Honore at rue St.-Roch, Metro: Tuileries)*. The church of St.-Nicholas-des-Champs *(third arrond., 252 rue St.-Martin, Metro: Arts et Metiers)*, justifiably proud of its 17th-century organ, shows it off with concerts from time to time. Aside from daily organ recitals at 5:45 p.m., Notre-Dame Cathedral (see "Historical Sites") has Sunday concerts. In the seventh arrond., the Parc du Champ de Mars, a long stretch of green extending from the Ecole Militaire to the Eiffel Tower, was once trampled by the marching feet of armed forces, but it now resounds with the pleasing beat of music from the numerous concerts given here in the summer. Popular for its arboretum, the Parc Montsouris *(in the 14th arrond. off avenue Reille, Metro: Cite Universitaire)*, has a bandstand where summer concerts are given; there's also a man-made lake, surrounded by a sculpture garden.

Nightlife

Videotheque de Paris ★★★
2 Grande Galerie, ☎ 01-40-26-34-30.
Metro stop: Chatelet/Les Halles.
Hours open: 12:30–8:30 pm Closed: Mon.
For one price, celluloid-mad Parisians and travelers can view a series of films or videos in the screening room of this art-house in the Forum des Halles shopping center. Also within the Videotheque are semi-private viewing cells where patrons can tailor their own programs from thousands of documentaries, newsreels and short subjects. A similar deal is offered at the Salle Garance in the Pompidou Center (see Museums and Exhibits); for FR25, you can move among the Salle's three theaters as many times as you want, hours are the same as the center. At the Cinematheque Francaise, *(16th Arr., Palais de Tokyo, 13 Avenue du President Wilson, ☎ 01-47-23-61-27, Metro: Alma-Marceau)* your admission price of FR25 entitles you to two movies and passage to the Palais de l'Image et du Son, a photography-film-and audio-visual museum at the same location. Admission: FR22.

Parks and Gardens

Jardin des Tuileries ★★★★
place de la Concorde.
Public transportation: 1, 8 or 12. Metro stop: Concorde or Tuileries.
Hours open: 7 a.m.–10 p.m. Special hours: Oct.–Mar., to 8 p.m.
A sizable part of the Tuileries was laid out in 1664 by Le Notre, and what was once the private enclave for the royal family is now a popular people's park. Spring is best, of course, and there are lovely views from the south end. Two museums in the park are the not-to-be missed Musée de l'Orangerie (see "Museums") and the no-less-important Jeu de Paume (designed by Antoine Stinco), which ceded its Impressionists to the Musée d'Orsay (see "Museums"); it has for several years become a salon for top contemporary artists (open noon–7 p.m.; Tues., until 9:30 p.m.; Sat.–Sun., 1–7 p.m.). Admission: free.

Jardin du Luxembourg ★★★
rue de Vaugirard.

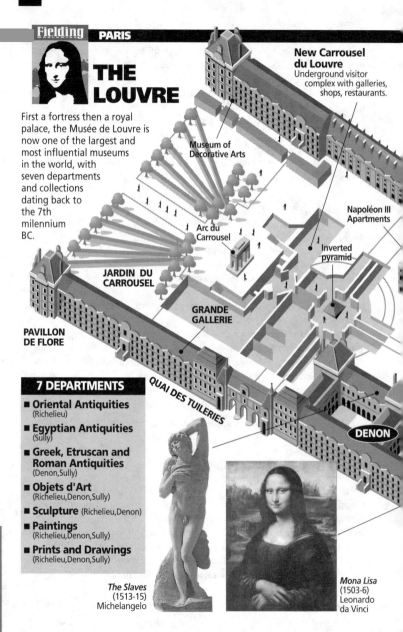

Fielding PARIS

THE LOUVRE

First a fortress then a royal palace, the Musée de Louvre is now one of the largest and most influential museums in the world, with seven departments and collections dating back to the 7th millennium BC.

New Carrousel du Louvre
Underground visitor complex with galleries, shops, restaurants.

Museum of Decorative Arts

Arc du Carrousel

Napoléon III Apartments

Inverted pyramid

JARDIN DU CARROUSEL

GRANDE GALLERIE

PAVILLON DE FLORE

QUAI DES TUILERIES

DENON

7 DEPARTMENTS

- **Oriental Antiquities** (Richelieu)
- **Egyptian Antiquities** (Sully)
- **Greek, Etruscan and Roman Antiquities** (Denon,Sully)
- **Objets d'Art** (Richelieu,Denon,Sully)
- **Sculpture** (Richelieu,Denon)
- **Paintings** (Richelieu,Denon,Sully)
- **Prints and Drawings** (Richelieu,Denon,Sully)

The Slaves
(1513-15)
Michelangelo

Mona Lisa
(1503-6)
Leonardo da Vinci

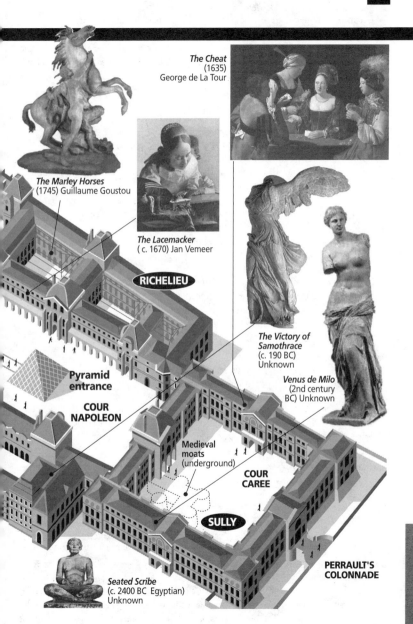

The Cheat
(1635)
George de La Tour

The Marley Horses
(1745) Guillaume Goustou

The Lacemacker
(c. 1670) Jan Vemeer

RICHELIEU

The Victory of Samothrace
(c. 190 BC)
Unknown

Venus de Milo
(2nd century
BC) Unknown

**Pyramid
entrance**

**COUR
NAPOLEON**

Medieval
moats
(underground)

**COUR
CAREE**

SULLY

Seated Scribe
(c. 2400 BC Egyptian)
Unknown

**PERRAULT'S
COLONNADE**

Public transportation: B. Metro stop: Luxembourg.
This 60-acre park is really the backyard of the Palais du Luxembourg, built in the
17th century for Marie de Medici (also headquarters for the Luftwaffe during the
Occupation) and now the French Senate. Romantic for strolling (but, please, not
on the grass!) Kids love riding the ponies and sailing the toy boats. Free band concerts on Sundays.

Jardin du Palais Royal   ★★★

place de Palais Royal, ☎ 01-42-60-16-87. enter at rue Montpensier
Public transportation: 1,7. Metro stop: Palais Royal-Musée du Louvre.
Hours open: 7 a.m.–11 p.m. Special hours: Winter to 8:30 p.m.
Protected from view by exclusive apartment houses, government offices and the
former palace of Cardinal Richelieu, this park offers privacy and serenity in the heart
of this busy district. Prerevolutionary arcades envelop the area, which is popular
with mothers and children. The only jarring elements, in my opinion, are the striped
Buren columns in the palace courtyard, some squat, some tall, which look to me like
hatboxes or ottomans that fell off a delivery truck. Admission: free.

Parc St.-Cloud   ★★

Between Pont de St.-Cloud and Pont de Sevres.
Public transportation: 10. Metro stop: Boulogne/Pont de St. Cloud.
Hours open: 9 a.m.–8 p.m.
On a hill above the left bank of the Seine, St.-Cloud is known for its park, designed
by Le Notre, from which there is an especially good view of Paris. Highlights of the
park include a 296-foot waterfall, the Grande Cascade and the Grande Jet, a 138-
foot fountain. Admission: free.

Shopping

Bazaar de l'Hotel de Ville   ★★

52 rue de Rivoli, ☎ 01-42-74-90-00.
Public transportation: 1, 11. Metro stop: Hotel de Ville.
Hours open: 9:30 a.m.–7 p.m. Special hours: Wed. until 10 p.m. Closed: Sun.
The basement of this department store is hardware heaven; whatever's broke, this
store will help you fix it. Everything from hammer and nails to electrical converters
is available here, and there's a knowledgeable army of salespeople to answer any
queries you might have.

Bouquinistes   ★★★

quai de Montebello.
Metro stop: Saint-Michel.
Hours open: 11 a.m.–7:30 p.m. Closed: Mon., Sun.
It's worthwhile to make a trip out to these bookstalls near Notre-Dame at least
once, even if you're not planning to buy. Naturally, there's a lot of junk, but who
knows? You might get lucky and find a first edition on your first run-through.

Discount Shopping Centers   ★★★

Various locations.
Outlets for new or hardly used designer clothing proliferate in Paris. Almost a mile
of brand-new clothing is sold for a song at the Marche du Temple, across from the
medieval Square du Temple *(second arrond., Carreau du Temple, off rue Dupetit*

Thouars); open 9 a.m.–noon, except Sundays. Only·top·of·the·line designer clothing, shoes and accessories for men and women are sold on consignment at **Catherine Baril** *(sixteenth arrond., 14 and 25 rue de la Tour;* ☎ *01-45-27-11-46); open 10 a.m.–7 p.m., Mon. 2–7 p.m., closed Sun.* If you can squeeze into an Alaïa, you can do so at considerable discount from **Reciproque**, a nest of consignment stores, at *89, 92, 95, 97, 101 and 123 rue de la Pompe,* in the 16th arrond., *open 10:30 a.m.–7 p.m., except Sun. and Mon.;* ☎ *01-47-04-30-28.* **Fabienne**, a consignment store for men only, also in the 16th arrond. *(77 bis, rue Boileau,* ☎ *01-45-25-64-26, open 10 a.m.–1:30 p.m and 3–7 p.m., closed Sun. and Monday, and Aug.),* features handmade shoes, clothing and accessories. At the four branches of **Tati** (one in the eleventh arron., at *13 place de la Republique, open 10 a.m.–7 p.m., Sat. to 7:30 p.m., closed Sun. and Mon.*), you might get jabbed by some elbows, but it's certainly worth a visit for undeniable bargains, in everything from fabrics to clothing; to say that it's always crowded is an understatement.

Flower and Bird Markets   ★★

place Louis Lepine, Ile de la Cite.
Public transportation: 4. Metro stop: Cité.
Hours open: 8 a.m.–7:30 p.m.
Flowers abound during the week (between the Cité Metro station entrance and the Seine River). On Sundays, it turns into a rather bland and ordinary bird market; you won't see anything you can't get at home.

Food Markets   ★★★

Various locations.
For either sightseeing or sustenance, Paris' specialty food markets are a must. All are closed Mondays, unless specified. Some of the best ones are the **Rue de Mouffetard** *(fifth arrond., Metro Cardinal Lemoine),* one of the city's oldest, bursting with local color and produce; **Rue de Buci** *(sixth arrond., Metro Mabillon, open 8 a.m.–7:30 p.m.),* food as well as flowers in the nearby **Carrefour de Buci** *(rue de Buci at rue Mazarine);* **Marche St.-Germain** *(rue Mabillon at rue Clement, Metro Mabillon, open 8 a.m.–7:30 p.m.);* **Marche Château-d'Eau**, an ancient covered market (vegetarians stay clear of this one) *(10th arrond., Metro Château d'Eau, open 8 a.m.–7:30 p.m.);* **Marche St.-Quentin**, historic, similar to old Le Halles market, lots of gourmet goodies *(10th arrond., 85 boulevard Magenta, Metro Gare de l'Est, open 8 a.m.–1 p.m. and 3:30–7:30 p.m.; Sundays to 1 p.m. only);* **Marche de Passy**, fresh foodstuffs and more *(16th arrond., Metro Passy);* **Rue Poncelet and Place des Ternes**, for meats and deli items *(17th arrond., off avenue des Ternes, Metro Ternes, open 8 a.m.–7:30 p.m.).*

Galignani   ★★

224 rue de Rivoli, ☎ *01-42-60-76-07.*
Metro stop: Tuileries.
Hours open: 9:30 a.m.–7:30 p.m. Closed: Sun.
Galignani is more than 300 years old, and is possibly the oldest English-language bookstore anywhere in Europe. There are best-sellers here, but it is known for big, glossy art books and calendars.

Gault

206 rue de Rivoli, ☎ *01-42-60-51-17.*
Metro stop: Tuileries.
Hours open: 10 a.m.–7 p.m.

A playland of marvelous ceramic houses, churches and buildings from France's varied regions. These make splendid home decorations and collector's items of surprisingly low cost. You can also have your name imprinted on the "building" of your choice. Made in St.-Paul-de-Vence by two brothers, Jean Pierre and Dominique Gault, each creation carries a certificate of authenticity. No credit cards.

Haute Couture   ★★★★

Rue du Faubourg Saint-Honore/Avenue Montaigne.

The hottest places for fashion, whether for Chanel classics or the razzle dazzle of Christian Lacroix, are in the bejeweled, over-cultured eight arrondissement. Many famous boutiques are within whispering distances of each other around the avenue des Champs-Elysées, some on avenue Montaigne or the rue du Faubourg Saint-Honore. Most are open daily except Sundays; opening times vary from 8–10 a.m., and they close between 6–7 p.m. Buy a hardly used designer ensemble at one of the consignment stores (see "Discount Shopping"), put on a haughty face, and browse. Or you can pretend they're museums and window-shop. Here are some addresses: **Christian Lacroix**, *73 rue du Faubourg St.-Honore* (☎ *01-42-65-79-08*), Metro: Champs-Clemenceau- average price for one of his creations is FR50,000; **Chanel**, *42 avenue Montaigne* (☎ *01-42-23-74-12*), Metro: Franklin D. Roosevelt—sales staff is fairly approachable; **Yves Saint-Laurent**, *5 avenue Marceau* (☎ *01-47-23-72-71*), Metro: Alma-Marceau—the aging enfant-terrible of the '60s still has the stuff.

Hotel Druot   ★★

9 rue Drouot, ☎ *01-42-46-17-11.*
Metro stop: Le Pelettier.
Hours open: 11 a.m.–6 p.m. Special hours: Closed from noon–2 p.m. Closed: Sun.

If you have a family treasure to sell, you can bring it to this auction house for appraisal at the times specified above; auctions are held several times daily. But most travelers will just want to watch the show or look at the varied objects d'art that will be going on the auction block. It's an interesting and different way to pass the day, and work on your French. Closed Aug.

La Samaritaine   ★★★

quai du Louvre and rue de la Monnaie. across from the Pont Neuf.
Public transportation: 7. Metro stop: Pont Neuf.
Hours open: 9:30 a.m.–7 p.m. Special hours: Tues.–Fri. until 8:30 p.m. Closed: Sun.

Supposedly the Sears of France—except that it's housed in an incredible glass-and-steel Art Nouveau building. Actually, "Samar" is four stores in one. Starting at the top, you'll be treated to a picture-postcard view of Paris that won't cost you a franc. There's also an inexpensive cafe that's open six months a year in good weather *(closed Apr.–Oct.).* The cafe-terrace is located in Building 2, on the 10th floor. Test out the equipment in the sporting goods department; the staff won't mind. You can get some advice on your cranky rental bike (or have your own fixed if you brought it with you). Practice some reverse chic: typical tradesmen and workers' clothing can be purchased here; it's up to you to put it all together, or surprise an amateur chef with an authentic chef's hat. A great way to remember Paris.

Louvre des Antiquaries ★★★

2 place de Palais-Royal, ☎ *01-42-97-27-00.*
Metro stop: Palais-Royal/Louvre.
Hours open: 11 a.m.–7 p.m. Closed: Mon.
A huge, three-story complex dedicated to the purchase and sale of antiques. As many as 250 shops representing many different types (Art Deco to maritime antiques) are housed here, plus a snack bar. High quality, but very expensive.

Paris Salvation Army ★★

12 rue Cantagrel, ☎ *01-45-83-54-50.*
Public transportation: C. Metro stop: Boulevard Massena.
Hours open: 9 a.m.–6 p.m.
If you want to see how Parisians clean out their closets, check out the thrift shop operated by this well-known organization. Stock changes daily.

Poilane ★★★★★

8 rue du Cherche-Midi, ☎ *01-45-48-42-59.*
Metro stop: Sevres-Babylone.
Hours open: 7:15 a.m.–8:15 p.m. Closed: Sun.
This shop sells the world-famous sourdough bread that everyone has heard about; lines form outside the shop early in the morning for fresh loaves, cookies and pastries. For ice cream and sorbets, you shouldn't miss **Berthillon**, *31 rue Saint-Louis-en-l'Ile (*☎ *01-43-54-31-61)*, Metro: Pont-Marie, with unusual flavors that put Baskin-Robbins to shame, such as marron glace, gianduja (hazelnut), kiwi and kumquat. *Open daily, except Mon. and Tues. from 10 a.m.–8 p.m.;* no cards. For equally unusual chocolates, try **Christian Constant**, *26 rue du Bac, seventh arrondissement, Metro: Bac (*☎ *01-42-96-53-53)*; here you'll find such far-out creations as bonbons with the essence of flowers, including jasmine, and others made with tea. Many of them are low in sugar. *Open daily from 8 a.m.–8 p.m.* On the same street, at *No. 44*, Lenotre (☎ *01-42-22-39-39)*, the King of patissiers, is also renowned for chocolates, including palets d'or with buttercream filling; there are shops all over town. *Open 9 a.m.–8 p.m., Mon.–Sat., Sun. to 1 p.m.* For gourmet goodies, the eighth arrondissement is host to a trio of greats who have been around since the 1800s. **Fauchon** (since 1886), at *26 place de la Madeleine, Metro: Madeleine (*☎ *01-47-42-60-11)*, is the most commonly known; besides prepared foods to go, there's a huge variety of exotic jams (sweet potato, jasmine petal), pastries, charcuterie and wines. Mail order to anywhere, and it also has a cafeteria. *Open daily, except Sun., 10 a.m.–7 p.m.,* all major cards. **Hediard** (1854), at *21 place de la Madeleine (*☎ *01-42-66-09-00), open daily, except Sun., 9 a.m.–6:30 p.m.;* and **Fouquet**, the oldest, (since 1852), at *22 rue Francois, first arrond., Metro: George V (*☎ *01-47-23-30-36), open daily, except Sun. from 9:30 a.m.–7 p.m.;* both have impeccable reputations for unusual and high-quality condiments, chocolates, pastry and packaged items. Hediard has a restaurant on the premises.

PARIS

Stamp Market   ★★

avenue Gabriel. Between avenue Marigny and Matignon.
Public transportation: 1,9. Metro stop: Franklin D. Roosevelt.
Hours open: 10 a.m.–6 p.m. Closed: Mon., Wed., Fri.
Even if you're not a collector, this outdoor market is fun. Pins and postcards as well
as stamps. Another interesting one is **Marche aux Vieux Papiers** ("Old Paper Mar-
ket"); it helps if you're knowledgeable or go with someone who is a collector *(in the
Paris suburb of St.-Mande, avenue de Paris, Metro St.-Mande Tourelle, open Wed.
only, from 10 a.m.–6 p.m.).*

W.H. Smith   ★★

248 rue de Rivoli, ☎ 01-42-60-37-97.
Metro stop: Tuileries.
Hours open: 9:30 a.m.–7 p.m. Special hours: Sat. to 7:30 p.m. Closed: Sun.
All the guidebooks to Paris and France you couldn't find overseas are available at
this famous bookshop. You can also pick up your magazines and thrillers here. Tick-
ets to cultural events can be purchased, as well; there's a tearoom upstairs.

Special Tours/Excursions

Bateaux Mouches   ★★★

Pont de l'Alma, ☎ 01-42-25-96-10.
Metro stop: Alma-Marceau.
Hours open: 10 a.m.–11 p.m.
Multilingual boat cruises on the Seine; they're very touristy, but can be fun if you
have a good sense of humor. Duration 90 minutes, boats leaving every 30 minutes;
winter departures 11 a.m., noon, 2:30 p.m., 4 p.m., 9 p.m. Lunch cruises Saturdays
and Sundays from Apr. 15-Nov. 15, departing 12:45 p.m.; FR300, FR350 on Sunday. Dinner cruise 8:30 p.m. daily, jackets and ties required; FR500. Admission:
FR35.

Bateaux Parisines Tour Eiffel   ★★

port de la Bourdonnais, ☎ 01-47-05-50-00.
Metro stop: Trocadéro.
Hours open: 10 a.m.–10:30 p.m.
Glass-topped boats (somewhat more luxurious than the Bateau Mouches) leave
every half-hour from the wharf near the Eiffel Tower. The usual tour lasts 90 min-
utes, but there's also a lunch cruise and a dinner cruise; jacket and tie required.
Admission: FR45.

Batobus   ★★

Various locations.
Hours open: 10 a.m.–7 p.m. Special hours: No winter service
A floating taxi service on the Seine with stops at the Eiffel Tower, Musée de'Orsay,
Louvre, Hotel de Ville and Notre-Dame. Individual tickets are steep, but a day pass
for FR60 is a scenic (and less frenzied) alternative to the mouches. Admission:
FR12.

Ticket Agencies

FNAC   ★★

Forum des Halles, Level 3, ☎ 01-42-86-87-12.

Metro stop: Chatelet/Les Halles.
Hours open: 10 a.m.–7:30 p.m. Special hours: Mon., 1–7:30 p.m.
If you plan to be in Paris for a reasonable length of time and intend to hit every play, concert and festival possible, the **Carte Alpha** (FR50 for one year) or the **Carte FNAC** (FR150 for three years) will lop 40 percent off of the price of your tickets. This money-saving package can be purchased from FNAC, a music- and bookstore entertainment center at the above location, with branches all over the city. It's also good to know that the **Kiosque Theater** *(eight arrond., 15 place de la Madeleine, Metro: Madeleine, no phone, open 12:30–8 p.m., Tues.–Sat., Sun. to 6 p.m., closed Mon.)* will sell you tickets for half-price; good only for the day of the show.

Museum Pass/Carte Musées et Monuments ★★★★
Various locations.
Here's a splendid way to see a lot for comparatively little: FR70 for one day, FR140 for three days, and FR200 for five days. The pass offers immediate entry to 65 museums and monuments (permanent collections only, not valid for special exhibitions), without waiting in long lines. You present your card, and voila, you're in. Here's a sampling of museums covered: the Louvre, Pompidou Center, the Musée d'Orsay, Cluny, the Crypt of Notre-Dame, and much more. You can obtain the pass from the participating museums, all Metro kiosks, and the Tourist Office Headquarters at *127 avenue des Champs-Elysées.* Travel agencies also often sell the pass in the United States and Europe.

Marne-la-Valee

Theme/Amusement Parks

Disneyland Paris ★★★★
Disneyland Paris, 30 minutes from Paris, ☎ *01-60-30-60-30. A4 E. from Paris, off at exit 14. Hours open: 10 a.m.–8 p.m. Special hours: Winter 10 a.m. to 6 p.m.*
The French version of the Magic Kingdom lies 20 miles east of Paris and employs some 12,000 people to keep it running. The name was recently changed from "Euro Disney" to "Disneyland Paris," but it remains the same less-than-successful story. The park contains most of what made the original famous: Main Street USA at the entrance, and the traditional gateway to Fantasyland: The Sleeping Beauty Castle (called a "Château" here). Attractions include It's A Small World, Pirates of the Caribbean, Indiana Jones, Big Thunder Mountain and Phantom Manor. Every evening, there is a fireworks show and the colorfully lit Main Street Electrical Parade. Lines are long for the most popular rides. As a concession to French tastes, wine is served. An RER A4 commuter train from the Central Paris station (Metro: Gare de Lyon) stops within strolling distance of the park (Marne-la-Vallee/Chessy). All-inclusive admission prices: FR195; under 12 FR150; after 5 p.m. FR150.

Seine-et-Marne

Historical/Architectural Sites

Château de Vaux-le-Vicomte ★★★★★
Maincy, ☎ *01-64-14-41-90.*
Located halfway between Fontainebleau and Vincennes (and 60 km from Paris), this great château employed many of the artists who were later to build, decorate

and landscape Louis XIV's palaces at Versailles, the Trianon and Marly. Here the combined geniuses of landscape gardener Le Notre, interior designer Le Brun and architect Le Vau are on perpetual show, as commissioned by the Sun King's arrogant finance minister, Nicholas Fouquet. It may, indeed, have been Fouquet's Folly; Louis, jealous of all the splendor (he thought he was being upstaged),threw him in prison, charging him with embezzlement. It's not on the usual tourist circuits, but Vaux is not to be missed by any true Francophile. If you are in town from May to October, don't miss the special "Candlelight Evenings" on Saturdays: the privately owned château is illuminated entirely by candlelight from 8:30–11:30 p.m. (FR75) There's also a fountain show on the second and last Saturday of each month. Hours: Apr.–Oct., 10 a.m.–6 p.m., Feb. 13–Mar, 11 a.m.–6 p.m.; Nov. 1-14, 11 a.m.–5 p.m.; Dec. 22–Jan. 4, 11–5 p.m. Admission to the gardens, and a carriage museum only, FR30. The cafeteria is open daily, 12:30–2:30 p.m. Admission: FR56.

Where to Stay

Hostels

Three Ducks Hostel   **FR90**   ★

6 place Etienne Pernet. ☎ *01-48-42-04-05. Take Metro line #8 to Commerce.*
Public transportation: 8. Metro stop: Commerce.

Definitely one of the cheapest places to stay in Paris, the Three Ducks Hostel is the scene for traveling youths and backpackers. While not exactly ideal for a peaceful night with the spouse, this place definitely exudes a bohemian, raucous attitude. A TV room, patio, kitchen and bar are in the building with laundry facilities next door. Summertime translates to reservations needed, barbecues and many young Americans drinking cheap beer. There is a 1 a.m. curfew, a lockout period from 11 a.m. to 5 p.m. and only cash is accepted for the 90 francs per bed price. This is also the embarkation point for the guided mountain bike tours of Paris offered in four languages and lasting six hours. It's a wonderful way to see the city and have some fun for FR120, including a bike and insurance.

Hotels and Resorts

Baltimore Westin Demeure Hotel   **FR1400–FR2200**   ★★★★★

88 Bis Avenue Kleber. ☎ *01-44-34-54-54, FAX: 01-44-34-54-44. Located equidistantly*
between the Eiffel Tower, the Arc de Triomphe and the Trocadéro on avenue Kleber, this
is one of the most centrally located hotels in the city.
Metro stop: Trocadéro.
Single: FR1400–FR2200. Double: FR1400–FR2200.

This luxury treasure is truly a jewel—if you can afford it! Be sure to ask for a room on avenue Kleber, where the balconies look out over the busy street and you can see the Eiffel Tower (the historical connection to the view is strong: the building was designed as a townhouse by Gustave Eiffel himself. The rooms are huge, most with a king-sized bed as well as a single, spacious bathroom, satellite television, etc. A nice, quirky touch is the complementary copy of *The Fifth Star*, a spy novel commissioned by the hotel (and prominently featuring the hotel) that is most notable for its quaint translation from French. Features: air conditioning in rooms, balcony or patio, in-room mini-bars, fitness center, in-room conference facilities. Credit Cards: All Major.Credit Cards: YE.

Castille Westin Demeure   FR600–FR3000   ★ ★ ★ ★ ★

37 rue Cambon. ☎ *949-7562, 01-44-58-44-58, FAX: 01-44-58-44-00.*
Public transportation: 1. Metro stop: Tuileries.
Double: FR600–FR3000.

Quite possibly the most sumptuous hotel in all of Paris, the Castille, formerly an annex of the Ritz (just up the street), completely renovated in 1994-1995, offers unparalleled luxury in the very center of the city. The Louvre is five minutes away, Chanel is next door, the place Vendome is one block over…many wealthy consumers stay in this palace just to be close to the couturier boutiques and shop til they drop. The 111 rooms and suites are all furnished with Bang and Olufsen TVs and stereo systems (two of each in the two-story duplex rooms and suites), each has a direct fax/modem line besides three telephones, and the service from the Concierge and staff of this hotel is the best there is. Fine dining on the patio of Il Cortile, the hotel's Italian restaurant, is available from 195 frances for the menu of the day. If you have the money to splurge, or you plan to spend a good deal of time in your room, for example if you're honeymooning in Paris in winter, this is where you belong. It doesn't get any better. Features: air conditioning in rooms, nonsmoking rooms, in-room safes, in-room minibars, in-room conference facilities. Credit Cards: All Major.

Domaine de la Tortiniere   FR455–FR870   ★ ★ ★

Les Gues de Veigne. ☎ *01-47-26-00-19.*
Rated Restaurant: *Domaine de la Tortiniere.*
Single: FR455–FR550. Double: FR665–FR870.

Proudly sitting on the top of a hillside overlooking the Indre River, this manor dates back to 1861. The Belle Epoque style is quite an imposing picture in the middle of a private 30-acre park. From the lush lawns below, the staircases lead to the terraces overlooking the property. The 21 modestly decorated rooms are equipped with TV, telephone and private bath; the choice rooms are equipped with private Jacuzzis. Guests dine in one of the two restaurants, and enjoy a nightcap in the intimate bar and lounge. A member of the Relais and Châteaux group of hotels. Features: wheelchair-access rooms, pool, tennis, houses, cottages or bungalows. Credit Cards: All Major.

Duc de Saint Simon   FR950–FR1450   ★ ★ ★

14 rue de St. Simon. ☎ *01-45-48-35-66, FAX: 01-45-48-68-25. Take Metro line #12 to Rue du Bac. Turn left on Boulevard St. Germain. Turn left on rue de St. Simon.*
Public transportation: 12. Metro stop: Rue du Bac.
Double: FR950–FR1450.

Enjoying a location among the gardens, one of this hotel's most appealing aspects is its quiet atmosphere. This 19th-century hotel's Swedish management maintains high standards and offers a warm welcome. It offers 34 bed chambers, each individually decorated with period furnishings and immaculately kept. Garden view balconies are available with some rooms. Antiques, paintings, floral arrangements and an overall charming ambience pervade the entire hotel. Although there are no dining facilities, there is a small bar. This charming hotel's increasing popularity makes reservations a must. Features: balcony or patio.

Eber Monceau Hotel   FR630–FR700   ★★★

18 rue Leon Jost. ☎ *01-46-22-60-70, FAX: 01-47-63-01-01. Take Metro line #2 to Courcelles. It lies near Parc Monceau.*
Public transportation: 2. Metro stop: Courcelles.
Single: FR630–FR700. Double: FR630–FR700.
As a member of Relais du Silence, this hotel focuses on providing a peaceful stay for its guests. There are just 18 guest rooms in this renovated, former bordello. While modest in size, they are attractively furnished and include a telephone, minibar, TV, radio and private bath with hair dryer. Families particularly enjoy the spacious two level suite with private balcony on the top floor. Guests linger around the bar and the breakfast area, both of which are near the reception area. Service oriented in every respect, the cordial staff is eager to please. Credit Cards: V, MC, DC, A.

Edouard VII   FR1000–FR1130   ★★★★

39 avenue de l'Opera. ☎ *01-42-61-56-90, FAX: 01-42-61-47-73.*
Public transportation: 3, 7, 8. Metro stop: Opera.
Single: FR1000. Double: FR1130.

This traditional hotel first opened near the Opera in 1885. Following many years of improvements, it now offers luxurious accommodations. There are 80 rooms, each individually decorated and adorned with beautiful furnishings and modern appointments. Situated above a busy avenue, the double windows deafen the noise while the balconies allow for good people watching. Each is equipped with a telephone, TV, minibar and private bath or shower. There are four suites available, and the hotel is wheelchair accessible. A French restaurant serves sumptuous meals, and the American style bar hosts jazz bands occasionally. The Edouard serves its business travelers and vacation travelers well. Features: wheelchair-access rooms, air conditioning in rooms, balcony or patio, in-room mini-bars, in-room conference facilities. Credit Cards: V, DC, A, E.

George V   FR1800–FR3900   ★★★★

31 avenue George V. ☎ *225-5843, 01-47-23-54-00, FAX: 01-47-20-06-49. Take Metro line #1 to George V. It lies on Avenue George between the Seine and the Champs-Elysées.*
Public transportation: 1. Metro stop: George V.
Single: FR1800–FR2300. Double: FR2500–FR3900.
This cosmopolitan hotel first lavished its guests with superior service in luxurious surroundings in 1928. Its latest improvements in 1992 continue its commitment to consistently high standards of maintenance. Guests delight in the dining options which include a gastronomic dream called Les Princes, a brasserie, a bar and a quaint tea room. All of the public areas are handsomely furnished and adorned with antiques, tapestries, sculptures and original paintings including Renoir's "Le Vase des Roses." The 260 plush accommodations are air-conditioned and include cable TV, radio, telephone, minibar, bath with bidet, hair dryer and robes and some rooms with a balcony. A full menu is available with 24-hour room service. Other services include hairdressing, baby-sitting, car rental, chauffeur, laundry, dry clean-

ing and concierge. A grand choice under skillful management. Features: air conditioning in rooms, balcony or patio, in-room conference facilities. Credit Cards: All Major.

Hotel Lido   FR850–FR970   ★ ★ ★

4 passage de la Madeleine. ☎ *528-1234, 01-42-66-27-37, FAX: 01-42-66-61-23. Take Metro line #8 or 12 to Madeleine. It lies between the Place de la Concorde and the Madeleine.*
Public transportation: 8, 12. Metro stop: Madeleine.
Single: FR850. Double: FR970.
A definite charmer, the Lido revels in its Right Bank location within close walking distance to many of the major sights and the Champs-Elysées. Distinctive characteristics include exposed wooden beams, beautiful antiques and a small garden. The 32 guest rooms come with a telephone, TV, minibar and private bath or shower with a hair dryer. About half of the rooms are air-conditioned. Although a bit cozy in size, the rooms are delightfully decorated in loving detail. Guests enjoy an included breakfast in the vaulted cellar. The smart, pleasant staff speaks English and guarantees an enjoyable stay. Features: air conditioning in rooms, in-room minibars. Credit Cards: V, MC, DC, A.

Hotel de Crillon   FR2450–FR3400   ★ ★ ★ ★ ★

10 place de la Concorde. ☎ *01-44-71-15-00, FAX: 01-44-71-15-02. Take Metro line #1, 8 or 12 to Concorde. It lies just north of Champs-Elysées.*
Public transportation: 1, 8, 12. Metro stop: Concorde.
Single: FR2450–FR2700. Double: FR3100–FR3400.
Originally constructed in the 18th century under orders of Louis XV, this classic palace rates as one of the grandest hotels in Paris. Ideally located on the Right Bank in picturesque surroundings, this hotel's prestige has attracted former guests such as Michael Jackson, Richard Nixon and countless other well known figures. Exquisitely designed public areas include a marble lobby, two restaurants, courtyard patio, tea room, sitting rooms and cocktail lounges. Guests are invited to utilize the 24-hour room service, 24-hour concierge service and available babysitting. Each of the 163 guest rooms is air-conditioned and equipped with a TV, telephone, radio, minibar, marble bath with hair dryer and some with a terrace and marble fireplace. Keen attention to detail in design, decoration, furnishings, maintenance and smart staffing have established this deluxe hotel as a hallmark of luxury. Features: air conditioning in rooms, balcony or patio. Credit Cards: All Major.

L'Abbaye Saint Germain   FR830–FR1450   ★ ★ ★

10 rue Cassette. ☎ *01-45-44-38-11, FAX: 01-45-48-07-86. Take Metro line #4 to St. Sulpice. Walk south on rue de Rennes, and turn left on rue Cassette.*
Public transportation: 4. Metro stop: St. Sulpice.
Double: FR830–FR1450.
Here is a beautiful conversion of a convent from the 1600s, a classic meld of the charm of an earlier day with the function of today. There are 46 guest rooms, four of which are suites. While a bit cozy in size, the chambers demonstrate taste in decorations and elegance in furnishings. Some room layouts include alcoves and other unusual architectural nuances. Rooms on the first floor are the most desirable,

opening onto the garden. The public areas display fine antiques and comfortable furniture. The small bar serves delightful concoctions in a relaxing, peaceful atmosphere typical of the hotel. A diligent and attentive staff complements this fine hotel, making it a popular choice for return visitors. Features: air conditioning in rooms, balcony or patio.

L'Hotel Guy Louis Duboucheron   FR950–FR2300   ★★★★

13 rue des Beaux Arts. ☎ 01-44-41-99-00, FAX: 01-43-25-64-81. Take Metro line #4 to St. Germain des Pres. Walk north on rue Bonaparte to rue des Beaux Arts.
Public transportation: 4. Metro stop: St. Germain des Pres.
Single: FR950–FR2300. Double: FR950–FR2300.

This exquisite hotel, adorned with antiques and lavish decorations with an emphasis on velvet, has been operating since 1900. There are just 27 cozy guest rooms here, each individually decorated in such styles as the Cardinale room with an abundance of purple and the art deco room with furniture from Mistinguett. Room #16 is notable, considering Oscar Wilde died there. All rooms have air conditioning, telephone, radio, TV, refrigerator and bath with hair dryer. The two top floor suites feature balconies overlooking the church of St. Germain des Pres. In addition to 24-hour room service, guests enjoy sumptuous cuisine in Le Belier, breakfast in the vaulted cellar and relaxing social evenings in the piano bar. Quite a transformation from the hotel of the early part of the century, this unpretentious and proud hotel continues to offer its guests exemplary service.

La Villa Saint Germain   FR800–FR1600   ★★★

29 rue Jacob. ☎ 01-43-26-60-00, FAX: 01-46-34-63-63. Take Metro line #4 to St. Germain des Pres. Walk north on rue Bonaparte to rue Jacob.
Public transportation: 4. Metro stop: St. Germain des Pres.
Double: FR800–FR1600.

Overflowing with character, La Villa is the creation of designer Marie Christine Dorner. A unique display of colors and materials, this hotel has found a unique style. There are 35 guest rooms of smallish size and avant garde design. Each has a TV and a telephone. The jazz club and bar downstairs feature live music, and the rooftop patio provides a peaceful retreat. Always popular with the chic crowd, reservations are a must.

Le Bristol   FR2500–FR4150   ★★★★★

112 rue du Faubourg Saint Honore. ☎ 01-53-43-43-00, FAX: 01-53-43-43-26. Take Metro line #1 or 13 to Champs-Elysées-Clemenceau. Rue du Faubourg lies parallel to Champs-Elysées to the north.
Public transportation: 1, 13. Metro stop: Champs-Elysées-Clemenceau.
Single: FR2500–FR2900. Double: FR3500–FR4150.

Sumptuous to Le Bristol has been a symbol of elegance since 1924. Situated in a seven story building in an exclusive downtown shopping district, this hotel serves many dignitaries visiting the nearby Elysee Palace. With a multimillion dollar refurbishment completed in 1994, it enjoys a lavish display of antiques, period furnishings, paintings and tapestries. The list of amenities and services includes a fitness center, enclosed pool, sun deck, sauna, solarium, beauty salon, business center, massage treatments, laundry and dry cleaning and concierge services. Guests enjoy fine dining at the gourmet restaurant and a suave social scene at the piano bar. The 195 accommodations are spaciously designed and include climate control, sitting area, safe, radio, TV, telephone, minibar and marble bath with hair dryer, telephone and robe. Some rooms are available with a balcony. A cordial and intelligent staff complements the fine tradition of this dignified hotel. Features: pool, air conditioning, balcony or patio, in-room safes, fitness center. Credit Cards: All Major.

Le Britannique   FR510–FR620   ★ ★

20 avenue Victoria. ☎ *01-42-33-74-59, FAX: 01-42-33-82-65. Take Metro line #1, 4 or 11 to Chatelet.*
Public transportation: 1, 4, 11. Metro stop: Chatelet.
Single: FR510. Double: FR620.
This former Quaker mission from World War I boasts a fine city center address. Unpretentious in attitude and style, it was refurbished in 1994 and decorated with a fine collection of antiques. Family operated, this hotel is composed of 40 guest rooms. Tastefully decorated, each comes with comfortable furniture, a minibar, cable TV and private bath with hairdryer. Although the staff doesn't speak much English, the genuine welcome and personal attention are easily understood. Features: balcony or patio. Credit Cards: V, MC, DC, A, E.

Le Raphael   FR1950–FR3450   ★ ★ ★ ★

17 avenue Kleber. ☎ *447-7462, 01-4-28-00-28, FAX: 01-45-01-21-50.*
Public transportation: 6. Metro stop: Kleber.
Single: FR1950–FR2450. Double: FR2450–FR3450.
Situated close to the Place Etoile and the Arc de Triomphe, this statement of refinement and quiet elegance was constructed in 1925. A peaceful atmosphere inside is created with the fine carved wood paneling, tapestries, period furniture, dated paintings and plush carpeting. Many high profile clients seek out this low profile, yet pampering and luxurious hotel. There are 87 rooms, each with air conditioning, TV, telephone, radio, minibar, safe and bath with hair dryer and robes. Forty of the rooms are suites, and nonsmoking rooms are available. There is a quiet restaurant and an English-style bar. A courteous staff provides 24-hour room service, concierge services, car rentals and laundry and dry cleaning. An ideal hotel for the discriminating guest preferring tasteful elegance and personal attention over glitz and glamour. Features: nonsmoking rooms, in-room safes, in-room minibars. Credit Cards: V, DC, A, E.

Les Marronniers   FR450–FR970   ★ ★ ★

21 rue Jacob. ☎ *01-43-25-30-60, FAX: 01-40-46-83-56. Take Metro line #4 to St. Germain des Pres. Walk north on rue Bonaparte to rue Jacob.*
Public transportation: 4. Metro stop: St. Germain des Pres.
Double: FR450–FR970.
A true gem, this hotel is located in the heart of St. Germain. Set back from the street, its garden atmosphere sets the scene for a peaceful stay. There are 37 guest rooms available, all comfortable and quiet. Rooms on the top floor are unique and offer glimpses of Saint Germain des Pres. In addition to the two lounges downstairs serving drinks, there is a glass enclosed veranda where breakfast is served. Guests

relax under the two chestnut trees for which the hotel is named and enjoy personal attention and service.

Montana Tuileries   **FR580–FR1050**   ★ ★ ★

12 rue Saint Roch. ☎ *01-42-60-35-10, FAX: 01-42-61-12-28. Take Metro line #7 to Pyramides. It lies off of rue de Rivoli and rue St. Honore.*
Public transportation: 7. Metro stop: Pyramides.
Double: FR580–FR1050.

Situated close to the Tuileries and the Louvre, this hotel offers a choice location and the peaceful advantages of its address on a small street. The 25 accommodations are well-kept and include a telephone, TV and private bath. All are individually styled with an accent on elegance. Two rooms feature balconies. Always a delightful experience, this little hotel is popular with value minded travelers who insist on a high level of service. Features: balcony or patio. Credit Cards: All Major.

Pavillon de la Reine   **FR1300–FR1950**   ★ ★ ★

28 place des Vosges. ☎ *01-42-77-96-40, FAX: 01-42-77-63-06. Take Metro line #1, 5 or 8 to Bastille. It lies near the Picasso and Carnavalet museums.*
Public transportation: 1, 5, 8. Metro stop: Bastille.
Single: FR1300–FR1500. Double: FR1500–FR1950.

With origins to the 1600s, this hotel overflows with character and charm. The 53 accommodations are tastefully decorated in Louis XIII style with antiques and attractive furnishings. Each is air-conditioned and has cable TV, telephone, minibar and a beautiful marble bath. Windows overlook a garden, a courtyard or a small sidestreet. There are 23 suites available in the form of duplexes. A cozy establishment with kind management. Features: air conditioning in rooms, in-room safes, in-room minibars. Credit Cards: All Major.

Plaza Athenee   **FR2300–FR3430**   ★ ★ ★ ★ ★

25 avenue Montaigne. ☎ *225-5843, 01-53-67-66-65, FAX: 01-53-67-66-66. Take Metro line #1 or 9 to Franklin D. Roosevelt. It lies between the Seine and the Champs-Elysées.*
Public transportation: 1, 9. Metro stop: Franklin D. Roosevelt.
Single: FR2300–FR2740. Double: FR3010–FR3430.

Glamour found in every detail, this elegant hotel attracts a large share of celebrities and those involved in the fashion world. A professional and discrete staff of 400 lavishes guests with service unmatched by any other hotel. Its 211 guest rooms are roomy and feature climate control, cable TV, radio, telephone, minibar and bath with bidet, hair dryer, robes and telephone. Some standard rooms come with a Jacuzzi and a balcony, and the suites exude Old World charm with period style furnishings. Guests enjoy casual drinks in the two celebrity-frequented bars, one of which was where Mata Hari was arrested. The hotel boasts two gourmet restaurants, Le Regence and Le Relais Plaza. Courteous services include concierge, secretary, babysitting, hairdressing, laundry, dry cleaning, car rental and travel assistance. The hotel's roots to the early 1900s are apparent in its distinguished attitude and personal service. Features: air conditioning in rooms, balcony or patio, in-room mini-bars, fitness center, in-room conference facilities. Credit Cards: All Major.

Regina   **FR1550–FR1900**   ★★★★

2 place des Pyramides. ☎ *01-42-60-31-10, FAX: 01-40-15-95-16. Take Metro line #1 or 7 to Palais Royal. It lies near the Louvre and the Jardin des Tuileries.*
Public transportation: 1, 7. Metro stop: Palais Royal.
Single: FR1550–FR1700. Double: FR1700–FR1900.

An ideal address for visiting the Louvre or a stroll through the Tuileries gardens, the Regina continues to be a classic symbol of luxury. Operating since 1904, it now offers 130 large accommodations with beautiful furnishings, cable TV, minibar, telephone, safe, fax and computer hook-up, bath with bidet and hair dryer and some with air conditioning, balcony and kitchenette. There are 15 suites and separate nonsmoking rooms available. A magnificent lobby with early century woodwork, two restaurants and a bar delight the senses. An efficient staff provides room service, turndown service, concierge service, laundry and dry cleaning, car rental and travel arrangements. A first class hotel all the way. Features: air conditioning in rooms, balcony or patio, nonsmoking rooms, in-room conference facilities. Credit Cards: All Major.

Relais Christine   **FR1530**   ★★★★

3 rue Christine. ☎ *01-43-26-71-80, FAX: 01-43-26-89-38. Take Metro line #4 or 10 to Odeon. It lies between Saint Germain des Pres and Notre Dame Cathedral.*
Public transportation: 4, 10. Metro stop: Odeon.
Single: FR1530. Double: FR1530.

Occupying a former monastery from the 16th century, the Relais Christine opened in 1979 with all of the comfort of a modern hostelry. The Old World charm lives on within the 50 guest rooms and the lovely public rooms. Each of the rooms displays fine period furnishings and antiques, standard with air conditioning, radio, telephone, cable TV, minibar and marble bath. Split level suites are available, and the ground floor room boasts a private terrace. The lounge and the breakfast room set a relaxing scene. Always courteous, the personable staff is sure to please. Features: air conditioning in rooms, in-room conference facilities. Credit Cards: All Major.

Ritz   **FR2600–FR4170**   ★★★★★

15 place Vendome. ☎ *01-43-16-30-30, FAX: 01-43-16-31-78. Take Metro line #8 or 12 to Madeleine. It lies two blocks south of the Opera.*
Public transportation: 8, 12. Metro stop: Madeleine.
Single: FR2600–FR3200. Double: FR3200–FR4170.

The definition of elegance, this hotel is one of the most famous hotels in the world. Founded by Caesar Ritz in 1898, it is unrivaled by any other hotel in luxury and service. Such public figures as Coco Chanel, Ernest Hemingway and the Duke of Windsor have resided here. With an emphasis on exclusiveness, the hotel has bullet-proof windows in some of the rooms, and there is no lobby (supposedly to discourage paparazzi gatherings). The 187 guest rooms have retained their original charm with modern appurtenances. Each is adorned with lovely antique furniture and brass beds along with cable TV, telephone, radio, minibar, safe, marble bath (Caesar Ritz was the first to include private baths in guest rooms) and some with Jacuzzi. L'Espadon is the hallmark restaurant. Guests also enjoy the garden terrace restaurant, several bars and 24-hour room service. Leisure facilities include a health club, indoor pool and squash court. Guests admitted to the Ritz Club may attend classes at the School of Gastronomy and are invited to utilize the concierge, hairdresser, baby-sitting and business services. A courteous, intelligent, multilingual staff wrote the book on service, making the entire experience here unforgettable. Features: air conditioning in rooms, fitness center, in-room conference facilities. Credit Cards: All Major.

Royal Monceau   FR2100–FR3200

37 avenue Hoche. ☎ *01-42-99-88-00, FAX: 01-42-99-89-90. Take Metro line #1, 2 or 6 to Charles de Gaulle-Etoile. It lies between the Arc de Triomphe and the Parc Monceau.*

Public transportation: 1, 2, 6. Metro stop: Charles de Gaulle-Etoile.
Single: FR2100–FR2600. Double: FR2600–FR3200.

Popular with business and vacation travelers alike, this distinguished hotel was built in 1928 and received its most recent renovations in 1993. The 220 guest rooms are spaciously designed and traditionally decorated with a pastel color scheme. Each is air-conditioned and standard with cable TV, telephone, radio, minibar and beautiful marble bath. In addition to 24-hour room service and a piano bar, dining options include the Italian restaurant, Il Carpaccio, a courtyard restaurant, Le Jardin, and a specialty restaurant, Les Thermes, in the health club. The two gourmet restaurants provide creatively presented cuisine and first-class service. Leisure facilities are well maintained and include a health club, indoor pool, sauna, Jacuzzi, Roman style baths, squash courts and massage treatments. A well-equipped establishment certain to please the seasoned traveler. Features: pool, air conditioning in rooms, sauna, in-room minibars, fitness center, in-room conference facilities. Credit Cards: V, MC, DC, A.

Saint James Paris   FR1450–FR1700

5 place du Chancelier Adenauer, avenue Bugeaud. ☎ *01-44-05-81-81, FAX: 01-44-05-81-82. Take Metro line #2 to Porte Dauphine. It lies between avenues Foch and Victor Hugo.*

Public transportation: 2. Metro stop: Porte Dauphine.
Single: FR1450. Double: FR1700.

Residing in a château with origins to the turn of the century, this hotel opened in 1987. A former club of the elite, it now treats its guests with refined service and attitude. There are just 48 spacious, comfortable accommodations with air conditioning, telephone, cable TV, minibar, safe and bath with bidet. Guests are greeted by the period decor and welcoming fruit basket. Thirty-four of the rooms are suites, and most offer garden views. Dining options include an English-style restaurant, a brasserie, room service and drinks in the library bar. The relaxing facilities include a fitness center with a sauna and a Jacuzzi, rooftop conservatory and lovely gardens. With more than 100 people on the courteous staff, guests here bask in the fine service. Features: sauna, fitness center. Credit Cards: All Major.

Université   FR550–FR1300

22 rue de l'Universite. ☎ *01-42-61-09-39, FAX: 01-42-60-40-84. Take Metro line #12 to Rue du Bac. Walk north on rue du Bac to rue de l'Universite.*

Public transportation: 12. Metro stop: Rue du Bac.
Double: FR550–FR1300.

This former 17th-century private residence is now a friendly hotel. Université is beautifully decorated with beamed ceilings and period furnishings. Each of the 27 guest rooms is attractively, individually decorated in comfortable style and comes with a TV and a telephone. Some feature balconies while others enjoy a spacious feeling with high ceilings. Guests are invited to enjoy the bar in the hotel. A welcoming staff assures a pleasant and carefree visit. Features: balcony or patio.

Low-Cost Lodging

Hotel du College de France   **FR500–FR550**   ★★

7 rue Thenard. ☎ *01-43-26-78-36, FAX: 01-46-34-58-29. Take Metro line #10 to Maubert Mutualite. It lies across the street from the College de France.*
Public transportation: 10. Metro stop: Maubert Mutualite.
Single: FR500–FR550. Double: FR500–FR550.

Situated on a quiet street in the heart of the Latin Quarter, this little hotel offers comfortable Left Bank lodging. There are 29 bed chambers, all of which are modestly decorated in similar, subtle colors. Each is well-kept and equipped with a telephone, TV and modern bath with a hair dryer. Those rooms on the top floors are the most desirable, with vistas of the towers of Notre Dame and exposed wood beams. While there is no restaurant, breakfast is served for FR35 in the breakfast room downstairs. The comfortable accommodations and the amiable, English speaking staff make this a well-visited hotel. Credit Cards: A.

Where to Eat

A. Beauvilliers   **$$$**   ★★★★

52 rue Lamarck ☎ *01-42-54-54-42.*
Metro stop: Lamarck-Caulaincourt.
Lunch: Noon–2 p.m., FR360–FR480.
Dinner: 7:15–10:30 p.m., entrées FR360–FR480.

An enchanting, terraced Montmartre restaurant with a flower and bibelot-filled dining room. There's a mood of luxury, but the cuisine is not complicated, with such offerings as grilled turbot, leg of lamb with herbs and cassoulet. For dessert, try the *millefeuille* with chocolate and pistachios. Closed: Sun. Amenities: outside dining, reservations required. Credit Cards: V, MC, A, E.

Apicius   **$$$**   ★★★★

122 ave. de Villiers ☎ *01-43-80-19-66.*
Specialties: langoustines tempura, roasted sweetbreads on a spit.
Lunch: Noon–2 p.m., FR400–FR560.
Dinner: 8–10 p.m., entrées FR400–FR560.

Chef Vigato's lively Apicius proves the theory that modern French cuisine need not be quirky and quixotic to be acceptable. There's even a hint of bistro fare served in this suave dining salon; cod and pigs' feet appear regularly. The chef is masterful with potatoes, whipping them in a creamy sauce accompanying the *ris de veau* (sweetbreads) *comme a la broche.* A dish of langoustines cooked tempura style is a surprise, and a delight. Chocolate is redefined in a puff-pastry dessert the chef calls "passion-choco." Closed: Sat., Sun. reservations required. Credit Cards: All Major.

Arpege   **$$$**   ★★★

84 rue de Varenne ☎ *01-45-51-47-33.*

Metro stop: Varenne.
Specialties: smoked lobster, candied tomato, game in season.
Lunch: 12:30–2 p.m., FR600–FR880.
Dinner: 7:30–10:30 p.m., entrées FR600–FR880.

Alain Passard's controversial restaurant is like performance art or graffiti on the Metro. You'll always find people who will rave about things that are disagreeable or incomprehensible, because it's "uncool" to admit you don't like something that's *au courant*. In any case, Arpege is ensconced in a second-story room that is a case of studied minimalism. Apparently, too much decor gets in the way of enjoying this interesting cuisine. Indeed, some dishes are splendid, while others are bizarre. The courses seem more interesting than the main choices, with sweets (candied tomato stuffed with a dozen flavors!) the weak link in the food chain. Haughty service, but the quality and prices are high. (Nobody seems to disagree with that!) Closed: Sat. Amenities: own baking, reservations required. Credit Cards: All Major.

Au Grain de Folie $ ★

24 rue de Lavieuville ☎ *01-42-58-15-57.*
Metro stop: Abbesses.
Specialties: guacamole, vegetarian platter, apple crumble.
Lunch: 11:30 a.m.–3 p.m., FR60–FR100.
Dinner: 6–11:30 p.m., entrées FR60–FR100.

One of Paris' handful of strictly vegetarian restaurants (albeit clouded with cigarette smoke), located in Montmartre. The mixed-veggie platter is served in good-sized portions; try the organic wine. Outdoor tables. Amenities: outside dining, own baking, reservations not accepted.

Au Pied de Cochon $$$ ★★

6 rue Coquilliere ☎ *01-42-36-11-75.*
Metro stop: Chatelet les Halles.
Specialties: Pied de Cochon Grille.
Lunch: 24 hours, FR220–FR350.
Dinner: 24 hours, entrées FR220–FR350.

A must for the first-timer. Beautiful turn-of-the-century decor, huge portions of (you guessed it) pig's feet and piles of shellfish served by bustling waiters to crowds of diners. Amenities: outside dining, cafestop, reservations recommended. Credit Cards: All Major.

Au Trou Gascon $$$ ★★★

40 rue Taine ☎ *01-43-44-34-26.*
Metro stop: Daumesnil.
Lunch: Noon–2 p.m., FR290–FR390.
Dinner: 7:30–10 p.m., entrées FR290–FR390.

This bistro, helmed by the talented Andre Dutournier (whose *ravioli de foie gras* once set Parisian tongues wagging), may be somewhat past its prime. But Dutournier can still perform the same tricks with several other dishes, including a belt-busting cassoulet, and robust Chalosse ham. Splendid! There's a fixed-price lunch for FR200. Closed: Sat., Sun. reservations recommended. Credit Cards: All Major.

Baracane $$$ ★★

38 rue des Tournelles ☎ *01-42-71-43-33.*

Specialties: southwestern cuisine, cassoulet.
Lunch: Noon–2 p.m., FR220–FR250.
Dinner: 7–11:15 p.m., entrées FR220–FR250.

One must get here early to get a good seat, as it's small and popular, especially at lunch, with its FR95 fixed-price menu (FR120 at dinner). The cuisine is from southwestern France, which means a hearty, delicious and fattening cassoulet, made here with confit of duck. Whatever the restaurant lacks in space, the chefs more than make up for it with the sizable portions on your plate. Closed: Sun. Amenities: cafestop, own baking, reservations recommended. Credit Cards: V, MC, E.

Benoit   **$$$**   ★ ★

20 rue St.-Martin ☎ 01-42-72-26-76.
Specialties: Coquilles St.-Jacques, braised beef "Grandmother-style."
Lunch: Noon–2 p.m., FR450–FR600.
Dinner: 7–10 p.m., entrées FR450–FR600.

A bistro with haute-cuisine prices and a polished atmosphere. It's a nice change to eat your marinated beef and vegetables while seated on velvet banquettes (instead of the usual wobbly, time-nicked chairs around tables covered with checked cloths). Sorry, no credit cards or fixed-price menus. The wine list is especially distinguished-you may find better bargains here than on the food menu. Closed: Sat., Sun.

Carré des Feuillants   **$$**   ★ ★ ★ ★

14 rue Castiglione.
Metro stop: Tuileries.
Specialties: friture d'anguilles, Pauillac lamb, Bazas beef.
Lunch: Noon–2 p.m., FR450–FR570.
Dinner: 7:30–10:30 p.m., entrées FR450–FR570.

Alain Dutournier's Carré des Feuillants is still an unqualified success, both with the public and critics (his other restaurant, Au Trou Gascon, has been bruised a bit by negative reviews). Some years back the savvy chef restored this 17th-century structure in the middle of a tony Paris neighborhood into yet another showcase of southwestern regional cooking. The specialties change often, depending on the dictates of his purveyors, but some perennial favorites have included cuts of beef from the prized Bazas cattle and veal with cepes. Closed: Sun. reservations recommended. Credit Cards: All Major.

Chartier   **$**   ★

7 rue du Faubourg Montmartre ☎ 01-47-70-86-29.
Metro stop: Rue Montmartre.
Lunch: 11 a.m.–3 p.m., FR62–FR82.
Dinner: 6–9:30 p.m., entrées FR62–FR82.

Enormous budget restaurant with Belle-Epoque decor. Service is a little rushed, and you have to share a table, but the prices are hard to beat. Once a bouillon, or soup kitchen, it's still a bastion of the working class. Basic French cuisine, three-course fixed price meals, including dessert. reservations not accepted.

Chez Elle   **$$$**   ★ ★

7 rue des Prouvaires ☎ 01-45-08-04-10.
Metro stop: Chatelet–Les Halles.
Specialties: Warm lentil salad with bacon.

PARIS

Lunch: Noon–2 p.m., FR190–FR240.
Dinner: 8–11 p.m., entrées FR190–FR240.

This unpretentious bistro, decorated with risqué photographs, doesn't take many chances with the menu, and that makes regulars happy. A salad of warm lentils with bacon starts off many a meal. The desserts are the deceptively light kind, including creme brulee and creme caramel. Closed: Sun. Amenities: outside dining, reservations recommended. Credit Cards: V, MC, A.

Chiberta $$$ ★★★★

3 rue Arsene Houssaye ☎ *01-45-63-77-90.*
Metro stop: Charles de Gaulle-Etoile.
Lunch: Noon–2:30 p.m., FR600–FR800.
Dinner: 7:15–10:30 p.m., entrées FR600–FR800.

Although this restaurant's name is Basque, the cuisine here is creative, rather than traditional, with an emphasis on seafood. Filets of fresh fish are often prepared with herbs and braised or barely singed in the pan. The desserts are also light and healthy, but by no means dull; try the seasonal frais de bois with honey ice cream and raspberry sauce or the fruit soup with honey and pineapple sorbet. Chiberta is a fashionable media hangout, orchestrated by chef Phillipe Da Sava. Closed: Sat., Sun. Amenities: happening bar, own baking, reservations required. Credit Cards: All Major.

Crous (University) Restaurant $ ★

Various locations.
Specialties: Three-course meals for FR15.
Lunch: 11:30 a.m.–1 p.m., FR15–FR38.
Dinner: 6–8 p.m., entrées FR15–FR38.

You don't really have to be a student to eat at these university cafeterias, you just have to be willing to stand in long, long lines. Once you get to the head of the queue, though, the reward is a three-course meal for as low as FR15 (with student I.D.) or FR30. Most of them keep regular hours during the week, some are open weekends and school holidays. **Crous**, at *39 ave. Georges Bernanos,* in the 5th arrondissement (☎ *40-51-36-00,* Metro: Port-Royal) will give you a comprehensive list, and sell you a book of tickets. Some locations include: *3 rue Mabillon (6e),* Metro: Mabillon; *13-14 rue Dareau, (14th e),* Metro: St.-Jacques; *Cours la Reine (8th e)* Metro: Champs-Elysées. Reservations not accepted.

Faugeron $$$ ★★★★

52 rue Longchamp ☎ *01-47-04-04-31.*
Metro stop: Iena or Trocadéro.
Lunch: Noon–2 p.m., FR430–FR550.
Dinner: 7:30–10 p.m., entrées FR430–FR550.

This well-established restaurant showcases Henri Faugeron's innovative cuisine amidst splendid surroundings. There are glittering chandeliers and rich velvet wall coverings. The spacious room is punctuated by a futuristic kitchen with a bridge from which the chef can observe his crew. Faugeron's cookery is a smooth melange of the grand as well as the modest in terms of ingredients: Try the potatoes mixed with truffles *(parmentier de truffes aux fines epices)* or a calf's head terrine. Closed: Sat., Sun. Amenities: own baking, reservations required. Credit Cards: V, MC, A, E.

Grand Vefour $$$ ★★★★

17 rue de Beaujolais ☎ *01-42-96-56-27.*
Metro stop: Palais-Royal.
Specialties: ravioles de foie gras, creme truffee, veal sweetbreads with wild rice and beans.
Lunch: 12:30–2 p.m., FR520–FR750.
Dinner: 7:30–10:15 p.m., entrées FR520–FR750.

The 200-year-old Grand Vefour has undergone a renovation of both its cuisine as well as its salon. The chef is Guy Martin, one of the youngest and brightest in the City of Light. He uses only the best ingredients, producing robustly flavored fare, with an innovative touch every now and then. The lush decor borders on Baroque, with restored murals from Napoleonic times, gilded woodwork, comfortable banquettes and fine old bas-relief ceilings. The many-mirrored walls, though, might dismay claustrophobes. We're grateful to the owner, Jean Taittinger, for helping restore this exalted house to greater glory. Closed: Sat., Sun. Amenities: own baking, reservations recommended. Credit Cards: All Major.

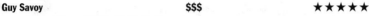

Guy Savoy $$$ ★★★★★

18 rue Troyon ☎ *01-43-80-40-61.*
Metro stop: Etoile.
Lunch: 12:30–1:30 p.m., FR570–FR700.
Dinner: 7:30–10:30 p.m., entrées FR570–FR700.

Guy Savoy is a whirling dervish: Proprietor of three additional bistros, he was able to refurbish the interior of this acclaimed restaurant in less than two months (after a blaze in 1993 wrought considerable damage). It's also hard to predict what will be on the menu, as dishes change often with the whim of this mercurial chef. What remains more or less constant (besides the high quality of the cuisine, the presentation and the service) is the wild game offered in season, usually winter. Recently, duck foie gras with sea salt made a splash on the scene. His apple tarts with ice cream are frighteningly good. Reserve weeks in advance. Closed: Sun. Amenities: own baking, reservations required. Credit Cards: V, A, E, A.

Jacques Cagna $$$ ★★★

14 rue des Grands-Augustins ☎ *01-43-26-49-39.*
Metro stop: St.-Michel/Odeon.
Lunch: Noon–2 p.m., FR460–FR630.
Dinner: 7:30–10:30 p.m., entrées FR460–FR630.

A longtime favorite with well-heeled locals and in-the-know expatriates, Jacques Cagna occupies one of the oldest buildings in Paris. The main dining room, with heavy antique timbers and wooden floors, is up one flight of stairs. The *turbot farci* and the John Dory with artichokes are splendid examples of melding delicious light flavors with color choices. If you top your meal with a *reine de saba* (a mouth-watering chocolate-fudge cake with English light custard), you might expire from ecstasy. Less costly than the big-name houses, and very pleasing gastronomically. Small, attentive staff. Closed: Sun. Amenities: own baking, reservations recommended. Credit Cards: All Major.

Joel Robuchon $$$ ★★★★★

59 avenue Raymond-Poincaire ☎ *01-47-27-12-27.*
Specialties: risotto of veal sweetbreads with truffles and parmesan.

Lunch: Noon–2:30 p.m., FR750–FR1200.
Dinner: 8–10:30 p.m., entrées FR750–FR1200.

You'll probably have to call the restaurant months before your arrival to eat here; there's a mile-long waiting list, as the amiable chef-proprietor Joel Robuchon occupies the highest place in the French culinary firmament. Only a lucky few pass through the portals of the two-story, turn-of-the-century house where he holds court. Interestingly, instead of a bar, there's a basement "smoking salon," where patrons can sit around puffing cigars and sipping cocktails, later returning for after-dinner drinks. Robuchon's cuisine involves ingredients you've encountered before, but in his hands, white beans are spun into creamed nectar, potatoes scale new heights, lamb sings and langoustines trill. A glance at the dessert cart (his metier is puff pastry) makes you want to say "I'll take one of each!" Ordering from the fixed-price menu (FR890–FR1200) here might ease the pain of decision-making. Closed: Sat., Sun. Amenities: own baking, reservations required. Credit Cards: V, MC, E.

Jules Verne $$$ ★★★★

Tour Eiffel, 2nd Floor ☎ *01-45-55-61-44.*
Metro stop: Trocadéro.
Specialties: crab souffle, milk-fed veal with spices.
Lunch: Noon–2:30 p.m., FR500–FR650.
Dinner: 7:30–10:30 p.m., entrées FR500–FR650.

Jules Verne occupies an upper tier of the Eiffel Tower (reached by private elevator), and it has such a glorious panorama that it's a wonder the chef even bothers to boil an egg. He does considerably more than that, however. Jaded Parisians used to snub patrons as tourists at the very mention of the place, but now they too are standing in the long lines waiting for a table. (Actually, it's often booked weeks in advance, so reserve early.) The crab souffle was splendid, as was the apple tarte with an apple cider sauce. There's a fixed-price lunch menu (except weekends) for FR290. Amenities: own baking, reservations required. Credit Cards: All Major.

L'Ambroisie $$$ ★★★★

9 place des Vosges ☎ *01-42-78-51-45.*
Metro stop: St.-Paul-le-Marais.
Lunch: Noon–2 p.m., FR650–FR900.
Dinner: 8–10 p.m., entrées FR650–FR900.

Co-owner and hostess Danielle Pacaud (husband Bernard is the chef) welcomes all patrons as if they are aristocrats, and you'll certainly feel like one, seated in an antique- and book-filled room decorated with exquisite taste. Chef Bernard is one of the champions of modern French cuisine, which he handles with a light, sure touch. His most celebrated dishes include a mousse of red peppers and delicate treatments of that once-scorned denizen of the deep, langoustines. His pastries, such as a bittersweet cocoa and vanilla ice-cream tarte, are in the Cartier class. Closed: Mon., Sun. Amenities: own baking. Credit Cards: V, E, A.

L'Etoile Verte $$ ★★

13 rue Brey ☎ *01-43-80-69-34.*
Metro stop: Charles-de-Gaulle/Etoile.
Specialties: scallops in coconut sauce, tarte aux pommes.
Lunch: 11 a.m.–3 p.m., FR125.

Dinner: 6:30–11 p.m., entrées FR125.
A simple eatery near a stellar neighborhood, the "Green Star" is always open, while others take their endless summer break. The rather plain dining room is often ablaze with creative flower arrangements. A vast a la carte menu with many choices is offered. Also daily specials and a FR60, three-course set meal, with beverage, dessert or cheese. Expect a long wait to get in. Credit Cards: All Major.

L'Incroyable $ ★

26 rue de Richelieu and 23 rue de Montpensier ☎ 01-46-96-24-64.
Metro stop: Palais-Royal.
Lunch: 11:45 a.m.–2:15 p.m., 5FR5.
Dinner: 6:30–8:30 p.m., entrées FR65–FR90.
It's incredible, but this restaurant near the arcade in the Palais Royale (it has two addresses) once charged the French equivalent of 65 cents for a three-course meal! That was back in the 1950s; today you can still get the same deal for $16. The presentation is attractive, and the quality is surprisingly high for the price. The apple tarte that is often offered as dessert is scrumptious. You can dine in either of two dining rooms or a courtyard. Closed: Sun. Amenities: outside dining, reservations not accepted.

La Bonne Franquette $$ ★★★★

18 rue Saint Rustique, Halfway between the Basilique Sacre Coeur and the Lapin Agile cabaret and Montmartre Vine down the hill.. ☎ 01-42-52-02-42.
Public transportation: 12. Metro stop: Abbesses.
Specialties: Escargots a l'ail Duck in wine sauce.
Lunch: 11 a.m.–2:30 p.m., FR50–FR150.
Dinner: 7–11:30 p.m., entrées FR50–FR150.
Set high atop the historic Montmartre hill, the Auberge de la Bonne Franquette has been a restaurant and formerly inn for over a century. It was a favorite hangout of Picasso and the other artists who lived just down the hill in the early 20th century, and earlier was painted by Vincent van Gogh ("La Guinguette," on display at the Orangerie). The food is traditional French, and while the place is not cheap, the ambience, helped along by the excellent house accordion player and guest cabaret singers and musicians, is the best of Paris. Amenities: outside dining, own baking, reservations recommended. Credit Cards: All Major.

La Cagouille $$$ ★★★★

12 place Constantin-Brancusi.
Metro stop: Gaite.
Specialties: baby mussels and scallops with leeks, shad in beurre blanc.
Lunch: Noon–2:30 p.m., FR280–FR380.
Dinner: 7–10:30 p.m., entrées FR280–FR380.
Located in the Place Brancusi, an offbeat neighborhood not known for quality restaurants, La Cagouille serves the freshest, and possibly the best, seafood in Paris, direct from ports all over France. Selections change daily, depending on what turns up, with a minimum of fuss; pure flavors are allowed to shine through. Owner Gerard Allemandou has also acquired a reputation for having the best Cognac selection around; some are very pricey, too. The fixed-price meals are FR250, including wine. Amenities: outside dining, reservations required. Credit Cards: All Major.

La Coupoule   **$$$**   ★★

102 boulevard du Montparnasse ☎ *01-43-20-14-20.*
Metro stop: Vavin.
Specialties: oysters, Indian lamb curry.
Lunch: 11:30 a.m.–2 a.m., FR220–FR400.
Dinner: 11:30 a.m.–2 a.m., entrées FR220–FR400.

Probably not the greatest food in the world, and the service can be abrupt (although if you're hungry, who needs charm), but it's a landmark. Shellfish selections from the stand-up bar are best. After 11 p.m., there's a supper menu for FR109 that includes oysters, steak and dessert. Fixed-price lunch, except Sundays, FR159. Amenities: happening bar. Credit Cards: All Major.

La Tour d'Argent   **$$$**   ★★★★

15 quai Tournelle ☎ *01-43-54-23-31.*
Metro stop: Sully-Morland.
Specialties: Pressed duck with orange sauce, peach flambée with Framboise.
Lunch: 12:30–2:30 p.m., FR800–FR1100.
Dinner: 8–11:30 p.m., entrées FR800–FR1100.

La Tour d'Argent remains a landmark, attracting North Americans and other outlanders, who comprise so much of its clientele. The spectacular penthouse views of the Seine and Notre Dame (illuminated at night) are the chief reasons for going; the food, in my opinion, is secondary (though the duck specialties are first rate!). Opposite the entrance is Comptoirs de la Tour, a smart boutique where you can purchase the restaurant's wares for sky-high prices. La Tour d'Argent is a Parisian fixture, and a costly one, especially after dark. You'll need a "tower of money" to dine here. Closed: Mon. Amenities: own baking, reservations required. Credit Cards: All Major.

Lasserre   **$$$**   ★★★★

17 avenue F.D. Roosevelt.
Metro stop: Champs-Elysées-Etoile.
Specialties: canard a l'orange.
Lunch: 12:30–2:15 p.m., FR500–FR800.
Dinner: 7:30–10:30 p.m., entrées FR500–FR800.

This venerable establishment has been on the scene for many a year, grew weary for a spell, and is now in good form again. The sumptuous decor is brightened by flowers, greenery, and a sliding roof that opens at the touch of a button to admit sunlight or moonbeams. Elegant touches consist of gold-rimmed plates, silver-necked carafes, antique-silver vases—everything is polished, including the service. Painfully high wine list. Reserve way in advance. Closed: Sun. Amenities: own baking, reservations required. Credit Cards: All Major.

Laurent   **$$$**   ★★★★★

41 avenue Gabriel ☎ *01-42-25-00-39.*
Metro stop: Champs-Elysées Clemenceau.
Specialties: Langoustines, veal kidneys with macaroni gratin.
Lunch: 12:30–2 p.m., FR600–FR1020.
Dinner: 8–11:15 p.m., entrées FR600–FR1020.

Classic and well known, also a bit set in its ways, Laurent nevertheless continues to draw business moguls, among others, for its singular, luxurious cuisine. A typical menu offering is a terribly rich (and pocket-picking) veal kidney topped with a pedestrian-sounding but delicious macaroni crust. Open in summer, the outside terrace is the stuff of pure romance. Closed: Sun. Amenities: happening bar, outside dining, own baking, reservations required. Credit Cards: All Major.

Le Bar a Huitres $$$ ★ ★ ★
112 boulevard du Montparnasse ☎ *01-43-20-71-01.*
Metro stop: Vavin.
Specialties: oysters, seafood platter for two.
Lunch: Noon–2 a.m., FR200–FR300.
Dinner: Noon–2 a.m., entrées FR200–FR300.
You can sit here until 2 a.m. and eat your fill of oysters and shellfish, or from a sea-food platter for two, which you can design to your taste from the varied menu. There are fresh fish dishes as well, including grilled sole meuniere, but most patrons prefer the other. There's a FR98 fixed-price menu at lunch, FR198 at dinner, with wine included. Patio seating available. Amenities: happening bar, outside dining, cafestop, reservations recommended. Credit Cards: All Major.

Le Grand Louvre $$$ ★ ★
Pyramide du Louvre ☎ *01-40-20-53-41.*
Metro stop: Palais Royal-Musée du Louvre.
Specialties: veal piccata with mushrooms.
Lunch: Noon–2:30 p.m., FR200–FR300.
Dinner: 7:30–10:15 p.m., entrées FR200–FR300.
Dining under the glass pyramid at the Louvre is not terribly expensive (especially for the FR170 fixed-price meal), and it certainly is atmospheric. The Southwestern-style cuisine was created by chef Andre Daguin. It seats 200, with room for 80 people in a private room. Closed: Tues. Amenities: happening bar, reservations required. Credit Cards: All Major.

Le Grizzli $$ ★ ★
7 rue St.-Martin ☎ *01-48-87-77-56.*
Metro stop: Chatelet-Le Halles.
Specialties: white bean salad with duck confit, veal stewed with cepes.
Lunch: Noon–2:30 p.m., FR190–FR230.
Dinner: 7:30–11 p.m., entrées FR190–FR230.
Bear-sized, hearty food from the Auvergne is served at this 90-plus-year-old estab-lishment. It's small, but there's a nice terrace for warm-weather dining. A fixed-price lunch is offered at FR110. Closed: Sun. Amenities: outside dining, cafestop, own baking, reservations recommended. Credit Cards: All Major.

Le Monde des Chimeres $$$ ★ ★
69 rue St.-Louis-en-I'lle ☎ *01-43-54-45-77.*
Specialties: sautéed chicken with 40 garlic cloves.
Lunch: Noon–2 p.m., FR270–FR300.
Dinner: 7–10:30 p.m., entrées FR270–FR300.
Expertly cooked, very authentic French family-style food is served here, in a house that's more than 200 years old. The highest-quality ingredients are used, and the menu runs the gamut from potted game meats to homemade desserts. There's a

fixed price meal for FR160. Well-chosen wine list. Closed: Mon., Sun. Amenities: own baking, reservations required. Credit Cards: V, MC.

Le Petit Plat **$$** ★★★

3 rue des Grand-Degres ☎ *01-40-46-85-34.*
Specialties: rabbit terrine in tarragon aspic, duck stew with prunes and juniper.
Lunch: FR60–FR175.
Dinner: 8–11 p.m., entrées FR160–FR175.

This bistro is highly touted, and with good reason—the food is wonderful. Excellent pastas and terrines, stews and roast chicken. You'll probably eat elbow-to-elbow with a stylish clientele. No table wine list. Closed: Mon., Sun. Amenities: own baking, reservations required. Credit Cards: V.

Ledoyen **$$$** ★★★★

carre Champs-Elysées ☎ *01-47-42-23-23.*
Metro stop: Champs-Elysées-Clemenceau.
Specialties: turbot roasted in biere de garde, smoked mussel and cream of cauliflower soup.
Lunch: 12:30–2 p.m., FR450–FR680.
Dinner: 7:30–10:30 p.m., entrées FR450–FR680.

One of Paris' most talked-about restaurants, this is a bastion of hearty Belgian favorites (including waffles and frites). It is situated in a parklike setting in the Carre des Champs-Elysées. Ghislaine Arabian, a female chef from Lille (in the northern reaches, by the Belgian border), has jaded Parisians clamoring for her beef stew with Gueze beer, turbot roasted in aged beer, and beer-flavored ice cream (cherry-flavored Kriek). French classics are also on the menu, including a sublime creme brulee, sans beer. Closed: Sat., Sun. Amenities: happening bar, own baking, reservations required. Credit Cards: All Major.

Les Noces de Jeanette **$$** ★★★★

14 rue Favart ☎ *01-42-96-36-89.*
Public transportation: 8, 9. Metro stop: Richlieu Drouot.
Specialties: Roquefort salad; salmon pate.
Lunch: 11 a.m.–2 p.m., FR60–FR120.
Dinner: 7 p.m.–midnight, entrées FR60–FR120.

Located just across the street from the historic Opera Comique, Les Noces de Jeannette (named after a particularly successful 19th century play) is decorated throughout the ground floor with posters from the theater and from early French movies. Upstairs are three separate dining rooms that may be booked for parties or groups, but you'll probably want to stay downstairs in the bistro section, where the delicious cuisine, the most traditional French available, can be yours for the excellent value 159-franc menu which includes entrée, main dish, cheese or dessert, aperitif before, wine during, and coffee afterwards. A steal in the heart of Paris' Opera district not to be missed. Amenities: own baking. Credit Cards: All Major.

Lucas-Carlton **$$$** ★★★★★

9 place de la Madeleine ☎ *01-42-65-22-90.*
Metro stop: Madeleine.
Lunch: Noon–2:30 p.m., FR580–FR900.
Dinner: 8–10:15 p.m., entrées FR580–FR900.

Lucas-Carlton remains one of Paris' more stylish restaurants and easily one of the most expensive. Alain Senderens' fixed-price menu is no bargain, unfortunately. The house itself is a venerable landmark with decor that goes back to the turn of the century. Chef-proprietor Senderens still maintains the magic of his craft, concocting such specialties as grilled and exotically spiced pigeon and ravioli stuffed with scallops. Upstairs, there's a private club for residents or frequent visitors to Paris; membership in the club is more cherished than enrollment in the Legion d'Honneur. Closed: Sun. Amenities: own baking, reservations required. Credit Cards: V, MC, A, E.

Michel Rostang $$$ ★ ★ ★ ★ ★

20 rue Rennequin ☎ *01-47-63-82-75.*
Metro stop: Ternes.
Specialties: truffles in season, petite chevres.
Lunch: Noon–2 p.m., FR550–FR710.
Dinner: 7:30–10 p.m., entrées FR550–FR710.

Possibly the brightest light in Michel Rostang's mini-culinary empire, this is also one of the more intimate havens in the city. The dining salon has a view of the chef and his busy kitchen, which is diverting and a little gimmicky. Lace curtains adorn the arched windows of the dining room, and textiled walls lend further softness; quiet music ripples the air. The Bresse chicken is his signature dish. Reserve a week in advance. Closed: Sun. Amenities: own baking, reservations required. Credit Cards: All Major.

Miravile $$$ ★ ★ ★

72 quai de l'Hotel -de-Ville ☎ *01-42-74-72-22.*
Specialties: salmon with herring, risotto with clams, chocolate-coffee mousse.
Lunch: Noon–2 p.m., FR220.
Dinner: 7–10:30 p.m., entrées FR220.

You'll pay only one price to eat here—FR220 will get you a delectable southwestern-style feast (not including wines, which can jack up your meal considerably). The dishes made with lobster, sardines and scallops are highly recommended. Elegant Italianate decor, outside terrace. Closed: Sun. Amenities: outside dining, own baking, reservations required.

Perraudin $$ ★ ★

157 rue St.-Jacques ☎ *01-46-33-15-75.*
Metro stop: St.-Michel.
Specialties: boeuf bourguignon.
Lunch: Noon–2:30 p.m., FR150.
Dinner: 7:30–10 p.m., entrées FR150.

Generations of starving students and their underpaid professors have made this country-style bistro their hangout for the FR60 three-course fixed-price lunch. At dinner, the fixed-price is FR100. Alas, the excellent wines are not included in either deal. Amenities: outside dining, reservations not accepted.

Polidor $$ ★ ★

41 rue Monsieur-le-Prince ☎ *01-43-26-95-34.*
Metro stop: Odeon.
Specialties: boeuf bourguignon, blanquettes du veau, rabbit in mustard sauce.
Lunch: Noon–2:30 p.m., FR90–FR170.

Dinner: 7 p.m.–1 a.m., entrées FR90–FR170.

One of Paris' national monuments, Polidor has been serving bistro food since 1845. Some of the more famous patrons have included Ernest Hemingway, James Joyce and Jack Kerouac. Fixed-price lunch FR55, dinner FR100. Amenities: cafestop, reservations not accepted.

Rendez-vous des Chauffeurs $ ★

11 rue des Portes Blanches ☎ *01-42-64-04-17.*
Metro stop: Marcadet-Poissoniers.
Lunch: Noon–2:30 p.m., FR48–FR75.
Dinner: 7–10 p.m., entrées FR48–FR75.

You'll find few tourists here, only neighborhood regulars enjoying the home-cooking of mom-and-pop owners Roger and Etiennette Lafarge. The produce is fresh off their own farm. Homemade desserts. Fixed-price meal at FR48. Closed: Wed., Thur.; reservations not accepted.

Taillevent $$$ ★★★★★

15 rue Lamennais ☎ *01-45-63-39-94.*
Metro stop: George V.
Lunch: Noon–2:30 p.m., FR530–FR720.
Dinner: 7–10 p.m., entrées FR530–FR720.

This Champs-Elysées area restaurant has been in the family of owner Jean-Claude Vrinat since its founding by his father in 1946, and, from that time, has enjoyed a long bask in culinary glory. The wine list itself dazzles with more than 500 choices. All details of creation and presentation are the province of chef Philippe Legendre, former apprentice to Joel Robuchon. His excellent kitchen produces such delights as Breton lobster sausage and a rabbit-and-spinach pie spiced with wild thyme. Guests enjoy all this largesse while seated on comfortable banquettes; reception is friendly, service smooth as silk. Closed: Sat., Sun. Amenities: own baking, reservations required. Credit Cards: V, MC, E.

Vivarois $$$ ★★★★

192 ave. Victor Hugo ☎ *01-45-04-04-31.*
Metro stop: Pompe.
Specialties: potato gallete with foie gras and truffles, duck with honey and spices, galantine of duck.
Lunch: Noon–2 p.m., FR410–FR690.
Dinner: 8–10 p.m., entrées FR410–FR690.

Prior to a few decorative changes a short time back, this restaurant was a study in modernity that some liked and many didn't. It's a little warmer now; the cuisine, however, has always been exemplary, as have the welcome and vigilance by Madame Jacqueline Peyrot. Certainly chef Claude is a virtuoso, concocting many dishes on the spur of the moment. Try the potato gallete with truffles and foie gras, if it's available. Closed: Sat., Sun. Amenities: own baking, reservations required. Credit Cards: All Major.

Barbizon

Le Bas-Breau   **$$$**   ★★★★

22 rue Grande, at the edge of the Forest of Fontainebleau. Located at Hotellerie du Bas-Breau. ☎ *01-60-66-40-05.*
Specialties: roast grouse, milk-fed veal chop, langoustines with fresh herbs.
Lunch: Noon–2 p.m., FR500–FR750.
Dinner: 7–9:30 p.m., entrées FR500–FR750.

You won't get out of this sumptuous hotel restaurant without spending a small fortune, but the flawlessly prepared classic cuisine eases the pain somewhat. Expect a romantic experience no matter what time of year you come—in winter a fire blazes in the elegant dining room; in summer and spring everyone eats outside in the courtyard. Game in season (mid-Aug.–Dec.) is a highlight. A fixed-price FR320–FR380 lunch, with wine, is offered weekdays. Amenities: outside dining, own baking, reservations required. Credit Cards: V, MC, A, E.

Directory

To and From

Paris is served by two international airports; Roissy-Charles de Gaulle and Orly. The former is to the northeast of the city; the latter to the southeast. There's no difference in terms of getting in and out of town; the airline you fly will determine which airport you use. Most transatlantic flights arrive at Charles de Gaulle. There are numerous options for entering the city from the airports, from direct buses to strategic points in town such as the Arc de Triomphe, to combined RER-Métro-bus passes that allow you to get to and from anywhere in the city from the airport with one ticket covering all three services for about FR40. Cabs take about 45 minutes to an hour to the center of town from either airport and cost between FR200 and FR300 depending on the time of day. You can also get to Paris from England on the Eurostar train using the Channel Tunnel, which will deposit you at Gare du Nord.

Tourist Offices

Bureau d'Acceuil Central, 127, avenue Champs-Elysées; ☎ *(33) 01-49-52-53-54.*
Gare d'Austerlitz; ☎ *(33) 01-45-84-91-70.*
Gare de l'Est; ☎ *(33) 01-46-07-17-73.*
Gare de Lyon; ☎ *(33) 01-43-43-33-24.*
Gare de Montparnasse; ☎ *(33) 01-43-22-19-19.*
Gare du Nord; ☎ *(33) 01-45-26-94-82.*
Eiffel Tower; ☎ *(33) 01-45-51-22-15.*

Rail Stations

The central information number for all of Paris' stations is ☎ *(33) 01-48-82-50-50*. There is a number for English-only speakers at ☎ *(33) 01-45-82-08-41*. The stations are each served by at least two Métro lines with the same name for the Métro station. Some of the complexes are huge; for example, at Gare de Montparnasse it can take you almost 20 minutes to get from the Métro platform to the platform from which your SNCF trains is departing if you are carrying bags. The following are the regions in France and Europe served by the six major stations:

Gare d'Austerlitz

The Loire Valley, the southwest (Bordeaux, the Paranoias), Spain and Portugal

Gare de l'Est

Eastern France (Champagne, Alsace, Lorraine), Luxembourg, Germany and Switzerland.

Gare de Lyon

Southern and southeastern France (Lyon, Provence, the Riviera).

Gare de Montparnasse

Brittany and TGV service to the southwest (Bordeaux and Toulouse).

Gare du Nord

Northern France, Britain, Belgium, and Holland.

Gare de St. Lazare

Normandy

Post Office

Main Post office: 52, rue du Louvre, 75001 Paris

There are numerous post offices throughout the city in every quarter. The ZIP codes in Paris are arrived at by adding the two-digit *arrondissement* number to 750; i.e. a Post Restante address in the eighth *arrondissement* would be 75008.

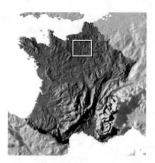

NEAR PARIS

Vaux-le-Vicomte combines monumental French gardens with 17th-century classical architecture.

What Makes Near Paris So French?

1. *Well, certainly not EuroDisney (now known as "Disneyland Paris"). The pseudonym doesn't disguise the fact its the wrong ears in the wrong place. It started out with a snowy-white image—no thrills, no alcohol. Forget it! Bowing to French tastes, wine was introduced along with some loops and corkscrews. Too little, too late. It's a loser—making France even more lovable!*

2. *Apuleius' Golden Ass in stained glass at the Chantilly estate.*

3. *The lily pond—ubiquitous in Monet's paintings—at his pink-stucco, green-shuttered house in Giverny.*

What Makes Near Paris So French?

4. *Louis XIV and the paintings he commissioned to depict himself as a Greek God (in his French dreams!), and his adoring family as lowlier gods and goddesses.*

5. Versailles, *the humble hunting lodge-turned-stupendously magnificent palace by Greek God Louis XIV.*

Within an hour or so of Paris are a number of great châteaux, one or two other attractions, some expansive parks and even farmland—incongruous in the region called Ile de France that is home to 10 million suburbanites. Information about each is given below, and although they each pertain to a town of sorts, you will find little else interesting enough to hold you away from Paris for more than a coffee or a quick meal. Most of these can be reached on the RER suburban trains, although in the case of Fontainebleau and Monet's house at Giverny you'll need to catch a cab from the station.

Versailles

Louis XIV, never known for shyness or restraint, once declared, *"L'Etat, c'est moi!"* meaning 'I am the state!' (Not as is often erroneously repeated, *"La Loi, c'est moi!"*, or I am the law, which rhymes better but wasn't uttered by the Sun King. His legacy of the Palace of Versailles certainly bears witness to such a megalomania. There are the paintings he commissioned of himself as a Greek god surrounded by his family, portrayed as lesser gods, and the unparalleled luxury and opulence of the palace and gardens, combined with the very way he selected (what was then an out-of-the-way place) and simply ordered, Captain Picard-like ("Make it so"), the construction of the greatest château in the world and a whole city around it. Employing the greatest architect (Le Vau), interior designer (Le Brun) and landscape gardener (Le Notre) of his time, Louis transformed the modest hunting lodge built in 1624 by Louis XIII into the single most magnificent palace on the globe. This is not an exaggeration. Even the laconic French, who have seen it all, take on a reverential tone when describing Versailles. *"C'est unique,"* they say with measured understatement, and it is. There's nothing like Versailles in the world, its ornate gilded sculpted ceilings and breathtaking Hall of Mirrors, its rows of oversized marble statues in the gardens, the "getaway" mini-palaces of the Grand and Petit Trianons, even the hamlet capricious Marie Antoinette had built so she could play at being a peasant girl.

Plan on spending an entire day at the palace. You'll enjoy a long walk around the gardens in between the main building with the state apartments and the Trianons. If you're really pressed for time concentrate on the state apartments, which are reached through a gallery of paintings called the *Gal-*

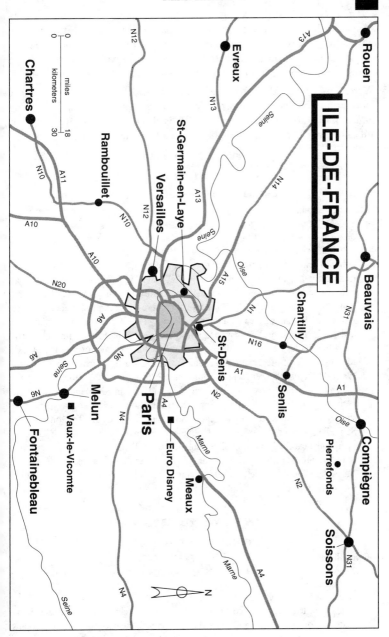

lerie de l'Histoire that shows in graphical form the passage of events and personages leading up to the creation of the palace. If you can visit during the summer, be sure to stay in the evening for one of the frequent *son et lumière* shows that light up the palace with lasers and the sky with fireworks. It's the nearest thing to being at one of the court balls in the 18th century.

Versailles is included on the Paris museum pass described above. For more information contact the tourist office at *7, rue des Réservoirs, 78000 Versailles;* ☎ *(33) 01-39-50-36-22.* Versailles is about nine miles west of Paris and can be reached on the RER-C line from Gare de Montparnasse.

What to Do

Yvelines

Historical/Architectural Sites

Château de Versailles   ★ ★ ★ ★ ★

> Versailles, ☎ 01-30-84-76-20. Rte N10 from Paris, park on place d'Armes
> Hours open: 9 a.m.–6:30 p.m. Special hours: Oct.–Apr. to 5:30 p.m.

In 1682, Louis XIV and his court left Paris for the Château de Versailles (once his father's hunting lodge), urging his nobles (none too gently) to live with him, effectively curtailing any plans of revolt. Louis XVI and Marie Antoinette lived here in untold splendor until forced to vacate by revolutionaries in 1789. Royalty is long gone, but the magnificence of this national treasure has been preserved. The palace was started by Louis Le Vau, and finished later by Jules Mansart. The gardens were laid out by Le Notre. You may look into the Grands Appartements (lavishly decorated by Charles Le Brun) and see your lovely self many times over in the Hall of Mirrors, scene of the Treaty of Versailles in 1919, which effectively ended World War I. Students, children, seniors admission FR26. Set away from the Château are the Grand Trianon, a tryst spot for Louis XIV and Madame de Maintenon, and the Petit Trianon, beloved by Marie Antoinette. She also tended a flock of pampered sheep in the Hamlet, directly behind it. Admission to the Grand Trianon is FR20; Sun. FR13; open daily, except Mon., 9:45 a.m.–noon and 2–5 p.m.; Petit Trianon, open daily, except Mon. from 2–5 p.m.; admission FR12; Sun. FR8. Note: From May through Sept., the price of your ticket includes the wondrous Grandes Eaux Musicales. You'll see the palace fountains spray and spout in concert with light, sound and music. (Sundays only, 4–6 p.m.) It's a glorious display; try not to miss it. Admission: FR40.

Where to Stay

Hotels and Resorts

Bellevue Hotel   **FR350–FR450**   ★ ★

> *12 avenue de Sceaux.* ☎ *01-39-50-13-41, FAX: 01-39-02-05-67. Close to the entrance of the château.*
> *Single: FR350. Double: FR450.*

A quaint little hotel with a convenient address on a lovely street for walking to the château. Constructed in 1850 and recently improved, the decor of the public rooms is modern and functional. Louis XV designs are prevalent in the 24 guest rooms, each equipped with TV, telephone, minibar and bath or shower. A small breakfast is served for FR40 in the lounge. Although a bit worn in areas and simple in furnishings, it's got character.Credit Cards: V, MC, DC, A.

Le Versailles   FR400   ★ ★

7 rue Ste-Anne. ☎ *01-39-50-64-65, FAX: 01-39-02-37-85. Near the entrance of the château.*
Double: FR400.

A very comfortable hotel situated close to the entrance of the château and the convention center, making it a solid choice for vacation and business travelers alike. The modern rooms, 50 in all, are well-designed with a good night's sleep in mind, but they are lacking in charm. All come with recently remodeled bathrooms. There is a garden and patio, and, while there is no restaurant, there are many dining facilities close by. Le Versailles provides consistently quality service in pleasant surroundings.Credit Cards: V, MC, DC, A.

Trianon Palace   FR1600–FR2400   ★ ★ ★ ★

1 boulevard de la Reine. ☎ *772-3041, 01-30-84-38-00, FAX: 01-39-49-00-77. Bordering the Château de Versailles.*
Single: FR1600–FR2100. Double: FR1900–FR2400.

The Trianon Palace is worth the indulgence even for travelers who plan on spending most of their time in Paris. This distinguished hotel first opened in 1910 and served as the headquarters for the Versailles Peace Conference in 1919. It was taken over by some Japanese investors in 1991 and overhauled with about $60 million worth of improvements. Pure magnificence is the result. Set in its own beautiful seven-acre park on the border of the château park, this palace defines luxury. There are 94 distinctive rooms, divided between the palace and the new building. From Old World to modern, each is decorated with antiques and attractive color schemes; standard amenities include cable TV, telephone, fax and computer hookups, minibar and spacious bath. An integral part of this hotel's reputation stands with its outstanding facilities, which include a medically supervised spa in the fitness center, indoor pool and tennis courts. No matter how one spends the day, be sure to wind up at least one evening dining in the gourmet restaurant, Les Trois Marches, and relaxing in the cozy piano bar. The smart staff provides 24-hour room service, baby-sitting and laundry service. An unforgettable experience in pampering and luxury found in few hotels. Features: pool, tennis. Credit Cards: All Major.

Where to Eat

La Flottille $ ★

Parc du Château, In the château park. ☎ *01-39-51-41-58.*
Specialties: Raw marinated fish with olive oil and anise; roast rack of lamb.
Lunch: Noon–3:30 p.m., FR90–FR115.

The only restaurant in the château park, this establishment was built in the late 19th century. A casual environment, the restaurant enjoys a location near the Grand Canal with outside tables. The brasserie serves snack foods all day, but the restaurant's dining room is popular with the lunch crowd. Various seafood dishes are

CHATEAUX OF ILE-DE-FRANCE

The Ile de France encompasses the city of Paris and has historically been the center of social, cultural and political power. With such intense focus on this relatively small geographical area, it is no surprise to find these châteaux surrounding the capital city in what was once undisturbed countryside and ideal hunting grounds for the upper classes on holiday.

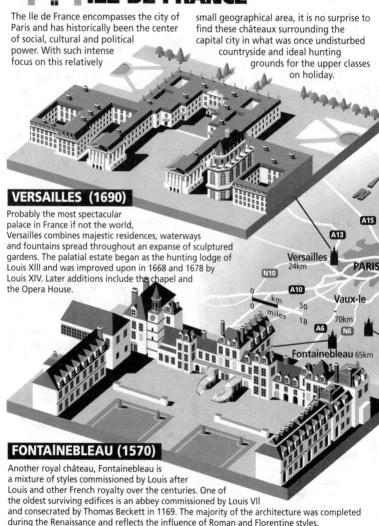

VERSAILLES (1690)

Probably the most spectacular palace in France if not the world, Versailles combines majestic residences, waterways and fountains spread throughout an expanse of sculptured gardens. The palatial estate began as the hunting lodge of Louis XIII and was improved upon in 1668 and 1678 by Louis XIV. Later additions include the chapel and the Opera House.

Versailles 24km — PARIS — A15 — A13 — N10 — A10 — Vaux-le — A6 — N6 — 70km — Fontainebleau 65km

0 km 30
0 miles 18

FONTAINEBLEAU (1570)

Another royal château, Fontainebleau is a mixture of styles commissioned by Louis after Louis and other French royalty over the centuries. One of the oldest surviving edifices is an abbey commissioned by Louis VII and consecrated by Thomas Beckett in 1169. The majority of the architecture was completed during the Renaissance and reflects the influence of Roman and Florentine styles.

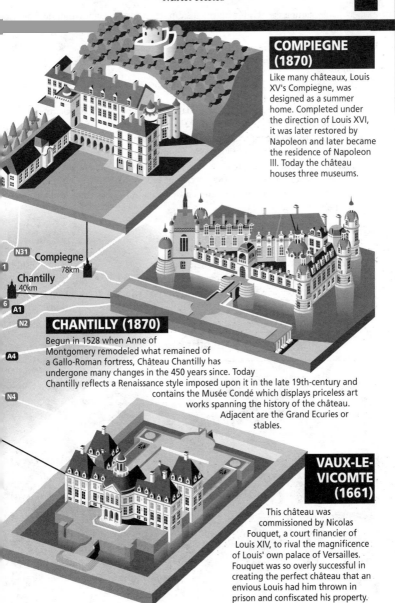

COMPIEGNE (1870)

Like many châteaux, Louis XV's Compiegne, was designed as a summer home. Completed under the direction of Louis XVI, it was later restored by Napoleon and later became the residence of Napoleon III. Today the château houses three museums.

N31 **Compiegne**
1   78km
Chantilly
40km
6 A1
N2

CHANTILLY (1870)

A4

Begun in 1528 when Anne of Montgomery remodeled what remained of a Gallo-Roman fortress, Château Chantilly has undergone many changes in the 450 years since. Today Chantilly reflects a Renaissance style imposed upon it in the late 19th-century and contains the Musée Condé which displays priceless art works spanning the history of the château. Adjacent are the Grand Ecuries or stables.

N4

VAUX-LE-VICOMTE (1661)

This château was commissioned by Nicolas Fouquet, a court financier of Louis XIV, to rival the magnificence of Louis' own palace of Versailles. Fouquet was so overly successful in creating the perfect château that an envious Louis had him thrown in prison and confiscated his property.

available starting at FR130 with the fixed-price menu. Amenities: outside dining, reservations recommended. Credit Cards: V, MC.

Les Trois Marches $$$ ★★★★★

1 boulevard de la Reine, In the Trianon Palace Hotel. Located at Trianon Palace. ☎ *01-30-84-38-00.*
Specialties: Foie gras with oysters; duck liver; lobster.
Dinner: 7–10 p.m., entrées FR175–FR300.

Considered one of the best restaurants in the region, Les Trois Marches attracts regular guests from Paris. Chef Gerard Vie, now using the most advanced facilities, serves his masterpieces in an intimate dining room during the cooler months and on the terrace in the summer months. In addition to his fabulous foie gras, salmon, braised pigeon and duck are always excellent choices. There are good wines for FR100 in his extensive and mostly pricey wine cellar. Fixed-price meals are FR270–FR750, with a lunch menu at FR260 on weekdays. Amenities: outside dining, reservations required. Credit Cards: V, DC, A.

Quai No. 1 $$ ★★★

avenue de St.-Cloud. ☎ *01-39-50-42-26.*
Dinner: 7:30–11 p.m., entrées FR70–FR180.

Model ships, barometers, wood paneling and seafood, of course. Popular dishes include fresh oysters, smoked salmon and sauerkraut with fish. Dispersed over two floors, the atmosphere at the Quai, one of the best values in Versailles, is pleasantly relaxed. Fixed-price meals start at FR120. Closed: Mon. reservations recommended. Credit Cards: V, MC.

Fontainebleau

Fontainebleau is Paris region's most impressive Renaissance château.

Like many of the great châteaux in France, Fontainebleau began life as a hunting lodge, this time in the 12th century, when the region was a favorite of the early Capetian kings. Besides the palace, which was largely built by François I (one wonders how he had time to work on Chambord, Blois and his other projects as well as this masterpiece) in the 16th century, the forest that the early kings hunted in is a 62,000-acre preserve crisscrossed with trails and paths that is a delight to explore. When you plan your visit to Fontainebleau be sure to allocate enough time for a leisurely stroll through its leafy glades.

The palace is a study in architecture and decoration through the ages, for even though François built the place in the early French Renaissance style, successive kings and even Napoléon used it as a retreat and placed their personal imprimaturs on the building—literally as well as figuratively; look for the insignia on the various eras' elements. The town surrounding the château built up in the 19th century when it was used as a cavalry base; it is charming but one gets the sense that it was thrown up somewhat post haste, which of course it was. The military continued to use the palace until this century, and between 1947 and 1967 it was the headquarters of NATO.

More information can be obtained on Fontainebleau from the Tourist Office at *31, place Napoléon Bonaparte, 77300 Fontainebleau;* ☎ *(33) 01-64-22-25-68.* The town is about 35 miles south of Paris on the A-6 autoroute, or it can be reached on the RER-A line form Gare de Lyon. Buses connect the station to the château (about two miles) every 15 to 30 minutes.

What to Do

Historical/Architectural Sites

Château de Fontainebleau ★★★★

Foret de Fontainebleau, ☎ *01-64-22-27-40. 45 minutes by train from Gare de Lyon*

Hours open: 9:30 a.m.–5 p.m. Special hours: Closed from 12:30–2 p.m. Closed: Tue.

Once the hunting lodge of Francois I and the scene of Napoleon Bonaparte's abdication, the Florentine-Romanesque château fronts one of the most beautiful national forests in France. Unlike Versailles, which is dominated by the tastes of Louis XIV, Fontainebleau luxurious galleries, ballroom, doorways and chapel reflect the individual styles of more than 30 kings, who used the palace as either a permanent or part-time residence. A FR32 ticket will get you into the Grands Appartements and the Salles Renaissances, which includes the Salle de Bal, designed by the Italian painter and architect Francesco Primaticcio, Napoleon's Appartements, and the Galerie Francois I, a riot of frescoes reflecting the human experience, as envisioned by Il Rosso Fiorentino. If you have time, tour the forest via bicycle; one company, **La Petite Reine** *(14 rue de la Paroisse,* ☎ *01-64-22-72-41)*, rents bikes for FR85 per day during the week, FR125 weekends. Admission: FR26.

Where to Stay

Hotels and Resorts

Grand Hotel de l'Aigle Noir   FR750–FR950   ★★★★

27 place Napoleon Bonaparte. ☎ *01-64-74-60-00, FAX: 01-64-74-60-01. About 3 km from the train station; across from the château.*
Double: FR750–FR950.
Albeit the most expensive hotel in town, its luxury is worth every franc. With a distinguished attitude and glamourous appearance, this former private mansion was converted into a hotel in the early 1700s. With views over the garden or of the château, the 57 guests rooms are delicately furnished with 18th-century reproduction furniture and blessed with climate control, cable TV, telephone, radio, minibar and private bath with hair dryer and robe. The most lavish rooms come with a balcony or Jacuzzi. Be sure to sample the fixed-price menu in the hotel's restaurant, Le Beauharnais, and relax in the piano bar for a casual drink. Leisure facilities abound, with a gym, indoor pool, sauna, massage services, indoor driving range and horseback riding offered at the hotel and tennis and golf facilities nearby. A very personable staff provides 24-hour room service, laundry service and concierge assistance. A well-rounded hotel with fabulous service, well-maintained facilities and luxury in every detail. Features: wheelchair-access rooms, pool, balcony or patio, nonsmoking rooms, fitness center. Credit Cards: All Major.

Hotel de Londres   FR230–FR500   ★★

1 place du General-de-Gaulle. ☎ *01-64-22-20-21, FAX: 01-64-72-39-16. Across from the Palace of Fontainebleau.*
Single: FR230–FR500. Double: FR230–FR500.
Occupying a choice location next to the Palace of Fontainebleau, this hotel exudes the warm welcome of a home. With origins to the days of the Second Empire, constant improvements over the years have still respected the stately 19th-century facade which boasts landmark status. There are 22 balconied rooms decorated in Louis XV style and modestly equipped with TV, telephone and bath. Breakfast is served for FR45, and other meals can be taken on the terrace with a fixed-price menu starting at FR130. Across from the Cour des Adieux, where Napoleon gave his farewell speech to his troops, this peaceful hotel creates an inviting ambience. Features: balcony or patio. Credit Cards: V, MC, DC, A.

Le Napoleon   FR600–FR700   ★★★

9 rue Grande. ☎ *01-64-22-20-39, FAX: 01-64-22-20-87. Across from the château.*
Single: FR600–FR650. Double: FR650–FR700.
Progressing a long way from its days as a coaching inn in the 1800s, Le Napoleon remains one of the most charming hotels in Fontainebleau. Enter through the lobby admiring the Asian rugs, attractive paintings, garden tea room and cozy bar just off the side featuring period furnishings. The 57 guest rooms are attractively decorated in pastel colors and equipped with TV, minibar, telephone and private bath or shower; request a room facing the courtyard, as they are quieter and more spacious. The restaurant, La Table des Marechaux, is known for some of the best dishes in town with fixed-price meals starting at FR130. A wonderfully formal hotel with unpretentious, courteous management at the helm. Credit Cards: V, MC, DC, A.

Where to Eat

Le Beauharnais   **$$**   ★★

27 place Napoleon-Bonaparte. ☎ *01-64-22-32-65.*
Lunch: Noon–2 p.m., FR155–FR200.
Dinner: 7:30–9:30 p.m., entrées FR155–FR200.

This is an elegant hotel restaurant with a garden setting, its serenity occasionally marred by conventioneers. Classic cuisine is served, with an emphasis on duckling, seafood and chocolate desserts. The fixed-price menus start at FR185. Amenities: outside dining, reservations required. Credit Cards: All Major.

Le Table des Marechaux   **$$**   ★★

9 rue Grande. ☎ *01-64-22-20-39.*
Lunch: Noon–2 p.m., FR125–FR175.
Dinner: 7–9:30 p.m., entrées FR125–FR175.

Surprisingly reasonable food is served at this luxurious restaurant in the Napoleon hotel. A generous fixed-price menu of classic dishes is available for only FR130. Even the dessert is an elaborately constructed affair, and a cheese platter is included (though wine isn't). Garden dining in good weather. Amenities: outside dining, own baking, reservations required. Credit Cards: All Major.

Chantilly

The castle at Chantilly is an anomaly; completely rebuilt in the late 19th century, it is a very precise replica of a Renaissance château that is only a century or so old. More interesting than the main building is the library (which houses the *Très Riches Heures du Duc de Berry*, the beautifully illustrated book of hours that dates from the early 15th century and provides the only written witness to the architecture of that time), and the Great Stables, built in 1721 and the only portion of the property to have lasted from the 18th century. More than 3000 horses are stabled in and around Chantilly, and the château is a national center for equestrianism and dressage. There is a very ho-hum museum of equestrianism, but the real treat is to watch the horses training for dressage shows.

For more information and for schedules of the horse shows contact the tourism office at *23, avenue du Maréchal Joffre, 60600 Chantilly;* ☎ *(33) 01-44-57-08-59.* The town is about 25 miles north of Paris and can be reached by road on the A-1 autoroute or by train on the RER-B line from Gare du Nord.

What to Do

Historical/Architectural Sites

Château de Chantilly   ★★★★

From the train station, walk down rue des Otages, and turn left at the end. About 15 minutes through the field. Or, take any bus from the station.

Once the throne of Louis XIV's cousin and general, the Conde, the Château de Chantilly sits on an artificial lake stocked with carp. A showcase of French Renaissance architecture, the original Grand Château was destroyed in the Revolution in an attack on such symbols of power and wealth. With the return of the Conde family in 1815, a mini-restoration led to the creation of the Petit Château. In 1830, the Duc d'Aumale inherited Chantilly from his uncle. In the years following (1875-1881), the main Renaissance château was rebuilt and now stands attached to the Petit Château. Shortly thereafter, the duc bequeathed the entire château and park to the Institute of France. His entire art collection, including works by Poussin, Watteau, Botticelli, Raphael and Fouquet, is seen in the Musée Conde. One of its most famous displays is its illuminated manuscript from the 15th century, showing the months of the year. The Musée Conde is in the Grand Château, which is to the right after entering the building. Both the Petit and the Grand Châteaux are *open daily, except Tues.; Mar.–Oct., 10 a.m.–6 p.m.; Nov.–Feb., 10:30 a.m.–12:45 p.m. and 2–5 p.m.; FR37.* Beyond the fountains are the incredible gardens, ingeniously designed by the royal landscaper, Le Notre. Different sections of the gardens were laid out in different centuries, from the French Garden in the 1600s to the English Garden in the 1800s. These gardens are a landscape architect's fantasyland, open from 10 a.m. to dusk; FR19; free with château visit.

Museums and Exhibits

The Grand Stables   ★★★

From the station, walk down rue des Otages and turn left at the end. Walk about 15 minutes through the field.

The Grand Stables at Chantilly were the idea of one Prince de Conde-Bourbon who believed he would be reincarnated as a horse. It once housed up to 240 horses and 500 hounds. There is now a Living Horse Museum with an in-depth exhibition of the history of the relationship of humans and horses, horse-race memorabilia, riding equipment and everything else any horse lover could possibly dream of. Dressage events (a show of elegance and fancy steps by tightly trained horses) are held at various times throughout the day. Races are held in June and other various times of the year. *Open Apr.–Oct., 10:30 a.m.–6:30 p.m., Wed.–Mon.; Nov.–Mar., 2–5 p.m.; FR45 (FR50 on weekends).*

Where to Stay

Hotels and Resorts

Hotel Campanile   FR268   ★★

route de Creil, N16. ☎ *16-44-57-39-24, FAX: 16-44-58-10-05. Less than 2 km north of town on the N16 towards Creil.*
Single: FR268. Double: FR268.

The sylvan surroundings of this hotel prove to be the most alluring reason to overnight here. Set on the edge of the forest outside Chantilly, this is a modern hotel opened in the 1980s. There are 50 well-furnished rooms functionally equipped with TV, telephone and private bath. Terrace dining overlooking the garden is available in the warm months, with meals starting at FR90. A well-managed hotel in a relaxing environment, the Campanile assures its guests of a good night's stay. Credit Cards: V, MC.

Low-Cost Lodging

La Caleche   **FR250**   ★

3 avenue du Marechal-Joffre. ☎ *16-44-57-02-55. On the avenue between the train station and the château.*
Double: FR250.
Decent lodging if one decides at the last minute to spend the night in town. Lying between the train station and the château, the location is definitely convenient. While not impressive in looks or feel, the 10 rooms do provide a simple night's lodging, and some of the rooms are equipped with private shower. The low price eases the basic-level standards. Credit Cards: V, MC.

Where to Eat

Le Relais Conde   **$$**   ★★

42 avenue du Marechal-Joffre, Across from the racetrack. ☎ *03-44-57-05-75.*
Dinner: 7–10 p.m., entrées FR105–FR140.
Occupying a building that once was a chapel, this charming restaurant sits across from the racetrack. The relaxed atmosphere of the several small dining rooms seems perfect for the horse-loving crowd that regularly dines here. An ideal lunch spot, the cassoulettes are popular appetizers, followed with one of the shellfish or meat dishes. The wine cellar is deep- and so must be your pockets. Fixed-price meals start at FR180. Closed: Mon. Amenities: outside dining, reservations required. Credit Cards: V, DC, A.

Le Tipperary   **$$**   ★★

6 avenue du Marechal-Joffre. ☎ *03-44-57-00-48.*
Specialties: Snail and shrimp stuffed ravioli.
Dinner: 7–10 p.m., entrées FR100–FR150.
A well-visited establishment, this small spot is in a 19th-century townhouse. Enjoy lunch at the outdoor tables or dinner inside the traditional dining room. Seafood dishes are plentiful, and the chef really knows his ravioli. The wine list is refreshingly affordable. Fixed-price menus start at FR160. Amenities: outside dining, reservations recommended. Credit Cards: All Major.

Compiègne

The château at Compiègne was a favorite haunt of Louis XV, as well as both Napoléons, so its decor and furnishings speak to a later, but still extravagant, age than that of Louis XIV. It is now a museum. Earlier history revolves around Joan of Arc, as in so many places in France, for it was here that she was captured and held prisoner before being burned at the stake by the British. The Armistice that ended World War I was signed in a railway carriage in a clearing in the forest here; 20 years later Adolf Hitler forced the French to sign another armistice, capitulating to his storm troopers, in the same carriage. Another military museum is the Musée de la Figurine, which displays the uniforms and equipment of soldiers from all ages and all countries on 100,000 small models. Finally, you may walk through the old town, pausing in front of the 15th-century City Hall, one of the last major Gothic buildings built in France before the Renaissance swept in, before stopping for a coffee and pastry at one of the inviting cafés.

For more information you can contact the Tourism Office at *place Hôtel de Ville, 60200 Compiègne;* ☎ *(33) 03-44-40-01-00.* The town is about 50 miles north of Paris and may be reached by car on the Lille-bound E-3 autoroute or by train from Gare du Nord.

What to Do

Historical/Architectural Sites

Château de Compiègne ★★

From the train station, cross the bridge over the river and head straight to place de l'Hotel de Ville. Continue to rue Magenta and turn left down any street to the château.
Hours open: 9:30 a.m.–5 p.m. Closed: Tue.

Built by Louis XV in the 18th century, this château was completed after his death. This became a palace o' romance for Louis XVI, and, later, Napoleon I. In 1770, teenage Louis XVI first met Marie Antoinette of Austria here, and later continued on to hold court at Versailles. In 1810, Napoleon I met his second wife, Marie Antoinette's niece, Marie-Louise, at Compiègne; their first meal together was in a dining room in the château which is visited during the guided tour. It was Napoleon III who brought the glory to Compiègne with his autumnal hunting season gala balls and week-long parties. On the tour, you'll see the secret door in the library of Napoleon I and get a look at the table where the son of Napoleon III etched the date in 1868 when his father wouldn't allow him to tag along on a hunting trip. Also in the château is the Car Museum and the Museum of Historical Figurines. The admission for the château covers both museums. Be sure to visit the Wagon du Marechal Foch in the surrounding forest, at Foret de Compiegne. Hitler danced his "jig of joy" here on June 22, 1940, after the French surrendered (He took particular delight in this venue, as it is the same spot the Germans signed the armistice to end WWI in 1918). This area is best explored by bike, available in town and at the entrance to the forest during peak tourist times. Admission: FR32.

Where to Stay

Hotels and Resorts

Château de Bellinglise   **FR600–FR1700**   ★★★★

Elincourt-Sainte-Marguerite. ☎ *03-44-96-00-33, FAX: 03-44-96-03-00. About 15 km from town in Oise.*
Single: FR600–FR1500. Double: FR675–FR1700.

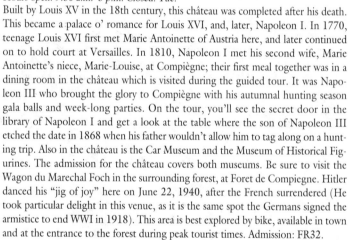

With all of the amenities of a cruise ship, minus the shuffleboard on the Lido deck, this hotel offers some fine leisure time. Active guests will love playing tennis, playing volleyball, burning up the running track and skeet shooting. After a grueling day of R&R, retreat to one of the 53 guest rooms in the former 16th-century château.

Each is handsomely furnished, quiet and equipped with satellite TV, VCR, telephone, minibar and private bath. Evenings mean socializing in the two lounges and bar after dinner in the restaurant. A traditional hotel situated in a wooded valley with two lagoons on the property, the entire facility is superbly designed. Features: tennis, in-room minibars, in-room conference facilities. Credit Cards: All Major.

Inns

Hostellerie du Royal-Lieu	**FR400**	★★★

9 rue de Senlis. ☎ *03-44-20-10-24, FAX: 03-44-86-82-27. About 2 km from town near the park land.*
Double: FR400.
Offering views over the sylvan park on the outskirts of town, this small hotel is the result of the time and effort spent by the friendly husband-wife owners. The 20 guest rooms and three suites, most with views over the lush garden, are lovingly decorated and looked after. Some even come with names such as Madame Butterfly and Madame Pompadour. Each room, whether decorated in such unique style or in period style, comes with TV, telephone and private bath. Breakfast is available for FR39, and meals in the rustic dining room start at FR200. A peaceful inn brimming with character. Credit Cards: V, MC, DC, A.

Where to Eat

Picotin	**$**	★★

22 place de l'Hotel-de-Ville, Near the Hotel de Ville. ☎ *03-44-40-04-06.*
While featuring a basically traditional menu, Picotin is also consistently good. There are a few inexpensive menus, all with delightful selections sure to please. A pleasant lunch spot or casual dinner choice. Amenities: happening bar, reservations recommended. Credit Cards: V, MC.

Rotisserie du Chat Qui Tourne	**$$**	★★★

17 rue Eugene Floquet, In the Hotel de France, in the old town. Located at Hotel de France. ☎ *03-44-40-02-74.*
Specialties: Lobster salad; duck; roast chicken.
Dinner: 7:15–9 p.m., entrées FR90–FR150.
The address of this restaurant is that of a building that has been here since 1665. With the rooms of the Hotel de France above, the dining room is just as charming-accented with lace, exposed wood beams and attractive floral prints. The fixed-price menus start at FR100 and tops out at FR210. Very attentive service makes this a delightful dining experience. Reservations recommended. Credit Cards: V, MC.

Giverny

If after seeing the extensive collection of Claude Monet's paintings in the Musée d'Orsay and the Musée de l'Orangerie, you want to get a more personal look at what inspired this great Impressionist, head for his home in Giverny. There, in a perfectly preserved pink stucco house (which cannot be toured, although you may look through the windows) surrounded by lush gardens and the famous lily pond he painted over and over again, Monet lived from 1883 until his death in 1926. The crowds are large at the small estate, and there is little to see other than the garden, but if you want to experience the play of light on the same plants and water the master saw, this is where you need to be. You can even buy seeds from the flowers in the garden in the gift shop to take home and plant—maybe you'll be inspired.

Monet's work did inspire a whole generation of young idealistic American painters, many of whom came to Giverny to study and work under their idol. The small Musée d'Art Américain, nearby the house, offers a collection of some of these painters' work.

Giverny, actually just inside the *département* of Normandy, is about 45 miles northwest of Paris and may be reached by train from Paris St. Lazare (alighting at Vernon and then a lengthy taxicab ride) or, preferably, by car on the A-13. For more information call the Claude Monet Foundation at ☎ *(33) 02-32-51-28-21*.

Claude Monet's house is now a museum honoring the famous artist.

What to Do

Museums and Exhibits

Claude Monet Foundation   ★ ★ ★ ★ ★

rue Claude-Monet, ☎ 02-32-51-28-21. Take a bus from the train station at Vernon for FR7. Hours open: 10 a.m.–6 p.m. Special hours: Open Apr.–Oct. Closed: Mon.

In 1883, Claude Monet rented a house in this small town of Giverny. He worked for 43 years here until his death. Considered the master Impressionist, he would paint the same scene several times, capturing the effects of light at different times of the day. Strolling through these gardens is a magical experience in itself—walking where Clemenceau, Renoir, Degas, Rodin, Cezanne and other friends of Monet walked. It's all here—the water lilies, the Japanese bridge, the weeping willows, the wisteria. The house is decorated in the pastel color schemes Monet knew, and his collection of Japanese prints adorns the walls. Nearby is the Museum of American Art, which houses the original works of the many American artists who studied here. One ticket covers the gardens, the house and the museum. A day here can be a wonderful and relaxing experience, but it can (and is more likely to be) a heavy dose of tourists in a very small area. Admission: FR35.

Monet's Gardens contain the water lilies and colors that the artist painted.

Parks and Gardens

Musée Claude Monet   ★ ★ ★ ★ ★

Giverny-Gasny, ☎ 02-32-51-94-65.
Hours open: 10 a.m.–6 p.m. Special hours: Closed from noon–2 p.m. Closed: Mon.

On the border of Normandy and the Ile de France, this is actually the house where the great Impressionist lived and where he painted some of his most memorable works. Among them are the Water Lilies series, which can be seen today in the Orangerie in Paris. Restored by American enthusiasts, Monet's pink-and-green house and famous gardens are now open to the public. On display in his studio are some rare Japanese prints from his private collection, but what you think are originals of his work are only reproductions. Still, you won't be disappointed; the decor within is a living canvas—even the kitchen is a sea of bright blue tiles. If you want to see the gardens alone, it will cost FR25; the most crowded months are May-June, when the curved, green Japanese bridge is covered in purple wisteria. Nearby, at *99 rue Claude Monet* (☎ 02-32-51-94-65), is the new Musée d'Art Americain Giverny, a fine museum filled with works by various Impressionist artists. Admission: FR35.

Where to Stay

Hotels and Resorts

Normandy   **FR325–FR375**   ★★

1 avenue Mendes-France. ☎ *02-32-51-97-97, FAX: 02-32-21-01-66. Northwest of Giverny, in Vernon.*
Double: FR325–FR375.
With so few choices for decent lodging near Giverny, this hotel's opening in 1990 was a welcome event. Situated in the center of Vernon, this simple hotel has 45 guest rooms, all comfortable and well-equipped. Request a room facing the back, as those are the quietest. The fine staff has already earned a reputation as being courteous, and the restaurant has become known for its hearty breakfasts. A smart lodging choice making visits to Giverny much more relaxing. Credit Cards: V, MC, A.

Inns

Hostellerie St.-Pierre   **FR550–FR645**   ★★

Chemin des Amoureux. ☎ *02-32-59-93-29, FAX: 02-32-59-41-93. About 30 km from Giverny, in St.-Pierre-du-Vauvray.*
Double: FR550–FR645.
On the banks of the Seine sits this small hotel in all of its design wonder. Triangular in layout, this half-timbered modern building in white resembles a classic Norman house, with a turret on one end. Quite an unusual sight from the exterior, the inside represents a more standard, functional approach to design. The 14 comfortable rooms are modestly decorated and equipped with central heating, TV, minibar, private bath, and most have a balcony overlooking the river. Guests relax in the sitting room or in the garden leading to the water before eating dinner in the dining room. While enjoying lovely views of the river, sit down to a delicious seafood dinner chosen from the fantastic specialty menu. The family owners deliver this experience with deft service. Credit Cards: V.

Where to Eat

Auberge du Vieux Moulin   **$$**   ★★

21 rue de la Falaise, Near Monet's house. ☎ *02-32-51-46-15.*
Dinner: 7:30–10 p.m., entrées FR70–FR110.
Residing in a late-19th-century mill, this address is within convenient walking distance to Monet's house. Enjoy your meal among original impressionist works hung on the walls of all of the small dining rooms. Besides fixed-price meals starting at FR140, salmon and various fowl dishes are featured on the a la carte menus. Closed: Sun. reservations not accepted. Credit Cards: V, MC.

Les Jardins de Giverny   **$$**   ★★★

Chemin du Roy, Near Monet's house. ☎ *02-32-21-60-80.*
Relax in this handsomely decorated, traditional dining room with rose garden views. The casual climate is ideal for the FR120 fixed-price lunches. For dinner, try the foie gras or any of the seafood dishes. Summer months practically require reservations. Closed: Mon. reservations recommended. Credit Cards: V, A.

Amiens

At 75 miles from Paris, Amiens is the farthest destination form the capital in this section, and it is worth noting that besides the world famous cathedral there is little of interest in the town. The cathedral itself, however, is well worth the trip, for it is considered by many to be the crowning glory of Gothic religious architecture in France (personally, I still prefer Chartres). The largest church in the country, it is 469 feet long and 140 feet high. The religious history of Amiens began in the fourth century, when a young Roman soldier took pity on a freezing beggar and, slicing his tunic in two with his sword, shared it with the man. Later ordained as a priest, the soldier would become St. Martin, bishop of Tours and one of the major developers of Christianity in France. While you're in the town you may want to visit the Musée de Picardie, the museum devoted to the history and culture of the region. It's not spectacular, but may be the only exposure you get to this *département.*

For more information contact the tourist office at *rue Jean-Catelas, 80000 Amiens;* ☎ *(33) 03-22-91-79-28.* Amiens can be reached on the N-1, or by train from Gare du Nord.

Where to Stay

Hotels and Resorts

Grand Hotel de l'Univers   **FR384–FR420**   ★★★

2 rue de Noyon. ☎ *03-22-91-52-51, FAX: 03-22-92-81-66. About 200 meters from the train station.*
Single: FR384. Double: FR420.
A modern four-story structure near the cathedral, this building was constructed in 1846. Traditional rooms are spacious, all 41 with satellite TV, telephone, minibar and bath. Some are furnished with antique tables and chairs. An elevator makes them all wheelchair accessible. Room service is available during most of the day, and there is a coffee shop on the first floor. A small bar and lounge is also in this Best Western-affiliated hotel. Breakfast costs FR50, and parking costs FR30. Features: wheelchair-access rooms, balcony or patio, in-room minibars. Credit Cards: All Major.

La Postillon   **FR300–FR500**   ★★★

16 place au Feurre. ☎ *03-22-91-46-17, FAX: 03-22-91-86-57. About 300 meters from the cathedral.*
Single: FR300. Double: FR500.

In an historical building a stone's throw away from the cathedral, Le Postillon offers fully equipped accommodations. There are 47 spacious rooms with varying levels of luxury and quiet (those in the back are the best). A lively pub keeps pouring until 2 a.m. Not particularly charming, but reliably efficient and friendly service. Features: wheelchair-access rooms. Credit Cards: All Major.

Where to Eat

Le Prieure   **$$**   ★★★

17 rue Porion, Near the cathedral. Located at Le Prieure. ☎ *03-22-92-27-67.*
Dinner: 7–9:30 p.m., entrées FR100–FR165.
In an 18th-century building, this hotel-restaurant serves its imaginative dishes in the dining room—complete with large aquarium. Let your palate pick up the freshness of the ingredients and the full flavor of the spices. Appetizers start at FR75, and fixed-price menus are FR125–FR200. Closed: Mon. reservations required. Credit Cards: DC, A.

Les Marissons   **$$**   ★★★★

68 rue des Marissons, Near the cathedral. ☎ *03-22-92-96-66.*
Specialties: Goose with honey; crayfish with tarragon sauce.
In one of the most beautiful sections of town sits this equally impressive restaurant. The knowledgeable staff serves Antoine Benoit's traditional dishes within this lovely building that once served as a shipyard in the 15th century; clement days translate to terrace dining. Pigeon is accented with black currants, salmon with crab coulis and lamb with garlic and thyme. The fixed-price meals start at FR135, during the week only. Jacket and tie required. Closed: Mon. Reservations recommended. Credit Cards: All Major.

NORMANDY

The cliffs at Etretat are spectacular at any tide, any season.

What Makes Normandy So French?

1. *William the Conqueror's clothing, reproduced and displayed upon a wax replica of Charlton Heston.*

2. *A propensity for eating death (the spoils of war, perhaps?) via various animal innards and lots of blood-drenched sauces–the foundation of this region's cuisine.*

3. *The spot where Flaubert wrote* Madame Bovary *in 1857.*

4. *Joan of Arc's barbecue site and bizarre memorial church that also encompasses restaurants and a food market.*

5. *A town legendary for a fig tree with some of Christ's blood drops stored within draws more thirsty pilgrims to its Benedictine distillery.*

A green, agricultural tapestry fraying at the edges of its rocky and history-fraught beaches, Normandy lies just northwest of Paris. Though quite small, the region has a 375-mile coastline and several major ports. With some of the heaviest rainfall in all of France, Normandy is lush and criss-crossed by many rivers, the mighty Seine among them, which finally reaches the sea in Normandy.

Normandy is served by four domestic airports, **Rouen**, **Le Havre**, **Caen** and **Cherbourg** as well as a small airfield at ritzy **Deauville/Trouville**. Many visitors arrive from England on **ferries** from Portsmouth and Southampton, alighting at Dieppe, Le Havre or Cherbourg. By road, Normandy is just a hop from Paris on the A-13 autoroute—Givérny, home to Monet, and Vernon are just over half-an-hour away, while you can reach Rouen in 90 minutes, Caen in two-and-a-half hours, and Cherbourg in about four hours. You may prefer to take the N-13, which besides being free of tolls affords a much prettier drive through the region.

History

Normandy is the site of perhaps more history per square mile than any other region—and in France, that's saying a lot. Beginning in the Dark Ages of the seventh and eighth centuries, the region repeatedly was plundered by Germanic and Saxon warriors who traveled across the relatively serene waters of what is now the English Channel to reach the region. The first people to firmly establish themselves, however, were the Scandinavian Vikings, who arrived in the ninth century. Unlike previous invaders, the Vikings built settlements to have their women and children. The name *Normandie* comes from the appellation then given to the Vikings—Norrmen or Norsemen, meaning literally the "men from the North."

By A.D. 911, the Normans had established a sufficiently lasting presence that King Charles the Simple of France recognized the region as an independent power in return for their pledge of allegiance to the French crown. Norman chieftain Rollon became the first duke of Normandie and made Caen his seat of power. During the next 300 years, Norman culture flourished, and the dukes created some of the most impressive architecture in Europe. Largely ecclesiastical, this includes numerous abbeys and cathedrals (often built for more political than divine motivations), among them the basilica at Lisieux, the cathedrals at Rouen and Bayeux, the twin abbeys of Caen, and of course, the most famous abbey-fortress of all—**Mont St. Michel**.

The Normans were aggressive warriors and they expanded their influence throughout Europe, and especially into England. By the 10th century, they had installed their own dynasty on the English throne, comprising a string of cousins of the dukes themselves. Meanwhile, in Normandy, the illegitimate son of the duke Robert the Devil, William the Bastard, was rising to power,

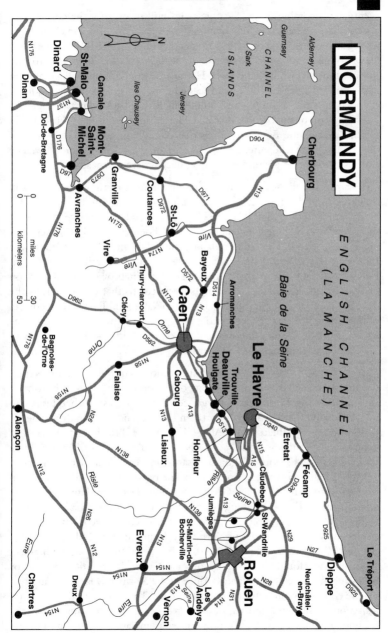

eventually becoming duke. A ruthless and brilliant warrior, he crushed the dissent that had begun to foment among some of his barons and became the undisputed ruler of the region. In England, an ailing King Edward the Confessor—William's cousin—designated the duke as his successor to the throne. Edward's right-hand man, Harold, swore to install William as king upon Edward's death, but instead made himself sovereign. William quickly rounded up an invasion force of 50,000 men and, backed by the pope and his newly compliant barons, defeated Harold in the Battle of Hastings in 1066, the last time England was ever successfully invaded. Harold himself died on the battlefield, after being struck in the eye by a Norman arrow. The story of the conquest is told in the magnificent **Bayeux Tapestry**.

William made his seat of power Caen, building a castle whose walls still stand today, and—in order to reverse his excommunication by the pope for marrying his cousin Mathilda—he also constructed the Abbaye aux Hommes/Eglise St. Etienne where he was buried. Following William, other Normans who became kings of England included Henry II and Richard the Lionhearted, whose lion heart is reputedly stored in the cathedral in Rouen. However, as England became a powerful country in its own right, the notion of a sovereign of one country being subservient to that of another, as the dukes of Normandy were still, became unworkable, and France took control of the region in 1204. This created a resentment that would fester over the next century or so, erupting in the 14th century with the 100 Years' War. This period was the bloodiest in Normandy's history.

More than 500 years later, the mid-20th century saw the Allied forces roaring across Normandy's beaches in one of the largest invasions in history on June 6, 1944. As World War II progressed, Hitler had established his Atlantic Wall" along the coastlines of northern Europe, and Normandy was heavily fortified. Nevertheless, the Allies, led by the British and Americans, determined that this was the spot to begin the reconquest of Europe from the Nazis. In 1942, a force of mostly Canadian troops had tried a landing at Dieppe, a major port in the northeast of the region, but the force was decimated by the heavily fortified German defenses. Two years later, on June 6, 1944, came D-Day. Beginning on the night of June 5 with advance paratrooper drops, Operation Overlord, as it was codenamed, saw 200,000 troops arrive on the beaches of Normandy during the first 24 hours. During the next 77 days, as 2 million Allied soldiers entered the region, the Battle of Normandy was fought and won by the Allies. A year later Hitler was dead by his own hand. The heroism and sacrifice of the Normandy landings and battles are commemorated throughout the region. There are countless cemeteries, monuments and museums, but I have found the most powerful testimony comes when I walk alone, in contemplation, along the beaches where tens of thousands of young men died during the battles. (See the D-Day Tour for a more complete history of the landings).

Much of Normandy was destroyed during the World War II, but a good deal of the region's patrimony remains. The Romanesque architecture in Caen, Bayeux and Rouen, is among the best in France, and even the reconstruction after the war is far from modern or ugly. Driving into and through the region from Paris, you pass dozens of small farming villages, crowded at first with Tudor-style wood-framed houses, then, farther to the north, houses built of stone. The Norman heritage is evident everywhere, as even the smallest village boasts a Romanesque church that dates back to the 11th or 12th century.

Cuisine

Normandy is the apple capital of France, and apples play a starring role in the region's cookery. It is not uncommon to find apples are the key ingredient in all three courses of a set-menu dinner. Apples also compose the main ingredient of the staple drink of the region: cider. *Cider* comes in two kinds—dry and sweet, and although it packs less of a punch than most wine (with an alcohol content of about five percent), it is nevertheless very definitely an alcoholic beverage. A stronger product, *pommeau*, is often served as an aperitif, and apple-based brandy, called *Calvados*, is one of the region's specialties. Not to be outdone by its rounder cousin, the pear, also grown in abundance, produces *poiré*, a pear cider.

Naturally for a coastal region, fish and seafood feature heavily on the menu. Whiting, sole and cod, are winter catches; mackerel, mullet and turbot appear during summer, while flounder and plaice are on the menu year-round. Also popular are wildfowl dishes, including roast pheasant and grouse especially in the fall, and poultry from staid chicken to duckling and goose. The region is a prime dairy-producing area, guaranteeing a tremendous variety of cheeses including the world-famous Camembert and Neufchatel cheeses.

Upper Normandy

Rouen

Victor Hugo called Rouen the "City of a Hundred Spires."

The capital of the Seine-Maritime département, Rouen suffered badly during World War II, but miraculously, much of its historic beauty remains. The old city center contains several hundred half-timbered houses, built in the 15th and 16th centuries, and still lived in and worked in today.

The most important and impressive sight in Rouen, however, is the cathedral **Notre Dame**. The first and greatest monuments built by the Normans, the cathedral was dedicated by William the Bastard in 1064. Paid for in large measure by the sale of indulgences to those wishing to eat butter during Lent, the cathedral is now one of the foremost examples of Gothic architecture in the country. Over the years Notre Dame has been witness to some momentous history—Joan of Arc was tried and sentenced to death here (and burned in the Place du Vieux-Marché down the street). Monet painted the cathedral's southwestern facade innumerable times in a well-known series of early Impressionist works.

The cathedral is but the foremost of the many churches in Rouen—Victor Hugo, who used to hang out here, called Rouen the "City of a Hundred Spires." Other famous writers worked often in Rouen, including native son Gustave Flaubert, who wrote *Madame Bovary* here in 1857.

What to Do

Historical/Architectural Sites

Eglise St.-Ouen ★★★

place du General de Gaulle, ☎ *02-35-08-13-90. At the end of rue de la Republique.*
Begun in 1318, this former abbey church symbolizes the peak of High Gothic style. The walls were opened to include more window space, with the weight of the roof being displaced onto a few key points with flying buttresses. The church is no longer used, which leaves the interior empty and larger in appearance. Take a break and relax in the grassy park by the stream, a perfect afternoon rest stop. Another church, Eglise Jeanne d'Arc, place du Vieux Marche, was completed in 1979 with a very questionable cement-and-wood facade. Outside is a cross marking the spot where Joan of Arc was burned as a heretic. Inside are beautiful stained-glass windows from the Eglise St.-Vincent after it was destroyed during WWII. Finishing off the church tour is the Eglise St.-Maclou, at place Barthelemy. This pure 15th-century Flamboyant Gothic was begun in 1437. Its decoration of the doors (from 1552), stairs and gallery, however, is of the Renaissance. A grand example of the evolution of the Gothic style, as compared to the cathedral. Across the street from the Eglise St.-Maclou is the Aitre St.-Maclou. This cloister served as the church's charnel house (a building used to store dead bodies and bones) during the Middle Ages, which was in high demand during the bubonic plague. Witness the preserved cat cadaver through a glass panel to the right of the entrance, which was buried alive in the building's walls to exorcise dead spirits. Open daily, 8 a.m.–9 p.m.; free admission.

Gros Horloge ★★

rue du Gros Horloge. From the train station, walk down rue Jeanne d'Arc about 300 yards. Turn left down rue du Gros-Horloge.
Hours open: 10 a.m.–5:45 p.m. Special hours: Closed 11:45 a.m.–2 p.m.
Climb this 14h-century clock for an awesome view of the city and a close look at the small clockworks museum. The area surrounding the clock tower is deluged with tourists trying to see the early Renaissance houses which make this area so charming (when the tourists aren't around). The tower closes at 11:45 a.m. on Wednesdays. Admission: FR6.

Notre-Dame Cathedral ★★★★★

place de la Cathedrale, ☎ *02-35-89-73-78.*
Built between the 12th and 16th centuries, this is one of the finest achievements in French Gothic architecture. Despite having been rebuilt after a ravaging fire in 1200, it is in the Lanceolate style. The facade, immortalized by Monet in his many paintings of the cathedral at different times of the day and in different lights, has undergone a major cleaning to spruce up the white. Incidentally, most of those Monet paintings are in Paris, although one remains in Rouen's Musée des Beaux-Arts. From the romanesque Tour St.-Romain to the Flamboyant Gothic Tour du Beurre (this Tower of Butter was paid for by those wanting the privilege of eating butter at Lent), the detail is impeccable. In the 19th century, the steeple was added, making it the tallest in France. Guided tours of the spacious nave are available for

FR14. *Open Mon., 9 a.m.–7 p.m.; Tues.–Sat., 7:30 a.m.–7 p.m.; Sun., 7:30 a.m.–
6 p.m. Mass is held Mon., 7 p.m.; Tues.–Fri., 8 and 10 a.m.; Sun., 8, 9 and 10:15
a.m., and noon.* Admission: free.

Tour Jeanne d'Arc　　　　　　　　　　　　　　　　　★★

rue du Donjon. Near the train station.
Hours open: 10 a.m.–5:30 p.m. Special hours: Closed noon–2 p.m. Closed: Tue.
This is the last remaining tour of the chateau where Joan of Arc was confined. Visit
the dungeon where she was tortured, which a few hundred years later was used by
the Gestapo to torture the French Resistance members. The information inside tells
of Joan's trial and the chateau's history, in French. Students free. Admission: FR6.

Museums and Exhibits

Musée des Antiquites　　　　　　　　　　　　　　　★★

198 rue Beauvoisine, ☎ 02-35-98-55-10. In Cloitre Ste-Marie.
Closed: Tue.
This former cloister houses relics from Gallo-Roman, Merovingian, Viking, Renaissance, Greek and Egyptian cultures. *Open Mon. and Wed.–Sat., 10 a.m.–12:30
p.m. and 1:30–5:30 p.m.; Sun., 2–6 p.m.* Students free. Other unusual museums
are throughout Rouen. The Musée Le Secq des Tournelles, at the Eglise St.-Lau-
rent, *rue Jacques Villon (☎ 02-35-88-42-92)*, fills the church with a large collection of wrought-iron objects including locks, keys, grill work, jewelry, candlesticks
and weapons from the third through 19th centuries. *Open Thurs.–Mon., 10 a.m.–
noon and 2–6 p.m.; Wed. 2–6 p.m.;* FR13, students free. Then there is the Musée
de la Ceramique, *1 rue du Faucon (☎ 02-35-07-31-74)*, displaying interesting
Norman ceramics. *Open Thurs.–Mon., 10 a.m.–noon and 2–6 p.m.;* FR13. The
Musée Flaubert et d'Histoire de la Medicine, in the Hotel-Dieu at *51 rue de Lecat
(☎ 02-35-15-59-95)*, is the birthplace of Gustave Flaubert, the author of Madame
Bovary. The bedroom where he was born, in addition to family furniture and pain-
inspiring medical paraphernalia, is on display. *Open Tues.–Sat., 10 a.m.–noon and
2–6 p.m.;* free admission. Admission: FR20.

Musée des Beaux-Arts　　　　　　　　　　　　　★★★

place Verdrel, ☎ 02-35-71-28-40. One block up from the Tour Jeanne d'Arc.
Hours open: 10 a.m.–6 p.m. Special hours: Closed noon–2 p.m. Closed: Tue.
Renovations completed in 1994, this grand building has one of the finest collec-
tions of fine art in France. Portraits by David, Delacroix, Gericault, Veronese,
Velasquez and Ingres are just some of the important works here. A version of
Monet's Rouen Cathedral, one of his most famous studies, is also here. Easily the
most in-depth display of works of French and Flemish artists from the 16th through
20th centuries. Admission: FR20.

Where to Stay

Bed-and-Breakfasts

Le Chateau   FR240–FR360   ★★★

place de l'eglise. ☎ *02-35-34-29-70. About 25 km northeast of Rouen. Take the N28 towards Neufchatel and turn right on the D919 towards Buchy. Turn right heading towards Bosc-Roger.*
Single: FR240. Double: FR360.

Guaranteed to satisfy anybody's desire for a charming bed-and-breakfast, this chateau lies across from the church in this small town. Set among the rolling green grass and the trees, this chateau is a healthy dose of tranquility. There are 4 guest rooms, all cheerily decorated and furnished with complementing wood furniture, overlook the grounds and come with a spacious, private bath. Request a room in one of the turrets on either side of the building, as those are the most charming. The gregarious owners serve a complimentary breakfast and offer ideas for a day's activities. Possibilities include touring the area on bicycle, hiking or taking advantage of the nearby tennis, swimming and golf. Le Chateau receives nothing but accolades from its guests. Credit Cards: Not Accepted.

Hotels and Resorts

Hotel de Dieppe   FR425–FR585   ★★

place Bernard-Tissot. ☎ *528-1234, 02-35-71-96-00, FAX: 02-35-89-65-21. Across from the train station.* Rated Restaurant: *Le Quarte Saisons.*
Single: FR425–FR495. Double: FR475–FR585.

Operating since the late 19th century, this hotel has been under the same family management for four generations. While maintaining its traditions and pride, the hotel is improved constantly to maintain the comforts of a modern facility. The compact rooms are decorated in period or contemporary decor, and each comes with a TV, telephone, bath and double-glazed windows to buffer the train noise. A small breakfast costs FR40, and the hotel restaurant, Le Quatre Saisons, is a reputable establishment that serves wonderful Norman dishes with a fixed-price menu starting at FR140. Cheerful and helpful, the staff gives a flawless performance. Credit Cards: V, MC, DC, A.

Hotel de la Cathedrale   FR225–FR375   ★★

12 rue St.-Romain. ☎ *02-35-71-57-95, FAX: 02-35-70-15-54. Across from the Archbishop's Palace.*
Single: FR225–FR310. Double: FR275–FR375.

An inexpensive hotel with a prime location across from the palace where Joan of Arc was tried and behind the cathedral. Behind the timbered facade lie 24 accommodations, each simply furnished and equipped with a TV, telephone and bath or shower. Good for a stopover, the facility is immaculately kept and conveniently located close to the town sights. Credit Cards: V, MC.

Inns

Le Moulin de Connelles   FR500–FR600   ★★★★

40 route d'Amfreville-sur-les-Monts. ☎ *02-32-59-53-33, FAX: 02-32-59-21-83. About 30 km south of Rouen. Take the A13 and exit at Louviers.*
Double: FR500–FR600.

Perhaps the most exquisite accommodations of all of Normandy, Le Moulin is the archetype for all other inns. Formerly a mill and then a private home, this luxurious small hotel sits on the edge of the Seine, as part of it lies over the softly flowing river. Within the classic, gabled Norman structure are 7 rooms and 6 suites (FR800), each plushly carpeted, decorated with subtle colors and standard with TV, telephone, minibar and excellent bathrooms. The choice rooms offer views over the river, as does the restaurant which serves sumptuous regional specialties with fixed-price menus starting at FR140. On-site facilities include a heated pool and a tennis court, and the gracious inn lends guests boats to casually tour the Seine. Le Moulin is conducive to changes in travel plans for guests who can't bear to leave this French Shangri-la. Features: pool, tennis. Credit Cards: All Major.

Where to Eat

Brasserie de la Grande Poste   **$**   ★

43 rue Jeanne-d'Arc. ☎ *02-35-89-67-44.*
Specialties: Steak and frites.
Lunch: 11 a.m.–11:30 p.m., FR45–FR75.
Dinner: 11 a.m.–11:30 p.m., entrées FR45–FR75.

You'll feel a bit like a French sardine in this packed-to-the-gills, old-fashioned brasserie, circa 1800-something. The street in front of it is appropriately aged, as well. Don't worry too much about missing any appointments, the raffish waiters hustle patrons in and out with alarming speed. Fixed price, weekdays, lunch only, FR60–FR90. The decorator who designed the Pascaline bistro, *5 rue de la Poterne, (*☎ *02-35-89-67-44)* seems to have been inspired by the Brasserie's authentic decor; robust cooking, entrées start at about FR50; fixed price menu from FR95. Open for lunch from noon to 2:30 pm, and dinner from 7:30 pm–11:30 pm. Accepts Visa only. Cafeterias: Flunch, *60 rue des Carmes (*☎ *02-35-71-81-81); Jumbo 11 rue Guillaume le Conquerant (*☎ *02-35-70-35-88).* Markets: place du Vieux Marche, Tuesday–Wednesday, Friday–Sunday from 7 a.m.–12:30 p.m. Credit Cards: V.

Gill   **$$$**   ★★★

9 quai de la Bourse. ☎ *02-35-71-16-14.*
Specialties: lobster stew with cider sauce, millefeuille (Napoleon-style pastry).
Lunch: Noon–2:15 p.m., FR200–FR350.
Dinner: 7–9:45 p.m., entrées FR200–FR350.

Situated on the waterfront, this cheerful, tasteful dining establishment (devoid of frills) is the finest restaurant in town. Gilles Tournadre's menu is contemporary, with the bright flashes of invention typical of the genre. At lunch weekdays and Saturdays, there's a set-price menu for FR195, including dessert. Closed: Sun. Amenities: own baking, reservations recommended. Credit Cards: All Major.

L'Ecaille   **$$**

26 rampe Cauchoise. ☎ *02-35-70-95-52.*
Specialties: St.-Pierre fish with pan-fried octopus in an oyster "jus," apple soufflé with Calvados.
Lunch: Noon–2 p.m., FR190–FR250.
Dinner: 7–10 p.m., entrées FR190–FR250.

A nautical theme runs through this cool green dining room with equally soothing decor. At this primarily seafood-oriented restaurant, the sauces and spices are kept to a minimum in order to accentuate the natural flavors of the fish and shellfish. Eating lightly has its reward, however; this way you'll be able to thoroughly enjoy the house-dessert apple soufflé with Calvados (apple brandy) sauce. The fixed-price menu starts at FR145, but it goes up from there. Closed: Mon. reservations required. Credit Cards: All Major.

Directory

To and From

Arrive by train from Paris St.Lazare (75 minutes one-way) or by car on the A-13 autoroute or the more scenic N-13 road.

Tourist Office

25 place de la Cathédrale; ☎ *(33) 02-32-08-32-40.*

Railway Station

place Tissot and rue Jeanne d'Arc; ☎ *(33) 02-35-98-50-50.*

Post Office

45 bis rue Jeanne d'Arc, 7600 Rouen; ☎ *(33) 02-35-08-73-66.*

Dieppe

A major port and the site of the closest beaches to Paris, Dieppe has a long history of maritime activity. The town was traded to the nearby abbey of Mont Ste. Cathérine-les-Rouen by Viscomte Goselin D'Arques de Cigare in 1030 in exchange for the princely sum of 5000 smoked herrings annually. It was from here that early colonial expeditions set sail to discover Newfoundland and establish French-speaking Canada, and from here that the explorer Verrazano launched the expedition that culminated with the discovery of Manhattan Island. Traders later used the port to import and export goods they transported to Brazil, Africa and the Far East. Dieppe still depends on the ocean for a living: it is one of the major ports connected by ferry to England, and commercial fishing remains its biggest industry.

Beginning in the late 18th century, the wealthy in Paris began to come to Dieppe for a "sea cure" that consisted of living for a time in the healthful ocean air. In 1824 the Duchesse de Berry, a Parisian aristocrat, took to the sea, and shortly afterwards, sea bathing began to become fashionable. The establishment of a number of hot-water baths solidifed Dieppe's standing as the number-one beachside resort of the era, and it began to attract English tourists, including the writer Oscar Wilde. The "beach," however, is not for those wanting a sun-splashed recumbent day on soft sand. Normandy's beaches are pebbly and narrow, more interesting for their marine life in the tidepools and the backdrop of tall, chalky white cliffs.

What to Do

Beaches

Beaches ★★

The white-cliffed beaches, although pebbly, are popular with French and British weekenders. These beaches were the sight of the attempted landing on Aug.19, 1942, by Canadian and other Allied troops. This failed operation, with more than 3500 men lost, convinced the Allied forces that a beach landing was near impossible. Thus, the next attempt didn't come until D-Day.

Historical/Architectural Sites

Canadian Cemetery ★★

In Hautot-sur-Mer. Take bus #6 in the direction of Carrefour du Vallon, and exit at rue des Canadiens.

On Aug.19, 1942, Dieppe was the main target of Operation Jubilee, the first sortie since 1940. More than 7000 men, mostly Canadians, landed on the coast. Heavy losses were incurred, including 3500 Canadians. There are 944 gravestones in this cemetery, each one bearing a unique poem or inscription in English, honoring the soldiers.

Eglise St.-Jacques ★★★

rue St.-Jacques. In the center of town.
Hours open: 8 a.m.–6 p.m.

Although this church was founded in the 13th century, it is mostly pure 14th-century Gothic, covered in moss. Supporting the central tower, the transept is the oldest part of the church. Take note of the beautiful portals and the elegant decoration on the inside.

Museums and Exhibits

Chateau de Dieppe ★★

Above the beach, ☎ 02-35-84-19-76. Above the beach.

On the cliffs above the beach is the 15th-century chateau, reconstructed unimpressively with red brick and tinted glass. Inside is the city museum, with a collection of paintings, maps, ivory and some colorful prints of George Braque. *Open Mon.–Sat., 10 a.m.–noon and 2–5 p.m.; Sun. 10 a.m.–noon and 2–6 p.m.; Sept.–May, closed Tues.* Admission: FR22.

Pubs and Bars

Le Brunswick

rue St.-Remy.

This British-run bar is a hip spot for young crowds, music and occasional concerts. A different pace is at the well-known, relaxed spot, Le Scottish, rue St.-Jacques. A subdued, smoky atmosphere with more than 100 brands of beer and whiskey. The casino, at 3 boulevard de Verdun is a glitzy gambler's haven, and Dieppe's only disco is inside (*☎ 02-35-82-33-60*).

Where to Stay

Bed-and-Breakfasts

Domaine de Champdieu   FR400–FR450   ★★★

Gonneville-sur-Scie. ☎ *02-35-32-66-82. About 14 km south of Dieppe via the N27. After Totes, take the D50 on the right, then the D203. Look for the signs for "Chambres d'Hotes."*

Single: FR400. Double: FR450.

Hidden in the countryside south of Dieppe, this B&B is a charming example of classic Norman style with its white facade with exposed dark wood. The interior is beautifully furnished with antiques and paintings- no comfort is forgotten. Breakfast is available for FR50, and sumptuous evening meals by candlelight are served for FR400. The gracious, English-speaking host will gladly direct you to nearby golf, tennis and the beaches. Features: country location. Credit Cards: Not Accepted.

Hotels and Resorts

Hotel Windsor   FR130–FR315   ★★

18 boulevard de Verdun. ☎ *02-35-84-15-23. On the seafront.*

Single: FR130–FR315. Double: FR130–FR315.

The Hotel Windsor offers the best value in this port town mainly used for Channel crossing. Originally built in the late 1800s, this former private house for one of Napoleon's men turned into a hotel in 1930. It has the best maintained accommodations in town, with 50 rooms in all. Most come with a private bath or shower, all come with TV and telephone. Each is modern, comfortable and functional. Those with sea views are definitely the best bets. There is a decent, Channel-view restaurant with fixed-price meals starting at FR100. Credit Cards: All Major.

La Presidence   FR340–FR560   ★★★

1 boulevard de Verdun. ☎ *02-35-84-31-31, FAX: 02-35-84-86-70. Next to the Municipal Casino.*

Single: FR340. Double: FR560.

Situated below the chateau, this classy hotel opens onto the sea with a wall of windows allowing the light to flood the interior of the panoramic restaurant. The 88 rooms are modern and include TV, telephone and private bath. The food is average, but the view is fantastic. Features: air conditioning in rooms. Credit Cards: All Major.

Where to Eat

A la Marmite Dieppoise $$$ ★★★

8 rue St.-Jean, Near town center. ☎ *02-35-84-24-26.*

Specialties: Fish and shellfish soup.

Dinner: 7:30–9:15 p.m, entrées FR115–FR175.

Creator of the creamy fish and shellfish soup bearing the restaurant's name, other delights include a wide array of seafood dishes. The welcome is genuine and the service attentive. Fixed-price lunch meals FR90–FR220. Closed: Mon. reservations required. Credit Cards: V, MC.

Le Port $$$ ★★★

99 quai Henri-IV, At the harbor. ☎ *02-35-84-36-64.*

Dinner: 6–9:30 p.m., entrées FR90–FR120.

As one might expect from a harborside restaurant, Le Port's menu is dominated by seafood. The traditional dining room borders on elegance that is almost intrinsic of the 19th-century building in which it lies. With appetizers starting at FR45, fixed-price menus start at FR100, and, for those carnivores, there are a few meat dishes. Closed: Wed. reservations recommended. Credit Cards: V, MC, A.

Directory

To and From

By sea from England, by train from Rouen (one hour one-way) or by car from Rouen on the N-27 road.

Tourist Office

quai du Carénge; ☎ *(33) 02-35-84-11-77.*

Post Office

2 boulevard Maréchal Joffre, 76200 Dieppe; ☎ *(33) 02-35-06-99-20.*

Rail Station

boulevard Clemenceau; ☎ *(33) 02-35-98-50-50.*

Fécamp

The small town of Fécamp, located on the Alabaster Coast between Dieppe and Le Havre, became famous in the sixth century as the site of a religious miracle. According to the legend, a few drops of Christ's blood had been collected from the body of the Saviour by Joseph of Arimathea (who had provided Jesus with a tomb) and stored in a hollowed-out fig tree. The tree washed up on the beach at Fécamp, and the drops of blood spilled on the ground, a natural spring began to bubble forth. The site quickly became an important destination for Christian pilgrims of the era. There's a small chapel on the site of the spring, while the fig tree is kept in the oversized 11th-century abbey of the Trinity.

Today, more pilgrims visit the town for the Bénédictine distillery. The bitter liqueur, made from a secret blend of 27 plants and herbs, is the town's number-one product and the distillery, formerly operated by Bénédictine monks, the number-one tourist destination. The Alexandre Le Grand you see commemorated throughout the town in street names and restaurants named after him is not the ancient Greek explorer, but the man who discovered the lost recipe for the liqueur in 1863 after it had been lost during the French Revolution. Fécamp also has a thriving fishing industry and is a particularly pretty seaside village, well worth a visit while you are Upper Normandy.

What to Do

Historical/Architectural Sites

Abbatiale de la Trinite ★★★

rue Jacques Huet, ☎ *02-35-28-53-88. Off of boulevard de la Republique.*
Hours open: 9 a.m.–7 p.m.

A massive 12th-century Norman Gothic abbey church, the nave is 127 meters long (as long as Notre-Dame in Paris). Don't let the worn facade deter you, the interior is brightly renovated and worth a visit. Inside the nave is the relic that supposedly carried the blood of Christ from Palestine to Fécamp- the trunk of a fig tree. Also noteworthy are the tombs of two of Normandy's dukes—Richard I and II. The view from the 210-foot high central tower is the best in town. Admission: FR15.

Museums and Exhibits

Musée Centre des Arts ★★

21 rue Alexandre-Legros, ☎ *02-35-28-31-99. Near the abbey.*
Hours open: 10 a.m.–5:30 p.m. Special hours: Closed noon–2 p.m. Closed: Tue.

This museum is in a shady park and arboretum. Regional art and objects of porcelain, ivory, paintings, furniture and earthenware. The ticket is also good for admission to the Musée des Terre-Neuves et de la Peche, across town at *27 boulevard Albert 1er (*☎ *02-35-28-31-99).* Learn about the adventures of Viking cod fishers who sailed for the Newfoundland and their boats, equipment and artifacts. *Open daily 10 a.m.–noon and 2–6:30 p.m.; Sept.–June, Wed.–Mon., 10 a.m.–noon and 2–5:30 p.m.* Boat rides with a local fisher run, giving a good view of town for 45 minutes. They run everyday in July and Aug. for FR50. Contact Promenade et Peches en Mer, *15 rue Vicomte (*☎ *02-35-28-26-65),* or the tourist office for more information. Admission: FR20.

Palais Benedictine ★★★

110 rue Alexandre Le Grand, ☎ *02-35-10-26-10.*

This is both a distillery and a museum dedicated to the Benedictine monks who used an elixir or regional plants and oriental spices as a healing agent. The 27 individual ingredients are exhibited to see and smell, as well as the final product. Rediscovered by Alexandre le Grand in 1863, this liqueur is often mixed with brandy. The 90-proof is available for sampling at the end of the tour. *Guided tours are given daily, 9:30 a.m.–6 p.m.; Sept.–Nov. and Apr.–June, 10 a.m., noon, 2 and 6 p.m.; Dec.–Mar., 10:30 a.m. and 3:30 p.m.* Admission includes sampling. Admission: FR25.

Where to Stay

Hotels and Resorts

Hotel-Restaurant D'Angleterre   **FR150–FR300** ★★

91-93 rue de la Plage. ☎ *02-35-28-01-60, FAX: 02-35-28-62-95. One block from the sea.*
Single: FR150–FR300. Double: FR150–FR300.

A close walk to the casino, this hotel dates back to the turn of the century. The 30 guest rooms are simply furnished and fairly spacious. All come with a TV, and most come with a private bath or shower. Breakfast is available for FR26. Credit Cards: All Major.

Inns

Auberge de la Rouge   **FR350**   ★★

> *Commune de St.-Leonard.* ☎ *02-35-28-07-59, FAX: 02-35-28-70-55. About 1 km south of Fécamp.*
>
> *Double: FR350.*

The 8 guest rooms attached to this restaurant are modest and comfortable. After a dinner of lobster or scallops in this local-favorite restaurant, retiring to one of these rooms tops off a wonderful evening. All come with private bath. Credit Cards: All Major.

Where to Eat

Auberge de la Rouge   **$$**   ★★★★

> *route du Havre, In St.-Leonard, about 1km south of Fécamp.* ☎ *02-35-28-07-59.*
>
> *Dinner: 7–9:30 p.m., entrées FR140–FR215.*

Just out of town, this little inn was built in 1894 as part of the postal service. Featured are several traditional and contemporary dishes—all using wonderfully fresh herbs and spices. Game specialties vary with seasons, but duck, lobster and various seafood dishes are always sumptuous. An intimate and relaxed setting with attentive, non-intrusive service. Closed: Mon. reservations required. Credit Cards: All Major.

Le Maritime   **$$**   ★★

> *2 place Nicolas-Selles, Between the old town and the port.* ☎ *02-35-28-21-71.*
>
> *Dinner: 7–9:30 p.m., entrées FR110–FR180.*

Hot with the locals, Le Maritime occupies two floors of a corner building. While the downstairs is more casual, the upstairs dining room offers seats with a view. Seafood dishes are big here, especially the fresh shellfish. Appetizers start at FR50, and fixed-price menus start at a very reasonable FR110. If it's good enough for the locals.... reservations recommended. Credit Cards: V, MC.

Le Viking   **$$**   ★★★★

> *63 boulevard Albert-1er, Near the sea.* ☎ *02-35-29-22-92.*

Soaking in a beautiful water vista, Le Viking sets the scene for an entirely enjoyable dining experience. While variations of cod are the chef's favorites, the fowl is just as impressive. Fixed-price menus are FR100–FR250, and a la carte meals are FR300. Varying hours, but usually open until 9:30 p.m.

Directory

To and from

> *By train from Rouen (75 minutes one-way) or by car from Dieppe on the D-925 coastal road or the D-926 road from Rouen.*

Tourist Office

> *113 rue Alexandre Le Grand;* ☎ *(33) 02-35-28-51-01.*

Rail Station

> *boulevard de la République;* ☎ *(33) 02-35-28-24-82.*

Le Havre

Founded by King Françoise I in 1517 as a seaport to replace the silted-up harbors of Honfleur and Harfleur, Le Havre sits at the mouth of the Seine River. It is one of the main entry ports for travelers and freight from England.

Le Havre was almost completely destroyed during World War II, and the rebuilding has left it one of France's ugliest cities. An important port for centuries and the second-largest port in the country, Le Havre has a great deal of infrastructure in the form of warehouses, railway depots and lines, oil refineries, and the like. There is a lot of traffic, especially container trucks boarding the ferries to England, and the air quality is thus quite poor. Discouraged? You should be. Although there is an excellent fine arts museum and a great view from the steeple of the church, the overall quality of Le Havre is that of grimy industry and ill-conceived, ugly post-war urban planning. Thanks to a new road bridge across the Seine estuary, it is easier than before to drive down to the **Flowered Coast**, which mitigates a little in Le Havre's favor. But I wouldn't recommend going out of your way to get here.

What to Do

Historical/Architectural Sites

Eglise St.-Joseph ★

boulevard Francois.
Hours open: 9 a.m.–7 p.m. Special hours: Closed noon–2 p.m.
With a bell tower nearly 325 feet high, the view over Le Havre is the best reason to stop in here. The spartan interior has square pillars supporting a lantern tower, and small stained-glass windows letting the light pour into the nave. Admission: free.

Museums and Exhibits

Musée des Beaux-Arts ★★★

boulevard Kennedy, ☎ *02-35-42-33-97.*
Hours open: 10 a.m.–6 p.m. Special hours: Closed noon–2 p.m. Closed: Tue.
Built entirely of glass and metal, this sophisticated museum houses an outstanding collection of works by Eugene Boudin. Other artists represented here include Monet, Pissarro, Renoir, Sisley and Dufy. Be sure to check out the Maison de la Culture du Havre (Cultural Center), at place Gambetta. In this unusual structure is a modern theater and cinema, showing plays, films and temporary exhibits. Admission is FR27 for the productions. Unfortunately, it's closed July 20–Sept. Admission: FR10.

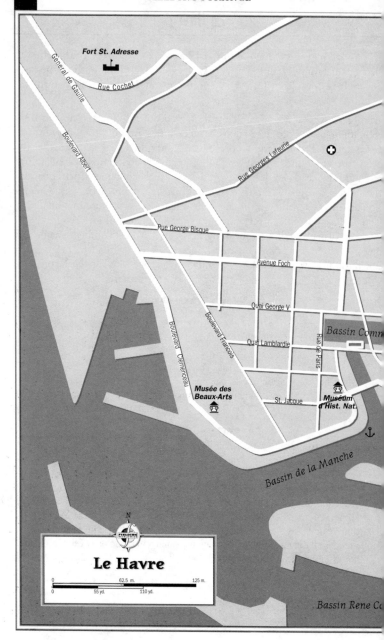

Fort St. Adresse

Rue Cochet

Général de Gaulle

Boulevard Albert I

Rue Geordes Lafaurie

Rue George Bisque

Avenue Foch

Quai George V

Boulevard François

Boulevard Clemenceau

Quai Lamblardie

Bassin Comm

Rue de Paris

Musée des Beaux-Arts

St. Jacque

Muséum d'Hist. Nat.

Bassin de la Manche

N

Le Havre

| 0 | 62.5 m. | 125 m. |
| 0 | 55 yd. | 110 yd. |

Bassin Rene C

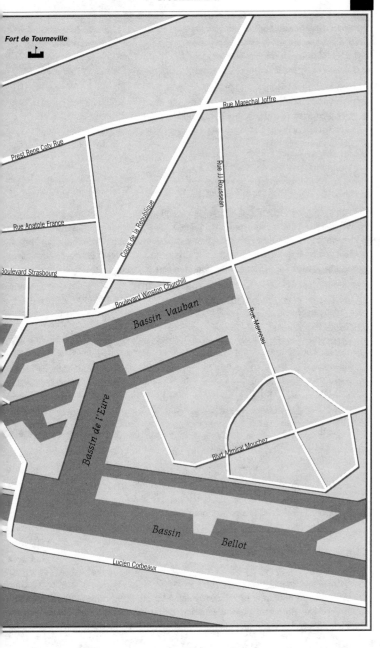

Where to Stay

Hotels and Resorts

Hotel Astoria   **FR240–FR260**   ★★

13 cours de la Republique. ☎ *02-35-25-00-03, FAX: 02-35-26-48-34. Opposite the train station.*
Single: FR240. Double: FR260.

An unpretentious hotel, ideal for an overnighter for those traveling by train. Constructed in the 1960s, this four-story building holds 37 rooms, each TV, telephone and bath. There is a restaurant with seafood dishes starting at FR53—definitely one of the most reasonably priced restaurants in town. While the rooms aren't all that special, the staff is sure to be helpful and friendly. Credit Cards: All Major.

Le Bordeaux   **FR300–FR500**   ★★★

147 rue Louis-Brideau. ☎ *02-35-22-69-44, FAX: 02-35-42-09-27. In the center of the port.*
Single: FR300–FR450. Double: FR350–FR500.

Facing the winter yacht basin, Le Bordeaux offers 31 modern, snug and soundproof rooms. Tastefully decorated, each comes with a TV, telephone, minibar and private bath. Although there is no restaurant, this is the best hotel in Le Havre. Breakfast is available for FR42. Features: in-room minibars. Credit Cards: All Major.

Le Mercure   **FR600–FR700**   ★★

chaussee d'Angouleme. ☎ *02-35-19-50-50, FAX: 02-35-19-50-99. Across from the Arts Center.*
Single: FR600. Double: FR700.

Near the ocean, Le Mercure's situation provides good views of the port's commerce docks. The 96 guest rooms, all decorated in the typical commercial fashion of a chain hotel, are large and well-furnished. Each comes with a TV, telephone and private bath. Highlighting the facility is the restaurant, Le Trois-Mats, where fixed-price meals begin at FR90. Breakfast costs FR52 extra. Credit Cards: All Major.

Where to Eat

La Chaumette   **$$$**   ★★★★

17 rue Racine. ☎ *02-35-43-66-80.*
Specialties: Lobster ravioli.

It doesn't get better than this in Le Havre. The supremely talented chef, Christine Frechet, works magic into her innovative dishes. She has mastered so many dishes, it would be foolish to single one out as her best. From lobster ravioli to skate with vinegar and celery, it is a gastronome's delight. *Closed Christmas eve–early Jan.; early May; and early Aug.–early Sept.* One might be tempted to arrange travel dates to Le Havre around the restaurant's schedule. Closed: Sun. Credit Cards: V, DC, A.

La Petite Auberge   **$$**   ★★★

32 rue Ste-Adresse. ☎ *02-35-46-27-32.*
Dinner: 7–9:30 p.m., entrées FR100–FR145.

A wonderful restaurant to linger over a good meal. Fixed-price meals from FR115, except Sat. dinner, make the experience that much more pleasant. Specialties include sole, lamb and filet mignon—of course, all accented with savory spices and sides. Deservedly popular, so call ahead for reservations. Closed: Mon. reservations required. Credit Cards: V, MC, A.

| **Le Monaco** | **$$** | ★★★ |

16 rue de Paris. ☎ *02-35-42-21-01.*
Dinner: 7:30–9:30 p.m., entrées FR70–FR150.
Guaranteed to be bustling, this contemporary restaurant features many exciting dishes. Try the smoked Norwegian salmon or the snails prepared in cider—both popular choices. Appetizers start at FR65, and the fixed-price meals begin at FR150. Pleasant service and atmosphere. reservations required. Credit Cards: All Major.

Directory

To and from

By sea from Portsmouth, England, by rail from Paris (two hours one-way), or by car from the east on the N-15 from Rouen, the A-13/A-15 autoroutes from Paris, or the D-940 from the Alabaster Coast.

Tourist Office

place de l'Hôtel de Ville; ☎ *(33) 02-35-21-22-88.*

Rail Station

cours de la République; ☎ *(33) 02-35-98-50-50.*

Post Office

rue Jules-Siegfried, 76600 Le Havre; ☎ *(33) 02-35-42-45-67.*

NORMANDY

Lower Normandy

Honfleur

On the opposite side of the Seine from Le Havre, the port of Honfleur dates from the early 11th century. The *Vieux Bassin* (old harbor) faces the sea without protecting jetties, and it forms the focal point of this charming town. The architecture is typical of northern fishing villages throughout Europe—tall, stone houses topped with grey slate roofs. The fishing industry is still going strong even though trade has been lost to Le Havre. You may catch a glimpse of carpenters building fishing boats down by the harbor using the same techniques and tools as their ancestors have done for hundreds of years.

Honfleur is known (primarily in Honfleur) as the birthplace of Impressionism. Boudin and Corot, whose work did indeed presage the coming of the true light-inspired Impressionists, painted canvases of the harbor here, and were succeeded by Monet himself, and today by countless amateur artists who outnumber the seagulls on the waterfront on a good day. Baudelaire lived here for a while, during which time he wrote the novel *Invitation au Voyage*.

Canadians will feel especially at home in Honfleur. The explorer Samuel de Champlain set sail from here on his way to discover the Great Lakes and Quebec. The town also was in the Canadian sector during the Allied invasion and liberation, and the chapel of Notre Dame de Grace is dedicated to all Canadians of Norman origin.

What to Do

Historical/Architectural Sites

Chapelle Notre-Dame-de-Grace   ★★★

Plateau de Grace. On top of the Plateau de Grace forested.

Besides the great views afforded from its hilltop location, the Notre-Dame is a lovely display of 17th-century architecture. As a final prayer point for many of the navigators who made the journey to North America, the chapel continues to be a well-visited site for pilgrims today. Of particular interest to Canadians, the north transept is dedicated to Canadians of Norman heritage. Admission: free.

Eglise Ste-Catherine   ★★

place Ste-Catherine. Near the old harbor.
Hours open: 9 a.m.–6 p.m. Special hours: Closed noon–2 p.m.

This church was rebuilt after the Hundred Years War by the local carpenters. The entire structure is built of timber from the local shipyards. Across the street is the belfry, also built of wood, and the neighboring houses are built in a similar fashion.

Museums and Exhibits

Musée Eugene Boudin ★★★

place Erik Satie, ☎ 02-31-89-54-00. Off rue de l'Homme de Bois.
Closed: Tue.

Many painters have flocked to this picturesque port, and now the tourists flock to this museum to see their work. Boudin's work, as the name implies, dominates this gallery. The works of many of his contemporaries are also represented in this impressive collection. *Open Wed.–Mon., 10 a.m.–noon and 2–6 p.m.; Oct–mid-Mar., Mon. and Wed.–Fri., 2:30–5 p.m. Closed Jan.–mid-Feb.* Admission: FR20.

Vieux Bassin ★★★★

At the harbor.

The best things in life are free. Stroll along the old harbor and soak in the picturesque scenery that has inspired many an artist. Through the masts of the pleasure crafts and fishing boats, look back at the slate-faced, narrow houses on the Ste-Catherine Quay. Notice the Governor's House and the Eglise St.-Etienne, all part of the rich townscape. Admission: free.

Where to Stay

Hotels and Resorts

Hostellerie Lechat FR350–FR450 ★★★

3 place Ste-Catherine. ☎ 02-31-89-23-85, FAX: 02-31-89-28-61. Near Saint Catherine's church.
Single: FR350–FR450. Double: FR350–FR450.

A popular establishment in Honfleur, this hotel is situated in a lovely square behind the harbor. The 18th-century Norman building is covered in ivy, with 22 exposed-beam rooms inside. Comfortable beds, with TV, telephone and bath accompanying. The rustic restaurant serves tasty regional food under its beamed ceiling, with local seafood highlighting the menu. There is also an American-style bar, serving good drinks and setting the welcoming social scene. A reliably quality hotel, with a handy location. Credit Cards: All Major.

La Ferme St.-Simeon FR750–FR2900 ★★★★

route Adolphe-Marais. ☎ 02-31-89-23-61, FAX: 02-31-89-48-48.
Single: FR750–FR1400. Double: FR2900.

A 17th-century manor house set in the park that is considered to be the birthplace of Impressionism. This Norman wood-and-slate house sits atop a hill, overlooking Le Havre and the Channel. There are 38 18th-century style rooms, each with marble bath, TV, telephone and minibar. The more peaceful rooms are available in the converted stables, while the more charming rooms are in the main house. The excellent facilities include tennis courts, heated indoor pool, sauna, solarium, fitness room, Turkish bath, whirlpools and massage services. Such a luxurious establishment as this is only complete with its excellent restaurant with terrace dining overlooking Le Havre and the Seine estuary. A FR95 breakfast and drinks are served in the bar. While some question whether the prices reflect the hotel's reputation more than the actual accommodations, this Relais and Chateaux rated hotel continues to be the leader in Honfleur. Features: pool, tennis, sauna, fitness center. Credit Cards: All Major.

Le Cheval Blanc   **FR390–FR600**   ★★

2 quai des Passagers. ☎ *02-31-81-65-00, FAX: 02-31-89-52-80. On the harborfront. Double: FR390–FR600.*

This harborfront hotel occupies a building which dates back to the 15th century. Run by a husband and wife duo, the reception is sure to be warm, and the accommodations are impeccably maintained. There are 35 rooms, about half with private bath. Room 34 offers the most comfort, with a couch, queen-size bed, table, chairs and Jacuzzi-style bathtub. All of the rooms are attractive and overlook the small port. The ultrafriendly owners make this inn a great overnight option. Credit Cards: All Major.

Where to Eat

L'Ancrage   **$**   ★★

12 rue Montpensier, At the harbor. ☎ *02-31-89-00-70.*

The setting is a two-story 17th-century building over the harbor. The fare is seafood- and a lot of it. Enjoy huge plates of seafood in a comfortably relaxed environment while keeping a few francs left in your pocket. Authentic Norman style food delivered by an hard-working staff. Closed: Wed. reservations recommended. Credit Cards: V, MC.

L'Assiette Gourmande   **$$$**   ★★★★

8 place Ste-Catherine, Across from the church. ☎ *02-31-89-24-88. Specialties: Prawns in caviar. Dinner: entrées from FR350.*

Honfleur's best chef is sitting pretty in his newly redecorated restaurant near the church. Stunning abilities combined with the freshest of ingredients has led Gerard to the top. Purposefully refraining from cream sauces, he has turned out incredible raspberry vinaigrettes, orange sauces, basil mussel sauces and other imaginative dressings for his succulent dishes. Desserts are equally impressive—in creation and presentation. Fixed-price menus are FR150–FR300. Closed: Tues. Amenities: outside dining, reservations recommended. Credit Cards: V, DC, A.

Restaurant L'Absinthe   **$$**   ★★★

10 quai de la Quarantaine. ☎ *02-31-89-39-00. Dinner: 7–9 p.m., entrées FR125–FR220.*

Locally popular because of its 17th-century dining room with exposed beam ceilings and stone walls, the generous portions of succulent fare served within are also well received. While seafood is the specialty, various dishes are available. During the warm months, meals may be taken on the terrace. Fixed-price meals begin at FR150. Jacket and tie required. Amenities: outside dining, reservations required. Credit Cards: All Major.

Directory

To and From

From Le Havre, over the new bridge.

Tourist Office

33 place Arthur Boudin; ☎ *(33) 02-31-89-23-30.*

Deauville/Trouville

These two cities that lie adjacent at the mouth of the tiny Touques river are like twin siblings who have become estranged. Although both had similar origins as sleepy fishing villages and both were favorite resorts during the rage of beach bumming in the 19th century, their fortunes took the towns in separate ways.

To put it bluntly, Deauville is the town who got all the money. In 1913, the legendary fashion designer Coco Chanel opened her first boutique here, and from then on it was posh all the way. Still the favorite of the jet-set, Deauville is a bona fide luxury resort, complete with private beaches, chic hotels, a flashy casino with spectacular cabaret, golf courses and loads of money. There are two horse-racing tracks (the town is twinned with Lexington, Kentucky, and takes its racing very seriously), and each year the town is overrun with Hollywood types during its annual **American Film Festival.** The beaches are sandy and broad, lined with a wooden boardwalk of the Atlantic City variety. Deauville also has a thriving nightlife. Besides the casino, there are several jammin' nightclubs and discos, rare in this region. Fittingly for its position, Deauville takes a decidedly snooty attitude towards Trouville. Although they are just half a mile apart, they cannot even be seen from each other, thanks to a modern condo complex Deauville built on a spit of land in the river estuary, seemingly to hide its poorer relative.

Across the river, poor Trouville tries its best to keep up with Deauville, but it has just simply fallen behind. At one time, Trouville was the most renowned beach resort in France, but that was oh, 150 years or so ago. King Louis-Phillipe popularized the spot, and the town businessmen, sensing an opportunity, planted lots of flowers and christened the coast *La Côte Fleurie* (The Flower Coast) in order to attract Parisian vacationers. Nowadays, the sheen has rubbed off, and while it still gets plenty of visitors, Trouville depends on its age-old fishing trade. Of course, for many people, myself included, the down-to-earth, even humble air of Trouville makes it far more attractive than ritzier Deauville. Another plus is that everything from food to lodgings is a good deal cheaper here. Trouville, too, has a casino, but while the carpets are a little worn, the minimum stakes are more manageable. If you prefer historic things, there are winding cobblestone streets and a charming Norman church, which Deauville lacks. Of course, the sand is just as sandy and the ocean is just as wet here as it is to the west.

What to Do

Historical/Architectural Sites

Louisiane Follies ★★

place Maréchal Foch, ☎ 02-31-87-75-00. In Trouville.

A fun spot to spend a couple of hours, the main gambling hall charges the entrance fee and imposes a dress code. The rest of the casino is more relaxed and amusing. Check out Bourbon Street and the other theme areas, where slot machines and games provide some low-key entertainment. Admission: FR70.

Nightlife

Casino de Deauville ★★

bd. Corniche, ☎ 02-31-13-31-14. In Deauville.

Hours open: 11 a.m.–3 a.m. Special hours: Weekends to 3:30 a.m.; winter, to 3 a.m.

From the sea, this fashionable gaming palace looks like a large vanilla ice-cream sundae. After indulging in baccarat, roulette and other games of chance, you can dine quite well in one of four restaurants or swim in a gleaming Olympic-size pool. During the racing season (July–Aug.), some salons may require formal dress, so don't forget your tuxedo or passport. High season is July 1–Sept. 15. Trouville's casino, the Louisiane Follies *(place Maréchal Foch, ☎ 02-31-87-75-00)* is not quite as fancy as Deauville's but it's a mite more fun. The decor is in good-humored bad taste, sort of like a gaming Disneyland, with Franco-American theme areas. The gambling-hall admission is FR70, collared shirts and pants are required. Free admission to play slot machines. Must be 18 years of age to play, and a passport is required. Open 11 a.m.–3 a.m. Admission: FR60.

Where to Stay

Hotels and Resorts

Beach Hotel **FR450–FR700** ★★★

quai Albert-1er in Trouville. ☎ 02-31-98-12-00, FAX: 02-31-87-30-29. In Trouville, near the water and the casino.

Double: FR450–FR700.

Guests relax in one of the 102 guest rooms, enjoying views of the port or the sea. The location is convenient to the casino, and there is a bar, pool and a solarium in the hotel. Wheelchair-accessible rooms are available. Decent breakfasts are served in the dining room. Inquire about the weekend packages for two. Credit Cards: All Major.

Carmen **FR180–FR340** ★★

24 rue Carnot. ☎ 02-31-88-35-43, FAX: 02-31-88-08-03. In Trouville, one block from the water, near the casino.

Single: FR180–FR340. Double: FR180–FR340.

Family-run, the rooms here vary from functional to moderate. Each of the 15 rooms comes with a TV, telephone, minibar and most with bath. Even the most basic room is comfortable and tidy. Meals from FR100 to FR200 are served in the welcoming restaurant, and breakfast costs FR32. The flower-filled courtyard puts on the home-like finishing touch. Credit Cards: All Major.

Hotel Normandy   **FR800–FR2000**   ★★★★★

38 rue Jean-Mermoz. ☎ 02-31-98-66-22, FAX: 02-31-98-66-23. In Deauville, across from the casino.
Single: FR800–FR2000. Double: FR800–FR2000.
Built in 1912, the Normandy has long been one of the premier hotels in Deauville. The traditional Norman structure flaunts its turrets, gables and sloping roofs, covering an entire block. Supremely popular with the wealthy on holiday from Paris, the chandeliers and columns on the inside and the neatly trimmed gardens on the outside combine to create an irresistible charm. There are 276 rooms, all furnished with antiques, TV, telephone, minibar, bath and scenic view; the most expensive rooms face the ocean. Extensive facilities include tennis courts, indoor pool, sauna, solarium, billiards and game rooms. There are two fine restaurants serving meals in the dining room or on the terrace. The level of service is unsurpassed. Features: pool, sauna, in-room minibars, fitness center. Credit Cards: All Major.

Hotel St.-James   **FR460–FR525**   ★★★

16 rue de la Plage. ☎ 02-31-88-05-23. In Trouville.
Single: FR460. Double: FR525.
Transformed into a hotel in 1957, this was originally built to be a private mansion in the 1830s. There are 14 rooms, each attractively decorated and including a private bath. Breakfast costs FR150, and traditional cuisine is served for FR160 and up. A quaint inn definitely worth a visit if staying the night in town. Credit Cards: All Major.

Le Continental   **FR360–FR400**   ★★

1 rue Desire-le-Hoc. ☎ 02-31-88-21-06, FAX: 02-31-98-93-67. In Deauville, about four blocks from the sea. Between the port and the casino.
Single: FR360–FR400. Double: FR360–FR400.
Basic and clean accommodations in one of the oldest buildings in town. The 42 chambers are comfortable and well looked after by the owner. Each comes with its own bath, TV and telephone. Though there is no restaurant, breakfast is served for FR32, and there is a bar in the hotel. Le Continental provides moderately priced and centrally located lodging. Credit Cards: All Major.

Le Royal   **FR1500–FR2000**   ★★★★★

boulevard Eugene-Cornuche. ☎ 02-31-98-66-33, FAX: 02-31-98-66-34. In Deauville, near the casino.
Single: FR1500–FR2000. Double: FR1500–FR2000.
The sister hotel to the Normandy, Le Royal belongs to the same family of hotels and casinos—the Lucien Barriere group. A traditional hotel, built in 1913, this stately hotel offers a more old-fashioned elegance. Palatial in appearance, it attracts big spenders who expect to be treated in a big spender manner. There are 298 rooms, varied in price depending on view, size (some are gigantic), amenities and whether there is a terrace or balcony. All are comfortably furnished with period pieces, satellite TV, radio, telephone and bath or shower. Leisure facilities include a heated pool, sauna, tennis, health club and game rooms. There are two restaurants, a grill and a bar. The large, courteous staff brings back the service of those grander days of yesteryear. Features: pool, tennis, sauna, fitness center.

Cabourg

Hotels and Resorts

Grand Hotel   **FR800–FR1300**   ★★★

promenade Marcel-Proust. ☎ *223-9862, 02-31-91-01-79, FAX: 02-31-24-03-20. On the seafront.*
Single: FR800. Double: FR1300.

Catch a glimpse to the past, the grand days of the late 19th century when this hotel's most famous guest stayed here- Marcel Proust. With a location directly on the beach, the Grand allows water views from most of its 68 rooms. The rooms are equipped with TV, telephone, private bath and some with balcony. Guests can reserve the Proust room, which has been restored to the days when he described it in his books. Connected to the casino, guests pass time gambling or drinking at the piano bar in the summer. There is a traditional restaurant with a loyal local following. Although the opulence of its earlier days has toned down a bit, there is a distinct air of elegance still lingering. Credit Cards: All Major.

Hotel de Paris   **FR200–FR350**   ★★

39 avenue de la Mer. ☎ *02-31-91-31-34. On a residential street in the center of town.*
Single: FR200–FR350. Double: FR200–FR350.

The Hotel de Paris occupies a building from the late 1800s, charmed by its five gables. Located in a residential area, a peaceful night's sleep is made easy. The 24 rooms with bath or shower, although elemental in furnishings, are comfortable and well-maintained. The family who looks after the hotel take pride in running a clean ship. Breakfast is served for FR30. Credit Cards: V.

Hotel du Golf   **FR600**   ★★★

avenue de l'Hippodrome. ☎ *02-31-91-27-57, FAX: 02-31-91-31-81. About 1 km from town center.*
Double: FR600.

Situated near the racetrack, the Hotel du Golf has the golf course out its back door. There are 40 bright, peaceful, modern rooms with private bath. There is a small pool in the back, and there is a restaurant and a grill in the hotel. Triples, quads and half and full pensions are available. Breakfast is included in the price. Features: golf. Credit Cards: All Major.

Where to Eat

Le Bistrot Gourmet   **$$**   ★

70 rue Gambetta. ☎ *02-31-88-82-52.*
Dinner: 7–11 p.m., entrées FR100–FR155.

A simple bistro specializing in seafood dishes; the quality is high for the price. Fixed-price menus start at FR115. Also worthy is Brasserie-Creperie Deauville-Trouville, *90 rue Eugene-Colas* (☎ *02-31-88-81-72)*, a multipurpose, two-story, democratic eatery with a pub *(open 9 a.m.–4 a.m.)*, a brasserie and cafeteria. Sandwiches (from FR30) full meals (FR55–FR85), crepes (FR30–FR55), ice cream, seafood. Fixed-price menus from FR80. Credit cards:Visa; reservations unnecessary. Open noon–3 p.m. and 6 p.m.–11 p.m. Closed Tues.–Wed. in June and mid-Oct. Closed: Tues. Amenities: cafestop, reservations recommended. Credit Cards: V, MC, A, E.

Le Ciro's $$ ★★

promenade des Planches. ☎ *02-31-88-18-10.*
Lunch: Noon–2:30 p.m., FR165–FR225.
Dinner: 7:15–10 p.m., entrées FR165–FR225.

Patrick Durant's regionally rich, creative cuisine is featured at this attractive, ocean-front, terraced establishment. Normandy cider and apples are liberally used to flavor fresh seafood, meat dishes and desserts. Gracious, intelligent service. Fixed-price FR180 menu. Amenities: outside dining, own baking. Credit Cards: All Major.

Le Petite Auberge $$ ★

7 rue Carnot. ☎ *02-31-88-11-07.*
Lunch: Noon–2 p.m., FR125–FR170.
Dinner: 7:15–10 p.m., entrées FR125–FR170.

A traditional bistro within a dice throw of the Casino. Well-prepared stews, shellfish and other uncomplicated dishes at decent prices. The fixed-price menu starts at FR120. Always packed with elbow-to-elbow diners. Also very popular with visitors is a brasserie across from the fish market, Les Vapeurs, *160 bd. Fernand-Moureaux* (☎ *02-31-88-15-24*), naturally serves fish and shellfish (mussels in cream, a specialty) and tons of it; open daily, except Wed., serving until 1 a.m. Outside dining in season. Main dishes start at FR90. Reservations recommended. reservations recommended. Credit Cards: V, MC, E.

Le Spinnaker $$ ★★

52 rue Mirabeau. ☎ *02-31-88-24-40.*
Specialties: turbot roasted with shallots, roasted lobster with cider vinegar, puff-pastry tart with apples.
Lunch: 12:30–2:30 p.m., FR155–FR220.
Dinner: 7:30–9:30 p.m., entrées FR155–FR220.

Centrally located, this restaurant is in a picturesque old Norman dwelling with a homey decor. The kitchen is as traditional as the ambience, with regional specialties interpreted by Pascal Angenard. Fixed-price meals start at FR160. Reservations recommended. Credit Cards: V, MC, A, E.

Directory

To and From

By train from Paris (about 2.5 hours one-way) or by car from the east along the coastal D-513 road or up from the A-13 autoroute, or as an excursion from Caen to the west on the D-513 road.

Tourist Office

place de la Mairie (Deauville); ☎ *(33) 02-31-88-21-43.*
22-36 boulevard F. Moureaux (Trouville); ☎ *(33) 02-31-88-36-19.*

Rail Stations

Both towns have a stop right in the city center; ☎ *(33) 02-31-88-28-80.*

Caen

The Norman capital city of Caen was almost completely destroyed during World War II. After suffering already heavy damage in the war's early years,

Caen was razed by fierce bombardment from Allied cruisers and battleships in the Battle of Normandy. According to the museum in town, fully 93 percent of the town's buildings were destroyed. An American soldier who witnessed the attack is widely quoted in the area thus: "It was the most frightening thing I have ever seen. One moment it was there; the next the whole town—parks, churches, shops—was gone."

Happily, today Caen is not the ugly monstrosity that so many Normandy towns became after postwar rebuilding. The center of town definitely has a modern feel, but the tall buildings are elegant and somehow warm. In addition, the three buildings that have dominated Caen for several centuries miraculously escaped the inferno and stand tall and imposing today. These are the ruins of William the Conqueror's castle and the twin abbeys that he and his wife built in exchange for lifting the papal sanction for marrying as cousins. The castle is right in the center of town and is used today mostly as a park and thoroughfare for the city's thousands of university students. The Abbaye aux Hommes, dedicated in 1064, is one of the best examples of Norman Romanesque architecture anywhere, despite having been rebuilt in the 18th century. Don't miss the reproduction of William the Conqueror's clothes, which are displayed on a Charlton Heston waxwork for some reason. Still used as a church, the monks' quarters were made a grammar school by Napoleon and now serve as City Hall. Across the street, the ruins of the Eglise St. Etienne still stand, and across town is the more modest Abbaye aux Femmes, where William's wife Mathilda is buried.

The Musée Pour La Paix combines detailed exhibits concerning the roles of Caen and Normandy in World War II, plus a thought-provoking examination of the need to create and maintain peace in our collective future.

Caen is a good place to base your visit to the Calvados region. It is young and hip thanks to the university, central location, being well-served by trains and buses. The city is rightfully proud of its cuisine, which stands out during hunting season.

What to Do

Historical/Architectural Sites

Abbaye aux Hommes/Eglise St.-Etienne   ★★★

place St.-Pierre, ☎ *02-31-30-42-01. Enter from place Monseigneur-des-Hameaux.*
Hours open: 8:15 a.m.–7:30 p.m. Special hours: Closed noon–2 p.m.

When William the Conqueror married his cousin, Mathilda of Flanders, he built this "Men's Abbey" to atone for his sins. It took only 12 years to complete, with the chancel, an example of early Norman Gothic, added in the 13th century. The nave and towers were parts of the original 11th-century abbey, Eglise St.-Etienne. William was buried here, but his tomb was destroyed during the War of Religion. Today, the abbey serves as City Hall. Tours leave daily at 9:30 and 11 a.m., and 2:30 and 4 p.m. for FR10. Visit the Abbaye aux Dames on the other side of town at *place de la Reine-Mathilde* (☎ 02-31-06-98-98). While no as impressive as the men's abbey, it is a fine example of Romanesque architecture founded by William's cousin-wife. The church attached to the abbey, Eglise de la Trinite, was recently restored. Tours of the crypt, transept and choir are available for free at 2:30 and 4 p.m. The church is open daily, 9 a.m.–noon and 2–6 p.m. Admission: free.

Jardin des Plantes ★★

5 place Blot, ☎ 02-31-86-28-80. Northeast of town, near the university.
Hours open: 8 a.m.–Sunset
A collection of plants, some medicinal, some poisonous, outside William's chateau. Within the walls of the ruins of the chateau are two museums. The recently renovated Musée des Beaux-Arts (☎ 02-31-85-28-63) contains a large collection of 17th-century Italian and French works and many 19th-century paintings of Caen by Monet, Boudin and Courbet. Open Wed.–Mon., 10 a.m.–6 p.m.; FR25. The other museum is the Musée de Normandie (☎ 02-31-86-06-24), which traces the regional archaeology and ethnology, and also has an exhibit on cider-making. *Open Wed.–Fri., 10 a.m.–12:30 p.m. and 2–6 p.m.;* FR10. While up here, be sure to catch the view from the ramparts over the city- the best part of the castle hill. Admission to both museums is free on Wed.

Museums and Exhibits

Caen Memorial ★★★★

Esplanade Eisenhower, ☎ 02-31-06-06-44; FAX 02-31-06-06-70.
Hours open: 9 a.m.–7 p.m. Closed: January 1–15.
Although there are other moving and informative exhibits, the highlight of this museum and memorial to peace is a series of spectacularly edited films (real footage interspersed with Hollywood interpretations) that try to explain "why we fight." Free admission for World War II veterans. Explanations in English. The museum is located northwest of Caen's city center on N13. Many signs point the way.

Closer to the center are two abbeys and a castle built by William the Conqueror and his wife, Queen Matilda, who made Caen their home base in the 11th century. The castle, the Chateau de Caen, Esplanade du Chateau, mostly in ruins, houses several interesting museums. **The Beaux Arts** (☎ 02-31-85-28-63) has a fine collection of 16th-, 17th- and 19th-century art, from the French and Italian masters to the French Impressionists. **Musée de Normandie** (☎ 02-31-86-06-24) is a showcase for the crafts and agricultural products of the region, including the famous Camembert cheese and Calvados apple brandy and cider. Spectacular views of the city can be seen for free from the castle ramparts. There's also a medieval herb garden on the grounds.

William and Matilda, who were cousins, built his-and-her Romanesque abbeys, the **Abbaye aux Hommes** and the **Abbaye aux Dames**, in order to appease the Church for marrying against its wishes. Will's abbey *(Esplanade Jean-Marie Louvel)* is notable for its church, the Eglise St.-Stephen, which houses the Conqueror's thigh bone, the only thing left of the great man after his tomb was desecrated by Huguenots in the 16th century (The church is open 8 a.m.–noon and 2–7:30 p.m.). His wife's remains lie in a black marble tomb in the choir of her abbey (place de la Reine Mathilde). Open 8 a.m.–6 p.m. Admission: FR61.

Bénouville
Museums and Exhibits

Sword Beach/Musée a Pegasus Bridge   ★★

Near the Pegasus Bridge, ☎ 02-31-44-62-64.
This museum recounts the stories of the British Parachute Brigade's operations on the Dives River. Major Howard's commando captured the Pegasus Bridge during the night of June 5–6, 1994, as a prelude to the landings. *Open mid-Mar.–May and early Sept.–Oct., 9:30 a.m.–12:30 p.m. and 2–6 p.m.; June–early July, 9:30 a.m.– 12:30 p.m. and 2–7 p.m.; early July–early Sept., 9 a.m.–7 p.m.; FR17.* While here, visit the **Café Gondree**, whose owners formed part of a resistance movement which aided the liberation. This was the first home liberated, and it is now a living museum. Stop in for a drink and peruse the memorabilia. A few kilometers away in Ouistreham is the **No. 4 Commando museum** *(☎ 02-31-96-63-10).* It details the story of the British and French liberators who attacked Sword Beach. The Musée du Mur de l'Atlantique, in a bunker on avenue 6 Juin, displays what was happening in the area before D-Day.

Colleville-sur-Mer
Museums and Exhibits

Musée Omaha   ★

Near the D514.
A small display focusing on the landing at Omaha Beach and the German occupation, this museum has a fine collection of war memorabilia. Included are the uniforms, weapons, photographs, propaganda and newspapers of the time.

Juno Beach
Historical/Architectural Sites

Juno Beach/Canadian Cemetery   ★★

Beny-sur-Mer-Reviers. At Beny-sur-Mer-Reviers, a few km south of Juno Beach.
In addition to the stone monument at the beach marking where General Charles de Gaulle came ashore shortly after the landings and the maple trees that were planted on the 50th anniversary throughout the area, the Canadian cemetery is nearby at Beny-sur-Mer-Reviers. Admission: free.

Where to Stay
Hotels and Resorts

Argouges   **FR280–FR500**   ★★

21 rue St.-Patrice. ☎ 04-31-92-88-86, FAX: 02-31-92-69-16. Single: FR280–FR300. Double: FR330–FR500.
Sheltered behind tall gates, a large courtyard and stone, semicircular staircase lead up to the 18th-century hotel's front entry. French doors in the gracious salon/ library lead out to the quiet back garden and terrace. The 25 guest rooms all have exposed beams; fabric covered walls; comfortable furniture; and private bathrooms.

Rooms have views of the garden or front courtyard. There are also two charming suites that have a small extra room for children. Additional guest rooms are provided in an equally delightful adjacent home. Breakfasts may be enjoyed in the intimate, elegant breakfast salon; on the back garden terrace overlooking the garden; or in the privacy of one's room. Breakfast is the only meal served. The hotel is open year-round. Features: in-room minibars. Credit Cards: All Major.

Chateau d'Audrieu   FR585–FR1200   ★ ★

Audrieu. ☎ *02-31-80-21-52, FAX: 02-31-80-24-73. From Caen, take the N13 east for about 28 km; then take the D158 for 5 km.*
Single: FR585–FR1200. Double: FR585–FR1200.

This chateau, set in a 50-acre park, offers the most luxurious accommodations at Audrieu. Its 21 well-appointed rooms are decorated with antiques and calla lilies, and all have private bathrooms. There is an excellent restaurant, and some of the produce, such as the raspberries, comes from the hotel's garden. A la carte dinners average FR350. Features: pool, country location. Credit Cards: All Major.

Ferme St. Simon   FR390–FR560   ★ ★ ★ ★

Route Adolphe-Marais. ☎ *02-31-89-23-61. Located just beyond Honfleur on the coastal road D513 in the direction of Deauville.*
Single: FR390–FR510. Double: FR440–FR560.

An old cider press is the focal point in front of this 17th-century Norman wood-and-slate house with flower boxes adorning every window. From the back patio, there is a view of Le Havre and the English Channel. The quality of the light and shimmering water has attracted artists to this hilltop inn, which is said to be the place where Impressionism was born at the end of the 19th century. In the garden, where famous painters set up their easels, 17 rooms have been added. Of these new rooms, three are suites, and, like the other 13 rooms and 13 suites, all have private bathrooms and are individually styled and decorated with fine antiques. Facilities include a solarium, massage service and whirlpool baths. The intimate restaurant has a beamed ceiling and flower arrangements at each table. Guests can also dine on the terrace, which has a view of the Seine estuary and Le Havre. The classic, yet simple cuisine is superb. Meals range from FR420 to FR550. Reservations for both the restaurant and hotel should be made well in advance. Features: wheelchair-access rooms, pool, tennis, sauna, in-room minibars, fitness center. Credit Cards: All Major.

Lion d'Or   FR400–FR470   ★ ★

71 rue St.-Jean. ☎ *02-31-92-06-90, FAX: 02-31-22-15-64. Located two blocks east of the tourist information center.* Rated Restaurant: *Lion d'Or.*
Single: FR400–FR430. Double: FR400–FR470.

Like an old French coaching inn, the Lion d'Or has a large open courtyard, a mansard roof, and lush flower boxes decorate the facade. Its 26 comfortable rooms, all with private bath, are set back from the street and around the cobbled, flower-filled courtyard. The beamed dining room, looking out on the courtyard, is famous for its cuisine. One meal is required of overnight guests. The restaurant has an extensive wine list, and there's an attractive bar with a fireplace. Meals cost from FR190 to FR320. Half-board rates are FR405 to FR530 (room, breakfast and a meal) per person, per day in season. Well renovated, it has retained its Old-World inn atmosphere. Credit Cards: All Major.

Novotel   **FR395–FR480**   ★★

avenue de la Cote-de-Nacre. ☎ *02-31-93-05-88, FAX: 02-31-44-07-28. Take the Caen Universit exit from the Caen Priphrique, north of Caen.*
Single: FR395–FR430. Double: FR465–FR480.
This hotel is located about 3 km north of the city center. Built in 1976, it is part of a nationwide chain with high standards. All of the 126 well-furnished rooms contain a single bed, a double bed and a bathroom, which makes them ideal for families. There are landscaped grounds, and the grill serves both French and international dishes, including the regional tripe a la mode de Caen. Features: wheelchair-access rooms, pool, air conditioning in rooms, nonsmoking rooms, in-room minibars. Credit Cards: All Major.

Relais des Gourmets   **FR350–FR550**   ★★★

15 rue de Geole. ☎ *02-31-86-06-01. Located at the foot of Chateau de Guillaume-le-Conquerant.* Rated Restaurant: *L'Ecaille.*
Single: FR350–FR505. Double: FR505–FR550.
A charming hotel in a great location near the Chateau. The reception area and lounges are filled with antiques, including a 13th-century closet. Its 24 spacious rooms, with private bath, are soundproofed; many have a view of the garden or the Chateau. Guests can dine on the hotel's terrace where an excellent seafood salad is served. There is also a high-quality restaurant next door, L'Ecaille, that faces the castle of William the Conqueror. Meals cost FR240 at both restaurants. Features: in-room minibars. Credit Cards: All Major.

Where to Eat

Daniel Turboeuf   **$$$**   ★★★

8 rue Buquet. ☎ *02-31-43-64-48.*
Specialties: roast pigeon with caramel sauce and pan-fried foie gras, apple tart in cider-butter sauce.
Lunch: Noon–2 p.m., FR300–FR400.
Dinner: 7- 9:30 p.m., entrées FR300–FR400.
Housed in an old dance studio, chef Daniel Tuboeuf's maison is fast becoming one of the leading restaurants in the city. Norman specialties are served, making good use of superb local ingredients. He combines the ubiquitous tripe with potatoes and apples, and bakes it into a luscious gateau. Excellent wine list. Set meals from FR125. Closed: Mon., Sun. Amenities: own baking, reservations required. Credit Cards: V, MC, E.

La Bourride   **$$$**   ★★★

15-17 rue du Vaugeux. ☎ *02-31-93-50-76.*
Specialties: pigonneau au sel et vanille, bourride des cinq poissons.
Lunch: 12:30–2 p.m., FR400–FR600.
Dinner: 7–9 p.m., entrées FR400–FR600.
Within a lovely half-timbered house across the port is the city's best restaurant. Built on bourride, a fish soup made with rich tomato and saffron stock (actually a southern specialty), the restaurant serves five different kinds. Chef Michel Bruneau also

cooks up a variety of Norman dishes, including a flavorful *andouille sausage melé*. Not to be missed are the desserts made from the famous local apples—including a definitive version of *tarte tatin*, a caramelized, upside-down apple tart. Closed: Mon., Sun. Amenities: own baking, reservations required. Credit Cards: All Major.

Le Petite Auberge   **$$**   ★
17 rue des Equipes-d'Urgence. ☎ *02-31-86-43-30.*
Lunch: Noon–2 p.m., FR65–FR75.
Dinner: 7–9 p.m., entrées FR65–FR75.
Norman specialties are served at this restaurant near the Church of St.-Stephen, at reasonable prices. The seafood and tripe are notable. The four-course fixed-price menus start at FR70. Tired of Norman dishes already? Amalfi, 201 rue Saint-Jean *(02-31-85-33-34)*, is a good pizza place that stays open until 11 p.m.; pies from FR60. Markets: pl. Courtonne, open daily, except Sun. and Mon., mornings only. Reservations recommended. Credit Cards: All Major.

Directory

To and From
By train from Paris (In just over two hours one-way) or by car on the A-13 autoroute or N-13 road, or on the N-175 road from Bretagne.

Tourist Office
place St. Pierre; ☎ *(33) 02-31-27-14-14.*

Rail Station
place de la Gàre (you'll need to catch a bus into the city center); ☎ *(33) 02-31-83-50-50.*

Post Office
place Gambetta, 14000 Caen; ☎ *(33) 02-31-39-35-93.*

Bayeux

   Dripping with history, Bayeux is the site of the best museum on the Battle of Normandy and also the **Bayeux Tapestry** (actually an embroidery), which tells the story of the other major battle that was to have a lasting effect on Europe—the conquest of England by William the Conqueror and the Battle of Hastings. The first major city to be liberated by the Allies—English soldiers took the city just one day after landing—Bayeux was spared the heavy fighting and intense bombardment that decimated Caen, its neighbor to the southeast. Bayeux has a feel of genuine history, although in the center of town, I find it seems somehow pretentious—the half-timbered buildings are just too perfect. Most of the town, however, is very beautiful as well as centuries old. The 11th-century cathedral completely dominates the skyline of Bayeux and the surrounding region. There is a well-organized pedestrian-path system and numerous narrow bridges cross and recross the river downtown.

Bayeux is a must-see stop for its historical attractions, but I wouldn't recommend staying overnight unless you are doing a scholarly paper on Mathilda's tapestry—no matter what time of the year, the town is filled with tourists.

What to Do

Historical/Architectural Sites

Cathedrale Notre-Dame   ★★★

5 rue Maitrise, ☎ *02-31-92-01-85.*

Consecrated in 1077 by William the Conqueror's brother, Bishop Odo, it reached its Gothic heights in the 13th century with the flying buttresses and spires atop the Romanesque towers. The 14th century saw the addition of side chapels; frescoes in the nave came were painted in the 15th century; and works of art were added through the 18th century. Structural reinforcing and touch-ups have been ongoing through present times. Informal tours of the nave and the crypt are offered in the summer. *Open July–Aug., Mon.–Sat., 8 a.m.–7 p.m., Sun. 9 a.m.–7 p.m.; Sept.–June, Mon.–Sat., 8 a.m.–noon and 2–7 p.m., Sun. 9 a.m.–12:15 p.m. and 2:30–7 p.m.* Admission: free.

Museums and Exhibits

Musée Baron Gerard   ★★★

place de la Liberte, ☎ *02-31-92-14-21.*
Hours open: 9 a.m.–7 p.m.

Before entering, take note of the plane tree in front, the Arbre de la Liberte (Tree of Liberty)—it was planted in 1797. Inside the museum is a wonderful collection of paintings, lace and porcelain. Two paintings to look for–David's "Le Philosophe" and Boucher's "La Cage." Another museum, the **Musée Diocesain d'Art Religieux**, in the Hotel du Doyen (next to the cathedral), contains religious artifacts including chalices, vestments and displays recounting several events in Normandy's history. If that's enough to draw you to its altar, the museum is *open daily, 10 a.m.–12:30 p.m. and 2–6 p.m. (until 7 p.m. July–mid-Sept.);* FR13. Admission: FR19.

Musée Memorial de la Bataille de Normandie   ★★★

boulevard Fabian Ware, ☎ *02-31-92-93-41. Across from the cemetery of Brittany.*
Hours open: 9 a.m.–7 p.m. Special hours: Sept.–May, 10 a.m.–12:30 p.m. and 2–6 p.m.

Near the largest British cemetery in Normandy, this museum details the 70-day Battle of Normandy. Recount the daily events of the war through old American, English, German and French newspapers. Accompanying these stories are photos, weapons and uniforms of the various troops. At the end, there is a 30-minute film, alternating in French and English, with footage from land, air and sea (worth the 30 minutes). Admission: FR28.

Musée de la Tapisserie de Bayeux   ★★★★

Centre Guillaume le Conquerant, rue de Nesmond, ☎ *02-31-92-05-48.*
Hours open: 9 a.m.–6:30 p.m.

The Bayeux Tapestry took more than 200 feet of cloth, endless spools of thread and lots of womanpower to relate the history of William the Conqueror's subjugation of

England in the Battle of Hastings in 1066. What is remarkable about it, other than its sheer size and amazing detail, is that the colors are still vivid after almost 1000 years. Your viewing of the tapestry, which is in five sections, is accompanied by a detailed audio-visual presentation in both French and English. In addition, a film in English in the second-floor cinema is shown every 40 minutes. Children, students, seniors FR13. It's unlikely that a tapestry will be woven to depict the 70-day battle for Normandy (Bayeux was never bombed), so we will have to make do with photos, news articles, and wax soldiers to comprehend what happened there from June to August in 1944. These can be seen at the **Memorial Museum of the Battle of Normandy**, *boulevard Fabian-Ware* (☎ *02-31-92-93-41*), *open 10 a.m.–12:30 p.m. and 2–6 p.m., Sept.–June. July–Aug., open 9 a.m.–7 p.m.*, with no lunch break. Admission FR20, children FR10. Just a few steps away from the museum is the **Bayeux War Cemetery**, where almost 5000 soldiers, mostly from Britain, and many from Germany, are buried. Admission: FR33.

Arromanches

Historical/Architectural Sites

Gold Beach/Musée du Debarquement ★★★

At the beach, ☎ *02-31-22-34-31. On the beach.*

Hours open: 9 a.m.–6:30 p.m. Special hours: Sept.–May, 9–11:30 a.m. and 2–5:30 p.m.

Port Winston, the artificial harbor created by the British in a day, lies offshore at Arromanches. It consists of 600,000 tons of concrete that was sunk in a semicircle to create a protected area for the unloading of the 2.5 million soldiers, 4 million tons of equipment and 500,000 vehicles. The museum shows how the harbor was created and how the Allied forces landed. Films, available in English, recount the events with actual film footage. It is closed for most of Jan. Near the museum (turn left to rue de la Batterie and take the steps up the cliff) is the **Arromanches 360-Degree Cinema**. An 18-minute film combines footage from D-Day with those of modern Normandy. *Open daily Oct.–Mar., 10 a.m.–5 p.m.; Apr.–Sept., 9 a.m.–7 p.m.; FR20.* Admission: FR24.

Museums and Exhibits

Musée du Debarquement ★★★★

place du 6 Juin, ☎ *02-31-22-34-31.*

One of the most amazing strategies in modern warfare was undertaken in this area on what became known as D-Day, June 6, 1944. British troops had brought in tons of material across the Channel at 4 miles an hour and constructed a makeshift port at Arromanches' modest little harbor to supply the Allied forces. Code-named Mulberry B, but nicknamed "Port Wilson," it was instrumental in the Allied victory. This museum documents the battle plans in detail. It's also worth shelling out FR20 to see the film *The Price of Freedom* at the Arromanches' 360-degree theater on a hill above the museum. Admission: FR32.

Omaha Beach

Historical/Architectural Sites

Omaha Beach/American Cemetery   ★★

Just above Omaha Beach.
Hours open: 9 a.m.–5 p.m.

The grounds of this American cemetery cover 200 acres of a coastal reserve. Filled with crosses and stars of David, the remains of 9386 soldiers are buried here on this American-owned property—a gift from the government of France. Admission: free.

Pointe du Hoc

Historical/Architectural Sites

Pointe du Hoc is one of Normandy's most-visited sites.

Omaha Beach/Pointe du Hoc   ★★★

From Bayeux, the road to Pointe du Hoc branches off to the right. Park in the lot, and walk to the cliffs.

A cross and a well-maintained landscape pay tribute here, allowing visitors to walk to the cliffs of the Atlantic Wall. It was on the beach below that 225 specially trained U.S. Rangers, led by Colonel James E. Rudder, began the ascent up the 100-foot sheer cliff. They took out the six 155-mm guns (which have a range of 10 miles) and fought off a counterattack for two days and nights—suffering 135 casualties before Allied help arrived. This site is one of the few sites in Normandy that really gives the impression of being a former battlefield. From the edge of the cliff, there is a fantastic view of the east coast of the Cotentin Peninsula.

Ste-Mère-Eglise

Museums and Exhibits

Airborne Troops Museum   ★★★

place du 6 Juin, ☎ *02-33-41-41-35.*

This museum is shaped like the parachutes that dropped fighting men from the 82nd U.S. Airborne Division in this town near Utah Beach on June 6, 1944. The operation was one of the first phases of "Operation Overlord," and the action liberated Ste-Mere-Eglise from the Germans. Within is the Douglas C-47 transport plane that flew the paratroopers in. *Open daily, Feb–mid-Nov., 9 a.m.–7 p.m.; mid-Nov.–mid Dec.; Sat.–Sun.* Admission: free.

Utah Beach/D-Day Landing Museum   ★★★

Utah Beach, ☎ *02-33-71-53-55. On Utah Beach, near Ste-Marie-du-Mont.*
Hours open: 9:30 a.m.–6:30 p.m.

Occupying a blockhouse near the American Commemorative Monument, this museum shows films and displays models showing how all of the troops, vehicles and equipment were brought ashore on June 6.

NORMANDY

Utah Beach has many exhibits and monuments depicting D-Day.

Utah Beach/Musée des Troupes Aeroportees   ★★★

place de 6 Juin, ☎ 02-33-41-41-35. About halfway between Cherbourg and Bayeux on the A13.
Hours open: 9 a.m.–7 p.m.

This museum houses a Douglas C47, the type of plane that dropped the paratroopers from the 82nd and 101st U.S. Airborne Divisions over the town on the night of liberation—one of whom got caught on the church steeple and played dead to avoid being shot by the Germans for several hours until the village was taken by the U.S. troops. There is a varied collection of memorabilia and war-related relics here, also. For a firsthand account of D-Day, talk with the museum's curator, who participated in the landing and, in 1975, married a French woman who had housed him in this town during the landings. Reduced off-season hours: Feb.–Mar. and Oct.–mid-Dec, 10 a.m.–noon and 2–6 p.m.; Apr.–May and mid-Sept.–late-Sept., 9 a.m.–noon and 2–7 p.m.; closed mid-Dec.–Jan. Admission: FR15.

Where to Stay

Hotels and Resorts

Churchill Hotel   FR285–FR425   ★★★

14-16 rue St.-Jean. ☎ 02-31-21-31-80, FAX: 02-31-21-41-66. In the center of old Bayeux.
Single: FR285. Double: FR325–FR425.

Built in 1986, the Churchill is a tasteful blend of traditional style and modern comforts. Residing on a pedestrian street in the center of old Bayeux, the restful nights here are what bring back the repeat guests. The 32 rooms are individually decorated, each with satellite TV, telephone and bath or shower. Breakfast is served for FR38, and the family prepared evening meals are excellent. Credit Cards: All Major.

Hotel du Luxembourg   FR350–FR450   ★★★

25 rue Bouchers. ☎ 02-31-92-00-04, FAX: 02-31-92-54-26. In the center of town.
Single: FR350. Double: FR450.

Considered by many to be the best hotel in town, part of the Luxembourg's building was a post office in the late 1800s. A Best Western affiliate, it has 22 rooms with TV, telephone and private bath. The restaurant, Les Quatre Saisons, is lavishly decorated with Louis XIII furnishings and elegant napery on the tables. There is also a bar and a disco that lasts until 4 a.m. in the basement. Breakfast is available for FR50. Features: in-room mini-bars. Credit Cards: All Major.

Le Lion d'Or   FR400–FR460   ★★★

71 rue St.-Jean. ☎ 02-31-92-06-90, FAX: 02-31-22-15-64. In the center of town.
Single: FR400–FR440. Double: FR400–FR460.

Le Lion d'Or is a renovated hotel that hasn't lost its Old World charm over the years. Reminiscent of an old coaching inn, there is a large garden courtyard with arched palms and a mansard roof. The balconied facade is dotted with overflowing flower boxes, peacefully set back from the street. There are 28 individually decorated rooms with TV, telephone and bath or shower. One meal is required of all overnight guests. Dining in the exposed beam dining room is a delight, with meals ranging from FR110 to FR320. Credit Cards: All Major.

Where to Eat

L'Amaryllis $ ★★

32 rue St.-Patrice. ☎ *02-31-22-47-94.*
An ideal choice for an intimate dinner at reasonable prices. This small establishment is unpretentious in decor and attitude. The entire ensemble makes for an enjoyable, peaceful dining experience. A solid three-course fixed-price meal is served for FR100—sure to leave the stomach satiated. Closed: Mon. Credit Cards: All Major.

Le Lion d'Or $$$ ★★

71 rue St.-Jean. ☎ *02-31-92-06-90.*
Specialties: Andouille sausage a la Bovary, squab stuffed with morels, braised sole in cider butter.
Lunch: Noon–2 p.m., FR150–FR200.
Dinner: 7–9:30 p.m., entrées FR150–FR200.
Classically prepared regional cuisine is served at this Old-World inn in the center of town. The beamed dining room features scenes from the Bayeux Tapestry and looks out on a pretty courtyard. A fixed-price FR110 menu is offered weekdays at lunch.
The Luxembourg Hotel, *25 rue Bouchers* (☎ *02-31-92-00-04*), has decent cuisine, not as acclaimed as the former, but in a much more elegant setting. Its fixed-price menu at FR99 is a good deal. Amenities: own baking, reservations required. Credit Cards: All Major.

Le Petit Normand $$ ★

35 rue Larcher. ☎ *none.*
Lunch: Noon–2:30 p.m., FR50–FR130.
Dinner: 7–10 p.m., entrées FR50–FR130.
Around the Cathedral of Notre Dame are two good eating choices. Le Petit Normand is one of the more popular lower-priced restaurants in town, with a medieval atmosphere. Fixed-price menus from FR50. About a half block away from the Cathedral is **Creperie Notre Dame**, *8 rue de la Juridiction* (☎ *02-31-21-88-70*), featuring crepes, sandwiches and light meals from FR30. You don't have to stay at **The Family Home** youth hostel, *39 Rue du General de Dais* (☎ *02-31-92-15-22*), to eat there (call to see if they have room for you); huge home-style meals prepared by Madame LeFevre are served at 7:30 p.m. for FR60, with wine from the family vineyards. The hostel is also located near the Cathedral, in a 17th-century building. Markets: regional foods, produce, etc., at Rue St.-Jean Wed. mornings, and at Place St.-Patrice on Sat. mornings. Amenities: own baking, reservations recommended. Credit Cards: V, MC, A, E.

Directory

To and From
By train from Paris and Cherbourg; by car from Caen on the N-13.

Tourist Office
Pont St. Jean (on the bridge!); ☎ *(33) 02-31-92-16-26.*

Rail Station
place de la Gàre; ☎ *(33) 02-31-83-50-50.*

NORMANDY

Post Office
   rue Larcher, 14400 Bayeux; ☎ *(33) 02-31-92-04-35.*

Cherbourg

There is even less reason to visit gritty Cherbourg than Le Havre—at least with the latter you might be on the way between two interesting points, whereas unless you're arriving by ferry from England, Cherbourg deserves a wide berth. The only reason it is featured in this guide at all is that you might in fact be arriving by sea and because it is, after all, a major regional city. Like most busy port cities, however, it is insufferably ugly and industrialized.

The naval port, still use by the French navy as a major base, dates back to the time of Napoleon Bonaparte. It is served by ferries from Portsmouth and Southampton in England and from Rosslare and Cork in Ireland, as well as transatlantic container ships. The port also became the major point of entry for military materiel for the Allied invasion of Europe following the liberation of Normandy. You can get a good view of the harbor and the entire city by driving up to the ancient Fort du Roulé, which today houses the Musée de la Libération. Another worthwhile excursion so long as you're here is a tour of the harbor aboard a motor launch.

What to Do

Historical/Architectural Sites

Eglise de la Trinite   ★★★
   place Napoleon, ☎ *02-33-53-10-63. On the south side of place Napoleon.*
   Hours open: 8 a.m.–5 p.m.
   With its foundations laid in the 11th century, the bulk of the work occurred from 1423 to 1504. It is one of the few historic buildings in Cherbourg, a shining example of the Flamboyant Gothic style. A modern addition is the stained glass, in rich reds and blues. A block north of boulevard Pierre Mendes France is the Eglise-de-Notre-Dame-de-Voeu, adorned with stained-glass windows depicting the life of St.-Mary from her birth to the Assumption and Coronation. Admission: free.

Museums and Exhibits

Musée Thomas-Henry   ★★

   rue Vastel, ☎ *02-33-44-40-22. In the Hotel de Ville (town hall).*
   Housed in the custom-built cultural center of the town hall, this museum contains works by many European artists, including Poussin, David and Vernet. Don't miss Murillo's Christ on Calvary nor Fra Angelico's altar panel. In the garden stands a statue of local artist, Jean-Francois Millet, with many examples of his work in the gallery. *Open May–Oct., Wed.–Mon., 10 a.m.–noon and 2–6 p.m.; Nov.–Apr., daily, 10 a.m.–noon and 2–5 p.m.* Admission: FR10.

Musée de la Liberation   ★★★
   Fort du Roule, ☎ *02-33-20-14-12. On Montagne du Roule.*
   Hours open: 10 a.m.–6 p.m. Closed: Mon.

Commemorating the liberation of Cherbourg from Nazi occupation and the Allied landings at Normandy, this museum sits atop the picturesque Montagne du Roule. The display includes Vichy propaganda, films, photos of the Germans surrendering, and artillery and other war-related artifacts. The view over the town and the port is reason enough to make the climb. Admission: FR2.

Where to Stay

Hotels and Resorts

Le Louvre   **FR240–FR320**   ★★

2 rue Henri-Dunant. ☎ *02-33-53-02-28, FAX: 02-33-53-43-88. In the center of town.*
Single: FR240–FR300. Double: FR260–FR320.
Convenient to the marina and town center, Le Louvre is one of the best values in Cherbourg. The furnishings are rudimentary, but there's plenty of space in the 42 soundproofed rooms. While there is no restaurant, breakfast is available for FR30.
Credit Cards: All Major.

Mercure Plaisance   **FR275–FR625**   ★★★

Gare Maritime. ☎ *02-33-44-01-11, FAX: 02-33-44-51-00. Bus #1 to the harbor.*
Single: FR275–FR610. Double: FR385–FR625.
Although it's a chain hotel, the Mercure offers the best lodging in Cherbourg. The expansive views of the harbor definitely earn it some points. It has 84 rooms, all with TV, telephone, minibar and bath or shower. Take time to sip on a drink at the bar, which opens onto the sea, and enjoy a fine seafood dinner in the restaurant, also offering water views. The amiable staff stays on its toes. Breakfast is available for FR50. Features: in-room minibars. Credit Cards: All Major.

Where to Eat

Cafe du Theatre   **$**   ★★

place du General de Gaulle, At the Theatre National de Cherbourg complex. ☎ *02-33-43-01-49.*
Dinner: 6–11 p.m., entrées FR60–FR85.
The choice café among the art and thespian crowd in Cherbourg, the fixed-price menu is a great value at FR70. Find a table in this bustling café, and settle in to enjoy some good food and even better people watching. There's a little of something here for everybody. Amenities: cafestop. Credit Cards: V, MC.

Chez Pain   **$$$**   ★★★★

59 rue au Ble. ☎ *02-33-53-67-64.*
Dinner: 7–10 p.m., entrées FR280–FR300.
To feel like you're in the thick of it all, sit down to a meal at this busy restaurant. A husband-wife duo keep the guests coming back for the warm welcome and consistently quality food. While not always dynamic, the dishes turned out are quite satisfying. Fixed-price menus are FR100–FR260. Closed: Sun. Credit Cards: V, A.

Le St.-Hours   **$$**   ★★★

59 rue au Ble, In the old town. ☎ *02-33-53-67-64.*
Dinner: 7:30–10 p.m., entrées FR90–FR210.
Considered one of the premier restaurants in Cherbourg, this establishment occupies the ground floor of a lovely 19th-century house. Appetizers start at just FR35,

and fixed-price meals start at FR130. Excellent seafood dishes and various cassoulets are the highlights of the menu. The restaurant closes July–early Sept. and mid-Dec.–late Dec. Closed: Sun. reservations recommended. Credit Cards: MC, A.

Directory

To and From
> *By sea from England or Ireland; by train from Caen (about an hour-and-a-half one-way); by car from the southeast on the N-13 or from the southwest on the D-904 road.*

Tourist Office
> *2, quai Alexandrell;* ☎ *(33) 02-33-93-52-02.*

Rail Station
> *Bassin du Commerce;* ☎ *(33) 02-33-57-50-50.*

Post Office
> *rue de l'Ancien Quai, 50100 Cherbourg;* ☎ *(33) 02-33-92-45-44.*

Mont St. Michel

Mont St. Michel is a wondrous mixture of history, art and legend.

The island abbey-fortress of Mont St. Michel is rightly considered one of the wonders of the Western world. Because of this around 850,000 visitors per year show up—keep that in mind when planning your trip.

History

The original oratory (a type of small chapel) was founded on the island in the early eighth century by St. Aubert, bishop of nearby Avranges. Legend has it that the bishop saw the Archangel Michael in a dream telling him to build him a shrine on the 264-foot (150-meters) high rock. It was not until the third such dream that Aubert got the message, and then only after The Archangel poked him in the head, leaving a permanent hole in his skull. Like the monasteries throughout medieval Europe, the abbey eventually became a self-contained community, with defenses against attack, villagers who produced much of the monks' material needs, and hordes of pilgrims and merchants. Between Aubert's first simple church and that, however, were centuries of continual construction and conflict that resulted in the hodge-podge of architectural styles found there today. As a result, Mont St. Michel features in both the Romanesque Architecture and Gothic Architecture tours in this book.

Aubert's chapel was replaced in the 10th century by a series of small chapels of which one survives today as the Notre Dame-sous-Terre, or Our Lady Underground; which is where the chapel is located. The main abbey church was built on the summit of the rock, supported by enormous buttresses and crypts beginning in the 11th century by the Benedictine monks. The first monastery buildings were begun at the same time, and over the following hundred years, especially under the supervision of Abbot Robert de Torigni, the monastic quarters were extended westwards and southwards. In 1204, King Phillipe of France annexed Normandy. In order to solidify his political support in the region, Phillipe provided funding for construction of the major portion of the monastery, a complex of six huge rooms, two on each of three floors, that were called *Le Merveil*, or the Marvel. These quarters became the monks' refectories and working rooms, as well as lodgings for the increasing number of pilgrims. The Marvel is an example of the earliest Gothic architecture in France, still very simple in design but moving away from the squat, solid look of the Romanesque style. During the 14th century, war with England made it necessary to protect the abbey, and the fortifications around the base of the island were added. The English did indeed lay siege to the island twice, once for 30 years, but were unable to conquer it. At the same time many of the houses around the base of the monastery were constructed, other buildings were being erected. These included storehouses and a parish church. In the 15th century, the abbey's chancel collapsed and was replaced with a flamboyant Gothic chancel and steeple. Consequently, the decidedly Romanesque nave adjoins the much lighter and fancier tower that now doubles the height of the rock. After its zenith in terms of architectural dominance and spiritual influence in the 16th century, the abbey went into decline, and some of its buildings fell into disrepair and even ruin. The church was damaged by fire in 1776, and after the Revolution, Napoleon turned the whole place into a prison. In 1874, the site became a national monument. Since then, work has gone on constantly to restore the abbey to its former glory. In 1969, a contingent of Benedictines returned to live in the abbey.

Visiting the Abbey

This is one of the rare occasions when a guided tour is absolutely indispensable—without it you'll fail to grasp the significance of much of what you're seeing around you. A basic tour lasting about an hour is included in the price of admission to the abbey, but you'd do better to shell out an extra FR22 and get the **Tour de Conférence**, a two-hour tour that explains things in more detail and gives you access to parts of the abbey that are off-limits to the one-hour circuit. You can wander around the rest of the island, with its one main street, countless narrow alleys and staircases, and fortifications, for free. Be warned, however, that the village is now a complete tourist trap: besides the restaurants listed here, there are numerous cheesy souvenir shops and the like. This part of the island is always more crowded than the abbey itself.

During summer and during school holidays, the site is absolutely overrun. If you must go during these times, your best bet is to stay overnight nearby (I recommend the Hotel Gué du Holme, described below) and try to arrive in the early morning so you can spend a good four or five hours looking around so that you get out before the real crush arrives.

One of the most attractive features of the site are the amazing tides in the bay. The tide comes in from as far as nine miles out at the speed of a horse's gallop, as the locals say, which is better than 15 miles an hour! Today, the causeway always stands above water, but in olden days the entire island was surrounded in a matter of minutes. It's still a most impressive sight to watch the mass of water rush in, and I strongly suggest trying to time your visit so you can be there about an hour-and-a-half before high tide. You should be extremely careful. I don't recommend that you slosh around in the tideflats which surround the island. The flats are treacherous enough themselves (they have the consistency of quicksands) but the tides have killer-strength. Every year three or four foolhardy tourists meet their deaths in the swirling waters.

What to Do

Historical/Architectural Sites

Abbaye du Mont St. Michel ★★★★★

Mont St. Michel, ☎ *02-33-60-14-14.*
Hours open: 9:30 a.m.–5 p.m. Special hours: Jan-Feb to 4:15 p.m., mid-May–mid Sept. to 6 p.m.

One of the most visited sights in France, this beautiful abbey atop a granite island (population: 120) was founded as a private chapel in the 8th century by Archbishop Aubert of nearby Avranches. By the mid-18th century, it had grown to its present size, serving as a monastery for a powerful order of Benedictine monks. It was also used as a prison after the Revolution. The island is connected to the mainland by a causeway, and you can reach the abbey via the Grande Rue, a twisty, 12th-century street that's a warren of tacky shops. Hour long guided tours of the abbey include

"The Miracle," a three-story Gothic "mini-monastery" built over a 16-year period in the 13th century. Tours in English are conducted daily every hour from 10 a.m. to noon; then again at 1:30 p.m. every hour until 5:30 p.m. Admission: FR56.

Where to Stay

Hotels and Resorts

Hotel Gue du Holme   **FR80–FR100**   ★★★★★

Le Bourg. ☎ *02-33-60-63-76, FAX: 02-33-60-06-77. Exit the main Caen-Rennes highway (N-175) on D-103, about one mile to St. Quentin-sur-le-Homme. Well signposted on the highway.*
Double: FR80–FR100.
Set in a tiny village of just 200 inhabitants a few steps from the 11th-century church, this hotel is one of my favorites in all of France. Naturally, this has more to do with the people than the accommodations; although the rooms are big and very comfortable, the walled garden is charming, the view of Mont St. Michel is precious, and the restaurant superlative. Your hosts Annie and Michel Leroux just couldn't be friendlier. Annie will engage you in conversation on just about any subject and do everything she can to make your stay more comfortable—when I arrived and the restaurant was closed she rushed around the corner to the local cafe and had them bring something over which she then put on the bill. Michel is an incredible chef who demonstrates his culinary skills on behalf of Normandy all over the world, and he is always willing to take a guest out to his favorite salmon-fishing streams just for fun. The village doesn't even appear on the map, it's so small, and there are only 10 rooms, so you'll really enjoy the peace and quiet, especially after a long day among the madding crowds of the abbey. Features: secluded garden atmosphere, air conditioning in rooms, country location. Credit Cards: All Major.

Hotel du Mouton-Blanc   **FR350–FR480**   ★★

Grande Rue. ☎ *02-33-60-14-08, FAX: 02-33-60-05-62.*
Between the sea and the basilica.
Single: FR350–FR480. Double: FR350–FR480.
A fantastic location midway up the village slope, this inn has selections dating from the 14th century and from the 1950s. There are 26 modest bedrooms, each with telephone, private bath and some with TV. The downstairs restaurant serves breakfast for FR45, and fixed-price meals from FR82. A charming Norman-style inn.
Credit Cards: All Major.

Les Terrasses Poulard   **FR300–FR1000**   ★★★

Grand Rue. ☎ *02-33-60-14-09, FAX: 02-33-60-37-31.*
Between the sea and the basilica.
Single: FR300–FR1000. Double: FR300–FR1000.
A combination of two village houses, one dating to medieval times and the other from the 1800s, this hotel blends well with its historic surroundings. Across from an 11th-century church, the hotel is bordered by the main street, the ramparts and a garden. Twenty-nine of the best rooms in town are here, with TV, telephone, mini-bar and bath or shower. Some of the more expensive rooms have fireplaces. The

bay-view restaurant specializes in seafood, with fixed-price menus starting at FR70. English-speaking staff. Credit Cards: All Major.

Where to Eat

La Mere Poulard   **$$**   ★★★★

Grand Rue, On the main street. ☎ *02-33-60-14-01.*
Specialties: any omelet.
Dinner: 7–9 p.m., entrées FR80–FR200.
Since 1888, La Mere Poulard has guarded its secret to its famous omelette created by Annette Poulard. Made over an oak fire in a long-handled skillet, these omelettes have attracted an incessant flow of customers. The beautiful location has also been a major draw. In addition to the egg creations, other traditional cuisine is served for a good share of your francs. Fixed-price menus start at FR160. reservations required. Credit Cards: All Major.

Le Manoir de la Roche Turin   **$$**   ★★★

Courtils, About 9km from the Mont. ☎ *02-33-70-96-55.*
Relax on the terrace with an aperitif, soaking in the view of Mont St. Michel. After enjoying the point of view off the Mont, retire to the lovely dining room for a variety of dishes highlighted by fresh fish. The husband-wife owners are sure to make your dinner a memorable one. Amenities: outside dining. Credit Cards: V, MC.

St.-Pierre   **$$**   ★★

Grand Rue, On the main street. ☎ *02-33-60-14-03.*
Enjoy terrace dining at this 15th-century building's brasserie-style restaurant. Pizza, pasta and meat dishes hover around FR180 with fixed-price menus starting at just FR80–FR160. Always an enjoyably relaxed experience set beneath the walls. Amenities: cafestop. Credit Cards: V.

Directory

To and From

By car on the D-97 spur off the N-176 between Brittany and Normandy. By train from Paris (four hours, via Rennes) or Caen (four-and-a-half hours, very slow line) to Pontorson, then bus connection. Also by charter bus from any major city in France.

Tourist Office

Just inside the only entrance to the island, the Porte Avancée. ☎ *(33) 02-33-60-14-30.*

Rail Station

(in Pontorson); ☎ *(33) 02-33-60-00-35.*

Post Office

Grand Rue, 50116 Mont St. Michel.

D-Day and the Battle of Normandy Tour

Introduction

The Allied invasion of Europe, known as "that great and noble undertaking," began with the D-Day landings on Normandy's beaches on the night of June 6, 1944. It ended 77 days later with the rout of the German 7th Army and marked the beginning of the end for the Nazis. This tour will take you to some of the most important sites where the fighting actually took place, the cemeteries where tens of thousands who made the supreme sacrifice are buried, and to a number of the many museums commemorating and interpreting the events of the summer of 1944.

Unlike most of the tours offered in this book, most of the sites on your route are within 50 or 60 miles of each other, so you may choose to base yourself in just one town, perhaps Caen or Bayeux, or else, if you take the tour at a very contemplative, if not leisurely pace, as you should and perhaps cannot avoid, you can stay at any number of bed and breakfasts in the small towns and villages along the way.

Following the 50th anniversary commemoration of the invasion in 1994 the Calvados, Manche and Orne Tourist Boards created their own self-guided tours of the region; eight in all: Overlord—The Assault, D-Day—The Onslaught, Objective-A Port, The Confrontation, Cobra—The Breakout, The Counter-Attack, The Encirclement, and The Outcome. These are fine tours, marked throughout the region with the distinctive two-tone seagull motif on signposts and route markers. Information for these tours is available from any of the tourist offices listed in the Normandy section of this book. But in order to complete them all, one would have to spend at least two weeks and travel hundreds of miles throughout the region, so I have created this tour to provide an overview of the events of that momentous time—the selection from among the many historical sites has been made based on their interest to the average visitor.

Background

As the Allies considered their plans to dislodge Hitler and the Third Reich from power, they decided to attack the Nazis at the peripheries of their territory—Africa, Italy and northwestern France. The proximity of England to northern France was crucial to successfully preparing for a massive invasion on a scale that had never before been seen, and thus that part of the plan quickly became the most significant. Since two-thirds of the invasion force was to be American, supreme command of the operation was given to General Dwight Eisenhower. Command of land forces went to the British General Sir Bernard Montgomery.

In 1942, the Allies had attempted an invasion at Dieppe, a strategic port in eastern Normandy. The operation was a disaster, as the strong German defenses decimated the largely Canadian forces with no significant German losses. The Allies learned an important lesson, however, namely that an attack on an established port was doomed to failure, and they decided to invade the continent on the open beaches of Normandy instead. The operation, conceived at the Quebec Conference in 1943, was code-named Overlord.

Hitler knew that an invasion was coming; it was impossible to hide the preparations for such a massive undertaking. The Germans had created what they called *Atlantikwall*, a line of coastal defenses that grew to include 10,000 reinforced-concrete bunkers and gun emplacements along the north coast of France, as well as their accompanying trenches, machine-gun posts, and miles of barbed wire, millions of mines on the beaches, and thousands of concrete obstacles designed to impede an Allied landing. Hitler was convinced that the Allies would attack at the narrowest point of the English Channel, at Pas de Calais, and he had ordered the strongest defenses to be placed there. Mindful of their experience in Dieppe, however, the Allies had decided to attack at a less-heavily defended stretch of coastline, as noted above. Nevertheless, they were happy to foster the German's delusion about the point of invasion. A campaign of deceit, code-named Operation Fortitude, was kicked off. Consisting of fake gliders and munitions dumps placed in plain view at airfields close to Calais, the plan even included a senior American general who was persuaded to walk around with his large white dog so he could be photographed by German spy planes. On the night of the invasion, planeloads of steel were dropped around Calais to create the radar image of an advancing armada. Operation Fortitude was so successful that even a month after the Normandy invasion 200 miles to the west, Hitler refused to redeploy his units at Pas de Calais, still believing the Normandy attack to be a diversion.

In the final days before the invasion, British and American bombers went on nonstop raids over the coastal defenses, attempting to soften up the Atlantic Wall before the attack. Even though Fortitude had worked so well, the fortifications of the attack zone were fearsome indeed and, as the Allies would find out soon enough, the bombing raids were only partially successful.

Bénouville

The invasion proper began in the evening of June 5. British paratroopers, arriving by parachute and glider, landed near the tiny village of Bénouville

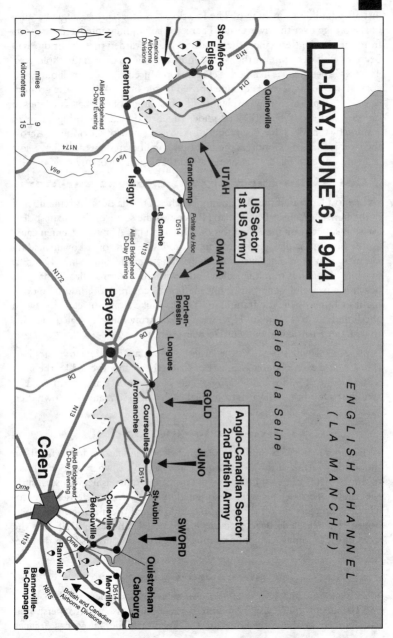

D-DAY, JUNE 6, 1944

Ste-Mère-Église

American Airborne Divisions

Carentan

Quineville

Allied Bridgehead D-Day Evening

N13

D14

UTAH

Isigny

Grandcamp

Vire

Vire

N174

La Cambe

D514

Pointe du Hoc

Allied Bridgehead D-Day Evening

N13

OMAHA

Port-en-Bressin

D6

Longues

**US Sector
1st US Army**

Bayeux

N172

D6

N13

Arromanches

Courseulles

D514

Benouville

Colleville

St-Aubin

Baie de la Seine

GOLD

JUNO

SWORD

**Anglo-Canadian Sector
2nd British Army**

ENGLISH CHANNEL
(LA MANCHE)

Caen

Orne

N13

Orne

Ranville

Banneville-la-Campagne

N815

Merville

D514

Ouistreham

Cabourg

British and Canadian Airborne Divisions

Allied Bridgehead D-Day Evening

N

miles

kilometers

0   15

0   9

just after midnight on June 6. The location was especially strategic because of the bridge over the river Orne. Thanks to last-minute intelligence reports from the French Resistance, the British were forewarned that the bridge had been set with dynamite by the Nazis, and were able to disarm the explosives. The **Musée des Troupes Aéroportés** (Paratroop Museum) has a small but good collection of materiel and equipment used by the first troops on the ground, as well as graphical displays explaining the first hours of combat. It is housed on the exact spot where the first glider touched down. The bridge, named *Pegasus* by the Allies, has been rebuilt in the exact style of the original. Across the river is the Café Gondrée, the first building liberated by the Allies, a sort of living museum filled with memorabilia that is still a working café.

Colleville-sur-Mer/St. Laurent-sur-Mer

The most famous of the five landing beaches, Omaha Beach is remembered in the film *The Longest Day*. Omaha Beach was the scene of the greatest devastation suffered by the Allied forces. The first U.S. Army servicemen came ashore here in the dawn hours of June 6, and were confronted by unyielding German firepower. The **Musée Omaha** has photographs of the initial assault, in which thousands of soldiers died in the withering German fire. Today, the beach is a peaceful, sandy strip, but memorials commemorating the bloody night of D-Day belie the tranquility. You can hike along the cliffs westward about an hour to Pointe du Hoc, where U.S. Army Rangers scaled the cliffs to take out a particularly potent German battery.

Also at Colleville-sur-Mer is the largest **U.S. military cemetery** in the region. Words—and even pictures—cannot describe the feeling evoked by the face-to-face sight of 9386 marble crosses laid out in perfect alignment on 172 acres just a few hundred yards from the beach where so many laid down their lives.

Ste-Marie-du-Mont

The other major U.S. landing-site, Utah Beach, lies farther to the north on the southern flank of the Contentin Peninsula. This is where the remainder of the 1st Army came ashore. They did not suffer quite as heavy losses, since the paratroopers (see below) had softened up the German defenses. Eventually these soldiers cut off the peninsula and secured the major port of Cherbourg. The **Musée du Débarquement**, located on Utah Beach itself, tells the story of the landings with photographs, vehicles and uniforms from the fateful night.

Ste-Mère-Eglise

A few miles inland from Utah Beach, this is the site where the U.S. 82nd and 101st Airborne Divisions, counterparts of the British paratroopers to the east, landed in the early hours of the invasion. The **Musée des Troupes**

Aéroportés (Paratrooper Museum) here focuses on the operations of the vanguard, especially the very first demolitions carried out behind the enemy lines in preparation for the beach landings a few hours later. There are dioramas on display as well as actual aircraft used in the assault.

Cherbourg

The isolation and subsequent liberation of the Cotentin Peninsula was an important milestone in the progress of the invasion. The **Musée de la Libération** offers a look at life in Normandy under Nazi occupation, as well as a detailed history of the 20-day campaign to free the peninsula and oust the Germans from their northernmost stronghold in France. After the American artificial port, the *Mulberry* sank (see below), Cherbourg became the main point of entry for U.S. forces.

Arromanches

At Juno Beach in Arromanches, the Canadian prong of the fivefold attack force came ashore. There are a number of memorials to the Canadian forces here. Gold Beach, the westernmost of the two British staging areas, also begins here. A museum called **Arromanches 360** offers a film and video presentation on the attack in the region, using nine screens to mix historical footage with present-day images.

Having learned their lesson from the Dieppe debacle two years earlier, the Allies knew they had to attack an open-beach area. But that meant they would not have a port at which to unload men and supplies in the days after the initial attack. Although 135,000 men and 20,000 vehicles came ashore on the five beaches, the Allies planned to use the area as the point of entry for a total of more than two million men and the millions of tons of supplies they would need in the campaign to liberate Europe. So they brought a port with them! Two artificial ports, in fact, codenamed *Mulberry A* and *Mulberry B*, were transported to the Normandy coast in one of the greatest feats of engineering of the war. The U.S. sector Mulberry was destroyed by a fierce storm before being fully completed, but the concrete pilings of the one at Arromanches, brought over at D-Day+3 and completed in just over a month, remain to this day. Initially, several obsolete ships, which had arrived under their own steam, were sunk to form a harbor. Then, prefabricated concrete components that had been towed from England were put in place to create a veritable port at which oceangoing supply ships could dock and unload material. The port was connected to the beach by means of floating causeways. The **Musée du Débarquement** at Arromanches, located on the seafront where the concrete components still loom ominously above of the water, tells the story of the bold strokes the Allies used to land their soldiers and equipment for the liberation drive.

Just a few miles from Arromanches is the German gun-emplacement at Longues-sur-Mer, where the artillery has been kept in place and you can see the formidable nature of the Atlantic Wall and the challenge it posed for the Allies.

Hermanville-sur-Mer

Ten thousand Allied troops were killed, wounded or disappeared in the first day of the invasion, along with a similar number of Nazis. There are dozens of cemeteries in the region where the dead heroes are buried. In this tiny fishing village is one of the most evocative of the British cemeteries. Containing just 986 graves (out of 19,000 in the Calvados region), and just yards from the first landing point, this cemetery provokes powerful emotions, and is a crucial stop to help you comprehend the magnitude of what happened here half a century ago.

Bayeux

The first city to be liberated in the invasion, by British troops on D-Day+1, Bayeux contains the biggest and best museum of the entire region. The **Musée Mémorial du Bataille de Normandie** has a comprehensive collection of vehicles, weapons, and uniforms used by the soldiers in the 77-day conflict, as well as hundreds of photographs and newspaper articles arranged chronologically to provide a step-by-step account of the battle. At the height of the fighting, approximately 1.5 million Allied troops were on the ground, slowly encircling the 7th German Army in a pincer movement around what is known as the Falaise pocket. The remaining 50,000 German troops surrendered on July 21, 1944. The battle saw 206,000 Allied casualties and 240,000 losses on the Nazi side. After it was over, German resolve in France was almost gone. Paris was liberated five days later, and although bloody fighting continued for another seven months, Hitler was finished from that point on.

Bayeux also contains the largest British cemetery in the region, with 468 graves and the names of 1807 soldiers whose remains were never found inscribed on the memorial there.

Caen

The city of Caen was completely destroyed during the intensive fighting. The Allies had hoped to capture Caen on the night of the invasion, but the Germans put up fierce resistance, and the city was crushed by heavy bombardments from Allied warships offshore. Furthermore, in order to facilitate the U.S. Force's capture of the Cotentin Peninsula, the British forces concentrated their operations around the city in the first days of the campaign in order to lure the German Panzer divisions to the area—a tactic that worked all too well. The city was liberated only after days of house-to-house fighting and after more than 90 percent of its buildings were razed. Perhaps this level of destruction is what inspired the museum there. Called **Le Mémorial—Un Musée pour la Paix** (A Museum for Peace), the center is a tribute to the forces of peace in the world, with a gallery dedicated to Nobel Peace Prize winners and displays honoring the nonviolent struggles of the world. The museum does, however, contain a lot of good information on the Battle of Normandy, especially as it affected the city itself.

BRITTANY

Vitré, a fortified town, is an easy excursion from Rennes.

What Makes Brittany So French?

1. Ex-stockbroker Gauguin–after dumping his job, wife and children–hung out and painted in Pont-Aven before setting sail for Tahiti.

2. The mysterious Carnac–site of prehistoric megaliths and alignments–is home to the world's oldest man-made buildings.

3. The magical lure of nomads who hung out in Brittany about 3000 years B.C.

4. A region with no grapes, but plenty of cider.

5. A drunken carpenter burned down most of the city of Rennes in 1720 and did not even help rebuild it.

The ancient and beautiful land of Brittany (*Bretagne* in French) stands apart from the rest of the country geographically as well as historically and socially. Consisting of the northwestern spear of France that thrusts out into the Atlantic Ocean and the western reaches of the English Channel, the region encompasses fully one-third of the French coastline, including countless bays and rocky inlets. Mont St. Michel (see the Normandy section), marks the eastern end of the region (and is still claimed by some in Brittany); the coastline follows a basically due west direction to Brest, then sweeps down towards the southeast until Western Loire begins at La Baule.

The only city with more than 200,000 inhabitants in the region is Rennes, the capital. Other major towns include Brest and Lorient. You can travel by air to these three cities as well as into airports at Nantes (actually part of Western Loire, but historically part of Brittany and located very close to the region), Dinard/St. Malo, Quimper and Lorient. Other visitors arrive at the ports of St. Malo or Brest from England or Ireland by ferry; there is good TGV service from Paris (2.5 hours one-way to Rennes or Nantes; four hours to Brest) and regular trains arrive from the Loire Valley to the south. By car, it's a straight shot into Brittany from the capital on the A81/A11 autoroute via Le Mans; this route will take you about four hours to reach Rennes. Other points of entry by automobile include the N-137 from the south, the N-157 into Rennes from the east, or the N-175 from Normandy via Mont St. Michel.

The most popular destinations in Brittany are located on the coast, each with its own distinct flavor. The Côte d'Emeraude and Côte de Granite Rose are the northern edge of the region, rich in shellfish and countless small pleasure ports on the relatively protected English Channel. Jutting out into the gray Atlantic, the coastline is rugged and harsh, yet powerfully beautiful. The southern portion of the coastline becomes softer and less wind- and rain-whipped as it descends into Western Loire. The coastal regions are collectively known as *armor*, from the ancient Breton word for sea, while the interior, which contains some of the most beautiful scenery in France, is the *argoat*, or "Land of the Forest." Much of the forest is gone now, replaced by pastures and farms, but there are still many patches of ancient woods, as well as expanses of rolling, hilly moorland.

History

A hundred centuries ago, a mysterious nomadic people ranged through Brittany, settling into permanent communities about 3000 years before Christ. Brittany is the site of more Stone Age relics than anywhere else in Europe. The earliest known megaliths are the burial site at Isle de Bono, which date from 3250 B.C. Two basic types of relics frequently are found in the region—*menhirs* and *dolmens*. Fans of Astérix the Gaul and followers of the ex-

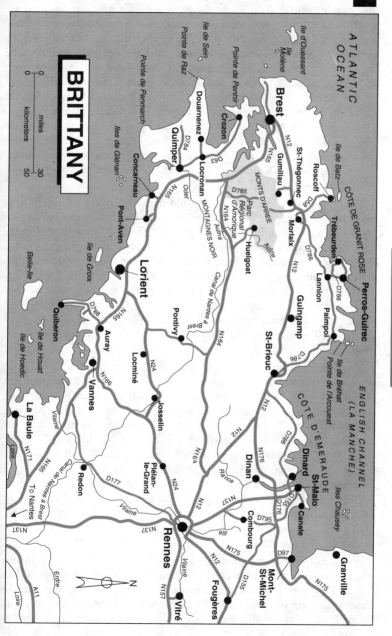

ploits of his pal Obélix will be familiar with these terms. The words come from Breton words: *men* (stone)-*hir* (long), and *dole* (table). A menhir is a tall stone set upright, weighing from one or two tons up to a hundred tons. A dolmen consists of two upright stones with a third placed laterally on the top, to form a sort of table. Archaeologists believe dolmens may have been used for sacrifices. When buried under rocks and dirt, the structures formed part of the burial chambers. Debate continues, but most scholars believe that these edifices may have been used in astronomical calculations. Many times, the stones are arranged in circles or other patterns, similar to Stonehenge in Britain. In fact, there are strong historical links between the Stone Age people of Britain and France. Prior to settling into permanent communities, people migrated back and forth across what is now the English Channel, then a swampy marshland.

The ties between Brittany and England remained strong during the next wave of settlement: the Celts, beginning about 500 B.C. Celtic civilization flourished until the arrival of the Romans just after the turn of the millennium. Conquering the region by A.D. 56, the Romans built upon many Celtic settlements, strengthening their hold on the region for the next 300 years. The fortifications at Le Yaudet, for example, show remains of the Celtic settlement there (called *Ploulec'h*) from the fourth-century B.C. as well as from the Roman era almost eight hundred years later. The Celts were a wild and fierce people and never subjected themselves willingly to the rule of Caesar. In the mid-fourth century, the Romans gave up trying to maintain a hold on Brittany and went home.

About this time, yet another wave of settlers came from Grand Bretagne to Bretagne. Fleeing the Saxon invasion of their island, the British brought with them the curious hodgepodge of beliefs that prevailed at the time. Welsh saints including Guirec and Tugdual began to evangelize Brittany, adding their Christian symbols to the Roman gods the Romans had left on the ancient megaliths (the earliest graffiti in the region?) and building the earliest churches and chapels. At the same time, the Druidic cult expanded in the region—the legend of King Arthur and Merlin the sorcerer is as strong in Brittany as in southwestern England. During this period, a distinct Breton identity was forged, including the Breton language. Breton is still spoken today, and in a revival to preserve the region's unique cultural identity, the language is taught in some schools. Also, you'll often see signs painted in both French and Breton, especially in the west.

In the face of greedy approaches from both France and England, the region, now ensconced as the Duchy of Brittany, held onto its independence for the next several centuries. During the 11th century, a series of mammoth castles and fortresses were built at the eastern end of the region to repel the French. The castles at Fougères, Vitré and Combourg are among the splenidly preserved fortifications that remain today. As so often happens, however, division came from within. In 1341, the Duke Jean III died with no heir apparent, so pro-English and pro-French factions within the duchy fell into a civil war that wracked the region for the next 40 years. This conflict, won by the pro-French side, marked the beginning of the end for an independent Brittany. It took another century (France being distracted by the Hundred Years War) but in 1488, Charles VIII defeated the Bretons at St. Aubrin-du-Cormier, and after a couple of arranged marriages between Breton duchesses and French royalty, the region finally became part of France in 1532. In 561 the capital was moved from Nantes to Rennes.

For the next 300 years, Brittany languished, its economic fortunes sinking until it was one of the poorest and most backward regions in France. During World War II, battles raged across much of the region, but postwar rebuilding has preserved Brittany's traditional ambience. The independence movement never completely waned, and in 1981, beginning with the presidency of François Mitterrand, the movement gained new strength. Mitterrand authorized Breton as a dual official-language, and worked to extend the TGV network into the region. Brittany is as modern and stable as the rest of France—although the strong, independent spirit of its people remains vibrant. The residents claim to be Bretons first and French second, and regional festivals and costumes endure, especially the tall lace headdresses called *coiffes* worn by women during the *pardons*—religious celebrations unique to Brittany.

Today, Brittany is the maritime center of France, accounting for most seagoing industry, be it shipping, fishing or pleasure boating. The area also is a major tourist destination for foreigners and French alike.

Cuisine

As might be expected, seafood abounds in Brittany. Oysters *(huitres)*, scallops *(coquilles de St. Jacques)* and small crabs *(araignées)* are served in every restaurant as well as sold by fishermen at roadside stands throughout the region. Fish and fish soup *(soupe de pecheur)* are also staples—often a restaurant will have a catch of the day that is just hours out of the water. Lobster is on the menu too, not cheap, but well-worth splurging at least once. Crayfish, shrimp and mussels round out the *fruits de mer* offerings. Fish and seafood tend to be prepared in light butter or cream sauces.

From Brittany come many of France's earthy vegetables—cauliflower, potatoes, onions and carrots. Such stalwart fare means dishes are hearty and wholesome rather than foo-foo. *Crêpes* (thin pancakes) are a staple of the Breton cuisine. A *crêperie* is a good place to get a light meal. Crêpes are often served with sweet jams and jellies and fruit preserves, but also with eggs. *Galttes* are thicker pancakes made from buckwheat and are served with any kind of savory dish.

Brittany's creperies are great spots for light meals.

Like Normandy, Brittany produces a lot of cider. There are no grapes the region—it's too cold and too damp—so the apple-based sparkling win is the *boisson* of choice with most meals. *Cidre brut* is the dry cider usual taken with meals; *cidre doux* is a sweeter drink to accompany desserts an crêpes.

Rennes

Rennes, the capital of the region, is the gateway to Brittany, where maje roads and railways converge. An ancient place, Rennes was founded by th Gauls and then developed by the Romans as a regional center of strategic im portance due to its location at the confluence of two major rivers, the Vilain and the Ile. The city today is somewhat schizophrenic. There is a small cen ter of original 16th-century houses built in the classic half-timbered medi eval style, but most of the town was burned to the ground in 1720 in raging fire started by a drunken carpenter. The great majority of the city's a chitecture is thus far more modern, some of it downright ugly. This includ several universities, although the students give the town a lively feel and thriving nightlife. Except for the Old Town and the museum of Brittan (which offers a good overview of the region's history from the prehistoric the present), there is little in Rennes to hold your attention. Most visito will be content with a stopover of a few hours before heading on to the re Bretagne.

BRITTANY

What to Do

City Celebrations/Events

ightfall Festival   ★★★

various locations, ☎ *02-99-79-01-98.*

Also called the Festival des Tombees de la Nuit, this bash is an eight-day welcome to summer, with poetry readings, storytelling, dancing, music and yummy Breton galletes, crepes, seafood and more. Event tickets cost FR35–FR150. Contact the **Office de Tourisme**, at *8 place du Marechal June, 35000 Rennes; FAX: 99-30-13-45.*

Historical/Architectural Sites

eux Rennes   ★★★

between quai Lamartine and rue St. Malo.

Blessedly unscathed by the great fire of 1720, this section of medieval Rennes consists of fine old homes that belonged to 17th-century nobles; many now have modern shops and chic restaurants on the premises. Note the predominant half-timbered style of architecture.

Museums and Exhibits

usée de Bretagne   ★★

20 quai Emile Zola, ☎ *02-99-28-55-84.*
Hours open: 10 a.m.–6 p.m. Special hours: Closed from noon–2 p.m. Closed: Tue.
This museum is devoted to the history of Brittany, going back as far as the Stone Age. Several galleries showcase Breton costumes, jewelry and furniture; others focus on megalithic monuments from Carnac and Locmariaquer. Right next door is the Musée des Beaux-Arts, with paintings from the 14th through the 20th centuries, including a few from the Pont-Aven school. Also on display are Quimper porcelain, as well as Egyptian, Greek and Etruscan artifacts. Hours are the same as the Museum of Brittany. Admission: FR15.

usée des Beaux-Arts   ★★

20 quai Emile Zola, ☎ *02-99-28-55-85. Near the canal.*
Hours open: 10 a.m.–6 p.m. Special hours: Closed noon–2 p.m. Closed: Tue.
A fine picture collection ranging from the 14th century to the present. Some Picasso, Gauguin and Rubens are found here. Most noteworthy is "The Newborn," by Georges de la Tour, an incredible display of color and lighting. In the same building is the Musée de Bretagne, providing information about the region's history and culture with displays on costumes, tools and traditions. A great introduction to the region. Admission: FR15.

Parks and Gardens

habor Garden   ★★★

rue Victor Hugo, near Notre-Dame-en-St.-Melanie.
Hours open: 7:15 a.m.–9:30 p.m.
A beautiful oasis, this 27-acre garden is a tribute to the art of French landscape design. Situated in what was once the garden of the Benedictine Abbey of Notre-Dame-en-St.-Melanie alongside it, the Thabor Garden has a section completely devoted to roses, as well as a traditional formal garden.

BRITTANY

Where to Stay

Hotels and Resorts

Central Hotel   **FR355**   ★★

6 rue Lanjuinais. ☎ *02-99-79-12-36, FAX: 02-99-79-65-76. Near the Rennes Cathedr.*
Double: FR355.

An air of elegance surrounds this hotel with origins from the late 1800s. Snuggle
in a back street location, the noise is kept to a minimum. There are 44 tidy gue
rooms, most of which have a private bath. Views from the windows are of the stre
or the courtyard. Car travelers will enjoy the off street parking in this town cent
situation. The helpful staff is very accommodating and speaks functional Englis
Credit Cards: V, MC, DC, A.

Hotel Angelina   **FR250–FR290**   ★ ★

1 quai Lamennais. ☎ *02-99-79-29-66, FAX: 02-99-79-61-01.*
Double: FR250–FR290.

Located above a fast-food restaurant, the noise from the traffic below can be a b
disconcerting. The 29 guest rooms are equipped with double windows to lessen th
noise, and each is comfortably attired with basic amenities. While some rooms hav
been graciously improved, some are still in need of a makeover; it's not tough t
overlook the roughness around the edges, though. The English speaking propr
etress greets each guest as an old friend, making the experience here worthy of th
two stars.

Mercure Centre Parc Colombier   **FR440**   ★

1 rue du Capitaine Maignan. ☎ *221-4542, 02-99-29-73-73, FAX: 02-99-30-06-3*
About 500 meters from the train station and 3 km from the airport.
Double: FR440.

This motor hotel, opened in 1973, provides decent overnight lodging for thos
seeking a quick getaway via train the next morning. There are 140 rooms, each wit
TV, radio, telephone, minibar and private bath. There is a restaurant and a bar i
the hotel, and a nightclub is just a short walk away. Lacking in character. Feature
wheelchair-access rooms, in-room minibars, in-room conference facilities. Cre
Cards: All Major.

Where to Eat

L'Escale   **$**

178 rue St.-Malo. ☎ *02-99-59-19-55.*
Dinner: 7:30 p.m.–midnight, entrées FR25–FR55.

L'Escale is a nice local hangout that's open late; it's a good spot for filling meals an
sweet and savory crepes. Also notable is **La Chope**, *3 rue de la Chalotais (*☎ *02-9*
79-34-54), also open until the witching hour, brasserie food from FR70; **Le Se**
ment de Vin, *bd. de La Tour-d'Auvergne (*☎ *02-99-30-99-30)*, wines and region
dishes, from FR75, open until 11 p.m. Closed: Mon., Tues. Amenities: cafesto
reservations recommended. Credit Cards: V, MC, E.

Le Corsaire   **$$$**   ★★ ★

52 rue d'Antrain. ☎ *02-99-36-33-69.*
Lunch: FR260–FR360.

Dinner: entrées FR260–FR360.

Located in an impressive town house in old Rennes, Le Corsaire is one of the city's top restaurants, with a one-star Michelin rating. Some of chef Luce's specialties include pan-fried langoustines with duck foie gras, and *coq au vin* with baby onions and *lardons* (bacon). The FR108 fixed-price menu is a good value. Closed: Mon. reservations required. Credit Cards: V, MC, DC, A, E.

e Palais $$$ ★★★

7 place du Parlement. ☎ *02-99-79-45-01.*
Lunch: Noon–2 p.m., FR350–FR450.
Dinner: 7–10 p.m., entrées FR350–FR450.

This clubby, woodsy and elegant dining establishment in the heart of old Rennes (near the Law Courts) is the domain of Marc Tizon, who presents choice seafood from the best purveyors in the region. Tizon bases many of his creations on unusual traditional recipes. His desserts are wonderful, including a warm chocolate cake with rum sauce or Breton butter cake with caramelized apples. Jackets required. Closed: Sun. Amenities: own baking, reservations required. Credit Cards: V, MC, A, E.

e Pire $$ ★★★★

18 rue du Mal-Joffre. ☎ *02-99-79-31-41.*

A husband-wife team that only gets better with time. While Madame Angelle assures your happiness in the dining room and courtyard, Marc Angelle is working magic in the kitchen. With the freshest of ingredients, he masters the traditional fare. Browse the extensive wine list for the perfect complement, or ask Madame Angelle for her insightful suggestions. Fixed-price menus start at FR110. Closed mid-late Aug. and late Dec.–early Jan. Closed: Sun. Amenities: outside dining, reservations required. Credit Cards: All Major.

Directory

o and From

By rail from Paris (two hours on the TGV) or by car from Paris on the A-11 autoroute or from Normandy by way of Mont St. Michel on the N-175. Rennes is a good starting point for a visit to the region, and can make a decent base for a tour of the interior.

ourist Office

pont de Nemours; ☎ *(33) 02-99-79-01-98.*

ail Station

place de la Gàre; ☎ *(33) 02-99-65-50-50.*

ost Office

27 boulevard du Colombier, 35000 Rennes; ☎ *(33) 02-99-01-22-11.*

St. Malo

The stunning walled port-city of St. Malo was founded on an island in the arbor mouth by the Welsh evangelist Maclou, who arrived (bringing the Gospel with him) during the sixth century. Although St. Malo is one of the remier tourist destinations in Brittany, the city has a long history of inde-endence, including an unsuccessful attempt to declare itself a separate republic, in the late 16th century. The immense fortifications that remai today bear witness to St. Malo's fiercely isolationist past. The city within th walls is called *intra-muros*. It was almost completely destroyed during Worl War II, but has since been scrupulously restored in the original architectur styles of the 15th, 16th and 17th centuries. Your first sight of this squat, gra city, with its tall granite houses will be one of your most memorable in all France.

Nowadays, the walled city is mostly a huge tourist trap. The ancient buil ings house restaurants and shops rather than whalers, explorers (Jacqu Cartier embarked on his discovery of Canada from St. Malo), and pirates o a break from terrorizing English traders. Nevertheless, you should spend couple of hours walking around the huge ramparts and wandering the laby rinthine streets. Watch out for huge crowds during summer, and don't e: pect to get a hotel room within the walls without a reservation made montl in advance. St. Malo has expanded well beyond its island, and there are number of worthwhile attractions in the rest of town, among them the 15tl century castle. You might also explore the beaches at low tide, when you ca walk out to the island of Grand Bé (where the writer Châteaubriand is bu ied) and Petit Bé Island, where you can tour an old fort that was once part the city's defenses.

Most of what is seen in St. Malo dates from the early 18th century.

What to Do

Historical/Architectural Sites

Fort National

Walk to it from Eventail Beach, at low tide only.

Special hours: Open daily, May-Sept. only.
This 17th-century fort built by Vauban is a 30-minute walk from the beach. Its imposing appearance warned would-be intruders to think twice before attacking the city; nowadays shutterbugs are daunted by the myriad photo opportunities from atop the walls. It must be attempted at low tide only, or you WILL be left stranded! Leaving St. Malo from the Champs-Vauvers Gate, cross the beach to the Grand Be, the burial island of the poet Châteaubriand; views from here are stupendous.

Petit Be National Fort ★★

Petit Be. Off of Port St.-Thomas, accessible at low tide.
Special hours: Closed late Sept.–Easter.
St. Malo's national fort, sometimes available for tours at low tide, makes for a nice visit. On the north point of land outside of the town center, it's a peaceful location for a stroll through a bit of history created by Louis XIV's military architect, Vauban, in 1689. Admission: FR10.

Ville Close ★★★★

Entrance through St.-Vincent's Gate. At the gate, take stairway to the right.
As a result of unceasing bombing attacks for two weeks in August 1944, most of the old walled city of St.-Malo was razed. Through local effort, historic buildings were gingerly taken apart and put back together again, a herculean effort. Now the number-one activity is to walk the fortified walls (which escaped destruction) from one end to the other, marked by towers and bastions. From the Bidouane Tower, you can see the National Fort, built by Vauban, which practically disappears at high tide. The Old City is separated from the suburbs and modern sprawl by an estuary. The entrance is at the St.-Vincent's Gate, near Esplanade St.-Vincent. Admission: free.

Museums and Exhibits

Château de St.-Malo ★★★

Between St.-Vincent and St.-Thomas Gates, ☎ 02-99-40-71-57.
Hours open: 10 a.m.–6 p.m. Special hours: Closed from noon–2 p.m. Closed: Tue.
Two museums of Malouin life and history are within this medieval Château, built between the 14th and 17th centuries. The great keep (the oldest part of the castle) houses the St.-Malo museum. Here you can read documents relating to the founding of the city and see exhibits encompassing ships and fishing. The highlight of a visit here, however, is the great view from the towers. Adjoining is the Quic-en-Groigne, where you'll see everything you just read about rendered in wax. Admission: FR16.

Special Tours/Excursions

Ile du Grand Be ★★

50 yards off the St. Malo coast.
A small island just off the coast where Châteaubriand is entombed, as his wish was to be buried near the waves and the wind. Take notice of the plaque behind the tomb, which is engraved with the words (in French, of course), "A great French writer wanted to rest here." In true Breton independent fashion, somebody drew a line through the word "French" and wrote "Breton." Attempt the walk to this

BRITTANY

island at any other time than low tide and it could be about six hours before you return.

Where to Stay

Bed and Breakfasts

La Korrigane   **FR400–FR800**   ★ ★ ★

39 rue le Pomellec. ☎ *02-99-81-65-85, FAX: 02-99-82-23-89. In the south section of town, near the harbor.*
Double: FR400–FR800.

A splendid turn of the century mansion, La Korrigane is guaranteed to enchant its guests with its classic charm. Situated among manicured gardens, within this lovely abode are 12 individually styled rooms. Each one is tastefully decorated with antiques and equipped with central heating, TV, telephone and a private bath or shower. Guests enjoy breakfast in the cozy garden and linger in the sitting rooms in the evenings. A fantasylike getaway. Credit Cards: V, MC, DC, A.

Hotels and Resorts

Hotel Atlantis   **FR350**   ★ ★ ★

49 chaussee du Sillon. ☎ *02-99-56-09-26, FAX: 02-99-56-41-65.*
Double: FR350.

Soak in the views offered by the many rooms overlooking the town beaches. There are 53 guest rooms of outstanding comfort featuring cool, bright designs. Rooms vary greatly in size and luxury, so it's wise to see the room prior to checking in. A tea room satiates the afternoon shift, and a sociable bar pours some tall drinks to the night crowd. One of the greatest delights here is enjoying breakfast on the terrace facing the sea—don't miss it. Credit Cards: V, A.

Hotel Elisabeth   **FR500–FR620**   ★ ★ ★

2 rue des Cordiers. ☎ *02-99-56-24-98, FAX: 02-99-56-39-24. Take bus #1, 2 or 3.*
Single: FR500–FR575. Double: FR540–FR620.

Quite a comfortable arrangement in the Elisabeth. Behind the 16th-century facade lie 17 guest chambers of contemporary comfort and convenience. Each comes with a TV, telephone and private bath, and many afford fine views of the harbor. A complimentary breakfast is included with the stay. The warm reception and courteous service make one immediately feel at home. Credit Cards: V, MC, DC, A.

Where to Eat

A la Duchesse Anne   **$$**   ★ ★

5 place Guy La-Chambre. ☎ *02-99-40-85-33.*
Specialties: grilled lobster "Duchesse Anne," fresh duck foie gras "a la maison," tarte tatin.
Lunch: 12:15–1:30 p.m., FR135–FR185.
Dinner: 7:15–9:15 p.m., entrées FR135–FR185.

Guests dine in an elegant, old-fashioned setting at A la Duchesse Anne—possibly St Malo's best restaurant. There are a few meat dishes available, but no-frills, classically prepared seafood is what this house does best. Prices are reasonable for what you get. A makeshift patio is set up for dining in the warmer months. Closed: Wed. Amenities: outside dining, own baking, reservations required. Credit Cards: V, MC.

Le Chalut   **$$**   ★★

    8 rue de la Corne-du-Cerf. ☎ *02-99-56-71-58.*
    Lunch: 12:30–2 p.m., FR95–FR155.
    Dinner: 7:30–10 p.m., entrées FR95–FR155.
    Le Chalet is a homey, unpretentious restaurant within the old city walls. Chef Jean-Philippe Foucat specializes in seafood dishes, and his sauces are interesting and savory. Fixed-price menus begin at FR95. Closed: Mon. Amenities: own baking, reservations required. Credit Cards: V, MC, A, E.

Le Petit Malouin   **$**   ★

    6 rue de la Veille Boucherie. ☎ *02-99-40-87-44.*
    Lunch: 11 a.m.–11 p.m., FR50–FR65.
    Dinner: 11 a.m.–11 p.m., entrées FR50–FR65.
    You can get good crepes here, both as a main course or for dessert, amid the surroundings of the picturesque Old City ramparts. For more crepes, try **Chez Chantal**, *2 pl aux Herbes (*☎ *02-99-40-93-97);* it's especially good for a mixed-seafood version. Visa accepted. How about a splurge? **Les Ecluses**, *gare maritime de la Bourse* (☎ *02-99-56-81-00),* in the port area, with great views of boats, is known for excellent lamb dishes and, of course, seafood, especially prawns. The fixed-price menu starts at FR94. Visa accepted. Closed: Sun. dinner, and Mon. Amenities: own baking, reservations not accepted.

Directory

To and From

    From Rennes by rail (one hour one-way) or by car on the N-137, or around the bay from Mont St. Michel on the D-176, or by ferry from England or Ireland.

Tourist Office

    esplanade St. Vincent; ☎ *(33) 02-99-56-64-48.*

Rail Station

    place de l'Hermine; ☎ *(33) 02-99-65-50-50.*

Post Office

    1 boulevard de la Tour d'Auvergne, 35400 St. Malo; ☎ *(33) 02-99-40-89-90.*

Dinard

Situated just across the mouth of the Rance estuary from St. Malo on the Emerald Coast, Dinard is proof to support the saying that getting there is half the fun. If you have the time, you should come from St. Malo by boat, across the harbor mouth—a great way to see the twin ports from the seafarer's perspective. Otherwise, drive over the *Barrage de Rance*, an engineering marvel (take the public tour, too) consisting of a hydroelectric plant that is powered by the surging tides and can be lifted hydraulically to permit ships to ply up river to Dinan.

Dinard has been a quasi-ritzy tourist spot as far back as the 19th century, and has a now somewhat dilapidated casino and several beautiful summer homes overlooking the bay. Be sure to take a walk along the Promenade du Clair-de-la-Lune, in moonlight if you can. You can then hike or drive around the peninsula through the tiny fishing villages of St. Lunaire, St. Briac and Lancieux, stopping off at the cliffs of Pointe de la Garde-Guérin or linger awhile at one of the sandy beaches if it's warm enough.

What to Do
Beaches

Plage de l'Ecluse

One of a trio of beaches, this beach, otherwise known as La Grande Plage, is surrounded by fashionable hotels and those who want to be seen. If it's sun, surf and crowds you seek, look no further. Another beach, La Plage de St.-Enogat, is backdropped by beautiful cliffs about 1 km west of La Grande Plage. The third beach, La Plage du Prieure, is about 1 km south of the main beach off of boulevard Feart. All three beaches will surely satisfy any fun-in-the-sun seeker.

Historical/Architectural Sites

Promenade du Clair de Lune ★★★

Along Baie du Prieure southwest from the Embarcadere.

Lined with semitropical vegetation and romantics holding hands, Dinard's most famous promenade offers vistas of St. Malo's old city across the water. The Plage de l'Ecluse, a lovely sandy beach, awaits at the end, with its calm shelter from the river and sea meeting at the crashing surf upon the rocks. On the far side of the beach, the path can be walked again, leading to Dinard's last beach, the Plage de St.-Enogat. Admission: free.

Museums and Exhibits

Musée du Pays

12 rue des Francais Libres, ☎ *02-99-46-81-05.*
Hours open: 2–6 p.m. Special hours: Easter–mid-Nov. only.

The museum is housed in the Villa Eugenie, a mansion built in 1868 for the Empress Eugenie, the wife of Napoleon III. Although she never spent time here, the mansion still remains. In the museum are artifacts tracing the history of the Dinard area and its development as a beach resort. A good rainy-day visit, considering any sunny days will be spent on the famous beaches here. Admission: FR15.

Where to Stay
Bed-and-Breakfasts

Manoir de la Duchee   **FR300–FR350**

La Duchee, Saint-Briac-sur-Mer. ☎ *02-99-88-00-02. Take the D786 towards Camping Municipal. Follow the signs.*
Single: FR300. Double: FR350.

A short drive through the countryside leads to this relaxing B&B outside of Dinard. Small in size and big in character, there are five comfortable rooms with TV and private bath. A duplex with a capacity for four persons is also available for FR500. The breakfast room, with exposed beams and attractive stonework, sets the scene for the complimentary breakfast. After starting the day with a tasty meal, there are horses and bikes to be ridden on the property, and there are sailing, swimming, tennis and golf facilities nearby. The service is friendly, and the accommodations are fit for any traveler who appreciates getting away from the city. Features: country location.

Hotels and Resorts

Le Grand Hotel **FR1000–FR1200**

46 avenue George-V. ☎ *02-99-88-26-26, FAX: 02-99-88-26-27. Near Saint-Servan Bay. Double: FR1000–FR1200.*
The premier hotel of Dinard, this hotel represents the grandeur of the 19th century and its architectural styles. Built in 1859, the five-story brick building is dotted with balconies off of the 63 guest rooms. Spaciously arranged, the rooms are furnished with period furniture and come with TV, telephone, minibar and beautiful, private bath. Relax with an aperitif in the bar before sampling the fixed-price menu in the restaurant starting at FR185. Recreational facilities include a heated pool and golf packages. A long living staple of quality accommodations in Dinard. Features: in-room minibars.Credit Cards: V, MC, DC, A.

Reine Hortense **FR1300** ★★★

19 rue de la Malouine. ☎ *02-99-46-54-31, FAX: 02-99-88-15-88. On the beach. Single: FR1300. Double: FR1300.*
The luxurious surroundings here originally pampered one of the Russian courtiers of the mother of Napoleon III. With only eight rooms, the atmosphere is intimate, and service is wonderful. Complementing the lavish public areas, the rooms are decorated in Louis XV or Napoleon III style. Each comes with a TV, telephone and private bath (one room has the silver-plated bathtub of Napoleon's mother). The only drawbacks, due to the size of this hotel, are there are no leisure facilities and breakfast is the only meal served. The accommodations and service are splendid. Features: beach location. Credit Cards: V, MC, DC.

Where to Eat

Altair **$$** ★★★

18 boulevard Feart, Near the beach. ☎ *02-99-46-13-58.*
Dinner: 7–9:30 p.m., entrées FR100–FR300.
Geared towards a relaxed, intimate crowd, the Altair sets a comfortable scene in an old-fashioned, country-style establishment. Warm months are ideal for lingering on the terrace. The breast of duck and the warm fish terrine are most excellent. The truly wonderful array of desserts is not to be missed. Fixed-price menus start at FR90 and are of generous proportions. Closed: Mon. Amenities: outside dining, reservations recommended. Credit Cards: All Major.

Le Petit Robinson **$** ★★★

38 rue de la Gougeonnais, About 3km southeast of town, in La Richardais. ☎ *02-99-46-14-82.*
Dinner: 7–9:30 p.m., entrées FR80–FR125.
Residing in a turn-of-the-century manor house, the cuisine includes attractively presented traditional fare. Seafood dominates the menu with everything from monkfish to lobster. A decent selection of wines rounds out the meal and the good conversa-

tion with the family owners. Fixed-price meals cost FR90–FR170. reservations required. Credit Cards: All Major.

Directory

To and From

By boat or by car from St. Malo.

Dinan

Dinan is situated above the Rance River within medieval ramparts.

Not to be confused with Dinard at the opposite end of the Rance river estuary, Dinan is one of the most charming and undiscovered towns of the Côte d'Emeraude area. In 1364, the French nobleman du Guesclin and the English cad Sir Thomas of Canterbury fought it out over the rights to the town, which was then an important river port in the textile industry. The Englishman backed down and Dinan's honor was saved.

Today, the medieval center of town is well-preserved and—unlike the more popular St. Malo—it is original. The Old Town is strategically built high above the river and is partially walled. From the 15th-century streets, you get a beautiful view of the river valley, and an even better one from the clock tower in the center of town. Naturally, Dinan has its 12th-century church and castle—what self-respecting Breton town wouldn't? You can walk down one of the steep footpaths to the little port, where the river is spanned by a Gothic-style bridge that, remarkably, still supports the traffic of today. A nice walk is along the bank of the river to the ruins of the 17th-century Abbaye St. Magloire at nearby Léhon.

What to Do

City Celebrations/Events

Fete des Remparts ★★

A biennial festival, the Fete des Remparts is on the first weekend of September (1996, 1998, 2000....). It's a grand display of medieval costumes, street musicians, duels and wild fun (☎ *02-96-39-75-40, for info.*). After-dark fun can be found at the young and lively **Bar au Prelude** (☎ *02-96-39-06-95*), which goes until 3 a.m. with cheap food, live music and great times.

Historical/Architectural Sites

Basilica St.-Sauveur ★★★

place St.-Sauveur. After entering the vieille ville through Port St.-Louis, turn right onto rue General de Gaulle, and follow the signs to the Jardin Anglais.
Hours open: 8 a.m.–6 p.m.
Reflecting more than 600 years' worth of work, the incongruous architectural styles of this church are immediately noticeable. The north transept has the cenotaph containing the heart of Du Guesclin, the 14th-century soldier who drove the English out of France. Its Romanesque portals, lavish 16th-century chapels and 15th-century Breton glass in the Evangelists' Window are just a few of the highlights of this basilica. The Jardin Anglais is a terraced garden and old cemetery offering great views, just behind the basilica.

Château de Dinan ★★★

Behind the walls of the old city.
Hours open: 10 a.m.–6:30 p.m. Closed: Tue.
Commanding the medieval ramparts of the old city, the château was begun by Duke John IV in the middle of the 14th century. The 15th-century towers project outwards for military purposes, and were able to withstand lengthy sieges. In the château is the local museum, displaying artifacts of Dinan's history, art and architecture. Temporary displays and sculpted tomb lids are seen in the Tour de Coetquen. Both museums are included in the château admission price.

Tour de l'Horloge ★★

rue de l'Horloge. In the heart of the old city.
Hours open: 10 a.m.–7 p.m. Special hours: Apr.–May, 2-6 p.m.
The clock tower, an historical monument dating back to 1498, has a bell donated by Anne of Brittany in 1507. The view from the 75-foot high top lays out the medieval streets and the surrounding countryside in jumbled detail. It's a fine view worthy of the few francs. Admission: FR10.

rue du Jerzual ★★

The sloping rue de Jerzual links the center of town with the port. It is flanked with old houses and 15th- and 16th-century shops where craftsmen have worked for centuries. Take time to stop in at some of the shops and appreciate the traditional crafts. La Porte du Jerzual, an ancient gate, lies at the street's end. Other interesting houses are on rue de l'Apport, place des Merciers and place du Guesclin.

BRITTANY

Where to Stay

Bed-and-Breakfasts

La Tarais   **FR250**   ★★

Calorguen. ☎ *02-96-83-50-59. About 7 km south of Dinan. Take the D12 towards Lehon, and then head to Calorguen. There will be signs.*
Double: FR250.

A lovely stone and brick country house on a village farm, La Tarais is charming in its simplicity. The product of a friendly Anglo-Dutch husband-wife duo, there are four rooms with bath kept in immaculate condition. While basic in furnishings, the understated effect works well here. The complementary breakfast is taken outdoors when it's warm or in the dining room at separate tables when the winter chill has arrived; other meals are available in the summer months. Possible activities include a pool and a tennis court nearby, scenic walks and a tour of Dinan. The multilingual owners make every guest feel at home. Features: country location. Credit Cards: Not Accepted.

Le Petit Moulin du Rouvre   **FR250–FR300**   ★★★

Sainte-Pierre-de-Plesguen. ☎ *02-99-73-85-84, FAX: 02-99-73-71-06. About 13 km east of Dinan. From the D794, take the N137 and the D10. Follow the signs once in the town.*
Single: FR250. Double: FR300.

Almost surreal in setting, this quaint B&B sits alone on the edge of a millpond among green grass and the shade of the trees. A stone mill, it provides waterside tranquility and intimacy. With just four small, attractive rooms with bath, guests enjoy the personal attention and conversation with the wonderful sweet proprietress. After starting off the day with a complementary breakfast, guests play golf at the nearby course or tour Dinan. Top off the day by dining on local specialties at the communal dinner table. Have a camera ready to capture this picturesque inn and its verdant surroundings. Credit Cards: Not Accepted.

Hotels and Resorts

D'Avaugour   **FR375–FR500**   ★★★

1 place du Champs-Clos. ☎ *02-96-39-07-49, FAX: 02-96-85-43-04. Near the ramparts in town. Take bus #34, 36 or 96.*
Single: FR375. Double: FR450–FR500.

Kudos to Madame Quinton for her lavish efforts in completely renovating an old building and creating this modern hotel. With some overlooking the ramparts and the square in the front, or the garden in the rear, the 27 rooms are furnished with beautiful reproductions and equipped with TV, telephone, minibar and private bath. Breakfast is available for FR45, and the hotel restaurant serves decent food in the garden every day; another restaurant opens for the summer, serving flavorful food from the grill. A stylish little hotel in the heart of town. Credit Cards: V, MC, DC, A.

Where to Eat

Chez La Mere Pourcel   **$$**   ★★★★

3 place des Merciers, In the center of Old Dinan. ☎ *02-96-39-03-80.*
Dinner: 7:15–10 p.m., entrées FR110–FR150.

One of the most enchanting settings in town, exposed wood beams, stone walls and leaded-glass create wonderful surroundings for an enjoyable taste of the regional cuisine. Deep, rich flavors abound in such dishes as red mullet, pigeon and rabbit. Choose from a well-priced selection of wines and flavorful desserts. Fixed-price menus start at FR90. Closed: Mon. Amenities: outside dining, reservations recommended. Credit Cards: All Major.

La Caravelle $$$ ★★★★

14 place Duclos. ☎ *02-96-39-00-11.*
Dinner: 7–9:30 p.m., entrées FR140–FR240.
Ignore the decor of this modern building—instead, savor the presentation, scent and taste of the inventive cuisine created by Jean-Claude Marmion. Your palate will always remember the John Dory with onions or green mustard; the game dishes are unmatched in Dinan; and the heavenly desserts can do no wrong. Service is cordial, attentive and unintrusive. Fixed-price menus start at FR125. reservations required. Credit Cards: All Major.

Les Jardins du Jerzual $ ★★

5 rue de la Chaux. ☎ *02-96-39-64-34.*
The huge menu here features such money savers as FR40 lasagna and many pastas from FR45. Many seafood dishes are available at low prices, too. Fixed-menus start at FR50. Another good refueling stop is near the **Les Jardins du Jerzual** at *15 rue du Petit Fort (*☎ *02-96-85-28-75).* A small crêperie with selections from FR10. In addition to dessert crepes, there are many others suitable for entrées (some with seafood). Closed: Mon. Credit Cards: V, MC.

Directory

To and From

By road along the banks of the river from St. Malo or Dinard.

Tourist Office

6 rue de l'Horloge; ☎ *(33) 02-96-39-75-40.*

Post Office

place Duclos, 22100 Dinan; ☎ *(33) 02-96-85-83-50.*

Côte de Granit Rose

The large promontory halfway along the northern coast of Brittany is known as the *Côte de Granit Rose*, or the Pink Granite Coast. This somewhat exaggerated name has its obvious roots in the blond-colored, smooth granite that dominates the coastline. The region offers little besides the spectacular coastline and some expensive spas offering seaweed cures (known as thalassotherapy), but it's well-worth making the drive on your way from the St. Malo area to Brest and Finistère. Sculpted by eons of tides and winds, the unusual rocks are most interesting at the stretch between Perros-Guirec and Trébeurden. From the former, you can take a short boat trip out to an ornithological reserve called Les Sept Isles (The Seven islands), where more than 15,000 pairs of seabirds, including puffins, nest.

To and From

> *Take the D-786 road west and exit at Lannion. From there drive along the D-788 to Perros Guirec, where you might stop for lunch. The road takes a circuitous route around the peninsula before returning you to Lannion.*

Brest

Brest is a thoroughly utilitarian port city, mentioned here mostly because it is a logical place to base yourself for a day or two while exploring the extreme northern peninsula of Finistère. Tucked inside the shelter of the Presqu'Ile de Crozon, Brest has a perfect natural harbor and has been France's chief naval base for more than 350 years. The harbor was the major port of entry for the Americans during World War I, and during World War II, the Nazis fortified Brest into a major U-boat base. The port was bombed to hell by the Allies and the rebuilt city is, like many ports, rather charmless and ugly.

Nevertheless, the medieval-era castle survived intact and is an interesting visit. Built from the 12th to 17th centuries, the castle stands on a site that had been used as a military installation. Today, the castle houses a good maritime museum. You can cross the River Penfeld via Europe's largest lifting bridge to the other side of the harbor and get a good panoramic view of the bustling port from the 16th-century Tour Tanguy.

What to Do

Historical/Architectural Sites

Château de Brest   ★★

> *rue de Siam,* ☎ *02-98-22-12-39. At the end of rue Siam.*
> *Hours open: 9 a.m.–6 p.m. Special hours: Closed noon–2 p.m. Closed: Tue.*

The château at Brest is the only building that survived the bombings during WWII. Now, it is the world's oldest active military institution housing the Musée de la Marine. With a collection of artifacts tracing the history and traditions of the town, it is rather unimpressive. However, the walk around the thick château walls offers splendid views of the Rhade and the naval harbor. Admission: FR24.

Museums and Exhibits

Musée de Beaux-Arts   ★

> *22 rue Traverse,* ☎ *02-98-44-66-27. Off of rue de Siam.*
> *Hours open: 10 a.m.–6 p.m. Special hours: Closed 11:45 a.m.–2 p.m.; Sun., 2–6 p.m.*
> *Closed: Tue.*

A large collection of art from the 16th through the 20th centuries, focusing on the works from the school of Pont-Aven. A good bet for a rainy day. Also on this free ride is the **Musée de la Tour Tanguy at place Pierre Peron** (☎ *02-98-45-05-31*). This 14th-century tower relives Brest's grand, pre-WWII days with dioramas, artifacts and photos. Round out a day of franc-free diversions by walking the Cours

Dajot promenade. First laid out in 1769 on the old ramparts, the views here are magnificent. The port activity, the Brest Channel (created by the melting of the glaciers and the rising sea level flooding the coastline) and the roadsted of 58 square miles fed by several estuaries are just a few of the sights. These views are the most scenic and interesting in Brest (and they're easy on the budget). Admission: free.

Oceanopolis ★★★

port de Plaisance, ☎ *02-98-34-40-40. Take bus #7 across from the train station, and exit at Oceanopolis.*

Europe's first sea center, Oceanopolis Brest is an ultramodern building shaped like a crab. Inside are aquariums and exhibits on the marine life of Brittany's coast, including everything from algae to seals. The imaginative displays also present incredible information on navigation, ocean dynamics, food chains and birds of the coast in their nesting places on the cliff face. *Open mid-June–mid-Sept., daily, 9:30 a.m.–6 p.m.; Oct.–May, Mon, 2–5 p.m., Tues.–Fri., 9:30 a.m.–5 p.m., weekends and holidays, 9:30 a.m.–6 p.m.* Admission: FR47.

Where to Stay

Hotels and Resorts

Mercure Hotel Continental   **FR350–FR480** ★★

24 rue de Lyon. ☎ *02-98-80-50-40, FAX: 02-98-43-17-47. About 500 meters from the train station.*
Single: FR350–FR440. Double: FR350–FR480.
This five-story hotel, opened in 1951 and last improved in 1990, offers good, basic accommodations. The 75 rooms are quiet and come with TV, telephone, minibar and private bath or shower. There is an average restaurant serving big meals and a bar in the hotel. Its convenience to the train station for tourists without an auto is one of its best features. Nothing much to write home about and nothing much to complain about at these prices. Features: wheelchair-access rooms, in-room mini-bars. Credit Cards: All Major.

Oceania Hotel   **FR460–FR790** ★★

82 rue de Siam. ☎ *02-98-80-66-66, FAX: 02-98-80-65-50. About 2 km from the train station.*
Single: FR460–FR690. Double: FR520–FR790.
With contemporary styles throughout most of the facility, the Oceania occupies a five-story building last renovated in 1989. The 82 rooms are mostly comfortable, but we recommend that you see the room before checking in as the decor varies widely. All come with TV, telephone, radio and private bath. The restaurant serves good meals, and there's a bar and lounge for evening relaxation. A decent hotel with moderate service. Features: wheelchair-access rooms, in-room conference facilities. Credit Cards: V, MC, DC, A.

Where to Eat

Le Frere Jacques   **$$** ★★

15 bis, rue de Lyon. ☎ *02-98-44-38-65.*
Specialties: prawn and oyster salad in warm vinaigrette.
Lunch: Noon–2 p.m., FR125–FR150.

Dinner: 7–9:30 p.m., entrées FR125–FR150.

The frere here is Jacques Peron, the affable chef-owner, who operates Brest's finest restaurant. Fresh fish and shellfish dishes are served in a comfortable dining room—some of them aggressively spiced. A fixed-price FR116 menu is offered. Closed: Sun. reservations required. Credit Cards: V, MC, E.

Le Nouveau Rossini   **$$**   ★★

22 rue du Commandant-Drogou. ☎ 02-98-47-90-00.
Specialties: roast pigeon breast with glazed turnips.
Lunch: Noon–2 p.m., FR100–FR175.
Dinner: 7–9:30 p.m., entrées FR100–FR175.

One of Brest's prettiest restaurants, Le Nouveau Rossini is in a newer section of the city, where chef Maurice Mevel can provide more space and patio dining for guests. Modern seafood cuisine, with an emphasis on natural juices and vegetables, is featured. Good wine cellar with vintages available by the glass. Fixed-price FR98 lunch menu weekdays and Sat. Brest also has some good creperies and places for light meals. **La Chaumine**, *16 rue J. Bart (☎ 02-98-45-10-70)*, open until 10:30 p.m., from FR80; **Creperie St.-Martin**, *3 rue Graveran (☎ 02-98-44-42-04)*, near the old quarter, three courses from FR55. Late-night pizzas (open to midnight) at **La Scala**, *30 rue d'Algesiras (☎ 02-98-43-11-43)*. Closed: Mon. Amenities: outside dining, reservations required. Credit Cards: V, MC, A, E.

Marina   **$**   ★★

16 rue de Siam. ☎ 02-98-80-09-61.

Only home-made repasts are served here. Pizza and zesty, flavorful pasta is what Marina knows—better than any other in Brest. A FR70 menu includes an entrée and a main dish. A fun, hip restaurant. Check out Le Soleil d'Or for those leafy cravings. This vegetarian restaurant offers filling meals at reasonable prices. A la carte main dishes start at FR40, with an entire meal costing about FR80. Located at *4 rue Graveran (☎ 02-98-43-61-94)*.

Directory

To and From

By train from Paris (four-and-a-half hours by TGV) or Nantes (four hours); by air on Air Inter from Paris; by car from eastern Brittany on the N-12 autoroute or from the Loire on the N-165.

Tourist Office

place de la Liberté; ☎ (33) 02-98-44-24-96.

Rail Station

place du 19 éme Régiment de l'Infantérie; ☎ (33) 02-98-80-50-50.

Post Office

rue de Siam, 29200 Brest; ☎ (33) 98-51-87-76.

Parc Régional d'Armorique

Occupying nearly half of the département of Finistère, this regional nature preserve is a wonderful place to stop the car and take a hike over the moors or along the coastline. The preserve contains the modest Monts d'Arrée mountains, and includes remains of ancient oak forests that figure in Arthurian legends. Megalith sites attest to the region's past. The main information center for the park is at Ménez-Meur. There are also nine small interpretive centers throughout the park, each one explaining historical and natural aspects of the region.

Parc Régional d'Armorique
☎ *(33) 02-98-21-90-69.*

Enclos Paroissiaux

While crossing the park, you will come across several villages combining examples of one of the most interesting phenomenons in Brittany—the *Enclos Paroissiaux*, or "Parish Closes." Dating from the 16th century, these lavish parish churches (and more) are completely out of proportion to the communities they dominate. Small villages, possessed of a religious fervor that especially marks Brittany (as well as a more terrestrial desire to compete with and better their neighbors once the fad took on), built these monuments, with construction taking place as long as 200 years. A typical *Enclos Paroissiau* consists of an ornate church, usually in a blend of Romanesque and Gothic styles, with an unusually ornate interior (hand-carved altar stones depicting scenes from the life of local saints, expensive stained glass windows, and big organs). Outside there is a *calvaire*, or Calvary, a large three-dimensional stone depiction of the Crucifixion, mounted on its own ornate colonnade. Other structures include a triumphal arch by which one enters the churchyard, the cemetery, the ossuary where the bones where kept after exhumation from the cemetery (in order to create a bridge between the living and the dead), and a separate chapel for funeral services. All this was considered obligatory in order for a village to claim a decent parish close. The best example is in Pleyben, but there are several sites throughout the park and the Val d'Elorn. You can pick up a guide to the major sites from any tourist office.

Quimper

The Celts who founded this city in western Brittany called the region *Cornouaille*, a clear homage to the Cornwall of southwestern England they left behind. Celtic culture flourishes today in Quimper perhaps more than in any other city in Brittany. Here, you will hear Breton spoken, the women often wear *coiffes* when they go to church on even a regular Sunday, and the local bookstores stock books written in Breton. The city's name in Breton is *Kemper*, which means confluence, referring to the two rivers: the Steir and Odet which still flow through the town center. The rivers are crisscrossed by dozens of bridges. Quimper came to prominence in the 10th- or 11th-centuries (no one is quite sure), when the legendary King Gradlon, founder of the lost city of Ys, moved his seat of power here after Ys disappeared beneath the waves. There is a statue of the king in the courtyard of the magnificent Gothic cathedral, which dates to the year 1240.

Quimper has been a major earthenware center since the 18th century.

Beginning at the cathedral and sweeping up away from the banks of the river is the Old Town, a charming place to wander among narrow streets crowded with crêperies, bookstores, and shops contained in half-timbered medieval houses. The city is famous for its beautiful hand-painted pottery, known as *Faïence*. The distinctive designs, often a pastoral scene contained within a yellow and blue border, have been handed down generation to generation since the late 17th century. Be sure to visit one of the local *faïenceries* and get a tour of the pottery works. Also not to be missed is a drive out to the windswept **Pointe du Raz**, the most rugged of Brittany's many wild coastal spots, and the most westerly point. Unfortunately the site has fallen victim to its own popularity—it receives more than 1 million visitors a year—and the area is completely denuded. A revegetation project begun in 1995 is achieving only minimal success. A better bet might be a trip to the Pointe du Van a few miles to the north. **Pointe du Van** is just as beautiful, if not more so, with far less tourist traffic—and unlike Pointe du Raz, there are no crêperies perched on the point to feed hungry visitors.

What to Do

City Celebrations/Events

Festival de Cornouaille   ★★

    Various locations, ☎ *02-98-53-04-05.*

This lively traditional music, dance and film festival is named after the medieval duchy of Brittany; Quimper was once its capital. It draws mobs from all over the country a week before the fourth Sunday in July. Tickets are FR35–FR200.

Historical/Architectural Sites

Cathedrale St.-Corentin ★★★

place St.-Corentin, ☎ *02-98-95-06-19.*
Hours open: 9 a.m.–6:30 p.m.
A handsome example of Gothic architecture, Quimper's Cathedral was built
between the 13th and 15th centuries and its dual spires were erected in the 1800s, paid for by contributions from the community. It is named after the city's first bishop, who became a saint supposedly because he subsisted on a single fish. Corentin's life is depicted in a sculpture on a 17th-century pulpit within the church. Admission: free.

Old Quimper ★★

Between the cathedral and the Odet.
The medieval town along the banks of the Odet is a charming place to stroll. Beautiful old houses with timber-frames and granite ground floors line the streets. Rue Kereon's lively atmosphere is a picturesque setting for shopping, and the Jardin de l'Eveche, (Bishop's Gardens) behind the cathedral, is a tranquil stop. Admission: free.

Museums and Exhibits

Musée Departemental Breton ★★

1 rue de Roi-Gradlon, ☎ *02-98-95-21-60.*
Hours open: 9 a.m.–6 p.m. Special hours: Oct.–May, to 5 p.m., except Sun.–Mon.
Hundreds of years' worth of regional life and lore is tastefully displayed, in this 16th-century bishop's palace. Exhibits include the inevitable Quimper ware, statuary, furniture and costumes. Admission: FR25.

Musée des Beaux Arts ★★★

40 place St.-Corentin, ☎ *02-98-95-45-20.*
Hours open: 10 a.m.–6 p.m. Special hours: Closed noon–2 p.m. Closed: Tue.
Holding their own among a decent collection of old masters (including Rubens'
Martyrdom of Saint Lucia) are a representative bloc of paintings from the 19th-century Pont-Aven school, including such artists as Haan, Serusier, Bernard and others. Contributions from the school's founder, Paul Gauguin, are noticeably missing, however. Admission: FR25.

Pubs and Bars

Ceilli Pub ★★

4 rue Aristide Briand, ☎ *02-98-95-17-61.*
Hours open: 10:30 a.m.–1 a.m. Special hours: Sundays, from 5 p.m.
Ceilli's is one of the few nightspots in town offering live Celtic music in a comfortable
atmosphere. You might be asked to join in an informal jam session. Admission: free.

Shopping

Faiences de Quimper HB Herriot ★★★

rue Haute, ☎ *02-98-90-09-36.*

Hours open: 9:30 a.m.–4:30 p.m. Special hours: Closed from 11:30 a.m.–1:30 p.m. Closed: Sat., Sun.

Vividly hand-painted pottery cast from Breton clay has been a proud local art form since the late 17th century, when the first workshop was established in Quimper. This venerable pottery factory conducts guided tours in English and French during the week from Mar.–Oct. Open to 5 p.m. on Fridays. Admission: FR15.

Where to Stay

Château

Château du Guilguiffin   **FR350–FR750**   ★★★

Landudec. ☎ 02-98-91-52-11. About 12 km west of town. Take the D784 towards Audierne. It is about 3 km before Landudec.
Double: FR350–FR750.
An absolutely enrapturing château fronted by a grand facade of 18th-century architecture. A respected establishment housing four guest rooms and two suites. Each room presents itself in proud style and comfort with very attractive bathrooms. The public drawing rooms and the lounge are evidence to the careful attention paid to tradition in design. Breakfast is included, and dinners are available in the dining room. A true example of the pride taken in individual ownership. Credit Cards: Not Accepted.

Hotels and Resorts

Le Griffon   **FR370–FR450**   ★★

131 route de Benodet. ☎ 02-98-90-33-33, FAX: 02-98-53-06-67. About 2 km south of town center and 4 km from the train station.
Single: FR370. Double: FR450.
Resting in peace on the edge of town, le Griffon has been operating since 1973. Meticulous maintenance and friendly service are the priorities here in this 49 room hotel. The bed chambers are fairly spacious and include a telephone and private bath or shower. Nonsmokers can request separate rooms. There is a heated, enclosed pool and a sauna in the hotel. Golf enthusiasts will find the golf course 5 km away very convenient. A good fixed price menu is available at Creach Gwenn, the on-site restaurant. A reliable choice for efficiency and comfort. Features: pool, sauna, non-smoking rooms. Credit Cards: V, DC, A, E.

Manoir du Stang   **FR515–FR850**   ★★★

La Foret Fouesnant. ☎ 02-98-56-97-37.
Single: FR515. Double: FR580–FR850.
To get to the courtyard that leads to the entrance of this ivy-covered manor house, travel down the long, tree-lined private avenue and under the stone tower gate. On the right are a formal garden and raised stone terraces leading to 25 acres of rolling woodland and a lake. The interior of the house is filled with ancient paneling and antique furniture. Guests are lodged either in the main building or in the older annex; the latter has a beautiful circular stone staircase. The 26 rooms (all with private bath) are decorated with silks and fine antiques. A maid in a starched lacy uniform and Breton cap brings a breakfast tray to each room in the morning. The dining room is furnished with Breton antiques, and the chef's specialty is grilled lob-

ster with tarragon. Fixed-price meals begin at FR170. Features: tennis. Credit Cards: Not Accepted.

Tour d'Auvergne · · · · · · · · · · · · FR245–FR490 · · · · · · · · · · ★★
13 rue Reguaires. ☎ *02-98-95-08-70, FAX: 02-98-95-17-31. One block from the Odet. Single: FR245. Double: FR410–FR490.*

With the advantages of a central location while still maintaining its quiet demeanor, this contemporary hotel houses 43 rooms. Most are available with a private bath or shower, and all come with a telephone. Be sure to check out the restaurant specializing in regional cuisine. Service in the restaurant and hotel is wonderful. Credit Cards: V, MC, A.

Where to Eat

L'Ambroisie · · · · · · · · · · · · · · · · SS · · · · · · · · · · · · · · · · · ★★
49 rue E.-Freron. ☎ *02-98-95-00-02.*
Lunch: Noon–2 p.m., FR15–FR200.
Dinner: 7–9:45 p.m., entrées FR150–FR200.

Not far from the cathedral but hidden slightly away, L'Ambroisie is an attractive restaurant decorated with art and fresh flowers. Chef Gilbert Guyon prepares wonderful crepes with seafood. A FR98 fixed-price lunch menu is offered (weekdays only). Some say Les Acacias, *88 bd. Creach'h-Guen* (☎ *02-98-52-15-20)*, is even better, at least more adventurous, and there's also a patio for dining. Seafood, great desserts, well-chosen wine list. A FR98 fixed-price lunch is offered. No lunch Sat., or dinner Sun. Closed: August 1-15. Amenities: own baking, reservations required. Credit Cards: V, MC, A, E.

Le Cafe des Arts · · · · · · · · · · · · · · S · · · · · · · · · · · · · · · · · · ★
4 rue St.-Catherine.
Lunch: 11 a.m.–1 a.m., FR60–FR100.
Dinner: 11 a.m.–1 a.m., entrées FR60–FR100.

On the other side of the river from the cathedral are several creperies and cafes. Cafe des Arts is an interesting hangout, with tasteful decor. Light meals start at FR20, and entrées start at FR60. If you backtrack to the cathedral, you'll find a simple creperie, serving generous portions, **Creperie du Frout**, *17 rue du Frout* (☎ *02-98-95-26-94)*, menus from FR40. Covered market: **Les Halles**, *rue St.-Francois*, has everything you need for stocking up, quick food stalls too; daily until 8 p.m., Sun. until 1 p.m. Closed: Sun. Amenities: cafestop, reservations recommended. Credit Cards: V, MC, A, E.

Le Capucin Gourmand · · · · · · · · · · · · SS · · · · · · · · · · · · · · · · · ★★
29 rue des Reguaires. ☎ *02-98-95-43-12.*
Specialties: snail ravioli with ginger, lobster ragout, creme brulee (ice cream).
Lunch: 12:15 a.m.–2 p.m., FR125–FR190.
Dinner: 7:15–10 p.m., entrées FR125–FR190.

Crowded but pleasant, this Michelin-starred restaurant is owned by Soisik and Christian Conchon, who prepare generously proportioned seafood and meat dishes. Popular prices as well, including a FR115 fixed-price meal. Closed: Sun. Amenities: own baking, reservations required. Credit Cards: V, MC, DC, E.

Le Parisien   **$$**   ★★★

    13 rue Jean-Jaures. ☎ *02-98-90-35-29.*

    Dinner: 7:15–9 p.m., entrées FR70–FR200.

The ambience and staff at this central restaurant make this one of the most pleasurable dining experiences downtown. The excellent menu selection includes lobster, beef, pasta and fish. Fixed-price menus start at FR100. A popular establishment, so be sure to reserve a table. Closed: Sun. reservations recommended. Credit Cards: V, MC.

Plonevez-Porzay

Manoir de Moellien   **$$$**   ★★

    On C10, 1 mile north of Locronan ☎ *02-98-92-50-40.*

    Lunch: Noon–2 p.m., FR255–FR320.

    Dinner: 7–9 p.m., entrées FR255–FR320.

For a traditional Breton experience, it's hard to beat this picturesque, well-kept, 17th-century stone hotel with a good restaurant attached. Sophisticated sea fare is served in the old-fashioned dining room. Fixed-price menus start at FR125 (except Sun.) Closed: Wed. Amenities: own baking, reservations required. Credit Cards: All Major.

Directory

To and From

    By rail from Paris (five hours by TGV, seven-and-a-half hours by more frequent regular train) or Nantes (three hours), or by car from the south on the N-165 or from the north through the Parc Régional d'Armorique.

Tourist Office

    place de la Résistance; ☎ *(33) 02-98-53-04-05.*

Rail Station

    avenue de la Gàre; ☎ *(33) 02-98-90-50-50.*

Post Office

    37 boulevard Admiral de Kerguélen, 29000 Quimper; ☎ *(33) 02-98-95-88-40.*

Locronan

Just a few miles north of Quimper is the small town of Locronan. Although Locronan is a definite tourist trap these days, the town is worth a visit of a few hours. Founded about 2500 years ago and originally a major center of the Druids, Locronan was Christianized by an itinerant Irish evangelist in the fourth century. The ensuing pagan-Christian cult is common throughout Brittany, but in Locronan it has given rise to an annual festival called the *Troménie*, held every July in honor of St. Ronan, the Irish evangelist. Every six years—unfortunately not again until 2001—there is a bigger bash called, yes, the *Grande Troménie*.

The town was a major sailcloth production center during the 16th and 17th centuries, and today a lot of fine granite houses from the Renaissance period surround the central 15th-century church. Louis XIV pulled his patronage from the town in the 17th century, however, and the town grew empty and quiet. Recently the town has rediscovered itself as a sort of life-sized museum.

What to Do
City Celebrations/Events

Grand Troménie   ★★★★

place d'Eglise.

Ronan, who at the time was an Irish hermit driven out of Ireland in the 5th century, is credited with Christianinzing Locronan. As part of his penitence, he ran four miles every day of his life and 7.5 miles on Sunday. Every six years, on the second Sunday of July, the town revives his memory with a colorful religious procession covering his same steps from the town center to the mountain. The women wear their rarely seen traditional costumes, often elaborately embroidered in silk brocade, and the churches display the symbols of their patron saints. The next Grand Troménie, unfortunately, is not until July of 2001.

Historical/Architectural Sites

Eglise St.-Ronan   ★★★★

place d'Eglise.

This picturesque stone church was built in the 15th century in honor of St. Ronan, an Irish missionary; his 5th-century tomb, with a figure of the saint carved from local granite, rests in the Le Penity chapel. Situated in the main square, the Eglise is one of the remaining structures left from Locronan's *age d'or* as a sailmaking empire. The area also teems with hand-weaving and wood-sculpting workshops.

Where to Stay
Hotels and Resorts

Hotel Bois du Nevet   FR220–FR280   ★★

route du Bois-de-Nevet-Locronan. ☎ *02-98-91-83-12, FAX: 02-98-91-83-12. About 1 km west of town.*
Single: FR220. Double: FR280.

Built in 1973, this hotel is a fine display of modern architecture. The contemporary style still retains hints of a rustic period. The 24 rooms and 11 suites are large and afford pleasant vistas of the countryside from the big windows. Each room comes with a private bath, and some have stairways leading to mezzanines. Breakfast is available for FR30, and half-board rates are from FR290 per person. This peaceful establishment is a wonderful meld of modern comforts and country atmosphere.
Credit Cards: V, MC, DC, A.

Inns

Hotel de la Plage   FR465–FR950   ★★★

Ste-Anne-la-Pallud. ☎ *02-98-92-50-12, FAX: 02-98-92-56-54. About 10 km from Locronan towards Plonevez-Porzay; at Ste-Anne-la-Palud.*
Double: FR465–FR950.

Just a few feet from the shore, this seaside inn is worth the short drive from town. A beautiful getaway choice, this Relais and Châteaux member attracts those travelers seeking pure tranquility and relaxation. There are 26 comfortable guest rooms

BRITTANY

decorated in traditional decor and equipped with central heating, TV, telephone, minibar and private bath. Four of the rooms are family rooms; although, there are no special facilities for children on the property. The choice rooms afford a view of the sea or the countryside and are filled quickly. The attractive public areas include a welcoming sitting room, a dining room and a conference room. Within the beautiful grounds are a pool, tennis court and bar hidden in a separate cottage. Don't miss enjoying one of the seafood dinners served by the incredibly talented kitchen. Two words describe the staff—warm and courteous. Features: wheelchair-access rooms, beach location, pool, tennis, fitness center. Credit Cards: V, MC, DC, A.

Concarneau

A sort of miniature St. Malo, Concarneau's central feature is the walled city located on a tiny island in the harbor. However, the visitor may be surprised to know that Concarneau is the number-one fishing port in France and the largest tuna-fishing port and canning center in Europe. Fittingly, the city has a decent **Musée de la Pêche** (Museum of Fishing).

The island in the harbor was inhabited by fishing people as far back as prehistoric times. Prior to the 10th century, the island's defenses consisted of moats around the village and an inner circle of spiked wooden fences. Captured by the English in 1348, the town was liberated by Duguescelin 30 years later, and became one of the most important fortified cities of the Duchy of Bretagne. After France and Bretagne were united through the marriage of the king and the daughter of the duke, the walled city was officially designated a royal stronghold. The walls were rebuilt in stone in 1451. By the mid-16th century, the *ville close* (walled city) had its own church and cemetery, a hospital, a marketplace and a large barracks. The civilian population lived on the mainland, and the island was connected to the shore by a bridge. Civilians took refuge within the walls in time of attack. Today, the only invaders are hordes of tourists, but the walled city has its drawbridge down and seems to welcome them heartily enough. The walk around the ramparts of the 360- by 110-yard enclosed village is a must. If you plan to eat or shop in Concarneau, you're better off waiting until you get back to the more modern part of town.

What to Do

City Celebrations/Events

Fete des Filets Bleus   ★ ★

The Blue Nets Festival, first held in 1905 to help the widows of Concarneau's sardine fishermen, occurs during the five days preceding the second-to-last Sunday in August. Witness traditional Breton costumes and dances, and get your fill of fish.

Historical/Architectural Sites

Ville Close ★★★

On the islet in the bay.

One of the first strongholds of the ancient county of Cornouaille, this hamlet is surrounded by ramparts dating back to the 14th century. Most of the current walls were built under the orders of Vauban, Louis XIV's architect. Take time to stroll along the granite ramparts, soaking in the views of the port, the town and the sea. In the city, rue Vauban and rue St.-Guenole are classic medieval streets, although tourist shops have taken over much of the street frontage.

Museums and Exhibits

Musée de la Pêche ★★★

rue Vauban, ☎ *02-98-97-10-20.*

Hours open: 9:30 a.m.–7 p.m. Special hours: Closed from 12:30–2 p.m.; winter, to 6 p.m.

Informative placards, old photographs and three-dimensional reconstructions painstakingly explain why Concarneau is France's third-largest shipping port. The museum also has models of exotic boats and ships, as well as an aquarium. A real education for kids—who, by the time they leave, will know how much work goes into making a tuna sandwich. Admission: FR30.

Where to Stay

Hotels and Resorts

Hotel des Sables Blancs   **FR180–FR300** ★★

plage des Sables-Blancs. ☎ *02-98-97-01-39, FAX: 02-98-50-65-88. About 2 km south of town center.*

Single: FR180–FR250. Double: FR190–FR300.

The kind owners of this hotel and restaurant warmly welcome all of the guests. While perhaps better known for the dining facilities, the 48 guest rooms are also quite pleasant. All of the cozy rooms are well kept and comfortable, and most come with private bath. Take advantage of the tasty breakfast available for 32 francs. Always a reliable seaside lodging option. Credit Cards: V, MC, DC.

Low Cost Lodging

Grand Hotel   **FR155–FR300** ★

1 avenue Pierre Gueguen. ☎ *02-98-97-00-28. On the quay in the center of port.*

Single: FR155–FR300. Double: FR155–FR300.

Very basic accommodations in a central location to the marketplace. There are 33 rooms, with the better half having private baths. Even with the most simple of amenities, the chambers are definitely comfortable. A hearty breakfast is available for 29 francs. Credit Cards: V, MC.

Where to Eat

Gandhi   **$** ★★

13 boulevard de Kerguelen. ☎ *02-98-64-29-50.*

For a break from the usual butter and garlic French fare, fill up on curry at this Indian restaurant. FR60 goes a long way here, and FR80 will graduate you to the big menu. Next to the cathedral is the **Creperie du Frout** (*17 rue du Frout;* ☎ *02-*

98-95-26-94). There's a filling FR40 menu and a wide variety of fillings. Or, another good value, **La Plenty** *(6 place St.-Guenole, in the ville close;* ☎ *02-98-97-03-31)* has plenty of dinners from FR20, which may be enjoyed in the secluded garden. Closed: Sun.

La Coquille   **$$**   ★

1 rue du Moros. ☎ *02-98-97-08-52.*

Specialties: lobster, clams.

Lunch: 12:30–1 p.m., FR105–FR145.

Dinner: 7:30–9:30 p.m., entrées FR105–FR145.

For harbor dining, this charming restaurant with high-beamed ceilings is a winner. It has great views of all the nautical action, especially from its rather snug patio. The fixed-price FR120 lunch menu is an excellent deal. Also worthwhile is the restaurant at the **Hotel des Sables-Blancs**, not far from the center of town, right on Sables-Blancs beach *(*☎ *02-98-97-01-39).* Good for simply prepared seafood, especially clams and lobster. The fixed-price menus start as low as FR80. Closed Nov.–Mar.; open until 9:30 p.m.; terrace dining. Even less expensive is **L'Escale**, *19 quai Carnot* *(*☎ *02-98-97-03-31),* seafood and meat dishes, menus from FR50. Market: pl. Jean Jaures, open daily 7 a.m.–1 p.m. Amenities: outside dining, reservations required. Credit Cards: All Major.

Le Galion   **$$**   ★ ★

15 rue St.-Guenole. ☎ *02-98-97-30-16.*

Specialties: blanquette (stew) of langoustines with asparagus, andouille sausage a la Breton.

Lunch: 12:30–2:30 p.m., FR105–FR155.

Dinner: 7:30–9:30 p.m., entrées FR105–FR155.

This is Concarneau's best restaurant. With granite walls and sturdy wooden beams, it is also one of the most atmospheric. Located in the old hamlet, the sea laps at it from all sides. In cold weather, with the fireplace roaring, it's a cozy place to dine. Owned and run by Henri and Marie Louise Goanac'h, it is an unpretentious establishment, and the seafood dishes are utterly fresh. The couple also operates a bistro, **L'Assiette du Pecheur**, nearby at #12 *(*☎ *02-98-50-75-84),* also specializing in seafood, with an FR85 fixed-price menu. Closed: Mon. Amenities: own baking, reservations required. Credit Cards: All Major.

Directory

To and From

By bus from Quimper or by car on the N-165 between Quimper and Lorient.

Tourist Office

quai d'Aiguillon; ☎ *(33) 02-98-97-01-44.*

Post Office

quai Carnot, 29900 Concarneau; ☎ *(33) 02-98-97-04-00.*

Pont-Aven

The home of artists since the late 19th century, Pont-Aven was once "a town of 14 mills and 15 houses," in the words of one local historian. Today, Pont-Aven is a perfectly beautiful small Breton town, with its requisite medieval church and imposing granite architecture, but the main attraction is definitely the art. There are currently some 40 private galleries in the town, as well as a fine museum tracing the development of the Pont-Aven School of post-Impressionist painting, which focuses on color, simplicity and an absence of perspective. Beware of the swarms of students on school trips that infest the area regularly, especially during school holidays.

Paul Gauguin

The most famous of the many painters who have made Pont-Aven their home and inspiration is without a doubt Paul Gauguin. A stockbroker and frustrated amateur painter, Gauguin lost his job in the financial crash in 1883, along with his desire—or willingness—to continue to live in respectable society. He abandoned his wife and family and took up painting fulltime, making his first visit to Pont-Aven in 1886. He lived there until 1890 in the Pension de Marie-Jean Gloanec, which remains to this day. His work focused on the simple Breton life and the local people's intense devotion to religion. One of his most well-known paintings, "The Yellow Christ," inspired by a crucifix in the nearby Trémalo chapel, portrays the Crucifixion taking place in Gauguin's contemporary Brittany farmland; this attempt to bring the remote and spiritual into everyday life was a constant theme in Gauguin's work. In 1891, after a stormy friendship with fellow pauper and troubled artist Vincent van Gogh, Gauguin moved to Tahiti, where he spent several years painting the indigenous people of the South Seas. He returned to Pont-Aven once more before returning again to Tahiti, where he died, bitter and unappreciated in 1903.

What to Do

Historical/Architectural Sites

Chapelle de Trémalo ★★

> *Bois de'Amour. About 1 km from the town center.*
> A well-marked trail leads you to this rustic chapel in the woods not far from the center of town. Inside, you'll find the wooden crucifix that inspired Gauguin to paint his famous "Le Christ Jaune" (The Yellow Christ). The tourist office at place de l'Hotel de Ville can provide you with a map and detailed directions to the favored settings of the Ecole de Pont-Aven artists.

Museums and Exhibits

Musée de L'Ecole de Pont-Aven ★★★

> *place de Hotel de Ville,* ☎ *02-98-06-14-43.*

Hours open: 10 a.m.–6:30 p.m. Special hours: Summer, to 7:30 p.m.

This splendid museum, devoted to the Impressionist style of painting developed by Paul Gauguin and his followers in the 1880s, does a quick change act about every three months. Unfortunately, works by the master rarely turn up here. Admission: FR25.

Where to Stay

Bed-and-Breakfasts

Le Chatel   **FR250**   ★★★

Riec-sur-Belon. ☎ *02-98-06-00-04. About 1 km east of town. Off of the D783 towards Riec-sur-Belon for about 800 meters, and there will be signs on the right.*
Double: FR250.

There aren't many times a traveler can boast about a night's lodging that was actually spent on a deer farm. Le Chatel affords that opportunity with its B&B set upon this deer farm. A collection of a number of small, enchanting buildings, this farm offers five guest rooms with shower or bath. Intimately designed with comfort and charm in apparent in every detail, the rooms provide a restful night's sleep. Breakfast is included, and nearby restaurants are available for other meals. Guests seeking more diversion than admiring the deer can enjoy nearby tennis, golf, horseback riding and beaches. Credit Cards: Not Accepted.

Pen Ker Dagorn   **FR240**   ★★★

Chemin des Vieux-Fours. ☎ *02-98-06-85-01. About 5 km south of town. In Croaz Hent Kergez, take the D77. In Nevez-Kerleun, turn left on C8 towards Port-de-Kerdruc. It's near the port of Kerduc on Chemin des Vieux Fours.*
Double: FR240.

A B&B deserving of its three stars for its charm and personal attention only found at a place of this small size. Stay for the two-day minimum at this lovely house in the country, shaded by well developed shrubbery and trees. There are just three rooms, each with its own bath or shower. All are spaciously comfortable, individually decorated and bright and airy. Start the day off with a wonderful breakfast for 30 francs, served by the charming couple who owns and manages the house. Leisurely afternoons can be spent at the nearby beaches, playing tennis, horseback riding, golfing, bicycling or touring Pont-Aven. A classic countryside getaway. Credit Cards: Not Accepted.

Inns

Moulin de Rosmadec   **FR400–FR470**   ★★★

On the Aven. ☎ *02-98-06-18-00, FAX: 02-98-06-18-00. In the middle of the Aven river.*
Double: FR400–FR470.

While there are just four accommodations to choose from at this restaurant with rooms, they are all worth it just for the setting alone. This 15th-century transformed mill provides an ideal setting for a peaceful night's sleep with the water flowing over the rocks below. The rooms are simply furnished and decorated in easy tones to create a comfortable setting. A meal in the delectable restaurant is not to be missed. Credit Cards: V, MC.

Where to Eat

La Taupiniere $$$ ★★★★

route de Concarneau, On the road towards Concarneau. ☎ *02-98-06-03-12.*
Some of the best food in Brittany is invented here by chef Guy Guilloux. With an
incredibly talented staff and attractive dining environment backing him up, Guil-
loux presents outstanding seafood and Breton ham specialties. While the prices
aren't pocketbook friendly, this is worth the splurge. FR220, FR320 and FR420
fixed-price menus are available. Jacket required. Closed: Tues. reservations
required. Credit Cards: V, MC.

Moulin de Rosmadec $$$ ★★★

Pont-Aven. ☎ *02-98-06-00-22.*
*Specialties: grilled Lobster "Rosmadec," roast turbot with prawn coulis, St.-Pierre fish
with artichokes.*
Lunch: 12:30–2 p.m., FR355–FR550.
Dinner: 7:30–9 p.m., entrées FR355–FR550.
Owners Monsieur and Madame Sebilleau converted a 15th-century mill into this
engaging hotel-restaurant. Antiques fill the dining rooms on two floors, and there's
garden seating in good weather. Excellent seafood from the southern coast is fea-
tured, as well as choice duck and chicken dishes. Inventive desserts, cheeses; highly
recommended. Fixed-price meals begin at FR150. Critics are buzzing about **La
Taupiniere**, *route de Concarneau* (☎ *02-98-06-03-12*), 4 km from the center on
D783. Guy Guilloux presents seafood in a modern vein; unusual desserts include
warm strawberries with pistachio ice cream. Open kitchen, pretty decor. Closed:
Wed. Amenities: outside dining, own baking, reservations required. Credit Cards: V,
MC, E.

Directory

To and From

By bus (Transports Caoudal; ☎ *(33) 02-98-56-96-72, or by car on the Lorien express-
way from Quimper.*

Tourist Office

place de l'Hôtel de Ville; ☎ *(33) 02-98-06-04-70.*

Carnac

Rivaling Stonehenge in its significance, Carnac is one of the world's greatest prehistoric sites. Unfortunately, the area containing the megaliths has
been crisscrossed by numerous roads, and a number of stones have apparently disappeared, but there are still 2792 great *menhirs*, each one carefully
placed by the Neolithic peoples who inhabited the area between 6000 and
4000 years ago. The stones are arranged in lines called alignments; the three
principal ones are the *Ménec* alignment, which contains 1169 stones, the
Kermario alignment, with 1029, and the *Kerlescan* alignment, which contains 594 stones. The precise purpose of the alignments is not known, but

BRITTANY

there is little doubt that these structures, the oldest man-made buildings in the world (predating the Great Pyramids of Egypt by, oh, 1000 years or so), were used for some kind of religious ceremonies as well as for astronomical studies. In addition to the alignments, Carnac is surrounded by a number of *dolmens* and burial sites. In order to fully appreciate the megaliths, it would be wise to pay a visit first to the museum, where you can see what archaeologists *do* know about them.

What to Do

Historical/Architectural Sites

Megaliths   ★★★

North of town. About 30 minutes north of town by foot.

Megalithic monuments were created by a culture from the Neolithic period, from about 4670 to 2000 B.C. This population was a settled people, growing crops, raising animals and producing pottery, baskets and other crafts. These practices contrasted with the hunter-gatherers of Paleolithic times. These megaliths, or menhirs, are single upright stones (some 13 feet high), most arranged in long rows called alignments and some supporting a horizontal slab on top of two stones. There are 2395 menhirs making up the three alignments, positioned in semicircles and parallel lines over a half of a mile. These stones and the markings on them have been considered abstract art, astrological calendars and religious monuments, just to name a few of the theories surrounding the mystery. Nobody will ever know the truth, that's part of the fun of visiting the stones.

Prehistoric Monuments/Menhirs   ★★★★

rue des Alignements. Head north from the town center on D196.

Carnac's prehistoric (4000–6000 B.C.) monuments stand out for their sheer size and diversity. Some of them are more than 12 feet high and weigh more than 300 tons. Although barriers have been erected around them (for good reason), all the important formations are placed within a few miles of each other. If you can spare at least three hours, you can visit as many of them as you can take. The more common stones are the stand-alone, upright menhirs, which are believed to have been erected to protect burial sites (from evil spirits?). Unique to the area are menhirs set in parallel lines, ending in a semicircle, called *cromlechs*. These may be remnants of ancient temples devoted to sun or moon deities. Not to be missed is the St.-Michel Tumulus, a 38-foot high mound of earth and rocks, which housed two ancient burial chambers. Marking the entrance to the Tumulus is a dolmen, two upright stones with another slab placed on top. Many of its effects can be seen in the Musée de Prehistoire nearby, and listed separately.

Tumulus St.-Michel   ★★

rue du Tumulus, ☎ 02-97-52-06-86. About a 5 minute walk from the Musée de Prehistoire.

The ashes of a tribal chief buried with his compatriots are buried in this mound, with modern tunnels allowing glimpses at the graves. This mound, or tumulus, was evangelized in the name of St.-Michael and topped with a chapel. Be prepared for a

45- to 90-minute wait during summer. The tour, in French, is every 15 minutes. *Open daily, 9:30 a.m.–7:30 p.m.; Sept.–Oct. and Easter–June, daily, 10 a.m.–noon and 3–6 p.m. Admission: FR7.*

Museums and Exhibits

Musée de Prehistoire   ★★★
10 place de la Chapelle, ☎ *02-97-52-22-04.*
Hours open: 10 a.m.–6:30 p.m. Special hours: Closed from noon–2 p.m. Closed: Wed.
A visit to this museum might clear up a few mysteries about the mute rock formations (megalithic monuments) that cover the Carnac landscape. Exhibits include crude stone weapons and tools, pottery, jewelry and reconstructed prehistoric carvings. Admission: FR32.

Where to Stay

Hotels and Resorts

Hotel Les Alignements   FR260–FR360   ★★
45 rue St.-Cornely. ☎ *02-97-52-06-30, FAX: 02-97-52-76-56. At the edge of town, near the Field of Megaliths.*
Single: FR260–FR360. Double: FR260–FR360.
Set on the edge of town, this hotel's location is most convenient for touring the prehistoric Field of Megaliths. Constructed in the early 1970s, this four-story building is home to 27 guest rooms. Last improved in 1991, the rooms are comfortable and come with TV, telephone and private bath. The choice rooms are those on the upper floors with balconies facing the garden in back. Those facing the street are equipped with double-paned windows to buffer the noise from below. Breakfast is available for FR39 and fixed-price meals start at FR100 in the contemporary restaurant. An ideal base for visiting the historic stones. Credit Cards: V, MC.

Lann-Roz   FR330–FR350   ★★
36 avenue de la Poste. ☎ *02-97-52-10-48, FAX: 02-97-52-03-69. Close to the sea.*
Single: FR330–FR350. Double: FR330–FR350.
A traditional hotel exemplifying the Breton style, this small establishment sits among flower gardens and green lawns. The pleasant demeanor of the family owners who manage this hotel makes each guest feel as though they are an old friend. There are 14 rooms, modestly yet comfortably attired and including TV, telephone and bath or shower. One of the biggest delights of staying here is relishing a sumptuous meal in the living room facing the grounds. Meals start at a reasonable FR100. A fantastic value. Credit Cards: V, MC, DC, A.

Le Diana   FR850–FR1100   ★★★
21 boulevard de la Plage. ☎ *02-97-52-05-38, FAX: 02-97-52-87-91. On the beach.*
Single: FR850. Double: FR1100.
Sit back, relax and enjoy the beachside location of this modern hotel. Drinks can be taken on the terrace, ideal for watching the bronzed bodies walk by or relaxing to the sound of the crashing waves. A heated pool and a rock garden are other alluring options for leisure during the day. The 30 guest rooms, although a bit small, are equipped with a kitchenette, sea-view balcony, radio, TV, telephone, minibar and bath or shower. Breakfast is served for FR80, and other fixed-price meals are avail-

able in the restaurant from FR250. Half-board rates are from FR390 to FR590.
Features: beach location.Credit Cards: MC, DC.

Where to Eat

La Caliorne $ ★★

8 rue de Colary. ☎ *02-97-52-92-05.*

A great snack stop with a menu starting at FR 60. Another quick-bite-to-eat place
is **Chez Yannick** *(8 rue du Tumulus;* ☎ *02-97-52-08-67).* Enjoy a galette from this
small creperie with secluded garden tables. Or, **Creperie Chez Marie** *(3 place de
l'Eglise;* ☎ *02-97-52-83-05)* serves galettes and crepes from FR25.

Directory

To and From

Carnac is on the road from Cornouaille into Western Loire, the N-165.

*Make it a stop on your way between Quimper and Vannes. The site is quite crowded dur-
ing school holidays but there are nice beaches in the village of Carnac, so you could well
make a day of it.*

Tourist Office

74 avenue des Druides; ☎ *(33) 02-97-52-13-52.*

Quibéron

Quibéron sits at the end of Quibéron Peninsula.

The beach resort town—and I mean a real beach resort town—of
Quibéron lies at the very end of the narrow Presqu'Ile de Quibéron. Presqu'Ile means literally almost island," i.e., a peninsula, but in this case the
name is apt, as the Quibéron Peninsula was an island as recently as 10,000

years ago. More recently, in the late 18th century, the town was a bastion of the counter-revolutionary forces, and in 1795 as many as 10,000 Royalists were massacred in an ill-advised attempt to invade the rest of France and restore the monarchy.

The town itself has everything you would expect in a bona-fide beach resort: there's a boardwalk, a cheesy casino, shops selling cheap souvenirs, pseudo art galleries selling uninspired watercolors, overpriced cafés, and so on. But if you're after a couple of days' R&R after touring the emotionally draining north of Brittany, hey, come on down. As you drive down the peninsula, you have a choice of the ocean to the right, the windswept, rocky *Côte Sauvage* (sauvage actually means wild, "not savage"), or the ocean to the west, where there are a number of sheltered, sandy beaches. The best beach, however, is in town, *La Grande Plage*.

What to Do

Beaches

Grand Plage   ★★★

> *On the western side of the handle of the peninsula.*
>
> Quiberon's grand plage is the main attraction in town. It's a long sandy beach with the dunes at your back and the tranquil blue in front. Relax in the sun—this is the reason you're here. Or, perhaps, it's the **Conserverie Belle-Iloise** (☎ *02-97-30-51-76*), on rue Kerne, that you seek. This new museum doles out information on the history of the town as a fishing port. Leave with an in-depth knowledge of fish-preserve preparation. *Open Mon.–Sat., 10–11:30 a.m. and 3–6 p.m.*; FR8. Admission: free.

Where to Stay

Hotels and Resorts

Ker Noyal   FR475–FR550   ★★★

> *rue de St.-Clement.* ☎ *02-97-50-08-41, FAX: 02-97-30-58-20. Near the beach.*
> *Single: FR475–FR550. Double: FR475–FR550.*
> This plush hotel in the middle of a sardine fishing port offers a relaxing, comfortable stay. Just a short walk from the beach, this hotel sits among beautiful gardens and walking paths. Within the two buildings are 102 rooms, each with a TV, telephone and private bath. While some of the rooms in the older building offer garden and sea views, those in the newer building have access to the terraces with lounge chairs. Regardless of which building the room is in, all are attractively decorated and immaculately maintained. Breakfast is served for FR50, and the two dining rooms offer fixed-price meals from FR200. A fine refuge with courteous, intimate service.Credit Cards: V, MC, DC, A.

Sofitel Thalassa   FR1400–FR1525   ★★★

> *pointe de Goulvars.* ☎ *02-97-50-20-00, FAX: 02-97-50-07-34. About 1 km east of town center, at the beach.*
> *Single: FR1400. Double: FR1525.*

Although part of a chain, the Thalassa, built in the 1970s, sets itself apart from other cloned hotels. At the end of the peninsula, this hotel boasts a fine beachside location. In its own little world, the hotel provides some peace and quiet on a well-equipped piece of property. There are 117 guest rooms and 16 suites; all are attractively decorated with quiet tones and equipped with a TV, telephone, minibar and spacious bath. Most have views over the sea or the plaza from the balconies. Recreational activities include swimming in the sea, swimming in the heated, indoor Olympic-size pool and playing tennis. Wind down the day with an aperitif in the lounge, and then dine on the terrace or in the dining room on some fantastic local seafood. Although a bit expensive, it's still one of the best choices in town. Features: pool, tennis, balcony or patio.

Where to Eat

La Goursen $$ ★★★

10 quai d' l'Ocean a Port Maria. ☎ *02-97-50-07-94.*
Dinner: 7–9:30 p.m., entrées FR90–FR175.
Bubbling with character, La Goursen is a bistro with origins from the turn of the century. Enjoy seafood specialties including sauerkraut, fish sausage and John Dory. The owner-chef is very receptive to any special requests. While there are no fixed-price menus available, the a la carte menu is reasonable. Reservations required. Credit Cards: V, MC.

Le Relax $$ ★★

27 boulevard Castero, Near the bay. ☎ *02-97-50-12-84.*
Dinner: 7–10 p.m., entrées FR70–FR110.
Come for the view alone—a beautiful panorama of the bay. A casual atmosphere in the dining room, with seafood dominating the menu. Fixed-price menus start at FR65–FR135. Reservations recommended. Credit Cards: V, MC, DC.

Le Thalassa $$ ★★★

Pointe de Goulvars, At the end of the headland. Located at Sofitel Thalassa. ☎ *02-97-50-20-00.*
Quite a respectable restaurant despite it being in a chain hotel. The well-practiced chef offers a bit of something for everybody. Choices of wine include some reasonably priced bottles. In addition to a FR200 fixed-price menu, there is a 500-calorie menu for FR200 that is excellent. Open until 9:30 p.m. Credit Cards: V, DC, A.

Directory

To and From

By train from Auray (only in July and August), or by car on the D-768, exiting from the N-165.

Tourist Office

14 rue de Verdun; ☎ *(33) 02-97-50-07-84.*

Rail Station

rue de la Gàre; ☎ *(33) 02-97-42-50-50.*

Post Office

place de la Duchesse Anne, 56170 Quibéron; ☎ *(33) 02-97-50-11-92.*

La Belle Ile-en-Mer

Even if you don't visit any other of Brittany's many islands, you should make the trip here, to the largest one. With a population of 4500, Bell Ile-en-Mer definitely lives up to its name, in all senses, which means "Beautiful Island on the Ocean." Lying nine miles off the southern tip of the Presqu'Ile de Quibéron, the island can be reached by ferry boat in a little over 45 minutes. You can also fly on a puddle-jumper from the mainland. Most people go by boat, arriving at Le Palais, the port and principal town. The island has its share of hotels and restaurants, as well as a golf course and a number of isolated beaches on the southern coast. Beware the treacherous tides, however, which are especially strong as they sweep around the island. The other main town is Sauzon, which can be reached by bus or on foot in a couple of hours.

What to Do
Beaches

Beaches   ★★★

Various locations.
About 6 km north of Le Palais is Sauzon, a tiny fishing port with quaint little houses and buildings. About 4 km past Sauzon is Pointe des Poulains, the northern tip of the island—a dramatic spot to overlook the bay, pounding waves and jagged rocks. The fort near the Grotte de L'Apothicairerie was home to Sarah Bernhardt for many years. Most famous, the Grotte (cave) is a cavern which the waves hit from both sides. It is officially closed due to many accidental deaths, but many visitors still climb down to it on calm, low-tide days. South on the D25 is the Aiguilles de Port-Coton, which Monet painted in 1886. Near Locamaria are several protected beaches, and just north of town is the Grands Sables beach, popular with swimmers and surfers. Admission: free.

Historical/Architectural Sites

Citadel   ★★

Le Palais, ☎ *02-97-31-84-17. In the port of Le Palais.*
Strengthened in 1682 by Vauban, a celebrated military constructor, this is the most prominent of the many fortifications on the island. Wander through the tunnels, passageways and chambers, and stop in the museum focusing on everything that has ever occurred related to Belle-Ile. *Open daily, 9:30 a.m.–7p.m.; May–June and Sept.–Oct., 9:30 a.m.–6 p.m.; Nov.–Apr., 9:30 a.m.–noon and 2–5 p.m.* Admission: FR28.

Where to Stay

Hotels and Resorts

Castel Clara Hotel   **FR860–FR1760**   ★★★★

Port Goulphar. ☎ *02-97-31-84-21, FAX: 02-97-31-51-69. On the southern shores, about 8 km from the harbor at Le Palais.*
Single: FR860–FR1050. Double: FR1100–FR1760.

A country-style inn of four stories, this hotel is a member of the Relais and Château, a symbol of tranquil lodging. Its beautiful location affords magnificent views of the sea from the balconied guest rooms. Enchanted by its lush garden setting, the many therapeutic amenities contributing to the total serenity found here include an indoor heated pool, sauna, two tennis courts, thalassotherapy center and solarium. Just a short distance away are golf, horseback riding and beaches. After dining at the superb in-house restaurant of the same name, guests retire to one of the 43 bed chambers in comfort. Each water view room comes with cable TV, telephone and spacious bath. This hotel offers the serenity of an inn, the amenities of a spa and the grand service of a resort hotel. Features: pool, tennis, air conditioning in rooms, sauna, balcony or patio, thalassotherapy. Credit Cards: V, MC, E, A.

Manoir de Goulphar   FR500–FR975   ★★★

Bangor. ☎ *02-97-31-80-10, FAX: 02-97-31-80-05.*
Single: FR500–FR515. Double: FR900–FR975.

This first-rate hotel, built in the 1970s, is perched on the Goulphar Harbor. Its peaceful rocky coast setting is a beautiful backdrop for this modern facility. There are 65 guest rooms, many with balconies overlooking the ocean and the harbor, equipped with comfortable amenities such as TV, telephone and private bath. Although a bit smallish, every square inch is designed with comfort. Fine service and attention are standard in the hotel and restaurant. Features: air conditioning in rooms, balcony or patio. Credit Cards: V, MC.

Inns

Le Clos Fleuri   FR400–FR500   ★★★

Bellevue, Route de Sauzon. ☎ *02-97-31-45-45, FAX: 02-97-31-45-57. About 500 meters from the port of Le Palais.*
Single: FR400–FR500. Double: FR400–FR500.

A rather new inn set among grassy grounds, this seaside hotel has a convenient location close to the harbor. There are 20 guest rooms, all modestly yet comfortably furnished in contemporary style. A good dining room serves breakfast, brunch, lunch and dinner at reasonable prices. Well accustomed to providing personal service, the staff strives to accommodate every need. Credit Cards: V, MC, DC, A.

Where to Eat

Castel Clara $$$ ★★

Port-Goulphar, A 45-minute trip by steamer from Quibéron. In Hotel Castel Clara. Located at Castel Clara. ☎ *02-97-31-84-21.*
Lunch: Noon–2 p.m., FR325–FR455.
Dinner: 7–9 p.m., entrées FR325–FR455.

The best view in town is from the tiny dining room of this well-known restaurant in a Relais & Château rated hotel. Yves Perou creates simply prepared seafood dishes using prime ingredients. His desserts are lovely. Along the Cote Sauvage, in the town of Sauzon, you'll find the **Roz-Avel**, *rue du Lt-Riou* (☎ *02-97-31-61-48*), featuring large, steaming portions of shellfish and fresh fish. The meat dishes are excellent too. There's a garden for warm weather dining. Generous fixed-price meals for FR95. Friendly service. Closed Wed. and Nov. 12-13. Amenities: outside dining, own baking, reservations required. Credit Cards: V, MC, E.

La Chaloupe   **$$**   ★

8 avenue Carnot. ☎ *02-97-31-88-27.*
Specialties: crepes, seafood.
Lunch: Noon–2 p.m., FR80–FR150.
Dinner: 7–11 p.m., entrées FR80–FR150.

For simple meals, including Breton crepes, this informal and friendly place is the best in town. The crepes start at FR12. Similar fare can be found at **Traou-Mod**, *9 rue Willaumez (*☎ *02-97-31-84-84)*, also in Le Palais; the crepes are sweet and savory, starting at FR10. Open daily from 11:30 am–midnight. Market: place de la Republique, 8 a.m.–1 p.m. Tue., Fri., Sat. Credit Cards: All Major.

Directory

Tourist Office
On the quay in Le Palais; ☎ *(33) 02-97-31-81-93.*

Post Office
port de Commerce, 56360 Le Palais-Belle Ile; ☎ *(33) 02-97-31-80-70.*

Vannes

At the top of the gulf of Moribahn lies the city of Vannes, once the capital of Brittany. Prior to that time, the port was the home of the Veneti, a seafaring tribe that dwelt in the region during pre-Roman times. After coming under Roman rule in 56 B.C. following an unusually well-documented sea battle at the mouth of the gulf, the port grew as a naval base for the various Caesars until the ninth century, when the first Duke of Brittany, Nominoë, made it his seat of power. Vannes was the home of the much beloved Duchesse Anne who, in spite of marrying the king and thus sealing Bretagne's fate as a region of France, is thought of as the mother of the Golden Age of the region. Vannes was also the site of the treaty between the duchy and the kingdom when the two became one. The town thus has a good deal of history to share, and was left relatively undamaged after World War II. Some portions of the old city walls survive, as do two of the venerable gates, the Porte-Prison and the Porte-Poterne. The cathedral dates from the 14th century, while the main covered-market, known as *La Cohue*, has parts that are a hundred years older still.

The town is a good base to explore the gulf and its many islands and beaches, it's also a good first point of entry or last stop into or before leaving Brittany. While you are there, be sure to make an excursion to the dark and mysterious Fôret de Paimpon (also referred to as the Fôret de Brocéliande), the last surviving portion of the original forest that once covered all of Brittany. You can reach the forest by traveling on the N-166 to the D-166 towards Rennes out of Vannes. During the time of Armorica, this forest was the haunt of Merlin the magician. The enchanted spring where Merlin met Vivian, Lady of the Lake, is reputed to be hidden somewhere within the forest—perhaps you will be the one to find it.

What to Do

Historical/Architectural Sites

Cathedrale St.-Pierre ★★

22 rue des Chanoines.
Hours open: 10 a.m.–7 p.m. Special hours: Closed 1–2 p.m.; Sun. Masses, 9:30, 11 a.m.
Walk through the red doors and carved portal of this granite Gothic facade into the 15th-century nave with small stained-glass windows, ornate white and gold altars and beautiful statues. Covering the nave is a heavy-ribbed vault from the 18th century, which hides the original timber roof. Admission to the treasury is FR3.

Old Town ★★★

Promenade de la Garenne.
The cobblestoned old quarter, closed off to car traffic, is protected from modern-day Vannes by its sturdy walls. The ducal palace of Vannes no longer exists, but from the promenade de la Garenne, a public park which used to serve as its gardens, you can view the fortified walls of the Old City from the Constable's Tower. Entering through the Porte St.-Vincent gate, you can visit the market square at place des Lices; some of the medieval buildings now house elegant shops. Still in use today, the square is the site of a food and crafts market on Wednesday and Saturday mornings. Occupying the old town's most prominent area is St.-Peter's Cathedral, with an unusual Italian-Renaissance style chapel, not common to this part of the world. Two museums, the **Beaux Arts** and the **Musée du Golfe et de la Mer**, are housed in La Cohue *(9-15 place St.-Pierre)*, both a marketplace and a court of law in the 14th century.

rue St.-Guenahel ★★★

On the opposite side of the park that is adjacent to the cathedral.
A stroll down rue St.-Guenahel gives one a view of typical Breton houses. Architectural features include half-timbering and second stories supported by diagonal timbers, especially evident in #17-19. At the bottom of the street is the heavily fortified Porte Prison (Prison Gate), which leads to the ramparts. Porte St.-Vincent (St.-Vicent's Gate), at the end of the street, opens to Place Gambetta and its inviting cafes beckoning an afternoon break.

Museums and Exhibits

Aquarium de Vannes/La Papilloneraie ★★★

Parc du Golfe, ☎ *02-97-63-74-84.*
About 15 minutes by foot from the center of town, these two unique museums are set in the Parc du Golfe. The **Aquarium de Vannes** *(☎ 02-97-40-67-40)*, in the shape of a huge shellfish, is full of re-created natural habitat tanks with many types of sea life. The electric eel is always popular, with its voltage meter showing visitors the strength of its electric wavelength. Admission is FR46, students FR26. Near to the aquarium is **La Papilloneraie**, on *rue Gilard (☎ 02-97-46-01-02)*, with a trop-

ical habitat reconstructed for hundreds of butterflies. Visitors pay FR30 to walk through the exhibit, in hopes of having a butterfly, or several, land on them. Both museums make for a fun afternoon. *Special hours are 9 a.m.–7 p.m. June through Aug. 9 a.m.–noon and 1:30-6:30 p.m. rest of year.*

Musée d'Archeologie/Vannes ★★★

2 rue Noe, ☎ *02-97-42-59-80.*

Hours open: 9:30 a.m.–6 p.m. Special hours: Oct.–Mar., from 2 p.m. Closed: Sun.

This medieval castle has a collection of prehistoric finds from sites all over the Gulf of Moribahn. You'll see weapons, tomb specimens, jewelry and personal effects proudly laid out over three galleries. Admission: FR20.

Special Tours/Excursions

Belle-Ile ★★★★

A 45-minute ferry trip from Port Maria in Quibéron, ☎ *02-97-31-81-93.*

Although often used as an excursion point from Quibéron, Belle-Isle is one of Brittany's largest islands, with hotels, a youth hostel, campgrounds and restaurants. Its shores and valleys have attracted many harried folk, including famous artists and actors (most notably, Sarah Bernhardt). The island was once owned by Nicolas Fouquet, Louis XIV's finance minister, who beefed up the already forbidding Vauban Citadel with cannons; unfortunately, he was arrested in Nantes on corruption charges before he could hole up there. The Citadel, with a museum and views from its ramparts, can be visited daily from 9:30 a.m.–7 p.m.; admission FR28. If you have time, you'll probably want to leave Le Palais, Belle-Ile's tourist sphere, for a driving, walking or cycling tour of the Cote Sauvage. Highlights include Sarah Bernhardt's old estate in Poulains Point (a half-hour walk from the port of Sauzon, northwest of Le Palais on D30). Port Donnant, the island's most beautiful, and least crowded, beach, is on this route (take D25), but it's unsafe for swimming. Admission: FR41.

Paimpont

Forest of Paimpont ★★★

45 km from Rennes, ☎ *02-99-07-84-23.*

The legend goes that Merlin the Magician and his amour, the fairy Viviane (The Lady of the Lake) lived within this forest together after the sorcerer retired from the spell-casting business. Just to be sure, Viviane kept him in a magic circle so he couldn't stray. It was also here that Joseph of Arimathea, original owner of the Holy Grail, lived, until he and the relic disappeared. You can cycle or walk to some of the more interesting sites, including Merlin's "tomb," and the Valley of No Return, where Fata Morgana would ensnare young men. There are real people who live here, however, in the town of Paimpont, which has been around since the Revolution. The tourist office provides guided tours, (FR15–FR35, depending on length) brochures and directions to the sights.

Where to Stay

Hotels and Resorts

Aquarium' Hotel   FR380–FR480   ★★★

Le Parc du Golfe. ☎ *02-97-40-44-52, FAX: 02-97-63-03-20. About 2 km from the town center near the Gulf of Moribahn.*
Double: FR380–FR480.

Quite a modern structure set outside of the town center in a more rural environment. Diversion at the hotel centers around the aquarium, the squash courts and the bowling and pool hall. A serendipitous tour by foot might take one along the path towards the gulf for a boat ride. The 48 accommodations are practical in furnishings and offer splendid views of the sea. There is bus service to and from town regularly. Features: wheelchair-access rooms. Credit Cards: V, MC, DC, A.

Image Ste-Anne   FR300–FR300   ★★

8 place de la Liberation. ☎ *02-97-63-27-36, FAX: 02-97-40-97-02. In the center of the Old Town.*
Double: FR300.

A leisurely walk through historic Vannes leads to this old country charmer. The old structure housing the 38 rooms shows its age in a somehow romantic, rustic manner. Each of the cozy, comfortable rooms comes with modest furnishings and private shower or bath. Dining in the restaurant is a reasonably priced, delightful affair with dishes including such specialties as duck and seafood. The kind staff treats the guests with respect and genuine helpfulness. Credit Cards: V, MC.

Manche Ocean   FR300–FR360   ★★

31 rue Lieutenant-Colonel-Maury. ☎ *02-97-47-26-46, FAX: 02-97-47-30-86. A short walk from the town center towards the train station.*
Double: FR300–FR360.

Subject to constant improvements, the Manche Ocean sits close to the train station and the town hall. The 42 rooms are well maintained and kept quiet with the double-paned glass windows. Spacious and comfortable, the private baths are attractive and include toiletries. A tasty breakfast is available, and half-board is from FR358 to FR400. Credit Cards: V, MC, DC, A.

Where to Eat

La Paella $ ★

7 rue Brizeux.
Specialties: Paella.
Lunch: Noon–2 p.m., FR40–FR55.
Dinner: 7–10 p.m., entrées FR40–FR55.

Paella is not exactly a local specialty, but this plain but friendly spot serves generous portions of the robust Spanish dish made with the region's great seafood for FR45–FR50, depending on the size. Indoor and outdoor dining. **La Varende**, *22 rue Fontaine* (☎ *02-97-47-57-52*), offers a FR98 set meal, seasonal dishes, crepes stuffed with seafood and good cider. *No lunch Sun., closed Mon., open until 10 p.m. in summer.* Market: pl. des Lices in the Old Town; *open Wed. and Sat. mornings until 1 p.m. Closed: Mon., Sun.* Amenities: outside dining.

Pressoir $$$ ★★

7 rue d'Hopital, 5 km north of the center on D767. ☎ *02-97-60-87-63.*
Specialties: roasted Breton lobster, red mullet and potato galette.
Lunch: Noon–2 p.m., FR250–FR345.
Dinner: 7–9:30 p.m., entrées FR250–FR345.

Somewhat away from the center of town, this highly rated establishment is out of the tourist sphere. It's well worth visiting for chef Bernard Rambaud's contemporary cooking; there's a definite Southern tone to it, with plenty of duck and pork products. Some of the set menus (at FR120 for lunch and FR180 for dinner) include foie gras and dessert. Closed: Mon. Amenities: own baking, reservations required. Credit Cards: V, MC, DC, A, E.

Regis Mahe $$$ ★★

place de la Gare. ☎ *02-97-42-61-41.*
Specialties: red mullet with aromatic herbs, chocolate tarte with ice cream and chicory sauce.
Lunch: Noon–2 p.m., FR300–FR400.
Dinner: 7–9:30 p.m., entrées FR300–FR400.

Regis Mahe's acclaimed cuisine combines traditional, regional seafood dishes with contemporary Provencal touches. He has brought the sunny south to the Breton coast with a menu full of fresh produce, fragrant herbs and fine olive oils. The restaurant is located near the train station, but that shouldn't deter you, as the dining room is tastefully decorated and supervised with a knowing hand by Madame Edith Mahe. The set menus begin at FR160 (lunch) including dessert. Closed: Mon. Amenities: own baking, reservations required. Credit Cards: V, MC, A, E.

Directory

To and From

By train from Paris (three-and-a-half hours), Quimper (two hours) or Nantes (75 minutes), or by car from the north or south on the N-165 or from Rennes from the east of the N-166.

Tourist Office

1 rue Thiers; ☎ *(33) 02-97-47-24-34.*

Rail Station

avenue Favrel et Lincy; ☎ *(33) 02-97-42-50-50.*

Post Office

place de la République, 56000 Vannes.

BRITTANY

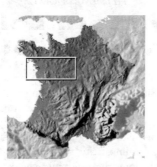

THE LOIRE

Azay le Rideau, built between 1518–1527, looks like a Gothic fortress.

What Makes The Loire So French?

1. *Châteaux, châteaux, châteaux–Renaissance mystique, feudal phenomena, scary-pants dungeons, push-up bra and stiff-upper-lip portraits, live donkeys, and hefty admission fees.*

2. *Loving son Louis XIII had his mama locked up in Blois. Two years later she waddled her way down a rope ladder, trod the moat, and escaped (though she did make up with her boy). A mother's love–who can explain it?*

3. *Fairytale author Charles Perrault allegedly used the Château of Usse as his setting for Sleeping Beauty.*

305

Western Loire (Pays de Loire)

Most of the time, visitors to the Loire region of France get as far as Tours or Orléans, fall in love with the châteaux, and never make it out to one of the prettiest and most interesting regions in the country—Western Loire. That's why I've put this region before the Loire Valley itself, and that's why I begin it with Nantes, the westernmost city, so hopefully you'll start out here and explore your way back along the Loire into châteaux country, allowing at least a few days to experience the joys of this area.

History

The history of Western Loire is turbulent. After the Romans conquered the area about 50 years before Christ, the marauding Visigoths and Franks waged war back and forth over the lower Loire, and the Gallic people, fed up with repeated attacks from every direction, began to fortify their cities and fight back. After the fall of the Carolingian empire towards the end of the 10th century, the county of Maine, with Angers as its major town, declared independence. The county quickly grew into the vassalage of Anjou. When the Anjouian ruler, Count Herbert II, died in 1062 without an heir, William the Conqueror of Normandy (he was still William the Bastard at the time), inherited the region. Resistance came from the residents led by the citizens of Le Mans, but their efforts did not have lasting success. About a century later, a strongman from the town of La Flèche overthrew Norman rule, and upon his death, his son Foulque V restored Anjouian rule. Foulque's son, Geoffrey Plantagenet, was married to William's granddaughter, so peace was established between the region and the Normans. The Plantagenets, by virtue of their connection to William, became kings of England, beginning with Henry II.

Henry II's son, Richard the Lionhearted, was next in line to the throne of England and the control of Anjou. His death in 1199 led to the region being incorporated into France (for a time), and the construction of new French forts at Angers and other Anjouian cities bordering on the then-independent Brittany. Louis IX tired of managing the region and gave it to his brother, restoring a measure of independence for another 250 years, but in 1481 France took over for good. About the same time, Nantes lost control of Brittany and was absorbed into the region, and so Western Loire became part of the French nation. Violence and strife continued, however, as residents of the Vendée area to the south of the region attempted a counter-revolutionary insurgency in the late 18th century. The uprising was brutally suppressed by the Parisian armies of the new revolutionary government in the Vendée

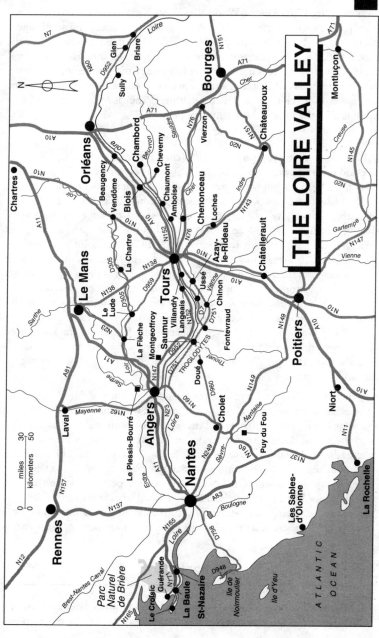

THE LOIRE VALLEY

War of 1793–1796. During World War II, St. Nazaire, on the coast, became a major Nazi submarine base. The Allies, alternately advancing south under Gen. George Patton (to sweep up to Paris) and bombing bridges over the Loire, inflicted huge damage on the area in order to oust Hitler's troops. Today, Western Loire is a modern yet beautifully tranquil region of France, with its own share of châteaux and much more, rolling hills and broad rivers, the lower Loire chief among them, that urges the visitor to come on just a little farther than she or he might have planned.

Cuisine

When you are in Western Loire, ask a chef or a waiter what the specialities are and he or she will answer, evasively, "Well, everything..." Not particularly helpful, perhaps, but it's true enough. The region reaches to the ocean, so fish and seafood, especially scallops, are plentiful. But this is also farming country, so fresh vegetables, from potatoes and tomatoes to asparagus, young green beans, and artichokes also abound. The quantity of pears grown here, is second only to Normandy, and Western Loire is the primary producer of cultivated mushrooms. Even cooking salt—from the flats at Guérande—is a specialty, and is often a listed ingredient on many menus à la carte. The two top chefs in the region I consulted, however, agreed that any dish in a *buerre blanc* sauce would have to get top billing. The white butter from the region was a favorite of Tsar Nicholas of Russia—he refused to take any other. Watch for fish or even chicken—the free-range chickens raised here under the *Loué* ("prized") label—are served with white butter sauce. Another specialty is *rilletes pork paté*, produced in the Sathre river region around Le Mans.

Wine-wise, Western Loire is a powerhouse, producing Muscadet, a dry white that is famous around the world, and the wines of the Saumur region. Saumur Champigny is a fruity red that goes well both with the meat dishes and the cheese dishes that are as popular here as anywhere in France. Using the traditional method (*mèthode traditionelle*—legally, it can't be called the Champagne method), the wineries of Saumur produce a sparkling wine that is quite delicious as an aperitif. Saumur Flammé is perhaps the best known, but there are Brut, Demi-sec, and even rosé and sparkling red varieties. The delicious Cointreau orange-liqueur is distilled in Angers, although oranges are not grown there. The region is also the birthplace of Guignolet cherry liqueur.

Nantes

The seventh-largest city in France and—along with Bordeaux to the south—portal to the west. Nantes is an exquisite city not to be missed if you are anywhere this side of Paris. There is endless discussion about whether the city is properly considered part of Brittany or part of Western Loire. Today, Nantes is the capital of the latter, but it was indeed part of Brittany until relatively recently, serving as capital for a time to Nominoë, first Duke of Bretagne, and other dukes.

Nantes became part of France in 1532, after peace was achieved by the marriage of Anne de Bretagne (who was born in the Château des Ducs de Bretagne here) into the French royal family. In 1598, King Henry IV signed the Edict of Nantes, granting religious freedom to Protestants and putting an end to the Wars of Religion. Henry IV apparently chose Nantes as the site of the treaty-signing because the city leaders were both virulently anti-Protestant and increasingly overtly separatist. Straddling the estuary of the mighty Loire, crisscrossed by two of its arms as well as the Erdre and the Sèvre, Nantes was originally built on several small islands. Today, the rivers run underground—the city's main boulevards follow the rivers' courses. The different neighborhoods are still referred to as the Ile *of this* and the Ile *of that*, including the Ile-Feydeau, where Jules Verne was born and where a small museum honors his literary exploits. The city became extremely wealthy during the 18th century with the *ebony trade*—a euphemism for the slave trade. Also known as the *triangle trade*, this was a three-legged route whereby Nantean ships carried French textiles and other goods to Africa to trade for slaves, who were then shipped to the Antilles and traded for sugar cane, which was brought back to Nantes and sold at a huge profit. The slave trade endured through the 17th and 18th centuries and evidence of the city's enormous wealth during this period is seen in the tall, opulent houses near the seafront.

During a visit to Nantes don't omit a tour of the cathedral. Although rather gloomy and unappealing on the outside, the cathedral's interior is one of the most pleasing in the region. The roof burned down about 20 years ago and when it was rebuilt, the inside of the building was completely restored (i.e., cleaned), and now the cavernous nave and choir are light and airy. Also worth shelling out a few precious francs for is an excellent dinner and evening tour on one of the riverboats that ply the Erdre and the Sèvre. For an even more delicious meal, visit the restaurant in the Domaine d'Orvault hotel in the suburb of Orvault, where the sumptuous cooking of chef Jean Bernard will certainly wow your palate. (**Restaurant Domaine d'Orvault**, *chemin des Marais-du-Cens, 44700 Orvault;* ☎ *(33) 02-40-76-84-02; FAX (33)02-40-76-04-21).*

What to Do

Historical/Architectural Sites

Cathedrale de St.-Pierre ★★

place St.-Pierre, ☎ *02-40-14-23-00. In the center of town.*

Hours open: 8:45 a.m.–7 p.m. Special hours: Closed noon–2 p.m.

Begun in 1434, the cathedral wasn't completed until 437 years later. Having survived everything from ravaging during the Revolution to bombings by the Allies in 1944, this survivor boasts the largest stained-glass window in France. Completely renovated after a fire in 1972, the interior white walls beautifully contrast with the stained-glass windows, which are best seen in the light of the morning. Visit the tomb of Francois II, duc de Bretagne, and his second wife and the museum of religions in the crypt. Admission: free.

Château des Ducs de Bretagne ★★

1 place Marc-Elder, ☎ *02-40-41-56-56. On the east side of town.*

Constructed by Francois II, this 15th-century château was once the seat of the dukes of Brittany. While not like the ornate palaces in the Ile de France, this is a heavily fortified castle. This is the site where the Edict of Nantes was signed in 1598, granting religious freedom to Protestants. Perhaps its most famous prisoner was Gilles de Retz, otherwise known as Bluebeard; he was burned at the stake after confessing to more than 100 murders. Behind the walls are two museums: The Musée des Salorges and the Musée des Arts Populaires Regionaux. The former was created in 1928 and contains exhibits on the different aspects of the commercial history of Nantes; the latter displays traditional Breton costumes and furniture. Both museums are included in the FR10 admission to the château. Admission: FR10.

Museums and Exhibits

Jules Verne Museum ★★★

3 rue de l'Hermitage, ☎ *02-40-69-72-52. At place M. Schwob; about 2 km southwest of the tourist office.*

Hours open: 10.a.m.–5 p.m. Special hours: Closed noon–2 p.m.; Sun., 2–5 p.m. only. Closed: Tue.

A refreshingly interesting museum with fantastic visuals centered around the characters and stories of the Nantes-born author. Included in the display are letters, photos and examples of Verne's works. Sunday admission is free, and students and senior citizens pay FR4. Admission: FR8.

Musée des Beaux-Arts ★★

10 rue Georges-Clemenceau, ☎ *02-40-41-65-65. East of place du Marechal-Foch. Closed: Tue.*

Filled with lesser-known works by famous artists, as well as a fine collection of provincial sculptures and paintings. Most notable are works by de la Tour, Kandinsky and Delacroix. *Open Mon. & Wed.–Sat., 10 a.m.–6 p.m. and Sun., 11 a.m.–6 p.m. Closed Tues.* Admission: FR30.

Where to Stay

Bed-and-Breakfasts

Château du Housseau   FR390–FR495   ★★★

Le Housseau. ☎ *02-40-30-21-95, FAX: 02-40-25-14-05. About 3 km northeast of Nantes. Take the autoroute, Pairs-Nantes, and exit at Beaujoire. Follow the signs to Le Housseau.*

Single: FR390–FR440. Double: FR450–FR495.

What a delight it is to drive up to this little château in the countryside, with its ivy-covered walls and white trim. While still convenient to town, this B&B retains its country roots. Set among green lawns and trees, there are five rooms found within this two-story structure. Each tastefully decorated room is touched with the warmth of home with matching bedspreads and curtains and equipped with TV, telephone, and bath or shower. Sunny mornings bring breakfast on the terrace beside the pool for FR50, and evenings brings dinner in the rustic dining room for FR200. Active guests find tennis and golf facilities nearby, and walking tours of town are easily done. With its close proximity to town, the Château du Housseau proves a good choice for all types of travelers. Features: country location. Credit Cards: Not Accepted.

La Plauderie   FR270–FR400   ★★★

1 rue du Verdelet. ☎ *02-40-02-45-08. Abou 25 km southwest of Nantes. Take the D751 towards Pornic. In Port Saint Pere, head left on D758 towards Bourgneuf-en-Retz. Double: FR270–FR400.*

Although a bit of a drive from Nantes, this house is worth the detour. Situated beside a church, it sits discreetly among secluded gardens. The madame of the house warmly welcomes guests to her three charming rooms with private shower or bath and hot tea-making facilities. The rooms are elegantly furnished to create a home-away-from-that-home-you-only-see-in-design-magazines feeling. After enjoying breakfast for FR35, guests depart for the nearby golf and tennis facilities and the beaches. This is the place where just reading a book on a bench among the gardens and trees outside the ivy-covered house seems enough. Credit Cards: Not Accepted.

Hotels and Resorts

Hotel Graslin   FR290–FR360   ★★

1 rue Piron. ☎ *02-40-69-72-91, FAX: 02-40-69-04-44. In the center of town across from the Graslin et Theatre.*

Single: FR290–FR360. Double: FR290–FR360.

The couple that owns and manages this hotel strive to keep high standards of maintenance and low prices. Modestly decorated, there are 47 rooms with satellite TV, telephone, radio, safe, private bath and some with minibar. An excellent combination of comfort and practicality, the rooms prove to be great for overnighting it. This central yet quiet facility is accented with many homelike touches, making it a reliable hotel choice in town. Credit Cards: V, MC, DC, A.

L'Hotel   FR360–FR400   ★★

6 rue Henry IV. ☎ *02-40-29-30-31, FAX: 02-40-29-00-95. At the top of place de la Duchesse-Anne; across from the Château des Ducs de Bretagne.*

Single: FR360. Double: FR400.

Across from the moats of the Château des Ducs de Bretagne sits this quality lodging choice. Crossing the threshold leads one to the antique-adorned lobby and the sitting area with comfortable furniture. There are 31 uniquely decorated rooms to choose from, and each comes with a TV, telephone, private bath and wood furnishings. Breakfast is available for FR37, and other meals and entertainment can be found nearby. A welcoming overnight choice for a diverse crowd of travelers. Credit Cards: V, MC, DC, A.

Where to Eat

La Cigale $ ★★★

4 place Graslin, Near the monuments; across from the Theatre Graslin. *02-40-69-76-41. Dinner: 6:45 p.m.–12:30 a.m., entrées FR65–FR80.*

The most famous brasserie in Nantes, La Cigale has occupied the same Belle Epoque building since 1895. Visited by all of the chic locals, the traditional fare and friendly service have made this a venerable hot spot. Stop by for a drink or the generous servings of seafood, beef, poultry and other specialties available with the FR70–FR130 fixed-price menus. A must-visit while in Nantes. Reservations recommended. Credit Cards: V, MC.

Le Domaine d'Orvault $$$ ★★★★

24 chemin des Marais du Cens, About 7km northwest on the N137 and D42, in nearby Orvault. *02-40-76-84-02.*
Dinner: entrées FR200–FR450.

One of the finest gastronomic experiences in the region, Le Domaine's Jean-Yves Bernard gives a purely stellar performance. From the freshest ingredients to the artistic presentation, each meal is nothing short of excellent. While the dessert selection is still improving, the wine list will be sure to please. Very professional service in a dark, subdued setting. Amenities: outside dining, reservations required. Credit Cards: V, DC, A.

Mon Reve $$ ★★★

route de Bords de Loire, Take the N751 9km east of Nantes. ☎ *02-40-03-55-50. Dinner: 7:30–9:30 p.m., entrées FR100–FR150.*

A verdant setting with rose garden, Mon Reve is a popular choice with locals. The FR200 fixed-price dinner is outstanding, and the a la carte dishes are equally impressive. Regional and creative cuisine are served from this multi-talented kitchen. Consistently quality food. Credit Cards: All Major.

Torigai $$ ★★★★★

Ile de Versailles, On the island just north of town center. ☎ *02-40-37-06-37.*
Combine a Japanese chef, his French wife and a romantic, riverside setting and the result is gastronomic heaven—also known as Torigai. A new taste lurks around every corner, as he combines his Japanese heritage with his French training. Remarkably light and exotic, the best part for your heart is the minimalist attitude he has towards fat. For an absolute steal, try the FR165 fixed-price lunch that includes wine. Service is equally impressive with an attentive, knowledgeable and cordial staff. Closed: Sun. Reservations required. Credit Cards: V.

Directory

To and From

> *By train from Paris (two hours on the TGV) or by car on the A-11 autoroute from Paris or the N-147 from the Loire Valley. You also can reach Nantes on Air Inter Europe and international flights from London.*

Tourist Office

> *place du Commerce;* ☎ *(33) 02-40-47-04-51.*

Rail Station

> *27, boulevard de Stalingrad;* ☎ *(33) 02-40-08-50-50.*

Post Office

> *place de Bretagne, 44000 Nantes;* ☎ *(33) 02-40-92-62-53.*

La Baule

Home of the "Most Beautiful Beach in Europe," La Baule is located on the Presqu'Ile de Guérande due east of Nantes and just past the delta where the River Loire empties into the Atlantic Ocean. The beach is truly stunning— six miles long, of fine sand, sheltered from the wind and the waves, and—the locals claim—the only major sandy beach in Europe that faces due south. This claim seems a little dubious, given the Riviéra, but the beach is none-theless magnificent.

La Baule did not exist 120 years ago. Before that there were just sand dunes where the town is now situated. The resort was the brainchild of a couple of Victorian-era Paris entrepreneurs who saw the possibilities and made use of the railroad that carried salt away from the nearby salt marshes. Unfortunately, the sea-front itself is marred by ugly modern apartment blocks, but most of the village itself is picturesque. Especially intriguing are the narrow, tree-lined streets lined with sumptuous seaside villas built by the Parisian and Nantean elite at the turn of the century—most are privately owned and several remain in the same families.

The town itself is a fine beach resort, but the surrounding area is really what makes it special. The *Presqu'Ile de Guérande* is named for Guérande, a charming *ville close* (walled town) that was the home of the Duchesse Anne de Bretagne. The peninsula is quite small and very flat; you could easily base yourself in La Baule without a car, and bike around. The whole area was his-torically part of Brittany—Nantes, of course was once Brittany's capital—and the architecture in Guérande shows it. The walled town is my favorite Old Town in western France—much more manageable and less touristy than St. Malo but more substantial than Concarneau. To the northeast of the town lies the **Parc Regional Naturel de Brière**. This nature reserve is centered around a 10,000-acre marsh that is home to thousands of migrating birds, as well as a resident population of herons, frogs (food for the herons) and wild boar. Within the park, strict building codes are in effect and the homes that lie inside its boundaries have thatched roofs, made from the reeds of the brière itself. There is a reconstructed village (**Kerhinet**) in the park, with a tiny museum (well-worth a visit) that explains the art of thatching.

Guérande was known in days gone by as the capital of the *Pays Blanc* ("White Country"). The name derives from the part of the marshy peninsula that for more than a thousand years has been home to a salt farm. How do you farm salt? Well, you can drive through the salt marshes and see. The tide is allowed to come in and then the sea water is sealed off by means of low, hand-built dikes. As the water evaporates, salt is crystallized and harvested by hand. In a good year the 200 or so salt farmers produce 10,000 tons of the stuff. Down the narrow point of the peninsula is the fishing port of Le Croisic, reached by driving (or riding) along the Côte Sauvage—not the truly wild coast we have seen in northern Brittany, but rocky and windswept and beautiful nonetheless. A severe storm demolished the harbor wall at Le Croisic in the fall of 1995, so you can see that the *côte* can get plenty *sauvage* at times. The aquarium at Le Croisic was built in the United States before being assembled in France, and has a tunnel where you walk under the water and look up at the sharks as they swim in slow circles above your head.

Where to Stay

Hotels and Resorts

Bellevue Plage   FR480–FR780   ★★★

27 boulevard de l'Ocean. ☎ *02-40-60-28-55, FAX: 02-40-60-10-18. Near the middle of the shoreline.*
Single: FR480–FR780. Double: FR480–FR780.
Here is a modern facility on a prime piece of land in the middle of the shoreline surrounding the bay. This small hotel houses 35 soundproofed rooms, each with air conditioning, TV and telephone. The decor is contemporary and improvements are constant. If the sun and fun seekers pass on the beach, the sailboats and the nearby golf, there is a solarium on the roof with grand views of the shoreline. Breakfast is available for FR50, and there are full restaurant facilities serving meals all day. Consistently a pleasant stay at a good value. Features: sailing, air conditioning in rooms, sauna. Credit Cards: V, MC, DC, A.

Castel Marie-Louise   FR750–FR1850   ★★★★

1 avenue Andrieu. ☎ *02-40-11-48-38, FAX: 02-40-11-48-35. Along the oceanfront.*
Double: FR750–FR1850.
A classic estate hotel situated along the waterfront, the Castel Marie-Louise is a distinguished member of the Relais and Châteaux group of hotels. Set among plush private gardens, this manor house offers expansive views of the beach from its secluded vantage point among the pines. The choice resort in La Baule, it offers 29 unique rooms, each exceedingly comfortable and handsomely furnished in different styles from rustic to Louis XV. All have the modern amenities including TV, telephone, minibar, spacious bath and some with balcony. Guests spend leisure time at

the beach, playing tennis or sipping drinks on the terrace and in the lounge. Every visitor should make reservations at the restaurant to enjoy one of the seafood specialties of the fine chef. How wonderful life is when seen from this prime estate. Features: wheelchair-access rooms, beach location, tennis. Credit Cards: All Major.

L'Hermitage   **FR2135–FR2420**   ★★★★

5 esplanade Lucien-Barriere. ☎ *02-40-11-46-46, FAX: 02-40-11-46-45. On the beach. Single: FR2135. Double: FR2420.*

A grand structure rising seven stories above the beach, this well-kept luxury hotel offers a plethora of rooms among opulent surroundings. Some balconied, the 215 rooms provide all of the modern amenities accented with attractive antique reproductions. Each room is air-conditioned and has a TV, telephone and minibar, and most offer great sea views. The facilities are well maintained and include a heated pool, 28 tennis courts, golf course, sauna, fitness center and children's activities during the summer. Take a pick from the three restaurants including a beach cafe, a grill and a more formal dining room which showcases fantastic seafood dishes prepared by the talented chef. Any lack of charm is compensated for by the grand scale of this operation. Features: beach location, pool, tennis, air conditioning in rooms, sauna, fitness center.Credit Cards: V, MC, DC, A.

Where to Eat

Castel Marie-Louise   **$$**   ★★★

1 avenue Andrieux, Along the oceanfront. Located at Castel Marie-Louise. ☎ *02-40-11-48-38.*

One of the few elegant restaurants in La Baule, the Castel Marie-Louise is housed in the first-class hotel of the same name. Some of the better dishes include lobster, salmon and ham. The wine cellar is respectable, and the desserts are exquisite. Fixed-price menus start at FR195 during the off-season. Exemplary service that is consistent with the entire hotel-restaurant staff. reservations recommended. Credit Cards: V, DC, A.

La Marcanderie   **$$**   ★★★★

5 avenue d'Agen, A few blocks from the beach. ☎ *02-40-24-03-12. Dinner: 7–9:30 p.m., entrées FR110–FR210.*

Once a private residence, chef Jean-Luc Giraud has established this as one of the best restaurants in town. Try the potato galette, scallops in cream sauce and a bottle of one of the fantastic cellared wines. The staff is diligent and happy to serve. Fixed-price menus from FR150 (weekdays only) to FR375. Jacket and tie required. Closed: Mon. reservations required. Credit Cards: V, A.

La Voile d'Or   **$$$**   ★★★★

14 avenue de la Plage, About 3km west in Pouliguen. ☎ *02-40-42-31-68. Dinner: entrées FR275–FR400.*

An ultra-chic establishment, the locals flock here for the traditional fare. Enjoy butter-roasted coquilles, John Dory and a bottle of wine from the decent collection while sitting on the bayside terrace. Consistently smart service. Fixed-price menus from FR120–FR300. Closed: Sun. Reservations required. Credit Cards: V, A.

THE LOIRE

Directory

To and From

> *The railroad ends at La Baule, but you can take the TGV all the way from Paris in three hours, or about an hour from Nantes. By car on the N-171 off the N-165 Nantes-Quimper expressway.*

Tourist Office

> *place de la Victoire;* ☎ *(33) 02-40-24-34-44.*

Rail Station

> *place de la Gàre;* ☎ *(33) 02-40-66-50-50.*

Post Office

> *place de la Victoire, 44500 La Baule.*

Angers

Angers, birthplace of the Anjou dynasties as well as the Plantagenet family that ruled England for a time, is a veritable royal city. The 13th-century castle dominates the city. One of the strongest forts in France at its time, the castle walls are studded with large, round towers, one every 100 feet at some points—17 towers in all. This massive fortress-castle is unusual in that it has two entrances—one facing the town, and one called the Gate of the Fields through which the king could enter somewhat discreetly. The castle was the site of so many battles during the Hundred Years' War that the Anjouians demanded that the king tear it down to remove the incentive for the English to keep attacking, but the crafty French monarch simply began slowly dismantling the towers, cutting their height by about 30 feet. The rocks were used to build a second inner wall, thus making the place even stronger. Also notable about the château (definitely built before the pleasure-palaces bearing the same name further up the Loire Valley) is the simultaneous use of slate and limestone, which gives the construction an almost Art Deco-style striped effect. Housed inside the castle is the "Tapestry of the Apocalypse," a 550-foot-long, world-famous depiction of the end of the world woven between 1375 and 1380. There are tapestries aplenty in Angers, including the collection of 15th- and 16th-century Flemish works housed in the former governor's lodge and, for those with a taste for the modern, the "Chant du Monde" ("Song of the World") tapestry created in 1957, which can be found in the Musée Jean Lurçat in the 12th-century St. John's Hospital. The hospital itself is an excellent example of the full development of the Gothic vaulting style, which evolved from the 12th-century Romanesque-style of architecture, passing through an intermediary phase known as Angevin vaulting. The hospital is located across the river from the Old Town, in a quartier known as *doutre*, which is rich in sights itself, including the 11th-century Abbaye de Ronceray.

There are other opportunities for art lovers in Angers, including the **Museum of David d'Angers**, the famous 18th- and 19th-century sculptor, and the **Fine Arts Museum**, both of which are entered on the same ticket. The former is housed in the beautifully restored nave of a Gothic church, topped with a glass roof that bathes the sculptures (mostly statues) in radiant, natural light. Nearby are the feudal châteaux of Serrant, Brissac, Plessis-Macé and Plessis-Bourré. If you have to choose only one, take Plessis-Bourré, a fairy-tale castles that sits in a wide, water-filled moat, reached by an imposing drawbridge. Built in the 17th century, the castle is especially interesting in that its exterior is quite stark, while the interior begins to display the extravagance and opulence we associate with the better-known works of the 18th-century to the north and east.

What to Do

Historical/Architectural Sites

Cathedrale St.-Maurice   ★★★

place Freppel, ☎ *02-41-87-58-45. Near the château.*
Hours open: 8 a.m.–5 p.m.

The vaulting of the nave of this cathedral, Angevin vaulting, symbolizes the transition from Romanesque to Gothic in the 12th century. This type of vaulting allowed for the construction of a single, wide, elegant nave as witnessed here. Try to arrive in the late afternoon, when the sun illuminates the interior through the beautiful stained-glass windows dating from the 12th through 16th centuries. At one time a rich collector of tapestries, the cathedral now displays its several remaining ones during the summer. Admission: free.

Château d'Angers   ★★★★

In the centre ville by the Loire.

Constructed in just 10 years, this château wasn't built as a party palace or a royal getaway; instead, its original purpose was to protect against the threatening Normans. While not exactly the image of a fairytale château, its 17 towers (now flattened) of alternating white freestone and dark schist, combined with its 981-yard long, 49-foot-high wall surrounding the perimeter, made a formidable position of defense. From the 17th to the 19th centuries, it stopped keeping people out and started keeping them in—when it served as a prison. Inside is one of the greatest pieces of art from the Middle Ages—the Apocalypse Tapestry. More than 550 feet long and 16 feet high, this is the oldest and most important tapestry to have been preserved. It was commissioned by the Duke of Anjou, Louis I, to upstage his brother, Charles V in 1375. Almost experiencing its own apocalypse, the tapestry once was used as a canopy to cover orange trees during frost and was later torn up during the Revolution. The 19th century brought semirestoration to the tapestry, all 77 pieces of it, and it now hangs in the château—slightly faded. *The entire château is open from 9 a.m.–7 p.m.; Sept.–Apr., 9:30 a.m.–12:30 p.m. and 2–6 p.m.* Admission is FR32; students FR20.

THE LOIRE

Museums and Exhibits

Galerie David d'Angers   ★★

33 rue Toussaint, ☎ *02-41-88-64-65. Near the cathedral.*
Hours open: 10 a.m.–6 p.m. Special hours: Closed noon–2 p.m. Closed: Mon.
Situated in a 13th-century church, the museum displays the sculptures of Pierre-
Jean David (1789–1856). The well-arranged collection presents statues, monu-
ments and busts of famous people of his time. All of these works were donated by
David to this, his native town. Also of interest in Angers is the **Musée des Beaux-
Arts**, adjacent to the **Musée David d'Angers**, *10 rue du Musée (☎ 02-41-88-64-
65)*, with an impressive collection of the masters' works from the 17th and 18th
centuries; *open Tues.–Sun., 10 a.m.–noon and 2–6 p.m., FR14.*

Musée Jean Lurcat   ★★★

4 boulevard Arago, ☎ *02-41-88-64-65. Near the river.*
Hours open: 9:30 a.m.–7 p.m. Special hours: Closed 1-2 p.m.
Founded in 1174 and used as a hospital for almost 700 years, this building how
houses the Jean-Lucrat Museum. Begun in 1957, the series of 10 tapestries called
Le Chant du Monde (The Song of the World) is a symbolic journey of his inspired
vision of the destiny of humans. Vibrant colors upon a black background, the self-
destruction and reconstruction of man is portrayed in a wild and mentally-challeng-
ing manner. *Sept.–May, 10 a.m.–noon and 2–6 p.m.; FR20.*

Where to Stay

Bed and Breakfasts

Château des Briottieres   **FR400–FR700**   ★★★

In Champigne. ☎ *01-41-42-00-02, FAX: 02-41-42-01-55. Abou 25 km north of
Angers towards Laval. At Montreuil-Juigne, turn right on D768 through Feneu to
Champigne.*
Double: FR400–FR700.
This three-story château is worthy of an overnight retreat outside of Angers. An aes-
thetic beauty, it houses nine guest rooms decorated in unpretentious elegance and
equipped with a telephone and private bath. Guests enjoy the scenic view over the
landscaped grounds from most of the rooms. In addition to the pool, other leisure
facilities include billiards, fishing and a sitting lounge. If more outdoor activities are
sought, just a short distance from the property are tennis, golf and horseback riding
facilities. At the end of the day, be sure to sample the gastronomic specialties served
at the communal dinner table for FR250. A gem of a private chateau with impeccable service from the courteous staff. Features: pool. Credit Cards: V, MC, E.

Hotels and Resorts

Hotel d'Anjou   **FR350–FR550**   ★★★

1 boulevard Foch. ☎ *02-41-88-24-82, FAX: 02-41-87-22-21. On the main boulevard,
near the big park.*
Single: FR350–FR550. Double: FR350–FR550.
Operating since 1850, this four-story Best Western-operated hotel has been renovated in 18th-century style. Guests are greeted by the kind staff in the reception
area, which displays attractive stained glass windows. There are 53 rooms kept in

pristine condition and equipped with TV, telephone, minibar and private bath. All are quite spacious, uniquely decorated and accented with fresh flowers. Be sure to sample the local dishes at the hotel's restaurant, La Salamandre, where a la carte meals average FR300. With its historic reputation for reliable accommodations, the d'Anjou has a loyal repeat crowd. Credit Cards: V, MC, DC, A.

Pavillon Paul Le Quere   **FR450–FR800**   ★★★★

3 boulevard Foch. ☎ *02-41-20-06-20, FAX: 02-41-20-00-20. On the main boulevard near the big park.*
Double: FR450–FR800.

With its townhouse origins dating to 1862, this rates as the finest establishment in Angers. Opened in 1992, its renovations were supervised by the Beaux-arts commission to assure every detail was perfect. The husband and wife duo have spent painstaking years to make this their ideal hotel and restaurant. There are just six rooms and four suites, each spaciously arranged and appointed with every convenience desirable. Even the baths, lavished in marble, are a pleasure to spend time in. There are two dining rooms, one in a glass rotunda and the other in a formal setting featuring marble and fireplaces. A visit to Angers wouldn't be complete without a meal enjoyed here, especially if one is a guest in the gracious hotel.

Inns

Château de Noirieux   **FR600–FR1250**   ★★★

26 route du Moulin. ☎ *02-41-42-50-05, FAX: 02-41-37-91-00. About 12 km from Angers off of the D52.*
Double: FR600–FR1250.

This château is one of those rare finds every well-heeled traveler seeks to keep quiet so as not to let the secret spot get spoiled by other visitors. Built in 1927, this small hotel first delighted guests in 1991. Located just a short distance from Angers among lush, immaculately maintained grounds, this idyllic spot affords views to the Loire. There are 19 rooms divided among three buildings, each with elegant furnishings, central heating, TV, telephone, minibar and private bath with hair dryer. Whether lingering in the lovely sitting rooms inside or lounging at the pool, Jacuzzi or tennis courts outside, guests find all of the facilities impressively well kept. Breakfast is served in the attractive dining room for FR70, and other meals are available starting at FR200. The courteous staff treats the guests to flawless service and welcomed pampering. Credit Cards: V, MC, DC, A.

Where to Eat

Le Logis   **$$**   ★★

9 place du Ralliement, Across from the Municipal Theater. ☎ *02-41-87-44-15.*
Dinner: 7:30–9:30 p.m., entrées FR100–FR150.

This conveniently located establishment puts quality dining in the heart of the action. The skill of the chef is best demonstrated with seafood dishes, although some meat dishes are on the menu. Appetizers start at FR80, and the fixed-price menus start at FR 120. Reservations are advised during summer months, considering the central location. Closed: Sun. Reservations recommended. Credit Cards: All Major.

Le Quere $$$ ★★★★★

> 3 boulevard Foch. ☎ 02-41-20-00-20.
>
> Le Quere retains its status as the leading restaurant in Angers. Paul Le Quere's delicate magic is worked in the kitchen while his wife, Martine, attends to the guests' every need. For FR200, the chef's special menu offers a generous meal well worth the price (weekdays only). A la carte meals tend to be expensive. Amenities: outside dining, reservations required. Credit Cards: V, DC, A.

Le Toussaint $$ ★★★

> 7 place du President Kennedy, Near the castle; on the same street as the cathedral. ☎ 02-41-87-46-20.
>
> Dinner: 7:45–9:30 p.m., entrées FR70–FR160.
>
> One of Angers' premier restaurants, chef Michel Bignon offers an excellent FR115 fixed-price menu, with the most expensive fixed-price at FR300. Try a memorable foie gras main course and an angelic soufflé glacé dessert. Relax with an after dinner drink, enjoying the second-floor view of the castle. Jacket required. Reservations recommended. Credit Cards: V, MC, A.

Directory

To and From

> By train from Paris (two-and-three-quarters hours) or Tours (one hour). By car on the A-11 autoroute from Paris and Le Mans or the N-152 from Tours.

Tourist Office

> place Kennedy; ☎ (33) 02-41-23-51-11.

Rail Station

> rue de la Gàre; ☎ (33) 02-41-88-50-50.

Post Office

> 1 rue Franklin Roosevelt, 49052 Angers.

Saumur

Saumur, birthplace of Coco Chanel, is one of the loveliest cities on the Loire. Begun on ancient foundations in the 14th century, Saumur's castle was one of the primary residences of the Dukes of Anjou; King Réne made it his home, during which period it was christened the "Castle of Love." It is possibly the most beautiful castle in all of France, thanks to its white stone, its fairytale-like towers topped by conical slate roofs, and its placement atop the escarpment beside the river, which gives it a spectacular view of the skyline for miles. The castle is stunning in any light, but if you can, catch a glimpse of it during sunrise or sunset, or at night, when it is illuminated. Nowadays, the lower level of the castle houses a museum dedicated to the decorative arts, while the upper floor is an internationally recognized museum of equestrianism with displays of harnesses and saddlery from around the world. Saumur is a major equestrian center, and there are frequent world-class shows and events held in and near the city. Originally a cavalry facility established in Saumur in 1814, the National Riding School is open to visitors.

Saumur's castle is stunning from any vantage point.

There are several sights to see within a few miles of Saumur. The *tuffaud* limestone that gives the château its white color was extracted from the escarpment to the east, and every building from manor house to outhouse is made of the same stone. Prized for its ease of sculpting, the limestone was shipped all over France, and even as far as Westminster Abbey in London. The process of mining the limestone from the cliffs has had a multiple-level effect on the area. Within the cliff, are dozens of miles of tunnels, and after these sat empty for many years the locals began to figure out ways to use them. Thanks to the dark and the damp, a primary use is for mushroom farming. Saumur and its surroundings account for 80 percent of cultivated mushrooms in France, and numerous *champignoneries* outside town are open to the public. There is even a **mushroom museum**, surely the only one in the world. Some caves are used as homes. Along with Granada in Spain, Saumur is one of two major troglodyte centers in Europe—and it is quite surrealistic to see a door open in the cliff as you pass and catch a glimpse inside of a fully furnished living room, complete with a television.

The caves also are used for wine cellars. I especially recommend a visit to the *Gratien & Meyer Winery*, just east of Saumur on the D-947, not least because there are guided tours in English. The winery has the primary local producer of "Saumur champagne" since 1864, and after the tour you get to taste the many varieties. Within the winery's 11 kilometers of subterranean passages and chambers are 9 million bottles of sparkling wine in various stages of fermentation. The winery's excellent mini-museum depicts the production process as it was 100 years ago.

To the west of Saumur, on the way to **Fontevraud** (see below) is the village of **Montsoreau**, another charming Loire hamlet that boasts an oversized château. This one is particularly lovely, as it sits practically in the river itself. Built during the 15th century, the castle was immortalized by Alexandre Dumas. It contains one of the most beautiful Renaissance staircases, built by Phillipe de Chambes, in the entire Loire region.

The Royal Abbey of Fontevraud, the major *tuffaud* limestone edifice in these parts, is one of the most impressive sights in France. The largest remaining abbatial community in Europe (even with one-fourth of its structure missing!), the abbey is in a near-perpetual state of renovation, but don't let that put you off—there's more than enough to see. The complex was founded in 1101 by a Benedictine monk, Robert of Abrissel. By 1115, the main abbatial church had been completed. Today, still standing in a state of perfect conservation, the cavernous nave and transept house the bodies of Richard the Lionhearted and Henry II, the kings of England, and two of their various wives. Also on view since a couple of years ago is the final resting-place of the abbey's founder, who was never canonized—due largely to some letters he wrote ruing having slept with nuns, albeit without giving in to temptation. Look carefully and you can see the outline of his body, Shroud of Turin-like, etched into the stone. Abrissels' vision was for a complete city. He created four monasteries on the site—one for men, one for contemplative nuns, one for "fallen women," and one used as a hospice for lepers. Each structure was self-contained, with cloister, dormitories and refectory, and today three are still standing. Numerous outbuildings and an immense kitchen/smoking house with a unique Romanesque/Byzantine stone roof kept the abbey functioning. The complex was so important that the pope came from Rome to dedicate it—the Vatican was so worried that the enormous order would begin to rival its power that it decreed the complex could not house more than 500 monks and nuns. In fact, however, at its peak the abbey—always under the rule of an abbess, even the men, by order of the founder—contained more than 1000 spiritual members, as well as hundreds of lay workers. Patronized by the *Plantagenets*, the order of Fontevraud grew to include more than 100 abbeys from Spain to England, all reporting to the abbess, who was a member of the Bourbon family. The monastic life continued for 700 years at Fontevraud. After the Revolution the abbey, like almost every other in France, became a prison. It continued as such until 1963, although the last remaining minimum security prisoners, who served as groundskeepers, did not leave until 1985. All the inner furnishings are gone, even in the main church, but the emptiness of the place only highlights its impressive architecture. The dormitories are now used for concerts, and the St. Lazaire leper hospice has been turned into a hotel and restaurant.

These are only some of the attractions near Saumur—it is well worthwhile spending several days exploring the region.

What to Do

Historical/Architectural Sites

Castle of Montsoreau ★★

In Montsoreau, ☎ *02-41-50-70-25. Southeast of Saumur off the D751.*
Hours open: 10 a.m.–6 p.m. Special hours: Closed noon–2 p.m. Closed: Tue.
Made famous by Dumas in La Dame de Montsoreau, this castle sits impressively on the banks of the Loire and Vienne rivers. Construction dates to the 15th century, with some additions in the 16th century. Also inside the castle is the Musée des Goums, relating history about the conquest of Morocco. Admission: FR22.

Château de Saumur ★★★★

Originally built by Philippe Auguste and Louis IX, the base for the château is a medieval fortress. In the 14th century, Louis I of Anjou built this fairy-tale structure on the remains of the fortress, and it later became known as the "castle of love" under King Rene's decorating in late Gothic style. In 1685, when the Edict of Nantes was revoked in 1865 at the time of the Wars of Religion, the château became a prison stronghold. It is said that Marquis de Sade (the original sadist) was held here during one of his prison stays. Three museums are housed in the château today: **Musée des Arts Decoratifs**, showcasing porcelain; **Musée du Cheval**, tracing the history of the horse from prehistoric times to present; **Musée de la Figurine et du Jouet**, miniature figures of everything imaginable. Admission to the entire château is FR33; *open Oct.–Mar., Wed.–Mon., 10 a.m.–noon and 2–5 p.m.; Apr.–June, daily, 9–11:30 a.m. and 2–6 p.m.; July–Sept., daily, 9 a.m.–7 p.m.* Admission: FR33.

L'Abbaye of Fontevraud ★★★

In Fontevraud., ☎ *02-41-51-71-41. Southeast of Saumur, off the D50.*
Hours open: 9 a.m.–7 p.m. Special hours: Oct.–May, 9:30 a.m.–noon and 2–6 p.m.
Tours in English, about one-hour long, take visitors through the abbey church, by the tombs of Henry II, Richard the Lionhearted, Eleanor of Aquitaine and Isabelle of Angouleme. A good photo-op is had with the view of the abbey from the south side of the town. Student admission is FR17. Admission: FR26.

Museums and Exhibits

Ecole Nationale d'Equitation ★★

rue de Marson, ☎ *02-41-53-50-60. In St.-Hilaire-St.-Florent.*
Opened in 1972, this modern establishment consists of five Olympic-size arenas, a vet hospital and stables for 450 horses. The stables have computerized feeding, and the manure is whisked away in a sewer to be sold as fertilizer to local mushroom growers. The National Riding School is centered here with the Cadre Noir (Black Squad) composing half of the instructors. Students here are taught the discipline, tradition, precision and decorum involved with French riding. The academy is

respected throughout France as an elite riding school for only the best. In Apr.–
Sept., tours leave between 9:30 and 10:30 a.m., FR30 (These are preferred, as the
Cadre Noir is usually training at this time). Afternoon tours are also available
between 2:30 and 4 p.m. Admission: FR30.

Mushroom Museum ★★

St.-Hilaire-St.-Florent, ☎ 02-41-50-31-55. About 2km west near the D751.
Hours open: 10 a.m.–7 p.m. Special hours: Open mid-Feb.–mid Sept.
The Musée du Champignon, or mushroom museum, gives tours of the local tufa
caves. These caves have the distinction of producing 75 percent of the total mushroom harvest in France. Since the humble beginnings in the time of Napoleon I, it
has progressed to produce about 120,000 tons of mushrooms per year. Worthy of
a lighthearted stopover. Admission: FR30.

Unique Museums

Various locations.
Saumur and its surroundings are home to three interesting, slightly offbeat museums. The **Musée du Masque "Jules Cesar,"** *rue de l'Abbaye* (☎ *02-41-50-75-26*),
has an excellent collection of carnival masks, including one of Whoopi Goldberg
and one of Francois Mitterrand, just to name a couple; *open daily, 10 a.m.–12:30
p.m. and 2:30–7 p.m; mid-Oct.–Mar., Sat.–Sun. only, 9 a.m.–noon and 2–6 p.m.;*
FR25. Just outside of town, in Turquant, is the **Musée des Pommes Tapees** *(☎ 02-
41-51-48-30).* Always wondered how to dehydrate apples? Wonder no more. Witness demonstrations of this popular 19th-century process, which later yields a fer-
mented alcoholic beverage. *Open June, Aug.–Sept., Tues.–Sun., 2:30–6:30 p.m.;
July 10 a.m.–noon and 2:30–6:30 p.m.* Admission FR20. On the other end of the
spectrum, back in town, the **Musée des Blindes** (Museum of Tanks) contains over
150 vehicles of war showing the development of the Armoured Corps since 1918
(including the 1918 Renault tank). On rue Beaurepaire *(☎ 02-41-67-20-96), 9
a.m.–noon and 2–6 p.m.;* FR20.

Where to Stay

Bed-and-Breakfasts

Beauregard   FR350–FR350 ★★

*22 rue Beauregard. ☎ 02-41-67-92-93. About 10 km northwest of Saumur on D751
towards Gennes.*
Double: FR350.
The pretty drive hints at what awaits on the small hill ahead—this lovely manor
house on the Loire. The pleasant couple who own this house greet their guests with
a warm smile and welcome. There are two rooms and one suite for four people, all
with private bath. With views of the Loire, the rooms are spaciously arranged and
beautifully decorated. Guests are treated to breakfast in the lovely dining room, and
other meals are available at nearby restaurants. The rural location is ideal for strolls
along the Loire and golf at the nearby course. A homey experience with personal
attention from the friendly owners. Credit Cards: Not Accepted.

Le Domaine de Mestre   **FR295**   ★★★

Fontevraud-l'Abbaye. ☎ *02-41-51-72-32, FAX: 02-41-51-71-90. About 12 km southeast of town on the D947 towards Chinon. Head towards Fontevraud-l'Abbaye. It lies between Montsoreau and Fontevraud.*

Double: FR295.

At one time this house was the farm of the monks of the local abbey. It now is one of the most beautiful B&Bs in the region. Its grand size allows for 11 rooms and one suite for three people. Each room is attractively decorated in traditional style and comes with private bath. Guests enjoy breakfast for FR35 and evening meals by reservation in the charming dining room featuring locally grown ingredients. Leisure activities are closeby and include tennis, golf and horseback riding. The English-speaking owners will gladly give directions to the nearby châteaux. A gracious house with commodious accommodations. Credit Cards: Not Accepted.

Hotels and Resorts

Anne d'Anjou   **FR390–FR495**   ★★★

32 quai Mayoud. ☎ *02-41-67-30-30, FAX: 02-41-67-51-00. At the foot of the château.*

Single: FR390. Double: FR495.

Situated at the foot of the château, this aged building served as a family home in the 18th century. The facade and the curving staircase with iron railing have received monument status. Recently renovated, the 50 guest rooms vary in decor and arrangement and include TV, telephone and private bath. It's a difficult choice between the rooms in the front facing the Loire and the rooms in the back facing the chateau. Some are done in contemporary style while others display old furnishings; the point of pride is room #102, with its classic paintings and Empire furnishings as part of the design Napoleon's architects devised. The distinguished restaurant, Les Menestrels, provides a delectable menu. A charming establishment that has pleased the likes of Ginger Rogers, Jean Marais and the Prince of Monaco. Credit Cards: V, MC, DC, A.

Le Prieure   **FR420–FR1350**   ★★★

On the D751. ☎ *02-41-67-90-14, FAX: 02-41-67-92-24. On the D751 towards Angers; about 8 km.*

Double: FR420–FR1350.

This former priory, dating to the 12th century, has been extensively renovated to become the modern establishment it is today. A Relais and Châteaux member, it sits on 60 acres of verdant grounds on top of a plateau. The 35 rooms provide comfortable furnishings, TV, telephone and minibar in fairly luxurious surroundings. Each room is individually decorated in traditional style. The grand reception area boasts a stone fireplace, fine wood furniture, crystal chandeliers and a cozy bar. With splendid views of the river, the hotel's restaurant of the same name serves divine fare with fixed-price menus starting at FR250; it's an experience no guest should miss. The relaxing surroundings make up for the slight dearth of character. Features: pool, tennis. Credit Cards: V, MC, A.

THE LOIRE

Where to Eat

Delices du Château $$ ★★★

Les Feuquieres, On the château property. ☎ *02-41-67-65-60.*
Dinner: 7–10:30 p.m., entrées FR100–FR150.

Occupying a 12th-century house within the château grounds, this restaurant affords fabulous views of the city. Chef Pierre Millon, son of a local vineyard owner, boasts of his deep cellar. The food is traditional with a flair of nouvelle introduced by the hands of the progressive Millon. Look for the FR180–FR300 fixed-price menus. reservations required. Credit Cards: All Major.

L'Escargot $ ★★

30 rue du Marechal Leclerc. ☎ *02-41-51-20-88.*
Dinner: 7–10 p.m., entrées FR60–FR100.

While nothing terribly inventive, the food and service here are reliable. With a name like this, one has to try the snails with garlic butter cassoulet. If not, fixed-price meals start at FR80 and are very filling. Solid, traditional, French. Reservations required. Credit Cards: V, MC, A.

Le Prieure $$$ ★★★★

D751, About 8km northwest of Saumur on the D751; in Chenehutte-les-Tuffeaux.
☎ *02-41-67-90-14.*

A breathtaking view from the terrace-dining room assures a pleasant couple of hours at this hotel-restaurant. With tasty appetizers, an outstanding wine list, and too many specialties to list, you can't go wrong. Fixed-price menus start at FR200–FR400. Amenities: outside dining, reservations required. Credit Cards: V, A.

Directory

To and From

By rail from Angers (half-an-hour) or Nantes (one hour) or by car just across the river from the N-152 between Tours and Angers.

Tourist Office

place Bilange; ☎ *(33) 02-41-40-20-60.*

Rail Station

avenue David d'Angers; ☎ *(33) 02-41-67-50-50.*

Post Office

rue Volney, 49413 Saumur; ☎ *(33) 02-41-51-08-05.*

Le Mans

Chief city of the Sathre river valley, Le Mans is known around the world for the 24-hour automobile race, which draws upwards of 300,000 people the third weekend in June every year to the city and was memorialized in the film *Le Mans*, starring the late Steve McQueen. Le Mans' automobile roots go deep—the first car to have its engine covered by a hood, *L'Obéissante* (The Obedient), was designed here by Amédée Bollée, a bell-founder by trade, in 1873. His son created the *Grand Prix*, which began in 1906. The 24-hour track-race was initiated in 1923. Today, Le Mans is a major production center for French automaker Renault, and it has one of the world's finest automobile museums.

But Le Mans has been an important city even before the birth of the automobile industry. The hilltop Old Town is surrounded by a Gallo-Roman wall built during the third century. The wall is the finest example of Roman fortification architecture in France, and certainly the oldest functional city wall in Europe. Henry II, first Plantagenet king of England was born here in 1133, as was John the Good, king of France, in 1319. Within the walls—called the *Vindunum* by the Romans—the Cathédrale de St. Julien dominates the skyline for miles around. The cathedral is the clearest example of the development of architectural styles in a religious building in France, more eclectic even than Mont St. Michel. Even the completely uninitiated will notice the stylistic differences in how the 11th-century nave walls are topped by the 12th-century roof, leading to the 13th–15th-century transept and choir. The stained-glass window collection rivals that of Chartres for beauty and comprehensiveness, as does the Romanesque-style portal, which tells the story of the childhood of Jesus Christ. If you have already visited Chartres or are going there next, you will notice how the same artisans traveled the medieval world plying their trade from site to site, often staying in one city for a decade or more, as was the case in Le Mans. An interesting feature of the building is that you can see the marks of individual stonemasons on each and every brick in the walls. The marks served to ensure that each worker was paid according to the work that he had done. Inside, the cathedral houses a collection of ecclesiastic treasures that includes a fragment of the True Cross. The exterior of the cathedral is notable for the double-barreled flying buttresses that seem to support the building in mid-air. This unusual construction helped reinforce the walls, which were rendered weak by so many windows. Most of the stained glass is original 13th-century work, although one pane dates from 1140. Even older—by about 4000 years—is the menhir situated outside cathedral outside. The oddly sculpted rock has stood in the same place since long before the area was evangelized in the first millennium AD. You will notice a small hole in the stone, the result of passersby poking their fingers into it for thousands of years—there is a saying in Le Mans that you haven't really been to the city unless you've touched the menhir.

The cathedral is the crowning glory of **La Vielle Ville**; the Old City. Le Mans is without a doubt the best-preserved medieval town in western France. You can wander through street upon street of 15th- and 16th-century half-timbered houses, all of which are still inhabited today. Fans of actor Gerard Depardieu will note that the classic *Cyrano de Bergerqac* was shot in old Le

Mans. Look out for the **House of the Red Pillar** and **Queen Berengaria's** house, which are two of the oldest.

What to Do

Historical/Architectural Sites

Cathedrale St.-Julien   ★★★

> *On top of the hill.*
>
> An explicit example of the architectural and design changes of the time, the cathedrale shines with its flying buttresses, portal, nave, choir and tombs. The afternoon light provides for a glorious light show through the stained-glass windows.

Museums and Exhibits

Musée de l'Automobile   ★★★

> *Circuit des 24 Heures du Mans,* ☎ *02-43-72-72-24. About 5 km south of town center.*
> *Hours open: 10 a.m.–7 p.m. Special hours: Oct.–May, to 6 p.m. Closed: Tue.*
>
> Detailing some of the products of France to the auto world, from classics to race cars, this museum is an auto lover's delight. There are also many audio-visual displays to entertain the non-automotively inclined. From a 19th-century steam-powered vehicle to recent innovations, it's all here—in the center of the 24-hour course. Admission: FR35.

Where to Stay

Hotels and Resorts

Arcade   **FR275–FR325**   ★★★

> *40 rue du Vert-Galant.* ☎ *02-43-24-47-24. On the banks of the Sarthe, a few kilometers from town center.*
> *Double: FR275–FR325.*
>
> A lovely location on the banks of the Sarthe, the Arcade sits just a few minutes from town center. Within the five-story structure are 95 contemporary rooms, with TV, telephone and air conditioning. Views from the rooms are of the courtyard or the river. Request a room on one of the upper floors, as they are more spacious. Facilities include a restaurant, bar, conference rooms and garage parking. The staff is very receptive to any request. Features: air conditioning in rooms. Credit Cards: V.

Chantecler   **FR230–FR250**   ★★★

> *50 rue de la Pelouse.* ☎ *02-43-24-58-53. Near the train station.*
> *Single: FR230. Double: FR250.*
>
> Thanks to a recent makeover, the Chantecler offers comfortable yet simple accommodations. With a central location near the train station, the soundproofing of the 32 rooms is a welcome feature. The rooms are basically furnished, well-attended and equipped with telephone and TV. A little relaxation is found in the restaurant and on the veranda. The hard-working staff doesn't miss an opportunity to offer a warm welcome. Half-board rates and parking are available. Credit Cards: V.

Concorde   **FR200–FR450**   ★★★

> *16 avenue du Gal-Leclerc.* ☎ *02-43-24-12-30, FAX: 02-43-24-85-74.*
> *Single: FR200. Double: FR450.*

In a central location near the old town, the Concorde offers 68 guest rooms. Each is well-kept, attractively furnished and equipped with modern amenities including TV and telephone. In addition to conference facilities and a peaceful courtyard, there is a fine restaurant. Half-board rates are available from FR310. Credit Cards: V, DC, A.

Where to Eat

La Cite d'Aleth $ ★★

7 rue de la Vieille Porte, In Le Vieux Mans. ☎ *02-43-28-73-81.*
This family-run creperie offers an extensive list of crepes and tasty side dishes. Inexpensive fixed-price menus are also available for under FR125. Another value-conscious stop is **La Mascotte** *(11 rue des Trois Sonettes;* ☎ *02-43-87-56-43).* The inexpensive fixed-price menus feature sausages and various grilled meats sure to please your arteries. Credit Cards: All Major.

Le Grenier a Sel $$ ★★★★

26 place de l'Eperon. ☎ *02-43-23-26-30.*
Recently improved, the dining room here sets an elegant scene underneath a mirrored ceiling. The stylish chef adds a twist to the mostly rustic fare, making the food here some of the best in Le Mans. Perhaps the experimentation envelope could be pushed a bit further to spice things up. Fixed-price menus start at FR120. Closed: Mon., Sun. reservations required. Credit Cards: V.

Directory

To and From
By train from Paris in less than an hour on the TGV. By car on the A-11 toll road from the capital or on the N-138 from Tours to the south.

Tourist Office
In the Hotel des Ursulines, rue de l'Etoile; ☎ *(33) 02-43-28-17-22.*

Rail Station
place 8 du mai 1945; ☎ *(33) 02-43-77-01-00.*

Post Office
58 rue Miroir, 72000 Le Mans; ☎ *(33) 02-43-50-52-52.*

Sathre Valley

The valley of the Sathre river south towards La Flèche and Angers is charming and well worth a one- or two-day visit. The region has its own beautiful châteaux at Châteauf-sur-Sarthe and at Malicorne, and an ideal way to see the sights is to rent a houseboat. In fact, a week's houseboat rental is a great Loire experience—you travel the Sathre, a tributary of the Loire, and navigate uncrowded locks and peaceful waterways from above Le Mans to Angers. Off-season prices for a week vary from $700 for a launch for two to four people to $3000 for a luxury motor yacht that sleeps 10. There are also weekend and five-day rates. For more information contact:

Les Croisières en Vallée de la Sarthe
☎ *(33) 02-43-92-31-31; FAX: (33) 02-43-92-04-44.*

The historical village at Asnières-sur-Vègre is a fine example of a medieval-era Western Loire community. The village looks too good to be true and, indeed, the houses have been completely rebuilt, but restoration occurred during the 16th century, after the War of Religion, so you're still seeing semi-authentic structures. This is as good a collection of red-tiled roofs as you'll see in France. You will note as you move from the extreme west to the more central region east of Angers that the roofing material changes from gray slate to red tile.

Also worth a visit is the *faïencerie* production village of Malicorne. The fine decorative pottery rivals porcelain for its lightness and beauty, and pieces have been handmade here since the 12th century. There is a museum dedicated to the art and guided tours (in English during summer) of the *ateliers* where the ceramic is made and painted. This town is also the site of the Sathre Valley's prettiest château, the **Château des Plessis Bourré** a 15th-century treasure that is privately owned and inhabited. The fortified home sits in the confines of a water-filled moat, reached by a bridge that is the Loire's finest.

Finally, stop by the **Abbaye de Saint Pierre-de-Solesmes** at Solesmes. After the Vatican II conference did away with Latin services in the Catholic church, Gregorian chants nearly became extinct. This abbey has preserved the hauntingly beautiful incantations—a mission of an associated order of these Benedictine monks in Spain is where the *Chant* CD that reached Number One around the world was recorded in 1994. At Matins at 9:30 a.m. and Vespers at 5:30 p.m., the public is invited to attend the service and hear the chants. The abbey itself consists mostly of 19th-century architecture, although the priory was begun in the year 1010 and the Chappelle de Notre Dame dates from the early 16th century. Although the tallest part of the buildings is only 100 years old, the abbey, nestled alongside the river and a weir, is strikingly beautiful. Especially ornate statuary, called Les Saints de Solesmes, are on display in both wings of the transept, depicting scenes from the life of Mary on the left and the Tomb of Christ on the right. An agreement between the monks and the town has strictly limited development in Solesmes—you will note that there are no souvenir shops near the abbey. A small guest house is located within the enclosure where men can stay for a few days of spiritual renewal, living and working with the monks under the same vows of silence and solitude—the Benedictine Rule—that the *pères* obey. It is wise to not only book in advance but to confer with the abbey as to whether you are a suitable candidate. The monks employ a strict screening procedure designed to ensure the harmony of their way of life. For more information contact:

Abbaye St. Pierre

F-72300 Solesmes

☎ *(33) 02-43-95-45-05; Minitel: 3615 SOLESMES.*

Solesmes is a good place to stay for the night in the valley or while on tour between Le Mans and Angers; try the **Grand Hotel de Solesmes** across the street from the abbey. It features an excellent restaurant and spacious rooms within the sound of the bells: ☎ *(33) 02-43-95-45-10, FAX: (33) 02-43-95-22-26.*

THE LOIRE

Royal Château
Country—Val-de-Loire

A region bigger than the nation of Belgium, the vast area of the central Loire valley is one of the most beautiful, best known, and heavily traveled areas in France. This is **Royal Château Country**, the valley of the kings, a lush land largely describing the arc of the Loire River, but extending north as far as Chartres, south as far as Bourges. Each city has its own magnificent Gothic cathedral, as if those looking toward the kingdom of heaven were trying to gird, or perhaps encroach upon, the unbelievable wealth and decadence of the earthly kings, who built homes for themselves beside and near the river that are not only ungodly but, in some cases, inhuman.

Here in Val-de-Loire is the 400-room hunting lodge of François I at Chambord; here is the floating château upon a bridge at Chenonceau that Henri II gave to his mistress Diane de Poitiers; here are the romantic, fairy-tale castles at Azay-le-Rideau and Chaumont. You have seen pictures of these opulent palaces—that's why you're coming here. You'll take pictures that will never convey the scale of these châteaux. You'll tell your friends when you get home of the lavish bed chamber of Louis XIV; your friends will yawn, uninterested, until they travel here and see for themselves that you were right. But this is a region of more than famous palaces. There are thousands of châteaux in the Loire Valley—several hundred are open to the public—as well as countless vineyards and caves, museums and churches. So go see the "must-sees" you've dreamed about, but don't rush off to another place without first spending some time driving aimlessly on the quiet country roads between Tours and Blois, far from the giant palaces and the gigantic crowds—you'll be surprised by the natural beauty you will discover.

History

The modern history of Royal Châteaux Country begins about the turn of the first millennium. After the Romans had conquered the region and the Gallo-Roman peace was established in the third century, the area sank into an age of barbarity. In a bloodthirsty fashion, first, the Merovingian, then the Carolingian powers held sway of the countryside. During the same centuries, an important new force was introduced to the region—Christianity. This central area of France was an important incubator for the new religion that, led at first by Saint Martin of Tours, was grafted onto the orderly Roman way of doing things. As the millennium rolled over once again, and the great feudal lords of the 10th and 11th centuries contested the ancient regions of Touraine, Orléanais and Anjou, the church counterbalanced their power with a strong ecclesiastical order still evident today in countless abbeys and churches built throughout the region. The Gothic cathedrals at Bourges and Charles were called "Bibles of Stone." Both of these great ecclesiastical structures were built about the same time as Notre Dame in Paris.

The turmoil of the Hundred Years War during the 15th century—when half of France belonged to England, and Normans, Burgundians and Plantagenets were at war with their fellow Frenchmen—sparked the beginning of the royal presence in the Loire Valley. The only true haven of the French crown, far enough away from the borders to be safe from invasion or capture, the Loire Valley became the home of the itinerant, underpowered, and dithering king Charles VII. Charles VII moved his court around the region, as was the custom of the medieval monarchs throughout the Middle Ages and well into the Renaissance. The presence of the crown gave prestige to a city and prompted the construction of many of the feudal forts and castles of the region. While huddled at Bourges, Charles VII was prodded into action by Joan of Arc, and the beginning of the end of the English presence in France—and the Hundred Years' War—came at Orléans. Once the war was over, France under Louis XI began to solidify its power and control over the country, with control emanating outwards from the Loire Valley. With the end of feudalism and the beginnings of a new class of entrepreneurs, traders and bourgeoisie, France country entered a new phase of prosperity. Later, trade with the New World spread the wealth around just a little. The Renaissance, a new movement, originating in Italy, with which Louis XI's son, Charles VIII, had become familiar and fond of during his campaigns there, began to find its way into France. The Renaissance brought a love of things fine and beauty for beauty's sake to the Loire Valley, where the crown was still based. At the same time, national unity and security reduced the need for the homes of kings and barons to be impregnable fortresses. First the kings, then the nobles, and finally the *nouveau riche* of the time began to convert their homes and rebuild in the new Renaissance style. Gothic, which had already replaced Romanesque, gave way to true Renaissance architectural style—wide windows, terraces and balconies and extravagant steeples and towers that were largely for show. These architectural details were often added to existing structures, sometimes creating odd results. Inside the châteaux, fine tapestries and carpets were complemented by ornate paneling, and works of art from within France and collected from around the world.

After the central government moved back to Paris and Ile de France, the Loire Valley maintained its status as a royal seat. Henry II, Louis XIV and monarchs all the way up to the Revolution spent a good deal of time at their various châteaux. After the demise of the monarchy, the region lost much of its prestige. Many of the greatest castles fell into disrepair or were even abandoned. Some have continued to be owned by the same family for five centuries or more. However, beginning in the 19th century, the French

CHATEAUX OF THE LOIRE

ANGERS

Built by St. Louis between 1228 and 1238, Château Angers holds an enormous medieval tapestry woven between 1375 and 1378, depicting the Apocalypse as found in the book of Revelation. The moats which were added by Louis XI in 1485 now serve as beautiful gardens surrounding the impressive fortress.

BRISSAC

Situated in a verdant park surrounded by cedar trees, Château Brissac retains some medieval characteristics from its original construction in 1455 which are all but covered with later Gothic remodeling. The château was never finished as work stopped in 1621 leaving it in an incomplete state.

MONTREUIL-BELLAY

Construction on this château spans a period of about 800 years thus lending the flavors of many architectural styles. Most evident is the work done between the 15th and the 19th centuries. The fortress which has long commanded the town of Montreuil-Bellay now offers views of the town and its environs as well as insight into the town's history.

SAUMUR

Towering over this city on the Loire, Château Saumur in its present form was constructed between the 14th and 16th centuries. Since the 16th century, the château has served many uses including the governor's residence, a prison, army barracks and it currently houses three museums.

THE LOIRE

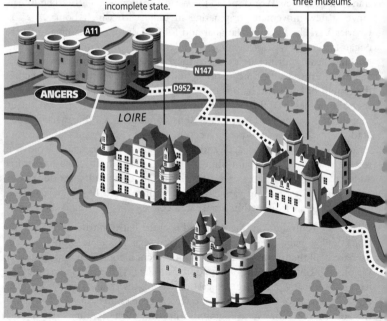

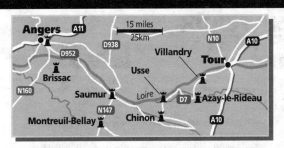

Tours to Orleans continued on next page

VILLANDRY

Only one tower of the original fortress remains after the 16th century remodeling of Château Villandry. While the interior contains decoration from subsequent centuries, the facade and gardens have been restored to the original style and splendor of their early days.

CHINON

This feudal castle is famous for the meeting held here in 1429 between Joan of Arc and Charles VII which is commemorated in a 17th century tapestry on display. While the château is in a state of disrepair, the castle walls are still in excellent condition and tower over the town.

USSE

Built in 1462 this château underwent a transformation during the next few centuries from a medieval fortress to the Renaissance palace that it is today. Château Usse sits on a cliff overlooking the Indre river and is surrounded by Chinon Forest.

AZAY-LE-RIDEAU

Designed to look like a Gothic fortress, Château Azay le-Rideau was only intended to be a summer residence. Built by a financier and his wife between 1518 and 1527, the château appears fortified while the interior affords complete luxury.

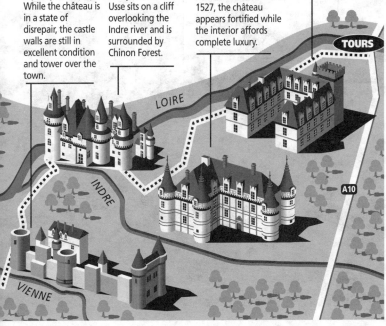

THE LOIRE

Fielding **FROM TOURS TO ORLEANS**

CHATEAUX OF THE LOIRE

AMBOISE

Château Amboise served as Leonardo da Vinci's studio during the last years of his life, and now it is believed to be his final resting place. Only a small part of the fortress survives, but the rich historical tradition is still evident in the Gothic architecture.

CHENONCEAU

Sitting across the Cher river, Château Chenonceau was originally built between 1513 and 1521 but has been revised and remodeled, keeping with the Renaissance style for hundreds of years. Governed over the centuries by the wives and mistresses of kings and nobility, the château reflects this feminine influence.

CHAUMONT-SUR-LOIRE

Originally built in a feudal style, Château Chaumont was twice severely damaged but rebuilt between l465 and 1510 in the Renaissance style which it still retains today. Surrounded by ancient cedars, the château is steeped in history and commands incredible views of the Loire.

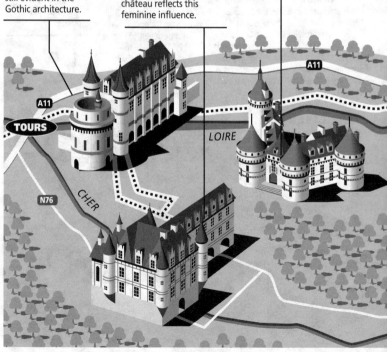

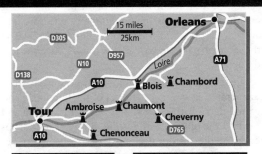

CHAMBORD

The history of massive Chateau Chambord began in 1518 with Francois I ordering the replacement of a small hunting castle with a grander residence. Believed to have been designed by Leonardo da Vinci, the construction was still not complete in 1547 when Francois I died nor in 1559 when his son Henry II died. This "unfinished" chateau contains 440 rooms and 365 fireplaces.

BLOIS

Important as a royal retreat until 1598 when Henry IV moved his court to Paris, Château Blois is still magnificent and awe inspiring. With only a small part of the original building intact, the château incorporates several centuries of architectural styles, including medieval, Gothic and Renaissance.

CHEVERNY

Built by Count Hurault de Cheverny between 1604 and 1634, this château is still owned by his descendants. Château Cheverny is magnificently constructed in asymmetrical style and features a kennel with capacity for 70 hunting dogs as well as a trophy room with over 2000 deer antlers.

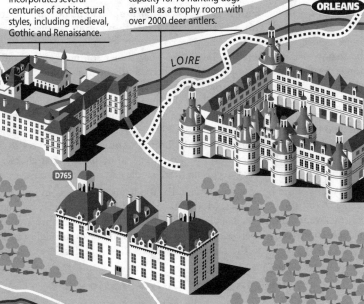

THE LOIRE

government began to recognize the historical significance of the region and its properties. With the government's assistance, many châteaux have been preserved for future generations. Restoration on some of the most important castles began early this century; collections of contemporary furniture and *objets d'art* were put together and placed in the monuments, and now the public can freely roam the incredible pleasure palaces that were once the lavish domain of kings and queens.

How you react to the châteaux of the Loire is an intensely personal matter. For some, the almost exaggerated Renaissance facades of the buildings, and the luxurious furnishings and decor within, are things of great beauty in and of themselves. Others will find the opulence disgusting, both in physical appearance and when viewed in the historical context of a time when debauched aristocratic excesses took place against a backdrop of abject poverty. Such visitors will prefer the clean lines of the earlier, Gothic-style building and the even purer, symmetrical form of the religious and military buildings that preceded the Renaissance, of which there are still many examples. Other visitors will contemplate the incredible community-wide faith and sacrifice that went into building the great cathedrals. Whatever your taste, there is something for everyone in Royal Château Country.

Cuisine

The Loire Valley is known as the *Garden of France*, so its no surprise to find tables stocked with a rich variety of mouth-watering simple dishes. From the deep soil away from the river come corn and spinach, as well as for the region's famous potatoes *au gratin*. The sandier soil nearer the Loire brings forth asparagus *(asperges)*, strawberries *(fraises)*, and mushrooms, which are grown on an industrial scale here. The kings used to come here to hunt, and game is often featured on the menu, especially in late fall. Wild duck, pheasant, quail, and grouse, as well as larger game including venison and wild boar *(sanglier)* abound. Fish dishes are renowned, especially salmon, which is making a comeback in the Loire and other regional rivers after years of absence. The cheeses of the Loire tend to be mostly goat cheeses, pleasant, but like most of the cuisine here, simple and unadventurous.

The wines of the Loire are legendary. Far too many to list here, in fact, but keep a lookout for Touraines, Montlouis, Vouvrays and Saumurs if you like light whites. Chinons, St. Nicolas-de-Bourgeuils, and Sancerres are among the best known reds. There are numerous wineries and caves throughout the region that are open to the public. Investigate a few and decide which are your favorite vintages.

Touring the Loire Valley

The best way to see the Loire Valley is to base yourself in one of the four main cities—Tours, Blois, Bourges and Orléans and make day trips. You might want to spend two or three days in Tours or Blois, and the same time in Bourges—that way you won't have so far to drive to the châteaux. If there ever was a region of France where you'll want a car, this is it—public transportation in the region is notoriously bad, and the bus tours are insufferable. The region is divided into six *départements*, but the best way to get information is through the tourist offices in the big cities, who are happy to provide information on surrounding sites. The addresses and telephone numbers for the main cities are given below under the city information itself.

Orléans

Capital of the region of Val-de-Loire, Orléans lacks the magnificent cathedrals of Bourges and Chartres, and is not close enough to many of the "must-see" châteaux to be the best central base for most people. Nevertheless, the city has a rich history, mostly centered around Joan of Arc, and enough to see and do to merit a night here on your journey through the Royal Valley.

Originally a Carnutian capital called Genabum, Orléans has always been prized for its strategic position on the river. After being conquered by Julius Caesar, the city was renamed Aurelianum, the name that eventually became Orléans. During the reign of Charlemagne, Orléans grew into a prestigious intellectual center that was home to some of the most important universities of the Middle Ages. During the 10th and 11th centuries, Orléans was the royal capital of the kingdom of France, and by the time the Hundred Years' War was in full swing, the city was coveted by the English, who laid siege to the city in 1428. The then-King Charles VII was hiding out in nearby Bourges when he was approached by Jeanne d'Arc, a young maiden who was convinced that she had been given the mission by God himself to drive out the English and restore Charles to the head of a powerful France. Charles first sent "Joan of Arc" to Poitiers to be examined by clerics, who determined that she was in fact inspired by God and not the devil, so Charles gave his approval for her to lead his men against the English besiegers at Orléans. On the 29th of April, 1429, Joan slipped into the city undetected by the English, lodging at the house of Jacques Boucher, treasurer of the Duke. After a skirmish on May 4, Joan led the army into battle a few days later, during which she was injured but refused to be taken back to the city; the French captured the boulevard des Tourelles and the main fort. The following day, according to the history now told, the two armies faced off again. Joan commanded that Mass be said on the battlefield, following which the English turned and fled. The victorious French (a victory for which the cowering Charles VII became Charles the Victorious) returned to the city, with Joan at the head of the procession. A fairly faithful replica of Boucher's half-timbered house that was destroyed in the Second World War (it's built with pieces of other 15th-century houses) occupies the site of the Maison de Jeanne d'Arc museum. It's one of a handful in the town and several in the country, and does a good job of explaining the life and times of la Pucelle—the Little Virgin.

SIDEBAR:

After the rout of the English at Orléans, Charles, still dithering, was urged by Joan to go to Reims to be crowned in the cathedral there, which he did. The next year, however, Joan was captured by the English and in 1431, at age 19, she was burned at the stake in Rouen, as a witch. She was canonized in 1920.

Each year in Orléans, a weeklong festival celebrates the martyr's life. A re-enactment of the victorious entry of Joan of Arc and the army into the city is the culminating moment. The residents of the city are understandably proud of their heroine, but they occasionally get just a little carried away. Describing the fireworks display that ends the celebration, the city brochure reads: "Orléans the faithful honors she who delivered it from oppression and by the message of Joan, in the inspiration always radiating from her spirit, makes a vibrant appeal to men of good will in favor of Peace." You get the picture.

Joan's presence is everywhere in Orléans, from the statue that dominates the Place du Martroi, to the stained-glass windows of the Cathédrale de Sainte-Croix. This is a disappointing cathedral compared to others in the region, its facade a shadowy replica of true Gothic-style sculpture created in the 18th and even 19th centuries. Between the cathedral, the river, and the place du Martroi lies the Old City, such as it is. The tourist office can give you a map to do a short walking tour. The most interesting places to linger include the History Museum, housed in a building called the *Hôtel Cabu*, the *Hôtel de Groslot*, a 16th-century mansion where four kings of France lived, and one, François II, died, and the *Museum of Fine Arts*, which displays French works from the 15th century to the present.

What to Do

Historical/Architectural Sites

Cathedrale Ste-Croix ★★

place Ste-Croix, ☎ *02-38-66-64-17. At the opposite end of place du General de Gaulle, on rue Jeanne d'Arc.*

Hours open: 8:15 a.m.–6 p.m. Special hours: Closed noon–1 p.m.

Begun in the High Gothic period, the construction of the Cathedral of the Holy Cross spanned from the 13th through the 16th centuries. After being partially destroyed in 1568 by the Protestants, the first Bourbon King, Henri IV, ordered reconstruction in a composite Gothic style, which took it into the 19th century. Yes, it's been bruised and battered, but it has survived valiantly. Stained-glass windows depict Joan of Arc's life, from her days of liberating Orléans to her death by burning. A guided tour of the crypt and the treasury reveals excavations of sections of buildings from the 13th century. The tour is free, but tips are always welcome. Admission: free.

Hotel Groslot ★★

place de l'Etape, ☎ *02-38-42-22-30. Around the corner from the Musée des Beaux-Arts.*
Hours open: 10 a.m.–5 p.m. Special hours: Closed noon–2 p.m.
Built in 1550 and expanded in the 19th century, this brick and stone Renaissance mansion is now the town hall. Four kings passed through here—Charles IX, Henri III, Henri IV and Francois II, who died here at age 17. The hotel's ornately decorated rooms and gardens are open to the public. Remains of the 15th-century chapel of St.-Jacques can be seen in the gardens. Worthy of the free visit.

Museums and Exhibits

Maison de Jeanne d'Arc ★★

3 place de Gaulle, ☎ *02-38-79-65-45. Off of place du Martroi.*
Hours open: 10 a.m.–6 p.m. Special hours: Closed noon–2 p.m.; May–Oct., 2–6 p.m. only. Closed: Mon.
A 1960s reconstruction of the house where Joan stayed during the 10-day siege of Orléans in 1429. Merely 17 years old at the time, she is known as the Little Virgin. This museum, one of many Joan of Arc museums in town, contains exhibits of period costumes, war weapons and models depicting the lifting of the siege. It's actually a great place for children to learn of her life, with an audiovisual show, suits of armor and the like. Admission: FR12.

Musée Historique ★★

place Abbe Desnoyers, ☎ *02-38-53-39-22. Near the intersection of rue de Bourgogne and rue de l'Empereur.*
Hours open: 10 a.m.–5 p.m. Special hours: Closed noon–2 p.m.; Apr.–Sept., to 6 p.m. Closed: Tue.
Within the Hotel Cabu, this museum is devoted to the archaeology and history of Orléans. The ground floor is the most impressive, with a collection of Gallo-Roman bronze animals and sculptures, along with statuettes which once adorned a pagan temple and were hidden from Christian zealots in the 4th century. Other floors display sculptures, souvenirs and artifacts from the Middle Ages through the classical period. Admission: FR12.

Musée des Beaux-Arts ★★★

1 rue Ferdinand-Rabier, ☎ *02-38-53-39-22. Near the cathedral.*
Hours open: 10 a.m.–6 p.m. Special hours: Closed noon–2 p.m. Closed: Tue.
Just across from the cathedral, the museum displays an in-depth collection of French works from the 17th to 19th centuries. See works by Pigalle, Correge, Le Nain, Watteau, Boucher, Delacroix and, most impressive, Cogniet's oil "Une Scene du Massacre des Innocents." The basement holds the modern art collection, with canvases by Picasso, Renoir, Monet, Miro, Braque and Dufy. Admission: FR17.

THE LOIRE

Parks and Gardens

La Source Parc Floral   ★★★

In Olivet, ☎ *02-38-49-30-00. About 10 km south of Orléans, in Olivet.*
Hours open: 9 a.m.–8 p.m. Special hours: Nov.–Mar., 2–5 p.m. only Closed: Fri.

Surrounding the Loiret spring, the source for the tributary of the Loire River, this 74-acre park cultivates many beautiful displays of flowers. Name your pleasure-tulips, daffodils and irises in spring; roses in early summer; roses again and dahlias in fall; and chrysanthemums at the end of the season in the exhibition hall—just to name a few. This huge park is ideal for picnicking and entertaining the kids with the playgrounds, miniature golf and endless pathways. Admission: FR20.

Where to Stay

Hotels and Resorts

Le Rivage   FR350–FR470   ★★

635 rue de la Reine Blanche. ☎ *02-38-66-02-93, FAX: 02-38-56-31-11. About 4 km north of Orleans, on the Loiret.*
Double: FR350–FR470.

A rather bland hotel in appearance, this white-fronted building is more noteworthy for its location on the banks of the Loire and its fine restaurant. The 17 compact guest rooms offer views of the river from the balconies, and each comes with central heating, telephone, TV, minibar and small bathrooms. The drawbacks are no elevator and thin walls. Highlighting the hotel is the exquisitely regional food prepared by two skilled chefs and served in the dining room and on the terrace. Working off the calories is made easy with the tennis court. An overall enjoyable experience heightened by the culinary expertise. Credit Cards: V, MC, DC, A.

Mercure Orleans Centre   FR450–FR550   ★★★

44-46 quai Barentin. ☎ *02-38-62-17-39, FAX: 02-38-53-95-34. On the river at Pont Joffre.*
Single: FR450–FR550. Double: FR450–FR550.

This multistory structure sits on the river in all of its modern glory. While not exactly a country château experience, the hotel is able to offer 109 rooms in comfort. Each is air-conditioned and equipped with telephone, minibar, radio, TV and bath. Guests lounge at the heated pool overlooking the Loire by day and socialize after dinner at the bar. Tennis and golf facilities are available within a short distance from the hotel. An efficient hotel with contemporary comforts. Features: wheelchair-access rooms, pool, air conditioning in rooms. Credit Cards: V, MC, A, YE.

Low-Cost Lodging

St. Martin   FR125–FR266   ★

52 boulevard Alexandre Martin. ☎ *02-38-62-47-47, FAX: 02-38-83-13-28. From place Albert, walk east on boulevard de Alexandre Martin.*
Single: FR125. Double: FR266.

Situated on the busy boulevard, this hotel still manages to provide quiet accommodations. All 22 rooms have a telephone, and about half come with a private bath and a TV. The chambers are well kept and modestly designed with simple furnishings.

It enjoys a location near good restaurants, shops and the sights of the town. A decent choice for overnighting it. Credit Cards: V, MC.

Where to Eat

La Loire   **$$**   ★★★

6 rue J-Hupeau. ☎ *02-38-62-76-48.*

The menu is sure to please most discerning guests—and at a good price, too. Value-priced, full-flavored dishes include oysters, fish and various complementing sides. Weekday fixed-price menus start at FR125, and others start at FR170. Of course, the gastronomic delights are always available a la carte. Closed: Sun. Credit Cards: V, A.

Les Antiquaires   **$$**   ★★★★

2-4 rue au Lin, Near the river. ☎ *02-38-53-52-35.*
Dinner: 7:30–10 p.m., entrées FR70–FR190.

A lovely building that was first built pre-Renaissance and still retains some of the original materials. A romantic fireside dining room hosts an intimate crowd for fixed-price meals starting at FR100 (weekdays only) through FR300. Flawless dishes featuring regional spices and game are the ticket to a satisfied palate; although, there is nothing here to disappoint. Closed: Mon., Sun. reservations required. Credit Cards: All Major.

Directory

To and From

By train from Paris in 75 minutes or by car on the A-10 autoroute from Paris or the autoroute, or N-152 along the river from Tours.

Tourist Office

place Albert 1er; ☎ *(33) 02-38-53-05-95.*

Rail Station

place Albert 1er; ☎ *(33) 02-38-53-50-50.*

Post Office

place du Général de Gaulle, 45031 Orléans; ☎ *(33) 02-38-77-35-14.*

Chamerolles

Less than 20 miles northeast of the city of Orléans in the forest is the charming town of Chamerolles, known as the capital of *La Banane des Parfume*. This somewhat unusual moniker given to the primary perfume-producing region in France has to do with the shape of the arc described between Chartres and this city, in which Paco Rabanne, Dior, Lancôme and numerous other parfumiers concoct their famous scents. The museum of *parfumerie* is housed in the 16th-century château of the city. The château is one of only three in France to still have a working drawbridge. The patterned brickwork and the giant sundial on the west side of the building complete the air of elegance, while the museum offers a comprehensive exhibit displaying the development of the perfume industry and the role perfume played in early French society, as well as an extensive collection of bottles from several centuries.

What to Do

Museums and Exhibits

Musée de Parfums   ★★★

N152, ☎ *02-38-39-84-66. About 30 km northeast of Orleans, in Chamerolles.*
Hours open: 10 a.m.–6 p.m. Special hours: Oct.–Mar., to 5 p.m.; closed Jan. Closed:
Mon., Tue.

Housed in a 16th-century château outside of Orléans is this perfume museum. The development, history and cultural importance of perfume are detailed on a tour through the beautiful rooms of the château. Admission: FR27.

St. Benoît-sur-Loire and Germigny

This powerful ecclesiastical twosome is located a couple of dozen miles to the southeast of Orléans on the banks of the river. You should try to arrive at sunset to view the abbey at St. Benoît-sur-Loire. Both the abbey and the Carolingian church at Germigny are excellent stops on the way back to town after an excursion to Camerolles or even Chartres.

The abbey and basilica in St. Benoît date from the 12th century. The floor mosaic was imported from Italy in 1531 but is believed to be original Roman work. The abbey is one of the few places in Europe where the Benedictine monks still perform the ancient Gregorian chants. The office is open to the public at noon from Monday to Friday and on Sundays at noon.

A little closer to Orléans is the tiny church at Germigny. The sanctuary was founded in A.D. 836, about the time the Veil of the Virgin was given to Chartres and thoughts of a cathedral began. The church was founded by Théodulfe, Bishop of Orléans, a close friend of Charlemagne. The Holy Roman Emperor himself dedicated the church in the 10th century as a favor to Théodulfe, bringing with him a gift from Rome of Byzantine mosaic. The only example in France of this glass-based artwork has been in the floor of the church for almost a thousand years. The mosaic is in such remarkably good condition because it lay undiscovered until the 19th century.

What to Do in Germigny

Historical/Architectural Sites

Basilica St.-Benoît   ★★★★

About 35 km southeast of Orleans, in St.-Benoît-sur-Loire.

Beholding the crypt of St.-Benedict, for whom the Benedictine rule is named, this basilica is looked after by the worshiping monks. Try to visit during Mass, weekdays at noon or Sundays at 11 a.m., to hear a Gregorian chant. Admission: FR15.

Eglise Germigny-des-Pres   ★★★

About 3 km from St.-Benoît-sur-Loire.
Hours open: 8:30 a.m.–sunset

Founded in 806 by the Bishop of Orléans, this small church displays the only Byzantine mosaic in France. Guided tours in French are available.

Chartres

If Orléans depends almost exclusively on Jeanne d'Arc to attract its visitors, Chartres is in the same boat with its cathedral, which is just about the only show in town but, oh, what a show! The queen of all Gothic cathedrals, the first, almost the biggest (Notre Dame of Paris would fit entirely inside its nave), the best preserved, the most mysterious, *la Cathédrale de Notre Dame de Chartres* is all these, and more. The cathedral is a living history book, telling of the medieval times in which it was constructed, as well as a testament to the strength of faith and human collaboration that made possible its construction. The cathedral has survived no fewer than eight fires, the Wars of Religion and the Révolution.

The mystery of Chartres begins with the ancient spring that today lies under the crypt of the cathedral. The waters were considered to hold magic curative powers by the druids who made the ancient city a center of the mysterious pre-Christian religion. When the region was evangelized during the third century, the Catholic founders—employing the same stratagem that worked for them all over the world—decided to integrate, rather than expunge, local beliefs. The first church in Chartres was built over the site of the spring, and by the ninth century, a fairly substantial Carolingian sanctuary stood on the site. In A.D. 876, Charles the Bald gave the city an extremely sacred relic, the Veil of the Virgin—a veil supposedly worn by Mary when the Archangel Gabriel announced to her that she was to bear the Son of God. The veil has been carbon dated to the first century; analysis has also shown that both the rough silk and the weave represent styles seen in 1st century Palestine. Of course, carbon-dating was not the test used to verify relics 1200 years ago—faith was all that was needed. The city fathers decided to build a great cathedral to house the relic and accommodate the growing streams of pilgrims. Work was begun in 1020 and completed some years later—the Romanesque cathedral was already, for its time, extremely large and significant in European Christendom. In 1194, the most disastrous of the fires struck the building, burning unchecked for three days and two nights. When it was all over, all Chartres mourned. The loss of their masterpiece, and especially the sacred relic, was a huge spiritual and economic blow to the city. After the embers had cooled, however, what was seen as a miracle took place. Three grubby, dehydrated priests emerged from the crypt, where they had taken refuge with the Veil, saving it from the inferno. On the spot, it was decided to rebuild the cathedral, but this time, in a show of gratitude for the miracle, the cathedral would *truly* be a masterpiece.

Today, the original 12th-century front, with its magnificent triple portal, as well as the crypt, still survive. The rest of the cathedral was rebuilt in just 60 years—in comparison Notre Dame de Paris took 170 years. It was an amazing community project: the records note that the entire region's population left their fields and houses and pitched in with the labor as well as the money to finance construction. Today the 13th-century cathedral is rightly thought of as Europe's finest Gothic masterpiece—and among other things, this cathedral was the first of such vast dimensions to use the new vaulting techniques, although compared to, say, Bourges to the south, it still has a somewhat heavy, earthly feel to it. The United Nations has designated the cathedral a site of international cultural heritage. So where to begin to describe its wonders? Inside, the nave rises to a staggering 121 feet. The labyrinth on the floor of the nave—where pilgrims traversed 851 feet of concentric circles in penitent prayer—is the only one of its kind still used in Europe, albeit today you'll often see New Age-type worshipers who seek "energy" from the earth and the heaven, a view tolerated but not condoned by the church. The amazingly ornate sculpted-screen, illustrating the lives of the Virgin Mary and Christ, around the choir was begun in 1514 by Jehan of Beauce and completed over several years by several Renaissance masters. The west (front) portal is the original 12th-century structure, but the mere fact that there are triple portals on both the north and south transept entrances is unique in the world, and they are of extraordinary artistic richness. The north portal is especially interesting in its depiction, in one portal, of the seasons of the year, the signs of the zodiac, and the main trade guilds of medieval Chartres. Perhaps the most remarkable thing about the cathedral is the fact that it is still a parish church, and if you live in the right neighborhood of the city, you have the right to be married or buried to the sound of its massive pipe organ.

The best-known and most impressive feature is the use of stained glass. There is no doubt that Chartres' *vitrains* represent the most important collection of stained glass in the world. Among the treasures are the three 12th-century windows above the west portal, which represent in just three panels the entire story of the Bible. The 12th-century window that adorns the south entrance to the ambulatory, known as Notre Dame de la Verrière illustrates, most unusually for the time, the Virgin appearing tender towards her son. The rest of the entire collection was crafted during the 13th century. In total, there is 26,900 square feet of glass. One window was donated in 1954 by the architects of the United States; another window was given as a token of reconciliation by Germany. Together, the stained-glass windows present in amazing detail the lives of Christ, the Virgin Mary, the saints and apostles, as well as various figures of the Old Testament. Only one window, the first to be installed when the cathedral was built, depicts the common man, showing the people of Chartres constructing the church.

Other than her cathedral, Chartres has little to offer. That is not to say that there is nothing to see. During the Middle Ages, as today, the city received countless pilgrims to the shrine, and the Old City—parts of it remarkably well preserved—was almost entirely dedicated to providing to the needs of the pilgrims. The most notable structures are the *lavadaires* of the old houses bordering the Eure river in Basse Chartres, where skins were washed before being turned into leather to make clothes and shoes for the pilgrims (the houses above them, incredibly, today are government-subsidized apartments for low-income residents). Other highlights include the Maison du Saumon, where fish was sold (now a restaurant), and next door, the House of the Spinning Sow, with an amusing wood carving telling a moral tale of the folly of trying to be what we are not, as well as a number of 15th- and 16th-century half-timbered houses. Next door to the cathedral is the former bishops' wine cellars, now an international museum of stained glass, with frequently changing exhibits (although they are of little interest other than to see how the craftsmanship of the 13th century has disappeared). Behind the cathedral's flying buttress-supported choir is a modest museum of fine art. Situated on a bluff overlooking the river, the museum features mostly local and regional exhibits.

Other churches in Chartres are worth visiting too. In most other cities, the abbatial church of St. Pierre would be considered a grand cathedral itself. St. Pierre was founded as an institution in the seventh century by Benedictine monks. Since it lay outside the city walls until the end of the 12th century, it has a heavily fortified keeplike belltower. The church of St. Andrew, on the banks of the river in the lower town, dates to the 12th century—the curious ruined arches are the remains of what was an arch over the river that supported the choir when the church was expanded in the 13th century. Also worth a look is the Museum of Agriculture, which houses excellent exhibits of farming tools and equipment from the Middle Ages to the present.

What to Do

Historical/Architectural Sites

Chartres Cathedral ★★★★★

place de la Cathedrale, ☎ 02-37-36-08-80.
Hours open: 7:30 a.m.–7:30 p.m. Special hours: Oct.–Mar., until 7 p.m.
Set on a hill above the Eure River, Chartres draws migrations of visitors to view its cathedral, an architectural poem begun in 1020, most of it destroyed by fire in 1194. The church's most precious relic, the Veil of the Virgin Mary (it's said Mary wore it while giving birth to Christ), was saved by loyal priests during the blaze. Rebuilt again by community effort after 25 years (quick work in those times), what you see today has been largely untouched since the 13th century. Among the hallmarks are the stained-glass windows, almost 30,000 square feet of them, removed in pieces twice during the world wars to save them from destruction. Tours are

given daily at noon and 2:45 p.m. by Malcolm Miller; the English architecture expert has been conducting them for more than 30 years. Admission: FR14.

Eglise St.-Pierre ★★

place St.-Pierre.

Originally a 7th-century Benedictine monastery (with the bell tower dating back to the period), the present structure dates to the Gothic years of the 12th and 13th centuries. The stained glass of the clerestory windows are the product of the 13th and 14th centuries.

St.-Andre Collegiale ★★

Near the river. From Rue du Cardinal Pie, take the stairs towards the river.

This Roman collegiate church closed in 1791 and was reduced to ruins in the early 19th century and the mid-20th-century. Concerts and other public events are now held in the remaining structures.

Museums and Exhibits

Centre International du Vitrail ★★★

5 rue du Cardinal-Pie, ☎ 02-37-21-65-72. From the cathedral's north portal, walk down the hill.

Hours open: 9:30 a.m.–6 p.m. Special hours: Closed noon–2 p.m.

This exhibition hall of stained glass hosts temporary shows and displays on stained glass. From the history of stained glass of the Middle Ages to the present, three exhibitions are held each year on medieval, Renaissance and contemporary styles. The half-timbered building in which the exhibitions are held was formerly a wine cellar in the 12th century. Quite an interesting look at the pride-and-joy craft of Chartres. Admission: free.

Musée des Beaux-Arts ★★

29 cloitre Notre-Dame, ☎ 02-37-36-41-39. Behind the cathedral.

Housed in the former Bishop's Palace, this collection focuses on the history of Chartres. Among its works are 16th-century enamels made for Francois I, Middle Age wooden sculptures and 17th-century harpsichords. A harpsichord festival is held every May. *Open Apr.–Oct., Wed.–Mon., 10 a.m.–1 p.m. and 2–6 p.m.; Nov.– Mar., 10 a.m.–noon and 2–5 p.m.* Admission: FR10.

Museum of Agriculture ★★

1 rue de la Republique, ☎ 02-37-36-11-30.

Hours open: 9 a.m.–6 p.m. Special hours: Sun., 10 a.m.–7 p.m.; closed 12:30–1:30 p.m. Closed: Sat.

Le Conservatoire du Machinisme et des Pratiques Agricoles, also known as Le Compa, first opened in 1990. The locomotive repair shed in which it is housed dates back to 1905. Displayed are fascinating exhibits on the industrialization of agriculture and the tools used. Tours are available in English. Student admission is FR15. Admission: FR20.

Where to Stay

Bed and Breakfasts

Château de Blanville   **FR600–FR800**

Saint-Luperce. ☎ *02-37-26-77-36, FAX: 02-37-26-78-02. About 12 km southwest of Chartres. Take the N123 and the N23 towards Nogent-le-Rotrou. Exit at Saint-Luperce. Once in the town, take the D114 towards Courville and follow the signs.*
Double: FR600–FR800.

Approaching this château through the iron gates, one gazes at the three story yellow structure with respect. Set back behind the flawlessly manicured shrubbery and gardens lies this 17th-century piece of architecture. As impressive as the facade, the interior houses the six charming guest rooms, each tastefully furnished and including a bath or shower. The young owners invite their guests to wander the house and linger in the sitting rooms, salons and library. All of the public areas are accented with 17th-century furnishings and beautiful antiques that add to the already wonderful charm. Breakfast is available for FR50, and dinners are available by reservation. A truly enjoyable experience from the moment one arrives to the almost sad moment one leaves. Features: pool.

Ferme du Château   **FR200–FR250**   ★ ★ ★

Leveville. ☎ *02-37-22-97-02. About 8 km northwest of Chartres. Take the N154 towards Dreux at Pont de Poisvilliers; exit towards Bailleau-L'Eveque on the D134.*
Single: FR200. Double: FR250.

Capturing great views of the spire of the Chartres Cathedral from all around the property, this lovely farmhouse sits beside a beautiful château. Describing this house as quaint is an understatement, as there are just two guest rooms. Handsomely decorated with attractive color schemes, the rooms are quite comfortable and include a bath or shower. Join the owners for a complimentary breakfast, and enjoy dinner and wine at the communal table for FR70 to FR100. Day tours might include the nearby cathedral, museums, Old Town or golf. No matter what activities the day brings, starting it off and winding it down at this small B&B makes it all that much more enjoyable. Credit Cards: Not Accepted.

Hotels and Resorts

Château d'Esclimont   **FR600–FR1900**   ★ ★ ★

Saint-Symphorien-le-Château. ☎ *02-37-31-15-15, FAX: 02-37-31-57-91. About 20 km from the cathedral.*
Double: FR600–FR1900.

Who could resist the invitation to relax at this Relais and Châteaux member hotel converted from a 16th-century Renaissance castle complete with turrets and moat? What more idyllic location than among 150 acres of parkland and trees? The 53 rooms are elegantly done in period style with modern amenities including TV, telephone and private bath. In addition to the helipad, facilities include an outdoor pool, two tennis courts and a beautifully kept garden. Dining options are plentiful with four restaurants from which to choose. Succumb to the temptation to relax in style and in nature. Features: pool, tennis, in-room conference facilities. Credit Cards: V.

Where to Eat

La Vielle Maison   **$$**   ★★★★

5 rue au Lait, In the old town. ☎ *02-37-34-10-67.*
Specialties: chicken and mushroom pie.

At the base of the cathedral, La Vieille Maison stands proud as one of the finest establishments in Chartres. Only using the freshest of ingredients, the full flavor of chef Bernard Roger's dishes shines through in every bite. One has trouble choosing which dessert to savor as the finishing touch. Fixed-price menus start at FR200. Jacket and tie required. Closed: Mon. reservations required. Credit Cards: V, DC, A.

Le Buisson Ardent   **$$**   ★★★

10 rue au Lait, In the historic center. ☎ *02-37-34-04-66.*
Dinner: 7:30–9:30 p.m., entrées FR100–FR150.

Offering dining on both levels, this restaurant is in an old two-story house that offers cathedral views from the second-floor tables. Traditional foods are the specialty, with a FR110 fixed-price menu offered weekdays. Standard fare made better by its charming surroundings. Closed: Wed. reservations recommended. Credit Cards: All Major.

Le Grand Monarque   **$$**   ★★★★

22 place des Epars. ☎ *02-37-21-00-72.*

So many dishes, so little time (or so few francs). While the style is decidedly traditional, the flavor is almost kinetic. The fresh ingredients and magical spices work together to create a taste explosion in classic dishes such as foie gras, paté and duck. A refreshingly affordable wine list tops off the whole experience. Fixed-price menus start at FR190–FR300. Amenities: outside dining. Credit Cards: All Major.

Directory

To and From

By train from Paris in under an hour (many Chartres residents commute to the capital) or by car from Paris or Orléans on the A-10 autoroute.

Tourist Office

place de la Cathédrale; ☎ *(33) 02-37-21-50-00.*

Rail Station

place Pierre Sémard; ☎ *(33) 02-37-18-59-00.*

Post Office

place de la Cathédrale, 28005 Chartres.

Bourges

The southeasternmost city in the Loire Valley, Bourges has a rich history that dates back to Celtic times. Founded as a fortified city in the Gallic kingdom of the Biturgies, and soon captured by the invading Romans, the strategic town sits on a promontory between two rivers and is thus easily defendable which only increased its importance under Caesar. Bourges became a royal domain in 1100 and later became an important venue during the Hundred Years' War. Towards the end of the 14th century, after Joan of Arc had met and moved the dithering King Charles VII here and ousted the British from France, the city rose to true prominence. Two men, both close to Charles VII, would become immensely important to the development of Bourges. One was Jean, Duke of Berry and Prince of France, who had the misfortune to have a brother, an uncle, a nephew and a son all become kings while the big prize never quite came his way. Jean decided to pretend that his duchy was a kingdom anyway, and he invested millions on lavish buildings to boost his prestige—the foremost of these is the cathedral, discussed below. The other pillar of Bourges was even more important. Jacques Coeur, finance minister to the king and the wealthiest merchant in France in the Middle Ages, made Bourges his home and his pride. Coeur was so wealthy from trading all over the world that he frequently loaned money to the crown. He was also a man of refined tastes, having traveled extensively in Italy just as the Renaissance was beginning. One of the most important buildings in Bourges is his palace, built atop the Gallo-Roman walls. (Many of the town's 15th-century elite got to build their homes on the wall; the ordinary people were relegated to the usual half-timber houses below, of which more than 400 survive.) Coeur's magnificent house was finished in 1453, and marks one of the first true Renaissance homes in France. The house featured Turkish baths, an indoor toilet, a floor plan that strayed from the typical serial chamber style of the time, and plenty of Renaissance-style decorative sculpting on the exterior octagonal tower.

Besides raising money for the expulsion of the English, Coeur also helped finance Bourges' cathedral, although later the great financier eventually fell afoul of the king and jealous nobles and was imprisoned for extortion. You have to feel a bit sorry for poor Bourges if you've already visited the cathedrals of Chartres, Paris and even Le Mans, but even if Bourges' cathedral doesn't have the soul of its sisters, the Cathédrale de St. Etienne has been classified as a world heritage site by the United Nations. Built at the same time as the cathedrals of Notre Dame in Chartres and Paris, this cathedral pushed the limits of the nascent Gothic style of architecture by incorporating a number of unusual features. The first and most obvious is the absence of a transept—there are a number of theories as to why, but the prevailing one is that the archbishop at the time was a brother of the archbishop in Paris, and he wanted to one-up him with the Bourges cathedral. By omitting a transept, as well as by making the side naves much lower than the main vaulted nave, the theory goes, the Bourges builders hoped to create the illusion of greater height than that of Notre Dame in Paris. The Cathédrale de St. Etienne does not have a great relic to attract pilgrims, as does Chartres; it is thought that St. Etienne was more of an educational center. This theory is supported by the presence of the quintuple portal on the west facade—the only one of its kind in France. The extra two portals gave the builders more room to depict in sculpture the biblical messages they wanted to convey. Especially interesting is the three-tiered depiction of the Last Judgement in the main portal, in which several priests and an archbishop are being cast into hell along with the other sinners. While not matching up to that of Chartres in quantity, the stained glass in the cathedral is equally important as a teacher. The Old and New Testaments are represented, along with several parables of Jesus, as well as the lives of the saints.

A new addition to the tour of the cathedral is the rood-screen, or *jubé*, on display in the basement, which is not really a crypt, since it is above-ground. Built in the 13th century, the sculpted stone screen that separated the nave from the choir is considered one of the foremost examples of French sculpture from the period. Unfortunately, the road-screen suffered great damage when it was torn down in 1758 to permit the people to see what the priest did during Mass. Many of the stones were used as masonry (!) for the 18th-century choir enclosure. The remains were discovered in the 19th and early 20th centuries, and after many years of restoration at the Louvre, what remains is on display. Also in the crypt is the tomb of Duke Jean.

If you take the guided tour you are shown the Romanesque faux-crypt that preceded the cathedral and, even deeper still, the true crypt of the Carolingian church that stood even earlier on the site. Outside the cathedral lie the Jardins des Prés Fichaux, lovely gardens with pools, fountains and early Renaissance-style landscaping.

Bourges is home to a number of worthwhile museums. These include the Estève Museum honoring the 20th-century painter Maurice Estève, housed in the Hôtel des Echevins atop the city walls. Inside the early 16th-century Hôtel de Cujas, the Berry Museum has good displays of Gallo-Roman relics and local sociology and history. The Museum of Decorative Art is located in yet another Renaissance palace called the Hôtel Lallemant. Bourges' Natural History Museum is less interesting. For a good look at the medieval heart of the city, head for the Rue Boubonnoux and look out for the House of the Three Flutes (the corner pillar is indeed sculpted to represent three flutes) on the corner of *Rue Joyeuse* (Happy Street), where the taverns and ladies of ill-repute were once found.

What to Do

City Celebrations/Events

Festival Printemps de Bourges ★★★★

22 rue Henri Sellier, ☎ *02-48-24-30-50.*

Held for one week during the school spring vacation at the end of April or the beginning of May, this festival showcases internationally renowned artists and many lesser-knowns. More than 100,000 tourists flock here for the folk, jazz, classical and rock concerts. The listed address and telephone number is of the organizing group. Some concerts are free, but some cost FR60–FR150. Bourges also plays host to the **Festival of Experimental Music** in June *(☎ 02-48-20-41-87)*. The **Ballades a Bourges** features music and dancing from mid July to late Aug.; FR50–FR90. From June–mid July is the **Festival of Jacques-Coeur** with music, dance and theater.

Cathedrale St.-Etienne is an astounding example of Gothic architecture.

Historical/Architectural Sites

Cathedrale St.-Etienne   ★ ★ ★ ★ ★

9 rue Moliere, ☎ 02-48-65-49-44. In the center of town.
Hours open: 8 a.m.–6 p.m. Special hours: Sun., noon–6 p.m.
Construction of this Gothic splendor began in the 12th century, converting a Romanesque structure into the widest Gothic cathedral in France. The west facade has five doorways, including one depicting parts of St.-Etienne's life and another re-creating the Last Judgment. Most of all, though, this cathedral is known for its 13th-century stained-glass windows—best viewed with binoculars to appreciate the deep, rich colors. The interior is marked by towering pillars rising 65 feet up and one long nave with no transept. Most similar to the Notre-Dame in Paris, the exterior's use of flying buttresses is an architectural student's ideal example of the classic Gothic style. The FR27 ticket to climb the north tower (fantastic views of the medieval quarter) also allows entry into the 12th-century crypt, where Jean de Berry (ruler of this duchy in the 14th century) rests. Admission: free.

Palais Jacques-Coeur   ★ ★

rue Jacques-Coeur, ☎ 02-48-24-06-87. On the south bank of the Yevre River.
Hours open: 9 a.m.–6 p.m. Special hours: Nov.–Mar., 10 a.m.–5 p.m. Closed: Tue.
At age 50, Jacques-Coeur had become a wealthy banker and finance minister in Bourges. He mastered the art of trading and pork barrel politics (He often lent

money to Charles "the conflict of interest" VII and his court, who in turn bought goods that he was importing.). However, his debtors became jealous and had him tossed in prison for extortion. Completed in 10 years, this grand palace is considered one of the best pieces of Flamboyant Gothic architecture. The interior is marked by vaulted ceilings, original paintings, tapestries and opulent detail. Its creator never had a chance to live in the completed masterpiece, as he escaped from jail after several years and died shortly thereafter. A 45-minute tour is given several times a day in French, with English booklets provided. Admission: FR27.

Museums and Exhibits

Museums   ★★★

Various locations.

A universal museum ticket is available for FR36 (students FR18), which includes admission to the Decorative Art Museum, the Esteve Museum and the Berry Museum, or individual admissions cost FR17. The **Decorative Art Museum**, housed in the 15th-century Hotel Lallemant *(6 rue Bourbonnoux;* ☎ *02-48-57-81-17)*, is a lovely display of tapestries, furniture, antiques and art dating back to the 16th century. In the **Hotel des Echevins** *(13 rue Edouard-Branly;* ☎ *02-48-24-75-38)*, the Esteve Museum is a display of the works of the local artist Maurice Esteve. Just as interesting is the mansion in which it is housed, which dates back to 1489. Finally, the **Berry Museum** is housed in the 16th-century Hotel Cajus *(rue des Arenes;* ☎ *02-48-70-41-92)*. Exhibited here are detailed displays of artifacts from prehistoric and Gallo-Roman times. All three museums are closed Sun. mornings; the Decorative Art Museum is closed Mon.; the Esteve and Berry are closed Tues.; open hours are 10 a.m.–noon and 2–6 p.m.

Where to Stay

Hotels and Resorts

Hotel d'Angleterre   FR385–FR420   ★★★

1 place des Quatre-Piliers. ☎ *02-48-24-68-51, FAX: 02-48-65-21-41. Across from the theater in the center of town.*
Single: FR385–FR420. Double: FR385–FR420.
Enjoying a central location, this hotel is one of the more-established hotels in town. An inviting reception area greets the guests before they retreat to one of the 31 guest rooms. Although a bit listless in style, the rooms are comfortable and well equipped with private baths. There is a Louis XVI style restaurant and a small bar downstairs. Inquire with the helpful staff about available golf packages. A reliable hotel choice sure to please the casual traveler. Credit Cards: V, MC, DC, A.

Hotel de Bourbon   FR450–FR620   ★★★

boulevard de la Republique. ☎ *02-48-70-70-00, FAX: 02-48-70-21-22. In the center of town.*
Double: FR450–FR620.
This former abbey offers a subtle blend of modern comfort and Old World style. There are 57 rooms and two suites available, all air-conditioned and well maintained. Wheelchair accessible rooms are also available. Guests relax while enjoying the fine meals served in the former Renaissance chapel. Leisure seeking guests can

arrange golf packages with the hotel. Always an excellent choice for a complete lodging and dining experience. Features: air conditioning in rooms. Credit Cards: V, MC, DC, A.

Inns

Auberge du Moulin de Chameron **FR330–FR650** ★ ★ ★

Charenton du Cher. ☎ *02-48-61-83-80, FAX: 02-48-61-84-92. About 40 km southeast of Bourges, between Bannegon and Neuilly.*

Double: FR330–FR650.

Although a bit of a drive from Bourges, this country hotel provides relaxing comfort upon arrival. A converted 18th-century water mill sets the scene as a small museum and restaurant now. The owner serves wonderful meals in the tented dining patio along the stream. In two more contemporary buildings lie the 13 guest rooms, all with heating, TV, telephone and bath or shower. Guests linger in the sitting rooms and the bar or find a little diversion swimming in the pool or fishing in the stream. A simply delightful experience in the countryside. Features: pool, country location. Credit Cards: V, MC, A.

Where to Eat

Jacques-Coeur **$** ★ ★ ★

3 place Jacques-Coeur, Across from the Palais Jacques-Coeur. ☎ *02-48-70-12-72.*

Specialties: fresh frogs' legs; scallops.

Dinner: 7:15–9:15 p.m., entrées FR90–FR130.

Sporting the medieval look, the building was actually built in 1947. With a consistently solid choice of dishes, chef Francois Bernard retains his reputation as a well-versed master of the traditional cuisine for which his restaurant is known. The wine cellar doesn't fall short of the demands of the discriminating guests. Fixed-price meals start at FR150. Reservations required. Credit Cards: All Major.

La Gueulardiere **$** ★ ★ ★ ★

In Berry-Bouy, about 8 km northwest off the D60. ☎ *02-48-26-81-45.*

Bourges locals drive the short distance to this favorite for the attractive design of the dining room and the exquisite cuisine. The specialties focus on seafood—such as the baked salmon with pine nuts. The excellent fixed-price menus start at FR100 during the week. Closed: Mon. Amenities: outside dining, reservations recommended. Credit Cards: V, DC, A.

Le Jardin Gourmand **$** ★ ★ ★

15 bis, boulevard Ernest-Renan. ☎ *02-48-21-35-91.*

Le Jardin Gourand resides in a lovely old townhouse, situated in a small garden. Curried lamb, poultry, salmon and many other respectable dishes are turned out here. While there is still a lot to refine, the chef has made a good showing and complements his dishes well with good wine selection. Fixed-meals start at FR100. Closed: Sun. Reservations recommended. Credit Cards: V, A.

THE LOIRE

Directory

To and From

> By train from Paris in two hours or Orléans in an hour, or by car from the north or south on the A-71 autoroute.

Tourist Office

> 21 rue Victor Hugo; ☎ (33) 02-48-24-75-33.

Rail Station

> place Général Leclerc; ☎ (33) 02-47-20-50-50.

Post Office

> 29 rue Moyenne, 18000 Bourges; ☎ (33) 02-48-68-82-82.

Route Jacques Coeur

Bourges prides itself on being the city at the center of France—at the heart—*le coeur de la France*. This goes along nicely with Jacques Coeur, the principal historical figure, of course, even if three tiny villages just to the south—Bruère-Allichamps, Vesdun and Soulzais-le-Potier—vie with each other for the honor of being the exact geographical center of the country. The tourist board has created a self-guided tour of the region called the Route of Jacques Coeur, with 18 stops along the way, that offers some châteaux every bit as interesting as their bigger cousins to the west, with only a fraction of the crowds.

To travel the entire route—which runs almost 100 kilometers from La Bussière in the north through Bourges to Culan in the south, covering 17 châteaux and an abbey, takes at least a week, and then at a frantic pace. You can decide for yourself based on interest and itinerary which parts of the route you want to follow, but here are three personal favorites that can all be visited comfortably in a day trip from Bourges.

Meillant

Like the other two châteaux described here, Meillant is privately owned and occupied year-round. Although not exactly a beautiful building, Meillant began life as a feudal castle in the 10th century. Gradually the castle evolved into a luxury home. First, the outside walls were demolished and the windows opened up, and first Gothic, then Renaissance elements, including one grossly exaggerated tower, were added. The result is sort of a visual cacophony, but it's a great way to see the evolution of building styles all in one place. The 16th-century chapel beside the main house has stained-glass windows created by the same craftsmen who made some of the Bourges cathedral's later panes.

Inside, the building contains sumptuous furniture and decorative ceilings and wall paneling, including a collection of 15th- and 16th-century *faïencerie* that is unrivaled outside a museum. A recent addition to the tour, housed in one of the stables, is an exhibition of quite attractive miniatures depicting life in the region from the Middle Ages to the present. The kids will like that part. There is also a modest automobile museum, with some good examples of the early Citröen and Renault cars of France.

Meillant is about five miles east of the N-144, about 20 miles south of Bourges.

Ainay-le-Viel

The château at Ainay-le-Viel is an example of the Renaissance style in so far as the house is concerned, but the octagonal defensive wall, which completely surrounds the house within a 30-foot-deep water-filled moat, is all 12th- and 13th-century fortification. The château suffered numerous sieges and attacks by the English during the Hundred Years' War, yet it was never breached. The nine towers gave defensive forces a 360-degree field of fire, and the drawbridge and portcullis, which were and are the only point of access, were virtually impregnable. The Bigny family, who bought the château in 1467, proceeded to tear down the donjon inside the walls. The comfortable Renaissance home was constructed in its stead. It features two Italian-style balconies that look straight out of *Romeo and Juliet.* Inside, the part of the home on tour is most notable for its 16th-century oratory, where extensive restoration work has uncovered 16th-, 17th- and 18th-century religious paintings on the walls underneath the 19th-century pattern.

The owners of the château over the years were a noble lot—Jacques Coeur himself owned the property for a time, along with two others on the route that bears his name—and their family mementoes are most interesting. Napoléon was good friends with Auguste Colbert, a previous owner, and there are numerous gifts he gave to the family, including a brace of flintlock pistols, accompanied by a letter written by the emperor himself. Also notable are a musical box and a pendant with a spider crafted in amber that belonged to Marie Antoinette. As part of the tour, you can climb among the towers and ramparts of one side of the courtyard.

Ainay-le-Viel is on the D-62 just south of St.Amand-Montrond, about 25 miles south of Bourges.

Culan

The château at Culan sits majestically on a promontory above the river, overlooking the countryside and the village over which its masters once lorded. Unusual for the region, in fact for the entire Loire Valley, the 13th-century château is unrestored (i.e., unchanged). The ramparts have all disappeared, but the south wall, with its featureless stone face and the three massive towers, bear witness to the defensive character of the property. The building features extremely rare early Gothic-style wooden framework, and interesting wooden roofs on the towers that were added in the 15th century. Inside the castle, a number of rooms are open to visitors, all filled with furniture and furnishings dating from the Middle Ages through the Renaissance period. The courtyard contains a medieval-style garden that has been recently restored to include plans and layouts that would have been familiar to gardeners during the Middle Ages.

Culan is located at the intersection of the D-997, D-943 and D-65 roads connecting Montluçon and La Chatre, about 35 miles south of Bourges.

Blois

Prior to the 15th century, Blois was home to a powerful clan of counts who busied themselves with fighting the counts of Orléans and of Anjou for control of the Loire River. They made their home in the medieval castle that dominated the city and the surrounding countryside, a fortress perched on a promontory overlooking the river. By the mid-15th century, the Orléannais had won the fight, and the duke, a brother of the king, settled in. After Charles VIII died without producing an heir, Louis, son of Orléans, became King Louis XII, and set to work transforming the fortress into a royal palace.

The castle, and the city, of Blois, remained, with neighboring Amboise, the main royal residence until Henri IV moved the court back to Paris in 1598. When Louis XIV built the summer palace at Versailles at the end of the 17th century and made it his center of operations, Blois' importance dwindled to almost nothing. In the intervening years, however, the city was the most important in France, and bears witness to that period with a wealth of monuments. The most interesting is the castle, which is a very clear example of the development of architectural styles of the era. The Gothic feudal hall was called the *Salle des Etats* and was built in the 13th century. The only portion of the fortress of that period to have survived, the hall was used for the business of government. Built in the 15th century by Louis XII, the adjoining wing was the first addition commissioned by the king, and it contains both late Gothic-style details along with the first signs of the Renaissance. Bricks were used in addition to stone, and the entranceway and chambers bear Louis' porcupine emblem. The salamander of François I adorns the 16th-century wing. Embodying the full force of the Renaissance movement the wing is dominated by a monumental octagonal staircase. The final wing, built by Gaston d'Orléans, who never became king, is constructed in a much more sober style, showing the influence of the classical period. The castle is filled with furniture and artwork from its various eras. A particularly interesting painting depicts the murder in the castle of the Duke of Guise at the hands of Protestant Henri III's assassins. Guise was a Catholic Henri who was suspected of coveting the throne.

The intriguing Old City of Blois rises up from the river to the shadows of the castle. The sector is full of stairways, alleys, and half-timbered houses, as well as the stone mansions of wealthier residents. These *hôtels particuliers* always followed a similar basic structure of a courtyard ringed by three wings with, up until the Renaissance, an exterior octagonal staircase. They also followed the decorative lead of the king who happened to be in residence at the château, although, in a few cases private mansions actually set the architectural trend. The foremost example of this is the enormous Hôtel d'Alluye, built for the financier Florimond Robertet in 1508, which contains what is believed to be the first straight-flight staircase ever built in France. You can walk up from the river to the castle, then just to the east you'll find the cathedral, interesting in that it was built in the 17th century (to replace the former structure that blew down in a storm) in the Gothic style, which had become outmoded in those days. Early nostalgia, maybe. Under the cathedral, the crypt, which can be visited by the public, dates to the 10th century. From the cathedral, take the winding alley called rue Pierre de Blois down to what was once the Jewish quarter, passing by a number of early Renaissance mansions that remain in private hands to this day.

What to Do

Historical/Architectural Sites

Château de Blois   ★★★★

Hours open: 9 a.m.–6:30 p.m. Special hours: Nov.–mid-Mar., 9 a.m.–noon and 2–5 p.m.

An eclectic composition of architectural styles from Gothic to 17th-classicism, the château at Blois watches over the Loire River. Constructed by Louis XII's men in late Gothic style, Francois I contributed the Renaissance touch, and Gaston of Orléans began work on the classical wing, never to be completed. Make use of the audiovisual display at the bottom of the staircase, tracing the château's history. The most elaborate wing is that of Francois I, with its spiral staircase, intricate ornamentation and his famous salamander symbol throughout. Highlighting the Louis XII wing are the paintings of Antoine Caron depicting the persecution of Thomas Moore. From the assassination of Henri de Guise to the death of Catherine de Medici to Marie de Medici not being allowed to leave the château under orders of her son, Louis XIII, who was only a teenager at the time, the château overflows with amusing and interesting history. A guided tour (usually available in English) is suggested to fully appreciate the history. Admission: FR32.

St.-Louis Cathedral   ★★

Old city. On the east side of the city.

Following the hurricane-destruction of the original Gothic structure in 1678, this 17th-century church was built. Named after Louis XIV, the crypt inside dates from the 10th century. Signage is, gratefully, in English, which makes this a worthwhile detour. The cathedral sometimes closes between noon and 3 p.m. Admission: free.

Where to Stay

Hotels and Resorts

L'Horset Blois Hotel   **FR410–FR490**   ★★★

26 avenue Maunoury. ☎ *02-54-74-19-00, FAX: 02-54-74-57-97. About 3 km from the train station, across from the Palais des Congres.*
Single: FR410–FR435. Double: FR450–FR490.

A first class establishment that first opened in 1988, this hotel's contemporary comforts are accented by the touches of classic French style. Attractive in every respect, the 78 guest rooms come with TV, radio, telephone, minibar and private bath. Nonsmokers enjoy separate rooms, and the hotel is also wheelchair-accessible. There is a restaurant serving quality food, and there is a cozy bar. Active guests are invited to take advantage of the nearby golf and tennis. Always a good alternative to the bigger chain hotels in town while still maintaining modern conveniences. Features: wheelchair-access rooms, nonsmoking rooms, in-room minibars, in-room conference facilities. Credit Cards: All Major.

Inns

La Malouiniere   **FR700–FR800**   ★★★

1 rue Berbard-Lorjou. ☎ *02-54-74-76-81, FAX: 02-54-74-85-96. About 5 km from the Blois train station, in Saint Denis Sur Loire.*
Single: FR700. Double: FR800.

With origins to the mid 1800s as a private residence, this quaint inn opened in 1990 in this charming riverside village. There are just eight individually designed rooms with TV, telephone, minibar, safe and private bath. A few rooms are available for nonsmokers, and there is one suite. Admire the vegetable garden and orchard, swim in the pool and swing the racquet on the tennis court. After a long day of vacationing, sit down to a quiet dinner in the restaurant. Definitely a charmer worthy of a relaxing visit. Features: wheelchair-access rooms, pool, tennis, nonsmoking rooms.Credit Cards: V, MC, E.

Pensions

Anne de Bretagne   **FR350**   ★★

31 avenue du Docteur Jean Laigret. ☎ *02-54-78-05-38, FAX: 02-54-74-37-79.*
Between the tourist office and the train station.
Double: FR350.

A simple pension with a little bit of character, it enjoys a location convenient for a walking tour of the town's sights. The 29 guest rooms are pleasantly decorated and always well kept; most are available with a private bath. The neighborhood bar next door pours some fine refreshments. With parking available on the street, this can make a good stopover for car travelers. Credit Cards: V, MC, DC, A.

Where to Eat

Au Rendez-Vous des Pecheurs   **$$**   ★★★★

27 rue de Foix, On the right bank of the Loire, just below the château. ☎ *02-54-74-67-48.*
Dinner: 7:30–9:30 p.m., entrées FR110–FR200.

Chef Eric Reithler, who studied under Guy Savoy in Paris, has brought new life into his fresh-fish specialties. Always pushing himself to new heights, he is passionate about his fish. With a changing menu, dependent on the fish availability in the markets, it's a new experience every time one dines here. Pick one of the many fine wines, with a concentration on the Loire regionals, to complement the dish. Fixed-price meals start at FR130. Closed: Sun. Reservations not accepted. Credit Cards: V.

La Peniche $ ★★★

promenade du Mail, Along the banks of the Loire. ☎ *02-54-74-37-23.*

This luxury barge, moored along the banks of the Loire, has the perfect atmosphere for enjoying the fresh seafood specialties. Gaze into the seawater fish tank or out at the river while shucking and sucking—oysters, that is. A relaxed setting, well-prepared seafood and friendly service. Fixed-price meals start at FR140 during the week. Closed: Sun. Reservations recommended. Credit Cards: All Major.

Le Medicis $$ ★★★

2 allee Francois 1er. ☎ *02-54-43-94-04.*
Dinner: 7–10 p.m., entrées FR110–FR200.

The dynamic menu at this charming inn is sure to include a good selection of fresh fish, as that's what the chef knows best. Fret not, the usual fare is also here—pigeon, foie gras and duck. Luscious desserts are the true delights. Fixed-price menus start at FR100. Reservations required. Credit Cards: All Major.

Directory

To and From

By train from Paris (one hour) or Tours (one hour), or by car on the N-152 between Orléans and Tours.

Tourist Office

3 avenue Jean Laigret; ☎ *(33) 02-54-74-06-49.*

Rail Station

place de la Gàre; ☎ *(33) 02-54-78-50-50.*

Post Office

5 rue Gallois, 41012 Blois; ☎ *(33) 02-54-44-68-58.*

Chambord

The granddaddy of them all, the largest residence in the Loire Valley, and the extravagant dream of three kings of France, the Château de Chambord evokes different reactions in visitors who see it for the first time down the mile-long, tree-lined approach. For me, the château is mostly grotesque, a monument to the opulent and irresponsible living and self-centeredness of the Renaissance monarchs. The 365 fireplaces in the building create a jumble of chimneys on the roof, and, together with the domes, spires and ornamental window frames, it results in a confusion of protuberances that is most often—charitably—described as resembling a miniature town. Nevertheless, Chambord is impressive just for its mass, and it is always included on the list of "must-sees" for most visitors.

Château Chambord is the culmination of the fantasies of three kings of France.

Playground of the Counts of Blois, a hunting lodge had been maintained at Chambord since at least the 12th century. After the Dukes of Orléans superseded their Blois rivals in influence and power, Duke Louis became King Louis XII. His son-in-law, François d'Angoulême, lived the profligate life of a royal daddy's boy, hunting often in the region around Blois and Chambord. When d'Angoulême became king at the age of 20, he decided to build a magnificent palace in his favorite part of the country. He demolished the old hunting lodge in 1519, and work began on the new château, according to designs partially conceived by Leonardo da Vinci. The young king was such a megalomaniac that he wanted to divert the faraway Loire to fill his moats, but in the end settled for the nearer Closson. Some 2000 workers labored nonstop on the building under two master masons, installing at least 700 stone salamanders, François' emblem. By 1537 the main keep, the four inner towers, and the terraces had been completed. François loved the place so much that he spent most of his time here, which meant the entire royal court was housed at Chambord. After his death in 1547, his son Henri II took up the project, adding the west wing and the chapel, although he moved the court around between Blois, Chenonceau and other châteaux. The palace was not finished until Louis XIV put the final touches on the building in 1685, more than 150 years after it was begun. The most sumptuous apartments are Louis XIV's quarters, including his ceremonial bed chamber. The most interesting architectural feature is the main staircase, almost certainly designed by Da Vinci, in a double helix form that permits one person to climb and another to descend without meeting. The lantern tower atop the staircase rises to 105 feet.

The interior of the château is more fully furnished today than it ever was when the kings used the place. When the royal court moved around, everything—furniture, tapestries, carpets, courtiers and staff—went with it. Chambord frequently sat empty for years at a time, especially during Louis XIV's reign. Today, a huge collection of contemporary furnishings and artwork—some of which was undoubtedly used in the palace during the 16th and 17th centuries—is on display in those few of the 400 rooms that are open to the public. Beginning in 1725, the castle was home to Stanislas Leszczynski, deposed king of Poland and father-in-law of Louis XIV. Twenty-three years later, the castle passed into the hands of Marshall Saxe; two years later the old warrior died, and after the Revolution the château was sold to increasingly less prosperous families, gradually falling into serious decline. It was declared a national monument in 1840, but was not purchased by the government until 1930. A massive renovation in the 1970s returned the château de Chambord to its former glory, even if the hordes of courtiers have now been replaced by hordes of tourists. Take a picnic when you visit and have lunch in the vast hunting park that surrounds the castle—the grounds are protected by a 20-mile-long stone wall. You might even catch a glimpse of one of the wild boar that roam freely throughout the park.

Chambord is at the intersection of the D-33 and D-112, about 12 miles east of Blois.

What to Do
Historical/Architectural Sites

Château de Chambord   ★★★★★
On the D33, 18 km east of Blois, ☎ *02-54-20-31-32.*
Hours open: 9:30 a.m.–6:15 p.m.
Where Chenonceaux shows a woman's touch, Chambord, in contrast, is a macho man's idea of a château; it's hefty and huge, with more than 400 rooms and 365 fireplaces. All this for a hunting lodge? Apparently, that's what Francois I had in mind, keeping thousands of workers busy for 18 years. Although he went broke several times, and couldn't pay ransom for two sons languishing in Spain, nothing deterred his grandiose plans. Among the many outstanding features are the terraced rooftops in the castle keep, and a cleverly designed double-spiral staircase (credited to Leonardo da Vinci). The 13,000-acre park surrounding the castle can be explored free of charge (but watch out for wild boar). *From Sept.–June, open until 5:15 p.m., closed from 12:15–2 p.m.* Admission: FR35.

Cheverny

Cheverny, itself an opulent luxury home, seems quite restrained in comparison to Chambord. It remains in the hands of the same family that built it 500 years ago, meaning that it has a (relatively) lived-in feel to it. The fur-

nishings all pertain to the château itself, and are thought to be the most im
pressive collection in the Loire region. Among the highlights are the 16th
century bed in the king's chamber, furnished entirely in contemporary Per
sian embroidery, possibly the world's most luxurious toilet, complete with a
lacquered commode, and the Hurault family's private collection of tapestries
and paintings, including works by Titian, Raphael, Rigault and other mas
ters.

The building will be familiar to readers of the *Tintin* series of comic books.
Swiss artist Hergé used it as the basis for Captain Haddock's home *Marlin
spike* (called *Moulinsart* in the French-language editions of the books). I
presents a classical facade in bright tuffaud limestone that is most pleasing to
view after the eyesore at Chambord. You can get an aerial view on the *Aere
Cheverny*, the largest hot-air balloon in the world, with a capacity of 30 pas
sengers. Incidentally, hot-air balloons, called *Montgolfières* in French, were
invented by the Montgolfières brothers in France in 1753. Another high
light of the visit to Cheverny is the feeding of the castle's pack of 70 fox
hounds (hunting is very much alive), a daily ritual that takes place at 5 p.m
in summer, 3 p.m. in winter.

Cheverny is at the intersection of D-765 and the D-52, about 15 mile
southeast of Blois.

What to Do

Historical/Architectural Sites

Château de Cheverny   ★ ★

Privately owned by the same family since its construction in the 17th century, this
château exhibits a symmetrical design in an almost uninviting manner. Two highlights include a kennel with more than 70 hunting dogs and a trophy room boasting
more than 2000 deer antlers. July and August brings a show complete with actors
fireworks and lasers for FR85. *Open June–mid-Sept., daily, 9:15 a.m.–6:45 p.m.
mid-Sept.–May, daily 9:15 a.m.–noon and 2:15–5:30 p.m.* Admission: FR31.

Chaumont

Completing the trio of famous "Cs" around Blois (Chenonceau more
properly belongs to Tours) is the château at Chaumont. In contrast to the
other recreational palaces of the region, Chaumont retains a decidedly mili
tary look and feel. A fortified castle has existed on this site high above the
Loire since the 10th century, when Eudes I of Blois was feuding with hi
counterpart Foulques in Anjou. The château was rebuilt in the 12th centur
by Count Thibaud V, and ownership descended through the generations o
the Amboise family until Peter d'Amboise took part in a rebellion agains
Louis XI in the mid-15th century. As punishment to d'Amboise, the kin
destroyed the castle. The present château was constructed beginning i
1469. It presents an appearance similar to the castle at Saumur: a squar

courtyard secured by four massive guard towers, with a single entrance guarded by two smaller towers, the portcullis and drawbridge over the moat (which still works today). The inner apartments, while having moved away from the *donjon* of yore, are very definitely Gothic in style, the Renaissance revolution came just a little too late for Chaumont. Catherine de Medici bought the place in 1550 for 120,000 pounds of gold. knowing that her wounded husband, King Henry II, didn't have long to live, de Medici wanted something to exchange with Henri's mistress, Diane de Poitiers, whom Henri had installed in Chenonceau. In 1559, the exchange was duly made. In the 18th century, Nicolas Bertin, the new owner, tore down the north wing, opening the courtyard and the apartments to the sun and the view of the river. In the late 19th century, the daughter of an extremely wealthy sugar magnate, married to what passed for a prince, "modernized" the château, giving it the luxurious decor still visible today. The princess also created the absurdly opulent stables for her horses, in which the hay was served in porcelain troughs and the horses dwelt in upholstered stalls.

Chaumont is a lovely castle in a gorgeous location, and it houses an interesting collection of medallions from the Louis XV era. The château is at the intersection of the D-751 and the D-114 on the Loire, about 20 miles southeast of Blois.

What to Do

Historical/Architectural Sites

Château de Chaumont ★ ★ ★

Easily accessible by train from Blois (from the train stop in Chaumont, about 2km up the hill), Chaumont was built during the rule of Louis XII by Charles d'Amboise. While the inside lacks any allure, the view from the grounds is magnificent. Horses are available for tours of the property for FR90 per hour. *Open Apr.–Sept., daily, 9:30 a.m.–6 p.m.; Oct.–Mar., daily, 10:15 a.m.–4:30 p.m.* Admission is FR27. Admission: FR31.

Beauregard

If you have time for just one more castle, visit the Château at Beauregard, at almost the exact geographical center of the triangle of the three "Cs" described above. Built beginning in 1545 by Jean du Thier, secretary of state to Henri II, the present castle is dominated by a central wing resting on seven arcades. The new owner, Paul Ardier, built the *Gallery of the Famous* in 1619. The most interesting feature of the castle, the magnificently paneled gallery displays portraits of 327 kings, queens, princes, popes, writers, scholars and generals of the day, painted by the artist Jean Mosnier of Blois. The entire floor of the gallery is tiled with Delft tiles depicting an army on the march. The original kitchen, restored to its historical condition, is also part of the visit.

THE LOIRE

Beauregard is on the D-765, about 10 miles southeast of Blois, halfway to Cheverny.

What to Do

Historical/Architectural Sites

Château de Beauregard　　　　　　　　　　　　　　　　　★ ★ ★

Hours open: 9:30 a.m.–6:30 p.m. Special hours: Closed noon–2 p.m.

In great contrast to the opulence of Chambord, Beauregard exudes more of an intimate ambience. Within the château is the largest portrait gallery in Europe, with the paintings all from the 17th century. Tours in English and French are available. Student admission is FR18. Admission: FR25.

Amboise

The charming town of Amboise, on the river just east of Tours, is utterly dominated by its massive château, and only about a fifth of the structure remains! The castle itself is steeped in Renaissance history. Louis XI lived in the building, as did Charles VII off and on. Charles VIII was born here, made it the primary royal residence, and died here as well. François I lived in the castle until Chambord was under construction, and both Anne of Brittany and Catherine de Medici spent time at the castle. Even Leonardo da Vinci, arguably more important to humanity in the long run than any of the various French kings and lords, spent time in the castle. Da Vinci is buried in the castle's chapel.

Wood and stone fortifications guarded the high bluff above the river since before the Middle Ages. Under King Clovis of the Franks, the castle was the scene of an armistice with the Visigoths (actually signed on the inhabited island of Ile de St. Jean below) in A.D. 503. After repeatedly being destroyed by the Normans, the castle was rebuilt as a serious medieval fortress in the 13th century. It belonged to Louis of Thouars for a while, but after he led a plot against the king, the castle was confiscated by the crown. Charles VIII was born in the castle, was engaged there to Margaret of Austria—who was three at the time and lived there until he sent her back to Flanders and married Anne of Brittany instead—and began the major expansion in 1491, heavily influenced by the new architectural styles of the Italian Renaissance that Charles VIII had seen while fighting in Naples. At its apogee, the castle was huge, able to house a court of three or four thousand people, with structure covering the entire plateau and anchored by two enormous towers (one of which survives), each large enough for horses and carriages to pass through on the ascent from the town. Unfortunately Charles cracked his head on a door frame in 1498 and died a few hours later. His successor, the Duke of Orléans, took the crown, took Anne of Brittany, and took the court to Blois, but the castle continued to be a part-time residence of the king and thus maintained its prestigious position. François I, occupied with the construction of Chambord, left it up to his wife to take care of the castle, as did Henri II, who was married to Catherine de Medici. After seeing the repression of the Conspiracy of Amboise—during which 1500 Huguenots were hung from its walls for plotting to kidnap the young king François II and force him (or actually his powerful mother Catherine) to crack down on the Dukes of Guise—the castle languished. In the late 18th century, it was owned by a grandson of Louis XIV, who built new apartments, but after the Revolution, the noble who was given the castle demolished most of it to sell the stone as building material. In the 19th century much of the remaining castle—two wings, two towers and the chapel—were restored, and in 1974, a private foundation bought it to preserve it for the future.

Containing a great collection of 16th-, 17th- and 18th-century furniture, the castle is in impeccable condition, and is very well presented. The foundation that administers it is committed to keeping the castle "alive." Fires burn in the fireplaces in winter, and anyone can rent the main hall or the beautiful terrace gardens with their unmatched views over the Loire (on a clear day you can see Tours to the east and Blois to the west) for a party or banquet. In the summer, visitors can watch an enjoyable period-show put on by the residents of the city. The show evokes the times of the three kings to have had most influence on the castle—Charles VIII, who built it; Louis XII, who repaired it after the Hundred Years' War; and François I, who kept it up in his youth—is put on by the residents of the city.

Elsewhere in Amboise, the most fun is to be had by wandering around the narrow streets gawking at the half-timber and Renaissance-style stone houses. The national **Musée de la Poste** contains some the rarest and earliest French stamps in existence, as well as displays describing the history of mail service in France. Another attraction perhaps of special interest to families traveling with children is the **Maison Enchantée**, a sort of toy museum with displays of children's classics including *Beauty and the Beast* and *Dr. Jeckyll and Mr. Hyde* "performed" by more than 200-foot-high mechanical dolls.

One of the most interesting visits anywhere in the Loire region is a stop a few miles south of the castle at the Clos Lucé manor house, where Leonardo da Vinci, the greatest mind the world had ever seen, lived out his final years. The house was given to da Vinci, along with a pension of 700 gold crowns a year, by King François I, who had invited him back from Italy. The great Florentine artist-architect-engineer, 64 at the time he moved to France in 1516, was no longer appreciated in Italy, and in François he had an appreciative audience and patron. The king visited regularly—a passage leading from the cellar of the manor supposedly leads to Amboise castle. Da Vinci brought with him his three favorite canvasses, the painting of a lady of Florence painted "*au naturel* to the order of the late Giuliano dei Medici," known to us as the "Mona Lisa," the "St. John the Baptists," which he finished at Clos Lucé, and the "Saint Anne." At the manor, da Vinci organized parties for the king and his court, helped design some of the châteaux of the area, including Chambord, and worked on drawings of his inventions. Four centuries before his time, da Vinci developed workable plans for the helicopter, airplane, parachute, military tank, suspension bridge and countless other inventions. There are no original drawings at the house (although some of the original furniture is displayed on the self-guided tour), but in the basement there are working versions of almost 40 of da Vinci's machines made according to his plans. Da Vinci died four years after arriving at Clos-Lucé and is buried in the chapel in the castle.

Just a mile outside Amboise on the road to Chenonceau is the *Pagode de Chanteloupe*, and interesting anomaly seemingly in the middle of nowhere. The last trace of the château de Chanteloupe, the pagoda combines the French Renaissance style of the late 18th century with the traditional shape of Chinese monuments. Built by the famous architect Le Camus for the Duke of Choiseul in 1775, the pagoda stands more than 150 feet tall. A climb to the top offers breathtaking views.

What to Do

Historical/Architectural Sites

Château d'Amboise ★★★★

On the D751, 35 km east of Tours, ☎ *02-47-57-00-98.*
Hours open: 9 a.m.–6:30 p.m. Special hours: 9 a.m.–noon., 2 p.m.–5 p.m. winter hours
Although visually imposing, the Château d'Amboise is known more for who lived in it than for its appearance. Charles VIII, who was born here (he also died here after hitting his head on a door frame), added the château's Italian-style embellishments; his royal apartments can still be visited today. Other royal residents were Francois I, the frustrated architect, and Mary, Queen of Scots. Highlights of the guided tour (in French) are the Tour de Minimes, with a circular ramp built to support chariots and/or multiple horsemen, and the site where Huguenots were hung from iron hooks after the Amboise conspiracy of 1560. There's a Son et Lumiere presentation in summer on Wed. and Sat. evenings; admission FR70. *Closed between noon–2 p.m. daily, except July–Aug.* Admission: FR33.

Clos-Luce ★★★

2 rue de Clos-Luce, ☎ *02-47-57-62-88.*
Hours open: 9 am–7 pm Special hours: Winter, 9 a.m.–6 p.m.
Leonardo da Vinci lived his remaining years peacefully in this brick manor house, as a guest of his patron, Francois I. It's furnished in the style he might have been accustomed to, and copies of some of his more fanciful inventions (at least during his lifetime) can be seen in the basement. A bookshop and children's museum are on the premises. Admission: FR35.

Pagode de Chanteloup ★★

South of town. About 2 km south of Amboise.

Special hours: Closed mid-Nov.–Feb.

Built in the 18th century, here lie the remains of the duke of Choiseul's château. The view of the valley is splendid.

Museums and Exhibits

La Maison Enchantée ★★★

7 rue du General Foy, ☎ 02-47-23-24-50. Near the château.
Hours open: 10 a.m.–7 p.m. Special hours: Nov.–Mar., 10 a.m.–noon and 2–6 p.m.
Always a fantastic treat for the kids and those of us who refuse to get old, this privately run museum displays more than 250 automated foot-high dolls. Miniature scenes are created and complemented with music—all the work of more than 13 years. Child admission is FR12. Admission: FR25.

Musée de la Poste ★

6 rue Joyeuse, ☎ 02-47-57-00-11. In the Hotel de Joyeuse.
Hours open: 9:30 a.m.–6:30 p.m. Special hours: Closed noon–2 p.m.
In the delightful 16th-century Hotel Joyeuse, this museum traces the history of mail carriers in France. Stamp collectors take interest in the collection of the first French stamps ever used, in the days when mail was only a royal privilege. *Oct.–Mar., 10 a.m.–5 p.m.;* students FR10.

Where to Stay

Hotels and Resorts

Domaine d'Houts de Loire FR650–FR1400 ★★★★

route de Herbault. ☎ 02-54-20-72-57. Northeast of Tours going 44 km on N152. From Onzain, follow signs for Mesland and Herbault. Rated Restaurant: *Domaine d'Houts de Loire.*
Single: FR650–FR900. Double: FR650–FR1400.

Southwest of Amboise, this is a converted 19th-century hunting lodge built for the Count de Rostaing. Now a delightful country hotel, it is within a wooded park with a tranquil lake, where swans glide by. To see the big picture, take a ride in its hot-air balloon. There are also paths for strolling within the woods, as well as swimming and fishing. Inside, the public spaces are laden with antiques. The hotel's 25 guest rooms and nine suites are beautifully decorated in pastel shades and have modern and traditional furnishings. The best suites are in the Sologne-style annex. All units have tile or marble combination baths with hair dryer and thick towels. Most look out on the countryside. Guests gather for drinks and peruse the tempting dinner menu in the elegant salon. The restaurant is gorgeous, with each table perfectly appointed. Garden dining is also available, and meals range from FR280 to FR400. Features: wheelchair-access rooms, pool, tennis, country location. Credit Cards: All Major.

Le Choiseul FR500–FR900 ★★★

36 quai Charles-Guinot. ☎ 02-47-30-45-45, FAX: 02-47-30-46-10.
Single: FR500–FR900. Double: FR500–FR900.
Situated on the banks of the Loire, this 18th-century hotel sits among private gardens and beautiful grounds. There are 32 plush guest rooms, intimately sized, air-conditioned and equipped with a TV, telephone, minibar and bath with hair dryer.

Garden view rooms are the most desirable. Guests have the choice of dining at two restaurants, one of which, Le Choiseul, offers peaceful garden views and succulent fare. A diligent and smart staff maintains these beautiful accommodations in a very businesslike manner. Features: pool, in-room mini-bars. Credit Cards: All Major.

Inns

Belle Vue   **FR220–FR320**   ★★★

12 quai Charles Guinot. ☎ *02-47-57-00-23. At the bridge crossing the Loire.*
Single: FR220. Double: FR320.
With wonderful vistas of the Loire, this charming inn offers attractive and comfortable rooms. All 34 chambers are furnished with modern comforts, including a telephone and private bath or shower. Breakfast is served on the outside terraces in the warm months and in the inside lounges the remainder of the year. Just below the châteaux, the Belle Vue consistently provides well maintained accommodations accented by its appealing location on the Loire. Credit Cards: V, MC.

Château de Pray   **FR550**   ★★★

route de Charge. ☎ *02-47-57-23-67, FAX: 02-47-57-32-50. About 2 km east of town on the D751.*
Single: FR550–FR650.
Originally a fortress from the mid 1200s, this building was converted into a manor during Renaissance times. Later transformed into a hotel, its most recent management has been kind with the flow of francs for restoration. Set among 25 acres of parks and gardens, this relaxing scene is home to 19 guest rooms. All are comfortable and modestly styled, with attractive wood furniture and practical amenities including private baths. A decent restaurant serves such specialties as salmon and rabbit, terrace dining available in the warm months. Antlers and various hunting trophies create the lodge type ambience that somehow seems so appropriate for the surroundings. Credit Cards: V, MC, DC, A.

Lion d'Or   **FR192–FR306**   ★★

17 quai Charles Guinot. ☎ *02-47-57-00-23, FAX: 02-47-23-22-49. At the base of the château.*
Single: FR192–FR306. Double: FR192–FR306.
With an address in the historic center of town, the Lion d'Or enjoys a location near the base of the châteaux. Many of the 23 modest guest rooms boast views of the Loire, and all are functionally furnished. Each comes with a telephone and private bath or shower. Breakfast is available for FR35, and good poultry, fowl and meat dinners are served in the dining room. This combination of 18th- and 19th- century sections of buildings has come together to create a fine inn. Credit Cards: V, MC.

Where to Eat

Le Choiseul   **$$**   ★★★★

36 quai Charles-Guinot, On the banks of the Loire, below the château. Located at Le Choiseul. ☎ *02-47-30-45-45.*
Housed in the Relais and Châteaux luxury hotel of the same name, this restaurant sits riverside. The talent in the kitchen works in harmony with the seasons, providing for a dynamic but consistently superb menu. An artful blending of traditional

foods with a nouvelle accent. Fixed-price menus start at a bargain FR200. Amenities: outside dining, reservations required. Credit Cards: V.

Le Manoir St.-Thomas $$ ★★★

place Richelieu, Between the Clos Luce and the château. ☎ *02-47-57-22-52.*
Dinner: 7:15–9:30 p.m., entrées FR120–FR150.

Upon entrance, one falls in love with the Renaissance building and garden. Upon sitting, one falls in love with the best food in Amboise. Refined to near perfection, the traditional dishes include oyster-stuffed ravioli, duck, lobster and sweetbreads. The wine list keeps improving with more smart acquisitions. Fixed-price menus start at FR200 for a four-course meal and FR300 for a seven-course meal. Jacket and tie required. Reservations required. Credit Cards: V, DC, A.

Pizzastro $ ★★

7 rue Leonard de Vinci. ☎ *02-47-30-55-15.*

For inexpensive Italian food, check out this small restaurant where the menu hovers around FR60. Or, for French food, look into **La Salamandre** at *1 quai Marechal Foch (*☎ *02-47-57-69-95).* Entrées start at FR40, and the desserts are tasty and just as cheap. Amenities: cafestop.

Directory

To and From

By train from Paris (two-and-a-half hours) or Tours (20 minutes) or by car on the N-152 from either Blois or Tours.

Tourist Office

quai du Général de Gaulle; ☎ *(33) 02-47-57-09-28.*

Rail Station

boulevard Gambetta (across the river, a good 20-minute walk to town); ☎ *(33) 02-47-23-18-23.*

Post Office

20 quai Général de Gaulle, 37400 Amboise; ☎ *(33) 02-47-57-08-80.*

Tours

The main city of the Loire region, Tours is a perfect base for much of your château exploring. Tours is also full of interesting sights in its own right, and a walking tour, especially through the brilliantly restored Old City, should not be omitted.

Religion played a large part in shaping the history of Tours. Already an important city, occupying the slice of land between the Loire and the Cher, in Gallo-Roman times, Tours was among the first French cities to be evangelized by St. Gatien in the third century. It was Gatien's successor, St. Martin, who brought true religious veneration to the city. The bishop of Tours for most of the fourth century, St. Martin has since given his name to several hundred French cities and thousands of churches around the world. At the abbey he founded, some of the most influential evangelists of early northern

Europe were trained, including St. Patrick of Ireland. If you are a Christian today, you almost certainly ultimately have St. Martin to thank. The 1500th anniversary of the bishop's death is in 1997, and the city planned a year-long celebration, including a visit by the pope. Even though St. Martin performed miracles in true apostolic fashion, the bishops who succeeded him were loath to promote his veneration (to their own detriment), and no shrine or monument was built to honor him for many years. Nevertheless the common folk from around Europe came in pilgrimage to honor the saint, as they do today, particularly from Germany, Switzerland and Belgium. Finally, in the 12th century, a massive basilica was built over his burial place. All that remains of the original basilica are the twin towers of Charlemagne and the Clock Tower. A new road traverses what was the original sanctuary, so you can see how huge it was. A new basilica, built in the 19th century, now covers St. Martin's remains.

The cathedral of Tours is not built on the scale of Chartres or Bourges to the east, but impressive nonetheless, with sweeping Gothic-style vaults and stained-glass some of which survive from the 13th century. Just up the street, Tours' château combines a hodgepodge of architectural styles ranging from Gallo-Roman walls to 19th-century apartments. The Dukes of Anjou lived in the 11th-century hall, while the ill-fated Duc de Guise has a 13th-century tower named after him. The Logis de Gouveneur was built in the 15th century. In the castle, a large diorama presents 31 scenes from the city's history featuring 165 wax figures. Another major church, the 13th-century church, St. Julien, was the only building near the bridge to escape bombing and subsequent fires during World War II. St. Julien's crypt houses a modest museum of Touraine wines. A much more interesting museum is the **Musée de la Compagnonnage**. *Les Compagnons* were—and still are—the skilled guildsmen, the artisans who in the Middle Ages built the great Gothic cathedrals of the region. Even now their skills are in great demand. The museum shows the craft work of stonemasons, carpenters, cabinetmakers, glaziers and sculptors from the 12th century to the present. In the former Bishop's Palace, built in the 17th and 18th century, long after St. Martin had gone to his great reward, you'll find a respectable fine arts museum, with displays of works of Rubens, Rembrandt and Degas, along with other artists from the 15th century to the present.

The old city of Tours had become a slum by the 1960s, but it was the site of one of the first and best restoration programs sponsored by the Culture Minister André Malraux. There are hundreds of immaculately restored half-timbered houses, ranging from modest workers' dwellings to soaring five-story merchants' homes around the Place Plumereau. This square, entirely ringed by 15th- and 16th-century houses, is situated near the university and is the center of Tours' café society and nightlife. Nearby is the other major museum of Tours, the *Musée Archaeologique et Historique de Touraine*. The exhibits are interesting if you are fond of fragments of pottery, but the building housing the museum, the *Hôtel Gouin*, a former silk merchant's house, is considered the finest Renaissance mansion in the city. Tours was the major silk-producing city in the country long before Lyons (which now completely dominates the industry). The mulberry trees that dot Tours are reminders of the once vibrant silk industry.

What to Do

City Celebrations/Events

Fetes Musicales en Tourraine   ★★★

A 10-day festival of music with worldwide musicians and singers. Eclectic concerts, food and dancing. One of the most pleasant times to be in Tours—also, the most crowded. Every June, call for more information. Admission: FR80.

Historical/Architectural Sites

Cathedrale de St.-Gatien   ★★★

5 place de la Cathedrale, ☎ *02-47-05-05-54. Left off boulevard Heurteloup.*
Hours open: 8 a.m.–6 p.m. Special hours: Closed 12:45–2 p.m.
This Gothic cathedral's construction spanned 250 years, with some sections of the two towers dating back to the 12th century. Its facade is made of the soft tufa stone, which is prevalent in this region. Some of the stained-glass windows, dating to the 13th century, are the hallmarks of its notoriety. The deep reds of the rose windows are of some of the best quality ever achieved in stained-glass. Inside is the 16th-century tomb of the children of Charles VIII. Under 18 FR15, under 13 free. Admission: FR27.

Eglise St.-Julien/Musée des Vins   ★★

16 rue Nationale, ☎ *02-47-61-07-93. Just off rue Colbert.*
In the vaulted wine cellars of the Abbey of St.-Julien is the Wine Museum. Although no samples are available, there is a fine display reflecting the history and the traditions surrounding wine. *Open mid-June–Sept., 9 a.m.–6:30 p.m.; Apr.–mid-June, Wed.–Mon., 9 a.m.–noon and 2–6 p.m.* Student admission is FR5. Admission: FR12.

Museums and Exhibits

Musée de l'Historial de Touraine/Château de Tours   ★★

25 quai d'Orleans, ☎ *02-47-61-02-95. Down rue Lavoisier.*
In a part of the ruins from the former château lies this wax museum with characters re-creating scenes from local history, including the death of Henry V, the hanging of the Huguenots and Charles VIII marrying Anne de Bretagne. Questionably interesting, but it's a good visual for learning the history of the region. Also nearby is an aquarium and an archaeological museum. Other museums of interest: **Musée de Compagnonnage**, *8 rue Nationale (*☎ *02-47-61-07-93)*, with edible paintings, Napoleon's face in bread, and châteaux of sugar, *9 a.m.–6:30 p.m.*, FR20; **Musée du Gemmail**, *7 rue du Murier (*☎ *02-47-61-01-19)*, art made of broken glass with artistic lighting, some signed by Picasso, *10 a.m.–6:30 p.m.*, FR25; **Centre de Cre-**

ation Contemporaine, *5 rue Racine (☎ 02-47-66-50-00)*, creative and contemporary works—not the usual fare. Admission: FR33.

Musée des Beaux-Arts ★★

18 place Francois Sicard, ☎ 02-47-05-68-73. South of the cathedral.
Hours open: 9 a.m.–6 p.m. Special hours: Closed 12:45–2 p.m. Closed: Tue.
Occupying the former episcopal palace, the Fine Arts Museum displays many works taken from the châteaux of Richelieu and (the former) Chanteloup. Included are works of Degas, Rembrandt, Delacroix and many others. Also displayed are a "Resurrection" and "Christ in Pars," by Mantegnas. The building itself and its gardens, with a 200-year-old cedar, are worth the stop. Admission: FR30.

Where to Stay

Hotels and Resorts

Alliance Tours Trois Riviere FR420–FR500 ★★★

292 avenue de Grammont. ☎ 02-47-28-00-80, FAX: 02-47-27-77-61. About 2 km south of town center.
Single: FR420. Double: FR500.
A modern hotel with the style of an 18th-century Loire Valley house set on the banks of the Cher. First opened in the 1970s, this distinguished hostellerie has established itself as the largest hotel in town. There are 110 rooms and six suites, all with TV, telephone, minibar, air conditioning and private bath. The quiet rooms are a meld of modern comforts and classic adornments with a cheerful color scheme. Public areas are handsomely attired, with the lobby boasting lovely crystal chandeliers. The lounge receives guests for drinks and breakfast, while the restaurant serves meals on its terrace. Guests are invited to stroll through the gardens or take a swim in the pool. A spacious hotel providing comfort and relaxation for an eclectic clientele. Credit Cards: V, MC, DC, A.

Hotel Jean Bardet FR650–FR1300 ★★★

57 rue Groison. ☎ 02-47-41-41-11, FAX: 02-47-51-68-72. About 1 km from town and 2 km from the Tours airport.
Single: FR650–FR1300. Double: FR650–FR1300.
Discovered behind the high walls and the acres of landscaped gardens, the Jean Bardet is a respected member of the Relais and Château society of hotels offering peaceful accommodations. The 21 guest rooms are decorated in a meld of period and contemporary styles yielding grand comfort and attractiveness. Each comes with a TV, telephone, minibar and marble bath. A wonderful dining room serves tasty meals, and a pool, nearby tennis, golf and water sports await to burn off the calories. An absolute delight in every manner, this white stone hotel, its landscaped park and its impeccable staff combine to make an excellent choice for any traveler. Features: pool, in-room minibars, fitness center. Credit Cards: All Major.

Hotel de l'Univers FR680–FR780 ★★★★

5 boulevard Heurteloup. ☎ 02-47-05-37-12, FAX: 02-47-61-51-80. About 200 meters from the train station.
Single: FR680. Double: FR780.

Famous around the turn of the century, this hotel pays tribute to some of its former guests with murals depicting such people as Winston Churchill, Thomas Edison, Ernest Hemingway, John D. Rockefeller and Rudyard Kipling. There are 85 attractive guest rooms with sitting areas, desks, cable TV, telephone and spacious, private bath or shower. The majority of the rooms, and the most desirable, face the interior gardens. Separate rooms for nonsmokers are available. Be sure to take dinner in the main dining room, La Touraine, with its wonderful fixed price menu starting at FR180. A thoroughly classy operation with attentive service. Features: wheelchair-access rooms, nonsmoking rooms, in-room conference facilities. Credit Cards: All Major.

Le Central   **FR180–FR340**   ★★

21 rue Berthelot. ☎ *02-47-05-46-44, FAX: 02-47-66-10-26. Off of the main boulevard, close to the river.*
Single: FR180–FR340. Double: FR180–FR340.
Set back from the street, Le Central is hidden among its gardens and trees. As its name implies, though, it enjoys a central location in town. The friendly family watching over the 41 rooms receives guests with genuine hospitality. The basic rooms are available with a sink and a bidet, with a shower or with a bath. Most come with a TV and a minibar, and all are comfortable and compact. Breakfast is available for FR30 in one of the two sitting rooms displaying 19th-century reproductions. A great base for a walking tour of town. Credit Cards: V, MC, DC, A.

Where to Eat

Jean Bardet   **$$$**   ★★★★★

57 rue Groison, A few minutes from the Loire. ☎ *02-47-41-41-11.*
Dinner: 7:30–9:30 p.m., entrées FR200–FR500.
An entire book could be written on the skills, inventiveness and precision of Jean Bardet. Known as the "prince of chefs" in Tours, he is a gastronomic godsend. Aperitifs are taken in the conservatory, and the beautiful dining rooms host the evening's taste of heaven. Oysters poached in muscadet, pan-roasted foie gras, guinea fowl or simple lobster—it is all taken to new heights of bold flavor. The desserts, as would be expected, are no less spectacular. A la carte dining can be expensive, and the fixed-price menus range from FR200–FR850. How much is one willing to pay for a slice of heaven? Jacket and tie required. Closed: Mon. Reservations required. Credit Cards: All Major.

Le Jardin du Castel   **$$**   ★★★★

10 rue Groison, On the banks of the Loire. ☎ *02-47-41-94-40.*
Specialties: oyster soup; pan-roasted prawns.
Dinner: 7:30–11 p.m., entrées FR100–FR300.
Formerly the second home of the director of the French Treasury, this 19th-century townhouse houses the elegant Jardin du Castel. In clement weather, meals can be taken in the enclosed garden or in the fireside dining room. The pan-roasted prawns are outstanding, as is the zucchini spaghetti with chive cream sauce. Excellent desserts are sure to please one's sweet tooth. Fixed-price menus are FR225–FR450. Closed: Tues. Reservations required. Credit Cards: V.

Les Trois Canards $ ★★

16 rue de la Rotisserie, In the old town, off place Plume. ☎ *02-47-61-58-16.*

A fun, casual restaurant popular with locals, "The Three Ducks" sports—you guessed it—a duck decor. Family run since 1934, this place has pleasantly served local cuisine at reasonable prices. The three-course fixed-price menu starts at FR50, and the FR75 menu features duck mousse, veal sautéed with onions and Saumur wine, salad and dessert. Always a pleasure. Closed: Sun.

Rotisserie Tourangelle $$ ★★★

23 rue du Commerce, In the commercial district, near the Hotel Gouin. ☎ *02-47-05-71-21.*

Specialties: Pike perch with sabayon.

Dinner: 7:30–9:45 p.m., entrées FR115–FR140.

This intimate restaurant, with garden dining in the summer, serves excellent food at value prices. Perhaps a rabbit and carrot salad followed by duck or fresh fish and completed with a refreshing sorbet. Excellent use of spices and regional ingredients, including wine in the many sauces. Fixed-price menus start at FR100–FR250. Closed: Mon. Amenities: outside dining, reservations required. Credit Cards: All Major.

Directory

To and From

By train from Paris (an hour TGV) or by car on the A-10 autoroute or N-10 national highway.

Tourist Office

rue Bernard Palissy; ☎ *(33) 02-47-70-37-37.*

Rail Station

3 rue Edouard Vaillant; ☎ *(33) 02-47-20-50-50.*

Post Office

1 boulevard Béranger, 37000 Tours; ☎ *(33) 02-47-60-34-21.*

Chenonceau

Chenonceau lacks the tree-lined avenue that leads to Chambord or the impressive views you see from castles that sit high above the river. You can't even see the château from the village that bears its name, or even from the parking lot at its base. As you finally approach on foot, the château appears to be an average Renaissance-style castle. Yet you view the château from the garden of Diane de Poitiers from the left, or from the garden of Catherine de Medici from the right, Chenonceau clearly emerges as the most spectacular château of them all. Built on an arched bridge that was itself built on the remains of a fortified mill, the castle spans the Cher river, and it seems to float above the water.

A ladies' pleasure palace, Chenonceau bears the mark of the several powerful women who owned and ran it. The main castle on the bank of the river was built in 1512 by Catherine Brinçonnet, wife of a financier. Acquired by the crown some years later, the property was given to Diane de Poitiers by King Henri II in 1547. Never shy about the fact that he had a lifelong mistress, Henri encouraged Diane as she laid out the garden and built the covered bridge over the river. After Henri died, Catherine de Medici, his widow, forced Diane to trade Chenonceau for nearby Chaumont, a swap that Diane was probably happy to accept—she left behind the unheatable castle over the river and set up residence at Chaumont, which brought with it a far higher income. At Chenonceau, Catherine transformed the gallery over the river with an Italian detailing and rebuilt part of the interior, installing one of the first straight-flight staircases of the time. Louise de Lorraine, Catherine's daughter-in-law, inherited the château in 1590 when the king died and turned it into a depressing shrine to her late husband, painting the ceilings black and white, and keeping only to her room. The next major influence was that of Madame Dupin, who hosted writers and philosophers there from 1739–1799. Thanks to Dupin's good standing with the villagers, the château was spared during the Revolution.

The castle tour takes you through most of the rooms, including the bed chambers of Catherine, Diane and Louise. Numerous pieces of furniture and works of art from the various time periods are on display. In one room, there is a collection of dozens of paintings and prints of the castle—it has always been a favorite of artists. The most interesting part of the visit is the tour of the kitchens, which are built deep into the recesses of the first two pylons in the riverbed. Beside the castle's main building there is a 13th-century round tower that now houses the gift shop. A waxwork museum that merits the rating of extra-cheesy completes the offering.

Chenonceau is on the N-176 road, about 15 miles east of Tours.

THE LOIRE

Château de Chenonceau's stunning beauty can be seen from the River Cher.

What to Do

Historical/Architectural Sites

Château de Chenonceau ★★★★★

D40, 35 km east of Tours, ☎ *02-47-23-90-07.*

In terms of pure beauty, it's usually a toss-up between the Château d'Azay-le-Rideau and this 16th-century stunner built on a bridge across the River Cher. Chenonceau's present design grew out of a total teardown accomplished by its second owners, Thomas Bohier (a financier) and his wife Catherine Briconnet, who acquired it in 1512. Actually, Bohier left all the details to Catherine, busy as he was with business affairs. Over the next 500 years, the château was added on to by a succession of women, royal and otherwise. The most famous decorators were Diane de Poitiers, paramour to Henri III, and Catherine de' Medici, Henri's scorned wife. Catherine couldn't very well blow up the bridge that Diane built, so she did the next best thing—covered it over with the vast (197-foot) black-and-white patterned gallery you see today. *Open Mar.–Sept., 9 a.m.–7 p.m. daily; mid-Sept.–mid-Mar., 9 a.m.–4:30 p.m. daily.* Admission: FR40.

Where to Stay

Château

Château de Chissay   FR450–FR890   ★★★

Chissay-en-Touraine. ☎ *02-54-32-32-01, FAX: 02-54-32-43-80. About 2 km from the Chissay-en-Touraine train station in Montrichard.*
Single: FR450–FR890. Double: FR520–FR890.

This small 15th-century châteaux opened as a hotel in 1986. The 31 rooms are styled in period decor and individually priced according to design and luxury. All come with central heating, telephone and private bath. There is an elevator making the rooms wheelchair-accessible. All meals are available in the restaurant and generous drinks and good conversation are served in the bar. This fantasy-like château is sure to charm the happy châteaux touring traveler. Features: pool. Credit Cards: All Major.

Inns

Du Bon Laboureur et Château   FR300–FR600   ★★

6 rue du Dr. Bretonneau. ☎ *02-47-23-90-02, FAX: 02-47-23-82-01. Near the château, in the town center.*
Single: FR300–FR500. Double: FR400–FR600.

Founded in 1800, this country-style inn, covered with ivy, resides in the heart of the town. With terraces overlooking the beautiful gardens and a small guest house in the back, there is a definite rustic feeling that has been respected during the improvements. Its 36 guest rooms are individually decorated and appointed with modern conveniences. Guests spend leisure time in the heated outdoor pool or at the tennis court. There are two restaurants serving both gastronomic delights and more informal fare. Traditionally courteous service and modern elegance make this a pleasant auberge. Features: pool, tennis. Credit Cards: All Major.

Hotel Ottoni la Roseraie   **FR255–FR465**   ★★★

7 rue du Dr. Bretonneau. ☎ *02-47-23-90-09, FAX: 02-47-23-91-59. In town center,*
about 1km from the train station.
Double: FR255–FR465.

La Roseraie sits among gardens a short way from the château. A sweet owner takes
pride in this little hotel, offering 18 guest chambers in charming style. All come
standard with central heating, telephone and cable TV. Guests can't help but linger
in the bright, sun-drenched dining terrace while enjoying breakfast, lunch or dinner. A captivating and relaxing experience.Credit Cards: V, DC, A.

Where to Eat

Au Gateau Breton   **$**   ★★

16 rue Bretonneau, Near the château. ☎ *02-47-23-90-14.*

Best visited in the warm months, the terrace dining is very inviting. Traditional,
regional cooking is prepared home-style and in copious amounts. Meat dishes are
prevalent, and the desserts are also available to go. Fixed-price menus range from
FR65–FR110. Amenities: outside dining, reservations required. Credit Cards: V, MC.

Du Bon Laboureur et Château   **$$**   ★★★

6 rue du Dr.-Bretonneau. ☎ *02-47-23-90-02.*
Specialties: turbot with hollandaise; braised rabbit with dried fruits.

Using vegetables from their own garden, the Jeudi family insists on the freshest of
ingredients. Always improving, the fresh fish, scallops and veal dishes have all come
a long way. The refined setting and attentive, cordial service makes the evening
quite pleasant. Fixed-price meals at FR200. Amenities: outside dining. Credit Cards:
All Major.

Loches

Loches is a fascinating town that has preserved its old, fortified center, of-
fering a continuous view of the development over the centuries of castle-
building in this region. The entire Old Town is contained within a fortified
wall that is 1100 yards long and has only two entrances. Built upon an easily
defensive promontory, the only weak point in the stronghold was the pla-
teau's link to the rest of the high ground, so it was there that the Counts of
Anjou constructed the massive medieval fortress in the 13th century. The
main donjon still stands, as do several guard towers and portions of the de-
fensive ditch, which the counts had hewn out of solid rock. At the other end
of the plateau is the completely separate, "new" château, begun at the end of
the 14th century atop the main northern watchtower of the first fortress.
The royal apartments are both medieval- and Gothic-style. It was here that
Joan of Arc convinced the still-dithering Charles VII to go to Rheims and be
properly crowned. Additions to the apartments are crafted with Renaissance-
style details commissioned by Charles VIII and Louis XII.

In between the two castles atop the plateau is the *Eglise St. Ours*, a Ro-
manesque church partially rebuilt with a vaulted Gothic-style arch and
porch. The "New Town," outside the fortified walls, is not new at all, but it

THE LOIRE

offers a pleasant hour or so strolling among medieval- and Renaissance-era houses.

Loches is about 20 miles southeast of Tours on the N-143.

What to Do

Historical/Architectural Sites

Château de Loches   ★★★

5 place Charles VII, ☎ 02-47-59-01-32. On top of the Loches hill.
Perched on the hilltop of this medieval town is the château and donjon. An integral part of this fortified city for centuries, construction occurred between the 13th and 17th centuries. Guided tours of the entire compound are available in French. *Open mid-Mar.–June and Sept., daily, 9 a.m.–noon and 2–6 p.m.; July–Aug., daily, 9 a.m.–6 p.m.; Oct.–Nov. and Feb.–mid-Mar., Thurs.–Tues., 9 a.m.–noon and 2–5 p.m.* Admission: FR18.

Eglise St.-Ours   ★★

1 rue Thomas Pactius, ☎ 02-47-59-02-36.
Hours open: 8 a.m.–7 p.m.
An intriguing example of Renaissance architecture, this church was constructed from the 10th through 15th centuries. Intricate details and beautiful adornments accent the intimate feeling throughout. Admission: free.

Villandry

Villandry is noted for the finest Renaissance gardens in France.

Villandry, the last major Renaissance château to be constructed in the Loire valley, was completed in 1536 by Jean le Breton, a finance minister of François I. The château's construction is distinctive not only because the architects were turning more toward classical sobriety, but because they also tried to inject a little variety by making the two wings not quite parallel to each other nor exactly perpendicular to the central wing, and by placing the main entrance door in a not quite symmetrical position. The building itself is nice, nothing fancy—a horseshoe-shape around a small open courtyard, surrounded by a moat, flanked by two classical outbuildings, topped by a single round tower containing some interesting 18th-century wood paneling, but not much else worth writing home about. What sets Villandry apart are its gardens for they are the finest Renaissance-style gardens in France.

Lovingly restored by a Spanish science professor who bought the château in 1906, the gardens are laid out on three levels. The first is the kitchen garden, echoing the ancestry of monks who produced vegetables for their consumption, but who honored God by laying their gardens out in orderly form. The nine squares each have a different geometrical pattern and are planted (twice a year) with colored vegetables such as blue leeks, red cabbage and beetroot, and green carrot tops. The second terrace is the ornamental garden, divided into two "salons" designed with low box-hedges and topiary. The one to the right as you walk up represents music, but far more interesting is the one on the right, which shows the phases of love. There is one square showing daggers and swords used in duels over women called "Tragic Love"; another showing fans and the horns of adultery called "Fickle Love"; another showing pure, simple hearts called "Tender Love"; and a fourth showing broken hearts called "Crazed Love." Passing further up through the third level, which is the water garden, dominated by a pond in the shape of a mirror, one comes to the belvedere, a balcony offering the best views of the ornamental garden and even the kitchen gardens.

Villandry is about 10 miles southeast of Tours on the D-751.

What to Do

Historical/Architectural Sites

Château de Villandry   ★★★

> A splendid château in the Renaissance style, major renovations in 1906 created what you see today. The highlight of the château are the gardens, which cover three levels of pools, flowers, vegetables, shrubs and neatly manicured flora and fauna. Check out the view of the designs in the gardens from the upper floors of the château. *The château is open May–mid-Sept., daily, 9 a.m.–6 p.m.; mid-Sept.–Apr., daily, 9 a.m.–5 p.m. The gardens are open daily, 9 a.m.–sunset.* Admission to the château and gardens is FR41; to the gardens only, FR27.

Azay-le-Rideau

One of the most popular châteaux in the Loire Valley, Azay-le-Rideau was originally a fortified keep guarding the ford across the Indre river. Charles VII, the dithering dauphin, passed by the castle in 1418 and found that the captain and 350 men had joined forces with the Burgundians, who were in turn allied with the English. The traitors made the mistake of jeering the young king-to-be, and in a fit of rage and more resolve than he would display until Joan of Arc lit a holy fire under his tail, Charles and his men retook the fort, hung all the soldiers, and burned the village and the castle. It was re-built in the developing Renaissance style with clearly defined horizontal and vertical lines by the wealthy financier Gilles Berthelot in 1518. Today, the château sits prettily on a tiny island in the middle of the gentle river. The castle is in the form of an "L," suggesting that it was intended to be completed with a third and possibly even a fourth wing; that was never built. Instead, a small tower punctuates the central south wing. Owned by the Biencourt family from 1787 to 1899, the château escaped destruction in the Revolution by dint of charity and politicking by the Marquis, but it almost met an unfortunate end in 1871. During this time it had been requisitioned by the Prussian army, and one night, a main chandelier in the kitchen fell to the floor, prompting the somewhat irrational Prince Charles Frederick of Prussia to believe the castle was under attack. In a frenzy, he ordered the castle to be burned and his men to evacuate. Fortunately, his officers brought him to his senses and the jewel was preserved. The interior of Azay-le-Rideau shows the incipient Italian influences on architecture of the time, with a straight-flight staircase and flat-paneled ceilings. It houses a modest collection of Renaissance furniture and Flemish tapestries from the 17th and 18th centuries.

Azay-le-Rideau is on the D-751, about 15 miles southwest of Tours.

What to Do

Historical/Architectural Sites

Château d'Azay-le-Rideau   ★★★★

On the D751, 20 km southwest of Tours, ☎ *02-47-45-26-61.*

Francois I, the flamboyant builder and party giver, appropriated this graceful château from his treasurer, Gilles Berthelot, piqued that his moneyman would dare to upstage him. Shades of Fouquet and Louis the XIV? Luckily for Berthelot, he disappeared before he could be thrown in prison, unlike the Sun King's hapless finance minister. The 16th-century castle invites comparisons with the Château at Chenonceaux: Its image is reflected in the Indre River, rather than the Cher, and it was designed by a woman, Berthelot's social climbing wife, Philippa, who built a straight, rather than spiral staircase (unusual for the times), just as Chenonceaux's first owner, Catherine Briconnet, did in 1512. *Open July–Aug., 9 a.m.–6:30 p.m.; Apr.–June and Sept., 9:30 a.m.–6 p.m., Oct.–Mar., 9:30 a.m.–5:30 p.m.; closed from 12:30–2 p.m.* Admission: FR32.

Chinon

The ruined château at Chinon was a superior castle when it was built and remains a superior castle even in its ruined condition today. It's a bit out of the way unless you're driving to or from Western Loire, but a visit is highly recommended.

The castle was enormous in its heyday, which came long after the first stronghold was established here in paleolithic times. After the Romans expanded, and the Visigoths fended off a siege in the third century, the site continued to be developed as a military fortress. Owned by the counts of Blois in the 10th century, the castle was given in a rare peaceful gesture to the Plantagenets of Anjou. Henri II, who became king of England, made Chinon his main residence and built an expansive fortress on the hilltop. Just the ramparts, four towers and a few rooms of the royal apartments survive today. The castle was to see its most historic time, however, during the period of King Charles VII, who at that time was just a dauphin, while his father, Charles VI, was still king but a prisoner of the English. Charles VII lived in the place almost continuously from 1427 to 1450, where he launched the tradition of French monarchs having an official mistress (from whom children were not bastards, but were considered legitimate) when he built his mistress Agnès de Sorel a house at the foot of the keep and himself a tunnel to visit her. In 1429, as he dithered, a young maiden from Lorraine called Jeanne d'Arc came to the castle bearing a divine message—that Charles was to reconquer France from the English. Forewarned of her arrival, Charles disguised himself as a mere vassal, and in the first proof of her saintly task, Joan went up to him immediately and said "C'est vous, le Roi" (It is you who are the king). Charles sent her off to Poitiers to have her head and hymen examined, and when she had been declared to be from God and not the devil, Joan of Arc led the battle that routed the English at Orléans. The big hall where she recognized Charles remains, marked by a commemorative plaque. There is also an excellent museum describing Joan's life and death in the *Tour de l'Horloge*. You can climb up and down the towers, including the central Coudray Keep, where you can descend into the spooky depths of the castle.

Chinon is high above the Vienne, and it offers breathtaking views over the lovely village below and the Vienne valley across the river. The château is about 30 miles southwest of Tours on the D-751.

What to Do

Historical/Architectural Sites

Château de Chinon ★★★

Take bus A or B from the train station.

Three separate strongholds overlooking the town, the Château de Chinon was where Charles VII and Joan of Arc first met. It was dismantled in the 17th century by Cardinal Richelieu to build the nearby town of Richelieu. The remains of the castle include the Château de St.-Georges, the Château de Mileu with the 14th-century clock tower, the royal apartments and gardens, and the Château du Coudray, where Joan of Arc stayed during her time at Chinon. *Open mid-Mar.–June and*

Sept., daily, 9 a.m.–6 p.m.; July–Aug., daily, 9 a.m.–7 p.m.; Oct., daily, 9 a.m.–5 p.m.; Nov.–mid-Mar., daily, 9 a.m.–noon. Admission: FR23.

rue Voltaire

Taking time to wander the medieval streets of Chinon is one of this town's greatest pleasures. One of the most typical streets is rue Voltaire, abounding with 15th- and 16th-century townhouses. Take a peek at #44, where Richard the Lion-Hearted died in 1199. The gabled houses with corner turrets and the 16th- and 17th-century mansions make this one of the most enchanting towns in the Loire Valley.

Where to Stay

Bed and Breakfasts

Hotel Diderot FR250–FR400 ★★★

4 rue Buffon. ☎ *02-47-93-18-87, FAX: 02-47-93-37-10. In the middle of town. Double: FR250–FR400.*

A three-story townhouse covered with ivy and punctuated with white trim and shutters, the Hotel Diderot is a statement of tastefully simple accommodations. With an address in the heart of town, it's convenient to the old château, the Grand Carroi and the church of St.-Maurice. There are 28 rooms, all immaculately kept and equipped with a bath or shower. Breakfast is available for FR40 and is served on the terrace in nice weather or in the rustic breakfast room. Repeat guests rave about the wonderful owners and the cozy accommodations guaranteed to be found here. Features: wheelchair-access rooms. Credit Cards: V, MC, DC, A.

Manoir de Montour FR360–FR360 ★★★

Beaumont-en-Veron. ☎ *02-47-58-43-76. About 5 km northwest of town. Take the D749 towards Avoine and Bourgueil until you reach Coulaine. Then head towards Savigny en Veron. Double: FR360.*

This house is aging like a fine wine—always changing a bit in character without ever losing its appeal. There are three rooms here, one of which is a suite for four persons costing FR460. All are quite spacious, comfortable and equipped with one welcomed addition, modern baths. Admire the fine display of wood and the attractive fireplaces throughout the house. Guests can take the complementary breakfast in their room, the garden or the dining room. The sweet proprietress will direct guests to the nearby pool, tennis, fishing, golf and horseback riding. A bright and airy establishment with a genuine homey feeling.

Hotels and Resorts

Le Chinon FR340–FR380 ★★★

Digue St.-Jacques. ☎ *02-47-98-46-46, FAX: 02-47-98-35-44. Across the river from the château. Single: FR340. Double: FR380.*

Built in 1988, this ultra-modern pyramidal building sits on the opposite bank of the river from the Château de Chinon. Very efficient in service and attitude, this hotel has 54 rooms, each comfortably arranged, carpeted and equipped with a TV, telephone and minibar. All come with a private balcony, but reserve one facing the château for a most attractive vista, especially in the misty early mornings. In addition to breakfast for FR40, the restaurant serves decent meals starting at FR70. The new-ness of this hotel can be very refreshing to those in search of modern comforts and uncharming to those in search of a quaint little hotel. Features: balcony or patio, in-room conference facilities.Credit Cards: V, MC, DC, A.

Inns

Château de Marcay   **FR500–FR1500**   ★ ★ ★

In Marcay. ☎ *02-47-93-03-47, FAX: 02-47-93-45-33. About 6 km south of town near the D49 and D116.*
Double: FR500–FR1500.
The owners flawlessly renovated this 15th-century château in 1971 to make this one of the finest hotels in the region. A member of the Relais and Châteaux, this charm-ing and peaceful château sits in a beautifully verdant setting amid private vineyards. Most of the 38 guest rooms are housed in the lovely château with the remainder in the separate and less charming pavilion. The spacious rooms in the main house fea-ture exposed-beamed ceilings and lavish antiques; each is equipped with a TV, tele-phone and a lovely marble bath. Some of the pampering rooms are even blessed with Jacuzzis. The wonderful experience continues in the dining room with its suc-culent regional cuisine and extensive wine list. Working off the calories is made easy with the heated pool and tennis court on the property. The efficient and courteous service completes the entirely enjoyable experience. Features: pool, tennis. Credit Cards: V, MC, DC, A, E.

Hostellerie Gargantua   **FR480–FR550**   ★ ★ ★

73 rue Voltaire. ☎ *02-47-93-04-71. Near the river.*
Single: FR480. Double: FR550.
This quiet, unassuming mansion, home to a bailiff in the 15th century, now houses 10 unique guest rooms. Each is differently and tastefully arranged; some are spa-cious and have a private bath, while others are lacking in amenities but low in price. Those with a view of the château are the best choices. Breakfast is best enjoyed, in the warm months, on the terrace with a grand view of the château. Also, be sure to enjoy a meal in the medieval dining room on a Friday or Saturday night when the waitresses dress to the period making it a very delightful experience; fixed-price meals start at FR100. A very flavorful hotel. Credit Cards: V, MC.

Where to Eat

Au Plaisir Gourmand   **$$$**   ★ ★ ★ ★

2 rue Parmentier, At the base of the château. ☎ *02-47-93-20-48.*
Specialties: pike with walnuts; steamed chicken with truffles.
Dinner: 7:30–9:30 p.m., entrées FR200–FR300.
Commanding a loyal following of gastronomic pleasure seekers from around the world, this small restaurant serves the best food in town. Intimate in every detail (only 30 seats), the staff is very accommodating. A salad of warm turnips and foie gras might lead to perch in a butter and wine sauce, an excellent local cellar wine and a sweet, rich dessert. Fixed-price meals start at FR175. Jacket and tie required. Closed: Mon. Credit Cards: V, MC.

Château de Marcay   **$$$**   ★★★★

Marcay, Take the D116 about 6km south of Chinon; in Marcay. ☎ *02-47-93-03-47.*
Specialties: freshwater perch with oysters and bone marrow with Chinon.
Dinner: entrées FR350–FR500.

Escape to the countryside to enjoy a fine meal while overlooking vineyards and gardens. Old World touches remain at this former 15th-century fortress, and the chef serves refined, traditional cuisine. Pigeon, poultry, seafood and game are all sure to delight. This isn't the place to hold back on the wine selection, as the cellar is one of the best in the region. The friendly staff is always helpful yet unobtrusive. Fixed-price menus start at FR140 during the weekday lunch and FR250 at other times. Reservations required. Credit Cards: All Major.

Jeanne de France   **$**   ★★

12 place General de Gaulle, In the main square. ☎ *02-47-93-20-12.*
A local hot spot, this pizzeria serves the best pizza, steaks and french fries in town. Contributing to the action are the jugs of wine that are popular with the young folks. Perfect for a relaxed, no frills evening. Closed: Wed.

Langeais

Langeais is included here mostly because it is a logical stop on the way back to Tours from visits to any of the preceding three châteaux or even the abbey at Fontevraud (see Western Loire), especially if you want to see the other bank of the river.

Built on the site of an ancient fortress, Langeais is a fine medieval castle that dominates the tiny village that bears its name, although it never quite compares to Chinon or Loches. Foulques Nerra, count of Anjou, built a fortress here in the 10th century. The central donjon, once housing the prison where the ruthless count kept his prisoners in metal cages, still stands. The main château was built between 1465 and 1467 by Louis XI. The main wall that faces the town is in remarkable shape, and has a working replica of the drawbridge that was once used to let in guests and keep out undesirables.

Louis gave the castle to François d'Orléans in 1466. François completed the construction by adding some loggias and extra guardhouses, but the most important work he did there was political. Charles VIII, the young king of France, was engaged to Margaret of Austria and Burgundy, while Anne of Brittany was engaged to Margaret's father Maximilian. François, fearing that this pair of unions would not provide the most stability to France, persuaded the king to break off the engagement so he could marry Anne instead. After this adroit diplomacy, François fell off a horse and broke his neck, on November 25, 1491, before the marriage could be celebrated. Two weeks later, the unappealing Charles VIII (he had asthma and 12 toes) and the long-suffering, pious Anne were married in the castle. Margaret, who had been engaged to Charles since she was three, returned empty-handed to Austria to face her irate father, who had lost France through his daughter and Brittany through his wife.

There are a fair amount of mementos of the marriage in the castle, along with an extremely comprehensive collection of authentic 15th-century furniture, artworks and tapestries gathered over 20 years by Jacques Siegfried, the last private owner of the château before it passed in the hands of a non-profit foundation. Langeais is about 15 miles east of Tours on the N-152 on the north (right) bank of the Loire.

What to Do

Historical/Architectural Sites

Castle de Langeais   ★★★

A fortress in every sense, the castle at Langeais stands imposingly over the town. With a fantastic location on the Loire, this formidable structure is contrasted on the inside with ornately decorated rooms. The dungeon ruins date back to the 9th century, with the present castle dating to 1465. Guided tours in English are available. *Open 9 a.m.–6:30 p.m.; mid-July–Aug., 9 a.m.–10 p.m.; Nov.–mid-Mar., 9 a.m.– noon and 2–5 p.m.* Admission: FR35.

THE LOIRE

POITOU-CHARENTES

La Rochelle is a fascinating port city.

What Makes Poitou-Charentes So French?

1. *Cognac, cognac, cognac. Merci, mon Dieu! Even the bit that evaporates during aging is called le part des anges (the angels' share). Have a zillion or more francs in your pocket? See if you can buy a drop still aging from the early 19th century!*

2. *Departure point for the Acadians who took off for Western Canada during the 18th century, were expelled and subsequently migrated down to Louisiana where they metamorphosed into "Cajuns." Who would've known that, come the 20th century, chef Paul Prudhomme would spice them into fame?*

3. *Many (most!) of the villagers in Archigny are cousins—make of that what you will.*

What Makes Poitou-Charentes So French?

4. *Land of the Futuroscope—go for the architectural kitsch and the high-tech cinemas.*

5. *The world's largest comic book fair is held each January in Angouleme—a center of cartoon production disguised as an unanimated little village.*

Sandwiched between the tourist-stomping grounds of the Loire valley and the equally popular wine country of Bordeaux is Poitou-Charentes, a beautiful and diverse region of western France—often widely overlooked by visitors, except perhaps for its cognac distilleries. The region around the city of Cognac is certainly worth a visit, especially if for a swallow or more of its illustrious hometown brew, but Poitou-Charentes has much more to offer. The start of the west's agricultural heartland, the region is mostly flat or gently sloping, exceptionally fertile, rich in history and Romanesque architecture. In addition, Poitou-Charentes possesses great sandy beaches along the Atlantic coast south of La Rochelle, itself the primary pleasure harbor on the west coast. Although it gets chilly in the early mornings and late evenings in winter, Poitou-Charentes is known for its year-round sunshine.

History

Poitou-Charentes' history is largely ecclesiastical and diplomatic rather than military. Nevertheless, three important battles that determined the course of France, and even Europe, took place in the region. Christianity was accepted here as early as anywhere in France, perhaps as early as the third century. A baptistry in the capital, Poitiers, dates the fourth century. Later, when the area was a major throughpoint on the pilgrims' route to Santiago de Compostela, countless Romanesque churches were built, and many still stand today. The first military victory for the region and for the cross came in A.D. 507, when the leader of the Gauls, Clovis, defeated a marauding Visigoth force that had invaded across the Pyrenees under Alaric II. Later, in A.D. 732, the relentless northward advance of the Moors from Northern Africa was finally halted and turned back in Poitou-Charentes when Charles "The Hammer" Martel defeated the Saracens. Although the Moors lingered in Spain for another 600 years their defeat at Poitou-Charentes marked the beginning of the end for their European empire.

Formerly a part of Aquitaine, the region's history was intertwined with that of England. When Eleanor of Aquitaine divorced the French King and married Henry II of Anjou (and England) in 1152, the region was part of her dowry. Poitou-Charentes was firmly part of England for almost a hundred years. Back in French hands by the 13th century, Poitou-Charentes was an occasional residence of the French Kings, but for the next three centuries it was a focal point of the English-French conflicts. The region's third major battle took place in 1365, and it was an ignominious episode for France that pitted the forces of the Black Prince against those of King Jean the Good at Nouaillé-Maupertuis. During the battle the French king was taken prisoner by the English. Joan of Arc, in her campaign to liberate France, was interrogated by religious leaders at Poitiers, and under her inspiration the region was returned to French rule. The British continued to hang around, however, and until the wars with Napoleon were a near constant presence and threat off the coasts of La Rochelle. Still, by the 18th century, the region had become a tranquil and stable provincial capital.

Poitou-Charentes' ties to North America, especially French-speaking Canada and Louisiana, are extremely strong. In the 18th century, French settlers left from ports up and down western France for the new territories in Canada. Expelled from a region in western Canada called Acadia in 1765 by the British, many of the Acadians, as they are called, migrated south to French-held Louisiana. The American term "Cajun" derives from a mispronunciation of the French "Acadian"). Others were returned to France where they wandered as refugees until settling in the Poitou-Charentes region. When you hear people refer to each other as "cousin" around the village of Archigny, it's because they *are* cousins—78 families were settled there after the *grand dérangement*. The region's commercial ties to French-speaking Canada continued to grow after peace was established there between France and England, however, and the 18th and 19th centuries saw a huge commercial growth of the coastal areas, especially the port of La Rochelle. Even today, Poitou-Charentes is in general a strong supporter of independence for Québec.

Cuisine

In a region as diverse as Poitou-Charentes, sweeping from the area just south of the Loire to the coast and down to Bordeaux, it is perhaps not surprising that the cuisine, too, is eclectic. The number one specialty is oysters—the *huitres* Marennes-Oléron harvested off the Poitou-Charentes coastline account for more than half the oysters in France, and it is possible to find restaurants in Poitiers or La Rochelle serving all-you-can-eat oysters for US$20. Another famous seafood specialty is *moules bouchot*—mussels grown on wooden stakes *(bouchots)* planted in the seabed. Best served in a *mouclade sauce* consisting of wine, cream and eggs, these delicious shellfish are found throughout the region. Poitou-Charentes also produces a quarter of France's lamb, so *agneau* is typically on the menu. In the Marias Poitevin marsh, specialties include *bouilliture d'anguilles* (eels cooked in a red wine sauce), *sauce aux lumas* (snails cooked in a red wine sauce), and *mojettes* (white beans cooked in butter). The region is not a major cheese producer; those that stand out are goat cheeses, including Chablis and chabichou.

Poitou-Charentes is not famed for its wines. Vintages are usually quite fruity and should be drunk young. The Loudun wines are very similar to Saumur vintage Loire wines. Haut-Poitou produces light white, rosé and red wines that are drunk very young. The Thouars red, white and rosé wines are served chilled (even the red), while Charente white, served with seafood under the name *blanc marine*, are the region's driest. Of course the major nectar of the region is cognac, which is discussed in more detail below. A favorite apèritif is pineau des Charentes, a blend of cognac and grape juice that comes in red, white or rosé varieties and is drunk chilled before a meal.

Poitiers

Poitiers, the capital of Poitou-Charentes, has a population of 100,000, of which 30,000 are students. Acknowledged as the "youngest" in France, Poitiers, during the school year, has a nightlife to prove it. Poitiers is also the home of Futuroscope, certainly the newest-looking architecture in France. There has been a university at Poitiers for more than 560 years. Founded by Pope Eugene IV in 1431, *l'Université de Poitiers* is one of the oldest in Europe. At the time, there were universities only in Bordeaux and Angers anywhere west of Paris. Granted royal patronage by King Charles VII a year after it was founded, the university first offered courses in civil law, canonical law, theology, medicine and art—noteworthy because the concept of "art for art's sake" was relatively new. Among the illustrious graduates of the university in the early days were Descartes, Rapin and the poet Rabelais. Nowadays, there are campuses all over the city, but the original 16th-century building, just a few blocks from the central square downtown, is still in use and houses, fittingly, a college of medieval studies.

The region was Christianized much earlier than northwestern France, beginning as early as the third century. The city lay on the major route of pilgrimage to Santiago de Compostela in Spain. Therefore, the churches and cathedrals in Poitou-Charentes are much more uniformly Romanesque than in other parts of the country. The premier example of the Romanesque style sits quietly right downtown in Poitiers, in the shadow of the cathedral and a stunningly ugly convention hall and planetarium—the fourth-century Baptistère St. Jean. Recent excavations have uncovered Roman ruins on the site, but the small church itself and the full-immersion font have stood unchanged for more than 1500 years. Just above the baptismal church, the Cathédrale de St. Pierre was commissioned in the 11th century by Eleanor of Aquitaine. It is a squat, extra-wide building, but its triple nave interior is cavernous and light. Though its stained glass pales in comparison to that at Le Mans or Chartres, the 12th-century *vitraines* are well worth studying. The pipe organ, made in the 18th century by Cliquot, was recently restored and is one of the finest of the Baroque period. The organ is used during Masses and occasionally for concerts. Perhaps the most stunning church in Poitiers, though, is the 11th-century Notre Dame la Grande in the main marketplace not far from the cathedral. Striking from afar for its conical Byzantine-style stone roofs, the church is most noteworthy for its stunning 12th-century facade. Using the same sculptural styles employed on the portals of many Romanesque cathedrals, the builders covered the entire front facade with an array of saints, beasts and other images that is unparalleled in a church of its size in France. The facade was originally painted in many colors. Today, during the summer, a sophisticated lighting-system recreates the color scheme each day at sunset.

The former palace of the Dukes of Aquitaine, now the Palais de Justice, bears a Napoleonic porch, but the rest of the exterior and all of the interior is constructed in 12th-century style. Especially impressive is the Salle du Roi, the massive central hall where feasts and meetings were held. Its three enormous fireplaces must have kept the dukes and all their courtiers nice and warm in the cold winter nights. Among all this architectural wonderland, don't forget the modern Musée St. Croix, built on the site of an abbey of the same name, which has a good regional collection of exhibits from prehistory to the Renaissance.

The Futuroscope theme park is, strangely, the crown jewel in Poitiers' collection of treasures—the region, in fact, calls itself "*Poitou-Charentes, pays du Futuroscope*," or "Poitou-Charents, land of the Futuroscope," as if the park were the number-one attraction. Well, actually it is, and it receives almost 3 million visitors a year. The park is dedicated to the visual image, consisting of several pavilions housing high-tech cinemas that use giant screens, 360-degree screens, and screens that go under your seat, plus moving seats, revolving seats, three-dimensional glasses and innumerable special effects to wow your senses. The lines are as long as those at EuroDisney—up to an hour-and-a-half in summer. It's worth a look just for the architecture, which is dissimilar to anything you'll see anywhere else, especially in rural France. One enormous building is constructed in the shape of a giant crystal, another appears to be a forest of giant glass tree trunks. Surrounding the park is a developing community of factories, colleges of engineering and aerospace studies, and housing, most of it constructed in the futuristic style.

For something much more historical, take a drive out around the many small villages surrounding Poitiers. Those of the Vienne river valley are especially enchanting. Head east on the N-151 to the village of Chauvigny, which is perched on a promontory overlooking the river. Built in the 15th century, the outer ramparts of the baronial castle are partially ruined, but in this case that only adds to their charm. The small inner fort, dating from the 12th century, is in much better condition. It houses a small but interesting museum of 19th-century industrial development, and hosts concerts during the summer.

From Chauvigny continue east to St. Sauvin, where a small monastery, the Abbaye de St. Sauvin, holds an unexpected treasure. The high ceilings of the nave in the abbatial church contain the wealthiest collection of 12th century frescoes in the world—the abbey is designated as a world heritage site by UNESCO. During the 15th century it was common for churches and abbeys that were, shall we say, second-class and thus built of less-than-perfect stone, to be plastered over on the interior and then given a fake, painted, set of perfectly aligned stones. It was not until 1835, and then quite by accident, that the fresco painting was uncovered. Perfectly preserved, the stunning display chronicles the Old and New Testaments in the nave, Christ in his glory in the Revelation of St. John in the porch, the Passion in the tribune, the lives of the early saints in the choir and, modestly, the lives of St. Sauvin and St. Cypien in the crypt (which is not open to the public). Looking up at the 700-year-old paintings on the roof, the fake stones painted on the walls and the fake marble on the columns, one gets the feeling that one is in a colorful art gallery rather than in a place of worship. The abbey is now home to the International Center for the Study of Muralism. For a good view of the exterior of the Romanesque complex, drive across the nearby 13th-century bridge. Then drive back across the river, and head north on D-11. Cross the river again at Nalliers, then make your way along the bank to St. Pierre-de-Maille. Turn right on the D-2 and drive to Angles-sur-L'Anglin.

The old baronial castle of Angles-sur-L'Anglin is situated on the promontory overlooking the river and the tiny village, at the bottom of which is the beautiful 12th-century church of St. Martin. Born in Angles in 1421, Cardinal Jean Balue became minister of finance for King Louis XI. As punishment for having defrauded the monarch, he was imprisoned for 10 years in his own invention, a tiny metal cage, called a *fillette*. For a change to happier considerations, drive back to St. Pierre and stop at the café overlooking the weir. After a cool drink, head on the D-2 road to La Puye. Turn right on the D-9, follow it until it crosses the D-3, which you will take (to the left) towards *Archigny*. Keep going for about five more miles and you will be in the heart of the *Forêt de Moulière*. Stop and take a walk before heading back to Poitiers for a well-earned dinner. The whole circuit is done comfortably in an afternoon.

What to Do

Historical/Architectural Sites

Baptistere St.-Jean   ★★★

    rue Jean Jaures.

    Dating from the 4th century, this polygonal, brick-and-stone structure is one of the oldest Christian buildings in France. This was the location of the baptisms of many of the first converts. Still in good condition, the interior contains frescoes of Constantine and Christ. *Open Apr.–Oct., 10:30 a.m.–12:30 p.m. and 3–6 p.m.; Nov.–Mar., 2:30–4:30 p.m. Closed Tues., except in July and Aug. Admission: FR4.*

Cathédrale St.-Pierre ★★★

place de la Cathédrale, ☎ *05-49-41-23-76. On the east side.*
Hours open: 8 a.m.–7 p.m.
With construction begun in 1162 by Henry II of England, this church was erected at the request of Eleanor of Aquitaine. While the exterior is unusually bland, the interior is highlighted by a grand organ and wonderful displays of light through the stained-glass windows. Note the 13th-century choir stalls—the oldest in France.

Notre-Dame-la-Grande ★★

place Notre-Dame-la-Grande, ☎ *05-49-41-22-56.*
Hours open: 8 a.m.–7 p.m.
Reflecting the Roman-Byzantine style, the facade hides the richly decorated interior. After many renovations, the frescoes and painted columns glimmer once again. Notice the biblical scenes carved into the doorway and the fresco of Christ and the Virgin Mary in the choir. Although not large in size as the name might imply, it is one of the great pilgrim churches. Admission: free.

Palais de Justice ★★

place Lepetit, ☎ *05-49-41-33-43.*
Hours open: 9 a.m.–6 p.m. Special hours: Closed noon–2 p.m. Closed: Sat., Sun.
Believed to be the site of Joan of Arc's examination by the council of theologians in 1429, the grand hall was a gathering point for the Dukes of Aquitaine. It was also here that Richard the Lion-Hearted was made *comte de Poitou* and *duc d'Anjou* in 1170. The lavish interior greatly contrasts the boring facade.

Museums and Exhibits

Musée St.-Croix ★★

61 rue St.-Simplicien, ☎ *05-49-41-09-53. Near the Baptistere.*
Hours open: 10 a.m.–6 p.m. Special hours: Closed noon–2 p.m.; closed holidays. Closed: Mon.
Local and Gallo-Roman history is recounted with artifacts from past centuries. Flemish art is the focus of the gallery of 17th- through 20th-century paintings. The Three Graces, a bronze by Maillol, highlights the collections. Admission: FR2.

Theme/Amusement Parks

Futuroscope ★★★★

In Chasseneuil, ☎ *05-49-49-31-10. About 7 km north of Poitiers. By car, take the A10 towards Paris-Chatellerault and take exit 18. Or, take bus #16 or 17 from the bus station.*
Hours open: 9 a.m.–6 p.m. Special hours: Closed Nov.–Mar.
Highlights of this high-tech amusement park include 360-degree Global Image, a theater that puts you in the middle of the action, the Cinema Dynamique, a theater with action seats that move along with the film, Kinemax, Europe's largest flat screen, and Tapis Magique, a theater with one screen in front and one on the floor. The entire park is an ingenious form of entertainment for both adults and children. Children admission is FR100. Admission: FR130.

Where to Stay

Hotels and Resorts

Château de Perigny   FR355–FR890   ★★★

In Perigny. ☎ *05-49-51-80-43, FAX: 05-49-51-90-09. About 15 km from town.*
Single: FR355–FR780. Double: FR400–FR890.

In a sylvan park-like setting, this chateau is a short drive from Poitiers. The 42 functional rooms are attractively decorated and have telephone, TV and private bath. The facilities, including pool, tennis courts and playground, are in good condition. In a city hotel market of mediocrity, the chateau is just a cut above the rest. Features: pool, tennis, sauna.Credit Cards: V, DC, A.

Hotel de L'Europe   FR300–FR480   ★★★

39 rue Carnot. ☎ *05-49-88-12-00, FAX: 05-49-88-97-30. Take bus #1, 2 or 9.*
Single: FR300–FR480. Double: FR360–FR480.

A coaching inn in its earlier days, this early 19th-century building annexed the stables and now has 88 guest rooms. The gardens and courtyard below, the rooms have TV, telephone, minibar and private bath. Contrasting the old-fashioned decor of the public areas, the rooms are quite contemporary due to recent and constant updates. Breakfast costs FR36, and parking is FR20. No restaurant. Credit Cards: All Major.

Where to Eat

Le Poitevin $ ★★

76 rue Carnot. ☎ *05-49-88-35-04.*

The locals' restaurant that is quickly becoming popular with tourists because of its inexpensive prices and tasty regional cuisine. Fixed-price meals start at just FR80. Another inexpensive choice is Le Chantegrille, place d'Armes *(☎ 05-49-01-74-00).* Enjoy a meat and fish plate with all-you-can-eat vegetables for just FR65. Open daily 11:30 a.m.–2 p.m. and 7–11 p.m. Closed: Sun.

Maxime $$ ★★★★

4 rue St.-Nicolas. ☎ *05-49-41-09-55.*
Dinner: 7:30–10 p.m., entrées FR125–FR200.

The finest place in town, Maxime offers a wide variety of set menus that are known for generous proportions. Some of the possible dishes include lobster, John Dory, foie gras and duck salad and duck breast. A smooth dessert and glass of wine are included. The fixed-price menus range from FR100–FR250. Closed Jan. 5–15; July 10–20 and Aug. 10–20. Closed: Sat., Sun. Reservations recommended. Credit Cards: V, A.

Pierre Benoist $$$ ★★★

La Croutelle, About 6km west on the N10, in Croutelle. ☎ *05-49-57-11-52.*
Specialties: lobster with foie gras sauce.
Dinner: 7:30–9:15 p.m., entrées FR225–FR350.

Dining on the outdoor terrace, overlooking the valley, is one of the most relaxing ways to spend a couple of hours in Poitiers. Pierre is a master of the traditional cuisine, and he uses his skills with a great variety of dishes. From calf's head to pigeon, he has established himself as a solid classical chef. The wine selection is excellent. Fixed-price meals start at FR175. Closed: Mon. Amenities: outside dining, reservations required. Credit Cards: All Major.

Directory

To and From

> *By train from Paris in an hour and a half, or by car on the A-10 autoroute from Orléans in the north or Bordeaux in the south.*

Tourist Office

> *8 rue des Grandes Ecoles;* ☎ *(33) 05-49-41-21-24.*

Rail Station

> *boulevard du Grand Cerf;* ☎ *(33) 05-49-58-50-50.*

Post Office

> *rue des Escossais;* ☎ *(33) 05-49-01-83-80.*

Angoulême

The quiet town of Angoulême is too far off the beaten track for most people, but it is home to some interesting sights. You can walk around the Old City on the ramparts built on top of fourth-century Gallo-Roman walls, and on a clear day you can see Cognac from the heights. The most imposing building in town is the 12th-century Cathédrale St. Pierre, which has one of the most important Romanesque facades in the country. Seventy-five characters illustrate the Ascension of Christ and the Last Judgement, while the decorations on the tympans depict Christ and the Apostles. A major paper-producing center during the 18th century, the city has become the center of production of cartoons *(bandes desinées)*. There is an excellent museum dedicated to the art form (of course Astérix, Obélix, Getafix and the rest of those pesky Gauls are well-represented) and each January the city hosts the largest comic-book fair in the world.

What to Do

Historical/Architectural Sites

Cathedrale St.-Pierre ★★★

> *place St.-Pierre,* ☎ *05-45-95-20-38.*
> *Hours open: 9 a.m.–7:30 p.m. Special hours: Sat., to 6:30 p.m.*
> Originally constructed in the 12th century, this magnificent structure was rebuilt in 1634 after destruction by the Calvinists. Paul Abadie, a 19th-century architect, improved on the detail, and, in the process, accidentally destroyed a 6th-century crypt. Take keen note to the characters on the facade depicting the Ascension and the Last Judgment. Possibly the finest example of Romanesque-Byzantine architecture in France. Admission: free.

Museums and Exhibits

Comic Strip Museum–CNBDI ★★★

> *121 rue de Bordeaux,* ☎ *05-45-38-65-65.*
> *Hours open: 10 a.m.–7 p.m. Special hours: Sat. & Sun., from 2 p.m. Closed: Tue.*
> Close to the distilleries of Cognac, the sleepy town of Angoulême is best known for its 17th-century paper mills, which today crank out reams of French comic strips

(Asterix, Tintin) for a voracious public. The city's best products are on view in the CNBDI (Centre National de la Bande Dessinee) building, an ultramodern structure with a series of mixed-media exhibitions that delight and inform. Featured are the original storyboards of many of your favorite French and international cartoon series, as well as videos and slide presentations that trace the history of this pop-culture form from its earliest origins. Admission: FR30.

Where to Stay

Hotels and Resorts

Hostellerie du Maine Brun   **FR400–FR750**

RN 141 Lieu-Dit la Vigerie. ☎ *05-45-90-83-00.*
Single: FR400–FR550. Double: FR550–FR750.

The stuff dreams are made of. Originally a flour mill built in the 14th century, this Relais and Chateaux hotel occupies part of 80 acres of private land. With deer and ducks roaming free on part of the land and production of cognac on the other, this park sets a relaxing scene for the hotel. The 20 guest rooms are individually decorated with antiques and modernized with TV, telephone, minibar and private bath. Although a bit worn around the edges, the spacious rooms are still the most luxurious in Angouleme. The restaurant serves beautifully presented fixed-price meals starting from FR180. The service is friendly and casual, adding to the relaxed atmosphere of this hostellerie. Features: pool, in-room minibars, fitness center, country location. Credit Cards: All Major.

Hotel de France   **FR390–FR590**   ★★

1 place des Halles. ☎ *223-9862, 05-45-95-47-95, FAX: 05-45-92-02-70. Near the train station, in the old town.*
Single: FR390–FR540. Double: FR440–FR590.

Within the old city's ramparts, this hotel occupies a building dating to the 16th century. The 90 high-ceilinged rooms contain cable TV, radio, telephone, minibar, bath and hair dryer. Nonsmoking rooms can be reserved. Rustic styles pervade the public spaces, with exposed wood and stone featured in the architecture. In addition to breakfast for FR50, there is room service and a restaurant and bar with fixed-price menus at FR150. Beautiful panoramas are granted from the terrace. Professional and efficient (perhaps too much so) service. Features: wheelchair-access rooms, nonsmoking rooms, in-room minibars. Credit Cards: All Major.

Where to Eat

La Ruelle   **$$$**   ★★★

6 rue des Trois-Notre-Dame. ☎ *05-45-92-94-64.*
Specialties: sole with crayfish and cucumbers, red mullet with saffron.
Lunch: Noon–2 p.m., FR250–FR300.
Dinner: 7:30–10 p.m., entrées FR250–FR300.

Unlike a lot of dining establishments run by couples, in this case, the wife is the chef while her husband keeps things running smoothly. Together, Jean-Francois and Veronique Dauphin have restored this ancient house to a fine gleam. The kitchen turns out inventive, ambitious cuisine; the poultry, seafood and organ meats are especially successful. Fixed-price menus are offered at FR160 (lunch, with wine), FR150 and FR205. Closed: Sun. Reservations recommended. Credit Cards: V.

La Vigerie

Le Moulin Gourmand $$$ ★ ★ ★

Lieu-Dit la Vigerie, Rte 141, 11 km west of Angouleme. Located at Le Moulin du Maine Brun. ☎ *05-45-90-83-00.*
Lunch: 12:30–2 p.m., FR175–FR360.
Dinner: 7:30–9:30 p.m., entrées FR175–FR360.

Many dishes here are made with the white cognac produced in the inn's own distillery, Moulin du Domaine de Maine-Brun. In the summer, dinner is served on the outdoor terrace facing a brook and a great forest of trees. Ignore the ferociously high a la carte menu, and concentrate instead on the three fixed price menus: FR180, FR280 and FR360. Amenities: outside dining, own baking, reservations required. Credit Cards: All Major.

Directory

To and From

By train from Poitiers (one hour) or Bordeaux (55 minutes), or by car on the N-141 from Cognac or the N-10 from Poitiers.

Tourist Office

2 place de St. Pierre; ☎ *(33) 05-45-95-16-84.*

Rail Station

place de la Gàre; ☎ *(33) 05-45-38-50-50.*

Post Office

place du Champ de Mars, 16000 Angoulême; ☎ *(33) 05-45-95-23-11.*

Le Marais Poitevin

The Marais Poitevin is actually a region, rather than a city, but is presented here since it can all be visited in a day. Between the city of Niort, north of La Rochelle, and the ocean, the former Gulf of Poitou—a swampy, marshy region—has been painstakingly reclaimed from the sea to create what the locals refer to as *La Venise Verte*—Green Venice. Extending over almost 200,000 acres, the Marais Poitevin is a charming rural region crisscrossed by hundreds of tiny canals and waterways, dotted with tiny villages, and home to a few thousand hardy *maraîchins* and countless species of fish, birds and other wildlife. The entire region is a natural park. Divided broadly into two halves, the *marais mouillé* (wet marsh) and the *marais déséché* (dry marsh), it is best explored aboard a flat-bottomed punt-like boat called a *pigouille* that can be rented at any of the villages. You also can explore the region by bicycle.

Beginning in the 11th century, the locals—initially monks who wanted to establish abbeys and create farmland to support them—have been digging canals and draining the fields in the area. The work still goes on, to keep the canals clear and repair those that are breached by the periodic high tides. Most of the canals are extremely narrow and rural, with beautiful houses along the banks, always with a boat moored nearby. The canal banks are planted with poplars, ashes, alders and willows, whose deep roots hold the soil together. You can rent the boats with or without a guide by the hour, half-day, or day in the villages of Coulon (the capital of the region and home to a museum explaining the creation of the canal system), La Garette, and Arçais, as well as in Damvix and Maillezais, which are actually across the border in the extreme southern tip of Vendée in Western Loire.

Directory

To and From

> *You can get to Niort from Paris or La Rochelle by train and then take a bus, or drive from Niort on the N-11 or N-148 then head into the Marais.*

Tourist Office

> *La Ronde (Courlon);* ☎ *(33) 05-49-27-82-44.*

La Rochelle

The fabulous port city of La Rochelle has been eclipsed as a commercial shipping center by Bordeaux to the south and Nantes to the north, but it is still a thriving maritime city, with the largest pleasure harbor on the Atlantic coast, boasting 3000 berths. There are four ports in La Rochelle—the pleasure port, the Old Harbor, the fishing harbor and the commercial deepwater port. The Old Harbor is guarded by famous twin 14th-century towers, and stand as a reminder to when La Rochelle was a wealthy and fiercely independent Aquitaine city.

Founded in the 10th century on a rocky islet in the natural harbor, La Rochelle quickly became a fishing port. In 1199, the village was given a town charter by Eleanor of Aquitaine, enabling it to collect taxes from the surrounding feudal villages. Always led by a strong mayor, the city played a crafty, independent role during the centuries-long conflict between England and France, never quite allying itself fully with either side and enriching itself at the expense of both. By the 15th century, the city had been encircled by massive ramparts and the entrance to its harbor was guarded by the St. Nicolas Tower and the Chain Tower—so called because a giant chain was stretched across the entry to prevent access to undesirable ships. The 15th century also saw the construction of the Lantern Tower, one of the oldest lighthouses in France, at which merchant ships were obliged to unload the arms and armament before entering the harbor.

Given its independent character, La Rochelle readily accepted the ideas of the Reformist movement sweeping across Europe during the 16th century, and became the center for Huguenot Protestantism in France. The rise of

Protestantism did not play well in Paris, and King Louis XIII sent Cardinal Richelieu—his enforcer of national unity—to La Rochelle to personally see that the city was brought into line. Richelieu laid siege to the city, and after 13 months La Rochelle was reduced to starvation and capitulated. Residents still speak proudly of their resistance to what they saw then as colonial oppression from France. Richelieu ordered the town's ramparts to be torn down, leaving only the twin towers, the Lantern tower, and a short stretch of rampart connecting them to defend against the British. The city fell into decline thereafter, and it was not until the 18th century, when trade with the New World in the form of the so-called Triangle Trade (slave trade), that La Rochelle again became prosperous.

While in La Rochelle, visit the towers. The best is the Lantern Tower, where you can climb the 162 steps to the original lantern chamber, viewing two centuries' graffiti etched into its walls by prisoners housed there over the years. The *Tour de la Chaine* (Chain Tower) has an interesting multimedia presentation on medieval life in the city, but only in French. After your tower tour, take an hourlong cruise around the harbor on the boats that depart from the quay by the Tour de la Chaine. Along the way, you will see the improbable Fort Boyard, a compact, oval fort rising out of the middle of the ocean. During the hostilities of the late 18th and early 19th centuries, British warships would wait just outside the harbor to sink the new warships the French had just built at La Rochelle. Occasionally, British ships even entered the harbor itself. Napoléon, tiring of this game, ordered construction of a fort with cannons that would cover the entire mouth of the bay. The fort took 50 years to build, however, and by the time it was finished, improved cannons had made it obsolete. It was used only as a prison.

Within the city are numerous Renaissance buildings including the *Palais de Justice*, *Chambre de Commerce* and the Gothic-to-Renaissance Town Hall. You enter the town by passing through the *Tour du Gros Horloge*, a fourth massive tower that remains from the pre-siege days. There are many museums in La Rochelle, as well as an aquarium, but your first stop should be at the *Musée du Nouveau Monde*, a museum devoted to La Rochelle's considerable ties to the New World. It houses exhibits of old maps, seafaring knickknacks, and trophies brought back from Canada by the first French explorers, as well as displays about the Acadiens. Interestingly, part of La Rochelle is paved with flat stones brought back from Newfoundland—they had been used as ballast by the ships that carried light-weight cargoes of beaver pelts from North America during the 18th century.

La Rochelle itself doesn't have much in the way of beaches, but there are plenty nearby. The best are on the south sides of the *Ile de Ré* and the *Ile d'Oléron* (the second largest island in France, after Corsica, with 20 beaches of fine, white sand), which can be reached by way of toll bridges, or the *Ile d'Aix*, which lies between them and can only be reached by boat. The last mentioned was the final home of Napoléon on French soil before being shipped of to St. Helena. There is a small museum in the house in which he spent his last few nights.

What to Do

Historical/Architectural Sites

Palais de Justice   ★★

10 rue du Palais.

Hearings are open to the public Mon. and Thurs. at 2 p.m. in this court of law which was completed in 1789, just before the Revolution. Another interesting 18th-century building is the Chambre de Commerce, formerly the stock exchange building. Finally, the Hotel de Ville (town hall), is at Place de l'Hotel de Ville (☎ *05-46-41-14-68*). Behind the Flamboyant Gothic wall is the Renaissance courtyard from the 16th century. The interior is opulently decorated with an abundance of chandeliers. *Open weekdays 9:30–11 a.m. and 3–5 p.m.; Sat. 2–5:30 p.m.; Oct.– Easter, weekdays 2:30–4 p.m.* Guided tours available in July and Aug. for FR20.

Towers   ★★★

Near the port.

Three towers are worthy of visiting for both an historical and a bird's-eye perspective of the town. Tour de la Chaine and Tour St.-Nicolas stand guard at the entrance to the port. To thwart attack by sea, a giant chain was strung between the two towers at night, forbidding enemy boat passage into the harbor. Climb both towers, soaking up the town history with displays strung along the ascent. A small section of the ramparts survived the destruction of Richelieu, and the Tour de la Lanterne (or Tour des Quatre Sergents, after the imprisonment of four sergeants here in the 1800s) is still connected. Climb to the top for the stellar view. *Tour de la Chaine is open Easter–Nov., 9:30 a.m.–noon and 2–6:30 p.m.; admission is FR20. Tour St.-Nicolas and Tour de la Lanterne are open Apr.–May and Sept., Wed.–Mon., 9:30 a.m.–12:30 p.m. and 2–6:30 p.m.; June–Aug., daily, 9:30 a.m.– 7 p.m.; Oct.–Mar., Wed.–Mon., 9:30–12:30 p.m. and 2–5 p.m.*

Museums and Exhibits

Musée du Nouveau-Monde   ★★★

10 rue Fleuriau, ☎ *05-46-41-46-50. In the Hotel Fleuriau.*
Hours open: 10:30 a.m.–6 p.m. Special hours: Closed 12:30–1:30 p.m. and Sun. morning. Closed: Tue.

Reflecting the history of the New World, the French paintings and sculptures give the French view of the history of North America. From the discovery of the Mississippi Delta in the 1600s through the purchase of the Louisiana territory, there's a little piece of Americana here for everybody. At *28 rue Gargolleau, the Musée des Beaux-Arts (*☎ *05-46-41-64-65)* houses a collection of art from the 17th through 20th centuries. Represented here are Rembrandt, Rubens, Delacroix and many others. *Open Wed.–Mon., 2–5 p.m.* Both museums are available with the same ticket. Admission: FR16.

Where to Stay

Hotels and Resorts

Hotel Champlain   **FR375–FR550**   ★★★

20 rue Rambaud. ☎ *05-46-41-23-99, FAX: 05-46-41-15-19. In town, France et Angleterre.*
Double: FR375–FR550.
Considered one of the city's best hotels, Le Champlain, operated by Best Western, occupies a former townhouse. The 36 stylish, comfortable rooms hint at an earlier day, and some overlook the flower garden. Those over the street are great for people watching, but the daytime noise makes afternoon naps difficult. All are well-equipped and have air conditioning and private bath. A small bar is also in the hotel. Features: air conditioning in rooms. Credit Cards: All Major.

Hotel Les Brises   **FR325–FR625**   ★★★

chemin de la Digne-Richelieu. ☎ *05-46-43-89-37, FAX: 05-46-43-27-97. Across from Port des Minimes.*
Double: FR325–FR625.
Across from Port des Minimes, Les Brises is in the most quiet and attractive location. The balconies on the front of the hotel provide excellent vistas. While character is not high on the list of priorities here, housekeeping is. The 48 wood-furnished rooms have TV, telephone and private bath. Uncommonly good breakfasts are worth the FR35. Garage parking is free. Credit Cards: All Major.

La Monnaie   **FR590**   ★★★

3 rue de la Monnaie. ☎ *05-46-50-65-65, FAX: 05-46-50-63-19. Across from the old harbor.*
Double: FR590.
A stately 17th-century hotel, Le Monnaie is in a quiet situation between the old harbor and the small beach. All of the 32 rooms are pleasant, but those on the ground floor facing the courtyard are the most spacious. Upper-level rooms offer glimpses of the water. The staff here is exceptional, providing unusually attentive service. Features: wheelchair-access rooms, air conditioning in rooms. Credit Cards: All Major.

Tour de Nesle   **FR250–FR400**   ★★

2 quai Louis-Durand. ☎ *05-46-41-30-72, FAX: 05-46-41-95-17. Near the main waterfront avenue.*
Single: FR250. Double: FR400.
Consider this hotel for its location near the waterfront. It's a good base for touring the old town and the harbor. The 28 rooms, though a bit compact, are well-maintained and available with a view of the canal and St.-Sauveur church. Continental breakfast is served in the small breakfast room. Credit Cards: V, MC.

Where to Eat

La Rena Bianca   **$**   ★★

9 rue Verdiere, Turn left off rue du Temple. ☎ *05-46-41-90-10.*
The locals' favorite for inexpensive seafood. There's a FR50 lunch menu and a FR70 menu that includes cheeses and dessert. FR55 will turn into mussels, chicken

curry and dessert. Another inexpensive choice is Les Comediens at the port. The set menus start at FR80, and the place is hoppin'.

Les Quatre Sergents $$ ★★★

49 rue St.-Jean-du-Perot, Near the port. ☎ *05-46-41-35-80.*
Dinner: 7:30–10 p.m., entrées FR100–FR200.

Originally an art nouveau greenhouse used to ripen bananas in the late 1800s, it now serves as a dining room. An incredibly extensive menu focuses on variety of seafood. The service is generally good. Fixed-price meals start at FR75. Closed: Mon. Reservations required. Credit Cards: All Major.

Richard Coutanceau $$ ★★★★

plage de la Concurrence, Near the casino. ☎ *05-46-41-48-19.*
Dinner: 7:30–9:30 p.m., entrées FR150–FR250.

Situated in a pine tree park, this is the premier restaurant in La Rochelle. Chef Richard Coutanceau applies his modernist approach to traditional dishes and gives them new life. From the fresh seafood to the exotic fowl, he will not accept inferiority. A FR200 set menu is a gift, with feuillete of oysters, fish, cheeses and creme brulée. The service is flawless. Closed: Sun. Reservations required. Credit Cards: All Major.

Directory

To and From

By train from Paris (three hours on the TGV), Bordeaux (two hours), or Poitiers (two hours), or by car on the A-10 autoroute between Bordeaux and the north to Niort and then on the N-11.

Tourist Office

place de la Petite Sirène; ☎ *(33) 05-46-41-14-68.*

Rail Station

boulevard Maréchal Joffre; ☎ *(33) 05-46-41-50-50.*

Post Office

place de l'Hôtel de Ville, 17021 La Rochelle; ☎ *(33) 05-46-30-41-30.*

Cognac

If you don't like cognac, there's little reason to come to this city, which is basically a small, sleepy wine-producing town that you have to make a special trip to reach. If you appreciate the heavenly golden nectar, though, this is indeed Nirvana.

Cognac (the drink) is based on the exceedingly average white wine that is produced in the region, an extremely large appellation that reaches from the Ile de Ré to Angoulême. Cognac was invented quite by chance, about 400 years ago, when one of the local wine makers experimented with distilling his wine for a second time. He discovered that the result was a smooth, much stronger liquor, that quickly became popular across 17th-century Europe. The first major distillery was the Otard house, set in a 16th-century château where the future King François I was born. It was the property of a Scotsman, Otard; several other distilleries were originally owned by Scots, including Hennessy and Martell.

What makes cognac different from other brandies, including Armagnac, besides the usual appellation factors such as soil, sun and grape, is the double-distillation process. The first distillation of the rather inferior wine, done in huge copper stills, yields a syrup containing about 30 percent alcohol. The second reduces it further to a stronger, thinner liquid, called *eau de vie*, which contains about 70 percent alcohol. Various different productions from the different vintages of the region include Grand Champagne, Petite Champagne (the distillers get to use the name because the soil is the same chalky stuff as in Champagne), Borderies, Fins Bois, Bons Bois, and Bois Ordinaires. The liquor is then stored in oak barrels for at least three years; some *eaux de vie* still in the *chais* (storehouses) date from the early 19th century. The tannins in the oak give the liquid its golden color. As much as three percent of the liquor evaporates during aging, this evaporation is known as *le part des anges* (the angels' share). The heady clouds of liquor fumes promote the growth of a black fungus on the casks and even the outside of the storehouses. The cellar master's expertise now comes into play, as he tastes (at the Hennessy distillery, for example) several thousand batches of *eau de vie* each year, ordering it to be moved into different barrels to fine-tune the taste and, ultimately, ordering the blending of the different nectars to make the cognac itself. There are five designations of Cognac; VS (Very Special), VSOP (Very Special Old Pale), Napoléon, XO and Paradis. Even a fairly ordinary VSOP will have more than 40 different *eaux de vie* blended together, including several selections that are more than 20 years old.

Cognac production is hugely important in the region—the distilleries, vineyards, bottle-makers and cask-makers employ most of the area's population. Over 95 percent of production is exported—cognac accounts for more foreign currency revenue than the entire automobile industry in France.

Besides the museum honoring the liquor, you'll want to visit a distillery or two. Besides Otard, for its historical value, I recommend Hennessy (which includes a boat ride across the river to get to the storehouse) and Rémy Martin (which has a miniature train ride through the vineyards) for unabashedly chauvinistic reasons—these are the only two houses left in French hands, the others having been bought out by British, Canadian and Japanese conglomerates. That's right, even Courvoisier. You can visit the distilleries of Camus, Courvoisier, Hennessy, Martell, Otard, Prince Hubert de Polignac, Rémy Martin and Renault-Bisquit. Each is a little different, all offer tasting and some give you a free nip bottle.

On your way to or from Cognac, stop in the ancient town of Saintes, near the autoroute. It's just another medieval town with cathedral, ramparts and museums, until you discover the first-century Roman amphitheater and triumphal archway, the latter rising in perfect condition in the middle of a park in the center of town.

What to Do

Museums and Exhibits

Musée du Cognac ★★

48 boulevard Denfert Rochereau, ☎ 05-45-32-07-25.
Closed: Tue.

Tracing the history of cognac, both the industry and the town, this museum includes exhibits, artifacts, art and sculpture. Since cognac is also the birthplace of the postcard, part of the museum displays old postcards and gives a bit of the history involved. *Open June–Sept., Wed.–Mon., 10 a.m.–noon and 2–6 p.m.; Oct.–May, Wed.–Mon., 2–5:30 p.m. only.* Admission: FR12.

Special Tours/Excursions

Distillerie d'Otard ★★★

127 boulevard, ☎ 05-45-82-40-00. At the Chateau de Cognac.
Hours open: 9:30 p.m.–5 p.m. Special hours: Closed from noon–2 p.m.

Housed in a medieval chateau that was the birthplace of Francois I, the Otard Distillery tour offers the most atmospheric tour. The presentation is conducted with a minimum of hard sell. Mini-bottles (like the kind you get in airplanes) are sold for FR15 each. **Hennessey**, *1 rue de la Richonne (☎ 05-45-35-72-72*, open weekdays 9 a.m.–5:30 p.m., free) offers a little boat ride across the Charente River to where their oak barrels are made; you'll also get a brief idea of the process of changing rotgut to nectar. Martell's tour offers free mini-bottles *(rue de Gate-Bourse, ☎ 05-45-36-33-33*, open weekdays, 9 a.m.–5 p.m.). **Remy-Martin's** distillery is out of the city center (about 5 km away), at **Domaine de Merpins**, *route de Pons, D732, ☎ 05-45-35-76-66*, and costs FR15, but it is the most comprehensive, with a blow-by-blow account of the whole process, also including a train ride and vineyard tour. Call to reserve. Note: All distilleries have different off-season hours, so call to confirm tour times. Admission: free.

Saintes

Historical/Architectural Sites

Arc de Germanicus ★★★

rue de l'Arc de Triomphe. On the east bank.

This Roman arch sits at what was formerly the entrance to the only bridge that crossed the lower Charente. Built in the first century, it stood with the bridge until 1843, when the bridge was destroyed. Originally on the West Bank, it avoided destruction by being dismantled and reassembled on the East Bank.

Cathedrale St.-Pierre ★★

Old town. In the old town district.

The dome above the south transept of the cathedral is all that remains from the former Romanesque church that used to occupy these grounds. Mostly constructed in the 15th century, the nave, aisles and organ date from the 16th century. Note the shallow dome of the tower and the Flamboyant Gothic main door. Although a bit incongruous in places, it remains a lovely piece of architecture amid the red-tiled roofs of the old town.

Roman Amphitheater ★★

West of town center. On the left bank.

Just a short walk west of town center, the Roman amphitheater has grown in beautifully with grass covering the steps. Built in the first century, it is distinguished as one of the oldest of the Roman world. Be sure to see the small fountain on the southern slope, dedicated to St.-Eustell, who was beheaded here.

Where to Stay

Hotels and Resorts

Le Valois FR360–FR520 ★★★

35 rue 14-Juillet. ☎ 528-1234, 05-45-82-76-00, FAX: 05-45-82-76-00. Near the post office.
Single: FR360. Double: FR520.

Noteworthy for anything but charm, Le Valois is a rigid, modern hotel. Through the doors of the beige facade, the interior manages to remain quiet despite the passing traffic outside. The 45 air-conditioned rooms contain TV, telephone, minibar and bath, all behind soundproof windows. Breakfast is the only meal served, but drinks flow all day in the bar. Other modest facilities include a sauna and a solarium. A very well-looked-after hotel. Features: air conditioning in rooms, sauna, in-room minibars. Credit Cards: All Major.

Inns

Hostellerie Les Pigeons Blancs FR280–FR450 ★★★

110 rue Jules-Brisson. ☎ 05-45-82-01-26, FAX: 05-45-82-20-33. About 1.5 km northwest of town center.
Double: FR280–FR450.

Named for the white pigeons that nest in the stone walls, this moss-covered inn used to function as a coaching inn in the 17th century. Family owned and managed, there are now seven rooms, each uniquely charming. All of the comfortable bedrooms are equipped with TV, telephone and bath. The restaurant, though, is the major attraction here, with delicious regional fare. Features: fitness center. Credit Cards: All Major.

Where to Eat

L'Echassier $$ ★★★★

72 rue de Bellevue, About 2km south on the route de St.-Brice. ☎ 05-45-32-29-04.
Chef Bernard Lambert has managed to attain an elegant yet personable atmosphere at L'Echassier. Formerly a student under the Troisgros chefs, he has developed into one of the leading chefs in the region. Guaranteed a greeting with a smile, the staff manages to be cordial and friendly while providing quick, attentive service. Some special dishes include snail ravioli, pigeon and various shellfish. Fixed-price menus start at FR140. Closed: Sun. Amenities: outside dining, reservations recommended. Credit Cards: All Major.

La Braserade　　　　　　　　　　　**$**　　　　　　　　　★★

23 rue du Pont Faume, Next to Les Halles. ☎ *05-45-82-00-45.*

Hearty fare includes meat and potatoes, steak and various meats and cheeses. From FR60 and up, the filling meals are a bargain. Another bargain is **Le Chantilly**, *146 avenue Victor Hugo.* Jammed with locals, the dishes vary but FR60 will usually get you meat, vegetables, cheese, fruit and, of course, wine. *Open noon–2 p.m. and 7–9 p.m., Mon.–Fri.; noon–2 p.m., Sat. Closed: Mon.*

Les Pigeons Blancs　　　　　　　　**$$**　　　　　　　★★★

110 rue Jules-Brisson, Less than 2kmm northwest of town center. ☎ *05-45-82-16-36. Dinner: 7–10 p.m., entrées FR150–FR300.*

In the hotel of the same name, this former post house has been in the same family since the 17th century. The family-run dining room guarantees a friendly reception and personal attention. The menu changes with the seasons and availability of ingredients, but the rack of pig and the lobster in wine are two specialties to look for. Fixed-price menus are FR125–FR300. Reservations recommended. Credit Cards: All Major.

Directory

To and From

By slow train from Angoulême (one hour) or Saintes on the main line (20 minutes) or by car on the N-141 between Saintes and Angoulême.

Tourist Office

16 rue du 14 Juillet; ☎ *(33) 05-45-82-10-71.*

Rail Station

place de la Gàre; ☎ *(33) 05-45-82-03-29.*

Post Office

2 place Bayard, 16100 Cognac; ☎ *(33) 05-45-82-08-99.*

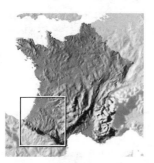

AQUITAINE AND THE SOUTHWEST

St. Emillion vineyards

What Makes Aquitaine and the Southwest So French?

1. *A trove of Stone Age relics—weapons, skeletons, cave paintings and such—provide evidence of mankind's earliest marks on this planet.*

2. *Aquitaine pâtés will make even the most diehard vegetarians drop to the ground and beg for engorged goose liver. Toss in those killer truffles or opt for some sheep-intestine stew.*

What Makes Aquitaine and the Southwest So French?

3. *Bordeaux—France's largest wine producing region—a district that even heaven is jealous of.*

4. *Lourdes—where St. Bernadette's beatific vision can be viewed beneath artificial lights and Plexiglas. Dying believers and other pilgrims flock to drink the waters, throw themselves on the shrine, or buy up unique souvenirs such as plastic Virgin Mary water bottles with pop-off heads.*

Relatively untrodden by foreign tourists (in comparison to the Loire region to the north and the Mediterranean coast to the west), the sweeping southwest of the country, encompassing Aquitaine and Midi-Pyrénées, is rich in history, culture, good weather and—of course—wine. Make your base the charming city of Toulouse, from which you can reach the Bordeaux vineyards, the Basque country around Biarritz, the Pyrénées or the eastern Mediterranean coast with equal ease. Wine lovers may choose to spend most of their time in Bordeaux; surfers may do as world-champion Kelly Slater has and visit the Atlantic beaches of the Gulf of Gascony; hikers and climbers may want something closer to the mountains of France's "most satisfying frontier." Or you may want to spend a couple of days in each corner of the region. From the 20,000-year-old cave paintings of the Dordogne to the tiny principality of Andorra, there's plenty to captivate you in this part of France.

History

This region exhibits some of the earliest traces of mankind to be found anywhere on the globe. Evidence of human settlement has been discovered in Les Eyzies-de-Tayac, dating back to 150,000 years ago. Pockmarked by natural caverns created when the rivers of the Massif Central wound their way through soft limestone plateaus towards the sea, the area provided a good natural habitat as paleolithic man began to build semi-permanent communities. Enormous quantities of Stone Age relics—tools and weapons, as well as skeletons and the world-famous cave paintings—have been found in the region.

Later history saw temporary unification of the region, along with much of Gaul, under Roman rule. Numerous Roman ruins remain, from amphitheaters that are still used today to the ruined foundations of villas and houses. After the collapse of the Roman Empire, the region began to fragment. The Basques, who had never accepted Roman rule much as they still refuse to accept centralized French or Spanish rule today, forged their own identity, as well as the Basque language. The Basque language is unique in Europe in that it is not descended from the Indo-European roots shared by other Eu-

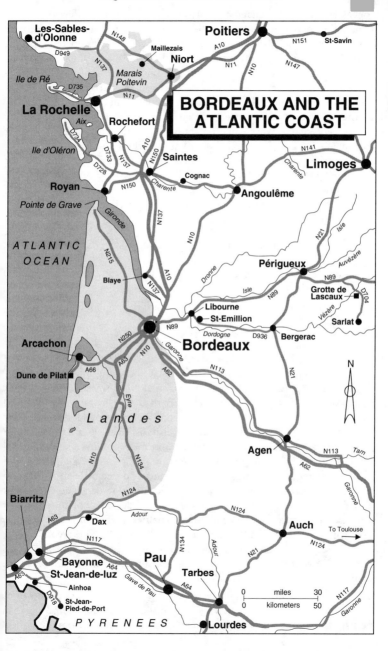

ropean languages. Language, too, played a major role in the development of Languedoc, of which Toulouse is the capital. The name of the region comes from Langue-d'oc (the language of "oc"), used to differentiate its people from the Langue-d'oïl spoken in northern France. Known as *Occitania*, this part of the country was independent both from France and from the Catholic church, having embraced an Asian version of Christianity called Catharism. The region was brought brutally into check in the mid-13th century by the forces of the King of France, an action endorsed enthusiastically by Pope Innocent III. Meanwhile on the west coast, Aquitaine held a major role in an even grander struggle, that between the English and the French. Eleanor of Aquitaine, who commanded an area that, at the time, reached from the Pyrénées to the Loire Valley, divorced Louis VII of France in 1152. Two months later, she married Henry Plantagenet of Anjou. When Henry II assumed the English throne, the entire region passed into the hands of the English crown, and the stage was set for the Hundred Years' War. Most of the region was returned to the French a century later, but Bordeaux and surrounding areas remained under English control for 300 years. During this period, numerous castles and fortified cities were built along the tense border, demarcated by the Dordogne river. It was not until the 15th century that the English were driven out. By that time, of course, their legendary taste for what they called "claret," the wines of the region, had transformed Bordeaux into the wine capital of the world.

Cuisine

The pâtés of Aquitaine are legendary. The best are *foie gras* made from the livers of ducks *(canard)* or goose *(oie)* that have been engorged by the force-feeding of corn. Rich and creamy pâté is made by farmers at their homes, where you can buy it a good deal cheaper than at restaurants. Truffles and cantarelle and cèpe mushrooms come from this region and also find their way into the pâtés. Meat, fowl and even fish dishes are invariably served in wine sauce around Bordeaux—*à la Bordelaise* means simply a sauce consisting primarily of wine and onions. Prunes are produced in Agen, and a specialty of the region is rabbit served with prunes and steamed carrots. Or you might try *cassoulet*, a stew based on white beans and sausage and containing either duck, pork or lamb. In the Basque region, dishes are often served *à la basquaise*, in a sauce heavy on garlic and tomatoes. In Toulouse and Languedoc, tripe, a stew made of sheep intestines, may not be to everyone's taste, but the sea snails stuffed with bacon, known as *cargolades*, are not to be missed. For your sweet tooth, try the *touron*, a flavored marzipan loaf made of almonds, pistachios, hazelnuts and fruit.

The wines of Bordeaux outshine the rest of this region, if not the world. There are numerous appellations, of which the *Médoc* and *Haut-Médoc* are perhaps the most venerated. Red wines are made primarily from the Caber-

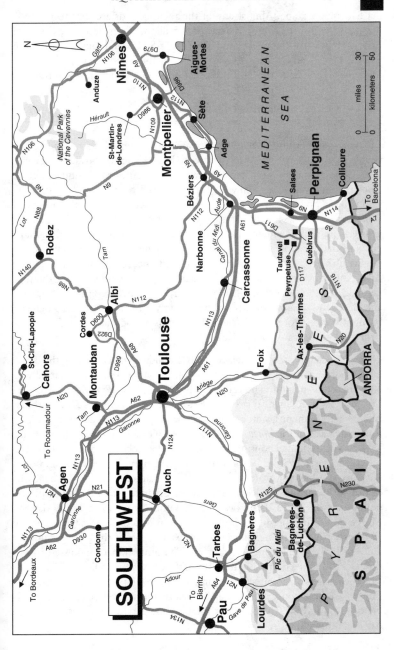

net Sauvignon grape. Almost any of the regional reds are sure to please—Margaux, St. Julien, Listrac, Lussac-St. Emillion, Côtes de Blaye, Côtes de Bourg, Bordeaux Supérieur and Graves-du-Sud stand out. Among the whites, Graves and Entre-Deux-Mers (from the region between the two main rivers) and Sauternes, Montbazillac and Loupiac are all worth trying.

Bordeaux

Once a quiet fishing port town surrounded by some better-than-average vineyards, Bordeaux has grown to become France's largest producer of wine, second-oldest trading port and fifth-largest city. After the conquest by the Romans, who were experts in viticulture, the port, then called *Bordiglia*, developed as a point of shipment for wine. However, when the English ruled Bordeaux, from 1154 to 1453, the town's fortunes really took off. The wine growers and shipping merchants reveled in their position as semi-official suppliers of the drink of Bacchus to the English (the English were, after all, at war with the rest of the country), and the city became immensely wealthy. After Aquitaine reverted to French control, there was no stopping the juggernaut. Wine exports to England and the rest of Europe continued to grow, and Bordeaux' role in the slave trade, along with Nantes and La Rochelle, brought it even more riches. It was during this period that the major reconstruction of Bordeaux took place.

The 18th century saw great classical-style buildings erected along the banks of the Garonne river, partially to show off the city's wealth and partially to hide the slums behind. The centerpiece is the massive *Esplanade des Quinconces*, a vast, tree-lined square adjacent to the *Quai Louis XVIII* that today is filled with fountains, statues, benches, pétanque courts, cafés and strolling tourists. Nearby is the *Place de la Bourse*, a smaller square flanked by two majestic classic buildings housing, on one side, the stock exchange, and on the other, the customs house. Bordeaux today is grimy and crowded and does not have the bustling waterfront traffic that marked its heyday. The 18th-century center is surrounded by a sprawling urban nightmare, along with the pollution, crime and all that goes with it. Within the city, you should visit the Musée de l'Aquitaine, which will give you an idea of how magnificent the city was during its prime, as well as an explanation of the strategic importance of the region throughout history. The other not-to-be-missed attraction is the Grand Théâtre, built by the architect Victor Louis in 1773-1780. The theater was an architectural example for the Grand Opera in Paris. Getting a ticket to a concert or play at Bordeaux' theater will be either impossible or prohibitively expensive, but the building is open to tours during the day on Saturdays.

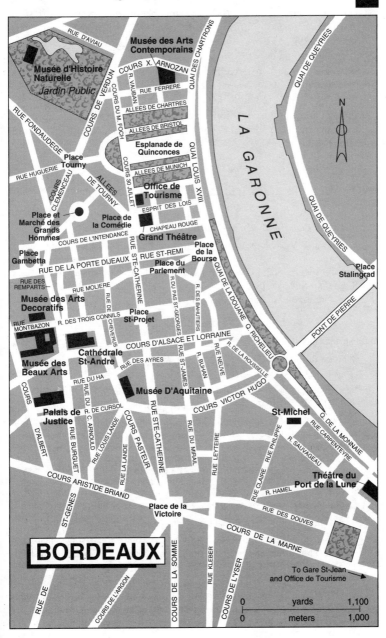

To educate yourself about Bordeaux wine, begin your research at the **Maison du Vin**, *1 cours du 30 Juillet;* ☎ *(33) 05-56-00-22-66*, a regional wine promotion house. You can taste some wines and ask questions of the staff whose job it is to encourage, not discourage you. Also offered are a 15-minute video presenting an introduction to Bordeaux wines, as well as courses (in French only) that give an overview of what it takes to be a connoisseur. You will be able to get advice on which of the hundreds of area châteaux to visit, as well as help making reservations to do so. The tourist office can also book guided-visits to the châteaux, making it relatively hassle-free for you to see some of the major producers.

What to Do

Historical/Architectural Sites

Grande Theatre ★★★

place de la Comedie, ☎ *05-56-44-28-41.*

The spectacular facade of this 18th-century building protects a jewel-box interior. Architect Victor Louis' creation inspired Charles Garnier to build the Paris Opera in a similar style in 1862. *Tours of the auditorium (FR25) are conducted by the tourist office July–Sept., at 10:30 a.m., 3 p.m. and 4:30 p.m., daily, except Mon., Sat. and Sun. Other months, Sat. only, at 3 and 4 p.m.*

Museums and Exhibits

Musée d'Aquitaine ★★★★

20 cours Pasteur, ☎ *05-56-01-51-00.*

Hours open: 10 a.m.–6 p.m. Closed: Mon.

A fantastic museum detailing the history of the region from prehistoric times through modern day. It contains reproductions of the Lascaux cave paintings, the 2nd-century B.C. Tayac treasure, 4000 Roman coins and a well-preserved statue of Venus. One of the best regional museums in France. Free admission on Wed. Admission: FR18.

Special Tours/Excursions

Maison du Vin ★★★

1 cours du 30 Juliet, ☎ *05-56-00-22-66.*

Hours open: 8:30 am–6 pm Special hours: Sat., 9 a.m.–5 p.m.

A wonderful wine resource, the Maison du Vin offers free tastings, maps and detailed information on wine tours of the surrounding regions, including the hard-to-get-into Château Mouton-Rothschild in Pauillac. Neophytes will also learn the do's and don'ts of tasting etiquette. Ask for the English version of the handy booklet, *Petit Guide des Vins.* Only open May–Oct. Another good resource is the tourist office, *12 cours du 30 Juillet (*☎ *56-00-66-00),* or **International Wine Tours**, *12 place de la Bourse (*☎ *56-90-91-28).*

Where to Stay

Hotels and Resorts

Claret   **FR495–FR600**   ★ ★

18 parvis des Chartrons. ☎ *05-56-01-79-79. Located near place Lainer at quai Louis SVIII; between rue Ferrere and Alle de Chartres.*
Single: FR495–FR550. Double: FR550–FR600.
What this newer, ultracontemporary hotel lacks in the way of charm, it makes up for in location, as it's right in the heart of the Cite Mondiale du Vin. It's a great choice for wine-loving visitors to Bordeaux. All of its 97 rooms have large private bath, comfortable beds and cable TV. Its business services are exceptionally good. Excellent breakfast buffets are served on the terrace overlooking the Cité and the ancient rooftops of Chartrons beyond. The traditional restaurant/bar is overpriced, but the sensational wine list is one of Bordeaux's best. Features: air conditioning in rooms. Credit Cards: All Major.

Grand Hotel Francais   **FR340–FR610**   ★ ★

12 rue du Temple. ☎ *05-56-48-10-35, FAX: 05-56-81-76-1. Located at cours de l'Intendance between rue Vital Charles and rue Grassi.*
Single: FR340–FR370. Double: FR370–FR610.
This renovated 18th-century five-story mansion with wrought-iron balconies has been upgraded, and it's now one of the best moderately priced hotels in Bordeaux. Accommodations include 35 soundproofed, spacious rooms with private bath, contemporary decor and amenities. Just breakfast is served. It is within walking distance of all of the city's major sights and shopping areas. Features: wheelchair-access rooms, air conditioning in rooms, balcony or patio, in-room minibars. Credit Cards: All Major.

Le Bayonne   **FR350–FR610**   ★

4 rue de Martignac. ☎ *05-56-48-00-88, FAX: 05-56-52-03-79. Located at cours de l'Intendance. It's between the Grand Theatre and Notre Dame.*
Single: FR350–FR460. Double: FR460–FR610.
In a restored 18th-century building the Bayonne is surprisingly one of the most up-to-date hotels in Bordeaux. The atmosphere of the 1930s has been retained in the decor, though many amenities have been added. Accommodations include 36 soundproof rooms with comfortable furnishings and color coordinated decor. There is no restaurant, but several good ones are nearby. Features: wheelchair-access rooms, air conditioning in rooms, in-room minibars. Credit Cards: All Major.

Mercure Château Chartrons   **FR690–FR1100**   ★ ★

81 cours St.-Louis. ☎ *05-56-43-15-00, FAX: 05-56-69-15-21. Located between rue Prunier and rue Barreyere near place Tournay.* Rated Restaurant: *Novamagus.*
Single: FR690–FR900. Double: FR900–FR1100.
Composed of several converted 19th-century wine warehouses, the Mecure Château Chartrons has a Victorian facade that belies its ultramodern, extremely luxurious interior. The 143 rooms and seven suites are equipped with every imaginable amenity, including high-tech bathrooms and soundproofing. A health club close by also avails its facilities to any guest of the hotel who wants to use them. On the premises are a bar, with an impressive array of local vintages sold by the glass, and a res-

taurant called Novamagus, where well-prepared regional meals begin at about FR1220 and reservations are recommended. There's also a bistro featuring simple regional dishes at moderate prices. Regularly scheduled tastings of fine Bordeaux are held in the hotel's own wine cellars. The desk will also book bus tours or arrange a car for touring the nearby châteaux. Half-board rates are FR490 (room, breakfast and a meal) per person, per day in season. Features: air conditioning in rooms, in-room minibars, fitness center. Credit Cards: All Major.

Sofitel Aquitania   FR580–FR1300   ★★

4 boulevard G. Domergue. ☎ *05-56-50-83-80, FAX: 05-56-39-73-7. Located near parc des Expositions and Palais des Congres.* Rated Restaurant: *Le Flore.*
Single: FR580–FR600. Double: FR600–FR1300.
Guests are greeted at this deluxe hotel in a marble and red-lacquered lobby with modern bronze sculptures. Its 205 rooms, all with private bath, are color-coordinated in warm tones. The lobby pub offers inexpensive meals, while the upstairs Le Flore restaurant with a terrace serves meals beginning at FR150. Also featured are conference rooms and a discotheque. Features: pool, air conditioning in rooms, nonsmoking rooms, in-room minibars. Credit Cards: All Major.

Where to Eat

Jean Ramet $$$ ★★★★

7-8 place J.-Jaures.
Specialties: pauillac lamb in season, Lampreys (eel) a la Bordelaise (Jan.–Apr. only).
Lunch: Noon–2 p.m., FR350–FR450.
Dinner: 7–10 p.m., entrées FR350–FR450.
Jean Ramet's superb but unpretentious Bordelaise cuisine is made with only the best seasonal ingredients available. The fresh fish, pigeon and lamb dishes are especially notable. The no-frills cuisine is matched by the dramatic yet clean-lined decor. Attentive service. Fixed-price FR150 lunch menu. Closed: Sun. Reservations required. Credit Cards: V, MC, A, E.

L'Alhambra $$ ★★★

111 bis, rue Judaique. ☎ *05-56-96-06-91.*
Lunch: Noon–2 p.m., FR100–FR200.
Dinner: 7–9:45 p.m., entrées FR100–FR200.

Chef Michel Demazeu's acclaimed, light, spa-type cuisine is surprisingly affordable for a restaurant with a three-star Michelin rating. Just ignore the a la carte menu and concentrate on the reasonable FR100 fixed-price lunch menu, which includes dessert. You won't be eating leftovers, and your entrée may be fresh seafood. The same deal at dinner is FR50 more. For an inexpensive meal that sticks to the ribs, try **Le Cafe Gourmand**, at *3 rue Buffon* (☎ *56-79-23-85*). The fixed-price lunches here are only FR60 and FR75. You can eat in the woodsy dining room or outside on a patio. The wines are extra, but worth trying. Closed: Sun. Amenities: own baking, reservations recommended. Credit Cards: V, MC, A.

La Chamade $$$ ★★★

20 rue des Piliers-de-Tutelle. ☎ *05-56-48-13-74.*
Lunch: 12:30–2 p.m., FR350–FR450.
Dinner: 7:30–10 p.m., entrées FR350–FR450.

Situated in a vaulted 18th-century cellar, La Chamade offers masterful cooking and an impressive collection of Bordeaux. Regional yet modern and light, the specialties include a marinated and grilled monkfish salad served with artichokes and poached duck with baby vegetables; simply prepared fish dishes are also featured. A popular FR180 fixed-price lunch menu includes cheese and dessert. Reservations required. Credit Cards: V, MC, A, E.

La Tupina $$$ ★★

6 rue de la Porte-de-la-Monnaie. ☎ *05-56-91-56-37.*
Specialties: rilletes of duck, foie gras.
Lunch: Noon–2 p.m., FR250–FR320.
Dinner: 8–11 p.m., entrées FR250–FR320.
Operated by one of Bordeaux's most talented chefs, La Tupina features regional cuisine with Southwestern origins, including plenty of duck—chef Xiradaki's specialty. The restaurant is in an 18th-century building with two cozy fireplaces, and many meals are cooked in them. There is a FR100 fixed-price lunch menu and the wine list suits every taste. Closed: Sun. Reservations recommended. Credit Cards: All Major.

Le Chapon Fin $$$ ★★★★

5 rue Montesquieu. ☎ *05-56-79-10-10.*
Specialties: crayfish ravioli with lime, veal sweetbreads with foie gras.
Lunch: Noon–2 p.m., FR450–FR510.
Dinner: 7:30–10 p.m., entrées FR450–FR510.
The leading restaurant in Bordeaux, Le Chapon Fin upholds its reputation with Catalonian-inspired cooking and a stellar wine cellar. The dining room has elegant turn of-the-century decor and lush plants; there's comfortable seating on several banquettes. Famous guests through the years have been Winston Churchill, Aristide Briand, Sarah Bernhardt and Toulouse Lautrec. A fixed-price FR150 lunch is offered. Closed: Mon., Sun. Amenities: outside dining, reservations required. Credit Cards: All Major.

Le Vieux Bordeaux $$$ ★★★

27 rue Buhan. ☎ *05-56-52-94-36.*
Lunch: Noon–2 p.m., FR300–FR420.
Dinner: 7–10 p.m., entrées FR300–FR420.
Reliable and steady, "Old Bordeaux" is practically a neighborhood institution. Recent renovations, however, include a sunny dining room looking out on a pool, where guests can enjoy such specialties as red peppers stuffed with fresh cod, a gratin of lobster with noodles, or turbot with buttery truffle sauce. Also featured are rich desserts laced with wine and vintage claret from the cellar. Closed: Sun. Amenities: outside dining, reservations required. Credit Cards: V, MC, DC, A, E.

Pavilion des Boulevards $$$ ★★★★

120 rue de la Croix-de-Seguey. ☎ *05-56-81-51-02.*
Lunch: Noon–2 p.m., FR420–FR500.
Dinner: 7–10 p.m., entrées FR420–FR500.
Chef Regis Franc excels at seafood and poultry dishes prepared with a minimum of fuss and heavy sauces. The desserts are creative and also carry on the naturalistic

theme. His wife, Nelly, is the hostess, and she presides over the two pristine dining rooms and the terrace. There's a FR200 fixed-price menu on weekdays, and the cellar has accessible prices. Closed: Sun. Amenities: outside dining, reservations required. Credit Cards: All Major.

Bouliac

Le St.-James   **$$$**   ★★★★

3 place C.-Hosteins, Seven km from Bordeaux on D10. Located at Le St.-James. ☎ *05-56-20-52-19.*
Specialties: roast Pauillac lamb, Lampreys a la Bordelaise, grilled pigeon.
Lunch: Noon–2:30 p.m., FR250–FR500.
Dinner: 7–10 p.m., entrées FR250–FR500.

Followers of Jean-Marie Amat's tasty interpretations of regional favorites flock to this small burg just outside of Bordeaux. The traditional cuisine featured at Le St.-James contrasts sharply with its utterly contemporary dining room. A FR160 (lunch) and FR220 (dinner) fixed-price menu is offered. Next door is a little bistro, appropriately called Le Bistroy, with off-putting, stark decor. A la carte only; FR150–FR200. Amenities: outside dining, own baking, reservations required. Credit Cards: All Major.

Eugenie-les-Bains

Les Pres D'Eugenie   **$$$**   ★★★★★

Eugenie-le-Bains. ☎ *05-58-05-06-07.*
Lunch: 12:30–2 p.m., FR500–FR600.
Dinner: 7:30–10 p.m., entrées FR500–FR600.

Within Michel Guerard's historic 19th-century spa-hotel is this restaurant offering a choice of cuisine minceur (sans heavy cream, accentuating natural flavors) or a slightly richer regional menu. Desserts on the latter are especially toothsome. Guerard owns two other establishments, **Maison Rose** and **Le Ferme aux Grives**. In the former, a smaller annex to the hotel, housing rooms and apartments, is a restaurant mainly used by guests. Le Ferme aux Grives is a satellite restaurant situated in a whimsically restored farmhouse. Delectable country cooking and a FR160 fixed-price three-course menu are featured, and there's also a cafe attached. Closed: Wed. Amenities: happening bar, outside dining, own baking, reservations required. Credit Cards: V, MC, A, E.

Directory

To and From

By train from Paris (three hours 15 minutes by TGV or overnight on the slow train), Nantes (four hours), or Toulouse (two-and-a-half hours), by plane on Air Inter Europe from any other major French city, or by car on the A-10 or N-10 road from the north or the A-62 or N-113 from the southeast.

Tourist Office

12 cours du 30 Juillet; ☎ *(33) 05-56-00-66-00.*

Rail Station

rue Charles Domerq; ☎ *(33) 05-56-92-50-50.*

Post Office

52 rue Georges Bonnac, 33000 Bordeaux; ☎ *(33) 05-56-48-87-48.*

Périgueux

Vielle Ville in Périgueux is lined with classic houses that exude quaint charm.

Now a rather quiet market town and regional administrative center that is often rushed through to get to the caves nearby, Périgueux relies heavily on its past to attract visitors. From the first to the third century the city was an important Roman capital, known as *Vesunna*. In the region of town called **La Cité**, you can see the few remaining vestiges of that period, including traces of an arena and a temple. La Cité remained the main hub through most of the 18th century, and the **Vielle Ville** is studded with classical-style houses and administrative buildings that sprung up when Périgueux became a Préfecture seat. The town then expanded, and today you can walk up the hill to the cathedral, which formerly stood apart, through busy streets crowded with fruit stalls and shops offering local gastronomic specialties including truffles and pâtés.

The cathedral in Périgueux is the largest in southwestern France, completely out of proportion to the size and importance of the city. A church has stood at the site of the Cathédral de St. Front since at least the sixth century, and the first cathedral was built in the 12th century. In the 19th century, massive renovation was undertaken by the architect Abadie, who also built the **Sacré Coeur** in Paris, and the result is a monolithic monster crafted of dazzling white stone. Combining Byzantine, Romanesque and Gothic styles into the essentially modern building, Abadie added 10 spires, five domes and turrets to the exterior of the building, while the inside is dominated by a huge Baroque altarpiece honoring the Virgin's Assumption. The other major site of interest in Périgueux is the **Musée du Perigord**. The museum houses an extensive collection of prehistoric artifacts, making it a good primer for a trip to the caves. There are burial remnants dating back 15,000 years, an extensive collection of Roman and Gallo-Roman mosaics, and other treasures from the days of Vessuna, as well as interpretive exhibits on the cave paintings.

What to Do

Historical/Architectural Sites

Cathedrale St.-Front ★★★

place de la Clautre, ☎ *05-53-53-23-62. In the medieval quarter.*

Hours open: 8:30 a.m.–7:30 p.m. Special hours: Closed noon–2:30 p.m.; open to dusk in winter.

Constructed to resemble a Greek cross, it was built from 1125–1150. The facade impresses with its 10 spires and five domes, while the interior exudes a feeling of emptiness. Admission to the 9th-century crypt and cloisters is FR15.

Museums and Exhibits

Musée du Perigord ★★★★

Cours Tournay, ☎ *05-53-53-16-42.*

Hours open: 10 a.m.–5 p.m. Special hours: Closed noon–2 p.m.; Apr.–Sept., to 6 p.m. Closed: Tue.

Easily one of France's most important museums, the Musée du Perigord houses an intriguing collection of artifacts from around the world dating back to prehistoric times. From mummies to Flemish paintings, the entire exhibit is informative and captivating. English reading guides are available. Admission: FR12.

Where to Stay

Hotels and Resorts

Hotel Bristol **FR255–FR335** ★★

37 rue Antoine-Gadaud. ☎ *05-53-08-75-90, FAX: 05-53-07-00-49. About 500 meters from the train station.*

Single: FR255–FR305. Double: FR285–FR335.

Four stories of modern hotel in the heart of the town. There are just 29 air-conditioned rooms, all clean and with TV, telephone and bath. A small bar and lounge is on the first floor. Breakfast costs FR35, but parking is free. Take advantage of the great location and explore the local restaurants and sights. Features: wheelchair-access rooms, air conditioning in rooms. Credit Cards: All Major.

Inns

Château des Reynats **FR450–FR800** ★★★★

In Chancelade. ☎ *05-53-03-53-59, FAX: 05-53-03-44-84. About 5 km northwest of Perigueux on D939.*

Single: FR450. Double: FR800.

Surrounded by a large park, this 19th-century château is a relaxing retreat in which every traveler to this region should indulge. The 37 rooms are supremely comfortable and amply spacious. All of the pampering amenities are here. On the property are tennis facilities and a pool, with golf nearby. Classic regional cuisine is prepared by a skilled kitchen staff for the stately dining room. Treat yourself to this heavenly pleasure. Features: wheelchair-access rooms, pool, golf, tennis. Credit Cards: All Major.

Where to Eat

L'Amandier   **$**   ★★

12 rue Eguillerie, Off place St.-Louis. ☎ *05-53-04-15-51.*

Fresh local cuisine at very reasonable prices. Lunch guests can order a FR50 set menu, and dinner guests can order a FR72 menu with soup, entrée and dessert. Another inexpensive choice is **Chez Pierrot** at *78 rue Chanzy (*☎ *05-53-53-43-22).* FR50 will turn into soup, entrée, dessert, fruit and wine in this very casual restaurant. Finally, there is **Le Fromage a Malices** at *3 rue Port de Graule (*☎ *05-53-04-47-44; near avenue Daumesnil).* Cheese is the specialty, with vegetables, meat and wine on the side. Set menus start at FR70.

L'Oison   **$$**   ★★★★

31 rue St.-Front ☎ *05-53-09-84-02.*
Dinner: 8–10 p.m., entrées FR125–FR250.

This restaurant first opened in this converted warehouse in 1982, and the locals have been faithful to it ever since. The respected chef, Regis Chiorozas, makes the most possible out of his fresh ingredients. His appetizers are some of the best in France, and the entrées are nearly flawless in preparation, cooking and presentation. A good yet affordable wine list. Set menus from FR135. Closed mid-Feb.–mid-Mar. and late June–early July. Closed: Mon. Reservations required. Credit Cards: All Major.

La Flambée   **$$**   ★★★

2 rue Montaigne ☎ *05-53-53-23-06.*
Dinner: 6–10 p.m., entrées FR100–FR150.

This family-run restaurant has been serving delicious food for many years in this 250-year-old building. Foie gras is the key dish here, prepared several different ways, and the lobster is picked from the restaurant aquarium. Always cordial and intensely knowledgeable, the staff knows how to serve. Fixed-price menus are FR130. Closed: Sun. Reservations recommended. Credit Cards: V, MC.

Directory

To and From

By train from Bordeaux (two-and-a-half hours) or Paris (via Limoges, seven hours) or by car on the N-89 road from Bordeaux.

Tourist Office

26 place Francheville; ☎ *(33) 05-53-53-10-63.*

Rail Station

rue Denis Papin; ☎ *(33) 05-53-09-50-50.*

Post Office

1 rue de 4 de Septembre, 24000 Périgueux; ☎ *(33) 05-53-53-60-82.*

Les Eyzies-de-Tayac

The sleepy village of Les Eyzies-de-Tayac was catapulted into world fame in 1940, when two boys searching for their lost dog, Robot, discovered the prehistoric cave paintings at Lascaux. Nowadays, the village is the center of the most impressive and extensive concentration of cave art in the world. Four major sites and a whole host of smaller caves surround the village, and it is the best place to base yourself for a look at prehistoric art. Start your visit at the **Musée Nationale du Prehistoire**, which is housed in a 16th-century castle overlooking the village. The museum is an essential stop before going on to the caves. Your tour of the exhibits of the bones, weapons, tools, carvings and drawings may provide you with your best glimpse of the treasures the caves conceal. Many caves have restricted access, and Lascaux, the main and most famous site, has been closed to the public since 1963.

Ever since their discovery, the caves have been a magnet to visitors, but the effect of thousands of breathing, sweaty bodies has upset the formerly sealed cave environment—increased moisture fosters the growth of microbes that damage the paint pigments. To preserve the fragile artworks, access to the primary cave site is limited to between 50 and 350 people per day. Consequently, reservations must be made weeks in advance.

The only major cave that is still open to the public is **Grotte de Font-de-Gaume**. The nearby **Grotte des Combarelles** contains etchings and carvings rather than paintings. If you can manage it, either of these sites is truly spectacular—it is a powerful experience to view artwork created more than 15,000 years ago.

If you cannot secure a reservation to visit a cave, then be sure to visit **Lascaux II**, a comprehensive reconstruction of the original cave that includes exact renditions of the paintings of bulls, bison, deer, horses and elk. Located only minutes from the Lascaux site, Lascaux II employs the tools, pigments and techniques that archaeologists believe were used in creating the original artworks. In addition to animal drawings, Lascaux contains geometric symbols and arrowlike designs that archaeologists believe were connected with ritual hunting magic.

What to Do

Historical/Architectural Sites

Cave Drawings   ★★★★

The Grotte de Font-de-Gaume is 1km away on the D47. The Grotte des Combarelles is about 2 km farther north.

The Grotte de Font-de-Gaume (*05-53-06-90-80*) contains 15,000-year-old paintings of prehistoric animals. Thanks to some youths in the 18th century, there is also a good look at some historic graffiti. Call well in advance to get tickets to enter the caves, as the number of visitors allowed is limited. Tours are available in English. *Open 9 a.m.–noon and 2–6 p.m.; Oct.–Mar., 9:30 a.m.–noon and 2–5:30 p.m. Closed Tues.* Admission FR31. The **Grotte des Combarelles** (☎ *05-53-06-90-80*) was discovered at the turn of the century. It contains more than 600 faint drawings of animals, seen by small guided tour. Again, tickets are hard to come by. *Open 9 a.m.–noon and 2–6 p.m.; Oct.–Mar., 10 a.m.–noon and 2–4 p.m. Closed Wed.* FR31.

Lascaux II   ★★★

In Lascaux, ☎ 05-53-53-44-35. In Lascaux.
A reproduction of the closed cave dwellings at Lascaux I, completely made of concrete. About 200 paintings span 130 feet of wall, depicting the drawings with great detail and respect for the originals. *Open Feb.–June and Sept.–Dec., 10 a.m.–noon and 2–5:30 p.m.; July–Aug., 9:30 a.m.–7 p.m. Closed Mon. Closed Jan.* Admission: FR45.

Museums and Exhibits

Musée National de Prehistoire   ★★★

On top of the cliffs, ☎ 05-53-06-97-03. On top of the cliffs.
Closed: Tue., Sun.
Start your tour of the city off with this museum. Located on the cliffs, it offers the best views of the city, and its collection helps prepare you for the cave paintings. Included here are weapons, tools, carvings and explanations of the caves and related history. *Open 9:30 a.m.–noon and 2–6 p.m.; Dec.–Mar., 9:30 a.m.–noon and 2–5 p.m.; closed Tues.* Admission: FR22.

Where to Stay

Hotels and Resorts

Les Glycines   **FR300–FR390**   ★★★

route de Perigueux. ☎ 05-53-06-97-07. On the D47.
Single: FR300–FR380. Double: FR340–FR390.
A four-acre garden inn that first opened its doors in 1862. Traditional decor and personal touches of the husband-wife owners make this a special little inn. The 25 rooms are comfortably furnished and have telephone and bath. Relax on the veranda with a cool drink, amid the gardens and the grape arbor. Fixed-price meals start at FR135 in the cozy restaurant. Half-board rates are FR380–FR420 per person. Features: pool. Credit Cards: All Major.

Inns

Hotel Cro-Magnon   **FR450–FR750**   ★★★

route de Perigueux. ☎ 05-53-06-97-06, FAX: 05-53-06-95-45. About 200 meters from the train station.
Double: FR450–FR750.
Secluded in a five-acre garden and enshrined in vines, this small hotel reflects old-fashioned style accented with modern comforts. The 22 inviting rooms are modestly furnished and equipped with TV, telephone and private bath. Two restaurants, one with an outdoor terrace, serve creatively prepared regional dishes and have fixed-price menus starting at FR130. Lounge around the pool, enjoy a cocktail in

the bar or explore the nearby attractions from this central base. Features: pool. Credit
Cards: All Major.

Le Centennaire   FR450–FR900   ★★★★

le Rocher de la Penne. ☎ *05-53-06-97-18, FAX: 05-53-06-92-4. On the outskirts of
town.*

Single: FR450–FR600. Double: FR600–FR900.

Known foremost for its restaurant, Le Centennaire is a two-story country inn that
has undergone major improvements to become the most charming hotel in the
area. Comfortable and well-equipped with modern conveniences such as TV, telephone, minibar and private bath, the 24 rooms are handsomely decorated. The leisure facilities include a pool, gym and sauna. The true Relais and Châteaux part of
the hotel–the restaurant–features the finest menu in the region. No self-respecting
gastronome could pass through Les Eyzies without indulging in a dinner here.
Closed Nov.–Mar. Features: wheelchair-access rooms, pool, sauna, fitness center.
Credit Cards: All Major.

Where to Eat

Cro-Magnon $$ ★★★

route de Perigueux ☎ *05-53-06-97-06.*

This small inn's dining room is worth visiting for the foie gras in terrine and the lobster with truffles. The small staff is known for their warm reception and personable
service. Set menus start at FR140. Dining on the garden terrace makes for a lovely
evening. Reservations recommended. Credit Cards: All Major.

Le Centennaire $$$ ★★★★★

Rocher de la Penne ☎ *05-53-06-97-18.*

Dinner: entrées FR250–FR350.

Roland Mazere's talent as a chef is unparalleled in this region. A wizard with modern, imaginative cuisine, his dishes explode in a symphony of tastes and light tex-
tures. Try the raw prawns in a truffle vinaigrette—an exploration in excellence.
Roland's wife makes every guest feel welcome and attends to every request in the
dining room and on the terrace. Set menus start at just FR220–FR475. Jacket
required. Reservations required. Credit Cards: V, MC, DC.

Directory

To and From

By train from Périgueux (20 minutes) or by car on the N-89 from Périgueux.

Tourist Office

place de la Mairie; ☎ *(33) 05-53-06-97-05.*

Rail Station

place de la Gàre; ☎ *(33) 05-53-06-97-22.*

Post Office

place de la Mairie, 24620 Les Eyzies-de-Tayac; ☎ *(33) 05-53-06-94-11.*

Rocamadour

The stunning cliffside village of Rocamadour, population 5000, receives 1.5 million visitors a year these days, more even than during its heyday as a pilgrim site during the Middle Ages. The little town is built into the side of a cliff in the Alzou canyon, with its main buildings and chapels clustered at the base of the rock, while a castle and ramparts guard it on top of the cliff. A long, long, winding flight of stone steps connects the two. Rocamadour was a tiny medieval village until 1166, when the perfectly preserved body of the early Christian hermit St. Amadour was unearthed near the chapel of Notre Dame. Amadour, rumor soon had it, was in fact Zacchaeus, a corrupt tax collector whom Jesus converted during his earthly ministry. Soon miracles began to happen in the village, always portended by the unmanned tolling of Notre Dame's bell. The site soon became a stop on the pilgrims' itinerary, rivaling Santiago de Compostela and Rome for importance. Pilgrims ascended the steps to the summit of the cliff on their knees, praying as they passed by the 12 Stations of the Cross on their way. Famous pilgrims of the time included Henri II and Louis XI, who made the pilgrimage twice. Today, pilgrims still mingle with the secular tourists, pausing to repeat the rosary on every stone step. Halfway up the route is a square surrounded by chapels, including the Notre Dame where St. Amadour was reburied. As at Mont St. Michel, there is one main-street in the village itself, and it is lined with tea rooms and cheesy souvenir shops.

Also at Rocamadour you'll find **La Féerie du Rail**, an amazingly intricate model village created by a local carpenter in his spare time over a 10-year period. In the adjacent hamlet of **L'Hospitalet**, which offers guests views of Rocamadour, you can tour the **Fôret des Singes**, a mini-zoo featuring only Barbary Apes, who seem to favor towns built on the side of crags—their other main public appearance is in Gibraltar.

What to Do

Historical/Architectural Sites

Chapelle Notre-Dame   ★★

    place St.-Amadour, ☎ *05-65-33-63-29. In the center of town.*
    Hours open: 9 a.m.–5 p.m.
    The site where the body of St.-Amadour was discovered, this cathedral also houses
    a statue of the Black Virgin on the altar. Although St.-Amadour's crypt is still below
    the church, the body's remains are in the Musée d'Art Sacree. Above the door leading to the cathedral is the sword that legend says belonged to Roland.

Foret des Singes   ★★

    l'Hospitalet, ☎ *05-65-33-62-72.*
    Barbary Macques, the monkeys indigenous to the Atlas mountains, will swing down
    and eat food out of your hands. A fun way to relax for a short while. *Open July and*

Aug., 10 a.m.–7 p.m.; Apr.–June and Sept., 10 a.m.–noon and 1–6 p.m.; Oct.–Nov., 10 a.m.–noon and 1–5 p.m.; Wed., Sat. and Sun. only in Nov. Child admission FR18. Admission: FR30.

Museums and Exhibits

La Feerie du Rail   ★★★

It took Robert Masseau more than 10 years to create this miniature model world. Depicting everything from a wedding to circus acts to active ski resorts, this fascinating piece of kinetic art delights adults and children alike. *Open mid-July–mid-Aug., daily, 9 a.m.–noon and 2–7 p.m.; mid-Aug.–mid-Nov. and Palm Sunday–mid-July, 10 a.m.–noon and 2–6 p.m.* Child admission FR10. Admission: FR28.

Where to Stay

Hotels and Resorts

Château de Romegouse   FR520–FR940   ★★★

N140. ☎ 05-65-33-63-07, FAX: 05-65-33-69-08. Take the N140 about 4 km southeast to Roumegouse.
Single: FR520. Double: FR790–FR940.
The isolated situation of this château surrounds the inn with 12 acres of parkland. Views of the Causse lend to the relaxing feeling of being removed from the touristy Rocamadour. There are 14 elegantly subdued rooms, equipped with TV, telephone, minibar and private bath. This Relais and Châteaux rated inn serves fixed-price menus from FR170 in its classic dining room. Breakfast is FR60. Two suites are available at FR1300 each. Features: in-room minibars, fitness center. Credit Cards: All Major.

Domaine de la Rhue   FR370–FR540   ★★★

In Rhue. ☎ 05-65-33-71-50, FAX: 05-65-33-72-48. About 6 km from town via the D673 and the N140.
Single: FR370. Double: FR540.
In a rustic environment outside of Rocamadour, this small but elegant hotel treats its guests to peaceful stays. The 12 chambers are exquisitely furnished with color-coordinated fabrics, exposed beams and stone walls. Hearty breakfasts can be taken outdoors in warm weather. Relax and stay awhile. Features: pool. Credit Cards: V, MC.

La Beau Site   FR340–FR460   ★★★

rue Roland-le-Preux. ☎ 05-65-33-63-08, FAX: 05-65-33-65-23. In the old town.
Single: FR340. Double: FR460.
Seize (even though it's a Best Western property now) the rare opportunity to spend the night in this cliff-hugging medieval-times village. Le Beau Site's traditional 15th-century charm is reflected in the exposed beams, exposed stone and huge fireplace in the reception area. The 42 rooms all have modern appointments, though. Some are air-conditioned, and include TV, telephone and private bath. Rear-terrace views of the valley are phenomenal. Family members prepare the regional cuisine in the restaurant with fixed-price menus starting at FR95. Breakfast costs FR49. Half-board rates are from FR250. Features: air conditioning in rooms. Credit Cards: All Major.

Sarlat

Hotels and Resorts

Hostellerie de Meysset   FR525–FR850

route des Eyzies. ☎ *05-53-59-08-29, FAX: 05-53-28-47-61. About 3 km north of Sarlat.*
Single: FR525. Double: FR850.
Blending in discreetly with local architectural styles, this hotel was built in 1970 in a three-acre park. Secure a room with a view of the countryside or one opening onto the private gardens. Two stories with 22 pleasant, comfortable rooms with private bath and telephone. Leisure activities are limited to strolls through the park, but the simplicity of the hotel is part of its charm. Warm weather means meals enjoyed on the outdoor terrace. Relaxed, casual atmosphere with a smiling staff. Features: country location. Credit Cards: All Major.

Hotel St.-Albert   FR230–FR310   ★★★

10 place Pasteur. ☎ *05-53-31-55-55, FAX: 05-53-59-19-99. Near the post office.*
Single: FR230. Double: FR310.
A combination of two hotels owned and managed by the same family, this establishment has a proud tradition of excellent service and welcoming accommodations. The St.-Albert was built in 1850 and served as a coaching inn. The Montaigne once had as a guest, who else, but the great French writer, Montaigne. The decor is predominantly modern with a gentle touches of traditional. St.-Albert's restaurant serves both hotels, making good use of fresh, local ingredients. Always keeping the guests happy, the owners socialize as much as possible. Credit Cards: All Major.

La Madeleine   FR325–FR400   ★★★

1 place de la Petite-Riguadie. ☎ *05-53-59-10-41, FAX: 05-53-31-03-62. In the middle of town.*
Single: FR325. Double: FR400.
La Madeleine's imposing stone building has been the symbol of touring hotels in Sarlat for many years. There are just 19 rooms, all with air conditioning, minibar, TV, telephone and bath. Traditional fixed-price dishes start at FR130 in the old-fashioned dining room. Half-board rates are FR380 to FR460. Features: air conditioning in rooms, in-room minibars. Credit Cards: All Major.

Souillac

Inns

Château de la Treyne   FR450

Lacave. ☎ *05-65-27-60-60, FAX: 05-65-27-60-70. Near the Dordogne River outside Souillac.*
Double: FR450.
A stately château that has resided on the Dordogne River since the 14th century. Although prices are steadily rising, the 14 rooms are still worth every franc. As debonair as ever, the large bed chambers, some with river views, are traditionally furnished and adorned with antiques. The firelit dining room sets a romantic scene for dinner, and the small bar beckons you for an after-dinner drink. Also part of the

hotel are a pool, tennis court and sauna. A loyal following returns to this inn, so reserve early. Features: pool, tennis, sauna. Credit Cards: V, MC.

Le Quercy FR200–FR270 ★★★

1 rue Recege. ☎ *05-65-37-83-56, FAX: 05-65-37-07-22. Near town center.*
Single: FR200. Double: FR270.

Following its complete overhaul, Le Quercy became a respectable little hotel. In a tranquil section of town, the 25 rooms are unpretentiously decorated and comfortably furnished. Request one with a private balcony overlooking the garden or the pool. The restaurant features a limited, but good, menu. Features: pool. Credit Cards: V, MC.

Where to Eat

Jehan de Valon $ ★★★

rue Roland-le-Preux, In the old town. Located at Le Beau Site. ☎ *05-65-33-63-08.*
In a medieval village nestled against the rock face, this restaurant is beautifully situated in the hotel Le Beau Site. The regional cuisine abounds with flavor and aroma. With recipes passed down through the generations of the Menot family, they have stayed true to the classic dishes while keeping the tastes alive. The family offers a warm reception to their beautiful inn. Set menus from just FR95. Reservations required. Credit Cards: All Major.

Sainte-Marie $$$ ★★★

place des Senhals, On the cliffs. ☎ *05-65-33-63-07.*
Dinner: entrées FR200–FR325.
Request a table on the terrace to absorb the views while dining on duck, foie gras and other delights. Service is generally efficient, and the atmosphere is relaxed. Set menus start at FR55–FR250. Reservations required. Credit Cards: V.

Directory

To and From

By train with great difficulty (changing at Sarlac or Brive, then St. Denis and then only arriving as far as three miles away), or by car on the N-20 from Toulouse.

Tourist Office

Hôtel de Ville; ☎ *(33) 05-65-33-62-59.*

Rail Station

Rocamadour-Padirac, three miles outside town; ☎ *(33) 05-65-33-63-05.*

Post Office

On the only street next to the tourist office, 46500 Rocamadour; ☎ *(33) 05-65-33-62-21.*

Cahors

Like so many other towns in France, Cahors rose to prominence on the basis of just one fortuitous happenstance, in this case, the election of Cahors resident Jean Duèze as Pope John XXII. Already a regional capital with its own university, the town boomed and grew into a banking center that became one of the most important in Europe. The town has always been a strategic location—the Romans fortified it, using the natural defenses of the Lot river. The 14th-century Pont Valentré, a fortified bridge that has never been captured, in spite of countless attacks and a siege of several months in 1580, made the city almost impregnable. Today, the town has a decent Romanesque cathedral, and some interesting 15th- and 16th-century houses. Cahors enjoyed a second surge of prominence when another native son, Léon Gambetta, became prime minister in the late 19th-century period of reconstruction after the Franco-Prussian war. The Romans called the wine of Cahors "black," and it is indeed a darker red than any you will see elsewhere, but quite delicious nonetheless.

From Cahors, you can make the circuit of the Célé and Lot rivers to the northwest, a pleasant trip along some beautiful gorges and canyons. You'll pass by the Grotte du Pech-Merle, a less well-known cave containing prehistoric paintings that is open to the public on a limited basis, and the Grotte Bellevue, which has no paintings but instead offers the fantastic artworks of nature in its stalagmites and stalactites. You can make the route in a day, but you'll probably want to stop overnight at Figeac, the outermost point from Cahors.

What to Do

Historical/Architectural Sites

Cathedrale St.-Etienne ★★★

place Chapou, ☎ *05-65-35-27-80.*
Hours open: 10 a.m.–6 p.m. Special hours: Closed noon–2 p.m. Closed: Mon.
The first church in France to be topped with domes, this Romanesque church was built in the 12th century and rebuilt between the late 1200s and 1500. Check out the characters on the north door and tympanum, depicting the Ascension. Also noteworthy is the cloister and the fresco-covered nave.

Pont Valentré ★★★

Lot River.
Cahors' picture-postcard bridge (built in the 14th century) is an enchanting sight, especially by moonlight. It's hard to believe this graceful structure, with seven pointed arches and crenellated parapets, defended the city from a number of attackers. Plans to build a complementary bridge are underway, as the Valentré is too narrow for vehicular traffic.

Cabrerets

Special Tours/Excursions

Grotte du Pech-Merle ★★★★

off D41 from Cabrerets, ☎ *05-65-31-27-05. From Cahors, take D653 (becomes D662) to D41*
Hours open: 9:30 a.m.–5:30 p.m. Special hours: Closed Nov. 1–Mar. 24.

This cave is the prehistoric version of Hollywood's Chinese Theatre, but with imprints of hands and feet dating back 20,000 years. Believed to have been used for religious ceremonies, the two-mile-long cave also bears wall paintings of recognizable animals and distinct carvings; saffron-hued stalactites hang from above. Found in 1922, this prehistoric cave is one of France's most important archaeological discoveries. Admission: FR42.

Where to Stay

Bed-and-Breakfast

Domaine de Labarthe　　　　　　　　FR350–FR500　　　　　★★★

Espere. ☎ *05-65-30-92-34.*
Double: FR350–FR500.

A red and brown tiled roof covers this sprawling mansion of white stone outside of Cahors. Amid trees and shrubs, there is a swimming pool and a plush lawn ideal for lounging around in good weather. Inside are three standard doubles, one of which has a TV, and one suite for three persons which has a kitchenette and telephone. The lovely park makes for a nice view from all of the well-maintained rooms. Breakfast is included in the price. Features: pool. Credit Cards: Not Accepted.

Hotels and Resorts

Château de Mercues　　　　　　　　FR665–FR1500　　　　　★★★

☎ *05-65-20-00-01, FAX: 05-65-20-05-7.*
Rated Restaurant: *Château de Mercues.*
Single: FR665–FR1100. Double: FR1100–FR1500.

Climb the curving staircase to this impressive stone château, built in the 13th century as a home to the counts of Cahors. Look no further for a castle. It's all here—corner turrets, suits of armor and natural air conditioning (open the windows). There are 25 rooms and nine suites are done in classic baronial style with exposed beams and half-timbered walls, giving a glimpse to the earlier days of the château. The most intriguing room is the "tower room," which has a ceiling that slides back to expose the shaft up the turret. Each comes with a private bath. The grounds boast two tennis courts, a pool and lovely gardens. Horseback riding facilities and a golf course are just a short drive away. Take time to visit the wine cellar under the front lawn that features their own label, and then sample a bottle in the restaurant with the duck or lamb. A classic Relais and Châteaux establishment. Features: pool, golf, tennis, horseback riding, in-room minibars. Credit Cards: All Major.

Where to Eat

Château de Mercues　　　　　　　　$$$　　　　　★★★

Mercues ☎ *05-65-20-00-01.*
Specialties: tarte with tomatoes, truffles and foie gras, chocolate-almond tarte.
Lunch: Noon–2 p.m., FR350–FR450.
Dinner: 7–10 p.m., entrées FR350–FR450.

You can't miss this imposing old castle by the Lot River, situated a few miles from Cahors. The sparkling cuisine, with plenty of sun-dried tomatoes, truffles and herbs, is prepared by Michel Dussau, who studied under the acclaimed Alain Ducasse of Le Louis XV in Monte Carlo. Many wines are from the castle's own vineyards. A fixed-price lunch is offered (except Sundays) for FR200. Amenities: outside dining, reservations required. Credit Cards: V, MC, A, E.

Le Balandre $$$ ★★★

5 avenue Charles de Freycinet ☎ 05-65-30-01-9.
Lunch: Noon–2 p.m., FR270–FR400.
Dinner: 7–9:30 p.m., entrées FR270–FR400.

The creative chef Gilles Marre has turned this period-decorated restaurant into one of the finest in Cahors. There is something to please everyone, from the classic eggs with foie gras and truffles or the locally raised lamb to the more inspired sea bass with mushrooms. No matter the choice, a selection of one of the local wines should accompany every meal. There is a fixed-price menu starting at FR220. Amenities: outside dining. Credit Cards: V, MC, A.

Marco $$$ ★★★

In Lamagdelaine, About 7 km northeast on the D653. ☎ 05-65-35-30-64.
Lunch: Noon–2 p.m., FR290–FR430.
Dinner: 7–9:30 p.m., entrées FR290–FR430.

Dining on the garden terrace when the warm weather is blessing Cahors adds to the already wonderful culinary experience presented by Marco. The parillada with lobster, monkfish, turbot, scampi and olive oil is a seafood lover's fantasy. There are also four poolside guest rooms available for rent. The fixed-price menu available weekdays and Saturday at lunch is FR125. Other set menus range from FR200–FR300. Amenities: outside dining. Credit Cards: All Major.

Laguoile

Michel Bras $$$ ★★★

Route de l'Aubrac ☎ 05-65-44-32-24.
Specialties: gargouillou of baby vegetables.
Lunch: Noon–2 p.m., FR235–FR385.
Dinner: 7–9 p.m., entrées FR235–FR385.

The town of Laguoile has been put on the map by Michel Bras, who is sort of a Gallic Euell Gibbons—a naturalist who has discovered the value of the earth's unheralded treasures, which he applies to his cooking. Whereas Gibbons would go on camping trips and gather roots, wild mushrooms and herbs and cook up semi-appetizing survival food, Bras, with his culinary skill, has turned the same techniques into an inspired enterprise. This is not a vegetarian restaurant, but meatless meals abound, including a *gargouillou* (stew) of baby vegetables, and wood mushroom tartes. You'd expect to dine in a rustic cabin, but it's situated in an ultramodern, concrete-and-glass building constructed on several levels, which is in stark contrast to the surrounding mountains. Pricey vintages share space with homemade herbal wines. Amenities: own baking. Credit Cards: MC, A, E.

Directory

To and From

By train from Paris (six hours) or Toulouse (an hour-and-a-half), or by car on the N-20 north from Toulouse.

Tourist Office

　　place Aristide Briand; ☎ *(33) 05-65-35-09-56.*

Rail Station

　　avenue Jean Jaurès; ☎ *(33) 05-65-22-50-50.*

Post Office

　　257 rue Wilson, 46000 Cahors; ☎ *(33) 05-65-35-48-96.*

Biarritz

Gambling, the beach, golf and thalassotherapy lure tourists to Biarritz.

The Basque seaside resort, Biarritz has been enveloped by the urban sprawl of Bayonne, the Basque commercial city, but if you visit the region, you'll definitely want to be in Biarritz. Once a whaling port the town became a popular seaside resort in the mid-19th century, when the Empress Eugenie, wife of Napoleon III, declared its mild winters and hot summers to her liking. Of course, everyone who was anyone in Europe followed her lead, and Biarritz the resort was born. Today it has just about everything you would want in a French beach resort. The long, golden, sandy beach still dotted with striped changing tents gives way to the rocky and waveswept Basque coast proper at its end. Pleasures include a ritzy casino, elegant tearooms, active nightlife, a golf course and something most European beaches do not have—great surfing. Biarritz is an ideal place to stop for a few days' rest and relaxation, whether you're taking in the sunrays on the beach, strolling along the seafront amid the many retirees who call it home, or walking out to the offshore Rocher de la Vierge amid a mild storm to feel crashing waves. The Empress built a summer home on a cliff above town; today the Villa Eugenie is the opulent Hôtel du Palais—you might stop in for a cup of tea to get a sense of how the other half lives.

What to Do

Beaches

Grande Plage   ★★

Grand Plage.

Known to be the best surfing beach in Europe, the Grande Plage attracts surfers from around the globe to its Professional Surfing Championship in September. Shops near the beach rent boards (about FR100 a day) and wet suits. Other good beaches are the plage Miramar, north of the Grande Plage, and a nude beach, the Pointe St.-Martin. Rocher de la Verge, southwest of the Grande Plage, is a magnificent, rugged promontory that's popular with tourists for great coastal views.

Historical/Architectural Sites

Hotel du Palais   ★★★

Grande Plage. On the Grande Plage.

While strolling along the Grande Plage, take a gander at the dominating Hotel du Palais. This palatial residence was built for the wife of Napoleon III, Empress Eugenie, who was the empress of France in the mid 1800s. Now a luxury hotel, King Edward VII stayed here in the early 1900s.

Nightlife

Casino Bellevue   ★★

place Bellevue.
Hours open: 5 p.m.–3 a.m.

Dominating Biarritz's best surfing and bathing beach, the Casino Bellevue, in an Art-Deco building, is a first-class entertainment center. You can have dinner at the excellent restaurant, quaff drinks at the piano bar and dance at its disco, La Plantation (*open 11 p.m.–4 a.m.*, admission FR70). Slots on the ground floor (FR5–FR10, casual dress), also video poker; upper floors for blackjack, roulette, baccarat and more (no jeans). Passport required for entry. Admission: FR70.

Where to Stay

Hotels and Resorts

Hotel Miramar   **FR1550–FR2700**

13 rue Louison Bobet. ☎ *05-59-41-30-00, FAX: 05-59-24-77-20. About 2 km from the train station, in the center of town.*
Double: FR1550–FR2700.

Oceanfront spa hotel with similar facilities to the Palais Hotel without as much luxury. A huge, modern facility, it's all here—indoor and outdoor pools, sauna, gym, solarium, hair salon and adjoining therapy facility. It boasts 126 air-conditioned rooms with cable TV, telephone, minibar, bath, hair dryer, robes and balcony views of the ocean. Indoor and outdoor dining are available at the two restaurants; late-night drinks at the bar. The less formal atmosphere proves to be a refreshing alternative. Features: pool, air conditioning in rooms, sauna, balcony or patio, in-room minibars, fitness center, in-room conference facilities. Credit Cards: All Major.

Melia   FR1110–FR1340   ★★★★

52 avenue de l'Imperatrice. ☎ *05-59-41-33-00, FAX: 05-59-41-33-99. Between the ocean and the golf course; about 20 minutes from the train station.*
Single: FR1110. Double: FR1340.

A dignified resort hotel dating back to the turn of the century. Surrounded by a park, the ocean and a golf course, this piece of property offers incredible views from most of the 71 rooms. All of the modern rooms have TV, telephone, minibar and bath. Nonsmoking rooms can be reserved. As the name implies, golf is a popular activity here, as are swimming and treatments at the nearby thalassotherapy institute. The restaurant's menu is highlighted by seafood, and the bar serves several specialty drinks. Breakfast is available for FR110. Features: wheelchair-access rooms, pool, golf, nonsmoking rooms, in-room minibars. Credit Cards: All Major.

Palais   FR1400–FR2650   ★★★★★

1 avenue ImpÈratrice. ☎ *05-59-41-64-00, FAX: 05-59-41-67-99.*
Rated Restaurant: *Le Grand Siecle.*
Single: FR1400–FR1950. Double: FR1800–FR2650.

Originally built in 1854 for the wife of Napoleon III, this oceanfront resort has attracted a crowd of international players accustomed to nothing but the best. A true palace in every respect, this grand hotel reflects strong Napoleonic influence with high ceilings and chandeliers, and the art nouveau decor complements the marble columns and staircases. The 128 elegant guest rooms have been luxurious enough to host such royal figures as Edward VII of England, Alfonso XIII of Spain and the Duke of Windsor. Each of the spacious, period-furnished rooms comes with cable TV, telephone, radio, minibar, refrigerator, spacious bath, hair dryer and robes. Request a room facing west to capture a sunset view over the ocean. Recreational facilities include a seawater swimming pool on the terrace, a sauna, a gym and a putting green. In addition to room service, dining and drinking options include three restaurants serving regional and international cuisine and an American-style bar. A truly deluxe hotel that every traveler to the Bordeaux region should take time to enjoy. Features: beach location, pool, air conditioning in rooms, in-room minibars, fitness center. Credit Cards: All Major.

Plaza Hotel   FR300–FR700   ★★

avenue Edouard VII. ☎ *05-59-24-74-00, FAX: 05-59-22-22-01. About 3 km from the train station, near the casino.*
Single: FR300–FR600. Double: FR320–FR700.

A traditional hotel, the Plaza's greatest asset is its convenient location to the casino. Built in 1928, the stained-glass windows and wrought-iron accents reflect its art deco style. The 60 soundproof rooms have TV, telephone, radio and private bath. Meals are served in the dining room and in the tavern. Breakfast costs FR49. Features: wheelchair-access rooms, in-room minibars. Credit Cards: All Major.

Inns

Château de Brindos   FR1000–FR1400   ★★★★

route de l'Aviation. ☎ *05-59-23-17-68, FAX: 05-59-23-48-47. About 2 km from town.*
Double: FR1000–FR1400.

Earning its four stars for atmosphere and attitude, the Château de Brindos sits lakeside in its own private park. There are 12 rooms here, each with TV, telephone and private bath. Guests linger in the firelit lounge, and later adjourn to the superbly romantic dining room for the excellent regional cuisine. Days are spent strolling around the lake, swimming in the pool or playing tennis. A brilliant example of a Relais and Châteaux hotel. Features: pool, tennis. Credit Cards: All Major.

Where to Eat

Cafe de Paris $$$ ★

5 place Bellevue, across from the Casino. Located at Cafe de Paris. ☎ *05-59-24-19-53.*
Lunch: Noon–2:30 p.m., FR400–FR600.
Dinner: 7–10:30 p.m., entrées FR400–FR600.

Recently refurbished, this former 19th-century stagecoach stop (the small hotel has 18 rooms) occasionally gets mud slung at it for some carelessly prepared meals. At these prices, that's alarming news. Be that as it may, when things are in working order, you can get some terrific regional specialties here. The dining room overlooks the Casino Bellevue and the ocean, which is a definite plus. Amenities: outside dining, reservations required. Credit Cards: All Major.

La Santa Maria $ ★

esplanade du Port Vieux ☎ *05-59-24-92-25.*
Hours: 9 a.m.–3 a.m., entrées FR42–FR70.

An informal bar-cafe perched on a cliff with a sea view, offering a grazing menu of Spanish tapas. Most items below FR60. If you want to graze in your hotel room later, go to Les Halles market on rue de Centre; open every day from 7 a.m. to 1 p.m. Amenities: cafestop, reservations recommended. Credit Cards: V.

Le Croque-en-Bouche $$ ★★

5 rue du Centre ☎ *05-59-22-06-57.*
Lunch: Noon–2 p.m., FR140–FR160.
Dinner: 7–10 p.m., entrées FR140–FR160.

With typical Basque generosity, this cheerful restaurant feeds a faithful clientele with high-quality delights (including morel mushrooms and foie gras) for only FR160. You're sure to find something you like from the quantity of choices available. Scrumptious desserts. Closed: Mon. Reservations required. Credit Cards: V, MC, A, E.

Le Vaudeville $ ★★

5 rue du Centre ☎ *05-59-24-34-66.*
Lunch: Noon–2 p.m., FR80–FR115.
Dinner: 7–11 p.m., entrées FR80–FR115.

You'd expect Rolls-Royce prices at this beautiful turn-of-the-century eatery; surprisingly, there's an FR87 set menu, including hors-d'oeuvres and dessert. The offal offerings (lamb kidneys, veal's head) are awfully good. Nicely priced wine list as well. Closed: Tues. Reservations required. Credit Cards: V, MC, E.

Directory

To and From

> *By train from Paris (five hours), by plane (like any true resort Biarritz has its own airport) from Paris on Air Inter Europe, or by car on the A-63 autoroute from the north or the A-64 autoroute from the west.*

Tourist Office

> *1 square d'Ixelles;* ☎ *(33) 05-59-24-20-24.*

Rail Station

> *Biarritz-la-égresse, about two miles out of town;* ☎ *(33) 05-59-24-00-94.*

Post Office

> *21 rue de la Poste, 64200 Biarritz;* ☎ *(33) 05-59-24-82-47.*

St. Jean de Luz

Even closer to the Spanish border and more charming than its neighbor Biarritz to the north, St. Jean de Luz is even more obviously Basque—there are posters in Euzkadi announcing *jai alai* competitions and bullfights. St. Jean de Luz, too, once made its living off whaling, but the citizens also turned to piracy, then tuna fishing, then tourism. The fishing harbor is still quite active, but the beach here is smaller than the one at Biarritz, although it is more sheltered from the wind due to the shape of the bay. The biggest thing that ever happened in St. Jean de Luz was the marriage of the young Louis XIV to Maria Teresa of Spain as part of a border treaty between the two countries. The church where the royal marriage took place in 1660, the Eglise St. Jean Baptiste, is still the main church in town. Today, a small museum recreates quarters where the king stayed before his wedding. Despite the town's small size, St. Jean de Luz offers all you would expect from a beach resort, including charter fishing, sailing, windsurfing, eating and drinking, and just plain old sunbathing.

What to Do

Historical/Architectural Sites

Eglise St.-Jean Baptiste   ★ ★

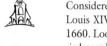

> *rue Gambetta.*

Considered one of the best Basque churches, the interior is pure magnificence. Louis XIV and the infanta Marie-Teresa of Spain were married in this church in 1660. Look for the plaque that marks the spot of the portal through which the married couple exited the church—it was sealed immediately following the ceremony. The three tiers of balconies were used for the separate seating that was mandated by the first Vatican council. One can't help but admire the splendor of the 17th-century altar and the joyous atmosphere of the entire church.

Museums and Exhibits

Maison Louis XIV Museum ★★

place Louis XIV, ☎ *05-59-26-01-56.*
The house in which Louis XIV stayed before his marriage, it has been recreated to resemble what it looked like at the time. Built in 1643 by a wealthy shipowner, it is still owned by his descendants. Guided tours are available. *Open June–Sept., Mon.–Sat., 10:30 a.m.–noon and 2:30–5:30 p.m. and Sun., 2:30–5:30 p.m.; July–Aug., to 6 p.m.* Admission: FR22.

Where to Stay

Hotels and Resorts

Hotel de Chantaco **FR600–FR1400** ★★★★

route d'Ascain. ☎ *05-59-26-14-76, FAX: 05-59-26-35-97. About 3 km from town center and 1.5 km from the beach.*
Single: FR600–FR1000. Double: FR900–FR1400.
Since the early days of this Basque mansion, this hotel has been widely popular with the well-to-do. Encompassed by a golf course in the middle of the countryside, the elegantly decorated public spaces feature stone fireplaces and period furnishings. The 24 guest chambers come with TV, telephone, minibar, bath, hair dryer and robes. Spread over the lush grounds are seven tennis courts and a pool. Excellent regional cuisine is served in the restaurant, with meals starting at FR250. Last renovated in 1986, the hotel's shine could use another buffing. Features: wheelchair-access rooms, pool, golf, tennis, in-room minibars. Credit Cards: All Major.

Melia Grand Hotel **FR700–FR1400** ★★★★

43 boulevard Thiers. ☎ *05-59-26-35-36, FAX: 05-59-51-19-91. About 2 km from the train station; near the beach.*
Single: FR700–FR1400. Double: FR800–FR1400.
Beachfront palace with an illustrious history dating back to 1925. After a recent and thorough series of renovations, it has re-established itself as the premier hotel of St.-Jean. It has 46 bright rooms, with the usual amenities and many looking towards the water. The former nightclub is now a fitness center, and the pool, bar and restaurant offer fine bay views. Palatial luxury on a small scale. Credit Cards: All Major.

Inns

La Deviniere **FR550–FR625** ★★★

5 rue Loguin. ☎ *05-59-26-05-51, FAX: 05-59-51-26-38. About 1 km from train station; near the port.*
Single: FR550. Double: FR625.
Originally a private townhouse dating from 1700, this antique-filled hotel has been modernized. Still as welcoming as ever, there are just eight rooms here. Each one is dignified and pretty, with telephone and private bath. Breakfast is the only meal served, for FR50.Credit Cards: V, MC, E.

Where to Eat

Chantaco **$$$** ★★★

Golf de Chantaco, Near the golf course. Located at Chantaco. ☎ *05-59-26-14-76.*
Dinner: entrées FR200–FR325.

An understated elegance is felt in the dining room overlooking the golf course and garden. Lightly textured dishes and flavorful spices are the keys to this restaurant's success. Pick one of the reasonably priced bottles to top off a relaxing evening. Set menus start at FR150 for weekday lunch to FR290 for dinner. Reservations recommended. Credit Cards: All Major.

Chez Maya   **$**   ★★★

4 rue St.-Jacques. ☎ *05-59-26-80-76.*
Dinner: 7–10 p.m., entrées FR50–FR100.

The best Basque food in town is found here at bargain prices. Well known by the locals for serving quality, authentic Basque dishes, Chez Maya offers appetizers from FR25 and set menus from FR85. A pleasant atmosphere, good service and generous proportions. Closed: Fri. Reservations recommended. Credit Cards: V, MC.

La Coupole   **$$$**   ★★★★

43 boulevard Thiers, Near the bay. ☎ *05-59-26-35-36.*
Specialties: local sole.
Dinner: entrées FR250–FR400.

Feast on the brilliant dishes of mostly seafood at this enchanting restaurant. The dining room sets one of the most attractive scenes for enjoying a meal that is upstaged only by the beautiful bay views out the window. From appetizer to dessert, it's hard to be disappointed by the meticulously prepared food here. Set menus from FR185. Amenities: outside dining, reservations required. Credit Cards: All Major.

Directory

To and From

By train from Biarritz (15 minutes) (and then connections to Paris), or by car on the A-64 autoroute that enters Spain.

Tourist Office

place Maréchal-Foch; ☎ *(33) 05-59-26-03-16.*

Rail Station

boulevard du Commandant Passicot; ☎ *(33) 05-59-26-02-08.*

Post Office

boulevard Victor Hugo, 64500 St. Jean de Luz; ☎ *(33) 05-59-26-01-95.*

Pau

The most important town in the mid-Pyrénées, Pau is located in a beautiful setting at the base of one of the major passes across the mountains. Formerly it was the capital of the independent duchy of Béarn (from where we get Bearnaise sauce), a part of the kingdom of Navarre, that once spread across both sides of the present Spanish-French border. Jean d'Albret inherited the region through marriage in 1484, and after ceding the southern half to the King of Spain, he passed the rest on to his son Henri II in 1527. Henri II's wife, the sister of François I, was a thorough Reformist (the family had been Protestant since Jean's conversion), and she ordered the château at Pau rebuilt in the Renaissance style, and created a renowned haven for thinkers, writers and artists. Jeanne d'Albret, Henri's daughter, traveled for 19 days from the north of France to give birth to her son in the castle; he was Henri of Navarre, who later claimed the French throne when his cousin Henri III died heirless. After converting to Catholicism, Henri IV took the French throne, preserving a good deal of Protestant freedom for his homeland. (For an excellent interpretation of these events, the film *La Reine Margot*, is available with English subtitles on video.)

After the tumultuous times of the Henris, Pau became a quiet regional town, enlivened by the coming of the nobility in the mid-19th century, which lasted only until they discovered Biarritz to the east, and then again in the late 19th century, when the bracing mountain air made the town a popular vacation destination for the English upper class. They, too, moved on, leaving behind a comfortable, peaceful town—well-worth a visit to see its castle, which houses a collection of the best preserved Renaissance-style Flemish tapestries in France, and the views of the mountains.

What to Do

Historical/Architectural Sites

Château de Pau ★★★

2 rue du Château, ☎ *05-59-82-38-19. On the west side of town.*
Hours open: 9:30 a.m.–5:15 p.m. Special hours: Closed 11:45 a.m.–2 p.m.
Dating back to the 12th century, this served as the residence of the viscounts of Bearn and the Kings of Navarre. It was also here that King Henri IV of France was born (look for the tortoise shell crib made for him). Remodeled in the 14th century, it was majorly refurbished four centuries later. Within the château is the Musée National du Château de Pau. Tours in French are offered several times every hour. Admission: FR27.

Museums and Exhibits

Musée des Beaux-Arts ★★

rue Mathieu-Lalanne, ☎ *05-59-27-33-02.*
Hours open: 9 a.m.–6 p.m. Special hours: Closed noon–2 p.m. Closed: Tue.
A varied collection of European paintings, featuring a display of Spanish sculptures. Famous artists, such as Degas, Boudin, El Greco and Zurbaran, are all represented here. Admission: FR10.

Where to Stay

Hotels and Resorts

Hotel Continental FR325–FR500 ★★★

2 rue du Marechal-Foch. ☎ *05-59-27-69-31, FAX: 05-59-27-99-84. Near the train station and the casino.*
Single: FR325. Double: FR500.
In a town with limited quality of hotels, the Continental, now run by Best Western, is as good as it gets. A traditional hotel with origins to the 1920s, its 80 rooms are

completely modernized with satellite TV, radio, telephone, minibar, bath and hair dryer. Some of the units are air-conditioned. The restaurant's a la carte menu begins at FR135. Breakfast costs FR40. Free garage parking. Features: wheelchair-access rooms, air conditioning in rooms, in-room minibars. Credit Cards: All Major.

Hotel de Paris   FR410–FR490   ★★★

80 rue Emile-Garet. ☎ *05-59-82-58-00, FAX: 05-59-27-30-20. Near Beaumont Park. Single: FR410. Double: FR490.*

Near Beaumont Park, the Paris offers quiet accommodations over a private courtyard. There are 41 rooms, all up-to-date and with TV, telephone, minibar and bath. Though there is no restaurant, a buffet breakfast is included in the price. Garage parking is free. Features: in-room mini-bars. Credit Cards: All Major.

Low-Cost Lodging

Hotel-Restaurant Corona   FR200–FR250   ★★

71 avenue du General-Leclerc. ☎ *05-59-30-64-77, FAX: 05-59-02-62-64. About 2 km east of town center.*
Double: FR200–FR250.

Comfortable and value-conscious accommodations. The Corona has 20 functional rooms with TV, telephone and bath. Semi-rustic decor created with exposed pinewood in the rooms. Meals begin at FR41 in the brasserie and at FR140 in the restaurant. Breakfast costs FR50 extra. Credit Cards: All Major.

Where to Eat

L'Agripaume $$ ★★★

14 rue Latapie ☎ *05-59-27-68-70.*
Dinner: 7–10:30 p.m., entrées FR75–FR175.

Featuring authentic Basque cuisine in an attractive, pastel dining room, L'Agripaume just improves with age. The foie gras, roast salmon, duck fillet and roast lamb are all favorites. An affordable selection of wines is a refreshing complement to the great value found in the authentic dishes. Set menus are FR75–FR400. Closed: Sun. reservations required. Credit Cards: V, MC.

La Table d'Hote $$ ★★★

1 rue du Hedas ☎ *05-59-27-56-06.*
Dinner: entrées FR125–FR250.

The inviting ambience designed by the owners who recently took over has changed the outlook of the entire establishment to keep pace with the exciting menus. A small but decent selection of wines is available from the cellar. The set menus are outstanding, ranging from FR75–FR150. Courteous service rounds out this thoughtfully reinvented establishment. Closed: Sun. Amenities: outside dining, reservations recommended. Credit Cards: V.

Pierre $$ ★★★

16 rue Louis Barthou ☎ *05-59-27-76-86.*
Specialties: all of the desserts.
Dinner: entrées FR175–FR325.

With fresh ingredients and careful attention to tradition with well-honed skills, chef Raymond Cassau serves consistently full-flavored cuisine. Some excellent main dishes include sole with mushrooms, salmon and white-bean cassoulet. Whatever your choice of dishes, the fruit-filled crepes always prove to be an excellent finishing touch. Unfortunately, no fixed menus available at time of printing. Closed: Sun. Reservations required. Credit Cards: All Major.

Directory

To and From

> *By train from Bayonne (an hour and three quarters), Paris (five hours), and Toulouse (four hours), or by car A-64 autoroute east to west or the N-134 road north to south.*

Tourist Office

> *place Royale;* ☎ *(33) 05-59-27-27-08.*

Rail Station

> *avenue Gaston Lacoste;* ☎ *(33) 05-59-30-50-50.*

Post Office

> *cours Bosquet, 64000 Pau;* ☎ *(33) 05-59-98-98-60.*

Lourdes

The most popular pilgrimage site in Christendom after Rome, Lourdes was just a tiny village in the foothills of the Pyrénées when the 14-year-old Bernadette Soubirous had 18 visions of the Virgin Mary in 1858. During her ninth vision, apparently, she scratched the ground and a spring emerged, flowing with waters said to have miraculous healing powers. The Catholic church authenticated Soubirous' visions, and the business started pouring in. Bernadette became a nun, canonized in 1933, and today Lourdes receives 5 million visitors each year, second in popularity only to Paris. The cave where the girl had her visions and the spring that still gushes forth may be visited, although you should expect long lines. Lines form to view the three basilicas, each more massive than the others, that honor St. Bernadette, as well as the Virgin Mary. At 4:30 p.m. daily, you can witness the Procession of the Blessed Sacrament and the Blessing of the Sick. Admittedly the high point of the pilgrimage, some people find this display of enormous faith uplifting, others see it as unrewarded desperation and somewhat macabre. But millions of people every year come to Lourdes from all over the world by car, by train, on chartered airplanes sometimes, and the villagers don't seem to mind.

What to Do

Historical/Architectural Sites

Grotto de Massabielle ★★★

> *Hours open: 6 a.m.–midnight*

The focus of the pilgrims to this area, this is the site that the Virgin Mary is said to have appeared 18 times to a poor shepherd girl, Bernadette Soubirous. Crutches from the miraculously cured hang on the walls, and millions of people have anointed themselves with water from the miraculous spring that cured Bernadette. Always well-visited, try to get here early in the morning.

More than 5 million visitors a year visit the basilicas and grotto at Lourdes.

Three Basilicas   ★★★

Above the grotto is the Basilique du Rosaire, built in 1889 in neo-Byzantine style. With the capacity to hold 4000 people, there are 15 chapels inside dedicated to the rosary. One story above is the crypt, reserved for silent prayer. The Upper Basilica, constructed in the 13th century but not consecrated until 1876, is capped with spires. *Both are open daily from 6 a.m.–7 p.m.* The third basilica is the Basilique Pius X. Built in 1958 in an underground bomb shelter, it actually won an international architecture prize upon completion. Within its 660-foot-long and 270-foot wide walls, 20,000 people can be accommodated—making it the world's second largest church (behind St.-Peter's in Rome). *Open daily 6 a.m.–6 p.m.*

Where to Stay

Hotels and Resorts

Galilee et Windsor   **FR450–FR550**   ★★★

10 avenue Peyramale. ☎ 05-62-94-21-55, FAX: 05-62-94-53-66. Near the grotto. Double: FR450–FR550.
This large facility boasts 169 rooms, all modernized while keeping the charm of the classic building. The quality of the rooms varies, but all are equipped with TV, telephone and bath or shower. Meals in the restaurant start at FR85, and breakfast is complimentary. Half-board rates are available. Features: air conditioning in rooms. Credit Cards: V, A.

Gallia et Londres   **FR600–FR700**   ★★★★

26 avenue Bernadette-Soubirous. ☎ 05-62-94-35-44, FAX: 05-62-94-53-66. Take bus #2.
Single: FR600. Double: FR700.
Built around the turn of the century, this classic hotel is immensely popular with pilgrimage groups. There are 90 rooms decorated in period style and equipped with TV, telephone and bath or shower. The hotel also boasts a bar, a pub and a secluded garden. Breakfast is included, and the restaurant offers good fixed-price menus starting at FR130. Half-board rates are available. Features: air conditioning in rooms, balcony or patio. Credit Cards: V, A.

Hotel Adriatic   **FR300–FR420**   ★★★

4 rue Baron Duprat. ☎ 05-62-94-31-34, FAX: 05-62-42-14-70. Take bus #2.
Single: FR300–FR370. Double: FR350–FR420.
Centrally located with easy access to the city's tourist sights, this 1950s hotel offers 85 traditionally decorated and well-kept rooms. Each comes with telephone and bath, and some have TV. Breakfast costs FR35, and the restaurant features meals starting at FR130. Features: in-room mini-bars. Credit Cards: V, MC.

Where to Eat

L'Ermitage   **$**   ★★★

boulevard de la Grotte et place Laurence. ☎ 05-62-94-08-42.
Only lunch is served at this French-Basque restaurant. Step inside and one feels part of a close-knit group of friends. Traditional regional recipes are the base for the flavorful dishes of salmon, duckling and beef. Fixed-price menus are FR75–FR200. Reservations recommended. Credit Cards: All Major.

Relais de Saux   **$$$**   ★★★

> route de Tarbes, About 3 km northeast of Lourdes on the N21; in Saux. Located at Relais
> de Saux. ☎ 05-62-94-29-61.
> Dinner: 7:15–9:30 p.m., entrées FR200–FR350.
> Surrounded by peaceful gardens, this Basque restaurant occupies an ivy-covered
> house from the 15th century. The elegant interior is highlighted by Louis XIV fire-
> places and rustic appointments, setting an enchanting mood for the delicious spe-
> cialties of duck, beef, lobster and other entrées. Only the best—and most
> expensive—ingredients are used to create the dazzling cuisine. Set menus start at
> FR160. Amenities: outside dining, reservations recommended. Credit Cards: V, A.

rue de la Grotte   **$**

> This touristic street is brimming with inexpensive restaurants. Menus from FR50
> are easily found in the cafes, pizzerias, brasseries and creperies. There's something
> here for everybody's pocketbook.

Directory

To and From

> By train from Bordeaux (three hours) or Toulouse (two-and-a-half hours), or by car on
> the N-21 road off the A-64 autoroute.

Tourist Office

> place Peyramale; ☎ (33) 05-62-42-77-40.

Rail Station

> avenue de la Gàre; ☎ (33) 605-2-37-50-50.

Post Office

> 31 avenue Maransin, 65100 Lourdes; ☎ (33) 05-62-94-00-00.

Parc National des Pyrénées

Created in 1967 to protect some of the most beautiful countryside in Eu-
rope, the Pyrénées National Park encompasses more than 62 miles of the
Spanish-French border. Within the long, narrow preserve, you'll find stun-
ningly beautiful meadows covered by snow in the winter and gorgeous wild-
flowers in spring and summer, and three peaks over 10,000 feet tall as well as
several crags that just miss that mark. The park is a haven for rare birds and
animals, including golden eagles, griffon vultures, chamois, marmots and a
dwindling population of Pyrenean brown bears. Also a hiker's paradise, the
park offers 217 miles of well-marked trails, ranging from gentle three-or
four-hour circuits to the monumental *Grand Randonée 10*, which crosses
the park as it reaches from the Atlantic to the Mediterranean coast. Numer-
ous *refuges* and *cabanes* dot the park for overnight stays. A *cabane* is an un-
manned hut with simple beds and not much else that you can stay in for free;
a refuge is not much more luxurious, but maintains a staff person on site and
costs FR66 per night. The guard/staff person also usually acts as chef, serv-
ing up hearty, carbohydrate-laden meals for about FR75 a person. If you

want something a little more comfortable, plan your route to start and end each day in one of the small villages in the park, all of which offer bed-and-breakfast accommodations.

For more information on the National Park, including maps, lists of accommodations, and safety tips for hikers, get in touch with the headquarters at:

Parc National des Pyrénées
  place de la Gàre, 65110 Cauterets; ☎ *(33) 05-62-92-52-56.*

Toulouse

Thanks to the 2.1 million population of Paris, a city like Toulouse can have only 360,000 inhabitants and still be the sixth-largest city in the country. Toulouse has all the accoutrements of a major urban center without the urban problems you might expect. In its early days, Toulouse was capital of the Visigoth kingdom, a strategic center connected to the Mediterranean by a low pass through the hills, to the Atlantic by the Garonne river. The fingers of valleys tapering out from the Pyrénées linked Toulouse to Spain. Between the ninth and the 13th centuries, Toulouse prospered as the capital of Raymond, dynasty of the Langue d'Oc people. During this time, the buildings you see today were begun. Toulouse is famous for its distinctive pinkish brick, made from the clay lining the river bed that's used instead of stone—the nearest quarries are 50 miles away. In the 13th century, the Capetians overran the city and the region, smothering what was a relatively cultured and forward-looking society. Toulouse entered a period of great intolerance and religious oppression, beginning with the eradication of the Cathars (see below). Over the next few centuries, the trend continued, as the Wars of Religion saw thousands of Huguenots perish in and around Toulouse, and the burning at the stake of Lucilio Vanini. The city prospered during this time, mainly as a result of trade in wool and other natural dyes that were used around the world.

Nowadays, Toulouse has returned to its more progressive roots. Home to the second-oldest university in France, founded in 1229, the city has a large student population and young feeling. Aircraft manufacturing has existed in Toulouse since 1917, and the city is home to the first successful jet, the Caravelle, as well as the Concorde, and more recently, the Airbus and the Ariane. You can walk the streets of old Toulouse, in a section just east of the river centered around Rue Metz, and see the impressive Renaissance-style mansions of 18th-century merchants, as well as the St. Sernin Basilica, the longest Romanesque church in the world. Also in Toulouse, you'll find L'eglise des Jacobins, a fine Gothic church built to underscore the Catholic church's primacy after the Cathar sect was stamped out, where St. Thomas

Aquinas' remains are housed. In addition, there are many fine museums. Don't forget to stop by the Place du Capitole on the other side of the river and watch life go by from one of the café terraces in front of City Hall. You are, after all, in the south of France where the pace is slow.

What to Do

Historical/Architectural Sites

Basilique St.-Sernin   ★★★

place St.-Sernin, ☎ *05-61-21-70-18.*

Hours open: 8 a.m.–6 p.m. Special hours: Closed noon–2 p.m.

The largest Romanesque structure in France, more than 115 meters long, was built in the 11th century and completed in the 12th century with the addition of the nave. The ambulatory inside is filled with chapels and 17th-century reliquaries. Above the 13th century crypt is the 18th-century tomb of St.-Sernin. The ambulatory and crypt cost FR10 and are open from 10–11:30 a.m. and 2:30–5 p.m. daily, except Sun. morning.

Eglise des Jacobins   ★★★

rue Lakanal, ☎ *05-61-22-21-92. In Old Toulouse.*

Hours open: 10 a.m.–6:30 p.m. Special hours: Closed noon–2 p.m.; Sun., open 2:30–6 p.m.

Begun in 1230 and completed in 1385, this church was the first Dominican (also known as Jacobins) convent, founded by St.-Dominic himself. This convent later became the founding institution of Toulouse University. In 1974, the 700th anniversary of his death, the ashes of St.-Thomas Aquinas were placed here. A magnificent structure, the Flamboyant Gothic design is highlighted by the vault in the apse and the spireless bell tower. Admission to the cloisters is FR10 (students free).

Where to Stay

Hotels and Resorts

Grand Hotel de l'Opera   **FR850–FR1300**   ★★★★

1 place du Capitole. ☎ *05-61-21-82-66, FAX: 05-61-23-41-04. About 1 km from the train station, across from the Opera.*

Single: FR850–FR900. Double: FR900–FR1300.

Opulence, luxury, elegance, grace—it's all here. On the lively place du Capitole, this stately hotel occupies a former 17th-century abbey that was deftly transformed into the award-winning establishment it is today. Early 19th-century antiques grace the public areas, and the 49 spacious rooms feature tasteful modern comfort. All are air-conditioned and contain TV, radio, telephone, minibar and bath; some of the balconied rooms overlook the square and the red-tiled roofs of the nearby buildings. Superb facilities include indoor and outdoor pools, health center, Turkish bath, sauna and massage services. The restaurant is outstanding, and there are two bars. Breakfast costs FR82. Unparalleled service and facilities. Features: wheelchair-access rooms, pool, air conditioning in rooms, sauna, in-room minibars, fitness center. Credit Cards: All Major.

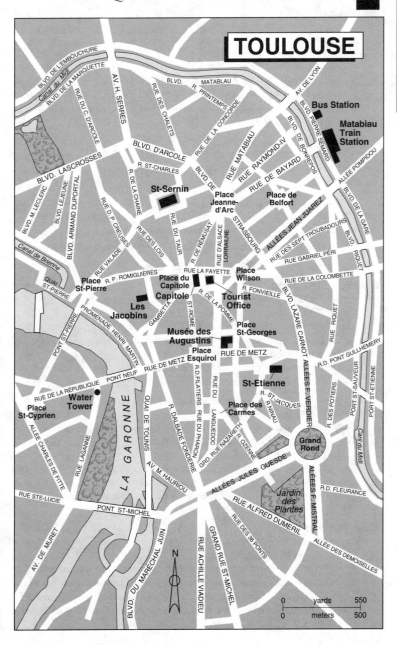

Hotel de Diane   FR390–FR515   ★★★

3 route de St.-Simon. ☎ *05-61-07-59-52, FAX: 05-61-86-38-94. About 5 km from town center.*
Single: FR390–FR455. Double: FR455–FR515.

Among five acres of park land, this 19th-century hotel is a great choice for guests seeking recreational activity. In addition to the on-site pool, tennis, squash and miniature golf are nearby. The 36 rooms contain satellite TV, telephone, bath and some with terrace. There is a decent restaurant and a bar in the hotel. Relaxed, friendly service. Features: pool, nonsmoking rooms. Credit Cards: All Major.

Hotel des Beaux-Arts   FR330–FR560   ★★★

1 place du Pont-Neuf. ☎ *05-61-23-40-50, FAX: 05-61-22-02-27. On the banks of the Garonne.*
Double: FR330–FR560.

This former 18th-century villa thrives in its central location on the banks of the Garonne. It manages to salvage some character from the cloned rooms, each quite comfortable with air conditioning, TV, telephone and private bath. Breakfast costs FR45, and other meals are served in the restaurant of the same name. Service is friendly and efficient. Features: air conditioning in rooms. Credit Cards: All Major.

Where to Eat

Brasserie des Beaux-Arts $$ ★★

1 quai de la Daurade, At the base of the Pont Neuf bridge. ☎ *05-61-21-12-12.*
Dinner: 7 p.m.–1 a.m., entrées FR75–FR125.

Part of a chain of excellent brasseries, the Beaux-Arts offers regional and seafood dishes. Focus is on fresh ingredients, careful preparation and precise use of spices. Terrace dining during the summer and late-night dining all year make this a popular spot with locals and tourists alike. Set menus from FR140. Amenities: outside dining, reservations recommended. Credit Cards: All Major.

Chez Emile $$ ★★

13 place St.-Georges. ☎ *05-61-21-05-56.*
Specialties: cassoulet.

Residing on one of the most beautiful squares in town, Chez Emile occupies two stories of a lovely building. Relax on the terrace in the summer and upstairs in the dining room the rest of the year. The menu is heavy with regional dishes, including fish, duck, cassoulets and other typical southwestern dishes. Set menus start at FR125 at lunch and FR190 at dinner. Closed: Mon., Sun. Amenities: outside dining, reservations recommended. Credit Cards: All Major.

Claude Ribardiere $$$ ★★★★

21 boulevard A. Duportal. ☎ *05-61-13-91-12.*
Dinner: entrées FR200–FR350.

An air of relaxed intimacy pervades this lovely restaurant and indoor garden terrace. Local and regional cuisine is prepared by the skilled hands of Claude Ribardiere. The bottles in the cellar are all excellent, and the service is always pleasant. Set menus from FR145 for lunch and from FR175 for dinner. Closed: Sun. Amenities: outside dining, reservations required. Credit Cards: All Major.

La Belle Epoque $$$ ★★★★

3 rue Pargaminieres. ☎ *05-61-23-22-12.*
Specialties: duck breast in paprika.
Dinner: entrées FR225–FR450.
An incredibly personable staff and a receptive chef who want to make every meal
perfect for each guest's tastes. Choices always include duck breast, veal, foie gras
and many other specialties. Speak with the chef for a specialized dish to satisfy your
individual palate. A refreshingly casual atmosphere. Set menus from FR200. Closed:
Sun. Reservations required. Credit Cards: All Major.

Les Jardins de l'Opera $$$ ★★★★★

1 place du Capitole ☎ *05-61-23-07-76.*
Specialties: rack of lamb; foie gras-stuffed ravioli.
Dinner: 8–10 p.m., entrées FR175–FR300.
Pure magnificence and elegance, the dining room is one of the most exquisitely
designed in all of France. Once seated, the cordial staff provides efficient, anticipatory service. Delicate balances are found with the ingredients, spices and sauces of
every dish. The perfection extends to the dessert menu and wine list. Set menus
range from FR200 at lunch to FR400 at dinner. Not one franc is wasted. Closed:
Sun. Amenities: outside dining, reservations required. Credit Cards: All Major.

Directory

To and From

*By train from Paris (five hours) or Bordeaux (two hours), or by car on the A-61/A-62
autoroute or the N-113/N-117 intersection.*

Tourist Office

Donjon du Capitole; ☎ *(33) 05-61-11-02-22.*

Rail Station

boulevard Pierre Sémard; ☎ *(33) 05-61-10-10-00.*

Post Office

9 rue Lafayette, 31000 Toulouse; ☎ *(33) 05-62-15-30-00.*

Albi

Like Toulouse, Albi is built almost entirely of the pinkish-red brick derived
from the clay in the Tarn river. And like Toulouse, it has a bloody history of
repression against the Cathars. A doctrine of spiritual purity and dualism
based on the view that the soul and spirit are good, while the body and earth
are bad, Catharism spread the south of France, particularly the southwest,
during the 12th and early 13th centuries. The sect was welcomed by ordinary people wearied by the oppressive materialism of the Catholic church,
and by the lords and dukes of Languedoc and Toulouse, who saw the church
as rivals to their earthly power. The Catholics, meanwhile, saw Catharism as
heresy, since its adherents shunned the sacraments and external trappings of
the church, including tithing. Centered in Albi, the heretics became known

as *Albigeois*, and the campaign to crush the sect, ordered by Pope Innocent III and enthusiastically supported by the king of France (who wanted earthly control of the region), was dubbed the Albigensian crusade. The Cathars did not fight, but instead took shelter in castles and natural refuges in the area, including a rocky pillar at Montsegur where, in the final stamp-out of the sect, the Catholics burned 250 Cathars in 1244. The Cathars were steadily massacred by the combined papal and Capetian forces.

Albi, as seen from the cathedral tower.

The imposing, almost threatening Cathédrale St. Cécile in Albi is a direct result of the Cathar inquisition. Built deliberately in a stern, foreboding style with impressive fortifications it was meant to affirm the dominance of the Catholic church and send a warning to the crushed citizens. Interestingly, within the church, the rood-screen, which was used to separate the clergy from the rest of the people during services, has survived—one of the few in France to remain—and today a witness to the once-fearsome authority of the church. Albi also was the birthplace of Henri Toulouse-Lautrec in 1864. The duke-turned-painter, Toulouse-Lautrec was crippled as a child and dead by 37, but his paintings sparked the growth of lithography. His work gave rise to a critical style of art that shone the light onto the dark corners of society, in his case, the seedy side of Paris nightlife and the despair and desperation of people engaged in everyday life. Toulouse-Lautrec's home is open to the public, but the prime attraction is the museum bearing his name, which houses an extensive collection of his oil paintings, pastels, drawings and also the sketches that were the basis for his famous posters.

What to Do

City Celebrations/Events

International Amateur Film Festival   ★

Syndicat d' Initiative, 19 place Ste-Cecile, ☎ 05-63-54-22-30.
Sometime between the last week of July and the first week of August, the city hosts a free film festival featuring aspiring Fellinis. Contact the Tourist Office for gratis tickets. Admission: free.

Historical/Architectural Sites

Cathedrale Ste-Cecile   ★★★★

rue de Castelviel, ☎ 05-63-54-15-11. Near the medieval center of town.
Hours open: 8:30 a.m.–5:30 p.m. Special hours: Closed 11:45 a.m.–2:30 p.m.
Built entirely of red brick, it was designed to serve as a fortified church in 1282 after heretics were banned from the city. Completed in 1392 and consecrated in 1480, ramparts and parapets outside complete the protection package. The interior is intricately decorated with brilliant Italian frescoes and accented by the stained-glass windows. In the summer, visit at 5 p.m. on Wednesdays to hear the booming organ or at night for a tour (FR18). Admission: FR2.

Museums and Exhibits

Musée Henri de Toulouse-Lautrec   ★★★

Palais de la Berbie, ☎ 05-63-54-14-09.
Hours open: 9 a.m.–6 p.m. Special hours: In winter, open Wed.–Mon., 10 a.m.–5 p.m.
The legendary artist who haunted Montmartre and painted its subjects so prolifically is well represented in this museum in a 13th-century archbishop's palace. Toulouse-Lautrec, who became crippled in his childhood, died very young of syphilis and alcoholism, but he left behind more than 30 posters of his favorite boho subjects, in addition to sketches, paintings and drawings from his early years. On the second floor are paintings created by his contemporaries, including Matisse, Dufy, Degas and Utrillo. If you have time, and are in town in July–August, his birthplace at *14 rue Toulouse-Lautrec in Vieil Alby* is open to visitors; the dwelling is still owned by his family. (Hours: 9 a.m.–noon; 3–7 p.m.) The Tourist Office, also in the Palais de Berbie, offers suggestions on walking tours of the Old City; open 9:30 a.m.–7 p.m., ☎ 05-63-49-48-80. Admission: FR20.

Where to Stay

Hotels and Resorts

Hostellerie St.-Antoine   **FR380–FR950**   ★★

17 rue St.-Antoine. ☎ 05-63-54-04-04, FAX: 05-63-47-10-42. About 75 km northeast of Toulouse; between the main post office and the theater.
Single: FR380–FR590. Double: FR590–FR950.
Owned by the same family for five generations, this 250-year old hotel is quiet, comfortable and centrally located. With its lovely walled garden, the hotel has an atmosphere not unlike a country estate. The lounge, which opens onto the garden, is decorated with some original artwork by Toulouse-Lautrec (the present manager's great-grandfather was a friend of the famous artist). There are 47 rooms, all

with tasteful furnishings, a scattering of antiques, TV and private bath. Especially noted for its breakfast, the hotel's restaurant also offers three fixed-price menus for FR150, FR200 and FR206. Half-board rates are FR390 to FR590 (room, breakfast and a meal) per person, per day in season. Features: pool, tennis, air conditioning in rooms. Credit Cards: All Major.

Hotel Chiffre — FR360–FR460 ★★★

50 rue Sere-de-Rivieres. ☎ *05-63-54-04-60, FAX: 05-63-47-20-61. About 1 km from train station; in the center of town.*
Single: FR360–FR460. Double: FR360–FR460.

An intimate two-story hotel, operating since 1890 and in the hands of the Chiffre family since 1918. The 40 rooms of this centrally located hotel come with TV, telephone and bath; only some are equipped with air conditioning. Request one of the quiet rooms over the inner courtyard. In addition to three fireplace lounges, there is a popular restaurant with fixed-price menus starting at FR100. Breakfast costs FR60. Free garage parking. Features: wheelchair-access rooms, air conditioning in rooms, in-room conference facilities. Credit Cards: All Major.

Inns

La Reserve — FR500–FR850 ★★★★

route de Cordes. ☎ *05-63-60-80-80, FAX: 05-63-47-63-60. Just outside of Albi; near the Tarn River.*
Single: FR500. Double: FR850.

This quiet country inn is situated in a five-acre park on the banks of the Tarn River. A Relais and Châteaux rated hotel, it offers 24 air-conditioned rooms with TV, telephone, minibar, private bath and some with terrace. All are uniquely decorated and perfectly comfortable. There are three suites available for FR1300. Leisure facilities include a heated pool, a tennis court and use of canoes and bicycles. Guests linger in the cozy lounge after a satisfying meal in the dining room. Breakfast is available for FR70. Sister hotel to the St.-Antoine. Features: pool, tennis, air conditioning in rooms, in-room minibars. Credit Cards: All Major.

Where to Eat

Le Jardin des Quartres Saisons — $$$ ★★★

19 boulevard de Strasbourg ☎ *05-63-60-77-76.*
Lunch: Noon–2 p.m., FR180–FR250.
Dinner: 7–10:15 p.m., entrées FR180–FR250.

The fish, seafood, and meat dishes change with the seasons at this pretty flower-filled restaurant, evocative of a spring garden. No matter what time of the year it is, though, you'll always be welcomed by the affable husband-and-wife team of Georges and Martine Bermond. Closed: Mon., Thur. Amenities: outside dining, own baking, reservations required. Credit Cards: A, A.

Moulin de la Mothe — $$$ ★★★

rue de la Mothe ☎ *05-63-60-38-15.*
Specialties: ham-stuffed squid in tomato coulis, perch fillets.
Lunch: Noon–2 p.m., FR240–FR340.
Dinner: 7–9:30 p.m., entrées FR240–FR340.

This riverside restaurant takes pride in its decor as well as its cuisine. Guests are served in a tastefully appointed dining room or in a garden in good weather. The excellent regional dishes are created by Michel Pellaprat, who selects the market-fresh produce he uses himself. Closed: Wed. Amenities: outside dining, own baking, reservations required. Credit Cards: V, MC, A.

Directory

To and From
> *By train from Toulouse (one hour) or Paris overnight, or by car on the A-68 autoroute from Toulouse or the N-112 road from the coast.*

Tourist Office
> *place Ste. Cécile;* ☎ *(33) 05-63-49-48-80.*

Rail Station
> *avenue Maréchal Joffre;* ☎ *(33) 05-63-53-31-64.*

Post Office
> *place du Vigan, 81000 Albi;* ☎ *(33) 05-63-48-15-56.*

Carcassonne

You will recognize the massive fortified city of Carcassonne if you saw Kevin Costner in *Robin Hood—Prince of Thieves.* Even in reality, Carcassonne does look more like a film set than an actual city. Although considered Europe's largest fortress, Carcassonne has been restored in the 19th century. Many visitors complain that Carcassonne looks too, well, new, but, nevertheless it is an imposing site. The medieval town is protected by two concentric rampart walls, with 52 towers between them. In their center is the main fort, which is ringed by moats and towers. Originally a Roman fortress, the city has endured its share of bloody conflict. Before being besieged by the Catholic-Capetian forces hunting Cathars in the 13th century, the city had its most glorious moment—and got its name—in the eighth century. Then held by the Moors, the city was besieged by Charlemagne for five years. The leader of the defenders, Carcas, the widow of a Moorish king, used trickery to hold off the attackers, including moving mannequins around the ramparts to create the impression of more soldiers than she actually had, and throwing out the city's last pig, which had been fed the last corn, to make Charlemagne believe there was still plenty of food. When Charlemagne finally gave up, however, she ordered the bells rung, leading the king to exclaim *"Carcas sonne!"* Translated as "Carcas is calling." Charlemagne's words were propitious—he returned to wait out an eventual treaty.

The city is overrun these days not by invaders, but by tourists, yet it is big enough that you can wander the streets imagining yourself holding out against besieging infidels. The nighttime illuminations of the fortress are especially beautiful.

What to Do

City Celebrations/Events

Festival de Carcassonne ★★★

Festival de la Cite, B.P. 236, 11005 Carcassonne, ☎ *05-68-24-33-13.*

Carcassonne fairy-tale medieval Cite is a lucrative income producer, and the town fathers have planned several events to further grease the wheels of commerce. The entire month of July is set aside for a performing-arts fete held at the Château Comtal. Tickets range from FR100–FR270, students, children FR55–FR90. For reservations, call ☎ *05-68-77-71-26.* The Bastille Day pyrotechnics show, which can be seen all over the city, probably beats any other July 14 festivity anywhere in France for spectacle. The two-week Medievales (mid-Aug.) takes visitors back to the more attractive aspects of the 12th century, with townspeople in authentic costumes hawking their wares (which you can buy). The Tourist Office, at *15 boulevard Camille Pelletan, place Gambetta (*☎ *05-68-25-07-04),* will supply details.

Historical/Architectural Sites

La Cité ★★★★

La Cite, ☎ *04-68-25-03-34.*
Hours open: 9 a.m.–6 p.m.

La Cite, Carcassone's upper town, is surrounded by a double set of walls (the inner walls are Gallo-Roman) and ramparts built by Louis IX and Philip the Bold (13th century). Guided tours of the highly atmospheric medieval town are given daily, literally hitting all the high points, including a walk on the ramparts and into the towers; it's recommended for the first-time visitor. Although entrance to the Cite is free, you'll have to pay a fee to get to see the inside of some of the main sights. These include the Château Comtal, the former 12th-century palace of the Trencavels that later became a fortress after Carcassonne fell under French rule (*open July– Aug. 9 a.m.–7 p.m.,* admission FR32; children, students FR20; for other times, check with the Tourist Office). There's no charge to visit the beautiful Romanesque-Gothic Basilique St.-Nazaire, where you can admire the vibrantly colored stained-glass windows. Within the church is the Siege Stone, relating the takeover of the city by the Crusaders, a 16th-century organ and the tomb of Bishop Radulf (*Guided tours in English, July–Aug., twice daily,* FR32; children, students FR20, ☎ *05-68-25-68-81).*

Where to Stay

Hotels and Resorts

Domaine d'Auriac **FR660–FR1300** ★★

route St.-Hilaire. ☎ *04-68-25-72-22, FAX: 04-68-47-35-54. Take D104 about 3 km southwest from Carcassonne to Auriac.*
Single: FR660–FR990. Double: FR990–FR1300.

Just outside Carcassonne, this 19th century manor was originally a country home. Rated as a Relais and Châteaux, it is probably the best place for food and lodging in the region. The ivy-covered inn is set within gardens with reflecting pools and flower-filled terraces. Within there are 23 rooms, all uniquely decorated and with private bathrooms. Several rooms have small salons. The dining room is lovely with elegant table settings (listed separately). In summer, meals are served beside the swimming pool on the terraces overlooking the beautifully landscaped gardens. Half-board rates are FR770 to FR980 (room, breakfast and a meal) per person, per day in season. Features: pool, golf, tennis, air conditioning in rooms, in-room mini-bars. Credit Cards: All Major.

Domaine d'Auriac   FR660–FR1300   ★ ★ ★

route de St.-Hilaire. ☎ *(68)25-72-22. About 4 km southwest of town.*
Double: FR660–FR1300.
A moss-covered country manor house built in the 1700s, it has been operating as a hotel since 1969. With some views over the park, there are 23 rooms with TV, tele-phone, minibar, private bath and hair dryer. Leisure facilities include a tennis court, pool and 9-hole golf course. Traditional cuisine is served in the dining room, and after-dinner drinks are savored in the bar. A Relais and Châteaux establishment. Features: pool, golf, tennis, air conditioning in rooms, in-room minibars. Credit Cards: All Major.

Hotel Dame Carcas   FR400–FR700   ★ ★ ★

15 rue St.-Louis. ☎ *275-2949, 05-68-71-37-37, FAX: 05-68-71-50-15. About 1 km from the train station, in the old city.*
Single: FR400–FR600. Double: FR500–FR700.
Behind the medieval walls, this hotel dates back to 1913. Somewhere behind the ivy-covered facade are 30 air-conditioned rooms. All are soundproof and with TV, telephone and private bath. There is a restaurant featuring a garden setting and a cozy bar in the hotel. A value-minded choice for those wishing to stay in the old city. Features: air conditioning in rooms. Credit Cards: All Major.

Hotel Montsegur   FR290–FR450   ★ ★ ★

27 allee d'lena. ☎ *05-68-25-31-41, FAX: 05-68-47-13-22. In the lower city.*
Single: FR290. Double: FR450.
A large 19th-century townhouse, behind a tree-lined, fenced garden. Even with all of the modern improvements, the owners have kept the place homey with antique adornments. There are 21 rooms with TV, telephone, bath and some with air con-ditioning. Reception is always open, and breakfast costs FR48. Credit Cards: All Major.

Hotel de la Cite   FR820–FR1250   ★ ★ ★

place de l'Eglise. ☎ *525-4800, 04-68-25-03-34, FAX: 04-68-71-50-1. From Porte Nar-bonnaise, take rue Mayrevieill to rue Porte d'Aude to rue St.-Louis.* Rated Restaurant: *La Barbacane.*
Single: FR820–FR900. Double: FR1100–FR1250.
In a former episcopal palace, this luxurious hotel is the most desirable place to stay within the ramparts of the Old City. Renovated in 1990 and reopened under new management, the hotel retains its medieval architectural heritage of thick stone walls and leaded Gothic windows. Passing through a vine-covered entrance, guests enter a long Gothic corridor and gallery leading to the grand lounge and the library. Much of the public space has elaborate woodwork, beamed ceilings and scenic views of the Old City. There are 23 rooms and three suites, providing every modern com-fort while keeping their Old-World style. Many rooms are furnished with antiques or reproductions and have views of either the city or an interior garden. Even the

simpler rooms are freshly painted and have tile baths. The hotel also features an attractive bar with a terrace and a baronial dining room (listed separately). Features: pool, air conditioning in rooms. Credit Cards: All Major.

Where to Eat

Brasserie Le Donjon $ ★★

4 rue Porte d'Avde. ☎ *05-68-25-95-72.*
Lunch: Noon–2 p.m., 86.
Dinner: 7–10 p.m., entrées FR86.
Operated by the Hotel Donjon nearby is this bustling, comfortable brasserie serving cassoulet and a reasonable FR85 set-price meal. Also within La Cite is a bistro, Les Coulisses du Theatre, in the Dame Carcas hotel, *15 rue St.-Louis (☎ 05-68-71-37-37), which offers an FR80 set-price lunch. Closed Sundays and from Sept. 15–Mar. 31.* **Market**: fruits and vegetables at *pl. Carnot, open Tues., Thurs., Sat. from 7 a.m.–1 p.m.* Amenities: outside dining, reservations recommended. Credit Cards: All Major.

La Barbacane $$$ ★★★★

place de l'Eglise, In Hotel de la Cite. Located at Hotel de la Cite. ☎ *05-68-25-03-34.*
Specialties: langoustines royales grilles, chou-fleur au caille de brebis.
Lunch: Noon–2 p.m., FR235–FR325.
Dinner: 7–9:45 p.m., entrées FR235–FR325.
Specialties of the region are given a nouvelle twist by the city's top chef Michel del Burgo, at La Barbacane, the baronial dining room in the ancient Hotel de la Cité. His desserts, which include a tomato stuffed like a baked apple and topped with ice cream, recall the interesting but bizarre creations of Alain Passard at Paris' controversial Arpege restaurant. Corbieres and Minervois wines. Prix-fixe lunch FR250, with wine. Closed: Mon. Amenities: own baking, reservations required. Credit Cards: V, MC, DC, A, E.

Auriac

Domaine d'Auriac $$$

route St.-Hilaire, About 5 km from Carcassonne, on D104. In Domaine d'Auriac. Located at Domaine d'Auriac. ☎ *04-68-25-72-22.*
Specialties: foie gras, cassoulet.
Lunch: 12:30–2 p.m., FR170–FR225.
Dinner: 7:30–9:15 p.m., entrées FR170–FR225.
Guests at this country inn just outside of the tourist bustle of Carcassonne are pampered with all kinds of luxuries, including chef Bernard Rigaud's lusty cassoulet (specialty of the house) served poolside in summer. The breads are all homemade and delicious. Comforting desserts. Amenities: outside dining, reservations required. Credit Cards: All Major.

Directory

To and From

By train from Toulouse (50 minutes), Marseilles (three hours), and Lyon (five hours), or by car on the N-113 road between Toulouse and the coast.

Tourist Office

    15 boulevard, Canmille Pelletan; ☎ *(33) 04-68-25-07-04.*

Rail Station

    Jardin St. Chenier; ☎ *(33) 04-68-47-50-50.*

Post Office

    40 rue Jean Bringer, 11000 Carcassonne; ☎ *(33) 04-68-25-05-96.*

Andorra

The smallest "nation" in Europe, Andorra is a semi-autonomous principality set in the Pyrénées that straddles the border between Spain and France. Andorra offers little to the visitor other than tax-free shopping (with higher prices that tend to cancel out the difference), the same beautiful mountain scenery that is to be had anywhere in the Pyrénées, and the chance to say you've been there. The tiny nation was formed as a political entity in 784 by decree of Charlemagne in gratitude to the citizens who helped battle the Moors, albeit unsuccessfully. Control over Andorra bounced around for several centuries, although the fiercely independent Catalan-speaking population remained studiously indifferent to events. Eventually an arrangement was concocted between the crown of France, which had come into the picture by marriage and inheritance, and the Church of Urgell, a Spanish denomination. Today, Andorra is a principality, along the lines of Monaco, with the French president and the Bishop of Urgell holding the role of co-princes. Andorra has its own popularly elected parliament and prime minister, and is represented in international affairs by Spain. By law, both Spanish *pesetas* and French *francs* are accepted in all stores in Andorra.

The capital of the principality is Andorra la Vella, a name that means "old" in Catalan. The town of 15,000 people is entirely given over to shopping. Electronics stores and perfumeries are the main feature. You can strike out in any of three directions (on one of the three main roads) to see the more charming mountain villages, each with its medieval church, steep-roofed houses, and sheep pastures.

Directory

To and From

    By train to l'Hospitalet, and then by bus (there are no train lines into Andorra), or by car on the N-20 road from Toulouse or the N-116 road from Perpignan, then the N-2 road into the principality. You will need to show a passport to enter Andorra.

Tourist Office

    22 avenue Doctor Villanova (Andorra la Vella); ☎ *(396) 202-14.*

Post Office

    1 carrer Pere d'Urg, Andorra la Vella, Andorra; ☎ *(396) 204-08.*

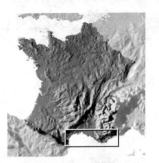

THE MEDITERRANEAN FROM SPAIN TO MONACO

Menton provides a calmer, less glamorous taste of the Riviera.

What Makes the Mediterranean Coast So French?

1. *F. Scott Fitzgerald penned* Tender is the Night, *and La Bardot kitty-katted in* And God Created Woman.

2. *Montpellier, site of Europe's first medical school, houses a library with the most grotesque full-color dermatology texts (i.e. freaks, freaks, freaks with half-faces, no faces, two-or-more faces!).*

461

What Makes the Mediterranean Coast So French?

3. *Bad, bad, drug-and-crime capital Marseilles is both the country's safest harbor and unsafest city.*

4. *St. Tropez—usually thought of as the Riviera's hottest beach resort—has no beach whatsoever!*

5. *The* **Cannes Film Festival**—*dating from 1946—is the film industry's annual May moment and a paparazzi shutter-flutter (was that Pamela Anderson Lee?).*

Ah, the south of France. Mystique still pervades the Mediterranean coast, making it the stuff of dreams for millions. Topless French women (there are none), unspoiled rocky coves bathed in brilliant sunlight (there are almost none), strolling members of the jet set meeting face-to-face on the promenade (they are usually elsewhere most of the year)—the Mediterranean conjures up images of magic and paradise for almost everyone.

Unfortunately, the dream is based on a reality that no longer exists. The heyday of France's Mediterranean coast occurred in the first half of this century, when F. Scott Fitzgerald and other American toffs decamped to the Riviera. Fitzgerald wrote the classic novel describing life there, *Tender is the Night*, and artists such as Pablo Picasso made the region their home and inspiration. But a long time has passed since Fitzgerald said, "On the summer Riviera ... whatever happened seemed to have something to do with art." Already by the 1950s, the novel was Françoise Sagan's *Bonjour Tristesse* (Hello Sadness), and the artists were early bad-boy nihilists such as Arman and Yves Klein, who blew up televisions and painted solid blue canvases. By the 1960s, the good times on the Riviera and most of the Mediterranean were coming to an end. Brigitte Bardot and the jet-set breathed new life—temporarily—and the coast rushed headlong to its boom, or more truthfully, its doom. Today, ugly 1970s hotel and apartment blocks crowd out the pastel-hued fishermen's cottages, the traffic is unbearable (St. Tropez doesn't even have a train connection) and everywhere is overcrowded. Even the water ranks among the most polluted in Europe. The beaches are naturally rocky east of Cap d'Antibes, so any sand you find is imported. The western, naturally sandy beaches are mostly private and fees are charged for their use.

All this is not meant to discourage you from visiting France's Mediterranean coast—after all, it's the country's number-one vacation spot, visited by tens of millions of people every year, including many French holiday-goers. I just want to put it into perspective. The reality is you'll have to fight with suffocating crowds during the summer, and even if you're camping, you'll pay $50 a night to pitch your tent. Sadly, the St. Tropez you saw in *And God Made Woman* is completely gone, replaced by a truly tacky, souvenir-selling

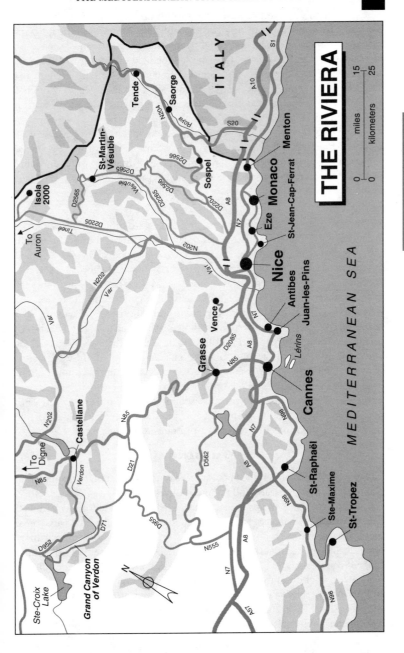

THE RIVIERA

beach resort. If you want to have a vacation sunning yourself on the beach, you will have a much better time for probably less money in Florida, Portugal, parts of the Caribbean, and certainly in other areas of France, such as on the Atlantic coast. If you want to come see the field of your dreams, however, it's still here under all the dross and exploitation. You can't get into the film festival at Cannes, but you can hang out on the streets and catch a glimpse of many Hollywood big shots. Even though you won't play Baccarat with David Niven (especially now that he's dead), you can afford to play slots for a while in the Grand Casino of Monaco. You can even drive or walk around Cap Ferrat and peer over high walls upon the villas where Fitzgerald and company once frolicked. If you come during winter you will indeed find that the Mediterranean coast was once a lovely, special place.

History

France's Mediterranean coast shares its history with other regions discussed in this book. The western coast lies at the edge of Languedoc and Rousillon, the eastern reaches include the coast of Provence. All areas were settled first by the Greeks, then by the Romans, who were attracted by the calm seaports and the trade ties they forged throughout the Mediterranean. The Franks invaded from the north after the fall of the Roman empire and the region was split into various feudal territories. Watchtowers and ruins of medieval forts bear witness to this period of splintered history, marked as much by bands of roving pirates as by organized hostilities. The western half of the coast came under the influence of the kings of Catalonia and Aragón in the 12th century, while the duchy of Savoy controlled the eastern portion a couple of hundred years later. King Réne of Anjou tried to unify the Mediterranean and bring it into his expanding territory, based in Western Loire, in the late 15th century. Finally, though not until 1860 for the most easterly part of the coast, the Mediterranean became part of France once and for all.

Cuisine

The traditional Mediterranean cuisine in France is based on the same ingredients as it is in other seabound regions—olives, garlic, spices and, of course, fish. *Bouillabaisse* is perhaps the specialty, a fish stew made from eel, mullet, red snapper and whatever else is in the catch of the day, flavored with tomatoes, olive oil and saffron. It is traditionally served with *rouille*, a garlic mayonnaise, and dry toasty croutons on the side. Another variety of fish soup is *bourride*, an even more garlicky, white-fish soup. *Daube de boeuf*, or *agneau*, is a stew of beef or lamb cooked with vegetables in red wine. *Ratatouille* is another hearty stew of onions, aubergines, zucchini, tomatoes and peppers, all cooked in olive oil and garlic. Also common are any type of fish or seafood dish, especially mussels *(moules)*, sea urchins *(oursins)* and octopus *(poulpe)*.

The wines of the south of France are undistinguished, although recently local vintners have been trying to improve the quality. After languishing as a mass-producer of vins de table for more than a century, the crescent-shaped region stretching from Banyuls on the Spanish border to Nice in the east, is returning to the production of the full-bodied, fruity red wines of yore. *Rivesaltes*, an appellation around Perpignan, produces sweet whites and rich reds; *Fitou* and *Coteaux* de Languedoc are among the newer reds that are trying to improve their quality; the rosés of Provence reach down to the coast farther east, and *Minervoix*, the easternmost region, produces pleasing wines such as *Saint Auriol, Daniel Domergue, Lastours* and *La Voulte Gaparets*.

Perpignan

Today a thoroughly French city in administration, language and geography, Perpignan still retains much of its Catalan culture, having become part of France for good only in the mid-17th century. In the 10th century this seaside city was the seat of power of the counts of Roussillon, but it reached the height of its glory three centuries later when it was transferred through marriage from the kings of Aragón to the kings of Mallorca. Under *Les Rois de Majorque*, Perpignan was the mainland capital of the small kingdom for just 68 years, long enough to construct the city's masterpiece, the Palace of the Kings of Mallorca, on a promontory separated from the river Têt by the town. The open courtyard now hosts concerts and theatrical performances, while during the day the Romanesque buildings, including the Great Hall where the kings dispensed mainland justice, can be toured along with a modest museum of local art. Begun in 1324 by the architect Sancho of Aragón and completed over the next two centuries by French builders, the Cathédrale St. Jean displays the city's trademark pebble-and-red-brick construction style. The bell that still sounds the hour at noon and calls the faithful to Mass was cast in the 15th century. The same architectural style is evident in buildings on the *rue de la Loge*, just down the street from the cathedral, where the Loge de Mer, Hôtel de Ville and Députation, the three most important government buildings in the city, stand in close proximity to one another.

Perpignan has a strong artistic heritage. The downtown square of place Hyacinthe Rigaud honors a 17th-century portrait painter who was born in the city; while Salvador Dalí, the eccentric surrealist who hailed from just across the border in Girona, said that Perpignan's station was the center of the universe and painted it often. The late 19th-century sculptor Aristide Maillol, known for his sensual, typically southern nudes, has works on display outside the Hôtel de Ville and in the place Aragón.

Within striking distance of Perpignan, you'll find the beaches and small seaside resorts of the Côte Vermeille at Carnet-Plage, St. Cyprien, and Argelès-sur-Mer. All are lively, sandy and sunny, and the water at all of these is vastly superior to that of the Côte d'Azur to the east.

What to Do

Historical/Architectural Sites

Cathédrale de St.-Jean ★★★

place Gambetta, ☎ *04-68-51-33-72.*
Hours open: 8 a.m.–7 p.m. Special hours: Closed noon–2 p.m.
Dating to the 14th and 15th centuries, the Cathédrale St.-Jean has a flat, red-brick-and-pebble facade. The interior is mostly lit with the light through the stained-glass windows, creating a rather dark ambience. Check out the pillar decorated with the decapitated head of Jean the Baptiste. For a small donation you can see the wooden crucifix in the south chapel realistically portraying Jesus' suffering. The whole experience is quite sullen. Admission: free.

Palais des Rois de Majorque ★★★★

avenue Gilbert Brutus, ☎ *04-68-34-48-29. Within the citadel.*
The oldest royal palace in France, this massive compound dates back to the 13th century. Built around a courtyard encircled by arcades, it is a fine display of civil and military architecture of the medieval times. Concerts and plays are now held in the courtyard. Besides the admiring the view, the chapels and the architecture, there is not much else offered here. The interior is of little interest, as it has been left fairly stark. *Open summer 9:30 a.m.–noon and 2:30–6 p.m.; off-season, 9 a.m.–noon and 2–5 p.m.* Admission: FR20.

Place de la Loge ★★★

This square hosts a few beautiful stone buildings. La Loge de Mer, built in 1397, once housed the Maritime Exchange and now holds onto only a part of the original Gothic design. Now home to a hamburger restaurant, the rest of the building was rebuilt in Renaissance style in 1540. Just a few feet away is the Hotel de Ville with its pebbled facade and wrought-iron gates. Sections of the interior courtyard date to the early 14th century, and the sculpture by Maillol was created in 1950.

Where to Stay

Hotels and Resorts

Park Hotel   **FR260–FR550**   ★★★

18 boulevard Jean-Bourrat. ☎ *04-68-35-14-14, FAX: 04-68-35-48-18. Across from the Jardins de la Ville.*
Single: FR260. Double: FR550.
A friendly family-run hotel facing the Jardins de la Ville, the Park Hotel is a well-visited overnight choice. With a private garden, the hotel has 67 air-conditioned rooms with TV, telephone, minibar and private bath. All are soundproof and luxuriously appointed since their renovations. Some, though, are still on the small side; be sure to request one of the refurbished ones. Breakfast costs FR38, and the res-

taurant has fixed-price menus starting at FR180. A very Catalonian influenced hotel. Features: air conditioning in rooms, in-room minibars. Credit Cards: All Major.

Villa Duflot   **FR540–FR700**   ★★★

109 avenue Victor-d'Albiez. ☎ *04-68-56-67-67, FAX: 04-68-56-54-05.*
Single: FR540. Double: FR700.
A modern villa-style hotel surrounded by a large park. The expansive hotel grounds buffer the noise from the nearby highway and city traffic. There are 24 large, air-conditioned rooms with all of the modern appointments. Average food is served in the restaurant, and there is a pool on the premises. One of the best hotels in Perpignan. Features: wheelchair-access rooms, pool, air conditioning in rooms. Credit Cards: All Major.

Where to Eat

Festin de Pierre   **$$$**   ★★★

7 rue du Theatre ☎ *04-68-51-28-74.*
Dinner: 7–9:30 p.m., entrées FR125–FR200.
Although the atmosphere can be a bit high-browed, the traditional food is excellent. Veal, poultry, red mullet and other classic dishes are served in the old-fashioned dining room. Set menus start at FR165. Closed: Wed. Reservations required. Credit Cards: All Major.

La Serre   **$**   ★★★

2 bis, rue Dagobert, In the center of old town. ☎ *04-68-34-33-02.*
In a convenient location in the historic center's hub, La Serre is a specialist in regional cuisine. Duck, poultry, mullet—it's all here and full of flavor and spice. The set menu at FR90 is one of the best bargains in town. Reservations recommended. Credit Cards: All Major.

Le Bourgogne   **$$$**   ★★★

63 avenue du Mal-Leclerc ☎ *04-68-34-96-05.*
Dinner: entrées FR200–FR325.
In an industry flooded with males, chef Teresa Morlans has established herself as one of the finest chefs in the region. Never stagnant with her menu choices, she continues to dazzle with her creatively skewed regional cuisine. Charming reception and attentive service. Set menus from FR175. Reservations required. Credit Cards: All Major.

Directory

To and From

By train from Paris (10 hours), Marseille (four hours), or Lyon (five hours), or by car on the A-9 autoroute on the way into Spain or the scenic route through the Pyrénées foothills from Toulouse on the N-20/N-116 roads.

Tourist Office

place Armand Lamoux; ☎ *(33) 04-68-66-30-30.*

Rail Station

rue Courteline; ☎ *(33) 04-68-51-10-44.*

Post Office

> *quai de Barcelone, 66000 Perpignan;* ☎ *(33) 04-68-34-40-65.*

Montpellier

A new city by French standards, where many communities in the south existed long before the Romans conquered them, Montpellier was founded in the late 10th century as an inland port connected to the ocean by the Camargue Canal and the Maguelone Lagoon. Montpellier achieved wealth in the 11th century as a primary port, trading with the eastern Mediterranean to import herbs and spices. The medicinal properties of the spices, combined with the knowledge of the Arabs and Jews migrating northward from Spain, led to the establishment in 1137 of the first medical school in Europe. The school was granted university status in 1289, and today the city is still a major university town. Fully one-quarter of its inhabitants are under 25 years of age, and there is animated daytime café society centered around the Place de la Comédie, known locally as *l'oeuf* for its oval shape. At night, Montpellier offers lively action.

The city was ravaged during the Wars of Religion, and little stands of the pre-16th century city other than two towers, *Tour de la Babote* and *Tour des Pins*, the last remnants of the original fortifications. Reconstruction during the 17th century, and development during the 18th century, has created a fine Renaissance-style town, with dozens of elegant *hôtels particuliers*, each with courtyard, spiral staircase, and loggia. A number are open to the public, including the *Hôtel des Tresoriers de la Bourse*, with its magnificent Louis XIII staircase, suspended on four corner pillars, as well as the *Hôtel des Tresoriers de la France*, and the *Hôtel Varennes*. On the eastern edge of downtown is the *Promenade de Peyrou*, a peaceful park from which one can see the sea and the remnants of the old aqueduct that once brought water to the city.

What to Do

Historical/Architectural Sites

17th-century residences   ★ ★

> *Various locations.*

Montpellier is best enjoyed by foot, with one's eyes admiring the incredible variety of architecture. From the new section of Antigone to the 17th-century mansions, it's all worth an afternoon walk. Some of the most noteworthy 17th-century mansions include the Hotel des Tresoriers de la Bourse, Hotel de Manse, Hotel Tresoriers de la France, Hotel Varennes and Hotel de Mirman. Watch for the Tour de la Babote off rue des Etuves and Tours des Pins near the cathedral.

place de la Comedie   ★★★

Place de la Comedie, also known as l'Oeuf, proves to be the best entertainment in the city with the best of all budget activities—people watching. Buzzing with young people, it's a great spot to grab a seat at an outdoor café watching all of the activity. Next to the Fontaine des Trois Graces is the 19th-century opera house, a beautiful structure. Down the esplanade is the opera and conference center reflecting the city's modern architecture. Day or night, the place de la Comedie is the heart of the action.

Where to Stay

Hotels and Resorts

Alliance Metropole   **FR620–FR675**   ★★★★

3 rue Clos Rene. ☎ *04-67-58-11-22, FAX: 04-67-92-13-02.*
Single: FR620. Double: FR675.
Subsequent to its renovations in 1991, this hotel rediscovered what made it such a grand hotel in the late 1800s. With the modern comforts of air conditioning and soundproofing, the 81 rooms are more sumptuous than ever. With 18th-century style furnishings, each comes with cable TV, telephone, minibar and beautiful marble bath. Those overlooking the interior courtyard garden are the most pleasant. There are four suites (FR750–FR950) and separate non-smoking rooms available. Regional dishes are served in the restaurant, and the bar is a cozy spot for an aperitif. One of the most diligent staffs ever put together. Features: air conditioning in rooms, in-room minibars, in-room conference facilities. Credit Cards: All Major.

Sofitel Anigone   **FR600–FR800**

1 rue des Pertuisanes. ☎ *04-67-65-62-63, FAX: 04-67-65-17-50. About 1 km from train station; in the business district.*
Single: FR600–FR700. Double: FR700–FR800.
The newest hotel in Montpellier, the Antigone opened in 1991 in a peaceful area of the business district. A multistory, streamlined structure offering a wealth of services. The 89 modern rooms are soundproof and fully equipped with air conditioning, cable TV, radio, telephone, minibar, bath and hair dryer. Nonsmoking rooms may be reserved. The eighth-floor restaurant provides the best panoramic view in town. Bar and grill service are available poolside. For modern comforts, the best choice in Montpellier. Features: wheelchair-access rooms, pool, nonsmoking rooms, in-room minibars, in-room conference facilities. Credit Cards: All Major.

Inns

Demeure des Brousses Hotel   **FR380–FR580**   ★★★

538 rue du Mas des Brousses. ☎ *04-67-65-77-66, FAX: 04-67-22-22-17. Just outside of town; 4 km from the train station.*
Double: FR380–FR580.
One word describes the atmosphere here—tranquil. A small hotel situated on the outskirts of town, this château style inn houses just 17 rooms. All of the attractive rooms come with TV, telephone, bath and hair dryer. Meals are enjoyed in the relaxed yet elegant dining room, with soothing nightcaps served in the bar. Expect a genuine welcome from the small, respectful staff. Credit Cards: All Major.

Where to Eat

L'Olivier $$ ★★★

12 rue Aristide -Olivier, Near the train station. ☎ *04-67-92-86-28.*

Dinner: 7:30–9:30 p.m., entrées FR125–FR275.

From the moment one enters this small establishment it's obvious that the emphasis is on personal attention. Warm smiles, respectful attention and personalized cuisine. The small menu is brimming with excellence—John Dory with artichoke hearts and cockles, sea bass with vegetables and many other feats of artistry. Set menus from FR140. Closed: Mon., Sun. Credit Cards: All Major.

La Tomate $ ★★

6 rue Four-des-Flammes ☎ *04-67-60-49-38.*

Since it opened in the 1970s, La Tomate has packed 'em in—tourists and locals. Known among the local crowd as the best value for French cuisine in town, the atmosphere is informal and friendly. Set menus start at FR55–FR115. For some decent Egyptian food, head for **Ramses** at *26 rue des Ecoles Laiques (* ☎ *04-67-60-30-05).* The Cleopatra plate is just FR50- a generously proportioned meal. Or, for system cleansing, head for the vegetarian delights at **Tripti Kulai** at *20 rue Jacques Coeur (* ☎ *04-67-66-30-51).* A sample platter starts at FR60, and a la carte items start at just FR15. Closed: Mon., Sun. Reservations recommended.

Le Chandelier $$$ ★★★★

3 rue Leenhardt, Near the train station. ☎ *04-67-92-61-62.*

Dinner: 7:30–9:30 p.m., entrées FR120–FR200.

A constantly changing specialty menu here might include prime-cut salmon, beef with violet shallot juice or mousse of smoked eel with mint-flavored mussels. The neoclassical decor provides an ambience of poetry and privacy with the splash of the small fountain in the background. The wine cellar keeps pace with the changing menu and holds a reserve of classics. Set menus start at FR120 and FR180 during the week for lunch and FR250 for dinner. Closed: Sun. Reservations required. Credit Cards: All Major.

Directory

To and From

By train from Toulouse (two hours) and Marseille (two hours), or by car on the A-9 coastal autoroute or the N-9 from the north.

Tourist Office

passage du Tourisme; ☎ *(33) 04-67-58-67-58.*

Rail Station

place Auguste Gilbert; ☎ *(33) 04-67-58-50-50.*

Post Office

place Rondelet, 34000 Montpellier; ☎ *(33) 04-67-34-50-00.*

Marseille

France's biggest port and second-largest city, capital of drugs, the Mob, street crime, and as grimy as Paris on a bad day, Marseille is not really a tourist destination. Nevertheless it has a certain attraction, perhaps because of its intrigue and its history of trading in men, materiel and money, something along the lines of *On the Waterfront*. Marseille is the biggest port in France in terms of trading ports, anyway and it is far and away the oldest. The Greeks established a settlement here, called Massilia, in the seventh century B.C. The Greco-local inhabitants built up a solid trading empire, expanding into the interior of Provence as well as farther along the shore to other ports. By the middle of the second century B.C., Massilia was a huge city for its time, run as an independent city-state. In 123 B.C. the city entered into a treaty with Rome, which served it well both commercially and in terms of protection from its envious Celtic neighbors. Massilia bet on the wrong side during the Roman civil war by backing Pompey. When Caesar emerged victorious, he burned and destroyed the city in 49 B.C.

Marseille's port continued to provide a safe harbor, although the original port silted up by the 11th century. During the Crusades, Marseille served as a naval harbor. When Provence became part of France in the late 15th century, the city's fortunes improved even more, and Louis XIII ordered more quays built in the 17th century, in time for a boom in business with the colonization of the Americas and other parts of the world. During World War II, Marseille was a major administrative center of the collaborationist Vichy government and the Nazis, and at the same time home to a strong Resistance, built around communist organizations and labor unions. Because of this, when the war ended, the American OSS (precursor to the CIA) gave organized-crime free reign to expand in the city in return for their stamping out the "Reds," which the Americans thought more dangerous. This, combined with the normal illicit business that always centers around a major port, as well as Marseille's historically independent attitude, resulted in the city becoming one of the most corruption- and crime-riddled areas of France.

The old port is pleasant for strolling with bustling activity on the small fishing boats that dock there. At the east end in the *Jardin des Vestiges*, remains of ancient Greek buildings can be seen. A third-century Roman ship excavated from the harbor is on display at the *Musée d'Histoire de Marseille*. At the other end of the old port is the site of a former Greek temple. More recent history can be seen in the basilica of Notre Dame de la Garde, built in the mid-19th century. The basilica's 150-foot bell tower topped with an enormous gilded statue of the Virgin Mary dominates the city skyline. Overlooking the port near the Fort St. Nicolas, the fortified Abbaye St. Victor, was begun in the 11th century. The abbey's most interesting feature is the crypt, believed to date from the fourth century, which contains catacombs used by early Christians to hide out, hold meetings and bury their dead.

The Historical Museum, the *Musée des Docks Romains*, display exhibits of the port as it was in the time of Caesar, while the Musée de Vieux Marseilles has a collection of paintings of the medieval city. The Musée des Beaux Arts contains more paintings illustrating the city's history. All are worth considering if you plan to be in the town for more than a few hours.

What to Do

Historical/Architectural Sites

Basilique St.-Victors   ★★

   quai de River-Neuve, ☎ 04-91-33-25-86.
   Hours open: 10 a.m.–6 p.m. Special hours: Closed 11 a.m–3 p.m. and Sun. 3–6 p.m.
Heavily fortified, the basilica was rebuilt in the 11th century. The crypt in the church, however, dates to the 5th century. The French Revolution saw this site used as a prison and barracks by rebels. Now, every Feb. 2, this church is visited as a pilgrimage site to commemorate the arrival of St.-Martha, St.-Mary Magdalene and Lazarus about 2000 years ago. Admission to the crypt is FR10.

Basilique de Notre-Dame de la Garde   ★★★

   place du Colonel Eden, ☎ 04-91-37-42-82. Bus 60 from Cours Jean Ballard
   Hours open: 7:30 a.m.–7 p.m. Special hours: Winter until 5:30 p.m.
This 19th-century church is Marseilles' Eiffel Tower, standing like a sentinel on its perch 531 feet above the city. Not particularly noteworthy either architecturally or historically, it has an amazing view from its terrace. Cafeteria on the premises. Admission: free.

Museums and Exhibits

Musée Cantini   ★★★

   19 rue Grignan, ☎ 04-91-54-77-75.
   Hours open: 11 a.m.–6 p.m. Closed: Mon.
An impressive array of international modern art is housed in this beautiful 17th-century mansion. On permanent view are 20th-century titans Francis Bacon, Balthus, Andre Derain and others. Exhibits change frequently, and the museum actively adds new acquisitions. Free admission Sun. morning. Admission: FR10.

Musée d'Histoire de Marseille   ★★

   square Belsunce, ☎ 04-91-90-42-22. In the Centre Bourse.
   Hours open: Noon–7 p.m. Closed: Sun.
Wander through archaeological excavations and learn about the history of an ancient Greek town. A boat from the 2nd century was discovered on the site in 1974 and has been freeze-dried where it is now situated. Another boat, this one 2500 years old, was discovered in 1993. Other displays feature old coins, pottery and other artifacts. Admission: FR10.

Musée des Docks Romains ★★

place Vivaux, ☎ *04-91-56-28-38. On the north side of the old port.*
Hours open: 11 a.m.–6 p.m.
Sitting on the site of the old Roman docks, this museum of Roman warehouses exhibits some of the 1st-century Roman warehouses and docks. These finds were made in 1947 during excavations prior to the building up of the area. Admission: FR10.

Musée du Vieux Marseille ★

2 rue de la Prison, ☎ *04-91-55-10-19. Behind the Hotel de Ville.*
Hours open: 11 a.m.–6 p.m. Closed: Mon.
Occupying the 16th-century Maison Diamantee, this ho-hum museum displays such exciting examples of Marseille's history as playing cards, the machines used to make the cards and various household items. Miscellaneous items are found throughout, but none justify paying the francs to enter. Admission: FR10.

Palais Longchamp ★★

boulevard Longchamp, ☎ *04-91-62-21-17.*
Hours open: 10 a.m.–5 p.m. Closed: Mon.
A trio of noteworthy museums are housed in the Palais Longchamp, a 19th-century building and multi-use complex, with a zoo, gardens and fountains. The jewel in the crown is the Beaux Arts, with a definitive collection of Italian, French and Flemish masters from the 16th through the 19th centuries (including Rubens, Watteau and Tiepolo). One entire salon is set aside for Honore Daumier, a Marseille-born painter and sharp-penned political caricaturist. There's a special museum for kids on the ground floor, with an adjoining natural history museum. Seniors, free. Admission: FR12.

Special Tours/Excursions

Château d'If ★★★

About 2 km south of the Port of Marseilles, ☎ *04-91-55-50-09.*
Hours open: 9 a.m.–7 p.m. Special hours: Winter to 5:30 p.m.
Just a short boat ride (FR60 round-trip) from the port of Marseille, this small isle is home to the formidable castle-prison immortalized in Dumas' *Count of Monte Cristo*. Originally a fortress, it eventually housed state prisoners, but not the fictional count. Admission for students and children is FR17. Admission: FR26.

Where to Stay

Hotels and Resorts

Concorde Prado   FR600–FR660   ★★★

11 avenue de Mazarques. ☎ *04-91-76-51-11, FAX: 04-91-77-95-10.*
Single: FR600. Double: FR660.
Popular with travelers who want to get away from the town center, this quiet hotel sits in a residential area near the harbor. The eight-story building sets design standards with its constant updating and attention to modern advances. Ascend in the bronze elevators to one of the 81 air-conditioned rooms. Each comes with a TV, telephone, minibar and private bath. Wining and dining options, in addition to room service, include a restaurant and an American-style bar. While the only recre-

ational facility here is a putting green, there are golf, tennis and horseback riding nearby. The hotel has a shopping gallery with 20 boutiques, a 600-person conference facility, various business services and dry-cleaning available. Features: air conditioning in rooms, in-room minibars. Credit Cards: V, MC, DC, A.

Concorde-Palm Beach   FR655–FR767   ★★★

2 promenade de la Plage. ☎ *04-91-16-19-00, FAX: 04-91-16-19-39.*
Rated Restaurant: *La Reserve.*
Single: FR655–FR687. Double: FR730–FR767.

A well-visited, beachfront hotel fronting Prado Bay, the Concorde is a modern four-story structure catering to both business travelers and vacation travelers alike. Guests enter through the large, bright lobby with the fireside bar and lounge adjoining. The two restaurant options are the grill, Les Voiliers, and the more formal restaurant, La Reserve. Terrace dining is offered in the warm months. The pool sits in the middle of the deck, adjacent to an umbrella-dotted terrace. The 145 air-conditioned rooms are a meld of cool colors, large windows, cane furnishings and large terraces opening onto the sea. A TV, telephone, minibar and private bath are standard in each. Helpful services include concierge, hairdressing and laundry. The management is attentive to the guests, if not always to the facilities. Features: beach location, pool, air conditioning in rooms, sauna, balcony or patio. Credit Cards: All Major.

Le Petit Nice Passedat   FR1000–FR1900   ★★★

16 rue des Braves. ☎ *04-91-59-25-92, FAX: 04-91-59-28-08.*
Rated Restaurant: *PassÈdat.*
Single: FR1000–FR1100. Double: FR1100–FR1900.

Easily the finest hotel and restaurant in Marseille, le Petit Nice occupies a residential-style villa from 1917. Situated behind a high wall and iron gates, this small Relais and Châteaux hotel sits among a row of private villas hugging the hill above the coast. The vantage point from this property offers fine sweeps of the coast and the islands. The public space keeps a fresh look, with the lobby, lounge, bar and seaside terrace inviting guests to linger and socialize. The 15 air-conditioned rooms have a TV, telephone, radio, safe, minibar, private bath, hair dryer and robes. The attractive restaurant serves creative cuisine to the tables with views of the rocky coast. A la carte meals start at FR450. A stunning location for this gem of the Marseille coast. Features: beach location, pool, air conditioning in rooms, sauna, balcony or patio, in-room safes, in-room minibars. Credit Cards: All Major.

Mercure Marseille Vieux-Port   FR500–FR850   ★★★

4 rue Beauvau. ☎ *04-91-54-91-00, FAX: 04-91-54-15-76.*
Rated Restaurant: *La Table du Roi.*
Single: FR500–FR620. Double: FR700–FR850.

Ideally located for visitors touring the town on foot, the Mercure Vieux-Port (formerly the Pullman Beauvau) overlooks the main thoroughfare at the Old Port. Originally opened in 1816, this hotel manages to stay surprisingly quiet considering its central location. In its earlier day, this grand hotel welcomed such guests as George Sand and Chopin. Since its major renovations in 1985, it now has 72 air-conditioned rooms with TV, telephone, minibar, tiled bath and hair dryer. The soundproofed rooms conjure up images of yesteryear with Provencal antiques and furnishings. There is no restaurant, but there is a snack bar and a cocktail lounge in the hotel, and there are many dining choices nearby. An above-average choice for a chain hotel. Features: beach location, air conditioning in rooms, nonsmoking rooms, in-room minibars. Credit Cards: All Major.

Sofitel Vieux Port   **FR630–FR960**   ★★★

36 boulevard Charles-Livon. ☎ *04-91-52-90-19, FAX: 04-91-31-46-52.*
Rated Restaurant: *Les Trois Forts.*
Single: FR630–FR780. Double: FR920–FR960.
On a promontory guarding the east entrance to the Vieux-Port, this Sofitel sits on leased land owned by the French navy and subject to reclamation at any time. The 127 guest rooms either overlook the boulevard or offer a beautiful panorama of the Old Port. Each of the rather commercially decorated rooms comes with air conditioning, TV, telephone, minibar and marble bath. The seven-story structure contains a rooftop restaurant, coffeeshop, snackbar, piano bar and poolside terrace. Most of the congenial staff speaks English. Features: wheelchair-access rooms, beach location, pool, air conditioning in rooms, nonsmoking rooms, in-room minibars. Credit Cards: All Major.

Where to Eat

Chez Fonfon   **$$**   ★★

140 rue deu Vallon des Auffes. ☎ *04-91-52-14-38.*
Specialties: bouillabaisse.
Lunch: Noon–2 p.m., FR175–FR250.
Dinner: 7–10 p.m., entrées FR175–FR250.
This simple restaurant, in an out-of-the-way location with its own bay, is noted for terrific bouillabaisse—some say the best in town. All fish dishes are impeccably fresh. Another good place for bouillabaisse and other seafare is **Chez Loury**, *3 rue Fortia, 1st er* (☎ *04-91-33-09-73*), but at a lower price; FR150 set meal (no dinner Sat.). Patio dining. Closed: Mon., Sun. Reservations recommended. Credit Cards: V, MC, A, E.

Jambon de Parme   **$$**   ★★

67 rue de la Palud. ☎ *04-91-54-37-98.*
Specialties: parma ham, scampi.
Lunch: Noon–2 p.m., FR140–FR200.
Dinner: 7–11 p.m., entrées FR140–FR200.
A wonderful change of pace, this stylish Italian restaurant offers Parma ham, pasta and veal dishes to a well-dressed clientele. Some of Marseilles' best families dine here regularly. French boudoir decor. Closed: Mon. Credit Cards: V, MC, DC, A, E.

Les Arcenaulx   **$**   ★★

25 cours d'Estienne-d'Orves. ☎ *04-91-54-77-06.*
Lunch: Noon–2 p.m., FR85.
Dinner: 7 p.m.–12:30 a.m., entrées FR85.
The intelligentsia gather at this elegantly appointed bookstore and restaurant offering a terrific lunch fixed-price lunch for only FR85 (except weekends). Light regional dishes, marvelous desserts. The best pastries and hot chocolate in town can be found at **L'Atelier du Chocolat**, *18 pl. des Huiles, 1st er* (☎ *04-91-33-55-00*), also light meals. Go for the FR80 set menu. For regional cooking at a low price, try

Panier des Arts, *3 rue Petit-Puits, 2nd eme* (☎ *04-91-56-02-32*), open until 10 p.m.; the fixed-price menu starts at FR70. Then there's **Chez Angele**, *50 rue Caisserie, 2nd eme* (☎ *04-91-90-63-35*), for pizza; lots of young people; FR60–FR100. Open until 11 p.m., closed Sun. nights and all day Mon. Nearby is **Le Roi du Couscous**, at *63 rue de la Republique* (☎ *04-91-91-45-46*), offering a veggie version of the North African semolina stew for FR40; other versions FR50–FR60. Closed: Sun. Amenities: outside dining, reservations recommended. Credit Cards: V, MC, DC, A, E.

Miramar
$$$
★★

12 quai du Port. ☎ *04-91-91-10-40.*
Specialties: bouillabaisse.
Lunch: Noon–2 p.m., FR355–FR450.
Dinner: 7–10 p.m., entrées FR355–FR450.
This is probably the best restaurant in town for traditional cooking. Bouillabaisse is the specialty, but any of the unusual fish dishes from the voluminous menu are guaranteed to satisfy. Also well known and popular is **Au Pescadou**, *19 place Castellane* (☎ *04-91-78-36-01*). A look at the tempting oyster display outside will make your mouth water. Featuring hundreds of varieties of fish, it's noisy and colorful. The fixed-price menus range from FR160–FR200. Closed: Sun. Amenities: outside dining, reservations required. Credit Cards: V, MC, DC, A, E.

Passedat
$$$
★★★

160 Corniche Kennedy, Anse de Maldorme, In Le Petit Nice. Located at Le Petit Nice.
☎ *04-91-59-25-92.*
Specialties: lamb carpaccio with basil, wolf fish "Lucie Passedat."
Lunch: Noon–2 p.m., FR235–FR375.
Dinner: 7–10 p.m., entrées FR235–FR375.
Located in one of Marseilles' best hotels, Passedat has won plenty of critical acclaim for its creative seafood everywhere but at home, where diners tend to be culinarily conservative. They probably don't know what to make of dishes such as *gateau de grenouilles aux pieds de porc* (cake of frogs' legs with pigs trotters). Perhaps with the higher than average prices charged, people are less willing to take chances. The service is also a little frosty. But it's hard to argue with the garden setting, overlooking the coastline and the outer islands. Closed: Sun. Amenities: outside dining, own baking, reservations required. Credit Cards: V, MC, A, E.

Villeneuve-les-Avignon

Aubertin
$$$
★★★

1 rue de l'Hopital, Across the Rhone from Avignon, 3 km northwest. ☎ *04-90-25-94-84.*
Lunch: Noon–2 p.m., FR250–FR330.
Dinner: 7–9:30 p.m., entrées FR250–FR330.
It's a good idea to reserve in advance, as this acclaimed restaurant has room for fewer than 30 lucky people; your reward is chef Jean-Claude Aubertin's springlike, creative cooking, largely devoid of heavy cream and oils. Terrace dining when the weather permits (more often than not). The fixed-price lunch menu starts at a reasonable FR150. Closed: Mon. Amenities: outside dining, own baking, reservations required. Credit Cards: V, MC, A, E.

Directory

To and From

> *By air from any city in France as well as many international destinations, by train from Paris (four-and-a-half hours) or Lyon (two-and-a-half hours), or by car on the A-7 or A-51 autoroute from the north, the A-55 autoroute from the west, or the N-8 road from the east and the Côte d'Azur.*

Tourist Office

> *4 La Canebière; ☎ (33) 04-91-13-89-00.*

Rail Station

> *boulevard Bourdet; ☎ (33) 04-91-08-50-50.*

Post Office

> *1 Hôtel des Postes, 13001 Marseille; ☎ (33) 04-91-90-31-33.*

St. Tropez

St. Tropez still attracts the trendy to its posh resorts.

The charming fishing village that St. Tropez once was fended off the worst excesses of the rest of the Mediterranean coast for longer than other towns, in part because no train line serves the town and also because it faced north and was not as attractive to sun worshipers. Outsiders began to arrive in 1862, when the painter Paul Signac came to stay and soon urged his fellow post-Impressionists, including Matisse, Bonnard and others, to come on down. Other artists and writers moved to the town in the 1920s, and between the wars St. Tropez had became a fashionable little resort. After World War II, during which the village saw heavy damage as a site of the southern Allied Army's landing, Brigitte Bardot filmed *And God Created Woman* in the town in 1956, and the hordes began to arrive. Given that St. Tropez is viewed as one of the beach resorts in France, the irony is that the town has no beaches—you have to drive a few miles to get to the Pampelonne coast to find parking, cram yourself next to other sunbathers on the sand, and pay an arm and a leg for a bottle of water or a cold beer.

The crowds drove Brigitte Bardot out of St. Tropez long ago, and nothing could induce me to visit except during the middle of winter. However, if you do stop in St. Tropez, the *Musée de l'Annonciade* contains an impressive collection of paintings by some of the artists who have lived here.

What to Do

Beaches

Tahiti Beach ★★★

route de Tahiti, Pampelonne, ☎ *04-94-97-18-02. In summer, take shuttle bus from Place de Lices.*

St. Tropez's public beaches, including the popular Plage des Graniers, are often pebbly and extremely crowded. For the real St. Tropez experience, you can lounge on a slender striped cushion for around FR80 a day at one of the private beach clubs on the tony Pampelonne strip (about 5 km southwest of the port of St. Tropez). Tahiti is one of the most fashionable, and your fee includes a chance to shell out more bucks for lunch (about FR700 for two), a massage and shower facilities. Admission: FR80.

Museums and Exhibits

Musée de L'Annonciade ★★★

place Grammont, ☎ *04-94-97-04-01.*
Hours open: 10 a.m.–8 p.m. Special hours: Winter until 6 p.m.; closed Nov. Closed: Tue.
Not surprisingly, most of France's leading modern artists have passed through St. Tropez at one time or another, often staying for long periods. This harborside museum contains an enviable collection of modern pieces by such masters as Paul Signac, Utrillo, Bonnard, Matisse, Roualt, Seurat and Maillol. The Naval Museum resides at the cliffside Citadel, high above town, at avenue Paul Signac. You can observe the poseurs in the cafés below from the balcony; bring a picnic lunch. Admission: FR25.

Nightlife

Les Caves du Roy ★★★

avenue Paul-Signac, ☎ *04-94-97-00-04. In the Hotel Byblos.*
Hours open: 11 p.m.–5 a.m. Special hours: Open June–Sept. only.
Like something out of the *Arabian Nights*, Les Caves du Roy's decor apes a Middle-Eastern pleasure palace, with mirrors and columns in abundance. The clientele is a mixture of wannabes and the seriously moneyed. Drinks start at FR135. Live music. Admission: free.

Pubs and Bars

Cafe de Paris ★★★

Quai Suffren, ☎ *04-94-97-00-56.*

Hours open: 8 a.m.–3 a.m. Special hours: Winter, to 7 p.m.
Varied offerings are available at this velvety boudoir in the heart of the port area.
You can shoot pool, have a coffee (reasonably priced) or a stiff drink (stratospheric)
in a makeshift turn-of-the-century bordello atmosphere. Always crowded.

Where to Stay

Hotels and Resorts

Byblos **FR1700–FR2870** ★★★★

avenue Paul-Signac. ☎ *04-94-56-68-00, FAX: 04-94-56-68-01. Located at the base of
the Citadelle, on Place de Lices, near Montee G. Ringrave.* Rated Restaurant: *Les Arcades.*
Single: FR1700–FR2260. Double: FR2730–FR2870.

This deluxe complex is situated on a hill above the harbor just a few minutes from
all the beaches. It has an exotic Moorish atmosphere, with tiling and mosaics set in
its patios and courtyards; within, nooks and niches are filled with antiques and
objects d'art, many from Lebanon. There are 60 rooms and 47 suites, each uniquely
decorated, with paisley brocades, rich mosaics and hammered brass. Some rooms
have a balcony overlooking an inner courtyard; others open onto a flowered terrace.
Standard features are double-glazed windows, telephone, TV and tile or marble
bathroom with robes and sunken tub. Accommodations also include 10 duplex
apartments built around a small courtyard with an outdoor spa. The hotel provides
such services as a beauty salon, 24-hour room service, same-day laundry and valet.
Its restaurant, **Les Arcades**, is only open for dinner. Prices range from FR280 to
FR400. Also featured are a Moorish-style bar, a nightclub and a disco. Features:
mountain location, pool, skiing, air conditioning in rooms, sauna, in-room minibars, fitness center. Credit Cards: All Major.

Domaine/Villa de Belieu **FR1800–FR4000** ★★★★★

Gassin on Route de St.-Tropez. ☎ *04-94-56-40-56, FAX: 04-94-43-43-34. Located
about 2 km north on Route de St.-Tropez, near the intersection of Gassin and Ramatu-
elle.* Rated Restaurant: *Restaurant Belieu.*
Single: FR1800–FR2000. Double: FR2000–FR4000.

A short drive from the center of St.-Tropez, this opulent hotel was converted from
a Mediterranean-style villa on the grounds of the Domaine de Bertaud-Belieu. This
estate has been producing grapes for wines for more than 2000 years. The villa is
Italianesque and the decor is pure Provence. All of the 12 rooms and five suites are
uniquely decorated in styles ranging from Rococo to Art Deco; many have antiques
and *trompe l'oeil* murals. All of the units are spacious and have private bath and
every modern convenience. Some have a balcony or private garden. The hotel also
provides a hairdresser, 24-hour room service, and a spa, styled after the Roman
baths, complete with sauna, Jacuzzi and gym. Guests are invited to visit the wine
cellar and the nearby golf course. The romantic **Restaurant Belieu** offers dining
outside under the stars as well as dining inside. In the wood-beamed restaurant,
tables are graced with French porcelain and antique silverware. The Provencal cuisine focuses on seafood, and the wines are the estate's best. Both lunch and dinner
are served daily, but reservations are required. Features: pool, golf, tennis, air con-

ditioning in rooms, sauna, balcony or patio, in-room minibars, fitness center. Credit Cards: All Major.

Ermitage   **FR450–FR890**   ★★★

avenue Paul-Signac. ☎ *04-94-97-52-33, FAX: 04-94-97-10-43. Located at the base of the Citadelle, on place de Lices, near Montee G. Ringrave.*
Single: FR450–FR700. Double: FR700–FR890.
Originally built as a private villa, this three-story hotel is a plush yet comfortable hideaway. It is next door to the Byblos, but it has a more relaxed atmosphere than its neighbor, and it is one of the few hotels with a sweeping view of old St. Tropez. The 29 rooms have been renovated and now have private bath and tastefully refurbished decor. There is a walled garden which is romantically illuminated at night. Within, a corner bar is situated near a wood-burning fireplace, adding to the cozy ambience. Breakfast is the only meal served. Features: in-room minibars. Credit Cards: All Major.

La Ponche   **FR750–FR2200**   ★★★

3 place Revelin. ☎ *04-94-97-02-53. Located at rue des Remparts.*
Rated Restaurant: *La Ponche.*
Single: FR750–FR900. Double: FR950–FR2200.
Situated in a fairly secluded part of central St. Tropez, this hotel was converted from a cluster of fishermen's cottages. Before it became a hotel, it had been a pub by the same name, frequented by Picasso. The hotel has a small beach and a plaza, which becomes a social center in the evenings, and the noise sometimes penetrates into the rooms. There are 18 spacious rooms, charmingly decorated with antiques and paintings; all rooms have a private bath; a few have a terrace facing the beach; two are suitable for families. The hotel has two dining rooms, featuring fresh seafood. Features: beach location, air conditioning in rooms, balcony or patio, fitness center. Credit Cards: All Major.

Le Yaca   **FR1000–FR2200**   ★★★

1 boulevard d'Aumale. ☎ *04-94-97-11-79, FAX: 04-94-97-58-50. Located between rue de la Citadelle and place des Remparts.* Rated Restaurant: *(No name given.).*
Single: FR1000–FR1200. Double: FR1200–FR2200.
The first hotel to be built in St. Tropez, Le Yaca dates back to 1722. Colette lived here in 1927, and pre-Impressionist painters, including Paul Signac, made this their home before that. The hotel is located off a narrow street in the old part of town. Inside, the high-ceilinged lobby looks out on an inner courtyard. Many of the hotel's 22 comfortable rooms, all with private bath, have handmade terra-cotta tile floors and massive ceiling timbers and look out on the courtyard. There is a restaurant on the premises. Features: pool, air conditioning in rooms. Credit Cards: All Major.

Residence de la Pinede   **FR1450–FR2915**   ★★★★

plage de la Bouillabaisse. ☎ *04-94-97-04-21, FAX: 04-94-97-73-64. Located about 1 km south on D98.* Rated Restaurant: *Residence de la Pinede.*
Single: FR1450–FR1850. Double: FR2700–FR2915.
Built in 1952, this chic resort hotel is tucked away in a grove of pine trees above its private beach. Rated as a Relais and Châteaux, it has attracted many celebrities. There are 42 spacious and comfortable rooms, which were recently remodeled and

redecorated in pastel colors. They all have small tile and marble bathrooms with hair dryer and thick towels. Other standard features are satellite TV, video, telephone and terrace overlooking the bay. The hotel also offers same-day laundry, 24-hour room service and a valet. The restaurant has excellent food, which is served in the dining room or on the terrace under the pine trees. Half-board rates range from FR1325 to FR1800 (room, breakfast and a meal) per person, per day in season. Features: wheelchair-access rooms, beach location, pool, water sports, air conditioning in rooms, balcony or patio, in-room minibars. Credit Cards: All Major.

Where to Eat

Bistrot des Lices   **$$**   ★ ★ ★

3 place des Lices ☎ *04-94-97-29-00.*
Specialties: risotto, pigs trotters, bourride (Provencal fish soup).
Lunch: Noon–2 p.m., FR125–FR200.
Dinner: 7:30 p.m.–12:30 a.m., entrées FR125–FR200.
Deceptively simple-looking, this establishment is actually a highly regarded local favorite, with a chic crowd (probably a celebrity or two), and a changing menu of Provencal favorites. There are several dining areas, a main room, a terrace facing the square, and a garden in the back. Amenities: outside dining, own baking, reservations required. Credit Cards: V, MC.

Château de la Messardiere   **$$$**   ★ ★ ★

avenue Roussel on the rte de Tahiti, 5 km southwest of St.-Tropez. In Château de la Messardiere. Located at Château de la Messardiere. ☎ *04-94-56-76-00.*
Lunch: Noon–2 p.m., FR350–FR550.
Dinner: 7–10:30 p.m., entrées FR350–FR550.
Fresh seafood and Asian spices are the hallmarks on the menu here. This restaurant, in a restored—and now very expensive—château, was once managed by the current St. Tropez restaurant king Christopher Leroy. Lunch is served by the pool (FR200 fixed price), dinner indoors in the country-French dining room. Leroy is now well established at **La Table du Marche**, an Art-Deco style bistro, with somewhat lower prices, *38 rue Clemenceau (*☎ *04-94-97-85-20),* open noon to 12:30 p.m. daily; specialties include roast Bresse chicken, steak and macaroni gratin and cheese souffles. Upstairs, a maximum of 20 people squeeze into **La Salle a Manger** (dinner only), giving it a dinner-party atmosphere. There's an a la carte menu (FR700–FR800), but most patrons leave it up to Christopher, who serves a FR500 set menu, which he changes nightly. Amenities: outside dining, own baking, reservations required. Credit Cards: V, MC, DC, A, E.

Lou Revelen   **$$**   ★

4 rue des Remparts ☎ *04-94-97-41-76.*
Lunch: Noon–midnight, FR95–FR200.
Dinner: Noon–midnight, entrées FR95–FR200.
The people at this port-side restaurant will serve you good set meals and treat you kindly. Perfect for the almost-midnight munchies. On the higher, budget-splurge end in this bargain-poor town are **Cafe des Arts**, on *pl. des Lices (*☎ *04-94-97-02-25),* a fashionable, see-and-be-seen establishment serving prix-fixe meals for FR190, with wine!! Also open until midnight. Lower still is the **Bar a Vins**, *13 rue des Feniers,*

where you can play billiards; prix-fixe FR180, wine by the glass, excellent food. Otherwise, there's the **morning fish market** *(rue du Marche)* and the **vegetable and fruit market** *(place aux Herbes)*, or the village market at place de Lices, Tuesday and Saturday mornings. Amenities: outside dining, cafestop. Credit Cards: All Major.

Residence de La Pinede   **$$$**   ★ ★ ★

place de la Bouillabaisse ☎ *04-94-97-04-21.*
Specialties: minestrone of roasted langoustines with basil.
Lunch: Noon–2 p.m., FR500–FR700.
Dinner: 7–10:30 p.m., entrées FR500–FR700.

This restaurant, within an ultra-posh celebrity hideaway, is helmed by Herve Quesnel, who was in charge of the kitchens at the Hotel Crillon in Paris. His cuisine, utilizing mostly local seafood, is cooked with a minimum of fuss, affording a maximum of natural flavors. He's ably assisted by sommelier Jean-Louis Rolland, who will guide you through the intricacies of his wine cellar. Dine indoors or on a terrace shaded by the pine trees that give the place its name. Smooth, anticipatory service. Amenities: outside dining, own baking, reservations required. Credit Cards: All Major.

Directory

To and From

By bus from Toulon or St. Raphael, or by car on the dead-end spur off the N-98 coastal road.

Tourist Office

quai Jean-Jourès; ☎ *(33) 04-94-97-41-21.*

Post Office

place A. Celli, 83990 St. Tropez; ☎ *(33) 04-94-79-47-30.*

Cannes

The town of Cannes owes its transformation from fishing village to world-famous resort to an outbreak of cholera. Although it would have happened sooner or later anyway, the town was "discovered" by Lord Brougham, a former Lord Chancellor of England, in 1834, when he could not travel on to Nice because of an outbreak of the disease there. He fell in love with the place, built a villa for himself, and returned every winter thereafter. The English and then French mucky-mucks soon popularized the place. The heart of Cannes is its boulevard de la Croisette, where the rich and famous can be spotted wheeling their Ferraris from hotel to casino to yacht harbor and back. One side of the boulevard is lined with lawns and towering palm trees, the other with expensive boutiques and elegant Belle Epoque-style hotels—including one, the Carlton, which truly epitomizes the Art Deco era, its twin domes having been modeled on the breasts of *La Belle Otero*, a well-known débutante of the mid-19th century. The city is perhaps best known for its International Film Festival, which began in 1946, and which gives the *Palme d'Or* to the best film of the year. Don't even think about trying to get tickets to the annual May event unless you have high connections in Hollywood. The Notre Dame de l'Espérance cathedral is a pleasing 17th-century structure, and there is an 11th-century watchtower bearing witness to the town's pre-jet set past. A boat trip to the twin *Iles de Lérins*, on one of which the "Man in the Iron Mask" (said to be Louis XIV's illegitimate brother) was imprisoned in the 17th century, is a good way to enjoy the view of the town and the coast while escaping the crowds. Cannes' beaches are justifiably famous for their fine white sand, but whenever the temperature rises above 60 degrees you'll find it impossible to get much more than a towel space's worth of room.

Cannes is best known for its annual film festival.

What to Do

City Celebrations/Events

Cannes Film Festival   ★ ★ ★ ★

   Palais des Festivals, 1 boulevard de la Croisette, ☎ *04-93-39-24-53.*
   Unless you have connections, or are there to hawk your own piece of celluloid, you won't be allowed to attend any screenings. That's the bad news. The good news is that no one will stop you from gawking all you want. Held the second and third week of May, every year since 1946.

Nightlife

Casino Municipale   ★ ★

   1 jetee Albert-Edouard, ☎ *04-93-38-55-26. Next to the Palais des Festivals.*
   Hours open: 5 p.m.–5 a.m. Special hours: Slots from 11 a.m.

Cannes' largest casino, the Municipale, shares Croisette space with the ultraposh **Palm Beach Casino** (☎ *04-93-43-91-12)* and the more intimate **Casino du Carlton** (in the Carlton International Hotel, *58 boulevard de la Croisette*). Slots, roulette, blackjack and more; **Jimmy's** nightclub on premises *(Wed.–Sun., 11 p.m.–6 a.m.)*. All three casinos require a passport; dressy attire required—no shorts or bathing gear. Admission: FR70.

Special Tours/Excursions

Ile St.-Honore/Ile St.-Marguerite ★★★★

Iles de Lerins, off the coast of Cannes, ☎ *04-93-39-11-82. Boats depart from the Gare Maritime, Vieux Port.*
Hours open: 7:30 a.m.–7 p.m.

Take refuge from all the Cannes glitz with a boat ride to the peaceful (except when invaded by tourists on weekends in summer), verdant Iles des Lerins. A short ride (just 20 minutes) away is the Ile Ste-Marguerite, which figures prominently in the claustrophobe's nightmare, Dumas' *Man in the Iron Mask*. The famous prisoner (who may have been Louis XIV's twin brother) in the crushing headgear was held for more than ten years in Cardinal Richelieu's Fort Vauban. You'll get to see the minuscule cell. The monks of the neighboring Ile Saint-Honorat (a 35-minute trip from Cannes) proffer homemade honey to a constant stream of visitors. Their monastery, Abbaye de Lerins, founded by Saint-Honore, has occupied the isle since the 12th century. Bring picnic lunches and bathing gear for secluded swimming on both islands. Although they can get crowded, the woodlands are big enough to share. They're best on weekdays and off-season. *Summer departures: every half-hour, 7:30 a.m.–7 p.m. Winter departures: 10 a.m.–5 p.m.* Round-trip for both islands is FR60; St.-Honorat round-trip only, FR45; Ste-Marguerite round-trip only, FR40. Admission: FR60.

Biot

Museums and Exhibits

Musée National Fernand-Leger ★★★★

Chemin Val-de-Pome, ☎ *04-93-65-63-61.*
Hours open: 10 a.m.–6 p.m. Special hours: Closed May 1, Jan. 1, Dec. 25. Closed: Tue.

This tiny hill town has been brought fame and prosperity as a result of the Fernand Leger Museum, which is located on its outskirts, a monument that merits all the attention it has attained worldwide. The collection, assembled by the artist's widow, is extraordinary, and the museum was expanded to accommodate the treasury of items. It's rare to see so many of Leger's excellent ceramics under one roof, as well as carpets, paintings, sketches, reliefs and even wire sculpture. If you have only seen Leger's two-dimensional art, this is a dramatic revelation of his wider visions. The building is airy and well-lighted, the front adorned with a vast mosaic across its entire facade. Students, children, seniors, FR20. Another popular attraction is **La Verrerie de Biot** *(Chemin des Combes,* ☎ *04-93-65-03-00)*, producers of *verre rustique*, jewel-toned glassware that's popular all over the country. *Open daily 10 a.m.–7 p.m.; Sun., 2–7 p.m.* Admission: FR32.

Theme/Amusement Parks

Marineland ★★

route de Biot, ☎ *04-93-33-49-49.*
Hours open: 11 a.m.–7 p.m.
Here, dolphins, seals and other aquatic residents perform three times daily at 2:30 p.m., 4:30 p.m., and 6 p.m., year-round. All the splashing really delights the kids. Admission: FR90.

Cagnes-sur-Mer

Museums and Exhibits

Maison le Colettes ★★

avenue des Colettes, ☎ *04-93-20-61-07.*
Hours open: 10 a.m.–6 p.m. Special hours: Mid-Nov-May, to 5 p.m. Closed noon-2 p.m. Closed: Tue.
This poignant museum is where Auguste Renoir spent his last years (1907–1919). Sadly crippled by arthritis, he could only paint by having his brushes tied to his fingers. You can see the wheelchair he was confined to, his coat and cravat, left as they were when he died. Along with the memorabilia, letters and photos on display are 10 of the great artist's canvases. In the garden sits one of his bronzes, entitled Venus. Admission: FR22.

Eze

Parks and Gardens

Jardin Exotique ★★★

rue du Château, ☎ *04-93-41-10-30.*
Hours open: 9 a.m.–8 p.m. Special hours: Winter until 6 p.m.
At the very summit of this hilltop village, you'll find the Jardin Exotique, part of an unoccupied old villa; the flora is deemed exotic for the region—cactus and other succulents abound. The prime appeal is the view; it's a wow. Admission: FR12.

Frejus-St.-Raphael

Theme/Amusement Parks

Aquatica ★

RN98, ☎ *04-94-52-01-01.*
Hours open: 9 a.m.–7 p.m. Closed: Sun.
Not far from the beach at Frejus (a short ferry ride from St.-Raphael) is this water park for those with an aversion to saltwater. Slides, three swimming pools and endless wet fun. Admission: FR95.

Where to Stay

Hotels and Resorts

Carlton Intercontinental FR1400–FR3690 ★★★

58 boulevard de la Croisette. ☎ *04-93-06-40-06, FAX: 04-93-06-40-25. Located between rue du Canada and rue Einesy.* Rated Restaurant: *La Cote.*
Single: FR1400–FR3000. Double: FR3200–FR3690.
Built in 1912, this luxurious hotel is immediately recognized by the twin gray domes at both ends of its facade and the Art Deco grand gate. Although the Carlton

has been modernized, it retains the feeling of a Belle Epoque hotel, and its service is superb. Its 326 rooms and 28 suites, all with private bath, are predictably lavish and comfortable. The ones at the front have a balcony that overlooks the sea and the Iles de Lrins. However, the views of the sunset from the rooms in the west wing are spectacular, and these rooms are much quieter. The hotel also has a 13-room penthouse—probably the most regal on the Riviera. Amenities include a well-equipped health club, with many spa facilities, as well as a private beach, where guests can check in directly from their yachts. Many guests at the Carlton are celebrities, especially during the annual film festival. Also offered is the Carlton Casino Club, on the 8th floor, which opened in 1989. La Cote restaurant (listed separately with the Carlton's other noted restaurant, La Belle Otero) is considered one of the most distinguished along the Riviera. Features: wheelchair-access rooms, beach location, water sports, air conditioning in rooms, balcony or patio, nonsmoking rooms, in-room minibars, fitness center. Credit Cards: All Major.

Fouquet's   **FR1100–FR1400**   ★ ★

2 rond-point Duboys-d'Angers. ☎ *04-93-38-75-81, FAX: 04-93-39-92-93. Located between rue d'Antibes and boulevard de la Croisette.*
Single: FR1100–FR1300. Double: FR1300–FR1400.

For a moderately priced hotel, Foquet's is a good choice. It's situated on a circular street with a number of other hotels several blocks from the beach. Each of its 10 comfortable rooms is decorated in bold colors and has private bath, hair dryer, dressing room and loggia. Very courteous service. Features: beach location, air conditioning in rooms, in-room minibars. Credit Cards: All Major.

Gray d'Albion   **FR1200–FR1600**   ★ ★ ★ ★

38 rue des Serbes. ☎ *04-92-99-79-79, FAX: 04-93-99-26-10. Located between boulevard de la Croisette and rue d'Antibes.* Rated Restaurant: *Le Royal Gray.*
Single: FR1200–FR1350. Double: FR1550–FR1600.

The smallest of the major hotels in Cannes, the Gray d'Albion is also one of the most luxurious. Centrally located near the convention center, it is in a nine-story modern building. The public areas have plenty of polished marble, high sheen woodwork, bronze and mirrors. There are 172 rooms and 14 suites. All units are spacious and have telephone, TV and video, as well as modern bath with hair dryer and toiletries. All are comfortably furnished with modern decor, and 14 were fully renovated recently. Although only a few rooms have a direct sea view, each has a private balcony. Also offered are a popular disco/piano bar/restaurant called Le Jane's, a private beach with water sports, a shopping arcade, an underground parking garage, the prestigious Le Royal Gray restaurants and a beach restaurant. Halfboard rates are FR725 to FR 1040 (room, breakfast and a meal) per person, per day in season. Features: beach location, water sports, air conditioning in rooms, balcony or patio, nonsmoking rooms, in-room minibars. Credit Cards: All Major.

Majestic   **FR1150–FR3800**   ★ ★ ★

14 boulevard de la Croisette. ☎ *04-92-98-77-00, FAX: 04-93-38-97-90. Between rue des Belges and rue des Serbes.* Rated Restaurant: *Le Sunset.*
Single: FR1150–FR1800. Double: FR3500–FR3800.

Built in 1926, this glamorous hotel is a favorite with celebrities during the annual film festival. Guests are greeted in an elegant, high-ceilinged, marble lobby and reception area. The public rooms have crystal chandeliers, tapestries, seasoned antiques and reproductions, as well as Oriental carpets, Louis XV silk furniture and potted palms. The 263 rooms and 24 suites, all with private bath, are also furnished with antiques and reproductions, offset by Oriental rugs and marble tables. The renovated rooms on the top floor are preferred as they offer an outstanding view of the harbor and the mountains. Outside is an overscale front patio with a pool in a palm grove. By the pool is a classic restaurant, Le Sunset. There are also a private beach with water sports and another restaurant and bar. Hotel services include a hairdresser, 24-hour room service, same-day laundry and valet parking. Features: wheelchair-access rooms, beach location, pool, water sports, air conditioning in rooms, in-room minibars. Credit Cards: All Major.

Martinez FR1300–FR3800 ★★★★

73 boulevard de la Croisette. ☎ *04-92-98-73-00, FAX: 04-93-39-67-82.*
Rated Restaurant: *La Palme d'Or.*
Single: FR1300–FR3200. Double: FR3250–FR3800.

Large and especially oriented to conventions, the Martinez is situated across the street from its private beach. In the 1930s this Art Deco hotel was world-renowned. After a period of decline, it was completely renovated by the Concorde hotel chain in 1982 and the results are impressive. There are 418 rooms and 12 suites; all have modern furnishings and costly up-to-date appointments; the marble baths feature hair dryer, robes and magnifying mirrors. In the garden, there is a cascading octagonal pool beside an outdoor terrace restaurant, J'Orangerie, which serves light, low-calorie meals. On its private beach are a restaurant, circular bar, cabanas and a water-skiing school. The hotel also has an award-winning restaurant, La Palme d'Or, and the pleasant L'Amiral bar extends to boulevard de la Croisette. Many services are offered, including same day laundry, valet and 24-hour room service. Features: beach location, pool, tennis, water sports, air conditioning in rooms, in-room minibars. Credit Cards: All Major.

Mimosas FR395–FR650 ★★★

rue Pauline. ☎ *04-93-61-04-16. Located just north of town center.*
Single: FR395–FR460. Double: FR460–FR650.

This attractive 1870s-style villa is located in a quiet, residential area about five blocks from the sea. The salons are comfortable with a mix of high-tech and Art Nouveau decor. Its 34 rooms, all with private bath, are modern, bright and spacious. Ten of the rooms have a private terrace. The gardens and pool are shaded by huge palm trees. There's a bar, but no restaurant. Mimosas tends to be fully booked during the summer; so it's advised to reserve early. Features: beach location, pool, balcony or patio, in-room minibars. Credit Cards: All Major.

Moliere FR350–FR600 ★

5 rue Moliere. ☎ *04-93-38-16-16. Located between boulevard de la Republique and d'Angers, just south of rue d'Antibes.*
Single: FR350–FR400. Double: FR560–FR600.

In a 19th-century townhouse, this hotel is conveniently located near the center of Cannes and just a five-minute walk to the sea. It has 45 bright and comfortable rooms, only some with private bathrooms with bath or shower. Most of the rooms are narrow, but they are all spotless. Many rooms have a terrace or balcony overlooking one of three pleasant flower gardens. There is no restaurant, but there is a cheerful breakfast nook. The Moliere is very popular in season and often full; therefore, it is recommended to reserve a room well in advance, especially during the film festival. Features: beach location, air conditioning in rooms, balcony or patio. Credit Cards: All Major.

Royal Hotel Casino   FR980–FR1850   ★ ★ ★

605 Ave. du General DeGaulle. ☎ *04-92-97-70-00, FAX: 04-93-49-51-50. Located near an artificial harbor, about 8 km from Cannes.* Rated Restaurant: *Le Fereol.*
Single: FR980–FR1300. Double: FR1300–FR1850.
This Las Vegas-style hotel was the first-and last-in France to have a casino directly on the beach. The interior is contemporary and plush with lots of marble. Accommodations include 180 modern rooms, most looking out toward the sea. All have TV, video, private bath and hair dryer. Amenities include same-day laundry service, valet, excellent facilities for business meetings and an hourly shuttle service to nearby Cannes. Le Fereol is highly recommended for its cuisine and also features dining on its outdoor terrace; reservations are required. The casino, open nightly from 8 p.m. to 4 a.m., offers blackjack, craps and roulette. In the bar lounge, shows are presented at 10 p.m. and 1 a.m. and feature a mix of nudity with music, feathers and Nevada-style choreography. Features: wheelchair-access rooms, beach location, pool, golf, tennis, air conditioning in rooms, nonsmoking rooms, in-room minibars, fitness center. Credit Cards: All Major.

Sofitel Le Mediterranee   FR940–FR1460   ★ ★

2 boulevard Jean-Hibert. ☎ *04-92-99-73-00, FAX: 04-92-99-73-29. Located at the edge of the old port, directly on the harbor at Quai St.-Pierre.* Rated Restaurant: *Le Palmyre.*
Single: FR940–FR1300. Double: FR1350–FR1460.
A favorite of the international yachting set, this sleek hotel stands directly on the harbor. Balconies overlook the bay, and there's a sun terrace. The 145 rooms are bright and comfortable and have contemporary decor, TV, refrigerator and marble bath with robes and hair dryer. The hotel's restaurant, Le Palmyre, has excellent food for the money, and there is also a viewful maritime lounge. Half-board rates are FR683 to FR955 (room, breakfast and a meal) per person, per day in season. Features: beach location, pool, air conditioning in rooms, balcony or patio, nonsmoking rooms. Credit Cards: All Major.

Victoria   FR680–FR1200   ★

rond-point Duboys-d'Angers. ☎ *04-93-99-36-36, FAX: 04-93-38-03-91. Located between rue Amouretti and rue d'Oran.*
Single: FR680–FR1200. Double: FR680–FR1200.
This small, stylish, modern hotel is nestled among the fancy boutiques on the main shopping street in the heart of Cannes. Guests are greeted in an English-style lobby, and there's a pleasant English bar. The 25 rooms, all with private bath, have period

reproductions, silk bedspreads, padded headboards, electronically controlled shutters, refrigerators and other amenities. Nearly half the rooms have a balcony overlooking a garden and pool. Features: beach location, pool, air conditioning in rooms, balcony or patio, in-room minibars. Credit Cards: All Major.

La Napoule

Hotels and Resorts

L'Ermitage du Riou   **FR810–FR1340**   ★★

boulevard Henery-Clews. ☎ *04-93-49-95-56, FAX: 04-92-97-69-05. Bordering the Riou River and the annes-Mandelieu golf course.*
Single: FR810–FR1000. Double: FR1000–FR1340.
This old Provencal-style house was turned into a seaside hotel in 1952. It has 41 large, comfortable rooms with Provencal furniture and ancient paintings. All rooms have a private bath, and many have a private terrace that overlooks the sea, harbor, river, golf course or swimming pool; those with a terrace looking out on the river are the quietest. The hotel also has a lovely garden, a solarium and a restaurant that specializes in seafood. Features: wheelchair-access rooms, beach location, pool, air conditioning in rooms, balcony or patio, nonsmoking rooms, in-room safes. Credit Cards: All Major.

Le Royal Hotel   **FR980–FR1900**   ★★★★

boulevard Henry-Clews. ☎ *04-92-97-70-00, FAX: 04-93-49-51-50. On the beach.*
Single: FR980. Double: FR1900.
Contemporary, glitzy style throughout. The 185 air-conditioned rooms have TV, telephone, minibar, bath and hair dryer. Be sure to reserve one with a view of the sea. Marble dominates the grand public spaces, all lavishly decorated. There is a good restaurant serving buffet and a la carte meals. The casino has all of the usual games, and the bar lounge features a Las Vegas-style dance show with the feathers, nudity and all. Valet, laundry and 24-hour room service are all on-site. Leisure facilities include a pool, golf course and tennis courts. A deluxe resort complex with first class service. Features: wheelchair-access rooms, beach location, pool, golf, tennis, air conditioning in rooms, in-room minibars. Credit Cards: All Major.

Where to Eat

Au Bec Fin   **$$**   ★★

12 rue 24-Aout ☎ *04-93-38-35-86.*
Lunch: Noon–2:30 p.m., FR85–FR120.
Dinner: 7–10 p.m., entrées FR85–FR120.
This rather plain family restaurant near the beach offers tasty southern-style seafood, salads and soups. The FR85 fixed-price menu includes dessert and cheese, and is undoubtedly a good value, but if you don't like what's offered, it won't hurt your wallet too much to order a la carte either. Nearby, at No. 15, and a bit cheaper still, is **le Monaco**, a popular spot that resembles the jeweled principality only in name. It's clean, and serves big portions of starchy dishes like couscous and paella. Fixed-price menu at FR80–FR100; entrées FR55–FR80. *Open daily, except Sun. for lunch (until 2 p.m.) and dinner (until 10 p.m.).* No credit cards, and reservations are required. Closed: Sun. Amenities: outside dining, reservations required. Credit Cards: All Major.

Cannes Beach   **$**   ★

La Croisette. ☎ *04-93-38-14-59.*
Lunch: Noon–2 pm, FR90–FR140.

Yes, you can be on a budget and have lunch on this precious beach. This one is very pleasant, not as flashy as others on the strip; mostly fish dishes. Amenities: outside dining, reservations not accepted. Credit Cards: V, MC, A, E.

Outdoor dining under the umbrellas is très chic in Cannes.

Carlton Intercontinental   **$$$**   ★★★★

58 La Croisette. ☎ *04-93-39-69-69.*
Lunch: Noon–2 p.m., FR300–FR450.
Dinner: 7–12:30 p.m., entrées FR300–FR450.

The posh Carlton Intercontinental has two excellent restaurants that play off each other. When you want light, inventive southern French cuisine, repair to **La Belle Otero. La Cote** *(☎ 04-93-68-91-68)* stays on the safe side by comparison, featuring well-loved classics that include the original Provencal pizza, pissaladiere, with anchovies, olives and onions. The elegant dining room beautifully blends Belle Epoque and Art Deco decor. *Closed Tuesdays and Wednesdays, and Apr.–Nov.* Fixed-price menus at FR220, FR370 and FR490. Amenities: outside dining, own baking, reservations required. Credit Cards: All Major.

La Palme d'Or   **$$$**   ★★★★

73 La Croisette, In Hotel Martinez. Located at Hotel Martinez. ☎ *04-92-98-74-14.*
Specialties: salad of pigeon with foie gras, pan-fried rouget filets with tapenade.
Lunch: 12:30–2 p.m., FR250–FR425.
Dinner: 7:30–10:30 p.m., entrées FR250–FR425.

The recently renovated Martinez is all the more impressive with the addition of this highly praised and elegant Provencal restaurant. The dining room and terrace face the hotel's eight-sided pool. Lobster, fresh fish from local waters (rouget, monkfish), plump olives and faultless produce play a substantial role in chef Christian Willer's La Croisette daily extravaganzas. *Closed: Mon., Tues.* Amenities: happening bar, outside dining, reservations required. Credit Cards: All Major.

Biot

Auberge du Jarrier   **$$$**   ★★

30 passage de la Bourgade. ☎ *04-93-65-11-68.*
Lunch: Noon–2 p.m., FR200–FR275.
Dinner: 7–9:30 p.m, entrées FR200–FR275.
Interesting Mediterranean-style cuisine moderne with an emphasis on seasonal produce is served in a garden when the weather permits, which is much of the time. The three-course fixed-price menus begin at FR250. Closed: Tues. Amenities: outside dining, reservations required. Credit Cards: V, MC, E.

Les Terraillers   **$**   ★★

11 route du Chemin-Neuf. ☎ *04-93-65-01-59.*
Working in a medieval potter's studio turned restaurant, chef Claude Jacques is a classicist who makes few concessions to "new" styles of cuisine; he prepares old chestnuts such as soufflé de coquilles St.-Jacques and sweetbreads with truffles to a grateful clientele. Such delicacies are served in the main dining room or on a terrace that unfortunately overlooks the street. Amenities: outside dining, reservations required. Credit Cards: V, A.

Cagnes-Sur-Mer

Le Cagnard   **$$$**   ★★★

rue Pontis-Long, In Hotel le Cagnard. Located at Le Cagnard. ☎ *04-93-20-73-22.*
Specialties: seafood ravioli with goat cheese, pan-fried foie gras with potatoes and truffles.
Lunch: Noon–2 p.m., FR200–FR300.
Dinner: 7–10:30 p.m., entrées FR200–FR300.
Within a remarkable medieval dwelling is this terrific hotel restaurant with a terrace where you can see the surrounding coastline; its retractable roof slides open to let the sunshine in. Inventive cuisine from Jean-Yves Johany with an emphasis on natural flavors, fresh fruit and vegetables. If you can't get into Le Cagnard, try **Restaurant des Peintres**, *71 montee Bourgade au Haut-de-Cagnes* (☎ *04-93-20-83-08*), for Alain Llorca's memorable, slightly Asian-flavored cuisine that changes with the seasons; specialties include bonito carpaccio and roast suckling pig. Fixed-price menu at FR200. Closed Wednesdays. Amenities: outside dining.

Eze

Château Eza   **$$$**   ★★★

Eze Village. ☎ *04-93-41-12-24.*
Specialties: provence vegetable platter with fresh coriander.
Lunch: Noon–2 p.m., FR250–FR350.
Dinner: 7–10 p.m., entrées FR250–FR350.
For those who are interested in this sort of thing, the lilting sounds of the chef minuet have been heard here recently, with Maxim-trained Bruno Cirino out and Andre Signoret in. He has adapted nicely, introducing his own innovations to the menu of Southern specialties (fresh fish, shellfish and lamb) and utilizing the finest produce.

THE MEDITERRANEAN FROM SPAIN TO MONACO

And the setting, an ancient village complex above the sea, remains as enchanting as ever. Accommodations here include six rooms and two suites, with luxurious decor and priceless antiques, most with a private entrance. Amenities: outside dining, reservations required. Credit Cards: All Major.

Château de la Chevre d'Or $$$ ★★★

rue de Barri. ☎ *04-93-41-12-12.*
Lunch: Noon–2 p.m., FR250–FR350.
Dinner: 7–10:15 p.m., entrées FR250–FR350.

Perched on a cliff high above the sea, this is the kind of place that's usually featured on "Lifestyles of the Rich and Famous." Chef Elie Mazot has the best credentials, having worked with the Troisgros brothers in Roanne. His pan-roasted langoustines in coconut milk and raspberry souffle are decadent, which they must be, in order to draw guests away from their cocktails on a terrace with such a heavenly view. A Relais and Châteaux rated establishment, it also offers 15 well-appointed rooms, some with a private terrace. Amenities: outside dining, reservations required.

Golfe Juan

Chez Tetou $$$ ★★

avenue des Freres-Roustand, a la plage. ☎ *04-93-63-71-16.*
Specialties: Bouillabaisse.
Lunch: Noon–2:30 p.m., FR400–FR475.
Dinner: 8–10 pm, entrées FR400–FR475.

Brigitte Bardot and other French starlets once hung out at this rustic cottage by the sea that still takes no credit cards and charges FR400 for a bowl of bouillabaisse, and FR100 for a plate of fruit. Other specialties on the small, unchanging menu include grilled langoustines. Closed: Wed. Amenities: outside dining, reservations required.

Directory

To and From

By train on the coastal line (Marseille about two hours, Monaco about 50 minutes), or by car on the N-98 coastal highway or the N-85 road from the north.

Tourist Office

1 boulevard de la Croisette; ☎ *(33) 04-93-39-01-01.*

Rail Station

1 rue de Jean Jaurès; ☎ *(33) 04-93-99-50-50.*

Post Office

22 rue Bivouac Napoléon, 06400 Cannes; ☎ *(33) 04-93-39-14-11.*

Nice

Nice can be nice if you know where to go. The capital of the Côte d'Azur is now France's fifth-largest city, and much is given over to drab suburbs of no interest whatsoever to the visitor. But the Old City, nestled at the foot of the hill crowned by the 12th-century ruins of the castle, retains a small-town Mediterranean feel. Nice's Old City provides a significant historical chroni-

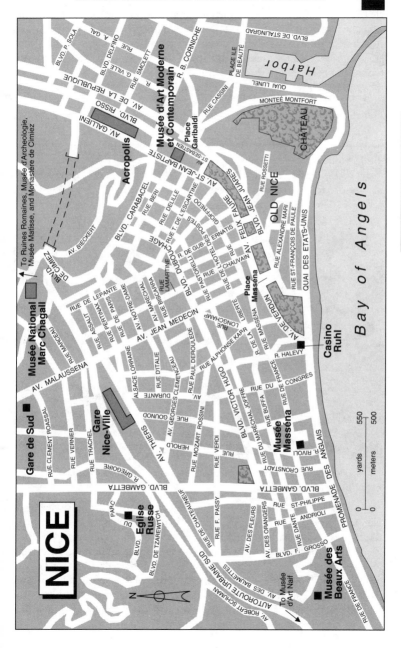

cle of the region. Founded by the Greeks some 500 years before Christ, the city, then known as Nikaia, was a major trading center before being taken over by the Romans 300 years later. After the Roman Empire declined, the area was subjected to invasions and attacks by all manner of seafaring Mediterranean peoples, until the late 10th century, when the Count of Provence drove out the Moors and annexed the city to his territory. In the 14th century, Nice became part of Savoy, the Italian duchy that plagued various French kings for centuries. France held the city twice, once at the beginning of the 18th, and again at the beginning of the 19th century. Louis XIV tore down the castle in 1706, which is why there are just ruins there now. Not until 1860, in a deal between Napoléon III and the Duke of Savoy, was Nice made part of France for good. By the mid-19th century, the city was a popular resort for European aristocrats, including heavyweights such as the widow of Tsar Nicholas I and Queen Victoria herself.

Nice: One's first thrill on the Riviera is the spectacular coastal view when arriving by plane or train.

The long Italian history of Nice gives the town a distinctly Italian feel. The tall, pastel-colored houses lining the port in the old town strongly resembles the houses on the harbors of Verona and Genoa. The Promenade des Anglais, built in the 19th century with funds raised from English residents, who loved their seafronts, is now a major boulevard, but a walk along it takes you from the Old Town past some of the more splendid hotels, until you come to the jewel of Nice's Belle Epoque era, the Hôtel Negresco. Farther up the hill, above the Old Town, you can wander through numerous museums, most honoring various painters who have lived and worked in the city. The

Musée Massena, Musée Matisse and Musée Marc-Chagall all have extensive collections of their namesake artists. The Musée des Beaux Arts houses a collection given to the city by Napoléon III in thanks for having approved his plan in 1860, as well as more recent works by Monet, Renoir and Sisley.

A walk down Promenade de Anglais reveals much of Nice's history.

What to Do

City Celebrations/Events

Carnavale   ★★★

Various locations, ☎ *04-93-87-16-28.*

Just before the somber days of Lent, the city lets out a long, collective whoop of abandon during the two-week Carnaval. It's a typically uninhibited bang-up flurry of parades, fireworks, yacht parades, balls, etc. It all ends with the burning (in effigy) of the King of Carnaval. Contact the Comite des Fetes (number above) at *5 Promenade des Anglais* for information on this and other annual festivities.

Museums and Exhibits

Musée Chagall   ★★★

avenue du Docteur Menard, ☎ *04-93-81-75-75.*
Hours open: 10 a.m.–7 p.m. Special hours: Open 10 a.m.–5:30 p.m. from Oct.–June. Closed: Tue.

This light-filled, modern museum houses more than 500 major works in several different mediums by the Russian-born artist, who lived the good life in Nice with his wife. On permanent exhibition are 17 startling canvases that make up the "Biblical Message" series. Even if you're tired of art museums by now, this complex is worth a visit if just for the fragrant, Mediterranean-style garden, with a cafe for musing. Admission: FR27.

Musée Massena   ★★★

65 rue de France, ☎ *04-93-88-11-34.*
Closed: Mon.

Formerly home to the Massenas, this splendid villa was constructed in 1900. Converted into this museum of regional art and local history, it still retains its lavishly beautiful ambience. In addition to paintings by Renoir, it also contains paintings by local artists and a display devoted to the Carnaval in Nice. Definitely worth a detour—just to admire the beauty. Admission: free.

Musée Matisse   ★★★

164 avenue des Arenes de Cimiez, ☎ *04-93-81-08-08. About 4 km north of town center. Hours open: 11 a.m.–7 p.m. Special hours: Open from 10 a.m.–5 p.m. from Oct.–Mar. Closed: Tue.*

Matisse loved Nice so much he spent more than 40 years here, painting and sketching. His donated work, including children's book illustrations, bronzes and fabric designs, fills several rooms of this museum, housed in one of Nice's oldest villas. His final work, *Flowers and Fruits,* is also displayed here. For a change of pace, visit the Cimiez archaeological museum, in the front of the villa; it's a repository of the latest finds from the ancient Roman settlement of Cemenelum, formerly centered in Cimiez. Admission: FR25.

Musée d'Art Moderne et d'Art Contemporain   ★★

promenade des Arts, ☎ *04-93-62-61-62.*
Hours open: 11 a.m.–6 p.m. Special hours: Fri. to 10 p.m. Closed: Tue.

Hundreds of pop-art, Neo-Realistic and avant-garde pieces are appropriately housed here, in this towering marble-and-glass museum, which is Nice's newest kid on the art block. There's a fairly large representation of American and Nicoise artists, including Warhol, Liechtenstein, Yves Klein and Cesar. Free admission Oct.–June. Admission: FR25.

Nightlife

Casino Roule/Jok Club ★★

Hotel Meridien, 1 promenade des Anglais, ☎ *04-93-87-95-87.*
Hours open: 5 p.m.–4 a.m. Special hours: Disco open from 11 p.m.
A mini Monte Carlo casino, with all the modern and traditional gaming conveniences. Bring a passport to gamble. Other facilities include a cabaret theater and Jok Club, a dressy disco for the well-heeled; no techno, house or hip-hop. (Admission to the disco is FR125.)

Parks and Gardens

Jardin Albert 1er ★★

promenade des Anglais.
Tolerant police have been known to look the other way when a local phenomenon, "fountaining," takes place in the city parks. This practice involves skinny dipping your way through Nice's extensive network of ornate, oversize fountains, usually in various states of inebriation. The Triton Fountain in the centrally located *Jardin Albert 1e* might be a good place to start; milder types can picnic here. Another park of note is the nearby **Esplanade du Paillon**, off place Massena. High up in the older section of town is **Le Château**, a piney refuge with a gorgeous view, named after the castle of the Savoy dukes (since demolished). It can be reached by elevator. *Open May–August, 10 a.m.–7:30 p.m., winter until 4:30 p.m.* Located east of Vieux Nice, via rue Rosetti. Currently, it's permissible to drink alcohol in all city parks and on the beach.

Pubs and Bars

Les 3 Diables ★★

2 Saleya, ☎ *04-93-62-47-00.*
Hours open: 7 p.m.–2 a.m.
This murky bar-cafe with earsplitting music is probably the most French among a slew of international-style nightspots. Drinks are FR17 and up. We've noticed a plethora of Irish-English live-music pubs throughout Nice, naturally frequented by English and American tourists. **Jonathan's**, at *1 rue de la Loge (*☎ *04-93-62-57-62)*, open 8 p.m.–12:30 a.m. daily except Mon., is a similar venue, but with a local clientele. Good, cheap beer. Admission: free.

Where to Stay

Hotels and Resorts

Beau Rivage FR700–FR1050 ★★★★

24 rue St.-Francois-de-Paule. ☎ *04-93-80-80-70, FAX: 04-93-80-55-77. Located just east of Le Jardin Albert-Ier, along promenade des Anglais.* Rated Restaurant: *Bistrot du Rivage.*
Single: FR700–FR970. Double: FR950–FR1050.
Located near the opera, this Belle Epoque hotel had Matisse and Chekhov as past guests. The five-story building on the beachfront walk was restored in the early

1980s, and the hotel now has a modern decor. Its 118 rooms have elegant Art Deco furnishings, marble bath, TV and soundproof windows. There's a restaurant on a deck looking out on the beach offering salads and light meals from May to September. The street-level Bistrot du Rivage is more formal, with excellent Mediterranean-style cuisine prepared year-round. Also offered is a private beach with bathing facilities. The service is excellent in every respect. Features: wheelchair-access rooms, beach location, water sports, air conditioning in rooms, nonsmoking rooms, in-room minibars. Credit Cards: All Major.

Château Eza   FR1200–FR3000   ★★★

rue de la Pise. ☎ *04-93-41-12-24, FAX: 04-93-41-16-64.*
Rated Restaurant: *Château Eza.*
Single: FR1200–FR1500. Double: FR1500–FR3000.

This cluster of medieval dwellings was made into a château by Prince William of Sweden, when he resided here. Its six spacious rooms and four suites have Persian rugs and huge marble bathrooms. This quiet, luxury hotel is a bit overfurnished, but the views are incredible—especially from the terrace. The Château Eza restaurant has two tiers for outdoor dining, as well as an indoor salon. This is a highly recommended, first-class restaurant. Both the restaurant and hotel are closed late October through early March. Features: beach location, air conditioning in rooms, in-room minibars. Credit Cards: All Major.

Château de la Chevre d'Or   FR1200–FR2600   ★★★★★

rue du Barri. ☎ *04-92-10-66-66, FAX: 04-93-41-06-72.*
Rated Restaurant: *Château de la Chevre d'Or.*
Single: FR1200–FR1400. Double: FR1500–FR2600.

This Relaix and Châteaux hotel is a well-preserved complex of medieval village houses that cling to a Riviera cliff. The interior is flawlessly decorated to maintain its 1920 neo-Gothic character, but it also added modern comfort—a helicopter was needed to transport the building materials. The 23 rooms all have private bathrooms and views of the coastline, plus some have private terraces. There is an incredible view from the lounge, which has French doors that open onto a terraced swimming pool. Classic French cuisine is served at the Château de la Chevre d'Or restaurant, which has a formal dining room and a terrace—both have breathtaking views. Cafe du Jardin serves simple meals such as fresh salads and fruit cocktails over the Mediterranean. The hotel is closed December through February. The main restaurant is closed on Wednesdays as well as December through February. Cafe du Jardin is closed on Tuesdays as well as mid-October through mid-April. Features: beach location, pool, air conditioning in rooms, balcony or patio. Credit Cards: All Major.

Elysée Palace   FR1000–FR1300   ★★★★

59 promenade des Anglais. ☎ *04-93-86-06-06, FAX: 04-93-44-50-40. Located on the promenade at rue Honore-Sauvan.*
Single: FR1000–FR1200. Double: FR1100–FR1300.

Opened in 1988, this ultramodern hotel is easily recognized by the huge bronze Venus tucked into one side, created by the Nice-born sculptor, Sacha Sosno. The Elysée Palace was built on the same site as the demolished 19th-century hotel with the same name. Inside, the public areas are spacious, with plenty of marble and decor reminiscent of the 1930s. There are 121 deluxe rooms plus 22 suites, all in contemporary decor with private marble bath. Most rooms offer a sweeping vista of the sea. The hotel has a gourmet restaurant, a dining terrace and a piano bar. Also featured are a rooftop pool with a city view, a hairdresser, a conference room and other facilities for business travelers. All guests are admitted to a private beach through the Beau Rivage, which is under the same Franco-American management. Half-board rates are FR515 to FR1050 (room, breakfast and a meal) per person, per day in season. Features: wheelchair-access rooms, beach location, air conditioning in rooms, sauna, in-room minibars, fitness center. Credit Cards: All Major.

Le Meridien   **FR1020–FR1850**   ★ ★ ★ ★

1 promenade des Anglais. ☎ *04-93-82-25-25, FAX: 04-93-16-08-90. Angled at the promenade and the park, Le Jardin Albert-Ier.* Rated Restaurant: *Cafe Jardin & La Terrasse. Single: FR1020–FR1650. Double: FR1250–FR1850.*

In a 10-story building in a great location, Le Meridien is a modern commercial hotel. Two escalators lead to a marble-floored lobby with shops. All of its 314 rooms have a sea view and are comfortable and well furnished. TV, trouser press, telephone, modern bath with hair dryer and thick towels are standard features. Highlights include a tea room and a piano bar as well as a sun deck and a rooftop pool with an exceptional view of the bay. The first-class fitness center provides a spa and hydrotherapy. Off the lobby is a small restaurant, Cafe Jardin, open from mid-September through late April for lunch only. La Terrasse is charming and elegant and offers excellent cuisine; however, it is only open from early May through mid-September. Another restaurant, L'Habit Blanc, is closed from July through August, as well as on Sundays and Mondays from June through September. Features: beach location, pool, air conditioning in rooms, balcony or patio, in-room minibars, fitness center. Credit Cards: All Major.

Negresco   **FR1200–FR2350**   ★ ★ ★ ★ ★

37 promenade des Anglais. ☎ *04-93-16-64-00, FAX: 04-93-88-35-68. Located between rue de Rivoli and rue de Cronstadt.* Rated Restaurant: *Restaurant Chantecler. Single: FR1200–FR1650. Double: FR1250–FR2350.*

Recently renovated, this turn-of-the-century landmark hotel is a national monument. Situated right on the seafront, the glamorous hotel was built in the French château style with a domed tower. Inside, the oval Royal Salon lobby is encircled with columns reaching to a stained-glass domed ceiling. Hanging from its center is the original crystal chandelier, designed and constructed by Baccarat. The floor is covered with the largest Aubusson carpet imaginable. Accommodations include 18 massive suites and 132 rooms. The suites are designed around different periods of French history (i.e., Romantic, Louis XIV, Empire, etc.). They have canopy beds, chandeliers, beautiful carpets and fine antique furniture. Many units have a balcony and/or sea view. The beautiful main dining room, Le Chantecler, is recommended whether you stay here or not. Guests enjoy an excellent brasserie, rooftop pool and private beach. Features: beach location, pool, air conditioning in rooms, balcony or patio, in-room minibars. Credit Cards: All Major.

Palais Maeterlinck   FR1300–FR3500   ★★★★

Basse Corniche. ☎ *04-92-00-72-00, FAX: 04-92-04-18-10. About 6 km east of Nice, along the Basse Corniche.* Rated Restaurant: *Le Melisande.*
Single: FR1300–FR1800. Double: FR2700–FR3500.

This sumptuous hotel was originally built as a private villa for Maurice Maeterlinck, the Belgian writer and winner of the Nobel Peace Prize for literature. Restored and enlarged, it is situated on nine acres of landscaped grounds east of Nice. Called the "jewel of the Cote d'Azur," it has stylish, eclectically decorated public areas- bathed in the sparkling Cote d'Azur light. Guests can admire lavish murals and paintings by Serge Megter. From the lofty hotel, they can take a funicular to the private, somewhat rock-strewn beach, complete with a marina. The swimming pool and garden terraces are near the sea. There is even a helipad on the grounds. All of the 22 rooms and six suites are elegantly furnished and have marble bath with robes and toiletries. Duplexes and apartments with kitchenettes are also available. Many units have huge terraces looking out on Cap d'Antibes or Cap-Ferrat. Le Melisande restaurant offers excellent French and international cuisine, with Provencal specialties and terrace. Buffet lunches are also served on the terrace. The restaurant is closed on Sunday and Monday evenings. Features: wheelchair-access rooms, beach location, pool, water sports, air conditioning in rooms, balcony or patio, nonsmoking rooms, in-room minibars, fitness center. Credit Cards: All Major.

Petit Palais   FR480–FR780   ★★

10 avenue Emile-Bieckert. ☎ *04-93-62-19-11. Located at avenue de Picardie in Carabacel, west of Palais des Congres.*
Single: FR480–FR680. Double: FR680–FR780.

This turn-of-the-century hotel is a 10-minute drive from the city center in the Carabacel residential district. It is the former home of Sacha Guitry, an early 20th-century French actor and director. Much of the original architecture of the creamy-white stucco mansion remains, as evident in the Florentine moldings and friezes. Inside, the public rooms have Italianate decor. There are 25 spacious rooms, with fine paintings, comfortable armchairs and excellent bathrooms. Many rooms have a private garden or terrace; others have a balcony affording a sea or city view. The management is friendly and helpful. Only breakfast is served. Features: secluded garden atmosphere, fitness center.

Splendid-Sofitel   FR690–FR1060   ★★★

50 boulevard Victor-Hugo. ☎ *04-93-16-41-00, FAX: 04-93-87-02-46. On the corner of rue Gounod and boulevard Victor-Hugo.* Rated Restaurant: *Le Concerto.*
Single: FR690–FR795. Double: FR790–FR1060.

Four blocks from the beach on a wide boulevard lined with large trees, this modern hotel is one of the most popular in Nice. It was built in 1964 on the site of the former Splendid, constructed in 1881 and the residence of the King of Wurtenberg. Accommodations include 115 rooms and 14 suites; all units have satellite TV, radio, private bath, hair dryer; most open onto balcony or large terrace. An excellent range of services is offered, including baby-sitting, a bank, barbershop, beauty salon, parking garage, solarium and travel agency. On the rooftop, there's a solar-heated pool with a panoramic view of the city, the sea and the surrounding hills. Le Concerto serves classic French cuisine, and light meals are available at the Topsail Bar, on the eighth floor, with a terrace. Half-board rates are FR555 to FR740 (room, breakfast and a meal) per person, per day in season. Features: wheelchair-access rooms, pool, air conditioning in rooms, sauna, balcony or patio, nonsmoking rooms. Credit Cards: All Major.

West-End   **FR430–FR1350**   ★★

31 promenade des Anglais. ☎ *04-92-44-14-00, FAX: 04-93-88-85-07. Located at the promenade and rue Rivoli.* Rated Restaurant: *L'Orangerie.*

Single: FR430–FR710. Double: FR930–FR1350.

In a prime location with outstanding sea views, the West-End is a traditional hotel that's been completely renovated. There are 126 modern rooms with bath, hair dryer and many with sea view. Also featured are a solarium and a private beach with water sports. L'Orangerie serves outstanding meals; for drinks, there's Le Shaker Bar with a terrace. Half-board rates are FR430 to FR930 (room, breakfast and a meal) per person, per day in season. Features: beach location, water sports, air conditioning in rooms, sauna, in-room safes, in-room minibars. Credit Cards: All Major.

Westminster   **FR500–FR1250**   ★★★★

27 promenade des Anglais. ☎ *04-93-88-29-44, FAX: 04-93-82-45-35. Located midway down the promenade at rue Meyerbeer.* Rated Restaurant: *Le Farniente.*

Single: FR500–FR1050. Double: FR850–FR1250.

Dating to 1880, this grand hotel along a famous promenade has been recently renovated but still retains Old-World touches. Guests are greeted in an impressive lobby with marble pillars, chandeliers and frescoes. There are 105 rooms with either modern or period furnishings; all have older tile and marble bath, TV, telephone and soundproof windows. Its gourmet restaurant has a view of the sea; its brasserie offers terrace dining. Both are known for their excellent cuisine. Half-board rates are FR500 to FR1200 (room, breakfast and a meal) per person, per day in season. Features: beach location, air conditioning in rooms, balcony or patio, in-room minibars. Credit Cards: All Major.

Windsor   **FR350–FR670**   ★★★

11 rue Dalpozzo. ☎ *04-93-88-59-35. A short walk from the promenade des Anglais, in the heart of Nice.*

Single: FR350–FR515. Double: FR530–FR670.

This moderately priced, family-run hotel is a charmer. In fact, it looks more like a villa than a hotel. Within, Oriental furnishings adorn the entrance hall, and there is an intimate drawing room with a fireplace. The 60 beautifully maintained rooms have bath or shower and French windows—many of which open onto a tropical garden and palm-fringed pool. Its fitness center offers a sauna, a Turkish bath and shiatsu massages. There are also an English-style pub and a Thai-style lounge. Half-board rates are FR390 to FR695 (room, breakfast and a meal) per person, per day in season. Features: beach location, pool, air conditioning in rooms, sauna, balcony or patio, in-room minibars, fitness center, country location. Credit Cards: All Major.

St.-Paul-de-Vence

Hotels and Resorts

Colombe d'Or   **FR950–FR1450**   ★★★

1 place du General-de-Gaulle. ☎ *04-93-32-80-02, FAX: 04-93-32-77-78. Located just south from the Foundation Maeght.* Rated Restaurant: *La Colombe d'Or.*
Single: FR950–FR1255. Double: FR1100–FR1450.

This legendary hotel has almost as much modern art as an art museum. There are a Leger mural on the terrace, a Braque dove by the pool, a Picasso and a Matisse in the dining room, and works by Chagall, Rouault, Dufy and Miro in the other public areas. The hotel's 16th-century ramparts which surround the hotel, gardens, terrace and pool, offer views over a landscape of cypress trees, red-roofed villas, palm trees and swimming pools. There are 15 rooms and 11 suites; all are full of antiques and have private bathrooms. Dining is available at La Colombe d'Or (listed separately) on the garden patio or inside. Guests can also enjoy an after-dinner drink in front of the fireplace in the lower "pit lounge." Reservations are recommended for accommodations as well as for meals. Half-board rates are FR700 to FR930 (room, breakfast and a meal) per person, per day in season. Art lovers will appreciate the hotel's close proximity to the Foundation Maeght. Features: pool, air conditioning in rooms, sauna. Credit Cards: All Major.

Le Hameau   **FR295–FR580**   ★★★

528 route de la Colle. ☎ *04-93-32-80-24, FAX: 04-93-32-55-75. Located on a hilltop at Hauts-de-St.-Paul.*
Single: FR295–FR480. Double: FR400–FR580.

On the outskirts of St.-Paul-de-Vence, this romantic Mediterranean villa is on a hilltop and has lovely views of the surrounding hills and valleys. Accommodations include 16 rooms and three suites, all with bath or shower. Most of the comfortable, whitewashed rooms have a small terrace or balcony that overlooks a vineyard. However, the rooms near route de la Colle can be noisy. Terraces of flowers and orange and lemon trees descend from the hotel, affording superb views of the village and the sea. Features: pool, air conditioning in rooms, balcony or patio, in-room minibars. Credit Cards: All Major.

Mas d'Artigny   **FR705–FR1830**   ★★★

route de la Colle. ☎ *04-93-32-84-54, FAX: 04-93-32-95-36. Located at des Hauts de St.-Paul; about 3 km from St.-Paul, at the end of a winding road.* Rated Restaurant: *Mas d'Artigny.*
Single: FR705–FR950. Double: FR1000–FR1830.

Somewhat like a sprawling Provencal homestead, this Relais and Châteaux rated hotel is in the outskirts of St.-Paul-de-Vence, on a 16-acre wooded hillside. Within the luxury resort are spacious public areas filled with a good mix of Mediterranean and period furnishings. In the lobby, there's a constantly changing exhibition of art. Accommodations include 53 spacious rooms and 19 suites, all with telephone, TV and tiled bath with robes and hair dryer. Many units have a balcony with a view of the sea, hills or town. Several of the suites have their own private swimming pool surrounded by a garden and hedges for privacy; these smaller heated pools are on a slope below the hotel's main pool. The restaurant serves good food and has a covered loggia above the pool. The bar has a viewful terrace. The staff is cordial, and English is spoken. Half-board rates are FR845 to FR1313 (room, breakfast and a meal) per person, per day in season. Features: pool, tennis. Credit Cards: All Major.

Villefranche-sur-Mer

Hotels and Resorts

Versailles   **FR580–FR860**   ★

avenue Princesse-Grace-de-Monaco. ☎ *04-93-01-89-56, FAX: 04-93-01-97-48. About five blocks west of the harbor.*
Single: FR580–FR680. Double: FR700–FR860.
Situated several blocks away from the harbor and outside the town center, this relatively modern hotel affords guests a perspective of the entire coastal area. There are 46 guest rooms and three suites with large windows and good views. All have bath or shower. The pool is particularly inviting; it's on a terrace and surrounded by palms and flowers. Guests can order breakfast or lunch on the rooftop terrace under an umbrella. The dining room has panoramic vistas, and meals begin at FR145. Half-board rates are FR845 to FR1313 (room, breakfast and a meal) per person, per day in season. Features: wheelchair-access rooms, beach location, pool, air conditioning in rooms, balcony or patio, in-room minibars. Credit Cards: All Major.

Welcome & Saint Pierre   **FR630–FR860**   ★★★

1 quai de l'Amiral-Courbet. ☎ *04-93-76-76-93, FAX: 04-93-01-88-81. Near rue de l'Eglise, at the old port.* Rated Restaurant: *St.-Pierre.*
Single: FR630–FR650. Double: FR820–FR860.
This six-floor villa looks down over the picturesque Villefranche port. The 32 rooms are small but comfortable and have bathrooms with bath or shower and balconies with sea or town views. Open fireplaces and fruitwood furniture in both the lounge and the restaurant add to their appeal. Serving excellent local cuisine, the restaurant is closed for lunch from July through August, except on weekends, and closed on Mondays from September through June. Half-board rates are FR480 to FR620 (room, breakfast and a meal) per person, per day in season. Features: beach location, air conditioning in rooms, balcony or patio, in-room minibars, in-room conference facilities. Credit Cards: All Major.

Where to Eat

Chantecler   **$$$**   ★★★★★

37 promenade des Anglais. ☎ *04-93-88-39-51.*
Specialties: sea bream filets with vegetables "a la grecque."
Lunch: 12:30–2:30 p.m., FR400–FR600.
Dinner: 7:30–10:30 p.m., entrées FR400–FR600.
Although the appointments are glamorous, the Chantecler is more of a showcase for its outstanding chef. Dominique Le Stanc is a purist and perfectionist—he buys the artichokes for such dishes as ravioli with langoustines from special farms. Terrific regional wine list; generous fixed-price menu for FR200 at lunch, including wine. Terrace dining in good weather. This is one of the finest hotel kitchens in France. Amenities: outside dining, own baking, reservations required. Credit Cards: All Major.

Chez Pipo $ ★

13 rue Bavastro. ☎ 04-93-55-88-82.
Specialties: Provencal chick-pea flour bread.
Dinner: 7–11 p.m., entrées FR10–FR75.

Socca, a paper-thin chickpea flour flat-bread, is a Provencal specialty, and it's the only thing this place serves. Wine available. You can also get socca and good pasta at **Nissa Socca**, 5 Sainte-Reparate (☎ 04-93-80-18-35), they serve wine and have outdoor seating. Closed Monday and all of January; no credit cards. If you want to splurge a little more, try the aforementioned **La Merenda** or **Brasserie de l'Union**, 1 rue Michelet (☎ 04-93-84-65-27), outdoor seating, local specialties, pasta, starting at FR95; open noon–2 p.m. and 7–9:30 p.m. **Flo**, 4 rue S.-Guitry (☎ 04-93-13-38-38), part of the Paris chain, is located in the old theater-casino. Some Provencal faves mixed in with choucroute alsacienne, etc. Open daily noon–3 p.m. and 7 p.m.–12:30 a.m.; fixed price menus start at FR90, with wine. **Outdoor market** at cours Saleya, open daily 7 a.m.–1 p.m. Amenities: outside dining, own baking, reservations not accepted.

Florian $$$ ★★★

22 rue A.-Karr. ☎ 04-93-88-86-60.
Specialties: filet of red mullet "grasse" style.
Lunch: Noon–2 p.m., FR330–FR500.
Dinner: 7–10 p.m., entrées FR330–FR500.

It may be staid and traditional, but that doesn't mean boring. Claude Gillon's cuisine is classic, but with a touch of Nicoise playfulness. The late-19th-century dining room is elegant and old-fashioned with mirrors and columns. Provencal wines. Six-course set menu at FR250; fixed-price lunch for FR190. Closed: Sun. Amenities: own baking, reservations recommended. Credit Cards: V, MC, E.

L'Ane Rouge $$$ ★★★

7 quai Deux-Emmanuel. ☎ 04-93-89-49-63.
Lunch: Noon–2 p.m., FR350–FR500.
Dinner: 7:30–9:30 p.m., entrées FR350–FR500.

So traditional is this restaurant that it has not moved with the times and provided a fixed-price menu. However, the largely seafood preparations are ultra-fresh and classically prepared. Guests are seated in the flamboyantly decorated salon or on the terrace, with colorful views of the port. Closed: Sat., Sun. Amenities: outside dining, reservations required. Credit Cards: All Major.

La Merenda $$$ ★★

4 rue de la Terrasse. ☎ none.
Specialties: pasta au pistou, red mullet filets, boeuf en daube.
Lunch: Noon–2 p.m., FR180–FR230.
Dinner: 7–9:30 p.m., entrées FR180–FR230.

There is no phone, it's open only four days a week, it's closed in February and August, and it makes no concessions to creature comforts. But the food is a wonderful collection of local favorites, some of them made at your minuscule table (there are only eight of them). You'll probably have to wait in line to get in. Closed: Mon., Sat., Sun. Reservations not accepted.

Nans-Les-Pins

Domaine de Châteauneuf $$$ ★★

N560, Logis de Nans. ☎ *04-94-78-90-0.*
Lunch: Noon–2 p.m., FR155–FR220.
Dinner: 7–10 p.m., entrées FR155–FR220.

This Domaine is the domain of Gilles Chirat, who worked with Michel Guerard, among other renowned chefs. He adds light, inventive touches to regional cuisine. Dine in the lovely garden, where you're close enough to hear the thwack of golf balls from the nearby Saint-Baume 18-hole course. Fixed-price menu, lunch only, FR170. Closed: Mon. Amenities: outside dining, own baking, reservations required. Credit Cards: All Major.

Directory

To and from

By train from Cannes (35 minutes) and Monaco (25 minutes), as well as to Paris via Marseille (seven hours), or by car on the N-7 coastal highway or on the N-202 road from the north. Also flights on Air Inter Europe from other major French cities as well as charter flights from abroad.

Tourist Office

avenue Thiers; ☎ *(33) 04-93-87-07-07.*

Rail Station

avenue Thiers; ☎ *(33) 04-93-87-50-50.*

Post Office

23 avenue Thiers, 06000 Nice; ☎ *(33) 04-93-88-56-80.*

St. Juan-les-Pins and Antibes

Situated on either side of the Cap d'Antibes peninsula, these two small towns and the beaches that connect them around the cape are where all the Riviéra glamor really began. This is where F. Scott Fitzgerald and his wife, Zelda, came and lived out their boozy, superficial lives, along with movie stars such as Rudolph Valentino, magnates such as Frank Jay Gould, and assorted deposed Russian aristocrats. This is where Fitzgerald based and began writing *Tender is the Night*—and even to this day, the area does have a certain flair. St. Juan-des-Pins, on the southern flank of the cape, is the epitome of modern decadence—although it would have been far too rowdy for Fitzgerald—packed with nightclubs with names such as V"oom-Voom" and "Whiskey-à-Go Go" that don't get going until after midnight. After Fitzgerald and his crew popularized the region, the area became a favorite stopover for American jazz artists, including Cole Porter and Louis Armstrong as well as those who had migrated to Paris—Josephine Baker, Dizzy Gillespie and others. Today there is an excellent jazz festival held every year in July under the pines of the resort that Gould began.

Rounding the cape, you pass golden beaches as well as the walled, wooded estates of millionaires, until you come to Antibes. Also a major resort, Antibes boasts a huge pleasure-harbor that is home-port to some of the world's most luxurious yachts, but one that has some history prior to the turn of the century. The Grimaldis (now of Monaco fame) built a castle here in the 12th century, long after the Greeks and then the Romans had inhabited the place they called Antipolis, of which only a tower and part of the keep stands today. Pablo Picasso was given the use of the castle as a temporary studio in 1946, and donated all 150 of the paintings and drawings he produced there to the town. The artworks are now on display in a museum inside the castle. Although there is more culture in Antibes than in St. Juan-des-Pins, the town is still a hedonistic center with crowds of rich folks and wanna-be-rich folks, as well as some nouveaux riche. Antibe's nightlife doesn't quite keep up with its neighbor to the south, but the action certainly is available.

What to Do

Museums and Exhibits

Musée Picasso/Château Grimaldi ★★★★

Château Grimaldi, place Marijol, ☎ *04-92-90-54-20.*

Hours open: 10 a.m.–6 p.m. Special hours: July–Aug. until 7 p.m.; closed Nov. 1-Dec. 10. Closed: Tue.

Housed in the Château Grimaldi is the Musée Picasso. Picasso was offered refuge here to paint and create for about six months in 1946. His sojourn resulted in more than 100 works of art, including ceramics, sculptures, lithographs, oils on paper and drawings, all of which he donated to the museum. It's located along the sea front in the former palace of the Grimaldi family. Also on display are works by other contemporary artists, including Leger, Miro and Caldero. Admission: FR20.

Nightlife

Clubs ★★★

Various locations.

The nightlife is almost impossible to avoid here—so here are a few of the most popular clubs in town: **Voom Voom**, *1 route Pinede (*☎ *04-93-61-18-71);* **Whiskey a Go Go**, *la Pinede (*☎ *04-93-61-26-40);* Le Pam Pam, *route Wilson (*☎ *04-93-61-11-05);* **Le Bureau**, *avenue de la Gallice (*☎ *04-93-67-22-74);* and **Joy's Club**, *avenue Dautheville (*☎ *04-93-67-78-87).*

Where to Stay

Hotels and Resorts

Belles-Rives **FR1500–FR2300** ★★★★

boulevard Baudoin. ☎ *04-93-61-02-79, FAX: 04-93-67-43-51. In St.-Juan-les-Pins. Double: FR1500–FR2300.*

One of the finest resort hotels on the coast, the Belles-Rives boasts grand panoramic views over the bay. The 41 guest rooms are individually decorated with period furniture and equipped with telephone, TV and bath. Facilities center around the water with a private beach, sailing, boating, water-skiing and other watersports. The restaurant serves dinners starting at FR360 on the bay-view terrace. Features: beach location, air conditioning in rooms, in-room minibars. Credit Cards: V, MC, A.

Hotel Juana
FR550–FR1600   ★ ★ ★ ★

avenue Gallice. ☎ *04-93-61-08-70, FAX: 04-93-61-76-60. At La Pinede, in St.-Juan-les-Pins.*

Single: FR550–FR900. Double: FR750–FR1600.

Brimming with charm, the Hotel Juana has been owned by the same family since 1931. While the 45 guest rooms are rather dark in decor, the old-fashioned style and comfort of earlier days is found here. Each room contains TV, telephone and bath or shower. With only a pine tree park in between, the beach is just a short walk away. There is a heated pool, a solarium and a terrace at the hotel. The restaurant serves excellent dishes, and 24-hour room service is available. Return to an era of class and sophistication at the Juana. Features: pool, air conditioning in rooms.

Hotel du Cap-Eden Roc
FR1500–FR3000   ★ ★ ★ ★ ★

boulevard J.F. Kennedy. ☎ *04-93-61-39-01, FAX: 04-93-67-76-04. South on boulevard du Cap and continue south on boulevard F. Meilland. Head west on boulevard Kennedy.* Rated Restaurant: *Pavillion Eden Roc.*

Single: FR1500–FR2300. Double: FR2300–FR3000.

Surrounded by 22 acres of gardens, this palatial hotel, built in 1870, is much like a country estate. The spacious public rooms have marble fireplaces, crystal chandeliers and richly upholstered armchairs. The 121 rooms and nine suites are exquisite, with luxurious period furnishings, and all of the rooms have private bath. The staff-guest ratio is an almost unheard of 3-to-1. There are exceptional views of both the gardens and the wide coastline from the hotel. Throughout the years, many celebrities have been seen, and can still be found, lounging by the swimming pool. The world-famous Pavillon Eden Roc, with its stylish restaurant overlooking the sea, snack bar, pool and cabanas, is near a rock garden apart from the hotel. Lunch is served on an outer terrace, under umbrellas and an arbor. Dinner specialties include bouillabaisse, lobster Thermidor and sea bass with fennel. Meals cost from FR500 to FR700, and reservations are required. Features: beach location, pool, tennis, water sports, air conditioning in rooms, fitness center. Credit Cards: Not Accepted.

Royal
FR390–FR640   ★ ★

boulevard du Marcechal-Leclerc. ☎ *04-93-34-03-09.*

Rated Restaurant: *Le Dauphin.*

Single: FR390–FR560. Double: FR490–FR640.

Built in the early 1900s, this is the oldest hotel in Antibes. The Royal has 37 rooms, all with private bath. It has its own beach with water sports, a café terrace in front with an extensive view and two restaurants and an English bar just off the lobby. Le Dauphin restaurant, open for lunch and dinner, specializes in seafood. Half-board rates are FR390 to FR490 (room, breakfast and a meal) per person, per day in season. Features: beach location, water sports. Credit Cards: All Major.

Where to Eat

Auberge Provencale $ ★★

61 place Nationale ☎ *04-93-34-13-24.*
Lunch: Noon–2 p.m., FR80.
Dinner: 7–10 p.m., entrées FR80.

One of the few budget offerings in town, the Auberge is an old favorite, with a fixed-price menu starting at FR80 (and for many of us, stopping there). Tasty, uncomplicated seafood and meat dishes. Nice people, too. Amenities: outside dining, own baking, reservations recommended. Credit Cards: V, MC, A, E.

Belles Rives $$$ ★★★★

boulevard du Littoral, At the bay. Located at Belles Rives. ☎ *04-93-61-02-79.*
Dinner: entrées FR300–FR475.

In one of the most tranquil resort hotels on the coast, this restaurant has seated more than its share of big names. Never dull, the kitchen, headed by Bernard Mathis, turns out fantastic international and French cuisine. From local waters, the sole, scallops and various shellfish are outstanding. The service, although distant at times, is very cordial. Set menus start at FR300. Amenities: outside dining, reservations required. Credit Cards: All Major.

La Terrasse $$$ ★★★

avenue Gallice, In Hotel Juana. Located at Hotel Juana. ☎ *04-93-61-08-70.*
Specialties: clam and squid canneloni in seafood sauce, millefeuille of wild strawberries with mascarpone cream.
Lunch: Noon–2 p.m., FR300–FR400.
Dinner: 7–10:30 p.m., entrées FR300–FR400.

There are two dining areas in the summer-only Hotel Jauna, with a forest of pines at its doorstep, but the most talked about is the beautiful al fresco La Terrasse, one of the best restaurants on the Azure Coast. Christian Morisset took over from the star-studded Alain Ducasse quite a while ago, but his stint with Roger Verge at Moulins ensured an easy transition. The cuisine remains essentially southern, with plenty of fresh seafood, fat goose liver and poultry, seasoned with fragrant herbs and garnished with the finest produce. The fixed-price menu at FR250 is a terrific deal. Closed: Wed. Amenities: outside dining, reservations required.

La Terrasse $$$ ★★★★★

avenue Gallice, La Pinede ☎ *04-93-61-20-37.*
Specialties: terrine of pigeon; cannelloni.
Dinner: 7:30–10:30 p.m., entrées FR300–FR600.

A trip back in time to the days of sophistication and elegance, this Art Deco villa paints the perfect backdrop for this gourmet restaurant. Best in the warm months, the restaurant is alive with the chic crowd dining on the terrace. The fresh ingredients combined with the culinary vision yield a rare gastronomic excellence. An ultra friendly staff will happily discuss the menu with you to decide what might please your palate the most. The set menus are a popular choice at FR500 and up for dinner (and, yes, a la carte is even more expensive). Amenities: outside dining, reservations required.

Les Vieux Murs $$ ★★★

avenue de l'Amiral-de-Grasse ☎ 04-93-34-66-73.
Lunch: Noon–2 p.m., FR150–FR250.
Dinner: 8–10 p.m., entrées FR150–FR250.

All the elements are here for an intimate evening of pure romance: a table for two
on a protected terrace facing the sea, under an arched ceiling in a 300-year-old
building. You want more? How about a bottle of regional wine from the excellent
cellars, and fragrant plates of fresh seafood cooked in unpretentious sauces. Fixed-
price menu at FR200. Another romantic spot, about 4 km out of town (take coast
highway N7), is the famous **La Bonne Auberge**, quartier La Brague (☎ 04-93-33-
36-65), which was founded by Jo Rostang in the '70s. It's now owned and man-
aged by son Philippe, who offers a democratic fixed-price menu for FR185. Sooth-
ing decor; seasonal, classic Southern-style cuisine. Closed Nov. 15-Dec. 15.
Amenities: own baking, reservations recommended. Credit Cards: V, MC, A, E.

Restaurant de Bacon $$$ ★★★★

boulevard de Bacon ☎ 04-93-61-50-02.
Specialties: bouillabaisse, chapon en papillote.
Lunch: 12:30–2 p.m., FR225–FR400.
Dinner: 8–10 p.m., entrées FR225–FR400.

The best bouillabaisse in France—some say the world—is served daily at this atmospheric restaurant on a promontory facing the Nice coastline. There's a wide variety
of unusual fish and shellfish dishes as well. For bouillabaisse in a grand setting, the
chic **Pavilion Eden Roc** restaurant, part of the Hotel du Cap-Eden Roc, bd. J-F-
Kennedy (☎ 04-93-61-39-01), also has a stellar view of the coast and an outdoor
terrace. A la carte FR470–FR600. Jacket required. Closed: Mon. Amenities: outside
dining, own baking, reservations required. Credit Cards: All Major.

Directory

To and From

By train to either place on the main coastal route, or by car on the circular peninsula road
just of the N-7 coastal highway.

Tourist Office

51 boulevard Guillamont (St. Juan-les-Pins); ☎ (33) 04-93-61-04-98.
11 place Général de Gaulle (Antibes); ☎ (33) 04-92-90-53-00.

Rail Station

avenue l'Esterel (St. Juan-les-Pins)
place Général de Gaulle (Antibes)

Post Office

rue Pauline, 06160 St. Juan-les-Pins
boulevard du Maréchal Leclerc, 06600 Antibes

Beaulieu-sur-Mer and St.-Jean-Cap-Ferrat

Situated on the north side of the tiny and exclusive Cap Ferrat peninsula,
the small town of Beaulieu-sur-Mer boasts uncrowded gravel beaches and

Kérylos, an unusual villa that is open to the public. Built between 1902 and 1908 for archaeologist Theodore Reinach, the villa reproduces an ancient Greek residence right down to mosaics and frescoes and benches and other furniture. You can walk around the peninsula from there, past the secluded and barely visible mansions of Somerset Maugham, Leopold II of Belgium and Gregory Peck, among other past and present owners, and you can admire the rocky coastline and the mountains that plunge into the sea just behind the cape. The most magnificent of all the mansions is open to the public, too, bequeathed to the *Institut de France* by Madame Baroness Ephrussi de Rothschild when she died in 1934. The villa itself is splendid enough, combining marble and typical terra-cotta simplicity to create an overall effect of great elegance, but it is the contents, that rival any museum outside the Louvre, that are most impressive. The Baroness had collected priceless Sèvre porcelain, artwork by Renoir and Sisley, tapestries, Oriental screens and ornaments, Persian carpets, Russian clocks and jewelry… and on and on.

For more information contact the tourist office in Beaulieu, *place de la Gâre;* ☎ *(33) 04-93-01-02-21.* You can take a train to Beaulieu (on the main coastal line) or drive there and around the cape on a circular road just off the main N-7 coastal highway.

What to do

St.-Jean-Cap-Ferrat

Historical/Architectural Sites

Villa Kerylos

rue Gustave-Eiffel, ☎ *04-93-01-01-44.*
Hours open: 3–7 p.m. Special hours: Oct.–Mar., Tues.–Sun., 2–6 p.m.
You may wonder what this "ancient" Greek villa is doing in the very French Riviera. Actually, it's only about 85 years old, built to exacting detail for an archaeologist, Theodore Reinach. Situated in a prominent spot facing the Baie des Fourmis, it contains faithful copies of Greek furnishings, amphorae and mosaics. It's closed in Nov. Admission: FR20.

Museums and Exhibits

Fondation Ephrussi de Rothschild ★★★

Chemin du Musée, ☎ *04-93-01-33-09. Near the tourist office.*
Hours open: 10 a.m.–7 p.m. Special hours: Sept.–June, to 6 p.m.;closed Nov.
This legendary estate belonged to the Baroness Ephrussi, a Rothschild, and is open to the public. The pastel-painted manse has furnishings fit for a queen (some of the antiques were Marie Antoinette's); there are original paintings by the likes of Renoir and Boucher, panels and screens from the Far East and priceless Sevres porcelain. The magnificent gardens, containing statuary from monasteries, churches and demolished palaces, keep local gardeners busy; the Institut de France is responsible for the water bill. Admission: FR38.

Where to Stay

Beaulieu-sur-Mer

Hotels and Resorts

Le Metropole   **FR700–FR2790**   ★ ★ ★ ★

15 boulevard du General Marechal Leclerc. ☎ *04-93-01-00-08, FAX: 04-93-01-18-51. On the corner of boulevard Mar. Leclerc and rue Paul Doumer.* Rated Restaurant: *Le Metropole.*

Single: FR700–FR1450. Double: FR1465–FR2790.

This huge white villa is situated among more than two acres of lush gardens bordering the sea. Rated as a Relais and Chateau, Le Metropole combines a *fin-de-siècle* Italianate style with ultramodern facilities. Its 50 luxurious rooms, all with private bath, are bright, handsomely furnished and have views that extend to St.-Jean-Cap-Ferrat. The hotel provide flawless service; the atmosphere is refined yet relaxed. There's a pool at the edge of the rocky coastline that's surrounded by flagstones, palm trees and parasols. Its restaurant, with a terrace overlooking the sea, however, is its centerpiece. Half-board rates are FR1465 to FR1925 (room, breakfast and a meal) per person, per day in season. Features: beach location, pool, water sports, air conditioning in rooms, sauna, balcony or patio, complimentary airport pickup service. Credit Cards: All Major.

Reserve de Beaulieu   **FR600–FR3500**   ★ ★ ★ ★ ★

5 boulevard du General Marechal Leclerc. ☎ *04-93-01-00-01, FAX: 04-93-01-28-99. Located about one and a half blocks south from Town Hall, near two churches.* Rated Restaurant: *La Reserve.*

Single: FR600–FR2600. Double: FR800–FR3500.

This pink-and-white palace, evoking an atmosphere of intimacy, luxury and elegance, is one of the most famous hotels on the Cote d'Azur. Guests tend to socialize around the main drawing room, which is like the living room of a lavish country estate. A number of the public lounges open onto a flower-filled patio courtyard, where there is alfresco dining when the wind is low. Because the hotel has been rebuilt in stages, its 40 rooms, all with private bathrooms, range widely in size and design. However, all rooms are exquisitely decorated and have a view of either the mountains or the sea. The large pool (heated Oct. through May) overlooks the beach and a small private harbor. The restaurant has a frescoed ceiling, parquet floors, Venetian crystal chandeliers and large windows facing the sea. Terrace dining is also offered. Half-board is required from May to September. Features: wheelchair-access rooms, beach location, pool, air conditioning in rooms, sauna, in-room mini-bars. Credit Cards: All Major.

Menton

Hotels and Resorts

Mediterranee   **FR350–FR500**   ★

5 rue de la Republique. ☎ *04-93-28-25-25, FAX: 04-93-57-88-38. Located where rue de la Republique meets rue Partouneaux.*

Single: FR350–FR460. Double: FR460–FR500.

This fairly new hotel in the center of town is just three short blocks from the beach. It has a modern decor and excellent conference and leisure facilities. Its 90 rooms, all with private bath, are attractively decorated. and include radios. The hotel has a rooftop terrace with chaise lounges and views of the sea. Half-board rates are from FR350 (room, breakfast and a meal) per person, per day in season. Features: wheel-chair-access rooms, beach location, air conditioning in rooms, in-room minibars. Credit Cards: All Major.

Napoleon   FR350–FR620   ★ ★

29 Porte de France. ☎ *04-93-35-89-50, FAX: 04-93-35-49-22. Located between the sea, mountains an Old Town; next to the Orly hotel.* Rated Restaurant: *No name given. Single: FR350–FR500. Double: FR520–FR620.*

This hotel is situated on a street shaded by palm trees. Inside, the main lounge, which has a bar, is more like a large living room and has 18th-century English and Italian furnishings. The 90 rooms all have a private bath and a balcony that overlooks either the sea or the Old Town. The pool is in a garden and stone terrace. Napoleon has a panoramic restaurant on the 6th floor that has been entirely refurbished. The restaurant is open to the public, and meals begin at FR150. Half-board rates are FR395 to FR445 (room, breakfast and a meal) per person, per day in season. Features: beach location, pool, air conditioning in rooms, balcony or patio, in-room minibars. Credit Cards: All Major.

Princess et Richmond   FR375–FR540   ★ ★

617 promenade du Soleil. ☎ *04-93-35-80-20. Located southwest on the promenade, near avenue du General-de-Gaulle. Single: FR375–FR435. Double: FR505–FR540.*

With a blue and white facade, this hotel is situated at the edge of the sea and yet is not far from the commercial center. Guests enjoy its panoramic garden terrace, where cocktails are served. There are 44 soundproof rooms with conservative furnishings and private bath. A continental breakfast is included with the room rate. The hotel has a minibus service to pick guests up at the train station or the airport. Sight-seeing tours are organized by the staff. Features: beach location, air conditioning in rooms, balcony or patio, in-room minibars. Credit Cards: All Major.

Roquebrune

Hotels and Resorts

Monte-Carlo Beach Hotel   FR2300–FR2550   ★ ★ ★

avenue Princesse-Grace, Monte-Carlo Beach. ☎ *04-93-28-66-66. Located at the border of Monaco; the avenue runs parallel with boulevard du Larvoltto.* Rated Restaurant: *La Pontiniere. Single: FR2300–FR2400. Double: FR2400–FR2550.*

Built in 1928, this lavish hotel was recently restored and has an Olympic-size pool. Its 44 rooms all have private baths, radios and loggias overlooking the sea. Accommodations also include a spacious circular suite above the lobby and seven bungalows. La Rivage offers light snacks and lunch for FR190 to FR300. An excellent lunch buffet for FR280 is served on the hotel's covered terrace, which affords sweeping views of the Cote d'Azur. La Potiniere reliably serves fine local fish grilled over a wood fire. Its dining room and terrace have sea views and excellent service, and prices range from FR350 to FR500. Features: beach location, pool, water sports, air conditioning in rooms, houses, cottages or bungalows, balcony or patio, in-room minibars. Credit Cards: All Major.

Roquebrune is a charming hilltop village with tortuously steep streets.

Victoria et de la Plage   **FR400–FR550**   ★★★

7 promenade Cap-Martin. ☎ *04-93-28-27-02, FAX: 04-93-28-27-02. Located at promenade de Schuman and promenade Cap-Martin.*

Single: FR400–FR500. Double: FR510–FR550.
This 1960s sea-level hotel is set behind a garden across from the Mediterranean. Its 32 rooms are well furnished and have classical decor, including silks and brocaded walls. All of the rooms have private bath with hair dryer, and 22 have a balcony. There is a main-floor bar, which is decorated with a sweeping mural of the Alps. Only breakfast is served. Features: beach location, air conditioning in rooms, balcony or patio. Credit Cards: All Major.

Vista Palace   FR950–FR1550

Grande Corniche. ☎ *04-92-10-40-00, FAX: 04-93-35-18-94. Located on the upper tier.* Rated Restaurant: *Le Vistaero.*
Single: FR950–FR1250. Double: FR1100–FR1550.
This deluxe hotel is perched 1000 feet up on the outer ridge of the mountains that run parallel to the coast, so its views of Monaco are spectacular. To enhance the panorama, the three-level hotel is cantilevered out into space and the seafront wall of almost every room is plate glass. There are 42 rooms and 26 suites, all with private bath, TV, telephone and many with a balcony. On the first level is a large reflecting swimming pool surrounded by subtropical plants and flowers. The hotel also features a solarium, massage parlor, Turkish bath, fitness center, indoor squash court and free shuttle service to Monte Carlo. The Mont Agel golf course is also within easy reach. Le Vistaero restaurant (listed separately) has a gorgeous sea vista and is open daily. Half-board rates are FR1145 to FR1300 (room, breakfast and a meal) per person, per day in season. Features: wheelchair-access rooms, beach location, pool, air conditioning in rooms, sauna, balcony or patio, in-room safes, in-room minibars, fitness center. Credit Cards: All Major.

St.-Jean-Cap-Ferrat

Hotels and Resorts

Clair Logis   FR260–FR600

12 avenue Centrale. ☎ *04-93-76-04-57. Located at the center of the peninsula, just north of avenue de Verdun.*
Single: FR260–FR400. Double: FR400–FR600.
A small, turn-of-the-century villa set in two acres of lush semitropical gardens. Each of its 18 spacious rooms has been refurbished and named after a flower, from mimosa to jasmine. All rooms have a private bath, and four have a large balcony. There is a ground-floor annex suitable for families. The most romantic accommodations are located in the main building; the rooms in the outlying annex are the most modern. Features: secluded garden atmosphere, balcony or patio. Credit Cards: All Major.

Grand Hotel du Cap-Ferrat   FR1300–FR5400

boulevard du General-de-Gaulle. ☎ *04-93-76-50-50, FAX: 04-93-76-04-52. Located at the southern tip of the peninsula.*
Single: FR1300–FR3900. Double: FR4000–FR5400.
A leading feature of this Belle Epoque palace is its location—it's hidden away in a 12-acre garden of semitropical trees and manicured lawns at the tip of Cap-Ferrat. Other hallmarks are its elaborate flowering terrace overlooking the sea and an Olympic-size, saltwater swimming pool, accessible via funicular railway from the

main building. The 59 luxurious rooms, each with a different decorative theme, are soundproof and have marble bath. Ten suites and a gorgeous honeymoon suite are also available. The hotel has a restaurant with a patio (listed separately), as well as an American-style bar opening onto the garden. The rates include a continental breakfast. Features: beach location, pool, tennis, water sports, air conditioning in rooms, in-room minibars, fitness center. Credit Cards: All Major.

La Voile d'Or   **FR1600–FR3400**   ★★★★

31 avenue Jean-Mermoz. ☎ *04-93-01-13-13, FAX: 04-93-76-11-17. Located at the south end of Port de Plaisance, near Capitaine Cook restaurant.* Rated Restaurant: *La Voile d'Or. Single: FR1600–FR3100. Double: FR3160–FR3400.*

On the edge of a little fishing port and yacht harbor, "The Golden Sail" affords panoramic views of the coast. The lounges, rooms and restaurant all open onto terraces, making this luxury hotel a romantic haven. There are 50 rooms and five suites; all are soundproofed and individually decorated with hand-painted reproductions of antiques, antique clocks and paintings. They also have baroque paneled doors, parquet floors and marble baths. The restaurant is highly recommended. Guests can gather on the canopied outer terrace for lunch and in the formal, stately dining room for dinner. The menu offers regional specialties and a few international dishes, as well as classic French cuisine. Features: beach location, pool, air conditioning in rooms, balcony or patio, in-room minibars, fitness center. Credit Cards: Not Accepted.

Where to Eat

Beaulieu-sur-Mer

African Queen   **$**   ★

Port de Plaisance.
Specialties: beef and lamb curry, pizza, ratatouille.
This movie-themed portside restaurant offers some exotic dishes along with the regional cuisine. Also good and reasonably priced (FR50–FR80) are several pizza offerings. American show-biz celebrities sometimes make an appearance here, or on the yachts that tie up nearby. Terrace dining for a view of the action. For more traditional fare, try **La Pignatelle**, *10 rue de Quincenet* (☎ *04-93-01-03-37*), with typical items including salade nicoise, fish soup and the like, from FR70. Amenities: outside dining, reservations recommended. Credit Cards: V, MC, E.

La Reserve   **$$$**   ★★

5 boulevard du Gal-Leclerc, In La Reserve de Beaulieu. Located at La Reserve de Beaulieu. ☎ *04-93-01-00-01.*
Specialties: sea bream with vegetables, langoustine risotto.
Lunch: Noon–2 p.m., FR300–FR400.
Dinner: 7–10:30 p.m., entrées FR300–FR400.
A few contemporary dishes add some modern tones to the otherwise classical cuisine served in this swanky dining room dripping with mirrors and gilt. Cocktails by the sea are usually *de rigeur* before sitting down to dinner, and that's easy to do as large windows look out on *la mer*. A pianist plays Chopin, adding to the unforgettable ambience. Some excellent desserts; ordinary wine list; terrace dining. Amenities: outside dining, reservations required. Credit Cards: All Major.

Le Metropole $$$ ★★★

15 boulevard du Gal-Leclerc, In Hotel le Metropole. Located at Metropole. ☎ *04-93-01-00-08.*

Specialties: roasted St.-Pierre fish with vegetables, mascarpone cheese with wild berries.

Lunch: Noon–2 p.m., FR250–FR400.

Dinner: 7–10 p.m., entrées FR250–FR400.

With glamorous turn-of-the-century decor, this hotel restaurant also has a wide terrace for dining above the sea. Delicious, though familiar southern French cuisine is served to a distinguished clientele. The service is soothing and utterly professional. Amenities: outside dining, reservations required. Credit Cards: V, MC, A, E.

St.-Jean-Cap-Ferrat

Grand Hotel du Cap-Ferrat $$$ ★★★

boulevard Gen. de Gaulle. ☎ *04-93-76-50-50.*

Specialties: trois petits salades de langoustines (shrimp, prawns and crayfish).

Lunch: Noon–2 p.m., FR350–FR400.

Dinner: 7–10 p.m., entrées FR350–FR400.

The mostly seafood dishes here are ethereally light, prepared with skill by Jean-Claude Guillon. The dessert carte is rather precious; he favors fruit infusions flavored with oddball herbs, such as a tarte with candied fennel (ugh) served with star-anise ice cream. This hotel dining room is elegant, but not forbidding, with professional service, and there's an outdoor patio. Amenities: outside dining, reservations required. Credit Cards: V, MC, DC, A.

Le Provencal $$$ ★★★

avenue D. Semeria. ☎ *04-93-76-03-97.*

Lunch: Noon–2 p.m., FR175–FR250.

Dinner: 7–11 p.m., entrées FR175–FR250.

This elegant, muraled restaurant, ablaze with flowers, is a laboratory for Jean-Jacques Jouteux's experimental cooking. One of his recent specialties was roasted St.-Pierre fish wrapped in a puff-pastry shell with figs. He enjoys high critical ratings. Fixed-price lunch menu at FR250. Closed: Mon. Amenities: outside dining, reservations required. Credit Cards: V, MC, E.

Monaco

There's probably no way to convince you not to go to Monaco. After all you've read about the tiny principality that is home to the world's oldest and most glamorous monarchy, after all you've seen on *Lifestyles of the Rich and Famous* about the millionaire set and the casino and the Bentleys, you've got to have a look, right? Well, don't say I didn't warn you. Today's Monaco was originally a Greek settlement, later taken over by the Romans. At the beginning of the 14th century, Monaco passed into the control of the Genoese empire, who sold it to the Grimaldi family. That's one way to become a king or a prince—buy yourself a kingdom. Today Monaco owes its survival as well as its prosperity to its Grand Casino, and other modern outfits that have since sprung up. Charles III, ruler of Monaco in the 19th century, was facing bankruptcy when he came up with a scheme to make some fast cash and built the Grand Casino on a rocky peninsula (now named Monte-Carlo in his honor). The place made money so fast that Charles III was soon able to abolish taxes for his people. The tax-free status of Monaco made it a grand place to live, and the town boomed, to the point that it is now dominated by high-rise apartment blocks rather than Belle Epoque-style hotels and casinos as you might have been led to expect. Every year it hosts the *Formula One* circuit for the *Grand Prix de Monaco* (on a street-course, obviously), as well as the professional rally drivers for the Monte Carlo Rally.

Monte Carlo's Grand Casino was built in 1878.

The "new" Grand Casino was built beginning in 1878 by Charles Garnier, who also designed the Paris Opera. You are free to go in and play the slot machines, but access to the gaming rooms costs FR80 just to watch. Mata Hari shot a Russian spy in this casino, Richard Burton proposed to Elizabeth Taylor (the second time) … the legends and the glamour just don't stop. Outside, you can watch the changing of the guard at the royal palace, a bit silly considering the entire principality covers less than three-quarters of a square mile, but, hey, that's tradition. One of the most interesting visits is to the automobile museum, called the *Monaco Top Cars Collection*, which houses Prince Rainier's personal collection of more than 100 of the most beautiful and exotic cars ever made.

What to Do

Historical/Architectural Sites

Palais du Prince ★★★

place du Palais, ☎ 00-377-92-25-18-31.

Hours open: 9:30 a.m.–6:30 p.m. Special hours: Closed Nov.–May.

Satisfy your desire to see how the "other half" lives. Only open during the summer, the royal family's home is open to the public. While the actual apartments are not open, the state rooms and opulent public rooms give one a glimpse at just how lavish a lifestyle it is. Witness the changing of the guard at 11:55 a.m. everyday. The Palace Museum, in one wing of the palace, holds artifacts from Napoleon and the principality of Monaco. Admission: FR30.

Museums and Exhibits

Monaco Top Cars Collection

les Terraces de Fontvieille, ☎ *00-377-92-05-28-56.*
Hours open: 10 a.m.–6 p.m. Special hours: Closed Nov. Closed: Fri.

The finest collection of cars in Europe. About 100 of the most beautiful, expensive, rare, fast cars to be found. The entire collection belongs to Prince Rainier. Highlighting the collection is the Rolls Royce that the Prince and the former Princess Grace (she died tragically in 1982) rode in on their wedding day and the car that won the Grand Prix of Monaco in 1929. Student admission FR15. Admission: FR30.

Musée de l'Oceanographie

avenue St.-Martin, ☎ *00-377-93-15-36-00.*

Founded by Prince Albert I in 1910, this aquarium is fed with sea water and displays an astounding array of sea life. There are about 3000 fish and related forms of life from around the world dispersed throughout 90 tanks. Director of the museum from 1957 to 1988, Jacques Cousteau established his research center here. The finest sea life exhibit in all of Europe. *Open Sept.–Oct. and Mar.–May, 10 a.m.–6 p.m.; Nov.–Feb., 10 a.m.–6 p.m.; June–Aug., 9 a.m.–8 p.m.* Admission: FR60.

Nightlife

Grand Casino   ★★★

place du Casino, ☎ *00-377-93-50-69-31.*

Designed by the architect of the Paris Opera, this casino was built in 1878. Styled in Belle Epoque, this opulent casino has hosted many royal figures and the international wealthy. The gaming rooms can be visited for a price, but the tables are reserved for the big spenders only. Slot machines are open to everybody. Less intimidating gambling can be found nearby at **Loews Casino**, *12 avenue des Spelugues* (☎ *93-50-65-00*) and **Le Cafe de Paris**, *place du Casino* (☎ *93-50-57-75*).

Where to Stay

Hotels and Resorts

Alexandra   **FR650–FR850**   ★

35 boulevard Princesse-Charlotte. ☎ *93-50-63-13, FAX: 92-16-06-48.*
Single: FR650–FR750. Double: FR780–FR850.

This *Belle Époque* hotel is in the center of the business district. Set on a busy street corner, its 19th-century design includes an elegant lobby with high ceilings. Alexandra's comfortably furnished 56 rooms all have private bathrooms and radios.

Breakfast is the only meal served. The hotel is open year-round. Features: air conditioning in rooms. Credit Cards: All Major.

Balmoral   FR400–FR850   ★★

12 avenue de la Costa. ☎ *93-50-62-37.*
Rated Restaurant: *(No name given.).*
Single: FR400–FR600. Double: FR550–FR850.
Balmoral is located on a cliff that overlooks the yacht harbor. This old-fashioned family hotel was built in 1898 by the grandfather of the present owner, Jacques Ferreyrolles. This is evident especially in the lounge, which has many family antiques. The guest rooms of this vintage hotel are like the public ones—homelike, immaculate and quiet. Approximately 50 of the 75 rooms have air conditioning, and all have sea views and private bathrooms. Many of the rooms have been renovated and an eighth floor was recently added. Breakfast is the only meal served, but snacks may be enjoyed in Balmoral. The hotel is open year-round. Features: beach location, air conditioning in rooms. Credit Cards: All Major.

Beach Plaza   FR700–FR1500   ★★★★

22 avenue Princesse Grace. ☎ *93-30-98-80, FAX: 93-50-23-14.*
Single: FR700. Double: FR1500.
The only hotel with a private beach, there are 305 rooms and nine suites (FR2100–FR4600). Each is spacious, attractively decorated and wonderfully comfortable. Leisure facilities are excellent, and a variety of recreational activities are offered. A nice alternative to the more pretentious 5-stars. Features: beach location, pool, in-room conference facilities. Credit Cards: All Major.

Hermitage   FR1100–FR2800   ★★★★★

square Beaumarchais. ☎ *92-16-40-00, FAX: 93-50-47-12.*
Rated Restaurant: *Belle ...poque.*
Single: FR1100–FR2300. Double: FR1400–FR2800.
Just a few minutes from the casino, this stunning *Belle Époque* hotel is perched on a cliff with views of the harbor and royal palace. The stately foyer retains its 1878 wood carvings, as well as its ornate stained-glass dome with an encircling wrought-iron balcony of ivy. The huge 220 rooms and 16 suites all have modern, private bathrooms, gleaming brass beds, and decoratively framed doors that open onto balconies. The units facing the harbor are captivating. Facilities include a gorgeous swimming pool and a fitness center. The stylish dining room has Corinthian columns, potted palms, glittering chandeliers and a marble terrace. Fixed-price menus begin at FR310. The Scorpion Bar is a chic nightspot with a piano bar. The hotel and restaurant are open year-round. Features: beach location, pool, air conditioning in rooms, balcony or patio, fitness center. Credit Cards: All Major.

Hotel de Paris   FR2700–FR3000   ★★★★★

place du Casino. ☎ *92-16-30-00, FAX: 92-16-38-49. Across from the casino.*
Single: FR2700. Double: FR3000.
Since 1865, the Hotel de Paris has been the leading choice of the aristocratic, the chic, the famous, the—well, you understand. Completely modern in conveniences, the decor is an opulent use of crystal, Louis XVI furniture and marble. The 206 rooms and 41 suites (FR5700) are pure luxury and comfort, with air conditioning,

minibar, TV, telephone and beautiful bath. Plush facilities include tennis courts and a heated indoor pool. Made famous in many movies, this elegant establishment continues to revel in its glory. Features: pool, tennis, air conditioning in rooms, in-room mini-bars. Credit Cards: All Major.

Loews   FR1400–FR2400   ★ ★ ★ ★

12 avenue des Spelugues. ☎ *93-50-65-00, FAX: 93-30-01-57.*

Rated Restaurant: *Le Foie Gras.*

Single: FR1400–FR2100. Double: FR1900–FR2400.

This casino resort lies on one of the most valuable pieces of real estate along Cote d'Azur. It contains the highest concentration of restaurants, bars and nightclubs in Monaco. Many celebrities are attracted to the hotel; even Prince Albert and Princess Stephanie show up for regular workouts in the seventh-floor health club. Besides the health club, there is the Monte Carlo Club and Monte Carlo Yacht Club where guests have access to such sports as tennis, golf, deep-sea fishing, sailing and scuba diving. After a day of exercising or shopping at one of the hotel's boutiques, guests can relax and enjoy a drink at the sunny Tahitian lobby bar or the more intimate Jockey Club. L'Argentin, a pampas-type restaurant, serves South American-style grilled meats and fish. There is also a formal gourmet restaurant, Le Foie Gras, for intimate dinners. The informal and nautical Le Café de la Mer is for breakfasts, snacks and light meals. The rooftop Le Pistou recreates the flavors of Provence. The hotel's entertainment highlights are included at the Folie Russe, a supper club with cabaret, and at the cavernous Grand Casino with a Las Vegas-style gaming room.

The 600 rooms in this entertainment extravaganza are tastefully and comfortably furnished. All rooms have sweeping panoramic views with private bathrooms. In addition, there are 35 luxurious suites with bright welcoming rooms and broad terraces. The hotel is opened year-round; however, Le Foie Gras is closed from January through mid-April and on Wednesdays during off-season months. For a large hotel, the hospitality level is superb. Features: wheelchair-access rooms, beach location, pool, golf, tennis, sailing, air conditioning in rooms, sauna, balcony or patio, in-room minibars, fitness center. Credit Cards: All Major.

Métropole Palace   FR1200–FR1950   ★ ★ ★ ★

4 avenue de la Madone. ☎ *93-15-15-15.*

Rated Restaurant: *Les Ambassadeurs.*

Single: FR1200–FR1500. Double: FR1600–FR1950.

In the heart of Monaco this hotel was rebuilt on the site of the original Métropole at Monte Carlo's "golden square." Its 123 rooms and 18 suites, all with private bathrooms, are handsomely furnished. Each room includes a radio, hypoallergenic pillows, a hairdryer and a full line of toiletries. The hotel's facilities and services include: an upscale restaurant, Les Ambassadeurs; a heated, seawater swimming pool; same-day and overnight laundry; 24-hour room service; baby-sitting; and valet parking. Métropole Palace and Les Ambassadeurs are open year-round. Features: wheelchair-access rooms, pool, air conditioning in rooms, in-room minibars. Credit Cards: All Major.

| **Mirabeau** | **FR1300–FR2000** | ★★★★ |

1 avenue Princesse-Grace. ☎ *92-16-65-65.*
Rated Restaurant: *La Caouple.*
Single: FR1300–FR1600. Double: FR1700–FR2000.
This attractive hotel, at the edge of the sea, is next to the Monte Carlo Casino. This landmark hotel has terraces with views of the Mediterranean and a lovely courtyard filled with plants. Its 99 guest rooms are well-decorated and have private bathrooms. Facilities include a swimming pool and parking garage. La Coupole restaurant, which is ranked one of the best on the Cote d'Azur, is capped with a glass canopy and has a fashionable bar. The hotel is open year-round. Features: beach location, pool, golf, tennis, air conditioning in rooms, balcony or patio, in-room minibars. Credit Cards: All Major.

Where to Eat

| **Le Cafe de Paris** | **$** | ★★★ |

place du Casino, Across from the casino. ☎ *92-16-20-20.*
Always a hot spot for people watching and casual, inexpensive food, this *belle époque* style brasserie is owned by the Societe des Bains de Mer. The international menus offer appetizers from FR50 and main dishes from FR90. After 2 a.m., the menu is limited. Stop by here on a late weekend night to see Monte Carlo in all its glory as the nouveau-rich and the nouveau-poor leave the casino. Amenities: cafés, reservations not accepted. Credit Cards: All Major.

| **Le Louis XV** | **$$$** | ★★★★★ |

place du Casino ☎ *93-30-23-11.*
Dinner: 8–10 p.m., entrées FR250–FR400.
Country cooking in an upscale, opulent, regal setting. Sounds odd, but it's a successful combination that attracts the most elite of crowds. The chef, Alain Ducasse, combines Provencal and Italian dishes to produce the most balanced and inventive rustic cuisine in the region. The wine list is practically endless with any bottle you could ever want—at prices you never would want. Fixed-price menus from FR630 for dinner. Closed: Tues. Amenities: outside dining, reservations required. Credit Cards: All Major.

| **Pizzeria Monegasque** | **$** | ★★★ |

4 rue Terrazzani ☎ *93-30-16-38.*
An eclectic crowd of locals patronizes this pizzeria. Quite plush for a pizza restaurant, the owner can throw around some of the big names who have dined here. Pizzas start at FR50, and main dishes, such as duck or carpaccio, start at FR70–FR110. A great spot for a late-night bite. Closed: Mon., Sun. Reservations not accepted. Credit Cards: All Major.

Directory

To and From

By train from Nice (25 minutes) and Cannes (70 minutes), or by car on the N-7 coastal road.

Tourist Office

2 boulevard des Moulins; ☎ *(00-377) 93-16-61-66.*

Rail Station

avenue Prince Pierre; ☎ *(00-377) 93-25-54-54.*

Post Office

place Beaumarchais, MC 98000 Monaco; ☎ *(00-377) 93-50-69-87.*

PROVENCE

Hill towns in Provence offer irresistible charm.

What Makes Provence So French?

1. *The oldest woman in the world, taking a drag off her (French) cigarette while reminiscing about the times she sold pencils to Van Gogh.*

2. *Vincent van Gogh's lopped-off ear lays pressed to the ground (decreed as "crazy" while alive, he was rediagnosed as "epileptic" après his death).*

3. *Cezanne, born and died in Aix-en-Provence—though his coat still hangs in Paris.*

4. *Black bulls, pink flamingoes, white pot-bellied horses and Carmarguais cowboys who hang bulls' horns above their cabanes to keep away evil spirits.*

5. *Julia Child.*

Mediterranean topography, cuisine, and culture begins in Provence, a region of sun, blue skies, small villages and, above all, vibrant colors. Van Gogh, one of the painters to be inspired by the region, reportedly said no one would believe him if he painted the colors realistically. Is that why he turned to post-Impressionism? Provence combines a stunning variety of towns, Roman ruins, perfumed hills and art museums. Let your fancy take you along narrow, twisting roads that connect the myriad picturesque Provençal villages, many perched impossibly on the sides of hills, ringed with olive groves, just waiting to be explored.

History

The mighty Rhône river splits Provence in two until it expands into the magnificent Camargue delta. The Rhône was all the Greeks needed in the sixth and fifth centuries before Christ to set up a brisk trading empire in this region. The artery that connected the Mediterranean sea with the interior was equally important to the Romans, who used it to expand their empire into Gaul, and built major cities on its banks at Nîmes and Arles, along with countless other smaller towns. Provincia, as the Romans called it, was the bastion of the Roman Empire in France until the fifth century, when the Barbarians, and the devastating effects of lead poisoning, drove the Caesars away. After the Franks and Visigoths lost their hold, Provence enjoyed several centuries of tranquility under the Counts of Provence, who came to be the Counts of Anjou, and Lorraine, and so on. The traditional Mediterranean triumvirate of wheat, olives and grapes fed the region's residents and brought them wealth. The Provençal people were unmoved by the chaos of the papal enclave at Avignon, and even the annexation of the region into France in 1481. Today, quiet Provence lives on much as it has for centuries.

Cuisine

The *cuisine provençale* is simple and delicious. Thanks to the temperate climate—five months of uninterrupted sunshine in summer, and mild winters—Provence is a garden paradise, producing melons, cherries, figs, asparagus and aubergines, as well as olives and herbs. *Ratatouille*, a hearty vegetable-based stew, is an important regional dish, and fish brought up from the nearby Côte d'Azur is a significant ingredient in many Provençal cooking pots. *Bouillabaise*, the fish stew discussed in the chapter on the Mediterranean, has also made its way up into the hills. Soups abound—one specialty is soup *de pistou*, based on a garlic and basil sauce known in other parts of the world as pesto. *Aïoli*, known elsewhere as *alioli*, a dip made from mayonnaise, garlic and olive oil, is served with hors d'oeuvres and bread. Fine wines such as *Châteauneuf-du-Pape* and *Côtes-du-Rhône* vie with innumerable acceptable *vins de table* for your attention, and a visit to Provence is

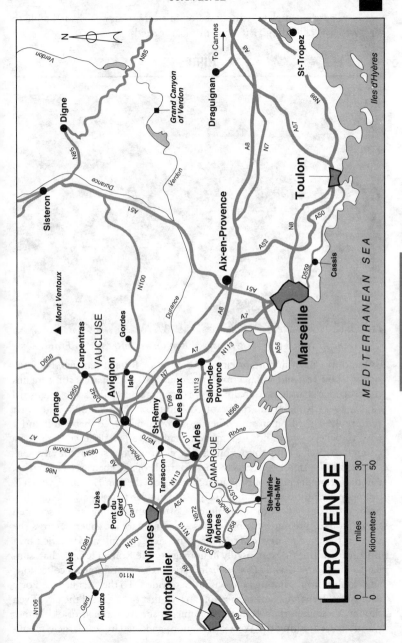

PROVENCE

not even nearly complete without a stop in a café to sit at a shaded table to sip *pastis*, the chilled *apéritif* made from anise seeds.

Nîmes

The Arena at Nîmes is the best-preserved Roman amphitheater in France.

One of the most important cities in France for Roman remains, Nîmes is rich in 2000-year-old architecture—the municipal coat of arms still contains the crocodile shackled to a palm tree that commemorated Caesar Augustus' victory over Cleopatra and the besotted Antony on the Nile. Built in the first century B.C., the Roman amphitheater is so well preserved that you'll find it hard to believe you're not in a modern stadium, especially if you are lucky enough to catch a bullfight or concert there during your stay in the city. Undoubtedly, the amphitheater is the best example of a Roman arena in France. Another stunning piece of Roman architecture is the *Maison Carré*, which is not a square house at all but actually a rectangular temple, also completely preserved, complete with finely fluted Corinthian columns and a sculpted frieze around three sides. It now houses a temporary art gallery. Across the street is the gaudy *Carré d'Art*, a glass-and-steel art museum designed by a British artist in 1993, supposedly in homage to the Roman temple that, similar to the *Centre Georges Pompidou* in Paris, presents multimedia collections and exhibits from paintings and sculpture to video. To the west lies the Porte Augustus, all that remains of the Roman wall that once girded the city. Even though these important Roman monuments survived, much of old Nîmes was destroyed during the Wars of Religion, and the city was largely rebuilt during the 17th and 18th centuries. The loveliest example of this classical reconstruction is the *Jardin de la Fontaine*, an elegant garden built around a natural spring that supplied the city with water before the Romans built their aqueduct and after they went mad and declined from using lead-lined pipes.

During the 17th-century reconstruction, Nîmes' economic fortunes began to rise, as the city became an important textile production center. An Austrian merchant, Levi Strauss, came up with the idea of making pants from the tough canvas the town produced for tent-making. The material was known as *bleu de Nîmes*, and the port from which most of the product made its way to the New World was Genoa, Italy, called *Génes* in French, hence "blue denim jeans."

What to Do
Historical/Architectural Sites

Les Arenes ★★★

boulevard Victor Hugo, ☎ *04-66-67-29-11.*
Hours open: 9 a.m.–6:30 p.m. Special hours: Oct.–May until 5 p.m.
A symphony of arches, the magnificent Roman amphitheater of Nîmes (1st century B.C.) once seated more than 20,000 spectators for the Saturday night gladiator follies. Today bullfights take center stage three times a year, in February, June and September. Concerts and theatrical events are also featured in summer. Not far away is the old Roman temple, **Maison Carré** *(place de la Maison Carré,* ☎ *04-66-67-29-11),* now used as an art museum. Its Corinthian-columned facade is remarkably preserved. *Open in summer, 9 a.m.–7 p.m., winter 9 a.m.–5:30 p.m.* In front of the Maison Carré is the three-year-old **Carré d'Art** *(*☎ *04-66-76-35-70),* an ultramodern reply to its classic cousin. Designed by Norman Foster, it is the city's newest cultural mecca, with a library, art galleries and rooftop restaurant. *It's open 11 a.m.–6 p.m.* Admission: FR22.

Parks and Gardens

Jardin de la Fontaine ★★★

quai de la Fontaine. At the end of the quai.
Special hours: Open to sunset; to 10 p.m. in summer.
Centered around the Neausus spring-fed fountain, this perfectly manicured garden offers grand views of the city—especially at the top where the Tour Magne stands. The Neausus spring, it is said, is the reason the Romans settled here. These gardens were laid in the 18th century, with the ruins of the Temple de Diane at the base. Spend some time taking a relaxing walk through, culminating in a climb up the tower (FR10). Admission: FR12.

Where to Stay
Hotels and Resorts

Hotel Imperator **FR530–FR1200** ★★★

quai de la Fontaine. ☎ *04-66-21-90-30, FAX: 04-66-67-70-25.*
Rated Restaurant: *L'Enclos de la Fontaine.*

Single: FR530–FR850. Double: FR850–FR1200.
This leading old hotel has been recently renovated, yet much of it retains its charming original character. Many of its 62 rooms have Provençal furniture, and all have private bath. The restaurant also serves lunch in an appealing rear garden. Half-board rates are FR730 to FR1200 (room, breakfast and a meal) per person, per day in season. Features: air conditioning in rooms, in-room mini-bars, fitness center. Credit Cards: All Major.

L'Orangerie   **FR300–FR500**   ★★

755 rue Tour de l'veque. ☎ *04-66-84-50-57. Located at boulevard Presidente-Allende.*
Rated Restaurant: *L'Orangerie.*
Single: FR300–FR390. Double: FR390–FR500.
A converted family estate surrounded by grounds with ancient plane trees. The 31 rooms are large and quiet. All have contemporary decor, private bathrooms, satellite TV and direct-dial telephones. Some have a balcony and view of the pool, while others look over the garden. The restaurant, with terrace dining, features regional dishes such as brandade with carpaccio. Reservations are recommended. Half-board rates are FR315 to FR370 (room, breakfast and a meal) per person, per day in season. Features: wheelchair-access rooms, pool, air conditioning in rooms, balcony or patio, in-room mini-bars. Credit Cards: All Major.

Le Cheval Blanc   **FR500–FR1900**   ★★★★

1 place des Arenes. ☎ *04-66-67-32-32, FAX: 04-66-76-32-33. Across from the arena.*
Single: FR500. Double: FR1900.
This impressive hotel once welcomed Picasso and Cocteau as its guests. Remodeled by Jean-Michel Wilmotte, the 35 soundproof rooms have TV, telephone, private bath and air conditioning. The decor occasionally includes attractive tapestries and murals. Public spaces are magnificent, with Provençal decor and handsome furnishings. Take dinner on the terrace overlooking the arena—an experience not to be forgotten. Breakfast costs FR70. Features: air conditioning in rooms. Credit Cards: All Major.

Inns

Le Louvre   **FR380–FR420**   ★★★

2 square de la Couronne. ☎ *04-66-67-22-75, FAX: 04-66-36-07-27. Between the train station and the arena.*
Single: FR380. Double: FR420.
This townhouse's guest list once included Thomas Jefferson. A preserved 17th-century villa, this well-established inn has 33 spacious rooms with TV, telephone and bath or shower. Reserve one overlooking the inner courtyard. While there is no restaurant in the hotel, breakfast is available for FR38 extra. Several restaurants are nearby. Credit Cards: All Major.

Lisita   **FR325**   ★★

2 boulevard des Arenes. ☎ *04-66-67-66-20, FAX: 04-66-76-22-30. Near the arena.*
Double: FR325.
A favorite spot for the Spanish matadors when bullfights are in town, this is a cozy little hotel. It has 30 smallish rooms, all modestly furnished and with private bath. The restaurant serves traditional fare in attractive surroundings. Credit Cards: All Major.

Where to Eat

Cheval Blanc   **$$$**   ★★

place des Arenes, In Hotel Cheval Blanc. Located at Cheval Blanc. ☎ *04-66-76-32-32.*
Lunch: Noon–2 p.m., FR200–FR255.
Dinner: 7–10:30 p.m., entrées FR200–FR255.
The dining room in the remodeled Hotel Cheval Blanc has been jazzed up, too.
Featured on the menu is tangy, modern, Mediterranean-inspired cuisine, with an
emphasis on fresh seafood. Exciting desserts; distinguished wine cellar. Both Coc-
teau and Picasso stayed at this prominent hotel. Closed: Sun. Amenities: own bak-
ing, reservations required. Credit Cards: V, DC, A.

Les Persiennes   **$$**

5 place de l'Oratoire ☎ *04-66-67-80-22.*
Lunch: 11:30 a.m.–2 p.m., FR75–FR100.
Dinner: 7–11 p.m., entrées FR75–FR100.
This place is a real find—generous with portions and *kind to your wallet.* The hors
d'oeuvres buffet is fresh, delicious and constantly replenished. It's yours for a fixed
price of only FR65. **Market**: Les Halles, between Rue Guizot and Rue de Halles,
open daily, 7 a.m.–1 p.m. Closed: Mon., Sun. Reservations recommended. Credit
Cards: V.

Notre-Dame-de-Vie

Moulin de Mougins   **$$$**   ★★★

424 Chemin du Moulin, On D3, 2 km southwest of Mougins. In Le Moulin de Mougins.
Located at Le Moulin de Mougins. ☎ *04-93-75-78-24.*
Lunch: Noon–2:15 p.m., FR255–FR400.
Dinner: 8–10 p.m., entrées FR255–FR400.
The moulin refers to the medieval olive mill that was fashioned into the great Roger
Verge's celebrated restaurant and small hotel. In the main dining room, the tables
are graced with only the best napery and tableware. There's also outdoor seating in
a garden under umbrellas. Verge has trained many chefs who have gone on to four-
star acclaim (Christian Morissot of La Terrace is one). Verge is famous for his "cui-
sine of the sun," light, inventive dishes based on classical recipes, using the produce
and bounty of Southern France. Today he has expanded his interests with a cooking
school and a boutique proffering a line of sauces and preserves. Verge has a smaller
restaurant, also a converted mill, **L'Amandier de Moulins**, *pl du Commandant-Lamy*
(☎ *04-93-90-00-91),* and much less expensive (FR160–FR220), with Joel Manson
presiding over the burners. Terrace dining on the upper level. Specialties: Bresse
chicken with lobster sauce, red mullet terrine. *Closed Wed., Sat. lunch, and Feb.* All
major cards. Another highly acclaimed spot (not related to Verge enterprises) is **Le
Relais a Mougins**, *pl. de la Marie (*☎ *04-93-90-03-47),* owned by Andre Surmain,
who made his fame at Lutece in New York. Entrées begin at FR58, the small bar
adjoining offers a FR75 set menu. Outdoor terrace, with view of village square. Spe-
cialties: Bresse pigeon in a potato crust, salade oasis with lobster and endive. *Open
daily, except Tues. lunch and Mon.* Amenities: outside dining, own baking, reserva-
tions required. Credit Cards: All Major.

Directory

To and From

> By train from Paris (four hours), Toulouse (three hours), and Marseille (two hours), or by car on the A-9 autoroute from the southwest, N-103 road from the northwest, A-9 from the northeast, or A-54 autoroute or N-113 road from the southeast.

Tourist Office

> 6 rue Auguste; ☎ (33) 04-66-67-29-11.

Rail Station

> avenue Feuchères; ☎ (33) 04-66-23-50-50.

Post Office

> 1 boulevard de Bruxelles, 30000 Nîmes; ☎ (33) 04-66-76-67-90.

Pont du Gard

The Romans constructed a 31-mile-long aqueduct from springs at Uzès to carry water to Nîmes, an amazing feat of engineering. But to get to Nîmes, they had to cross the Gard river, which lies at the bottom of a deep river valley. No problem for the Roman hydrologists—they constructed the monumental bridge called *Pont du Gard* that still stands today, and which is capable of carrying water although it no longer does so. The Romans themselves wrote that this bridge was the most concrete proof of the supremacy of their empire and their culture. Standing 160 feet tall and spanning 1000 feet across the river, the bridge was the tallest and one of the longest ever built by Roman engineers. Constructed on three levels, with 52 arches in the top level that supported the water channel, the bridge consists of blocks of stone weighing up to six tons that were lifted into place with a system of pulleys and winches, along with the muscle-power of many slave laborers. Archaeologists estimate that the bridge carried water for as long as 500 years.

To get to Pont du Gard, catch a bus in Nîmes or follow the signposts off the A-9 autoroute north from Nîmes.

Avignon

This lovely city owes its stunning, rampart-enclosed beauty to the popes of the Catholic church, who made Avignon the capital of Christianity in the 14th century. The fortifications of the Papal Palace reflect the violent nature of medieval-era religious life, which, in feudal, factionalized Italy, was what drove the Holy See here in the first place. Wanting to escape the pressures of political Rome, and certainly urged on by the manipulative King Phillipe IV of France, Pope Clement V stunned Rome by moving the seat of the church to Avignon in his native France in 1309. The Holy See had owned land in the area since the 13th century and, building upon the relatively modest Episcopal residence, Clement V set about constructing a palace for himself that would become one of the grandest in Europe. Both the Old Palace, largely constructed between 1334 and 1342 by Pope Benedict XII, and the new Palace, built by Clement VI between 1342 and 1352, featured classic military-style architecture—all those papal treasures to protect from infidels—and the fortress-palace is buttressed by 10 towers, the tallest standing more than 160 feet high. Benedict XII was a former Cisterian monk, thus his section of the palace is centered around a cloister, its austere, sober construction stands as testimony to the emphasis he placed on spiritual worship. By contrast, Clement VI believed the best way to honor God was for the ecclesiastical leadership to live in luxury, and his portion of the palace reflects this, with a huge courtyard for parties (it now houses the famous Avignon festival), ornate ceramic tiling in his study, and frescoes painted by the greatest Italian artists of the time, including Simone Martini and Matteo Giovanetti. In order to further consolidate the power of the church in Avignon, Pope Clement VI bought the city from the Countess of Provence in 1348. During the instability of the Hundred Years' War, Pope Innocent VI reinforced and expanded the palace's ramparts and defenses, so that at its peak the structure covered 150,000 square feet. Unfortunately, the visitor today will have to imagine the finery that once furnished the palace and content him or herself with studying the architecture, as the Revolution saw all the contents destroyed or looted.

Avignon was home to seven official popes from 1309 to 1377, when Gregory IX died in Rome. Thus began the famous schism in Christianity, when Urban VI was elected pope in Rome by local leaders of the church, while the other cardinals elected Clement VII, who continued to live in Avignon. For the next 37 years there was a pope in Rome and an anti-pope in Avignon, and sometimes even a third pope in Pisa, all claiming supremacy and excommunicating each other. The confusion reigned until 1417, but even after the Papacy was unified and returned to Rome, Papal Legates continued to represent the church in Avignon, which remained the property of the church until 1791.

The song goes "*Sur le pont d'Avignon, on y dansait...*" (On the bridge of Avignon we used to dance), but the dancing actually used to take place on an island under the bridge's central span. A famous landmark, the *Pont St. Bénézet* was reputedly begun by a shepherd boy, Bénézet, in 1177. At the time of its construction, the 22-arch bridge was the only stone bridge across the Rhône, and it was a vital link for trade as well as for the Catholic Cardinals who built their villas in Villeneuve. All but four of the arches were washed away by flood waters in the 17th century, and since then, the bridge has stood, whimsically, leading halfway across the river. There is a tiny chapel, the *Chapelle St. Nicolas*, at the end. Today, you use another bridge to get across to Villeneuve, but it is worth the trip to visit the complex of the 15 cardinals' villas, which were integrated with an abbey and fortress to make a grand structure that is a fine counterpart to the Papal Palace. Also on this side of the river is the *Chartreuse du Val de Bénédiction*, a Carthusian monastery erected in the 14th century by Pope Innocent VI to honor the decision of the Carthusian Order's leader to reject his election to Popehood.

Avignon's St.-Bénézet Bridge is a popular rendezvous spot for lovers.

During the Papal years, Avignon grew wealthy, and a walk around the maze of narrow streets surrounding the palace reveals fine mansions and houses. Hidden among the town are numerous venues for some of the more than 400 plays that are performed during *Festival Off*, the companion celebration to the original *Festival d'Avignon*, Europe's most important drama-and-dance festival, held concurrently from early July to early August.

What to Do

City Celebrations/Events

Festival d'Avignon ★★★

Bureau du Festival, 8 bis rue de Mons, ☎ *04-90-82-67-08.*
Hours open: 9:30 a.m.–11 p.m.
Stimulating dance, theater, film and drama accentuate this important festival held mid-July–early Aug., with performances at the Palais des Papes and various cultural centers; tickets FR95–FR200, also some free events. A fringe festival, called "Off" (July 9–Aug. 3), is slightly cheaper, irreverent and daring; contact Festival Off at *place du Palais (*☎ *04-90-82-28-62).*

Historical/Architectural Sites

Chartreuse du Val de Benediction ★★★

60 rue de la Republique, ☎ *04-90-25-05-46. In Villeneuve-les-Avignon.*
Hours open: 9:30 a.m.–5:30 p.m. Special hours: Apr.–Sept., 9 a.m.–6:30 p.m.
This charterhouse, founded in 1356 by Pope Innocent VI, was the most important Carthusian monastery in France. On the way in, notice the plaques which mark the height the flood waters reached in 1840 and 1856. Once inside, wander through the labyrinth of chambers, halls, cells and cloisters. Key sights include the tomb of Pope Innocent VI and the Coronation of the Virgin by Charonton. Student and senior admission is FR14. Admission: FR25.

Château des Papes ★★

In Châteauneuf-du-Pape.
Built by the Avignon popes in the 14th century as a country seat, the castle now lies in ruins. The best excuse to visit is to soak in the stellar views of the Rhone Valley, Avignon and the surrounding vineyards, which produce one of the Rhone's finest wines, Châteauneuf-du-Pape, thanks to the popes who planted the original vineyards.

Fort St.-Andre ★★★

On the hill, ☎ *04-90-25-55-95. In Villeneuve-les-Avignon.*
Guarding watch above the town is Fort St.-Andre. Founded in 1360 to symbolize strength to the powers across the river, it protected the Benedictine abbey and the town. The remains of the fort and the abbey may be wandered in their almost eerie surroundings of a day gone by. *Open Apr.–Sept., daily, 9 a.m.–noon and 2–6:30 p.m.; Oct.–Mar., daily, 10 a.m.–noon and 2–5 p.m. Also of interest might be the Musée Municipal Pierre de Luxembourg, rue de la Republique (*☎ *04-90-27-19-66) and the Tour Philippe le Bel, rue Montee de la Tour (*☎ *04-90-27-49-68). The* museum houses mostly religious articles and paintings taken from the Chartreuse

during the Revolution. The tower, best climbed for the view, was built in the 14th century to serve as an entryway to the town. All of the historical sights can be visited with one 45-franc ticket available at any of the attractions. Admission: FR20.

Avignon's Palais des Papes has 10 stout towers surrounding a courtyard.

Palais des Papes   ★★★★

place du Palais-des-Papes, ☎ *04-90-27-50-74.*
Hours open: 9 a.m.–7 p.m. Special hours: Winter, to 5 p.m. or 6 p.m., depending on month.

If the Palais du Papes looks imposing, standing stalwart above the walled city, it was meant to be that way. The fortress-residence of the Avignon popes is awesome with its thick brick walls topped by 10 stout towers surrounding a central courtyard. Life was tough in the 14th century, and, if you weren't prepared, you'd be easily overwhelmed by blackguards, thieves and thugs. The empire building began in earnest in 1309, when Pope Clement V decided to move the papal court from Rome to Avignon. The Palais was added on to until the court returned to Rome in 1377. The interior is graced by Gobelin tapestries and frescoes by Simone Martini. Guided tours are given in English daily at 10 a.m. and 3 p.m., admission FR53. North of the Palais is the Petit Palais, former home of the Archbishop of Avignon, and now a museum brimming with treasures from the Renaissance and sculpture and painting from the School of Avignon (15th through early 16th centuries). *Open daily, except Tues., 9:30 a.m.–6 p.m.* Admission: FR16; children, students, seniors FR8. Sundays free in winter. Admission: FR42.

Synagogue   ★★★★

place Juiverie, ☎ *04-90-63-39-97. In Carpentras.*
Hours open: 10 a.m.–5 p.m. Special hours: Closed noon–3 p.m. Closed: Sat., Sun.
Founded in 1367, this is France's oldest synagogue. Since its inception, it has undergone reconstruction in the mid-1700s and in the mid-1900s. A modest build-

ing, it is across from the Hotel de Ville, with a Hebrew-inscribed plaque marking the building. After ringing the bell and getting in, look for the paneled sanctuary on the first floor and the ground-floor oven used to bake matza until the turn of the century. This oven and the women's baths have remain completely unchanged. Admission: free.

Where to Stay

Hotels and Resorts

Danieli   **FR350–FR490**   ★

17 rue de la Republique. ☎ *04-90-86-46-82.*
Single: FR350–FR450. Double: FR390–FR490.
An intimate hotel with an Italian flair, the Danieli offers 29 rooms. The softly toned chambers, accented with a bit of Art Deco style, feature contemporary furnishings, TV, telephone and private bath. The Italian character is glimpsed in the baronial staircases and structural arches. A light breakfast is served for FR40. A bit of charm is thrown in with this value-minded hotel. Credit Cards: All Major.

Europe   **FR610–FR1500**   ★ ★ ★

12 place Crillon. ☎ *04-90-14-76-76, FAX: 04-90-85-43-66.*
Rated Restaurant: *La Vielle Fontaine.*
Single: FR610–FR650. Double: FR650–FR1500.
Once the home of the Marquis de Graveson, this 16th-century mansion has been operating as a hotel since the late 1700s. The salons are graced with Aubusson tapestries, lovely antiques and original pieces of art. Retreat to any of the 47 air-conditioned guest rooms, decorated with period furnishings and offering TV, telephone and marble bath. Overlooking the town and the Palais des Papes, the three rooftop suites are splendid displays of refined elegance. The experience here is capped with a meal in the hotel restaurant, La Vielle Fontaine, which serves fixed-price meals from FR200 in the dining room and in the inner courtyard. A grand hotel with an intimate feeling aroused by the charming staff. Features: pool, air conditioning in rooms, balcony or patio, in-room minibars. Credit Cards: All Major.

La Mirande   **FR1300–FR2100**   ★ ★ ★

4 place de l'Amirande. ☎ *04-90-85-93-93, FAX: 04-90-86-26-85.*
Rated Restaurant: *La Mirande.*
Single: FR1300–FR1400. Double: FR1400–FR2100.
An exquisite hotel housed in a former cardinal's palace dating back to the 17th century, it sits across from the Palais des Papes. Opened in 1990, this magnificent piece of architecture beholds a private garden, lavish salons and 20 elegant rooms. Each of the rooms is individually styled with a plethora of antiques, original art and complementing fabrics. The rooms are also equipped with cable TV, telephone, minibar, safe, air conditioning, robes, hair dryer and toiletries. The well-maintained communal facilities include a sauna, a Jacuzzi and a solarium. The restaurant beckons with its flavorful food, attentive service and intimate surroundings; perhaps a late-night cocktail from the bar to close out a wonderful evening. The only choice for deluxe accommodations in Avignon. Features: wheelchair-access rooms, air con-

ditioning in rooms, sauna, in-room safes, in-room minibars, fitness center. Credit Cards: All Major.

Vonnas

Hotels and Resorts

Georges Blanc   **FR800–FR1700**   ★★★★

Vonnas. ☎ *04-74-50-90-90, FAX: 04-74-50-08-80.*
Rated Restaurant: *Georges Blanc.*
Single: FR800–FR1000. Double: FR1500–FR1700.

Reason alone to visit Vonnas, Georges Blanc's Relais and Châteaux 19th-century country inn sits on the banks of the romantic River Veyle. The 30 air-conditioned guest rooms vary from basic to luxurious, and each has a private bath. Leisure time is spent on the tennis courts, playing golf and swimming in the heated pool. The culinary masterpieces created by George Blanc are among the finest in the world. From appetizers of frog legs, to any wine from the select list to the superb desserts, every course is gastronomic euphoria. Reservations are required for a chance to experience this legend. Features: pool, tennis, air conditioning in rooms. Credit Cards: All Major.

Where to Eat

Christian Etienne   **$$**   ★★★★

10-12 rue de Mons.
Specialties: Vegetables Provençal.
Lunch: Noon–2:30 p.m., FR350–FR500.
Dinner: 8–10:30 p.m., entrées FR350–FR500.

Besides being one of the best restaurants in town (and one of the oldest), Christian Etienne also has one of the most enviable locations—his patrons face the Palais des Papes while they dine. And what dining! The small but smart menu offers an ever-changing cornucopia of tastes and flavors. The fixed-price meals are perhaps the most creative; one features an entire menu of Provençal vegetables. Marvelous fish and shellfish dishes are available as well. Closed: Sun. Amenities: outside dining, own baking, reservations recommended. Credit Cards: V, MC, A.

Hiely-Lucullus   **$$**   ★★★★

5 rue de la Republique.
Specialties: turbot in a white wine sauce with palourdes, pan-fried langoustines with vegetables.
Lunch: Noon–2 p.m., FR140–FR310.
Dinner: 7:30–9:45 p.m., entrées FR140–FR310.

For many years this was the domain of master chef Pierre Hiely. Although he's semi-retired, the quality of the classic cuisine has not changed a whit. No less talented people are still running a tight ship (the place looks like one), and the prices are democratic. Only four-course fixed-price meals are available (from FR140–FR310), but there's enough variety in each one to satisfy the fussiest diners. At lunch (except Sundays), the FR130 menu includes wine. Closed: Mon. Amenities: own baking, reservations required. Credit Cards: V, MC, E.

Le Petit Bedon   **$$$**   ★

70 rue Joseph Vernet ☎ *04-90-82-33-98.*
Lunch: Noon–2 p.m., FR100–FR150.
Dinner: 7–10:30 p.m., entrées FR100–FR150.

You might see chefs from the top-flight restaurants eating here on their days off;
most of them secretly enjoy the good, simple cooking and the easy prices. What's
more, the people are nice and the surroundings are pleasant. The sparkling fish
dishes are especially worth ordering; affordable wine list. Closed: Sun. Reservations
recommended. Credit Cards: V, MC, DC, A.

Tache d'Encre   **$$$**   ★ ★

22 rue des Teinturiers ☎ *04-90-85-46-03.*
Lunch: Noon–2 p.m., FR50–FR90.
Dinner: 7:30–12 p.m., entrées FR50–FR90.

For a pleasant evening out, this popular club-restaurant offers a decent meal with
some scintillating live music (but nothing too extreme). The set menus are less
FR100; lunch is an even better deal, with three courses a FR50. Call the club for
show information. Avignon has some excellent pastry shops. **Simple Simon**, *27 rue
de la Petite Fusterie* (☎ *04-90-86-62-70*), is an all-French speaking "Olde
English" tea shop, and it's open until 2 a.m. in summer; cakes, pastries, meat pies,
etc., FR50–FR150. **Les Felibres**, *14 rue Limas* (☎ *04-90-27-39-05*), lunch only,
serves up books with tea and pastries, also regional cooking, FR130–FR150. The
town's covered food market is at place Pie; *open 8 a.m.–1 p.m. daily, except Mon.*
Amenities: happening bar, cafestop, own baking, reservations recommended. Credit
Cards: V.

Directory

To and From

*By train from Paris (four hours), Lyon (two hours), or Marseille (an hour and a half), or
by car from any direction, just off the A-9 and A-7 autoroutes as well as the N-7, N-570,
and N-580 highways.*

Tourist Office

41 cours Jean Jaurès; ☎ *(33) 04-90-82-65-11.*

Rail Station

porte de la République; ☎ *(33) 04-90-82-50-50.*

Post Office

avenue du Président Kennedy, 84000 Avignon; ☎ *(33) 04-90-86-78-00.*

Carpentras

Even before Avignon's independent period, first from Provence, then from
France, the town of *Carpentras*, just to the north, belonged to the Vatican,
along with a small region called the *Comtat Venaissin*. During the Middle
Ages, the city became a relative haven for Europe's Jews. The Jews bought
protection from the popes, who decreed that it was wrong to physically harm
the "flesh and blood of Christ." Nevertheless, although it was better than
being killed in other parts of France and Europe, the Jews were confined to a

ghetto called *la carrière*, which until its expansion, permitted by the popes in 1741, consisted of a single street locked at both ends at night. Here you can visit the oldest synagogue in France, dating from 1367, as well as the 14th-century kosher bakery and *mikva* bath house. When Provence became part of France and the Jews were subjected to violence throughout the country, (as well as when the Jews were driven out of Spain and Portugal at the end of the 15th century), Carpentras became a major population center for *les juifs*, and the Jewish community remains strong in the area today.

Carpentras is about 12 miles northeast of Avignon on the D-938 road.

Châteauneuf-du-Pape

Not content with the Papal Palace in Avignon, Pope John XXII built himself a summer retreat in this small village. Erected between 1316 and 1333, the castle was destroyed by the retreating Nazis in 1944, but the vineyards planted in the 14th century are still going strong, and *Châteauneuf-du-Pape* has become one of the world's most famous wines. You can get a beautiful view over the Rhône valley from the castle ruins, and you can tour many of the vineyards and caves in the area. For more information contact the tourist office, *place du Portail,* ☎ *(33) 04-90-83-71-08.*

Châteauneuf-du-Pape is about 10 miles north of Avignon off the D-942 road.

Arles

Vying with Nîmes for the title of *La Rome Française,* Arles offers more variety than its competitor to the north. Strategically situated at the point at which the Rhône splits into two branches, the city was an important Celtic settlement when the Greeks invaded and colonized it in the sixth century B.C. Later the city became an important base for the Roman expansion into Provence. General Marius used prison-labor to dig a canal from the town to the sea, which immediately made Arles a major port on the route to Roman territories in Spain. In 49 B.C. Caesar built the fleet he used to crush Marseilles at Arles. As the Roman network of roads expanded, Arles became a major crossroads, and eventually became the capital of Gaul until the decline and fall of the empire. Today, the Roman presence is most evident in Arles. The oldest is the Roman theater, called the *Théâtre Antique.* It was built in the first century B.C. but when the theater declined in importance, it was partially dismantled for building material in the fifth century. Converted into a fort in the ninth century, the theater eventually obliterated buildings and gardens, and was excavated in the 19th century. Today just one twin column, called *Les Deux Veuves* (the Two Widows), is all that stands, although there are various pedestals, capitals, and sections of columns scattered around the site, which is still used for concerts. Most of the significant remains are in the *Musée Lapidaire d'Art Païen* (the Museum of Pagan Art). The amphitheater, built in about A.D. 75 under the rule of the Emperor Vespasian, seated 20,000 spectators and was one of the largest arenas in France. Three of its original four towers remain, as do the pits and chambers where gladiators and wild animals were kept before being sent out onto the sand to fight and die. The arena was used as a fort towards the end of the Roman empire, and is thus partially dismantled and modified, but it is still in excellent condition. Today, it is used for bullfights and concerts, although spectators are seated in modern steel-bleachers. The final major Roman relic you should visit in Arles is the *Thermes de Constantin*, the baths built in the fourth century. Housed in the now-vanished *Palais Constantin*, the baths were the largest in the region, consisting of cold, warm, and hot baths, as well as wrestling facilities and steam rooms—all the features of a modern gym 1500 years ago.

The Arles amphitheater is used for concerts and bullfights.

PROVENCE

More recently, the 12th century saw construction of the *Eglise St. Trophime*, a very respectable Romanesque-style church with an ornate, carved portal that is one of the finest in Provence, and superb Romanesque- and Gothic-style sculpted cloisters. The church was constructed of stone taken from the *Théâtre Antique*. Artists have always been drawn to Arles, and the city has a wealth of art to show for it. The **Museum of Pagan Art** and the adjacent **Museum of Christian Art** offer contrasting views. In the basement of the latter, you can visit the *Cryptoporticus*, a kind of cellar used to level the ground for the Roman Forum that was once situated above, and inspect the early Christian sarcophagi on display there. More sarcophagi are to be found in the *Alyscamps*, a tree-lined walkway on the site of an ancient burial ground where centuries ago several broken and complete sarcophagi were arranged in mysterious pattern. Vincent van Gogh painted the Alyscamps during his sojourn in Arles, beginning in 1888. During one of his fits (diagnosed after his death as epilepsy) Van Gogh cut off an ear and was treated in the hospital in Arles, which is now a museum devoted to the artist's life and work. (A year later, in the nearby village of St. Rémy-en-Provence, where the prophet Nostradamus was born, Van Gogh shot himself and died). Another splendid museum is the *Museon Arlatan*, created in 1904 by Nobel Prize-winning poet Frédéric Mistral, devoted entirely to regional art and culture. Less enthralling, the *Musée Réattu* is devoted to local artist Jacques Réattu, although it also houses some Picasso sketches, as well as work by more modern Provençal artists.

What to Do

City Celebrations/Events

Rencontres Internationales de la Photographie ★★★

10 rond point des Arenes, ☎ *04-90-96-76-06.*
Special hours: July only
Shutterbugs the world over flock to this festival of photography held every July. Gallery exhibits, slide presentations, workshops and other events are open to the public at reasonable prices (FR10–FR30). If you think your work is up to snuff, bring your samples along for a consultation. The Arles Festival, also in July, is a monthlong drama, music and dance extravaganza made even more dramatic by being staged in the city's impressive Roman ruins (see "Historical Sites"). Admission: FR30.

Historical/Architectural Sites

Eglise St-Trophime ★★★★

place de la Republique.
Combining a 12th-century Romanesque facade with Romanesque and Gothic cloisters, the Eglise St-Trophime stands on the site of many former churches. It is named after St-Trophime, a bishop of Arles around the 2nd to 3rd centuries. Noted for its medieval carvings, the cloisters are made of two Romanesque galleries from the

12th century and two Gothic galleries from the 14th century. *The church is open daily, 8 a.m.–7 p.m. The cloister is open daily, 9:30 a.m.–12:30 p.m. and 2–7 p.m. Admission is FR18; students, FR10. Admission: FR20.*

Roman Amphitheater   ★★★★

Rond-Point des Arenes, ☎ *04-90-96-03-70.*

Hours open: 8:30 a.m.–7 p.m. Special hours: Contact tourist office for winter hours. Closed: Mon.

All of Arles' important ancient Roman sites are within walking distance of each other, and an all-inclusive ticket called Forfait 2 (FR30; children FR20) can be purchased at the Tourist Office at *boulevard des Lices (*☎ *04-90-18-41-20).* Hours for all sites are the same. The amphitheater, still in use today for summer bullfights and for outdoor concerts during the Arles Festival in July, was built in the first century. Much of the structure is still intact, and as many as 20,000 people can be seated in the arena. Once used as a fortress, it has three towers, or donjons, that can be climbed for a definitive view of the area. Emperor Augustus' Roman Theater, at *rue du Cloitre (*☎ *04-90-96-93-30),* should actually be called "The Two Corinthian Columns," because they are the only remains of the first-century theater-fortress-quarry. A semicircular seating area within the complex is an important Arles Festival venue. Also worth visiting are the thermae, or **Baths of Emperor Constantine**, within the old imperial palace, at *rue Dominique Maisto, near the rue du 4 Septembre.* The baths date from the fourth-century A.D. Admission: FR15.

Museums and Exhibits

Musée Arlaten   ★★★★

29 rue de la Republique, ☎ *04-90-96-08-23.*

Closed: Mon.

Established in 1904 by the poet Frederic Mitral, using money won with his Nobel Prize, this was a display of his love for the region. Set in the 16th-century Hotel Laval-Castellane, this museum focuses on the everyday items related to Provençal life. Among its collection is a letter from Theodore Roosevelt to Mistral (in French), furniture, costumes, wigs and other objects centered around everyday life in Provence. *Open July–Aug., 9 a.m.–12:30 p.m. and 2–6 p.m.; Nov.–Feb., 9 a.m.–noon and 2–4:30 p.m.; Apr., 9 a.m.–12:30 p.m. and 2–6:30 p.m.* Student admission, FR7. Admission: FR15.

Musée Réattu   ★★★

Rue du Grand Prieure, ☎ *04-90-49-37-58.*

Hours open: 9 a.m.–7 p.m. Special hours: Call tourist office for winter hours.

This Rhone-side museum is dedicated to native son, Jacques Réattu (1760–1833). The museum contains Réattu's collection, including some of the painter's own work, as well as pieces by modern artists such as Rousseau (whose work takes up one entire salon), Gauguin, Leger, Utrillo, Dufy and Picasso. The drawings and etchings you'll see of Picasso's were made in Arles in the 1970s—the master was so fond of the area that he generously donated them to this museum. Other highlights are modern sculptures and 16th-century Arras tapestries. Admission: FR15.

Musée d'Art Chretien ★★★

rue Balze. Near the Hotel de Ville.
Hours open: 9 a.m.–6 p.m. Special hours: Closed 12:30–2 p.m.
This museum of Christian art occupies a 17th-century Jesuit chapel, featuring an excellent collection of 4th-century sarcophagi. Once inside the museum, descend into the Cryptoporticus, the store rooms carved in the 1st century B.C. as the base of a Roman forum. These rooms were not excavated until the 1900s. Admission: FR15.

Musée d'Art Paien ★★★

place de la Republique.
Hours open: 9 a.m.–6 p.m. Special hours: Closed 12:30–2 p.m.
The Museum of Pagan Art sits in a former 17th-century church, showcasing objects discovered during excavations of the theater. Findings from Roman times include the damaged statue of Augustus, Apollo's altar and a copy of the cast of the Venus of Arles, which now sits in the Louvre. Marble sarcophagi and some 4th-century mosaics are also displayed. Admission: FR15.

Where to Stay

Hotels and Resorts

Calendal   **FR180–FR400**   ★

22 place Pomme. ☎ *04-90-96-11-89.*
Single: FR180–FR200. Double: FR290–FR400.
This relaxing hotel has 27 large rooms with classic Provençal decor. Most of the antique-adorned rooms afford views over the garden, and all come with telephone and private bath. A small breakfast is served for FR29. A good choice for a comfortable overnighter. Credit Cards: All Major.

D'Arlatan   **FR385–FR695**   ★★

26 rue du Sauvage. ☎ *04-90-93-56-66, FAX: 04-90-49-68-45.*
Single: FR385–FR450. Double: FR385–FR695.
This hotel is tucked away on a small street in the center of town near the Place du Forum, within easy walking distance of all the city's major sights. Built in the 15th century on the ruins of an old Constantine palace, the structure still has parts dating back as far as the fourth century. It is a quaint hotel ornamented with antiques and coordinated fabrics. The well-appointed and charming rooms are furnished with regional antiques and tapestries. Modern amenities include a TV, telephone, minibar and private bath. Request a room overlooking the palm-lined garden and the pond. An understated charmer, as discovered by the many loyal return clients. Features: air conditioning in rooms, in-room conference facilities. Credit Cards: All Major.

Jules César   **FR650–FR1000**   ★★★★

7 boulevard des Lices. ☎ *04-90-93-43-20, FAX: 04-90-93-33-47.*
Rated Restaurant: *Lou Marques.*
Single: FR650–FR800. Double: FR820–FR1000.
Considered by many to be the premier hotel in Arles, the Jules César opened in 1929 in a converted 17th-century convent. Ideally located in the town center, this Relais and Châteaux establishment is situated amid the gardens, buffering it from

any of the noise caused by its downtown location. It offers 49 ultra-spacious rooms, each quite comfortable and equipped with TV, telephone, minibar and air conditioning. After an aperitif in the bar, choose from one of the two restaurants for a reasonably priced dinner. The courteous and discreet staff is eager to serve. Features: pool, air conditioning in rooms, in-room mini-bars. Credit Cards: All Major.

Bourg-en-Bresse

Hotels and Resorts

Le Logis de Brou   **FR220–FR380**   ★★

132 bd. de Brou. ☎ *04-74-22-11-55, FAX: 04-74-22-37-30.*
Single: FR220–FR300. Double: FR300–FR380.
A good overnighter in the center of town, this four-story boxlike hotel was built in 1968. Amid landscaped grounds, the 30 rooms can get a bit loud with the busy road just outside the property. All of the rooms are comfortable and simply furnished with antique reproductions, standard with TV, telephone and private bath. A small breakfast is available for FR35, and parking costs FR50. Credit Cards: All Major.

Prieure   **FR400–FR600**   ★★

49-51 boulevard de Brou. ☎ *04-74-22-44-60.*
Single: FR400–FR500. Double: FR500–FR600.
The two French sisters who own this little hostellerie have established it as the most charming place in town. Surrounded by an acre of lovely gardens within 400-year-old stone walls, there are 14 guest rooms with TV, telephone and private bath or shower. Each room is furnished in Louis XV style and restfully quiet. Spring brings the wafting aromas of the blooming flowers into all of the public areas. Credit Cards: All Major.

Roanne

Hotels and Resorts

Troisgros   **FR700–FR1600**   ★★★

place du Tilleul. ☎ *04-77-71-66-97, FAX: 04-77-70-39-77. At the train station.* Rated Restaurant: *Troisgros.*
Single: FR700–FR800. Double: FR1200–FR1600.
Famous for its restaurant, this train-station hotel is divided into two sections. The older wing was improved and offers modern rooms with a view of either the garden or the square. The newer wing has contemporary rooms with views of the indoor garden. All of the 19 rooms are air-conditioned and include TV, telephone and private bath. Breakfast starts at FR18. Enjoy a meal in the restaurant of this 14th-century Relais and Châteaux inn. Closed Feb. Features: air conditioning in rooms. Credit Cards: All Major.

Inns

Artaud Hotel Restaurant   **FR180–FR380**   ★★

133 avenue de la Liberation. ☎ *04-77-68-46-44, FAX: 04-77-68-46-44. In Le Cocteau. Take N7 for about 3 km from Roanne.*
Single: FR180–FR290. Double: FR180–FR380.

Attached to this suburban restaurant are 25 lovely rooms. Unpretentious and well-appointed, all come with TV, telephone and bath or shower. Breakfast costs FR33. Warm reception that lasts throughout the stay. Credit Cards: V, MC.

Where to Eat

Hostellerie des Arenes $ ★★

62 rue de Refuge. ☎ *04-90-96-13-05.*
Specialties: pizza, duck with green peppercorns, seafood vol-au-vent.
Lunch: Noon–2 p.m., FR65–FR85.
Dinner: 7–9 p.m., entrées FR65–FR85.
On the rue du Refuge near the dual amphitheaters, this homey refuge is thankfully not too touristy, although it's packed tight most nights with hungry diners. The mood is convivial, especially on summer nights when the terrace is open. Pizza is a specialty, but it's expensive. The fixed-price menus (starting at FR75) are a good buy. Closed: Tues. Amenities: happening bar, outside dining, own baking, reservations required. Credit Cards: V, MC.

L'Olivier $$$ ★★★

1 bis, rue Reattu. ☎ *04-90-49-70-74.*
Lunch: Noon–2 p.m., FR250–FR350.
Dinner: 7–9:15 p.m., entrées FR250–FR350.
This is one of Arles' best restaurants, and it's accessible to all via a generous set of fixed-price meals, especially on weekdays, when it's only FR140. You won't get cast-offs either, nor will you leave hungry. The four-course repast includes soup, a fish course, a choice of meat or poultry, ending with one of its excellent desserts. Closed: Mon., Sun. Amenities: outside dining, reservations recommended. Credit Cards: A.

La Guele du Loup $$ ★★

39 rue Arenes. ☎ *04-59-96-96-69.*
Specialties: grilled fish, goat cheese salad.
Lunch: Noon–2 p.m., FR180–FR200.
Dinner: 7–11 p.m., entrées FR180–FR200.
You go through a leafy entranceway overgrown with ivy to get to this tastefully decorated basement restaurant run by friendly people. A fixed-price lunch and dinner are offered for only FR85. Closed: Mon. Credit Cards: All Major.

Le Vaccares $$ ★★★

place du Forum, entrance rue Favorin. ☎ *04-90-96-06-17.*
Specialties: lamb with tapenade, rabbit with rosemary.
Lunch: Noon–2 p.m., FR100–FR165.
Dinner: 7:30–9:30 p.m., entrées FR100–FR165.
Everyone gets a bird's-eye view of the goings-on in the market square while dining at this cheerful restaurant. Chef Bernard Dumas serves wonderful traditional specialties such as *tapenade* (olive paste with capers, anchovies and olive oil) with Camargue lamb, and herbed mussels. His aioli garlic sauce with anything is not to be missed. Fixed-price menus range from FR165 to FR300. Closed: Mon. Amenities: outside dining, own baking, reservations required. Credit Cards: V, MC.

Directory

To and From

> *By train from Toulouse (three-and-a-half hours), Avignon (for connections to Paris and Lyon, 20 minutes), and Nîmes (20 minutes), or by car on the N-113 road between Nîmes and Marseille or the N-570 road from Avignon.*

Tourist Office

> *place de la Républic;* ☎ *(33) 04-90-18-41-20.*

Rail Station

> *avenue P. Talbot;* ☎ *(33) 04-90-82-50-50.*

Post Office

> *5 boulevard des Lices, 13200 Arles;* ☎ *(33) 04-90-18-41-00.*

Les Baux-de-Provence

The abandoned city of Les Baux sits atop a rocky spur that thrusts out into the *Val d'Enfer* (Valley of Hell), a jumbled landscape said to be inhabited by witches and goblins. In the 11th century, the Lords of Baux were the most powerful clan in Provence, and they built the château atop the promontory, along with the ramparts, the *Porte Eguyières*, and the *rue de Trencat*, the ruins of which can all be viewed today, along with the ruined 17th-century town hall. By the mid-16th century, the stronghold had become a bastion of Protestantism and this, combined with its independent ways, moved Louis XIII to rout the Lords or Baux and tear down the castle. The town has never again been inhabited, although the shepherds from the area celebrate Midnight Mass on Christmas Eve in the ruined Eglise St. Vincent each year. A tiny village nestles at the foot of the rock, replete with tea rooms, postcard stands, and the man who collects your FR10 to climb up to the ruins. *Les Baux* gave its name to bauxite, first discovered here in 1822.

Les-Baux-de-Provence is about 10 miles northeast of Arles, reachable by rare bus or by car on the D-17 road.

What to Do

Historical/Architectural Sites

Citadel of Les Baux ★★

> *Cité Morte,* ☎ *04-90-54-55-56.*
>
> *Hours open: 9 a.m.–7:30 p.m.*
>
> The citadel, the stronghold of medieval lords who held a powerful sway over the area, is now a huge ruin. Unoccupied for more than 400 years, it overlooks a mass of sun-bleached rocks that make up the hellishly named Val d'Enfer (Infernal Valley) and, below that, the small town of Les Baux. You can climb a precarious stairway to a viewing tower and visit an archaeological museum on your way in or out of the site. Admission: FR32.

PROVENCE

Where to Stay

Hotels and Resorts

La Benvengudo FR495–FR690 ★★

Vallon de l'Arcoule. ☎ *04-90-54-32-54, FAX: 04-90-54-42-58.*
Single: FR495–FR535. Double: FR620–FR690.

Just a short walk from the village center, this hotel is aptly named for the Provençal word for welcome. A converted 19th-century farmhouse amidst neatly manicured shrubbery and trees, it's now locally owned and operated by a family that used to work for another nearby hotel. They keep the 17 rooms, with TV, telephone and private bath, tidy and fresh looking. The peaceful surroundings inspire guests to linger on the terrace or take advantage of the pool and tennis court. The inn serves wonderful fixed-price meals starting at FR225. The small staff assures a welcoming and pleasant stay. Features: pool, tennis, air conditioning in rooms, balcony or patio. Credit Cards: All Major.

Mas d'Aigret FR450–FR900 ★★

Les Baux. ☎ *04-90-54-33-54, FAX: 04-90-54-41-37.*
Rated Restaurant: *Mas d'Aigret.*
Single: FR450–FR570. Double: FR745–FR900.

A clear day means sweeping views towards the Mediterranean from the terrace of this completely restored farmhouse. The 14 attractive rooms have TV, telephone, minibar and private bath. Most sport private terraces, and two are partly built into the surrounding rock. The restaurant is also carved out of rock and serves excellent regional dishes. The unique use of the environment and the comfortable accommodations make this a worthwhile stopover. Features: pool, balcony or patio, in-room minibars. Credit Cards: All Major.

Oustau de Baumaniere FR900–FR1350 ★★★

Val d'Enfer, Les Baux, Maussane-les-Alpilles. ☎ *04-90-54-33-07, FAX: 04-90-54-40-46.*
Rated Restaurant: *Oustau de Baumaniere.*
Single: FR900–FR1150. Double: FR1100–FR1350.

This virtual mecca for gastronomic pilgrimages was considered by many to be the best country restaurant in all of France in its earlier days. While some think the restaurant has slipped a bit since the founder passed on the reins, most critics still consider this a rare example of perfection in French fare. The 11 rooms and 13 suites dating from the 16th and 17th centuries are found in four separate houses. Rather simple in design, each air-conditioned room comes with a TV, telephone, minibar and private bath. Active guests enjoy tennis, horseback riding and swimming, and golf is a short drive from the hotel. While the accommodations aren't the big attraction here, the restaurant and the surroundings keep the guest registry full. Features: pool, tennis, air conditioning in rooms, in-room minibars. Credit Cards: All Major.

Where to Eat

L'Oustau de Baumaniere $$$ ★★★

Val d'Enfer. ☎ *04-90-54-33-07.*
Specialties: ravioli with truffles, leg of lamb in a puff-pastry crust.
Lunch: Noon–2 p.m., FR250–FR450.
Dinner: 7–9:30 p.m., entrées FR250–FR450.

Located in the "Infernal Valley" below the eerie ruined castle of Le Baux, this restaurant was the celebrated enclave of Raymond Thuilier, who died several years ago at the age of 96. His grandson, Jean-Andre Charial, who had plenty of practice helping the old man run the restaurant, is now fully in charge, and does an admirable job. The dining room is a high-ceilinged salon, while the quiet terrace (which patrons undoubtedly prefer) overlooks the castle. Charial has added lighter touches to the classic menu, with plenty of local produce and fresh seafood. The noted wine vaults feature an unbelievable 90,000 bottles, including some very rare (and expensive) vintages. Closed: Wed. Amenities: outside dining, reservations required. Credit Cards: All Major.

Mas d'Aigret   **$$**   ★ ★

Les Baux de Provence, 13520, Below the Old Town on D27A. Located at Mas d'Aigret. Located at Mas d'Aigret. ☎ *04-90-54-33-54.*

Lunch: Noon–2 p.m., 90.

Dinner: 7–9 p.m., entrées FR90.

Unfortunately, British journalist Pip Phillips and his wife, Chantal, no longer own this unprepossessing small inn, which had a personality with a capital "P" (for Phillips?). But it's still worthy for the FR90 fixed-price lunch (on weekdays only, which is too bad), including wine. Regional seafood is the specialty. This is a deal that's hard to beat, especially in this notoriously pricey tourist area. Amenities: outside dining, own baking, reservations recommended. Credit Cards: All Major.

Plaine de la Camargue

Just south of Arles, as the two branches of the Rhône, *Le Grand Rhône* and *Le Petit Rhône*, diverge and make their way to the sea, lies the vast marshy delta of the Camargue, a creation of the 20 million cubic-meters of sand, silt and gravel brought down by the rivers each year. Shaped by the receding of the sea over millennia and the fierce mistral winds that frequently whip across the region, the Camargue is divided roughly into three parts—the salt-producing marsh near the village of Salin-de-Giraud, the cultivated region reminiscent of the Marais Poitevin to the north, and the nature reserve in the south. The most famous inhabitants of the 370-square-mile area are black bulls, pink flamingoes, small, white pot-bellied horses, and the guardiens or herdsmen that tend them. The marshes are home to diverse species of flora and fauna, and the region can be explored on guided horseback or on mini-safari. At the edge of the ocean is the tiny village of *Les Stes. Maries-de-la-Mer*, where a church is the site of an annual pilgrimage in May by Gypsies. The pilgrimage honors the arrival in A.D. 18 of Mary Magdalene, Martha, the sister of the Virgin Mary, and the resuscitated Lazarus, where they were met by a Gypsy named Sarah, now the patron saint of Gypsies. Beautiful, deserted white beaches stretch eastwards from the village, including a nudist beach about four miles out.

The Camargue is south of Arles towards the ocean, reached by the D-570 road. Information is available at the tourist office in *Les Stes. Maries-de-la-Mer, 5 avenue van Gogh,* ☎ *(33) 04-90-97-76-49.*

Aix-en-Provence

The colorful gardens of Provence have inspired artists for centuries.

Formerly the capital of independent Provence, Aix-en-Provence is one of the larger towns in the region (population 150,000), and hosts the renowned *International Festival of Lyrical Art* and music each year in July, during which the city becomes Europe's musical capital. The city began life in 122 B.C., when a Roman army commanded by Sextius defeated the Franks at Entremont and set up camp around Aix' hot and cold springs. Aquae Sextiae, as it was called, developed in a medium-sized provincial town under the Romans, until it was destroyed by the Lombards in the late sixth century. The resilient town rebuilt, and in the 12th century hit the big time when the Counts of Provence made it their capital. Good King René, the last in the line, and an enlightened and cultured man for his time, infused Aix with the artistic strengths it still possesses, completing the cathedral and funding literature and the arts, as well as supporting the university. When Provence was annexed to France in 1486, Aix retained a strong, independent character and was governed autonomously by its own parliament. Eventually Paris tired of Aix' headstrong ways and stripped it of its regional administrative authority just before the Revolution. Fortunately, the town has preserved many of the most beautiful 17th- and 18th-century buildings that sprung up during its prosperous time as a provincial capital. Most of these can be seen in the lovely Old City. Called the *City of a Thousand Fountains*—no doubt an exaggeration—Old Aix contains many charming squares that indeed have many beautiful fountains, as well as ornate facades and doorways protecting the elegant classical-style. Now lined with as many cafés as houses, *Cours Mirabeau* is the most pleasant of the Old Quarter streets. The *Cathédrale St. Sauveur*, not far away on *rue de la Roque*, contains a fourth-century baptistry, 16th-century doors made of walnut, and a late 15th-century triptych by Nicolas Froment of the Burning Bush, featuring none other than Good King Réne himself.

Of the many artists who have lived and worked in Aix-en-Provence, the most famous is Paul Cézanne, who was born here in 1839 and died here in 1906. His studio, L'Atélier de Cézanne, is preserved as it was at the time of his death. A more far-reaching view of his work is on display at the Musée Granet, where a room devoted to Cézanne contains the "Still Life with Sugarbowl," "Nude at the Mirror" and "Bathers," as well as several renditions of the *Montagne Ste. Victoire*, which lies nine miles east of the city. Most of Cézanne's work is at the Musée du Quai d'Orsay in Paris. The museum also has worthwhile displays of fine art and archaeology, while the Musée de la Tapisserie displays tapestries from throughout the ages.

What to Do

Historical/Architectural Sites

Cathedrale St-Sauveur ★★★

 rue Gaston de Saporta, ☎ *04-42-23-45-65.*

Hours open: 8 a.m.–6 p.m. Special hours: Closed noon–2 p.m. Closed: Tue.

An eclectic medley of architectural styles from the 5th through 18th centuries. Quite and interesting piece of work, the main Gothic centerpiece was built between the 13th and 14th centuries. The carved panels of the main portal, in remarkable condition, date back to the 16th century. Also worth viewing is "The Burning Bush," a triptych by Nicolas Froment from the 15th century, in the nave.

Museums and Exhibits

Musée Granet ★★

place St-Jean-Marie-de-Malte, ☎ 04-42-38-14-70.

Hours open: 10 a.m.–6 p.m. Special hours: Closed noon–2 p.m. Closed: Tue.

Housed in a 17th-century priory of the Knights of Malta, the works of local artist Francois Granet (1775–1845) constitute the majority here. Also represented are Cezanne, Ingres, Delacroix and Caravaggio. Much of the work is by minor artists; however, the collection is still enjoyable. Admission: FR18.

Musée des Tapisseries ★★★

28 place des Martyrs de la Resistance, ☎ 04-42-21-05-78.

Hours open: 9:30 a.m.–6 p.m. Special hours: Closed noon–2 p.m. Closed: Tue.

Within this 17th-century Archbishop's Palace, the three series of tapestries from the 17th and 18th centuries decorate the walls. The "Adventures of Don Quixote" by Notoire, "The Grotesques" by Monnoyer and "The Russian Games" by Leprince comprise the collection. Admission: FR14.

Music

International Music Festival ★★★★

Palais de l'Ancien Archeveche, ☎ 04-42-21-14-40.

Hours open: 9 a.m.–7 p.m.

Some of the world's greatest opera stars, chamber orchestras and guest soloists perform annually at this world-famous festival (July). Performance venues include the Cathedrale de St-Saveur, the Musée des Tapisseries and the Theatre d l'Archeveche. Tickets (FR250–FR1000) should be purchased several months ahead of time. Less high-brow entertainment can be enjoyed (it's easier on the wallet, too) in the second week of June, when the Aix en Musique is in full swing. Jazz, rock, and alternative musicians, as well as classical performers pop up in unlikely places, and many events are free of charge. There's also a dance festival (Tickets FR250–FR250) of some renown, also held throughout the month of July. Call the tourist office for information.

Nightlife

Le Mistral ★★

3 rue Frederic Mistral, ☎ 04-42-38-16-49.

Hours open: 11 p.m.–6 a.m.

A popular student hangout with live music until the rooster crows. **Le Scat**, at 11 rue Verrerie (☎ 04-42-23-00-23), is, as its name implies, a jazz club; highly recommended, also in the FR80 range, and patrons don't have to scat until dawn; closed Sun. Gay Aix repair to **La Chimere** for dancing and drinking; outside the city limits

at *route d'Avignon* (☎ *04-42-23-36-28), open 10 p.m.–6 a.m.; closed Mon*.
Admission: FR80.

Where to Stay

Hotels and Resorts

Augustins   **FR496–FR1200**   ★

3 rue de la Masse. ☎ *04-42-27-28-59, FAX: 04-42-26-74-87.*
Single: FR496–FR696. Double: FR592–FR1200.
A majestically restored 12th-century convent, this converted hotel boasts vaulted
ceilings, terra-cotta floors and stained glass windows. Keeping true to its heritage,
the reception area is located in a small chapel, and the other public areas are decorated with original paintings. The 32 air-conditioned guest rooms are modestly decorated and include TV, telephone, minibar and private bath. The two rooms with
private terraces facing the bell tower are the best choices. Weather permitting,
breakfast is taken in the garden for FR50. A small, close-knit staff pays personal
attention to each guest. Features: air conditioning in rooms, balcony or patio. Credit
Cards: All Major.

Le Pigonnet   **FR650–FR1500**   ★★

5 avenue du Pigonnet. ☎ *04-42-59-02-90, FAX: 04-42-59-47-77.*
Rated Restaurant: *Le Patio.*
Single: FR650–FR700. Double: FR750–FR1500.
Surrounded by gardens on the edge of town, Le Pigonnet charms guests with its
Provençal architecture. The view might look familiar to art aficionados, Paul
Cézanne painted the Mountain of Sainte Victoire from this garden. Taking advantage of the lovely setting, breakfast is served under the veranda overlooking the
courtyard and the reflecting pool, and dinner is also available outside or in the restaurant. The 49 air-conditioned accommodations are all constantly updated and
include cable TV, telephone, minibar and private bath or shower. The central location proves handy to the health club, horseback riding, golf and tennis nearby. The
deft staff gives a flawless performance. Features: pool, air conditioning in rooms, in-
room minibars. Credit Cards: All Major.

Villa Gallici   **FR800–FR1700**   ★★★★

18 avenue de la Violette (impasse des Grands Pins). ☎ *04-42-23-29-23, FAX: 04-42-96-
30-45.*
Single: FR800–FR1100. Double: FR1100–FR1700.
Considered one of the most stylish hotels in town, the Gallici was established in
1992, occupying a 1940s villa. A true gem of the Provence region, it sits tranquilly
among landscaped gardens, olive trees and oleanders. The facade, although from
the 1940s, reflects the architecture typical of the area in the 18th century. Within
are just 15 rooms, each decorated with 18th-century themes and lavishly furnished.
The standard appurtenances include air conditioning, TV, telephone, minibar, safe
and plush bath. Two of the best rooms come with private Jacuzzis. While there is
no restaurant on the premises, a lunch buffet from the nearby Le Clos de la Violette
is served poolside when the weather permits. Reservations should be made if any

hope of experiencing this divine pleasure exists. Features: wheelchair-access rooms, pool, air conditioning in rooms, in-room safes, in-room minibars.

Where to Eat

L'Arbre a Pain $ ★

4 rue Emeric David ☎ *04-42-38-32-41.*
Specialties: Vegetarian specialties.
Lunch: 11 a.m.–2:30 p.m., FR40–FR60.
Dinner: 6–11 p.m., entrées FR40–FR60.

Vegetarian specialties, including Mediterranean salads and complete meals for under FR50. Pleasant surroundings. Not vegetarian, but also a good buy, is **La Table Provence**, *13 rue Marechale Joffre (* ☎ *04-42-38-32-41) open for lunch only, noon–2 p.m.; closed Sunday,* features a three-course meal with wine and dessert, for FR65. In the center of town, the place **Richelme** is the site of a produce market *open Tuesday, Thursday and Saturday, 7 a.m.–1 p.m.* Not far away is a flea market with food stalls, on place de Verdun. Supermarkets worth scouring are **Monoprix**, *25 cours Mirabeau (Mon.–Fri., 8:45 a.m.–8:30 p.m.)* and **Casino** *(1 ave. de Lattre de Tassigny, near the blvd. de la Republique, closed Sunday, 9 a.m.–8:30 p.m.).* Closed: Sun. Amenities: cafestop, reservations not accepted.

Le Bistro Latin $$ ★★

18 rue Couronne ☎ *04-42-38-22-88.*
Specialties: chartreuse of mussels, rabbit.
Lunch: Noon–2 p.m., FR120–FR150.
Dinner: 7–10:30 p.m., entrées FR120–FR150.

Classic bistro cookery in one of the friendliest places in town; there's always a nice welcome here. The entrées are popularly priced, but the set menus have the greatest appeal. Three courses, including dessert, go for as little as FR90 (at lunch). Aix's most historic eatery is *Les Deux Garcons, 53 cours Mirabeau (* ☎ *04-42-26-00-51),* a brasserie where Cezanne, Camus and other famous folks whiled away the time. Prices (FR200 average) are high for the simple fare offered, but it's good for coffee or espresso (FR10–FR15). Reservations recommended. Credit Cards: V, MC, A, E.

Le Clos de la Violette $$$ ★★★

10 avenue de la Violette ☎ *04-42-23-30-71.*
Specialties: sea bream with eggplant in wine sauce, scallops with artichokes.
Lunch: Noon–1:30 p.m., FR400–FR510.
Dinner: 7:30–9:30 p.m., entrées FR400–FR510.

One of Aix's top chefs, the energetic Jean-Marc Banzo, prepares bright, regional dishes in this beautiful walled villa in a suburban location. There are several dining areas, but the most favored spot is a garden that's a riot of blooms in summer. Market-fresh produce, lamb, oysters and Mediterranean seafood are often featured on his seasonal menus. Excellent cellar with local wines and creative fruit-based desserts. The FR185 fixed-price lunch is a bargain. Jacket required. Closed: Sun. Amenities: outside dining, own baking, reservations required. Credit Cards: V, A.

Les Freres Lani $$$ ★★★

22 rue Leydet ☎ *04-42-27-76-16.*
Lunch: Noon–2:30 p.m., FR250–FR400.

Dinner: 7–10:30 p.m., entrées FR250–FR400.

Behind an unobtrusive facade hides this restaurant with food that has people buzzing with excitement. Joel Lani is an inventive chef of the highest order, concocting a fresh palette of flavors from the best local produce. Amenities: own baking, reservations required. Credit Cards: V, MC, A, E.

Directory

To and From

By train from Marseille (40 minutes, connections to everywhere), Nice (three hours) or Cannes (two-and-a-half hours), or by road on the A-8 autoroute from the east or west or the A-51 autoroute from Marseille or the north.

Tourist Office

2 place du Général de Gaulle; ☎ *(33) 04-42-16-11-61.*

Rail Station

avenue Victor Hugo; ☎ *(33) 04-91-08-50-50.*

Post Office

2 rue Lapierre, 13100 Aix-en-Provence; ☎ *(33) 04-42-16-01-50.*

Grasse

Formerly a tanning center that just happened to be surrounded by hills covered with fields of lavender, roses, mimosa and other flowers, Grasse lurched into prominence in the 16th century when Cathérine de Medici declared her fondness for scented gloves and the fashion for perfume rapidly caught on. A good place to start your discoveries of the world of fragrance is at the **Musée Internationale de la Parfumerie**, where displays explain the 4000-year history of perfume making. Nowadays, most commercial fragrances are made mostly of chemical essences, but the best—and most expensive—still blend as many as 300 actual fragrances, including some created by the complex and laborious process known as *enfleurage*. In this process, flowers are enveloped in layers of fat, which absorb the scent of the flower then after several months are dissolved with alcohol. When the alcohol evaporates, the essence of perfume is what is left. Three of the oldest perfume houses in the world, **Fragonard**, **Molinard** and **Galimard**, are in the town; each offers tours and visits. The unspoiled town, which has views of the coast but not the crowds, holds a rose festival in May and a jasmine festival in August. If you make the town your first (or last) stop in Provence you can take the amazingly twisty and scenic N-85 road through the Alpes d'Haute Provence to or from Grenoble and Lyon.

What to Do

Museums and Exhibits

Musée International de la Parfumerie   ★★★

8 place du Cours, ☎ *04-93-36-01-61.*

Detailing the complete history of perfume-making, this museum follows the process from extraction techniques to marketing the final product. Besides the 4000 years of historical tales, there is a garden on the rooftop where jasmine, lavender, mint and thyme are grown. Another prize in this museum is the jeweled travel case that belonged to Marie Antoinette. *Open 10 a.m.–7 p.m.; Oct. and early Dec.–May, Wed.–Sun., 10 a.m.–noon and 2–5 p.m.* Admission: FR15.

Where to Stay

Hotels and Resorts

Hotel du Patti   **FR300–FR400**   ★★★

place du Patti. ☎ *04-93-36-01-00, FAX: 04-93-36-36-40. In the old town.*
Single: FR300. Double: FR400.

Ideally situated in the center of old town, this hotel continues to receive nothing but compliments from its guests. The 50 rooms are immaculate, comfortable and well-equipped. From the waitpersons in the restaurant to the housekeepers in the hotel, service is always courteous and with a smile. Half-board available. Features: air conditioning in rooms. Credit Cards: V, DC, A.

Panorama   **FR310–FR500**   ★★★

2 place du Cours. ☎ *04-93-36-80-80, FAX: 04-93-36-92-04.*
Single: FR310. Double: FR400–FR500.

Centrally located, this modern hotel offers 36 well-appointed rooms. Some of the better (and more expensive) rooms have balconies and good views. All are equipped with TV, telephone and bath, and some have air conditioning. While there is no restaurant, room service is available. Features: air conditioning in rooms, balcony or patio. Credit Cards: DC, A.

Inns

Les Aromes   **FR380–FR480**   ★★

route de Cannes. ☎ *04-93-70-42-01. About 1 km south of town center; near the high-way.*
Single: FR380. Double: FR480.

Enjoying seclusion from the nearby highway noise, Les Aromes is hidden behind an encircling wall and courtyard. Designed in Provençal style, this modern facility has just seven rooms. Each comes with TV, telephone and bath, and half-board is included. Breakfast is served for FR25. Credit Cards: V, MC, A.

Where to Eat

L'Amphitryon   **$$**   ★★★

16 boulevard Victor-Hugo. ☎ *04-93-36-58-73.*
Dinner: 7:30–9 p.m., entrées FR100–FR225.

Along with the rest of the buildings on this street, this structure was a 19th-century stable. Completely modernized, the restaurant serves the best food in Grasse. With major influence from southwestern France, the chef prepares such dishes as foie gras, duckling and fish stew in red wine. The service is friendly and generally efficient. Fixed-price menus range from FR110–FR225. Closed: Sun. Reservations recommended. Credit Cards: All Major.

Maitre Boscq **$$** ★★

13 rue de la Fontette, In the old town. ☎ *04-93-36-45-76.*
Dinner: entrées FR140–FR200.

In the beautiful old town section of town sits this small restaurant. Try the garlic and sage soup with one of the many flavorful, aromatic main dishes. A warm reception and casual atmosphere. Set menus from FR105. Closed: Mon. Reservations recommended. Credit Cards: V, A.

Directory

To and From

By bus from Cannes or by car on the N-85 road from Cannes.

Tourist Office

palais des Congrès, 22, Cours Cresp; ☎ *(33) 04-93-36-66-66.*

Post Office

place de la Foux; 06310 Grasse.

PROVENCE

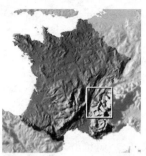

LYON AND THE ALPS

The French Alps are a challenge for skiers and mountain climbers.

What Makes Lyons and the Alps So French?

1. *Lyon's superstar international chefs, including Saint Paul Bocuse.*

2. *Lyon, again–this time as the bravest resistance center of World War II.*

3. *French Alps for serious skiers and mountain climbers (Alpinism is a sport, not a dis-ease–usually).*

4. *Evian, from under the ground, and Chartreuse, from atop the mountains.*

5. *Annecy, named France's cleanest city, and home of Cecelia–globetrotting dog-turned-mail-art who just won't die.*

.om the great city of Lyon, which the Romans made the capital of their vast Gallic empire, the Rhône Valley stretches eastward, rising until the landscape explodes in the angry furrows and ridges, peaks and valleys of the French Alps. Best known as a skiing area, the mountains are home also to some of the most challenging climbs in the world—*serious* mountain climbing known as Alpinism. The center of winter sports for the world, the French Alps have played host to the Winter Olympics no fewer than three times since their inception in 1924. In the inaugural games at Chamonix, Canada showed Switzerland what-for in the sport of ice hockey, beating the Swiss 33-0. In 1968 at Grenoble, local hero Jean-Claude Killy took all three alpine event gold medals, while in 1992 Albertville was the triumphant demonstration to the world of the entire region's prowess and competence. This competence has seen Lyon dominate as a European center of finance for 400 years, but also has established Grenoble as a high-tech center located in a pristine environment. The region highlights the hardy spirit of its inhabitants in year-round attractions that range from skiing, hiking, swimming, thermal spas, art museums (in even the smallest valley towns) and a natural beauty unmatched anywhere.

This chapter deals with the towns in the Alps that are worthy of a visit at any time of year, and offer more than simply skiing. The nature of the skiing industry in the French Alps is such that one is able to obtain considerably better prices through a tour operator by purchasing a package that includes flights, ground transfers, accommodations, lift passes and even equipment rental, than if you were to put together a trip yourself. The names and telephone numbers of some of the major resorts are given at the end of the chapter for your convenience.

History

From very early times man learned to adapt to the mountains. Towns in the valleys of the Alps have existed since prehistory, from fishing communities on the lakes to sheep-farming villages higher up. The Romans recognized the importance of the region as both a natural barrier and a natural passageway between modern-day Italy and France, and set about conquering the Alps before expanding northwards into Gaul from their Mediterranean settlements. They made Lyon the hub of their road network and the capital of the "Three Gauls." The Alpine region itself was historically divided into two provinces, both of which were formerly independent states, the *Dauphiné* and *Savoie*. The Dauphiné, covering the northern part of the region, centered around Grenoble, became part of France as early as 1349. It's most memorable contribution to the history of France was perhaps giving its name to the heir to the throne, *dauphin* now being a term used to designate the king-to-be. The region took the name first, from the son of one of the feudal dukes, who was called "dolphin" in English, or *dauphin*. As with Wales in

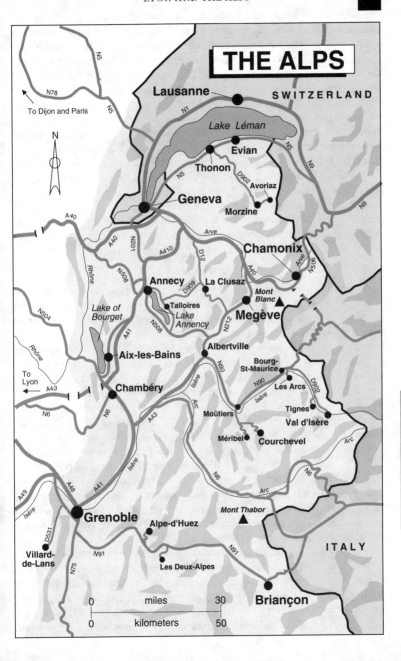

THE ALPS

To Dijon and Paris

N

SWITZERLAND

Lausanne

Lake Léman

Evian

Thonon

Avoriaz

Geneva

Morzine

Arve

Chamonix

Annecy

La Clusaz

Mont Blanc

Talloires

Megève

Lake Annecy

Lake of Bourget

Albertville

Aix-les-Bains

Bourg-St-Maurice

To Lyon

Les Arcs

Chambéry

Tignes

Moûtiers

Val d'Isère

Méribel

Courchevel

Grenoble

Mont Thabor

Alpe-d'Huez

ITALY

Villard-de-Lans

Les Deux-Alpes

Briançon

| 0 | miles | 30 |
| 0 | kilometers | 50 |

Britain, the heir to the throne of France traditionally ruled the region of the Dauphiné before acceding to the throne, so the term Dauphin was often applied to the prince. Savoie, on the other hand, did not come peaceably into the French fold, and did not come at all until 1860. The dynasty began in the 10th century, expanding its rule over the centuries and establishing its seat of power in Chambéry in 1232. The Savoie duchy grew to include all the territory from Lyon to Turin and from Bern to Nice, an incredibly strategic area that covered both sides of the Alps, with their trans-Alpine routes, as well as control of significant Mediterranean ports. The kings of France long coveted the region, and the dukes moved across the mountains to Turin in 1563 to avoid greedy French ambitions, but it was not until the Savoie rulers took control of Sardinia and Sicily in 1713, and then of all Italy in 1859, that France was able to get a piece of the pie. In a deal whereby the French king helped Duke Vittorio Emmanuele II of Savoie oust the Austrians from Lombardi in exchange for the house of Savoie relinquishing its possessions west of the Alps (a treaty that was confirmed by popular vote in Nice and Provence), the last piece of the French national map was put into place.

Cuisine

In a country where cuisine is of the utmost importance everywhere, Lyon reigns undisputed as the gastronomic capital. There are more three-star Michelin restaurants in Lyon than in Paris, and people regularly travel from New York or Tokyo just to eat a $250 meal in the restaurant of one of the world's finest chefs, many of which simply bear the name of the wizard himself. Nevertheless, it is possible to eat for less than an arm and a leg in Lyon and the Alps and still enjoy the region's mouth-watering food and drink. In Lyon traditional restaurants known as *bouchons* serve up a hearty cuisine based largely on pork products—*saucissons chauds* is sliced sausage with potatoes, tripes and other offal plates including *pied de veau* (cow's feet), and *tablier de sapeur*. In the Alps, cheese is the number one ingredient. An import from Switzerland, *raclettes*, is a communal dinner where you heat strips of cheese on a grill at the table and eat them with cold cuts and boiled potatoes, while *fondue* is a pot of melted cheese into which you dip vegetables and pieces of meat on long metal forks. Potatoes *au gratin* originated here, and anything *au gratin dauphinois* means it is served with a crust of browned melted cheese. Cheeses for eating, which tend to be rich and creamy, include St. Marcellin, Beaufort and Reblochon, and the strongest of the region, Tomme. The icy mountain streams and glacial lakes bring forth plenty of delicious trout *(truite)*, which is most delicious when served as *truite meuniere*, that is, in a creamy butter sauce with almonds. The wines of the Côtes du Rhône are found here as well as in Provence, and the Beaujolais Nouveau, discussed in the next chapter, makes its way into the region with great ceremony in November. Other fine wines include whites such as Apremont,

Marignan and Chignin, and reds including Montmelian and St. Jean-de-la-Porte. *Chartreuse*, a liqueur produced by monks in the Alpine monastery of the same name, is the local digestif of choice, while spring water sold under the *Evian* name emanates from a source deep underneath the small eponymous town.

Lyon

Lyon offers tourists more subtle charm than ostentation.

France's third-largest city (second-largest if you count the suburbs, as Lyonnais do and Marseillais tend not to), Lyon is probably the most livable of all French cities. Lyon offers formidable museums and a rich cultural life, a healthy economy, wonderfully efficient local transportation, and is within easy reach of the Alps (within sight of them on a clear day), the Mediterranean coast, and even Paris (only two hours away by TGV). In fact, Lyon's superb geographic position was what led the Romans to establish it as a center of their empire. Located at the confluence of the Rhône and Saone rivers, Lyon was originally a Celtic, then a Gallic settlement. When the Romans advanced, the town became one of the first base camps Julius Caesar established for his conquest of Gaul. As the empire expanded to the north, the nearby city of Vienne became the regional capital, but by 43 B.C. Caesar Augustus had granted cityhood to the town now called *Lugdunum*, after a Celtic god, Lug. Before long, Lyon's development began to outpace Vienne's. Agrippa was the ruler who designated Lugdunum as the meeting point for the major roads that united the far-flung reaches of the Roman's

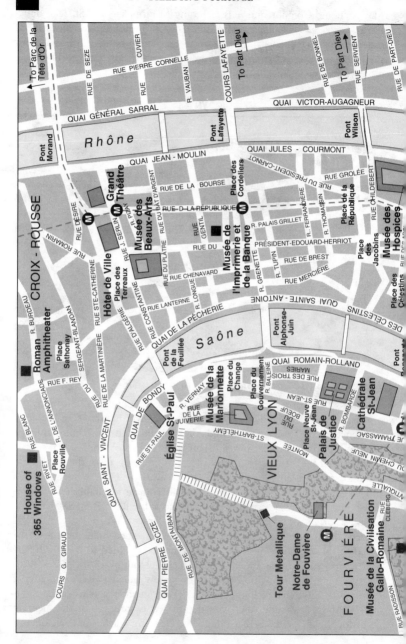

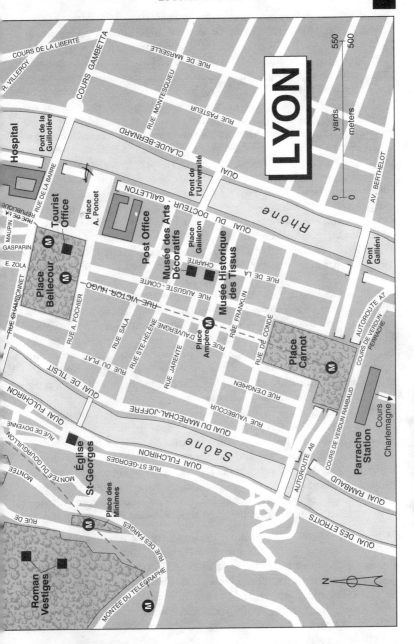

LYON

territories in Gaul, Lyon was the hub for routes leading to Saintes, Orléans, Rouen, Chalon, Amiens, Belgium, Geneva and Arles. The Roman remains in Lyon are quite rich, though somewhat disappointing for a city of its size. They are mostly concentrated on the Fouvière Hill, which derives its name from *forum vetus*, or Old Forum, which was built there. There was also a new forum, the baths, the capitol, the circus, the amphitheater and at least one temple. What has been excavated and is on display (and in use) today are the twin theaters, a larger outdoor theater seating around 13,000 people, that was used (for theater performances), and a smaller, covered Odeon that seated about five thousand people (for concerts and speeches). The entire site is open to the public for free, and next to it is the excellent Musée de la Civilization Gallo-Romaine, with an extensive collection of artifacts. The exhibits include the Claudian Tables, bronze tablets with a transcription of the speech given by Claudius in A.D. 48 that granted full citizenship to the residents of Gaul, along with the right for the citizens to become senators. Also on the Fouvière hill are the Basilique de Notre Dame de Fouvière and the Tour Métallique, the city's most distinctive landmarks until the Crédit Lyonnais skyscraper in Centre de Part-Dieu was built. From Place Bellecour below, these two monuments together look gaudy and juxtaposed, like something in a Disney park. And indeed, the tower—a sorry imitation of the Eiffel Tower in Paris—seems just plain dumb today, although when it was erected at the turn of the 20th century it was all the rage. The basilica is worth a second look. Even if you don't ache to see the Roman site, take the funicular to the top of the hill (the cost is part of a regular Metro ticket) and visit the basilica. Constructed beginning in 1870 by the residents of the city to keep a vow made to the Virgin Mary if she would deliver them from the Prussian invaders, the basilica holds the distinction of being the only Christian church in France not actually owned by the church. Now administered by a public foundation, it is open to the public. Its four towers bear the names of the four cardinal virtues (one the towers can be climbed by way of a 300-step circular staircase), and the exterior was crafted to look fortified as a symbol of the Virgin's protection. The interior is sumptuously ornate, all gilded and painted paneled-ceilings and statuary, rather reminiscent of a ballroom. From the terrace surrounding the basilica, you get a magnificent view of the city, with vistas as far as the snow-topped distant Alps.

Christianity arrived in Lyon about the middle of the second century, and was not welcomed by the Romans. Saint Pothinus and Saint Blandina were among 50 Christians fed to the lions in Lyon's circus in A.D. 177. Twenty years later Saint Irenæus went to the same death. Martyrdom only serves to strengthen a cause, however, and by the year A.D. 250, aided by the arrival of new missionaries from Rome, and under the tolerance of Constantine, Christianity began to flourish. The city was the first bishopric in France; its head was called the Primate of Gaul. The religious hierarchy was the dominant force in Lyon for the next 10 centuries, until the kings of France took over. During this period, the town began construction of Lyon's most beautiful church, the Primatiale St. Jean, which was begun in 1192 on the site of an early baptistry, traces of which are still visible. The western facade bears 280 medallions sculpted in classic Romanesque fashion with holy, profane and just plain bizarre figures mixed freely together. Among St. Jean's highlights are the 14th-century astronomical clock, which shows the dates of religious festivals through the year 2019, and a small amount of 13th-century stained glass. The cathedral is in the heart of *Vieux Lyon*, the district that sweeps around the foot of the hill on the west bank of the Saone. This area contains some of the most impressive Renaissance-style mansions in France, a testament to the wealth Lyon enjoyed during her boom years. Beginning in the 15th century, as the royal court under François I, and later, as the emerging bourgeoisie, developed a taste for fine things, Lyon grew to be the foremost silk-producing center in Europe. By the 16th century more than 10,000 people were employed in the silk trade, along with many more in the manufacture of velvet and satin. The merchants built the tall houses in this district, and some with especially noteworthy architectural features are found on rue St. Jean, rue du Boeuf, and rue Juiverie. The rue du Boeuf is home to the **Musée Historique de Lyon**, which contains exhibits detailing how the city grew during the Renaissance period. The **Musée de la Marionette** is devoted to one of the period's most important cultural contributions, the Lyon puppet.

Across the river on the Presqu'Ile, now the heart of the modern city, most of the silk manufacture took place. Beginning just north of the place Terreaux, the land rises in a district called Croix Rousse, which was where the *canuts*, or silk workers, lived and worked in appalling conditions that gave rise to numerous revolts during the 17th and 18th centuries. At the **Maison des Canuts** on rue d'Ivry there is a display that details just how bad the working conditions were, as well as a demonstration of the traditional weaving methods. Next door to each other on rue de la Charité, are the **Musée Historique des Tissus** (the Historical Museum of Textiles) and the **Musée des Arts Decoratifs**, which both house fine examples of the canuts' production, as well as tapestries and silks from around the world with examples from early Christian times to the present. At the same time that silk merchants were bringing fame and fortune to the city, banking and printing were growing in importance. You can see a history of both at the **Musée de l'Imprimerie**. With the advent of the printing press, the printing industry was born. As printing took hold in Lyon, new ideas, especially those brought by the Reformation, were easily circulated and the city became quite progressive. But progressiveness had its costs, especially during the Wars of Religion and the counter-Reformation, when Lyon suffered for its cultural permissiveness. Today, Lyon continues to be a center of publishing. The same ideological factionalism brought Lyon further trouble during the Revolution, as the citizens of Lyon debated about how to participate in the upheaval. This hesitation prompted revolutionaries in the rest of the country to declare the entire city counter-revolutionary and Lyon was sacked. Thousands of people were beheaded at the guillotines in the place Terreaux, one of the two principal squares on the Presqu'Ile, the other being the massive and empty place Bellecour, where today you'll find the main tourist office. At one end of place Terreaux is the Hôtel de Ville, an ornate 17th-century palace. At the other end is the Opéra de Lyon, a neoclassical building topped with a modern metallic barrel-shaped roof since being renovated in 1993, a project that has displeased almost everyone in the city. It's not hard to see why. In the middle of the square is a huge fountain, designed by Bartholdi, of Statue of Liberty fame, depicting a river goddess riding her watery horses amid great waves and spray. Housed in a former 17th-century Bénédictine convent on one side of the square is Lyon's most important museum, the Musée des Beaux Arts. It contains the largest and most significant collection after the Louvre in Paris, and it is the pride of the city. Highlights include the antiquities wing, which has Egyptian mummies and Etruscan and Cretian statuettes that date from 2000 B.C., the sculpture exhibit with works by Rodin, Bourdelle and Malliol, among others, and the two-floor collection paintings with examples from every French, Dutch, English and Spanish Old Master you've ever heard of, as well as many more modern works. Call before you go to make an appointment to tour the Cabinet d'Arts Graphiques, which houses more than 4000 etchings and working-sketches from artists including Delacroix, Picasso, Degas and Rodin.

Between place Terreaux and place Bellecour is an extensive, mostly pedestrian area that is home to most of the city's shopping and nightlife. Also nearby is another museum not to be missed, the Musée de la Résistance et la Déportation, one of the most important archives in France recording the Nazi occupation and the efforts of the resisters to undermine it. Lyon's cuisine is known as the best in France, and there are a number of otherworldly restaurants in the pedestrian area, including Léon de Lyon, Christian Bourillot and Villa Florentine (the top of the heap, Paul Bocuse, is outside the city at Collognes-au-Mont-d'Or). Any of these will easily set you back US$300 or more for a dinner for two. A cheaper alternative are the *bouchons*, traditional working people's restaurants that serve up good, hearty food at more down-to-earth prices.

What to Do

Historical/Architectural Sites

Basilique Notre-Dame de Fourviere ★★★★

Fourviere Hill, ☎ 04-78-25-51-82. On the hill.

Hours open: 8 a.m.–6 p.m. Special hours: Oct.–Mar., closed noon–2 p.m.
Completed in 1896, this basilica was built to fulfill a vow taken by the
during the Franco-Prussian War of 1870. The interior reflects the classic
of the period, with beautiful marble and mosaics. While offensively lavish to
it still possesses some inner beauty that deserves appreciation. At least ma
climb, if for no other reason, for the view.

Old Forum ★★★

Fourviere Hill. Above the old city.
Hours open: 7 a.m.–9 p.m. Special hours: Mid-Sept.–mid-Apr., 7 a.m.–7 p.m.
Next to the Musée Gallo-Romain are the two rebuilt Roman theaters. These are the
largest of the preserved ruins and are still in use for concerts of all sorts.

Primatiale St-Jean ★★★

place St-Jean, ☎ 04-78-42-11-04.
Begun in 1180, construction halted in 1268 because of religious fighting and never
resumed again. Witness the unusual towers atop the building, incongruous in
design. Inside, look for the Flamboyant Gothic chapel, the 12th-century stained
glass and the astronomical clock that sounds off at noon, 2 and 3 p.m. Within the
treasury are rare jewels and silk, available for viewing for FR16. *The cathedral is
open Mon.–Fri., 7:30 a.m.–noon and 2–7:30 p.m.; Sat.–Sun., 2–5 p.m. The treasury is open Wed.–Sun., 9:30 a.m.–noon and 2–6 p.m.*

Theatres Gallo-Romains ★★★★

17 rue Cleberg, ☎ 04-78-25-94-68.
Still in use today for everything from rock music to opera, these dual amphitheaters
date back to the times of the Romans (43 B.C.). Both are in remarkable repair; the
larger Grand Theatre is the oldest of its kind in France. Below the theaters is an
excellent archaeological museum, the Musée Gallo-Romain, showcasing an Alad-
din's cave of ancient money, jewelry, mosaics and weapons. *The museum is open
Wed.–Sun., 9:30 a.m.–6 p.m. Admission: FR20; students FR10; under 18 free.*

Museums and Exhibits

Maison des Canuts ★★★★

10-12 rue d'Ivry, ☎ 04-78-28-62-04. About 1km up the hill from Place des Terreaux.
Instituted by the Guild of Silk Workers (known as *canuts* in French), this museum
details the rich history of silk-weaving in Lyon. Witness demonstrations of the local
weaving techniques or spend some francs on some silk souveniers. *Open Mon.–Fri.,
8:30 a.m.–noon and 2–6:30 p.m.; Sat., 9 a.m.–noon and 2–6 p.m.* Admission:
FR10.

Musée Gadagne ★★★★

12 rue de Gadagne, ☎ 04-78-42-03-61.
Hours open: 10:45 a.m.–6 p.m. Special hours: Fri., to 8:30 p.m. Closed: Tue.
Two museums are within this 16th-century building. The **Musée Historique de
Lyon** traces the history of Lyon with displays of paintings, pottery, furniture, pewter
and various other products of the city. An interesting Roman sculpture display is on
the first floor. If puppets pique your interest, the **Musée de la Marionette** is the
place for you. Founded by Laurent Mourguet, the creator of the most famous of

French marionettes called Guignol, this museum displays a wide array of puppets. In addition to representative puppets from other regions of France, there are collections from Italy, Russia, Belgium, Turkey and Indonesia. Admission: FR20.

Musée Historique des Tissus ★★★

34 rue de la Charite, ☎ *04-78-37-15-05.*
Hours open: 10 a.m.–5:30 p.m. Closed: Mon.

Lyon was once the center of the silk industry, and after seeing the dazzling display of antique and contemporary embroideries and tapestries here, you'll want to go out and buy a loom and start spinning yourself. The **Musée Lyonnais des Arts Decoratifs** next door is a worthy complement to its fabulous neighbor. Both museums are included on one ticket and share the same hours. Admission is free on Wed. Admission: FR26.

Musée de l'Imprimerie ★★

37 rue de la Poulaillerie, ☎ *04-78-37-65-98.*
Hours open: 9:30 a.m.–6 p.m. Special hours: Closed noon–2 p.m. except on Fri. Closed: Mon., Tue.

The Museum of Printing showcases some of the history of the industry that came here in the late 15th century. Some of the first books printed, including a page from the Gutenberg Bible, are displayed along with related tools of production. Admission FR20.

Musée de la Resistance et de la Deportation ★★★★

14 avenue Berthelot, ☎ *04-78-37-65-98.*
Hours open: 9 a.m.–5:30 p.m.

Situated in a building that was used by the Nazis for torturing prisoners, this museum recounts the French resistance to German occupation. It also tells of the history of the people deported to concentration camps. Student admission FR10. Admission: FR20.

Musée des Beaux Arts ★★★★

Palais St-Pierre, 20 place des Terreaux, ☎ *04-78-28-07-66.*
Hours open: 10:30 a.m.–6 p.m. Closed: Mon., Tue.

Lyon's fine-art museum is a mini-Louvre, and much more accessible. It is located in a former convent dating back to the 17th century. On the ground floor there's an impressive collection of Egyptian and Near Eastern antiquities. A multi-period assemblage of paintings, drawings and sketches fills the galleries on the next two floors. Objets d'art and sculpture round out the collection, including some important Rodin pieces in the courtyard. At the time of this writing, some exhibits may have been closed due to renovation. The **Musée d'Art Contemporain**, which once shared space with the Beaux Arts, has moved from the Palais to quai Charles de Gaulle, near the Jardin Tete d'Or. Admission: FR20.

Where to Stay

Bed-and-Breakfast

Saint-Colomban Lodge   FR350–FR450   ★★

7 rue du Hetre-Pourpre. ☎ *04-78-33-05-57.*
Single: FR350. Double: FR400–FR450.

A great escape to a peaceful residential neighborhood just outside of Lyon. Surrounded by a private park, there are five attractive rooms within this contemporary lodge. Furnished with pine, the amenities include satellite TV, telephone and private bath. Sunny weather translates to complimentary breakfast on the terrace; otherwise, the tables in the lounge are set. Reserved evening meals are served at the communal table for FR100, including wine. While there are no recreational facilities on the property, golf and tennis are found nearby. A good base for touring Lyon while remaining a bit removed. Credit Cards: Not Accepted.

Hotels and Resorts

Cour des Loges   **FR880–FR1700**   ★ ★ ★

6 rue du Boeuf. ☎ *04-72-77-44-44, FAX: 04-72-40-93-61.*
Rated Restaurant: *Tapas.*
Single: FR880–FR1100. Double: FR980–FR1700.

In a Renaissance setting, encased within the walls of Old Lyon, this hotel occupies four houses from the 14th, 17th and 18th centuries. The decor is a stunning contrast of modern and old; for example, old stone walls and massive beams stage a backdrop for bright fabrics, chrome, glass and dried flowers. There is also an interior courtyard with Florentine arcades and hanging gardens. Inside, the 53 guest rooms and 10 suites are beautifully furnished and equipped with double windows to buffer city noises; automatic shutter to block out the light; televisions that offer CNN; minibars that are well-stocked with complimentary beverages and snacks; and videocassette recorders. Unfortunately, the accommodations are expensive and surprisingly small. In some cases bathrooms are located on a terraced level in the room—not for the modest. Tapas is the hotel's informal, intimate restaurant that offers excellent light fares. The hotel also offers a bar, lounges, an indoor swimming pool, a Jacuzzi, a dry sauna, terraced gardens, a basement wine cellar and a private garage. Services include valet and 24-hour room service. The hotel and restaurant are open year-round. Features: wheelchair-access rooms, pool, air conditioning in rooms, sauna, nonsmoking rooms. Credit Cards: All Major.

Pullman Part-Dieu   **FR560–FR900**   ★ ★

129 rue Servient. ☎ *04-78-63-55-00, FAX: 04-78-63-55-20.*
Rated Restaurant: *L'Arc-en-Ciel.*
Single: FR560–FR620. Double: FR660–FR900.

Occupying the top floors of the Credit Lyonnais Tower in the center of the business district, the Pullman is the tallest hotel in Lyon. Above the seven-story lobby are the 245 rooms, each comfortable and functionally furnished in typical commercial hotel style. The soundproof rooms are air-conditioned and include TV, telephone, radio, minibar, bath and hair dryer. There are two suites and separate nonsmoking rooms. In addition to the grill, there is a 30th-floor restaurant and bar offering the best panorama in town. Meals begin at FR115 in the grill and FR250 in the restaurant. The views compensate for any lack of character. Features: air conditioning in rooms, sauna, nonsmoking rooms, in-room minibars. Credit Cards: All Major.

Pullman Perrache   **FR490–FR900**   ★ ★

12 cours de Verdun. ☎ *04-78-77-15-00, FAX: 04-98-37-06-56.*

Rated Restaurant: *Les Belles Saisons.*

Single: FR490–FR820. Double: FR820–FR900.

This 19th-century renovated hotel is near the Perrache train station and offers some of the best 123 rooms in Lyon. They're outfitted with plush fabrics and inviting colors, and open onto hallways with Oriental runners, 19th-century furniture and painted jardinieres. The hotel is a monument to art nouveau. The rooms, all with private bathrooms, have been redecorated in a traditional style. They include many improvements like soundproofing and air conditioning. There are also shops, a piano bar and a winter garden in the hotel. The hotel and restaurant are open year-round. Features: wheelchair-access rooms, air conditioning in rooms, nonsmoking rooms, in-room minibars. Credit Cards: All Major.

Tour Rose   FR950–FR1650   ★★★

22 rue de Boeuf. ☎ *04-78-37-25-90, FAX: 04-78-42-26-02.*

Rated Restaurant: *La Tour Rose.*

Single: FR950–FR1200. Double: FR1200–FR1650.

In the heart of the old town, the rooms and restaurant occupy a former Renaissance convent. There are just 12 rooms, all individually and luxuriously attired. All of the terraced rooms are named after Lyonnais silk companies whose lavish fabrics are part of the furnishings. The three hanging gardens and the views of Lyon add to the relaxing atmosphere. The dining room in the former chapel is reason alone to visit this inn, one of the best in Lyon. Features: air conditioning in rooms. Credit Cards: All Major.

Inns

Hostellerie Beau Rivage   FR500–FR820   ★★★★

2 rue de Beau-Rivage. ☎ *04-74-56-67-27.*

Rated Restaurant: *Beau Rivage.*

Single: FR500–FR700. Double: FR700–FR820.

This Relais and Châteaux inn offers 20 well-furnished rooms decorated in an old-fashioned way, and all have private bathrooms. One of the accommodations is a former apartment with lots of space and a renaissance decor. The cuisine is exceptional and traditional, and garden dining is available. Meals cost FR180 to FR435. The inn and restaurant are open year-round. Features: air conditioning in rooms, in-room minibars. Credit Cards: All Major.

Hostellerie du Vieux Perouges   FR390–FR1100   ★★★★

place du Tilleul. ☎ *04-74-61-00-88, FAX: 04-74-34-77-90.*

Rated Restaurant: *Hostellerie du Vieux Pèrouges.*

Single: FR390–FR700. Double: FR700–FR1100.

This inn is a handsome and lavishly restored group of 13th-century timbered buildings. Its museum-caliber interior is furnished with polished antiques; cupboards with pewter plates; iron lanterns hanging from medieval beams; glistening refectory dining tables, stone fireplaces; and wide plank floors. Its 15 comfortable rooms, all with private bathrooms, are beautifully decorated with regional antiques and a few have their own garden. The 13 annex houses are simply decorated, but quite pleasant and perhaps more appealing since they are less expensive. The restaurant is run in association with Le Manoir, where overnight guests are accommodated. The food is exceptional, especially when it's served with the local wine. Meals cost FR130 to FR390, excluding breakfast, which is FR60 and is served on a covered terrace perched on top of the tower. The inn and restaurant are closed on Wednesdays from November through March. Half-board rates are FR650 (room, breakfast and a meal) per person, per day in season. Credit Cards: All Major.

Lyon has many excellent bistros and cafés.

Where to Eat

Alain Chapel $$$ ★ ★ ★

on N83, 19 km north of Lyon. ☎ *04-78-91-82-02.*
Lunch: Noon–2 p.m., FR480–FR650.
Dinner: 7–9:30 p.m., entrées FR480–FR650.

Alain Chapel died five years ago, but this legendary restaurant and small hotel is still
pulling its weight. The restaurant is run by Philippe Jousse, who had worked with
Chapel since the 1980s, and he still adheres to the same classic techniques employed
by the master. Jousse has continued to buy fish from Brittany and eggs and vegetables from local farmers. Many familiar dishes remain, including lobster salad and
chicken cooked in a bladder, but Jousse has added a few interesting innovations,
including rabbit with *foie gras en gelée.* Closed: Mon. Amenities: outside dining,
own baking, reservations required. Credit Cards: V, MC, DC, A, E.

Bernachon $ ★ ★ ★

42 cours F.D.-Roosevelt. ☎ *04-78-52-23-05.*
Lunch: 8 a.m.–1 p.m.
Dinner: entrées FR50.

Here you'll find the best hot chocolate in the world (great for breakfast) made from
house-roasted cocoa beans; also offered are bonbons and pastries, as well as daily
lunch specials. Closed: Mon., Sun. Amenities: own baking, reservations not
accepted.

Christian Bourillot $$$ ★ ★ ★ ★

8 place des Celestins, In the second arrondissement. ☎ *04-78-37-38-64.*
Dinner: 7–10 p.m., entrées FR200–FR400.

Still the same restaurant it has been for years—and that's a wonderful thing. A wonderful sampling of Lyonnais cuisine from the traditional menu and exciting international flavors from the more nouvelle menu. The staff makes every guest feel
welcomed, and they shower each one with unobtrusive attention. An incredible collection of bottles in the cellar. Set menus start at FR200–FR400 on the weekdays.
Closed: Sun. Reservations required. Credit Cards: All Major.

Hostellerie du Vieux Perouges $$

*place du Tilleul, 35 km northeast of Lyon on D84, near Merimeux. Located at Ostellerie
du Vieux Perouges.* ☎ *04-74-61-00-88.*
Lunch: Noon–2 p.m., FR145–FR185.
Dinner: 7–9 p.m., entrées FR145–FR185.

A very touristy, but beautifully preserved inn from the 14th century, restored in the
half-timbered style common to the area. The menu is quite good, appropriately traditional *(truffle terrine Brillat-Savarin, carp a l'ancienne)* and rather expensive.
Fixed-price meals range from FR175 to FR400, and an unusual after-dinner liqueur
is offered, called Ypocras, whose recipe supposedly dates to the Middle Ages.
Closed: Wed. Amenities: own baking, reservations required. Credit Cards: V, MC, E.

La Mere Brazier $$ ★ ★

12 rue Royale.
Metro stop: Croix-Paquet.

Specialties: artichoke hearts with foie gras, quenelles de brochet, Bresse chicken "demi-deuil."
Lunch: 12:30–2 p.m., FR175–FR200.
Dinner: 8:30–10 p.m., entrées FR175–FR200.

This restaurant was the first dining establishment owned by a woman chef to receive three stars from Michelin. Located in the old silk-makers section of town, it is run by Madame Brazier's daughter-in-law and one of her granddaughters, and although it's lost two of those stars, people still come for dishes invented by the venerable patronne. The dining room is as warm and cozy as the welcome, but sometimes the food, which is hardly haute cuisine, lacks flavor, which is unfortunate at the high, high prices (Fixed-price meals start at FR330). Closed: Sun. Reservations recommended. Credit Cards: All Major.

La Pyramide $$ ★★★

14 avenue F. Point. ☎ *04-74-53-01-96.*
Lunch: 12:30–2:30 p.m., FR155–FR380.
Dinner: 7–9:30 p.m., entrées FR155–FR380.

For years now, Patrick Henrioux has been the guiding light of this venerable kitchen that became a legend under the late Fernand Point. Henrioux pleases the loyal patrons who supported him, after a rough transition period, by keeping the old favorites on the menu, while drawing a new crowd with lighter, inventive creations. These dishes reflect his southern roots, and include a salad of prawns with aromatic herbs, and bonito grilled with ginger; but you'll probably never find a better *quenelles de brochet* anywhere. There's a terrace for dining in the summer months. Closed: Wed. Amenities: outside dining, own baking, reservations required. Credit Cards: All Major.

La Tour Rose $$$ ★★

22 rue du Boeuf. ☎ *04-78-37-25-90.*
Metro stop: St.-Jean.
Lunch: Noon–2 p.m., FR250–FR350.
Dinner: 7:30–10:30 p.m., entrées FR250–FR350.

This inn and restaurant is a multilevel structure incorporated into a medieval convent in Lyon's Old Town. Favored by the arts community, it is the baby of chef, caterer and party planner Philippe Chavent. His inventive cuisine employs ingredients that shouldn't really work, but do, due to good instincts, solid technique (he worked under Paul Bocuse), luck, or a combination of all three. The menu changes frequently, but to give you an idea, one item that appeared not too long ago was snails and creamed carrots molded into a cake. Asian flavors and spices are often employed, including ginger, seaweed, sesame oil and hibiscus flowers. The desserts are delicate and different. One problem is that all this innovation comes at a price: It's very expensive, but he's made up for that by opening a wine bar, **Comptoir du Boeuf**, at *2 place Neuve-Saint-Jean* (☎ *04-78-92-82-35*), which serves hearty dishes from FR150. Wines by the glass, terrace dining. Closed: Sun. Amenities: happening bar, outside dining, reservations recommended. Credit Cards: All Major.

Le Bouchon de Fourviere $ ★★

9 rue de la Quarantine. ☎ *04-72-41-85-02.*

Lunch: FR65–FR130.
Dinner: entrées FR65–FR130.

Welcome to bouchon country—Lyon has legions (well, quite a few) of middling to excellent bistros all over town with hearty cooking at easy prices. La Bouchon de Fourviere appeals to journalists; three course set meals include dessert; also in the 4th eme is **La Conciergerie**, *44 quai P.-Scize* (☎ *04-78-83-23-39*), prix-fixe FR45; open until 11 p.m.; In the 2nd eme the best choice is **Chez Sylvain**, *4 rue Tupin* (☎ *04-78-42-11-98*), a traditional old hangout for local families, prix fixe FR74, FR85 and FR95, lunch only, terrace dining, excellent desserts, no credit cards. Closed July 19–Aug. 19. Others in the area are **Le Bistrot de la Minaudiere**, *7 rue de la Poulaillerie* (☎ *04-78-37-32-96*), prix-fixe FR60; open until 10 p.m.; **Chez Rabatel**, *pl A-Gourju* (☎ *04-78-37-14-98*) is part of La Voute-Chez Lea, founded by Mere Lea, one of the better known female restaurateurs; regional menu items as low as FR54; open until 9 p.m. Closed: Sat., Sun. Amenities: cafestop, reservations not accepted.

Le Fedora $$ ★★

249 rue M.-Merieux. ☎ *04-78-69-46-26.*
Lunch: Noon–2 p.m., FR190–FR230.
Dinner: 7:30–10 p.m., entrées FR190–FR230.

Chef Daniel Judeaux, who opened this restaurant in 1978, once worked at Maxim's in Paris and then under Paul Bocuse. Once serving classic Lyonnaise specialties, he changed his focus some time ago and now features creative seafood and shellfish dishes, accompanied by good wines. You can eat in the recently spiffed-up dining room or at tables set up in the garden. The fixed-price menu starts at FR160, with wine. Closed: Sun. Amenities: outside dining, own baking, reservations required. Credit Cards: All Major.

Le Vivarais $$

1 place du Dr.-Gailleton. ☎ *04-78-37-85-15.*
Specialties: chicken liver poached in bouillon, raspberry tart, pear tart.
Lunch: Noon–2 p.m., FR180–FR230.
Dinner: 7–10:15 p.m., entrées FR180–FR230.

This *bouchon* (bistro) is favored by well-heeled members of Lyon's business community, who can expect unstinting quality at reasonable prices. Robert Duffaud, the chef, worked for years with Alain Chapel, and he believes in procuring the freshest ingredients possible from the best suppliers in town. You can taste a wide sampling of his skill in the FR100 fixed-price menu, which often includes a local sausage served with Le Puy lentils. Closed: Sun. Reservations required. Credit Cards: All Major.

Leon de Lyon $$$ ★★★★

1 rue Pleney. ☎ *04-78-28-11-33.*
Metro stop: Hotel-de-Ville.
Lunch: Noon–2 p.m., FR250–FR325.
Dinner: 7:30–10 p.m., entrées FR250–FR325.

Second only to Paul Bocuse in stature, chef Jean-Paul Lacombe may truly be the culinary lion of Lyon, now that the former is frequently absent. An inventive artisan, Lacombe takes humble Lyonnaise favorites such as pigs' feet and stuffs the meat into a potato, together with foie gras, truffles and champignon mushrooms. His dining room is tasteful and comfortable, with leather chairs and pretty stained-glass windows. The service is self-assured, and the reception is welcoming.

Other top-class establishments are **Nandron**, *26 quai J.-Moulin* (☎ *04-78-42-10-26*), popular with wealthy businesspeople; sublime *quenelles de brochet* with sauce Nantua, quail eggs *en cocotte* with truffles, Bresse chicken grandmere; *open daily, except Sat. from noon–2 p.m. and 7:30–10 p.m. Closed July 24–Aug. 23,* all cards, reservations recommended. Metro: Cordelier. **Pierre Orsi**, *3 pl. Kleber* (☎ *04-78-89-57-68*), is the perfect place for a birthday, anniversary or any sentimental occasion. The chef makes everyone feel welcome, and the waitresses in long floral-printed dresses take their jobs very seriously. Turn-of-the-century decor; specialties include Bresse pigeon with garlic, and wild mushrooms and lobster in puff pastry. *Open daily, except Sun. evening; 12:15–1:30 p.m. and 8–9:30 p.m., closed Aug. 10–20.* Metro: Place Kleber. Jacket and tie required. Closed: Sun. Amenities: own baking, reservations required. Credit Cards: V, MC, A, E.

Marche du Quai St-Antoine $

quai St-Antoine.
Metro stop: Hotel de Ville.
Lunch: 8 a.m.–noon.
Fill a picnic basket with cheese, sausages, fruit and veggies from this daily farmer's market facing the Rhone River. Just north of the city center, the Parc de la Tete d'Or is so big (300 acres) that there's more than enough space to enjoy your meal in relative peace and quiet. Closed: Mon.

Restaurant Paul-Blanc $$ ★★★

rue P.-Blanc. ☎ *04-74-04-04-74.*
Lunch: Noon–2 p.m., FR175–FR225.
Dinner: 7–9:30 p.m., entrées FR175–FR225.
Bruno Maringue is seemingly content with carrying on the classic traditions of his grandfather, Paul Blanc. And why not? The crayfish ravioli or fricassee of chicken with morel mushrooms in cream are reason enough for many to return, again and again. Closed: Tues. Amenities: outside dining. Credit Cards: V, MC, DC, A, E.

Collonges-au-Mont d'Or

Paul Bocuse $$$ ★★★★★

50 quai de la Plage, 25 km north of Lyon via N51. ☎ *04-72-27-85-85.*
Lunch: Noon–2 p.m., FR255–FR475.
Dinner: 7–10 p.m., entrées FR255–FR475.
This world-famous establishment is located in a sprawling converted house on the banks of the Saone River, a 15-minute car trip from Lyon. Paul Bocuse has long been known as the culinary lion of the region, but because of many other business ventures, he is often out of the country, leaving the restaurant to be run by his long-time associates, Roger Jaloux and Christian Bouvarel. This disturbs many critics, who claim these absences have led to indifferent service and amateurishly prepared dishes. Be that as it may, it does not lack support from fans (you have to book way ahead of time). His classic creations are still extremely popular, including Bresse

LYON AND THE ALPS

chicken served in a pig's bladder or truffle soup under a puff-pastry beret. Jacket and tie required. Amenities: own baking, reservations required. Credit Cards: All Major.

Condrieu

Beau Rivage $$$ ★★★

2 rue Beau-Rivage, N86, 18 km from Vienne. In Beau Rivage. Located at Beau Rivage.
☎ *04-74-9-52-24.*
Lunch: Noon–2 p.m., FR230–FR300.
Dinner: 7–9:15 p.m., entrées FR230–FR300.

A romantic ivy-covered inn and restaurant with a terrace overlooking the Rhone River. Reynald Donet's marvelous cooking follows traditional lines, including *quenelle de brochet* with lobster salpicon, and roast lamb with foie gras (in season). The fixed-price lunch is a bargain at FR180. Amenities: outside dining, own baking, reservations required. Credit Cards: All Major.

Directory

To and From

Lyon is served by national and international flights at the Santolas airport, by TGV connections to anywhere in the country as well as Italy and Switzerland, and is on the main A-6/A-7 autoroute between Burgundy and Provence.

Tourist Office

There are several around the city, of which the main branch and the easiest to find is at: place Bellecour; ☎ *(33) 04-78-42-25-75.*

Rail Stations

Two TGV stations serve the city. Part-Dieu is further out to the east; the main station is Perranche at:
place Carnot; ☎ *(33) 04-78-92-50-50.*

Post Office

place Antonin Porcet; ☎ *(33) 04-72-40-65-22.*

Vienne

Set on a sunny bend in the Rhône river, Vienne was a sleepy Allobrogian village when the Romans conquered it at the beginning of the first century B.C., 60 years before Caesar invaded Gaul. Vienne became an administrative capital long before Lyon assumed the role, and today the town contains many remnants of its important past. The most significant of these are the Temple d'Auguste et Livie, an almost entirely preserved rectangular temple built in 25 B.C.; the Théâtre de Cybèle, a mostly ruined temple to the goddess Cybele, whose worship involved ritualistic orgies, the Théâtre Romaine, a huge amphitheater seating 15,000 people that is currently used for a July jazz festival, and the pyramid from the Roman Circus that was once the centerpiece of the chariot racetrack. Two museums, the Musée Lapidaire and the Musée des Beaux Arts et d'Archaeologie, house relics and objects found at the ongoing archaeological dig that continuously uproots the town. A major site is at St. Romain-en-Gal, part of the old Gallo-Roman city but now a separate commune across the river. The remains of villas, temples, baths, sewers, heating systems, mosaics and other treasures have all been found here and are housed in a rich Musée Archaeologique.

In the more recent past, when the Romans declined and once the Franks took over in the sixth century, Vienne became an important religious fiefdom of the Holy See, causing conflicts between the church and France until the latter took possession of the city in 1349. The most important vestige of this period is the Cathédrale St. Maurice, constructed during the transition from Romanesque to Gothic styles between the 12th and 16th centuries. This unusual cathedral features a gigantic nave with three equilateral aisles, and no transept. A smaller church, the Eglise St. Pierre, is less impressive overall but has parts dating to the fifth and sixth centuries.

Vienne is about 10 miles south of Lyon and can be reached on the A-7 autoroute or the N-86 highway.

What to Do

Historical/Architectural Sites

Cathedrale St-Maurice   ★★★

place St-Maurice. Off rue Clementine.

Constructed from the 12th to 16th centuries, this medieval church is a combination of Romanesque and Gothic architecture. The west front demonstrates the Flamboyant Gothic while the inside is dotted with Romanesque sculptures, has three aisles and lacks a transept. One of Vienne's most interesting pieces of architecture.

Temple d'Auguste et Livie   ★★★

place du Palais.

Strategically placed in the middle of town is this graceful temple, built in 25 B.C. (the Romans conquered the city in the first century B.C.) with well-preserved Corinthian columns. Another temple, dedicated to the goddess Cybelle, lies in ruins nearby, off the place de Miremont. A working amphitheater, the Theatre Romain, based at the foot of Mont Pipet, off rue de Cirque, is used today for rock concerts and the Jazz a Vienne festival, which takes place in the first two weeks of July. The theater seats about 8000 people; when it was first built, more than 13,000 gladiatorial spectators were accommodated. A FR25 multi-use ticket (FR20, students) will get you into the city's main attractions; purchase your ticket at the theater, *open 10 a.m.–5 p.m., Wed.–Mon., Sun. from 1:30–5:30 p.m.*

Museums and Exhibits

Musée Lapidaire   ★★★

place St-Pierre, ☎ *04-74-85-20-35. In the southern part of town.*

Within the Eglise St-Pierre, a church with 5th-century origins, the Musée Lapidaire showcases stone carvings and various architectural pieces from ancient Roman to medieval times. *Open Apr.–mid-Oct., Wed.–Mon., 9 a.m.–1 p.m. and 2–6:30 p.m.; otherwise, Wed.–Sat., 10 a.m.–noon and 2–5 p.m. and Sun., 2–5 p.m.* Admission: FR10.

LYON AND THE ALPS

Musée des Beaux Arts et Archeologie ★★

place St-Pierre, ☎ *04-74-85-20-35. Near the Eglise St-Pierre.*
A fine collection of Gallo-Roman pieces combined with 17th- and 18th-century
works from minor artists of the region. Open Apr.–mid-Oct., Wed.–Mon.; mid-
Oct.–Mar., Wed.–Sun.

Where to Eat

L'Estancot $$ ★★

4 rue de la Table-Ronde ☎ *04-74-85-12-09.*
Dinner: entrées FR70–FR150.
A popular little restaurant with regional dishes served in a relaxed atmosphere.
Another inexpensive choice is **Pagode d'Or** *(25 rue de la Charite;* ☎ *04-74-53-39-
18)* serving Japanese, Chinese and Vietnamese cuisine. Sit with a group and watch
the food cooked right in front of you. *Closed Mon. lunch and Tues. dinner.*
Another, more expensive, choice is **Magnard** at *45 cours Brillier (*☎ *04-74-85-10-
43).* Traditional cuisine with a variety of seafood, poultry and meats from FR125–
FR250 and less expensive set menus. *Closed: Sun.*

La Pyramide Fernand Point $$$ ★★★★★

14 avenue Fernand Point ☎ *04-74-53-01-96.*
Dinner: 7–9:30 p.m., entrées FR150–FR375.
Founded by the late, great chef Fernand Point in 1923, the tradition of excellence
has been faithfully followed. Classic and nouvelle dishes are served here, many still
dressed with Point's famous sauces. Some of the specialties include a prawn salad,
the roast kid stuffed with red pepper and a fresh cod. The deft staff will gladly recommend a bottle of wine from the astonishingly rich cellar. Guests are guaranteed
to leave the table in a jovial mood—heavier in the belly and lighter in the wallet. Set
menus start at FR250. Closed: Wed. Reservations required. Credit Cards: All Major.

Le Bec Fin $$ ★★★

7 place St-Maurice, Across from the cathedral. ☎ *04-74-85-76-72.*
Dinner: 7–9 p.m., entrées FR75–FR150.
An unpretentious establishment with some of the best food in town. Ideal for lunch,
the weekday menu is a good value, and the proportions are more than generous.
Steak and freshwater fish are the staples here and are sure to please every time. The
a la carte dishes are varied and include such dishes as foie gras and duckling. Set
menus are FR110–FR240. Jacket required. Closed: Mon. Reservations recommended. Credit Cards: V, MC.

Grenoble

Situated at the meeting point of three valleys as well as the Isère and Drac
rivers, Grenoble has had the luxury to spread out. Today, Grenoble is a modern city and is clearly both an administrative capital and a major economic
and trade center. Once the capital of the Dauphiné region, Grenoble wears
its authoritative role well. For the best view of the city, take the télépherique
from the river to the Bastille fortress located 1640 feet above the city. Built

during the 16th century and reinforced during the 19th century, the fort protected the approaches to the city. Stroll down to the Institut de la Géographie des Alpes, founded by geologist Raoul Blanchard in 1908, and peruse his 13-volume treatise on the western Alps. You can continue walking back down to the town through parc Guy Pape and the Jardin des Dauphin until you come to the Musée Dauphinois, a charming regional museum devoted to local customs and crafts that is housed in a 17th-century convent. Across the river is the place St. André, the heart of the medieval city, on one side of which is the 13th-century Eglise St. André and the 15th-century Palais de Justice. As befitting a modern city, Grenoble has two excellent art museums, the Musée de Grenoble, which specializes in modern artists including Picasso, Matisse and Chagall, and the Centre National d'Art Contemporain, with temporary exhibitions by contemporary artists. Nearby is the Chartreuse monastery, where the liqueur of the same name is manufactured—reputedly, only three monks at any one time know the list of 130 ingredients. Also close by on the N-91 highway east out of town is Alpe d'Huez, mentioned here not as a ski resort but as the yearly site of the most grueling climb in the Tour de France bicycle race.

What to Do

Historical/Architectural Sites

Chartreuse Distillery ★★★★

10 boulevard Edgar Kofler, ☎ *04-76-05-81-77. About 20 minutes north in Voiron.*
Founded by St-Bruno in 1084, the original monastery is not open to the public, as the monks live in seclusion. However, the distillery and museum are open to all. First produced by the monks in the early 1600s, the Chartreuse liqueur is a mixture of 130 ingredients, which only three monks now know. Tour the distillery, and sample a bit of the famous liqueur at the end. The museum educates visitors about the life of the monk. *The distillery is open July–Aug., 8 a.m.–6:30 p.m.; Sept.–Oct. and Easter–June, 8–11:30 a.m. and 2–6:30 p.m.; Nov.–Easter, Mon.–Fri., 8–11:30 a.m. and 2–5:30 p.m. The museum is open Easter–Oct., 9:30 a.m.–noon and 2–6:30 p.m.* Admission FR12.

Fort de la Bastille ★★★★

On the hill. Take the telepherique from quai Stephanie-Jay.
Erected in the 16th century as a point of defense, the fort is perched 263 meters above town. While the fort itself is of little interest, there is a Musée de l'Automobile inside with a decent exhibition of cars and related pieces. Still, the best reason to take the cable car ride to the top is the unmatched view over the city. *The telepherique operates from 10 a.m.–midnight from Apr.–mid-Sept.; Nov.–Mar., to 6 p.m.* One-way tickets cost FR22 and round-trip tickets cost FR32. Take it to the top and meander back down the hill along the numerous footpaths.

place St-Andre ★★★

place St-Andre. Near the Isere.

The heart of the medieval city, place St-Andre is watched over by two of Grenoble's oldest buildings. Built in the 13th century, the church is made completely of brick. The Palais de Justice reflects three different styles: a Gothic middle, a Renaissance section to the right and a combination of Gothic and Renaissance to the left. A great square to begin a leisurely stroll around the city.

Museums and Exhibits

Musée Dauphinois   ★★★★

30 rue Maurice Gignoux, ☎ *04-76-85-19-00. On the hill below the Bastille.*
Hours open: 9 a.m.–6 p.m. Special hours: Closed noon–2 p.m., closed Tue. Closed: Tue.
One of the country's finest museums devoted to regional art, the Dauphinois is housed in a 17th-century convent. In addition to the permanent display of furniture, tools, paintings and pictures of the region, there are changing exhibits. It is a fantastic introduction to the heritage and lifestyle of the mountain people. Admission: FR15.

Musée de Grenoble   ★★★

5 place de Lavalette, ☎ *04-76-63-44-44.*
Hours open: 11 a.m.–7 p.m. Special hours: Open until 10 p.m. on Wed. Closed: Tue.
Along with lesser-known Picassos, the Musée de Grenoble features an array of Renaissance and Baroque art, Egyptian art and modern works by Chagall and Matisse. Wed. admission is free. Another museum housing temporary displays is the **Centre National d'Art Contemporain**, built by Gustave Eiffel, at *155 cours Berriat* (☎ *04-76-21-95-84).* As the name implies, some interesting, changing exhibits focus on contemporary art. Admission: FR25.

Where to Stay

Hotels and Resorts

Alpotel   FR450   ★★★

12 boulevard du Mal-Joffre. ☎ *04-76-87-88-41, FAX: 04-76-47-58-52. In the middle of town, on a main boulevard.*
Double: FR450.
A member of the Mercure chain of hotels, the quality here is consistently high and the service professional and courteous. Comfortable and constantly updated, the 88 modern rooms are air-conditioned and well-appointed. The bar and the restaurant are always good for creative cuisine and a lively atmosphere. Centrally located, the Alpotel proves to be a handy choice. Features: wheelchair-access rooms. Credit Cards: All Major.

Hotel d'Angleterre   FR460–FR540   ★★★

5 place Victor-Hugo. ☎ *04-76-87-37-31, FAX: 04-76-50-94-10. On the edge of Grenoble's largest square/park.*
Single: FR460. Double: FR540.
With the best address in Grenoble, this hotel opens onto the largest square in town. Behind the attractive facade lie 70 air-conditioned rooms, the best of which overlook the square. Soundproof, the rooms have TV, telephone, radio, minibar and private bath. The public areas are handsomely furnished and decorated with wood-

grained walls. Breakfast is the only meal served, for FR45. Some family rooms are available for FR650. Credit Cards: All Major.

Park Hotel   **FR600–FR1200**   ★★★★

10 place Paul-Mistral. ☎ *04-76-85-81-23, FAX: 04-76-46-49-88. In the center of town. Single: FR600–FR1000. Double: FR700–FR1200.*

Grenoble's leading hotel, situated by a park in the town center. The contemporary style pervades the 50 bedrooms and salons, with attractive furnishings and wood paneling throughout. The rooms are soundproof, comfortable and equipped with TV, telephone, minibar and air conditioning. The bar and billiard room are recent additions that add to the already impressive facility. Highly trained and professional, the staff is the best in town. Features: mountain location, in-room conference facilities. Credit Cards: All Major.

Where to Eat

L'Escalier   **$$$**   ★★★★

6 place de Lavalette, In the old town. ☎ *04-76-54-66-16.*
Specialties: prawns in filo pastry.
Dinner: entrées FR175–FR275.

While the crowd may be a bit pretentious, the cuisine is truly wonderful. After admiring the presentation of the lovely dishes, the first bite will confirm that there is nothing lacking in the food here. The thoughtful menu even includes a low-calorie section. Of course, the typically rich, full-textured dishes are still available. Ask owner Alain Girod to recommend a wine to accompany such dishes as puff-pastry tart of lamb's brains and oyster essence or prawns in filo pastry. Set menus from FR120 at lunch. Closed: Sun. Reservations required. Credit Cards: All Major.

La Poularde Bressane   **$$**   ★★★

12 place Paul Mistral, Across from the Parc Paul-Mistral. ☎ *04-76-87-08-90.*
Dinner: 7:30–9:45 p.m., entrées FR80–FR175.

A chic crowd keeps this elegant restaurant going. While focusing on traditional cuisine, the chef ventures out sometimes with the results being excellent contemporary cuisine. It's always a pleasure to discover some new creation of his and complement it with one of the regional wines. Set menus from FR120. Closed: Sun. Reservations required. Credit Cards: V, DC, A.

Le Berlioz   **$$**   ★★★

4 rue Strasbourg ☎ *04-76-56-22-39.*
Dinner: 7:30–10:30 p.m., entrées FR125–FR200.

Francoise Legras keeps things interesting here by changing the menu monthly, featuring different regional specialties. The wonderful dishes featured keep locals coming back to see how she outdoes herself every month. Always a good bet are the roast duck in spicy honey sauce, the marinated halibut and the slow-cooked lamb. Some great lesser known wines are available. Set menus from just FR83 at lunch and FR115 at dinner. Closed late Apr.–early May and mid-July–mid-Aug. Closed: Sun. Reservations required. Credit Cards: V, A.

LYON AND THE ALPS

Directory

To and From

> By train from Paris (three hours) or Lyon (an hour-and-a-half), or by road at the end of the A-9 autoroute from Lyon or the A-9 from the north or N-75 highway from the south.

Tourist Office

> 14 rue de la République; ☎ (33) 04-76-42-41-41.

Rail Station

> place de la Gàre; ☎ (33) 04-76-47-50-50.

Post Office

> 7 boulevard Maréchal-Lyautey, 38000 Grenoble; ☎ (33) 04-76-43-53-31.

Aix-les-Bains

Once the poshest of the Alpine resorts, Aix-les-Bains is centered around natural hot springs that were first exploited by the Romans. In the basement of the modern-day Thermes Nacionaux you can see vestiges of the Roman baths, constructed in the first century. The full "cure" is available only to those bearing a doctor's prescription, but several elements are open to the public for a moderate fee. The spa is actually the most popular in France. Across from the baths is the Temple of Diana, a restored second-century temple that now houses the Musée Archéologique et Lapidaire, containing a small collection of Roman artifacts. This resort town was popularized by Napoléon III in the mid-19th century, and underwent a typical Belle Epoque expansion (and subsequent decline) that has left it with an aging but elegant casino and some charming hotels around the town center, as well as a small museum, the Musée Faure, containing some Impressionist works as well as sculptures by Rodin, and other treasures. The big business now—besides the spa—is the lake. Lac du Bourget is a major center for waterskiing, windsurfing, and even sunbathing in the summer. Boats leave at regular intervals to the Abbaye d'Hautecombe on the other side. This Bénédictine abbey containing the mausoleum of the Savoie dynasty can also be reached by circumnavigating the lake by car.

What to Do

Historical/Architectural Sites

Abbaye d'Hautecombe ★★★★

> Grand Pont, ☎ 04-79-54-26-12. Boats depart from the Grand Pont daily. There are from 2–5 boats daily; 2.5 hours; FR60.
> Catch the morning boat to this abbey on a promontory protruding into the lake. Rebuilt in the 19th century in the Troubadour Gothic style, it houses the tombs of the princes of Savoy. Gregorian chants are the highlight at the daily mass at noon and at the Sunday mass at 9:15 a.m. *Open Mon. and Wed.–Sat., 10–11:30 a.m. and 2–5 p.m.; Sun., 10:30 a.m.–noon and 2–5 p.m.* Also accessible by car. Admission: free.

Musée Faure ★★★

boulevard des Cotes, ☎ *04-76-61-06-57. On top of the hill.*
An outstanding collection of Impressionist paintings with works by Pisarro, Renoir, Rodin, Cezanne and Sisley. *Open Mon. and Wed.–Fri., 9:30 a.m.–noon and 1:30–5:45 p.m.; Sat.–Sun., 9:30 a.m.–noon and 1:30–6:45 p.m.* The view over town is a nice extra. Near the baths is the Temple of Diana, with its small display of Gallo-Roman works and relics. Admission: FR20.

Thermes Nationaux ★★★

place Maurice Mollard, ☎ *04-79-35-38-50.*
Hours open: 3–9 p.m.
The structure was built in 1857, and the new baths were started in 1934. Take a tour of the modern baths which includes a visit to the ancient Roman baths beneath the structure. While only French citizens may receive the full treatment here, a few different water massages are available for various prices. Tours cost FR15 and leave Mon.–Sat., 3 p.m. Nov.–Mar. on Wed. only at 3 p.m. Admission: FR15.

Where to Stay

Hotels and Resorts

Le Manoir **FR300–FR550** ★★★

37 rue Georges-1er. ☎ *04-79-61-44-00, FAX: 04-79-35-67-67. In the Parc du Splendide-Royal.*
Single: FR300. Double: FR550.
Encompassed by gardens and trees, Le Manoir's 73 rooms reflect the rustic decor of the entire hotel. Provencal furniture is featured in the rooms, and each includes TV, telephone, bath and many with balconies. After breakfast for FR48 on the terrace (weather permitting), a short walk will lead to the thermal center. Enjoy dinner in the fireside dining room featuring meals starting at FR140. Features: pool, balcony or patio, fitness center. Credit Cards: V, MC, DC.

Inns

Hotel Ariana **FR550–FR850** ★★★

avenue de Marlioz. ☎ *04-79-61-79-79, FAX: 04-79-61-79-61. Near the Marlioz Institute.*
Single: FR550. Double: FR850.
On the outskirts of town, the Ariana offers a relaxing environment centered around guests using the spas. The 60 rooms, although a bit small, are relaxing and equipped with TV, telephone, radio and bath. Some rooms are available with balconies overlooking the surrounding park grounds. Built in 1983, the contemporary decor is evident in the white marble and abundant use of wood, metal and attractive furniture in the public areas. The restaurant is excellent, and breakfast is served for FR65. Features: pool, air conditioning in rooms. Credit Cards: V, MC, DC, A.

Where to Eat

Adelaide **$$$**

avenue de Marlioz. ☎ *04-79-88-08-00.*
Dinner: entrées FR200–FR400.

The relaxing atmosphere of this restaurant is heightened on the lovely terrace. While enjoying the peaceful surroundings, the cordial staff will tell you of the specials which often focus on seafood. While the menu is a bit overpriced for what is served, the cuisine is slowly catching up. Set menus from FR200–FR315. Reservations required. Credit Cards: All Major.

Davat $$ ★★★

au Grand Port, At the port where the steamers dock. Located at Hotel Restaurant Davat. ☎ *04-79-63-40-40.*
Dinner: 7:30–9:30 p.m., entrées FR145–FR260.
Formerly a 19th-century lakeside residence, this inn houses a fine restaurant. The traditional cooking is popular for its full flavors and heavy textures. Keeping with the classic theme, the service is friendly and the smiles genuine. The meals here are among the best values in town, with set menus at FR100–FR250. Closed: Mon. Reservations required. Credit Cards: V, MC.

Lille $$ ★★★

au Grand Port, At the port where the steamers dock. Located at Lille. ☎ *04-79-63-40-00.*
Dinner: 7:30–9 p.m., entrées FR140–FR255.
In the family for four generations, this lakeside inn houses a charming little restaurant. Assured of a warm reception and a solid meal, guests here walk away having enjoyed the experience from start to finish. Traditional dishes, such as pike mousse and cassoulet, are served by a very friendly staff who know the meaning of courtesy, politeness and attention. The set menus are FR145–FR360. Closed: Wed. Reservations required. Credit Cards: All Major.

Directory

To and From
By train from Paris (three hours) and Lyon (an hour-and-a-quarter), or by road on a spur off the A-41 autoroute.

Tourist Office
place Maurice Mollard; ☎ *(33) 04-79-35-05-92.*

Rail Station
place de la Gàre; ☎ *(33) 04-79-85-50-50.*

Post Office
avenue Victoria, 73100 Aix-les-Bains; ☎ *(33) 04-79-35-05-92.*

Chambéry

Nestled in the valley between Chartreuse and Bauges mountain ranges, Chambéry is a gateway for all traffic across the Alps. Consequently the Counts of Savoie made it their capital in 1232. In order to protect themselves from the encroaching of the king of France, the counts moved to Turin in 1563, but Chambéry retains a quiet charm as if it is well aware of its important past. Finished in the 13th century and restored in stages through ʾ 19th century, the Château des Ducs de Savoie is the main legacy of the dukes. The main entrance to the castle, the Porte de l'Eglise St. Dominic, dates from the 15th century. The Sainte Chapelle inside was the home of the famous Sainte Suaire until the dukes moved across the Alps to Turin and the relic took its present name of the Shroud of Turin. Rebuilt in the 19th century after suffering heavy fire damage, the chapel retains its flamboyant architecture, while the interior is decorated in beautiful *trompe l'oeuil* friezes. The steeple contains 70 bells that can call the faithful to Mass in a range of six octaves. Better known than the Chambéry castle is the Fontaine des Eléphants, a whimsical fountain that was erected by civic leaders in 1838 in memory of a favorite local son, the Count de Boigne, who was involved in several taxing massacres in India in the early 19th century, and gave part of his spoils to the city upon his return. Nearby is the excellent Musée des Beaux Arts, which houses a terrific collection of Italian paintings by such artists as Titian, Tintoretto and Lutto. A less interesting museum is the nearby Musée Savoisien, maintained in a former Franciscan convent. The museum includes displays depicting the city and the region's past, including a large archaeological exhibit consisting mostly of pottery fragments. The most interesting visit in town, besides the chapel in the château, is the Musée des Charmettes, the house where Jean-Jacques Rousseau lived in "happiness and innocence" (according to him) with his mistress Madame de Warens from 1736 to 1742.

What to Do

Historical/Architectural Sites

Château des Ducs de Savoie   ★★★

rue Basse du Château, ☎ *04-79-33-42-47.*
Special hours: Open only Mar.–Dec.
Built in the 14th century, only parts of this building can be visited. One section, the adjoining Ste-Chapelle, was built in the 15th century to house the Holy Shroud, the cloth believed to have covered the crucified Christ. Although the shroud was taken to Turin in 1860, the chapel is still worth a visit for the view atop the Round Tower. Most of the remaining parts of the château are used for city administrative purposes. Five guided tours are offered in the high season at various times. In the low season, tours are on Sat. at 2:15 p.m. and Sun. at 3:30 p.m. Admission: FR25.

Fontaine des Elephants   ★★★★

boulevard de la Colonne and Rue de Boigne. At the intersection of the two streets.
The most famous monument in the city, this fountain hovers over the intersection of the two streets. Created in 1838 in honor of General de Boigne, there are four elephants spouting occasional spurts of water underneath a victory column. General de Boigne was a local businessman who was honored after spreading some of his monies made in the East Indies on the town.

Museums and Exhibits

Musée Savoisien   ★★★

boulevard du Theatre, ☎ *04-79-33-44-48. Near the fountain.*
Hours open: 10 a.m.–6 p.m. Special hours: Closed noon–2 p.m. Closed: Tue.

LYON AND THE ALPS

Sitting in a 13th-century monastery, the Musée Savoisien boasts a rich archaeological collection. Local findings include 13th-century wall paintings, pottery and jewelry. Admission: FR20.

Musée des Beaux-Arts   ★★★★

place du Palais du Justice, ☎ *04-79-33-44-48. North of the fountain.*
Hours open: 10 a.m.–6 p.m. Special hours: Closed noon–2 p.m. Closed: Tue.
Behind the Louvre, this has the second largest collection of Italian paintings in France. Boasting an extensive collection from the 14th to 18th centuries, such greats as Titian, Lutto and Tintoretto are all represented here. A sizeable French collection also makes a showing here. Admission: FR20.

Musée des Charmettes   ★★★

chemin des Charmettes, ☎ *04-79-33-39-44. About 2km southeast of town.*
Hours open: 10 a.m.–6 p.m. Special hours: Closed noon–2 p.m.; Oct.–Mar., to 4:30 p.m. Closed: Tue.
Situated in the house where Jean-Jacques Rousseau lived with his lover, Madame de Warens, this museum is a reconstruction of the interior of the house as he lived in it. Enjoy the view of Chambéry from the garden and a show depicting his life here (July and Aug. only). A bus leaves from the tourist office at 2:30 p.m. in July and Aug. Admission: FR20.

Where to Stay

Hotels and Resorts

Hotel des Princes   FR260–FR400   ★★★

4 rue de Boigne. ☎ *04-79-33-45-36, FAX: 04-79-70-31-47. In the center of town.*
Single: FR260. Double: FR400.
In the lovely old town of Chambery, the 45 rooms here are the best in town. Greeted in a reception area with an exposed beam ceiling, it's obvious that Old World elegance still exists. The comfortable, soundproof rooms are pretty and come with TV, telephone and private bath. Breakfast is served for FR33, and guests enjoy a restaurant and a bar and lounge in the hotel. Simple but more than adequate. Features: mountain location, air conditioning in rooms. Credit Cards: All Major.

Le France Hotel   FR320–FR440   ★★

22 faubourg Reclus. ☎ *04-79-33-51-18, FAX: 04-79-85-06-30. In the center of town.*
Single: FR320. Double: FR440.
A modern, sleek establishment with good mountain views from the balconies of some of the 48 rooms. Soundproof and air-conditioned, the rooms come with TV, radio, telephone and bath. Breakfast is the only meal served (FR45), and there is a small bar in the lobby. Features: mountain location, air conditioning in rooms, in-room minibars. Credit Cards: All Major.

Novotel Chambéry   FR450–FR480   ★★★

Le Motte Servolex. ☎ *04-79-69-21-27, FAX: 04-79-69-71-13. About 2 km north of Chambery, near La Motte Servolex off of the autoroute.*
Single: FR450. Double: FR480.
Just north of Chambéry, this hotel is convenient for travelers by car who are just passing through. Definitely a chain hotel, the 103 air-conditioned rooms are all

comfortable, spacious clones, with TV, telephone, minibar and private bath. Breakfast costs FR52, and meals are available in the bar and the grill from FR130. Free on-site parking. Features: mountain location, air conditioning in rooms, in-room minibars. Credit Cards: All Major.

Where to Eat

L'Essentiel $ ★★★

183 place de la Gare, Across from the train station. ☎ *04-79-96-97-27.*
Specialties: scallops; ravioli.
Dinner: 7–10:30 p.m., entrées FR50–FR125.
One of the newest additions to Chambéry, L'Essential is quickly establishing itself as a winner. A family affair in the kitchen and the dining room, many inviting dishes are turned out. Most exciting is the dynamic menu that changes with the seasons and the availability of ingredients at the market. Seafood, duckling and pigeon are among the few staple dishes. As with most family restaurants, the reception and personal attention keep guests coming back for more. Set menus start at FR100. Reservations recommended. Credit Cards: All Major.

La Chaumiere $ ★★★

14 rue Denfert-Rochereau, Near the Theatre Dullin. ☎ *04-79-33-16-26.*
Dinner: 7–10:30 p.m., entrées FR60–FR125.
Follow the locals here for the best set menu in Chambéry from FR90–FR180. Enjoy such traditional dishes as foie gras, fresh fish, duckling and red mullet. Especially nice during summer months, the outdoor terrace fills quickly. A good value all around, the wine menu is equally affordable. An intimate affair with pleasant service. Closed: Sun. Credit Cards: V, MC.

Les Princes $$ ★★★★

4 rue de Boigne. ☎ *04-79-33-45-36.*
Dinner: entrées FR200–FR375.
It's a package deal here. With the price of a meal, one can take advantage of the intelligent staff, the respectable wine cellar and the skilled chef—all wrapped up in beautiful surroundings. The cuisine is a new look at classic—a lighter touch. Set menus are from FR165. Reservations required. Credit Cards: All Major.

Directory

To and From

By train from Paris (seven hours) or Grenoble (55 minutes), or by car on the N-6 highway from Lyon or A-41 autoroute from Grenoble.

Tourist Office

24 boulevard de la Colonne; ☎ *(33) 04-79-33-42-47.*

Rail Station

place de la Gàre; ☎ *(33) 04-79-85-50-50.*

Post Office

square Paul Vidal, 73000 Chambéry; ☎ *(33) 04-79-96-69-15.*

Annecy

One of the most picturesque towns in a region chock-full of them, Annecy sits at the northern end of Lac Annecy, surrounded on all sides by snow-capped mountains. Known as the Pearl of the Alps, the lake is pristine, and the town itself has won the title of cleanest city in France, and has been voted the most beautiful garden city several times as well. Memorialized by Cézanne in a famous painting called, unremarkably, "Le Lac d'Annecy," the old Town, with its cobbled streets, houses, and churches dating from the 16th and even 15th centuries, is indeed beguiling. Split into two sections by the Thiou Canal, one of the town's most photographed features is the tiny Palais de l'Ile, a 12th-century mansion once used as a prison but now housing a small history museum. The castle of the Counts of Geneva, begun in the 12th century and expanded from the 14th to the 16th centuries, has turreted walls and towers that may be climbed for a good view of the town, while the Bishop's Palace on rue Ste. Claire is an interesting example of 17th-century cold-weather architecture. The main feature of Annecy, however, is undoubtedly the lake, which can be hiked around, swum in by the hardy during summer, and enjoyed by boat. A boat trip to the tiny village of Talloires on the lakeshore is highly recommended as the best way to see the beautiful scenery of the area, including the 15th-century Château de Duingt which, sadly, is not open to the public. Also nearby, just west of the town is Mont Semnoz; its summit, called the Crêt de Châtillon (a modest to strenuous hike), offers superb views of the valley and nearby Mont Blanc.

What to Do

Historical/Architectural Sites

Château d'Annecy   ★★★★

On the hill, ☎ *04-50-33-87-31.*

Hours open: 10 a.m.–6 p.m. Special hours: Closed noon–2 p.m. Tues.; open daily July - Aug. Closed: Tue.

Worthy of a visit for the fantastic vista alone, the Château d'Annecy also houses the Musée d'Annecy within its 13th-century walls. Regional art and archaeological pieces are on permanent display with interesting temporary exhibits passing through. Admission: FR20.

Palais de l'Isle   ★★★

canal du Thiou, ☎ *04-50-33-87-31. In the old town.*

Hours open: 10 a.m.–6 p.m. Special hours: Closed noon–2 p.m.; in off-season, closed Tues.

A 12th-century prison on a small island in the canal du Thiou. Today there is a small museum tracing local history within its walls. Admission: FR20.

Where to Stay

Hotels and Resorts

L'Imperial Palace   **FR800–FR1200**   ★★★★★

32 avenue d'Albigny. ☎ *04-50-09-30-00, FAX: 04-50-09-33-33. Across a corner of the lake from the center of town.*
Double: FR800–FR1200.

This grand lakeside palace dates to the turn of the century. Made over into the contemporary establishment it is today, it offers splendid views of the lake and the mountains. The 98 huge rooms have balconies or terraces, and come with all of the plush amenities possible. Two restaurants are here, the elegant La Voile and the more casual Brasserie du Parc. Other facilities include a bar, casino, jazz club, beauty center and recently added pool with removable roof. All of this is just a short walk from the heart of town. Features: wheelchair-access rooms, mountain location, pool.

Inns

Demeure de Chavoire   **FR750–FR1000**   ★★★★

71 route d'Annecy. ☎ *04-50-60-04-38, FAX: 04-50-60-05-36. About 3 km west of Annecy.*
Single: FR750. Double: FR1000.

Just outside of Annecy, this cozy inn houses the most charming accommodations in the area. With all of the touches of home and then some, the 13 intimate rooms have names instead of numbers to complement the unique decor of each one. All come with TV, telephone, minibar and private bath. It's the little things that larger hotels miss, such as chocolates by the bed, that make this place so irresistible. Tranquil and adorned with antiques, this little inn's cheerful attitude is carried on by the supremely courteous staff. Features: mountain location, in-room minibars. Credit Cards: All Major.

Where to Eat

Au Lilas Rose   **$**   ★★

passage de l'Eveche, In the center of the old town. ☎ *04-50-45-37-08.*

A casual restaurant with a wide variety of dishes, including fondue, lamb and even pizza. Fixed menus start at just FR45. Another franc-saver is the **Restaurant Le Phenix Imperial** at *8 rue Poquier* (☎ *04-50-45-48-57*). A rare find in France—Vietnamese food. Main dishes start at FR25, as do the tasty desserts. *Open 11:45 a.m.–1:30 p.m. and 6:30–11 p.m.; closed Mon.*

Auberge de l'Eridan   **$$$**   ★★★★★

13 vieille route des Pensieres, Lakeside in the small town of Veyrier-du-Lac. ☎ *04-50-60-24-00.*
Dinner: 7–9:30 p.m., entrées FR200–FR400.

Chef Marc Veyrat continues to reign as the finest chef in the region. In this lakeside château completely refurbished to suit the visionary ideals of the chef-owner, the restaurant flourishes as one of the best in the world. A naturalist by passion, Marc only uses the freshest ingredients, including rare mountain berries, in his carefully crafted cuisine. Every dish on the menu, from the pike perch sausage to the pork gelee with caviar, dazzles the critics, the refined client and the layperson. Reservations are a must to have the privilege to be seated in this gallery of masterpiece cuisine. Set menus from FR500. Closed: Tues. Credit Cards: All Major.

Le Belvedere $$$ ★★★★

7 chemin du Belvedere, About 2 km from Annecy, on the route de Semnoz. Located at Le Belvedere. ☎ *04-50-45-04-90.*
Dinner: 8–9:30 p.m., entrées FR145–FR250.

In business for more than two decades, Le Belvedere continues to dazzle its loyal clientele. Dining is best in the summer months when the views of the lake and town are enjoyed from the terrace. Any time of year, however, the food is spectacular. Fresh and imaginative, the chef focuses on seafood dishes such as sea bass with wild mushrooms and scallops soup. It's all finished off nicely with light and sweet desserts and a late harvest wine. Set menus are from FR200–FR350. *Closed mid-Oct.– early Dec. and early Apr.–mid-Apr. Closed: Mon.* Amenities: outside dining, reservations recommended. Credit Cards: V, MC.

Directory

To and From

By train from Paris (four hours), Lyon (two hours), or Grenoble (two hours), or by car on the A-41 autoroute from Lyon and Chambéry or the N-508 highway from the A-40 autoroute from the west.

Tourist Office

1 rue Jean Jaurès; ☎ *(33) 04-50-45-00-33.*

Rail Station

place de la Gàre; ☎ *(33) 04-50-33-59-00.*

Post Office

4 rue des Glières, 74000 Annecy; ☎ *(33) 04-50-33-67-00.*

Chamonix

Located at the foot of Mont Blanc, Chamonix is a dizzying town—dizzying in altitude, in beauty, and in price. Nevertheless it is *de rigeur* to make the trip here, even if you visit no other site in the Alps. Nothing else compares to Chamonix. Nearby is the Glacier des Bossons, known as the Mer de Glace, a nine-mile-long glacier shifting more than 300 feet every year, which you can reach on foot in a couple of hours or by special-service train. There are *télépheriques* to several nearby peaks, but the most impressive excursion, by far, is the cable-car ride to the top of the 12,605-foot crest of the Aiguilles de Chamonix. The round-trip ride (allow four hours to give yourself some time at the top) costs a heady FR160, and you'll likely feel light-headed in the thin air at the summit, but the views of Mont Blanc and the rest of the Alps—on both sides of the France-Italy border—are unbeatable. Countless hiking routes radiate from the town; all are well-marked and detailed in a map available at the tourist office. Nearby are numerous ski runs; the French national team trains here, and the first Winter Olympics were held here in

1924. Chamonix is also the site of the National Mountaineering School and the Alpine Museum, as well as the point of departure of the first recorded ascent of Mont Blanc (15,676 feet) by Dr. Michel Paccard and Jacques Balmat on August 8, 1786.

Chamonix lies at the foot of Mont Blanc, Europe's highest peak.

What to Do

Special Tours/Excursions

Téléphérique Aiguille du Midi ★★★★★

Hours open: 6 a.m.–5 p.m. Special hours: Winter, 8 a.m.–4:45 p.m.
Until you're past the halfway point of this trip (7544 feet, at the Plan de l'Aiguille), you'll be singing the verses "…where little cable cars, climb halfway to the stars…" But soon enough, you will be seeing stars, and the words will freeze on your lips, as the altitude changes drastically upon reaching the craggy needle, the Aiguille du Midi. At 12,606 feet, this is the highest cable-car ride in the world, affording the intrepid with uninterrupted views of Mont Blanc and the Vallee Blanche, Europe's largest glacier (unless obscured by clouds). After a brief recovery, you can hike back to town (one way is FR134, round-trip FR160) or continue on to Italy (you'll need a passport) for FR240. Don't forget to wear warm clothes, and try to get an early start. Two shorter and less-harrying excursions are to a four-mile-long glacier: the **Mer de Glace** (*04-50-53-12-54*, May–Sept., 8 a.m.–6 p.m.), reached by rack railway next to the main station, at avenue de la Gare.

Sports and Recreation

Chamonix Mountain Bike ★★

138 rue des Moulins, ☎ *04-50-53-54-76.*
Hours open: 9 a.m.–7 p.m. Special hours: Winter, closed noon–2 p.m.

This outfit arranges mountain bike tours at FR2500 and up and daily bike rentals for FR100. For hiking tours as well as bike tours, contact **Compagnie des Guides** *(190 place de l'Eglise,* ☎ *04-50-53-00-88);* bike tours are quite a bit cheaper and shorter (two hours in length, FR600, available July–Aug.). These experienced guides will take you on hiking trips to Mont Blanc and other locations during the summer months for FR500–FR2500.

Where to Stay

Hotels and Resorts

Hotel Mont-Blanc FR550–FR1300 ★★★

62 allee du Majestic. ☎ *04-50-53-05-64, FAX: 04-50-55-89-44.*
Single: FR550–FR775. Double: FR830–FR1300.
A beautiful hotel faintly reflecting the Belle Epoque period, this resort hotel dates to the turn of the century. Its location in the center of Chamonix is sheltered by its gardens, creating a peaceful environment for the 43 rooms. The mountain-view rooms sport pinewood paneling and satellite TV, telephone, radio, minibar and bath. After a meal in the restaurant, the Matafan, guests warm up with a soothing drink in the bar until 1 a.m. Amenities include a year-round heated outdoor pool, sauna, tennis court and shuttle bus to the ski slopes in the winter. The accommodating staff works hard to keep this one of the finest hotels in town. Features: pool, tennis, sauna, in-room minibars. Credit Cards: V, MC, DC, A.

Jeu de Paume FR680–FR1250 ★★★

705 route du Chapeau, Le Lavacher. ☎ *04-50-54-03-76, FAX: 04-50-54-10-75.*
Single: FR680–FR970. Double: FR970–FR1250.
Situated in the village of Lavancher, this small hotel snuggles against the mountains with views of Chamonix and the Vallee d'Argentiere. Built in traditional chalet style, this charming hotel has 22 rooms with TV, radio, minibar, private bath and some with balcony. Five of the rooms are suites, and all are wheelchair-accessible. Dining and drinking options include a restaurant, bar and 24-hour room service. Leisure facilities include an indoor pool, sauna, tennis court and skiing and golf facilities nearby. A shuttle bus whisks guests into Chamonix for other restaurant choices and shopping. Peaceful surroundings, comfortable accommodations and personal service. Features: mountain location, pool, tennis, skiing, in-room minibars. Credit Cards: All Major.

Inns

Albert 1er FR570–FR920 ★★

119 impasse Montenvers. ☎ *04-50-53-05-09, FAX: 04-50-55-95-48.*
Rated Restaurant: *Albert 1er.*
Single: FR570–FR690. Double: FR690–FR920.
This chalet-style hotel received its name in 1905 when King Albert of Belgium stayed here on a holiday. Since its inception at the turn of the century, this four-story hotel has stood out as one of the choice hotels in Chamonix. Recently renovated in a Tyrolean style, there are 30 charming rooms, each comfortable and well-equipped with TV, telephone and bath. Although a bit smallish, many of the rooms open up to views of the mountains from their private balconies. The reception is

genuinely warm, and the tasty breakfasts of warm rolls, honey and homemade yogurt start the guests off right for their active days in the Alps. In addition to the pool, sauna and gym in the hotel, there are fantastic golf, tennis and skiing facilities nearby. A superb Alpine chalet. Features: mountain location, pool, tennis, skiing, sauna, balcony or patio, fitness center. Credit Cards: All Major.

Au Bon Coin **FR214–FR380** ★★

80 avenue de l'Aiguille-du-Midi. ☎ 04-50-53-15-67.
Single: FR214–FR330. Double: FR260–FR380.

This hotel is very French as well as alpine. It has 20 clean and well-kept rooms, all with private bathrooms. Many have views of the surrounding mountainside, as well as terraces. This place is tranquil and there is private parking as well as a garden. The hotel and its restaurant are closed May through June and October through mid-December. Features: mountain location, skiing, balcony or patio. Credit Cards: All Major.

Where to Eat

Albert-1er **$$** ★★★

119, imp. du Montenvers. ☎ 04-50-53-05-09.
Lunch: 12:30–1:30 p.m., FR145–FR255.
Dinner: 7:30–9:30 p.m., entrées FR145–FR255.

Chef Pierre Carrier skillfully combines luxury ingredients like caviar, truffles and the purest virgin olive oils with only the finest local fish, cheeses and produce. Many of his dishes are truly inspired, including a chocolate dessert in a bluish cream made from gentian flowers. His wife, Martine, presides over the handsome dining room paneled in wood with windows facing a picture-postcard vista of the surrounding mountains. A special, romantic experience. Amenities: own baking, reservations required. Credit Cards: All Major.

Atmosphere **$$** ★★

113 place Balmat. ☎ 04-50-55-97-97.
Lunch: Noon–2 p.m., FR100–FR175.
Dinner: 7:30–11 p.m., entrées FR100–FR175.

Atmosphere, as its name implies, offers a socko view of Mont Blanc, as well as a delicious, untrendy menu (including a FR100 fixed-price meal) and friendly service. For fondue, *raclette* (potatoes, cheese, pickles) and grills in a traditional mountain setting, head for the well-known **La Tartiffle**, *87 rue des Moulins (☎ 04-50-53-2-02);* fixed-price menus start at FR75. *Open daily, except Tues., until 11 p.m.* Cheaper still is a cafeteria, **Le Fonds des Gires**, *350 Ave. du Bois du Bouchet (☎ 04-50-55-85-76),* with menus from FR45. Sandwiches are available at **Poco Loco**, *45 rue du Dr. Paccard;* in season open until 2 a.m. Reservations required. Credit Cards: All Major.

Directory

To and from

By train from Paris (eight hours), Lyon (four hours), or Annecy (two-and-a-half hours), or by car on the N-506 highway or from Italy under the Mont Blanc tunnel.

Tourist Office

place du Triangle de l'Amitié; ☎ (33) 04-50-53-00-24.

LYON AND THE ALPS

Rail Station

    avenue de la Gàre; ☎ *(33) 04-50-53-00-44.*

Post Office

    place Jacques Balmat, 74400 Chamonix; ☎ *(33) 04-50-53-15-90.*

Ski Resorts

Courchevel 1850

☎ *(33) 04-79-08-00-29.*

Where to Stay

Hotels and Resorts

Byblos des Neiges   **FR1500–FR3560**   ★★★★

    au Jardin Alpin. ☎ *04-79-00-98-00, FAX: 04-79-00-98-01.*
    Rated Restaurant: *Byblos des Neiges.*
    Single: FR1500–FR1650. Double: FR2040–FR3560.
    In this ski town known as much for its high taste and high profile as it is for its high
elevation, the Byblos des Neiges blends in perfectly. A virtual snow palace in the forest, this tops the list of luxury hotels in Courchevel. A subtle blend of rustic and
contemporary, the hotel opened in 1984 as one of the largest in town. Features
include fireplace lounges and chic boutiques, an indoor pool, sauna, Jacuzzi, Turkish bath, fitness center with massage services, hair salon and heated garage. The 78
plush rooms have TV, telephone, radio, minibar and bath; most come with loggia
and panoramic windows to open up the snug space. There are two restaurants, one
featuring elaborate seafood platters and the other serving lunch buffets, and a piano
bar. Concierge, laundry, dry cleaning and room services are efficiently provided.
The luxury of a first class hotel and the relaxed ambience of a ski town meld to make
this the best choice for accommodations in all of Courchevel. Features: wheelchair-access rooms, pool, sauna, in-room minibars, fitness center. Credit Cards: All Major.

Inns

Bellecote   **FR1000–FR1750**   ★★★

    route de l'Altiport. ☎ *04-79-08-10-19, FAX: 04-79-08-17-16.*
    Single: FR1000–FR1250. Double: FR1250–FR1750.
    Located near the Bellecote run, this seven-story chalet sits on a solid stone foundation. Recognized for its quality construction of the exterior, the interior showcases
interesting objects the owner imported from Afghanistan and the Himalayas. In
addition to the exotic objects adorning the 53 wood-paneled rooms, each comes
with TV, telephone, minibar, bath and terrace. Its central location affords easy
access to the ski slopes, and there is a heated indoor pool, a health club and a sauna.
The restaurant offers full meals from FR330 in the elegant dining room. An impressive establishment with a warm, friendly ambience. Features: mountain location,
pool, skiing, sauna, in-room minibars, fitness center. Credit Cards: All Major.

Hotel des Neiges   **FR1000–FR1750**   ★★★

    Courchevel 1850. ☎ *04-79-08-03-77, FAX: 04-79-08-18-70.*
    Single: FR1000–FR1250. Double: FR1250–FR1750.

This Relais and Châteaux winter hotel thrives at its location next to the ski slopes. Omnipopular with the film world, the lively atmosphere sets the scene in the fireside piano bar, cocktail lounge and restaurant. Peace and relaxation are easily found in the 42 guest rooms which are accented with antiques, TV, telephone, radio and private bath. The hotel also has a terrace, sauna and Jacuzzi. Des Neiges welcomes an international crowd seeking a social yet relaxing environment. Features: mountain location, skiing, fitness center. Credit Cards: All Major.

La Sivoliere   **FR725–FR1870**   ★★★

quartier Les Chenus. ☎ 04-79-08-08-33, FAX: 04-79-08-15-73.
Rated Restaurant: *La Sivoliere.*
Single: FR725–FR1000. Double: FR1000–FR1870.
Under the snow-covered pines, La Sivoliere's warmth and welcome have attracted such distinguished guests as the Spanish royal family. While small in size compared with other neighborhood hotels, this modern establishment is big on character. Along with the coordinated fabrics, smart furnishings and fireplaces, the public areas are lavished with 18th- and 19th-century antiques. The 32 intimate and functional bedrooms are elegantly furnished, and the modern conveniences include TV, telephone and bath. After carving up the ski slopes with those parallel lines, relax in the tea room or wind down with the gym's sauna and steambath. Breakfast is served for FR75, and the dining room delights with full meals from FR200. Features: mountain location, skiing, fitness center. Credit Cards: All Major.

Where to Eat

Chabichou   **$$**   ★★★

quartier Les Chenus. ☎ 04-79-08-00-55.
Lunch: Noon–2 p.m., FR200–FR275.
Dinner: 8–10 p.m., entrées FR200–FR275.
There have been quite a few changes made to this well-known chalet-style hotel-restaurant: It's been remodeled recently, it's now open all year (it used to close from Apr.–Dec.), and prices have come down considerably. Cuisine of the Savoie region is served either on the terrace or in the dining room with big picture windows and a glass roof; wherever you dine, the views are amazing, especially in winter. Amenities: happening bar, reservations required. Credit Cards: V, MC, DC, A, E.

La Chalet de Pierres   **$$**   ★★

au Jardin Alpin, Near the Verdon ski slope. ☎ 04-79-08-18-61.
Specialties: charcuterie, pommes frites.
Lunch: Noon–10 p.m., FR130–FR155.
Dinner: Noon–10 p.m., entrées FR130–FR155.
Inexpensive for the area, and highly popular with the pre- and après-ski crowd, who can swish in directly from the Verdon ski slope outside. It's a two-story establishment with a terrace and fireplaces. Good protein-rich meat dishes are served to get the blood going (steaks, chicken) as well as daily specials, and there's a dessert bar. Less expensive is the **Bel Air 1650**, at the top of the Montriond lift (☎ 04-79-08-00-93), with hearty set meals for a little over FR100. Amenities: outside dining, cafestop, reservations required. Credit Cards: V, MC, E.

Le Bateau Ivre **$$** **★★**

quartier Les Chenus, In La Pomme de Pin. Located at La Pomme de Pin. ☎ *04-79-08-02-46.*
Lunch: 12:30–2:15 p.m., FR175–FR300.
Dinner: 7:30–10 p.m., entrées FR175–FR300.

The gracious, capable Jacob family runs this two-star restaurant in an American-owned hotel in the French Alps, and so far the partnership is working well, with the owners staying out of the Jacobs' way. The mountain views from the terrace are stunning, as are Jean-Pierre Jacob's modern French dishes, including calf's sweetbreads with potatoes and a chocolate mousse soufflé. Regional wines (Roussette de Savoie). Amenities: outside dining, own baking, reservations required. Credit Cards: All Major.

Les Deux Alpes

Where to Stay

Hotels and Resorts

Chalet-Hotel Mounier **FR350–FR700** **★★★**

P'tit Polyte. ☎ *04-76-80-56-90, FAX: 04-76-79-56-51. Near town center; P'tit Polyte.*
Single: FR350. Double: FR700.

From the process of booking a room through checking out, the staff is an absolute pleasure. All of the 48 rooms in this stone chalet are superbly comfortable. Some include balconies. Guaranteed to feel at home, great attention has been paid to the soft touches and details. Plush facilities include Turkish baths, indoor pool, Jacuzzi, solarium and billiard room. All of this and an impressive restaurant that is only getting better. Features: wheelchair-access rooms, mountain location, skiing. Credit Cards: V, MC.

La Berangere **FR550–FR850** **★★★**

At the base of the slopes. ☎ *04-76-79-24-11, FAX: 04-76-79-55-08. At the foot of the ski slopes.*
Double: FR550–FR850.

A Relais and Châteaux member, le Berangere sits directly on the ski slopes. A four-story structure with 59 rooms, the facility is well-equipped. All of the rooms have cable TV, radio, telephone, bath, hair dryer and balcony. Some rooms are set aside for nonsmokers. Watch the skiers do the downhill swoosh as you dine in the restaurant. Or, if you are one of those skiers, return to the hotel to relax in the heated pools, Jacuzzi, sauna and fitness room. The hotel closes in May, Oct. and Nov. Features: wheelchair-access rooms, mountain location, pool, skiing, sauna, balcony or patio, nonsmoking rooms, fitness center. Credit Cards: All Major.

Megeve

☎ *(33) 04-50-21-27-28.*

Where to Stay

Hotels and Resorts

Chalet du Mont d'Arbois **FR1130–FR1700** **★★★**

route du Mont-d'Arbois. ☎ *04-50-21-25-03, FAX: 04-50-21-24-79.*
Rated Restaurant: *Chalet du Mont d'Arbois.*

Single: FR1130–FR1520. Double: FR1520–FR1700.

Two words to describe this Rothschild-family chalet—rustic and luxurious. Built in 1928, Nadine de Rothschild designed the interior and runs the entire show. Overlooking Megeve, the chalet offers fine views from the 20 well-appointed rooms that are furnished with bleached pine, antiques, comforters, TV, radio, telephone, bath and some with balcony. The public rooms reflect the rustic side of the chalet, with exposed beam ceilings, fireplaces and antiques. The house restaurant serves the best gourmet meals in town, and the wine list features some bottles from the Rothschilds' vineyards in Bordeaux. The accommodations, service and food make it worthy of its Relais and Châteaux status. Features: mountain location, pool, tennis, skiing, air conditioning in rooms. Credit Cards: All Major.

Fer a Cheval　　　　　　　　　　**FR675–FR1000**　　　　　　★★

36 route du Cret-d'Arbois. ☎ *04-50-21-30-39.*
Rated Restaurant: *Fer a Cheval.*
Single: FR675–FR820. Double: FR845–FR1000.

Two connected mountain chalets compose this popular, town-center hotel, designed in traditional Savoy style. Busy in the summer with the mountain sightseers and busy in the winter with the skiers, this hotel keeps a full guest list. The 30 rooms are comfortable and spacious, each with TV, telephone and bath. The fireside lounge warms the winter folk with hot tea, and guests can also enjoy meals there. The sauna and Jacuzzi await after a long day of fun in the snow, and the lovely garden and pool are revealed to the summer visitors. The restaurant serves meals starting at FR240 in the old-fashioned dining room. An intimate mountain atmosphere with friendly service from the small, efficient staff. Closed from Mid Apr.–June and Mid Sept.–Dec. Features: wheelchair-access rooms, mountain location, pool, skiing, air conditioning in rooms, sauna. Credit Cards: All Major.

Méribel

☎ *(33) 04-79-08-60-01.*

Where to Stay

Hotels and Resorts

Hotel l'Antares　　　　　　　　**FR1600–FR2560**　　★★★★★

Le Belvedere. ☎ *04-79-23-28-23, FAX: 04-79-23-28-18. Near the ski slopes.*
Single: FR1600–FR2450. Double: FR1940–FR2560.

This is as good as it gets. Opened in 1991, this purely deluxe hotel pampers its well-heeled guests with luxury only found in the mystical Alps. Within this château are 76 guest rooms with air conditioning, satellite TV, telephone, private bath and some with en-suite Jacuzzi. The 16 uniquely decorated suites all come with double hearth fireplaces. Highly polished marble and wood lavish the four-story lobby and atrium, with similar decor throughout the public spaces. In addition to three restaurants and a piano bar, there is an indoor/outdoor pool, four Jacuzzis, massage treatments and hair styling. Ideal for those "skiers" seeking the post-skiing comforts more than the skiing itself. Features: mountain location, pool, skiing, air conditioning in rooms, balcony or patio. Credit Cards: All Major.

Méribel caters to the well-heeled with several sophisticated ski resorts.

Hotel le Chalet   **FR1630–FR2460**   ★★★★★

Le Belvedere. ☎ 04-79-23-28-23, FAX: 04-79-00-56-22. About 3 km from the village
center; at the foot of the slopes.
Single: FR1630–FR1950. Double: FR1660–FR2460.

Just across from the slopes, this ski chalet is the product of the personal attention the husband and wife owners have devoted to creating the ideal ski chalet. Completely built of pine, it opened in 1989 and quickly became one of the best hotels in town. The 35 rooms all feature a fireplace, balcony, plush carpets, TV, radio, telephone and large bath. Even the kids will appreciate the thoughtfulness of the playroom and the film shown each afteroon. Modern facilities include a heated pool, Jacuzzi and sauna. Every ski lover's dream. Features: mountain location, pool, skiing, sauna, balcony or patio. Credit Cards: All Major.

| **Mont Vallon Hotel** | **FR1200–FR2400** | ★★★★ |

Méribel-Mottaret. ☎ *04-79-00-44-00, FAX: 04-79-00-46-93. In Le Mottaret; about 6 km south of Meribel.*
Double: FR1200–FR2400.

Providing easy access to the 3 Valleys ski complex, Mont Vallon is a huge ski-hotel. There are 90 comfortable, elegant rooms with TV, telephone and large bath. Four of the eight suites come with fireplace. Dining options include two restaurants, and the piano bar is a pleasant way to wind down the evening. Leisure facilities include a heated pool, sauna, Jacuzzi, whirlpool, gym and squash court. Even with this many rooms and facilities, it manages to keep an intimate atmosphere. Features: wheelchair-access rooms, mountain location, pool, skiing, sauna, fitness center. Credit Cards: All Major.

Val d'Isere

☎ *(33) 04-79-06-06-60.*

Where to Stay

Hotels and Resorts

| **Christiana Hotel** | **FR950–FR1700** | ★★★ |

At the mountain. ☎ *04-79-06-08-25, FAX: 04-79-41-11-10. Next to the ski slopes.*
Double: FR950–FR1700.

Operating since 1952, the Christiana has one of the best situations in town. Just a short walk from the ski slopes, the 68 rooms are equipped with telephone, bath and balcony. Relax with an international group of skiers in one of the three lounges, one of which has a fireplace. The restaurant and bar are lively and reasonably priced. A sauna and a hydrotherapy center finish out the facilities. Features: wheelchair-access rooms, mountain location, pool, skiing, sauna. Credit Cards: All Major.

| **Hotel Val d'Isere"** | **FR980–FR1800** | ★★★★ |

At the ski slopes. ☎ *04-79-06-08-30, FAX: 04-79-06-04-41. At the foot of the mountain.*
Single: FR980–FR1250. Double: FR1400–FR1800.

The most luxurious hotel in Val d'Isere. It is a modern facility with extensive facilities. There are 52 rooms with cable TV, telephone, radio, bath and hair dryer. The best rooms have a VCR, minibar and balcony. One can spend the entire day inside the hotel and not get bored. There is a heated pool, gym, Jacuzzi, sauna and adjacent water therapy center. No matter how the day is spent, be sure to return for a meal in the elegant dining room, and wind down the night in the piano bar. The hotel closes from early May through June and Sept. through Nov. Features: moun-

tain location, pool, skiing, sauna, balcony or patio, in-room minibars, fitness center.
Credit Cards: All Major.

Val Thorens

☎ *(33) 04-79-00-08-08.*

Where to Stay

Hotels and Resorts

Fitz Roy Hotel   **FR1800–FR2500**   ★★★★

☎ *04-79-00-04-78, FAX: 04-79-00-06-11. Near town center.*
Double: FR1800–FR2500.
This ski resort hotel offers 37 country style rooms, not missing a beat with elegance
and service. Each spacious, cozy room has TV, telephone, radio, minibar, balcony
and bath with whirlpool. Three of the seven suites have a fireplace (FR2700–
FR4800). Guests seeking a little relaxation enjoy the fitness room, pool, saunas and
beauty center. The restaurant, although not as impressive as the hotel, serves inventive dishes at reasonable prices. A Relais and Châteaux rated hotel. Features: wheelchair-access rooms, mountain location, pool, skiing, in-room minibars, fitness
center. Credit Cards: All Major.

Le Sherpa   **FR500–FR500**   ★★★

☎ *04-79-00-00-70, FAX: 04-79-00-08-03.*
Double: FR500.
Tranquility is assured at this slope-side hotel. The 42 rooms are fully equipped and
boast lovely views from the balconies. A sauna, Jacuzzi, solarium and lounge bar top
off the excellent amenities. Decent food at good prices in the restaurant. The room
rates listed are for half board. Features: skiing, sauna, country location. Credit Cards: MC.

Other Ski Resorts

Albertville
☎ *(33) 04-79-32-04-22.*

Les Arc
☎ *(33) 04-79-41-55-45.*

Avoriaz
☎ *(33) 04-50-74-02-11.*

Châtel
☎ *(33) 04-50-73-22-44.*

Les Houches
☎ *(33) 04-50-55-50-62.*

Les Saisies
☎ *(33) 04-79-38-90-30.*

CENTRAL FRANCE

Spectacular Gorges du Tarn winds 50km from Ispagnac to Millau.

What Makes Central France So French?

1. *Some of the best whitewater rafting in Europe combined with narrow gorges, big-horned sheep and griffon vultures.*

2. *Hot- and cold-running Vichy to cure everything from rheumatism to sex manias (try the cold).*

3. *Volcanic mountains and unadorned châteaux.*

4. *One of France's most prized and revered Black Madonnas (don't seek her out—she'll find you).*

5. *Robert Louis Stevenson hiked Cevennes with his faithful donkey in 1878.*

Central France is a remote, mountainous region that has largely escaped modernization and tourist hell. The Massif Central, a huge plateau of hard granite crisscrossed with volcanic mountain ranges, forms the heart of this region, which encompasses the administrative regions of Auvergne, Limousin and the northern Rhone valley. The extreme altitude seems to set the central area apart from the rest of the country; the French are joyously rediscovering the region and working hard to preserve both its natural beauty and independent character. Small towns dotted on the hillsides have not changed in centuries, the châteaux to be found here are feudal and defensive, unadorned by Renaissance frippery; the churches and cathedrals somber Romanesque, not lofty Gothic as elsewhere. You can get to the center of the region, Clermont-Ferrand, easily by train, but in order to get around elsewhere you'll need a car. The most attractive feature of the area is its natural beauty—the rolling hills and volcanic lakes don't attract the Alpinists of the Pyrénées nor the skiers of the Alps. The region is usually uncrowded, peaceful, and perfect for hiking and breathing the clean mountain air. A luxury for the visitor who has only two or three weeks to see the major sights of the country, Central France is a treat for those who take the time for an extended visit.

History

Site of a great Gallic victory over the Romans at Clermont-Ferrand in 52 B.C., the region was nevertheless brought under Roman control before the birth of Christ. It was one of the first regions of France penetrated by the Gospel, and soon developed into a center of Christianity. The bishop of Puy-en-Velay was one of the first pilgrims to visit the tomb of St. James in Spain, and following his path came hundreds of thousands of others from across Europe. The Middle Ages saw the route across the high mountain-plateau become an important rallying and departure point for pilgrims. At the same time, the relative stability of the region made it attractive to a new generation of Roman leaders—the popes. The first Crusade was ordered and set off from Clermont-Ferrand at the end of the 12th century. Because of its distance from the borders and its rugged landscape, the region remained securely in the hands of the French during the conflicts with England, held during the Hundred Years' War first by the Duke of Berry, then by King Charles VII, although he preferred the home comforts of the Loire for his residence. During the apogee of the monarchy of united France, Central France remained a sleepy backwater, its small agricultural communities unchanged by the Renaissance and even relatively unscarred by the Revolution. For a brief period, the area's hot springs attracted bourgeoisie visitors from Paris during the 19th century, but even in Vichy, center of the spa craze, the hubbub soon died down and today the city remains largely as it was 100 years ago. Vichy was the site of the most significant historical period in the region in the 20th century, when the French government fled there after the

Nazis took Paris and voted to collaborate with the German invaders rather than fight to the end. This took place even as Lyon, just to the southwest, was becoming the center for the Resistance. Since the end of the war, Central France has lapsed back into its quiet agricultural ways, notwithstanding the tire industry at Clermont-Ferrand, and remains one of the most tranquil regions in the country.

Some of the finest cheeses in the country come from Central France.

Cuisine

As befitting a down-to-earth country region, the cuisine of Central France is unassuming, hearty and wholesome. Lamb *(agneau)* is served often in the south, where sheep pastures abound; in the northwest and near Clermont-Ferrand, big game, such as venison and wild boar, is more common. You won't find the foo-foo US$20 entrées and *nouvelle cuisine* of Paris and Lyon here, but the region has some specialties that will hit the spot after a day's hiking in the hills. *Truffade*, a cheese-smothered potato dish, is a staple, as is salted pork with lentils, *bourriol*, stuffed cabbage and *potée Auvergnate*, a hearty meat-and-vegetable soup. Some of France's finest cheeses come from the region, including those of the Cantal appellation, of which *fourme* gave its name to *fromage* overall. *St. Nectaire*, loosely translated as holy nectar, is another favorite. The wines of the region are not spectacular, but Saint Pourçain and Courent among the whites and Boudes among the reds are acceptable local vintages.

Clermont-Ferrand

Built in the center of the volcanic region and itself on an extinct volcano, Clermont-Ferrand echoes the dark hues of the basalt-strewn volcanic fields—the majority of the city's buildings are constructed of black basalt rock. The city was an important Celtic settlement before the arrival of the Romans, capital of the Arverni tribe that gave its name to the region of Auvergne. Here Julius Caesar suffered one of the most significant defeats of his conquest of France there at the hands of the chieftain Vercingétorix in 52 B.C. (the great Gallic leader is immortalized in a statue in the *place de Jaude*), but Caesar returned later the same year to take control of the city for good.

A cathedral has stood in Clermont-Ferrand since the fifth century, on the site where the imposing Cathédrale de Notre Dame de l'Assomption now stands. Built in the 13th century in black lava rock, whose strength enabled craftsmen to create especially slender Gothic-style pillars, the exterior of the dark-colored building takes on a haunting, almost sinister look. The main facade and the two spires are much more recent, constructed in the mid-19th century, but much of the stained glass is from the 12th to 15th centuries. Close by is an even older religious temple, the Basilica de Notre Dame du Port, built around 1150 in unmistakably sober and somber Romanesque style. The city was such an important site to early Christianity that in 1095 the Catholic church held a major synod in the city, culminating in the order to reconquer the Holy Land of Pope Urban II. This marked the beginning of the First Crusade, which resulted in the capture of Jerusalem three years later.

Clermont-Ferrand's more modern history is much more urbane. In about 1830, a partnership between two local merchants, Aristide Barbier and Edouard Daubrée, launched the manufacture of agricultural machinery and rubber belts and hoses—the start of the Michelin tire empire, which is still based in the city. In 1891, Barbier's grandsons, André and Edouard Michelin, invented the removable bicycle tire, and in 1895 the pneumatic car tire; the company has since given the world the steel-belted and radial tires, and, of course, the chubby Michelin Man.

Among the city's many museums, the Musée de Ranquet and the Musée des Beaux Arts are the two that pay homage to Blaise Pascal, the 17th-century child prodigy and genius who wrote some of France's most important philosophy and science treatises of the era.

What to Do

Historical/Architectural Sites

Basilique de Notre-Dame-du-Port ★★★

> *rue du Port,* ☎ *04-73-91-32-94. In the northeast section of the old town.*
> *Hours open: 8:30 a.m.–7 p.m.*

This Romanesque 12th-century basilica is identified by its four radiating chapels and octagonal tower. Within the volcanic-rock walls is the crypt beholding the black Madonna. Stop by in the morning to see the interior at its best through the light of the stained-glass windows.

Cathedrale de Notre-Dame-de-l'Assomption ★★★★

> *rue de la Cathedrale,* ☎ *04-73-92-46-61. On the top of rue de Gras.*
> *Hours open: 2–7 p.m. Special hours: Sun., 9:30 a.m.–7 p.m.*

Built from dark volcanic stone in the 13th century, this cathedral is one of the finest examples of Gothic architecture in France. Phenomenal peaked arches on the outside and impressive stained-glass windows on the inside. The contrast of the illuminated windows against the dark interior is awesome. Tours of the windows are given in French during the summer months. A not-to-be-missed sight in Clermont-Ferrand.

Museums and Exhibits

Musée des Beaux-Arts ★★★

> *rue du Seminaire,* ☎ *04-73-23-08-49.*
> *Hours open: 10 a.m.–6 p.m. Closed: Mon.*

This former 18th-century convent was renovated in 1991 and transformed into the Musée des Beaux-Arts. Within this vibrant structure are minor but interesting works dating back to the 1400s and miscellaneous artifacts from the 1100s. Although not carrying any of the big names, it manages to keep an afternoon's interest. Admission: FR21.

Musée du Ranquet ★★★

> *34 rue des Gras,* ☎ *04-73-37-38-63. Near the cathedral.*

Situated in the 16th-century mansion called the Architects' House, the Musée du Ranquet features regional history with a variety of displays. From Pascal's calculating machine to wooden furniture to shoes that used to be worn by the people of Auvergne, the museum relays a good story of local heritage. While the admission

price is right, the interest is questionable. *Open June–Sept., 10 a.m.–noon and 2–6 p.m.; Oct.–May, to 5 p.m.; closed Sun. morning and Mon.* Admission: FR12.

Where to Stay

Hotels and Resorts

Gallieni Hotel   FR210–FR330   ★★

51 rue Bonnabaud. ☎ *04-73-93-59-69, FAX: 04-73-34-89-29. South of the historic center of town.*
Single: FR210–FR300. Double: FR250–FR330.

An inexpensive motor hotel, just south of the historic town's center. There are 80 rooms with TV, telephone, minibar and private bath. All of the rooms are comfortable and modern, with the original design from the 1970s. Meeting facilities accommodate up to 170 people. Breakfast is FR40, and the hotel restaurant, La Charade, offers a good, value-minded menu. Credit Cards: All Major.

Mercure Centre Gergovie   FR360–FR485   ★★

82 boulevard Gergovia. ☎ *221-4542, 04-73-34-46-46, FAX: 04-73-34-46-36. About 2 km from the train station, facing the Puy-de-Dome.*
Single: FR360–FR440. Double: FR400–FR485.

Centrally located near the beautiful Jardin Lecoq, this multistory hotel opened in 1972. Formerly the Altea Hotel, it has 124 rooms. The chambers are soundproof and kept radiantly clean. Each is equipped with TV, telephone, minibar and private bath or shower. La Retirade, the hotel restaurant, serves great food from FR115, and there is a bar. Always a safe, albeit not so charming bet as a chain hotel. Features: wheelchair-access rooms, in-room minibars, in-room conference facilities. Credit Cards: All Major.

Where to Eat

Gerrard Truchetet $$ ★★★

Rond-Point de la Pardieu. ☎ *04-73-27-74-17.*
Dinner: 7–9:30 p.m., entrées FR125–FR250.

No hype, no pomp—just straightforward, good food. A modest establishment with a warm welcome and no fluff. Consider the goat cheese, any of the salads or any other home-cooked special. The generous set menu starts at FR110 for lunch during the week and FR145 for dinner. Closed: Sun. Reservations recommended. Credit Cards: V.

Jean-Yves Bath $$ ★★★★

place du Marche St.-Pierre. ☎ *04-73-31-23-23.*
Dinner: 7:30–9:15 p.m., entrées FR100–FR225.

The second floor of this building is occupied by the modern dining room of chef Jean-Yves Bath. It is here that such dishes as rabbit salad, fish salad, roast calf's head and lobster vinaigrette are served by the professional staff. Following these original dishes, any number of exquisite desserts may be ordered to complete the entire "Bath experience." Set menus are FR160 for weekday lunch and FR260 for dinners. On the street level, the brasserie offers more cost-conscious meals in copious amounts. One might have steak, fish or some other quickly prepared meal while sipping on wine served by the glass. This popular bistro stays busy until 1 a.m. Closed: Sun. Reservations required. Credit Cards: All Major.

Le Clave   **$$**   ★★★

> *10-12 rue St.-Adjutor, In the center of town.* ☎ *04-73-36-46-30.*
> *Dinner: 8–10:30 p.m., entrées FR100–FR150.*

As one of the leading chefs in Central France, Jean-Claude Gerard serves his loyal clientele well. Favorite dishes include foie gras, Atlantic perch and rabbit on shredded salad. While he is creating in the kitchen, the owner of this 19th-century house walks the two dining rooms putting a smile on everybody's face as he chats with each table. Set menus start at FR150. Valet parking is available. Reservations required. Credit Cards: V, MC.

Directory

To and From

> *By train from Paris (three-and-a-half hours), Lyons (three hours), or Bordeaux (six hours), or by car on the A-71/A-72 autoroute between Lyons and the north.*

Tourist Office

> *69 boulevard Gergovia,* ☎ *(33) 04-73-93-30-20.*

Rail Station

> *avenue de la Union Soviétique,* ☎ *(33) 04-73-92-50-50.*

Post Office

> *1 rue Louis Renon, 63000 Clermont-Ferrand;* ☎ *(33) 04-73-30-63-00.*

Parc Naturel Régional des Volcans d'Auvergne

The government of France recognized the significance of the natural beauty of the volcanic mountains of Auvergne long ago, and by 1967 the Regional Natural Park of the Auvergne Volcanoes had been formed to preserve the natural scenery as well as the tiny mountain villages that dot the mountain slopes. Undisputed king of the crests here is Puy-de-Dôme, a 5000-foot-high volcano that erupted as recently as 4000 years ago. The mountain's summit is less than 10 miles from Clermont Ferrand. To hike the mountains requires a considerably longer journey. The summit is nearly always in or above the clouds, although the enterprising tourist officials of the region have attempted to make good of this by marketing the *mer de nuages* effect when you can see only the tops of nearby mountains emerging from the clouds. On a rare clear day, you can see for miles in every direction, including a vast swath of the Chaîne des Puys range that covers one-eighth of the country. The ruins of a Roman temple to the god Mercury lie on the mountain's summit.

Le Puy de Dôme is only the most majestic peak of the park; it encompasses three entire mountain ranges, and you could easily spend several days hiking in the area. More information can be had at the tourist office in Clermont-Ferrand, as well as at the Centre d'Acceuil du Puy de Dôme on the slopes of the big mountain itself.

Vichy

Depending on how close a student you are of French history, you may recognize the name of Vichy either from the collaborationist government of half of France under the Nazis that was seated here, or from the spring-water bearing its name that is sold around the world. Since Roman times, this small town on the banks of the Allier river has been famed for its hot- and cold-water springs, which are reputed to cure all manner of ailments including rheumatism, arthritis and even indigestion. The ruins of a medieval castle that once guarded the fort still stand beside the river; under Henri IV the town grew in importance as a strategic crossroads.

In the 17th century, the rich and famous of Paris began to come to the town to take "the waters," as they still do today. Louis XIV's daughters were known to favor the site, and when Napoléon III came here in the 1860's, Vichy's fortunes were assured. The building boom of the latter half of the 19th century spawned a number of ornate galleries and hotels around the spas (including one named for the emperor himself), the **Galleries du Parc** surrounding the **Parc des Sources**, which was originally part of the 1889 Paris Exhibition, and the Grand Casino, built in 1865. Vichy's infamous period as the seat of the French state began in July 1940, when the French government, having fled Paris when the Nazis took it, convened in the Opera House to figure out what to do. The decision, by a vote of 569-80, was to abolish the Troisième République and form a puppet government, which, led by Maréchal Petain, danced to Hitler's tune until the end of the war, sending thousands of Frenchmen and women into the hands of the Gestapo. It is from the Collaborationists that the infamous Jean Le Pen, leader of the ultra-right-wing party Front National, which has recently taken 20 percent of the vote in French elections, emerged.

Not surprisingly, the French, ashamed of this black period in their history, have chosen not to commemorate the Vichy government, so you'll have to rely on the tales of elderly residents, who can be coerced into talking with *un verre* of something in one of the cafés, if approached politely.

It is impossible to take a cure in Vichy without a reservation made long in advance and a good deal of money. Nevertheless, you can visit the *Halle des Sources* in the park and sample the *eau curative*, about FR10 for a cupful, or at the source Celestins on boulevard Kennedy, where you can drink a less pungent mineral water for free. Since the creation of an artificial lake in the town by damming the Allier in the 1960s, Vichy is a center of water sports. A day-long pass to the Centre Omnisports costs around FR100 and gets you access to the swimming pools, windsurfing, canoeing and even golf.

What to Do

Nightlife

Opera House/Casino ★★★

1 rue du Casino, ☎ *04-70-59-90-55.*

Six operas are staged during the summer in this beautiful opera house for which tickets can be purchased on the side of the building at rue du Parc. Within the same building is the Grand Casino, attracting an international crowd of big franc spenders.

Parks and Gardens

Parc de Sources/Hall des Sources ★★

rue du Parc, ☎ *04-70-98-95-37. Bordered by rue du Parc, rue du President Wilson and rue du Casino.*

The heartbeat of Vichy, this park hosts the Hall of Sources at the north end. It is here that four of the springs emerge from the ground, spewing hot, sulfur-tasting water. Fill up a cup for FR9 and toast to your health—if you can handle the taste. Admission: free.

Sports and Recreation

Centre Omnisports ★★★★

off pont de Bellerive, ☎ *04-70-59-51-00. On the promenade next to pont de Bellerive. Hours open: 9 a.m.–6 p.m. Special hours: Closed noon–2 p.m. Closed: Sun.*

An astounding sports facility offering such diversions as windsurfing, canoeing, kayaking, golf and fencing. "Pass'sports" are available for FR50 for a half-day, FR100 for a full day and FR500 for a week. Check out the swimming pool near the campground across the river for more affordable exercise at FR13.

Where to Stay

Hotels and Resorts

Aletti Palace Hotel FR600–FR850 ★★★★

3 place Joseph Aletti. ☎ *04-70-31-78-77, FAX: 04-70-98-13-82. About 500 meters from the train station.*

Single: FR600–FR730. Double: FR660–FR850.

Built in 1910, this restored hotel and spa sits in a park across from the casino. From the moment one steps through the grand entrance to the moment one opens the door to the Belle Epoque rooms, it is obvious that this is what luxury is meant to be. There are 54 air-conditioned rooms with cable TV, telephone and private bath. All are attractively furnished, and some have balconies with excellent town views. There are suites and nonsmoking rooms available. Dining and drinking are made easy with two restaurants and a bar in the hotel. Other facilities include a business center, pool, fitness room and sauna. In the area, golf, tennis, water-skiing, windsurfing, fishing and boating are easily accessible. Skilled management and staff at the Aletti cater to your every need. Features: wheelchair-access rooms, pool, sauna, nonsmoking rooms, fitness center, in-room conference facilities. Credit Cards: All Major.

Les Celestins   FR760–FR1400   ★★★★

111 avenue des Etats-Unis. ☎ *04-70-30-82-00, FAX: 04-70-30-82-01. About 1 km from train station; near the golf course.*
Single: FR760–FR900. Double: FR1100–FR1400.

A luxury hotel and spa "cure center," the Les Celestins is next to an 18-hole golf course. An impressive resort complex, there are 131 air-conditioned rooms with satellite TV, radio, telephone, minibar, bath and hair dryer. Twelve magnificent suites are available for FR1600 to FR2100. Not only is there 24-hour room service, there are three restaurants to cure your hunger. The hotel bar dishes out nightly entertainment. In addition to the indoor and outdoor pools, the adjacent cure center offers beauty treatments, massage services, a whirlpool, solarium, fitness room and spa facilities with medical check-ups. The most elaborate arrangement in Vichy. Features: pool, sauna, thallasotherapy, fitness center, in-room conference facilities.

Pavillon Sevigne Vichy   FR530–FR1110   ★★★★

10-12 place Sevigne. ☎ *04-70-32-16-22, FAX: 04-70-59-97-37. About 1 km from the train station.*
Single: FR530–FR960. Double: FR700–FR1110.

Once the home of Madame of Sevigne, this resort occupies an imposing 17th-century mansion. Wonderful improvements have made the accommodations as inviting as ever, while keeping the Old World feeling alive. There are 47 Empire-style rooms, some with balcony, equipped with cable TV, telephone, minibar and bath or shower. Breakfast costs FR75. The Napoleon III style restaurant is one of the finest in Vichy, as would be expected at a Relais and Châteaux rated hotel of this calibre. Features: wheelchair-access rooms, balcony or patio. Credit Cards: All Major.

Where to Eat

Brasserie du Casino $ ★★★

4 rue du Casino ☎ *04-70-98-23-06.*
Dinner: 7–10 p.m., entrées FR70–FR120.

One of Vichy's most happening spots, this brasserie has been booming since it opened in the 1920s. It's also one of the prettiest brasseries with wood paneling, copper and Art Deco styling. While it's busiest at lunch, a visit at night is rewarded by live piano entertainment. The food, value-priced, features the typical brasserie fare, such as steaks, soups, sweetbreads and fish. Fixed-price menus are FR100–FR140. Closed mid-Feb.–early Mar. and Nov. Closed: Wed. Reservations recommended. Credit Cards: All Major.

L'Alambic $$ ★★★★

8 rue Nicholas-Larbaud ☎ *04-70-59-12-71.*
Specialties: ravioli of frogs' legs with herbs.
Dinner: 7:30–10 p.m., entrées FR130–FR190.

An energetic talent in the kitchen, Jean-Jacques Barbot keeps the 20 seats in his restaurant full by sticking to his proven successes. Serving the best food in town, Barbot specializes in ravioli with frogs' legs, roast pigeon and the freshest of seafood. The desserts created by his wife are no less impressive, with the winner remaining the gratin of pears with toasted almonds. Set menus from FR170. Make every effort to be in one of those 20 seats during your visit to Vichy—they're the best seats in town. Closed: Mon. Reservations required. Credit Cards: V, MC.

Directory

To and From

By train from Paris (three-and-a-half hours) or Clermont-Ferrand (25 minutes), or by car on the D-906 road between Clermont-Ferrand and Moulins.

Tourist Office

19 rue du Parc; ☎ *(33) 04-70-98-71-94.*

Rail Station

place de la Gàre; ☎ *(33) 04-70-97-21-00.*

Post Office

place Charles de Gaulle, 03200 Vichy; ☎ *(33) 04-70-30-10-75.*

Le Puy-en-Velay

Situated in a formerly extremely active volcanic region, now the confluence of the young Loire and the Borne rivers, Le Puy evokes images of the violent eruptions of eons past. Scattered in the fertile and tranquil basin around Le Puy are towering, jagged rock pinnacles that look as if they are still being thrust up from beneath the earth's surface, as well as rocky promontories and basalt outcroppings, remnants of cooled lava flows. Long a religious cross-roads since the Bishop Gotescalk made one of the first recorded pilgrimages to Santiago de Compostela in Spain in 962, the town is home to many sanctuaries, including several perched atop the rocky pinnacles. The most impressive of these is the Chapelle St. Michel d'Aiguilhe, which the bishop built atop a sliver of volcanic rock towering more than 250 feet above the town. The steep climb offers a rewarding view of the entire basin. At the top is the chapel, which has resisted the weather and gravity for almost 1000 years, and contains a rare 10th-century wooden crucifix and frescoes dating from the 12th century. An equally impressive view can be had from the terrace atop the Rocher Corneille, another climbable volcanic protrusion topped by a 52-foot statue of the Virgin Mary.

The lower levels of the town are dominated by the Cathédrale Notre Dame, first built in 430 on the site of a Roman temple. The present cathedral was begun during the 10th century, with major restoration work carried out in the 19th century. The altar is the home of one of the most celebrated Black Madonnas in France; this one is a replica of the original, created in the 12th century in the Middle East and brought back by Louis IX during the Crusades, but destroyed in the Révolution. Puy-en-Velay has been a center for lace-making since the 17th century, reaching its peak in the 19th century. Housed in the Musée Crozatier is an excellent display on the history of lace, including the needlepoint variety that was eclipsed by bobbin lace in the early 20th century. The prime exhibit is an unfinished lace square with 500 bobbins still attached.

Nearby Puy-en-Velay is the Château Polignac, a medieval fortress built atop a lava promontory that was left 300 feet above the valley floor by the erosion of the surrounding soil. The impregnable fortress was home to a family of lords that ruled the valley for more than four centuries, falling into decline only in the 19th century. An attractive excursion for a hike and picnic is Lake Bouchet, 13 miles to the southwest of town, its crystal-clear water contained in a perfectly circular volcanic crater atop the mountain.

What to Do

Historical/Architectural Sites

Cathédrale de Notre-Dame   ★★★★

place du For, ☎ *04-71-05-44-93. On top of rue des Tables.*
Hours open: 9 a.m.–6 p.m.
Originally the site of a Roman temple, this cathedral was begun in the 5th century and continued until the end of the 12th century. Today, witness the Romanesque structure accented with Byzantine adornments. It is the Black Madonna for which this cathedral is known, however; admire it upon the baroque high altar. Also of importance are the Romanesque frescoes in the transept and the Bible of Theodolphus, a document from Charlemagne's era, in the transept. Admission to the cloisters is FR16; *open Wed.–Mon., 9 a.m.–noon and 2–6 p.m.* Admission: free.

Chapelle St-Michel-d'Aiguilhe   ★★★

On top of Rocher St-Michel, ☎ *04-71-02-71-32.*
Built by the Bishop of Le Puy in 962 after one of the first pilgrimages to Santiago de Compostela, this chapel is set on what used to be the vent of an old volcano. After the 80-meter climb up 268 steps, gaze upon the 19th-century bell tower (the original one was destroyed by lightning in the 13th century) and the mosaic facade about the doorway. *Open mid-June–mid-Sept., daily, 9 a.m.–7 p.m.; mid-Sept.–mid-June, daily, 10 a.m.–noon and 2–5 p.m. Dec.–Feb., only in the afternoon.* Admission: FR5.

Château de Polignac   ★★

About 5 km northwest of town.
Special hours: Open summer only.
Formerly the residence of the Polignac family, which wielded major power in the area from the 11th through 14th centuries, the remains of the château sit on this volcanic rock. An interesting countryside detour in the summer.

Rocher Corneille   ★★★

above the cathedral, ☎ *04-71-04-11-33. At the north end of the old town.*
At this volcanic rock above the town and cathedral, a 23-meter-high statue of the Virgin Mary was erected in 1860 (made of melted-down cannons from the Crimean War). Every kilometer of the view is worth the walk up the rock from behind the cathedral. *Open May–Sept., daily 9 a.m.–7 p.m; Oct.–Mar., Wed.–Sun., 10 a.m.–5 p.m.; Apr., Wed.–Sun., 9 a.m.–6 p.m.; Closed Dec. and Jan.* Admission: FR10.

Museums and Exhibits

Musée Crozatier ★★★

Jardin Henry Vinay, ☎ *04-71-09-38-90. At the southern end of the Jardin Henri Vinay. Special hours: Closed Feb. Closed: Tue.*

A unique combination of archaeological relics and handicrafts of local artisans. In addition to a major display of lace, there are paintings from the 14th through 20th centuries, highlighted by works from Rubens. *Open May–Sept., Wed.–Mon., 10 a.m.–noon and 2–6 p.m.; Oct.–Jan. and Mar.–Apr., Wed.–Mon., 10 a.m.–noon and 2–4 p.m. Admission: FR12.*

Where to Stay

Bed and Breakfasts

Le Pre Bossu FR350–FR480 ★★★

In Moudeyres. ☎ *04-71-05-10-70, FAX: 04-71-05-10-21. About 25 km southeast of Le-Puy-en-Velay, in Moudeyres.*
Double: FR350–FR480.

In a remote village outside of Le Puy, Le Pre Bossu is a little gem among fields of wildflowers. Built in 1969, its stone facade and thatched roof blend in perfectly with the neighboring houses. The public spaces are highlighted by the exposed beams, wood floors and cozy fireplace. The antiques and fresh flowers put on the finishing, rustic touches. There are 10 rooms, half with bath and half with shower, simply equipped with central heating and a telephone. Casual gatherings are in the bar and the TV lounge. Breakfast, lunch and dinner are all outstanding. This farmhouse is a worthwhile detour, if at least for the food. Credit Cards: V, MC, A.

Hotels and Resorts

Hotel Chris'Tel FR260–FR400 ★★★

15 boulevard Alexandre-Clair. ☎ *04-71-02-24-44, FAX: 04-71-02-52-68. Near the Jardin Henry-Vinay.*
Single: FR260. Double: FR400.

A short walk from town center, this modern hotel offers 30 comfortable rooms. Each balconied room has a TV, telephone, desk and private bath. Functional yet appealing. Breakfast, the only meal served in the dining room, costs FR40. A warm welcome from the small staff. Features: balcony or patio. Credit Cards: All Major.

Where to Eat

Le Bateau Ivre $$ ★★★

5 rue Portail d'Avignon ☎ *04-71-09-67-20.*
Dinner: 7:30–10 p.m., entrées FR90–FR110.

Within this 19th-century house is the small husband-wife owned restaurant. Regional specialties are prepared with a home-cooked flair that can be a refreshing change after dining on so many fancy dishes at other establishments. Salmon, lamb and lobster are just a few of the featured dishes. Fixed-price meals start at FR100 during the week. Warm reception and big smiles from this hard-working couple. Closed: Mon., Sun. reservations recommended.

Pizzeria Pepino $ ★★

9 rue Vibert, Near place du Breuil. ☎ *04-71-09-13-25.*

Lunch: Noon–2 p.m.
Dinner: 7:30–11 p.m.

A relaxing pizza place with pies from FR35. Other set menus include salad, a meat dish and dessert from FR50. Big proportions and a friendly atmosphere. Another informal stop is **Cafe Le Palais** at *27 place du Breuil (☎ 04-71-09-01-81).* Good, cheap bites start at FR45 for the plate du jour. Food only at lunch, noon–2 p.m. Ice cream and drinks are served until 1 a.m. Closed: Mon.

Directory

To and From

By train from Lyon (two-and-half hours) and Clermont-Ferrand (two hours), or by car on the N-88 road from Lyon.

Tourist Office

place du Breuil; ☎ *(33) 04-71-09-38-41.*

Rail Station

place Maréchal Leclerc; ☎ *(33) 04-36-35-35-35.*

Post Office

8 avenue de la Dentelle, 43000 Le Puy-en-Velay; ☎ *(33) 04-71-07-02-00.*

Les Gorges

The central region is one of the wateriest in all France, with volcanic lakes and rivers everywhere. But the best water experience is found in the gorges, of which the Tarn and Jonte gorges are the most spectacular and most popular. Several companies offer whitewater rafting trips down the rivers, many based in Puy-en-Velay. The village of La Malène on the D-907 highway is a good starting point for rafting expeditions. Les Gorges du Tarn is ranked as the best remaining untamed river canyon in Europe, a 15-mile trip down a narrow gorge that reaches 2000 feet at its deepest point. A drive southeast from Le Puy takes you into the area, and abundant wildflowers and wildlife—from big-horned mountain sheep to the once almost-extinct griffon vulture—can be seen from any of the twisting roads. From the D-907 highway that winds along the northern rim of the canyon, turn off on the D-995 climb the hairpins for a few miles, turn off again on the D-46, and you will find Pointe Sublime (its real name), one of the most spectacular vista points of the region.

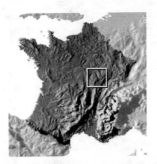

BURGUNDY

Romanesque abbeys reveal Burgundy's medieval heart.

What Makes Burgundy So French?

1. *Louis XIV's doctor prescribed wine for his royal patient's dyspepsia (bet you get Rolaids or Mylanta!).*

2. Boeuf bourgiugnon, coq au vin, escargots and Dijon *mustard (now you know how Louis came down with that dyspepsia!).*

3. *Chablis, one of the world's most famed wine-producing villages.*

4. *The world's first photograph, created by Joseph Nicephore Niecpe, in 1816, of his home near Chalon-sur-Saone.*

5. *The world's most important wine auction, in Beaune, each year.*

615

Burgundians like to think of their region as the heart of France. They make a good argument—the region is certainly one of the richest in history, architecture, art, gastronomy and modern economy. Today *Bourgogne*, as it is called in French, is best known for its excellent wines, and perhaps for the mustard that bears the name of its capital, Dijon. But the role that the region played in the development and history of France was absolutely crucial, and the legacy of the power, wealth and influence of Burgundy is still evident today in its monasteries, castles, towns and villages. Positioned between Champagne and Alsace-Lorraine to the north, Lyon to the south, the Massif Central to the west, and the Alps to the east, Burgundy is a land of rolling green hills grazed by world-famous Charolois cattle, charming villages, plates of steaming *coq au vin*, glasses of the *nouveau beaujolais* and more—much more.

History

After the rupture of the Carolingian empire with the signing of the Treaty of Verdun in A.D. 843, resulting in the split of France and Central Europe between Charlemagne's grandsons, the Kingdom of France began to take shape and solidify. At the time, powerful independent states such as Bretagne and Aquitaine maintained their near-independence on the Atlantic coast, while the Holy German Empire grew ever more powerful to the east. This left a vacuum in between, and the eastern area of modern France became the scene of many struggles for power over the centuries. During the Middle Ages, a third great power of medieval continental-Europe rose to power in the region—the rapidly growing, wealthy Catholic church.

In the 10th, 11th, and 12th centuries religious authority in Burgundy gained more strength here than in any other region. The *Bénédictines* built abbeys and churches hither and yon, the legacy of which you can see today in the prime ensemble of Romanesque-style ecclesiastical architecture throughout France. Cluny, in the heart of Burgundy, was the center of the religious power base, closely followed by Vezelay. The Cistercians, a sub-sect of the Bénédictine order, expanded their influence in the south of the region, building the great abbey at Fontenay in 1118, and other churches and monasteries throughout the region. Religious authorities collected tithes and dispensed the law of God and the church with equal fervor.

The great religious leaders would hold enormous power again during the Renaissance, this time over the whole of France, as appointed clergymen such as Cardinal Mazarin and the biggest of them all, Cardinal Richlieu, appointed by the crown, acted as virtual prime ministers, using the church as a means of control and building sumptuous apartments and palaces for themselves alongside the austere Bénédictine and Cistercian accommodations. Beginning in the 14th century, the Dukes of Burgundy launched a run in

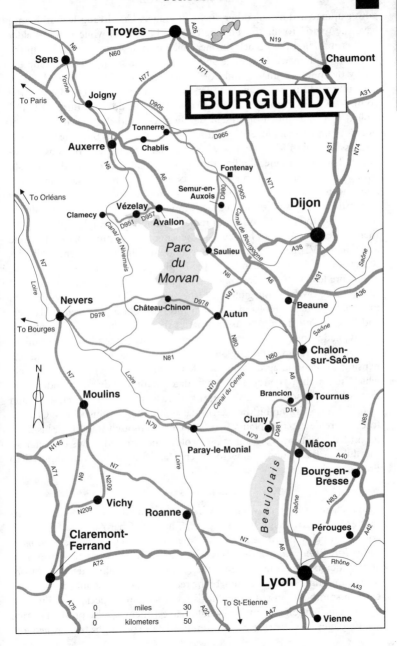

power unmatched by any other duchy in France. Good King Jean of France gave the region to his son Phillipe the Bold in 1364, while Phillip's elder brother inherited the French throne. Phillipe soon acquired Flanders in the north through marriage, and he and his successors set about expanding the duchy by annexing small chunks of French territory. The combined wealth and culture of Burgundy and Flanders was considerable, and by the time the country collapsed into the Hundred Years' War, the dukes of Burgundy controlled almost as much of present day France as did the crown. The most overt attempt to take over the entire country was early on, when Jean the Fearless, cousin of King Charles VI, attempted a coup d'état but was assassinated. The next in line, Phillipe the Good, initially sided with the English, who already controlled Aquitaine and Normandy through the Plantagenet line, and France was reduced to a small section of the Loire Valley. Shortly after Charles VII was confronted by Jeanne d'Arc, she managed with divine help to rally the people and begin the expulsion of the English. Phillipe, either suddenly coming to his senses or sensing the tide turn, allowed Jeanne and Charles VII to travel through Burgundy to Champagne, where Charles was crowned—after he abandoned the English, the war was soon over. Phillipe swore loyalty to the crown and set about continuing the expansion and economic growth of Burgundy. By the time he died, the duchy included most of present-day Holland, Belgium and Luxembourg, as well as Flanders and Picardy and Burgundy itself. Charles the Bold, the next Duke of Burgundy, had none of the finesse of Phillipe. He attempted by military might to expand his realm, attacking Switzerland (where he was routed), and dispensing with an old agreement for safe passage with independent Lorraine, which he sought to conquer to consolidate the Burgundy and Flanders portions of his territory. By this time, the French crown had had enough, and Louis XI (not without his own territorial ambitions) sent his armies. Charles' forces were defeated at Nancy in 1476. Charles himself was killed, his body found half eaten by wolves in an ice-cold, muddy pond. Thus the reign of the dukes of Burgundy came to an end, and the region was annexed to France.

Cuisine

The cuisine in Burgundy reflects what the region is known for—its wine, its mustard and, to a slightly lesser extent, its lean Charolais beef. The dish you've probably heard of, and which remains the region specialty *numéro un*, is *boeuf bourgiugnon*. Basically just a stew, the dish has class from lean and tender beef, marinated first, then cooked slowly in red wine. Mushrooms, onions and bacon complete the recipe. *Coq au vin* is another favorite, chicken smothered in red wine. Snails *(escargots)* are a specialty of Burgundy—originally the grape pickers would harvest them as a by-product during the vendage; now they are grown commercially. You might try *escargots à la*

Bourguignonne, snails prepared and served in their shells with garlic, parsley and butter. *Minute steak Dijonnaise* is sure to please meat lovers and mustard connoisseurs. The cheeses of Burgundy include Epoisses and Saint-Florentin for those who can't handle the hard stuff, Pipo Crem' and Bleu de Bresse for lovers of blue cheeses, and Bouton de Culotte (literally, "panty spot") and Cendré d'Aisy for the true aficionados.

Burgundian wines first earned renown during the 15th century, when the duchy was at the height of its power. The wines are still among the most esteemed in the world today, and with good reason—they are rich, earthy, fruity and full. After the Révolution, Napoléon rewrote the laws governing appellations, so today a daunting number of different wines are produced in the region. In some cases, such as the Clos la Roche, the appellation belongs uniquely to one vineyard. In simple terms, the regions are divided as follows. In the northeast around the city of the same name and extending almost to Auxerre are produced Chablis. From Dijon south is the Côte de Nuits, and immediately south of that the Côte de Beaune. Together these two make up the Côte d'Or. The town of Beaune hosts the most important wine auction in the world every year. A patchy non-contiguous region west of Châlons-sur-Saone produces the Côte Chalonnais wines, while the large area to the south, centered northeast of Mâcon, produces Mâconnais. Further south still, reaching almost to Lyon, is the Beaujolais region, which produces a rich, extremely fruity wine that has benefitted of late from a hype-marketing campaign wherein the "beaujolais nouveau" is rushed to restaurants around the world in time for the stroke of midnight on the third Thursday of November each year. The grapes used in Burgundy are mainly chardonnay for the whites of Chablis, and pinot noir for the region's reds. Gamay is the grape that produces Beaujolais and Mâconnais.

Auxerre

Auxerre is a charming mid-sized town that typifies Burgundy. Surrounded by gently rolling hills covered with fertile vineyards, and filled with religious history, the town is a port of sorts—the river Yonne is navigable—and was an important Roman settlement on the road from Lyon to Boulogne. The most interesting of the town churches you should visit is the Abbaye St. Germain. St. Germanus was the successor to St. Martin in the early effort to evangelize Gaul. He was born in the town in A.D. 378, became its first bishop, and died in A.D. 448. The wife of Clovis, first Christian king of Gaul, is thought to have erected a small basilica over St. Germanus' tomb in the early sixth century. In A.D. 841, the new church was built on the foundation of the basilica. This church had an outer nave to the west and a crypt to the east—the ninth-century crypt is still in place. Within the crypt, the site of the original tomb is covered by a ceiling held up by Gallo-Roman columns, and you can see a fifth-century carving depicting Christ, as well as extremely faded eighth-century frescoes—the oldest in France—showing early bishops of Auxerre. Expanded again in the 12th century, the abbey now boasts a beautiful Romanesque-style bell tower as well.

Another sight in Auxerre is the *Cathédrale St. Etienne*. Completed in the mid-16th century after three centuries of construction work, the cathedral has a good collection of 13th-century stained glass, as well as an 11th-century fresco showing Christ in glory on horseback in the crypt. The choir is archetypal Gothic-style, all lightness and heavenward-looking latticework. You can climb the tower for a good view of the town before setting off to wander through the winding medieval-era streets.

What to Do

Historical/Architectural Sites

Abbaye St-Germain ★★★★

2 place St-Germain, ☎ *03-86-51-09-74.*

Founded by Queen Clothilde, wife of Clovis, this 6th-century abbey was built on the site where St-Germanus was buried in 448 A.D. Reaching its heights in the Middle Ages, it was pillaged during the Wars of Religion by the Huguenots. Tours of the crypts and the 9th-century frescoes are every half-hour. *Open June–Oct., 1–6:30 p.m.; Nov.–mid-May, 10 a.m.–noon and 2–5:30 p.m.* Free admission Wed. Admission: FR20.

Cathédrale St-Etienne ★★★

place St-Etienne, ☎ *03-86-52-23-29.*

Hours open: 9 a.m.–6 p.m. Special hours: Closed noon–2 p.m.; Sun., open 2–6 p.m. only.

Constructed during the 13th century and completed in the 16th century, this cathedral demonstrates the flamboyant Gothic style. The interior's refined Gothic decor is punctuated by the stained-glass rendition of Joan of Arc and the 13th-century stained glass behind the altar. Visit the 12th-century manuscripts in the treasury and a beautiful fresco of Christ atop a horse in the crypt. Admission to the crypt and to the treasury is FR25 each. Admission: free.

Where to Stay

Hotels and Resorts

Le Normandie FR260–FR350 ★★

41 boulevard Vauban. ☎ *03-86-52-57-80, FAX: 03-86-51-54-33. On the town outskirts.*

Double: FR260–FR350.

A short walk from the cathedral, le Normandie's vine-covered facade fronts 47 rooms. Meticulously clean, the rooms have TV, telephone, radio and bath. All are quiet, but those facing the garden are the most appealing. The public areas are a meld of antique furnishings and modern conveniences. Small but well-maintained, the fitness room has a sauna. There is a bar and a small garden in the hotel, and

there are several dining options nearby. Breakfast costs FR30, and parking is FR24.
Features: fitness center. Credit Cards: All Major.

Inns

Le Maxime   **FR450–FR590**   ★★★

2 quai de la Marine. ☎ *03-86-52-14-19, FAX: 03-86-52-21-70. On the banks of the Yonne River.*
Double: FR450–FR590.
Family-run 19th-century hotel on the banks of the Yonne. The owners have person-alized the conservative decor of the 25 pleasant rooms. Each comfortable room comes with TV, telephone and bath. Request one with a river view. Breakfast can be taken in the lounge or in the bedrooms, and the bar, Le Cave de Bourgogne, fea-tures a rustic decor with exposed beams and copper pots. There is no restaurant here, but there are several nearby. Credit Cards: All Major.

Sens

Hotels and Resorts

Croix Blanche   **FR275**   ★★

9 rue Victor-Guichard. ☎ *03-86-64-00-02, FAX: 03-86-65-29-19. Near the cathedral.*
Double: FR275.
The value-minded rates for these 25 functional rooms are appealing. Its location is convenient for touring the town on foot. Its restaurant continues with the value theme, serving decent fare. Two solid stars. Credit Cards: V, MC.

Paris et Poste   **FR360–FR540**   ★★★

97 rue de la Republique. ☎ *03-86-65-17-43, FAX: 03-86-64-48-45. Near town center.*
Double: FR360–FR540.
Should one decide to overnight it in Sens, this is the best bet. Reliable quality since the refurbishments. The 18 rooms vary in size, but all are comfortable and air-con-ditioned. Quaint restaurant with consistently good food. It's all so...predictable (possibly because it's Best Western-affiliated). Features: air conditioning in rooms.
Credit Cards: All Major.

Where to Eat

Jean-Luc Barnabet   **$$**   ★★★

14 quai de la Republique, In the center of old town. ☎ *03-86-51-68-88.*
Dinner: 7–9:30 p.m., entrées FR175–FR300.
This lovely 17th-century house sits in the middle of old town. Within its charming walls, Jean-Luc and Marie Barnabet have come together to build one of the best classic restaurants in town. Not limited to just the traditional recipes, though, they have added their own interpretations to these classic dishes, pushing them to new heights. A nice vault of wine includes an impressive list of chablis. Together, these two have efficiently and elegantly created a restaurant that only improves with age. Set menus from FR300. Closed: Mon. Amenities: outside dining, reservations rec-ommended. Credit Cards: V.

La Salamandre   **$$**   ★★★

84 rue de Paris. ☎ *03-86-52-87-87.*
Dinner: 7:30–10 p.m., entrées FR150–FR300.

Serving the best seafood in town, La Salamandre continues to make a strong showing as one of the finest restaurants in Auxerre. Strong on tradition and pure ingredients, the chef's best dish is the charlotte of smoked fish on potato salad. Other shellfish dishes are quite impressive, especially the lobster and the oysters. Set menus from FR100 during the week and from FR140 on weekends. Reservations recommended. Credit Cards: V, A.

Le Jardin Gourmand   **$$**   ★★★★

56 boulevard Vauban. ☎ *03-86-51-53-52.*
Dinner: 7:30–9:30 p.m., entrées FR80–FR175.

Commanding a faithful contingent, chef Pierre Boussereau serves market dependent cuisine that constantly changes. Depending on ingredient availability and the seasons, the menu changes at least seven times a year. And what could be more pleasant than eating on the terrace or in the Louis XVI dining room? His wine cellar is a virtual stockpile—with more than 300 different wines, including 50 different chablis. His meticulous attention to fresh, pure ingredients assures outstanding flavor every time. Set menus start at FR120–FR320. Closed: Mon. Amenities: outside dining, reservations required. Credit Cards: V.

Directory

To and From

By train from Paris (two hours), Lyon (four hours), or Dijon (one hour), or by car on the N-6 highway just off the main A-6 autoroute into Burgundy.

Tourist Office

quai de la République; ☎ *(33) 03-86-52-06-19.*

Rail Station

rue Paul Doumer; ☎ *(33) 03-86-46-50-50.*

Post Office

place Charles Surugue, 89011 Auxerre; ☎ *(33) 03-86-48-57-21.*

Chablis

One of the most famous wine-producing villages in the world, Chablis has a quiet, self-confident feel to its winding streets. Filled with stone houses, Chablis is shaped by Le Serein (Calm River) that flows through its center. You can visit the wine caves, enjoy a wine festival in February or November, or just sip a glass in a café where it is guaranteed to taste better than anywhere else in the world.

Chablis is about 11 miles east of Auxerre on the D-965 road.

Tonnerre

The main attraction of Tonnerre is the mysterious spring that gushes forth in the middle of town. The *Fosse Dionne* produces an enormous quantity of water, so much so that it has never been explored. The spring is surrounded by an 18th-century washing site converted into a small plaza.

Tonnerre is about 10 miles past Chablis on the D-965 road.

Dijon

The ancient capital of the Duchy of Bourgogne and now the capital of the region, Dijon is a vibrant modern city with color and history to spare. Famous for its coarse-grain mustard, Dijon is also a gastronomic center par excellence. One of the hallmarks of the reign of the dukes was a love of things artistic, especially in the case of Phillipe the Good, and the connection to Flanders enabled the dukes to bring artists from the north to spruce up their homes and buildings. The clearest legacy of this is the use of glazed, colored tiles on the roofs of buildings, a practice that endured through the prosperous 17th and 18th centuries, when numerous elegant *hôtels partculiers* were built by wealthy merchants. But there are other, more subtle revelations of the patronage of the Dukes of Burgundy, including the tomb of the first Duke Phillip by Jean de Marville, and the altar of the Chartreuse de Champmol, a five-year work by Jean de Beaumetz, sculptures by Claus Sluter and paintings by Melchior Broederlam, and the work of Malouel, the most renowned of the Burgundy-Flemish painters, whose masterpiece "Pietà" hangs in the Louvre in Paris. The centerpiece of Dijon is the Palais des Ducs, rebuilt in the 17th century as the parliament building. The elegant classical-style building now houses the city's *Musée des Beaux Arts*, the richest repository of the Gothic-style art the dukes supported. The guard room is the most important *salle* in the museum, housing the tombs of Phillip the Bold and John the Fearless, masterpieces of 14th-century sculpture with the effigy of the deceased on top and an ornate and intricate carving of the procession of mourners wending their way around the sides of the tomb. The tombs were in the Chartreuse until it was mostly destroyed in the revolution, but you can still see the portal of the chapel and an ensemble known as the "Well of Moses" by Sluter, who did the most sculpture on the tombs. You could easily spend all day in the museum, but don't forget to wander Dijon's narrow streets admiring the mansions of the Renaissance. If you can handle another cathedral, you'll find the Cathédrale St. Michel has an 11th-century crypt topped with 13th- to 15th-century superstructure. The 13th-century Gothic-style Eglise de Notre Dame, close to the center of town, is a better bet, having kept some of its original gargoyles, including an owl that you touch for good luck—today the owl's face is completely rubbed away. Notre Dame also contains a 14th-century clock with moving figures that spring to mechanical life at the chime of the hour.

What to Do

Historical/Architectural Sites

Eglise St-Michel   ★★★★

place St-Michel, ☎ *03-80-63-17-85. A few hundred meters east of the Musée des Beaux-Arts.*

Considered to have one of the most beautful Renaissance facades in France, the church was begun in the 15th century in the Flamboyant Gothic style. Notice the mythological and biblical scenes above the portal, where angels are seen with pagan figures. Tours are available from 3–6 p.m. on weekdays at no charge, but donations are always appreciated. Admission: free.

Eglise de Notre-Dame   ★★★

place Notre Dame, ☎ *03-80-30-11-77. One block north of the Palais des Ducs.*

Constructed in the Burgundian Gothic style between 1220 and 1240, the facade is covered with 19th-century gargoyles that replaced the originals. On the way in, stop and rub Dijon's bird, the owl, for good luck. Once inside, seek out the 11th-century Black Virgin statue and the 1946 tapestry celebrating the city's liberation from German occupation in 1944. The bells of the clock are rung by a figure of a man, his wife and their two children.

Palais des Ducs/Musée des Beaux-Arts   ★★★★

place de la Liberation, ☎ *03-80-74-52-70. In the center of town.*
Hours open: 10 a.m.–6 p.m. Special hours: Sun., 10 a.m.–12:30 p.m. and 2–6 p.m. Closed: Tue.

Formerly the palace where the Dukes of Burgundy held court, the present building is mostly the product of the 17th century, as it was reconstructed for the parliament. The Musée des Beaux-Arts now occupies the east wing, and the Hotel de Ville sits in the west wing. There is an excellent collection of works by Flemish artists, including some by Picasso, Braque and the 14th-century triptych by Jacques de Baerze. Not to be missed is the guard room, which contains the decorated tombs of Jean the Fearless and his wife, Marguerite de Baviere and Philippe the Bold. Admission is free on Sunday. Admission: FR15.

Where to Stay

Bed-and-Breakfasts

Chateau de Longecourt   FR700   ★★★★

In Longecourt-en-Plaine. ☎ *03-80-39-88-76. About 18 km southeast of Dijon. Take the D996 or D968 towards Saint-Jean-de-Losne. In Longecourt, it's on the place de la Mairie.*
Double: FR700.

Earning its fourth star for the warm reception and service, this pink-brick, turreted chateau stands proud. Circumnavigated by a tranquil moat, the peace is protected. Three of the antique-furnished rooms have private bath and toilet, and the other two have private bath but share a toilet. Request the Catherine de Medici room. Breakfast is included, and wine-accompanied dinner is at the communal table for FR250. Credit Cards: Not Accepted.

Le Relais de Chasse — FR340–FR400 ★★★

In Chamboeuf. ☎ *03-80-51-81-60, FAX: 03-80-34-15-96. About 18 km southwest of Dijon. Take A31, exit Nuits-St-Georges. Take N74 to Gevrey-Chambertin, then left on D31 towards Chamboeuf. After the church, turn left on first private drive.*
Double: FR340–FR400.

Overlooking a beautiful park, this sandstone-color house resides in a small country-side village. The four large bedrooms are individually decorated and furnished with antiques; each one has private bath. A light breakfast of breads, cheeses and jams is served on the garden terrace in warm weather. No other meals are served, but several quaint restaurants are nearby. Minimum stay is two nights. Credit Cards: Not Accepted.

Hotels and Resorts

Best Western du Chapeau Rouge — FR460–FR725 ★★★★

5 rue Michelet. ☎ *528-1234, 03-80-30-28-10, FAX: 03-80-30-33-89. Behind the cathedral; about 500 meters from the train station.*
Single: FR460–FR560. Double: FR610–FR725.

A landmark hotel in a former Cardinal's home, this is Dijon's most comfy stay. Ideally located near the cathedral, amid beautiful medieval houses. This Best Western affiliate has kept on the ball, with constant improvements to the 31 rooms. All of the units come with TV, telephone, minibar and private bath; some have Jacuzzi. The decor is traditional, with floral wallcoverings and old-fashioned furniture. Meals range from FR200 to FR300 in the restaurant. While nothing luxurious, there is a bit of classic character here. Credit Cards: All Major.

Hotel Sofitel la Cloche — FR510–FR600 ★★★

14 place Darcy. ☎ *221-4542, 03-80-30-12-32, FAX: 03-80-30-04-15. In the commercial center of town; about 500 meters from the train station.*
Single: FR510. Double: FR600.

Dating from the early 1400s, this building is an historical monument. Prominently situated near Dijon's main square, la Cloche rises five stories above town. The 80 rooms offer unobstructed views, soundproof windows, air conditioning, satellite TV, telephone, minibar and bath. The lobby-level bar welcomes many tourists and locals to its discreet social scene. Beneath the stone vaults is the cellar restaurant, Jean-Pierre Billoux, in all of its expensive glory. Credit Cards: All Major.

Ibis Central — FR300–FR350 ★★

3 place Grangier. ☎ *03-80-30-44-00, FAX: 03-80-30-77-12. Across from the post office.*
Single: FR300. Double: FR350.

Presiding over a busy, central square, this 1926 hotel is one of the more acceptable hotels in the Ibis chain. The 90 rooms have made the best of modernization, with soundproof windows, air conditioning, TV, telephone and bath. The restaurant is uncommonly pleasant, with good views and intimate dinners. Credit Cards: All Major.

Where to Eat

Jean-Pierre Billoux — $$ ★★★★

14 place Darcy, In the center of town. ☎ *03-80-30-11-00.*
Specialties: terrine of pigeon; guinea fowl with capers.

Dinner: 7:30–9:30 p.m., entrées FR180–FR270.

With an emphasis on rustic, almost country-style cuisine, Billoux still throws in a hint of contemporary flavor to his dishes. Almost simple in preparation, he has redefined such specialties as farm chicken, guinea hen, frogs' legs and other staples in traditional French cuisine. His sommelier has built an incredible wine cellar to keep pace with the magic worked in the kitchen, and there are actually some affordable bottles from which to choose. Set menus are FR240 during the week and FR450 on weekends. Every franc is well spent at this Relais and Chateaux restaurant. Jacket and tie required. Closed: Mon. Reservations recommended. Credit Cards: All Major.

La Toison d'Or $$ ★★★

18 rue Sainte Anne, In the old town. ☎ *03-80-30-73-52.*
Dinner: 7–9:30 p.m., entrées FR100–FR170.

This elegant restaurant is run by a wine company, which, first and foremost, translates to an excellent wine cellar. Within the walls of this classic Burgundian-style house is served some of the best food in the region. Some sample dishes include smoked salmon, sweetbreads in truffle cream and turbot baked with bone marrow. In addition to the dining room, there is a small wine museum through which you may tour in English. The set menus at this dining complex start at FR150. Reservations required. Credit Cards: All Major.

Le Rallye $$ ★★★

39 rue Chabot-Charny, In the middle of the old city. ☎ *03-80-67-11-55.*
Dinner: 7:30–9:30 p.m., entrées FR85–FR225.

Within the stone walls of this 18th-century building lies a traditional restaurant with all of the classic fare. The husband-wife duo operates this establishment in the spirit of an earlier time. The welcome is genuine, and the meals are solid. Look for the steamed turbot or the terrine of duck with pistachios. Set menus start at FR95–FR225. Closed late Feb.–mid-Mar. and most of Aug. Closed: Sun. Reservations required. Credit Cards: All Major.

Directory

To and From

By train from Paris (three hours), Lyons (two hours), or Strasbourg (four hours), or by road on the A-6 autoroute from Paris or Lyon or the A-31 autoroute from Champagne and the north.

Tourist Office

34 rue des Forges; ☎ *(33) 03-80-44-11-44.*

Rail Station

cour de la Gàre; ☎ *(33) 03-80-41-50-50.*

Post Office

place Grangier, 21000 Dijon; ☎ *(33) 803-0-50-62-19.*

Avallon

A strategic fortified town on a rocky promontory overlooking the Cousin river since before the Romans invaded, Avallon is still a cold and defensive-looking town. Invaded and besieged repeatedly during the years, Avallon has had good reason to stay that way. The ramparts that encircle the city give a good view over the valley. A highlight is the 12th-century Romanesque-style Eglise St. Lazare, which has an ornately carved portal similar to the left portal at Chartres, displaying the signs of the zodiac along with the different labors of each month. The statuary contained within the nave retains some of its original polychrome painting. The best of Avallon, however, is the Musée de l'Avallonais, containing a surprisingly good collection of art from through the ages. Highlights include a second-century Roman mosaic depicting Venus, and a series of emotive etchings called "Misère" depicting Christ's agony executed by the early 20th-century artist Georges Rouault.

What to Do

Historical/Architectural Sites

Eglise Collegiale St-Lazare ★★★

rue Bocquillot. South of the bell tower.
Hours open: 8:45 a.m.–7 p.m. Special hours: In the winter, to 6 p.m.
Built in the 11th century on the site of a 4th-century sanctuary dedicated to St-Mary, the nave was augmented in the 12th century. The church was named after a piece of St-Lazare's skull was donated to the church in the year 1000. Above ground, there are two richly decorated portals (a third was destroyed when the original clock tower collapsed), and below ground is a 4th-century crypt.

Museums and Exhibits

Musée de l'Avallonais ★

place de la Collegiale, ☎ *03-86-34-03-19. Behind the tourist office.*
Hours open: 10 a.m.–6 p.m. Special hours: Closed 12:30–2 p.m.; May–mid-Sept. only.
Closed: Tue.
Founded in 1862, this hodgepodge museum displays prehistoric and Gallo-Roman art, statues and jewelry and modern-day religious art. Rather poorly arranged, the artifacts may be of interest to some visitors. Admission: FR15.

Where to Stay

Inns

Chateau de Vault-de-Lugny FR650–FR1600 ★★★★

Vault de Lugny. ☎ *03-86-34-07-86, FAX: 03-86-34-16-36. About 5 km northeast of Avallon. Take D957 northeast and turn right in Pontaubert. Follow the signs.*
Single: FR650–FR950. Double: FR700–FR1600.
A noble symbol of luxury, this Relais and Chateaux rated chateau was constructed in the 16th century. Owned and managed by a father-daughter duo, it flourishes on 100 acres of stream-fed property complete with a 13th-century tower and a moat. With this kind of wonderful isolation, tranquility is assured. The 12 rooms are rich with traditional decor and have TV, telephone, minibar and private bath. Old World elegance is defined in the Renaissance suite with canopy bed, stone fireplace, beamed ceiling, oak table and antique furnishings. Lunch and dinner are served to guests only in the candlelit dining room, and the salon-bar is very inviting. Fairy-tale

writers couldn't dream up something this good. Features: wheelchair-access rooms, tennis, in-room minibars. Credit Cards: V, A.

Hostellerie de la Poste   FR650–FR900   ★★★

13 place Vauban. ☎ *03-86-34-06-12, FAX: 03-86-34-47-11. About 1 km from train station, in the center of town.*
Single: FR650. Double: FR900.

With a guest list that has included Napoleon, Eisenhower and Kennedy, la Poste has been luring guests since 1707. The 2 two-story buildings now sit where the inn, stables and outlying houses originally were. Decorated in period style with antiques, tapestries and some canopy beds, the 30 rooms have TV, telephone and bath. Freshly renovated, la Poste is positioned to last a few more centuries. Credit Cards: All Major.

Moulin des Ruats   FR300–FR650   ★★★

Vallee du Cousin. ☎ *03-86-34-07-14, FAX: 03-86-31-65-47. About 4 km from Avallon, in the Cousin Valley.*
Double: FR300–FR650.

A picturesque old mill on the banks of the Cousin River, it has been a hotel since 1924. After years of adjustments, it now has 26 comfortable rooms with pretty, country decor. Those in the side building are a bit more modern but still attractive. Basic amenities include telephone and bath; some have river-view balconies. Delicious food is served on the terrace in warm months and in a dining room with river views the rest of the year. Friendly, personal service. Credit Cards: All Major.

Where to Eat

Moulin des Ruats $$$ ★★★★

D427, About 3.5 km out of town on the D427, at Vallee du Cousin. ☎ *03-86-34-07-14.*
Dinner: 7–9 p.m., entrées FR200–FR400.

A successful combination of a beautiful location on the banks of the Cousin River and excellent original cuisine, the Moulin des Ruats. Take advantage of the setting during warm months and take dinner on the terrace. The food is delightfully thoughtful; try the sweetbread, snails or any of the succulent fish. Desserts are delectable, and the wine cellar is improving with the years. Set menus from FR150 for weekday lunch and FR225 for dinners. Closed: Mon. Amenities: outside dining, reservations required. Credit Cards: V, DC.

Restaurant Le Morvan $$ ★★★

7 route de Paris, On the edge of town, off the N6. ☎ *03-86-34-18-20.*
Dinner: 7–9 p.m., entrées FR130–FR225.

Pleasantly located on the outskirts of town, this restaurant occupies an attractive 18th-century inn boasting a pretty park view. Regional cuisine is prepared with great care, including dishes such as duckling, fresh fish and sweetbreads. All of the food is impressive. Set menus start at FR130–FR225. Closed: Mon. Reservations required. Credit Cards: All Major.

Directory

To and From

By train from Paris (three hours) and Auxerre (one hour), or by car on the N-6 highway, parallel to the A-6 autoroute, from Auxerre.

Tourist Office

    4 rue Boquillot; ☎ *(33) 03-86-34-14-19.*

Rail Station

    place de la Gàre; ☎ *(33) 03-86-34-01-01.*

Post Office

    9 rue des Odebert, 89200 Avallon; ☎ *(33) 03-86-34-13-50.*

Vézelay

Vézelay's Basilica of Sainte-Madeleine is surrounded by gorgeous countryside.

While at Avallon you should visit the abbey at Vézelay. A Bénédictine abbey had been on the site at the top of the hill in the tiny village since the ninth century, but things changed dramatically when the abbey received the relics of St. Mary Magdalene (her remains, more or less) from a church in St. Maximin in Provence in the 11th century. In order to accommodate the huge numbers of pilgrims, who often visited the site before continuing on to Santiago de Compostela in Spain, a much larger basilica was built. The result is one of the finest examples of Romanesque-style religious architecture in France. The crypt dates back to the original Carolingian abbey, although the vault was replaced in the late 12th century. One of the highlights is the tympanum, a carved entranceway from the narthex into the nave, dating from 1120 to 1135, that depicts the risen Christ shining light upon his faithful. The facade of the basilica was completed about the same time, and has a large 13th-century stained-glass ensemble. The 13th-century Tour de St. Michel, to the right of the facade, is named after a statue of the archangel it contains. The interior of the basilica is most instructive for those interested in religious architecture of the middle ages. The nave is early 12th-century Romanesque, using alternating light and dark stones to create an unusual striped effect in the round transverse arches. Built just 50 years later, the choir has the Gothic-style vaulting that was then so modern. The chapter house and the cloister are the last remnants of the monastic buildings. In the late 13th century, unscrupulous town leaders back in St. Maximin spread a rumor that the relics of Magdalene were still in Provence, and although the Catholic church continued—and continues—to proclaim that what you see in the crypt are in fact Mary Magdalene's last earthly remains, Vézelay's fortunes declined soon afterwards, and until the basilica was restored in the mid-19th century it had fallen into disrepair.

Vézelay is about nine miles east of Avallon on the D-957 road.

What to Do

Historical/Architectural Sites

Basilique Ste-Madeleine

On top of the hill.
Hours open: 7 a.m.–6 p.m. Special hours: Closed Sun. until 1 p.m.
Founded in the 9th century under Charlemagne, the Christians flocked here in the 11th and 12th centuries to see the alleged remains of Mary Magdelene. Upon entry, notice the tympanum above the center portal, dating to 1125, which displays Christ, the apostles, evangelists and zodiac signs. In 1120, the nave caught fire during the pilgrimage and killed more than 1000 worshipers. The most impressive time to visit is on a Tues. or Fri. night between 9 and 10:30 p.m (July and Aug. only) when the church is illuminated. Guided tours upon written request. Admission: free.

Where to Stay

Hotels and Resorts

Hotel Poste and Lion d'Or   FR250–FR590   ★★

place du Champ-de-Foire. ☎ *03-86-33-21-23, FAX: 03-86-32-30-92.*
Single: FR250–FR320. Double: FR340–FR590.
Once an 11th-century basilica, this site later served as a post office and now a traditional country inn. Overlooking the valley, there are 48 attractive rooms with TV, telephone and private bath. The dining room serves exceptional food with fixed-price meals starting at FR140. Formerly the Poste et Lion d'Or Hotel, this is considered to be a local historical monument. Credit Cards: All Major.

L'Esperance   FR350–FR1500   ★★★

St-Pere-sous-VÈzelay. ☎ *03-86-33-39-10, FAX: 03-86-33-26-15.*
Rated Restaurant: *L'EspÈrance.*
Single: FR350–FR1000. Double: FR1100–FR1500.
A country manor house just outside town, this Relais and Chateaux inn houses 36 uniquely decorated rooms in three separate buildings. Situated by a stream and a large garden, the setting is tranquil and rustic. Comfortable and small, the rooms come with TV, minibar, telephone, radio and private shower or bath. The suites in the millhouse are the most lovely, especially number 31, which has a private staircase and a living room. The renowned restaurant is one of France's best. Leisure facilities are limited to a gym and a pool. The tradition of accommodating and respectful service has been carried on by the courteous staff and management. Closed Jan. Features: pool, tennis, air conditioning in rooms, fitness center. Credit Cards: All Major.

Le Pontot   FR550–FR850   ★★

place du Pontot. ☎ *03-86-33-24-40, FAX: 03-86-33-30-05.*
Single: FR550–FR600. Double: FR550–FR850.
In a town of limited lodging options, Le Pontot bodes well with its 10 rooms. Formerly a fortified medieval chateau from the 15th century, this central hotel enjoys a location near the Basilica Ste-Madeleine. The individually decorated rooms come with telephone, radio and private bath—simple yet sumptuous. Sunny mornings awaken guests with breakfast in the garden, while the elegant blue salon warms its guests with breakfast on the chilly days. A quality choice for those with reservations. Credit Cards: All Major.

Where to Eat

Cheap Eats $ ★★

Near rue St-Etienne. ☎ *03-86-33-35-57.*
The best creperie in town, **L' Auberge de la Coquille** *(81 rue St-Pierre;* ☎ *03-86-33-35-57)* offers tastily-stuffed crepes, galettes and salads from FR30. *Open daily 11:30 a.m.–9:30 p.m.; closed mid-Nov.–mid-Feb.* Another bargain spot is **A la Fortune du Pot** *(place du Champ de Foire).* Some healthy dishes are on the menu starting at FR60. *Open weekdays, noon–2:30 p.m. and 6–9 p.m.; weekends, noon–5 p.m.* Finally, the town's main brasserie, **Le Vezelien**, closes in Feb. *(*☎ *03-86-33-25-09).*

Marc Meneau **$$$**

St-Pere-sous-Vezelay, Take the D957 about 3 km southeast of Vezelay. Located at
L'Esperance. ☎ *03-86-33-39-10.*
Dinner: 7:30–9:30 p.m., entrées FR290–FR400.

The finest establishment in Burgundy and one of the top restaurants in France,
Marc Meneau sits in the enchanting hotel L'Esperance. Chef Meneau is a self-
taught culinary wizard serving guests in beautiful glassed-in dining rooms. Making
his work appear effortless, every one of his dishes is the result of careful selection of
ingredients, detailed preparation, perfect cooking and artful presentation. He can
do no wrong with his appetizers, entrées and desserts. Add to this rare display of
perfection a fine bottle of wine, and it's a gastronomic experience like no other.
While not a bargain, the relativity of quality of food to price is appropriate. Fixed-
meals start at FR300 for weekday lunch and FR560 for dinners. Closed: Tues. res-
ervations required.

Fontenay

Burgundy's other great monastery is harder to visit but well worth the trip.
In 1098, a group of Bénédictine monks, disenchanted by what they saw as
the extravagance of the great monastery at Cluny (now in ruins, the monas-
tery was among the most powerful in Europe at the time), founded the Cis-
tercian order, dedicated to poverty and simplicity. In 1112, a young
Burgundian noble of great intelligence and drive joined the order and built it
up into one of the largest orders in Europe, with 167 abbeys established in
his lifetime, and more than 700 by the 17th century. He was canonized as St.
Bernard in 1174, just 21 years after his death. The monastery at Fontenay is
a notable example of the stern, austere doctrines of the order, its Abbey
Church barren of all decorations, the long dormitory unheated, its chapter
house and scriptorium featuring only the most functional of ribbed vaulting.
Used as a paper mill after the Révolution, the abbey was purchased by a non-
profit foundation in the early 20th century and restored to its original con-
dition. While it lacks the authenticity of Vézelay, which has been in use as a
sanctuary for 1000 years, Fontenay offers a revealing look at the harsh life of
the 12th-century monk.

Fontenay is about 30 miles northeast of Avallon on the D-32 spur, off the
D-905 road.

What to Do

Historical/Architectural Sites

Abbaye de Fontenay ★★★★

On the D32, ☎ *03-80-92-15-00. Northeast of Avallon and northwest of Dijon off of the*
D905.
Hours open: 9 a.m.–6 p.m. Special hours: Closed noon–2 p.m.

The oldest remaining Cistercian foundation in the country, this abbey was founded
by Bernard de Clairvaux in 1118. Enjoying a fantastically sublime location in the
forest, peace and tranquility is found. During the Revolution, the abbey was sold

and converted into a paper mill. Around the turn of the century, it was restored to its original state under new ownership. Guided tours are given in French, with English brochures available.

Historical tours help visitors envision the former glory of the abbey at Cluny.

BURGUNDY

Châlon-sur-Saone

The unassuming town of Châlon-sur-Saone has always been an important trade center. Here, the Saone becomes a serious river, navigable down to the Rhône and points south. There is archaeological evidence that the Romans imported wine here from Naples before they had grape vines up and going in Gaul. Nowadays, the city is home to a major heavy-engineering firm and a nuclear power plant. You won't visit for the industry, or even the cathedral, which is a perfectly fine Romanesque-to-Gothic structure with a Carolingian crypt. The number-one attraction in this town is the **Musée Nicéphore Niepce**. If the name says nothing to you, consider heading on, but if you recognize the inventor of photography, the museum is a shrine. There is evidence that the 11th-century Arab scientist El Hazen understood the principles of camera obscura, and in the 15th century Leonardo da Vinci pondered the problem, as well as various 18th century scientists who attempted to engrave an image using light. Success came to Joseph Nicéphore Niecpe, who was born in this town in 1765. He was an inventor and draftsman, and already had invented an internal combustion engine in 1807 when he decided he was going to figure out how to make a camera. It took him three years, but on May 28, 1816, he succeeded in making and fixing a positive image—of his house just south of town—creating the world's first photograph. The museum has Nicéphore Niecpe's original instruments and experiments, as well as documents and archives, producing a fascinating history of early photography. Unfortunately, that first print no longer exists.

What to Do

Historical/Architectural Sites

Eglise St-Vincent ★★

quai des Messageries. Up the river from the Musée Niepce.
At the heart of the medieval town, the Eglise St-Vincent reflects a medley of architectural styles. Built on the ruins of a temple dedicated to Mercury, this cathedral sits close to the banks of the River Saone. Take note of the detailed stonework in the choir and the beautiul wooden statues.

Museums and Exhibits

Musée Nicephore Niepce ★★★

28 quai des Messageries, ☎ *03-85-48-41-98. On the banks of the River Saone. Closed: Tue.*
Named for the man who invented photography, this museum occupies an 18th-century house on the banks of the Saone. Tracing the history of photography, it displays equipment from the 1800s, some of the early photographs and a fine collection of contemporary photos. The lunar camera used with the U.S. Apollo space program is also included here. *Open July–Aug., Wed.–Mon., 10 a.m.–6 p.m.;*

Sept.–June, Wed.–Mon., 9:30–11:30 a.m. and 2:30–5:30 p.m. Child admission is
FR5; Wed. admission is free. Admission: FR10.

Where to Stay

Bed-and-Breakfasts

Les Buissonnets   **FR270–FR380**   ★ ★ ★

102 grande rue. ☎ *03-85-91-48-49. About 12 km northwest of Chalon-sur-Saone. Exit
the autoroute at Chalon Nord, then take N6 towards Chagny. About 3 km past Champ-
forgeuil, head left towards Fontaines.*
Double: FR270–FR380.

Surrounded by a private park, this lovely house is watched over by the welcoming
husband and wife owners. Beautifully furnished with antiques and color coordinated fabrics, the three rooms come with private bath. Adjacent to the salon, the
dining room serves complementary breakfast and dinner (FR150 with wine) at sep-
artate tables. Visit the nearby village for a relaxed day of touring. Credit Cards: Not
Accepted.

Hotels and Resorts

St-Georges   **FR425**   ★ ★

32 avenue J.-Jaures. ☎ *03-85-48-27-05, FAX: 03-85-93-23-88. Across from the train
station.*
Double: FR425.

An updated, provincial hotel convenient to the train station and the town center. All
48 rooms are air-conditioned and include modern amenities; most have bath.
Although a bit compact, they are impeccably kept. The service is attentive. Features:
air conditioning in rooms. Credit Cards: All Major.

St-Regis   **FR500**   ★ ★

22 boulevard de la Republique. ☎ *03-85-48-07-28, FAX: 03-85-48-90-88. Between old
town and the train station.*
Double: FR500.

Well-situated between the train station and the old town, the St-Regis is an old
faithful now part of the Best Western family. Nothing showy, just 38 air-conditioned rooms equipped with modern amenities and decorated in contemporary
style. There is a decent restaurant, as well as a bar and a few lounges. Half-board
rates are FR340–FR550. Features: air conditioning in rooms.

Autun

Hotels and Resorts

Les Ursulines   **FR340–FR560**   ★ ★

14 rue Rivault. ☎ *03-85-52-68-00, FAX: 03-85-86-23-07. Located between boulevard
Mac-Mahon and rue Dufraigne. Between the Cathedral and Tour des Ursulines.* Rated
Restaurant: *Ursulines.*
Single: FR340–FR450. Double: FR450–FR560.

A former convent, this quiet hotel has views of the countryside and the mountains
of the Morvan. Accommodations include 38 rooms, all with lively decor and
thoughtfully equipped. There are a restaurant, wine cellar and courtyard. Features:
wheelchair-access rooms. Credit Cards: All Major.

St-Louis **FR300** ★★

6 rue de l'Arbalete. ☎ *03-85-52-21-03, FAX: 03-85-86-32-54. Near town center.*
Double: FR300.

Since its first days as a 17th-century coaching inn, th St-Louis has developed into a
comfortable hotel. Classically French, there are 52 well-scrubbed rooms, most with
bath, TV, telephone and minibar. The Napoleonic Chamber boasts two canopied
beds and a fireplace. Relax in the sun-drenched garden during the day, and start off
the evening with dinner in the restaurant. As charming as it was in the 1800s when
Napoleon stayed here. Credit Cards: All Major.

Where to Eat

Didier Denis **$$** ★★★★

1 rue du Pont ☎ *03-85-48-81-01.*
Dinner: 7:30–9:45 p.m., entrées FR175–FR225.

The energetic and insightful Didier Denis skillfully blends classic cuisine with a
modern hand. He makes the most complicated dish appear simple—the tastes are
unhindered by any unnecessary meddling with the fresh and pure ingredients. The
gracious hosts give the warmest of receptions to every guest that has the pleasure of
dining here. Pick any one of a number of excellent bottles from the cellar. Set
menus from FR90. Closed: Mon. Reservations required. Credit Cards: V.

Ripert **$$** ★★★

7 place St-Vincent, Near the cathedral. ☎ *03-85-48-89-20.*
Dinner: 7–9 p.m., entrées FR100–FR200.

Reliably quality fare based on the availablity of ingredients at the market. Chef Alain
Ripert presents a new menu daily, making dining here an interesting, flavorful experience every time. Perhaps a foie gras, leg of lamb or fresh fish will highlight the
menu. No matter what the special of the day is, one can be sure Ripert will put a
new twist on it, using his culinary creativity to the guests' benefit every time. Set
menus start at FR100–FR125. Closed: Mon., Sun. Reservations recommended.
Credit Cards: V.

Directory

To and From

By train from Dijon (half an hour) or Lyon (70 minutes), or by car at the intersection of
the N-6 road and A-6 autoroute south of Dijon.

Tourist Office

boulevard de la République; ☎ *(33) 03-85-48-37-97.*

Rail Station

rue de la Gàre; ☎ *(33) 03-85-50-01-01.*

Post Office

22 place de Beaune, 71100 Châlon-sur-Saone.

Beaune

Beaune is a living demonstration of the history of Burgundy. The vines that
now produce the world's most beloved red and white wines were originally
planted and maintained by monasteries and abbeys. As the cloisters and ab-

beys became more luxurious, abbots and monks sold off their land to raise money for finer things. At the same time, the newly wealthy local bourgeoisie invested in wineries, and by the 16th century, the wineries of the region were all in the hands of merchants and the wines were gaining fame around the world.

All, that is, except for 130 acres. This is the vignoble still belonging to the Hôtel Dieu, the magnificent 15th-century hospital in Beaune. This stunning jewel is a Gothic-style building with a monumental colored-tile roof and elegant interior decor, ironwork, gables and beams. The hospital was founded in 1443 by Nicolas Rolin (1377–1461), who as chancellor to Phillip the Good, was one of a time-honored class of French financiers who made fortunes for their rulers as well as themselves. Rolin came from humble beginnings but rose to be Phillipe's right hand man, credited with negotiating a peaceful transition for the duchy, from supporting the English during the Hundred Years' War to being a prestigious part of France after the war ended. At age 66, perhaps seized with guilt for his own excesses, Rolin founded a free hospital for the poor and guaranteed it a perpetual income from a 3200-acre estate of woodland, farmland and vines. Today the Hôpital de Dieu, a monument, survives on the last remaining vines, whose superb wines are sold at auction the third Sunday in November in a three-day celebration and wine festival that is one of the most important in the country. The hospital cared for the indigent sick until 1971—a total of 520 years, under the same foundation founded by Rolin. The buildings are filled with original furniture and equipment, such as jars of woodlouse powder and shrimps' eyes in the apothecary, kitchen utensils and even old medical personnel uniforms on the mannequins in the various dioramas. Inside, one of the most beautiful and significant Gothic-style artworks in existence can be found. "The Last Judgment" was painted by Roger van der Weyden between 1443 and 1451. Still in remarkable condition, the painting includes incredible detail and depth of emotion. In the prudish 19th century the naked figures in the painting (the dead awaiting judgment) were given clothing, but the masterpiece was later restored to its original glory.

Beaune is located halfway between Dijon and Châlon-sur-Saone at the junction of the A-6 and the A-31 autoroutes.

What to Do

Historical/Architectural Sites

Hotel Dieu ★★★

place de la Halle, ☎ *03-80-24-45-00. North of Chalon-sur-Saone.*
Founded in the 15th century, this still partially functioning hospital gives a fascinating glimpse at late medieval life. Tour the halls, wards and various rooms of this Gothic building. A good English brochure is available at the entrance. *Open Apr.–*

mid-Nov., daily, 9 a.m.–6:30 p.m.; mid-Nov.–Mar., daily, 9 a.m.–11:30 a.m. and 2–5:30 p.m. Student admission is FR20. Admission: FR25.

Where to Stay

Hotels and Resorts

A la Cote St-Jacques   **FR720–FR1750**   ★★★★

14 faubourg de Paris. ☎ *03-86-62-09-70. Located on the N6 leading to Sens; between the Yonne River and rue faubourg St.-Jacques.*
Single: FR720–FR1000. Double: FR1170–FR1750.

With its adjoining golf course, this hotel attracts a following of swinging enthusiasts. In addition to golf, there are tennis courts, croquet and a pool. Nearby are the racetrack and the stadium for even more of the sporting theme. The 165 rooms are done in pastel colors, spacious and come with TV, telephone, minibar and private bath. Breakfast is served for FR90, and other meals are available in the dining room with scenic views. A very leisurely hotel. Features: wheelchair-access rooms, pool, golf, tennis, air conditioning in rooms, sauna, in-room minibars. Credit Cards: All Major.

La Poste   **FR500–FR1000**   ★★

1 boulevard Georges-Clemenceau. ☎ *03-80-22-08-11, FAX: 03-80-24-19-71. Located about 45 km south of Dijon; opposite Le Cap at rue du Faubourg-Bretonniere.*
Single: FR500–FR750. Double: FR750–FR1000.

In a building dating back to 1660, this hotel is located on the busy ring-road that follows Beaune's ancient walls. In recent years, La Poste has undergone a complete renovation, including the addition of double-paned windows to eliminate the traffic noise from rooms facing the boulevard. The lobby and bar have retained their old-world ambience, but the 21 rooms are more contemporary in their decor, all with brass beds and well-equipped bathrooms. The rooms in the front of the hotel overlook both the impressive ramparts and a noisy intersection that the soundproof windows don't quite keep at bay. For complete quiet, ask for a room at the back, where there is a view of the vineyards on nearby slopes. The in-house restaurant is reliable for traditional Burgundian dishes. Also featured are a billiard room and garage parking for guests. Features: air conditioning in rooms, in-room minibars. Credit Cards: All Major.

Le Cep   **FR500–FR1000**   ★★★

27 rue Maufoux. ☎ *03-80-22-35-48, FAX: 03-80-22-76-80. Located opposite La Poste, between Rempart des Dames and rue Vivant-Gardin.*
Single: FR500–FR600. Double: FR600–FR1000.

A restored Renaissance mansion, Le Cep is located in the heart of town. In the public areas, heavy-beamed ceilings, old gilt-framed portraits and fresh flower arrangements create an atmosphere of character and elegance. A massive stone staircase leads from the interior roofed courtyard to the upper floors, and arched galleries overlook the courtyard on each floor. Accommodations include 49 large, comfortably furnished, elegantly decorated rooms with thick carpets and highly polished antiques; each room is different and has a marble bath. The former wine cellar, a cozy room with a low, arched stone ceiling, is used as a breakfast room when the weather does not permit breakfast outdoors in the courtyard. Features: wheelchair-access rooms, air conditioning in rooms. Credit Cards: All Major.

Inns

Lameloise   **FR600–FR1500**   ★★

36 place d'Armes. ☎ *03-85-87-08-85. Located on the square at boulevard de la Libert.*
Rated Restaurant: *Lameloise.*
Single: FR600–FR1100. Double: FR1100–FR1500.
Surrounded by a walled, tree-filled garden, this 15th-century three-story stone mansion has a country atmosphere, despite its central setting in the town. Inside, the decor is essentially modern, with 18th- and 19th-century furnishings are used as accents. There are 20 rooms of various sizes, all with private bath, and some with a terrace overlooking the vineyards. This Relais and Chateau rated inn has an exceptional restaurant, and reservations are required. Features: air conditioning in rooms.
Credit Cards: All Major.

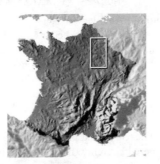

CHAMPAGNE

Vintners have produced wine in the Champagne region since Roman times.

What Makes Champagne So French?

1. Champagne–*a designation given* only *to sparkling white wine produced in the* Sacred Triangle.

2. *The* Sacred Triangle–*Reims, Epernay and Chalone-sur-Marne.*

3. *About 200 million bottles of* champagne *produced annually according to the* méthode traditionelle–*making the world a happier* (much happier) *place.*

4. *The* Sacred Triangle.

5. Champagne.

Despite the best efforts of the wine-makers in this part of the country to protect their trademarked name from being applied to all sparkling wines, millions of people around the world are unaware that there is even a place called Champagne. Yet *la Champagne* exists, a region that is home to the so-called Triangle Sacré, the "Sacred Triangle" where *real* champagne (liquid ecstacy to some) is produced. This is the Mecca for lovers of bubbly just as Cognac is the pilgrimage for connoisseurs of fine brandy. Yet there really is more to do in Champagne than simply visit the caves of Moët and Chandon and sample the elixir. The towns that produce champagne as well as the little villages, with half-timbered churches, hold much to interest visitors.

History

Now a quiet region bordering peacefully on Belgium, separated only by the dense and ancient Ardennes forest, Champagne has a bloody and confrontational past. Although the tribes that inhabited the region when the Romans invaded adapted to and accepted Roman rule readily, Champagne was first torn apart by war when Attila the Hun came pillaging in the middle of the fifth century. A combined force of Roman, Frankish and Visigoth armies routed the invader in a battle at Champs Cataluniques. Later that century, the region "crowned" the first Christian king in France when Clovis was baptized at Reims; all French kings except for three were subsequently crowned there. Violence continued—thousands died in the Wars of Religion, and it was here that king Louis XVI, fleeing the Révolution with his family, was arrested, before losing his head to the guillotine. In 1870, a major battle between the French of Napoléon III and the Prussian army ended in defeat for the French; Napoléon's downfall followed soon after. Like Alsace-Lorraine to the east, Champagne was devastated during World War I; the Battle of the Marne was one of the bloodiest and most deadly of the conflict. Barely a generation later, Hitler's Nazis motored unopposed through Luxembourg and Belgium and around the end of the Maginot Line to begin their conquest of France in Champagne. Since the end of World War II, the region has achieved a peaceful lifestyle, and now champagne production as well as wheat and sugar beet farming to the south reign as the king industries.

Cuisine

For a sparkling white wine to be called champagne, it must be produced in an area of 84,000 acres mostly contained in the Sacred Triangle marked by the cities of Reims, Epernay and Châlone-sur-Marne. Vintners have been producing wine in the region since Roman times—indeed, some caves have been in business since then—but the sparkling, double-fermented wine we know as champagne has only been around since the end of the 17th century. Today, some 200 million bottles of the stuff are produced every year; that's

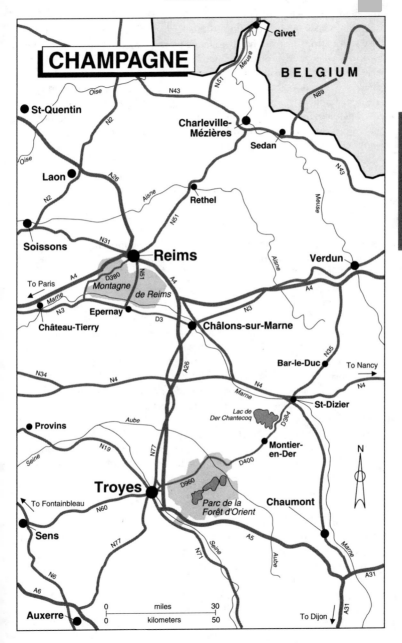

the genuine article, not counting *mouseaux* or *crémant*, which are similar sparkling wines made according to the *Méthode Traditionelle*, but produced elsewhere. Not surprisingly, champagne plays a major role in local cuisine. It is drunk as an apéritif or to celebrate, just as in the rest of the world, and is served with any plate from fish to sorbet. It is also used in cooking, some specialties including *volaille au champagne* (chicken cooked in champagne), *rognons* (kidneys), *civet d'oie* (goose stew), and several fish dishes. Other *champagnois* dishes include *andouilettes*, sausages common throughout the north of the country, smoked ham, and trout either stuffed or *à la Ardennaise*, that is, in a ham and cream sauce.

Reims

Reims (often written *Rheims* in English; rhymes with "rhymes") forms one corner of the Sacred Triangle and is known to most people the world over precisely and only for being a producer of *le champagne*. But Reims has earned its place in history. The site of the coronation of most of France's kings, Reims was a stabilizing and unifying force in the French political and social landscape from the 13th through 19th centuries. Its roots as a center of power go even deeper than that—Caesar conquered the region held by the Remes tribe and the city that developed became the capital of the Romans' Belgica province. The Remes were cooperative with their new masters, and in the middle of the fifth century, the united Roman, Visigoth and Frankish forces repelled the armies of Attila the Hun, whose westward advance was halted outside the city. The Romans soon declined, and the new leader of the Franks, King Clovis, showed a shrewd appreciation of the burgeoning influence of the church when he was baptized as a Christian here in 498 by the bishop, St. Remigius. A church had been erected on the site of a former Roman temple as early as A.D. 401, but in 1211, the present monumental Gothic-style cathedral was begun. Built in the style introduced at Chartres, it was expanded and embellished with even more ornate details, even lighter lines, and even more prominent windows. The nave at Reims is also taller than the one at Chartres. The most interesting and best-known feature of the cathedral are the sculpted angels included with the saints and kings sculpted on the building's exterior; the sculptors chose to give the angels a happy countenance, and one in particular, known as the "Smiling Angel of Reims," has a positively mirthful expression and has become the symbol of the city. Clovis' baptism is now considered the first coronation at Reims, although he had pronounced himself king long before, but his baptism sparked a trend that was continued in the coronation of Louis VIII in 1223. From that ceremony until the coronation of Charles X in 1824, all but three of France's kings were anointed by the Bishop of Reims in the cathedral. Perhaps the most significant baptism was that of Charles VII who had to be positively shoved into it by Joan of Arc in 1429. From the 17th century, when a king-to-be was to be crowned, he spent the night before the ceremony in the Bishop's palace, known as the Palais du Tau. Tau is Greek for the letter "T," and it referred to the shape of the building, built to represent the crosses then carried by Roman Catholic bishops. The palace now houses a museum that contains original sculpture from the cathedral (much has been replaced over the years) as well as 15th-century tapestries depicting Clovis' baptism, and coronation robes worn by some of the kings. Also significant is the Basilique St. Rémi, begun in the year 1007, although much restored since then. The basilica is notable for the unusual proportions of the interior—400 feet long by only 85 feet wide. The transepts are original 11th-century construction; the choir dates from a century later.

A major battleground during World War I, Reims was occupied by the Germans for four years, and was almost completely destroyed. By the end of the war, only 60 houses out of 15,000 remained habitable, and the cathedral had been badly damaged. A generation later, when the Allies routed Hitler's armies in western Europe, General Dwight Eisenhower accepted the surrender of the Germans in Reims, and the schoolroom, immortalized in journalism classes everywhere as the "little red schoolhouse" (called the *Salle de Reddition*), is open to the public and houses a museum explaining the last days of World War II. After World War II, much of the restoration work on the cathedral was financed by the Rockefeller Foundation. Work continued until 1966, when Reims held a 1500th anniversay bash to celebrate the baptism of King Louis. An impressive sight remaining from Reims' deep history is the Porte Mars, the massive triple triumphant arch built by the Romans in the third century. A number of small champagne houses in Reims offer tours of their facilities, including Taittinger, Pommery and Ruinart, although you would probably be better served touring one of the larger houses in Epernay.

What to Do

Historical/Architectural Sites

Basilique St-Remi ★★★

53 rue St-Simon, ☎ *03-26-85-31-20. On the southeast side of town.*
Hours open: 10 a.m.–6 p.m. Special Hours: Closed noon–2 p.m. Closed: Tue.

Less visited but quite an outstanding achievement, this is a Gothic renovation of a Carolingian Romanesque church. The nave, the transepts, the aisles and one of the towers dates from the 11th century. The interior is like an airplane hangar, 400 feet long, but only 85 feet wide. St-Remi, the bishop of Reims from 459 to 533, rests in the elaborately carved tomb behind the altar. His baptism of Clovis is credited with introducing Catholicism to the French. Next door is the **Abbaye St-Remi**, *53 rue Simon* (☎ *03-26-85-23-36*), which houses a rich collection of Carolingian and

Merovingian artifacts, religious art and military uniforms. *Open Mon.–Fri., 2–6:30 p.m., Sat.–Sun., 2–7 p.m.*; FR10. Admission: free.

Cathédrale Notre Dame ★★★★

place du Cardinal Lucon.
Hours open: 7:30 a.m.–7 p.m.

Built between 1211 and 1294, the Cathédrale Notre Dame is a Gothic marvel. It has abundant sculpture and statuary ("The Smiling Angel") and six stained-glass windows by Chagall that replaced a few of the many that were destroyed in World War II. At sunset, you can view the Rose Window atop the center doorway of the west facade; from here, you can see in greater detail the sculpted forms of the Virgin, the 12 apostles and a band of angels. Next door is the **Palais du Tau**, the archbishop's palace, with a Gothic chapel, and the Salle, a banquet hall where just-crowned monarchs would hold sumptuous banquets. Today it houses a tapestry-rich Treasury, including the baptismal tapestry belonging to Clovis, King of the Franks, and Charlemagne's talisman, a relic reportedly from Christ's cross (*open 9:30 a.m.–6:30 p.m.*; admission FR27, students, seniors FR17, children FR7). This year, the city is doing a major clean-up in preparation for the 1500-year anniversary of Clovis' baptism, which will be celebrated in the cathedral. Admission: free.

Porte de Mars ★★★

place de la Republique. Off boulevard Foch.

Built in 200, this served as the western gate of ancient Reims, once the largest in the Roman Empire. It was erected in honor of Augustus, two centuries after his death. Towards the center of town is the place Royal, the most royal of Reims' squares. A statue of Louis XV stands in the center, replaced after the revolutionaries tore it down in a demonstration against royalty. Admission: free.

Museums and Exhibits

Musée des Beaux-Arts ★★

8 rue Chanzy, ☎ 03-26-47-28-44. Near the Basilique St-Remi.
Hours open: 10 a.m.–6 p.m. Special Hours: Closed noon–2 p.m. Closed: Tue.

Housed in the former abbey of St-Denis, this provincial art gallery has a decent collection of works from the 16th through 20th centuries. Cranach, both elder and younger, are strongly represented here with the dozen or so portraits of German princes, which the museum has owned since it first opened. Other well-knowns here include Monet, Renoir, Gauguin, David, Delacroix, Matisse, Pissarro and many others. A fine collection but the facility could use some sprucing up. Admission: FR10.

Palais du Tau ★★★

place du Cardinal Lucon, ☎ 03-26-47-81-79. To the right of the cathedral.
Hours open: 9:30 a.m.–6:30 p.m. Special Hours: Sept.–June, closed 12:30–2 p.m.

Built in 1690, the Tau Palace Museum is the former archbishop's palace. Within its spacious rooms are tapestries, sculptures and artifacts that once adorned the cathedral. Also displayed are the velvet and gold vestments worn by Charles X, the last king to be crowned here. Other items of interest include the 9th-century Talisman of Charlemagne, the 12th-century coronation chalice and the collar of the Order of the Holy Ghost. Admission: FR27.

Salle de la Reddition ★★

12 rue Franklin Roosevelt, ☎ 03-26-47-84-19. On the north side of town, across the tracks.
Closed: Tue.

On May 7, 1945, the Germans surrendered to General Dwight Eisenhower, the Allied Supreme Commander, in this schoolroom. Two days later, the Germans surrendered to the Russians in Berlin, with V.E. Day (Victory in Europe) splitting the difference—May 8th. The room now exhibits Allied maps, photos and newspapers from the end of the war. *Open Wed.–Mon., 10 a.m.–noon and 2–6 p.m.; Oct.– Apr., 2–6 p.m.* Admission: FR10.

Special Tours/Excursions

Krug ★★★

5 rue Coquebert, ☎ 03-26-89-44-20. Between boulevard Lundy and rue de la Justice. Special Hours: By appointment only. Closed: Sat., Sun.

The three stars is for the tour only—the champagne is pure five stars. Even though tour arrangements need to be made in advance, it is worth it to have visited the maker of the best champagne in existence. Krug, the most prestigious house in Champagne (Moet et Chandon, known for its Dom Perignon, is more famous— but Krug is considered by most the greatest champagne producer of all time), is focused on making wine, not attracting tourists. However, if you take the time to plan a tour, you will get a glimpse at what sets this champagne apart from the rest. Only producing about 500,000 bottles annually, it's definitely an example of "quality not quantity." Learn about the Grande Cuvee, a blend of 40 to 50 wines from 6 to 10 vintages, and the small oak barrels used for the first fermentation. A perfected process by a discreet wine maker—it's worth learning from the best.

Mumm ★★

34 rue du Champ-de-Mars, ☎ 03-26-49-59-70. At rue de Savoye.

Owned by Seagrams, Mumm is very adept at marketing, making this a very tourist-friendly house. The champagne is known for its fruitiness with low levels of acidity. Its best is the Cuvee Rene Lalou 1985, made from half chardonnay and half pinot noir. An impressive building, the 1920s house is surrounded by trees. Inside are ultramodern facilities geared to impress its visitors. The tour lasts about one hour and includes a walk through the cellars—with 35 million bottles—and a tasting at the end. *Open Mar.–Oct., daily; Nov.–Feb., Mon.–Fri.* Admission: FR20.

Pommery ★★★★

5 place du General-Gouraud, ☎ 03-26-61-62-56. Between rue des Crayeres and boulevard Henry-Vasnier.

Within this large Victorian building of red brick, gray stucco and white stone are the cellars of Pommery. One of the few that still grows most of its own grapes, it is known for its delicate champagnes. At the top of its list is the Cuvee Speciale Louise Pommery. The tour, descending over 100 steps and back up, shows off its Roman cellars, its 20,000-gallon oak barrel dating to 1904 and its skylights that were carved out in Roman times. A very polished presentation for a refined champagne house. Open May–Oct., daily; Nov.–Apr., Mon.–Fri.

Ruinart ★★★

4 rue des Crayeres, ☎ *03-26-85-40-29. At rue du Chemin-Vert.*
Said to be the oldest commercial winery in the region, this winery was founded by the nephew of a monk who learned his techniques from Dom Perignon. The limestone cellars are magnificent landmarks that date back to the second century B.C. Call ahead to ask if an English-speaking tour will be given. Admission: free.

Taittinger ★★★★

9 rue St-Nicaise, ☎ *03-26-85-45-35. Between rue d'Ay and boulevard Victor-Hugo.*
This family operation is housed in a large building encompassed by trees and flowers. Well-known for the high percentage of chardonnay used in its bubblies, they usually have a rich aroma and complex taste. Tours take you through limestone cellars from Roman times and the vestiges of the former abbey and church. Tastings are provided to small, interested groups. *Open Mar.–Nov., daily; Dec.–Feb., Mon.–Fri.* Admission: FR18.

Where to Stay

Hotels and Resorts

Boyer les Crayeres FR1000–FR1800 ★★★★★

64 boulevard Henry Vasnier. ☎ *03-26-82-80-80, FAX: 03-26-82-65-52. About 5 km from the airport.*
Single: FR1000–FR1800. Double: FR1000–FR1800.

An elegant hotel occupying a beautiful chateau in a private 17-acre landscaped park. The public spaces are opulently decorated, with high ceilings, antiques and beautiful potted palms throughout. The 16 guest chambers are individually decorated with period style furnishings, and each comes with TV, telephone, minibar, radio, hair dryer and private bath. Two of the rooms come with a terrace, and one boasts a fireplace. There is a tennis court on the edge of the property, an English style bar in the hotel, and massage and hairdresser services are available to your room. Unrivaled by any other in the region, the grand restaurant in this Relais and Chateaux rated hotel is not to be missed by anybody visiting the Champagne area. Features: tennis, in-room conference facilities. Credit Cards: All Major.

Grand Hotel des Templiers FR1000–FR1400

22 rue des Templiers. ☎ *03-26-88-55-08, FAX: 03-26-47-80-60. Just outside of town center.*
Single: FR1000. Double: FR1200–FR1400.
With an emphasis on tranquility, this cozy 19th-century mansion was converted into a hotel in 1987. After a day in the countryside tasting champagne, the 19 rooms here are just what the peace and relaxation doctor ordered. Elegantly decorated and spaciously designed, the rooms are accented with antiques and have TV, radio, telephone, minibar, marble bath and hair dryer. The spa facilities include a heated indoor pool, Jacuzzi, sauna and steam bath. Superb lounges, smartly furnished and well maintained. While not as lavish as the Boyer, the more subdued

atmosphere lends a distinctly romantic feeling. Features: pool, sauna, fitness center.Credit Cards: V, MC, DC.

Hotel de la Paix   FR370–FR600   ★

9 rue Buirette. ☎ *03-26-40-04-08, FAX: 03-26-47-75-04. Located between the train station and the Cathedral; at place Drouet d'Erlon.*
Single: FR370–FR420. Double: FR400–FR600.

A contemporary Best Western hotel in a perfect setting near the imposing Sube fountain. On the grounds are a garden with a swimming pool and a chapel. All of its 105 rooms have private bathrooms and comfortable beds. Some also have garden views. The hotel has a brasserie/tavern, which serves excellent dishes, including grills, oysters and seafood. Meals begin at FR85. Features: pool, air conditioning in rooms, nonsmoking rooms, in-room minibars. Credit Cards: All Major.

L'Assiette Champenoise   FR505–FR770   ★★

40 avenue Paul-Vallent-Couturier. ☎ *03-26-84-64-64, FAX: 03-26-04-15-56. Located about 6 km from Reim's center; take autoroute A4 westbound, exit at Tinqueux.* Rated Restaurant: *L'Assiette Champenoise.*
Single: FR505–FR770. Double: FR545–FR770.

In a chateau just outside Reims, this acclaimed hotel is set among century-old trees. It is a former private Norman estate, and some of the present structure dates from 1896, although much of it was constructed in the 1980s. Its 60 rooms have private bath and are luxuriously furnished. The hotel restaurant is locally renowned and features both classical and innovative French cooking. Half-board rates are from FR715 to FR1000 (room, breakfast and a meal) per person, per day in season. Features: wheelchair-access rooms, pool, sauna, in-room minibars. Credit Cards: All Major.

Mercure Reims Cathedrale   FR370–FR475   ★★

31 boulevard Paul Doumer. ☎ *221-4542, 03-26-84-49-49, FAX: 03-26-84-49-84. About 1.5 km from the train station, adjacent to the Marne Canal.*
Single: FR370–FR430. Double: FR400–FR475.

Formerly the Altea Champagne, this centrally located hotel sits on the banks of the Marne Canal. One of the biggest hotels in Reims, it has 124 air-conditioned rooms with TV, telephone, minibar and bath. There are several lounges, a restaurant and a bar in the hotel. Fixed-price meals cost from FR100. A good choice for travelers by car, considering its proximity to the autoroute and the free parking. Credit Cards: All Major.

Low Cost Lodging

Grand Hotel du Nord   FR265–FR320   ★★

75 place Drouet d'Erlon. ☎ *03-26-47-39-03, FAX: 03-26-40-92-26. In the center of town; exit at Reims-Centre.*
Single: FR265–FR275. Double: FR290–FR320.

Although in the heart of place Drouet d'Erlon, the 50 rooms are kept quiet with good soundproofing. Each contains a TV, telephone, minibar and private bath. There is also a comfortable TV lounge, popular with the late night crowd. This value choice puts you near all of the major sights and in the middle of the activity of the cafés, movie theaters and boutiques. Features: in-room minibars. Credit Cards: All Major.

Where to Eat

Boyer **$$$** ★★★★

64 boulevard Henry Vasnier, In Hotel Boyer-Les-Crayeres. Located at Boyer-Les-Crayeres. ☎ *03-26-82-80-80.*

Lunch: Noon–2:30 p.m., FR200–FR300.

Dinner: 7:30–10:30 p.m., entrées FR200–FR300.

A very French, and very rich, clientele patronize the Boyer family's acclaimed establishment, isolated within a private estate and chateau in the heart of the city. Gerard Boyer breezily combines humble dishes such as pig's feet with a noble stuffing of foie gras and cepes. The desserts are inventive, softly textured and dizzyingly sweet, especially the ice creams. What's to drink? Champagne, of course! Reserve as far back as a month for weekend dining. Le famille Boyer also owns a bistro, **Au Petit Comptoir**, *17 rue de Mars (* ☎ *03-26-40-58-58)*, helmed by a Boyer acolyte, Fabrice Maillot. He prepares hearty cuisine at people prices, and the crowds love it. Seating is on comfy booths, or on a patio; the champagne is reasonably priced. *Open until 10:30 p.m., no lunch Sat., closed Sun. and Aug. 8–23*. Entrées FR170-180. Closed: Mon. Amenities: own baking, reservations required. Credit Cards: All Major.

Le Chardonnay **$$** ★★

184 avenue d'Epernay. ☎ *03-26-06-08-60.*

Lunch: Noon–2 p.m., FR145–FR185.

Dinner: 7–10 p.m., entrées FR145–FR185.

This former Boyer cottage is now owned and run by Jen-Jacques Lange, who offers a scaled down version of Gerard Boyer's exceptional cuisine. Prices are also much lower, especially the set menus that start at FR140, with affordable wines. Dishes include quail stuffed with mushrooms and a *feuillete* of frogs' legs and leeks. Gracious service and atmosphere. Amenities: own baking, reservations required. Credit Cards: V, MC, DC, A, E.

Le Continental **$$** ★★

95 place Drouet-d'Erlon. ☎ *03-26-47-01-47.*

Specialties: sole, duck with black-currants.

Lunch: Noon–2 p.m., FR115–FR170.

Dinner: 7–10 p.m., entrées FR115–FR170.

Tricked out like a little bonbon box, this popular restaurant and brasserie serves excellent duck, foie gras and seafood. Perhaps the crowds like the FR98 fixed-price menu, too. Amenities: happening bar.

Le Florence **$$** ★★

43 boulevard Foch. ☎ *03-26-47-12-70.*

Specialties: lobster in champagne sauce, pigeon salad with lentils.

Lunch: Noon–2 p.m., FR175–FR200.

Dinner: 7–9:30 p.m., entrées FR175–FR200.

Once the turf of Jean-Pierre Maillot, the kitchens of this late-19th-century house turned restaurant are in the capable hands of chef Laurent Helleu. Champagne figures heavily in the seasonal menu, as well as in the cellar. Closed: Sun. Amenities: outside dining, reservations required. Credit Cards: All Major.

Les Brisants $$ ★

> *13 rue de Chativesle.* ☎ *03-26-40-60-41.*
> *Lunch: Noon–2:p.m., FR75–FR125.*
> *Dinner: 7 p.m.–midnight, entrées FR75–FR125.*

For people with champagne tastes and a beer budget, this attractive spot might fit the bill. Four course menus, meat dishes and starchy stretchers are available for FR75. Patio dining available. Also good is **Le Colibri**, *12 rue Chanzy, near the Cathedral,* *(*☎ *03-26-47-50-67)* with menus starting at FR60. *Open until 10:30 pm.* Self-service cafeteria at **La Coupole**, in front of Les Brisants, *(*☎ *03-26-47-86-28)* entrées from FR50. Markets: **place du Boulingrin**, *Wed.–Sat, 8 a.m.–2 p.m., ave. Jean Jaures, Sunday morning, 8 a.m.–1 p.m.* Amenities: outside dining. Credit Cards: V.

Monchenot

Auberge du Grand Cerf $$ ★★

> *On N51, 10 km from Reims. In Hotel Auberge du Grand Cerf. Located at Auberge du Grand Cerf.*
> *Specialties: salmon terrine with oysters, pigs trotters stuffed with calf's sweetbreads.*
> *Lunch: Noon–2 p.m., FR150–FR200.*
> *Dinner: 7–9:30 p.m., entrées FR150–FR200.*

Classic cuisine served in a pretty garden or pastel-painted dining room. Extensive wine list with choice champagnes. Fixed-price FR175 lunch offered weekdays and Sat. Closed: Sun. Amenities: outside dining, reservations required. Credit Cards: V, MC, A, E.

Directory

To and From

> *By train from Paris (an hour and a half), Strasbourg (four hours), or Metz (three hours), or by car on the A-4 (from Paris) or A-26 autoroute, or N-51 highway.*

Tourist Office

> *2 rue Guillaume de Machault;* ☎ *(33) 03-26-77-45-25.*

Rail Station

> *boulevard Joffre;* ☎ *(33) 03-26-88-50-50.*

Post Office

> *rue Olivier-Métra, 51100 Reims;* ☎ *(33) 03-26-88-44-22.*

Epernay

There is really no reason to come to Epernay other than for the champagne—the main source of income for this town of 30,000. Epernay has the highest per capita income in France, although I wouldn't swear to how equitable the distribution might be. Since champagne rules in Epernay, I'd like to explain the champagne process in a little more detail.

The Romans, in Champagne as elsewhere, turned viticulture into big business in Epernay. The chalky soil and other factors had always aided in the production of mediocre still (non-sparkling) white wines, and because of the cold weather, the fermentation often stopped and restarted in spring, giving the wines a slight effervescence. According to local folklore (less partial historians have it quite differently), a Bénédictine monk named Dom Perignon, cellar keeper at the city's abbey, experimented with deliberately fermenting the wine a second time, and thus created the bubbly as we know it. He is said to have exclaimed upon trying his concoction, "Brothers, come quickly! I am drinking stars!" Nowadays, the process in Champagne and elsewhere (where it is called *Méthode Traditionelle*) begins with a normal fermentation of the rather bitter grapes, at around 70 degrees F, in oak barrels or stainless steel vats. The resulting wine is siphoned off and then blended with other years' productions, according to the cellar master's wisdom. Just before bottling, the wine is *liqueur de tirage*, the secret potion of sugar, cognac and yeast. The bottles are stored in a cool place for at least several months, and often for several years. In Epernay and Reims, the bottles are stored in the hundreds of miles of limestone tunnels under the cities, where the constant temperature takes one variable out of the production equation. During storage, the bottles—all 200 million of them—are turned by hand, and gradually inverted, by professionals known as *remueurs*, to move the thick sediment to the neck of the bottle. When the yeast converts the sugar to alcohol and carbon dioxide, the sediment is removed in a process called *dégorgement*, where the neck of the bottle is plunged into freezing brine, and the solid mass of dead yeast cells is extracted. A final dash of sugar, called *liqueur d'expédition*, is added and the wine is rebottled. The metal cap under the wire holding the cork on was originally placed there to prevent rats from eating the corks when the bottles were being shipped overseas.

Now in partnership with the Cognac house Hennessy, the giant house Moët et Chandon is the largest producer and owns the brand name Dom Perignon, as well as Pommery, Ruinart and Mercier (as well as Luis Vuitton luggage and Christian Dior perfumes). The best visits are to the Moët or Mercier cellars, both on avenue de Champagne downtown. The former is a slightly snooty affair, true to Moët's character; the latter offers a lot more whizz-bang, including a train ride through the tunnels, and the world's largest wine barrel, which was displayed at the 1889 World Exhibition in Paris. (A larger Cognac barrel, which also debuted at the Exhibition, is now in Wisconsin, holding beer).

What to Do

Museums and Exhibits

Musée du Vin de Champagne   ★★

13 avenue de Champagne, ☎ *03-26-51-90-31.*

Hours open: 10 a.m.–6 p.m. Special Hours: Open only Mar.–Oct.; closed noon–2 p.m. Closed: Tue.

CHAMPAGNE

Displaying everything related to champagne, from early wine bottles, to various paraphernalia to clothes worn by the wine-makers. Either a great introduction to this wine region or a boring recap of everything you've already seen.

Special Tours/Excursions

De Castellane ★★★★

57 rue de Verdun, ☎ 03-26-55-15-33. Off avenue de Champagne; towards the river.
Hours open: 10 a.m.–6 p.m. Special Hours: Closed noon–2 p.m.
One of the more interesting tours given, it has a certain country flair. In addition to the tour of the bottling rooms and cellars, there is a museum on champagne making, a butterfly garden and a fine collection of old champagne labels. Climb to the first tier of the tower for a grand view over town. Oh, the champagne—try the Cuvee Royale or the pinot noir Commodore—both are excellent.

Mercier ★★★★

70 avenue de Champagne, ☎ 03-26-54-71-11. At rue de Lorraine.
Special Hours: Dec.–Mar., closed Tues.–Wed.
The ultimate in champagne tour entertainment. Epernay's most futuristic building houses this house that was founded in 1858. Well-known in France, this house is owned by Moët et Chandon. After viewing a film on the making of champagne, visitors climb aboard a glass elevator, passing figures acting out the process on their way down to the cellars. The tour through the cellars is aboard a laser-guided train, and it passes by the world's largest wine barrel, which was featured at the 1889 World's Fair in Paris. A fantastic, showy, modern learning process. Admission: free.

Moët et Chandon ★★★★

18 avenue de Champagne, ☎ 03-26-54-71-11. At rue Jean-Chandon.
Special Hours: Nov.–Mar., Mon.–Fri. only.
Definitely the most well-known of the champagne houses, the elegant building and tour are impressive. Founded by Claude Moet in 1743, it produces more than 20 million bottles per year—with most sold abroad. The best bottle is the vintage Dom Perignon, the name most people associate with fine champagnes. One of the best in the region, the tour is visitor-friendly, with informative multilingual guides taking the groups through the stately building. The visit is concluded with a tasting.

Where to Stay

Bed-and-Breakfasts

Chateau du Ru Jacquier FR400–FR400 ★★★

Igny-Comblizy. ☎ 03-26-57-10-84, FAX: 03-26-57-11-85. About 20 km southwest of Epernay. Take the N3 towards Chateau-Thierry, and turn left on D18 towards Dormans for about 7 km.
Double: FR400.
A lovely two-story chateau, the corner turrets press towards the sky, adding to its fairy-tale appearance. Deer and horses graze on the surrounding land, among citrus trees and lush shrubbery. Inside, a wooden staircase meanders up to the six comfortable, attractive guest chambers. Five of the rooms come with a bath, and one comes with a shower. After a complimentary breakfast outside, there is trout fishing on the property, and the golf course, mountain biking and cellar visits are nearby. Or, for

the romantics, fall in love again while enjoying a ride in the horse-drawn carriage. End the day with a good FR150 dinner in the well-appointed dining room. Experience the charm only a small chateau could deliver. Credit Cards: Not Accepted.

Hotels and Resorts

La Briqueterie   **FR600–FR1500**   ★★★★

route de Sezanne. ☎ *03-26-59-99-99, FAX: 03-26-59-92-10. In Vinay, about 7 km south of Epernay of N51.*
Single: FR600–FR1400. Double: FR710–FR1500.
Among 10 beautifully landscaped acres, La Briqueterie is a classic country-style hotel. Family owned and operated for many years, the inn reflects the fresh attitude and new life infused by the owner's daughter. The 42 spacious rooms feature deep-pile carpeting, marble baths, cable TV, telephone, radio, minibar and terrace. There are two suites available for FR1410. The dining room features excellent regional dishes and a large selection from the wine cellar. An indoor pool, sauna and fitness room round out the facilities, and supervised children's programs provide a break to parents. Professional and always smiling, the staff is a pleasure. Features: wheelchair-access rooms, pool, sauna, fitness center. Credit Cards: All Major.

Royal Champagne   **FR700–FR1400**   ★★★

Bellevue. ☎ *03-26-52-87-11, FAX: 03-26-52-89-69. About 9 km north of Epernay, in Champillon.*
Single: FR700–FR1400. Double: FR700–FR1400.
Rising above the town, this hilltop hotel occupies a former coaching inn dating back to 1788. A fantastic vantage point to survey the hillside vineyards and the Marne Valley. This Relais and Chateaux rated hotel charms its guests with the heavenly comfort of its 30 rooms. All of the immaculate rooms contain cable TV, telephone, minibar, bath and hair dryer. A peaceful night's sleep is assured in any of them, thanks to the removed location of the hotel. There are two restaurants boasting extensive lists of the bubblies. Golf and tennis facilities are closeby. The staff is fresh and attentive. Features: balcony or patio, in-room minibars, country location. Credit Cards: All Major.

Where to Eat

Chez Pierrot   **$$$**   ★★★

16 rue de la Fauvette, At rue des Nommois. ☎ *03-26-55-16-93.*
Dinner: 7–9:30 p.m., entrées FR125–FR225.
An intimate bistro with a loyal chic following. Regional cuisine is prepared home-style and includes sausage, salmon, lamb and other favorites carefully prepared with the finest of local ingredients. Champagne is available by the glass, and the knowledgeable staff will gladly assist in choosing the right one to accompany your meal. Closed: Sun. Reservations recommended. Credit Cards: All Major.

Les Berceaux   **$$$**   ★★★

13 rue Berceaux, In the center of town. ☎ *03-26-55-28-84.*
Dinner: 7–9:30 p.m., entrées FR120–FR200.
This brick-fronted building punctuated with flower boxes was a coach house in the 1800s. Within the building now is a wine bar, a restaurant and a hotel. Excellent

regional food is served by the owner-chef and his wife. Try the snail cassoulet, the quail eggs with foie gras or the sole soufflé. Lobster and crayfish may be picked from the aquarium, and it can all be rinsed down with one of the fine bottles of champagne or wine from the cellar. These bottles may be sampled by the glass at the wine bar. Set menus from FR150. Reservations recommended. Credit Cards: All Major.

Royal Champagne   **$$$**   ★ ★ ★

On the N51, About 5km north on the N51, in Champillon. ☎ *03-26-52-87-11.*
Dinner: 7–9:30 p.m., entrées FR225–FR375.

This Relais and Chateaux establishment boasts expansive views over the countryside vineyards. The in-house chef has reinterpreted regional cuisine, blessing his patrons with a reliable menu of rich in a la carte specialties. Whether it's his filet of turbot or his sweetbreads, the predictability of regional food has disappeared. Revel in the variety and celebrate with one of the 150 champagnes on the extensive wine list. Set menus start at FR230 for lunch and FR370 for dinner. Reservations recommended. Credit Cards: All Major.

Directory

To and From

By train from Paris (an hour and a half), Reims (20 minutes) and Strasbourg (four hours), or by car on the N-3 highway from Château-Tierry (the exit from the A-4 autoroute from Paris) or the N-51 road from Reims.

Tourist Office

7 avenue de Champagne; ☎ *(33) 03-26-55-33-00.*

Rail Station

cours de la Gàre; ☎ *(33) 03-26-88-50-50.*

Post Office

place Hughes Plomb, 51200 Epernay; ☎ *(33) 03-26-53-31-60.*

Châlons-sur-Marne

Châlons-sur-Marne is the third corner of the Sacred Triangle, but it offers neither the glorious cathedral of Reims nor the high-class champagne cellar tours of Epernay. Nevertheless the town has a certain charm, mostly due to its well-preserved and well restored Old Town, filled with half-timbered houses and crisscrossed by peaceful canals. Châlons-sur-Marne has a rich ecclesiastical heritage, too, and two of its churches in particular are worth visiting. The Eglise de Notre Dame-en-Vaux, standing in the center of town, was built in the 12th century and is a masterpiece of Romanesque and, later, Gothic-style architecture. The stained glass, in distinctive Champagne green (as opposed to Chartres blue), was crafted from the 13th to the 16th centuries. The belltower contains 56 bells, quite an earful at any hour, but especially impressive when bell-ringing concerts are underway. Mass is celebrated with Gregorian chants on Sunday mornings. Next door to the cathedral is a small museum, the Musée du Cloitre de Notre Dame-en-Vaux, which contains the original 12th-century sculpted cloisters. The other major church in the town is the Cathédrale St. Etienne, which displays several architectural styles from the Romanesque crypt to the Gothic nave and the Baroque portal. It also contains 13th- to 16th-century stained glass. (The most impressive window depicts *St. Stephen's* martyrdom.) The treasury holds a display of 12th-century glass, allowing you to see the craftsmanship of the time up close.

What to Do
Historical/Architectural Sites

Cathédrale St-Etienne ★★★★

rue de la Marne, ☎ 03-26-64-18-30.
Hours open: 9 a.m.–sunset
Begun around 1235, the cathedral was actually consecrated by Pope Eugene III in the 12th century. An eclectic display of architecture, the body is Gothic, the tower is Romanesque and the facade is Baroque. Renaissance and medieval stained glass is what this cathedral is famous for. Just as Chartres' glass is known for its blues, Chalon is known for its green tints. The most impressive windows are those of the Renaissance, in the side chapels on the south side, depicting scenes from the Creation, Paradise, Passion and the lives of Christ and the Saints. Admission: free.

Eglise de Notre-Dame-en-Vaux ★★

place Tissier.
Hours open: 10 a.m.–7 p.m. Special Hours: Closed noon–2 p.m.
Originally a small chapel, it was transformed into this four-story Gothic after a collapse of the chapel's ceiling. In addition to the Romanesque towers on the sides, the church boasts 56 bells—considered the greatest chimes in Europe. While inside, look up at the glowing 13th- and 16th-century rose windows, arranged in the same pattern as those at Chartres. Gregorian mass is at 9:30 a.m. on Sun. Admission: free.

Museums and Exhibits

Musée du Cloitre ★★

rue Nicholas Durand, ☎ 03-26-64-03-87. Next to Notre-Dame.
Hours open: 10 a.m.–6 p.m. Special Hours: Closed noon–2 p.m.; Oct.–Mar., to 5 p.m. Closed: Tue.
Dating to 1170, the cloister was destroyed in 1759 during the Revolution, and many of its sculptures were damaged. Displayed here are the excavated sculptures which have been reconstructed. "The Four Evangelists," the "Washing of the Feet" and the "Marriage in Cana" constitute part of the 12th-century works. Admission: FR20.

Where to Stay
Hotels and Resorts

Aux Armes de Champagne **FR500–FR800** ★★★

31 avenue Luxembourg. ☎ 03-26-69-30-30, FAX: 03-26-66-92-31. About 10 km east of Châlon-sur-Marne on the N3.
Single: FR500–FR800. Double: FR500–FR800.

Worth the short drive from Chalon, this hotel sits in the middle of L'Epine. Across from the Our Lady of the Thorn church, the 35 rooms overlook either the town or the garden. Constant improvement and maintenance has kept these soundproof rooms in shipshape, with modern amenities such as TV, telephone, minibar and bath or shower. The restaurant uses ingredients from regional food markets to prepare the traditional dishes. Discreet, courteous, anticipatory service. Features: in-room minibars.Credit Cards: MC.

Inns

Hotel d'Angleterre   **FR430–FR500**   ★★★★

19 place Monseigneur Tissier. ☎ *03-26-68-21-51, FAX: 03-26-70-51-67. Near the center of town.*
Single: FR430–FR450. Double: FR450–FR500.
Behind the stone facade of this small hotel are 18 rooms overseen by the house chef and owner, Jacky Michel. Some offer visuals of Notre-Dame-en-Vaux. Rooms are decorated in pastels and contain a TV, telephone, minibar and bath or shower. Jacky's cuisine is the best in town, and the wine selection complements his work in perfect harmony. Fixed-price meals start at FR170. His genuine welcome instantly makes you feel at home. Features: in-room minibars. Credit Cards: All Major.

Where to Eat

Au Carillon Gourmand   **$$**   ★★★

15 bis, place Monseigneur Tissier, Near the church of Notre-Dame-en-Vaux. ☎ *03-26-64-45-07.*
Lunch: Noon–2 p.m.
Dinner: 7:30–10:30 p.m., entrées FR100–FR175.
Friendly service, a solid menu, attractive surroundings and low prices. This centrally located restaurant keeps a faithful following by sticking to the basics. The pigeon and chicken liver pie is a reliable source of palatable pleasure. An affordable list of fine wines is available. Set menus start at just FR80. Closed: Mon. Reservations recommended. Credit Cards: V.

Aux Armes de Champagne   **$**   ★★★

In L'Epine, About 9 km from town. ☎ *03-26-69-30-30.*
An enchanting restaurant focusing on traditional cuisine and straightforward cooking styles. With the ingredients picked fresh from the markets, the menu changes weekly. Within the elegant surroundings, patrons feast on the ever-changing delights delivered to their tables by a deft staff. Set menus start at FR195, and a la carte menus constantly change. Reservations recommended. Credit Cards: V, MC.

Jacky Michel   **$$$**   ★★★★

19 place Monseigneur Tissier, Across from the Notre-Dame-en-Vaux. Located at Hotel Angleterre. ☎ *03-26-68-21-51.*
Dinner: 7:30–9:30 p.m., entrées FR175–FR300.
Residing in a lovely stone-fronted re-creation of a building destroyed in WWII, the restaurant shows off the culinary mastery of chef Jacky Michel. Whether it's the duck carmelized with honey and Chinese spices or the veal kidneys with red wine sauce, his magical touch is present in every dish. Just as remarkable is the wine cellar

that features a grand selection of Bordeaux, Burgundy and, of course, Champagne. A FR160 set menu is available during the week, and the weekend menus start at FR210. Closed Christmas holidays. Closed: Sun. Amenities: outside dining, reservations required. Credit Cards: All Major.

Directory

To and From

By train from Paris (an hour and a half), Reims (half an hour), and Strasbourg (three and a half hours), or by car on the D-3 road off the A-4 autoroute from Reims or on the N-3 road from Verdun in Alsace-Lorraine.

Tourist Office

3 quai des Arts; ☎ *(33) 03-26-65-17-89.*

Rail Station

avenue de la Gàre; ☎ *(33) 03-26-88-50-50.*

Post Office

94 rue de la Marne, 51000 Châlon-sur-Marne.

Troyes

A jewel of a city, Troyes is filled with half-timbered houses in its champagne cork-shaped center, where you can sit at a café terrace far away from the crowds that swarm the Sacred Triangle. Troyes was once a major trade center, holding fairs called *foires* that made it the commercial capital of northern Europe in the Middle Ages. Today, Troyes is France's capital of French knitwear, and there is an excellent Hosiery Museum (Musée de la Bonneterie) displaying stockings from the 16th century to the present. The other main museum in town (give the Musée d'Art Moderne a miss; it's only worthwhile feature is a single Rodin) is the Maison de l'Outil et de la Pensée Ouvrière, the "Tool and Workers' Thoughts Museum." Maintained in a beautifully restored 16th-century half-timbered house, the museum holds a true treasure-trove of woodworking tools from the ages. Troyes has many beautiful churches—don't miss the Eglise St. Madeleine, dating from the 12th century, which has one of the few existing rood screens in France; the Basilique St. Urbain, built by Pope Urban VI beginning in 1262; the Eglise St. Nizier, with a brightly colored Burgundy-style tiled roof; the Eglise St. Jean-au-Marché, begun in the 13th century and site of the marriage of Henry V of England and Cathérine in 1420; and not least, the Cathédrale St. Pierre et St. Paul, begun in the 13th century and now very worn on the outside but containing a Gothic feast for the eyes.

For an excursion from Troyes, take D-960 road east about 15 miles to the Lac et Fôret d'Orient, an expansive nature reserve with several lakes in addition to the main artificial one, where you can enjoy hiking and watersports.

What to Do

Historical/Architectural Sites

Basilica Ste-Urbain ★★

rue Clemenceau, ☎ *03-25-73-02-98.*

Called the "Pantheon of Champagne," this church was founded by Pope Urban IV, a native of Troyes, in 1261. Its amazingly uniform interior was constructed in less than 30 years, and the 13th-century stained-glass windows are lovely. Perhaps most interesting, though, are the gargoyles on the exterior. Admission: free.

Cathédrale St-Pierre et St-Paul ★★★

1 place St-Pierre, ☎ *03-25-80-90-12.*
Hours open: 10 a.m.–6 p.m. Special Hours: Closed noon–2 p.m.

Built from the 13th through the 17th centuries, this Flamboyant Gothic stone cathedral is a masterpiece. Although much of the intricate carvings were destroyed during the Revolution, it now contains 112 stained-glass windows (covering about 16,000 square feet) and one of the longest naves in France. The tower, though, has remained unfinished since the 16th century. The *son-et-lumiere* program, a free sound and light show, is given on Fri. and Sat. nights from late June–mid-Sept. The treasury is open only in summer, Tues.–Sun., 2–6 p.m., FR10. Admission: free.

Eglise St-Jean ★★★

rue Champeaux, ☎ *03-25-73-02-98.*

This church saw the marriage of Catherine of France to Henry V of England in 1420. Begun in the 13th century, it was rebuilt after the fire in 1524. In addition to the 15th-century fresco of the Last Judgment in the chancel, two big bells, the ones that fell from the belfry in 1911, are on display. Another church is the Eglise St-Nizier, lying in the quarter behind the cathedral. This late-Gothic and Renaissance church is reflective of the period in the region when colored-tile roofs were popular.

Eglise Ste-Madeleine ★★

rue de la Madeleine, ☎ *03-25-73-02-98.*
Hours open: 10:30 a.m.–5 p.m. Special Hours: Closed noon–2 p.m.

Built in 1150, this is the oldest church in Troyes. The most impressive feature is its stone jube, or rood screen, a structure built to separate the nave from the chancel. (It is one of seven in all of France.) The richly colored stained-glass windows, from the Champagne school of artisans, date from the 16th century. Worthy of stopping in, but nothing to go out of the way for.

Museums and Exhibits

Maison de l'Outil et de la Pensee Ouvriere ★★★

7 rue de la Trinite, ☎ *03-25-73-28-26. In the center of town.*
Hours open: 9 a.m.–6:30 p.m. Special Hours: Closed 1–2 p.m. Open at 10 a.m. on Sat. and Sun.

The Museum of Tools and Crafts is situated in the 16th-century Hotel de Mauroy. Similar to Dad's tool shed, the museum displays an extensive collection of hand tools dating back to the 18th century. From carpenters to blacksmiths, the tools of the trades are found here. English brochures are available at the entrance. Admission: FR30.

Municipal Museums ★★★

Various locations.

If planning on visiting more than one of the city-run museums, check into the museum pass (FR40), which covers all of the following museums. Keep in mind, too, that Wednesdays are free. The **Musée de l'Art Moderne**, *place St-Pierre (☎ 03-25-76-26-80)*, is to the right of the cathedral. It displays 4000 works by many of the masters, incuding Degas, Braque, Cezanne, Dufy, Picasso, Gauguin, Rodin and Matisse, among others. There is also a sculpture garden and a fine display of African sculptures. *Open Wed.–Mon., 11 a.m.–6 p.m.*; FR20. The **Musée des Beaux-Arts**, *21 rue Chrestien-de-Troyes (☎ 03-25-42-33-33)*, is housed in the former Abbaye St-Loup. In this museum is one of the largest private collections ever given to the country. In addition to a varied display of archaeological finds, weapons, jewelry and sculptures, a fine collection of paintings from the 15th through 20th centuries is here. *Open Wed.–Mon., 10 a.m.–noon and 2–6 p.m.*; FR20. The **Musée Historique de Troyes et de la Champagne**, *rue de Vauluisant (☎ 03-25-42-33-33)*, is in the 16th-century Hotel de Vauluisant. Here are religious artifacts, sculptures, paintings and documents related to the history of Troyes. In the same building is the Musée de la Bonneterie (Hosiery Museum). Troyes' famous hosiery industry is well represented here, with stockings, gloves and hats that gave Troyes its successful start in the 16th century. *Both museums in the Hotel are open Wed.–Sun., 10 a.m–noon and 2–6 p.m.*; FR20.

Special Tours/Excursions

Walking Tours ★★★★

Throughout town.

The true charm of Troyes is found wandering the streets—enjoying the beautiful, half-timbered buildings. Around the Musée de l'Histoire are many 16th-century mansions, or hotels, worthy of peeking in whenever possible. Stroll through the pedestrian quarter via *ruelle des Chats* (Cat's Lane), and stop for crepes and a drink at one of the many cafés near place du Marechal Foch, named after the WWI French general. Most of the buildings in town date from after 1524, the year a fire destroyed most of the town.

Where to Stay

Hotels and Resorts

Grand Hotel and Patiotel　　　　　**FR270–FR435**　　★★

4 avenue Joffre. ☎ 03-25-79-90-90, FAX: 03-25-78-48-93. Across from the train station.

Single: FR270–FR365. Double: FR320–FR435.

Sitting across from the train station, this hotel and restaurant complex was built in the 1930s as the Grand Hotel. The final stages were added in 1987, with the creation of the attached Patiotel. Sharing a lobby, breakfast room, garden and pool, the two hotels share common space but offer different rooms with different prices. With 102 rooms between the two hotels, those in the Grand are more traditional, spacious and equipped with minibars and attractive furniture. Those in the Patiotel are smaller and more commercially styled but offer garden views. In the complex are five restaurants, ranging from tavern style to almost elegant. The lower room rates listed are for the Patiotel, and the higher rates are for the Grand. Credit Cards: All Major.

La Poste   **FR400–FR550**   ★★★★

35 rue Emile Zola. ☎ *03-25-73-05-05, FAX: 03-25-73-80-76. About 1 km from the train station, in the town center.*
Single: FR400. Double: FR550.
From the staff to the rooms, la Poste is a first-rate hotel. The 28 rooms, although a bit small, are the most comfortable and attractive rooms to be found in Troyes. Each contains satellite TV, radio, telephone, minibar, hair dryer and beautiful bath. The hotel has a bar and three restaurants: La Table Gourmande, serving classical French fare; Le Carpaccio, with pizza and pasta; and Le Bistrot, specializing in seafood. Breakfast costs FR50 extra. The only leisure facility is a heated pool. A fine display of tasteful luxury in every respect. Features: pool, in-room conference facilities. Credit Cards: All Major.

Le Relais St-Jean   **FR450–FR650**   ★★★

49 rue Paillot-de-Montabert. ☎ *03-25-73-89-90, FAX: 03-25-73-88-60. In the center of the historic district.*
Double: FR450–FR650.
Opened in 1990 in the heart of the historic district, this hotel sits near the Eglise St-Jean. With its contemporary style, it is the most modern and well-equipped hotel in town. The 22 rooms are air-conditioned and contain TV, telephone, minibar and private bath. There is a bar in the hotel. A calm and stately establishment with personal attention from the staff. Features: wheelchair-access rooms, air conditioning in rooms. Credit Cards: All Major.

Where to Eat

Le Bourgogne   **$$**   ★★★

40 rue du General-de-Gaulle ☎ *03-25-73-02-67.*
Dinner: 7:15–9:15 p.m., entrées FR90–FR200.
The two brothers who own this restaurant have honed their talents well to make this one of the finest choices in Troyes. Expanding on the regional favorites, they are sure to use only the freshest ingredients to draw out the full flavor from every dish. They boast an excellent wine cellar certain to satisfy the toughest connoisseur. A very pleasant experience. Closed: Sun. Reservations required. Credit Cards: V, MC.

Le Valentino   **$$**   ★★★★

11 cour de la Rencontre, In the old section of town, across from the town hall. ☎ *03-25-73-14-14.*
Dinner: 7:30–9:45 p.m., entrées FR110–FR180.
Considered the finest restaurant in Troyes, Le Valentino has solidly established itself as the king of seafood. Personally buying the fish every morning at the markets, he starts with only the best seafood and ends with only the best dishes. Whether it's his raw salmon in olive oil and dill seed or his lobster with orange juice-flavored butter sauce, his visionary skills are evident. The wine cellar keeps pace with the changing specialties and offers some affordable bottles. Set menus are FR160–FR350. Jacket

and tie required. Closed: Mon. Amenities: outside dining, reservations recommended. Credit Cards: All Major.

Directory

To and From

> *By train from Paris (an hour and a half) or Mulhouse (three hours). Troyes has always been a crossroads. Listed clockwise from the south, you can reach the city by car on the N-77, N-60 or N19 highways, or on the A-26 or A-5 autoroutes.*

Tourist Office

> *16 boulevard Carnot;* ☎ *(33) 03-25-73-00-36.*

Rail Station

> *avenue Maréchal Joffre;* ☎ *(33) 03-25-73-50-50.*

Post Office

> *place Général Patton, 10000 Troyes;* ☎ *(33) 03-25-73-50-50.*

Colombey-les-Deux-Eglises

Near both Burgundy and Lorraine, this small village is the final resting place of Général Charles de Gaulle, the stern architect of modern France. Born in Lille, farther to the north, he and his wife bought a small house in Colombey-les-Deux-Eglises in 1933 for a summer retreat. Badly damaged during World War II, it was not until De Gaulle led the Free French to victory over the Nazis (with considerable help from the Allies) that he was able to restore the house, called *La Boisserie*. He moved to the house permanently after his final retirement from public life in 1969, and died here on November 9, 1970. He is buried in a simple tomb in the single church in the village, a site visited by thousands of pilgrims every year, and which sees ceremonial Mass sponsored by the government on each anniversary of his death. The village landmark is the huge Cross of Lorraine erected on its outskirts in the general's memory. His house is now a small museum dedicated to his life.

Colombey-les-Deux-Eglises is about 35 miles east of Troyes off the D-60.

ALSACE AND LORRAINE

Strasbourg is a picturesque town surrounded by water.

What Makes Alsace and Lorraine So French?

1. *The home of quiche Lorraine—what would American cocktail hours and thaw-to-impress lunches be without it?*

2. *Nancy's Musée de l'Ecole with reputedly the world's largest collection of Art Nouveau works (the movement began here)—plus the city is a great place to pick up underwear in a pinch.*

3. *A town named "Metz" is pronounced "mess," but isn't really one at all.*

663

What Makes Alsace and Lorraine So French?

4. *A town named "Bitche," pronounced like you think, was one during various wars. At the Citadel your head will be outfitted with a suspicious-looking helmet that gives off infrared signals, multilingual commentary, and smell- and sound-arama. Good luck!*

5. *Birthplace of August Bartholdi (Colmar), creator of the Statue of Liberty.*

The neighboring regions of Alsace and Lorraine constitute France's northeast border with Germany, Luxembourg and Switzerland. Nestled between the Vosges mountains to the south and west and Germany's Black Forest to the north and west, the region is often the coldest in France. Nonetheless the glorious scenery of forests, lakes and rivers make it one of the most popular vacation spots for Europeans. Relatively undiscovered by Americans, other than veterans returning to the sites of the great battles of both World Wars, the region is full of history and natural beauty and is well-worth a sojourn of a few days or even more.

The wedding of "L'ani Fritz" is staged in Alsace's Marlenheim.

History

Alsace-Lorraine has one of the bloodiest histories in France, as countless intra-European wars have raged back and forth across its borders. Paradoxically, the very first invasion of the region by the Romans passed relatively peacefully. The Celtic tribes living in the area swiftly made peace with the Romans, who brought great engineering and cultural wealth to the region. The Romans also tolerated the ancient religions of the indigenous inhabitants. The Roman remains at Metz and the cross-border archaeological park

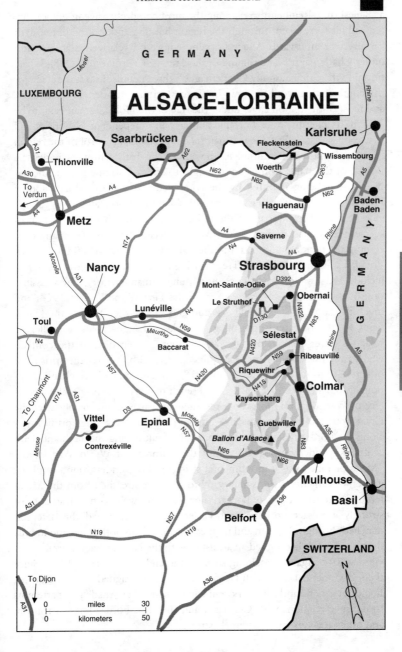

at Bleiesbruck-Reinheim, are among the most comprehensive in France. Attila and his force swept through the region burning and looting in the sixth century, yet afterwards Alsace-Lorraine enjoyed a relatively stable period under Charlemagne. The signing of the Treaty of Verdun in A.D. 843, partitioning the empire among Charlemagne's three grandsons, set the stage for the conflicts that would follow. Louis the German invaded 15 years later, and most of the region came under the rule of the Holy German Empire by A.D. 870. The duchy of Lorraine and certain independent bishoprics and cities not withstanding, the German rulers maintained control of the region for the next several centuries. At the end of the 15th century, Charles the Bold (not the Bald) of Burgundy sought to annex Lorraine, but he died at Nancy after being defeated by the combined forces of the duchy and of France. Gradually, France gained a foothold in the region, and bit by bit, Alsace-Lorraine became part of the united country, much to the chagrin of successive German regimes. The rivalry between Paris and Germany concerning the region continued into the 19th century, until 1870 the Franco-Prussian war ended with the Treaty of Frankfurt that redrew the border to include Alsace and much of Lorraine within German territory. The assassination of the Archduke of Austria set off the First World War in 1914, and much of the region, especially Verdun and the Marne, became the killing fields of trench warfare, poison gas attacks and high-explosive artillery—weapons never seen before in war. Millions of men died in the conflict, which ended when the Americans joined forces with the French, British and other Allies to defeat the Kaiser in 1918. Lorraine and Alsace changed nationality again, back to French. The French military leaders (notably Secretary of War Maginot) foresaw a resurgent Germany immediately after the Great War, and began a massive building program, creating fortifications along the border that echoed feudal castles built during the 12th and 13th centuries. Under construction until the outbreak of World War II, the "Maginot Line" was a monumental string of forts, underground bunkers, gun emplacements, turrets and watchtowers that stretched from the Mediterranean to the Belgian border. Fortifications were concentrated most strongly in Alsace-Lorraine, but Hitler simply sidestepped the defenses, marched through Belgium and trapped the forts from both sides, and in only days, the French had signed an armistice with the Nazis. Alsace-Lorraine was German once again, remaining so until the end of the war in 1944. Since then, beginning at once with De Gaulle's policies designed to unify Europe, France in general and Alsace-Lorraine in particular have made great attempts to improve relations with Germany, and the cross-border links in tourism and other areas are now extremely strong.

Cuisine

The cuisine of the region is Germanic in its names, major ingredients and its hearty carbohydrate content. *Choucrout* (pickled cabbage) is served with all manner of things, including various kinds of *saucisson* (sausage), fish and even *volaille* (poultry). In Alsace, *baeckeoffa* is a specialty—a stew of pork or lamb with potatoes and herbs served in the dish it simmered in for the last few hours. Potatoes are everywhere—in omelettes, as side dishes, and even in to some sausages. Lorraine brings forth *Quiche Lorraine* and *potée Lorraine*, another hearty pork-and-cabbage based stew. The region is crisscrossed by countless rivers and streams, thus fish dishes are extremely popular. Specialties include *carpe à la juivre*, *truite frite* and others. *Fromage blanc*, a whipped-cream cheese, is used often and liberally in desserts and breakfast, while *tarte à la quetsche* (a plum pie) and *kougelhopf* top the list of pastries.

The wine route of Alsace is a pleasing excursion of a day or two between Strasbourg and Colmar in the Vosges foothills. The favorites are the whites *sylvaner*, *pinot blanc*, *Moselle*, *riesling*, *muscat d'Alsace*, *tokay d'Alsace* and the red *pinot noir*. All, even *pinot noir*, are served chilled. In Lorraine, *schnapps* made from yellow plums called *Mirabelles*, as well as cherries, pears, currants and almost any other fruit are the digestif of choice or the perfect drink to warm you up on a cold afternoon. The region is the top beer-producing and beer-drinking region in France.

Nancy

Historically capital of the Duchy of Lorraine, Nancy was founded in the 11th century, making it a new city by French standards, but you have to look quite hard to see anything that dates back beyond the 17th or 18th centuries. The violent history of the city has obliterated much of its architecture. The first duke of Lorraine, Gérard d'Alsace, built a fort on the dry strip between two marshes of the Meurthe River. When Charles the Bold of Burgundy seized the region in the 15th century, the people of the duchy and the city revolted, and Charles was forced to return from a failed expedition in Switzerland to lay siege to the city. He failed again, and died at the scene, and the Dukes of Lorraine were back in charge. Soon after, much of the Ducal Palace was destroyed by fire, and the palace wasn't rebuilt until the 17th century. Two wings, designed very differently by two different architects, are all that remain today, with Renaissance decorations on the doorways. Also in the 17th century, Duke Charles III ordered construction of the "New Town" designed on a series of rectangles. Of the old town, only some walls, one gate tower, and the haphazard layout of the streets can be seen today. At the end of the 17th century, after having seen Versailles, Duke Leopold ordered the Palais du Gouvernement built at the end of the Place de la

Carrière (the word in this case meaning "jousting competition" rather than "quarry"). Finished in 1753, it was designed by Mansart, builder of Versailles.

Place Stanislas, Nancy, features decorative ironwork.

Before the palace was finished, Leopold died and his successor, François I, finally gave in to the long-standing French desire to have Lorraine, trading it for Tuscany in Italy. In order to ease the transition and to assuage an old man's broken ego, King Louis XV appointed his father-in-law, Stanislas, who had, not once but twice, been deposed as king of Poland, to run the duchy as a semi-autonomous province. When Stanislas died, the duchy would become completely French. Louis counted on this happening soon—after all, in 1738 Stanislas was already in his sixties. Much to Louis' chagrin, Stanislas lived to the ripe old age of 89, and Louis only survived him for eight years. (There is a certain poetic justice in this: Louis was married to Marie, Stanislas' daughter, at age 15 because he was in ill-health and the lords of France thought he would die soon without an heir. In fact, they had 10 children and he lived to be 64.) All this was to the eternal good of Nancy, however, as Stanislas turned out to be a *bienfaisant,* or "do-gooder," as the people of the city called him, and he built one of the most magnificent 18th-century city centers in France, as well as instituting free legal and medical service for the poor, a free public library, and a host of other social programs. The centerpiece of his legacy is the Place Stanislas, an elegant and perfectly proportioned square at the center of the city where there was once barren land between the Old and New Towns. Designed by the architect Emmanuel Héré and with extensive ironwork by master craftsman Jean Lamour, the square is ringed with grand buildings now housing the Hôtel de Ville, Musée des Beaux Arts, fancy restaurants, and the tourist office. Two magnificent statues depicting Neptune and his wife Amphitrite guard two corners, while in the middle of it all is a statue of Stanislas himself. Stanislas, aware of his tenuous position with the ever more impatient Louis, put a statue of the king there; you can also see the royal coat of arms throughout the complex as he made sure to show his loyalty to the crown. The Arc de Triomphe, an imposing three-arch gateway to the square, leads to Place de la Carrière, at the other end of which is the Palais du Gouvernement. Stanislas had a new, symmetrical facade put on the houses down both sides of the street, and built a huge new *hôtel*, now the *bourse*, to match the mansion of the Beauvau family that now houses the superior court. The entire ensemble of buildings that Stanislas created has been classed as a World Heritage Site by the United Nations.

Besides the Museum of Fine Arts, the star of which is a painting of the death of Charles the Bold by Delacroix, there is a decent Musée Historique de Lorraine, with engravings and archaeological finds that help explain the history of Nancy and Lorraine prior to the 15th century. The must-see attraction in Nancy, however, is the Musée de l'Ecole de Nancy. This museum is the largest collection anywhere of Art Nouveau, the turn-of-the-century art movement that swept across Europe before being swallowed up by Art Deco. The movement was led by Nancy artisans and artists such as Emile Gallé, who founded the School of Nancy. A true Renaissance man, Gallé was a master glassworker, ceramicist, painter, botanist and woodworker. Other influential artists include Louis Marjorelle (ironworker), Jacques Gruber (stained glass) and Eugène and Auguste Vallin (cabinetmakers). Gallé's vision was to create an association of "art-based" industries. Today, while the flowing curves and nature-inspired mass-produced furniture and furnishings the movement produced were influential, it is the hand-crafted gems on display at the museum that are truly astonishing. Straight lines were definitely out with the Ecole de Nancy, and Mother Nature was in. Desks, bureaus lamps, and ornaments are all sculpted to evoke or copy animals and plants,, including the opium poppy these men began to smoke, and water plants such as lilies and lotuses. Fish, frogs, deer and butterflies were other favorites. Splicing together materials was also important, including the use of metal as decoration on wooden furniture and the three (or more) layers of glass fused in one of Gallé's lamps, or the 600 types of woods the Vallin brothers used in creating beautiful inlaid pictures on dressers and desks. Set in a period house that was owned by Gallé the museum also features a garden filled with plants that once inspired the artist. This museum is a don't-miss stop for anyone who studies or appreciates art and the boldness of visionary artists.

What to Do

Historical/Architectural Sites

place Stanislas ★★★★

In the center of town.

A stunning square in the middle of town, place Stanislas is the source of life for Nancy. Bustling with the activity of the camera-armed tourists, this square is named after a Polish king from the 18th century, Stanislaw Leszczynski (perhaps his last name didn't roll off the tongue quite as easily). It is on this square that the Hotel de Ville (city hall) and the Arc de Triomphe (with the tourist office below) sit. As any reputable square would have, there are also several popular restaurants and stores surrounding the square. Walk through the Arc de Triomphe to place de la Carriere, with the Palais du Gouvernement on the far end.

Museums and Exhibits

Musée Historique Lorrain/Palais Ducal ★★★★

64 Grande Rue, ☎ 03-83-32-18-74. In the heart of the old town.
Closed: Tue.

The Musée Lorrain remains one of the finest museums in France. Housed in the Palais Ducal, it contains a wide array of relics and art relating a deep history of Europe. More specifically, it also traces the region's history from the Gallo-Roman days. Tapestries, paintings, sculptures and artifacts from the area and the ducal palace are on display. One entire floor is reserved for Jacques Callot, the Nancy-born engraver. From Jewish history in France to 17th-century works from the masters, this museum offers a broad historical experience. *Open Wed.–Mon., 10 a.m.–6 p.m.; mid-Sept.–Apr., Wed.–Mon., 10 a.m.–noon and 2–7 p.m.* Admission: FR20.

Musée de l'Ecole de Nancy ★★★★

36 rue du Sergent, ☎ 03-83-40-14-86. About 2 km southwest of the city center.
Hours open: 10 a.m.–6 p.m. Special Hours: Closed noon–2 p.m.; Oct.–Mar., to 5 p.m. Closed: Tue.

Grasp the true roots of Nancy-style art as created by its greatest master—Emile Galle—the founder of the Ecole de Nancy. Housed in a lovely turn-of-the-century building, this museum struts its contributions to the Art Nouveau movement. Included are jewelry, furniture, glass and iron works, all used creatively to counter the bland, stagnant works that were produced prior to the reactionary movement. Admission: FR20.

Musée des Beaux-Arts ★★★★

3 place Stanslas, ☎ 03-83-85-30-72. In the center of town.
Hours open: 10:30 a.m.–6 p.m. Special Hours: Mon., noon–6 p.m. only. Closed: Tue.
Within the walls of this magnificent 18th-century mansion is a delightful collection of 17th-century paintings and modern works. Artists represented include Delacroix, Matisse, Dufy, Bonnard, Modigliani and Rubens. Italian baroque, rococo and contemporary artists are well showcased with such greats as Ribera, Tintoretto and Car-

avaggio. Adding to the wonderful variety is the collection of crystal vases and lamps. Admission: FR20.

Where to Stay

Hotels and Resorts

Grand Hotel de la Reine FR730–FR2000 ★★★★

2 place Stanislas. ☎ *03-83-35-03-01, FAX: 03-83-32-86-04.*
Single: FR730–FR840. Double: FR1200–FR2000.
On the beautiful Stanislaus square, this imposing hotel occupies an 18th-century mansion that is an historical monument. One of the most exceptional establishments in the region, its 50 rooms are decorated in grand Louis XV style, with the choice ones overlooking the square. All contain telephone, minibar and private bath. Some boast Venetian-style chandeliers and draped testers over the bed. Serving classic and nouvelle cuisine, the hotel restaurant has found a balance between elegance and functional. The hotel also has a bar and lounge. Supremely chic. Features: wheelchair-access rooms, in-room minibars, in-room conference facilities. Credit Cards: All Major.

Mercure Nancy Centre Thiers FR475–FR625 ★★★

11 rue Raymond Poincare. ☎ *03-83-39-75-75, FAX: 03-83-32-78-17. Near the train station.*
Double: FR475–FR625.
Catering to business and holiday travelers alike, the Mercure Nancy Centre Thiers (formerly the Altea Thiers) is a towering hotel near the place Stanislas. A modern facility opened in 1975, it has 190 soundproof rooms with air conditioning, cable TV, telephone, radio, minibar, bath and hair dryer. Nonsmoking rooms are available. Facilities are limited to a small gym, 250-person meeting facilities and a business center. The restaurant and popular bar are excellent. As is typical of most executive hotels, the staff is very efficient and professional. Features: wheelchair-access rooms, air conditioning in rooms, nonsmoking rooms, fitness center, in-room conference facilities. Credit Cards: All Major.

Inns

Hotel Choley FR140–FR280

28 rue Gustave Simon. ☎ *03-83-32-31-98, FAX: 03-83-37-47-73. Near town center.*
Single: FR140. Double: FR140–FR280.
A small inn charmed by the family owners who live here. The third generation of the Choley family runs this inn, which has a wonderful collection of antiques and art. The 20 simple rooms are individually decorated with period pieces, but only eight come with private bath. Old musical instruments and a nostalgic billiard table give the firelit salon its classic character. Good home-style cooking costs FR150 in the restaurant. Accommodations here give the most character for the franc. Credit Cards: V, MC.

Where to Eat

Café Foy $$ ★★★

1 place Stanislas, In the center of town. ☎ *03-83-32-21-44.*
Dinner: 7–9:30 p.m., entrées FR90–FR150.

A café for two seasons—on and off season, that is. Summertime means terrace seating, a high-brow clientele and live classical music sometimes. The rest of the year the café is returned to the more informal, local crowd. No matter what the season, the regional food in the upstairs Restaurant Le Foy is excellent. Set menus there start at FR125–FR200. Closed: Wed. Reservations recommended. Credit Cards: V.

La Gentilhommiere $$ ★★★

29 rue des Marechaux. ☎ *03-83-32-26-44.*
Dinner: 7–10 p.m., entrées FR110–FR180.

Occupying the house where Victor Hugo's father once lived, this restaurant is full of history and tradition both in the building and in the cuisine. Madame Bouillier runs a happy ship with a helpful staff ready to serve. In the warm months, take your meal of pigeon or duck or some other specialty on the terrace. Set menus from FR160. Closed: Sun. Reservations required. Credit Cards: All Major.

Le Capucin Gourmand $$ ★★★

31 rue Gambetta, Near place Stanislaus. ☎ *03-83-35-26-98.*
Dinner: 7:30–10 p.m., entrées FR125–FR250.

Classically set in an old house in the center of town, Le Capucinn Grand offers a respectable lineup of dishes. Whether it's the reliable quiche Lorraine or the fresh fish, a meal here is best finished with one of the phenomenal desserts created by the chef's son. A family affair, the wife keeps things running smoothly in the pleasant dining room. An excellent wine cellar puts on the finishing touches to a wonderful package. Set menus from FR180. Closed: Mon., Sun. Reservations required. Credit Cards: V, A.

Directory

To and From

By train from Paris (three hours), Strasbourg (one hour), or Metz (40 minutes), or by car on the A-31 autoroute from Burgundy in the south or connecting to the A-4 autoroute from Paris.

Tourist Office

14 place Stanislas; ☎ *(33) 03-83-35-22-41.*

Rail Station

place Thiers; ☎ *(33) 03-83-56-50-50.*

Post Office

8 rue Pierre-Fourier, 54000 Nancy; ☎ *(33) 03-83-39-27-10.*

Metz

Metz (pronounced mess) has a long, rich history you can see for yourself depicted in its entirety in stone throughout the town. Amazingly, despite being burned down, conquered, bombed and battled over repeatedly, Metz is filled with buildings and houses from all eras. The Eglise St. Pierre-aux-Nonnains, rescued from service as a military storehouse, dates from the fourth century, and is believed to be the oldest church in France. Metz was first settled by the Romans and rose to prominence as a crossroads of the major east-west and north-south highways of northern Gaul. Roman Metz boasted an amphitheater that was northern Gaul's largest, seating 25,000 people. Water was piped to the city along two aqueducts, today a major portion remains. Partly thanks to a lucky find, the Musée d'Art et d'Historie of Metz (also known as the Cour d'Or) has the best Gallo-Roman collection in France. When the original art museum was being expanded, workmen digging in the basement uncovered Roman baths right underneath. Now, the vast collection of Roman pottery, tombstones, mosaics, jewelry, heating system components, and other artifacts is housed in a thematic string of galleries inside the excavated baths. The walls of the rooms are the *tempidarium*, *frigidarium* and *caldarium*, and the quantity and quality of the exhibits gathered from Metz and its surroundings is phenomenal. The museum continues through a 15th-century barn, also inside, in which are housed Merovingian-era carvings and exhibits through the Middle Ages. There is also a somewhat-interesting fine arts wing.

The rest of Metz history is outside. After Attila the Hun routed the Roman defenses and overran the city in A.D. 451 through the early Middle Ages, Metz was the capital of the Merovingian kingdom of Austrasia, which reached to present-day Luxembourg and the Netherlands. (An interesting side note is that the city was never part of Germany until the late 19th century; the name is not Germanic, as it seems, but a corruption of *Mets*, itself an abbreviation of Mediomatriques, the name of the tribe indigenous at the time of the Roman conquest.) Although most of Lorraine was a stable duchy by the turn of the second millennium, Metz remained independent and allied with the Holy Roman Empire, and in the 12th century, the city declared itself a sovereign Republic. About the same time, construction began on the great Cathédrale St. Etienne. While not as exquisite as Chartres, the cathedral is definitely one of the most interesting in France. By the early 13th century, five churches lined the place d'Armes. Two churches that stood a few feet from each other at almost right angles were joined to form the basis for the cathedral. The result is a truly magnificent Gothic cathedral that took 300 years to build—Metz had been annexed to France in by Henri II in 1552 by the time the cathedral was completed. The original columns of the two churches, done in distinctly different styles, form the four corners of the intersection of the towering 140-foot-high nave and the transept, which are joined together in uncomfortable angles and bizarrely-shaped vaults. The cathedral has the greatest area of stained glass in France, some 60,000 square feet, and the greatest proportion of stained glass to surface area—there is more glass than stone. The glass ranges from the 13th to the 20th century, providing a collection unique in the world. The great masters of the 16th and 17th century signed their windows next to the anonymous work of the original medieval *compagnons.* Stained-glass panes were crafted by true artists including Herman von Münster, Valentin Bousch and Theobald von Lixheim. Some of the finest modern stained-glass windows also adorn the church, including a series by Bissière, depicting the crucifixion, and the first stained glass mounted in a church by the great artist Marc Chagall, showing Jacob wrestling with the angel and dreaming of the ladder, Jeremiah and scenes from Genesis. Other interesting modern stained glass in Metz includes the work by film-maker Jean Cocteau at the Romanesque church of St. Maximin, off rue Mazelle.

Outside the cathedral, in the place des Armes, is an ensemble of classical-style buildings built in the 18th century to house the Hôtel de Ville, the Corps de Gard (guard house), and Parlement (meant to house the King's governor, but used as a law court). Thus the four powers were all present—the government, the church, the military, and the law. Built at the same time as Stanislas' elegant palace in Nancy, military Metz' great Renaissance construction-style was more somber and plain. The same period saw the construction of the Opera and Théâtre complex, as well as numerous offices and apartments. On the tiny Ile Petit Saulcy in the middle of one of the two branches of the River Moselle, is the Temple Neuf, the most striking evidence of Metz' annexation to Germany. The Prussians invaded Lorraine in August 1870. Metz held out until falling in October and becoming formally part of Germany the next year. Fully 40 percent of the population emigrated to Nancy, still part of France, and the Prussian Emperor (and King) Wilhelm II moved thousands of people into Metz. Built in Rhenish style from dark stone that clashes with the golden sandstone composing every other building in the city, the enormous temple was designed to stamp Second Reich rule on the city. The German administration built houses and other buildings in Metz, too, the most notable of which are the monumental train station and mansions nearby.

In the years before World War I the city was steadily fortified and armed by the Germans, and in 1914 Metz became the launching site for a major flank of the invasion of France that was turned back only 30 miles east of Paris by Maréchal Joffre, leading to four years of trench hell in and around much of northeastern France. After the war, Metz rebuilt, but the citizens preferred to restore the elegant Renaissance-style houses of the 17th and 18th century rather than tear them down. Germany invaded again and occupied the city again from 1940 to 1944, and more damage was inflicted in the two-and-a-half month battle to liberate the city, but the restoration effort only intensified. The result is a city that looks unscarred in spite of its war-filled history, with the third-highest ratio of open space to people in France (25 square meters of parkland for each inhabitant) and strong sense of depth and character.

What to Do

Historical/Architectural Sites

Basilique St-Pierre-aux-Nonnais ★★★

rue de la Citadelle, ☎ *03-87-39-92-00. From the esplanade, take the stairs in the southeast corner.*

Hours open: 2–6 p.m. Special Hours: Oct.–Mar., Sat.–Sun., 2–5 p.m. only. Closed: Mon., Sun.

Rumored to be the oldest church in France, the facade and part of the walls date to the 4th century. The beginnings of the church are from the 7th century, when it was first a convent. Mainly functioning as a cultural center today, the large assembly hall called the Arsenal is the focal point of the structure. Admission: FR10.

Cathédrale St-Etienne ★★★★

place d'Armes, ☎ *03-87-75-54-61. On the hill above the Moselle in the old town.*
Hours open: 9 a.m.–6:30 p.m. Special Hours: Closed noon–2 p.m.

A meld of two separate churches, this cathedral was created in the 13th century in the Gothic style. Setting this glorious work apart from others are the 6500 square meters of stained-glass windows and the modern windows, some of which were designed by Chagall. Admission to the crypt FR12. Tours available in summer months. Admission: FR20.

place d'Armes ★★★

Next to the cathedral.

Surrounding this Louis XV-style square are the Hotel de Ville, the Corps de Gard, the Law Courts (formerly the parliament building) and the cathedral. The warm yellow tones of many of the buildings in town mimic the rare stone used to build the cathedral, which is now reserved for restoration of churches and public buildings.

place de la Comedie ★★★★

Northwest of the cathedral.

This 18th-century square was the site of many of the guillotine executions. These days it is the address for the **Opera-Theatre** *(*☎ *03-87-75-04-96).* Opera, dance, plays and ballet are staged here throughout the year. Tickets can be reserved by calling ☎ *03-87-75-40-50.*

Museums and Exhibits

Musée d'Art et d'Histoire ★★★

2 rue du Haut-Poirier, ☎ *03-87-75-10-18. Near the cathedral.*
Hours open: 10 a.m.–5 p.m. Special Hours: Closed noon–2 p.m.

Partly housed with Roman baths discovered during construction in 1935, the core of the museum is within a 15th-century granary and a 17th-century convent. Tour parts of the Roman aqueducts, the baths and the fine collection of art and relics from Gallo-Roman days to the Middle Ages. Student admission FR15; free admission Wed. and Sun. morning. Admission: FR20.

Where to Stay

Hotels and Resorts

Hotel Royal   **FR460–FR1200**   ★ ★ ★

23 avenue Foch. ☎ *888-4747, 03-87-66-81-11, FAX: 03-87-56-13-16. Near train station.*
Single: FR460–FR960. Double: FR520–FR1200.

Fully modernized, the interior of this 1906 stone facade provides a choice of styles in the 63 bedrooms. Most are contemporary and simple, while others are more classically luxurious. Standard appurtenances include TV, telephone, radio, minibar and bath. Some rooms are reserved for nonsmokers. There are two restaurants, a bar and a lounge. Most of the handsomely furnished public spaces have exposed beam ceilings, and the basement-bar has exposed stone. Breakfast is served for FR65. Very attentive service. Credit Cards: All Major.

Mecure-Centre   **FR370–FR420**   ★ ★ ★

29 place St- Thiebault. ☎ *221-4542, 03-87-38-50-50, FAX: 03-87-75-48-18. About 200 meters from the train station.*
Single: FR370–FR420. Double: FR370–FR420.

This chain hotel sits between the train station and the pedestrian district. All of the 112 air-conditioned rooms are constantly updated and include cable TV, telephone, radio, minibar, bath and hair dryer. Four suites are available at FR630 each. There are a restaurant, bar and meeting facilities in the hotel. While not particularly interesting, the hotel does provide consistently quality accommodations. Features: wheelchair-access rooms, in-room minibars, in-room conference facilities. Credit Cards: All Major.

Novotel-Centre   **FR480–FR520**   ★ ★ ★

place des Paraiges. ☎ *03-87-37-38-39, FAX: 03-87-36-10-00. About 1 km from the train station; near the cathedral.*
Single: FR480. Double: FR520.

A former Sofitel turned Novotel in 1988, this facility sits in the heart of the historic St-Jacques quarter. Although it's a chain hotel, the 120 rooms here are considered the best in Metz. All of the air-conditioned rooms come with cable TV, telephone, radio, minibar, bath and hair dryer. There are three suites for FR890 each. In addition to the poolside snack bar, there is a grill-restaurant open from 6 a.m. to midnight with meals beginning at FR150. A very modern, efficient hotel. Features: wheelchair-access rooms, pool, in-room minibars, in-room conference facilities. Credit Cards: All Major.

Where to Eat

A la Ville de Lyon   **$$**   ★ ★ ★

7 rue des Piques, In the center of the historic town. ☎ *03-87-36-07-01.*
Dinner: 7–10 p.m., entrées FR100–FR150.

This former coaching inn located in the cathedral district is the address for one of the region's most interesting restaurants. Guests dine beneath the fantastic vaulted ceilings of this beautiful building that has been a restaurant since the late 1800s and is now an historic monument. It is here that such tasty dishes as basil-scented lamb, pigeon with bordeaux and salmon in anise are carefully prepared and artfully served. The set menus are a great deal in comparison to the a la carte menus, with the best value at just FR100. Closed: Mon. Reservations required. Credit Cards: All Major.

La Dinanderie **$$** ★ ★ ★

2 rue de Paris, Just north of the cathedral, on the outskirts of town. .☎ 03-87-30-14-40. Dinner: 7–9:45 p.m., entrées FR110–FR170.

The atmosphere is warm in this 17th-century building where chef Claude Piergiorgi quietly does his work. Constantly pushing himself to improve, his menus often change to suit the season and the availability of ingredients. The a la carte dishes are always tempting and might include fresh salmon, veal or poultry. The fixed-price menus are equally attractive and generously priced from FR160. Desserts are one of the greatest joys here, as is the wine—albeit expensive. Service is cordial and efficient. Closed: Mon., Sun. Credit Cards: V, MC, A.

Directory

To and From

By train from Paris (three hours), Strasbourg (an hour and a half), or Nancy (one hour), or by car at the intersection of the A-4 Verdun-Germany and A-31 Nancy-Luxembourg autoroutes.

Tourist Office

place d'Armes; ☎ *(33) 03-87-55-53-76.*

Rail Station

place Général de Gaulle; ☎ *(33) 03-87-63-50-50.*

Post Office

1 place Général de Gaulle, 57000 Metz; ☎ *(33) 03-87-56-73-00.*

Verdun

Still surrounded by thick walls, fortified gateways and towers, Verdun wears the armor once necessary during its war-filled past. Strategically located on the bank of the Meuse river, Verdun was founded with the construction of a Gallic fort in the first century. Over the centuries, the town has been the site of more conflict than most places on the globe, notably during the World War I battle that lasted almost a year-and-a-half and cost the lives of 700,000 men. The seeds of the conflict—in fact, some historians argue, of all conflict in Europe—were sown here in A.D. 843 when the three grandsons of Charlemagne signed the Treaty of Verdun dividing the empire into three parts. Charles the Bald received control of Gaul, Lothair kept the central region (northern Italy, Provence, the Rhineland, the Netherlands, Belgium), and Louis the German ended up with the eastern German portion of the empire. Louis the German launched the first "Franco-German" war in A.D. 858, when he invaded after Lothair's death.

The upper town of Verdun was besieged by the Duke of Brunswick in 1792, eventually falling to occupation after several weeks. The town was besieged and occupied again during the Franco-Prussian War, at the end of the 19th century, setting the stage for the battle of World War I. In 1914, the major action was at the *Battle of the Marne*, to the south, but that attack quickly was bogged down in the mud and stalemate of trench warfare. The Germans decided to enter through Verdun and outflank the French defenders. The attack came on February 21, 1916. Using all the tools of modern warfare—aircraft, long-range heavy artillery, poison gas and mobile cannons—the Germans pounded Verdun for four straight days before capturing the strategic *Douaumont Fort*. The fort is now a museum with tours of the buildings and the surrounding battlefields, where some of the bloodiest fighting occurred when the French retook it in October 1916. General Pétain (the same man who a generation later would capitulate to the Nazis) took over the defenses of the city, and by summer it was clear the Germans were going nowhere. They tried to effect a pincer movement, with savage, three-month battles for control of the key points—Dead Man's Hill, Hill 304, and the Eparges Promontory—but everywhere the Germans took a fort or a hill, they were stalemated in the face of dogged French opposition. Eventually the tide turned and the Germans were slowly driven back until the war ended in 1918 with the rout of the Germans before the remaining French and American forces. Key sites to see around the city include the Douaumont Fort, as well as the Ossuaire de Douaumont, where the remains of 130,000 unidentified soldiers of both sides are buried; Fort Vaux, another defensive position taken by the Germans in the early days of the battle and recaptured at the cost of thousands of lives a few months later; the Tranchée des Bayonettes, a trench where an entire battalion of French infantrymen from the 137th Regiment, waiting with fixed bayonets to "go over the top," was buried alive in a flurry of exceptionally accurate German heavy-artillery fire; Fleury-devant-Douaumont, a village that was overrun by the Germans on June 23 and retaken by the French on August 18, leaving nothing but a few grassy mounds and a modern chapel commemorating the site; as well as the Musée de la Citadelle Militaire in Verdun itself, which provides a thorough explanation of the battles.

What to Do

Historical/Architectural Sites

Citadelle de Verdun ★★★

rue de Ru, ☎ *03-29-86-62-02. About 10 min. outside of town center.*
Erected on this site of a former 12th-century abbey, the Citadelle de Verdun now houses the Musée de la Citadelle Militaire. Through an audiovisual display including a ride in an electric tour car, the role of Verdun in World War I is brought to life. The tour encompasses a small section of the 7 km of underground tunnels. English-language tours are available. *Open mid-Apr.–Dec., daily, 9:30 a.m.–noon and 2–5:30 p.m.; July–Aug., to 7 p.m. Admission: FR30.*

Fort Douaumont and Fort Vaux ★★★

On the banks of the Meuse, ☎ *03-29-88-32-88. North of the city.*
The two forts involved in the Battle of Verdun in 1916-1917, Fort Douaumont and
Fort Vaux were two heavily fortified compounds involved in the bloodshed. Learn
of the thousands of lives lost, the famous carrier pigeon that delivered the Raynal's
last message for help and the underground caverns. Tours are available throughout
the year. *Open daily 9 a.m.–6:30 p.m.; mid-Sept.–Dec., 9:30 a.m.–noon and 1–
5:30 p.m.; Jan.–Mar., 10 a.m.–noon and 2–4:30 p.m.; Apr., 9:30 a.m.–6 p.m.*
Admission: FR15.

Tranchee des Baionnettes ★★

Near the fort.
Special Hours: Always open.
Discovered a few years after the war, this was the trench where France's entire 137th
Regiment perished—bayonets in hand. It was found when a passerby noticed bayo-
net ends poking out of the ground. Also near the fort is the Ossuaire de Douaumont, which contains the bones of more than 100,000 French and German
soldiers. Peek through the windows of the structure at the piles of bones and the
names of soldiers lost enscribed on the wall. *Open daily 9 a.m.–6:30 p.m.; Oct.–
Nov., 9 a.m.–noon and 2–5 p.m.; Jan.–Mar., 9 a.m.–noon and 2–5:30 p.m.; Apr.,
9 a.m.–6 p.m.* Admission: free.

Where to Stay

Hotels and Resorts

Hotel Bellevue FR170–FR360 ★★★

1 Rond-point du Marechal-de-Lattre-de-Tassigny. ☎ *03-29-84-39-41, FAX: 03-29-86-
09-21. Across from the botanical gardens.*
Single: FR170. Double: FR360.
Family-run, the Hotel Bellevue is centrally located across from the botanical gardens. The 72 rooms, most with bath, have TV and telephone. Simply designed,
comfort and cleanliness are keys here. Breakfast is available for FR38, and the restaurant serves dinner only, for FR115 and up. Credit Cards: All Major.

Le Coq Hardi FR380–FR650 ★★★

8 avenue de la Victoire. ☎ *03-29-86-36-36, FAX: 03-29-86-09-21. Near the Meuse
River.*
Single: FR380–FR520. Double: FR220–FR650.
Built in 1827, this large hotel is composed of four attached houses. This half-timbered structure sits on the banks of the Meuse River. The salon is dotted with
antiques and centerpieced by a Renaissance fireplace. The 40 air-conditioned
rooms, most with private bath or shower, contain a TV and a telephone. The dining
room serves traditional cuisine in a relaxed atmosphere. From the greeting to the
goodbye, the staff exudes a very personal welcome feeling. Credit Cards: All Major.

Inns

Chateau des Monthairons FR400–FR750 ★★★

In Les Monthairons. ☎ *03-29-87-78-55, FAX: 03-29-87-73-49. In Les Monthairons,
about 13 km south on D334.*

Double: FR400–FR750.

Situated in a huge park on the banks of the Meuse, this restored chateau has 21 rooms. Three suites are available for FR1000 to FR1200 each. Very distinguished in decor, the large rooms feature high ceilings and spacious baths. After a tasty breakfast, canoeing on the river is a pleasant way to spend the day, and horseback riding is nearby. The Chateau's quiet location provides a peaceful getaway. Credit Cards: All Major.

Where to Eat

Chateau des Monthairons   **$$$**   ★★★

Monthairons, About 13km south on the D334, in Monthairons. Located at Chateau des Monthairons. ☎ 03-29-87-78-55.
Dinner: 7:30–10 p.m., entrées FR175–FR300.

In the neighboring village sits this relaxing chateau on the banks of the Meuse River. As part of a 19th-century Renaissance-style chateau, a sense of tranquility pervades its setting in the park. The summer months are the most pleasant, as the garden dining is most romantic. Wild game, seafood and traditional dishes are featured on the menu here. A good bottle of wine is assured from the well-stocked cellar. Set menus from FR160–FR350. Amenities: outside dining, reservations required. Credit Cards: V, A.

Le Coq Hardi   **$$**   ★★★

8 avenue de la Victoire. ☎ 03-29-86-36-36.
Dinner: 7:30–9:30 p.m., entrées FR100–FR175.

One of the most enchanting dining rooms in the region is found in this hotel-restaurant. With a painted ceiling, Louis XIII furnishings and beautiful place settings, sitting down to dine is a regal experience. Specialties here are mostly regional, with duck and foie gras consistently appearing on the menu. Fixed-price menus start at FR195–FR450. While the food is outstanding, the dining room alone is worth the visit. Closed: Thur. Reservations required. Credit Cards: All Major.

Directory

To and From

By train (the station was built by Gustave Eiffel) from Metz (an hour and a half), or by car off the A-4 autoroute from Metz.

Tourist Office

place de la Nation; ☎ (33) 03-29-86-14-18.

Rail Station

place Maurice Genovoix; ☎ (33) 03-29-45-50-50.

Post Office

avenue de la Victoire, 55100 Verdun; ☎ (33) 03-29-83-45-58.

Bitche

You may have visited the troglodytes in the Loire Valley, but if you visit the fortress-town of Bitche, just a few miles from the German border, you'll spend most of your day underground. The most visible feature of the city is the Citadel. Built on a rocky hilltop where a castle has stood since the 12th century, the present impregnable citadel was built by Vauban from 1681 until 1683. Partially razed a few years later, the castle was rebuilt by Louis XV in 1741. With its defensive system of bastions, moats and towering, unpierced walls, the massive fortress was designed to hold off attackers and withstand the ravages of the time; it eventually became an air raid shelter that offered protection from even 20th-century firepower. Most of the fortress was constructed underground with passageways and chambers hewn out of solid rock. The visit to the Citadel is one of the most innovative in France. Upon entering, the visitor dons a special helmet (operated by infrared signals) that provides commentary in English, French or German, as well as music and the sounds of battle and even aromas from the different eras in the fortress' history (baking bread, gunpowder, the stables, etc.). Two of the largest chambers are small museums, one contains a display of art and culture from *Pays de Bitche* from prehistory onwards, the other shows the development of the fortress itself, including plans and historical documents.

After a couple of hours in the bowels of the Citadel, have lunch and then visit the Fort Simershof, one of the largest and the best-preserved of the Maginot Line positions, which will take you into the heart of the hills outside Bitche and into the underground city that was home to 820 men at any one time. Built in a feverish nonstop construction project lasting from 1929 to 1938, the fort contains five kilometers of underground tunnels and chambers, and eight main gun emplacements, with 65mm and 75mm cannons capable of hitting targets as far as 12 kilometers away. The Simserhof Fort is the only one of hundreds of emplacements on the Maginot Line to be in perfect working condition. Visitors enter through the munitions entrance on the 60cm-gauge electric train used to transport the giant shells and other supplies into the fort, through double fortified doors guarded by machine gun nests and anti-tank cannons that still have their guns in place. The giant electric plant, consisting of four 175-kilowatt generators, the air-filtration plant, the kitchens and even the infirmary and morgue are all as they were when the fort was built, and all are displayed as they would have functioned. The most impressive element of the tour is the elevator ride to the top of one of the artillery blocks, where the massive and then ultra-modern retractable-guns were operated by a crew of a dozen men each. The huge machines of war still rise and rotate just as they did in preparation for the impending war with Germany. Since France was loath to construct such fearsome defenses along the frontier with a friendly neighboring country, the Maginot Line ended at the Belgian border and Hitler's army just marched around it, attacking from the rear while other German troops pushed into the heart of France. During the first three days of the German invasion Simserhof fired some 30,000 rounds in defense of smaller, neighboring forts, until its commander and troops finally emerged and surrendered to the Nazis five days after the armistice. The fort was used as storage by the Nazis, and some of its equipment was cannibalized for the *Atlantikwall*. It was retaken by the U.S. Third Army in 1944 and, having escaped major damage, was restored. The public tour is long and somewhat harrowing, as one begins to understand the incredible genius and invention that men have employed in the business of destroying one another. It is highly recommended as both a complement to the Citadel, an earlier era's Simserhof, and as an object-lesson in human history and sociology.

Bitche is surrounded by one of the most beautiful natural regions in France, the Parc Naturel des Vosges du Nord, a giant nature reserve listed by the United Nations as a "Global Biosphere Reserve." Numerous small villages, lakes, and woods await exploration, and the region also offers a world-class golf course, the 12th-century troglodytic fort Falkenstein (means "eagle's rock") in the hills outside the village of Phillipsbourg, and the carnivorous plant called the sundrew *(drosera)* that hides out in peat bogs. The miles of hiking trails, are perfect for anyone seeking some peace and quiet in a natural setting. Even if you visit Bitche only for the day, however, make the trip to the Royal St. Louis Glassmakers at St. Louis-lès-Bitches, just a few miles out of town. Glassmakers had been established in the tiny hamlet since the 16th century and, beginning in 1767, the royal glassworks were founded, quickly becoming the world's most renowned producer of fine lead-crystal—a newly discovered technique. At its peak in the last century the factory employed over a thousand people, and owned the entire village of St. Louis-lès-Bitches. Now just 350 men and women work at the plant, which is owned by Hermès. You can take a tour and watch the creation of fine crystalware—each performed by hand, with 25 or more steps then visit the showroom and museum to gawk at the finest examples of the work, or even buy a service, if you have your Gold Card with you.

Directory

To and From

> By train from Strasbourg (one hour) or Metz (two hours), or by road on the N-62 highway between Sarreguemines, and then the A-4 autoroute to Metz or Hageunau, and the A-4 autoroute to Strasbourg.

Tourist Office

> Hôtel de Ville; ☎ *(33) 03-87-06-16-16.*

Rail Station

> rue de la Gàre; ☎ *(33) 03-87-96-00-18.*

Post Office

> 25 rue de Sarreguemines, 57230 Bitche; ☎ *(33) 03-87-96-05-42.*

ALSACE AND LORRAINE

Strasbourg

Strasbourg shopkeepers prepare for Nöel celebrations.

Located halfway between Paris and Prague, and since 1949 the seat of the Council of Europe, Strasbourg calls itself the "Crossroads of Europe." Indeed, its name comes from the early German *Strateburgum*, or "City of Roads." Located at the meeting point for countless roads, rail lines, and waterways linking France to Germany and Central Europe as well as the Baltic, Strasbourg has both benefitted and suffered from its position over the years. Since Roman times, when the legions established a military camp in the area, Strasbourg has enriched itself from international trade, first in wheat and wine, then in the exchange of ideas through the printing press, and now as a major point of transfer for both goods and services from one side of Europe to the other. Strasbourg is one of the European Community's three capitals along with Brussels and the Hague. The strategic "crossroads" location has brought its share of strife, too. Attila the Hun invaded and looted the city during the fifth century, the religious tension between Protestants and Catholics saw the Thirty Years' War take its toll, and Strasbourg was in German hands from 1870 to 1918 and again from 1940 to 1944. Partly due to all this conflict, Strasbourg has an air of even-handedness. The cathedral has served as both a Protestant and a Catholic place of worship; squat, heavy Germanic architecture shares room with French elegance and open squares, and the city gave birth to the first of the Romance languages. The Strasbourg Oaths, sworn to each other by Charles the Bald and Louis the German, grandsons of Charlemagne, in A.D. 842, had to be in a language that both could understand; the bastardized Latin text used by each is thought to be the earliest written example of the ancestor of modern French.

The old city of Strasbourg, known as "Petite France" from a former hospital, is in the center of the city on an island surrounded by canals. To get a good view of the old 16th- and 17th-century houses that were once the homes of fishermen and tanners, take a boat trip round the island—the boat ride provides a much better perspective than the mini-train. From the water, you also will see the historic covered bridges with their watchtowers, mills, and the rest of the island. The jewel of Old Town as well as the city is the **Cathédrale Notre Dame**, masterpiece of flouncy, lattice-work Gothic-style architecture built in pinkish sandstone beginning in 1176. The 466-foot-high steeple was the tallest church spire in the world for 500 years. The west facade and the north and south portals have excellent sculptures, although the statues of the Church and the Synagogue, represented as women, are copies. The depiction of the wise and foolish virgins of Jesus' parable is most acclaimed—the Seducer seems to have won out over the Foolish Virgin, as she has begun to unbutton her dress. Inside is a monumental 16th-century astronomical clock, which offers a popular chiming ceremony each day at 12:30 p.m. when a mechanical rooster crows for St. Peter, Death and Christ and the Apostles. Next door to the cathedral is a wonderful museum called the **Musée de l'Oeuvre Notre Dame**. Dedicated to the cathedral, the museum contains the architects' original working drawings, the original medieval statuary, and the oldest stained glass (10th century) in existence. In the place de la Cathédrale is the Pharmacie du Cerf, supposedly the oldest in France, having opened for business in the 16th century. The **Palais des Rohan**, the 18th-century palace built by Robert de Cotte, houses the **Musée des Beaux Arts**, the **Musée Archaeologique** and the **Musée des Arts Decoratifs**. Of these, the last is the most worthwhile, partially contained in the State Apartments of the palace, and displaying one of the best collections of ceramics and crystal in France.

What to Do

Historical/Architectural Sites

Cathédrale de Notre-Dame   ★★★★

place de la Cathédrale, ☎ *03-88-32-37-92.*

Hours open: 10 a.m.–6 p.m. Special Hours: Closed from noon–2 p.m. Closed: Tue.

Strasbourg's Gothic-Romanesque cathedral is a stunner. Besides a plethora of lacy stone carvings, statues and a vividly colored rose window, it is memorable for the Astronomical Clock that strikes daily at 12:30 p.m., releasing a mechanical tableaux retelling the denial of Christ by St. Peter (FR5 to see the clock). For incomparable views of the city, you can climb partway up the 471-foot spire for FR12. Admission: FR15.

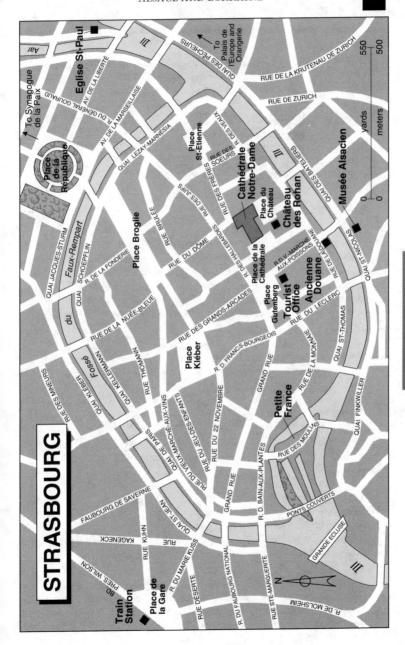

STRASBOURG

Train Station

Place de la Gare

Eglise St-Paul

To Synagogue de la Paix

Place de la République

To Palais de l'Europe and Orangerie

QUAI DES PÊCHEURS

RUE DE LA KRUTENAU DE ZURICH

RUE DE ZURICH

AV. DE LA LIBERTÉ

AV. DE LA MARSEILLAISE

R. DU GÉNÉRAL GOURAUD

QUAI JACQUES-STURM

Faux-Rempart

QUAI SCHOEPFLIN

R. DE LA FONDERIE

Place Broglie

RUE BRULÉE

RUE DU DÔME

RUE DES JUIFS

RUE DES FRÈRES

RUE DES HALLEBARDES

RUE DES SOEURS

R. DES VEAUX

Place St-Étienne

Cathédrale Notre-Dame

Place du Château

Château des Rohan

Musée Alsacien

QUAI DES BATELIERS

QUAI LEZAY-MARNESIA

Place de la Cathédrale

R.D.V.-MARCHÉ-AUX-POISSONS

Place Gutenberg

Tourist Office

Ancienne Douane

RUE DE LA DOUANE

QUAI ST-NICOLAS

RUE DE LA NUÉE-BLEUE

QUAI KELLERMANN

RUE THOMANN

RUE DES GRANDS-ARCADES

RUE DU LECLERC

Place Kléber

R.D. FRANCS-BOURGEOIS

GRAND RUE

RUE DE LA MONNAIE

QUAI ST-THOMAS

Fossé

QUAI KLÉBER

RUE DES MINEURS

QUAI DE PARIS

RUE DU VIEUX-MARCHÉ-AUX-VINS

RUE DU JEU-DES-ENFANTS

RUE DU 22 NOVEMBRE

Petite France

RUE DES MOULINS

QUAI FINKWILLER

FAUBOURG DE SAVERNE

QUAI ST-JEAN

KAGENECK

RUE KUHN

BD. PRÉS. WILSON

R. DU MARIE KUSS

R. DÉSERTE

R. DU FAUBOURG NATIONAL

RUE STE-MARGUERITE

GRAND RUE

R.D. BAIN-AUX-PLANTES

PONTS COUVERTS

GRANDE ÉCLUSE

R. DE MOLSHEIM

N

550 500 yards meters 0

Aar

Palais de Rohan   ★★★

2 place du Chateau, ☎ (03) (88) 52-50-0. Just south of the cathedral.
Hours open: 10 a.m.–6 p.m. Special Hours: Closed noon–1:30 p.m.; Sun., 10 a.m.–5
p.m. Closed: Tue.

Built between 1732 and 1742, this building served as a residence for the city's car-
dinal-princes. It is a striking example of the decorative elegance of the 18th century
and is considered one of the finest achievements in French design. Its beautiful
rococo interior houses three museums. The **Musée des Arts Decoratifs** includes the
re-created apartments of the former residents and a collection of ceramics and other
decorative pieces. The **Musée Archeologique** focuses on finds from Neolithic times
through 800 A.D., including pots, tools, weapons and jewelry. The **Musée des
Beaux-Arts** rounds out the museums here. It covers Italian, Dutch, Flemish and
French artists including Corot, Giotto, Kalf- mostly works from the 17th and 18th
centuries. Admission to each museum is FR15, or to any two museums FR22.

Palais de l'Europe   ★★

avenue de l'Europe, ☎ 03-88-41-20-29. In the northeast section of town. Take bus #3,
13 or 23.
Special Hours: Tours at 2:30 p.m., except when in session. Closed: Sat., Sun.

Headquarters of the Council of Europe and meeting place of the European Parliament, free tours are given except when the parliament is in session. Across the street
is the **parc de l'Orangerie**, with shaded paths, playgrounds and swan-filled lakes. In
addition to boat rentals on Lac de l'Orangerie (☎ 88-61-07-89, FR37 per half-
hour), free evening concerts are often held here in the summer. Admission: free.

Petite France   ★★★★

Around rue des Dentelles, rue de la Monnaie, rue des Moulins and the canal.

With its half-timbered houses and quaint lanes, la Petite France is the colorful historic core of Strasbourg. This quarter was named for a hospital that stood here in
the 16th century. Once the home of fishermen, millers and tanners, the houses are
beautifully reflected in the waters of the Ill (straight from a postcard). The Ponts
Couverts (Covered Bridges) utilize towers that were used for defense in the 13th
century. The arms of the Ill were given locks, allowing shipping from the Rhine to
reach every canal-side shop. Especially charming is rue du Bain-aux-Plantes. Admission: free.

Place Gutenberg   ★★

Off rue des Grandes Arcades.

One of the oldest squares of Strasbourg, this was the political center in the 14th–
16th centuries. The Hotel du Commerce, the former town hall and now the site of
the chamber of commerce and the tourist office, was built in 1582, in beautiful
Renaissance style. David d'Angers created the statue in the center of the square; it
is of Guttenberg who perfected his printing press in Strasbourg in the 1400s.

Synagogue de la Paix   ★★★

16 avenue de la Paix. About 300 meters northeast of place de la Republique.

This synagogue replaced the one burned down by Nazis in 1940. Rebuilt in 1958
with the Centre Communautaire (Jewish community center), part of it was vandal-
ized by neo-Nazi militants in late 1992. Nearby, at place de la Republique, there

had been a Jewish cemetery in the Middle Ages. In 1349, 2000 Jews were accused of causing the Black Plague by tainting the wells, and they were burned alive. Later, on this square, the Palais du Rhin was used as an imperial palace by Kaiser Wilhelm I. There is a war memorial in the center of the square for those killed in WWI.

Museums and Exhibits

Cathedral Quarter

place de la Cathédrale. At place de la Cathédrale and rue Merciere.
Not only is this an ideal spot from which to admire the cathedral, there are two especially attractive buildings here. The Pharmacie de Cerf is the oldest pharmacy in France, with its ground floor dating from the 15th century. On another corner is the Maison Kammerzell, built about the same time as the pharmacy. Admire the lovely Renaissance details in the sculpted wood. From here, explore the surrounding streets, such as rue Merciere, place du Marche-aux-cochons-de-lait (that's right, Suckling-Pig Market Square) and rue des Cordiers. There are many half-timbered beauties to be admired up close. Admission: free.

Musée d l'Oeuvre Notre-Dame

3 place du Chateau, ☎ 03-88-52-50-00.
Hours open: 10 a.m.–6 p.m. Closed: Mon.
In order to preserve the ancient sculptures adorning the Cathedral, many of them were replaced, and the originals housed in this museum. The regional art and medieval stained glass are also worth seeing.

Special Tours/Excursions

Circuits en Bateau

The Quai, place du Chateau. behind the Cathédrale de Notre-Dame
Hours open: 9 a.m.–9 p.m. Special Hours: Night tours March-Oct. only.
Covered barges ply the Ill River and surrounding canals daily for picturesque views of the city. The duration is usually about two hours; students, children FR19.50. Longer Rhine river cruises (as long as four hours) are offered May-Sept.; dining available. For information ☎ *(03) 88-32-75-25.* Admission: FR37.

Where to Stay

Hotels and Resorts

Comfort Hotel Plaza   **FR400–FR530**   ★★

10 place de la Gare. ☎ 03-88-15-17-17, FAX: 03-88-15-17-15.
Rated Restaurant: *La Cour de Rosemont.*
Single: FR400–FR500. Double: FR450–FR530.
A modern six-story hotel dating to the 1950s, the Comfort Hotel Plaza wears a traditional interior fronted by a rather sleek facade. Very popular with groups, the hotel has 78 comfortable guest rooms with TV, telephone, radio, minibar and bath or shower with hair dryer. The decor is traditional, and the housekeeping is meticulous. There are two restaurants in the hotel, one of which caters to the business lunchtime crowd with sidewalk tables and the other to the more formal dinner crowd with specialty game dishes. Formerly part of the Best Western chain, this facility is still reminiscent of a commercial hotel in appearance; this makes for a qual-

ity hotel with modern amenities and characterless ambience. Features: in-room minibars. Credit Cards: All Major.

Hotel Regent Contades   FR550–FR1200   ★★★★

8 avenue de la Liberte. ☎ *03-88-15-05-05, FAX: 03-88-15-05-15.*
Single: FR550–FR1000. Double: FR800–FR1200.
Although opened in 1987, this hotel has quickly become a leading symbol of luxury in Strasbourg. With the premier address in town, this three-story establishment sits between the cathedral and the Council of Europe. A fine example of traditional style, the public areas showcase Asian rugs, original art and fresh flowers in a well-orchestrated display of design prowess. There are 44 rooms decorated with soothing color schemes, coordinated furnishings and subdued lighting. Modern amenities include TV, radio, telephone, minibar, safe and tiled bath with hair dryer and robes. Breakfast is the only meal served in the dining room, with 24-hour room service and nearby restaurants making up for the lack of dining options in the hotel. Get wet in the sauna and whirlpools, and soak in the rays in the solarium. Attentive and cheerful, the staff proves to be one of the greatest assets to this service oriented hotel. Features: sauna, in-room safes, in-room minibars. Credit Cards: All Major.

Hotel des Rohan   FR350–FR620   ★★

17-19 rue du Maroquin. ☎ *03-88-32-85-11, FAX: 03-88-75-65-37. About 50 meters from the cathedral.*
Single: FR350–FR375. Double: FR375–FR620.
A well-appointed hotel in a choice location near the cathedral. The structure is a restored four-story building with origins from the 17th-century. Within are 36 smallish, elegant rooms decorated either in Louis XV style or with pine paneling in a more rustic decor. All are well-equipped with cable TV, telephone, radio, minibar and private bath with hair dryer. Although breakfast is the only meal served, the staff is happy to make recommendations for nearby restaurants. A peaceful establishment offering tasteful and comfortable lodging. Features: nonsmoking rooms, in-room minibars. Credit Cards: All Major.

Monopole-Metropole   FR360–FR520   ★★

16 rue Kahn. ☎ *03-88-14-39-14. About 200 meters from the train station.*
Single: FR360–FR580. Double: FR440–FR520.
Residing on a quiet side street, this is a very traditional Alsatian hotel, as evidenced by the brick and stone facade. Within the doors lie the contemporary lobby spotted with antiques and statues and a salon featuring oil paintings and antique objects behind glass. The 94 rooms are decorated in modern or traditional style and come with satellite TV, telephone, radio, minibar and private bath or shower. Breakfast is served in the high-ceilinged dining room for FR60, and there are a few sitting lounges throughout the hotel. Once family owned, the hotel is now operated by the Best Western chain. Features: nonsmoking rooms, in-room minibars. Credit Cards: All Major.

Regent Petite France   FR800–FR1320   ★★★★

5 rue Moulins. ☎ *03-88-76-43-43, FAX: 03-88-76-43-76.*
Rated Restaurant: *Le Pont Tournant.*
Single: FR800–FR1200. Double: FR1200–FR1320.

ALSACE AND LORRAINE

Formerly an ice factory on the edges of the Ill River, the Regent still displays the old steam machinery in the Ice-Making Museum. Opened in 1992, this unique structure actually touches ground on both sides of the river. The spacious marble lobby is smartly furnished with leather seating and accented with small palms. Just beyond are the reputable restaurant and the sociable cocktail lounge. The 72 air-conditioned rooms are modern and include satellite TV, telephone, radio, minibar and private bath with hair dryer and robes. The postmodern decor gives the old building a little twist. Room service is available 24 hours if the beds are too comfortable to leave. A well-appointed choice in a very scenic section of town. Features: wheelchair-access rooms, air conditioning in rooms, nonsmoking rooms, fitness center. Credit Cards: All Major.

Obernai

Hotels and Resorts

A la Cour d'Alsace   FR430–FR780   ★★★

3 rue du Gail. ☎ *03-88-95-07-00, FAX: 03-88-95-19-21. In the old section of Obernai, near the Strasbourg airport.*
Single: FR430–FR740. Double: FR520–FR780.
Converted from a 17th-century manor house that once was home to local barons, this hotel first opened its doors in 1984. The 43 rooms are individually decorated and contain TV, telephone, safe, bath and hair dryer. Overlooking the gardens, there are two restaurants and a bar in the hotel. It keeps its modern look fresh with constant maintenance and updating. Features: wheelchair-access rooms. Credit Cards: All Major.

Where to Eat

Buerehiesel $$ ★★★

4 parc de l'Orangerie. ☎ *03-88-61-62-24.*
Lunch: Noon–2:30 p.m., FR155–FR300.
Dinner: 7–9:30 p.m., entrées FR155–FR300.
Set in a large park near the Council of Europe headquarters, this restaurant is a juxtaposition of the old and the new, with modernized Alsatian cuisine served in a typical wine route farmhouse. Signature dishes include baby frogs' legs served with onion-stuffed spatzle and mousse of celeriac with caviar. Although it's rated as one of the best restaurants in the country, a few of chef Antoine Westermann's culinary experiments fall flat from poor conception, and the serving staff sometimes looks like they need a boost in morale. Closed: Tues. Amenities: own baking, reservations recommended. Credit Cards: All Major.

Le Crocodile $$$

10 rue d l'Oure. ☎ *03-88-32-13-02.*
Lunch: Noon–2 p.m., FR200–FR300.
Dinner: 7–9:30 p.m., entrées FR200–FR300.
A handsome restaurant, Le Crocodile is all aglow with burnished woods, tasteful flower arrangements and natural light. The tables are spaced discreetly apart, so you never feel hemmed in, even when it's crowded, which it often is, being the number-one spot in town. The food reflects the rich bounty of the Alsace region, with plenty

of pork dishes, including pig's trotters and black truffles stuffed in a caul "crepe," as well as typically French classics such as pressed duck, artichokes and mushrooms. Those who want to eat lightly can do so on a myriad of fresh fish dishes (turbot, perch) with delicately cooked vegetables. Le Crocodile is also noted for its wine cellar, which can push your bill into the stratosphere. Jacket and tie required. Closed: Mon., Sun. Reservations required. Credit Cards: All Major.

Maison Kammerzell $$ ★★

16 place de la Cathédrale. ☎ *03-88-32-42-14.*
Specialties: Choucroute.
Lunch: Noon–3 p.m., FR100–FR165.
Dinner: 7 p.m.–1 a.m., entrées FR100–FR165.
This brasserie would be more appropriately named the "House of Choucroute," as it serves several versions of this local standby, a stew of cabbage cooked in white wine, usually served with a slew of pork parts, sausages and potato. Other dishes are served as well, of course, including chicken with noodles or fresh fish, but it's really not for vegetarians. Don't miss the unusual plum-and-brandy sorbet. The building the Maison is lodged in, a Hansel and Gretel structure built in the 15th century, is lovingly cared for inside and out by the owners. Amenities: outside dining, cafestop, reservations required. Credit Cards: All Major.

Winstub Strissel $ ★

5 place de la Grande Boucherie. ☎ *03-88-32-14-73.*
Lunch: 10 a.m.–2 p.m., FR55–FR70.
Dinner: 7–11 p.m., entrées FR55–FR70.
Informal and inexpensive, this winstub serves wines by the glass along with typical Alsatian dishes. The king of the winstubs is **S'Burjerstuewel** (also called "Yvonne's Place"), *10 rue du Sanglier (*☎ *03-88-32-84-15);* it's good for a splurge (dinner for two is FR175–FR230) and the local specialties that go with wine, including Alsatian white cheese *(bibbeleskas),* stuffed pig's stomach, and cheesecake. We'll break our rule of eating as the natives do by mentioning this pizza place, because it's so popular with students, and the prices are right—there's a wide variety of toppings, also salads, pasta and desserts. For Alsatian-style pizza, try this mouthful: **Auberge** (that's the easy part) **du Flammekueche Burg**, *19 rue des Veux (*☎ *03-88-35-35-85),* where they bake the pies in wood-burning ovens; *open until 11:30 p.m.,* entrées FR60 and up. Back to tradition, try **Au Pont Saint Martin**, *15 rue des Moulins (*☎ *03-88-32-45-13),* for a taste of choucroute (cabbage cooked with white wine and pork, served with potatoes) for FR65 or equally good baekoffe (no cabbage, several kinds of meats) for FR80. *Open daily, noon–2:30 p.m. and 6–11 p.m. Closed: Mon., Sun.* Amenities: cafestop, reservations not accepted.

Directory

To and From

By train from Paris (four hours), Nancy (an hour and a half), and Metz (an hour and a half) (Frankfurt, Zurich, and Brussels are all within three hours), or by car on the A-4 autoroute or N-4 highway from the west or the N-83 highway from the south. Also international air service on Air France and other carriers and domestic flights on Air Inter Europe.

Tourist Office
   17 place de la Cathédrale; ☎ *(33) 03-88-52-28-28.*

Rail Station
   place de la Gàre; ☎ *(33) 03-88-22-50-50.*

Post Office
   5 avenue de la Marseillaise, 67000 Strasbourg; ☎ *(33) 03-88-52-35-20.*

Colmar

Boat trips along Petite Venise offer scenic glimpses of Colmar.

Colmar is an ancient trading city that grew rich on the wine trade during the 13th century, reaching its peak of prosperity in the 16th century, when the elegant houses lining the canal quarter were built. The city's Old Quarter is wonderfully well-preserved, and a boat trip in summer along the canals known as "Petite Venise" is a great way to see the old houses of the wine merchants and tanners. The unique attraction of Colmar is its wealth of art and art museums. Chronologically, the richness begins with the Eglise Dominicains, a Gothic-style church housing the 1473 painting "La Vierge au Buisson de Roses" (The Virgin of the Rose Hedge), a religious masterpiece by Martin Schöngauer, a native of the city. Continuing on to the Unterlinden Museum, one finds another great religious work produced 50 years later, the monumental "Issenhein Altarpiece" painted in 1512 by Matthias Grünewald for an Antonite convent just outside the city. The depiction of the suffering of Christ on the cross and the anguish of his followers gathered around him is considered one of the most significant explanations of contemporary theology. The museum also houses a collection of Rhenish paintings from the 14th to the 17th centuries, as well as displays of costumes and everyday objects from the Middle Ages and Renaissance Alsace. The next stop is the museum located at the birthplace of August Bartholdi, creator of the Statue of Liberty and countless massive public-space sculptures in the 19th century. There is a life-sized ear from Liberty, as well as models of his statues of famous French generals and politicians, including the "Lion of Belfort," a commemoration of the Resistance of the nearby city to the Prussian invasion in the late 19th century.

What to Do

Historical/Architectural Sites

Eglise St-Martin   ★★

place de la Cathédrale. In the center of Old Colmar.
Hours open: 8 a.m.–5 p.m.
The largest church in town, this church was begun in 1230 and completed in 1315. Notable is the choir, erected by William of Marbourg, and the 230-foot-high steeple. Also, compare the sculptures above the main entrance—the Last Judgment reflects Gothic, and the scenes of St-Nicolas are Romanesque.

Eglise des Dominicains   ★★★

place des Dominicains, ☎ 03 (89) 41-27-20.
Hours open: 10 a.m.–6 p.m. Special Hours: Apr.–Oct. only.
View Martin Schongauer's "Virgin of the Rosebush," one of Colmar's most famous works. Painted in 1473 in Flamboyant Gothic with a Renaissance finish, it's beautifully illuminated by the 14th-century stained-glass windows. Admission: FR8.

Maison Pfister   ★★★

11 rue des Marchands, ☎ 03-89-41-33-61.
A civic building erected in 1537, this is one of the most decorative houses in Colmar. Admire the oriel window and wooden balconies on the outside; there's a wine boutique on the ground floor. Continue across St-Peter's Bridge into Petite Venice, a lovely canal-striped section of town with well-restored half-timbered houses on surrounding streets. Perfect for a late-afternoon stroll.

Museums and Exhibits

Musée Bartholdi   ★★

30 rue des Marchands, ☎ 03-89-41-90-60. Near the Musée Unterlinden.
Hours open: 10 a.m.–6 p.m. Special Hours: Closed noon–2 p.m.; closed Jan.–Feb. Closed: Tue.
Birthplace of August Bartholdi, creator of the Statue of Liberty, this museum is filled with memorabilia of New York City's honorary citizen. The plans, scale models and related items of the statue are presented here, along with other artifacts related to the history of Colmar. Check out the life-size model of Liberty's ear on the top floor. Admission: FR20.

Musée d'Unterlinden   ★★★

place d'Unterlinden, ☎ 03-89-20-15-50. At place de la Sinne.
Hours open: 9 a.m.–6 p.m. Special Hours: Nov.–Mar. to 5 p.m.

Once a Dominican convent built in 1232, this is one of the most visited French provincial museums. Assembled here is an impressive collection of religious art from the 14th–17th centuries. The jewel in its crown is Mathias Grunewald's "Issenheim Altarpiece." Painted around 1510, this is an immense altar screen with multiple panels. It depicts various religious scenes, including St-Anthony visiting St-Paul, the Temptation of St-Anthony, the Crucifixion and the Resurrection. A powerful piece of art—considered one of the greatest Christian paintings of the Middle Ages. Other attractions include works by Picasso and Monet, as well as a collection of weapons, ironworks and costumes. *Nov.–Mar. to 5 p.m., Wed.–Mon., 10 a.m.– noon and 2–6 p.m.* Admission: FR28.

Special Tours/Excursions

Josmeyer

78 rue Clemenceau, ☎ *03-89-27-01-57. Take D417 about 5 km southwest of Colmar.* Within this half-timbered house topped with a red-tile roof, tastings and sales are in the golden stone-carved cellars. Some of the best wines here are the Rieslings, the Pinot Gris and the Gewurtzraminers. The highlights here are on vintages, which the wine-maker says gives the wine its charm. On Saturdays, tastings are held in the morning only.

Where to Stay

Hotels and Resorts

Hostellerie Le Marechal   **FR450–FR550**

4-5 place des Six-Montagnes-Noires. ☎ *03-89-41-60-32. Near the River Lauch.* *Single: FR450. Double: FR550.*
Great effort has gone into the restoration and connecting of the three 16th-century houses that make up this old-fashioned hotel and its virtual maze of corridors. The 30 unique rooms are smallish and decorated in cheerful, attractive colors. All rooms have a TV, telephone, minibar, bath and either a fan or air conditioning; views come in the form of the river or the park. Suites with Jacuzzis are FR1000 to FR1400. Atmospheric meals are served canalside in the summer and in the firelit dining room in the winter. Breakfast for FR60. Credit Cards: All Major.

Husseren-les-Chateaux   **FR400–FR600**

rue du Schlossberg. ☎ *03-89-49-22-93. About 9 km south of Colmar, in Husseren-les-Chateaux.*
Double: FR400–FR600.
Set just a short drive south of Colmar, this hotel is perched on a countryside hill. The views of the Vosges countryside and the surrounding vineyards are splendid. Comfortable and cheery, the 35 air-conditioned rooms have all of the standard conveniences and come with mezzanines. Facilities include an indoor pool, sauna, solarium and game room. Features: wheelchair-access rooms, pool, air conditioning in rooms, sauna.

La Fecht   **FR300–FR400**

1 rue de la Fecht. ☎ *03-89-41-34-08, FAX: 03-89-23-80-28. At the edge of the old town.*
Single: FR300. Double: FR400.

At the edge of the old town sits La Fecht, a small hotel with 39 rooms. Well-maintained and rather spacious, the rooms have TV, telephone, radio, minibar and bath. A sauna and an attractive terrace are also in the hotel. Good meals start at FR95 in the restaurant. Guests with cars appreciate the garage parking. Features: wheelchair-access rooms. Credit Cards: All Major.

Terminus Bristol   FR425–FR750   ★★★

7 place de la Gare. ☎ *03-89-23-59-59, FAX: 03-89-23-92-26. Near the train station. Single: FR425–FR475. Double: FR500–FR750.*

Despite its central location near the train station, the Terminus manages to remain relatively quiet. Behind the red sandstone facade are 70 rooms, both modern and provincial in decor. Each room has a TV, telephone, minibar and bath. Regularly improved, the look is kept new and the facilities kept in top condition. Alsatian fare is served at the hotel restaurant, and there is an adjoining bar. Breakfast costs FR50. The Terminus does a brisk business. Features: wheelchair-access rooms. Credit Cards: All Major.

Riquewihr

Inns

Le Sarment d'Or   FR225   ★★★

4 rue du Cerf. ☎ *03-89-47-92-85, FAX: 03-89-47-99-23. In town center. Double: FR225.*

Among the medieval buildings that draw the tourists to this town, this little hotel sticks with tradition while offering modern comforts. Above the firelit restaurant are the 10 rooms, individually decorated and comfy-cozy. All of the up-to-date conveniences are here, as well as its small-size charm. Credit Cards: V, MC.

Where to Eat

Au Fer Rouge $$ ★★★★★

52 Grand Rue. ☎ *03-89-41-37-24.*
Specialties: braised sole; perch with sauerkraut.
Dinner: 7–9:30 p.m., entrées FR150–FR275.

In the heart of Colmar, this timbered building sits peacefully reminding those who pass of a much simpler day. Within these walls, however, the cuisine has patrons thanking the culinary gods for living in these days of invention. The dishes served here have escaped any traditional boundaries to become some of the finest examples of the benefits of a creative spirit in the kitchen. Just a few of the wondrous works include filet of beef with tarragon, ballottine of quail and wild duck. The service, however, has remained true to the graciousness of yesteryear. Set menus from FR210 during the week and FR320 on weekends. *Closed Jan. and early–mid-Aug. Closed: Mon.* Reservations required. Credit Cards: All Major.

La Maison Rouge $ ★

9 rue des Ecoles. ☎ *03-89-23-53-22.*
Lunch: Noon–2:30 p.m., FR58–FR79.
Dinner: 6:30–9:30 p.m., entrées FR58–FR79.

Two-level charmer with a patio upstairs is a good deal for Alsatian specialties at budget prices; prix-fixe menu, four courses at lunch for FR60. For more of the same, try

Le Bec Fin, *8 place du Marche* (☎ *89-41-73-76*), this intimate spot has ice cream and tea and light meals like quiche (FR40) as well; prix fixe FR85. *Open 10 am–10 pm, closed Monday.* **Monoprix Cafeteria**, *4 Quai de la Sinn*, across from the Unterlinden Museum (☎ *03-89-41-22-57*), self-service, prix-fixe FR30–FR55; *open 7:30 a.m.–9:30 p.m., closed Sunday.* Markets: place de l'Ancienne Douane, Thursday mornings, place St.-Joseph, Saturday mornings. The aforementioned Monoprix is also a well-known supermarket chain. Amenities: cafestop, reservations recommended. Credit Cards: V, MC, A, E.

La Maison des Tetes $$ ★★★

19 rue des Tetes, in the old town. ☎ *03-89-24-43-43.*
Dinner: 7–9:30 p.m., entrées FR80–FR200.

The facade of this 17th-century Gothic style restaurant is known for the sculptured heads in front. It is these sculptures for which the restaurant is named ("House of Heads"). The dining rooms are just as lovely, with wood beams and stained glass in use. The traditional cuisine perfectly melds with the atmosphere, often including freshwater fish or fillet of beef. A good selection of wines at reasonable prices complements the inexpensive set menus from FR100. Closed: Mon. Amenities: outside dining, reservations required. Credit Cards: All Major.

Rendez Vous de Chasse $$ ★★★★

7 place de la Gare, At the train station. Located at Terminus-Bristol. ☎ *03-89-41-10-10.*
Dinner: 7–10 p.m., entrées FR120–FR200.

A first-rate establishment from top to bottom, the Hotel Terminus-Bristol hosts this fine restaurant. Sink into this pampering, luxurious setting and decide between dishes such as duckling foie gras and pike perch. The main dishes and the desserts are season-sensitive and may vary, which makes for an interesting meal every time. The wine list includes many reasonably priced bottles to accompany the meal. Set menus from FR180. Closed: Tues. Reservations recommended. Credit Cards: All Major.

Schillinger $$$ ★★★

16 rue Stanislas. ☎ *03-89-41-43-17.*
Specialties: ravioli with smoked duck foie gras, duckling with lemon sauce.
Lunch: Noon–2:15 p.m., FR250–FR350.
Dinner: 7 p.m.–9:30 p.m., entrées FR250–FR350.

The familiar dishes of Jean Schillinger remain, although his Robuchon-trained son, Jean-Yves, is now more or less in charge of the kitchen. The latter's classically oriented cuisine encompasses all the regions of France and includes such dishes as duck with lemon sauce. At Schillinger's, you'll find extravagant decor and polished service. **Au Fer Rouge**, Patrick Fulgraff's restaurant in Old Town, *52 Grand-Rue (03-89-41-37-24)*, comes close to Schillinger in quality, but with a more Alsatian focus. Specialties include roast suckling pig and pike perch with sauerkraut and bacon. A la carte FR200–FR350, fixed-price FR210 weekdays and Saturday lunch. *Open noon–2 p.m. and 7 p.m.–9:30 p.m.; no dinner Sun., closed Mon., and Jan. 16–Feb. 3. Closed: Mon.* Amenities: own baking, reservations required. Credit Cards: All Major.

Illhaeusern

L'Auberge de l'Ill   **$$$**   ★★★★★

Rue de Collonges, Located 19 km from Colmar on N83. In the Hotel des Berges. Located at Hotel des Berges. ☎ *03-89-71-83-23.*

Specialties: duck in aspic with goose liver.

Lunch: Noon–2 p.m., FR350–FR455.

Dinner: 7 p.m.–9:30 p.m., entrées FR350–FR455.

You won't have to worry about missing the turnoff to this temple of gastronomy—lots of signs point to it, as if it were Disneyland. Attached to a delightful small inn on the River Ill, the Auberge is run by the Haeberlin brothers: chef Marc and host and restaurant designer Jean-Pierre. Marc's robust cooking makes good use of the region's rich bounty, including baby cabbage, duck, pheasant and goose; sometimes whole dinners are arranged around goose parts, from gizzard to leg. Unusual creations featured on the recent menus have been a grenouille ragout with choucroute-stuffed baby cabbage. Wonderful ice-creams and desserts. Due to its exemplary reputation, you must reserve weeks in advance. Closed: Tues. Amenities: own baking, reservations required. Credit Cards: All Major.

Directory

To and From

By train from Paris (six hours), Lyon (four-and-a-half hours) and Strasbourg (half an hour), or by road on the A-35 autoroute or N-83 highway between Strasbourg and Basle, Switzerland.

Tourist Office

4 rue des Unterlinden; ☎ *(33) 03-89-20-68-92.*

Rail Station

place de la Gàre; ☎ *(33) 03-89-41-66-80.*

Post Office

36 avenue de la République, 68000 Colmar; ☎ *(33) 03-89-41-19-19.*

Mulhouse

Lacking the picturesque quarters of half-timbered houses of other Alsatian towns, Mulhouse's industrialization is its strength—and it contains the highest concentration of worthwhile industrial museums in France. An independent city during the 13th century, Mulhouse (the name itself means "millhouse") was part of Switzerland from the early 17th century, only joining France in 1798, after the Révolution and after the rest of Alsace. Mulhouse was a textile-production center by the mid-18th century, and pioneered the creation of printed textiles. In 1812, the Dollfus et Mieg Mill became the first in France to convert to steam power. Today, industry continues to dominate the city, with a massive Peugeot plant on the outskirts.

The museum tour begins with the **Musée de l'Impression** sur Etoffes, the textile-printing museum, which traces the development of the industry from its inception in 1746 in Mulhouse through the present. Nearby is the Musée de Papier Peint, the wallpaper museum. Before setting out to the museums outside the center of town, visit the **Musée Historique**, which gives a broader perspective on the history of the city, enhanced by the 18th-century former Hôtel de Ville in which it is housed. The **Musée de l'Automobile** is a true jewel, based on the collection of the Schlumpf brothers, local mill owners. More than 500 cars are exhibited, providing a comprehensive look at the development of the automobile in France and around the world. The highlight for most aficionados is the collection of 123 Bugattis, the most important in the world. The **Musée Français du Chemin de Fer**, the railway museum, is almost as impressive, housed on the tracks of a former mainline terminal station. From the steam locomotive built by Stephenson in 1846 to the powerful monsters of the 1950s, as well as a collection of rolling stock including Imperial and royal carriages, this is a rich display of the history of rail transportation in France. If you have time, drive a few miles north to Ungersheim, where the Ecomusée d'Alsace presents living displays of Alsace countryside and farming from through the ages. A series of minifarms show the development of agriculture in the region, as well as displays of traditional rural crafts.

Mulhouse is half an hour by train or about 30 miles by road south of Colmar.

What to Do

Historical/Architectural Sites

★★

Musée Historique

place de la Reunion, ☎ *03-89-45-43-20. In the old town, near the marketplace. Hours open: 10 a.m.–6 p.m. Special Hours: Closed Noon–2 p.m. Closed Tues.*
Within the walls of the Hotel de Ville is the Musée Historique and its displays tracing regional history. The Hotel, in Renaissance style, dates to the 16th century and is worthy of a visit to snap some photos of the frescoes and outside stairway. A good starting point for a tour of the old town. Admission: FR20.

Museums and Exhibits

★★★★

Ecomusee

Chemin Grosswald, ☎ *03-89-74-44-74. North of Mulhouse off the A35, in Ungersheim. Special Hours: Closed Jan.–early Feb.*
A reconstructed Alsatian village, this outdoor museum was opened in 1980, dedicating itself to local heritage. About 40 houses were saved from demolition by being completely recreated in this small village. Walk the streets and witness the skills of the blacksmiths, bakers and various craftspersons in action. *Open late Feb.–Apr., 11 a.m.–5 p.m.; May and Oct., 10 a.m.–6 p.m.; June–Sept., 9 a.m.–7 p.m.; Nov.–Dec., 11 a.m.–5 p.m.* Student admission FR45; child admission FR30. Admission: FR52.

★★★

Musée de l'Automobile

192 avenue de Colmar, ☎ *03-89-42-29-17. Hours open: 10 a.m.–5:30 p.m. Special Hours: Closed Tues.*
Showing the combined collection of the Schlumpf brothers, this museum features more than 400 vintage cars, covering the keystones of the European auto industry.

ALSACE AND LORRAINE

On display are more than 120 Bugattis, custom-made Ferraris, Rolls Royces and a steam-powered Jacquot. They're all given gemstone treatment by the French government. For automobile buffs, this is Mecca. But why stop here? At the Musée **Francais du Chemin de Fer**, *2 rue Alfred Glehn (☎ 89-42-25-67)*, the focus is on steam engines, locomotives and more cars. Fire engines and pumps, too. *Open 9 a.m.–6 p.m., winter 10 a.m.–5 p.m.*, admission FR43, children FR20. Admission: FR56.

Musée de l'Impression sur Etoffes ★★

3 rue des Bonnes-Gens, ☎ 03-89-45-51-20. Next to the post office.
Concentrating on textiles and fabric printing, the Museum of Textile Printing contains more than eight million pieces of cloth from around the world. Machines from the past that printed cloth and related articles are proudly displayed. Mon., Wed. and Fri. are printing machine demonstration days at 3 p.m. *Open May–Sept., daily, 10 a.m.–noon and 2–6 p.m.; Oct.–Apr., Wed.–Mon., 10 a.m.–noon and 2–6 p.m.* (Museum closed for restoration is expected to re-open by press time.) Admission: FR25.

Where to Stay

Hotels and Resorts

Bourse   FR340–FR480   ★★

14 rue de la Bourse. ☎ 03-89-56-18-44. Located at avenue du Mar. Joffre; near the stock exchange, train station and place de la Republique.
Single: FR340–FR400. Double: FR450–FR480.
Conveniently located, this hotel offers quiet rooms, about half of which overlook an inner courtyard. The decor of the rooms ranges from old-fashioned to contemporary; most bathrooms are modern. There is no restaurant, and the hotel is open year-round. Features: nonsmoking rooms. Credit Cards: All Major.

Bretonnerie   FR400–FR825   ★★

22 rue Sainte Croix de la Bretonnerie. ☎ 03-48-87-77-63, FAX: 03-42-77-26-78. Take metro line #1 or 11 to Hotel de Ville. Walk north on rue de Archives to rue Sainte Croix de la Bretonnerie.
Public transportation: 1, 11. Metro stop: Hotel de Ville.
Single: FR400–FR690. Double: FR620–FR825.
This quiet hotel occupies a tall 17th-century mansion that once housed French aristocrats. While staying true to the building's heritage by keeping the stone walls, exposed wood beams and period furniture, it possesses the comforts of modern day. There are 31 guest rooms, all of which are generously sized and attractively furnished. Each comes with a minibar and a safe. Breakfast is served in the medieval-times basement displaying wood tables and high backed chairs under a vaulted ceiling. Take note that this popular choice is closed for part of August. Credit Cards: All Major.

Hotel du Parc   FR650–FR1300   ★★

26 rue de la Sinne. ☎ 03-89-66-12-22, FAX: 03-89-66-42-44. Located between the Square Steinbach and avenue Clemenceau. Rated Restaurant: *Hotel du Parc.*
Single: FR650–FR900. Double: FR990–FR1300.

The premier address of Mulhouse, this beautifully restored Art Deco building recaptures the glamour of the 1930s. The 76 rooms are well equipped, and all have private bath. Guests are treated to live music at teatime. There is also a sleek Art Deco bar called Charlie's, and a restaurant that offers quality lunches and dinners as well as after-theater suppers. Features: air conditioning in rooms, nonsmoking rooms, in-room minibars. Credit Cards: All Major.

Low Cost Lodging

Grand Hotel Jeanne d'Arc   **FR350–FR450**   ★

3 rue de Jarente. ☎ *03-48-87-62-11, FAX: 03-48-87-37-31. Take metro line #1 to St. Paul. It lies near rue de Turenne.*
Public transportation: 1. Metro stop: St. Paul.
Single: FR350–FR450. Double: FR350–FR450.
A standard hotel which proves to be one of the better value choices in the area. The 36 guest rooms are slightly worn and ecclectically decorated, with a telephone, cable TV and tidy bath. Return visitors appreciate the location near the many shops, the place des Vosges and the Picasso Museum. Breakfast is available for FR40 per person. Credit Cards: V, MC, DC, E.

Where to Eat

Aux Caves du Vieux Couvent   **$$**   ★

rue du Couvent. ☎ *89-46-28-79-33.*
Lunch: Noon–2 p.m., FR50–FR198.
Dinner: 7 p.m.–9:30 p.m., entrées FR50–FR198.
Popular with locals, this informal restaurant offers hearty regional specialties at reasonable prices. Also good is **Wistuwa** (Wine Bar) **zum Mehlala**, *7 rue d'Illzach (*☎ *89-59-41-32),* near local movie houses; its desserts are particularly notable. *Open noon–11 p.m.;* prices start as low as FR45. Amenities: cafestop. Credit Cards: V, A.

Restaurant de la Poste   **$$**   ★★

7 rue General de Gaulle. ☎ *03-89-44-07-71.*
Specialties: raw smoked eels, supreme de sandre, moule de fromage blanc, sorbet myrtilles.
Lunch: Noon–2 p.m., FR142–FR192.
Dinner: 7–10 p.m., entrées FR142–FR192.
One of Mulhouse's best restaurants, with an established reputation, featuring good seafood dishes and a wine cellar. The fixed-price menu is a steal at FR130. reservations required. Credit Cards: V, MC, E.

ALSACE AND
LORRAINE

CORSICA

Calvi is one of Corsica's most popular resorts.

What Makes Corsica So French?

1. *Napoleon was born here.*

2. *The grand paintings at Musée Fesch.*

3. *Napoleon's life story is displayed in his original home-turned-museum.*

4. *Bonifacio, the citadel, once home to the French Foreign Legion.*

5. *The chichi beaches at Palombaggia and Pinarello.*

The rocky island of Corsica, called La Corse in French, is France's most independent region geographically, topographically, and culturally. Variously described as "Island of Beauty" (by the Greeks), a "mountain in the sea" by the poet Ratzel, "everything fascinating" by the sculptor César, and a place where "everything shimmers, everything is colorful, everything is bathed in light" by Henri Matisse, the island has kept a separate identity and language since becoming part of France in 1768. Partly due to its reluctance to embrace France as its motherland, and partly due to the sometimes violent separatist movement, Corsica has never become an overexploited tourist destination. Nevertheless it is one of the most wonderful regions of France to visit, full of history from prehistoric man to Napoléon, natural beauty such as crystal clear waters and snow-capped mountains, traditional ways of life and quiet farming villages.

History

The third-largest island in the Mediterranean after Sicily and neighboring Sardinia, Corsica, at just 113 by 51 miles, has had more than its fair share of history through the ages. The island is one of the richest repositories of megaliths and evidence of prehistoric man in the world. Some 5000 years ago ancient builders raised menhirs and dolmens here that rival those of Carnac for their number and quality of preservation. From the 258 megaliths collectively known as the Palaggio near the village of Sartène on the road between Ajaccio and Bonifacio, to the statues, dating to 4000 B.C., found in 1946 at Filitosa a few miles north), which are the earliest known sculptural art in Europe, the island is a living museum to our ancestors. The next chapter in Corsica's history is reputed to have taken place some 3000 years later, when Ulysses supposedly sought safe harbor in what is now Bonifacio during his long journey home described in Homer's *Odyssey*. By about 550 B.C. the Greeks had settled the island, establishing trading posts and building communities in the same locations that are now the island's major cities. *Kalliste* was the ancient Greek name for Corsica, meaning Beautiful Island, a moniker that has recently been readopted by the region's tourist board.

In the latter part of the first millennium after Christ, Corsica, like much of Europe, was a possession of the Holy Roman Empire. It was placed under the administration of the Bishop of Pisa by the Pope in 1077, a time when the different bishoprics were virtual fiefdoms. The rival Genoa bishopric clamored for equity in the distribution of what was seen to be a potentially valuable possession, with its strategic position for trade in the Mediterranean, so the pope acquiesced and reapportioned part of the island to the Genoese. For the next 500 years or so the rival Italian kingdoms played tug-of-war with the island, with Genoa gradually getting the upper hand, but the growing population, tired of outside influence wherever it came from, grew increasingly independence-minded. The 1550s saw the first major armed struggle for self-determination on the island, as the Corsicans, led by Sampiero Corso rose up against the Genoese. After seeking and receiving the assistance of French King Henri II (who was always ready to put a wrench in Genoa's works), the islanders defeated the Genoese army in 1553. Independence lasted only a few years, however, and by 1560 the Genoese were back in charge and Corso was martyred for the cause. Things remained the same way for another 200 years or so, until the second of Corsica's great national heroes, Pascal Paoli, led a new revolt against the Italians in 1754. This was Corsica's one and only true period of independence, but it lasted just 15 years. French politics had changed in the intervening two centuries, and they favored the side of the Genoese this time. Genoa, glad to be rid of what was increasingly a thorn in its side, sold the island to Louis XV for 40 million francs in 1768, and the French stamped out the rebellion and annexed the island the following year. That same year saw the birth in Ajaccio of Corsica's most famous, but by no means favorite, native son, and after rising to military prominence during the Révolution, Napoléon returned to stamp out a new threat to French rule led by Paoli and the English army in 1792. Ever since, the Corsicans have resented French administration, and separatism has ebbed and flowed through the intervening years to the rhythm of the island's economic and social fortunes. The past 20 years have seen a resurgence in the movement, as the economy has soured and a new wave of immigration—supported by Paris but resented by the Corsicans—has seen the island's demographics turn even darker skinned than previously. Corsican—a dialect of Italian—is still spoken along with French, and occasional car bombings and assassinations attest to the strong sense of independence felt on the island. Visitors should not fear to come to Corsica, however; violent acts are the exception, not the norm, and tourism is a mainstay of the economy and generally respected by the residents.

Cuisine

Food and drink in Corsica are typically Mediterranean, based largely on olives, seafood and fresh produce. Corsican *bouillabaisse* differs from its mainland cousin in the extent of herbs and spices used to flavor the soupy stew, while *figatelli*, *fritelli*, *lonzo* and *coppa* are all typical Corsican *charcuterie* products. Wild boar *(sanglier)* is a specialty; poultry in myrtle and fresh river trout are not to be missed. Cheeses are mainly produced from goat's milk (roasted kid is a delicious early summer dish); *brocchiu* being the most popular. This goat cheese is also used to stuff ravioli, vegetables including artichokes, and omelettes. Wines produced on the island use a different selection of grapes than on the mainland; Nielluccio in Cap Corse and Patrimonio, Sciarello, known as "the grape that cracks between the teeth," around Ajaccio, and Vermentino around Figari and Porto Vecchio. Cap Corse, Patrimonio, Calvi, Ajaccio, Sartène, Figari and Porto-Vecchio are the local *appellations controlées*, producing mostly robust, fruity red wines as well as a smaller variety of whites that go well with the omnipresent fish and sea-food dishes served throughout the island.

Traveling to Corsica

The island is located about 100 miles off the coast, southeast of the eastern end of the Mediterranean coast. Air Inter Europe and Air Corse fly to Ajaccio and Bastia year-round and Calvi and Figari (serving Bonifacio) in summer. Flight times are about an hour and a half from Paris, 40 minutes from Marseille, and half an hour from Nice. Ferry service from Marseille, Toulon and Nice takes anywhere from five to 10 hours, depending on the ship used and the weather conditions encountered. The primary carrier is SNCM, which can be contacted at *12, rue Godot-de-Mauroy, 75009 Paris;* ☎ *(33) 01-49-24-24-24*, or booked through a travel agent.

Ajaccio

Ajaccio, capital of Corsica, is situated in a natural basin overlooking one of the Mediterranean's most beautiful natural harbors. Although Napoléon never returned here after 1804, the general is present everywhere in the city, with an annual celebration of his birth, a museum displaying his life in the town hall, another museum at his birthplace, and street names everywhere honoring the island's most famous native son.

Napoléon was born in the city on August 15, 1769 to Charles-Marie Bonaparte, (who had fought in the campaign for independence from Genoa but was loyal to the French by the time "Napoleone" was born), and Letizia Romolino. It was perhaps inevitable that he should become a military genius, since he was sent to military school in France at the tender age of 10. He served as a sublieutenant in the artillery from 1765, followed by a year as a lieutenant in the Corsican guard, and in 1792 he became a captain in the French army. After enduring the Terror after the Revolution with no small discomfort—his family was exiled from Corsica, which used the confusion to attempt independence with the aid of the British. After Napoléon himself led the forces to recapture the island he was at first promoted to brigadier general then—after Robespierre went to the guillotine— declared a Terrorist. In 1795, however, rehabilitated, he managed the defense of Paris against a royalist counterrevolutionary force, and from then on his ascendance in the military would know no bounds. The following year he married Josephine Tascher de la Pagerie, then set off on the Italian campaign that would turn him into a world famous general. In a year he had split the Italians from their Austrian allies, defeated both, and returned to Paris in triumph. Already coveting absolute power, he saw that the Directory government of the time was still too strong for him to topple, and, biding his time, set off to conquer Egypt. He accomplished this with little trouble, set up a modern government in Egypt, conquered Turkey, and returned to France with a stronger hand (and a weaker opposition), seizing power in 1799. In 1804 he made himself emperor Napoléon I, in a famous ceremony at Notre Dame cathedral in Paris where he snatched the crown out of the pope's hands and placed it on his own head. He soon quashed another Italo-Austrian attempt at resistance and made himself king of both countries, as well as of Spain, placing his brothers as viceroys of his far-flung territories.

The tide began to turn from about 1809, however, as the peoples of Europe (in some cases actively encouraged by Napoléon's siblings, who were relatively populist governors), supported by the English—whom he had never conquered—and the same factions within France that had never welcomed the Revolution, began to align themselves together against him. He resisted furiously both on the battlefield and in the political arena for another half dozen years, until the Battle of Waterloo put an end to his reign in 1815. He sailed for exile on St. Helena in July of that year, where he died on May 5, 1821, apparently of stomach cancer.

One of the ironies of Napoléon's life is that the Maison Bonaparte, his natal house that is now a museum, was requisitioned for a time in 1793 by Hudson Lowe, an Englishman who would eventually be his jailer on St. Helena. Besides the Napoleonic history in Ajaccio the Musée Fesch is well worth a visit—the art museum is considered to house the best collection of Italian works in France outside Paris. The collection, largely assembled as the spoils of war during Napoléon's first Italian campaign by his unscrupulous uncle, Cardinal Fesch, contains pieces by Boticelli, Titian and Veronese, among others. To go even further back in history, drive south of town on the N-196 to Filitosa, where the megalithic statues mentioned above are to be found. On the way back to town you can take the slower, but spectacular coast road around the point to the Golfe d'Ajaccio; there are numerous secluded sandy beaches to be explored as well as the Iles Sanguinaires—a string of tiny, blood red islands capped by ancient forts and lookout towers.

What to Do

Historical/Architectural Sites

Cathédrale Notre-Dame de la Misericorde   ★ ★ ★

rue St-Charles, ☎ 04-95-21-07-67. At the intersection of rue St-Charles and rue Forcioli Conti.

Hours open: 7 a.m.–6:30 p.m. Special hours: Closed 11:30 a.m.–3 p.m.; Sun., morning only.

Napoleon was baptized in 1771 in the marble baptismal font near the entrance of the church. The cathedral is just as famous for Delacroix's painting "Vierge au

Sacre-Coeur," hanging on the wall near the altar. Masses may be attended on Sat. at 6:30 p.m. and Sun. 8:30 and 10 a.m.

Museums and Exhibits

Maison Bonaparte ★

rue St-Charles, ☎ *04-95-21-43-89. In the old town, at place Letizia.*
Hours open: 10 a.m.–5 p.m. Special hours: Closed noon–2 p.m.
While this is the house where Napoleon was born and lived out the first nine years of his life, the national museum housed here has little to do with him. The furniture isn't from his period, the knick-knacks aren't from his period and the remaining displays are of questionable interest. Closed Sun. afternoon and Mon. morning. Admission: FR20.

Musée Fesch ★★★★

52 rue du Cardinal Fesch, ☎ *04-95-21-48-17.*
Hours open: 9:30 a.m.–6 p.m. Special hours: Closed 12:30–3 p.m. Closed: Mon.
A grand collection of 14th- to 19th-century Italian primitive paintings- second only to the Louvre. Named after Napoleon's uncle, Cardinal Fesch, the museum is highlighted by a Titian and Veronese's depiction of the rape of Leda. In Oct.–Apr., open 9:30 a.m.–noon and 2:30–6 p.m. Next to the museum is the Chapelle Imperiale, built by Napoleon III in 1855 to hold the tombs of the Bonaparte family. In addition to the tombs, the Bibliotheque Municipal inside contains books dating back almost 500 years. Admission: FR25.

Musée Napoleonien ★★

place Foch, ☎ *04-95-21-48-17. In the Hotel de Ville.*
Hours open: 9 a.m.–5:30 p.m. Special hours: Closed noon–2 p.m.
To complete the Napoleonic tour, the Salon exhibits memorabilia from the little man. Featuring medals, paintings and various relics, the entire museum is contained within two rooms. Admission: FR5.

Where to Stay

Hotels and Resorts

Eden Roc **FR500–FR1200** ★★★★

route des Iles Sanguinaires. ☎ *04-95-51-56-00, FAX: 04-95-52-05-03. At kilometer 8 on the autoroute.*
Double: FR500–FR1200.
Clinging to the hillside just above the gulf and the Iles Sanguinaires is this imposing hotel under the Best Western banner. There are 45 rooms with views of the gardens, the golf course or the water. All of the large rooms, although a bit worn around the edges, are modern and include TV, telephone and private bath. Recreational facilities are well-maintained, including a health club, tennis courts, spa and pool; water sports are at the small beach. The gourmet restaurant specializes in local seafood. Cheerful and courteous, the staff treats every guest to impeccable service. Features: beach location, pool, tennis, fitness center, in-room conference facilities.
<small>Credit Cards: All Major.</small>

Fesch **FR310–FR375** ★★★

7 rue Fesch. ☎ *04-95-21-50-52, FAX: 04-95-21-83-36. In the center of the old city.*

CORSICA

Double: FR310–FR375.

Designed by a local group of artisans, the medieval decor of this hotel is accented by sheepskin furnishings. On the small side, but comfortable, the 77 air-conditioned rooms are functional and quieted by the double-glazed windows. Half-board rates from FR490. A fantastic location in the heart of the old city. Features: air conditioning in rooms. Credit Cards: All Major.

La Dolce Vita   FR420–FR940   ★★★

route des Iles Sanguinaires. ☎ *04-95-52-00-93, FAX: 04-95-52-07-15. At kilometer 8 on the autoroute.*
Double: FR420–FR940.

Across from the beach just outside of town, La Dolce Vita sprawls over a pine-shaded lawn and flowered terraces. As one might guess from the name, the decor is Italianate, and the 32 rooms are modestly furnished, including private bath. Traditional fare with a distinctly Corsican accent is served in the restaurant. Attentive service in a subdued atmosphere. Features: beach location, pool. Credit Cards: All Major.

Where to Eat

L'Amore Piattu $$ ★★★

8 place du Gale-de-Gaulle, At Diamant II. ☎ *04-95-51-00-53.*
Dinner: 7:30–10 p.m., entrées FR125–FR200.

The modernized atmosphere and new terrace give new life to this seaview restaurant. How refreshing it is to see the attention to detail paid by the owner-chef Marie-Louise Maestracci. Whether it's chatting with guests or preparing one of her wonderful dishes, she gives it her full attention. She bases her menu on the finds at the market but usually features an array of seafood creations. Purely delightful in every respect. Set menus from FR220. Closed: Sun. Amenities: outside dining, reservations recommended. Credit Cards: V.

Restaurant de France $$$ ★★★

59 rue Fesch, Near the Old Quarter. ☎ *04-95-21-11-00.*
Dinner: 7–9 p.m., entrées FR125–FR250.

It's usually the sign of a good meal when the locals are regulars. This traditional restaurant features three-course meals with lamb, fresh fish, poultry and various other local favorites. Venture in to dine with the casual group of locals who have made this one of the best undiscovered restaurants in town. Closed: Sun. Credit Cards: All Major.

Directory

To and From

Ajaccio is at one end of the railway that traverses the island from north to south (roughly); you can catch a train northwards, but the city will probably be your arrival and departure point on the island. By road you can with relative ease make your way south to Bonifacio on the N-196, north to Corte and Bastia on the N-193, or take much smaller roads elsewhere on the island.

Tourist Office

place Maréchal Foch; ☎ *(33) 04-95-21-40-87.*

Rail Station

    rue Jean Jérôme Levie; ☎ *(33) 04-95-23-11-03.*

Post Office

    13 cours Napoléon, 20000 Ajaccio; ☎ *(33) 04-95-51-84-75.*

Bonifacio

Impossibly perched on the heights of a narrow limestone promontory that is France's most southern point, old town Bonifacio huddles inside a fortified wall that dates from the 12th century, built by the Genoese when they controlled the island. The imposing citadel was the headquarters for the famous French Foreign Legion from 1963 to 1983 and still houses a garrison of the notoriously tough brigade that will take anyone from any country who wants to enlist and leave behind a previous life. The views from the old town are breathtaking; neighboring Sardinia, just nine miles away, looks close enough to touch. Those with vertigo will want to select their café or restaurant carefully up here, however, for some parts of the town are literally on the edge of the limestone cliffs that drop several hundred feet to the ocean below. Descending to the harbor the town loses none of its charm, as the port is filled with working fishing boats as well as yachts and small ferries that ply the straights separating Corsica and Sardinia. You might take a cruise to Italy, or else explore the Lavezzi or Cavallo islands, deserted and impossibly beautiful and just a few miles away. There are not a lot of "cultural" activities to do in Bonifacio, but the quiet charm and stunning beauty of the town makes it well worth a visit.

What to Do

Historical/Architectural Sites

Citadelle   ★★★★

    Upper town. At the tip of the peninsula. At the Montee Rastello and Montee St-Roch stairs.

Within the walls of this citadel, the Ville Haute (Upper Village) can be wandered by foot. Within the gates at place d'Armes, find the Bastion of the Standard. Within, you can learn about the history of Bonifacio and see the weight and pulley sytem used in the raising of the drawbridge. *Open mid-June–mid Sept., 9 a.m.–7 p.m.* Admission is FR15. Farther in among the narrow streets is the **Eglise Ste-Marie Majeure**. This Romanesque church was constructed in the 14th century and has received countless facelifts since then. Now a conference hall, the interior's Renaissance style is exemplified in the baptismal font. The marble altar at the front dates back to the 17th century. Under the large porch is the cistern that used to hold water for the community for use in emergencies.

CORSICA

Museums and Exhibits

Aquarium ★★

71 quai Jerome Comparetti, ☎ 04-95-73-03-69. Near the marina.
Hours open: 10 a.m.–7 p.m. Special hours: Open to midnight in July–Aug.; closed Nov.–
Mar.

Just off the touristic promenade lies this small aquarium. There are about 12 tanks holding marine life specific to the Strait of Bonifacio. Sandy beaches and coves are discovered on the north side of the Sound. Look for Plage de l'Arinella and Plage de la Catena. Admission: FR20.

Where to Stay

Hotels and Resorts

Hotel Genovese — FR1300–FR1500 ★★★★

Quartier de Citadelle. ☎ 04-95-73-12-34, FAX: 04-95-73-09-03. In the upper city's
ramparts.
Double: FR1300–FR1500.

Actually built into the old city's ramparts, Le Genovese occupies a former legionnaires' barracks. A first class complex overlooking the bay and the port. It's small enough, with 14 rooms, to keep the personal touch, and luxurious enough to satisfy those in need of pampering. Opulence, in the strongest sense of the word, describes the plush rooms with peach fabric wall coverings and private bath. There is no restuarant, but breakfast is available. The hotel also has a romantic bar. A longtime favorite with the crowd seeking discreet luxury. Credit Cards: All Major.

La Caravelle — FR600–FR1200 ★★★

35 quai Comparetti. ☎ 04-95-73-00-03, FAX: 04-95-73-00-41. On the harbor.
Single: FR600. Double: FR1200.

Right in the thick of the activity of the marina, La Caravelle manages to stay relatively quiet. It offers 30 air-conditioned rooms with TV, telephone and private bath; the modern decor stays fresh with the constant improvements by the caring management. The popular restaurant brims over with tourists. As the saying goes, "The three most important aspects of a successful restaurant (and hotel, in this case) are location, location and location." Features: tennis, air conditioning in rooms. Credit Cards: All Major.

Where to Eat

La Caravelle — $$$ ★★★

at the harbor ☎ 04-95-73-06-47.
Dinner: 7:30–11:30 p.m., entrées FR200–FR350.

Boasting lovely frescoes, this dining room sets the most pleasant dining atmosphere in Bonifacio. The cuisine is daring—sometimes falling short, but usually impressive. The signature dish has become the lobster ravioli soup, which only barely taps the natural skills of La Caravelle's chef. Even though it's the best food in town, the prices could be lower. The set menu is FR150. Amenities: outside dining, reservations required. Credit Cards: All Major.

Stella d'Oro — $$$ ★★★

7 rue du Gal-de-Gaulle ☎ 04-95-73-03-63.

CORSICA

Dinner: 7:30–11 p.m., entrées FR125–FR300.
Popular with the locals, Stella d'Oro is a hallmark of Bonifacio. Could there be a
Bonifacio without this popular gathering place? The regulars keep this restaurant
going, serving tasty fish dishes at inflated prices. Any of the fresh catches will cer-
tainly satisfy. Set menus from FR95–FR150 for lunch. Reservations recommended.
Credit Cards: All Major.

Directory

To and From

*The town is not easy to reach; there is no train service, and the roads (the N-196 from the
northwest and Ajaccio, and the N-198 from the northeast and Aleria and Bastia) are slow
and very winding, but nothing good comes without sacrifice, right?*

Tourist Office

place de l'Europe; ☎ *(33) 04-95-73-11-88.*

Post Office

place Carrega, 20169 Bonifacio; ☎ *(33) 04-95-73-01-55.*

Porto Vecchio

The Golfe de Porto Vecchio is one of the most beautiful bays on Corsica,
looking out to the Mediterranean from the eastern coast just 20 miles from
Bonifacio. It's an expensive place to stay, popular with the jet set whose
yachts crowd the small harbor, and you might want to make the day trip
from another base but, whether you stay the night or just pass through, you
won't fail to fall in love with the natural beauty of the coastline in this part of
the island. The town itself doesn't have much to offer other than the fact
that it is a very beautiful and charming Mediterranean fishing port (!)—the
citadel built to defend the bay by the Genoese is not one of Corsica's more
interesting ones— but the nearby beaches, especially at Palombaggia and
Pinarello, are spectacular. Lined with cork trees, made of white sand, brilliant aquamarine water, and ringed by red cliffs, these beaches are the epito-
me of rest and relaxation, Mediterranean style. Not a bikini top in sight, but
a glass of cold wine never more than 50 meters away. Paradise!

Where to Stay

Hotels and Resorts

Grand Hotel de Cala Rossa   **FR450–FR2200**   ★★★★

route Cala Rossa. ☎ *04-95-71-61-51, FAX: 04-95-71-60-11. About 8 km north of
Porto-Vecchio, in Cala Rossa.*
Single: FR450. Double: FR2200.
Lush gardens, contemporary interior design and pampering luxury are the corner-
stones of the Grand Hotel. While the 50 soundproof rooms vary in price, all are
plush, lavishly equipped and flawlessly maintained. Begin the day with breakfast out-
side, just off the beach, including croissants, homemade jams, juice, coffee and tea.
Sailing, water-skiing and fishing are just a few of the activities at the beach—best to

be enjoyed during the shoulder seasons with fewer tourists. The restaurant's chef has perfected his local dishes in the magnificent dining room. Make the detour to this leading hotel and restaurant. Features: beach location, tennis, water sports, fitness center. Credit Cards: All Major.

Moby Dick   **FR400–FR1200**   ★★★

Baie de Santa Giulia. ☎ *04-95-70-43-23, FAX: 04-70-01-54. About 8 km south of Porto-Vecchio.*
Single: FR400. Double: FR1200.
On a jetty dividing the sea and a lake is the beached Moby Dick. There are 44 rooms, bright, well-equipped and radiantly clean. A fantastic spot from which to watch the sunset, as the rooms boast views of the sea and the mountains. The restaurant specializes in what any restaurant surrounded by water would—seafood. It's worth at least one night's stay here, at least for the stellar location. Features: beach location, tennis. Credit Cards: All Major.

Where to Eat

Le Flamboyant   **$$$**   ★★

route de Bonifacio ☎ *04-95-70-12-06.*
Dinner: 7–10 p.m., entrées FR175–FR275.
The amiable staff and pleasant, welcoming atmosphere always make dining here a joy. Simple, solid dishes are best represented with the seafood. A tempting list of desserts rounds out an enjoyable meal. Limited choice of wines. Set menus from FR105. Credit Cards: All Major.

Regina   **$$$**   ★★★★

On the N198, About 3 km north on the N198. ☎ *04-95-70-14-94.*
Dinner: 7–10:30 p.m., entrées FR200–FR350.
Only premium ingredients are used for this grand-affair cuisine. Very showy in the presentation yet impressive beneath the surface. Crab gratin, lobster lasagne and veal mignon top the list, with less complicated but more enjoyable dishes such as fresh fish hidden in between. Peruse the menu—there's a solid base of quality dishes. The cellar is the last word on wine on all of Corsica. The FR200 set menu is the best value. Amenities: outside dining, reservations required. Credit Cards: All Major.

Directory

To and From
By car only, on the N-198 from Bonifacio north up the east coast.

Tourist Office
place de l'Hôtel de Ville; ☎ *(33) 04-95-70-10-36.*

Post Office
rue Leclerc, 20137 Porto Vecchio; ☎ *(33) 04-95-70-18-77.*

Bastia

Bastia itself is a bustling port city and about as modern as Corsica gets. The main harbor and downtown area are predominantly 19th century, although most of the city, destroyed in the Second World War, is horribly modern and concrete. The highlights aside from the port are the **place St. Nicolas**, café central during the day and the nightlife hub when the sun goes down; the **place de l'Hôtel de Ville**, bordered on each side by beautiful 17th-century churches; and the 16th-century Genoese citadel. Bastia is used more as a base for exploring **Cap Corse**, the northern promontory that stretches almost 30 miles into the blue Mediterranean while never exceeding eight miles in width. You can drive the tortuous D-80 around the entire cape in a day, heading off on any of the even tinier roads to a number of priceless mountain villages. Among the most interesting (going clockwise around the Cap) are **Pozzo**, from where you can strike out on foot to the summit of 3000-foot **Monte Stello**, where spectacular 360º views of Corsica and Elba await you; **Centuri**, near the tip of the cape on the west side, where fresh fish makes for an excellent meal at any time and in any establishment; and **Canari**, a village dominated by the 12th-century Pisan church of Santa María Assunta.

What to Do

Historical/Architectural Sites

Cap Corse　　　　　　　　　　　　　　　　　　★★★★

Haute Corse. In Cap Corse, north of Bastia.

Located on the northern tip of Corsica, this part of the island is about 40 km long and 10 km wide. A bit of land jetting out above Bastia, the interior is mountainous and the coastline magnificent. Take your camera and capture the beautiful, small villages of Erbalunga, a clifftop town, Centuri, a fishing settlement, Nonza, a black sand beach and medieval town, and Patrimonio, with a hilltop church.

Museums and Exhibits

Musée Ethnographique Corse　　　　　　　　★★

place du Donjon, ☎ 04-95-31-09-12. Inside the Citadelle.
Hours open: 9 a.m.–5 p.m. Special hours: Closed noon–2 p.m.

The Ancien Palais des Gouverneurs (Former Genoese Governors' Palace) is home to this mediocre museum of anthropology. Detailing peasant life and local history, the 18th-century rebel flag is the crown jewel of this collection of military and civilian artifacts. In the palace's garden is a World War II German submarine turret that was captured by the French resistors. Admission: FR10.

Shopping

Terra Vecchia　　　　　　　　　　　　　　　★★★

off place St-Nicolas. South of place St-Nicolas.

With the place de l'Hotel de Ville hosting the open-air market, this section's old buildings provide a great opportunity to meander the streets. Near the Hotel de Ville is the Oratoire de l'Immaculee Conception, on rue Napoleon. Stop in and peek at the modest exhibit of religious art within this 16th-century building. On another side of the Hotel de Ville is the Eglise St-Jean Baptiste. Commanding a picturesque location over the old port, this 17th-century church is accented by its two towers.

Where to Stay

Hotels and Resorts

Castel Brando   **FR350–FR500**   ★★★

20 Erbalunga. ☎ *04-95-33-98-05, FAX: 04-95-32-08-01. About 10 km north of Bastia on D80; in Erbalunga.*
Single: FR350. Double: FR500.
In the heart of a quaint fishing village north of Bastia, Castel Brando is just a few minutes from the sea. A transformed 19th-century mansion, it is done in handsome light colors. It boasts 16 large rooms, pleasantly furnished in country style and well-equipped with large baths and kitchenettes. Linger over the complimentary breakfast served under the palmed terrace, and cool off in the Roman bath-style pool. An easy trip into Bastia, this makes a good base for exploring the area while enjoying a peaceful location. Credit Cards: All Major.

Pietracap   **FR300–FR700**   ★★★★

20 route de San Martino. ☎ *04-95-31-64-63, FAX: 04-95-31-39-00. Just north of Bastia, in Pietranera.*
Single: FR300. Double: FR700.
Nestled in a hillside olive grove north of Bastia, Pietracap is an ultramodern hotel. The 42 rooms are generously sized, with modern furnishings and balconies opening to the garden and the sea. All are air-conditioned and fully equipped with the most up-to-date conveniences. There is a bar but no restaurant. Bicycles may be rented here, and there is a pool. The best choice for a quiet night's stay. Features: pool, balcony or patio. Credit Cards: All Major.

Posta Vecchia   **FR350**   ★★★

quai des Martyrs. ☎ *04-95-32-32-38, FAX: 04-95-32-14-05. Near the port.*
Double: FR350.
Rather chic in attitude and style, the Posta Vecchia was converted into a hotel in 1978. Exposed wood beam ceilings lend a rustic feeling to the 49 rooms. Equipped with the standard amenities, soft touches include the floral wallpaper and bedcovers. Request a larger room in the main house overlooking the port. The congenial staff can recommend local restaurants. Credit Cards: All Major.

Where to Eat

La Citadelle   **$$$**   ★★★

5 rue du Dragon. ☎ *04-95-31-44-70.*
Dinner: 7:30–10:30 p.m., entrées FR200–FR300.
Typically regional atmosphere and far from typical cuisine. Although the focus of the chef lies with desserts, his skills are omnipresent in all of his dishes. Wonderful Corsican favorites are always on hand, ready to be completed with one of the outstanding desserts from the multi-talented kitchen. The service is efficient and generally friendly. Set menus from FR130 for lunch. Closed: Mon. Amenities: outside dining, reservations required. Credit Cards: V, A.

Le Romantique   **$$$**   ★★★

4 bis, rue du Pontetto, At the old port. ☎ *04-95-32-30-85.*
Dinner: 7:30–11 p.m., entrées FR150–FR275.

As the name suggests, this is a romantic little portside restaurant with one of the best female chefs in the Mediterranean. Her great variety of menus makes for an interesting visit every time. She flourishes with regional fare and ventures out with some exciting dishes. Her limited but excellent wine list features some traditional bottles. Guaranteed to make you smile, her reception and service is wonderful. Set menus from just FR100. Reservations recommended. Credit Cards: All Major.

Directory

To and From
By train from Ajaccio (three hours) or by road on the N-198 from the south.

Tourist Office
place St. Nicolas; ☎ *(33) 04-95-31-00-89.*

Rail Station
place de la Gàre; ☎ *(33) 04-95-32-60-06.*

Post Office
avenue Maréchal Sebastiani, 20200 Bastia; ☎ *(33) 95-31-00-60.*

Calvi

Genoese Citadelle offers spectacular views of Calvi and the sea.

A pleasant Corsican and Mediterranean port town but by no means among Corsica's best, Calvi has become one of the most popular destinations on the island. In summer it is very crowded, but if you can make it in June to the free jazz festival the crowds are much more palatable. Topped by an imposing 16th century citadel and the Cathédrale de St. Jean Baptiste, that dates from the same period, Calvi has long been a staunchly Catholic and military

CORSICA

town. Today the citadel, although partially open to the public, is home base for one of the elite units of the French Foreign Legion. The presence of Napoléon is felt once again in this town, with street names and statues honoring the general, since his family dwelt here briefly after being forced out of Ajaccio and before fleeing the island altogether. The main street is called Christophe Colomb, a testament to the Calvi delusion that Columbus was born here. The beach areas around town tend to be expensive (that is, the bars and restaurants that line them) you might do better to drive or take the small-gauge railway north towards Ile Rousse and stop at one of the many beautiful and secluded beaches and inlets along the way.

What to Do

Historical/Architectural Sites

Eglise St-Jean Baptiste ★★★

place d'Armes. In the citadelle, near the Palais des Gouverneurs.
Built in the 13th century and reconstructed in the 16th century, the church is noteworthy for its interior. Glance up at the screened pews that were used by the local elite women to hide from any suggestive glares from peasant men. Next to the altar, this ebony statue of Christ was recognized as having saved Calvi from the Saracens when it was carried around town prior to their unexpected retreat.

Genoese Citadelle ★★★

On the promontory.
Clinging to a granite promontory behind the ramparts and fortifications, the citadel offers spectacular views of the town and sea. The welcome center inside the gates offers videos on local history and guided tours in English. Just above the entrance to the citadel is the Palais des Gouverneurs, at place du Donjon. Built in the 13th century, the Caserne Sampiero, as it is known, now houses the barracks for the Foreign Legion. Tours of the Citadelle are at 10 a.m., 4:30 and 6:30 p.m., Easter–September. Tour and video, FR50.

Where to Stay

Hotels and Resorts

Hotel Villa **FR800–FR1800** ★★★★

chemin de Notre Dame de la Serra. ☎ *04-95-65-10-10, FAX: 04-95-65-10-50. Above town.*
Single: FR800. Double: FR1800.
Opened in 1992, the Hotel Villa has quickly become Calvi's leading hotel. Snuggled on a hill above town, it has splendid views over the citadel and the bay. The 25 air-conditioned rooms command high rates—and justifiably so. Ever so spacious, the contemporary rooms are highlighted by walk-in closets, beautiful furnishings and balconies. Public spaces display a fine collection of original paintings and sculptures. Dine on the terrace in the warm months, overlooking the pool and gardens. The entire indulgent package is a worthwhile splurge. Features: pool, tennis, air conditioning in rooms. Credit Cards: All Major.

Le Signoria   **FR500–FR950**   ★★★★

route de la Foret de Bonifato. ☎ *04-95-65-23-73, FAX: 04-95-65-33-20. About 5 km outside of Calvi.*
Single: FR500. Double: FR950.

This 17th-century inn looks out on the mountains beyond the eucalyptus and olive groves. An intimate spot, there are just 10 room in the main house and the annex. Delightfully decorated, each one reflects the personal touch of the management's effort to keep this inn as homey as it is. Leisure facilities on the property include a pool and a Turkish bath. Nearby are boat rentals, tennis and horseback riding. Relax over an apertif in the bar before sitting down to a meal in the intimate dining room, recognized for its creative use of local ingredients. A delight to all of the senses, heightened by the anticipatory and courteous staff. Features: pool. Credit Cards: All Major.

Where to Eat

L'Ile de Beaute   **$$$**   ★★★

quai Landry, On the quai. ☎ *04-95-65-00-46.*
Dinner: 7–10 p.m., entrées FR200–FR325.

In a lovely setting on the quai, this restaurant has been given new life with the aquisition of a young chef. Taking advantage of the local industry, fresh seafood is the featured cuisine. Taste the fish and shellfish skillfully prepared and perfectly presented with imaginative spices and sauces. Set menus from FR95 at lunch and FR350 at dinner. Hours extended during the summer. Amenities: outside dining, reservations required. Credit Cards: All Major.

U Spuntinu   **$$**   ★★★

route de Bonifato, On the town outskirts. ☎ *04-95-65-07-06.*
Dinner: 7:30–11 p.m., entrées FR125–FR225.

Come back to an earlier time, when food was simple, solid and reasonably priced. Enjoy country-style cooking at this unpretentious establishment where the owner-farmer uses ingredients from his own farm. Whether it's stew, poultry or goat, there is a welcome down-home attitude about this entire operation that emanates in the generous meals. A hearty reception and a satisfied stomach are assured. Reservations recommended. Credit Cards: DC.

Directory

To and From

By train from Bastia (three hours) or Ajaccio (five hours), or by road on the N-193 from the north and east or the narrow and slow D-51 up the coast from the south.

Tourist Office

port de Plaisance; ☎ *(33) 04-95-65-16-67.*

Rail Station

place de la Gàre; ☎ *(33) 04-95-65-00-61.*

Post Office

boulevard Wilson, 20260 Calvi; ☎ *(33) 04-95-65-10-40.*

CORSICA

LANGUAGE
Pronunciation Tips

Whereas in English we place more emphasis on some syllables than on others, French is spoken without all those ups and downs.

The consonant at the end of a word is normally not pronounced, thus the s is not pronounced in anglais (English).

On, en, and an have nasal sounds.

Pronounce vowels as follows: a = *ah*, e = *euh*, é = *ay*, è = *eh*, i = *ee*, o = *oh*, u = *ew* (as in dew, with pursed lips), oi = *wa*.

G (before i and e) and j are pronounced like the *s* in leisure.

Nouns in French are considered either masculine or feminine, with little apparent logic. The articles *a* and *the* are *un* and *le* for masculine nouns and *une* and *la* for feminine nouns, while *les* is the plural form of the for all nouns.

ENGLISH	FRENCH
Encounters	*Les rencontres*
Hello (Good morning/afternoon)	*Bonjour*
Good evening	*Bonsoir*
Good night	*Bonne nuit*
Good-bye	*Au revoir*
Excuse me	*Excusez-moi*
Sorry	*Pardon*
Please	*S'il vous plaît*
Thank you	*Merci*
Yes/No	*Oui/Non*
Pleased to meet you	*Enchanté*
How are you?	*Comment allez-vous?*

ENGLISH	FRENCH
Mr. or Sir	*Monsieur*
Mrs., Madam, Ma'am	*Madame*
Miss	*Mademoiselle*
Do you speak English?	*Parlez-vous anglais?*
I don't speak French	*Je ne parle pas français*
I don't understand	*Je ne comprends pas*
I understand	*Je comprends*
I don't know	*Je ne sais pas*
Who?	*Qui?*
What?	*Quoi?*
Where?	*Où?*
Where is/are... , please?	*Où est/sont . . . , s'il vous plaît?*
Where are the toilets?	*Où sont les toilettes?*
Where is the bank?	*Où est la banque?*
I need to change money	*J'ai besoin de changer de l'argent*
When?	*Quand?*
How?	*Comment?*
Why?	*Pourquoi?*
What's your name?	*Comment vous appelez-vous?*
My name is . . .	*Je m'appelle . . .*
I'm American/British/Canadian	*Je suis Américain/Anglais/Canadien*
I live in New York	*J'habite New York*
Careful!	*Attention!*
Help!	*Au secours!*
What time is it?	*Quelle heure est-il?*
It is 10 o'clock	*Il est 10 heures*
noon	*midi*
midnight	*minuit*
yesterday	*hier*
today	*aujourd'hui*
tomorrow	*demain*
tonight	*ce soir*
morning	*matin*

ENGLISH	FRENCH
afternoon	*après-midi*
Transportation	*Le transport*
train	*le train*
station	*la gare*
track	*la voie*
platform	*le quai*
car	*la voiture*
seat	*le siège/la place*
departure	*départ*
arrival	*arrivée*
the information office	*le bureau de renseignement*
the baggage checkroom	*la consigne*
a ticket	*un billet*
a supplement	*un supplément*
first/second class	*première/deuxième classe*
a connection	*une correspondance*
a sleeping car	*un wagon-lit*
a couchette	*une couchette*
the bus	*le bus*
the bus stop	*l'arrêt de bus*
the subway	*le métro*
the subway station	*la station de métro*
(to the) left/right	*(à) gauche/droite*
straight ahead	*tout droit*
north/south/east/west	*nord/sud/est/ouest*
near/far	*près/loin*
The post office	*La poste*
a stamp	*un timbre*
a postcard	*une carte postale*
envelopes	*des enveloppes*
by air mail	*par avion*
The hotel	*L'hôtel*
a room	*une chambre*

ENGLISH	FRENCH
with one bed/two beds	*avec un lit/deux lits*
with bath/shower/toilet	*avec bains/douche/toilettes*
key	*clé*
elevator	*ascenseur*
ground (first) floor	*rez de chaussée*
second floor	*premier (ler) étage*
A tour of the city	*Une visite de la ville*
a city map	*un plan de ville*
museum	*musée*
admission ticket	*billet d'entrée*
free admission	*entrée libre*
open/closed	*ouvert/fermé*
street	*rue*
cathedral	*cathédrale*
church	*église*
basilica	*basilique*
a (private) mansion, townhouse	*un hôtel (particulier)*
garden	*jardin*
bridge	*pont*
tower	*tour*
ramparts	*remparts*
covered market	*halles*
castle/château	*château*
Shops/stores	*Boutiques/magasins*
I would like...	*Je voudrais...*
to buy	*acheter*
to see	*voir*
to try on	*essayer*
the dress	*la robe*
the skirt	*la jupe*
socks	*les chaussettes*
shoes	*les chaussures*
the hat	*le chapeau*

ENGLISH	FRENCH
the handbag	*le sac*
the necktie	*la cravate*
the shirt	*la chemise*
the trousers	*le pantalon*
It's too big/small/long/short	*C'est trop large/petit/long/court*
That's good/bad	*C'est bon/mauvais*
How much (is it)?	*(C'est) combien?*
expensive/inexpensive/cheap	*cher/pas cher/bon marché*
Can I pay with this credit card?	*Puis-je payer avec cette carte de crédit?*
Colors	***Les couleurs***
red	*rouge*
green	*vert*
blue	*bleu*
black	*noir*
white	*blanc*
yellow	*jaune*
brown	*marron*
pink	*rose*
Illness/pharmacy	***Maladie/pharmacie***
I'm sick	*Je suis malade*
I'm cold/hot	*J'ai froid/chaud*
I have a headache/stomachache	*J'ai mal à la tête/mal au ventre*
I need a doctor	*J'ai besoin d'un médecin*
medicine	*les médicaments*
It hurts here	*Cela me fait mal ici*
Where is the pharmacy?	*Où est la pharmacie?*
I need...	*J'ai besoin...*
aspirin	*d'aspirine*
Band-Aids	*de pansements*
toothpaste	*de dentifrice*
razor blades	*de lames de rasoir*
shaving cream	*de mousse à raser*

ENGLISH	FRENCH
To telephone	***Téléphoner***
the telephone	*le téléphone*
Hold the line	*Ne quittez pas*
to call collect	*téléphoner en PCV*
Who's calling?	*De la part de qui?*
To drive	***Conduire***
driver's license	*permis de conduire*
Fill the tank, please	*Le plein, svp.*
the oil	*l'huile*
the tires	*les pneus*
detour	*déviation*
dead end	*impasse*
toll	*péage*
yield right	*priorité à droite*
slow down	*ralentir*
one way	*sens unique*
no entry	*sens interdit*
keep right/left	*serrez à droite/gauche*
exit	*sortie*
no parking	*stationnement interdit*

ENGLISH	FRENCH
The restaurant	***Le restaurant***
I'm thirsty	*J'ai soif*
I'm hungry	*J'ai faim*
I would like to reserve	*Je voudrais réserver*
a table for two	*une table pour deux*
the menu	*la carte*
the fixed-price menu	*le menu*
tasting/sampling	*dégustation*
sampling of dishes throughout the meal	*menu dégustation*
the wine list	*la carte des vins*
the bill/check	*l'addition*
tip included	*service compris (s.c.)*

ENGLISH	FRENCH
drink (not) included	*boisson (non) comprise*
all you can eat	*à volonté*
a cocktail/aperitif	*un apéritif*
cheers!	*tchin-tchin!*
cocktail snack	*amuse-gueule/amuse-bouche*
enjoy your meal	*bon appétit*
light appetizer (before l'entrée)	*hor d'oeuvre*
the appetizer	*l'entrée*
the main course	*le plat principal*
the dish of the day	*le plat du jour*
French onion soup	*gratinée*
cheese (tray)	*(plateau de) fromage*
breakfast	*le petit déjeuner*
lunch	*le déjeuner*
dinner	*le dîner*
a spoon	*une cuillère*
a fork	*une fourchette*
a knife	*un couteau*
red/white/rosé wine	*vin rouge/blanc/rosé*
a beer	*une bière*
some coffee	*du café*
some water	*de l'eau*
a bottle of	*une bouteille de*
a glass of	*un verre de*
a cup of	*une tasse de*
ice cube	*glaçon*
egg	*oeuf*
butter	*beurre*
jam	*confiture*
bread	*pain*
buttered bread	*tartine*
herbal tea	*infusion, tisane*
tea	*thé*

ENGLISH	FRENCH
Fish	*Poisson*
anchovies	*anchois*
Mediterranean striped bass	*bar/loup*
pike	*brochet*
fresh cod	*cabillaud*
plaice/flounder	*carrelet*
hake	*colin/merlu*
sea bream	*daurade*
halibut	*flétan*
haddock	*églefin, aiglefin*
smoked haddock	*haddock*
herring	*hareng*
lamprey eel	*lamproie*
burbot	*lotte*
sea-perch	*loup de mer*
mackerel	*maquereau*
whiting	*merlan*
dry, salted cod	*morue*
perch	*perche*
ray fish	*raie*
(smoked) salmon	*saumon (fumé)*
red mullet	*rouget*
tuna	*thon*
trout	*truite*
cooked in white wine with onions and shallots	*marinière*
Shellfish	*Coquillages*
seafood	*fruits de mer*
crustaceans	*crustacés*
by weight	*selon poids*
when available	*selon arrivage*
crab	*crabe, tourteau*
shrimp	*crevettes*

ENGLISH	FRENCH
jumbo shrimp	*gambas*
crayfish	*écrevisses*
lobster	*homard*
spiny lobster	*langouste*
Norwegian lobster	*langoustine*
mussels	*moules*
oysters	*huîtres*
meaty, flat oysters	*belons*
elongated oysters	*fines de claires*
cultivated oysters	*marennes*
scallops	*(coquille) St-Jacques*
little scallops	*pétoncles*
land snails	*escargots*
frog's legs	*cuisses de grenouille*
Meat	***Viande***
beef	*boeuf*
steak	*bifteck*
rib steak	*entrecôtes*
fillet steak	*tournedos*
skirt steak	*bavette*
thick tenderloin steak	*chateaubriand*
sirloin steak	*faux-filet*
choice piece of tenderloin	*filet mignon*
roast beef	*rosbif*
rumpsteak	*rumsteck*
thick, round fillet steak	*tournedos*
grilled meat	*grillade*
beef stew	*pot-au-feu*
meatball (also fishball)	*boulette*
bone	*os*
lamb	*agneau*
mutton	*mouton*
leg of lamb or mutton	*gigot*

ENGLISH	FRENCH
chop/cutlet	côte/côtelette
rack of, ribs	carré de
pork	porc
cold cuts, pâtés, cured meats (usually pork-based)	charcuterie
pig products	cochonnailles
pig's feet	pied de cochon
ham	jambon
shoulder	épaule
slice	tranche
bacon/bacon cubes	lard/lardons
sausage/dried sausage	saucisse/saucisson
veal	veau
scallop, slice of meat or fish	escalope
Organ meats	**Abats**
sweetbreads	ris
kidneys	rognons
liver	foie
fatted goose or duck liver	foie gras
tongue	langue
brain	cervelle
gizzard	gésier
tripe (intestines)	tripes
blood	sang
Poultry and game	**Volaille et gibier**
chicken	poulet
chicken breast	blanc de poulet/volaille
drumstick	cuisse de poulet
duck/duckling	canard/caneton, cannette
sliced duck steak	magret de canard
duck cooked in its own fat	confit de canard
quail	caille
turkey/young turkey	dinde/dindonneau

ENGLISH	FRENCH
goose	*oie*
guinea fowl	*pintade*
pigeon/young pigeon, squab	*pigeon/pigeonneau*
rabbit/young rabbit	*lapin/lapereau*
hare	*liévre*
jugged hare	*civet de liévre*
saddle of hare or rabbit	*râble*
venison	*cerf, chevreuil*
wild boar	*sanglier*
Preparations	***Préparations***
baked	*au four*
fried	*frit*
grilled	*grillé, au gril*
skewered and grilled	*brochette*
in the covered pan or baking dish	*á la casserole*
in the frying pan	*á la poêle*
with lemon and parsley after being sautéed	*á la meunière*
in the oven	*au four*
boiled	*bouilli, à l'eau*
steamed	*à la vapeur*
simmered	*mijotée*
wrapped in parchment or foil	*en papillote*
dumpling	*quenelle*
stew	*ragoût*
smoked	*fumé*
roast	*rôti*
braised	*braisé*
flamed	*flambé*
raw	*cru*
extra rare	*bleu*
rare	*saignant*
medium rare-medium	*à point*

ENGLISH	FRENCH
well done	*bien cuit*
minced or ground	*haché*
stuffed/stuffing	*farci/farce*
breaded	*pané*
seasoned, flavored	*assaisonné*
mixed herbs	*fines herbes*
spice (spiced)	*épice (épicé)*
garlic	*ail*
pepper (peppered)	*poivre (poivré)*
salt (salted)	*sel (salé)*
mustard	*moutard*
parsley	*persil*
parsley and garlic	*persillade*
basil	*basilic*
cinnamon	*cannelle*
dill	*aneth*
tarragon	*estragon*
chives	*ciboulette*
shallots	*echalots*
garnish	*garniture*
covered with	*nappé de*
with buttery cream sauce	*blanquette*
with an egg riding horseback	*à cheval*
with mushrooms, perhaps also bacon and potatoes	*forestier*
Vegetables and garnishes	***Légumes et garnitures***
raw cut vegetables	*crudités*
shredded	*en julienne*
artichoke	*artichaut*
asparagus	*asperge*
avocado	*avocat*
eggplant	*aubergine*
broccoli	*brocoli*

ENGLISH	**FRENCH**
mushrooms	*champignons*
types of wild mushrooms	*cèpes, pleurotes*
truffles (pungent, high-priced mushrooms)	*truffes*
cauliflower	*chou-fleur*
Brussel sprouts	*choux de Bruxelles*
cucumber	*concombre*
watercress	*cresson*
spinach	*épinard*
fennel	*fenouil*
beans	*haricots*
string beans	*haricots verts*
corn	*maïs*
leeks	*poireaux*
peas	*petits pois*
peppers	*poivrons*
potatoes	*pommes (de terres)*
French fries	*pommes frites*
thin fries	*pommes allumettes*
baked	*pommes au four*
sliced and baked with milk and cheese	*pommes dauphinoises*
with cheese and browned	*pommes gratinées*
steamed or boiled	*pommes vapeur*
tomato	*tomate*
noodles	*nouilles*
pasta	*pâtes*
rice	*riz*
green salad	*salade verte*
types of lettuce	*batavia, laitue, frisée, mache, romaine*
salad dressing	*sauce*
oil and vinegar dressing with herbs and mustard	*vinaigrette*
Desserts	***Desserts***
moulded lady fingers and custard cake	*charlotte*

ENGLISH	FRENCH
thin custard	crème anglaise
caramel custard pudding	crème caramel
sweetened whipped cream	crème chantilly
thin pancake	crêpe
sweets	entremets
custard pie (may also be a tart)	flan
black forest cake: chocolate, cream, candied cherries	forêt-noir
cake, tart	gâteau
waffle	gaufre
pancake, flat cake or pastry	galette
Genoese sponge cake	génoise
ice cream	glace
cold chestnut cream dessert	mont-blanc
pastry	pâtisserie
sherbet	sorbet
pie, tart	tarte
pie	tourte
with fruit purée	au coulis
Fruits	**Fruits**
apricot	abricot
pineapple	ananas
banana	banane
black currants	cassis
cherries	cerises
lemon	citron
small tangerine/tangerine	clémentine/mandarine
strawberries/wild strawberries	fraises/fraises des bois
raspberries	framboises
blueberries	myrtilles
blackberries	mûres
coconut	noix de coco
grapefruit	pamplemousse

ENGLISH	FRENCH
peach	*pêche*
pear	*poire*
apple	*pomme*
plum	*prune*
grapes	*raisins*
raisins	*raisins sec*
Nuts	***Noix***
almonds	*amandes*
peanuts	*cacahouètes*
cashews	*cajoux*
chestnuts/small chestnuts	*marrons/châtaignes*
hazelnuts	*noisettes*
walnuts	*noix*

ENGLISH	FRENCH	ENGLISH	FRENCH
Days of the week	***Jours de la semaine***	**Days of the week**	***Jours de la semaine***
Sunday	*dimanche*	Thursday	*jeudi*
Monday	*lundi*	Friday	*vendredi*
Tuesday	*mardi*	Saturday	*samedi*
Wednesday	*mercredi*		
Months	***Mois***	**Months**	***Mois***
January	*janvier*	July	*juillet*
February	*février*	August	*août*
March	*mars*	September	*septembre*
April	*avril*	October	*octobre*
May	*mai*	November	*novembre*
June	*juin*	December	*décembre*
Numbers	***Chiffres***	**Numbers**	***Chiffres***
one	*un*	six	*six*
two	*deux*	seven	*sept*
three	*trois*	eight	*huit*
four	*quatre*	nine	*neuf*
five	*cinq*	ten	*dix*

ENGLISH	FRENCH	ENGLISH	FRENCH
eleven	*onze*		
twelve	*douze*		
thirteen	*treize*		
fourteen	*quatorze*		
fifteen	*quinze*		
sixteen	*seize*		
seventeen	*dix-sept*		
eighteen	*dix-huit*		
nineteen	*dix-neuf*		
twenty	*vingt*		
twenty-one	*vingt-et-un*		
twenty-two	*vingt-deux*		
thirty	*trente*		
forty	*quarante*		
fifty	*cinquante*		
sixty	*soixante*		
seventy	*soixante-dix*		
seventy-five	*soixante-quinze*		
eighty	*quatre-vingts*		
ninety	*quatre-vingt-dix*		
one hundred	*cent*		
five hundred	*cinq cents*		
one thousand	*mille*		

HOTEL INDEX

A

A la Cote St-Jacques, *638*
A la Cour d'Alsace, *689*
Albert 1er, *592*
Aletti Palace Hotel, *609*
Alexandra, *518*
Alliance Metropole, *469*
Alliance Tours Trois Riviere, *374*
Alpotel, *580*
Anne d'Anjou, *325*
Anne de Bretagne, *360*
Aquarium' Hotel, *302*
Arcade, *328*
Argouges, *232*
Artaud Hotel Restaurant, *543*
Au Bon Coin, *593*
Auberge de la Rouge, *216*
Auberge du Moulin de
  Chameron, *355*
Augustins, *551*
Aux Armes de Champagne, *656*

B

Balmoral, *519*
Baltimore Westin Demeure
  Hotel, *158*
Beach Hotel, *226*
Beach Plaza, *519*
Beau Rivage, *497*
Beauregard, *324*
Belle Vue, *370*
Bellecote, *594*
Belles-Rives, *506*
Bellevue Hotel, *184*
Bellevue Plage, *314*
Best Western du Chapeau Rouge,
  625
Bourse, *698*
Boyer les Crayeres, *648*
Bretonnerie, *698*
Byblos des Neiges, *594*
Byblos, *479*

C

Calendal, *542*
Carlton Intercontinental, *485*
Carmen, *226*
Castel Brando, *713*
Castel Clara Hotel, *297*
Castel Marie-Louise, *314*
Castille Westin Demeure, *159*
Central Hotel, *264*
Chalet du Mont d'Arbois, *596*
Chalet-Hotel Mounier, *596*
Chantecler, *328*
Chateau d'Audrieu, *233*
Château d'Esclimont, *349*
Château de Bellinglise, *194*
Château de Blanville, *349*
Château de Brindos, *436*
Château de Chissay, *378*
Château de la Chevre d'Or, *498*
Château de la Treyne, *429*
Chateau de Longecourt, *624*
Château de Marcay, *385*
Château de Mercues, *432*
Château de Noirieux, *319*
Château de Perigny, *396*
Château de Pray, *370*
Château de Romegouse, *428*
Chateau de Vault-de-Lugny, *627*
Château des Briottieres, *318*
Chateau des Monthairons, *679*
Château des Reynats, *422*
Château du Guilguiffin, *282*
Château du Housseau, *311*
Chateau du Ru Jacquier, *653*
Château Eza, *498*
Christiana Hotel, *599*
Churchill Hotel, *240*
Clair Logis, *514*
Claret, *417*
Colombe d'Or, *502*
Comfort Hotel Plaza, *687*
Concorde Prado, *473*
Concorde, *328*
Concorde-Palm Beach, *474*

Cour des Loges, *569*
Croix Blanche, *621*

D

D'Arlatan, *542*
D'Avaugour, *274*
Danieli, *535*
Demeure de Chavoire, *589*
Demeure des Brousses Hotel,
  469
Domaine d'Auriac, *456*
Domaine d'Auriac, *457*
Domaine d'Houts de Loire, *369*
Domaine de Champdieu, *213*
Domaine de la Rhue, *428*
Domaine de la Tortiniere, *159*
Domaine de Labarthe, *432*
Domaine/Villa de Belieu, *479*
Du Bon Laboureur et Château,
  378
Duc de Saint Simon, *159*

E

Eber Monceau Hotel, *160*
Eden Roc, *706*
Edouard VII, *160*
Elysée Palace, *498*
Ermitage, *480*
Europe, *535*

F

Fer a Cheval, *597*
Ferme du Château, *349*
Ferme St. Simon, *233*
Fesch, *706*
Fitz Roy Hotel, *600*
Fouquet's, *486*

G

Galilee et Windsor, *445*
Gallia et Londres, *445*
Gallieni Hotel, *606*
George V, *160*
Georges Blanc, *536*

RESTAURANT INDEX

INDEX

Q

International Conversions

TEMPERATURE

To convert °F to °C, subtract 32 and divide by 1.8. To convert °C to °F, multiply by 1.8 and add 32.

Fahrenheit	Centigrade	
230°	110°	
220°		
210°	100°	Water Boils
200°		
190°	90°	
180°	80°	
170°		
160°	70°	
150°		
140°	60°	
130°		
120°	50°	
110°	40°	
100°		
90°	30°	
80°		
70°	20°	
60°		
50°	10°	
40°		
30°	0°	Water Freezes
20°	-10°	
10°		
0°	-20°	
-10°		
-20°	-30°	
-30°		
-40°	-40°	

WEIGHTS & MEASURES

LENGTH

1 km	=	0.62 miles
1 mile	=	1.609 km
1 meter	=	1.0936 yards
1 meter	=	3.28 feet
1 yard	=	0.9144 meters
1 yard	=	3 feet
1 foot	=	30.48 centimeters
1 centimeter	=	0.39 inch
1 inch	=	2.54 centimeters

AREA

1 square km	=	0.3861 square miles
1 square mile	=	2.590 square km
1 hectare	=	2.47 acres
1 acre	=	0.405 hectare

VOLUME

1 cubic meter	=	1.307 cubic yards
1 cubic yard	=	0.765 cubic meter
1 cubic yard	=	27 cubic feet
1 cubic foot	=	0.028 cubic meter
1 cubic centimeter	=	0.061 cubic inch
1 cubic inch	=	16.387 cubic centimeters

CAPACITY

1 gallon	=	3.785 liters
1 quart	=	0.94635 liters
1 liter	=	1.057 quarts
1 pint	=	473 milliliters
1 fluid ounce	=	29.573 milliliters

MASS and WEIGHT

1 metric ton	=	1.102 short tons
1 metric ton	=	1000 kilograms
1 short ton	=	.90718 metric ton
1 long ton	=	1.016 metric tons
1 long ton	=	2240 pounds
1 pound	=	0.4536 kilograms
1 kilogram	=	2.2046 pounds
1 ounce	=	28.35 grams
1 gram	=	0.035 ounce
1 milligram	=	0.015 grain

Order Your Guide to Travel and Adventure

Title	Price	Title	Price
Fielding's Alaska Cruises and the Inside Passage	$18.95	Fielding's Indiana Jones Adventure and Survival Guide™	$15.95
Fielding's America West	$19.95	Fielding's Italy	$18.95
Fielding's Asia's Top Dive Sites	$19.95	Fielding's Kenya	$19.95
Fielding's Australia	$18.95	Fielding's Las Vegas Agenda	$16.95
Fielding's Bahamas	$16.95	Fielding's London Agenda	$14.95
Fielding's Baja California	$18.95	Fielding's Los Angeles	$16.95
Fielding's Bermuda	$16.95	Fielding's Mexico	$18.95
Fielding's Best and Worst	$19.95	Fielding's New Orleans Agenda	$16.95
Fielding's Birding Indonesia	$19.95	Fielding's New York Agenda	$16.95
Fielding's Borneo	$18.95	Fielding's New Zealand	$17.95
Fielding's Budget Europe	$18.95	Fielding's Paradors, Pousadas and Charming Villages of Spain and Portugal	$18.95
Fielding's Caribbean	$19.95	Fielding's Paris Agenda	$14.95
Fielding's Caribbean Cruises	$18.95	Fielding's Portugal	$16.95
Fielding's Caribbean on a Budget	$18.95	Fielding's Rome Agenda	$16.95
Fielding's Diving Australia	$19.95	Fielding's San Diego Agenda	$14.95
Fielding's Diving Indonesia	$19.95	Fielding's Southeast Asia	$18.95
Fielding's Eastern Caribbean	$17.95	Fielding's Southern California Theme Parks	$18.95
Fielding's England including Ireland, Scotland and Wales	$18.95	Fielding's Southern Vietnam on Two Wheels	$15.95
Fielding's Europe	$19.95	Fielding's Spain	$18.95
Fielding's Europe 50th Anniversary	$24.95	Fielding's Surfing Australia	$19.95
Fielding's European Cruises	$18.95	Fielding's Surfing Indonesia	$19.95
Fielding's Far East	$18.95	Fielding's Sydney Agenda	$16.95
Fielding's France	$18.95	Fielding's Thailand, Cambodia, Laos and Myanmar	$18.95
Fielding's France: Loire Valley, Burgundy and the Best of French Culture	$16.95	Fielding's Travel Tool™	$15.95
Fielding's France: Normandy & Brittany	$16.95	Fielding's Vietnam including Cambodia and Laos	$19.95
Fielding's France: Provence and the Mediterranean	$16.95	Fielding's Walt Disney World and Orlando Area Theme Parks	$18.95
Fielding's Freewheelin' USA	$18.95	Fielding's Western Caribbean	$18.95
Fielding's Hawaii	$18.95	Fielding's The World's Most Dangerous Places™	$21.95
Fielding's Hot Spots: Travel in Harm's Way	$15.95	Fielding's Worldwide Cruises	$21.95

To place an order: call toll-free 1-800-FW-2-GUIDE
(VISA, MasterCard and American Express accepted)
or send your check or money order to:
Fielding Worldwide, Inc., 308 S. Catalina Avenue, Redondo Beach, CA 90277
http://www.fieldingtravel.com
Add $4.00 per book for shipping & handling (sorry, no COD's), allow 2–6 weeks for delivery